THE MARIN COUNTY
BREEDING BIRD ATLAS

12/25/93

Tata,

Hope this book brings you
countless hours of enjoyment.

Love,

Dave, Nancy & Asheley

THE MARIN COUNTY BREEDING BIRD ATLAS

A Distributional and Natural History of Coastal California Birds

W. David Shuford

Illustrations by Keith Hansen and Ane Rovetta
Maps by Dewey Livingston
Photographs by Ian Tait

California Avifauna Series 1

*Bushtit
Books*

A Project of Point Reyes Bird Observatory

Dave Shuford

Keith Hansen
1990

Publisher's Cataloging-in-Publication Data
Shuford, W. David, 1949–
The Marin County breeding bird atlas: a distributional and natural history of coastal California birds.
p.   cm.
Includes bibliographic references and index (p.   )
1. Birds—California—Marin County.   2. Bird populations—California—Marin County—Geographical distribution.
3. Marin County (Calif.)—Natural history.   I. Title.
QL684.C2.S58   1993   598.2'9794'62   92-81834

ISBN 0-9633050-0-X

Library of Congress Catalog Card Number: 92-81834.

Published by   BUSHTIT BOOKS
                  P.O. Box 233
                  Bolinas, CA 94924

Printed in the United States of America by Braun-Brumfield, Inc., Ann Arbor, Michigan.

Designed and typeset by Susan Goldhaber Murray.
Cover design by Susan Claire Peaslee.

Printed with soy-based inks on acid-free, recycled paper.

The Marin County Breeding Bird Atlas is a project of:

POINT REYES BIRD OBSERVATORY, 4990 Shoreline Highway, Stinson Beach, CA 94970. Founded in 1965, Point Reyes Bird Observatory is a nonprofit membership organization dedicated to conducting ecological research, interpreting research results to the public, and providing a scientific basis for conservation of wildlife and their habitats. Funding is supplied by research grants, contracts, and individual contributions. Skilled volunteer work is the backbone of many PRBO projects, including the one upon which this book is based. PRBO provides credible, fact-based information and guidelines for policy issues and public and private environmental stewardship. Our studies of birds, marine mammals, and their habitats often involve issues of national and international significance, such as oil spill impacts, wetlands conservation, wildlife/fisheries conflicts, and population threats to neotropical migrants.

Suggested citations (whole book or individual species accounts):

Shuford, W. D. 1993. *The Marin County Breeding Bird Atlas: A Distributional and Natural History of Coastal California Birds.* California Avifauna Series 1. Bushtit Books, Bolinas, Calif.

Peake, H. 1993. Hooded Oriole. In W. D. Shuford. *The Marin County Breeding Bird Atlas: A Distributional and Natural History of Coastal California Birds*, 405–408. California Avifauna Series 1. Bushtit Books, Bolinas, Calif.

To the late David Gaines,
my first bird mentor and an inspirational teacher, naturalist, and conservationist,

To Stuart Johnston,
a born naturalist who knows the birds so well and who lives as wild and free
as any of them, or us,

To Bob Stewart,
who not only started the Marin atlas project
but as a teacher has probably opened the eyes of more budding naturalists in
Marin County than anyone else,

and, of course,
To my Family.

Contents

CONTENTS

CONTENTS

CONTENTS

Marin Breeding Bird Atlas Contributors

Cosponsors—Point Reyes Bird Observatory and Marin Audubon Society

Overall Coordinator 1982, Compiler, and Editor—W. David Shuford

Overall Coordinator 1976 to 1978—Robert M. Stewart

Area Coordinators 1982—Betty Burridge (Tomales Area), Scott Carey (Novato Area), Bill Lenarz (South Marin), Dave Shuford (West Marin)

Computer Entry and Summary—Bill Lenarz

Species Account Authors—John R. Arnold (Northern Mockingbird), Edward C. Beedy (Tricolored Blackbird), A. Sidney England (Black-chinned Sparrow, Sage Sparrow), Geoffrey R. Geupel (Wrentit), Walter D. Koenig (Acorn Woodpecker), Holly Peake (Hooded Oriole), Helen M. Pratt (History of Marin County heron and egret colonies), Stephen I. Rothstein (Brown-headed Cowbird), W. David Shuford (153 species), Robert M. Stewart (Wilson's Warbler), and Pamela L. Williams (Northern Oriole).

Reviewers—Edward C. Beedy (landbirds, main text), Pete H. Bloom (diurnal raptors), Seth Bunnell (Spotted Owl), Scott Carey (landbirds), Harry R. Carter (seabirds), David F. DeSante (main text), Richard A. Erickson (short species accounts), Jules G. Evens (rails, Osprey), Sam Fitton (Hooded Oriole), Gordon I. Gould, Jr. (Spotted Owl), Stephen L. Granholm (landbirds), Roger D. Harris (Pileated Woodpecker), Paul R. Kelly (Clapper Rail), Bill Lenarz (landbirds, main text), M. Robert McLandress (waterfowl), Joseph Morlan (short species accounts), Gary W. Page (shorebirds), Helen M. Pratt (egrets and herons), Steve Simmons (Wood Duck), William J. Sydeman (seabirds, Pygmy Nuthatch), Irene C. Timossi (landbirds), Brian J. Walton (Peregrine Falcon), Jon Winter (owls).

Marin Breeding Bird Atlas Participants

Debbie Ablin, Julia Allen, Sarah Allen, Jane Anderson, Philip Ashman, Audubon Canyon Ranch Research Associates, Stephen F. Bailey, Nancy Barbour, Steve Barbour, Brenda Barten, Jim Bartholomew, Joan Basore, Dennis Beall, Max Beckwith, Gordon Beebe, Ted Beedy, Lori Belton, Irene Biagi, Steve Bobzien, Betty Boyd, Warren Bray, Joan Breece, Tony Briggs, Patty Briggs, Betty Burridge, Leanne Bynum, Kurt Campbell, Jean Canepa, Scott Carey, Barbara Chase, Frank & Carolyn Christian, Peter Colasanti, Carolyn Corey, Robin Dager, Rosamond Day, Dave DeSante, John Dillon, Peter & Louise Dolcini, Doug Ellis, Michael Ellis, Jules Evens, Carter Faust, Mike Fennell, Mary Fishman, Barbara Ford, Carol Fraker, Mary Gillman, Helen & Richard Glassman, Terry Goldblatt, Jon Goodchild, Steve Granholm, Nancy Hanson, Tony Harrow, Kristi Hein, Luanna Helfman, Emmy Hill, Bob Hogan, Craig Hohenberger, David Holway, Joan Howard, Ken Howard, George Hugenberg, Doug Judell, Bill Keener, John Kipping, Kathy Kipping, Gerry Kleynenberg, Elsa Konig, Bob Lampee, Robert H. Laws, Jr., Rick LeBaudour, Bill Lenarz, R. A. Lewis, Stephen M. Long, Tom Love, Shirley McArdell, Flora Maclise, Gary McCurdy, Grace McMichael, Bill Manolis, Marie Mans, Buck Marcussen, Gloria Markowitz, Leah Marks, Mary Mayer, Sarah Mayer, Audrey Miller, Stephen H. Morrell, Brenda Myron, Patricia & Anthony Napolitan, Adeene Nelligan, Dan Nelson, Don Neubacher, LaVerne Nickel, Marcia Nute, Gary Page, Carmen Patterson, Holly Peake, Susan Claire Peaslee, Treet Pellitier, PRBO's Palomarin Staff and Volunteers, Charlotte Poulsen, Lina Jane Prairie, Helen Pratt, Alton ("Bob") Raible, Elaine & Tom Reale, Liza Riddle, Inez Riney, Mary Louise Rosegay, Ane Rovetta, Allen Royer, Corinne Ryan, Mary Ann Sadler, Barbara Salzman, Susan Sanders, Phil & Margaret Schaeffer, Bob & Ruth Scott, Bob Seely, Sid & Nancy Shadle, Marianne Shepard, Dave Shuford, Dianne Sierra, Sue Smith, Vernon Smith, Eric Sorenson, Bruce Sorrie, Barry Spitz, Spring Bird Count Participants (Even Cheaper Thrills, Pt. Reyes Peninsula, & South Marin—Appendix A), John A. Sproul, Jr., Rich Stallcup, Jean Starkweather, Lynne Stenzel, Robert M. Stewart, Nick Story, Helen Strong, Tim Sullivan, Ian Tait, Lynn Tennefoss, Gil Thomson, Carol Thoney, Noel Thoney, Irene Timossi, Dorothy Tobkin, Beverly Treffinger, Ed Vine, Pat Welsh, Bette Wentzel, Janet Wessel, Jack Whetstone, Jim White, Diane Williams, Pam Williams, Summer Wilson, Claire Wolfe, Michael Wolfe, Keiko Yamane, Vincent S. Yoder, Florence Youngberg, Bob & Carol Yutzy, Mark Zumsteg. Many other people contributed additional observations via the above participants or directly to the coordinators.

Acknowledgments

Financial support for the atlas project was provided by generous contributions from an anonymous donor, Golden Gate Audubon Society, Marin Audubon Society, Marin County Fish and Game Fund, Marin Municipal Water District, Andrea Meyer, Sequoia Audubon Society, Lynne Stenzel, and, especially, the general membership of Point Reyes Bird Observatory. The board, administration, and staff of Point Reyes Bird Observatory provided tremendous logistical and moral support throughout the evolution of the project from the initial stages of field work through the completion of the book. Special thanks to Gary Page for granting me an extended leave from my duties in PRBO's Coastal and Estuarine Program to work on this book. Successive Executive Directors—Jane Church, Burr Heneman, and Don McCrimmon—lent their full support to the project, and Laurie Wayburn's commitment at a crucial stage enabled the completion of the final product you hold in your hands.

Janet Kjelmyr, Lisle Lee, Michelle Morris, Meg Sanders, Meg Simonds, Janice Tweedy, and, particularly, Susan Goldhaber Murray and Liz Tuomi were invaluable in crafting my handwritten or hastily typed text and tables into a polished manuscript . . . bless their souls. Susan Claire Peaslee was a godsend in rising well above the call of duty to deftly manage the early and middle stages of book production and copyediting . . . I can't thank her enough. Liz Tuomi contributed additional copyediting skills and along with Pam Williams and Susan Goldhaber Murray proofread all of the manuscript. Mary Anne Stewart skillfully copyedited the entire final version of the manuscript. Edris Cole, Dianne Sierra, and Meryl Sundove proofread the spellings of observer names. Thanks to Bertha Rains for an initial literature search, and to Karen Hamilton for locating and obtaining many hard to find references and for providing cataloging data for the finished book. Many thanks to Julia Gennert for pasting up the illustrations on the typeset manuscript. Helen and Paul Green generously provided a true home away from home when I needed to spend innumerable days and nights researching literature at the Biology Library at U.C. Berkeley. Special thanks to Scott Carey, Doug Judell, Bill Lenarz, Bob Stewart, Irene Timossi, and Jules Evens for spending enormous amounts of time in the field and sharing their vast knowledge of Marin County breeding birds. Many thanks to the numerous Marin County landowners who provided access to their lands without which our field work would have suffered greatly.

Jules Evens (rails and Osprey), Allen Fish (diurnal raptors), Roger Hothem (herons and egrets), John Kelly (herons and egrets), Gary Page (Snowy Plovers), Helen Pratt (herons and egrets), and Dave DeSante, Geoff Geupel, and Bruce Sorrie (Palomarin landbirds) kindly provided data from their studies. L. Richard Mewaldt provided much of the material in the White-crowned Sparrow account. Sheila Hershon searched the files of the California Center for Wildlife for breeding records of Western Screech Owl in Marin County during the atlas period. Numerous others supplied essential facts and figures. Dennis Beall drew the base map used to construct the atlas map for each species. Many thanks to Keith Hansen, Dewey Livingston, Ane Rovetta, and Ian Tait for their patience in waiting for my plodding writing to catch up with their inspirational artwork which graces these pages. When all of the above was said and done, Susan Goldhaber Murray used her remarkable blend of computer skills, problem solving abilities, artistic talents, and great patience to craft the text into a well organized and aesthetically pleasing book, for which she should be duly proud. Speaking for the birds as well, I give final and heartfelt thanks to all those listed above, or not, who in one capacity or another volunteered their time because of a deep concern for birds and their environment.

Illustrations

Preface

The contents of this book evolved over a long period, at first expanding in scope, only later to contract. Beyond the grid-based distribution maps, there is no set formula (nor should there be) as to what warrants inclusion in a breeding bird atlas, or as to whether it even need be a book: some county atlas projects have been published as short papers in local ornithological journals (e.g., Klimkiewicz & Solem 1978). State or provincial atlas books published in North America have ranged from compilations of computer data printouts (Adamus 1987) to full-scale books for Vermont (Laughlin & Kibbe 1985), Ontario (Cadman et al. 1987), and New York (Andrle & Carroll 1988). These three books and their counterparts from other countries include extensive introductory and interpretive material along with species accounts accompanying the maps that provide detail on such topics as habitat preferences, various aspects of the species' breeding biology, and historical trends of populations. The increasing inclination of writers to use natural history information to provide a framework for understanding distributional patterns is followed by this author as well.

Although some would argue that the maps should be the highlight of an atlas book—after all, they are usually the main data generated by the field work—they are lifeless abstractions without an understandng of the intricate web of niche requirements that each species must meet for survival, and without survival there is no distribution or map. Hence, the reader will encounter a strong ecological bent in the material contained in this atlas. The stage is set for interpreting the maps, the species accounts, and the facts and concepts elucidated by the atlas project by first describing Marin County's geographic and geologic setting, the seasonal oceanic and climatic cycles affecting birds here, and the county's principal bird habitats—the realm in which the mundane, dramatic, and poignant events of the lives of our breeding birds unfold. Also, a historical perspective is emphasized in describing changing land use practices, bird population trends, and how the concept of the bird atlas has transformed the way we approach distributional studies.

A great deal of additional material written for this book had to be left out because of time, space, and financial considerations. The original intent was to broaden the discussion of bird distribution patterns to include all of coastal northern California, and to provide additional species accounts for other species of birds that breed elsewhere in this region but not in Marin County. Much of this material was contributed by others and I lament its loss from the present publication and the diversion of many peoples' talents from other projects. Their mark was left on this book nonetheless.

Ralph Hoffmann (1927) in his enchanting, but now underappreciated, field guide, *Birds of the Pacific States*, remarked that "one cannot have too many good bird books." The author will feel the long effort of writing was well worth it if but a few readers deem the present book to be in that category. True satisfaction, though, will come only if some acquire, in part through reading, a deeper appreciation and fascination with our winged companions that motivates them to be better stewards of the Earth. May we be lucky enough to meet in nature's heartland and share its many pleasures together.

Dave Shuford
Bolinas, California
March 1993

A tiny fuss-budget of a Bushtit scolds a prowling Scrub Jay while its partner warily peers from the nest hole. Drawing by Keith Hansen, 1990.

INTRODUCTION

Lest the uninitiated reader be led to believe that the problems of distribution of the birds of California are in the main solved and fully presented in this work, may we quickly disillusion him.

— Joseph Grinnell and Alden H. Miller,
The Distribution of the Birds of California

UNTIL THE LATE 1960s, bird distributions were traditionally mapped using random observations from scattered sources, often collected over lengthy periods of time. In addition, breeding distribution maps usually did not distinguish between records of a species based solely on presence during the breeding season and those backed with positive proof of breeding. Even when aided by knowledge of species' habitat needs, this manner of mapping was largely a subjective process. Numerous judgments had to be made when encountering the inevitable gaps in the record in seemingly suitable habitat or isolated occurrences in habitats of questionable suitability. Usually a great deal of uncertainty remained over whether the pattern of distribution plotted was partly an artifact of uneven knowledge of the area in question, whether breeding records were sufficiently documented, or whether the actual distribution had changed over the course of the extended period of data collection. These problems were especially acute where observers were few but could not be overcome even in areas, such as Great Britain, with a very high proportion of observers in the population and a history of ornithological exploration stretching back for centuries. The lack of an adequately documented record of changes in the distribution and abundance of highly visible species such as birds has been particularly frustrating for conservationists and managers. With subjective mapping methods using data from the entire historical record, only the most dramatic changes in distribution and abundance were noticeable. Often an awareness of a reduced distribution or population decline was apparent only during the later stages, when conservation efforts were the most difficult to implement.

All this changed in the late 1960s when avian distribution studies were revolutionized by the simple concept of the breeding bird atlas—a compilation of accurate distribution maps for all the bird species in a particular geographical area under study. At the outset, the area is divided with a uniform grid of equal-sized atlas blocks (rectangles or squares). These blocks are initially the basic units of field study and ultimately the mapping units for bird distribu-

tion. In addition to noting presence or absence, field workers record for each species the highest category of breeding evidence they observe, based on well-defined criteria for possible, probable, and confirmed breeding. By conducting thorough field work in each of these blocks during a several-year period (usually five years), the current details of avian distribution can effectively be frozen in time. Complete coverage of *all* blocks over a *short* time span avoids the main weaknesses of earlier mapping studies and enables changes in distribution to be easily documented by replicating the work in future years.

Historical Background of Breeding Bird Atlases

Ferguson-Lees (1976), Robbins (1982), and Laughlin et al. (1982) have summarized the history of mapping bird distributions. Phillips' (1922-1926) *A Natural History of the Ducks* was the first serious attempt to map the distribution of a large number of birds. In North America, the first books to map selected species were *Birds of New Mexico* (Bailey 1928), *Florida Bird Life* (Howell 1932), and *The Distribution of the Birds of California* (Grinnell & Miller 1944). In Europe, the first attempts to map bird distribution over broad areas were the *Birds of the Soviet Union* (Dement'ev & Gladkov 1951-1954), *A Field Guide to the Birds of Britain and Europe* (Peterson et al. 1954) and the *Atlas of European Birds* (Voous 1960). In North America, *The Birds of Canada* (Godfrey 1966) and *Birds of North America* (Robbins et al. 1966) were the pioneer works in this vein.

The concept of mapping distribution with the aid of a grid had its origin with a German botanist, Heermann Hoffmann, who in 1860 published the first grid-derived maps of certain plants in central Europe. Although ornithologists began on a subjective basis to use grids to plot the distribution of certain bird species in Britain in the 1950s (Norris 1960, Prestt & Bell 1966), the main impetus for the current atlas movement was the publication by the Botanical Society of the British Isles of the *Atlas* of the *British Flora* (Perring & Walters 1962). This work systematically mapped the distribution of the British flora by 10-km squares. Things have never been quite the same since, as British bird students jumped into the objective comprehensive atlasing of breeding birds with a passion. The pilot project covering three counties in England began in 1966 and was published as the *Atlas of Breeding Birds of the West Midlands* (Lord & Munns 1970). Following close on its heels was the awe-inspiring effort of *The Atlas of Breeding Birds of Britain and Ireland* (Sharrock 1976), where over 10,000 observers completed field work from 1968 to 1972 in each of the 3682 10-km atlas squares covering all of Britain and Ireland! While the British field work was still in progress, other European atlas projects were initiated and subsequently multiplied profusely until by 1981 at least 16 European countries had completed or started atlas projects (Robbins 1982). Avian atlasing soon spread to other continents as well, and atlasing already had been applied to map the distribution of other life forms ranging from marine algae to a host of marine and terrestrial invertebrates. Not ones to rest on their laurels, the British soon began and completed an atlas of winter bird distribution (Lack 1986). They are also currently working toward the completion of their second breeding bird atlas that will resurvey all of Britain and Ireland.

In North America the first recognition of the importance of grid-based mapping of bird distribution came in the 1960s (Skarr 1967, 1969) and resulted in the publication of *Montana Bird Distribution: Preliminary Mapping by Latilong* (Skarr 1975). Montana was divided into 47 1°-blocks of longitude and latitude, and maps were constructed for each species. Although different categories of breeding evidence were presented where applicable, the initial latilong study differed in several important ways from most other atlas projects. First, the size of the blocks was very large compared with breeding bird atlas blocks—a latilong in Montana is nearly 100 times as large as a 10-km square. Secondly, species were initially mapped in a latilong if they occurred in any season, not just the breeding season (see Skarr 1980). Lastly, and perhaps most importantly, observations were used from the entire historical record of Montana ornithology rather than from a fixed and limited number of years. Preliminary latilong projects have also been published for Colorado (Kingery & Graul 1978), Wyoming (Oakleaf et al. 1979), and Utah (Walters 1983).

The first North American atlas work (patterned closely on the European models) was initiated in 1971 on a county-by-county basis by the Maryland Ornithological Society, and the first work was published as the *Breeding Bird Atlas of Montgomery and Howard Counties, Maryland* (Klimkiewicz & Solem 1978). As in Europe, the idea quickly spread. The number of full-state or provincial atlas projects underway or completed in North America swelled

from 10 in 1981 (Laughlin et al. 1982), to 26 in 1986 (Sutcliffe et al. 1986), to 33 in 1990 (Smith 1990). The accuracy and conservation value of distribution studies has increased dramatically with the ascendancy of avian atlas projects.

A Perspective on the History of Avian Distribution Studies in California

The bulk of the data on California's avifauna—especially in regard to breeding birds—was collected in the early to mid-1900s by professional ornithologists from the Museum of Vertebrate Zoology at the University of California, Berkeley, under the direction and inspiration of Joseph Grinnell, his students, and his associates in the Cooper Ornithological Society. A large part of the data collected came from field work organized to document the distribution of the vertebrate fauna in less well known areas of California, particularly in areas in danger of rapid change caused by human encroachment, but also in protected parks. Most of the important distributional studies were published as monographs either in the University of California Publications in Zoology or the Pacific Coast Avifauna series. The culmination of this work resulted in the publication of the landmark *The Distribution of the Birds of California* (Grinnell & Miller 1944), supplemented by *An Analysis of the Distribution of the Birds of California* (Miller 1951). All subsequent California workers have owed an enormous debt to the 1944 publication. Though now out of date in many respects, it still stands as the single most important reference on the distribution of California birds.

In the last 40 years, professional field ornithology has shifted away from an emphasis on distributional and taxonomic studies toward ecological and experimental work, often on single species. Although some professional ornithologists in California still contribute important distributional studies, a host of amateur field ornithologists are presently in the forefront of updating and expanding our knowledge of California's avifauna. Much of the recent distributional work has been published in the seasonal reports of both the Middle and Southern Pacific Coast regions of *American Birds*, in articles in *Western Birds* (formerly *California Birds*), or in regional distribution books or annotated checklists. Much information is scattered in numerous papers in a variety of scientific journals; and a vast store of unpublished knowledge is on file with the regional editors of *American Birds*, university museums, government agencies, and in individual field workers' notebooks.

As with past avifaunal studies in California, most recent work has suffered from concerted effort in certain areas at the expense of others. First, the distribution of observers in California, as elsewhere, is very clumped—most are concentrated close to population centers on the coast and in the Central Valley. Secondly, recent amateur enthusiasm for searching for migrants, hence increasing one's chances for sighting rare birds, has further concentrated observers. The discovery in the 1960s that rarities can be found relatively frequently in isolated habitat patches on the coast or in desert oases is the prime example of this phenomenon. Though amateur ornithologists in California have added an enormous amount in recent years to our knowledge of vagrants and to migrational phenomena in general, until very recently there has been a notable lack of interest in breeding birds.

There have been few attempts to map bird distributions throughout California. Grinnell and Miller (1944) were the first to map a selected number of the state's breeding species to elucidate subspecific ranges. Subsequently, Garrett and Dunn (1981) mapped selected breeding species in southern California, and 'Grenfell and Laudenslayer (1983) mapped the summer and/or winter distribution of 340 species of birds in all of California. Unitt (1984) and Roberson (1985) mapped breeding distributions in California in San Diego and Monterey counties respectively. All these authors relied on subjective methods to map approximate breeding ranges, using largely presumptive evidence of breeding. The Marin atlas project is the first to objectively plot the distribution of all breeding species in any area of California based on systematically collected data.

The fine-scale distribution data and supplemental natural history information of the *Marin County Breeding Bird Atlas* can be used by local conservationists as an aid to preserving and protecting our remaining valuable wildlife habitats. On a larger scale, perhaps this beginning will stimulate others to start atlas projects in other counties and eventually all of California. Indications are that the Marin atlas may already have played that role—as of 1991 there are atlas projects underway (or completed) in 12 other California counties (Table 1, Figure 1; Manolis 1991). It is to be hoped that more bird students will seize this opportunity to conduct field work with conservation ramifications foremost in their minds. The human horde presses heavily on our remaining wildlands, and a basic understanding of the distribution, abundance, and habitat requirements of all our native fauna is essential for protecting our heritage of biological diversity.

History of Breeding Bird Studies in Marin County, California

In the late 1870s and early 1880s, C.A. Allen, living then in Nicasio or San Geronimo, published several short notes on breeding birds in Marin County (e.g., Allen 1881). The Mailliard brothers, Joseph and John W., contributed the most to the early knowledge of Marin's avifauna, primarily from field work near their ranch in the San Geronimo

Valley. Their work bore fruit in numerous papers published from 1881 to at least 1938 (see Grinnell 1909, 1924, 1939) and the accumulation of a large specimen and egg collection eventually housed at the California Academy of Sciences (Mailliard 1924b). Records of Allen's and earlier ones of the Mailliards' attributed to Nicasio may in fact refer to specimens collected some miles away (Mailliard 1924b). J. Mailliard's 1900 paper first summarized knowledge of the status of landbirds in Marin County. The first publication to report the status of all species of the county's avifauna was Stephens and Pringle's (1933) *Birds of Marin County*. They compiled information primarily from records of the Audubon Association of the Pacific (now Golden Gate Audubon), derived mostly from observations from 56 field trips to various places in southern Marin from 1919 to 1933. They also used information from Grinnell and Wythe's (1927) *Directory to the Bird-life of the San Francisco Bay Region* and unpublished observations of several active observers. Additions and corrections to the Marin list were published in 1936 (*Gull* 18, No. 6). Limited additional information on Marin's breeding birds has been published in avifaunal works of broader geographic scope (e.g., Grinnell & Miller 1944, Miller 1951), as occasional notes (e.g., Ralph & Ralph 1958), as part of single-species studies (e.g., Page & Stenzel 1981), or as part of seasonal field note summaries of local or national Audubon Society publications (e.g., *The Gull, Audubon Field Notes, American Birds*). Even as the number of observers in the area grew greatly from the 1950s to the early 1970s, and access improved with better roads and the establishment of numerous parks, little effort was focused on breeding birds. At the time, observers focused much of their field work on the coast, particularly on Point Reyes, and mostly on migrational phenomena, seasonal abundance patterns, Christmas Bird Counts, and single-species studies. Breeding birds took a back seat.

The picture of Marin County's breeding avifauna painted by work prior to the atlas project was a sketchy one. Initial observer coverage was focused on central and southern Marin, with minimal field work from Point Reyes (see Shuford 1986). Early records from the drier portions of the county around Novato were almost unheard of. The small geographic focus, few observers, and difficulty of travel are reflected in the earlier lists of Marin's breeding birds. Interpretation of Mailliard's (1900) summary of the status of landbirds in Marin County indicated he had knowledge at the time of about 89 species of landbirds breeding here. Similar interpretation of Stephens and Pringle's (1933) list suggests they knew then of 96 species of breeding landbirds. Even including 4 species (Purple Martin, Violet-green Swallow, Bank Swallow, and Western Bluebird) considered as breeders in Marin by Mailliard (1900) and 3 species (Northern Harrier, American Robin, and Tricolored Blackbird) by Grinnell and Wythe (1927), as of 1933

Table 1. Information on county breeding bird atlas projects in California as of 1991 (see Figure 1; Manolis 1991).

County	Project Years	Block Size[1]	Number[2] of Blocks	Block[3] Coverage	Project Coordinators	Sponsoring Groups
Sacramento	1988–1992	5 km	138	all	Tim Manolis	Sacramento Audubon
Marin	1976–1982	2.5 km	221	all	Dave Shuford Bob Stewart	Point Reyes Bird Observatory Marin Audubon
Sonoma	1986–1991	5 km	185	all	Betty Burridge	Madrone Audubon
Napa	1989–1992	5 km	79	all	Bill Grummer Mike Rippey	Napa-Solano Audubon
San Francisco	1991–1992	5 km	20	all	Stephen F. Bailey	Sequoia Audubon S.F. Bay Bird Observatory Golden Gate Audubon
San Mateo	1991–1995	5 km	74	all	Rick Johnson	
Santa Clara	1988–1992	5 km	168	all	Bill Bousman	Coyote Creek Riparian Station
Santa Cruz	1987–1991	5 km	72	all	David Suddjian	Santa Cruz Bird Club
Monterey	1988–1992	5 km	364	70 quads (154 priority, 210 nonpriority blocks)	Becca Serdehely	Monterey Peninsula Audubon
San Luis Obispo	1989–1993	5 km	409	78 quads (175 priority, (234 nonpriority blocks)	Mildred Comar	Morro Coast Audubon North Questa Audubon
Orange	1985–1990	5 km	111	all	Peter DeSimone Silvia Gallagher Nancy Kenyon	National Audubon Sea and Sage Audubon
San Bernardino	1987–1992	5 km	224	sampling of 2106 potential blocks	Barbara Carlson	Kerncrest Audubon Pomona Valley Audubon San Bernardino Valley Audubon
Riverside	1990–1994	5 km	144	sampling of 740 potential blocks	Barbara Carlson	San Bernardino Valley Audubon

[1] Block sizes are indicated by the length of one side of a square block (or its equivalent); the area of a 2.5 km block is 6.25 km² and of a 5 km block is 25 km². Marin County's 2.5 km blocks were derived by directly subdividing USGS 7.5 minute topo maps; the 5 km blocks from all other counties were derived from the Universal Transverse Mercator (UTM) grid.

[2] May or may not include partial blocks.

[3] Coverage schemes: 1) most counties—all blocks, 2) Monterey and San Luis Obispo counties—all blocks in certain accessible areas (priority blocks) and quads (each with 1 priority and 3 nonpriority blocks) in more remote areas, and 3) San Bernardino and Riverside counties—stratified random sampling (varying by area from 1 of 6 to 1 of 12 potential blocks) plus selected specialty blocks.

Figure 1. Map of California highlighting the 13 counties with breeding bird atlas projects that are completed or in progress (see Table 1).

there was knowledge of only 103 species of breeding landbirds in Marin County. Adding the 22 species of waterbirds that Stephens and Pringle indicated were breeding in the county gives a total of 125 species of confirmed or suspected breeding birds in Marin County in 1933. For some species, breeding evidence was based largely on assumptions and limited data. For example, the evidence of California Thrasher in the county was based solely on a single aural record (Mailliard 1900, Stephens & Pringle 1933). By 1951 there were indications of at least 8 additional breeders in Marin (Grinnell & Miller 1944, Miller 1951) for a total of 133 breeding species in the county. This total is about 82% of the number of breeding species known from Marin County at the time of this writing (see Results and Discussion p. 51). These numerical comparisons tell only part of the story. Initially many species were considered breeders without sufficient documentation, and knowledge of the countywide distribution and abundance of most species was fragmentary at best.

Origin of the Marin County Breeding Bird Atlas Project

In 1976, Bob Stewart, then the landbird biologist at Point Reyes Bird Observatory, was inspired by the publication of the seminal *Atlas of the Breeding Birds of Britain and Ireland* (Sharrock 1976). Encouraged by Chandler Robbins and the progress of Maryland's atlas work, Bob initiated a proposed three-year project to map the breeding distribution of all bird species in 221 atlas blocks (2.5-km square equivalents) in Marin County, California. At that time, small-scale breeding bird atlas work was in its formative stages. The only other projects underway in North America were in Maryland and Massachusetts. There was no precedent whatsoever in California or the West. The initiation of atlas work in California, even on this tiny scale, can be viewed as an important landmark in light of the history of previous avifaunal work in the state.

Uninterrupted chaparral, redwood forest, mixed evergreen forest, and marshland graced Mount Tamalpais and the Corte Madera shoreline in presettlement times. Drawing by Ane Rovetta, 1989.

UNDERSTANDING BIRD DISTRIBUTION

Efforts to develop broad distributional principles and categories commonly run beyond the facts and violate the essentially statistical character of distributional data. There is an urge to create simplified concepts, perhaps unwittingly as paths of least intellectual resistance. These become lines of escape from exhaustive factual comprehension.

— Alden H. Miller,
An Analysis of the Distribution of the Birds of California

SINCE THE LOCAL AVIFAUNA is a product of thousands of years of evolution, it stands to reason that any study of bird distribution must start with a solid understanding of each species' biology and the environment to which the birds have adapted. A host of climatic, topographic, and geologic factors interact on a local scale to provide a suite of habitats available for birds. The trick to unraveling the puzzle of bird distribution is to grasp the factors that influence the habitat selection of each species. This is not an easy task. All bird distributions are constantly changing, at least on a local scale, whether in response to a varying environment or in response to varying competition and/or predation influences from other species. In addition, a bird may reach the limit of its distribution though seemingly suitable habitat continues uninterrupted. Today biologists believe that landbirds generally select habitats according to the structure of plant communities, rather than selecting particular species of plants (e.g., Verner & Larson 1989) though exceptions exist and many factors are at play. Foraging seabirds are generally distributed with respect to various water masses with characteristic ranges of temperature and/or salinity, with the added constraint of the need for protected, isolated terrestrial habitat for breeding. For these reasons, the overview below emphasizes the seasonal cycles of weather and ocean currents that interact with the local topography and geology, which in concert shape the breeding habitats to which Marin County's avifauna has adapted. We will see that Marin County's geographic position and evolutionary history place it in an area of exceptional oceanic productivity and varied terrestrial plant communities. Consequently, it is home to a large and varied breeding avifauna.

Marin County Topography

Marin County's setting and topography are important determinants of local weather patterns and plant distribution. Marin County lies at 38°N along the California coast just north of the Golden Gate at the mouth of San Francisco Bay. The county is roughly diamond shaped and covers 588 square miles—it is the fourth smallest of California's 58 counties. Its long axis runs northwest to southeast, and it is bounded by the Pacific Ocean on the west, the Golden Gate on the south, San Pablo and San Francisco bays on the east, and the low rolling hills of the Sonoma County "borderlands" on the north (Figures 2 and 3).

Though seemingly uniform from the surface, the Pacific Ocean off our shores can be divided into several zones useful for describing the distribution of sea-going birds (see Shuford et al. 1989). *Neritic* describes waters over the continental shelf, which off Marin varies from about 20 to 25 miles in width, extending just seaward of the Farallon Islands and Cordell Bank. The neritic zone can be subdivided into inshore and offshore zones. The inshore zone reaches from the shoreline to a line beyond which the bottom is too deep for a diving seabird to exploit—a depth of about 230 feet. The offshore zone extends from that depth to the seaward edge of the continental shelf. *Oceanic* describes waters of the deep ocean from the continental slopes beyond the continental or insular shelves—the true home of pelagic seabirds.

Marin's shoreline is dissected by several bays, lagoons, and estuaries: Tomales Bay, Abbott's Lagoon, Drake's and Limantour esteros, and Bolinas Lagoon on the outer coast; and several tongues of San Francisco Bay, most notably Richardson Bay, on the east. On the outer coast most of the shoreline rises abruptly to steep cliffs, except for occa-

7

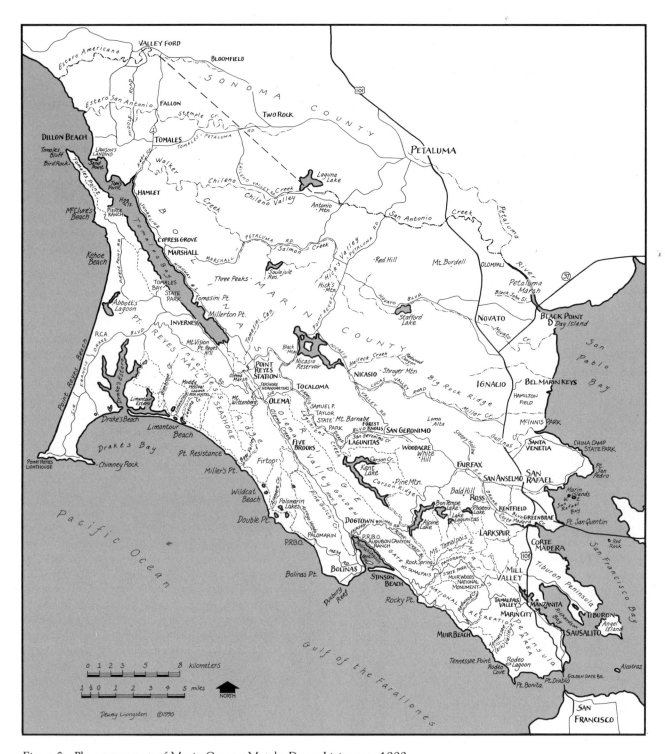

Figure 2. *Place name map of Marin County. Map by Dewey Livingston, 1990.*

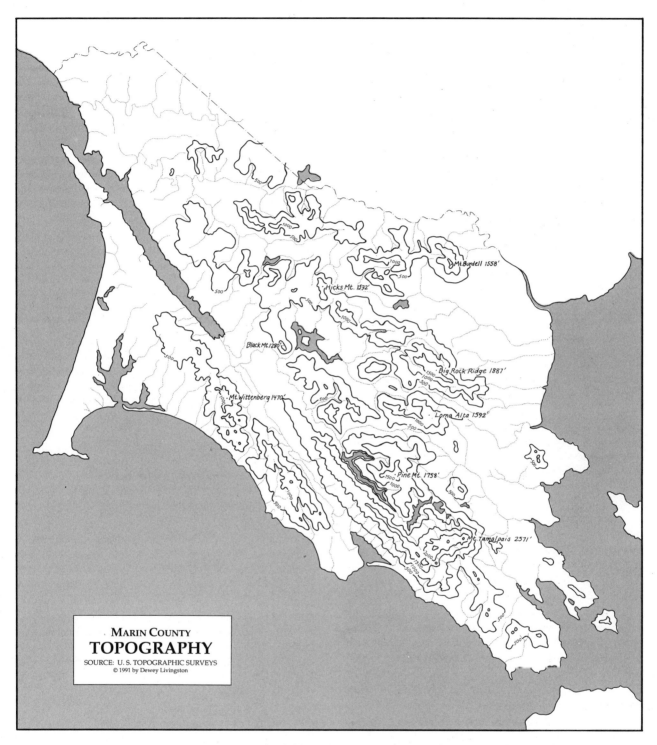

Figure 3. Topographic map of Marin County. Dark solid lines show 500 foot topographic contours; thin dotted lines mark stream drainages. Map by Dewey Livingston, 1991.

sional small pocket beaches and the long beaches fronting Drake's Bay and the west side of the Point Reyes peninsula. Along the eastern bayshore, marshlands and reclaimed former marshlands cover alluvial plains, particularly near Novato. Otherwise Marin's uplands consist predominantly of hilly and low mountainous terrain. The most prominent peak is Mount Tamalpais, a sacred Miwok refuge with the famed profile of the Sleeping Lady, which reaches a height of 2571 feet at its East Peak. Other high peaks are Big Rock Ridge (1887 ft.), Pine Mountain (1758 ft.), Loma Alta (1592 ft.), Mount Burdell (1558 ft.), Hicks Mountain (1532 ft.), Mount Wittenberg (1407 ft.), and Black Mountain (1280 ft.). Although these peaks are not impressive as mountains go, they are rather steep; the flank of Mount Tamalpais rises 2000 feet in a little over a mile starting at sea level at Stinson Beach.

In the pattern typical of the Coast Range mountains, Marin County's major ridges run northwest to southeast roughly paralleling the coastline. Toward the coast these ridges are clothed primarily with conifer forests, mixed hardwood forests, and coastal scrub. Inverness Ridge stretches the length of the Point Reyes peninsula, reaching a height of 1407 feet at Mount Wittenberg. On the east, the ridge rises rather steeply from Tomales Bay and the Olema Valley. On the west, the southern portion of the ridge descends rapidly to steep cliffs and rocky shoreline. The northern portion of the ridge, around Drake's and Limantour esteros, descends to low rolling hills and pastureland, flanked by a long beach and dune system set off by the steep cliffs and rocky shoreline of the Point Reyes headlands and Tomales Point. From the Golden Gate low grass- and brush-covered hills of the Marin Peninsula ascend to the north to Mount Tamalpais. The rest of the south central part of the county is dominated by several roughly parallel ridges, the most prominent being Bolinas Ridge, Carson Ridge, Loma Alta, and Big Rock Ridge. Smaller parallel ridges emanating from those larger ridges and from Mount Tamalpais separate Marin's larger towns and cities lying in small valleys along the San Francisco and San Pablo bayshores. The heavily forested southern ridges grade to the north into much smaller, less well defined ridges covered largely with grasslands and a patchwork of brush and hardwood forest. To the extreme northwest along the drainages of Estero de San Antonio and Estero del Americano, the low rolling hills are clothed almost entirely in grasslands, as are lowlands on outer Point Reyes.

Unlike most of the northern California coast, Marin has no major rivers draining its landmass. Instead the numerous canyons give rise to many small permanent and intermittent streams that flow into small valleys between the hills and then into the ocean. Natural freshwater ponds or lakes are very rare in Marin, as in most of the Coast Range. The largest of these is Laguna Lake, a seasonal lake,

on the Marin-Sonoma border in Chileno Valley. The only other notable natural freshwater ponds are several near Double Point north of Palomarin on the Point Reyes peninsula. Marin Municipal Water District, however, has impounded water in seven sizable reservoirs: Alpine Lake, Bon Tempe Lake, Kent Lake, Lake Lagunitas, Nicasio Reservoir, Phoenix Lake, and Soulajoule Reservoir. The only other large impoundment is North Marin Water District's Stafford Lake. Numerous small diked stock ponds dot the grassy hills of the cattle and sheep ranches, mostly in the central, northern, and western parts of the county.

The topography of the coastal ridges exerts a profound effect on local weather. Varied coastal relief influences local rainfall patterns countywide, as discussed in greater detail below. The only major gaps in the ridge system are in the Estero lowlands near Tomales (which connects with the Petaluma Valley of southern Sonoma County), the Nicasio gap near the reservoir of the same name, and the Muir Woods gap. These gaps funnel winds and coastal fog eastward, moderating the summer climate of adjoining inland areas relative to other areas blocked from major air movements by high ridges. Evidence of the strong winds in these gaps can be readily seen in the wavelike top of the wind-sculptured bay laurel forest below Nicasio Reservoir. The influence of Marin's varied relief on microclimate reaches beyond its effect on large-scale air movement and rainfall. Local differences in slope, exposure, temperature inversions, cold air drainage, and ground water levels also have marked effects on vegetation.

Geology and Soils

Marin County's most infamous geologic feature, the San Andreas Fault, slices the earth's crust under Bolinas Lagoon, the Olema Valley, and Tomales Bay. This fault— known chiefly as the source of the great 1906 San Francisco earthquake—separates two areas of strikingly different geologic history, now juxtaposed by displacement along the fault of several hundred miles or more. To the west on the northward moving Pacific Plate, the Point Reyes peninsula has a base of Cretaceous (at least 84 million years old) granitic rock overlain with relatively young (4-26 million years old) marine sedimentary deposits of the Cenozoic age. To the east on the North American Plate lie the intensely folded and faulted rocks of the Franciscan complex, including Mesozoic (136 million years old) marine sandstones and shales, chert, sea floor volcanic rocks (mainly greenstone), serpentine, and unusual metamorphic rocks.

As a result of its complex geologic setting and history, Marin County hosts many soil types (Kashiwagi 1985). Contrasts in soil types are most apparent on opposite sides of the San Andreas Fault since their respective origins and histories are so different. The distribution of distinctive soil types appears to explain much of the overall distribution of Marin County's conifer forests. A thin, relatively barren soil derived from serpentine rock is one of the exceptional types found locally east of the San Andreas Fault. Although serpentine soils are extremely harsh and support few species, they harbor a number of endemic species and genetically distinct populations of plants (Kruckeberg 1984). Serpentine soil also supports a unique chaparral community, with generally sparser and stunted shrubs favored by certain chaparral birds. Although soils may be important determinants locally, topography and microclimate generally play a greater role in influencing broad patterns of plant distribution and hence bird distribution.

Climate

Seasonality

Many transplanted Easterners bemoan the "lack of seasons" in coastal lowland California. Despite the relatively low variation between summer and winter temperatures along the coast, there are marked seasonal changes in weather, though these contrast greatly with patterns typical of the rest of temperate North America. Marin County and much of lowland California enjoy what is termed a Mediterranean climate because of its similarity to that of the eastern Mediterranean region—a climate found in only a handful of areas in the world. Seasonally we experience "a desert in summer, a sodden, dripping landscape in winter, and a glory of wildflowers in spring" (Major 1977). Zonally this is a subtropical climate combining some of the worst features of arid and humid climates. The basic features of this climate—tempered significantly along the coastline by cool ocean waters—are (1) hot and arid summers and cool and humid winters, so that (2) the supply of water and the need of water for plant growth are exactly out of phase, (3) the growing season is limited by cool winter temperatures and summer drought, and (4) native vegetation is lush in the spring when higher temperatures occur temporarily with an adequate water supply and either is desiccated or fails to grow in summer (Major 1977). In other words we have two major seasons: a distinct cool, rainy season when the grassy hills turn green and a dry, hot summer when the hills turn golden brown. Spring is characterized by increasing warmth at the end of the rainy season and a profusion of wildflowers that begin to bloom in earnest in February and March. Many people also remember spring, not so fondly, by the long stretches of intensely windy days. Summers on the outer coast are generally characterized by cool ocean breezes and recurring overcast or fog, and inland by clear skies and hot days. Fall is a period of relatively calm and prolonged warmth grading into the cooler rainy winter. Here flowers bloom at almost any season and the limited fall color, from the few deciduous trees and shrubs, lingers into November and December.

Temperatures

Winter temperatures in Marin County are generally mild because warm air masses usually accompany the frequent winter rainstorms. Nevertheless, the pervasive dampness gives the impression of cooler temperatures than those recorded. Frosts may be frequent locally, but snow dusts the higher ridges only every few years. Summer temperatures can exceed 100° F at interior sites. Mean monthly temperatures vary greatly between sites in Marin County, particularly among coastal and interior stations (Table 2).

The narrow zone along the shore west of the low coastal ridges has an equitable maritime climate—that is, average temperatures vary little from month to month. For example, on outer Point Reyes, mean January and July temperatures vary by only about 4° F (Table 2). Winter temperatures on the outer coast remain warmer than those inland because of the proximity of heat-retaining ocean waters, whereas summer temperatures are depressed by cool ocean breezes and to a lesser degree by reduced solar radiation during frequent episodes of persistent fog. Summer temperatures on the outer coast may occasionally reach those of the interior, but hot days are few and cool days abound. For perspective, summer temperatures on the coast in the San Francisco Bay Area "are among the coldest within the continental limits of the U.S., yet air temperatures rise so rapidly inland that within 60 miles of the ocean the maximum temperatures are comparable with any in the U.S. outside the Sonoran-Mohave Desert region" (Patton 1956). With every 10-mile increment from the coast, mean monthly temperature increases 3° F in July and August, and over the same distance the daily maximum increases about 4.5° F from June through August. In contrast to the outer coast, January and July mean temperatures in the interior of Marin County vary by almost 20° F (Table 2). Although summer temperatures in the interior of Marin often hover over 90° F, they too are moderated to an extent, relative to inland lowland regions of the state, by the proximity of the ocean and San Francisco and San Pablo bays.

Precipitation

On the central California coast, precipitation falls primarily as rain, with about 95% of the yearly total compressed into the seven-month period from October through April (Table 3). Yearly rainfall on the coast generally decreases from north to south. Because the moisture-laden air of ocean-generated storms must rise when encountering Marin's broken, low mountainous terrain, rainfall varies greatly over the short distances between recording stations (Table 3, Figure 4). Although rainfall is relatively high on the coastal slope, much moisture passes inland. In fact,

Table 2. Air temperature (degrees F) at selected Marin County sites.

	MEAN Jan	MEAN Jul	MIN–MAX FOR ALL YEARS	YEARS OF DATA
Hamilton Field[1]	46.5	65.5	23–106	25
Point Reyes[2]	49.5	53.6	30–98	42
San Rafael[3]	49.5	67.8	26–110	30
Mt. Tamalpais[2]	43.7	69.0	19–100	25
Kentfield[3]	46.7	67.0	17–112	30
Corte Madera[4]	47	62	22–108	20

[1] Data from U.S. Air Force/Air Weather Service
[2] Data from U.S. Weather Bureau (1934).
[3] Data from National Oceanic and Atmospheric Administration (1982).
[4] Data from Marin Municipal Water District

some of the wettest areas of Marin are on the east side of the first or second coastal ridges, as exemplified by the county's highest average precipitation at Kent Lake. While nearly rain-free summers are expected, winter rainfall may vary dramatically over the course of one rainy season or among years. Even in good rainfall years, a very dry early winter can be followed by an extremely wet late winter or vice versa. The period of atlas field work fortuitously encompassed dramatic extremes of yearly rainfall. The atlas project began with (up to that time) the state's worst recorded drought in 1975–76 and 1976–77 and culminated with the deluge of 1981–82, highlighted by the now-legendary flood of 4 January 1982, when almost the whole county was afloat (Table 3). Rainfall in California tends to peak and dip on approximately a five- to six-year cycle, though not usually reaching these extremes (Michaelson 1977). The amount of rainfall in California is a function of anomalies in sea surface temperature in the North Pacific Ocean as discussed in greater detail below.

Pacific Ocean Air and Current Cycles

Publications by Patton (1956), Gilliam (1962), Major (1977), and Ainley (1990) portray a dynamic interaction between the forces of air, sea, and land. Seasonal (and long-term) changes in the ocean currents and air masses of the Pacific Ocean drive the weather cycles in coastal California. Weather systems move across the Pacific from west to east fueled and modified by the direction of the rotation of the earth, the overall clockwise circulation of water in the North Pacific (Gyre), and the presence of the North Pacific High about halfway between California and Hawaii. This large high pressure system, with clockwise circulating winds, moves northwest in the spring and summer as the

Northern Hemisphere warms up and southeast in fall and winter as it cools. The clockwise circulation of water in the North Pacific Gyre sends cool surface waters of the California Current south along our coastline year round. This boundary current is one of the most productive stretches of ocean in the world. It appears to be responsible for the largely temperate character of the local breeding marine avifauna (in an otherwise subtropical region) and the large variety and number of breeding seabirds (Ainley & Boekelheide 1990). The main flow of the California Current is about 125 to 310 miles offshore; another more variable zone occurs close to shore where flow of the current is altered by bottom and coastal topography. Also a deep, warmer countercurrent (below 650 feet in depth) flows northwest along our coast. On the surface west of the California Current are found warm subtropical waters of relatively high salinity and rather depleted nutrients.

Bolin and Abbott (1963) described three phases of the annual cycle of ocean circulation directly off northern California: the Davidson Period (Nov–Feb), the Upwelling Period (Feb–Sep), and the Oceanic Period (Sep–Oct). Timing, intensity, and duration of these three phases varies from year to year, as do weather patterns and ocean productivity. The Davidson Period commences with the cessation of northwest winds and upwelling in the fall (see below). At this time the deep countercurrent reaches the surface and flows northward along the immediate coast—landward of the southward-moving California Current—in a band about 50 miles wide. Because the North Pacific High has dropped southward at this time, the rainy season commences as storms are no longer deflected northward and now reach our coast. These counterclockwise-circulating low-pressure storm systems bring prevailing winds

UNDERSTANDING BIRD DISTRIBUTION

Table 3. Average yearly rainfall during the California water-year (Oct–Sep) at selected Marin County stations. Seasonality and annual variation of rainfall depicted by patterns at Kentfield. Data primarily from California Department of Water Resources (1980).

Location	Elev. (ft.)	Data Period	Average (in.)	Range (in.)
Pt. Reyes Lighthouse	510	62 yrs; 1879–1944	19.57	9.56–47.45
Inverness	150	14 yrs; 1951–1968	36.65	23.80–48.15
Palomarin*	240	17 yrs; 1967–1983	35.93	15.82–61.15
Nicasio	205	16 yrs; 1960–1975	37.16	21.50–57.85
Novato Fire House	18	17 yrs; 1957–1979	25.08	10.19–42.20
Hamilton Field	0	24 yrs; 1934–1963	25.90	12.37–47.84
Kent Lake	360	16 yrs; 1960–1975	66.00	36.14–116.20
Woodacre*	430	31 yrs; 1951–1983	45.45	17.02–79.12
San Rafael Natl. Bank	25	105 yrs; 1872–1976	36.85	15.01–67.43
Kentfield*	80	92 yrs; 1896–1983	47.86	21.41–88.63
Mt. Tam 1 mi. S	950	39 yrs; 1898–1958	35.26	12.81–74.50
Muir Woods*	170	15 yrs; 1966–1983	40.71	18.26–66.21
Mill Valley	10	11 yrs; 1957–1975	33.69	18.48–58.02
Tiburon	400	13 yrs; 1958–1979	29.31	12.81–47.26

* Supplemental data directly from recording station; all data from PRBO's Palomarin Field Station courtesy of Dave DeSante and Geoff Geupel.

AVERAGE MONTHLY AND YEARLY RAINFALL AT KENTFIELD

Oct	Nov	Dec	Jan	Feb	Mar	Apr	May	Jun	Jul	Aug	Sep	Total
2.70	5.58	8.77	10.63	8.37	6.44	2.88	1.33	0.30	0.04	0.04	0.58	47.86

YEARLY RAINFALL TOTALS AT KENTFIELD
DURING YEARS OF THE MARIN COUNTY BREEDING BIRD ATLAS

1975–76	1976–77	1977–78	1978–79	1979–80	1980–81	1981–82
22.54	23.40	62.58	38.42	56.83	30.14	81.75

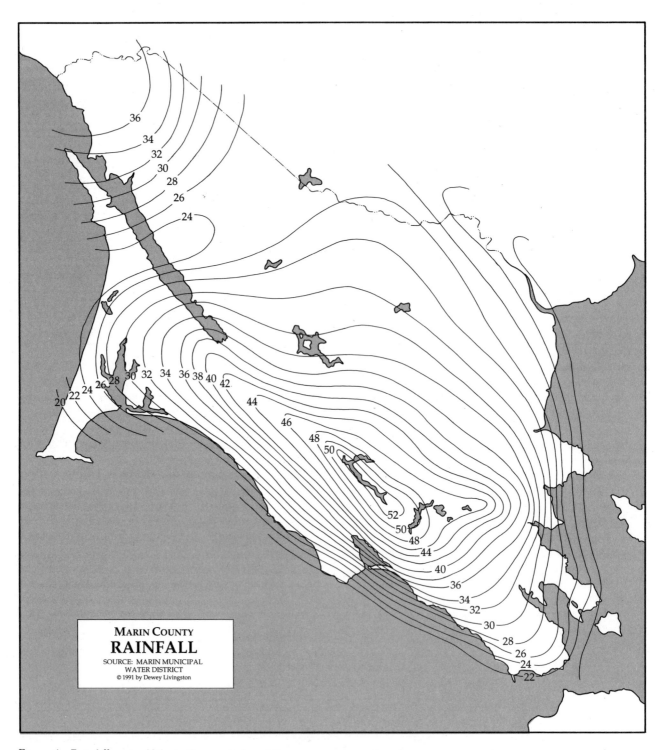

Figure 4. Rainfall map of Marin County. Isohyetal lines connect areas of similar average annual rainfall (inches per year). Map by Dewey Livingston, 1991.

from the south as they approach the coast. The Davidson Current is reinforced by these southerly winds (and other factors) until prevailing winds shift to the northwest in February and March. Because flowing water (or air) tends to move to the right in the Northern Hemisphere (reacting to the Coriolis force caused by the rotation of the earth), water flowing northward in the Davidson Current tends to pile up along the coast. This causes water to sink—a phenomena called downwelling—and to be replaced by water from offshore. Although surface temperatures are relatively warm for winter time, they decline through the period because the heavy storms of the season mix waters to a considerable depth and partially because solar radiation decreases seasonally. The frequent winter storms often hit land with high, gusty winds. Between storms, weather can vary from cool, clear days, to variable overcast, to occasional periods of ground fog—particularly inland. Winter also occasionally blesses us with very warm springlike days.

The onset of the Upwelling Period coincides with the northward movement in spring of the North Pacific High, which again deflects storms to the north. Exceptionally, summer rain reaches us from rare fragments of tropical storms that move north from the vicinity of Baja California or from ocean storms that pass by an infrequently weakened North Pacific High. Warming of the interior at this time sets up a low-pressure system inland. The resulting high- to low-pressure gradient causes winds to intensify. Prevailing winds are from the northwest due to their origin from the clockwise-rotating North Pacific High and deflection to the right by the Coriolis force. Periods of intense winds will alternate with calm spells, but high winds dominate the weather of this period. Winds pick up in the morning to reach late afternoon maxima; high velocities often extend into predawn hours. From March to August, winds on nearby Southeast Farallon Island on average attain speeds greater than 16 mph on about one-third of all days and on almost one-half of all days from April to June. Velocities typically reach 35–40 mph and maxima exceed 55 mph (Ainley 1990). The mean wind velocities from April through June of 25.7 mph (n = 18 yr.) at Point Reyes and 18.8 mph (n = 4 yr.) at Southeast Farallon Island are the highest values of any three-month period at these stations (Calif. Dept. Water Resources 1978). Another important characteristic of these winds is their steadiness. Winds flow continuously from the west for every hour from May to September except in the early mornings of June to August when winds flow from the south or west-southwest (Patton 1956).

These strong northwesterly spring winds increase the flow of the cool California Current and move water along the immediate coast south and offshore, again because of the Coriolis force causing movement to the right. The water moving offshore is replaced from below by cool

nutrient rich waters. This process, called upwelling, is restricted to within 12 to 30 miles of the coast, along our narrow continental shelf. Surface temperatures reach the low of the annual cycle during peak winds and upwelling from April through June. Moist ocean air passing over the cool upwelled waters gives rise to periods of intense coastal summer fog described in more detail below. Although upwelling continues through the spring and summer, solar warming causes sea surface temperatures to rise. The nutrient-rich surface waters—supplied by both the strengthened California Current and local upwelling—stimulate high productivity of the food chain of algae, zooplankton, fish, and ultimately seabirds (Ainley 1990). Marin County lies within the region of maximum upwelling along the West Coast (stretching from Cape Blanco, Oregon, to Point Conception, California), and Point Reyes is a particularly important upwelling center. Upwelling occurs progressively later in the season from south to north along the California coast (Bakun 1973), and ocean productivity and weather patterns lag as well. Breeding seabirds time their nesting, as do arriving migrant seabirds, to take advantage of this seasonal peak of food abundance in late spring and summer. Although upwelling occurs during the same general period each year, there is considerable year-to-year variation in timing and intensity (Ainley 1990). Consequently, the timing and success of seabird breeding can vary greatly—some years many species do not breed at all. The processes affecting upwelling are complex and not well understood (D.G. Ainley & W.J. Sydeman pers. comm.). Although years classified as cold-water years generally signify high ocean productivity/high breeding success (vice versa for warm-water years), this is not always the case. The timing of spring winds can be as important as their intensity—prolonged periods of intense winds and upwelling can sometimes be too much of a good thing, disrupting the productivity at the base of the food chain. Even some years with strong upwelling can be warm-water years.

During July and August, northerly winds lessen as we grade into the relatively calm, relatively fog-free Oceanic Period of September and October. With the cessation of strong winds, upwelling slackens and the California Current slows down. This is a period of rather passive onshore movement of warm nutrient-depleted waters that raise sea surface temperatures sharply to their annual high. Skies vary from clear to overcast during this period, with relatively infrequent coastal fog, while temperatures remain warm throughout the county and are the warmest of the year on the immediate coast. This lag in the occurrence of seasonal high temperatures is another characteristic of the equitable coastal climate. This period is the West Coast equivalent of Indian Summer. As fall progresses and air temperatures drop, the North Pacific High moves farther south, setting the stage for the return of winter storms and the start of another yearly cycle.

Climatic Extremes

Although the preceding paragraphs describe the typical annual weather cycle, extreme conditions arise when shifts in global air and water circulation cause a breakdown in the normal pattern (see Ainley 1990). A classic example of this was the now famous El Niño event of 1982–83. The term El Niño ("the child") was first applied to the warm countercurrent that normally occurs off Peru around Christmastime, heralding the end of the fishing season. El Niño now generally denotes the unusually persistent warm-water conditions that occur every two to seven years in the Peru Current brought about by atypical circulation patterns in the tropical South Pacific. For reasons not completely understood, the normally persistent easterly trade winds near the equator slacken or reverse. Instead of warm water piling up along the coast of Asia, as it usually does, it flows back in a long period wave toward the east, bringing unusually warm water to the coast of South America. In very strong El Niño events, the warm water moves up the California coast with a much strengthened countercurrent. Usually during such events upwelling winds subside, summer fog is infrequent, and winter rainfall is extremely high. An El Niño event is usually followed by "anti-El Niño" weather that is unusually windy, dry, and cold. Other atypical meteorological events can transport warm nutrient-poor waters northward along the California Coast, strengthening the Davidson Current and simulating El Niño-like conditions including high rainfall.

Coastal Summer Fog

Besides stimulating the food chain, upwelling plays an important part in the cycle of summer fog. Although rain is virtually nonexistent here in the summer, humidity along the shore is the highest of the year. Most people refer to the condensation clouds that dominate coastal summer weather as "fog," though in actuality they are low stratus clouds. Moisture in the air moving in off the open ocean condenses when it cools as it passes over the upwelled nearshore waters. Although this fog can occur at the surface of the ocean or land, moving landward it usually forms predominantly in a belt 500 to 2300 feet above sea level. Although summer fog can blanket virtually all of Marin County, most of it is blocked from penetrating inland by the higher coastal ridges, except where gaps or low-lying areas occur. Summer fog is a dominant seasonal feature of the seaward side of the Marin Peninsula, the west slope of Bolinas Ridge in the Mount Tamalpais area, and particularly the Point Reyes peninsula west of Inverness Ridge; to the north, fog penetrates through the low-lying hills near Tomales inland to about Hicks Valley. Except near Sausalito and Tiburon, summer fog is infrequent along the Marin shoreline of San Francisco and San Pablo bays, though "tule fog"—formed by the cooling of humid air over chilled land—often envelopes this area in winter.

A characteristic of the coastal air column that also greatly affects weather is an inversion layer usually lying at an altitude of about 2300 to 4400 feet. Both above and below this zone air gets cooler with increasing altitude. In contrast, within the inversion layer air gets warmer with increasing altitude. There is also an abrupt transition from moist to dry air low in the inversion layer. As moist ocean air moves onto land it rises, cools off, and moisture condenses as stratus clouds up to the height of the base of the inversion layer, where the air is too warm to allow for condensation. This phenomenon explains why summer views from the top of Mount Tamalpais frequently show just a few ridges peeking through a sea of fog enveloping the rest of the county. As a result, in summer the tops of Mount Tamalpais and other high ridges experience warmer temperatures than nearby lowlands because they are within the tempered inversion layer and bathed in sunny skies above the stratus layer.

Although upwelling is thought of as the driving force behind summer fog, the origin of the air approaching us is also critical. Normally cool air moving in from the northwest over the ocean is ideal for fog production, but occasionally a tongue of high pressure moves over land, and warm air off the continent reaches us from the north or northeast. In this situation, despite upwelling, the ocean cannot cool the warm air sufficiently to produce fog, and the inversion layer may come down to ground level, further hindering the process. The inversion layer also explains why we rarely have summer thunderstorms, even with a copious supply of moist air. This layer blocks air movement to the altitudes necessary for the production of thunderheads, except under the conditions mentioned above when the inversion comes down to ground level.

Summer fog ebbs and flows on a daily cycle. It is most intense at night, dissipates normally in the morning or early afternoon as the air warms, and increases again in the late afternoon as the air cools. It typically ebbs and flows on a several-day cycle as well. While the immediate coast is enjoying cool temperatures, the interior of Marin may be baking in 90-plus-degree weather, with temperatures frequently soaring over 100 degrees further inland in the Central Valley. As temperatures rise in the interior, the low-pressure system there intensifies, causing cool coastal air to flow inland, bringing moist air off the ocean and increasing fog along the coast. As the interior cools over several days, the inflow of air slackens, as does the intensity of coastal fog, until the interior heats up again, renewing the cycle. Although summer fog is often credited with keeping temperatures on the immediate coast low, there is evidence that advection of cool air off the ocean is five to six times more important in lowering temperatures than is loss of solar radiation blocked by the stratus layer (Patton 1956).

Like rainfall, the intensity of summer fog increases from south to north along the California coast, with a corresponding increase in the extent of coast redwood forest. It has been stated or implied that coastal summer fog is the crucial element that maintains coast redwood forests by supplying large amounts of water in the form of "fog drip" when moisture condenses as the air collides with the tall, massive trees and falls to the ground like rain. In actuality, redwoods grow primarily in protected coastal valleys where ground fog, wind, and fog drip are not particularly common. Fog drip is heaviest along ridge crests at the level of maximum stratus layer and where trees are exposed to moisture-laden winds. Fog drip per se is not the limiting factor in the occurrence of redwoods. Rather, the combination of high summer humidity, year-round cool temperatures, and low evapotranspiration, along with a high water table and the alluvial soils of coastal valleys, all provide a nourishing environment for these awesome trees.

Locally, however, fog drip does provide significant additional moisture. Oberlander (1956) measured 2 to 60 inches of precipitation from fog drip at various exposures on the San Francisco Peninsula. The highest measurements, under an exposed tanbark oak, showed more precipitation from fog than is normally recorded in an entire rainy season. Parsons (1960) recorded 9.8 inches beneath a Monterey pine in the Berkeley Hills, and Azevedo and Morgan (1974) recorded 1.4 to 16.7 inches at several sites in the low mountains south of the Eel River Valley, Humboldt County. Much of the precipitation fell during a few heavy fog drip periods. Since rainfall is next to nil in summer, fog drip and humid air are important determinants of the types of plant communities growing within the coastal zone. There the importance of summer moisture is reflected in the dense, rank ground cover beneath Marin County's Douglas fir, Bishop pine, and bay laurel–dominated mixed evergreen forests. Forests in the interior of Marin, away from the consistent penetration of summer fog, usually have very sparse understories or ground cover because of the lack of ground moisture during the summer. The types and distribution of plant communities found in Marin County are described in the pages that follow.

The wind-sculpted California bay forest leaning inland at the Nicasio gap. Drawing by Ane Rovetta, 1989.

MARIN COUNTY
BREEDING BIRD HABITATS

Strip the world of its blossoms, and the higher forms of life must come to a speedy termination. Thus we see the flower playing a wonderfully important part in the cosmos around us . . . the instrument by which Nature brings about the fullness of her perfection in her own good season.

— Mary Elizabeth Parsons,
The Wild Flowers of California

MARIN COUNTY hosts a diverse array of habitats for breeding birds. Most of these habitats equate with the county's plant communities described below. Others do not, and these additional habitats are described briefly in a section following the plant community descriptions.

Marin County Plant Communities

Evolutionary history, varied topography, unusual soils and geology, and wide differences in local climate over short distances have combined to provide Marin County with a diverse flora and a large number of plant communities arranged in a patchy mosaic over the landscape (Figure 5). Marin County hosts eleven major plant communities, of which six can be subdivided into fifteen associations. Consequently, the county is endowed with habitat that supports a wide variety of breeding birds. Because birds generally base their habitat choice on the structure of plant communities rather than on particular plant species (e.g., Verner & Larson 1989), the following descriptions emphasize structure over floristics. These descriptions are condensed from Shuford and Timossi's (1989) *Plant Communities of Marin County, California*, to which the reader is referred for greater detail. The communities and associations described can, of course, grade into one another to varying degrees. The edges of plant communities (ecotones) often support a high diversity of bird species.

Mixed Evergreen Forest

This is the predominant forest type in Marin County and is characterized by closed-canopy stands of several species of broadleaved evergreen hardwoods. Conifers may occur in varying numbers and in some cases may dominate. Because it occupies a broad range of slope, moisture, and elevational gradients, this community is quite variable,

occurring in three main associations that may grade into one another. Mixed evergreen forest grows throughout most of the hilly and mountainous terrain of Marin County.

Coast Live Oak–California Bay–Madrone Forest. This association is dominated by one or more of these evergreen hardwood species: coast live oak *(Quercus agrifolia)*, California bay *(Umbellularia californica)*, and madrone *(Arbutus menziesii)*. California buckeye *(Aesculus californica)* and black oak *(Quercus kellogii)* may be important locally. Dominant trees at maturity average 30 to 80 feet in height. In drier conditions, a true understory is reduced or lacking entirely, with scattered saplings of the dominant trees forming the understory where it exists. In most intermediate conditions, poison oak *(Toxicodendron diversilobum)* and toyon *(Heteromeles arbutifolia)* are important understory components. In moister conditions, especially toward the immediate coast, this forest association can have a well-developed understory of sword fern *(Polystichum munitum)*, huckleberry *(Vaccinium ovatum)*, California hazelnut *(Corylus californica)*, poison oak, and currant *(Ribes spp.)* about 3 to 6 feet in height. This association occurs at low to moderate elevations throughout most of the county.

Tanbark Oak–Madrone–Live Oak–Douglas Fir Forest. This mixed evergreen association is dominated, in varying proportions according to site, by tanbark oak *(Lithocarpus densiflorus)*, madrone, Douglas fir *(Pseudotsuga menziesii)*, coast live oak, and canyon live oak *(Quercus chrysolepis)*. California bay, coast redwood *(Sequoia sempervirens)*, California nutmeg *(Torreya californica)*, and chinquapin *(Castanopsis chrysophylla* var. *minor)* occur locally. At maturity, dominant trees average 30 to 80 feet and occasionally reach 120 feet. This forest is generally rather open under the canopy as the understory consists of scattered saplings of

19

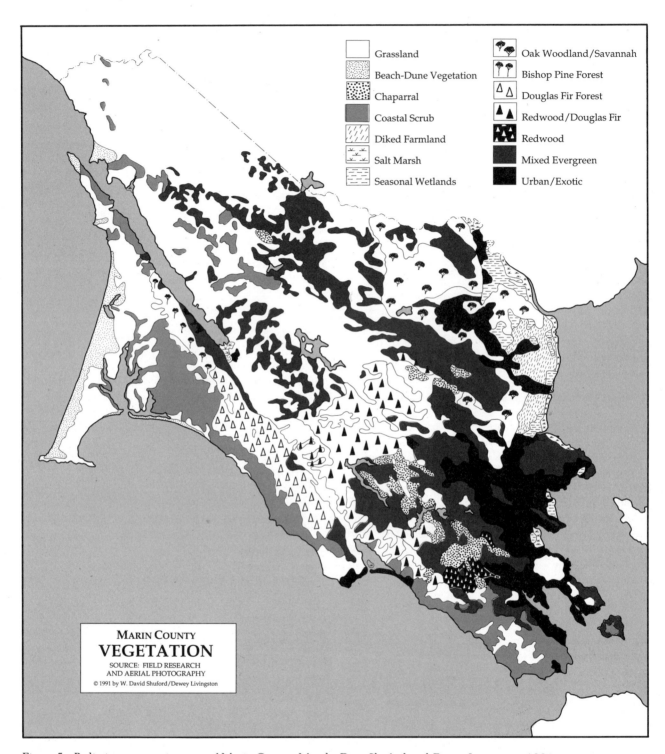

Figure 5. *Preliminary vegetation map of Marin County. Map by Dave Shuford and Dewey Livingston, 1991.*

Oak woodland and oak savannah stand watch on Mount Burdell, Novato. Drawing by Ane Rovetta, 1989.

the dominant trees. This association occupies mid to high elevations on Mount Tamalpais and surrounding ridges and, to a limited degree, Inverness Ridge.

Douglas Fir Forest. This closed-canopy forest is dominated by Douglas fir, which in mature stands averages 100 to 160 feet in height. There may or may not be a secondary canopy of coast live oak, California bay, and blue blossom *(Ceanothus thyrsiflorus)* averaging 25 to 65 feet in height. In most cases there is a dense understory about 4 to 8 feet in height, consisting of huckleberry, salal *(Gaultheria shallon)*, sword fern, California hazelnut, poison oak, red elderberry *(Sambucus callicarpa)*, and thimbleberry *(Rubus parviflorus)*. In Marin County, Douglas fir forest grows mostly on the southern and central portions of Inverness Ridge and locally throughout the Mount Tamalpais and Lagunitus Creek watersheds. In these latter areas, Douglas fir most frequently mixes with coast redwood or with trees of the tanbark oak-madrone-live oak-Douglas fir forest described above.

Oak Woodland and Oak Savannah

In contrast to the mixed evergreen forest, typical oak woodland and oak savannah have open canopies, grassy ground cover below and between the trees, and a predominance of deciduous, rather than live oaks. Oak woodland is distinguished by tree cover greater than 30%, whereas oak savannah consists of isolated trees. The characteristic tree of Marin's oak woodlands and oak savannah is valley oak *(Quercus lobata)*. Although there is no true understory, scattered shrubs such as manzanita *(Arctostaphylos spp.)*, ceanothus *(Ceanothus spp.)*, poison oak, and several species of herbaceous thistles may occur, especially on the edges. The grassy ground cover consists of species characteristic of valley grassland, described below. On deeper

soils on valley floors, valley oaks at maturity vary in height from 30 to 100 feet, whereas smaller oaks grow on shallower soils on steeper slopes. Blue oak *(Quercus douglasii)*, a characteristic tree of oak woodland and oak savannah in hills of the interior Coast Range, grows locally in Marin only in Novato on Mount Burdell and near Black Point. Oak woodland and oak savannah generally occupy relatively dry areas in the interior of Marin County, especially around Novato north of Big Rock Ridge and east of Hicks Valley. A lack of recruitment of sapling oaks threatens the long-term survival of California's oak woodlands and oak savannahs.

Bishop Pine Forest

This forest is one of a number of relict, fire-adapted, closed-cone pine communities that grow in disjunct stands along the California coast. Bishop pine *(Pinus muricata)* is the dominant tree, usually thriving in pure, even-aged stands that reach 60 to 70 feet in height at maturity. Bordering the pines are limited stands of live oak, California bay, tanbark oak, madrone, California buckeye, and wax-myrtle *(Myrica californica)*. The understory of the pines is usually a dense shrub layer about 4 to 8 feet high consisting of huckleberry, salal, coffeeberry *(Rhamnus californica)*, chinquapin, and two species each of manzanita and ceanothus. On deeper soils where the pines reach their greatest stature, the shrub layer is taller and often parklike, with many grassy openings between the shrubs and pines. On steeper slopes and rockier soils, the shrub layer grows as continuous low dense cover. In Marin County, bishop pine forest thrives primarily on granitic soils on the north end of Inverness Ridge on the Point Reyes peninsula. Five

21

*Gnarly bishop pine forest at Tomales Bay State Park.
Drawing by Ane Rovetta, 1985.*

small stands grow on gravelly, sandstone-derived soils east of the San Andreas Fault on Bolinas Ridge and in the vicinity of Carson Ridge (Millar 1986).

Coast Redwood Forest

The essence of the coast redwood forest is a towering canopy of coast redwoods averaging 100 to 130 feet in height, with exceptional trees reaching 250 feet. California bay and tanbark oak may form a subcanopy 50 to 65 feet high. California bay is consistently found along moist drainages, while tanbark oak is found on the edges or in occasional sunny openings in the forest. The understory consists primarily of California hazelnut, huckleberry, western azalea *(Rhododendron occidentale)*, wood rose *(Rosa californica)*, thimbleberry, and patches of sword fern, and is generally open except where it is locally dense along streams. This forest occurs primarily east of the San Andreas Fault in areas of high year-round humidity, hence mostly in the zone of persistent summer fog. Redwoods are widespread on the Mount Tamalpais and Lagunitas Creek watersheds, and are local from there north to the north slopes of Big Rock Ridge.

Grassland

California's grasslands were formerly dominated by perennial bunch grasses, interspersed with numerous annuals. Today these grasslands are dominated by introduced European annuals whose spread was aided and abetted by stock grazing and dry-land farming. Although overall introduced annual grasses now dominate our grasslands, native perennial bunch grasses still persist locally on the immediate coast. Grasslands are widespread in Marin, particularly in the northwestern region of the county. There are two major types of grassland in California and in Marin County: coastal prairie and valley grassland.

Coastal Prairie. Coastal prairie has also been called the *Festuca-Danthonia* grassland after the dominant genera of grasses in this community in California. The dominant species in ungrazed sites on Point Reyes are the perennial bunch grass hairgrass *(Deschampsia holciformis)*, the low-growing form of coyote brush *(Baccharis pilularis* ssp. *pilularis)*, the native biennial grass California brome *(Bromus carinatus)*, sheep sorrel *(Rumex acetosella)*, and bracken fern *(Pteridium aquilinum* var. *pubescens)*. Scattered bushes of the low-growing coyote brush and bracken ferns are characteristic of grassland on the immediate coast but become scarcer inland. The scattered brush and ferns and the mix of perennial and annual grasses give the coastal prairie a more varied structure than that of interior valley grasslands. Typical stands of coastal prairie are less than about one and one-half feet high. There are marked differences between grazed and ungrazed sites. Grazing decreases the average height of plants threefold, reduces the percent cover of perennial and biennial species, and reduces the percentage of native species (Elliott &

Wehausen 1974). Coastal prairie flourishes in the moist coastal zone shrouded by persistent summer fog, and its distribution seems to parallel that of breeding Grasshopper Sparrows (see species account).

Valley Grassland.   The perennial bunch grass that originally dominated the valley grassland was needlegrass *(Stipa pulchra)*. Among others, two major associates were the rye grasses *Elymus glaucus* and *E. triticoides. Stipa pulchra*–dominated grassland now occurs very locally on Mount Tamalpais. Valley grassland over most of the rest of the drier interior of Marin County is dominated by introduced annual grasses and forbs such as wild oats *(Avena fatua* and *A. barbata)*, soft chess *(Bromus mollis)*, ripgut grass *(B. diandrus)*, fescues *(Festuca* spp.), and filaree *(Erodium* spp.). Today valley grassland appears to have fewer species and a less varied structure than coastal prairie. Valley grassland has one or two often dense layers up to about three feet high. On very disturbed or over-grazed sites, one or a few species may predominate, and local patches of noxious introduced thistles often thrive. Valley grassland predominates in the drier portions of the county.

Coastal Beach-Dune Vegetation

Dune communities here reside in a narrow zone above the wave-washed beaches, primarily on Point Reyes. There is a noticeable zonation of plants from the beach inland as a function of both changing physical gradients—exposure to salt spray and sandblasting by persistent onshore winds—and of the length of successional history on stabilized dunes.

Northern Beach Association.   Close to the beach the dunes are covered mostly with perennial grasses, usually less than two feet tall, and a number of low-growing perennial herbs. The latter are generally prostrate, ever-green, and succulent as adaptations to the salty air, strong winds, and shifting sands. The prominent grasses are the perennial American dune grass *(Elymus mollis)* and the introduced European beach grass, or marram grass *(Ammophila arenaria)*. Associated low-growing herbs include sea rocket *(Cakile maritima)*, sand-verbena *(Abronia latifolia)*, silver beach weed *(Ambrosia chamissonis)*, *Atriplex leucophylla*, beach morning glory *(Calystegia soldanella)*, ice plant *(Carpobrotus chilense* and *C. edulis)*, and lupines *(Lupinus* spp.), particularly moving landward. The amount

Beach and dunes at Limantour Estero strand lapped this day by the gentle surf of Drake's Bay. Drawing by Ane Rovetta, 1984.

23

A mosaic of grassland, mixed evergreen forest, and chaparral clothing Big Rock Ridge just east of the Big Rock.
Drawing by Ane Rovetta, 1989.

of plant cover can reach 100% but generally averages about 10%–25%. The introduction for "dune stabilization" of the European beach grass has caused the development of a steep-sided foredune parallel to the beach and abutting a series of wind-molded dunes and coastal swales oriented perpendicular to the beach and coast. Formerly foredunes rose gradually to the landward perpendicular dunes that had many openings among them connected to the beach.

Northern Dune Scrub. Landward, a dune scrub association about three to five feet high occupies the older, more stable dunes. This association is characterized by a number of perennial lupines (*Lupinus albifrons, L. arboreus, L. rivularis,* and *L. chamissonis*), mock heather (*Haplopappus ericoides*), and the low-growing, small-leaved form of coyote brush (*Baccharis pilularis*). These shrubs, mixed with other subshrubs and perennial and annual herbs, usually form an open canopy.

Northern Coastal Scrub

Northern coastal scrub or "soft chaparral" is a two-layered, herb-rich, evergreen shrub community that grows on the lower slopes of hills in the summer fog zone along the immediate coast. It consists of two major associations:

Coyote Brush–Sword Fern Scrub. Coyote brush (*Baccharis pilularis* ssp. *consanguinea*) dominates this association, which has a closed or open overstory about three to seven feet tall. Other important overstory shrubs depending on site and exposure are poison oak, California hazelnut, blue blossom, coffeeberry, thimbleberry, and, in the spring and summer, cow parsnip (*Heracleum lanatum*). The understory varies from a dense, tangled interwoven thicket of ferns along with low woody and herbaceous perennials

and annuals to a more open one devoid of ferns. Western sword fern usually dominates the understory at denser and moister sites, but California blackberry (*Rubus ursinus* and/or *R. vitifolius*), salal, western bracken fern, huckleberry, bush monkey-flower (*Mimulus aurantiacus*), and Douglasiris (*Iris douglasiana*) may be important components along with grasses, sedges (*Carex* spp.), rushes (*Juncus* spp.), and other forbs. This association is widespread on the lower ocean-fronting hills the length of the county, particularly on north-facing slopes.

Coastal Sage–Coyote Brush Scrub. This is a one-layered coastal scrub association dominated by coastal sage (*Artemisia californica*) about two to four feet high with lesser amounts of coyote brush, poison oak, bush monkey-flower, California blackberry, western bracken fern, grasses and forbs, and, in some areas, lupines. Open areas among the bushes in many areas are either bare or rocky soil or, more frequently, are covered with grasses and forbs. Spanning the length of the county on south-facing slopes, this association is most widespread on the southern end of the Point Reyes peninsula and east of the San Andreas Fault from Bolinas Lagoon south to the Golden Gate.

Chaparral

Dense chaparral scrub arises from poor rocky soils on drier inland hills. Dominant chaparral species are evergreen, densely branched, woody summer-dormant shrubs with small thick stiff leaves. Chaparral is highly adapted to fire and regenerates quickly. The shrubs in this community generally form a single dense, intertwining, almost impenetrable overstory layer with a sparse ground cover below.

24

Chaparral associations vary with slope, sun exposure, elevation, soil, and fire history. Chaparral grows here only east of the San Andreas Fault, primarily on Mount Tamalpais, Pine Mountain/Carson Ridge, and Big Rock Ridge. Marin's hills support four chaparral associations:

Chamise Chaparral. Chamise *(Adenostoma fasciculatum)* dominates this association, forming almost unbroken stands on hot xeric sites, usually on south- or west-facing slopes and ridges. Chamise here reaches a height of three to six feet at maturity. Manzanita and ceanothus occur infrequently in this association.

Manzanita Chaparral. Manzanita shrubs three to six feet high dominate this association. Typical manzanita species of the chaparral are Cushing manzanita *(Arctostaphylos cushingiana)*, hoary manzanita *(A. canescens)*, and Marin manzanita *(A. virgata)*. Manzanita and chamise chaparral often alternate on east- and west-facing slopes— for example, along the Old Railroad Grade near the West Point Inn on Mount Tamalpais.

Mixed Chaparral. Mixed chaparral consists of an almost even mix of manzanita, chamise, buck brush *(Ceanothus ramulosus)*, and interior live oak *(Quercus wislizenii var. frutescens)* ranging from three to ten feet high. It abounds on mesic sites, where it usually grades into mixed evergreen forest on shady slopes or in draws. Other shrubs of this association are chaparral pea *(Pickeringia montana)*, coffeeberry, and ceanothus *(Ceanothus sorediatus* and *C. foliosus)*.

Serpentine Chaparral. This association is restricted to biologically harsh serpentine soils. There the shrub canopy is broken with bare ground and rock outcrops, and shrubs generally are dwarfed or stunted, often reaching only about one and one-half to three feet in height. Characteristic shrubs are leather oak *(Quercus durata)*, Jepson's ceanothus *(Ceanothus jepsonii)*, Tamalpais manzanita *(Arctostaphylos montana)*, and Sargent cypress *(Cupressus sargentii)*. Elsewhere it may grow as a fairly large tree; but on Carson Ridge, Sargent cypress grows amid the chaparral as a striking dwarf forest ten to fifteen feet high. Serpentine chaparral occupies extensive areas along the Pine Mountain Fire Road on Carson Ridge and on Mount Tamalpais on Serpentine Knoll and on the Benstein Trail above Potrero Meadows.

Coastal Salt Marsh

Salt marsh is restricted to the upper intertidal zone of protected shallow bays, estuaries, and lagoons. Vertical zonation of saltmarsh plants reflects elevational gradients that affect the frequency and duration of tidal flooding. Bordering the mudflats are pure open stands of cordgrass *(Spartina foliosa)* about one and one-half to three feet tall. Landward, cordgrass is replaced at the mean high water level by thick mats of low-growing salt marsh dominated by pickleweed *(Salicornia virginica)*, generally about four to eighteen inches in height. Other characteristic plants of the upper pickleweed zone are alkali heath *(Frankenia grandifolia)*, marsh rosemary *(Limonium californicum)*, jaumea *(Jaumea carnosa)*, plantain *(Plantago maritima)*, and saltgrass *(Distichlis spicata)*. On isolated mounds or along natural levees of tidal sloughs not subject to frequent flooding grow clumps of gumplant *(Grindelia humilis* or *G. stricta)* and dock *(Rumex occidentalis)* up to about three feet tall. In the grasslandlike upper border of the salt marsh,

A toe hold of coastal salt marsh on the shores of San Pablo Bay abutting the mixed evergreen forest, grassland-blended hills of China Camp State Park. Drawing by Ane Rovetta, 1989.

25

saltgrass and spergularia (*Spergularia* spp.) mix with other salt-tolerant natives and introduced species. Where salt marshes historically graded primarily into brackish marsh and then into freshwater marsh, grassland, or shrub communities, today most salt marshes abruptly abut dikes and roadsides. In brackish situations the marsh is dominated by various forms of bulrush (*Scirpus* spp.) and cattails (*Typha* spp.).

An estimated 60%–95% of the marshland in the San Francisco Bay system has been lost to filling and diking (Nichols & Wright 1971, Josselyn 1983). Remnant stands of salt marsh still persist in Marin County at a number of sites along the shores of San Francisco and San Pablo bays and on the outer coast in the upper reaches of Tomales Bay, Limantour and Drake's esteros, and at Bolinas Lagoon.

Coastal Riparian Forest

In Marin County, willow- and alder-dominated riparian groves border small streams and the edges of ponds and freshwater marshes, where the trees merge with marsh vegetation. Typical overstory trees of our riparian forests are red alder *(Alnus oregona)*, white alder *(A. rhombifolia)*, arroyo willow *(Salix lasiolepis)*, yellow willow *(S. lasiandra)*, big-leaf maple *(Acer macrophyllum)*, and box elder *(A. negundo* ssp. *californicum)*. Near stream and marsh edges willows colonize recently deposited soils and are tolerant of some flooding. Because they reproduce vegetatively, willows often form pure stands with overstory height averaging 10 to 15 feet. Landward, willows usually intergrade with alders, which may provide an overstory canopy 30 to 40 feet high or may grow in pure stands of similar height.

The riparian understory may include saplings of the overstory trees and thickets of California blackberry or Himalaya-berry *(Rubus procerus)* interspersed with a thick herbaceous ground cover. Under natural conditions, alder groves may sometimes have little understory or ground cover, but cattle often eliminate the low vegetation under both alders and willows by grazing and trampling. Riparian forests may grade into a number of other communities. In stream canyons, moisture-loving, shade-tolerant California bay trees may mix with or replace the typical riparian dominants. With the spread of human influence, riparian communities in Marin County, as elsewhere, have been lost or degraded at an alarming rate. Alder and willow riparian thickets are still widespread in drainages on the outer coast, but few remain in the urbanized corridor near the bayshore of eastern Marin.

Freshwater Marsh

Bulrush-Cattail Marsh. Typical freshwater marsh thrives in shallow standing or slow-moving water on the edges of ponds, lakes, or streams. Cattail and California bulrush *(Scirpus californicus)* border open water in mixed association with each other, or in pure stands, averaging five to eight feet high. Assemblages of other marsh species, usually about one and one-half to five feet high, grow in shallower water or damp soil. These include rushes *(Juncus* spp.), sedges *(Cyperus eragrostis* and *Carex* spp.), spike rush *(Eleocharis* spp.), curly dock *(Rumex crispus)*, sheep sorrel, water parsley *(Oenanthe sarmentosa)*, and the bur-reed *Sparganium eurycarpum.* The county's largest freshwater marsh and willow riparian stand is located at Olema Marsh.

Riparian forest of Olema Valley flanked by Douglas fir forest, mixed evergreen forest, and grassland on Inverness Ridge. Drawing by Ane Rovetta, 1989.

Riparian growth hemming in the view of pond turtles at Five Brooks Pond. Drawing by Ane Rovetta, 1985.

Coastal Swale.   Another type of freshwater marsh grows primarily along the outer coast where water reaches the surface in depressions in coastal prairie or among dunes. Water channels are choked with water cress *(Nasturtium officinale)*, water parsley, and marsh pennywort *(Hydrocotyle ranunculacea* and *H. verticillata)* ranging up to 1½ feet in height. In shallower water or on saturated mud, the swale may be dominated by pure stands up to 4 feet high of the bulrush *Scirpus microcarpus* or slough sedge *(Carex obnupta)*. On drier ground grow clumps of various grasses, interspersed with plants such as marsh checkerbloom *(Sidalcea rhizomata)*, bog lupine *(Lupinus polyphyllus* var. *grandifolius)*, Siberian montia *(Montia sibirica)*, the monkeyflower *Mimulus guttatus*, and poison hemlock *(Conium maculatum)*. Riparian-like patches of wax-myrtle, 6 to 12 feet high, sometimes border swales. Coastal swales in damp meadow soil may be dominated by clumps of rushes and sedges mixed with grasses.

Exotic Plants

Exotic plants have been introduced widely in California and Marin County. In urban and suburban settings, ornamental plants, whether alone or mixed with native species, provide shade and beauty for human inhabitants and food and shelter for wildlife. Many exotics have escaped and become naturalized in native communities with varying effects. Some introduced plants are inconspicuous immigrants sharing the resources with dominant native species, whereas other aggressive exotics have pushed out and replaced the rightful heirs of our plant communities. As noted above, Mediterranean annual grasses have entirely changed the character of our native grasslands, and European beach grass has altered both the structure and flora of dune communities. The range and extent of effects that introduced plants have had on the native flora and on the birds and other native wildlife that depend on them are very incompletely known.

Of the many introduced species naturalized in the county, only the most conspicuous, widespread, or offensive ones are mentioned here. Many species of *Eucalyptus* have been introduced to California—the most common and widespread is bluegum eucalyptus *(E. globulus)*. Extensive stands, planted originally as windbreaks and woodlots, now grow as small patches of forest in what formerly were almost treeless expanses of grasslands in Marin County. Mature eucalyptus groves may form towering canopies reaching over 100 feet skyward. The volatile oils produced by eucalypts preclude the establishment of a rich understory flora. The most frequent understory plants are sapling eucalypts, blackberries, and in some areas, the exotic and blanketing German ivy *(Senecio mikanioides)*. Eucalyptus groves have shown only a limited ability to invade forest edges and are most successful in penetrating grasslands and brush communities. Planted Monterey cypress

(Cupressus macrocarpa) forms a similar (though infrequently self-generating) community of lesser stature around farmyards, mostly on the outer coast.

Scotch broom *(Cytisus scoparius)* and French broom *(C. monspessulanus)* are widely naturalized along the county's disturbed roadsides. French broom has been especially successful in invading native communities of brush, open woodland, and grassy hillsides. Other conspicuous invaders are the showy white-plumed jubata (Andean) grass—a close relative of the less invasive pampas grass—and gorse *(Ulex europaeus)*, a dense thorny shrub that is difficult to eradicate.

Disturbed fields and roadsides usually support thickets of introduced annual weeds, some of which may reach 6 to 10 feet in height. Conspicuous in such areas are sweet fennel *(Foeniculum vulgare)*, poison hemlock, wild oat *(Avena fatua)*, teasel *(Dipsacus sativus)*, and other weedy herbs and exotic grasses of disturbed valley grassland.

While many exotics are here to stay, extensive monitoring and eradication efforts are needed to ensure the future integrity of our distinctive native flora and plant communities. When known, the extent of use by breeding birds of exotic plant species and communities is described in the species accounts.

Additional Breeding Bird Habitats

Breeding birds may use a number of habitats beyond the standard plant communities, but these can usually be described verbally without resort to a formal classification scheme. For example, rocky cliffs may provide nest sites for White-throated Swifts, Cliff Swallows, Common Ravens, and Rock Wrens. Rocky sea stacks, wave-battered cliffs, and offshore islands are home to bustling colonies of storm-petrels, cormorants, gulls, alcids, and scattered pairs of oystercatchers. Human structures may supply nesting shelter for a variety of birds, including American Kestrels, Pacific-slope Flycatchers, Black Phoebes, several species of swallows, American Robins, European Starlings, House Finches, and House Sparrows, among others. Although a pair of Killdeer may select for their nest site the worn pebbles along a stream margin, they seem equally at home incubating their eggs in similar substrate in driveways or on gravel roofs. Ponds may furnish the requisites for species such as Pied-billed Grebes or American Coots that build floating nests.

For many species of landbirds the nesting habitat and the foraging habitat are one and the same. Other species may conceal their nests near the edge in one plant community and forage in an adjoining community or in the

Bishop pines lean outward from Mount Vision toward Tomales Bay. Drawing by Ane Rovetta, 1989.

surrounding air space. Different species of swallows may have distinct and fairly easily described structural requirements for nest sites, as well as presumably distinct, but not so easily described, air space requirements for foraging. Most seabirds breed on islands or steep mainland cliffs and forage considerable distances at sea. Ducks often nest in upland areas but forage in aquatic habitats and soon lead their young there as well. Similarly, herons and egrets select relatively predator-proof nesting sites high in trees, on islands, or in marshes over water and may forage in nearby or distant wetlands. Hence it is not possible to classify each species by preference for one or several habi-

tats, any of which will satisfy all their needs at a given time. Not only may a single species be dependent on more than one habitat while nesting, but its habitat needs also may change during the course of the breeding season. Habitat descriptions and preferences beyond those portrayed here can be found in the individual species accounts; discussion of species membership in various bird communities can be found in the Results and Discussion section (p. 61). Changes in land use that may have affected the suitability of various habitats in Marin County for breeding birds are discussed in the section that follows.

Grass-covered hills with mixed evergreen forest filling draws above Nicasio Reservoir. Drawing by Ane Rovetta, 1989.

HISTORY OF LAND USE
IN MARIN COUNTY

How can you expect the birds to sing when their groves are cut down?

— Henry David Thoreau,
Walden

FOR THOUSANDS of years people we now call Coast Miwoks lived lightly on the land in Marin and part of adjacent Sonoma County. In aboriginal times their entire population numbered about 2000 persons (Kelly 1978). These Native Americans subsisted by harvesting the abundant sea life, stream-dwelling fish, upland game, and a variety of fruits, berries, seeds, and roots that supplemented their staple of acorns. Although relatively little is known of their history, by all accounts they lived in harmony with nature, preserving the bounty that greeted them when they first occupied these lands.

This way of life was destined to pass as the seeds of enormous change were sown in the late 1500s and early 1600s by the arrival of the earliest European explorers—Drake, Cermeño, and Vizcaino—on Marin's shores. In 1776 the Spanish established a mission and *presidio* in San Francisco, and in the same year traveled north to explore parts of what we now call Marin County (Munro-Fraser 1880). The next wave of expansionism broke with the founding of the San Rafael mission in 1817. Forced evangelization of the native population soon led, via demoralization and disease, to the disintegration of their culture (Kelly 1978). By 1851 or 1852 only about 250 Coast Miwoks remained.

The demise of native wildlife populations—and even whole ecosystems—at the hands of the invading Europeans was equally swift. Exploitation of the forests began almost as soon as Europeans visited these shores. The first commercial logging was established in Larkspur in 1816 to cut cordwood for Spanish troops at the *presidio* (Fairley 1987). In the 1820s and 1830s Yankee whalers and trading ships visiting San Francisco Bay laid anchor at Sausalito for wood and water. Wood was needed in quantity to fuel the whaler's trypots, and the mission in San Rafael undoubtedly used wood extensively for various activities during its tenure from 1817 to 1834.

With the secularization of the missions in 1834, timber was a big attraction on the new land grants at Rancho Corte Madera del Presidio (1834) and Rancho Sausalito (1836). Much of Marin's shoreline along San Francisco Bay was heavily forested, and the wood was quickly harvested. Early logging concentrated on the lower slopes of Mount Tamalpais, in the bottoms of canyons where giant redwoods grew and where timber could be easily transported via ships on the bay. Marin's first sawmill was built in Cascade Canyon on the Tamalpais slope in about 1836 (Munro-Fraser 1880, Mason & Park 1975, Fairley 1987). Although some of the timber supplied local needs, such as construction of ranch buildings and fuel for brick kilns, most was shipped to San Francisco—redwood for wharf pilings and warehouses, other trees for cordwood to heat city buildings. Cordwood was also cut in the Novato area, where oak and bay were the dominant trees. Attesting to the rapidity of exploitation, all the choice redwoods were felled in Mill Valley by 1852, when a steam mill was moved to Bolinas, though at the time Corte Madera was still being actively logged (Fairley 1987).

Fueled by the boom of the Gold Rush, the 1850s to 1870s were the era of greatest timber exploitation. Lumbering concentrated then near Bolinas and on the north slopes and ridges of Mount Tamalpais. Dogtown became a major logging and lumber center, beginning with its first mill in 1851 (Fairley 1987). By 1880 about 15 million board feet of lumber had been cut near Bolinas (Munro-Fraser 1880, Fairley 1987). Logging continued in the Bolinas area throughout the nineteenth century. Much of it was to supply cordwood for San Francisco houses and, after 1875, to fuel steam locomotives. Large amounts of cordwood also came from the north slopes of Mount Tamalpais, from which it was shipped to Ross Landing (Corte Madera); some was burned at San Quentin prison, but most was sent to San Francisco. Tanbark oak was cut for its bark, used to tan hides, and the remainder was sold for cordwood (Rothwell 1959). Extensive woodcutting in this area also supplied railroad ties and heavy studding for the White's Hill tunnel of the North Pacific Coast Railroad, fence posts for big ranches being subdivided for dairy farms, and cordwood for the steam engines of the second Pioneer Paper Mill on Papermill Creek (Rothwell 1959, Fairley 1987).

Logging continued in the lower drainage of Lagunitas Creek until 1903, when the supply of old-growth timber was just about exhausted (Fairley 1987). Except at Muir Woods, ultimately all the old-growth timber on Mount Tamalpais fell to the woodsman's ax and saw. The introduction of oil (1902), gas, and electricity ended the supremacy of cordwood and relaxed, somewhat, the intense pressure on Marin's forests. Around 1918, a second round of cutting occurred in the area to be flooded by Alpine Dam. A mill operated in the lower Lagunitas Creek drainage until 1951; the site was flooded with the completion of the Kent Lake dam in 1953. Between 1946 to 1951 this mill sawed over 21 million board feet of lumber (Fairley 1987). Much timber was cut on Inverness Ridge in the late 1950s and 1960s, and the last logging in the county, on Bolinas Ridge above Dogtown, was shut down by court order in 1969 (Mason 1981, D. Livingston pers. comm.).

We'll never know the full effect of all this logging on the county's birdlife, but it must have been tremendous. The loss of most of the old-growth forest on the slopes of Mount Tamalpais, largely in a period of fifty years, must have displaced great numbers of birds breeding in these habitats. One can only speculate, but it seems very likely that the populations of largely old growth–dependent species such as the Spotted Owl must have plummeted during this period. Great fires (usually human caused), such as those in 1929 and 1945, were similarly destructive (Fairley 1987), but the return of nutrients to the soil in these cases undoubtedly speeded recovery.

Logging also filled the creeks and estuaries in downstream drainages with silt, altering these habitats profoundly. Boat traffic was restricted in Bolinas Lagoon, Tomales Bay, Corte Madera Creek, and Richardson Bay by the silt from logging and to a lesser degree, in most cases, from plowing of fields (Munro-Fraser 1880, Rothwell 1959, Melbostad 1969, Mason & Park 1975, Fairley 1987). Sedimentation from these sources, dredging of channels and harbors, leveeing of tidal marshes, and, particularly, the transport into San Pablo Bay of debris from the massive hydraulic mining in the Sierra Nevada from 1853 to 1884 all increased the amount of tidal marsh in Marin County (Atwater et al. 1979, Josselyn & Buchholz 1984). Nevertheless, the extent of historic expansion of tidal marsh habitat has been far outweighed by losses. In fact, tidal marsh habitat in the greater San Francisco Bay estuary has decreased historically by 60% to 95% (Nichols & Wright 1971, Atwater et al. 1979). As of 1984 only

about 32% of the tidal marsh habitat that existed in Marin County in 1850 remained (Josselyn & Buchholz 1984). Large tracts of tidal marsh were first diked off around Novato and San Rafael in the late 1800s, with diking accelerating in the 1900s, particularly after 1940 (Atwater et al. 1979, Josselyn & Buchholz 1984). Since 1974, several projects have restored some of these marshes to tidal action, though the total acreage is small compared to habitat lost.

The effect on bird populations of these losses of tidal marsh habitat has been great, though little documented except for certain species. Loss of salt marsh is the main reason for the decline of the endangered California Clapper Rail, and marsh loss and fragmentation currently threaten populations of salt marsh–breeding Black Rails and Song Sparrows (see accounts). Many other birds that use these habitats for breeding, foraging, or roosting have likewise been affected.

Fortunately, many birds reside in the seasonal wetlands formed by the alteration of tidal marshes. But these wetlands are also being lost rapidly to urban encroachment (Granholm 1989). Between 1956 and 1988, 61% of the seasonal wetlands in south San Francisco Bay were lost. From 1975 to 1988, 35% of the remaining seasonal wetlands in San Francisco Bay were lost and 10% of those in San Pablo Bay. During the latter period, Marin County lost 9% of its seasonal wetlands, and in the foreseeable future it will lose an additional 13% if all currently planned projects are implemented. The impact on birds inhabiting seasonal wetlands is obvious.

The damming of Marin's streams for municipal water supplies beginning in 1873 (Fairley 1987) may have doomed breeding American Dippers in the Lagunitas Creek watershed (see account). But on the whole, the loss of streamside and upland habitat to inundation has been balanced by the expansion of aquatic habitat and the accretion of some marshland. Female Common Mergansers and their broods now ply the waters of Kent Lake while Pied-billed Grebes, American Coots, Marsh Wrens, Red-winged Blackbirds, and Song Sparrows suspend their nests in marshy fringes of many of the county's eight major reservoirs. In contrast to these upstream benefits to birds, it seems likely that loss of fresh water downstream must have degraded some of Marin's important wetlands.

Agricultural uses have also taken their toll on the land. Although various crops have been grown in Marin, cattle and, particularly, dairy ranching have dominated the agricultural economy since the early days of white settlement. With the establishment of the San Rafael mission in 1817, large herds of Mexican longhorn cattle ranged freely on the land, to be annually slaughtered for their hides and tallow (Mason & Park 1975, Fairley 1987). In 1834 the San Rafael mission owned 4500 cattle (Mason & Park 1971). With the secularization of the missions that year, thousands of cattle soon roamed the large land grants throughout the county. In response to the boom of the Gold Rush the dairy industry prospered, particularly on the lush grasslands of Point Reyes. In 1870 Point Reyes boasted the largest dairy operation in California (Mason & Park 1971); the assessor's rolls reported 25,390 cows—the highest number for any county in the state (Fairley 1987). Overgrazing was noticed as early as the 1850s in coastal areas of California (Heady 1977). The introduction of alien grasses, dry-land farming practices, and year-round concentrated grazing all combined to drastically alter native grasslands from ones dominated by perennial bunch grasses to ones dominated by exotic annual grasses (see Bird Habitats section p. 22). The effects of these changes on bird populations are undocumented but must have been great.

Agricultural practices have also inadvertently fostered the pervasive expansion of species such as the European Starling (introduced) and Brown-headed Cowbird (native) that have adversely affected many native hole-nesting and cup-nesting landbirds, respectively (see accounts). Grazing and land clearing (for various purposes) have reduced and degraded Marin County's riparian habitat, though to an unknown degree as no inventories have been taken.

Direct exploitation of the region's wildlife also exacted a heavy toll. In fact, Stine (MS) concluded that the California game trade "is the foremost example of rapid commercial plunder of a region's wildlife to be found on this continent." The demise or decline of coastal populations of whales; sea otters, fur seals, and other pinnipeds; anadromous fish; shellfish; and upland game such as tule elk, grizzly and black bears, and various furbearers has been relatively well documented (Grinnell, Dixon, & Linsdale 1937; Skinner 1962; Stine MS). Less is known of impacts on bird populations. Nevertheless, Grinnell et al. (1918) concluded that in California "beyond question waterfowl and upland game birds have both on the average decreased by fully one-half within the past forty years."

Perhaps the first extensive exploitation of the region's bird populations was at the Farallon Islands, where Russian sealers harvested the meat and eggs of breeding seabirds. Between 1812 and 1827 they annually killed 5000 to 10,000 seabirds, peaking at 50,000 in 1828 (Stine MS). The Russians skinned the birds and shipped the dried meat to Fort Ross, where it was a highly prized food item. Fort Ross also served as a supply center for fur operations in Alaska and Kamchatka. The Russians at Fort Ross in 1827 and 1828 shipped nine sea lion bladders containing hundreds of pounds of insulating feathers of Farallon seabirds to Nova Arkangelsk (Sitka) in Russian America (Stine MS).

The intensity of exploitation of wildlife resources accelerated with the rapid increase of the human population at the time of the Gold Rush. The commercial harvest of Common Murre eggs on the Farallon Islands from 1848

to the early 1900s had a devastating effect on populations of murres and most other species of seabirds breeding on those islands (Ainley & Lewis 1974). There appears to be no record of exploitation of seabird colonies on the Marin County coastline, but it seems unlikely that any large rookery went unmolested at a time of unrestrained harvesting practices. Market hunting rapidly depleted populations of waterfowl, shorebirds, and Clapper Rails around San Francisco Bay (Grinnell et al. 1918). One observer thus described the decline in duck numbers in the Marin County area: "In 1876 ducks were very plentiful in all the marshes from Sausalito north to Petaluma, Napa and Vallejo. In those days it was easy for a boy to kill from twenty to thirty ducks in a day's shooting and very much larger bags were obtained by experienced hunters. Today [1913], in the region between Sausalito and Novato, I think it is safe to say there is not one duck in the marsh now where there were a hundred then" (Grinnell et al. 1918). Egrets were also shot for their feathers, in demand by the millinery trade, leading to their near extinction in the Bay Area at the turn of the century (see accounts). Although measures to protect wildlife were passed in California as early as 1852, it was not until 1913 with the prohibition on the sale of game in the state and the passage of the Federal Migratory Bird Treaty Act that wildlife began to be given a semblance of the protection we see today (Grinnell et al. 1918).

As enlightenment spread regarding the need to conserve our exploited wildlife resources, the "indirect" impacts of an expanding human population continued to negatively affect the county's birdlife. These impacts fall into two broad categories: direct conversion of wildlife habitat to industrial, agricultural, and residential uses; and indirect contamination or degradation of habitat from human activities. Marin County's population is now concentrated in the eastern urban corridor along Highway 101, dominated by light industry, service-oriented businesses, residential neighborhoods, and their attendant impacts. Rural West Marin has a ranching- and tourist-based economy, with much of the land there set aside in federal or state parks or protected by agricultural zoning (Figure 6). Throughout most of its history the county's population and development have concentrated along the shores of San Francisco and San Pablo bays because of the easy transportation links to nearby population centers. From 323 inhabitants at the time of the first census in 1850, the county's population has grown exponentially to 230,096 people in 1990 (U.S. Bureau of the Census). The postwar boom saw the population expand dramatically from 52,907 people in 1940 to 206,038 in 1970. The impacts on the land have followed a similar pattern, as detailed above, with regard to the loss of tidal marshes and seasonal wetlands.

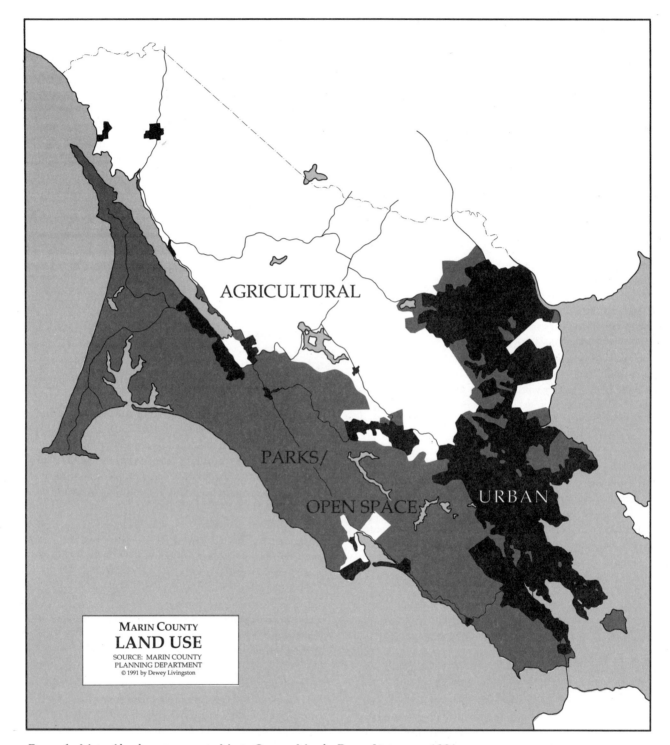

Figure 6. Map of land use patterns in Marin County. Map by Dewey Livingston, 1991.

The impact of a human population is a function not only of population size, but also of the affluence of that population and the disruptiveness of the technologies providing the goods consumed (Ehrlich & Ehrlich 1990). The impacts of technology were observed and decried early in Marin County's history with respect to logging (see Munro-Fraser 1880). More subtle and insidious impacts soon began to be noted. Beginning in 1884, the second Pioneer Paper Mill on Lagunitas Creek dumped the waste water, laced with acid and dyes, from its pulp vats into a brick sewer and then directly into the creek below. These wastes caused heavy silt to form in the creekbed from Taylorsville to Tomales Bay. The mill owners expressed concern over this problem but had found no solution when the mill was forced to close its doors in the financial crisis of 1893 (Rothwell 1959).

More recently, our high consumption rates were ultimately responsible for major oil spills in 1971, 1984, and 1986 that despoiled Marin's coastline and killed or debilitated thousands of birds (Smail et al. 1972, PRBO 1985, Page et al. 1990). Chemical contaminants from urban, agricultural, and industrial activities have been detected in the tissues of many species of waterbirds in San Francisco Bay, often at levels known to impair reproductive success (Ohlendorf et al. 1988, Ohlendorf & Fleming 1988). The demise of Peregrine Falcon and Osprey populations, here and throughout the country, are among the foremost indicators of pesticide pollution in our environment, warning of the direct threats to humans as well from our misuse of technology. These are but a few examples of advanced technologies gone awry as detected in birds.

Fortunately a strong environmental movement coalesced in Marin County in the 1960s and 1970s to fight unrestricted development and to preserve large (and small) tracts of land such as Point Reyes National Seashore and the Golden Gate National Recreation Area. While our local environmental victories are impressive, and should be duly lauded, much remains to be done. Even though the county's population has begun to stabilize through restrictive zoning, traffic continues to increase from the relentless population expansion of nearby counties, and our as-yet-unchecked affluent lifestyle keeps on affecting wildlife. Protecting land and wildlife here in Marin is not enough as the effects of our lifestyles range way beyond county borders. What new habitat changes will our breeding birds face as nesting time approaches yet again with each revolution of the Earth around the sun?

*Turkey Vultures lazily soar over grassland and mixed evergreen forest on the hills surrounding Soulajoule Reservoir.
Drawing by Ane Rovetta, 1985.*

TIMING OF BREEDING

Yet the coming and going of the birds is more or less a mystery and a surprise. We go out in the morning, and no thrush or vireo is to be heard; we go out again, and every tree and grove is musical; yet again, and all is silent. Who saw them come? Who saw them depart?

— John Burroughs,
Wake-Robin

THE BREEDING SEASONS of birds are typically timed to take advantage of periodic (often mild) conditions so that the young hatch out when appropriate foods are abundantly available (Welty & Baptista 1988). The inherited rhythms of breeding roughly match the seasonal rhythms of the environment as adaptions not only to food supply or mild weather, but in some cases to availability of vegetative cover, nest sites, nest materials, or avoidance of predation or competition. As ultimate factors driving adaptation, these necessities do not always proximally trigger the unfolding of events in the breeding cycle. Some of the more important proximate factors that actually trigger the initiation or termination of breeding include day length, temperature, rainfall, and food availability. In some cases environmental conditions may act as both ultimate and proximate factors influencing the timing of breeding. Only rarely will a single factor determine the annual breeding schedule of a species.

The timing of breeding for a single species can vary with latitude or altitude, between local populations breeding in different habitats, and from year to year. Moreover, nesting phenology can vary greatly among many species in the same area. Some species may not breed at all in a given year unless certain environmental conditions are met. An understanding of variability in the timing of breeding, though fascinating in its own right, has practical value in aiding the planning of a strategy for a breeding bird atlas project and in interpreting its results. Without a knowledge of the timing of local breeding events it is difficult to know when to concentrate field work to best advantage or how to interpret the significance of observations collected during atlas field work.

Patterns of variation in the timing of breeding of birds are generally attributable to variation in the natural environment, though the linkage between timing and particular causative factors is not often clear. In one regard, the climate on the central California coast seems to exhibit little seasonal variability as we experience relatively mild temperatures year round. On the other hand, we do have distinct rainy and dry seasons. Moreover, rainfall patterns here can vary greatly both within the rainy season and among years, while ocean conditions can also vary tremendously from year to year. Taken as a whole, our climate influences not only the timing and length of the breeding season but also the annual variation in these parameters.

From his studies of the timing of breeding in the Sacramento Valley, Davis (1933) concluded that on the whole, flesh-eating species tended to start breeding before omnivorous and insectivorous species, which generally preceded vegetable and seed-eating birds. These patterns seem to hold for the coast as well, though for either region there are numerous exceptions. Another pattern that seems to apply in most areas is that year-round resident species tend to breed before summer residents, though again there are exceptions. For example, California Quail tend to initiate egg laying here in May (PRBO files, D. Shuford pers. obs.), well after most other year-round residents and after some summer residents such as Allen's Hummingbirds, Orange-crowned Warblers, and Wilson's Warblers do (see below).

Because Marin County's climate is so mild, the breeding season here is lengthy. Two of the earliest breeders are hummingbirds. Anna's Hummingbirds (year-round residents) come into breeding condition in late November and early December before the winter solstice, when day length approaches the shortest of the year (Pitelka 1951a, Williamson 1956). Nesting itself commences in December and probably reaches a peak in January and February, the coldest and generally the wettest months of the year. Rainfall seems to be the main climatic factor influencing the inherent rhythm of the breeding cycle. Once males begin to come into breeding condition, a period of consecutive days of rainfall, rather than the actual amount, seems to abruptly increase territorial establishment and the commencement of other breeding activities. These adaptations seemingly ensure breeding in a period when food plants are most numerous. Allen's Hummingbirds arrive in the San Francisco Bay area in mid- to late January and begin to lay eggs in early to mid-March (rarely by mid-Feb; Pitelka 1951a). Thus this hummingbird also begins nesting in the rainy season, and its arrival here seems to be timed to coincide with the initiation of blooming of particular nectar-producing plants, presumably stimulated by winter rains and early spring warmth (see account).

Great Horned Owls are also very early nesters and begin laying eggs here in February (M. Cohen in litt.). Great Blue Herons commence egg laying at Audubon Canyon ranch from early to mid-February, and their initiation of first clutches may peak from early to late March (Pratt 1974). Killdeer may lay eggs here in early March (D. Shuford pers. obs.). Spotted Owls, Red-tailed Hawks, and Red-shouldered Hawks all are incubating eggs at least by mid- to late March (PRBO files). Clapper Rails begin laying in Marin County by early March (Evens & Page 1983), Scrub Jays at least by mid-March (PRBO files), and salt marsh-breeding Song Sparrows by late February or early March (Johnston 1956a, D. Shuford pers. obs.). Many resident landbirds begin egg laying in late March or early April, including Chestnut-backed Chickadees, Plain Titmice, Bushtits, Bewick's Wrens, Wrentits, Savannah Sparrows, upland-breeding Song Sparrows, and White-crowned Sparrows (PRBO files, Johnston 1956a, Geupel & DeSante 1990). Several resident waterbirds—Double-crested Cormorants, Mallards, and American Coots—begin egg laying in late March to early April (Ainley & Boekelheide 1990, D. Shuford pers. obs.). Overall, April and May appear to be the peak months for egg laying here for both landbirds and waterbirds.

For summer residents (migrants), the timing of breeding in Marin County corresponds roughly to the timing of spring arrival here (Table 4). For most species there is about a four- to five-week lag between first arrival of males and egg laying of females. For example, Orange-crowned Warblers arrive here in late February to early March and begin egg laying by at least early April (PRBO files), and Wilson's Warblers arrive in late March and begin egg laying in late April (Stewart & Darling 1972, Stewart 1973). There are of course a number of exceptions to this rule. American Goldfinches, though resident in the county, are largely absent from Point Reyes until late March. Despite this relatively early arrival, American Goldfinches do not begin to nest on Point Reyes until the third to fourth week of May (PRBO files), presumably because nesting and hatching of young is timed to coincide with the maturation of abundant seed crops. In the Sacramento Valley, American Goldfinches can start laying eggs in late April (Davis 1933), presumably because seed maturation is early in that region's dry, hot climate. Most species that glean insects from foliage can start breeding earlier than seed eaters because of the relatively early bloom of insect populations. The relationship of the arrival of aerial insectivores such as swallows to timing of breeding is deceptive.

Tree Swallows start to arrive in Marin County in numbers in mid- to late February (Table 4), but do not begin laying eggs on Point Reyes until early May (PRBO files). Although adults can survive during rainy weather early in the spring, by subsisting on berries or perhaps traveling some distance to find insects (see account), young can not; total failure of nests has been documented here during unseasonal rains in June (Stewart 1972).

Also because of our mild climate, many species here can raise two or even three broods a year, particularly resident landbirds (DeSante & Baptista 1989, Geupel & DeSante 1990, G.R. Geupel & D.F. DeSante pers. comm.). Although most landbird young have fledged by late July, nests of some species such as Barn Swallows may be active until late August or, rarely, early September (B. Baez & D. Shuford pers. obs.), and American Goldfinches, rarely, are still feeding fledged young in mid-September (J.G. Evens pers. obs.). Young of many of our species of breeding seabirds fledge in August and September or even later (Ainley & Boekelheide 1990). The Ashy Storm-Petrel provides an extreme example of an extended breeding season. At the Farallon Islands, Ashies lay eggs mostly from early May to late August (sometimes later), and young fledge from early September to mid-November and, rarely, through December. Although data are lacking for this region, Red Crossbills elsewhere in their breeding range are known to breed in any month of the year (see account).

Given this great variability in timing of nesting, what are the factors that initiate or terminate breeding? Of the proximate factors, day length seems to have the greatest influence through its effect on the waxing and waning of gonadal development (Welty & Baptista 1988). As noted above for the Anna's Hummingbird, rainfall is a contributing factor to the initiation of breeding. Mewaldt and King (1977) concluded that warm temperatures and dry weather in the prenesting period advanced breeding in White-crowned Sparrows and cool rainy weather delayed it. Also in White-crowned Sparrows the timing of termination of breeding is directly related to the amount of winter rainfall during the previous year, such that breeding extends later into the summer after winters of heavy rainfall (DeSante & Baptista 1989). Presumably increased rainfall prolongs the growing season of green plants upon which grazing insects depend and hence the availability of these insects for the sparrows to feed their young. In arid parts of their range, California Quail breed irregularly depending on the amount of winter rainfall preceding the spring nesting season (Leopold et al. 1976). In dry years, quail are inhibited by chemicals (phytoestrogens) in stunted forbs and grasses, and few or no young are produced during the short breeding season. In contrast, in wet years lush forb growth supplies large amounts of seeds for quail consumption, stimulating vigorous and extended breeding (young hatched as late as September). Although the initiation of

Table 4.   Arrival dates of Marin County landbirds with comparisons to other regions of California. Data reported as average arrival date (x̄), number of years with data (n), and the span of first arrival dates (range). Lack of data for particular species may reflect infrequent records of the species, poor coverage of appropriate habitat, or difficulty of distinguishing individual migrants from birds of smaller resident populations.

	Palomarin[1], Point Reyes 1967-1989 x̄ (n) range	Marin County[2] ~1900-1980 x̄ (n) range	Berkeley Area[3] 1911-1947 x̄ (n) range	Northern California[4] 1972-1984 x̄ (n) range	Southern California[5] 1972-1984 x̄ (n) range
Vaux's Swift	- -	- -	- -	4/6 (6) 3/26-4/19	4/12 (15) 4/4-4/19
Black-chinned Hummingbird	- -	- -	- -	3/26 (5) 3/11-4/9	3/25 (10) 2/25-4/11
Allen's Hummingbird	2/5 (19) 1/24-2/27	2/5 (27) 1/16-2/28	2/13 (30) 1/29-2/24	- -	- -
Olive-sided Flycatcher	4/17 (18) 4/13-4/26	4/18 (23) 4/7-4/30	4/19 (30) 3/28-5/5	4/14 (6) 4/9-4/22	4/12 (14) 3/19-4/29
Western Wood-Pewee	5/15 (11) 4/24-6/7	- (4) 4/14-4/26	5/1 (13) 4/18-5/8	4/15 (6) 4/9-4/21	4/13 (14) 4/3-4/24
Pacific-slope Flycatcher	3/27 (16) 3/18-4/8	3/25 (16) 3/11-4/5	3/26 (32) 3/12-4/9	3/22 (5) 3/12-4/4	3/14 (5) 3/2-3/22
Ash-throated Flycatcher	4/26 (13) 4/10-5/9	- -	- -	4/9 (5) 4/2-4/15	3/31 (15) 3/22-4/9
Western Kingbird	- -	4/5 (5) 4/1-4/11	- -	3/23 (5) 3/2-3/31	3/14 (14) 3/5-4/3
Purple Martin	- -	4/7 (13) 3/6-4/30	- -	- -	- -
Tree Swallow	2/13 (19) 1/20-3/8	2/22 (12) 2/3-3/5	- -	- -	- -
Violet-green Swallow	2/25 (18) 2/9-3/19	2/21 (11) 2/6-3/13	- -	- -	- -
N. Rough-winged Swallow	3/19 (15) 3/8-3/31	3/7 (7) 2/29-3/15	- -	- -	- -
Cliff Swallow	3/24 (18) 3/12-4/10	3/18 (16) 3/9-3/29	3/22 (11) 3/5-4/7	- -	- -
Barn Swallow	3/15 (14) 2/24-4/8	3/11 (14) 3/5-3/19	- -	- -	- -
House Wren	- -	- -	3/21 (21) 3/4-4/6	- -	- -
Swainson's Thrush	4/27 (19) 4/19-5/4	4/26 (20) 4/15-5/4	4/24 (32) 4/14-5/5	4/21 (5) 4/18-4/28	4/21 (15) 4/6-5/1
Solitary Vireo	- -	- (4) 3/20-4/5	- -	4/1 (6) 3/22-4/9	3/27 (15) 3/14-4/10
Warbling Vireo	3/26 (21) 3/15-4/3	3/25 (20) 3/13-4/6	3/25 (30) 3/9-4/6	3/21 (6) 3/13-3/31	3/11 (15) 3/1-3/20
Orange-crowned Warbler	3/6 (22) 2/27-3/16	3/4 (15) 2/18-3/16	3/3 (29) 2/21-3/14	- (4) 2/26-3/8	- -
Yellow Warbler	- -	4/18 (5) 4/8-4/23	4/16 (30) 4/7-5/2	4/6 (6) 3/21-4/17	4/2 (15) 3/24-4/12
Black-throated Gray Warbler	- -	4/14 (8) 3/31-4/27	- -	4/4 (5) 3/30-4/14	3/24 (15) 3/11-4/7
Hermit Warbler	- -	- -	- -	4/16 (5) 4/13-4/20	4/16 (15) 4/7-4/24
MacGillivray's Warbler	4/20 (12) 4/9-4/30	4/18 (9) 4/3-4/30	4/12 (18) 4/3-4/26.	4/11 (6) 4/8-4/14	4/1 (15) 3/18-4/17
Wilson's Warbler	3/25 (23) 3/16-4/5	3/24 (27) 3/10-4/8	3/22 (32) 3/11-4/3	3/19 (6) 3/17-3/20	3/13 (15) 3/3-3/23
Yellow-breasted Chat	- -	- -	- -	- -	4/13 (15) 4/4-4/24
Western Tanager	- -	- -	- -	4/13 (5) 4/3-4/22	4/13 (15) 4/7-4/17
Black-headed Grosbeak	4/14 (18) 4/5-4/21	4/13 (34) 4/4-4/26	4/13 (37) 4/4-4/21	4/3 (6) 3/28-4/8	3/26 (15) 3/22-4/1
Lazuli Bunting	- -	4/28 (6) 4/21-5/2	4/22 (30) 3/30-5/7	4/18 (5) 4/14-4/22	4/5 (15) 4/1-4/15
Chipping Sparrow	- -	4/14 (7) 4/2-4/24	4/15 (10) 3/29-4/26	- (4) 3/20-4/12	- -
Black-chinned Sparrow	- -	- -	- -	- -	3/28 (15) 3/10-4/24
Grasshopper Sparrow	- -	4/21 (5) 4/2-4/30	- -	- (3) 4/1-4/18	- -
Brown-headed Cowbird	3/28 (13) 3/3-4/14	3/30 (6) 3/17-4/14	- -	- -	- -
Hooded Oriole	- -	3/29 (13) 3/16-4/13	- -	3/19 (6) 3/5-3/30	3/10 (15) 2/27-3/24
Northern Oriole	- -	4/3 (6) 3/24-4/7	- -	3/16 (6) 3/10-3/20	3/14 (15) 3/5-3/21
American Goldfinch	3/30 (13) 3/23-4/6	3/24 (8) 3/2-4/6	- -	- -	- -

[1] Data from PRBO's Palomarin Field Station courtesy of Dave DeSante and Geoff Geupel.
[2] Data compiled by the author from various sources and personal field notes.
[3] Data from Weston (1948).
[4] Data from summaries in seasonal reports of the Middle Pacific Coast Region of American Birds.
[5] Data from summaries in seasonal reports of the Southern Pacific Coast Region of American Birds.

breeding in Tricolored Blackbirds usually coincides with rainfall or flooding of rice fields in the Central Valley, nesting appears to be triggered by an abundance of food (see account).

Most Farallon seabirds seem to be primed by photoperiod to both initiate and terminate egg laying (Ainley & Boekelheide 1990). Food abundance still appears to have some effect on timing of breeding though. In years when initiation of egg laying is late, laying by seabirds may begin en masse when prey appear. Also second and replacement clutches of seabirds are most frequent in years when a high level of breeding success indicates abundant food. The fact that species with the most similar diets breed at the same time also suggests prey availability strongly affects the timing of breeding of seabirds, though the complexities of the pathways linking upwelling, prey availability, and timing of breeding are still poorly understood.

Year-to-year variability in the timing of initiation or termination of breeding differs greatly among species. At Palomarin, timing of initiation of breeding in Wrentits, as measured by mean clutch completion dates of first nesting attempts, varied only from 19 to 30 April over six years (Geupel & DeSante 1990). The timing there of termination of breeding by White-crowned Sparrows, measured as the mean clutch completion date for the latest 10% of nests, ranged from 25 June to 20 July over seven years (DeSante & Baptista 1989). Timing of breeding of Farallon seabirds can vary greatly from year to year, and under extreme conditions virtually all females of species such as Brandt's Cormorants, Pelagic Cormorants, and Pigeon Guillemots fail to lay any eggs (Ainley & Boekelheide 1990). The variation in the timing of commencement of breeding for various Farallon seabirds is indicated by the range among years of mean clutch initiation dates: Brandt's Cormorant (28 April–6 June), Pelagic Cormorant (22 May–12 June), Western Gull (only 3–14 May), Common Murre (9 May–9 June), and Pigeon Guillemot (20 May–17 June). In addition to the seabirds mentioned, Marin County hosts a number of other species that will not breed unless certain food supplies are available. Long-eared Owls, Short-eared Owls, and Black-shouldered Kites will not remain to breed unless certain rodents occur in abundance; Red Crossbills will only breed in years of plentiful conifer seeds; and various dabbling ducks may fail to breed locally when small wetlands dry up during droughts.

These patterns of variation in the timing of breeding of a wide range of species further demonstrate that most if not all species have each adopted a different strategy to exploit their environment. It is clear from the length of the breeding season on the California coast, the great year-to-year variation in timing of breeding in certain species, and the lack of breeding by some species in particular years that efforts to document patterns of breeding distribution of our avifauna are best spread each year over many months and over enough years to sample a broad range of environmental conditions. The Marin atlas project was fortunate enough to span some of the wettest and driest years in the county's history and consequently provided information on how both extremes affected bird distribution here.

METHODS EMPLOYED IN THE MARIN ATLAS

The detection of a pattern or test of a hypothesis can be no better than the data on which it is built.

— John A. Wiens,
The Ecology of Bird Communities

Grid System

THE GRID SYSTEM chosen in 1976 for the *Marin County Breeding Bird Atlas* was roughly comparable to the metric grids used in Europe at that time. Following the lead of North America's first atlas project in Maryland (Klim-kiewicz & Solem 1978), a grid system was overlain on 7.5-minute U.S. Geological Survey topographic maps of Marin County. Each of the 17 topo maps covering Marin County (Figure 7) were divided into 24 equal-sized blocks. Because some of these topo maps included large portions of the ocean, San Pablo or San Francisco bays, or land in adjacent Sonoma County, a total of 221 blocks formed the basic atlas grid of Marin County (Figure 8). Each of these block was assigned a specific numerical code. Though slightly rectangular in shape (about 1.4×1.7 miles on a side), each one of our basic blocks is roughly equivalent in area to a metric block 2.5 km on a side. The basic blocks were also lumped together for later data analysis into groups of four and again into groups of sixteen to facilitate direct comparisons of the Marin atlas data with data from other atlas projects with larger basic block sizes. At the latitude of Marin County (38° N) our basic block, 4-block units, and 16-block units are slightly larger in area (1.02 times) than 2.5-km, 5-km, and 10-km squares, respectively. For all practical purposes, though, our block units are directly comparable in size to their respective metric equiva-lents. Although comparability with other atlas projects is desirable, the comparison of the Marin atlas that will be of most benefit will be that with itself when repeated at a future date.

Blocks along the outer coastline, the shorelines of San Francisco and San Pablo bays, and the Sonoma County border did not conform to the basic grid system. Those blocks were slightly larger or smaller than a basic block and were of necessity irregular in shape. Parts of blocks were merged with adjacent blocks to facilitate future data com-parisons among blocks of roughly equivalent size. This

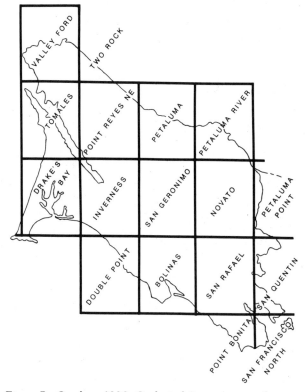

Figure 7. Overlay of U.S. Geological Survey topographic map grid on a Marin County map, forming the basis for the Marin County Breeding Bird Atlas grid (Figure 8).

avoided, for example, a comparison of a block comprised of 90% land and 10% ocean with a block that has 20% land and 80% ocean. Merging of blocks in this manner has precedence in the first atlas project, the *Atlas of British Flora* (Perring & Walters 1962). Besides bringing odd blocks into closer conformity of size and composition, this method had the practical application, in some cases, of providing direct access to all of a block from one place. For

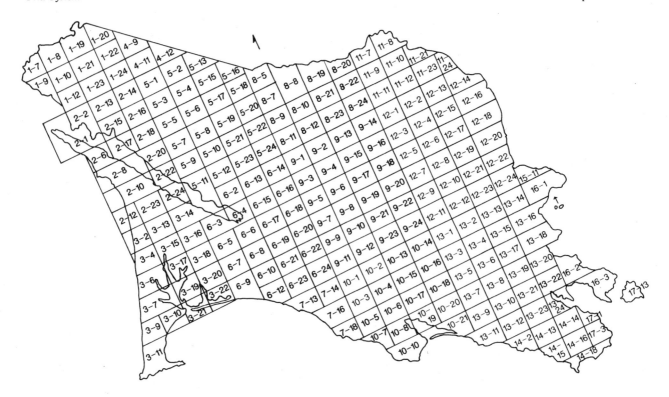

Figure 8. The basic Marin County Breeding Bird Atlas grid with 221 numbered blocks. Blocks were created by dividing each of 17 7.5-minute USGS topo maps (see Figure 7) into 24 equal-sized blocks; parts of some irregular-sized blocks were merged with adjacent ones to bring blocks into closer conformity of size. A basic Marin block is roughly equivalent in area to a metric block 2.5 km on a side.

example, if the grid system had been applied rigidly along Tomales Bay, either an observer would have had to drive long distances around the bay to get access to parts of a block on the opposite side of the bay, or else two different observers would have had to cover the separate parts of the block. With our convoluted coastline, either method—using a rigid grid system or one that merged parts of blocks—would have created blocks of different sizes or shapes. The latter method was chosen as a matter of practicality and should pose no problem if the same exact grid is used when the atlas project is repeated in the future.

Participant Instruction and Block Assignments

From 1976 through 1978, Bob Stewart was the sole coordinator of the Marin County Breeding Bird Atlas Project. The atlas was advertised in the *Point Reyes Bird Observatory Newsletter* and widely in local Audubon Society and conservation newsletters. In 1976 and 1977 several organizational workshops were held. Participants were instructed on how to conduct field work in their blocks and were provided with refresher sessions on bird songs and nest-finding strategies. One or more blocks were assigned to each participant based on his or her available

time and ability. From 1979 through 1981, there was a hiatus in atlas work. This author became the overall coordinator in 1982 for the final field season of the atlas project. In that year workshops and advertisements were conducted in the same manner as in previous years. Likewise, the vast majority of participants that year were solicited through personal contact. In 1982, regional coordinators were solicited to organize participants in four areas encompassing all of Marin County. Betty Burridge (who now organizes the Sonoma County Breeding Bird Atlas Project) was coordinator for 17 blocks in the Tomales area, Scott Carey for 43 blocks in the Novato area, Bill Lenarz for 61 blocks in southern/eastern Marin, and Dave Shuford for 100 blocks in the West Marin area. An effort was made to maintain contact with participants throughout each field season.

In all years each participant was provided with the following:

1. Instruction sheets detailing the objects of the atlas project, how and when to conduct field work, and how to record the required data.

2. A topo map (or photocopy) of his or her atlas block(s) and adjacent blocks; the location of the blocks(s) was outlined on an attached map of Marin County.

PRBO MARIN COUNTY BREEDING BIRD ATLAS PROJECT

NAME: Doug Ellis   19 82

ADDRESS: P.O. Box 155 Eldridge, Ca.   ZIP 95431   BLOCK # 5-13

Name	A.O.U.#	Po	Pr	Co	Name	A.O.U.#	Po	Pr	Co	Name	A.O.U.#	Po	Pr	Co
Pied-billed Grebe	006				American Coot	221				Hairy Woodpecker	393			
Ashy Petrel	108				Black Oystercatcher	287				Downy Woodpecker	394			FY
Double-crested Cormorant	120				Snowy Plover	278				Ash-throated Flycatcher	454			FY
Brandt's Cormorant	122				Killdeer	273			D	Black Phoebe	458			FY
Pelagic Cormorant	123				Western Gull	049				Western Flycatcher	464		S	
Great Blue Heron	194				Common Murre	030				Western Wood Pewee	462		S	
Green Heron	201				Pigeon Guillemot	029				Olive-sided Flycatcher	459			
Great Egret	196				Band-tailed Pigeon	312				Horned Lark	474		T	✱
Snowy Egret	197				Rock Dove	313.1				Violet-green Swallow	615			
Mallard	132				Mourning Dove	316		T		Tree Swallow	614			ON
Pintail	143				Barn Owl	365				Rough-winged Swallow	617			
Cinnamon Teal	141				Screech Owl	373		T		Barn Swallow	613			ON
Ruddy Duck	167				Great Horned Owl	375				Cliff Swallow	612	✓		
Turkey Vulture	325	✓			Pygmy Owl	379				Purple Martin	611			
Sharp-shinned Hawk	332				Burrowing Owl	378				Steller's Jay	478		D	
Cooper's Hawk	333				Spotted Owl	369				Scrub Jay	481			FY
Red-tailed Hawk	337	✓			Saw-whet Owl	372				Common Raven	486			FY
Red shouldered Hawk	339	✓			Poor-will	418				Common Crow	488	✓		
Marsh Hawk	331				White-throated Swift	425				Chestnut-backed Chickadee	741			NY
Osprey	364				Anna's Hummingbird	431		T		Plain Titmouse	733		D	
Sparrow Hawk	360	✓			Allen's Hummingbird	434		T		Common Bushtit	743			FY
California Quail	294		T		Belted Kingfisher	390	✓			White-breasted Nuthatch	727			
Ring necked Pheasant	309.1				Red-shafted Flicker	413				Red-breasted Nuthatch	728			
Virginia Rail	212				Pileated Woodpecker	405				Pygmy Nuthatch	730			
Sora	214				Acorn Woodpecker	407				Brown Creeper	726			
Black Rail	216													

Po=Possible; Pr=Probable; Co=Confirmed   Enter Criteria Code in Correct Column

Name	A.O.U.#	Po	Pr	Co	Name	A.O.U.#	Po	Pr	Co	Name	A.O.U.#	Po	Pr	Co
Wrentit	742		S		Purple Finch	517		S		**Rare Possibilities**				
Dipper	701				House Finch	519			FY	Black-crowned Night Heron	202			
House Wren	721				Pine Siskin	533			FY	American Bittern	190			
Winter Wren	722				American Goldfinch	529			FL	Wood Duck	144			
Bewick's Wren	719			FY	Lesser Goldfinch	530				White-tailed Kite	328			
Long-billed Marsh Wren	725				Red Crossbill	521				Swainson's Hawk	342			
Rock Wren	715				Rufous-sided Towhee	588			FY	Golden Eagle	349			
Mockingbird	703				Brown Towhee	591		D		Prarie Falcon	355			
California Thrasher	710				Savannah Sparrow	542		S		Peregrine Falcon	356			
Robin	761		D		Grasshopper Sparrow	546		S		Clapper Rail	210			
Hermit Thrush	759				Lark Sparrow	552		D		Common Gallinule	219			
Swainson's Thrush	758		T		Rufous-crowned Sparrow	580				Tufted Puffin	12			
Western Bluebird	767		T		Oregon Junco	567.9		DD		Long-eared Owl	286			
Golden-crowned Kinglet	748				Chipping Sparrow	560				Short-eared Owl	287			FL
Loggerhead Shrike	622				White-crowned Sparrow	554				Vaux Swift	298			
Starling	493			FY	Song Sparrow	581			FY	Black-chinned Hummingbird	429			
Hutton's Vireo	632		S							Nuttall's Woodpecker	328			ON
Warbling Vireo	627		S							Western Kingbird	447		T	
Orange-crowned Warbler	646		NY							Cassin's Kingbird	448			
Yellow Warbler	652									Willow Flycatcher	466			
Black-throated Gray Warbler	665									Bank Swallow	616			
Hermit Warbler	669									Yellow-breasted Chat	683			
MacGillivray's Warbler	680									Hooded Oriole	505			
Yellowthroat	681									Lawrence's Goldfinch	531			
Wilson's Warbler	685		S							Black-chinned Sparrow	565			
House Sparrow	688.2									Sage Sparrow	574			
Western Meadowlark	501.1		FY											
Red-winged Blackbird	498		FY											
Bullock's Oriole	508		FL											
Brewer's Blackbird	510		DD											
Brown-headed Cowbird	495													
Black-headed Grosbeak	596													
Lazuli Bunting	599		S											

Figure 9. A representative field recording card from the Marin County Breeding Bird Atlas. See Table 5 for various codes used to denote Possible (Po), Probable (Pr), and Confirmed (Co) breeding evidence.

Table 5. CRITERIA FOR POSSIBLE, PROBABLE, AND CONFIRMED BREEDING CODES entered on Marin County Breeding Bird Atlas field cards (Figure 9).

POSSIBLE BREEDING – this code should be entered in the first column (PO) of the Atlas Card.

Bird recorded in the breeding season in possible nesting habitat but no other indication of breeding noted. Take 1 May through 31 July as the breeding season for most species. Summering, nonbreeding adults such as gulls in a dump when you *know* there is no gullery in your block, migrant shorebirds and warblers, should NOT be included.

PROBABLE BREEDING – codes entered in second column (PR).

S   Singing male present (or breeding calls heard) on more than one date in the same place. It is a good indication that a bird has taken up residence if the dates are a week or more apart.

T   Bird (or pair) apparently holding territory. In addition to singing, chasing of others of the same species often marks territory.

D   Courtship and display; or agitated behavior or anxiety calls from adults, suggesting probable presence of nest or young nearby; brood-patch on trapped female or cloacal protuberance on trapped male.

N   Visiting probable nest-site.

B   Nest building by wrens and woodpeckers. Wrens may build many nests and woodpeckers, although they usually drill only one nesting cavity, may also drill roosting holes.

CONFIRMED BREEDING – codes entered in third column (CO).

DD   Distraction display or injury feigning, coition. Agitated behavior and/or anxiety calls are "D" only.

NB   Nest building by any species except wrens and woodpeckers.

UN   Used nest found. These must be carefully identified if they are to be used. Some nests (like those of Northern Oriole) are persistent and very characteristic. Others are more difficult to identify correctly.

FE   Female with egg in the oviduct.

FL   Recently fledged young (including downy young of waterfowl etc.). This code should be used with caution for species such as Starlings and swallows that may move some distance soon after fledging. Recently fledged passerines are still dependent on parents and being fed by them.

FS   Adult carrying fecal sac.

FY   Adult(s) with food for young. Some birds (gulls, terns, and birds of prey) continue to feed their young long after they've fledged and may move considerable distances. Also some birds (like terns) may carry food long distances to young in a neighboring block. Be careful especially on the edge of a block. Care should be taken to avoid confusion with courtship feeding (D).

ON   Adult(s) entering or leaving nest-site in circumstances indicating occupied nest. *Not generally used for open nesting birds.* The correct code would be "N" if you simply see a bird fly into or out of a bush or tree and do not find the nest. It should be used for hole nesters as when a bird enters a hole and remains inside, changes over at a hole, or bird leaves hole after having been inside for some time.

NE   Nest and eggs or bird setting and not disturbed or egg shells found below the nest. If you find a cowbird egg in a nest, it's NE for cowbird and NE for the host nest.

NY   Nest with young or downy young or downy young of waterfowl, quail, waders, etc. If you find a young cowbird with the other young, it's NY for the cowbird and NY for the host species. Since parents often lead downy young for considerable distances, care should be taken if such records are close to the edge of the block.

3. Atlas recording card(s) to be filled out in the field or immediately afterwards (Figure 9).

4. A breeding category sheet (Table 5)—a slightly modified form of the one used in the Maryland county atlas project (Klimkiewicz & Solem 1978), originally derived from the British categories (Sharrock 1976).

5. The assurance that the locations of all sightings of rare breeding birds would, at the discretion of the observer, be kept confidential and protected on maps (see Data Summary p.48).

In 1982—the final year of fieldwork—participants were provided with photocopies of the previous years' atlas card(s) for their block(s) if there had been any prior coverage. They were further instructed on how to obtain adequate coverage of their blocks (see below). In addition, observers were asked to keep records of the total number of hours they spent in the field collecting atlas data. That year, area coordinators contacted all participants around 1 June. At that time, if some observers already had been able to cover their block(s) adequately, they were encouraged to help with other areas still in need of coverage. If participants felt they would not have time to finish the necessary field work in their block(s), another observer was assigned to help complete the coverage that season. Adequacy of coverage was judged qualitatively by the overall coordinator as described below. In addition to regular communication between area coordinators and participants, close contact was maintained between area coordinators and the overall coordinator.

Gathering Additional Information

Because different methods work best for gathering data on certain groups of species, or because a diversity of methods can enhance data collection for all species, a number of additional methods were employed to gather data that supplemented the standard atlas procedures. These strategies included the following:

1. *Owling routes.* With the realization that owls and poorwills would be inadequately covered compared with other species, special owling routes were drawn up in 1977 and 1982 and assigned to various nocturnal enthusiasts. These routes were of varying length and covered virtually all the major roads in the sparsely inhabited parts of the county. Several walking routes were also covered along trails in the Inverness Ridge area of the Point Reyes National Seashore and within the Mount Tamalpais watershed.

2. *Spring Bird Counts.* Following the tradition of the Christmas Bird Counts (CBC) published in the National Audubon Society journal *American Birds*, three Spring Bird Counts (SBC)—Southern Marin, Point Reyes Peninsula, and Even Cheaper Thrills—were conducted in Marin County in May or early June in various years beginning in 1978 (Appendix A).

Aside from seasonal timing, these counts were conducted in an identical manner to the CBCs, except that, in addition to counting the number of individuals of each species, each area leader assigned the highest category of breeding observed that day (Table 5) to each potential breeding species in an area. To channel some of this energy into the atlas project, the Marin atlas grid was overlain on the South Marin SBC circle in 1977 and over all three SBC circles in 1982. Each of the area leaders, many of whom were already atlas participants, was provided with all the information given to regular atlas participants along with atlas cards for all the blocks or partial blocks that fell within his or her normal SBC area. In addition to collecting the standard numerical and breeding information described above, area leaders were also asked to fill in all breeding evidence for each individual atlas block in their area. This resulted in large amounts of atlas data being collected on single days, and sometimes parts of blocks being covered by the SBC team that otherwise might not have been covered by the atlaser already assigned that block.

3. *Casual observations.* Besides using the systematic atlas data collected in specified blocks from 1976 through 1978 and in 1982, other available data were incorporated in the data base. In advertisements and instructions to participants, everyone was encouraged to submit additional data on breeding evidence for any species (especially rare or unusual ones) that were observed in an atlas year but not in an assigned atlas block. Available data were also solicited for the intervening years of 1979 through 1981, when no organized effort was made to cover atlas blocks. Individuals particularly active in those years were contacted directly and asked to submit from their field notes and memories any and all specific breeding bird sightings. All such observations were given the same scrutiny as atlas card data; a determination of the exact location and type of breeding evidence observed was necessary to correctly assign records to specific atlas blocks.

4. *Breeding seabirds surveys.* Fortuitously, in 1979 and 1980 personnel from the U.S. Fish and Wildlife Service conducted censuses of breeding seabirds along the entire California coast and subsequently published the information as the *Catalog of California Seabird Colonies* (Sowls et al. 1980). Breeding site data from Marin County that had not already been confirmed during atlas work were extracted from that publication (or field notes and maps on file at the California Academy of Sciences in San Francisco) and assigned to the appropriate atlas block. U.S. Fish and Wildlife Service personnel resurveyed breeding seabirds on the central and northern California coast in 1989 (Carter et al. 1990, 1992). These 1989 data were not

used to construct the atlas maps but were used to supplement the knowledge of distribution and abundance discussed in the species accounts.

Determining Adequacy of Coverage

Determining when data of sufficient quality have been collected in individual blocks or in all blocks in a region is a perplexing problem facing all atlas projects. Although it would be ideal to confirm breeding for all species in each block, that goal is unrealistic. On the other hand, atlas coordinators must attempt to maximize the return of field effort given limitations in the number and ability of observers, time available, and access problems or other logistical constraints.

On a practical level, an atlas coordinator must decide when an observer should be shifted to cover another block because additional time spent in the original block will yield few new species or instances of confirmed breeding evidence. More importantly, an atlas project can establish scientific credibility only if there is confidence that field work has documented a high proportion of the species actually breeding in each block. Otherwise there will always be the nagging doubts, rife in preatlasing days, as to whether the distribution patterns or population trend indicated is real or just an artifact of insufficient coverage.

Other Atlases

A number of methods have been used to assess adequacy of coverage in other atlases, and all have their shortcomings. Two popular measures, used singly or in combination, assume adequate coverage in a block when a certain number of species (and sometimes confirmed breeders) have been recorded or when a certain number of field hours have been logged. In Vermont, the initial experience of atlas committee members indicated that most of the state's blocks contained 100 breeding species (Laughlin & Kibbe 1985, Kibbe 1986). With this knowledge they selected 75 species recorded in a block (and 35 confirmed breeders) as the level of acceptable coverage, assuming that number would represent 75% of the species actually in most blocks. In practice 75 species was only 60%–65% of the 120 or more species they later found in some blocks. The New York atlas initially defined adequate coverage as 76 breeding species per block with half (38) confirmed as breeders; they later dropped the 50% confirmation requirement (Andrle & Carroll 1988). Ontario originally set an adequate coverage standard of 16 hours of field work with the expectation that the effort would identify 75% of the breeding species in a block (Cadman et al. 1987). Because expectations were not met, coverage goals were modified. Based on experience and estimates of habitat diversity in each block, coordinators estimated the total number of

species breeding in each. Retaining the minimum requirement of 16 hours of field work, adequate coverage was then set at establishing breeding evidence for 75% of the estimated number of breeding species.

Setting either an arbitrary number of species detected or field hours spent as the measure of adequate coverage is problematic. Because habitat diversity, and hence the number of breeding species, may vary greatly among blocks, a preselected regionwide goal of species detection will set unrealistically high or low expectations for many blocks. A minimum number of hours of field work is an inadequate standard because observers varying in field skills will consequently differ in the number of species they can detect in a given time period. Even when observer skills are comparable, the number of hours needed to detect the same number of birds may also vary greatly among blocks as habitat diversity, ruggedness of terrain, or ease of access varies.

In combination with species and field time goals, Smith (1982) suggested measuring adequacy of coverage by plotting the number of new species detected in each of the three breeding categories against time spent in each new visit to a block. Termination of coverage was recommended when the plotted curves leveled off as returns diminished with time spent. This method relies on the probably unrealistic assumption that most observers will keep accurate records, graph them, and correctly interpret the results; regardless, this method, like others, will falter because of observer variability. No matter how much time is spent to compensate, observers with poor skills in identifying bird songs will plateau at lower species totals than will more skilled observers.

Kibbe (1986) suggested using an ACID (Adequate Coverage Identification) test to evaluate when observers' efforts became ineffective and it was time to move on to another block. Coverage in this scheme is scored by adding the products of three times the number of species with confirmed breeding evidence, two times the number with probable evidence, and one times the number with possible evidence (ACID score = $[3 \times CO] + [2 \times PR] + PO$). The assumption is that as complete coverage is approached, scores change less and less between successive surveys. With skilled observers this method may actually measure "adequate" coverage, but scores of some observers may peak at too low a level because they are not recording difficult-to-detect species. Because the score is most sensitive to increases in the number of confirmed species, an observer may detect most of the breeding species long before the ACID score begins to level off. Thus practicality would suggest moving skilled observers to new blocks long before their scores peaked, if finding most breeding species is a higher priority than establishing confirmed breeding evidence for all of them.

Raynor (1983) suggested assessing coverage by first plotting the number of species found in each block against an informed estimate of the number of breeding species probably present in each block. The informed estimate is made after the first atlas year and is based on identification of habitats in each block (from maps or other data), knowledge of habitat preferences of expected breeding birds, lists of species in nearby blocks with similar habitats, and personal knowledge of the block or similar habitats in the same area. The informed species estimate can be revised or updated annually if coverage continues; also results can be evaluated against the estimate and can be used to revise it. Once the expected number of species is estimated for each block, calculations can be made of ratios of the total number of species (or confirmed species) recorded to expected species (T/EX or CO/EX). These ratios can be plotted as percentages and classified to define quality of coverage. For example, the range of values calculated can be partitioned into three equal categories corresponding to good, fair, and poor coverage. Raynor (1983) proposed a very high standard of listing 95% of the expected species and confirming 57% as a goal for adequate coverage of a block. Although his method is intuitively appealing, it is not without pitfalls. The main drawback is that refining estimates over time—based on the assumption that with good coverage, counts and estimates will tend to converge—may lead to a self-fulfilling prophecy. If the species list exceeds the estimate, the estimate will be revised upward, but if the list is low and remains low after further work is conducted, the estimate will likely be revised downward. In other words, once coverage has been qualitatively deemed *adequate* on some level the estimate will be revised to fit the actual number of species recorded. This is not a *test* of adequate coverage. Rather, it fits data to what one assumes from past knowledge or current field work is the "real" number of species breeding in a block. Although scientifically fortified with plots and correlations, the linchpin of this method is the accuracy of the estimation of breeding species. Sophisticated data analysis will not suffice if the estimates of expected species have low accuracy. The people estimating must have a very extensive knowledge of local habitat distribution, habitat preferences of expected breeding birds, and a fair amount of prior distributional knowledge of the birds being studied. In atlases covering large geographical areas various sub-coordinators are likely to make the species estimates for the blocks in their subregion. Hence coverage standards may vary with subregions as coordinators vary in knowledge or a tendency to be conservative or liberal in their estimations of expected breeding species.

The only way to accurately test for adequate coverage is to send a highly qualified observer—well versed in local bird songs and willing to hike, if need be, to all available habitats—to a block with prior coverage and see if he or she can add many new species. If after a day in the field the observer adds little to the breeding list, it seems fair to assume that the block has been adequately covered. Because of limits to observer numbers, ability, and time, such a test is usually not possible for most blocks. On the other hand, such a test is advised for blocks with lower species totals than other adjoining blocks with similar habitats and even for a certain percentage of randomly selected blocks in various subregions of the atlas area.

The Marin Atlas

We did not use any a priori standard of coverage nor were data from Marin atlas blocks formally compared to a standard, score, or test. Rather, we assessed adequacy of coverage in the Marin County Breeding Bird Atlas Project on an empirical block-by-block basis in a manner similar to that later used in Ohio (Rice & Peterjohn 1986). The overall coordinator carefully weighed the data for each block just prior to and during the final year of atlas field work in 1982. From the basis of knowledge of habitat preferences of expected species and the habitats known or expected to be found in each block, species lists from data cards for each block with some coverage were scrutinized. Species that were likely still to be found were highlighted on cards sent back to observers, who were asked to specifically look for those species in the appropriate habitats. To further ensure adequate coverage of all blocks, and to prioritize the assignment of blocks to participants in the final atlas season, each area coordinator was given a list of all blocks in their area qualitatively divided into the following categories: (1) blocks not covered at all, (2) blocks needing much work, (3) blocks needing moderate work, and (4) blocks needing spot checking. Blocks in the last category appeared already to have been covered "adequately." Nevertheless, considering that one or more species are almost inevitably missed in every block, no matter how well covered, participants were asked to look for additional species in these blocks when they had reason to suspect that a species had been missed.

Although throughout the project we emphasized to observers the importance of obtaining as much evidence of confirmed breeding as possible, we placed a higher priority in the final year of at least establishing presence in each block of as many of the expected species as possible. This approach was taken to ensure that our data would best represent the distribution of each species. We did not want to miss the presence of species in undercovered blocks at the expense of spending too much time confirming breeding of more species in blocks where most expected species had already been found. We assumed that if we spent enough time to document the presence of most species that the natural by-product would be the observation of considerable evidence of confirmed breeding.

Mop-up efforts were targeted for blocks in the "needing moderate work" category. Skilled observers sent to such blocks for one-time intensive visits generally added only a few species. The use of mop-up observers to randomly sample a small number of blocks is highly recommended as a true hands-on test of adequate coverage. The success of mop-up efforts also bolstered confidence in the lists of expected species generated for blocks where such observers were not used.

In the last year, many blocks were covered for the first time, basically by the technique of block-busting, now widely promoted by most atlas projects. Area coordinators or other skilled observers with excellent birdsong identification skills and the willingness to hike off the beaten path covered these blocks on at least two field days separated by about two weeks to a month. For comparison, block-busting *teams* in some state atlas projects with larger block sizes than those in Marin averaged about 10 to 20 hours per block (Laughlin & Kibbe 1985, Andrle & Carroll 1988). It was felt that our blocks were of such small size that an observer could easily hike to visit all the major habitats in one day. The second visit ensured probable breeding status for many species based on hearing or seeing individuals at the same site over time. Confirmed breeding evidence was usually found for many species on the second visit, which we tried to time for the period when many recently fledged young were just out of the nest and still being fed by parents.

Other methods noted above geared toward specific groups, such as owls and seabirds, enhanced our ability to achieve adequate coverage. Mop-up efforts or Spring Bird Count help also had the advantage of obtaining independent coverage of many blocks. This enhanced coverage because observers with *different* skills worked a block, and some individuals were likely to visit areas of the block not covered by another observer. Given the pitfalls of the many methods of assessing coverage described above, there is no reason to suspect that our atlas necessarily suffered by the lack of an a priori standard of coverage.

Data Summary

After the completion of atlas field work in 1982, the overall atlas coordinator made a final check of all atlas cards for accuracy and asked original observers for details about unusual or questionable sightings. The most frequent question asked was not whether the observer felt the species in question was identified correctly, but whether the species was observed in "appropriate habitat" at the right time of year. After being satisfied that all observations on the data cards were correct to the best of the coordinator's knowledge, the data were transferred from the atlas cards onto species summary sheets. Each summary sheet had a listing of all atlas blocks and three

columns to check off possible, probable, or confirmed breeding. The number of blocks that had evidence for the three categories was totaled and checked. Bill Lenarz then entered all the atlas data from the species sheets into computer files and checked the breeding category totals against those done by hand. Data were summarized for all species and all blocks, including the 2.5-, 5-, and 10-km block equivalents. Data presented below are from the 2.5-km block equivalents. Lenarz also wrote additional computer programs for more detailed analyses currently slated for future publication.

Before the 1982 field season, preliminary species maps were made by hand, using all the 1976 to 1981 atlas data and the symbols of breeding evidence subsequently portrayed on the final maps (see Content of Species Accounts p. 73). Copies of these maps were given to the regional coordinators to illustrate the detail of the final maps, to point out gaps in our knowledge, and to provide encouragement to coordinators and atlas participants. After the completion of data collection in 1982, final maps were constructed by adding to the preliminary maps all the information from the checked species sheets. For each species, dots on the map were counted and checked against the species sheets and, if necessary, adjustments were made. It is likely that a very few errors in mapping were made, but this should not affect the overall pattern of distribution of common species. Maps of rarer species were checked and double-checked against the species sheets. For several rare and sensitive species, the locations of breeding records were protected by moving the dots on the map by one to two blocks; such maps were labeled accordingly (see Content of Species Accounts p. 73).

Quantitative Data on Abundance

Although no organized effort was made to estimate the abundance of each species in each block as part of the atlas project, data on the abundance of birds in Marin County collected for other purposes were summarized or identified. Sources of this data included the following:

1. *Spring Bird Counts.* Data from the three SBCs described above are presented in Appendix A.

2. *Breeding Bird Survey routes.* Data from the two 24.5-mile USFWS Breeding Bird Survey routes established in Marin County are summarized in Appendix B. Eleven years of data from the period 1972 to 1986 were used from the Fairfax 083 route; coverage dates ranged from 8 May to 14 June (median 2 June). Seven years of data from the period 1975 to 1986 were used from the Point Reyes 071 route; coverage dates ranged from 3 to 22 June (median 11 June).

3. *Breeding Bird Census plots.* Data on abundance of Marin County birds collected on Breeding Bird Census plots along the coast (1951–1990) and published in *Amer-*

ican *Birds* or the *Journal of Field Ornithology* were *not* summarized, but the names, locations, and citations of the published accounts of these plots are listed in Appendix C.

4. *Breeding seabird colony surveys.* Numbers of seabirds estimated at various colonies in Marin County by USFWS personnel (Sowls et al. 1980; Carter et al. 1990, 1992) were summarized and accompany the seabird accounts.

5. *Heron and egret rookery surveys.* Data on the numbers of herons and egrets breeding at various Marin County rookeries (Pratt 1983, p. 103 this volume) are presented in tabular form with the appropriate species accounts.

6. *Nesting Osprey surveys.* Data on the number of Ospreys nesting at Kent Lake in the Marin Municipal Water District (Evens 1991) accompany the Osprey account.

7. *Common Yellowthroat surveys.* Data on numbers of Saltmarsh Common Yellowthroats from surveys of the San Francisco Bay area (Hobson et al. 1986) supplement the Yellowthroat account.

In addition, after the atlas work was completed, estimates were made of the relative abundance of each species in an "average" block. These qualitative estimates were based on the author's detailed field notes on abundance gathered while exploring habitats in virtually all parts of Marin over an eight-year span from 1975 to 1982. These abundance estimates per average block were used in conjunction with the atlas distribution data to make estimates of the relative abundance of each species countywide as presented in each species account (see Content of Species Accounts p. 73).

Coastal scrub, grassland, and riparian forest lend a soft-looking texture to the landforms of the Rodeo Lagoon valley and Wolf Ridge west of "Hawk Hill." Drawing by Ane Rovetta, 1989.

RESULTS AND DISCUSSION

. . . all nature is so full, that that district produces the greatest variety which is most examined.

— Gilbert White, 1768

Atlas Coverage

FIELD WORKERS covered all 221 blocks in the *Marin County Breeding Bird Atlas* grid. The amount of time spent on field work was tallied only in 1982, when about 92 observers logged over 2800 hours afield. In only a few blocks was coverage considered unsatisfactory. In one case, coverage was compromised because we were denied access to private land comprising all of one block along the Estero del Americano; but observers were able to at least sample most habitats in that block via kayak.

For all atlas blocks combined, possible breeding accounted for 33.4% of all records, probable for 34.0%, and confirmed for 32.6%. Although these data fall short of the ideal of confirming all species as breeders in all blocks, they are consistent with our efforts to obtain accurate distribution maps by documenting the presence of most breeding species in each block (see Adequacy of Coverage p. 46). Excluding nightbirds, we probably found some evidence of breeding for 90%–95% of all species actually breeding in most blocks. Owls, poorwills, and other secretive species such as rails were not surveyed as well as other species, but their basic distribution patterns were established. For example, the Great Horned Owl was recorded in about two-thirds of the potential blocks though it likely occurred in almost all of them. Nonetheless, the owl's atlas map clearly shows that it breeds throughout the county; notably, a high proportion of the blocks without documentation of Great Horned Owl were away from roads, where coverage was scant. Extraordinary efforts would have to have been made to bring the completeness of data collection for nocturnal birds up to that of diurnal species. Since the basic distribution patterns of nocturnal species were established, the expenditure of such effort seems warranted only in the case of Endangered or Threatened species such as the Spotted Owl (see account).

Patterns of Species Richness of the Breeding Avifauna

During the field work for the *Marin County Breeding Bird Atlas*, we found breeding evidence for 157 species of birds. For 143 of these we established confirmed breeding evidence. Of the remaining 14 species, 9 species—Blue-winged Teal, Rhinoceros Auklet, Tufted Puffin, Northern Pygmy-Owl, Burrowing Owl, Vaux's Swift, California Thrasher, Yellow-breasted Chat, and Red Crossbill—still lack confirmed breeding evidence. Currently, all of these species except Burrowing Owl, Yellow-breasted Chat, and Red Crossbill probably breed in the county annually in small numbers.

Of the 14 species that remained unconfirmed during the years of atlas field work, 5 species were confirmed breeding in the county at other times: Northern Shoveler was confirmed subsequent to atlas work, both Common Poorwill and Rock Wren prior to atlas work, and both MacGillivray's Warbler and Black-chinned Sparrow both before and after the atlas period. An additional 6 species not recorded during atlas field work have been confirmed as breeders in the county: Peregrine Falcon both prior to and after atlas work; American Avocet after atlas work; Spotted Sandpiper both prior to and after atlas work; and Greater Roadrunner, Cassin's Kingbird, and American Dipper all prior to atlas work. Of these, Greater Roadrunner has been entirely extirpated from the county, and American Dipper appears to have been extirpated here as a breeder. In recent years, Dippers have been recorded in the county only as irregular migrants or winter visitants; it is possible they may still breed here irregularly in high runoff years, though recent summer records are lacking.

In all, in historical times Marin County has supported at least 163 species of breeding birds—154 based on confirmed evidence and 9 based on suspected evidence. Including naturally irregular/irruptive breeders such as Long-eared Owl, Black-chinned Sparrow, Red Crossbill, and Lawrence's Goldfinch, but excluding extirpated breeding species (Greater Roadrunner and American Dipper), extralimital breeders (Say's Phoebe, Cassin's Kingbird, and Northern Parula) or otherwise very infrequent breeders (Double-crested Cormorant, American Avocet, Spotted Sandpiper, Burrowing Owl, Short-eared Owl, and Yellow-breasted Chat), the county's breeding avifauna currently numbers about 152 more or less regularly breeding species.

A number of additional species not mentioned above may also have bred here historically and either went undetected or were inadequately documented; some of these may once have been part of the regular breeding avifauna (see Species of Unclear Breeding Status or Potential Breeders pp. 429–434). Certain other species breeding elsewhere in the San Francisco Bay Area are the most likely potential future colonizers to Marin County. One of the most likely species to soon become established is Wild Turkey which was introduced to the county in 1988.

Based on the number of blocks in which they were recorded, 20 of the 157 breeding species during the atlas period were classified as nearly ubiquitous in their distribution here, 15 as very widespread, 17 as widespread, 10 as fairly widespread, 9 as somewhat local, 23 as local, and 63 as very local (Table 6). A ranking of the 157 species by their Overall Population Index yielded 5 species with extremely large populations, 15 with very large populations, 12 with large populations, 18 with fairly large populations, 6 with moderate-sized populations, 19 with small populations, and 82 with very small populations (Table 7). The two methods of ranking species—by distribution and a combination of distribution and abundance—each showed a disproportionate number of species with relatively restricted distributions and relatively small populations. These patterns are typical of many avifaunal assemblages that have been studied (e.g., Wiens 1989).

Countywide, the number of breeding species recorded per block ranged from 22 to 84 and averaged 56.7 (SE = ± 0.79) (Figure 10). Sixty-two percent of the blocks had between 50 to 70 species each. The areas of the county that tended to have the highest breeding species richness per block were the south-central interior ridges (Figure 11) with a mix of hardwood, conifer, scrub, and grassland habitats. On the whole, blocks in the grassland-dominated regions of outer Point Reyes and around Tomales supported the lowest species richness. Habitat diversity was not measured, but it undoubtedly would have shown a positive relationship with species richness per block.

Recognizing that comparisons of species richness between areas of different size, or where data were collected differently, poses some problems (Wiens 1989), it is still instructive to compare the size of Marin's breeding avifauna with that of other regions. Preliminary comparisons show that the species richness of the entire Marin County breeding avifauna is roughly similar to that of most other counties in coastal northern California (Shuford in prep.). Comparisons also show that the breeding avifauna of Marin County (latitude about 38°, 588 square miles) is greater than that of interior areas at roughly the same latitude of similar or even much greater size. At about 38°45' latitude, Yolo County encompasses 1034 square miles, ranges from about 100 to 3000 feet in elevation, and extends from the east slope of the Interior Coast Range across the west side of the Sacramento Valley floor. Yolo County has a breeding avifauna of about 133 species

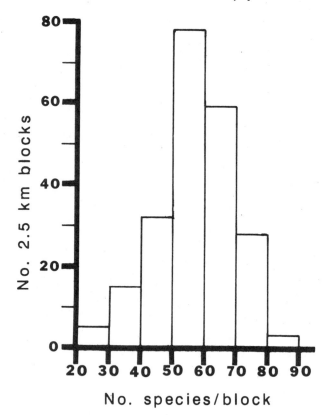

Figure 10. Frequency distribution of the number of species found per atlas block.

(Gaines & Beedy 1987). At about 37°45' latitude, the west slope of the Yosemite region is roughly the size of Yolo County, ranges from about 1200 to over 13,000 feet on the west slope of the Sierra Nevada, and currently supports about 141 species of breeding birds (Gaines 1988). The east slope of the Yosemite region, roughly equal in size to the west slope, ranges from the Sierran crest down the east slope to about 6400 feet in the Great Basin and currently sustains about 149 species of breeding birds. The combined Yosemite region spanning the west and east slopes harbors about 187 species of breeding birds. It is not surprising that the greater Yosemite region supports a more numerous breeding avifauna than Marin County, considering that the former is much larger, ranges over almost 12,000 feet in elevation, and straddles two of California's major biogeographical regions, the Sierra Nevada and the Great Basin. Further atlas work in California will provide needed insight into patterns of breeding bird species richness in this diverse state.

The number of breeding species in Marin County's avifauna compares favorably even with a few states and provinces in North America: Kentucky (164 species), Arkansas (157), Delaware (157), Mississippi (153), Prince Edward Island (146), and Hawaii (131) (DeSante & Pyle 1986). Clearly, Marin County supports a large avifauna for its size. This can be attributed to the county's diverse array

RESULTS AND DISCUSSION

Table 6. Relative distribution ranking of all species recorded on the Marin County Breeding Bird Atlas. Species are listed in descending order, by the number and percentage of total blocks (No. - %) in which they were detected, with respect to the seven categories of the Relative Distribution Index (RDI); see Content of Species of Accounts (p. 75).

NEARLY UBIQUITOUS

Scrub Jay (214-96.8)
Turkey Vulture (213-96.4)
Red-tailed Hawk (213-96.4)
Mourning Dove (212-95.9)
California Quail (208-94.1)
Bushtit (207-93.7)
House Finch (207-93.7)
Bewick's Wren (205-92.8)
Barn Swallow (203-91.8)
Cliff Swallow (202-91.4)
California Towhee (201-91.0)
Allen's Hummingbird (198-89.6)
American Robin (197-89.1)
Chestnut-backed Chickadee (195-88.2)
Rufous-sided Towhee (195-88.2)
European Starling (194-87.8)
Brewer's Blackbird (193-87.3)
Song Sparrow (192-86.9)
Orange-crowned Warbler (191-86.4)
Dark-eyed Junco (188-85.1)

VERY WIDESPREAD

Hutton's Vireo (184-83.2)
Wrentit (182-82.4)
Violet-green Swallow (177-80.1)
Purple Finch (177-80.1)
Brown-headed Cowbird (173-78.3)
American Goldfinch (173-78.3)
Red-winged Blackbird (172-77.8)
Common Raven (170-76.9)
Western Bluebird (170-76.9)
American Crow (169-76.5)
Black Phoebe (167-75.6)
Warbling Vireo (164-74.2)
Anna's Hummingbird (163-73.8)
Pacific-slope Flycatcher (163-73.8)
Wilson's Warbler (161-72.8)

WIDESPREAD

Steller's Jay (154-69.7)
Pine Siskin (151-68.3)
Ash-throated Flycatcher (150-67.9)
Great Horned Owl (149-67.4)
Killdeer (146-66.1)
Downy Woodpecker (145-65.6)
Lesser Goldfinch (145-65.6)
House Sparrow (144-65.2)
Northern Flicker (143-64.7)
Swainson's Thrush (137-62.0)
Western Wood-Pewee (136-61.5)
Western Meadowlark (135-61.1)
Tree Swallow (132-59.7)
Plain Titmouse (129-58.4)
Black-headed Grosbeak (129-58.4)
Northern Oriole (129-58.4)
Brown Creeper (128-57.9)

FAIRLY WIDESPREAD

Lark Sparrow (124-56.1)
Horned Lark (123-55.6)
American Kestrel (122-55.2)
Band-tailed Pigeon (117-52.9)
Lazuli Bunting (115-52.0)
Savannah Sparrow (115-52.0)
Mallard (110-49.8)
N. Rough-winged Swallow (104-47.0)
Olive-sided Flycatcher (96-43.4)
Grasshopper Sparrow (96-43.4)

SOMEWHAT LOCAL

Chipping Sparrow (93-42.1)
Rock Dove (90-40.7)
Acorn Woodpecker (86-38.9)
White-crowned Sparrow (85-38.5)
Hairy Woodpecker (82-37.1)
Western Kingbird (74-33.5)
Belted Kingfisher (73-33.0)
Nuttall's Woodpecker (72-32.6)
Northern Mockingbird (67-30.3)

LOCAL

White-breasted Nuthatch (59-26.7)
American Coot (58-26.2)
Red-shouldered Hawk (56-25.3)
Winter Wren (56-25.3)
Cinnamon Teal (52-23.5)
Rufous-crowned Sparrow (52-23.5)
Osprey (49-22.2)
Northern Harrier (48-21.7)
Hermit Thrush (48-21.7)
Western Screech-Owl (42-19.0)
White-throated Swift (42-19.0)
Golden-crowned Kinglet (42-19.0)
Pygmy Nuthatch (40-18.1)
Loggerhead Shrike (40-18.1)
Red-breasted Nuthatch (39-17.6)
Golden Eagle (38-17.2)
Common Yellowthroat (38-17.2)
Cooper's Hawk (36-16.3)
Pied-billed Grebe (34-15.4)
Black-shouldered Kite (34-15.4)
Barn Owl (34-15.4)
Marsh Wren (34-15.4)
Northern Saw-whet Owl (32-14.5)

VERY LOCAL

House Wren (29-13.1)
Pileated Woodpecker (28-12.7)
Green-backed Heron (24-10.8)
Purple Martin (24-10.8)
Black-throated Gray Warbler (23-10.4)
Yellow Warbler (22-10.0)
Ruddy Duck (20-9.0)
Yellow-rumped Warbler (19-8.6)

Virginia Rail (17-7.7)
Spotted Owl (16-7.2)
Blue-gray Gnatcatcher (16-7.2)
Rock Wren (15-6.8)
California Thrasher (15-6.8)
Tricolored Blackbird (15-6.8)
Hooded Oriole (15-6.8)
Northern Pintail (14-6.3)
Western Gull (14-6.3)
Great Blue Heron (12-5.4)
Vaux's Swift (12-5.4)
Western Tanager (12-5.4)
Red Crossbill (12-5.4)
Pelagic Cormorant (11-5.0)
Snowy Plover (11-5.0)
Hermit Warbler (11-5.0)
Gadwall (10-4.5)
Sora (10-4.5)
Black Oystercatcher (10-4.5)
Pigeon Guillemot (10-4.5)
Blue-winged Teal (9-4.1)
Ring-necked Pheasant (9-4.1)
Black-necked Stilt (9-4.1)
Solitary Vireo (8-3.6)
MacGillivray's Warbler (8-3.6)
American Bittern (7-3.2)
Sharp-shinned Hawk (7-3.2)
Black Rail (6-2.7)
Great Egret (5-2.3)
Wood Duck (5-2.3)
Common Merganser (5-2.3)
Clapper Rail (5-2.3)
Red-breasted Sapsucker (5-2.3)
Black-chinned Sparrow (5-2.3)
Brandt's Cormorant (4-1.8)
Northern Shoveler (4-1.8)
Sage Sparrow (4-1.8)
Lawrence's Goldfinch (4-1.8)
Common Murre (3-1.4)
Common Moorhen (2-0.9)
Northern Pygmy-Owl (2-0.9)
Burrowing Owl (2-0.9)
Long-eared Owl (2-0.9)
Common Poorwill (2-0.9)
Yellow-breasted Chat (2-0.9)
Ashy Storm-Petrel (1-0.4)
Double-crested Cormorant (1-0.4)
Snowy Egret (1-0.4)
Black-crowned Night-Heron (1-0.4)
Canada Goose (1-0.4)
Rhinoceros Auklet (1-0.4)
Tufted Puffin (1-0.4)
Short-eared Owl (1-0.4)
Say's Phoebe (1-0.4)
Northern Parula (1-0.4)

Table 7. Abundance ranking of all species recorded on the Marin County Breeding Bird Atlas. Species are listed in descending order in seven categories with respect to their Overall Population Index (OPI); see Content of Species Accounts (p. 75).

EXTREMELY LARGE POPULATION

Cliff Swallow (1010)
Warbling Vireo (984)
Song Sparrow (960)
Orange-crowned Warbler (955)
Dark-eyed Junco (940)

VERY LARGE POPULATION

Red-winged Blackbird (860)
Scrub Jay (856)
Mourning Dove (848)
House Finch (828)
Bewick's Wren (820)
Barn Swallow (812)
Wilson's Warbler (805)
California Towhee (804)
Allen's Hummingbird (792)
American Robin (788)
Chestnut-backed Chickadee (780)
Rufous-sided Towhee (780)
European Starling (776)
Brewer's Blackbird (772)
Wrentit (728)

LARGE POPULATION

Violet-green Swallow (708)
Purple Finch (708)
American Goldfinch (692)
Swainson's Thrush (685)
Pacific-slope Flycatcher (652)
Turkey Vulture (639)
Red-tailed Hawk (639)
California Quail (624)
Bushtit (621)
Pine Siskin (604)
Ash-throated Flycatcher (600)
Lesser Goldfinch (580)

FAIRLY LARGE POPULATION

House Sparrow (576)
Savannah Sparrow (575)
Hutton's Vireo (552)
Western Meadowlark (540)
Brown-headed Cowbird (519)
Plain Titmouse (516)
Black-headed Grosbeak (516)
Northern Oriole (516)
Brown Creeper (512)
Western Bluebird (510)
American Crow (507)
Black Phoebe (501)
Lark Sparrow (496)
Horned Lark (492)
Anna's Hummingbird (489)
Steller's Jay (462)
Great Horned Owl (447)
Killdeer (438)

MODERATE-SIZED POPULATION

White-crowned Sparrow (425)
Western Wood-Pewee (408)
Band-tailed Pigeon (351)
Lazuli Bunting (345)
Common Raven (340)
Mallard (330)

SMALL POPULATION

Downy Woodpecker (290)
Olive-sided Flycatcher (288)
Grasshopper Sparrow (288)
Northern Flicker (286)
Chipping Sparrow (279)
Rock Dove (270)
Tree Swallow (264)
Acorn Woodpecker (258)
American Kestrel (244)
Winter Wren (224)
Western Kingbird (222)
Nuttall's Woodpecker (216)
N. Rough-winged Swallow (208)
Northern Mockingbird (201)
White-breasted Nuthatch (177)
American Coot (174)
Hairy Woodpecker (164)
Cinnamon Teal (156)
Common Yellowthroat (152)

VERY SMALL POPULATION

Belted Kingfisher (146)
Hermit Thrush (144)
Marsh Wren (136)
Western Screech-Owl (126)
Pygmy Nuthatch (120)
Red-shouldered Hawk (112)
Rufous-crowned Sparrow (104)
Osprey (98)
Northern Harrier (96)
Black-throated Gray Warbler (92)
White-throated Swift (84)
Golden-crowned Kinglet (84)
Loggerhead Shrike (80)
Red-breasted Nuthatch (78)
Pied-billed Grebe (68)
Black-shouldered Kite (68)
Barn Owl (68)
Yellow Warbler (66)
Northern Saw-whet Owl (64)
House Wren (58)
Yellow-rumped Warbler (57)
Western Gull (56)
Pileated Woodpecker (56)
Pelagic Cormorant (55)
Green-backed Heron (48)
Purple Martin (48)
Blue-gray Gnatcatcher (48)

Tricolored Blackbird (45)
Hooded Oriole (45)
Pigeon Guillemot (40)
Golden Eagle (38)
Great Blue Heron (36)
Cooper's Hawk (36)
Virginia Rail (34)
Snowy Plover (33)
Spotted Owl (32)
Rock Wren (30)
California Thrasher (30)
Brandt's Cormorant (28)
Northern Pintail (28)
Black-necked Stilt (27)
Great Egret (25)
Western Tanager (24)
Hermit Warbler (22)
Common Murre (21)
Ruddy Duck (20)
Black Oystercatcher (20)
Ring-necked Pheasant (18)
Black Rail (18)
MacGillivray's Warbler (16)
Solitary Vireo (16)
Clapper Rail (15)
Red Crossbill (12)
Vaux's Swift (12)
Gadwall (10)
Sora (10)
Blue-winged Teal (9)
Sage Sparrow (8)
American Bittern (7)
Snowy Egret (7)
Sharp-shinned Hawk (7)
Black-crowned Night-Heron (6)
Common Poorwill (6)
Wood Duck (5)
Common Merganser (5)
Red-breasted Sapsucker (5)
Black-chinned Sparrow (5)
Northern Shoveler (4)
Lawrence's Goldfinch (4)
Ashy Storm-Petrel (3)
Common Moorhen (2)
Rhinoceros Auklet (2)
Tufted Puffin (2)
Northern Pygmy-Owl (2)
Long-eared Owl (2)
Yellow-breasted Chat (2)
Double-crested Cormorant (1)
Canada Goose (1)
Burrowing Owl (1)
Short-eared Owl (1)
Say's Phoebe (1)
Northern Parula (1)

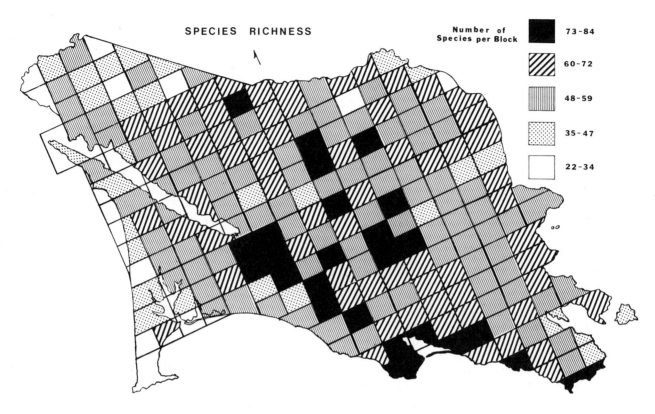

Figure 11. Map of countywide patterns of species richness of breeding birds.

of habitats, resulting from varied topography and the sharp moisture and temperature gradients over the short distance from the cool, moist coast to the hotter, drier interior.

Distributional Highlights of Atlas Work

The atlas field work documented distribution patterns for a number of Marin County's breeding species that probably would not have been predicted beforehand. Foremost among these was the distribution pattern here of the Grasshopper Sparrow. McCaskie et al. (1979) considered the Grasshopper Sparrow an uncommon to rare breeding species in northern California as a whole, and in preatlas days that classification seemed to fit Marin County as well. Thorough coverage of our previously little-birded grasslands revealed Grasshopper Sparrows breeding in over 10% of all atlas blocks and the vast majority of blocks near the coast with extensive grassland (atlas map and Figure 5). The concentration of breeding Grasshopper Sparrows in the moister, less disturbed grasslands toward the immediate coast matched the pattern noted along the San Mateo County coast in the 1960s and 1970s (D.F. DeSante pers. comm.); in contrast, Sibley (1952) had reported most nesting records in the south San Francisco Bay region were from the Inner Coast Range, 20 to 25 miles from the coast. Before the atlas period, the Cooper's Hawk was a species

very rarely reported in Marin County in the breeding season, but we now know it is a secretive but regular breeder here in broadleaved mixed evergreen forests.

Of course a number of rare or newly established breeders were documented nesting in the county for the first time during the atlas years. Among others, these included American Bittern, Common Merganser, Sharp-shinned Hawk, Black Rail, Black-necked Stilt, Short-eared Owl, Say's Phoebe, and Northern Parula. The first and subsequent breeding records of Red-breasted Sapsucker in the county documented the existence of a disjunct breeding population here (Shuford 1986). The atlas also provided documentation of the distribution of several species that, directly or indirectly as a result of activities of an expanding human population, have become well established here in appropriate habitat in the last few decades. These include Northern Mockingbird, European Starling, Brown-headed Cowbird, and Hooded Oriole. The reader is encouraged to comb the species accounts for other noteworthy breeding records or distribution patterns uncovered by the atlas work.

The previously little surveyed region of the county around Novato proved to support rather widespread breeding populations of species characteristic of the Inner Coast Range, such as Nuttall's Woodpecker, Western Kingbird, and Northern Oriole, and a restricted population of a formerly unknown breeder in the county—Blue-gray Gnatcatcher. That the Novato area also supported populations of such species as Olive-sided Flycatcher, Pacific-slope Flycatcher, Steller's Jay, Chestnut-backed Chickadee, Brown Creeper, Wilson's Warbler, and Purple Finch indicated that all of the county is tempered to some degree by the cool and moist coastal climate. Although hinted at by previous work (Orr 1937, Miller 1951), the slopes of Mount Tamalpais and some surrounding ridges proved to host the county's only or main breeding populations of Solitary Vireo, Yellow-rumped Warbler, Black-throated Gray Warbler, Hermit Warbler, and Western Tanager. The chaparral on Carson Ridge proved to be an important habitat in the county for Common Poorwill, California Thrasher, Rufous-crowned Sparrow, Sage Sparrow, and, irregularly, Black-chinned Sparrow. A number of waterbirds (ducks, rails, and shorebirds) were added to the county's breeding list, but the restricted breeding distribution of most of them documents the limited extent of freshwater, brackish, and saline wetlands in the county.

A number of other studies conducted concurrently with or subsequently to the atlas project have provided valuable data for the county on the distribution and abundance of breeding seabirds (Sowls et al. 1980, Carter et al. 1990), herons and egrets (Pratt 1983, p. 103 this volume), Black Rails (Evens et al. 1989), Snowy Plovers (Page & Stenzel 1981), Ospreys (Evens 1989), and Common Yellowthroats (Hobson et al. 1986). Quantitative data on an array of Marin's breeding birds has been contributed by Spring Bird Counts, Breeding Bird Plots, and Breeding Bird Surveys (Appendixes A–C).

Composition of the Breeding Avifauna

The 163 species of Marin County's breeding avifauna represent 43 families of birds. Of these, 41 are aquatic species (including Osprey, Belted Kingfisher, and Ameri-

can Dipper), and 122 are landbirds. All of the waterbirds can be found in Marin County year round, although 22 species have substantially greater populations in winter and 7 species have substantially greater populations in summer (Table 8). Of the landbirds, 30% (37) are summer residents (breeding migrants) and 70% (85) are year-round residents, although at least 23 of these are generally more numerous in winter (Table 9). Of 154 wintering landbird species recorded for Marin County (Shuford 1982), 67% (103) are year-round residents (including 15 species of lingering summer residents) and 33% (51) are wintering migrants (including lingering individuals of 13 species of typically passage migrants). These patterns of a relatively high percentage of resident species and a moderate percentage of summer and winter resident migrants are typical of the central and southern coast and foothill regions of California (Tangren 1977). On the whole, these regions tend to have relatively moderate temperatures and rainfall. Areas in California with a high percentage of summer residents and a low percentage of winter residents (e.g., high mountains) tend to have relatively low June and December temperatures and relatively high precipitation. Areas with a high percentage of winter residents and a low percentage of summer residents (e.g., Central Valley and southern deserts) tend to have relatively high June and December temperatures and relatively low precipitation. Areas with a high percentage of both summer and winter residents (e.g., northern Sacramento Valley) tend to have large amounts of June rainfall coupled with mild winters, whereas areas with low percentages of both of these components (e.g., some southern California mountains) tend to have relatively low June precipitation and relatively more severe winters (Tangren 1977).

Miller (1951) partitioned California's breeding birds into four avifaunal groupings—one of Boreal (conifer) affinity and three of Austral (lowland, nonboreal) affinity.

Table 8. A list of 41 species of waterbirds breeding in Marin County, California, with annotations on seasonal status; all species occur year round to some degree. List includes one extirpated breeder—American Dipper.

Pied-billed Grebe*	Northern Pintail*	Snowy Plover*
Ashy Storm-Petrel	Blue-winged Teal**	Killdeer*
Double-crested Cormorant	Cinnamon Teal**	Black Oystercatcher
Brandt's Cormorant	Northern Shoveler*	Black-necked Stilt**
Pelagic Cormorant	Gadwall*	American Avocet*
American Bittern*	Common Merganser*	Spotted Sandpiper*
Great Blue Heron	Ruddy Duck*	Western Gull
Great Egret**	Osprey**	Common Murre*
Snowy Egret	Black Rail*	Pigeon Guillemot**
Green-backed Heron**	Clapper Rail	Rhinoceros Auklet*
Black-crowned Night-Heron	Virginia Rail*	Tufted Puffin*
Canada Goose*	Sora*	Belted Kingfisher
Wood Duck*	Common Moorhen*	American Dipper*
Mallard	American Coot*	

* Relatively more numerous in winter.
** Relatively more numerous in summer.

Table 9. Classification of seasonal status of 122 species of breeding landbirds in Marin County, California. List includes one extirpated breeder—Greater Roadrunner—and three extralimital breeders—Say's Phoebe, Cassin's Kingbird, and Northern Parula.

YEAR-ROUND RESIDENTS
(85 Species)

	Hairy Woodpecker	Common Yellowthroat	Pacific-slope Flycatcher
Turkey Vulture	Northern Flicker*	Rufous-sided Towhee	Ash-throated Flycatcher
Black-shouldered Kite	Pileated Woodpecker	California Towhee	Cassin's Kingbird
Northern Harrier*	Black Phoebe	Rufous-crowned Sparrow	Western Kingbird
Sharp-shinned Hawk*	Say's Phoebe*	Lark Sparrow	Purple Martin
Cooper's Hawk*	Horned Lark	Sage Sparrow	Tree Swallow
Red-shouldered Hawk	Steller's Jay	Savannah Sparrow	Violet-green Swallow
Red-tailed Hawk*	Scrub Jay	Song Sparrow	N. Rough-winged Swallow
Golden Eagle	American Crow	White-crowned Sparrow*	Cliff Swallow
American Kestrel*	Common Raven	Dark-eyed Junco*	Barn Swallow
Peregrine Falcon*	Chestnut-backed Chickadee	Red-winged Blackbird	House Wren
Ring-necked Pheasant	Plain Titmouse	Tricolored Blackbird*	Blue-gray Gnatcatcher
California Quail	Bushtit	Western Meadowlark*	Swainson's Thrush
Rock Dove	Red-breasted Nuthatch*	Brewer's Blackbird	Solitary Vireo
Band-tailed Pigeon*	White-breasted Nuthatch	Brown-headed Cowbird	Warbling Vireo
Mourning Dove	Pygmy Nuthatch	Purple Finch	Orange-crowned Warbler**
Greater Roadrunner	Brown Creeper	House Finch	Northern Parula
Barn Owl	Rock Wren	Red Crossbill*	Yellow Warbler
Western Screech-Owl	Bewick's Wren	Pine Siskin	Black-throated Gray Warbler
Great Horned Owl	Winter Wren*	Lesser Goldfinch	Hermit Warbler**
Northern Pygmy-Owl	Marsh Wren	American Goldfinch	MacGillivray's Warbler
Burrowing Owl	Golden-crowned Kinglet*	House Sparrow	Wilson's Warbler
Spotted Owl	Western Bluebird		Yellow-breasted Chat
Long-eared Owl*	Hermit Thrush*		Western Tanager
Short-eared Owl*	American Robin*	**SUMMER RESIDENTS**	Black-headed Grosbeak
Northern Saw-whet Owl	Wrentit	(37 Species)	Lazuli Bunting
White-throated Swift	Northern Mockingbird		Chipping Sparrow
Anna's Hummingbird	California Thrasher	Common Poorwill**	Black-chinned Sparrow
Acorn Woodpecker	Loggerhead Shrike	Vaux's Swift	Grasshopper Sparrow
Red-breasted Sapsucker*	European Starling	Allen's Hummingbird	Hooded Oriole
Nuttall's Woodpecker	Hutton's Vireo	Olive-sided Flycatcher	Northern Oriole
Downy Woodpecker	Yellow-rumped Warbler*	Western Wood-Pewee	Lawrence's Goldfinch

*   Relatively more numerous in winter than summer.
** Small numbers regularly winter.

Members of these avifaunas have similar centers of distribution and often similar areas of origin as species. The four avifaunas are classified as follows:

1. *Boreal avifauna.* Species of northern derivation or distribution centered in coniferous forest areas and habitats.

2. *Great Basin avifauna.* Chiefly Great Basin and Great Plains species. This avifauna in California is concentrated east of the Sierran crest in grassland, sagebrush, piñon-juniper woodland, riparian woodland, and aquatic and semiaquatic environments.

3. *Sonoran avifauna.* Desert-dwelling species and those that range into the state from the Southwest and Mexico. In California, this avifauna occupies mostly Colorado and Mohave desert habitats of desert scrub, arid woodland, riparian woodland, and marshes.

4. *Californian avifauna.* Lowland species that are essentially confined to the state or are centered there and have their most continuous and dense populations in California. These species are found principally in oak woodlands, riparian forest, chaparral, and marshlands west of the Cascade-Sierra axis.

In addition, California's breeding avifauna hosts a large list of unclassified forms, chiefly species of marine environments, species of general continental or holarctic distribution, and species or races of widespread western North American distribution.

Marin County's avifauna is generally dominated by Boreal and Californian forms. Nonetheless, the Boreal and the combined Austral elements are of similar importance here at the species level, while Austral (mostly Californian) elements predominate at the racial and combined (species and race) levels (Table 10). The Boreal avifauna provides Marin with 27 species and 13 races; the Californian avifauna, 11 species and 33 races; the Great Basin avifauna, 11 species and 3 races; and the Sonoran avifauna, 5 species and 1 race. Only four Great Basin species (Western Meadowlark, Brewer's Blackbird, Northern Oriole, and Brown-headed Cowbird) and no Sonoran species were classified as having fairly large or larger populations in the county (cf. Tables 7 and 10), further indicating the minor contribution of these avifaunas to that of Marin County. The 27 Boreal species of Marin's avifauna are matched by 27 species of Austral origin; the 13 Boreal races compare to 37 Austral races.

Miller (1951) stressed the greater importance in California of the strong west-east moisture gradient versus the weaker north-south moisture and temperature gradient in influencing the differentiation of the state's Boreal avifauna. Similarly, the strong west-east (coast-interior) moisture and temperature gradients in Marin County are the prime factors affecting regional distribution of the county's avifauna, Boreal or non-Boreal. As detailed above, the county has two main climate zones: (1) a coastal zone of relatively high winter rainfall, cool summer temperatures, and high summer humidity from summer fog and (2) an interior zone with less rainfall, higher summer temperatures, and lower summer humidity. These climatic zones correspond to two main biogeographical regions of the county with differing avifaunas (Figure 12). The coastal zone has a dominant Boreal avifaunal element and the interior zone a dominant Austral/Californian element. Inverness Ridge, Bolinas Ridge, Mount Tamalpais, and several other spur ridges in central Marin have similar avifaunas because they share many species that prefer the conifer forests or dense mixed evergreen forests that predominate in the moist coastal zone. Characteristic landbirds of the coastal zone are Band-tailed Pigeon, Spotted Owl, Northern Saw-whet Owl, Hairy Woodpecker, Pileated Woodpecker, Olive-sided Flycatcher, Red-breasted Nuthatch, Pygmy Nuthatch, Winter Wren, Golden-crowned Kinglet, Hermit Thrush, Wilson's Warbler, and Pine Siskin. The upper slopes of Mount Tamalpais and nearby ridges support another subset of Boreal species. These areas have relatively high winter rainfall but are sheltered from intense summer fogs by either an inversion layer of warmer air at higher elevation or by the barrier of adjacent coastal ridges. In these somewhat drier areas, the conifer and mixed conifer forests are more open and hence support such boreal species as Solitary Vireo, Yellow-rumped Warbler, Western Tanager, and a non-Boreal but allied species, Black-throated Gray Warbler. All of these are lacking from Inverness Ridge, except Yellow-rumped Warbler, which breeds there in smaller numbers than on Mount Tamalpais.

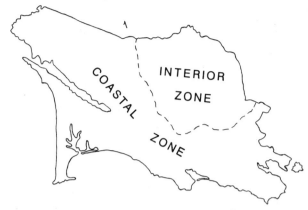

Figure 12. Preliminary map of the two main biogeographical regions of Marin County.

The avifaunas of outer Point Reyes and the Tomales area are also similar to each other. Although lacking most of the true conifer birds, their combined avifauna is primarily just a depauperate subset of that of the Boreal/coastal avifaunal region of Marin County. Hence, the Point Reyes/Tomales area should be included in that avifaunal region rather than in the Austral/interior region of Marin. The outer Point Reyes/Tomales area shares with the conifer-dominated coastal areas species such as Swainson's Thrush, Savannah Sparrow, Grasshopper Sparrow, White-crowned Sparrow, Pine Siskin, and American Goldfinch that are lacking or breed in smaller numbers in the drier interior of Marin.

The other true biogeographical region of Marin County is the oak woodland–dominated area from north of San Rafael through Novato to the Sonoma County line and west to around Hicks Valley. This Austral/interior region of Marin County supports a primarily Austral/Californian avifauna. Characteristic members of the avifauna of this region are Western Screech-Owl, Nuttall's Woodpecker, Plain Titmouse, White-breasted Nuthatch, House Wren, Blue-gray Gnatcatcher, and Lesser Goldfinch. As noted above, even in this region the coastal influence is felt as such Boreal species as Steller's Jay, Chestnut-backed Chickadee, Brown Creeper, Wilson's Warbler, Dark-eyed Junco, and Purple Finch are rather widely distributed, though more locally than on the immediate coast.

Miller (1951) divided California geographically into a number of faunal districts, provinces, and areas. He included the conifer-dominated areas of Marin County, as well as outer Point Reyes, in the Central Coast District of the Coastal Province of Boreal avifaunal regions of the state. He included the rest of Marin, including the Tomales area, in the San Francisco Bay District of the Californian Province of Austral avifaunal regions of the state. His inclusion of the Tomales area in the San Francisco Bay district, while at the same time including outer Point Reyes in the coastal Boreal province, seems unwarranted because of the number of moist habitat–adapted species found in

RESULTS AND DISCUSSION

Table 10. Avifaunal affinities of Marin County's breeding birds, after Miller (1951).

BOREAL AVIFAUNA (27 species)

Canada Goose[a]	Pygmy Nuthatch	Wilson's Warbler
Common Merganser	Brown Creeper	Western Tanager
Northern Pygmy-Owl	Winter Wren	White-crowned Sparrow
Spotted Owl	Golden-crowned Kinglet	Dark-eyed Junco
Northern Saw-whet Owl	Swainson's Thrush	Purple Finch
Red-breasted Sapsucker	Hermit Thrush	Red Crossbill
Olive-sided Flycatcher	Solitary Vireo	Pine Siskin
Steller's Jay	Yellow-rumped Warbler	
Chestnut-backed Chickadee	Hermit Warbler	
Red-breasted Nuthatch	MacGillivray's Warbler	

[a] A small population probably of introduced stock.

AUSTRAL AVIFAUNA

Great Basin Avifauna (11 species)

Blue-winged Teal	White-throated Swift	Brewer's Blackbird
Black-necked Stilt	Say's Phoebe[b]	Brown-headed Cowbird[c]
American Avocet	Rock Wren	Northern (Bullock's) Oriole[a]
Common Poorwill[a]	Western Meadowlark	

[a] Race in Marin of Californian affinity.
[b] Single extralimital breeding record.
[c] Race in Marin of Sonoran affinity.

Sonoran Avifauna (5 species)

Greater Roadrunner[a]	Northern Mockingbird[c]	Hooded Oriole[c,e]
Cassin's Kingbird[b]	Black-chinned Sparrow[d]	

[a] Extirpated.
[b] Single extralimital breeding record.
[c] Populations expanded into residential plantings in Marin in last few decades.
[d] Race presumed in Marin of Californian affinity.
[e] Race in Marin of Californian affinity.

Californian Avifauna (11 species)[a]

California Quail[b]	Plain Titmouse	Hutton's Vireo
Anna's Hummingbird	Bushtit	Tricolored Blackbird
Allen's Hummingbird	Wrentit[b]	Lawrence's Goldfinch
Nuttall's Woodpecker	California Thrasher	

[a] California Condor perhaps formerly bred in Marin.
[b] Race in Marin of Boreal affinity.

UNCLASSIFIED SPECIES (109 species)

Pied-billed Grebe	Wood Duck	Sharp-shinned Hawk[a]
Ashy Storm-Petrel	Mallard	Cooper's Hawk
Double-crested Cormorant	Northern Pintail	Red-shouldered Hawk[c]
Brandt's Cormorant	Cinnamon Teal	Red-tailed Hawk[d]
Pelagic Cormorant	Northern Shoveler	Golden Eagle
American Bittern[d]	Gadwall	American Kestrel
Great Blue Heron[c]	Ruddy Duck[b]	Peregrine Falcon
Great Egret	Turkey Vulture[d]	Ring-necked Pheasant
Snowy Egret[d]	Osprey	Black Rail[c]
Green-backed Heron[c]	Black-shouldered Kite	Clapper Rail[c]
Black-crowned Night-Heron	Northern Harrier	Virginia Rail

(Continued)

Table 10. *(Continued)*

UNCLASSIFIED SPECIES *(Continued)*

Sora
Common Moorhen
American Coot
Snowy Plover[c]
Killdeer
Black Oystercatcher
Spotted Sandpiper
Western Gull
Common Murre
Pigeon Guillemot
Rhinoceros Auklet
Tufted Puffin
Rock Dove
Band-tailed Pigeon[c]
Mourning Dove[d]
Barn Owl
Western Screech-Owl[c]
Great Horned Owl[a]
Burrowing Owl[d]
Long-eared Owl
Short-eared Owl[a]
Vaux's Swift[a]
Belted Kingfisher[d]
Acorn Woodpecker[c]
Downy Woodpecker[c]
Hairy Woodpecker[a]

Northern Flicker[d]
Pileated Woodpecker[a]
Western Wood-Pewee[a]
Pacific-slope Flycatcher[a]
Black Phoebe[c]
Ash-throated Flycatcher[d]
Western Kingbird[e]
Horned Lark[c]
Purple Martin
Tree Swallow
Violet-green Swallow[a]
N. Rough-winged Swallow
Cliff Swallow
Barn Swallow
Scrub Jay[c]
American Crow[d]
Common Raven[d]
White-breasted Nuthatch[c]
Bewick's Wren[a]
House Wren[d]
Marsh Wren[c]
American Dipper[a]
Blue-gray Gnatcatcher[c]
Western Bluebird[c]
American Robin
Loggerhead Shrike[c]

European Starling
Warbling Vireo[d]
Orange-crowned Warbler
Northern Parula
Yellow Warbler[c]
Black-throated Gray Warbler[e]
Common Yellowthroat
Yellow-breasted Chat[d]
Black-headed Grosbeak
Lazuli Bunting[e]
Rufous-sided Towhee[c]
California Towhee[c]
Rufous-crowned Sparrow[c]
Chipping Sparrow[b]
Lark Sparrow[b]
Sage Sparrow[c]
Savannah Sparrow[c]
Grasshopper Sparrow[d]
Song Sparrow[c]
Red-winged Blackbird[c]
House Finch[d]
Lesser Goldfinch[c]
American Goldfinch[c]
House Sparrow

[a] Race in Marin of Boreal affinity.
[b] Race in Marin of Great Basin affinity.
[c] Race in Marin of Californian affinity.
[d] Race of general western distribution.
[e] Species of general western distribution.

both the outer Point Reyes and Tomales areas. On the other hand, a number of species with interior affinities occur in the Tomales area to a limited or greater extent but are essentially lacking on outer Point Reyes. These species include Nuttall's Woodpecker, Western Kingbird, Lark Sparrow, and Northern Oriole. Quantitative analyses using matching coefficients and cluster analysis (Johnson & Cicero 1986, Taylor & Smith 1986), or other multivariate techniques, are needed to refine the subjectively described regions of avifaunal similarity in Marin County and perhaps to elucidate others.

Marin County Breeding Bird Communities

Knowledge of the requirements of individual species as described in the species accounts probably provides the most insight into species' distribution patterns. Looking at species' relationships may stimulate additional discussion of both local and broad-scale distribution patterns. For this reason, the county's nesting avifauna has been grouped into 22 main breeding bird communities (Table 11). Wiens (1989) has indicated that published definitions of biotic communities range from discrete, closely integrated assemblages of species that possess properties paralleling those of individuals, to the fortuitous overlapping of species responding independently to environmental conditions, to any set of organisms living near each other about which it is interesting to talk (Wiens 1989). The listing of species in Marin's bird communities implies no relationship among the species, or lack thereof, but simply that species in a particular community are likely to co-occur in similar habitats with a fair degree of certainty.

An important lesson learned from the exercise of categorizing Marin's birdlife into communities is that it is a difficult and not entirely satisfying task. Marin County, and California in general, are characterized by a diverse array of habitats arranged in a patchy mosaic over the landscape. Consequently, Marin hosts many single habitat specialists, many multihabitat generalists, and many edge-adapted species. Because many species may use several habitats, linger on the edge of two or more, or fall anywhere along the continuum among these strategies, they are difficult to categorize as to community affiliations. Hence, such species may not be listed as primary members of any community, but rather as secondary or tertiary members of several communities.

Most aquatic species of necessity use more than one habitat type—one for foraging and another for nest sites. For these species the foraging habitat is the community of which they are considered primary members. Among landbirds, raptors often use open habitats to forage in and nearby forests or cliffs for foraging perches, shelter or roost sites, and nest sites. Such species include Turkey Vulture,

Black-shouldered Kite, Red-shouldered Hawk, Red-tailed Hawk, Golden Eagle, American Kestrel, Peregrine Falcon, Barn Owl, Great Horned Owl, Northern Pygmy-Owl, and Long-eared Owl. Aerial insectivores such as swifts and swallows forage almost exclusively on the wing but must come to earth to nest. Among Marin's landbirds it is possible to list quite a number of strongly edge-adapted species or multihabitat generalists. These include California Quail, Mourning Dove, Common Poorwill, Anna's and Allen's hummingbirds, Northern Flicker, Black Phoebe, Western Kingbird, Scrub Jay, American Crow, Common Raven, Bushtit, Western Bluebird, American Robin, Northern Mockingbird, Loggerhead Shrike, European Starling, Lazuli Bunting, California Towhee, Rufous-crowned Sparrow, Lark Sparrow, Red-winged Blackbird, Tricolored Blackbird, Brewer's Blackbird, Brown-headed Cowbird, House Finch, Pine Siskin, the three goldfinch species, and House Sparrow. The large number of such species and the abundance and widespread distribution of many of them attest to the success of a generalist or edge-adapted lifestyle.

Factors Limiting Species Richness of the Avifauna

A great number of factors influence the number of species that breed in a given area, but several of these are of paramount importance (MacArthur & Wilson 1967, Wiens 1989). The pool of species available to colonize an area is a function of the distance from source populations, the size of source populations, and the dispersal ability of those species. Clearly, if populations of potential colonizers are isolated from an area by long distances, are small in size, and have poor dispersal abilities, they are unlikely to provide colonizers or become established if they arrive in the area in question. The availability of suitable habitat, nest sites, shelter, or other resources also influences the ability of an area to support colonizers that do reach the area. Local extinction (extirpation) can also reduce the number of breeding species, whether by unpredictable chance events such as volcanic activity, forest fires, or droughts or by competition with similar species or from predation.

At present the size of the Marin County breeding avifauna seems limited largely by availability of suitable breeding habitats. Many species of waterbirds that have bred elsewhere in the San Francisco Bay Area and potentially could colonize Marin County (see Potential Breeders pp. 429–434) occur here on a regular basis in winter or during migratory periods (Shuford et al. 1989). Presumably if suitable habitats were available in the county, some of them would establish themselves as breeders here. On the other hand, some species may be poor colonizers because of strong attachment to traditional breeding

Table 11.   Species membership of twenty-two Marin County breeding bird communities. Primary, secondary, and tertiary membership assigned by subjective assessment of species' relative abundance among habitat types and with respect to other members of a particular community. Many additional species may be found in the Urban/Suburban Community depending on the mix of native and exotic vegetation. Community use codes—N = nesting, F = foraging, E = use of edge of community—may apply to single species or a whole community. Nesting and foraging codes designate species that use a particular habitat for only one of those needs; in terrestrial habitats, all species that lack N and F codes satisfy both breeding and foraging needs in their respective habitats.

OCEANIC (PELAGIC) WATERS COMMUNITY (F)

Primary Members
Ashy Storm-Petrel
Rhinoceros Auklet
Tufted Puffin

Secondary Members
Western Gull
Common Murre

NERITIC (CONTINENTAL SHELF) WATERS COMMUNITY (F)

Primary Members
Brandt's Cormorant
Pelagic Cormorant
Western Gull

Common Murre
Pigeon Guillemot

Tertiary Members
Rhinoceros Auklet
Tufted Puffin
Osprey

ESTUARINE WATERS AND TIDAL FLAT COMMUNITY (F)

Primary Members
Great Blue Heron
Great Egret
Snowy Egret
Black-crowned Night-Heron
Osprey
Western Gull

Secondary Members
Mallard
Northern Pintail
Clapper Rail (E)
Snowy Plover
Killdeer (E)
Belted Kingfisher
American Crow (E)
Song Sparrow (E)

Tertiary Members
Double-crested Cormorant
Canada Goose
Peregrine Falcon
Brewer's Blackbird (E)

COASTAL SALT MARSH COMMUNITY

Primary Members
Mallard
Northern Harrier
Black Rail
Clapper Rail
Savannah Sparrow
Song Sparrow

Secondary Members
Northern Pintail
Cinnamon Teal

Tertiary Members
Black-necked Stilt (N,E)
Barn Owl (F)
Common Raven (F)

COASTAL BEACH AND DUNE COMMUNITY

Primary Members
Snowy Plover
Western Gull (F)
Common Raven (F)
Horned Lark
White-crowned Sparrow
House Finch
American Goldfinch

Secondary Members
Northern Harrier
Killdeer
Song Sparrow
Brewer's Blackbird
Brown-headed Cowbird

GRASSLAND COMMUNITY

Primary Members
Turkey Vulture (F)
Red-tailed Hawk (F)
Mourning Dove (F)
Great Horned Owl (F)
Western Kingbird (F)

Horned Lark
American Crow (F)
Common Raven (F)
Western Bluebird (F)
European Starling (F)
Lark Sparrow

Savannah Sparrow
Grasshopper Sparrow
Red-winged Blackbird (F)
Western Meadowlark
Brewer's Blackbird (F)
Brown-headed Cowbird (F)

(Continued)

Table 11. *(Continued)*

GRASSLAND COMMUNITY *(Continued)*

Secondary Members
Black-shouldered Kite (F)
Northern Harrier (F)
Golden Eagle (F)
American Kestrel (F)
Rock Dove (F)
Barn Owl (F)
Loggerhead Shrike (F)
Tricolored Blackbird (F)

Tertiary Members
California Quail (E/F)
Burrowing Owl
Short-eared Owl
Black Phoebe (E/F)
Say's Phoebe (F)
Lazuli Bunting (E/F)
California Towhee (E/F)
Rufous-crowned Sparrow (E)

Chipping Sparrow (E/F)
Northern Oriole (E/F)
House Finch (E/F)
Pine Siskin (E/F)
Lesser Goldfinch (E/F)
American Goldfinch (E/F)
Lawrence's Goldfinch (E/F)

NORTHERN COASTAL SCRUB COMMUNITY

Primary Members
California Quail
Allen's Hummingbird
Scrub Jay
Bushtit
Bewick's Wren
Wrentit
Rufous-sided Towhee
Song Sparrow
White-crowned Sparrow
Brown-headed Cowbird
American Goldfinch

Secondary Members
Great Horned Owl (E)
Western Bluebird (E)
Swainson's Thrush
European Starling (F)
Orange-crowned Warbler
Wilson's Warbler
California Towhee (E)
Rufous-crowned Sparrow
House Finch (E)

Tertiary Members
Mourning Dove (F)
Anna's Hummingbird
Northern Flicker (F)
American Robin (E/F)
Lazuli Bunting (E)
Black-chinned Sparrow
Brewer's Blackbird (E)
Purple Finch (E)
Pine Siskin (F)

FRESHWATER POND OR LAKE COMMUNITY

Primary Members
Pied-billed Grebe
Great Blue Heron (F)
Mallard (F)
Cinnamon Teal (F)
American Coot

Secondary Members
Great Egret (F)
Snowy Egret (F)
Green-backed Heron (F)
Black-crowned Night-Heron (F)
Wood Duck (F)

Northern Pintail (F)
Gadwall (F)
Ruddy Duck (F)
Osprey (F)
Virginia Rail (E/F)
Sora (E/F)
Killdeer (E/F)
Black-necked Stilt (F)
Belted Kingfisher (F)
Black Phoebe (E/F)
Song Sparrow (E/F)
Red-winged Blackbird (E/F)
Brewer's Blackbird (E/F)

Tertiary Members
Canada Goose (F)
Blue-winged Teal (F)
Northern Shoveler (F)
Common Merganser (F)
Common Moorhen (F)
American Avocet (F)
Spotted Sandpiper (E)

FRESHWATER MARSH COMMUNITY

Primary Members
Northern Harrier
Virginia Rail
Sora
Marsh Wren
Common Yellowthroat
Song Sparrow
Red-winged Blackbird

Secondary Members
Great Blue Heron (F)
Mallard
Cinnamon Teal
American Coot
Black Phoebe (E)
Tricolored Blackbird

Tertiary Members
American Bittern
Black Rail
Common Moorhen
Short-eared Owl

FRESHWATER STREAM COMMUNITY (F)

Primary Members
Great Blue Heron
Belted Kingfisher

Secondary Members
Green-backed Heron

Wood Duck
Mallard
Cinnamon Teal
Gadwall
Killdeer (E)
Song Sparrow (E)

Red-winged Blackbird (E)
Brewer's Blackbird (E)

Tertiary Members
Common Merganser

(Continued)

Table 11. *(Continued)*

COASTAL RIPARIAN FOREST COMMUNITY

Primary Members
Red-shouldered Hawk
California Quail (E)
Mourning Dove
Great Horned Owl
Anna's Hummingbird
Allen's Hummingbird
Downy Woodpecker
Hairy Woodpecker
Western Wood-Pewee
Pacific-slope Flycatcher
Black Phoebe (E)
Tree Swallow (N)
Steller's Jay
Scrub Jay
Chestnut-backed Chickadee
Bushtit
Bewick's Wren
Swainson's Thrush
American Robin
Wrentit

European Starling
Warbling Vireo
Orange-crowned Warbler
Yellow Warbler
Wilson's Warbler
Black-headed Grosbeak
Rufous-sided Towhee
Song Sparrow
Brown-headed Cowbird
Purple Finch
American Goldfinch (E)

Secondary Members
Green-backed Heron
Wood Duck
Northern Saw-whet Owl
Belted Kingfisher
Nuttall's Woodpecker
Northern Flicker
Ash-throated Flycatcher
American Crow (N)

Plain Titmouse
Winter Wren
Western Bluebird (E)
Hutton's Vireo
Common Yellowthroat
Lazuli Bunting (E)
California Towhee (E)
Red-winged Blackbird (E)
Northern Oriole
House Finch (E)
Pine Siskin
Lesser Goldfinch (E)

Tertiary Members
Cooper's Hawk
Red-breasted Sapsucker
House Wren
MacGillivray's Warbler
Yellow-breasted Chat

MIXED EVERGREEN FOREST COMMUNITY

Primary Members
Cooper's Hawk
Band-tailed Pigeon
Great Horned Owl
Northern Saw-whet Owl
Anna's Hummingbird
Allen's Hummingbird
Downy Woodpecker
Hairy Woodpecker
Western Wood-Pewee
Pacific-slope Flycatcher
Ash-throated Flycatcher
Steller's Jay
Scrub Jay
Chestnut-backed Chickadee
Bushtit
Brown Creeper
Bewick's Wren
Swainson's Thrush
American Robin (E)
Hutton's Vireo
Warbling Vireo
Orange-crowned Warbler
Wilson's Warbler
Black-headed Grosbeak
Dark-eyed Junco
Purple Finch

Secondary Members
Black-shouldered Kite (N,E)
Red-shouldered Hawk (N,E)
Red-tailed Hawk (N,E)
American Kestrel (N,E)
California Quail (E)
Mourning Dove (N,E)
Western Screech-Owl
Spotted Owl
Acorn Woodpecker
Northern Flicker (N,E)
Olive-sided Flycatcher
Violet-green Swallow (N)
Plain Titmouse
Red-breasted Nuthatch
White-breasted Nuthatch
Pygmy Nuthatch
Winter Wren
Golden-crowned Kinglet
Western Bluebird (N,E)
Hermit Thrush
Wrentit
European Starling (N)
Solitary Vireo
Yellow-rumped Warbler
Black-throated Gray Warbler
Western Tanager

Lazuli Bunting (E)
Rufous-sided Towhee
California Towhee (E)
Chipping Sparrow (N,E)
Lark Sparrow (N,E)
Song Sparrow
Brown-headed Cowbird (E)
House Finch (N,E)
Pine Siskin

Tertiary Members
Great Blue Heron (N)
Great Egret (N)
Snowy Egret (N)
Black-crowned Night-Heron (N)
Wood Duck
Turkey Vulture (N)
Northern Pygmy-Owl
Long-eared Owl (N)
Red-breasted Sapsucker
Tree Swallow (N)
American Crow (N)
Common Raven (N)
Northern Parula
White-crowned Sparrow (E)
American Goldfinch (E)

(Continued)

Table 11. *(Continued)*

BISHOP PINE FOREST COMMUNITY

Primary Members
- Northern Saw-whet Owl
- Allen's Hummingbird
- Hairy Woodpecker
- Pacific-slope Flycatcher
- Steller's Jay
- Chestnut-backed Chickadee
- Pygmy Nuthatch
- Brown Creeper
- Bewick's Wren
- Wrentit
- Wilson's Warbler
- Rufous-sided Towhee
- Dark-eyed Junco
- Purple Finch
- Pine Siskin

Secondary Members
- Mourning Dove (E)
- Spotted Owl
- Great Horned Owl (E)
- Violet-green Swallow (N)
- Bushtit
- Winter Wren
- Swainson's Thrush
- European Starling (N)
- Hutton's Vireo
- Song Sparrow
- White-crowned Sparrow (E)

Tertiary Members
- Osprey (N)
- California Quail (E)
- Band-tailed Pigeon
- Anna's Hummingbird

- Northern Flicker (E)
- Pileated Woodpecker
- Olive-sided Flycatcher
- Purple Martin (N)
- Tree Swallow (N)
- Red-breasted Nuthatch
- Golden-crowned Kinglet
- Western Bluebird (E)
- Hermit Thrush
- American Robin (E)
- Orange-crowned Warbler
- Yellow-rumped Warbler
- California Towhee (E)
- Chipping Sparrow
- Brown-headed Cowbird
- House Finch (E)
- Red Crossbill
- American Goldfinch (E)

COAST REDWOOD FOREST COMMUNITY

Primary Members
- Spotted Owl
- Northern Saw-whet Owl
- Allen's Hummingbird
- Hairy Woodpecker
- Pileated Woodpecker
- Pacific-slope Flycatcher
- Steller's Jay
- Chestnut-backed Chickadee
- Red-breasted Nuthatch
- Brown Creeper
- Winter Wren

- Golden-crowned Kinglet
- Hermit Thrush
- Wilson's Warbler
- Dark-eyed Junco
- Purple Finch
- Pine Siskin

Secondary Members
- Band-tailed Pigeon
- Vaux's Swift (N)
- Olive-sided Flycatcher
- American Robin

Tertiary Members
- Great Blue Heron (N)
- Great Egret (N)
- Snowy Egret (N)
- Turkey Vulture (N)
- Osprey (N)
- Sharp-shinned Hawk
- Pygmy Nuthatch
- Hermit Warbler
- Red Crossbill

DOUGLAS FIR FOREST COMMUNITY

Primary Members
- Band-tailed Pigeon
- Spotted Owl
- Northern Saw-whet Owl
- Allen's Hummingbird
- Hairy Woodpecker
- Pileated Woodpecker
- Olive-sided Flycatcher
- Pacific-slope Flycatcher
- Steller's Jay
- Chestnut-backed Chickadee
- Red-breasted Nuthatch
- Pygmy Nuthatch
- Brown Creeper
- Winter Wren
- Golden-crowned Kinglet
- Wilson's Warbler

- Dark-eyed Junco
- Purple Finch
- Pine Siskin

Secondary Members
- Bushtit (E)
- Hermit Thrush
- American Robin
- Wrentit
- European Starling (N)
- Yellow-rumped Warbler
- Lazuli Bunting (E)
- Rufous-sided Towhee
- Chipping Sparrow (N,E)
- Song Sparrow
- Brown-headed Cowbird (E)
- Red Crossbil

Tertiary Members
- Great Blue Heron (N)
- Great Egret (N)
- Turkey Vulture (N)
- Osprey (N)
- Sharp-shinned Hawk
- California Quail (E)
- Northern Pygmy-Owl
- Acorn Woodpecker (N,E)
- Red-breasted Sapsucker
- Purple Martin (N)
- Bewick's Wren
- Swainson's Thrush (E)
- Orange-crowned Warbler (E)
- Northern Parula
- Hermit Warbler
- White-crowned Sparrow (E)

(Continued)

Table 11. *(Continued)*

OAK WOODLAND AND OAK SAVANNAH COMMUNITY

Primary Members
Red-tailed Hawk
Mourning Dove
Anna's Hummingbird
Western Screech-Owl
Great Horned Owl
Acorn Woodpecker
Nuttall's Woodpecker
Ash-throated Flycatcher
Western Kingbird
Violet-green Swallow
Scrub Jay
Plain Titmouse
Bushtit
White-breasted Nuthatch
Bewick's Wren

Western Bluebird
European Starling
Orange-crowned Warbler
Chipping Sparrow
Brown-headed Cowbird
Northern Oriole
Lesser Goldfinch

Secondary Members
Turkey Vulture
Black-shouldered Kite (N)
Red-shouldered Hawk (N)
Golden Eagle
American Kestrel
California Quail
American Crow (E)

House Wren
Blue-gray Gnatcatcher
Hutton's Vireo
Lazuli Bunting (E)
Rufous-sided Towhee (E)
California Towhee (E)
Lark Sparrow (N,E)
Western Meadowlark
House Finch

Tertiary Members
Long-eared Owl (N)
Lawrence's Goldfinch

CHAPARRAL COMMUNITY

Primary Members
California Quail (E)
Common Poorwill
Anna's Hummingbird
Scrub Jay
Bushtit
Bewick's Wren
Wrentit
California Thrasher
Rufous-sided Towhee
Rufous-crowned Sparrow (E)
Sage Sparrow

Secondary Members
Turkey Vulture (E)
Mourning Dove (E)
Great Horned Owl (E)
Orange-crowned Warbler
Lazuli Bunting (E)
California Towhee (E)
Brown-headed Cowbird
Lesser Goldfinch (E)

Tertiary Members
Ash-throated Flycatcher
Blue-gray Gnatcatcher (E)
Black-chinned Sparrow

EUCALYPTUS GROVE COMMUNITY

Primary Members
Great Horned Owl
Allen's Hummingbird
Olive-sided Flycatcher
Chestnut-backed Chickadee
Bewick's Wren
American Robin
Northern Oriole
House Finch
Pine Siskin
American Goldfinch

Secondary Members
Red-shouldered Hawk (N)
Red-tailed Hawk (N)
Mourning Dove (N)
Downy Woodpecker
Northern Flicker

Western Kingbird (N,E)
Tree Swallow (N)
Scrub Jay
American Crow (N)
Common Raven (N)
Bushtit
Brown Creeper
Western Bluebird (N,E)
Swainson's Thrush
European Starling (N)
Lazuli Bunting (E)
California Towhee
Song Sparrow
Dark-eyed Junco
Brown-headed Cowbird (E)
Purple Finch
Lesser Goldfinch

Tertiary Members
Great Blue Heron (N)
Great Egret (N)
Black-shouldered Kite (N)
California Quail
Pacific-slope Flycatcher
House Wren
Winter Wren
Warbling Vireo
Chipping Sparrow
White-crowned Sparrow (E)

WEEDY FIELD COMMUNITY

Primary Members
California Quail
Mourning Dove
European Starling
California Towhee

Song Sparrow
Red-winged Blackbird
Brewer's Blackbird
Brown-headed Cowbird
House Finch

Pine Siskin (F)
Lesser Goldfinch (F)
American Goldfinch

(Continued)

Table 11. *(Continued)*

WEEDY FIELD COMMUNITY *(Continued)*

Secondary Members
Black-shouldered Kite (F)
Northern Harrier
Red-tailed Hawk (F)
American Kestrel (F)
Great Horned Owl (F)
Black Phoebe (E/F)
Bewick's Wren
Western Bluebird (F)
Rufous-sided Towhee
Western Meadowlark
House Sparrow

Tertiary Members
Mallard (N)
Northern Pintail (N)
Cinnamon Teal (N)
Northern Shoveler (N)
Gadwall (N)
Ring-necked Pheasant
Barn Owl (F)
Northern Flicker (F)
Western Kingbird (F)
Bushtit (F)
Loggerhead Shrike

Common Yellowthroat
Lazuli Bunting
Tricolored Blackbird

URBAN/SUBURBAN COMMUNITY

Primary Members
Rock Dove
Mourning Dove
Anna's Hummingbird
Northern Mockingbird
European Starling

California Towhee
Brewer's Blackbird
Brown-headed Cowbird
House Finch
House Sparrow

Tertiary Members
Hooded Oriole

AERIAL COMMUNITY (F)

Primary Members
Violet-green Swallow
Cliff Swallow
Barn Swallow

Secondary Members
Tree Swallow
N. Rough-winged Swallow

Tertiary Members
Peregrine Falcon
Vaux's Swift
White-throated Swift
Purple Martin

CLIFF, SLOPE, BLUFF, OR BANK COMMUNITY (N)

Primary Members
Brandt's Cormorant
Pelagic Cormorant
Black Oystercatcher
Western Gull
Common Murre
Pigeon Guillemot
Belted Kingfisher

Secondary Members
White-throated Swift
Pacific-slope Flycatcher
Black Phoebe
N. Rough-winged Swallow
Cliff Swallow
Barn Swallow
Common Raven
Rock Wren
Bewick's Wren

Tertiary Members
Ashy Storm-Petrel
Turkey Vulture
Peregrine Falcon
Rhinoceros Auklet
Tufted Puffin
Rock Dove

grounds. For example, Canada Geese (apparently from captive stock) have only recently become established as breeders in the San Francisco Bay Area (Lidicker & Mc-Collum 1979), including Marin County, although they have long wintered in the region (Grinnell & Wythe 1927, Grinnell & Miller 1944).

Many species of landbirds that breed elsewhere in California pass through Marin County as regular migrants or strays (Shuford 1982), but the few that have established themselves in Marin in recent decades either were formerly habitat limited or were introduced species expanding into vacant niches. Northern Mockingbirds and Hooded Orioles have both expanded their breeding ranges in California as a whole during this century. Both began to breed in Marin County as their statewide population numbers increased and the residential plantings they favor in this part of their range became available with the expanding human population (see accounts). Brown-headed Cowbirds also expanded into the San Francisco Bay Area, including Marin County, by exploiting habitat changes caused by extensive livestock grazing and other human habitat modifications. Introduced Rock Doves, European Starlings, and House Sparrows also expanded to exploit unoccupied niches (or were better competitors) in agricultural, pastoral, or urban/suburban habitats made suitable by human endeavors.

Extralimital breeders such as Cassin's Kingbird and Say's Phoebe have bred here only once each, presumably because of a lack of suitable breeding habitat. Although the breeding record of Cassin's Kingbird is also the only record of the species for the county, the Say's Phoebe is fairly common here each year in winter and thus provides a large pool of potential colonizers. It is unclear whether the Northern Parula is limited here by a lack of suitable habitat or by the fact that few potential colonizers stray from their eastern breeding grounds. Other species with small or irregular breeding populations in Marin such as American Avocet, Spotted Sandpiper, Burrowing Owl, Short-eared Owl, and Yellow-breasted Chat are probably limited by suitable habitat (e.g., lack of many ground squirrels to provide burrows for Burrowing Owls); colonizers are in short supply only for the Chat.

One species that very likely is absent as a breeder in Marin County because of its limited dispersal ability is Mountain Quail. Mountain Quail breed in the outer Coast Range both to the north and south of Marin County (Grinnell & Miller 1944), and seemingly suitable habitat

is available on Mount Tamalpais and elsewhere in Marin. However, Mountain Quail disperse on foot, and the closest breeding population in Sonoma County is cut off from Marin County by a large stretch of unsuitable grassland and marshland habitat along the border of the two counties. It is not clear if Blue Grouse, which also breeds in Sonoma County, has not colonized Marin County because of poor dispersal capabilities or because of unsuitable climatic or habitat factors. Red-breasted Sapsuckers formerly were thought to reach their breeding limit on the California coast in central Mendocino County but are now known to breed in small numbers in Sonoma and Marin counties (Shuford 1986). Limited observer coverage of the southern part of the coastal breeding range suggests that these small sapsucker populations formerly may have gone undetected, but then again the species may have colonized from the regular wintering population in this region, an option not available to Blue Grouse. Now that it is extirpated in the county, the Greater Roadrunner is as unlikely as the Mountain Quail to recolonize Marin County. The Roadrunner appears to be constrained by its limited dispersal abilities, the small size of the nearest breeding populations, and the inhospitability of the intervening habitats between Marin and source populations, rather than by lack of suitable breeding habitats in Marin. The American Dipper, another extirpated breeder and currently an irregular winter visitant here, seems unlikely to recolonize because of habitat degradation caused by damming of the one known former breeding stream.

The lack of a breeding population of a particular species may also be due to the time lag between extirpation and recolonization. Double-crested Cormorants formerly bred on the outer coast of Marin County and only recently have recolonized that area (see account), at a time when the coastal California breeding population as a whole was increasing. The potential pool of colonizing cormorants was large because of the species' presence in Marin year round, but nevertheless it took several decades to become reestablished here as a breeder. Peregrine Falcons formerly bred all along the Marin County coastline but were extirpated when the species' population crashed in the 1970s from reproductive failures caused by pesticide pollution. Peregrines recolonized Marin in 1990. The time lag between extirpation and recolonization may have been a function of both a limited pool of colonizers and chance factors that led to reestablishment of breeding populations in other counties before Marin.

CONSERVATION APPLICATIONS

Come now, let us make a truce with the children of life, and share with them the good things which we plentifully enjoy. There is happiness enough for all; and some of us there are who cannot be happy unless all are.

— William Leon Dawson,
The Birds of California

The birds and animals, trees and grasses, rocks, water and wind are our allies. We need to see them with our hearts as well as our minds, to let them speak to us of where we have come and where we are going, of three-and-a-half billion years of shared evolutionary travel, of our place on this planet.

— David Gaines,
Birds of Yosemite and the East Slope

How to Use This Book as a Conservation Tool

IT IS ONE THING to state that a breeding bird atlas will be useful for conservation or management but quite another to articulate exactly how to put it to its best use. Perhaps it is appropriate to start by stating what a breeding bird atlas will *not* do. An atlas will not substitute for environmental impact statements and reports involving studies of local habitat needs of birds or potential human impacts on birds at specific sites, particularly if local conditions have changed between the time of atlas work and these studies. Because an atlas tries to document the distribution, and sometimes abundance, of all species of birds in an area, it cannot be expected to be as accurate as similar studies that concentrate on single species (e.g., Page & Stenzel 1981 for Snowy Plovers) or small groups of closely related species of birds (e.g., Sowls et al. 1980 and Carter et al. 1990 for seabirds). An atlas will, however, if conducted and written with care, serve as a very important reference tool to conservationists, consultants, and managers. All atlases should first and foremost provide an accurate picture of distribution of most bird species in the chosen area and thus should serve as the primary reference that defines which breeding species are of restricted distribution there. These are the species that should be given special consideration in any development, mitigation, habitat enhancement, or habitat acquisition projects. Because species of limited range also often occur in small numbers, it should not be assumed that such species were found during the atlas years in every atlas block in which they actually breed. Hence, when a habitat is threatened with degradation, specific searches should be made for relatively rare species found in equivalent habitats in nearby blocks, based on the assumption that some such species missed in the initial atlas work may be found if additional effort is made.

The further usefulness of an atlas book will then depend on the types and extent of additional information provided to supplement the atlas maps of each breeding species. This will of course vary from atlas to atlas. Because the present book documents each species' current and former status, it lends a historical perspective to evaluations of the need for protection of species. For example, all other things being equal, greater consideration should be given to protection of a species that has already declined in numbers, especially if it is in trouble throughout its entire range. The extensive information on habitat, nesting, and food requirements will not only acquaint the reader with basic breeding needs of any species but will also direct them to further, more detailed literature. Information on population threats will also alert the reader to problems various species have faced in the past or might face in the future. In short, an atlas book can be most useful as a source of detailed information upon which decisions can be based. Often those decisions will require further field work and literature research, as rarely will this or any other atlas book provide all the information needed to understand and deal with a specific environmental problem.

Identification of Breeding Bird Species of Special Concern

A number of birds that breed in Marin County can be found on various lists of species that warrant or need consideration for protection at the state or national level (Table 12). Populations of these species are declining to various degrees and in extreme cases face possible extinction. At present only state and federally Threatened or

Table 12. Species or subspecies of birds that breed in Marin County that are currently listed as Endangered, Threatened, or of management concern in this region by state or national organizations.

FEDERAL AND STATE ENDANGERED[1, 2]

American Peregrine Falcon
California Clapper Rail

FEDERAL THREATENED[1]

Northern Spotted Owl
Western Snowy Plover (coastal population)

FEDERAL CANDIDATE[3], Category 2

Black Rail
California Horned Lark
Loggerhead Shrike
Saltmarsh Common Yellowthroat
Bell's Sage Sparrow
San Pablo Song Sparrow
Tricolored Blackbird

FEDERAL MANAGEMENT CONCERN[4], Region 1
(California)

Black Rail
Snowy Plover
Olive-sided Flycatcher
Loggerhead Shrike

STATE THREATENED[2]

California Black Rail

STATE SPECIES OF SPECIAL CONCERN[5]

Ashy Storm-Petrel
Double-crested Cormorant
Osprey
Northern Harrier
Sharp-shinned Hawk
Cooper's Hawk
Golden Eagle
Snowy Plover
Rhinoceros Auklet
Tufted Puffin
Burrowing Owl
Long-eared Owl
Short-eared Owl
Purple Martin
Yellow Warbler
Saltmarsh Common Yellowthroat
Yellow-breasted Chat
San Pablo Song Sparrow
Tricolored Blackbird

AUDUBON BLUE LIST[6]

American Bittern
Northern Harrier
Sharp-shinned Hawk
Cooper's Hawk
Red-shouldered Hawk
Short-eared Owl
Loggerhead Shrike
Grasshopper Sparrow

---

[1] U.S. Fish and Wildlife Service (1989a), Federal Register.
[2] Calif. Dept. Fish and Game (1991a).
[3] U.S. Fish and Wildlife Service (1991).

[4] U.S. Fish and Wildlife Service (1987b).
[5] Calif. Dept. Fish and Game (1991b).
[6] Tate (1986).

Endangered species are afforded special legal protection, although many Candidate or Forest Service "sensitive" species are treated on federal lands as if they were "listed." Other management categories of concern are just that—they express concern over apparent declines in species' populations but do little to protect them beyond raising awareness, an important first step. Although these protection efforts should be lauded, they may not do enough. Are the state and federal levels the only valid ones for consideration of protection of species? Biodiversity has recently become a fashionable concept to promote, but should we try to enhance biodiversity just at the state and federal level and not at the county level or even in our backyards? Should we settle for small populations of species in distant parts of our state and nation, when with protection viable populations could exist as well in our own neighborhoods? Preservation and enhancement of habitats is now also an often championed approach to retaining biodiversity, but

again why not at the local as well as the state and federal levels? These topics will be hotly debated in the years to come.

As a starting point for consideration of preservation of biodiversity of breeding birds in Marin County, it seems logical to first promote protection of all the species that breed in the county that have already been given a state, federal, or other national management designation (Table 12). This study also identifies an additional preliminary list of Marin County Breeding Bird Species of Special Concern (Table 13), not on any state or national list, that should at a minimum be given consideration for protection at the county level. An emphasis is placed on the preliminary nature of the Marin list and the need for refining it, as others will undoubtedly disagree with the author over which species to include on the list or if such a county list is even needed. The species in Table 13 are regular native breeding species with overall population indices in the lower 25% of those calculated for all species recorded in the atlas project (Table 7). They are vulnerable because they nest here in very small numbers, generally in restricted, often imperiled, habitats or are colonial nesting species that concentrate at very few sites. Some species falling in the lower 25% of population indices were excluded from the list because they were irregular or extralimital breeders (Canada Goose, Blue-winged Teal, Say's Phoebe, Northern Parula, Black-chinned Sparrow, Red Crossbill, and Lawrence's Goldfinch) or had small recently established populations in human-created habitat (Hooded Oriole).

If we are to maintain viable diverse communities of birds in Marin County, it is clearly necessary to protect extensive areas of the full range of the county's natural habitats. Fortunately much of our land has already been preserved in parks or open space (Figure 6). The effect of habitat fragmentation on bird populations is now a trendy topic in ecological and conservation circles, but our knowledge of these effects is still in its infancy. In that light, it seems prudent to err on the side of caution and preserve

large rather than small areas of habitat. The bird habitats in Marin County that most deserve protection are ones that conservation efforts are also currently focused on elsewhere in the state and nation—wetlands, marshlands, and riparian forests. Of the 63 species from the county on various management lists (Tables 12 and 13), 51% are marsh-dependent species, other waterbirds, or seabirds; 21% are miscellaneous landbirds; 19% are raptors (two species are also marsh dependent); 5% are chaparral-dependent species; and 5% are riparian-dependent species. As discussed in the land use section, loss or degradation of important habitats in the county is very evident. Many of these species, particularly those dependent on wetlands, face uncertain futures without preservation or enhancement of their habitats.

The knowledge presented in this and other scientific studies can inform concerned citizens, but only if they repeatedly and forcefully express the value and importance that wildlife plays in enhancing their lives will habitat preservation and enhancement efforts succeed.

Trail winding through the dimly-lit understory of the Douglas fir forest on Inverness Ridge. Drawing by Ane Rovetta, 1986.

Table 13. A preliminary list of Breeding Bird Species of Special Concern in Marin County. Does not include species already given state, federal, or national protection or recognition (see Table 12).

BRANDT'S CORMORANT – county breeding population concentrated at only six colonies; vulnerable to disturbance at colonies and oil pollution.

PELAGIC CORMORANT – breeding population well scattered along the coast but particularly vulnerable to nearshore oilspills in breeding season.

GREAT BLUE HERON – currently breeding at only seven colonies and numbers breeding in county have declined in recent years; vulnerable to loss of wetlands, disturbance at colonies, and pesticide contamination.

GREAT EGRET – currently breeding at only five colonies; dependent on dwindling wetlands and vulnerable to pesticide contamination and disturbance at colonies.

SNOWY EGRET – virtually entire county breeding population concentrated at one colony; dependent on vanishing wetlands and vulnerable to disturbance and pesticides.

GREEN-BACKED HERON – a very small population dependent on overgrown borders of streams and marsh edges; threatened by degradation and loss of riparian and freshwater marsh habitats.

BLACK-CROWNED NIGHT-HERON – entire county breeding population concentrated at one colony; dependent on shrinking wetlands and vulnerable to disturbance at colonies and pesticides.

WOOD DUCK – very small population dependent on freshwater ponds and streams with overgrown borders; numbers apparently reduced over former times.

NORTHERN PINTAIL – very small breeding population dependent on freshwater, brackish, and saline wetlands for breeding.

NORTHERN SHOVELER – currently known to breed in the county at only one managed freshwater wetland.

GADWALL – very small breeding population dependent on scarce freshwater and brackish marshes and ponds.

COMMON MERGANSER – very small breeding population on reservoirs and streams.

RUDDY DUCK – very small breeding population in freshwater ponds and marshes.

VIRGINIA RAIL – very small breeding population restricted to freshwater marshes.

SORA – very small breeding population restricted to freshwater marshes.

COMMON MOORHEN – very small breeding population dependent on limited freshwater ponds, sloughs, and marshes.

BLACK OYSTERCATCHER – very small breeding population restricted to rocky shores primarily on the outer coast; intertidal food supply vulnerable to oil pollution.

BLACK-NECKED STILT – very small breeding population restricted to a few freshwater and brackish wetlands along the San Francisco and San Pablo bay shorelines; vulnerable to heavy metal contamination.

AMERICAN AVOCET – has attempted to breed a few times in brackish or freshwater wetlands along the San Francisco and San Pablo bay shorelines; vulnerable to heavy metal contamination.

COMMON MURRE – currently breeding in the county at only four colonies; populations have been severely reduced in recent years by oil pollution, gill netting, and severe El Niño.

PIGEON GUILLEMOT – breeding population well scattered along coast but particularly vulnerable to nearshore oilspills in breeding season.

NORTHERN PYGMY-OWL – inexplicably scarce as a breeding bird in the county; dependent on clearings in conifer and mixed evergreen forests.

COMMON POORWILL – very small breeding population restricted to chaparral-covered ridges.

VAUX'S SWIFT – very small breeding population apparently dependent on fire-hollowed nesting snags in conifer forests.

RED-BREASTED SAPSUCKER – very small disjunct breeding population dependent on moist conifer forests and bordering riparian zones.

PILEATED WOODPECKER – very small breeding population dependent on old-growth or mature second-growth conifer forests.

ROCK WREN – very small population breeding at few sites; may be vulnerable to predation as is the Farallon population.

BLUE-GRAY GNATCATCHER – very small breeding population restricted mostly to live oak woodlands.

CALIFORNIA THRASHER – very small breeding population restricted to a few chaparral-covered ridges.

SOLITARY VIREO – very small breeding population restricted to relatively dry open mixed evergreen woodlands on Mount Tamalpais and vicinity.

HERMIT WARBLER – very small breeding population inhabits Douglas fir or mixed Douglas fir/redwood forests on Mount Tamalpais and nearby ridges.

MACGILLIVRAY'S WARBLER – very small breeding population inhabits brushy riparian borders mostly on the coastal slope.

WESTERN TANAGER – very small population breeding in relatively open Douglas fir or mixed evergreen hardwoods on Mount Tamalpais and nearby ridges.

CONTENT OF SPECIES ACCOUNTS

Birds . . . had many magical properties . . . they were thought to know the secret of all living things, to have great foresight, and to fill with wisdom the hearts of those who took the trouble to learn their language and listen.

— Laurens van der Post,
A Story Like the Wind

THE SPECIES ACCOUNTS section of the book provides basic, though detailed, information for all of Marin County's breeding birds. The key sections of each account include (1) an atlas distribution map, (2) atlas data accompanying the map, and (3) the species account text. These materials are presented in a standardized format as described below.

Atlas Breeding Distribution Maps

A distribution map is presented for each species that was confirmed or believed to breed in Marin County during the period of atlas field work, 1976 to 1982. Species lacking atlas maps were found breeding in Marin County prior to or after the period of atlas field work. Each map has the atlas grid of 221 blocks overlain on a standard map of Marin County. Broken lines within the county boundaries denote major roads—further orientation can be obtained by reference to the place name map of Marin County (Figure 2).

Three symbols are used within the blocks of the atlas maps to denote the three categories of breeding evidence (Table 5):

- ○ — Possible Breeding
- ◑ — Probable Breeding
- ● — Confirmed Breeding

Blocks lacking any of the above symbols indicate that no evidence of breeding was observed in that block for that species during the period of atlas field work. Asterisks in certain blocks of the map for Nuttall's Woodpecker denote records of that species in late June and July indicative of postbreeding dispersal; these data demonstrate the importance of completing field work before the postbreeding period (which varies among species) to ensure that atlas maps accurately portray *breeding* distribution.

The symbol *P* next to the map of several rare and sensitive species denotes that locations of breeding records have been protected by moving dots on the map by one to two blocks in any direction (see Data Summary p. 48).

Key to Abundance and Distribution Data Accompanying Atlas Maps

This key describes the information that accompanies the atlas map preceding the species account text, with examples for a colonial nesting species—Great Blue Heron—and a solitary nesting species—Swainson's Thrush (Figure 13). Accounts for former, or recently documented, breeding species of course lack atlas maps or data and therefore are preceded only by information on former or current seasonal status.

Seasonal Status

Information is presented on whether a breeding species occurs in Marin County as a year-round resident or only as a summer resident (Figure 13). For year-round residents, periods of peak occurrence (if any) are indicated and whether the species occurs primarily in a seasonal role other than as a breeder. For example, the seasonal status of the Sharp-shinned Hawk is "Occurs year round, though almost exclusively as a winter resident and transient from Sep through Apr; numbers swell substantially during fall migration from Sep through mid-Nov." Information is also provided on the periods when colonial waterbirds gather at their breeding colonies (e.g., Great Blue Heron, Figure 13).

Breeding Status

This section gives a verbal description of the relative abundance of the species in an average block and its distribution countywide, based, respectively, on categories of the Fine-Scale Abundance Rating and the Relative Distribution Index listed below. In addition, the overall population size of the species in the county is described by the verbal categories of the Overall Population Index also listed below. For example, Swainson's Thrush (Figure 13) is termed "a *very common* [Fine-Scale Abundance Rating = 5], *widespread* [Relative Distribution Index = 137] breeder; overall breeding population *large* [Overall Population Index = 685]."

73

Great Blue Heron *Ardea herodias*

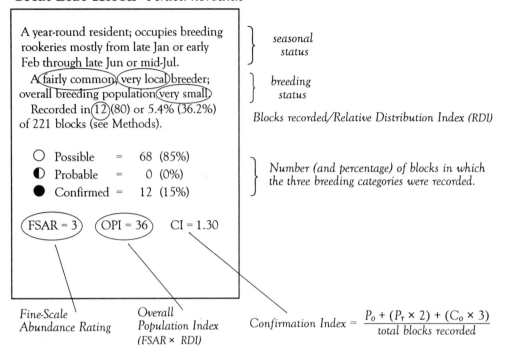

A year-round resident; occupies breeding rookeries mostly from late Jan or early Feb through late Jun or mid-Jul. } *seasonal status*

A fairly common, very local breeder; overall breeding population very small. } *breeding status*

Recorded in 12 (80) or 5.4% (36.2%) of 221 blocks (see Methods). *Blocks recorded/Relative Distribution Index (RDI)*

○ Possible   = 68 (85%)
◐ Probable   = 0 (0%)
● Confirmed = 12 (15%) } *Number (and percentage) of blocks in which the three breeding categories were recorded.*

FSAR = 3   OPI = 36   CI = 1.30

Fine-Scale Abundance Rating

Overall Population Index (FSAR × RDI)

$$\text{Confirmation Index} = \frac{P_o + (P_r \times 2) + (C_o \times 3)}{\text{total blocks recorded}}$$

Swainson's Thrush *Catharus ustulata*

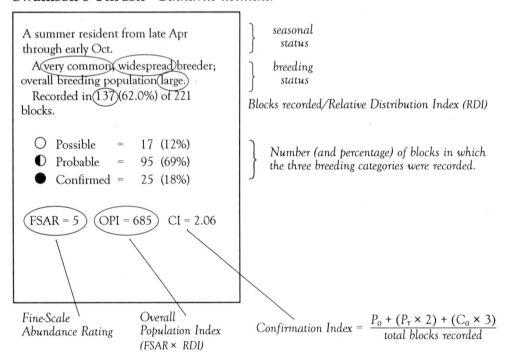

A summer resident from late Apr through early Oct. } *seasonal status*

A very common, widespread breeder; overall breeding population large. } *breeding status*

Recorded in 137 (62.0%) of 221 blocks. *Blocks recorded/Relative Distribution Index (RDI)*

○ Possible   = 17 (12%)
◐ Probable   = 95 (69%)
● Confirmed = 25 (18%) } *Number (and percentage) of blocks in which the three breeding categories were recorded.*

FSAR = 5   OPI = 685   CI = 2.06

Fine-Scale Abundance Rating

Overall Population Index (FSAR × RDI)

$$\text{Confirmation Index} = \frac{P_o + (P_r \times 2) + (C_o \times 3)}{\text{total blocks recorded}}$$

Figure 13. Examples of data presented with the atlas map of each breeding species during the Marin County Breeding Bird Atlas project. Data presentation is slightly different for colonial breeders (e.g., Great Blue Heron above) than solitary breeders (e.g., Swainson's Thrush above) because most colonies have been located and their size determined (see text). The circled abundance and distribution terms are the verbal equivalents (from index scales, p. 75), respectively, of the circled FSAR, RDI, and OPI values below them.

74

Blocks Recorded

For each species, the number of atlas blocks in which it was recorded is listed along with what percentage of the total number of blocks (221) that represents. Because we felt we documented most, if not all, heron and egret colonies, for those species, data on blocks recorded is listed first as the number of blocks with confirmed breeding based on known active colonies. Following in parentheses is the number of blocks in which these wetland-dependent species were recorded, as an indication of the importance of foraging habitat away from colonies and often outside the atlas block where actual nesting activities were centered (e.g., Great Blue Heron, Figure 13). Similarly, for herons and egrets, the percentage of "total" blocks is listed first as the percentage of *confirmed* to total blocks and in parentheses as the percentage of recorded to total blocks. Since the atlas grid did not sample most foraging habitat of breeding seabirds, the number of blocks recorded (and percentage of total blocks) for those species is based on only the number of blocks with active colonies.

Fine-Scale Abundance Rating (FSAR)

For all but colonial waterbirds, this rating qualitatively defines the abundance of a species (based on notes and impressions gathered by the author over a number of years) in an "average" atlas block in which it was recorded. The scale from 1 to 7 is based on the number of pairs an observer would expect to encounter by sight and/or sound while on foot during four hours afield in one block during prime daily or nightly hours of activity for the species during the height of its breeding season. Because the categories were assigned qualitatively, they may be off by plus or minus one (or more?) category. For colonial waterbirds, rating categories are assigned based on average population sizes of known colonies in Marin County during the atlas period (Tables 14-17). The categories (numbers seen/4 hrs) and their verbal equivalents are based on a log scale like that used by DeSante and Ainley (1980):

1	< 1 pair	very rare (irregular; does not occur every year)
		rare (regular; occurs yearly)
2	1-3 pairs	uncommon
3	4-9 pairs	fairly common
4	10-27 pairs	common
5	28-81 pairs	very common
6	82-243 pairs	abundant
7	> 243 pairs	very abundant

Relative Distribution Index (RDI)

For all but colonial waterbirds, this index is a measure of the relative breeding distribution of a species in the county based simply on the number of blocks in which it was recorded during the period of atlas field work. The index for colonial waterbirds is the number of blocks with active

breeding colonies. For example, the Great Blue Heron (Figure 13) has a Relative Distribution Index of 12 (blocks with colonies) even though it was recorded in a total of 80 blocks. The total number of potential blocks in the county (221) in which a species could occur were divided into seven categories with verbal equivalents:

1-31 blocks	very local
32-62 blocks	local
63-93 blocks	somewhat local
94-124 blocks	fairly widespread
125-155 blocks	widespread
156-186 blocks	very widespread
187-221 blocks	nearly ubiquitous

Overall Population Index (OPI)

This index is derived by multiplying the Fine-Scale Abundance Rating for a species times the number of blocks in which it was recorded during the atlas project (times blocks with colonies for colonial waterbirds). The range of actual values—from 1 to 1010—was divided into seven categories with verbal descriptions:

1-146	very small population
147-290	small population
291-434	moderate-sized population
435-578	fairly large population
579-722	large population
723-866	very large population
867-1010	extremely large population

Breeding Criteria Categories

For each of the three Breeding Criteria Categories of Possible (○), Probable (◑), and Confirmed (●) there is listed the number of blocks in which that category was recorded and, in parentheses, the percentage of the total number of recorded blocks (of all categories) that figure represents. Colonial waterbirds are treated the same as other species even though they probably were confirmed in most, if not all, the blocks they were breeding in.

Confirmation Index (CI)

This index is a measure of how difficult each species was, relative to other species, to confirm as a breeder. The index for each species was derived by multiplying the number of blocks with Possible evidence of breeding by 1, the number of blocks with Probable evidence by 2, and the number of blocks with Confirmed evidence by 3. These three products were then summed and divided by the total number of blocks in which the species was recorded. Though used for a different purpose, our Confirmation Index is similar mathematically to the "ACID" (Adequate Coverage Identification) test used by some to evaluate whether an atlas block has received enough observer coverage (Kibbe 1986, p. 46 this volume).

Content of Species Account Text

Although the atlas maps do stand alone in documenting the breeding distribution of each species, they do not provide information that might help to explain the observed distribution or a knowledge of habitat and foraging requirements necessary for conservation efforts. These functions are served by the species account text. Selected (but detailed) biological/ecological, distributional, and historical information is presented in three standard sections: (1) Ecological Requirements, (2) Marin Breeding Distribution, (3) Historical Trends/Population Threats (sometimes combined with section 2), and a fourth infrequently used Remarks section. The accounts primarily are meant to be informative and to point the reader in the right direction when additional information is needed. They are by no means meant to be the last word on the subject.

Because an attempt has been made to standardize the accounts and make them accessible, without sacrificing detail, the reader may be under the illusion that most aspects of each species' breeding ecology are well known. This is far from the case. Much still needs to be known about the basic biology of even the most common and well-studied species. The species accounts vary greatly in length for the simple reason that the amount of information available varies widely among species. The reader is cautioned to interpret and use this information carefully. If information is critical for the conservation efforts of a species, primary sources should be consulted directly and, if possible, local studies should be undertaken.

Although an effort was made to use information from local studies whenever possible, the data presented in the species accounts may have been collected far from Marin County or even outside California, and its applicability may suffer accordingly. The reader may wonder why the text provides detail on aspects of a species ecology derived from distant studies when in fact local studies are available. Such information is presented because insight often comes from comparing the biology of the same species in different habitats. A classic example of this is Bob Stewart's comparative studies of Wilson's Warblers at Palomarin on the Point Reyes National Seashore and at Tioga Pass in the Sierra Nevada (see account). The comparative approach works on the local level as well. I did not realize that a basic habitat requirement of breeding Wilson's Warblers in Marin County was moist, low dense cover until I observed them breeding here in moist stands of coastal scrub that lacked the canopy of Douglas fir, bishop pine, alder, or willow typically associated with their more widespread forested breeding haunts here.

Although the accounts focus on the important aspects of each species ecology, they *cannot* begin to convey adequately the grace, spirit, intensity, drama, humor, or exhilarating beauty of our feathered friends and their lives. Much of avian essence can be captured in prose and poetry, as such authors as Dawson (1923) and others have so admirably demonstrated, but much cannot. One has to experience birds in the raw, on their own terms. The accounts that follow may in some small way transmit an appreciation for the ecological factors that are important to birds, but only by spending time with the birds themselves can we appreciate their importance, and that of the rest of the natural world, to our lives.

Ecological Requirements

The more one knows about the basic breeding biology of a species, the better able one is to interpret its pattern of distribution. Nevertheless, an understanding of certain aspects of the ecology of breeding birds appears more crucial in this regard. Hence, particular ecological requirements have been emphasized here and others have been deliberately ignored, even though the latter factors might provide additional insight as well. Each species account tries to describe the range of local habitats the species occupies for breeding, special features of the habitat(s) it needs, where it locates its nest, what type(s) of nest it builds and of what materials, what kinds of food it requires, and what foraging styles it uses to obtain its food. For all but habitat requirements, information on seasonal, sex-, and age-related variation in nesting and foraging requirements are presented when available. Various biological characteristics of each species such as types of breeding displays or clutch size are *not* presented because they do not bear directly on the issue of niche requirements and because this information is already summarized in such standard references as Harrison (1978) and Ehrlich et al. (1988).

Marin Breeding Distribution

This section gives a verbal description of the species' breeding distribution, any geographical trends of distribution or abundance in the county, and any factors that might help explain the observed distribution. Also included are specific documented records from the period of atlas field work, though particularly noteworthy records from outside that period are occasionally listed as well. The format of these "representative" breeding records is as follows: (breeding code, date of observation, and observer initials). For example, a record (NY 5/22-28/82 —TO) would read that a nest with young was under observation from 22 to 28 May 1982 by Typical Observer. Breeding codes (Table 5) joined by a slash indicates that more than one type of breeding behavior was observed on the same date, whereas codes joined by a hyphen indicates that different categories of breeding evidence were observed over a period of days or weeks.

Historical Trends/Population Threats

Although the historical record of changes in the distribution and abundance of birds in Marin County and California as a whole is incomplete, any and all apparent population trends are discussed, from the local to the widespread. The main historic sources consulted were Mailliard (1900) and Stephens and Pringle (1933) for Marin County; Grinnell and Wythe (1927) and Sibley (1952) for the San Francisco Bay Area; and Grinnell and Miller (1944) and Remsen (1978) for California as a whole. Robbins et al. (1986) and the corresponding unpublished Breeding Bird Survey data for California collected by volunteers of USFWS provided information on recent bird population trends. Additional sources are other avifaunal works, published papers or reports on particular species or species groups, and the published seasonal reports and/or unpublished data on file with the editors of the Middle and Southern Pacific Coast regions of *American Birds*.

Remarks

This section is a catch-all used very infrequently and only when important or interesting material about a species did not fit conveniently into any of the three main subdivisions of the species accounts (e.g., Brown-headed Cowbird account).

Observers

The following individuals are cited in the text for their specific observations: Peg Abbott (PA), Sarah G. Allen (SGA), Carol Annable (CA), Bob Baez (BoB), Janice Barry (JBa), Hal Barwood (HBa), Dennis Beall (DnB), Max Beckwith (MB), Gordon Beebe (GBe), Edward C. Beedy (ECB), Laurence C. Binford (LCB), Barbara Binger (BBi), Tupper Ansel Blake (TAB), Gerald Brady (GB), Aubrey Burns (ABu), Stan Camiccia (SCa), Scott Carey (ScC), Harry R. Carter (HRC), Pam Cleland (PCl), Marna Cohen (MC), Peter Colasanti (PCo), Chris Cutler (CCu), Dave DeSante (DDeS), Jules G. Evens (JGE), Carter L. Faust (CLF), Marc Fenner (MFe), Shawneen E. Finnegan (SEF), Richard Franz (RFz), Steve Gellman (SG), Al & Wilma Ghiorso (A&WG), Manuel & Lillian Gorin (M&LG), Keith Hansen (KH), Rob Hansen (RH), Roger D. Harris (RDH), Roger Harshaw (RHa), Burr Heneman (BHe), Jim Higbee (JH), Emmy Hill (EH), David A. Holway (DAH), Ken Howard (KeHo), Stuart Johnston (SJ), John P. Kelly (JPK), Shirley & Mike Kelly (S&MK), John Kipping (JKip), Gerry J. Kleynenberg (GJK), Rick LeBaudour (RLe), Bill Lenarz (BiL), Phil Lenna (PL), R. A. Lewis (RAL), John Lovio (JLo), Gary F. McCurdy (GFMc), Flora Maclise (FMa), Grace McMichael (GMcM), Eugene Y. Makishima (EYM), Bill G. Manolis (BGM), Gloria Markowitz (GMk), Peter J. Metropulos (PJM), Andrea Meyer (AM), Grace Miller (GMi), Joseph Morlan (JM), Marina Gera Nell (MGN), Don Neubacher (DNe), Ed O'Connor (EO), Gary W. Page (GWP), Linda Parker (LP), Carmen J. Patterson (CJP),

Holly Peake (HoP), Susan Claire Peaslee (SCP), Alan Pistorius (AP), Point Reyes Bird Observatory personnel (PRBO), Helen Pratt (HPr), William M. Pursell (WMP), Alton "Bob" Raible (ARa), C. J. Ralph (CJR), Jean M. Richmond (JMR), Ane Rovetta (ARo), David Ruiz (DRu), R. J. Ryder (RJRy), Ellen Sabine (ESa), Mary Ann Sadler (MAS), Barry Sauppe (BS), Phil & Margaret Schaeffer (P&MSh), Dave Shuford (DS), David Sibley (DaS), Dianne Sierra (DSi), Sue Smith (SSm), Bruce Sorrie (BSo), Barry Spitz (BSp), Rich Stallcup (RS), Jean Starkweather (JSt), Lynne E. Stenzel (LES), Robert M. Stewart (RMS), Roger Stone (RSt), Helen Strong (HS), Merl Sturgeon (MeS), Meryl Sundove (MSd), Ian Tait (ITa), Gil Thomson (GiT), Irene Timossi (ITi), Dorothy Tobkin (DT), Beverly Treffinger (BTr), Wayne & Susan Trivelpiece (W&ST), Bill Tyokodi (BTy), Ed Vine (EV), Nils Warnock (NW), Anne & John West (A&JWe), Ralph S. Widrig (RSW), Pamela L. Williams (PLW), Jon Winter (JW), Peg Woodin (PWo), Keiko Yamane (KY), Mark Zumsteg (MZ), Clerin Zumwalt (CZ).

Abbreviations

The following abbreviations are used for frequently used literature citations: AB = *American Birds*, formerly *Audubon Field Notes* (AFN); ABN = "American Birds Notebooks"—data on file with the regional editors of the Middle Pacific Coast Region of *American Birds*; ACR Report = Audubon Canyon Ranch Report; JFOs = *Journal of Field Ornithology Supplement*; (G&M 1944) = (Grinnell & Miller 1944); (G&W 1927) = (Grinnell & Wythe 1927); (S&P 1933) = (Stephens & Pringle 1933). The following abbreviations are used in the listing of representative breeding records in the Marin Breeding Distribution section or elsewhere in parentheses in the text of the species accounts:

Ave.	=	Avenue
CDFG	=	California Department of Fish and Game
E, W, N, S	=	compass directions
ft.	=	foot (feet)
in.	=	inch(es)
km	=	kilometer(s)
mi.	=	mile(s)
Mt.	=	Mount
PRNS	=	Point Reyes National Seashore
Rd.	=	Road
SP	=	State Park
St.	=	Street
USFWS	=	U.S. Fish and Wildlife Service
USFS	=	U.S. Forest Service
yd.	=	yard(s)
yr.	=	year(s)

Coast redwoods towering above the lush, ferny understory at Samuel
P. Taylor State Park. Drawing by Ane Rovetta, 1989.

SPECIES ACCOUNTS

Grebes
Family *Podicipedidae*

PIED-BILLED GREBE *Podilymbus podiceps*

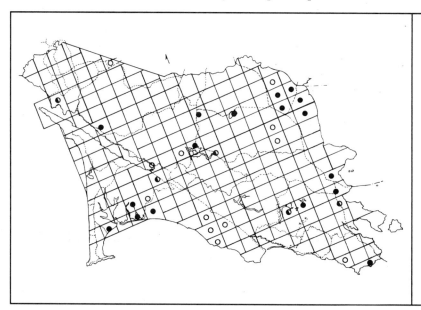

Occurs year round, though primarily as a winter resident from Sep through Mar.
   An uncommon local breeder; overall breeding population very small.
   Recorded breeding in 34 (15.4%) of 221 blocks.

○ Possible = 12 (35%)
◑ Probable = 5 (15%)
● Confirmed = 17 (50%)

FSAR = 2   OPI = 68   CI = 2.15

Ecological Requirements

These floating submersibles are breeding inhabitants of Marin County's marshy-edged freshwater ponds and lakes, freshwater marshes with open water, and, sparingly, brackish water impoundments. In much of their range, Pied-billed Grebes also nest on sloughs and marshy areas of slow-flowing rivers. Occasionally, they breed on estuarine waters with slight tidal fluctuations (Palmer 1962, Johnsgard 1987), but there appear to be no reports of nesting in this habitat in coastal California. Infrequent sightings of birds on estuarine waters in summer (e.g., 3 birds at Drake's Estero 23 Jun 1981 —DS) may represent breeders foraging away from nesting ponds or perhaps oversummering nonbreeders. Of major importance in all breeding habitats is the availability of fairly dense emergent vegetation used for nest construction, anchorage, or concealment. Breeding ponds range in size from ½ to more

than 100 acres and in depth from a few inches to 10 feet (usually less than 3-5 ft.); smaller ponds (1-5 acres) are used most frequently (Bent 1919, Johnsgard 1987).

Pairs are generally solitary while nesting. They defend a small area around the nest site, but they will feed with other nesting Pied-billeds in deeper, open-water areas of ponds and marshes (Glover 1953a). These grebes build nests that are sodden masses of decaying aquatic vegetation. They usually conceal the nests in varying amounts of emergent vegetation but still allow for underwater approach; sometimes they locate nests in open water (Miller 1942, Glover 1953a, Stewart 1975). Nests are usually anchored to, or built up around or among, dead or growing reeds, rushes, or, infrequently, bushes, logs, or dead trees. The nests are not rigidly anchored as some rooted plant stalks always project through them, preventing drift, yet allowing enough up-and-down play to accommodate changing water levels (Miller 1942). In shallow water, Pied-billeds usually build their nests up from the bottom. Below water level, the nest foundation is a bulky mass of vegetation culminating above water in a smaller hollowed platform in which the female lays the eggs. Nest materials are a wide variety of available dead, and sometimes green, materials including cattail flags, rushes, sedges, grasses, algae, and, if the nest is in shallow water, occasionally mud. Although they lay eggs in only one nest, Pied-billeds construct two to several nest structures, and they may continue to add considerable nest material during incubation.

Pied-billed Grebes capture their aquatic prey in their bills by foot-propelled pursuit dives of short duration in shallow water; by picking individual items from the water's surface; by skimming the surface for masses of floating invertebrates; or even by snatching insects from the air (Johnsgard 1987). Overall, the North American diet is about 46.3% insects (especially damselflies, dragonflies and nymphs, grasshoppers, water boatmen, backswimmers, waterbugs, predaceous diving beetles, flies, and hymenoptera), 27% crayfish, 24.2% fish (especially catfish, eels, perch, and sunfish), and 4.1% other crustaceans (brine shrimp, crabs, shrimp, etc.) (Wetmore in Palmer 1962 and Johnsgard 1987, n = 174). Other food items include frogs, salamanders, snails, leeches, spiders, and seeds and soft parts of aquatic plants. The stout bills and heavy jaw musculature of Pied-billed Grebes are well adapted for killing heavy-bodied fish, as well as crayfish and frogs, which they eat in greater proportions than do other species of North American grebes (Zusi & Storer 1969). For unknown reasons, grebes ingest their own feathers. Perhaps the feathers function to prevent bones in the stomach from passing into and puncturing the intes-

tine, to retain bones in the gizzard until they can be digested, or to promote the regurgitation of pellets (Jehl 1988). Hatching is asynchronous. Initially, young often ride on their parents' backs, where they are sometimes fed, and remain there when the adults dive at signs of danger (Palmer 1962).

Marin Breeding Distribution

During the atlas period, Pied-billed Grebes were patchily distributed in Marin County, reflecting the distribution of suitable ponds and marshes. Representative breeding locations were Nicasio Reservoir (NB-FL 5/16-7/17/82 — DS); Phoenix Lake (FL 6/16/76 —RMS); a brackish pond at Spinnaker Point, San Rafael (NE Jun 1982 —HoP); and a freshwater pond above Rodeo Lagoon (FL 7/27/82 —DS).

Historical Trends/Population Threats

The number of Pied-billed Grebes breeding in Marin County has undoubtedly increased in historical times because of the impoundment of streams for cattle and human water needs, since natural freshwater ponds and marshes are rare here and in coastal California in general. For California as a whole, numbers of Pied-billed Grebes have likely decreased because of loss of most of our wetlands. Numbers of Pied-billed Grebes were relatively stable on Breeding Bird Surveys in California from 1968 to 1989 (USFWS unpubl. analyses). Since the early 1980s, government agencies and private groups in California have made management decisions leading to increasing areas of permanent and summer-flooded wetlands for waterfowl, and Pied-billed Grebes will undoubtedly benefit from these new habitats (M.R. McLandress pers. comm.).

Storm-Petrels
Family *Hydrobatidae*

ASHY STORM-PETREL   *Oceanodroma homochroa*

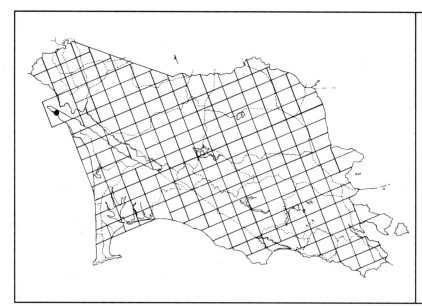

A year-round resident on pelagic waters (peak Sep–Jan); petrels occupy the Farallon Island colony (and probably Bird Rock, Marin Co.) almost year round (irregular late Nov–early Dec).

A fairly common, very local breeder; overall breeding population very small.

Recorded in 1 (0.4%) of 221 blocks (see Methods).

○	Possible	=	0	(0%)
◑	Probable	=	0	(0%)
●	Confirmed	=	1	(100%)

FSAR = 3   OPI = 3   CI = 3.00

Ecological Requirements

Adapted to a lifetime at sea, during the breeding season these diminutive ocean waifs obtain their sustenance from the edge to about 15 miles seaward of the continental shelf within the cool waters of the California Current—waters strongly influenced by coastal upwelling (Ainley et al. 1974; Briggs et al. 1987; Ainley & Boekelheide 1990, Chap. 4). From spring to fall, Ashy Storm-Petrels in this region most consistently frequent the warm side of thermal fronts bordering upwelled waters (Briggs et al. 1987).

Ashy Storm-Petrels nest in loose colonies on islands and offshore rocks. Pairs occupy cavities among loose rocks of talus slopes, in stone walls, in caves, or under driftwood (Bent 1922, Dawson 1923, Ainley et al. 1974). Petrels usually occupy breeding sites for a few days one to two weeks prior to egg laying before finally settling down to the chores of their lengthy breeding season (W.J. Sydeman pers. comm.). Generally females lay the single egg on the floor of the cavity, though occasionally they place it on a rough foundation of weeds or pebbles (Bent 1922). Characteristics of nesting islands selected by the petrels are suitable nest cavities, a lack of terrestrial predators, and reasonable proximity to productive ocean feeding grounds. Nonetheless, the presence of avian predators, particularly the Western Gull, affects colony attendance patterns and other aspects of the biology of these petrels. At the Farallon Islands, Ashy Storm-Petrels approach their nesting grounds only under the cloak of darkness and make fewer visits on full-moon nights than on new moon-nights (Ainley & Boekelheide 1990, Chap. 4). As adaptations to avoid predation, adults feed their chicks more frequently and chicks fledge more often during dark phases of the moon; most chicks that fledge during light phases of the moon do so on overcast nights. When disturbed, storm-petrels also discharge foul-smelling oil from the mouth and nostrils, presumably another antipredator defense.

Ashy Storm-Petrels usually occur solitarily at sea, but large numbers sometimes gather around concentrations of food, which they may locate by their well-developed sense of smell. Foraging birds hover on outstretched wings and patter on the sea's surface with outspread webbed feet, then catch their prey by dipping, surface seizing, or shallow plunges. They forage during the day and also probably extensively at night (Ainley & Boekelheide 1990, Chap. 3), as suggested by their consumption of some crustaceans that ascend to surface waters mostly at night (McChesney 1988). While feeding chicks, Ashy Storm-Petrels at the

81

Farallon Islands prey mainly on small fish and euphausiids, and to a limited degree on other crustaceans (decapods and amphipods) and cephalopods (McChesney 1988, n = 30); they are also known to scavenge and consume fish oil (Ainley et al. 1974, Ainley 1984a). Admirably suited to the vagaries of finding food far at sea or to the uncertainties of returning landward during adverse weather, adults often spend several days away at sea during nesting. Upon returning to nesting sites, they feed small young an energy-rich stomach oil or, later in the season, partially digested prey. Because adults attend their eggs and young infrequently and irregularly, the incubation and nestling phases are long and variable, even by seabird standards.

Marin Breeding Distribution

Ashy Storm-Petrels breed in Marin County at Bird Rock off Tomales Point, the northernmost locale in the species' breeding range where nesting has been confirmed. These petrels were first confirmed breeding there on 3 July 1972 when an adult was found incubating an egg in a rock crevice; a petrel chick found there on 23 August 1969, though unidentified, was undoubtedly this species (Ainley & Osborne 1972). Sowls et al. (1980) found them still breeding there during the atlas period as did Carter et al. (1992) in 1989 (see below).

An adult Ashy Storm-Petrel with a brood patch was captured in a mist net on the night of 5–6 August 1989 in the vicinity of suitable crevice-nesting habitat on an offshore islet in Van Damme Cove, Mendocino County; additional evidence of breeding is needed to substantiate this probable extension of the breeding range 85 miles north of Bird Rock (Carter et al. 1992).

Historical Trends/Population Threats

Although long-term data are lacking, the Marin County breeding population of Ashy Storm-Petrels probably has always been small. Ainley and Osborne (1972) initially estimated a maximum of 20 to 24 birds nesting on Bird Rock in 1972, but Ainley and Whitt (1973) later revised the estimate downward to 10 birds. During the atlas period, Sowls et al. (1980, NE 7/1/79) estimated the breeding population on Bird Rock at 14 birds. A higher estimate of 74 petrels breeding there in 1989 was attributed to greater effort expended that year than in others to determine the size of this colony (Carter et al. 1992).

Virtually all of the northern and central California breeding population of Ashy Storm-Petrels is concentrated on the Farallon Islands (Sowls et al. 1980, Carter et al. 1992). A population estimate at the Farallones of 4000 birds in 1972 (Ainley & Lewis 1974) has also been reported by other workers (Sowls et al. 1980, Carter et al. 1992), but additional censusing efforts are needed to assess the accuracy of this estimate and the trend of the regional population (H.R. Carter & W.J. Sydeman pers. comm.). The Ashy Storm-Petrel is currently a Bird Species of Special Concern in California (Remsen 1978, CDFG 1991b).

Ashy Storm-Petrels breeding at Bird Rock are vulnerable to disturbance by humans crossing from Tomales Point at low tide or by boat. Occasional intruders, however, are quite unlikely to even notice these furtive, nocturnal cavity-dwellers, though they would undoubtedly disturb other nesting seabirds. Coulter and Risebrough (1973) detected high pesticide levels and eggshell thinning in Ashy Storm-Petrels at the Farallon Islands, but breeding biology studies have not disclosed any adverse effects of this contamination (Ainley & Lewis 1974; Ainley & Boekelheide 1990, Chap. 4). Perhaps the greatest threat to the species would be a catastrophic event at sea. An oil spill to the south in Monterey Bay, where thousands of Ashies concentrate in fall, could inflict severe, perhaps irreparable, damage to the population (Ainley 1976, Sowls et al. 1980, Roberson 1985).

Cormorants
Family *Phalacrocoracidae*

DOUBLE-CRESTED CORMORANT   *Phalacrocorax auritus*

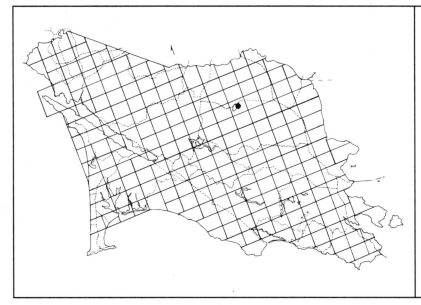

A year-round resident; numbers swell (at least on Pt. Reyes estuaries) from Aug through Dec. At Farallon Islands (and S.F. Bay bridges), birds occupy nest sites mostly from mid- to late Mar (rarely beginning early Apr) through Aug (rarely Sep). In poor food years, Farallon birds desert colonies during midseason.

A very rare, very local breeder; overall breeding population very small.

Recorded in 1 (0.4%) of 221 blocks (see Methods).

○ Possible	=	0	(0%)
◑ Probable	=	0	(0%)
● Confirmed	=	1	(100%)

FSAR = 1   OPI = 1   CI = 3.00

Ecological Requirements

The West Coast version of this piscivorous phalacrocorid was originally dubbed the Farallon Cormorant, despite being the only one of our locally breeding cormorants that makes its living in both estuarine or inshore waters and inland lakes, reservoirs, and rivers.

Farallon Island breeders feed within about 20 to 50 miles of the colony in nearshore coastal waters and in estuaries and lagoons on Point Reyes and in San Francisco Bay (Ainley & Boekelheide 1990, Chap. 3). Although most foraging waters are no more than about 35 feet deep, Double-crests apparently can, if need be, dive foot-propelled from 65 to 260 feet, intermediate depths for diving seabirds. Pelagic and Brandt's cormorants generally are deeper divers. Double-crested Cormorants usually feed singly or in small flocks of less than 20 but sometimes up to hundreds of birds (Bartholomew 1942). Smaller flocks are often roughly circular in formation and coalesce by swimming after diving. Larger flocks arrange themselves in long, compact lines perpendicular to the direction of movement of schooling fish and "leapfrog" (by swimming or flying) to the front of the flock after surfacing from dives. In marine waters along the West Coast, Double-crests feed mostly on schooling fish found from the surface to near (but not on) flat sand or mud bottoms (Ainley et al. 1981; Ainley & Boekelheide 1990, Chap. 3). They also feed somewhat over rocky or gravelly substrates (Lewis 1929, Palmer 1962). Farallon breeders feed almost exclusively on neritic and estuarine fish, predominately two species of surfperch (Embiotocidae) and in particular the shiner surfperch *(Cymatogaster aggregata)* (Ainley et al. 1981; Ainley & Boekelheide 1990, Chap. 3, n = 2815). At the Farallones, the diet of Double-crests varies little between years and overlaps little with that of Brandt's or Pelagic cormorants. Overall the Double-crested Cormorant feeds primarily on a wide variety of marine and freshwater fish, usually of no commercial value (Lewis 1929, Palmer 1962, Robertson 1974, Ainley et al. 1981). Other dietary items include shrimp, squid, salamanders, frogs, and watersnakes, whereas crayfish may be important at some inland sites. Crabs, mollusks, seaworms, aquatic insects, and other invertebrates are likely first consumed by the cormorants' fish prey. The young are fed by regurgitation and, if possible, they creche (gather together in clusters) after leaving their nests but before fledging.

On the California coast, nest sites of Double-crests are more varied than those of Pelagic or Brandt's cormorants. Double-crests nest on the moderately steep, rocky slopes of offshore islands or rocks; on inaccessible mainland cliffs; in trees; and on structures such as bridges, wharf pilings, abandoned dredges, and electrical power towers. At inland sites (and sometimes coastal salt ponds), birds nest near fresh water, in trees, usually surrounded by water, or on islands, where the nest may be placed on the ground; on rock ledges or pinnacles; or in bushes or trees (Bent 1922, Lewis 1929, Palmer 1962, D. Shuford pers. obs.). Tree nests may be in crotches or well out on horizontal limbs and range to over 100 feet above the ground. Double-crests are highly colonial except where the availability of suitable nest foundations precludes closer spacing. Where Double-crests cohabit nesting islands with Brandt's Cormorants, Double-crests often nest on the steeper, more broken terrain of higher slopes, crests of ridges, and summits of rocks or islands (Dawson 1923; Ainley & Boekelheide 1990, Chap. 6). A prime requisite of Double-crested Cormorants' nest sites appears to be at least one side of the ground or rock falling abruptly away (Bent 1922). On the other hand, Double-crests tend to avoid the narrow shelves of precipitous cliffs inhabited by Pelagics (Dawson 1923; Ainley & Boekelheide 1990, Chap. 6).

The bulky, cup-shaped body of a Double-crested Cormorant nest is composed primarily of coarse sticks and twigs when available. Otherwise seaweed, kelp, dead tules, and weed stalks are typical substitutes. The large stick nests found in trees may serve as much as landing platforms as they do egg baskets for these heavy, ungainly landing craft (Ainley 1984b). Various soft materials such as grasses, straw, seaweed, moss, green leaves or conifer sprays, bark strips, and feathers (along with the odd bone, dead crab, or human artifact) are incorporated in the wall of the nest or form a pseudolining (Bent 1922; Dawson 1923; Palmer 1962; Ainley & Boekelheide 1990, Chap. 6). Items such as plastic rope, packing tape, paper, cigarette butts, rags, and even a gun holster have been found in nests on the girders of the San Rafael–Richmond Bridge, Contra Costa County; one nest there was built on a hubcap (R.P. Henderson & M. Rauzon pers. comm.)! Nests built on the remains of previous years' nests may become quite large from the addition of material throughout the nesting season and over the course of many years.

Marin Breeding Distribution

The only Marin County breeding record for Double-crested Cormorants during the atlas period was of a single nest observed in a California bay tree amidst a Great Blue Heron colony on an island in Stafford Lake, Novato, in the breeding season of 1978 (ScC). The only two known colonies of this cormorant in the county were established

on the outer coast prior to and subsequent to the atlas project (see below).

Historical Trends/Population Threats

Formerly, a nesting colony (size unknown) was located in Marin County on a flat shelf of the cliff at Point Resistance, about one mile north of the ocean end of Bear Valley; nests with large young were observed there on 30 May 1929 (Bolander & Bryant 1930). Surveys in 1979 and 1980 of seabirds breeding on the outer coast of California revealed no colonies of Double-crested Cormorants in Marin County (Sowls et al. 1980), but repeat surveys in 1989 found a new colony of 14 birds on 5 June at Dillon Beach Rocks (Carter et al. 1992).

Breeding populations of Double-crested Cormorants in California declined during historical times at the Farallon Islands because of disturbance from commercial collectors harvesting Common Murre eggs and from island occupants (Ainley & Lewis 1974; Ainley & Boekelheide 1990, Chap. 6), on islands off southern California and the west coast of Baja California because of pesticide contamination and human disturbance (Gress et al. 1973), and in interior California because of disturbance from lake development and recreation (G&M 1944, Sowls et al. 1980). Eggshell thinning has also been documented at the Old Arcata Wharf, Humboldt County (*fide* Sowls et al. 1980).

Ainley and Lewis (1974) suggested that marine breeding populations of Double-crested Cormorants failed to recover from their decline because populations of their prey base—the Pacific sardine *(Sardinops caerulea)*—were over-exploited by humans in the late 1940s at a time of unfavorable environmental conditions. The sardines were replaced by the northern anchovy *(Engraulis mordax)*, a possibly less desirable prey of the cormorants. Recent dramatic increases of Double-crested Cormorants in California, despite no rise in sardine populations, suggest that other factors may also have been limiting the cormorants. The Farallon population of this cormorant began to recover slightly in the 1970s (Ainley & Boekelheide 1990, Chap. 6), declined substantially after the 1982–83 El Niño Southern Oscillation event, but by 1989 had increased to about 1140 breeding birds (Carter et al. 1992). Channel Island populations, which may have declined substantially since the turn of the century, now also are increasing (Carter et al. 1992). Breeding numbers in San Francisco Bay—swelled greatly by the establishment (primarily since 1984) of colonies on bridges—totaled 2789 birds in 1989 to 1991, representing 37% of the northern and central coastal California population (Carter et al. 1992, H.R. Carter pers. comm.). Numbers on the outer coast of this region alone increased from 1466 birds in 1979 to 1980, to 4785 in 1989, as a result of expansion at old colonies and the establishment of 11 new ones (Carter et al. 1992). Numbers of Double-crested Cormorants also increased on

Breeding Bird Surveys in California from 1968 to 1989, though they were relatively stable from 1980 to 1989 (USFWS unpubl. analyses). These trends presumably reflect changes in the population of the interior, where most BBS routes are located.

Because of continentwide population declines, the Double-crested Cormorant was placed on the Audubon Society's Blue List from 1972 to 1981 (Tate 1981) and on its Species with Special Concerns list in 1982 (Tate & Tate 1982). Although numbers now appear to be increasing widely (e.g., Tate 1986, Carter et al. 1992), this cormorant is still considered a Bird Species of Special Concern in California (Remsen 1978, CDFG 1991b).

BRANDT'S CORMORANT *Phalacrocorax penicillatus*

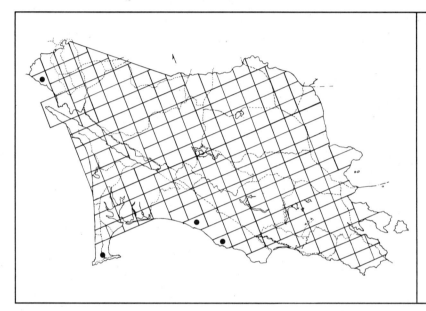

A year-round resident; numbers depressed somewhat on ocean waters from Dec through Apr. Farallon Island (and probably Marin) breeders occupy nesting colonies starting mid- to late Mar (extremes early Mar and early May) through Aug (rarely through Sep and Oct). In poor food years, few birds occupy nest sites and all desert early in the season.

A very abundant, very local breeder; overall breeding population very small.

Recorded in 4 (1.8%) of 221 blocks (see Methods).

○ Possible	=	0	(0%)
◑ Probable	=	0	(0%)
● Confirmed	=	4	(100%)

FSAR = 7   OPI = 28   CI = 3.00

Ecological Requirements

Flight lines of Brandt's Cormorants merge with multispecies feeding flocks, alerting birds and humans alike to the bountiful productivity of the ocean waters near California's seabird breeding colonies. The Brandt's Cormorant is one of two strictly marine cormorants breeding along the California coast and inhabiting waters over the continental shelf. Of the two, its distribution indicates it is the most characteristic of the cool upwelling waters of the California Current (Ainley & Boekelheide 1990, Chap. 5). Brandts feed primarily in nearshore waters, but also well offshore and in deep coastal bays. The importance of these different foraging areas to Farallon Island breeders varies seasonally and yearly (Ainley & Boekelheide 1990, Chap. 3). Although breeders range up to 50 miles from the Farallon colony on feeding trips (Ainley & Boekelheide 1990, Chap. 3), foraging birds seldom stray more than 6 miles from land, except in transit (Briggs et al. 1987).

Brandt's Cormorants make relatively deep, foot-propelled foraging dives. Along the mainland coast, they forage over sand and mud bottoms at depths of about 30 to 200 feet and offshore over rocky bottoms, as well, apparently up to about 400 feet in depth (Ainley & Boekelheide 1990, Chap. 3). Brandts use equal proportions of schooling and nonschooling prey and show great dietary diversity. A study of their diet up and down the Pacific Coast indicates that although the majority of their prey live on or just above the bottom over both rocky and flat substrates, appreciable numbers range from mid-depths to the surface and others hide in the substrate (Ainley et al. 1981). Brandts vary their feeding habits from north to south along the West Coast. To the north in areas of overlap with Pelagics, Brandts eat the same prey as Pelagics, but they feed just above rocky substrate or near substrate without relief, whereas Pelagics feed primarily in rocky substrate. To the south, in areas where Pelagics are absent, Brandts feed almost exclusively in rocky habitat or near rocks on flat bottoms (Ainley et al. 1981).

Brandt's Cormorants are gregarious foragers. In years of high oceanic productivity (rockfish abundance), they tend to feed in large flocks, often with Western Gulls and

Common Murres; in unproductive years they feed in smaller flocks by themselves (Ainley & Boekelheide 1990, Chap. 3). Brandts prey on a wide variety of marine fish and occasionally take octopus and market squid. At the Farallon Islands, the diet is dominated by midwater schooling rockfish, mainly *Sebastes flavidus* and *S. jordani*. Other important prey are flatfish (bothids and pleuronectids), Pacific tomcod *(Microgadus proximus)*, midshipmen *(Porichthys notatus)*, and spotted cuskeels *(Chilara taylori)* (Ainley et al. 1981; Ainley & Boekelheide 1990, Chap. 3, n = 11,190). In most years, dietary diversity is low because of the reliance on juvenile rockfish, but in unproductive (usually warm-water) years it is higher. In cool-water years, the pre-egglaying diet is more diverse and overlaps little in species composition with the later-season diet. Overlap of the Brandt's Cormorant diet with that of the Double-crested Cormorant is minimal, though slightly greater in warm-water years. At the Farallon Islands, Brandt's and Pelagic cormorants eat many of the same prey species (except in warm-water years), because they both rely heavily on juvenile rockfish, though Pelagics tend to take smaller-sized prey. Like our other cormorants, Brandts feed their young by regurgitation, and the young creche (gather together) before and after leaving the nest and before fledging (Carter & Hobson 1988).

Brandts form the largest and densest colonies of our locally breeding cormorants where they nest on offshore islands, sea stacks, and inaccessible mainland cliffs. Where Brandts' colonies overlap with those of Double-crested Cormorants, Brandts often prefer the gentler terrain of high, rounded shoulders of rock; gradual, sloping inclines; and flat tops of rocky islands (Bent 1922, Williams 1942). Although Brandts occasionally nest on wide ledges or niches on a cliff face, these sites are never as precarious as those chosen by Pelagic Cormorants. Brandt's Cormorants build large, bulky, cup-shaped nests that solidify from compaction and the accumulation of fecal droppings. Nests are generally built on the rotted debris and guano of the previous year's effort, but, rarely, they expand to tall cylinders with yearly additions of material. Typical nest materials are land plants such as Farallon weed, grasses, and mosses and marine plants, including algae, eelgrass, and surfgrass (Bent 1922; Dawson 1923; Palmer 1962; Ainley & Boekelheide 1990, Chap. 5).

Marin Breeding Distribution

During the atlas period, Brandt's Cormorants bred at six colonies along the outer coast of Marin County (NE, Sowls et al. 1980; Table 14, Figure 14). In 1989, the total number of occupied colonies remained the same, but the small colony at the "Sonoma–Marin County Line" was abandoned and a new colony was established at Bird Rock, off Tomales Point (Carter et al. 1992).

Historical Trends/Population Threats

Partial surveys in 1969 to 1972 estimated a total of 1330 Brandt's Cormorants were breeding at three sites along the Marin County coast (Ainley & Whitt 1973). From complete surveys, numbers of this cormorant breeding in the county totaled 3204 birds in 1979 to 1980 (Sowls et al. 1980) and 1935 birds in 1989 (Carter et al. 1992). The recent change in local population size may in part reflect differences between the two survey periods in oceanographic conditions, which can dramatically affect the number of Brandt's Cormorants that breed in a given year (Ainley & Boekelheide 1990, Chap. 5). Also, because part or all of the birds at a colony often shift breeding locations among years, Carter et al. (1990) stressed the importance of assessing population trends over large rather than small areas.

During the mid-1880s, the Brandt's Cormorant population at the Farallon Islands declined drastically from disturbance caused by commercial egg collectors gathering Common Murre eggs, but cormorant numbers there have since increased dramatically (Ainley & Lewis 1974). Numbers of Brandt's Cormorants attempting to breed at the Farallones in the 1970s and 1980s have fluctuated greatly from year to year, reflecting varying oceanographic conditions and hence food supplies (Ainley & Boekelheide 1990, Chap. 5). On the central and northern California coast as a whole, estimates of the population size of this cormorant varied from 58,290 breeding birds at 61 sites in 1979 to 1980 (Sowls et al. 1980) to 54,029 birds at 71 sites in 1989 (Carter et al. 1992). Sowls et al. used a 1979 PRBO estimate for the South Farallon Islands of 28,000 Brandt's that Ainley and Boekelheide (1990) revised to about 19,000.

Populations of Brandt's Cormorants on the Channel Islands have also declined historically, first from human disturbance and later presumably from the accumulation of pesticides as indicated by eggshell thinning (Hunt et al. 1979). Chick deformities that often result from pollutants are rarely observed at the Farallon Islands (Hobson & Carter 1988). Significant numbers of Brandt's Cormorants are caught in gill nets (H.R. Carter pers. comm.), but few die during oil spills (Page et al. 1990).

Table 14. Numbers (not pairs) of marine birds nesting on the outer coast of Marin County in 1979 to 1980 (Sowls et al. 1980) and 1989 (Carter et al. 1992). Colony names are listed in order from north to south (see Figure 14). X = present, but no count. See Sowls et al. (1980) for prior preliminary survey data for the Marin coast.

	Ashy Storm-Petrel		Double-crested Cormorant		Brandt's Cormorant		Pelagic Cormorant		Black Oystercatcher [a]		Western Gull [b]		Common Murre		Pigeon Guillemot		Rhinoceros Auklet		Tufted Puffin		Totals	
	1979	1989	1979	1989	1979	1989	1979	1989	1979	1989	1979	1989	1979	1989	1979	1989	1979	1989	1979	1989	1979	1989
"Sonoma-Marin County Line"	-	-	-	-	12	-	134	84	4	5	16	14	-	-	40	25	-	-	-	-	206	128
"Dillon Beach Rocks"	-	-	-	14	190	18	186	143	6	3	12	32	-	-	40	20	-	-	-	-	434	230
Tomales Point	-	-	-	-	-	-	134	141	-	3	2	6	-	-	8	-	-	-	-	-	144	150
Bird Rock	14	74	-	-	-	55	8	37	2	6	228	168	-	-	30	115	-	3	-	-	282	488 [c]
"Elephant Rock Complex"	-	-	-	-	-	-	16	-	-	-	-	8	-	-	12	28	-	-	-	-	28	36
Point Reyes	-	-	-	-	2400	1522	808	266	10	6	62	178	16,500	15,155	120	616	-	6	6	4	19,906	17,753
Coast Campground South	-	-	-	-	-	-	-	-	-	-	-	-	-	-	-	63	-	-	-	-	-	63
Point Resistance	-	-	-	-	150	46	104	-	2	-	20	8	7500	3518	60	50	-	-	-	-	7836	3622
Millers Point Rocks	-	-	-	-	194	114	60	59	-	1	34	30	-	358	10	55	-	-	-	-	298	617
Double Point Rocks	-	-	-	-	258	180	16	9	2	-	24	8	13,000	4464	40	22	-	-	-	-	13,340	4683
Stinson Beach to Rocky Point	-	-	-	-	-	-	-	-	-	-	-	6	-	-	-	-	-	-	-	-	-	6
Gull Rock Area	-	-	-	-	-	-	28	9	2	1	4	6	-	-	2	7	-	-	-	-	36	23
Muir Beach Headlands to Tennessee Cove	-	-	-	-	-	-	34	42	2	1	-	20	-	-	X	34	-	-	-	-	36+	97
Bird Island	-	-	-	-	-	-	-	-	-	1	2	56	-	-	4	5	-	-	-	-	6	62
Point Bonita	-	-	-	-	-	-	60	95	-	-	4	10	-	-	X	66	-	-	-	-	64+	171
Bonita Cove	-	-	-	-	-	-	20	2	-	-	2	6	-	-	X	2	-	-	-	-	22+	10
Point Diablo Bluffs and Needles	-	-	-	-	-	-	64	15	-	-	16	34	-	-	X	-	-	-	-	-	80+	49
Totals	14	74	-	14	3204	1935	1672	902	30	27	426	590	37,000	23,495	366+	1108	-	9	6	4	42,718	28,188

[a] Black Oystercatcher – two breeders were also found on the Marin Islands during USFWS seabird surveys inside San Francisco Bay in 1990 (Carter et al. 1992).

[b] Western Gull – about 230 breeders were found at 12 Marin County sites inside San Francisco and San Pablo bays during USFWS baywide surveys in 1990 (Carter et al. 1992); see text.

[c] Total number of breeding seabirds at Bird Rock in 1989 includes 30 unidentified alcids found there.

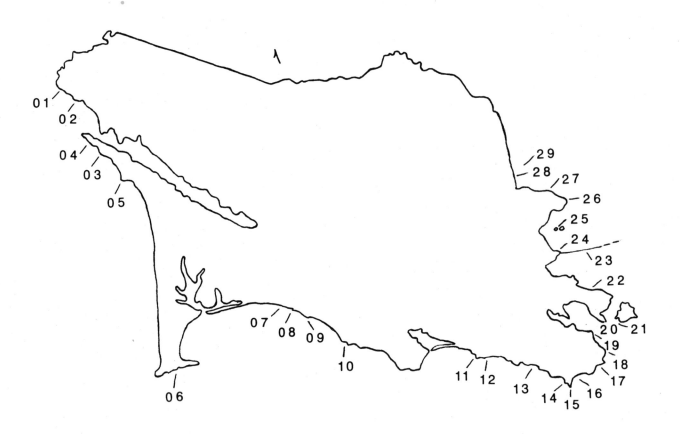

Colony codes used are:

01 = "Sonoma-Marin County Line"	11 = Stinson Beach to Rocky Point	21 = Angel Island
02 = "Dillon Beach Rocks"	12 = Gull Rock Area	22 = Bluff Point to Paradise Cay
03 = Tomales Point	13 = Muir Beach Headlands to Tennessee Cove	23 = Richmond-San Rafael Bridge
04 = Bird Rock	14 = Bird Island	24 = Point San Quentin
05 = "Elephant Rock Complex"	15 = Point Bonita	25 = Marin Islands
06 = Point Reyes	16 = Bonita Cove	26 = The Sisters and Point San Pablo
07 = Coast Campground South	17 = Point Diablo Bluffs and Needles	27 = Rat Rock
08 = Point Resistance	18 = Yellow Bluff	28 = Southwest San Pablo Bay Duck Blinds
09 = Millers Point Rocks	19 = Sausalito Point Area	29 = Marin County-West San Pablo Bay Ship
10 = Double Point Rocks	20 = Peninsula Point and Cone Rock	Channel

Figure 14. Map of marine bird colony sites in Marin County. See Carter et al. (1992) for detailed colony maps and standard California and USFWS colony codes (not used here).

PELAGIC CORMORANT　*Phalacrocorax pelagicus*

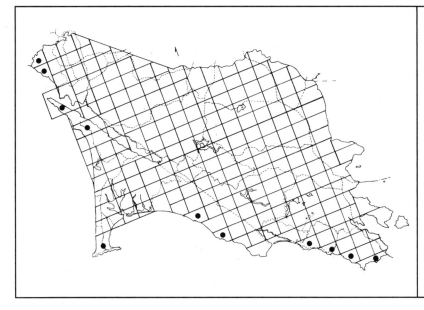

A year-round resident. Pelagics occupy breeding cliffs at the Farallon Islands (and probably Marin) in high numbers mostly from Mar (extremes Dec or Jan and Apr or May) through Aug (rarely to early Oct). In poor food years, birds fail to lay eggs or desert nests as early as Jun or Jul.

A very common, very local breeder; overall breeding population very small.

Recorded in 11 (5.0%) of 221 blocks (see Methods).

○	Possible	=	0 (0%)
◖	Probable	=	0 (0%)
●	Confirmed	=	11 (100%)

FSAR = 5　　　OPI = 55　　　CI = 3.00

Ecological Requirements

These sleek iridescent cormorants choose lofty, precarious nest sites free of acrophobics. In the watery realm, they are exclusively marine inhabitants, but despite what their name implies they occupy nearshore waters within 12 miles (mostly within 6 mi.) of mainland or island shores (Briggs et al. 1987).

Like Brandts, Pelagic Cormorants are foot-propelled divers that perhaps reach 400 feet in depth. In contrast to Brandts, Pelagics typically feed alone on solitary nearshore prey that hide in rocky reef substrates (Ainley et al. 1981; Ainley & Boekelheide 1990, Chap. 3). In years of high ocean productivity and superabundant prey, Pelagics at the Farallon Islands tend to feed in the company of small multispecies flocks of seabirds on midwater schools of rockfish. The Brandt's Cormorant account contains further comparison of the feeding niches of these two species. The diet of the Pelagic Cormorant is most similar to the Pigeon Guillemot, another species feeding mostly in rocky substrates (see account). The predominant prey of Pelagic Cormorants at the Farallon Islands are several species of sculpin (cottids), juvenile rockfish (mostly *Sebastes flavidus* and *S. jordani*), and a mysid shrimp *(Spirontocaris sp.)*; other fish, crustaceans, octopuses, and marine worms are minor components of the diet there (Ainley et al. 1981; Ainley & Boekelheide 1990, Chap. 3, n = 6839). Juvenile rockfish are most important in cold-water years, and sculpins in warm-water years. Like our other cormorants, Pelagics feed their young by regurgitation.

Of the California cormorant clan, Pelagics are the daredevils, nesting on narrow ledges and niches of precipitous cliffs and sea caves on coastal bluffs or offshore rocks and islands. Because these sites are limited, Pelagic Cormorant colonies are generally smaller and looser aggregations than those of Brandt's and Double-crested cormorants (Sowls et al. 1980, Carter et al. 1984). Presumably because of the precariousness of cliff nests, Pelagics cement them to the ledge by their own excrement. Nests are often semicircular, rather than round, where they abut the cliff face, but like Brandts' nests, they rarely become large from yearly reconstruction and additions. Nest materials include seaweeds, grasses, mosses, and, rarely, sticks, with dry grasses and, occasionally, feathers used as a lining (Bent 1922; Dawson 1923; Palmer 1962; Ainley & Boekelheide 1990, Chap. 6).

Marin Breeding Distribution

During the atlas period, Pelagic Cormorants bred in 14 main colony sites along the outer coast of Marin County (NE, Sowls et al. 1980; Table 14, Figure 14). In 1989, the number of colony sites was reduced to 12 by the abandonment of the "Elephant Rock Complex" and Point Resistance colonies (Carter et al. 1992).

Historical Trends/Population Threats

Partial surveys in 1969 to 1972 estimated 800 Pelagic Cormorants were breeding at four sites along the Marin County coast (Ainley & Whitt 1973). Based on complete surveys, numbers of this cormorant breeding in Marin declined from an estimated 1672 birds in 1979 (Sowls et al. 1980) to 902 in 1989 (Carter et al. 1992). At the Farallon Islands, numbers of breeding Pelagic Cormorants vary greatly from year to year depending on oceanographic conditions and food supply (Ainley & Boekelheide 1990, Chap. 6). In particularly poor food years, virtually the whole population there may desert their nests early in the breeding season—1989 was such a year. Hence, the low numbers at Marin County colonies in 1989 are probably indicative of short-term variation in ocean conditions in the Gulf of the Farallones rather than a long-term decline of the cormorant population. Again, because Pelagic Cormorants, like Brandts, frequently shift colony sites, population trends should be assessed for large rather than small

areas (Carter et al. 1990). Sowls et al. (1980) estimated a breeding population of 15,458 Pelagic Cormorants at 166 sites along the central and northern California coast in 1979 to 1980, whereas Carter et al. (1992) estimated 11,658 birds at 169 sites (including 1 in S.F. Bay) in 1989 to 1990. Population trends between the two surveys varied among several large segments of the coast.

Numbers of Pelagic Cormorants breeding on the Farallon Islands declined in the late nineteenth century because of disturbance but subsequently increased (Ainley & Lewis 1974). Pelagic Cormorants generally are less vulnerable to disturbance than are Brandt's or Double-crested cormorants because they are more widely dispersed in less accessible nesting sites.

Nesting cormorants must be ever watchful for the predatory shenanigans of Western Gulls. Drawing by Keith Hansen, 1989.

Bitterns and Herons
Family *Ardeidae*

AMERICAN BITTERN *Botaurus lentiginosus*

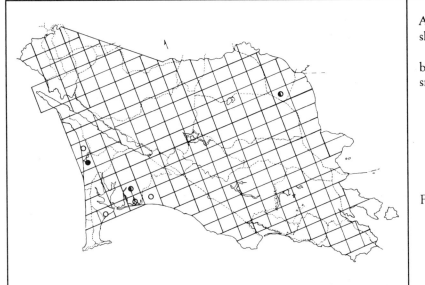

A year-round resident; numbers swell slightly from Sep through Apr.

A very rare (perhaps rare), very local breeder; overall breeding population very small.

Recorded in 7 (3.2%) of 221 blocks.

○ Possible	=	4	(57%)
◑ Probable	=	2	(29%)
● Confirmed	=	1	(14%)

FSAR = 1   OPI = 7   CI = 1.57

Ecological Requirements

With their frozen sky-pointing postures, cryptic reedlike coloration, and booming, ventriloqual calls, American Bitterns can be difficult to spot in their breeding haunts of freshwater marshes and coastal swales. They prefer cattail and tule marshes over much of the range, but their main requirement seems to be dense marsh vegetation within the first two to three feet of the ground. Although American Bitterns breed in brackish and saltwater marshes elsewhere in North America (Bent 1926, Palmer 1962), there appear to be no definitive breeding records for these habitats in coastal California; Bitterns do frequent them at other seasons, however.

American Bitterns are solitary feeders that usually hunt from a standing or slow walking position (Hancock & Kushlan 1984). They hold their bills low and strike with a quick jab while wading through water or low marsh, or while peering down from a bank or a perch in marsh vegetation. American Bitterns also walk quickly or run in tall grass, gleaning insects from grass stems or flycatching them from the air. Overall, the diet includes about 20.3% fish, 19.0% crayfish, 23.1% aquatic and land insects, 20.6% frogs and salamanders, 9.6% mice and shrews,

5.5% snakes, and 2.2% crabs, spiders, and miscellaneous invertebrates (Palmer 1962). Geographic and seasonal variation in the diet has been noted.

Unlike most of the heron and egret clan, American Bitterns breed solitarily. They usually locate their nests in wet places in a marsh; they build them up as much as eight inches above shallow water or mud, or they lodge them in marsh vegetation (Bent 1926, Palmer 1962). Nests are also found occasionally on dry ground in grassy meadows or hayfields (though in proximity to marshlands) or on floating islands in lakes. Concealment is provided by surrounding vegetation, but more often than not the nest is open above rather than screened by arched-over stalks; new growth may further seclude the nest as the season progresses. The nest is a small, flat platform made of materials such as dead cattail flags, bulrushes, other sedges, rushes, and reeds, as well as grasses, weeds, or small sticks; eggs may sometimes be laid practically on bare ground. Young hatch asynchronously and are fed by regurgitation. Circumstantial evidence suggests that young may move to a second nearby platform after 20 days of age and that previous years' nests may sometimes be reused (Palmer 1962).

91

Marin Breeding Distribution

The only confirmed breeding record for American Bittern in Marin County was a sighting of two recently fledged young at Abbott's Lagoon on 28 July 1981 (DS) in an area where adults had been seen throughout the breeding season. The rarity here of Bitterns in the breeding season seems largely attributable to the scarcity of extensive fresh-water marshes.

Historical Trends/Population Threats

American Bitterns probably always have been scarce breed-ers in Marin County, but they may have declined with the historic loss of freshwater marshes, particularly around San Pablo and San Francisco bays. The American Bittern was included on the Audubon Society's Blue List in seven years from 1976 to 1986 (Tate 1981, 1986; Tate & Tate 1982). Numbers of American Bitterns were relatively sta-ble on Breeding Bird Surveys in California from 1968 to 1989 (USFWS unpubl. analyses).

GREAT BLUE HERON *Ardea herodias*

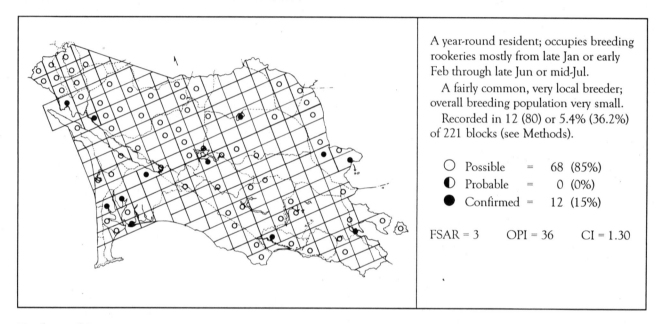

A year-round resident; occupies breeding rookeries mostly from late Jan or early Feb through late Jun or mid-Jul.

A fairly common, very local breeder; overall breeding population very small.

Recorded in 12 (80) or 5.4% (36.2%) of 221 blocks (see Methods).

○	Possible	=	68	(85%)
◑	Probable	=	0	(0%)
●	Confirmed	=	12	(15%)

FSAR = 3　　　OPI = 36　　　CI = 1.30

Ecological Requirements

Great Blue Herons are stately denizens of shallow tidal and freshwater feeding grounds and adjacent uplands. Great Blues have the widest range of foraging habitat of Marin's breeding herons and egrets. To seize unsuspecting prey, they most commonly stand still or wade slowly in the shallow waters or along the shores of estuaries, lagoons, bays, freshwater ponds, streams, and, less frequently, tide pools; they also perch in nearshore kelp beds in the Monterey Bay area, riding the swells (Roberson 1985). Less frequently, in aquatic habitats, they hover over water and stab at prey below, dive into water from the air headfirst, drop into water from perches feet first, float or swim on the water's surface stabbing at or picking up prey, wing-flick to disturb prey, and dash after prey with their wings used for balance, lift, or braking (Hancock & Kushlan 1984). Additional aquatic, shoreline, or terrestrial

feeding techniques include pecking, probing, and even flycatching. Great Blues spend a fair amount of time stalking, poised motionless, in pastures and fields in search of rodents (especially pocket gophers), lizards, and insects. Although they forage mostly during the day, Great Blues also feed at night, especially in tidal habitats (Han-cock & Kushlan 1984). In some areas, especially on islands, Great Blues visit human habitations for scraps of food put out for them. Great Blues forage singly or in aggregations and in some circumstances defend feeding territories (Pratt 1980). It has been suggested that colonial nesting Great Blues will follow one another to exploit food that is unevenly distributed and concentrated in areas of temporary abundance. However, adult birds at the Audubon Canyon Ranch rookery on Bolinas Lagoon do not appear to follow other herons on foraging flights;

instead they land where other herons are already feeding or go to familiar feeding grounds (Pratt 1980). Long-distance foraging flights are common in Ciconiformes, and some authors believe Great Blues may fly up to about 50 miles to feeding areas. Although most adults departing the Audubon Canyon Ranch rookery go to Bolinas Lagoon to feed, many fly out of sight in several directions to unknown foraging areas (Pratt 1980). See Marin Breeding Distribution section for the extent of the foraging range in the county.

Overall in the U.S., this heron's diet is about 71.6% fish, 8.9% crustaceans, 8.2% insects, 4.7% mice and shrews, 4.2% amphibians and reptiles, and 2.5% miscellaneous animal and vegetable matter (Palmer 1962). Most vegetable fare is probably taken incidentally, but Great Blues apparently eat the seeds of water lilies. They also capture marshbirds as large as Black-necked Stilts and Clapper Rails (Palmer 1962, Hancock & Kushlan 1984); rails are particularly susceptible to herons and egrets when forced out of marshes at high tides (Evens & Page 1986).

Great Blues breed in small to large colonies or, rarely, solitarily. In Marin County, they place their nests high in large trees such as redwoods, Douglas fir, California bay, coast live oak, and eucalyptus, often in mixed colonies with Great Egrets (Pratt 1983). In mixed heronries, Great Blues typically, but not invariably, nest in the highest parts of trees (up to 130 ft., Bent 1926), with other species below them (Palmer 1962). In other areas, Great Blues also nest in shrubs, on the ground, on tule platforms, on rock ledges or sea cliffs, and on duck blinds or other artificial structures. Nests are flat platforms of sticks with inner shallow, saucer-shaped depressions. They may vary considerably in bulk since they are reused repeatedly; nest material is added throughout incubation and early in the nestling phase. The nests may be lined with fine twigs, mosses, pine needles, reeds, weed stalks, marsh grasses, or leaves (Bent 1926, Palmer 1962, H.M. Pratt pers. comm.). The young hatch asynchronously and are fed by regurgitation.

Marin Breeding Distribution

During the atlas period, Great Blues were confirmed nesting in 12 colonies scattered throughout Marin County (Pratt 1983; Table 15, Figure 15, and atlas map). Only two of these colonies (at Nicasio Reservoir and Drake's Head) were newly discovered by atlasers. Great Blues have also nested at several other sites either prior to or after the atlas period (Pratt p. 103 this volume; Table 15, Figure 15). Although most local heron colonies are adjacent to estuaries, Great Blues forage throughout the lowlands of Marin in the breeding season. In contrast, the other colonial breeding herons and egrets forage primarily in the estuaries and marshes along Marin County's bay and ocean shores (see atlas maps).

Historical Trends/Population Threats

Grinnell and Miller (1944) did not list any breeding sites for Great Blue Herons in Marin County, but this was undoubtedly because of limited coverage in this area. Pratt (1983) reported the known history of Marin County colonies, noting that the Audubon Canyon Ranch colony was "well established and active in 1941." Although data are lacking, it seems likely that heron populations have been reduced by the historic loss of extensive marshlands in the San Francisco Bay system. Pratt (p. 103 this volume) describes a decline in Great Blue numbers in Marin since 1968. For California as a whole, numbers were relatively stable on Breeding Bird Surveys from 1968 to 1989 (USFWS unpubl. analyses). Disturbance at nesting colonies can cause abandonment (Werschkul et al. 1976), and pesticide contamination poses threats to reproductive success (see Hancock & Kushlan 1984).

Table 15. Numbers of breeding *pairs* of Great Blue Herons at 16 Marin County colonies from 1967 to 1991 (see Figure 15). U = Nest counts unavailable—herons may or may not have been nesting. In addition, at least one heron nest was at an inaccessible site off Bel Marin Keys Boulevard, Novato, in 1985 (based on the sound of large young being fed).

	1967	1968	1969	1970	1971	1972	1973	1974	1975	1976	1977	1978	1979
Audubon Canyon Ranch	50	62	55	50	44	46	58	48	45	40	41	43	35
De Silva Island	0	0	0	0	0	0	0	0	0	0	0	0	5
Drake's Head	U	U	U	U	U	U	U	U	U	U	U	U	U
Home Bay	U	2	3	U	U	U	U	U	U	U	U	U	U
Inverness Park	U	U	U	U	U	16	0	U	4	3	4	3	U
Nicasio Reservoir	U	U	U	U	U	U	U	U	U	U	U	U	U
Nick's Cove	U	U	U	23	U	U	U	23	28	23	24	16	U
North San Pedro Road	0	0	0	0	1	1	1	0	0	1	2	1	4
Phoenix Lake	0	0	0	0	0	0	0	0	0	0	0	0	0
Sand Point	U	U	U	U	U	U	U	25	7	U	U	U	U
Schooner Bay A & B	U	U	U	U	U	U	15	15	12	9	0	7	7
Stafford Lake	8	U	U	5	U	U	5	14	21	U	21	19	16
Olema	U	U	U	26	U	19	0	0	0	0	0	0	U
Bolinas-Fairfax Road	U	U	U	U	U	U	U	U	U	U	U	U	U
Smiley's "Preserve"	0	0	0	0	0	0	0	0	0	0	0	0	0
West Marin Island	U	U	U	U	U	U	U	U	U	U	U	U	0

	1980	1981	1982	1983	1984	1985	1986	1987	1988	1989	1990	1991
Audubon Canyon Ranch	33	27	26	13	16	18	21	18	13	16	9	7
De Silva Island	5	3	0	0	1	4	3	3	7	6	9	9
Drake's Head	U	U	11	3	4	1+	U	U	3	U	0	0
Home Bay	0	1	0	0	0	U	U	U	0	U	0	0
Inverness Park	12	8	6	3	6	U	U	U	10	U	7	9
Nicasio Reservoir	U	U	6	6	5	U	U	U	13	0	0	U
Nick's Cove	18	15	15	19	16	U	12	0	0	0	0	0
North San Pedro Road	4	3	2	2	4	U	U	U	8	16	21	17
Phoenix Lake	0	0	0	1	U	U	U	U	0	U	0	U
Sand Point	U	16	13	10	12	U	7	U	8	13	18	16
Schooner Bay A & B	7	3	0	0	0	U	U	U	0	U	0	0
Stafford Lake	27	23	27	29	28	30	31	U	30	27	32	16
Olema	U	U	U	U	U	U	U	U	U	U	U	U
Bolinas-Fairfax Road	U	U	U	U	U	U	U	U	U	1	1	1
Smiley's "Preserve"	0	0	0	0	0	0	0	· 0	0	0	6	10
West Marin Island	0	0	1	0	0	0	0	0	0	0	1	2

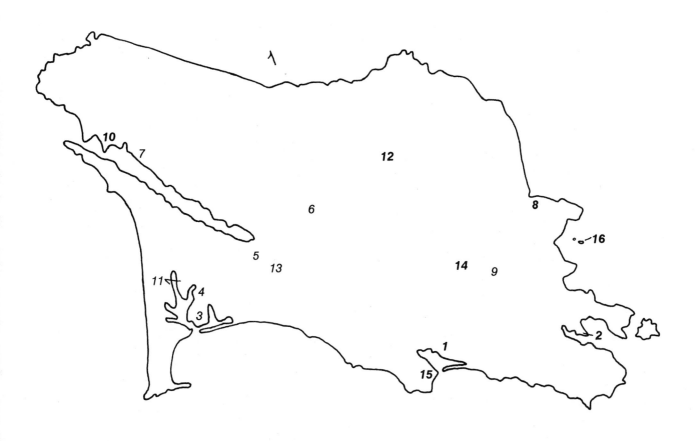

Colony codes used are:
1 = Audubon Canyon Ranch
2 = De Silva Island
3 = Drake's Head
4 = Home Bay
5 = Inverness Park
6 = Nicasio Reservoir

7 = Nick's Cove
8 = North San Pedro Road
9 = Phoenix Lake
10 = Sand Point
11 = Schooner Bay A & B
12 = Stafford Lake

13 = Olema
14 = Bolinas-Fairfax Road
15 = Smiley's "Preserve"
16 = West Marin Island

Figure 15. Map of heron and egret colony sites in Marin County. Rookeries denoted by bold numbers were known to be active in 1991; all other sites were active prior to 1991 (see Tables 15 and 16).

95

GREAT EGRET *Casmerodius albus*

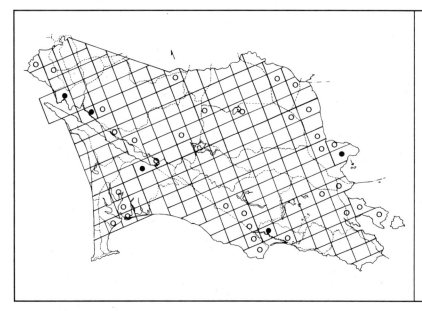

Occurs year round, though numbers swell substantially when birds occupy breeding rookeries, mostly from mid-Mar (rarely mid-Apr) until late Jul to mid-Aug.

A very common, very local breeder; overall breeding population very small.

Recorded in 5 (37) or 2.3% (16.7%) of 221 blocks (see Methods).

○	Possible	=	32 (86%)
◑	Probable	=	0 (0%)
●	Confirmed	=	5 (14%)

FSAR = 5   OPI = 25   CI = 1.27

Ecological Requirements

Great Egrets present elegant lines and exude a ghostly aura as they forage in a variety of shallow-water habitats, including estuaries; lagoons; bays; saltwater, brackish, and freshwater marshes; as well as ponds and streams, irrigation ditches, and wet meadows. In Marin County, breeding Great Egrets prefer estuarine and bay habitats. They use inland freshwater habitats and pasturelands only to a limited degree compared with Great Blue Herons (see atlas maps).

Great Egrets feed singly or in groups and form large aggregations at concentrations of prey. Solitary birds vigorously defend foraging sites. Aggressive encounters occur when gregariously feeding birds attempt to steal prey captured by other individuals (Hancock & Kushlan 1984). Great Egrets forage primarily by slowly walking in shallow water, along shorelines, or in dry habitats; they also poise motionless to dart out and seize prey from a crouched posture with their heads drawn in. Infrequent foraging tactics include startling or activating prey by vibrating their feet in water (moving their feet up and down on the substrate) or by wing flicking. Great Egrets also forage actively by hovering over the water and stabbing at prey below, by flying along and periodically reaching into the water to pick up prey, or by diving into the water from the air headfirst. More complex foraging tactics include foot paddling while flapping the wings violently up and down; and periodically hopping from the water, stabbing prey brought to the surface. Great Egrets also glean insects from

plants. They feed primarily on fish, frogs, salamanders, snakes, snails, crustaceans, insects, small mammals, and, occasionally, small birds. Fish usually comprise the bulk of the diet in the wet season, but there is considerable local variation (Palmer 1962, Hancock & Kushlan 1984). Great Egrets specialize in capturing small to medium-sized rails forced from cover at high tides (Evens & Page 1986). Birds apparently travel considerable distances to forage. In the breeding season, Great Egrets frequently fly along the shoreline northwest of Bolinas, presumably commuting from the nesting colony at Audubon Canyon Ranch on Bolinas Lagoon to alternate feeding grounds at Limantour and/or Drake's esteros (Shuford et al. 1989).

Great Egrets breed solitarily or, more often, in small to large colonies, often in association with other species of wading birds. In Marin County, they nest in tall trees (redwoods, Douglas firs, eucalyptus, California buckeyes), often alongside Great Blue Herons (Pratt 1983; see Great Blue Heron account). Elsewhere, they sometimes nest low to the ground in small willows or on bent-down bulrushes (Bent 1926, Palmer 1962). Nests are flat platforms of sticks or tule stalks and are usually flimsier and flatter than those of Great Blue Herons; nests from previous years may be reused. Many nests lack a lining or cavity, but sometimes they are considerably hollowed and are well lined with fine twigs, vines, or weed stems. The young hatch asynchronously and are fed by regurgitation.

Marin Breeding Distribution

During the atlas period, Great Egrets nested at five colonies along the Marin County shoreline (Table 16, Figure 15, and atlas map).

Historical Trends/Population Threats

From the 1880s to the 1890s, Great Egret numbers in California were greatly reduced by hunters for the feather trade. They began to recover by 1911, and by 1943 the species was "common in the remaining suitable portions of its former range" (G&M 1944). Numbers probably failed to reach historic levels because of the extensive loss of the state's wetland habitat. Great Egrets reappeared in the San Francisco Bay Area in 1924 (Stoner 1934), and in Marin County with seven birds at Bolinas on 7 May 1929 (Stoner 1934) and one bird at Drake's Estero on 7 June 1931 (Stephens 1931). The birds at Bolinas were likely breeding then at what is now known as Audubon Canyon

Ranch (Pratt 1983). Human insensitivity was still evident in July 1955, when 53 egrets (mostly Greats, a few Snowies) were "wantonly slaughtered ... by rifle-bearing target shooters" at West Marin Island; the culprits were arrested (AFN 10:51). The West Marin Island rookery had been active for "many years" prior to this incident (Ralph & Ralph 1958). Pratt (p. 103 this volume) describes recent trends in numbers of Great Egrets at Marin County colonies. On the whole, Great Egret numbers increased on Breeding Bird Surveys in California from 1968 to 1989 (USFWS unpubl. analyses).

Great Egrets reproduced poorly in the late 1960s and early 1970s because of DDT-induced eggshell thinning (Faber et al. 1972, Ives 1972, Pratt 1972), but since then a decrease in the rate of egg loss during incubation suggests the species is recovering (Pratt 1974). Disturbance at colonies can, of course, cause abandonment.

Table 16. Numbers of breeding pairs of Great Egrets at five Marin County colonies from 1967 to 1991 (see Figure 15). U = Nest counts unavailable—egrets may or may not have been nesting. See Pratt (1983) for numbers of Great Egrets seen on or feeding near West Marin Island, 1973 through 1981.

	1967	1968	1969	1970	1971	1972	1973	1974	1975	1976	1977	1978	1979
Audubon Canyon Ranch	70	74	86	85	85	96	99	96	85	65	84	88	98
Inverness Park	0	0	0	0	0	0	0	0	3	4	12	2	U
Nick's Cove	U	U	U	0	U	U	U	5	15	13	6	12	U
Sand Point	U	U	U	U	U	U	U	0	0	U	U	U	U
West Marin Island	U	U	U	U	U	U	U	U	U	U	U	U	58

	1980	1981	1982	1983	1984	1985	1986	1987	1988	1989	1990	1991
Audubon Canyon Ranch	103	148	150	97	110	113	98	113	113	102	91	100
Inverness Park	1	0	0	0	0	U	U	U	1+	U	0	0
Nick's Cove	6	5	0	0	0	0	0	0	0	0	0	0
Sand Point	U	6	13	19	19	U	20	U	20	25	25	49
West Marin Island[1]	11	75	107	190	139	84	160	89	66	79	119	90

[1] On-site counts found 155 pairs in 1990 and 131 pairs in 1991 (R.L. Hothem/USFWS pers. comm.); counts from this site reported in table from these and previous years were taken from a boat.

SNOWY EGRET *Egretta thula*

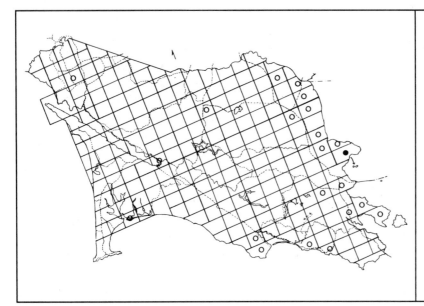

A year-round resident; birds occupy breeding colonies mostly from mid-Mar through mid-Aug.

A very abundant, very local breeder; overall breeding population very small.

Recorded in 1 (22) or 0.4% (10.0%) of 221 blocks (see Methods).

○	Possible	=	21 (95%)
◐	Probable	=	0 (0%)
●	Confirmed	=	1 (5%)

FSAR = 7   OPI = 7   CI = 1.09

Ecological Requirements

These dashingly handsome little egrets with "golden slippers" forage in a variety of shallow saltwater, brackish, and freshwater habitats comparable to those frequented by their larger cousin the Great Egret. Snowies also occasionally forage in pastures and fields and, like Cattle Egrets, will follow cattle and other livestock to pick up insects disturbed by their grazing (Palmer 1962, Hancock & Kushlan 1984). In the breeding season in Marin County, Snowy Egrets forage primarily in tidelands and marshlands along the San Francisco and San Pablo bayshores near their only regular nesting colony (see atlas map).

Snowies are extremely active feeders "moving about with great show of nervous energy, yet much poise and grace" (Palmer 1962). They also have the most diverse repertoire of foraging behaviors of any heron or egret so far studied (Hancock & Kushlan 1984). Snowies typically feed in conspecific or multispecies flocks, principally while walking slowly or quickly or while standing. They are especially adept at startling or attracting prey by vibrating their legs and yellow feet, by scratching their toes across or inserting them into the substrate, or by moving their feet up and down on the substrate. In addition, Snowies attract fish by placing their bills in the water and rapidly opening and closing them. Snowies are also accomplished aerial foragers. From flight they periodically reach into the water for prey, trail their toes in the water, and while hovering stab at prey below or pat, stir, or rake the water with their feet. Snowies also dash about rapidly, extending their wings for a few seconds at a time, with short flights interspersed. Their gentle looks belie their kleptoparasitic tendencies. I

have watched Snowies chase White-faced Ibis at Los Baños wildlife refuge and force them to drop crayfish, which the Snowies promptly ate. Their diet includes small fish, crustaceans (especially crayfish), frogs, lizards, snakes, worms, snails, insects, and, occasionally, small rodents (Palmer 1962).

Breeding Snowies are highly colonial, and they typically nest with other species of egrets or herons. Only occasionally do pairs breed alone. At the only well-established Marin County colony at West Marin Island, Snowies nest at varying heights in live oak and buckeye trees, in coastal scrub, and on the ground (Pratt 1983, H.M. Pratt & R. Hothem pers. comm.). Birds breeding irregularly at Audubon Canyon Ranch nest 60 to 70 feet up in coast redwood trees (H.M. Pratt pers. comm.). Throughout their range, nests usually are situated from the ground to 30 feet up (most 5-10 ft.) in a variety of trees; various bushes, cacti, and broken-down reeds and bulrushes also serve as nest supports (Bent 1926, Palmer 1962). The typically elliptical, somewhat loosely woven nest has a foundation of sticks and a rather flat body of twigs with a shallow cavity. Nests are sometimes lined with finer twigs, stalks of marsh plants, or rootlets. On occasion, birds construct no nest and instead lay eggs in a depression in the broken and matted-down tules of the previous year. Dead canes, reeds, rushes, tules, sage, holly, birch, and other plants may be used in the nest depending on availability. Snowies probably do not, or only infrequently, reuse former nests, although they may use the same site and sticks from other old nests in construction of the new one (Palmer 1962). Young hatch asynchronously and are fed by regurgitation.

Marin Breeding Distribution

Snowy Egrets breed consistently in Marin County in large numbers only at the West Marin Island rookery (Table 17, Figure 15, and atlas map). About five pairs nested at Audubon Canyon Ranch in 1969, 1988, and 1989; four pairs nested there in 1990 and 1991 (Pratt 1983, H.M. Pratt pers. comm.).

Historical Trends/Population Threats

Snowy Egrets were locally common in California prior to 1880, but because of the ravages of plume hunters they declined to the brink of extinction by the early 1900s (G&M 1944). By 1908 they were recorded again, and by 1943 they were fairly common in favored places (G&M 1944), though as late as 1932 a bird seen at Richardson Bay, Marin County, was still worthy of note in the *Condor* (Swanton 1933). Snowy Egrets probably have not recov-

ered to historical population levels because of the extensive loss of California's wetlands. At the time of Ralph and Ralph's (1958) visit to the active Snowy Egret colony at West Marin Island in 1957, local residents claimed that Snowies had been established there "for at least five years." See Great Egret account regarding a slaughter of 53 egrets, including a few Snowies, on West Marin Island in July 1955. Pratt (p. 103 this volume) describes recent trends in the West Marin Island Colony. On the whole, Snowy Egret numbers increased on Breeding Bird Surveys in California from 1968 to 1989 (USFWS unpubl. analyses). In San Francisco Bay, Snowy Egret eggs show concentrations of organochlorine pesticide residues and mercury, but below "critical" levels that cause adverse effects on reproduction (Ohlendorf et al. 1988). Monitoring of Bay Area colonies should be continued as reproductive failure in Idaho colonies has been linked to DDE contamination (Findholt 1984). Like our other colonial nesting waders, Snowy Egrets are also highly susceptible to nest loss from disturbance.

Table 17. Estimates of the number of breeding pairs of Snowy Egrets and Black-crowned Night-Herons on West Marin Island from boat censuses from 1979 to 1991.

	1979	1980	1981	1982	1983	1984	1985	1986	1987	1988	1989	1990	1991
Snowy Egrets[1]	262	U	325	500	400	400	161	126	239	212	245	300	277
Black-crowned Night-Herons[2]	98	U	109	80	89	54	79	40	41	35	61	37	45

[1] On-site counts found 463 pairs in 1990 and 487 pairs in 1991 (R.L. Hothem/USFWS pers. comm.).
[2] On-site counts found 306 pairs in 1990 and 294 pairs in 1991 (R.L. Hothem/USFWS pers. comm.).

GREEN-BACKED HERON *Butorides striatus*

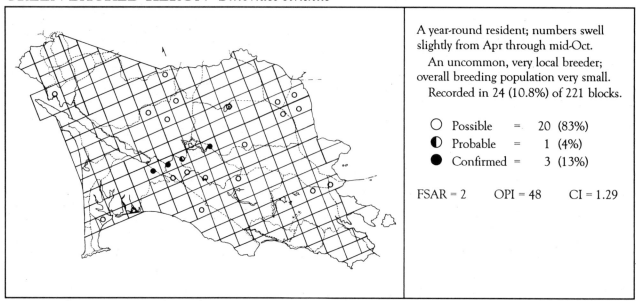

A year-round resident; numbers swell slightly from Apr through mid-Oct.

An uncommon, very local breeder; overall breeding population very small. Recorded in 24 (10.8%) of 221 blocks.

○	Possible	=	20	(83%)
◐	Probable	=	1	(4%)
●	Confirmed	=	3	(13%)

FSAR = 2   OPI = 48   CI = 1.29

Ecological Requirements

This compact, dapper heron blends in well with the forested margins of the quiet waters of streams, ponds, and freshwater marshes. Green-backed Herons use brackish marshes and estuarine borders to a limited extent in California, as they do commonly elsewhere, but most breeding birds here inhabit freshwater habitats. They forage mostly by day but also sometimes at night; at coastal sites, the timing of foraging bouts may vary with tidal heights (Hancock & Kushlan 1984). Green-backs are patient feeders. They usually stand crouched and motionless on a branch or rock, or they walk slowly along the shoreline waiting to stab their prey. Birds also flycatch from a standing position and startle prey by vibrating their feet in water or by raking their toes across the substrate. More active foraging techniques include launching from a perch feet first, or from the air headfirst, into the water, and floating or swimming on the surface of the water while securing prey. They even hang from branches while stabbing in the water. Green-backed Herons also ingeniously place items such as bread and feathers on the water's surface to lure in prey (Lovell 1958, Sisson 1974). In many situations they vigorously defend feeding territories (Palmer 1962, Hancock & Kushlan 1984). Their diet includes small fish, crustaceans, aquatic and land insects, amphibians, reptiles, other invertebrates, and small mammals (Palmer 1962, Hancock & Kushlan 1984).

In Marin County, Green-backed Herons nest solitarily. Elsewhere, they also nest in small groups or, rarely, large colonies; they rarely mix with other species for nesting. Nests are placed in a variety of situations. These include from on the ground to up to 30 feet in trees in dry woods or orchards; in low trees (most 10–15 ft.) or bushes over or near water; or amid marsh vegetation (Bent 1926, Palmer 1962). Nests vary from round to oval and from very flimsy platforms (usually new nests) to very tightly woven, bulky structures (mostly old, reworked nests). Green-backed Heron nests built on the foundations of other species' nests, such as those of Black-crowned Night-Herons or crows, are usually rather flimsy. The body of the nest is built of twigs or, rarely, of coarse weeds, reeds, or cattails. It is commonly unlined or lined with finer twigs, vines, and bits of reeds or other plant material. The young hatch asynchronously and are fed by regurgitation.

Marin Breeding Distribution

The spotty breeding distribution of Green-backed Herons in Marin County during the atlas period reflected the limited distribution of their preferred breeding habitat. Representative nesting locations were Nicasio Reservoir (NB 5/9/81 —JE) and just north of Inverness Park (FL 7/18/82 —DS). An earlier breeding record was of a nest with three young observed at San Anselmo Creek in Ross on 5 July 1935 (*Gull* 17, No. 7).

Historical Trends/Population Threats

Loss and degradation of marsh and riparian habitats must have greatly reduced the state's historic populations of this heron. On the whole, numbers of Green-backed Herons increased on Breeding Bird Surveys in California from 1968 to 1989, though numbers were relatively stable from 1980 to 1989 (Robbins et al. 1986, USFWS unpubl. analyses).

BLACK-CROWNED NIGHT-HERON *Nycticorax nycticorax*

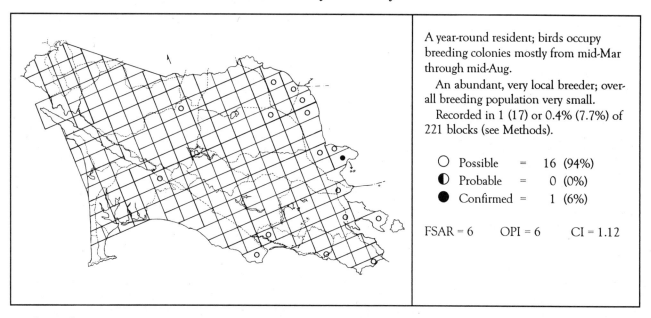

A year-round resident; birds occupy breeding colonies mostly from mid-Mar through mid-Aug.

An abundant, very local breeder; overall breeding population very small.

Recorded in 1 (17) or 0.4% (7.7%) of 221 blocks (see Methods).

○	Possible	=	16 (94%)
◑	Probable	=	0 (0%)
●	Confirmed	=	1 (6%)

FSAR = 6　　　OPI = 6　　　CI = 1.12

Ecological Requirements

The handsome portly profiles of Black-crowned Night-Herons appear posed for the painter at their communal daytime roosts and nesting colonies. The seasoned naturalist need not raise binoculars in the fading light of dusk to identify their eerie silhouettes as these herons give their characteristic *wok-wok* calls while flying out to feed in a variety of shallow marine and freshwater habitats, including bays, estuaries, tidal flats, lagoons, freshwater ponds, and marshes.

Unlike our other herons and egrets, Black-crowned Night-Herons are primarily nocturnal or crepuscular foragers. Although they occasionally come out to feed in broad daylight, they usually do so only on overcast or foggy days. They forage either solitarily, maintaining exclusive feeding territories, or in aggregations, and they usually hunt their prey from a poised stance or from a slow stalking gait (Hancock & Kushlan 1984). While standing or walking, they sometimes put their heads under an opened wing, which may reduce glare, making prey more visible, or attract prey to the shade of the wing. Additionally, Black-crowns occasionally hover over water, stabbing at prey below; dive headfirst into water; and float or swim on the water's surface, stabbing or picking up prey. On occasion they also rapidly open and close their bills in algae-covered water to attract prey (Palmer 1962).

The diet is diverse and varies with locality. Overall in the U.S. it consists roughly of 51.5% fish, 22% crustaceans (shrimp and crayfish), 16% aquatic insects, 6% frogs, 3% rodents, and the remainder mostly spiders and worms; other food items include tadpoles, snakes, salamanders,

mollusks, marine annelids, vegetable matter, and small birds (Palmer 1962, Wolford & Boag 1971). While walking around in colonies of nesting waterbirds, Black-crowns will take the young of terns, other herons, and ibises (Hancock & Kushlan 1984). At one locale, Black-crown young were initially fed shrimp, followed by fish after the young reached three weeks of age (Palmer 1962).

Black-crowned Night-Herons nest in small to very large colonies, usually with other herons or egrets. Nest sites are diverse and range in height from the ground to 160 feet up in trees. Colonies are variously located in trees or brush in mainland or island woodlands, forests, or swampland; in old orchards or in city parks; in stands of cattails and tules and on floating dead vegetation anchored to emergent cattail stalks; and on the ground among tufts of tall grass on islands (Bent 1926, Palmer 1962). Black-crowns at Marin County's West Marin Island colony build their nests mostly in coastal scrub but also in California buckeye trees (H.M. Pratt & R. Hothem pers. comm.). Nests vary from rather frail platforms to solid, bulky structures (sometimes deeply cupped) that are used for several years. Coarse twigs, sticks, reeds, or weed stalks make up the body of the nest, while finer materials such as small twigs or rootlets form the lining or are woven into the top; sticks from old nests are reused in the construction of new ones.

Marin Breeding Distribution

Black-crowned Night-Herons currently nest in Marin County only at West Marin Island (Pratt 1983; Table 17, Figure 15, and atlas map).

101

Historical Trends/Population Threats

Little information is available on the historical status of this species throughout California, though Grinnell and Miller (1944) termed it "formerly abundant, now greatly depleted locally." Moffitt (1939a) reported that about 25 pairs of Black-crowned Night-Herons nested in Marin County in live oaks and California bays on the north end of Belvedere Island from at least 1918 to 1938. He expressed concern at that time over the fate of the colony because of recent nearby house building and brush clearing. That colony is no longer extant, and the birds probably abandoned it because of further human encroachment soon after Moffitt's report. Disturbance to colonies can, of course, cause abandonment (Tremblay & Ellison 1979). Ralph and Ralph (1958) observed Black-crowns breeding at the West Marin Island rookery, which had been active for "many years." It is unknown if all, part, or any of that colony was established by emigrants from the Belvedere Island colony. Pratt (p. 103 this volume) describes recent trends in the West Marin Island colony. On the whole, Black-crowned Night-Heron numbers were relatively stable on Breeding Bird Surveys in California from 1968 to 1989 (USFWS unpubl. analyses).

The Black-crowned Night-Heron was included in the Audubon Society's Blue List from 1972 to 1981 (Tate 1981) and on its list of Species with Special Concerns in 1982 (Tate & Tate 1982). It was down-listed to a Species of Local Concern in 1986 (Tate 1986). In addition to habitat loss and disturbance, organochlorine (and mercury) contamination poses a widespread threat to Black-crowned Night-Heron populations, including Bay Area colonies, but so far it has had only limited local effects on their reproductive success (Ohlendorf et al. 1978, 1988; Custer et al. 1983; Findholt 1984).

Whether foraging or attending young, Black-crowned Night-Herons exude unwavering concentration. Photograph by Ian Tait.

RECENT POPULATION TRENDS OF MARIN COUNTY HERON AND EGRET COLONIES

Helen M. Pratt

The history of Marin County's heron and egret colonies was previously chronicled by Pratt (1983). Ongoing monitoring of these colonies provides additional information on the population trends of Great Blue Herons, Great Egrets, Snowy Egrets, and Black-crowned Night-Herons. See Pratt (1983) for census methods. The recent initiation of a monitoring program of heron and egret colonies throughout much of the San Francisco Bay Area (J. P. Kelly pers. comm.) should provide a broader perspective with which to evaluate future population trends of the Marin colonies.

Great Blue Heron

Since the high of 62 pairs in 1968, the Great Blue Heron population at Audubon Canyon Ranch has declined by about 89% (Table 15). During the past 25 years, various other colonies were newly formed, first discovered, abandoned, or have increased or decreased in size. Preceding the discovery of the Drake's Head and Nicasio Reservoir colonies, a countywide census in 1974 revealed 125 heron nests. In 1982, the first year after all the notable colonies were discovered, 107 nests were counted. In 1989, the nest count was 79, though additional birds were nesting then at Inverness Park, where poor visibility through the trees precluded a census. Thus the overall heron population in Marin County has declined since 1968, largely attributable to the drop in numbers at Audubon Canyon Ranch and the abandonment of the Nick's Cove and Schooner Bay colonies. Recent events at the Stafford Lake colony—the county's largest in 1990—may presage further declines of the Marin heron population. The Stafford population declined by 50% from 1990 to 1991. Also in 1991, all nests there failed because a temporary lowering of the water level in the lake, to enable repair of the irrigation system of the neighboring golf course, apparently allowed raccoons to invade the colony (H.M. Pratt pers. obs.).

Great Egret

The Great Egret population at Audubon Canyon Ranch has increased since 1967 (Table 16). In two instances, sharp declines from one year to the next—from 85 pairs in 1975 to 65 in 1976 and from 150 pairs in 1982 to 97 in 1983—occurred the year following raccoon predation on the colony. After installation of raccoon barriers at the base of nesting trees prior to the 1984 nesting season, the Audubon Canyon Ranch population has since remained at a plateau of about 100 to 110 pairs. On West Marin Island, the Great Egret population has fluctuated widely since the first census there in 1979 (Table 16).

Snowy Egret

Like those of Great Egrets, Snowy Egret numbers on West Marin Island have fluctuated widely since 1979—from a low of 126 pairs in 1986 to a high of 500 pairs in 1982 (Table 17). Such fluctuations are characteristic of Snowy Egrets at other colonies as well (e.g., Thompson et al. 1979). Determinations of general population trends would require coordinated censuses over a wide area.

Black-crowned Night-Heron

Based on counts from a boat, the Black-crowned Night-Heron population on West Marin Island has decreased since the first census in 1979 (Table 17). A fire on the island in July 1981 may have been responsible for a decline from 109 nests that year to 80 in 1982. Night-heron nests are hidden deep within the coastal scrub, and probably most of them are impossible to see from a boat. Figures from these censuses may be too inaccurate to be useful. Recent on-site counts provide better population estimates (see Table 17).

Waterfowl
Family *Anatidae*

CANADA GOOSE   *Branta canadensis*

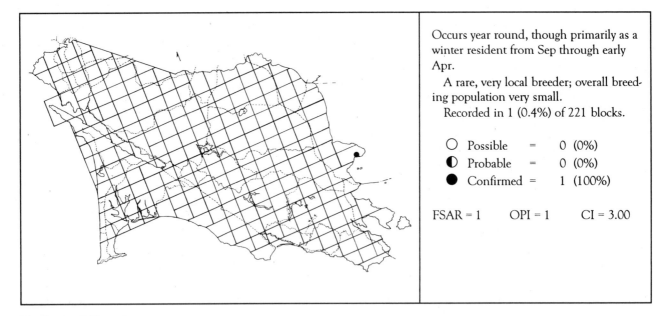

Occurs year round, though primarily as a winter resident from Sep through early Apr.

A rare, very local breeder; overall breeding population very small.

Recorded in 1 (0.4%) of 221 blocks.

○ Possible	=	0	(0%)
◐ Probable	=	0	(0%)
● Confirmed	=	1	(100%)

FSAR = 1   OPI = 1   CI = 3.00

Ecological Requirements

The echoing sounds of geese calling in flight overhead stir nostalgic feelings for times when California was wilder and untrammeled. The only native subspecies of Canada Goose known to breed in California is the Western, or Great Basin, Canada Goose, *Branta canadensis moffitti* (see Bellrose 1980). As native breeders, "Honkers" are presently restricted in California to the Modoc Plateau, Great Basin Desert, and valleys of the adjoining Klamath, Cascade, and Sierra Nevada mountains (G&M 1944). There they breed on the marshy borders of freshwater and alkaline lakes, reservoirs, streams, and in extensive marshes and wet meadows. In recent years, birds (probably mostly or entirely from plantings) have begun breeding locally in a wild state in the San Francisco Bay region on estuarine borders or islands, and at reservoirs, where they may also mix with domestic birds (see below). Captive birds established in California are largely *B. c. moffitti*, especially stock from near Reno, Nevada (M.R. McLandress pers. comm.).

Canada Geese nest in a greater variety of sites than all other species of waterfowl (Palmer 1976a, Bellrose 1980). They sometimes give the appearance of being semicolonial nesters, but this seems to reflect the concentration of birds at limited suitable nesting sites rather than inherent social

tendencies of the species; they do sometimes nest in or near California or Ring-billed gull colonies (Palmer 1976a). The nest site must be firm and dry and include freedom from disturbance, cover for the nest, and unobstructed visibility in all directions for the incubating bird (sometimes island nests may be in woods or under scrub). Nearby must be a guard site for the gander (up to 0.25 mi. away on open terrain), a grazing area (usually close at hand, but up to 1–5 mi. away), and proximity to permanent water (to which the young are led). Nests are usually within a few feet of water, and about 90% are within 50 yards; exceptionally, a nest may be 300 yards from water. Canada Geese nest most frequently on islands or islets. They also commonly select hummocks on peninsulas, lakeshores, streamsides, or in marshes or fields; mats of bullrushes in marshes, or the tops of muskrat or beaver houses; haystacks; dikes and ditch banks; gravel bars, talus slopes, river bluffs, ledges, or cliffs; clusters of low scrubby growth, stumps, or trees (particularly in abandoned nests of herons, Ospreys, and other hawks); and a variety of elevated artificial structures, including washtubs, tires, wicker baskets, wooden boxes or platforms, and anchored floating rafts. The female forms the nest scrape in the earth or other soft substrate by "wallowing" and collects twigs, reeds, weed stems, and grasses for the base and rim from, at most, a few feet from the nest (Dawson 1923, Palmer 1976a, Bellrose 1980).

Canada Geese feed primarily by grazing in marshes, meadows, and fields; they forage in cultivated fields more often on autumn staging areas and wintering grounds than on spring or summer habitats. Aquatic feeding is incidental except in coastal birds. They feed by tipping up in water, mainly when grazing forage is scarce, and, rarely, by diving from the surface (Palmer 1976a). Breeding birds feed singly or in flocks away from nesting territories. They feed mostly during the day, but also at night during periods of fattening (McLandress & Raveling 1981a) or when they are unable to secure adequate food during daylight hours because of shortages or excessive disturbance while feeding (M.R. McLandress pers. comm.). The diet of breeding birds includes mainly the shoots, foliage, stems, seeds, roots, and rhizomes of grasses, sedges, and aquatic plants, berries, and cultivated grains (particularly succulent, high-protein sprouts and mature seed heads). Insects, crustaceans, mollusks, and fish form a minor part of the diet, and perhaps all but the latter are consumed when attached to food plants. Canada Geese shift from a winter diet of mostly corn or other carbohydrates to a diversity of food items in spring before migrating (McLandress & Raveling 1981a,b). Although they still continue to eat some corn, protein-rich new-growth grass is important for laying on fat stores necessary for the migration and breeding effort. Females may have to obtain minerals (perhaps some from snail shells), and possibly protein, for egg formation from food sources on the breeding grounds. Goslings also need high-protein grass for growth (M.R. McLandress pers. comm.).

Marin Breeding Distribution

The only known breeding location for Canada Geese in Marin County was at West Marin Island near San Rafael. During the atlas period, an adult was seen there from a boat in the spring/summer of 1982 (HPr). Goslings seen nearby at McNear's Beach by Point San Pedro in May or June of 1982 (DT) may have come from a nesting attempt on West Marin Island, the Sisters (small islets directly off Pt. San Pedro), or from any of a number of duck blinds along the shoreline to the north. Subsequently, nesting was confirmed on West Marin Island by the observation there of a nest with eggs on 27 March 1983 (PCl) and two adults with two goslings on the water close to the island on 24 May 1983 (HPr et al.). A semidomestic flock also lived nearby at Peacock Gap golf course. In recent years, non-breeding oversummering individuals or escapees have occasionally been seen during the breeding season at various Marin County locations. A flock of up to 35 birds at Bolinas Lagoon in June and July each year since 1984 may represent birds dispersing after breeding at sites elsewhere in Marin County or the San Francisco Bay Area (Shuford et al. 1989).

Historical Trends/Population Threats

The Canada Goose was first recorded nesting on the California coast in 1932 when two pair bred at Crystal Springs Reservoir, San Mateo County (*Bird Lore* 35:112, Moffitt 1939b). It is now well established as a breeder in small numbers at several sites around San Francisco Bay (Lidicker & McCollum 1979) and appears to be increasing (ABN). It seems likely that most, if not all, coastal nesting records pertain to birds of introduced stock for the following reasons: (1) the major gap in the breeding range between the main California population in the northeastern corner of the state and that of the recently established population in the Bay Area, Suisun Marsh (1970s), the Delta (1980s), and Yolo County (1970s) (M.R. McLandress pers. comm.); (2) the strong attachment to traditional breeding grounds (Palmer 1976a); and (3) the ease with which this species adapts to captivity. It is also possible that a few winter residents pioneered a new breeding outpost on their own, perhaps as cripples from hunting casualties. The current coastal population may have originated from birds bred in captivity in the Bay Area in the early 1900s from eggs collected at Lake Tahoe (Grinnell et al. 1918); from a semicaptive flock of *B. c. moffitti* that has bred at Lake Merritt, Oakland, since at least 1954 (AFN 10:276, AB 27:913); or from captive stock derived from near Reno, Nevada, and released in Suisun Marsh, the Delta, or the Sacramento Valley. Released birds from captive stock from the Tahoe-Reno area seem to adapt to the mild conditions of Bay marshes and will probably continue to increase until hunters perceive numbers to be great enough to hunt (M.R. McLandress pers. comm.).

WOOD DUCK *Aix sponsa*

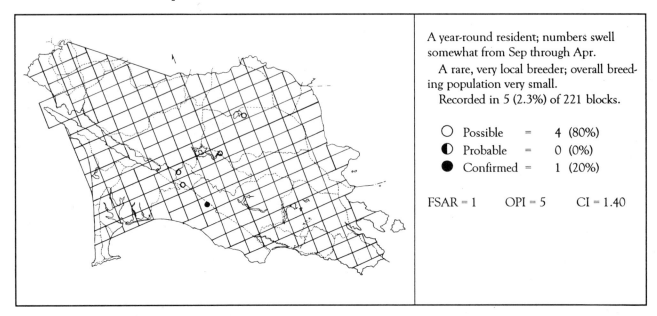

A year-round resident; numbers swell somewhat from Sep through Apr.

A rare, very local breeder; overall breeding population very small.

Recorded in 5 (2.3%) of 221 blocks.

○	Possible	=	4 (80%)
◑	Probable	=	0 (0%)
●	Confirmed	=	1 (20%)

FSAR = 1   OPI = 5   CI = 1.40

Ecological Requirements

Gaudily bedecked male Wood Ducks and their cryptic mates are wary recluses of the quiet waters of ponds, slow-flowing streams, wooded swamps, marshes, and reservoirs that provide overhanging secluding, woody vegetation along their margins. Wood Ducks rarely venture into deep open or fast-flowing waters. In most cases, they seem to prefer smaller water bodies to larger lakes and rivers for nesting (Naylor 1960). Wood Ducks are the most woodland- and forest-inhabiting of our local breeding ducks. Expert at flying between trees or through their crowns, Woodies use tree trunks and branches for perches, nest sites, and part of their foraging beat. In Marin County, riparian, broadleaved evergreen, mixed coniferous, or coniferous forests surround the wetlands used for nesting. Prime feeding areas are shallow (<1 ft. deep) or contain much floating or emergent vegetation as substrate for invertebrates (Drobney & Fredrickson 1979). Decomposing deciduous leaves provide excellent substrate for the midge larvae and other invertebrates important in the diet of Wood Ducks, particularly egg-laying females and growing ducklings (M.R. McLandress pers. comm.). A diversity of habitats is important to Wood Ducks to provide them with a broad array of plant and invertebrate foods (Landers et al. 1977). As well as providing foraging needs, ideal habitat for brood rearing and summer molting should include a spreading brushy overstory for concealment from above; small open-water passages; and scattered fallen dead limbs, trees, stumps, exposed roots, or muskrat houses for perching (Palmer 1976b).

Pairs or small groups of Wood Ducks generally feed from the surface in shallow water. They prefer to forage in wooded wetlands, though they occasionally feed along nonwooded shorelines next to open water (Drobney & Fredrickson 1979). Foraging birds move constantly and rapidly, using sizable areas during the course of feeding. There is no evidence that birds are attached to specific feeding areas or that they establish feeding territories. Woodies forage primarily by pecking at foods on the surface or by surface dabbling and, infrequently, by subsurface dabbling or bottom feeding (Drobney & Fredrickson 1979). Rarely, they dive to catch fish (Palmer 1976b). While afloat or ashore, Wood Ducks are adept at catching nearby airborne insects (Palmer 1976b) and probably glean others from emergent vegetation, stumps, logs, and water margins (Landers et al. 1977). In fall and winter, they prefer to procure acorns and other mast from shallow flooded swamps and bottomlands, but they also search for these foods under trees, and even among shrubbery, in upland forests (Palmer 1976b, Bellrose 1980). At times they fly into trees twined with grapevines and snatch the grapes from arboreal perches. Wood Ducks sometimes also feed in fields of corn, wheat, or other cereal grains, and, at least in Ohio, in farmers' hog lots.

The diet from fall through early spring is about 90.2% vegetable matter and 9.8% animal matter (Mabbott in Palmer 1976b, n = 399). In South Carolina, vegetable foods account for over 90% of the diet in all months except March, when they comprise 77% (Landers et al. 1977, n = 200). In Missouri, animal foods comprise about one-third of the diet of males in spring (n = 55) and of males and females in fall (n = 40) (Drobney & Fredrickson 1979). In preparation for breeding, females enter a period of hyperphagia, when they concentrate on protein-rich invertebrates and spend twice as much time feeding as do males (Drobney & Fredrickson 1979; Drobney 1980, 1982). During the breeding season in Missouri, consumption of animal foods by females averages about 58% (n = 60) and reaches a peak of 79% (n = 20) during laying (Drobney & Fredrickson 1979). Females of breeding pairs there eat more invertebrates, a greater diversity of invertebrates, and more aquatic (vs. aquatic-associated and nonaquatic) invertebrates than do males. The latter difference is perhaps attributable to the fact that males are more alert to their surroundings while foraging and therefore feed from a more erect posture. Hence they might be expected to feed more on fallen branches and tree trunks than do females, which feed more on or below the water's surface. The shift of Woodies from eating mostly aquatic invertebrates in spring to mostly nonaquatic invertebrates in fall may be a result of changing availability (Drobney & Fredrickson 1979) or perhaps more time spent foraging in upland areas when mast and fruit crops have ripened. The young initially eat almost exclusively animal matter (mostly insects), but by six weeks of age they have gradually switched to a diet comparable to that of adults (Palmer 1976b, Bellrose 1980).

The main vegetable fare includes the seeds and other parts of aquatic plants and the seeds, nuts, and fruits of trees; fleshy fruits may be important in summer (Palmer 1976b, Landers et al. 1977, Drobney & Fredrickson 1979). Acorns may be a particularly important food in fall and winter, depending on the crop. Animal foods consist primarily of aquatic and land insects and other invertebrates. Important items are adult and larval dragonflies, damselflies, mayflies, midges, caddisflies, crane flies, horse flies, beetles, and true bugs; less important are other insects, spiders, snails and slugs, isopods, crustaceans, and, very rarely, amphibians, fish, and mice.

Wood Ducks nest in natural cavities of trees, in Northern Flicker or Pileated Woodpecker cavities more or less enlarged by the decay of wood, in wooden and metal nest boxes, in barns (in hay) and abandoned camps, and in hollow trees (especially fallen ones) (Palmer 1976b). In Merced County, Wood Ducks use natural cavities in trees, since woodpecker (even flicker) cavities there are too small, though most use wooden nest boxes erected in the last 16 years (S. Simmons pers. comm.). Exceptionally, Wood Ducks prospect for nests in chimneys, or nest in crevices or fissures in rocks; one very unusual twig and leaf nest they used was supported by small branches high in a tree (Palmer 1976b). No nest material is added to the nest cavity except down (Bellrose 1980). The eggs are laid (and initially covered by debris) in a depression hollowed or

scratched out by the female in the soft, dry rotted wood or in other bits of bark, twigs, and leaves that have fallen into the cavity or have been brought in by squirrels (Bent 1923, Dixon 1924, Palmer 1976b, Bellrose 1980). Wood Ducks prefer nest boxes with sawdust spread on the bottom of the cavity (S. Simmons pers. comm.). They also prefer nest trees over water or in open stands along small streams or ponds, though they sometimes nest in dense woodlands and up to 200 yards from water (Dixon 1924, Naylor 1960, Palmer 1976b, Bellrose 1980). In Merced County, Wood Ducks most readily accept nest boxes close to and facing the water since they typically fly along waterways and are more likely to see nest holes so situated (S. Simmons pers. comm.). A preference is shown for nest boxes on vertical or forward-leaning trees. The height of natural cavities in trees ranges from 2 to 65 feet above the ground (Bellrose 1980). In California, 12 natural nest sites (in willows, cottonwoods, or valley oaks) ranged from 6 to 30 feet above the ground, and 10 of these were below 15 feet (Dixon 1924). In Illinois, the height of 158 nest cavities ranged from 6 to 55 feet above the ground (Bellrose et al. 1964). The average height there was 25 feet, but nests over 30 feet were actually preferred, based on occupancy rates relative to availability. Wood Ducks will use nest cavities year after year and are most likely to use previously occupied nests. Females prefer entrance holes as small as they can easily pass through, and there are instances of females cracking an egg still in the oviduct while squeezing through a narrow crevice (Dixon 1924)! Frequently, more than one female will "dump" eggs in the same cavity (Palmer 1976b, Bellrose 1980). In Merced County, up to 62 eggs have been dumped in a single nest box, and as many as six different females have laid in the same box on the same day (S. Simmons pers. comm.)! Egg dumping occurs there mostly from the middle to the end of the nesting season and may involve mostly juvenile females. Only rarely will two female Wood Ducks incubate in the same cavity or will one lay jointly with another species of cavity-nesting duck (Palmer 1976b, Bellrose 1980).

The day after the young hatch, the female coaxes them to spring out of the cavity and flutter to the ground or water by calling to them from the entrance cavity, a nearby limb, or from below. After first leading the young to water, the female is likely to keep moving them (Bellrose 1980). Females and broods may move to a series of ponds, traveling as much as 1.5 miles directly from an initial open nest pond to a vegetated one. Before developing flight capabilities, they may journey as far as 4 miles to another watershed. In areas of rivers and oxbow lakes, broods may move an average of 1.5 to 3 miles in the first two days after leaving the nest and a maximum of 6.5 miles in four days (Smith & Flake 1985). Wood Ducks sometimes produce two broods in a season, a rare phenomenon in North

American waterfowl (Bellrose 1980). The production of two broods in a season by banded females has been noted repeatedly in Merced County (S. Simmons pers. comm.).

Marin Breeding Distribution

Although seen at scattered locations in Marin County during the atlas period, Wood Ducks were confirmed breeding only once. A female with two downy young was observed on 5 May 1980 at Mill Pond on the Stewart Ranch about two miles south of Olema (DS). Had we contacted the California Department of Fish and Game during our atlas work, we undoubtedly would have confirmed nesting of more Wood Ducks. Fish and Game initiated a pilot nest box program by erecting 152 boxes throughout the state from 1952 to 1956 (Naylor 1960). Of the 5 boxes in Marin County, at least 2 were occupied "immediately" by pairs of nesting Wood Ducks; on the basis of a photograph in Naylor (1960:247), these were apparently at Mill Pond. Of 12 nest boxes in Marin in the 1960s, Wood Ducks "used" 1 at Mill Pond in 1967, 3 of 7 along Lagunitas Creek (19??), and 2 of 4 along Olema Creek in 1966 (MeS *fide* GiT). California Department of Fish and Game personnel also put up 3 nest boxes at Nicasio Reservoir in both 1983 and 1984, but as of 1991 it is not known if Wood Ducks have nested in them yet. In the 1970s, females with small young were seen on Pine Gulch Creek, on Mill Pond, and on Papermill Creek north of Tocaloma (EO). Adults with small young were seen at Five Brooks Pond in the Olema Valley from late May through July each year from 1987 through 1989 (ABN).

Historical Trends/Population Threats

In Marin County, Wood Ducks formerly "nested" on Gallinas Creek in 1872 or 1873 and occurred along Papermill and Lagunitas creeks up to about 1886 (G&W 1927). Mailliard (1911) observed that Wood Ducks were "plentiful" in Marin County in the 1870s and 1880s, but that they were "extremely scarce" there in 1910. Grinnell and Wythe (1927) considered them extirpated in the San Francisco Bay region. Numbers also declined throughout California, with a low ebb in 1915; thereafter, numbers increased at least through 1943 (G&M 1944, Naylor 1960). Naylor (1960) attributed the early declines to overshooting from sport hunting, to market hunting (especially for the valuable, highly colored feathers of the male), and to habitat destruction. The latter included draining and reclaiming marshes, dredging and mining activities, along with clearing of riparian vegetation resulting in the loss of nesting cavities. Though recent nest box programs will likely aid their recovery, it is doubtful that Wood Ducks will ever regain their former "abundance," given the history of habitat degradation and continuing increases in human development and recreational uses of waterways. Pesticides from agricultural runoff may also be affecting the supply of aquatic insects that are crucial during the nesting season (S. Simmons pers. comm.). Numbers of Wood Ducks were relatively stable on Breeding Bird Surveys in California from 1968 to 1989 (USFWS unpubl. analyses).

MALLARD *Anas platyrhynchos*

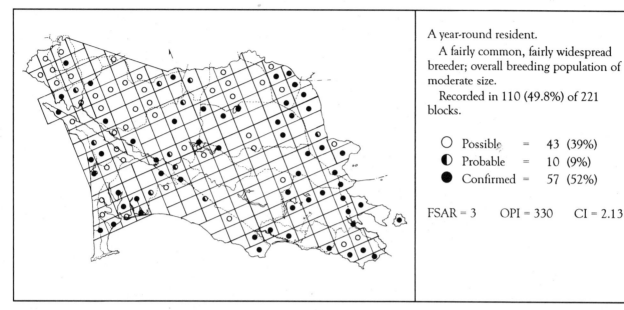

A year-round resident.

A fairly common, fairly widespread breeder; overall breeding population of moderate size.

Recorded in 110 (49.8%) of 221 blocks.

○ Possible   =   43 (39%)
◐ Probable   =   10 (9%)
● Confirmed =   57 (52%)

FSAR = 3   OPI = 330   CI = 2.13

Ecological Requirements

Mallards, our most familiar and adaptable ducks, frequent a wide variety of shallow freshwater ponds, marshes, sewage ponds, reservoirs, slow-moving streams, and brackish marshes and estuaries. Mallards need wetlands for resting and loafing, feeding, waiting, and brood rearing; they also require upland nesting sites with good cover (Dzubin 1969). Wetland feeding sites are generally near to, but up to five miles from, nesting areas (M.R. McLandress pers. comm.). An important requisite for breeding is space and freedom from interference from conspecifics. Although the home range throughout the whole breeding cycle may include up to six to ten ponds, the pair soon localizes its activity to one or two ponds (or a part of a large pond). This waiting area is a temporarily exclusive territory from which the male chases intruding pairs (and pursues lone females), especially during the brief period (13–22 days) just prior to laying until early incubation (Titman 1983). The male defends his mate from other males intent on forced copulation, and he alerts her to the presence of potential predators, allowing her to feed with a minimum of interruption during a period when she has special nutrient requirements. An important function of the waiting area is the reestablishment of the pair bond whenever the female is away from the nest (Dzubin 1969). Territories sometimes overlap, but more than one pair are usually not seen at the same place at the same time; some males move beyond the territory once the female begins incubating.

Breeding Mallards feed primarily in shallow water by tipping up for aquatic plants in marshes and for mast in flooded swamps. Although capable of diving for food, they rarely do so (Palmer 1976a). They also feed in agricultural crops such as corn, rice, or waste grain in stubble fields, especially from late summer through winter. In addition, they may obtain grain during breeding from ephemeral ponds in tilled land (Swanson et al. 1979). On warm summer nights, hens and broods may feed after dark on concentrations of emerging midges and mayflies (Swanson & Sargeant 1972). The diet overall consists of about 90% vegetable matter, including the stems and, particularly, the seeds of aquatic plants, cultivated grains, and mast (McAtee in Palmer 1976a, n = 1578). Animal matter comprises 10% of the diet in the form of aquatic insects (caddisfly larvae, dragonflies, damselflies, predaceous diving beetles, water boatmen, mosquito larvae, and midge larvae), earthworms, snails, crustaceans, tadpoles, fish eggs, and, rarely, frogs and small fish (Palmer 1976a, Swanson et al. 1979). Mallards obtain a significant part of their energy and lipid (fat) requirements for reproduction at sites occupied prior to arrival on the breeding grounds (Krapu 1981). The protein for egg formation, however, is obtained principally from the diet during the nesting period. Females spend more than twice as much time foraging during the laying period as do males (Dwyer et al. 1979). During laying, females increase their consumption of animal matter to about 70%; snails are important then for both protein and calcium (Krapu 1979; Swanson et al. 1979, n = 15). See Northern Shoveler account regarding the importance of fat reserves for egg formation. Young

Mallards switch from an initial exclusive dependence on invertebrates to vegetable fare when they are about half grown (M.R. McLandress pers. comm.).

Mallards are catholic in their choice of nest sites but generally prefer upland sites to marshes (Bellrose 1980). Availability of fairly dense cover about two feet high appears to be the main requirement. Nests range from a few feet to as much as a mile and a half away (Palmer 1976a, Bellrose 1980). Reports of most nests being within 100 to 350 yards of water (Dzubin & Gollop 1972, Palmer 1976a, Bellrose 1980) are likely an artifact of extensive research in the pond-studded prairie pothole regions of the U.S. and Canada. At Grizzly Island in the Suisun Marsh, nest densities are highest about one-half mile (or as far as possible) from water (M.R. McLandress pers. comm.). The distance of nests from the water is related not only to the dispersion of water, but also to the availability of nesting cover close by and the intensity of harassment of females by males as a function of population density (Dzubin & Gollop 1972). Because of these considerations, the closest water to the nesting site is not necessarily the pond used as a waiting site or the pond to which the brood is moved at hatching.

Typical nest sites include weed fields, hayfields and pastures, grain stubble fields, grassy and weedy edges of roadsides, weedy and brushy levee and ditch banks, dense marsh vegetation (sometimes over water), small islands, under piles of brush, under fallen logs in dense brush, under clusters of trees, and, less frequently, in heavy timber at the base of a large tree (Bent 1923, Palmer 1976a, Bellrose 1980). Atypical sites include tree crotches up to 25 feet above the ground, on tree limbs, in hollows of trees, on stumps, on muskrat houses or fallen logs, in old magpie nests, on the understructure of a bridge, and in a box on a barn roof. Mallards also accept artificial nest baskets, especially those located three to four feet over water in areas free of heavy vegetation (Bellrose 1980). The female forms the nest bowl in plant litter (already in place or gathered at the site) or in moist earth and adds pieces of marsh plants,

weeds, and grasses reachable from the nest. Most nests have a distinct canopy or cover, either natural or bent over the nest by the female (M.R. McLandress pers. comm.). After hatching, the female may lead the precocial young overland to more than one body of water; distances traveled by hens and broods may be up to three and a half miles in two days, and five miles in nine days (Dzubin & Gollop 1972, Palmer 1976a, Bellrose 1980). In large ponds and marshes, several stretches of shoreline are used during this period. The factors responsible for brood movement are unclear (Dzubin & Gollop 1972). They probably involve searching for favorable food and cover and moving to more permanent ponds and may be influenced by drying of wetlands, food shortage, and disturbance.

Marin Breeding Distribution

During the atlas period, the Mallard was the most numerous and widespread duck nesting in Marin County. It bred at freshwater sites scattered throughout the interior, at brackish marshes along the coast, and on the San Francisco and San Pablo bayshores. In urban-suburban settings, the breeding status of free-flying birds can be difficult to establish because of the presence of domestic stock and their hybrids and of "self-tamed," unconfined wild birds on the same ponds with truly wild stock. Fortunately, these considerations did not pose problems in establishing breeding in particular blocks because wild Mallards were such widespread breeders. Representative nesting locations were a pond by the beach at Limantour Estero (FL 4/8/80 —DS); Bahia Drive ponds near the Petaluma River mouth, Novato (NE 6/7/80 —DS); and Nicasio Reservoir (FL 7/18/82 —DS).

Historical Trends/Population Threats

In the period 1968 to 1989, populations of breeding Mallards were increasing in California (Robbins et al. 1986, USFWS unpubl. analyses).

NORTHERN PINTAIL *Anas acuta*

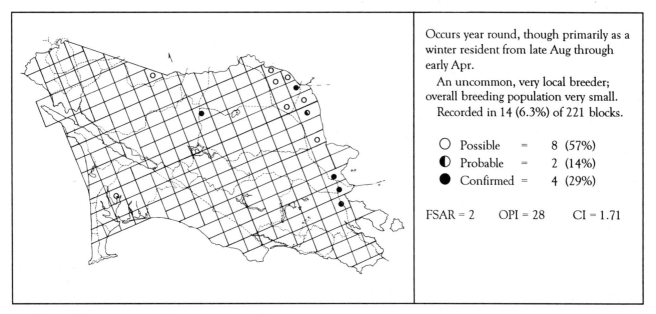

Occurs year round, though primarily as a winter resident from late Aug through early Apr.

An uncommon, very local breeder; overall breeding population very small. Recorded in 14 (6.3%) of 221 blocks.

○ Possible	=	8	(57%)
◑ Probable	=	2	(14%)
● Confirmed	=	4	(29%)

FSAR = 2   OPI = 28   CI = 1.71

Ecological Requirements

These sleek, elegant ducks characteristically nest in open country that contains many scattered small bodies of water (Palmer 1976a)–typically shallow, temporarily flooded basins harboring an abundance of aquatic invertebrates for foraging and brood-rearing habitat (Krapu 1974a). Ephemeral spring ponds, vernal pools, and flooded uplands are particularly attractive (M.R. McLandress pers. comm.). Apparent adaptations by Pintails to the use of ephemeral wetlands are smaller clutches, shorter incubation periods, and shorter fledging periods than Mallards and Gadwalls (Bellrose 1980, M.R. McLandress pers. comm.). Surprisingly, open flooded areas are used, seldom near trees. In Marin County, breeding Pintails mostly frequent wetlands in or near extensive brackish marshes along the bayshore, though they sometimes also use inland bodies of water. How the niches of the Mallard and Gadwall differ from that of the Pintail in Marin County is not clear, though Pintails are fussier in their choice of wetlands and appear to choose larger, but shallower bodies of water. Compared with other dabbling ducks, Pintail drakes are highly mobile and least attached to their waiting sites or "activity centers" (Palmer 1976a). Drakes will chase other females and loaf or feed with other drakes while their mates are at their nests. With this low level of aggression, many individuals can use preferred ponds.

Pintails prefer to feed in very shallow water at the surface or by tipping up (Palmer 1976a). Rarely, large numbers of Pintails will dive for preferred foods (Miller 1983). Their long necks and tipping feeding style enable them to sift seeds and benthic invertebrates from the detritus and sediments on or near the bottoms of ponds (Krapu 1974a). They also pick seeds or invertebrates from concentrations on the water's surface (Krapu 1974a, Euliss & Harris 1987). While foraging, they tend to spend more time tipping up than moving, then move quickly over short distances between tip-ups (Eadie et al. 1979). Pintails also feed extensively in rice, corn, and stubble fields on waste grain, though primarily in fall and winter (Bellrose 1980). Pintails often feed in both agricultural fields and wetlands at night (Euliss & Harris 1987, Miller 1987).

The diet in North America is about 87.2% vegetable and 12.8% animal (Mabbott in Palmer 1976a, n = 790), but percentages vary and animal matter sometimes predominates geographically or seasonally. For example, in the Central Valley the fall diet of Pintails is 97% or more vegetable matter, but by mid- to late winter it may be about 30%–85% animal matter (Connelly & Chesemore 1980, Euliss & Harris 1987, Miller 1987). Vegetable fare consists largely of the seeds of pondweeds, sedges, alkali bulrush, grasses, smartweeds, and several species of "moist soil plants" such as brass buttons, fat hen, swamp timothy, and purslane (Palmer 1976a, Miller 1987, M.R. McLandress pers. comm.). Animal fare includes various aquatic insects (midge larvae, water boatmen, caddisfly larvae, dragonfly and damselfly larvae and nymphs, predaceous diving beetles, mosquito larvae), earthworms, snails and other mollusks, crustaceans (brine shrimp, crabs, crayfish, shrimp), and, very rarely, miscellaneous items such as frogs and fish (Krapu 1974a,b; Palmer 1976a; Swanson et al. 1979; Miller 1987). Pintails arrive on the breeding grounds with large fat reserves necessary for the reproductive effort (Krapu 1974a). In North Dakota, breeding female Pintails in insect-rich habitats consume 79% animal matter compared with 30% by males (Krapu 1974b). Overall in various habitats, females consume 60% animal foods, reaching a peak of 77% during laying, when there is the greatest need for calcium (from snails) and protein. See Northern Shoveler account regarding the importance of fat reserves for egg formation.

Pintails choose relatively dry, open nest sites with low or sparse vegetation and generally nest farther from water than other ground-nesting ducks (Duncan 1987). In Alberta, most nests are from 0.6 to 1.2 miles from water, with some as far as 1.9 miles from water; many nests are also on pond edges or on islands. The low average distances of nests from water in other studies (about 200 yds. or less) may be because nest searches were conducted close to water (Duncan 1987) or because studies were in areas with extensive pond systems, where it is difficult for birds to nest far from water (M.R. McLandress pers. comm.). Female Pintails apparently nest far from water to reduce the probability of predation, rather than to avoid harassment by males near ponds as some authors have suggested (Duncan 1987). Spacing in available upland areas seems to be more important than vegetation for nest site selection (M.R. McLandress pers. comm.). Although Pintails may select nest sites in bare earth, they more often choose sites near, or in, some vegetation, such as weeds, grasses, brush clumps, low willows, or beds of marsh plants (Palmer 1976a, Bellrose 1980). They generally avoid timbered or extensive brushy areas. In the brackish Suisun Marsh, Pintails often nest in the cover of pickleweed two to three feet high (M.R. McLandress pers. comm.). More than

other species of waterfowl, Pintails use farmland habitats such as stubble fields, hayfields and pastures, roadsides, fallow fields, grain fields, and field edges for nesting (Palmer 1976a, Bellrose 1980). Females lay their eggs in a natural or hollowed-out depression lined with grass, bits of straw, weed stems, leaves, sticks, or mosses mixed with down (Bent 1923). Pintail hens usually lead their broods farther overland to water than other puddle ducks, and frequently from one pond to another (Bellrose 1980).

Marin Breeding Distribution

During the atlas period, most nesting Pintails in Marin County were found in wetlands along the San Francisco and San Pablo bay shorelines. Representative nesting localities included Spinnaker wetlands, San Rafael (FL 5/6/80 –DS); Bahia Drive ponds near the Petaluma River mouth, Novato (FL 6/16/79 & 6/14/80 –GiT); and fish-breeding ponds near the Cheese Factory, Hicks Valley (FL 6/21 & 7/14/82 –DS, ScC). The presence of a pair of birds at a freshwater pond at the head of Home Bay, Drake's Estero, on 17 June 1981 (DS) suggested that Pintails may occasionally breed along the outer coast of Marin County.

Historical Trends/Population Threats

Formerly, Pintails were not known to breed in Marin County (G&W 1927, S&P 1933, G&M 1944), but they were probably overlooked because of limited observer coverage since small numbers were known to breed then around San Francisco Bay (G&M 1944). Numbers of Northern Pintails were relatively stable on Breeding Bird Surveys in California from 1968 to 1989 (USFWS unpubl. analyses).

BLUE-WINGED TEAL *Anas discors*

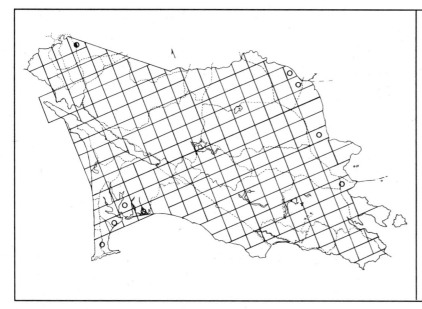

Occurs year round, though primarily as a spring transient from late Jan through Jun (mostly Apr-Jun).

A very rare (perhaps rare), very local breeder; overall breeding population very small.

Recorded in 9 (4.1%) of 221 blocks.

○	Possible	=	8	(89%)
◐	Probable	=	1	(11%)
●	Confirmed	=	0	(0%)

FSAR = 1   OPI = 9   CI = 1.11

Ecological Requirements

This dapper eastern counterpart of the Cinnamon Teal occurs irregularly in the breeding season in Marin County in shallow, marshy-edged ponds, in freshwater marshes, in slow-moving streams and sloughs, and, sparingly, in brackish water impoundments. The drake defends both his waiting site and his mate (Palmer 1976a). Both the hen and the drake stay within a circumscribed site, which may contain more than one water area; the drake prefers to wait at the one nearest the nest. Other nearby areas are used for communal feeding. Blue-winged and Cinnamon teal overlap broadly in habitat use and are often found in each other's company. Both species prefer to feed in very shallow water, usually with much emergent or floating vegetation (Bent 1923, Palmer 1976a). Although both species feed frequently in both open water and among emergent vegetation, Blue-wings feed more often in open water than Cinnamons do; both species feed to a limited degree on mudflats on pond edges (Connelly & Ball 1984). At times, Blue-winged Teal feed over deep water on emerging aquatic insects or on invertebrates using the substrate of vascular plants that extend to the surface (Swanson et al. 1974). Blue-wings sometimes gather to feed at night on emerging insects that concentrate in large numbers on the water's surface at the approach of darkness. Both of these teal species feed mostly near the surface by prolonged immersion of part or all of the bill below the water's surface (eye above water) or by picking items off the surface. To a limited degree, they feed by immersing the head past the eye or by tipping up, but they seldom dive (Swanson et al.

1974, Palmer 1976a, Connelly & Ball 1984). They also visit grain fields in the fall (Bent 1923).

The Blue-winged Teal diet year round is about 70% vegetable matter and 30% animal matter (Mabbott in Palmer 1976a, n = 319). Vegetable food consists mainly of seeds of grasses and sedges, and seeds, stems, and leaves of pondweeds. Animal foods include aquatic insects (midge larvae, caddisfly larvae, nymphs of damselflies and dragonflies, predaceous diving beetles, water boatmen, mosquito larvae), mollusks (mostly snails), various small crustaceans, and a few spiders, water mites, and, very rarely, fish (Swanson et al. 1974, 1979; Palmer 1976a). As with other dabbling ducks, dietary changes occur seasonally. Animal matter is particularly important in the breeding season when it can amount to 89% (increasing from 45% in spring to 95% in summer) of the diet of males and females combined (Swanson et al. 1974, n = 107). At that time, females feed more intensely and consume more animal matter (more snails, less crustaceans) than do males. In North Dakota, consumption of animal matter (especially midge larvae and snails) by females (n = 20) peaks at 99% of the diet during laying, when calcium and protein needs are high for egg formation (Swanson et al. 1974, 1979; Krapu 1979). See Northern Shoveler account regarding the importance of fat reserves for egg formation. The Blue-winged Teal diet also varies considerably between local habitats (Swanson et al. 1974). Compared with Green-winged Teal, Blue-wings feed more on animal matter and more heavily on vegetative parts of plants than on seeds (Bellrose 1980). Relative to Shovelers, Blue-wings

113

eat larger crustaceans (Swanson et al. 1974). Unlike other dabbling ducks, Blue-winged Teal feed on amphipods that concentrate on the terminal buds and other parts of vascular plants.

Blue-winged Teal typically nest in dry sites with fairly tall, dense grass, in sedge meadows, in brackish marshes of cord grass and salt grass, or in hay or alfalfa fields (Bent 1923, Palmer 1976a, Bellrose 1980). They also occasionally nest on soggy ground, on islands, in dense cattail growth, and in cavities in and upon muskrat houses. Nest sites range from the water's edge up to a mile away, but average roughly 125 feet from water (Bellrose 1980). The nest may be set well into a dense clump of rank grass on the surface or may be sunk in a cavity flush with the ground (Bent 1923). The nest bowl is lined with fine dead grass (less frequently with cattail blades or other wetland vegetation in damp places) and the obligatory down; growing grass often arches over the nest cavity. Females with broods may travel overland about 100 to 1600 yards (maximum 2.25 mi.) from the nest site to water but once established are more likely to remain at a site than are many other species of ducks (Bellrose 1980).

Marin Breeding Distribution

Blue-winged Teal occur in Marin County in small numbers most years in May and June (DS), but the species has not yet been adequately documented to breed here. Documentation is difficult to obtain because of the species' relative scarcity in Marin, the great similarity of female Blue-winged Teal and the much commoner Cinnamon Teal, and the tendency of these two species to hybridize in the wild (Harris & Wheeler 1965; relatively frequent sightings of males showing apparent hybrid characters —ABN). During the atlas years, we obtained suggestive evidence of nesting by observations of a female Blue-winged/Cinnamon–type female and downy young accompanied by a male Blue-winged Teal on Americano Creek on the Marin/Sonoma County border near Valley Ford, Sonoma County, on 10 June 1977 (CJP), and at the Bahia Drive ponds near the Petaluma River mouth, Novato, on 14 June 1980 (GiT) (but see comments below). During the atlas period, there were also scattered sightings of male Blue-winged Teal on Point Reyes and in wetlands along the San Pablo and San Francisco bay shorelines.

Atlasers in California should be very cautious about interpreting the significance of observations of male Blue-winged Teal accompanying female Blue-winged/Cinnamon Teal and young. First of all, Blue-wings likely breed one to two months later than Cinnamon Teal (M.R. McLandress pers. comm.). Secondly, male Cinnamon Teal attend females with young only infrequently (5%-

10% of broods), and Blue-winged Teal probably do so even less frequently since they are one of the northern ducks, which tend to have weak pair bonds. Blue-winged Teal males in these cases may be ready to mate, but the hens were likely mated earlier in the season to Cinnamon Teal males, hence the offspring would be Cinnamon Teals (M.R. McLandress pers. comm.). Even the observation of a *carefully identified* Blue-winged Teal female with young, even if attended by a male Blue-winged Teal, is not positive proof of nesting of this species because of the uncertainty of parentage. Nesting of Blue-winged Teal in areas of marginal occurrence of that species within the heart of the range of the Cinnamon Teal can probably best be considered valid only after a number of carefully identified Blue-winged Teal females have been seen with broods, thus lessening the likelihood that all sightings represented offspring of mixed-species pairs.

Historical Trends/Population Threats

Grinnell and Miller (1944) did not consider the Blue-winged Teal a breeding species in coastal northern California, although they did list a 21 June record for Arcata, Humboldt County. Recently, McCaskie et al. (1979) considered the species a rare to uncommon breeder on the northern California coast. This reported change in status may simply be the result of more thorough recent coverage of this region, but other evidence suggests a possible range expansion. Wheeler (1965) and Connelly (1978) reported that from the 1930s to the 1960s, Blue-winged Teal pioneered new breeding areas and increased in numbers on the Pacific Coast, especially north of California. On the other hand, the species' notorious tendency to abandon drought-stricken areas to pioneer newly available habitat far from the center of its breeding range (Bellrose 1980) perhaps explains periodic influxes that occur in Marin County and elsewhere along the northern California coast that might be interpreted as a true range expansion. For example, in May and June of 1980, one observer (DS) saw 23 Blue-winged Teal in Marin County compared with about 1 to 4 birds per year in several other years, with roughly equivalent time spent in the field. Similarly, Johnson and Yocum's (1966) report of a ratio of 42 Blue-winged Teal males to 36 Cinnamon Teal males at Lake Earl, Del Norte County, from 1 June to 20 July is certainly not typical of most years since Yocum and Harris (1975) considered Blue-wings to be rare breeders in that region. Numbers of Blue-winged Teal on Breeding Bird Surveys in California did increase from 1968 to 1989 but were relatively stable from 1980 to 1989 (USFWS unpubl. analyses).

CINNAMON TEAL *Anas cyanoptera*

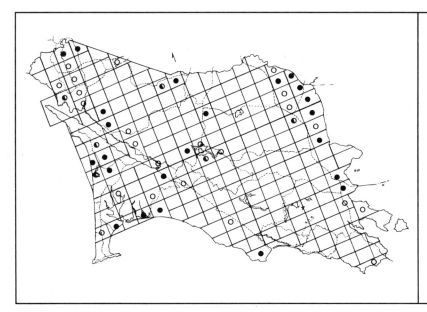

Occurs year round, though primarily as a spring transient from Jan through May (especially Mar and Apr) and secondarily as a summer resident from May through Sep.

A fairly common, local breeder; overall breeding population small.

Recorded in 52 (23.5%) of 221 blocks.

○	Possible	=	23 (44%)
◐	Probable	=	6 (12%)
●	Confirmed	=	23 (44%)

FSAR = 3   OPI = 156   CI = 2.00

Ecological Requirements

The stunning Cinnamon Teal drakes and their cryptic mates are studies in contrast in the freshwater and brackish ponds and marshes they inhabit. Their lifestyles, habitat preferences, and foraging methods are so similar to those of their primarily eastern congeners, the Blue-winged Teal, that the reader is referred to the descriptions in the preceding account. The Cinnamon Teal diet is roughly 80% vegetable matter, mostly seeds and other parts of sedges, pondweeds, and grasses; and 20% animal matter, divided about equally between aquatic insects (beetles, true bugs, damselflies, dragonflies, larval midges, etc.), and mollusks (snails and small bivalves) (Martin et al. 1951, n = 59; Mabbott in Palmer 1976a, n = 41). Like other dabbling ducks (see accounts), Cinnamon Teal appear to change their diet seasonally and consume more animal matter in summer (especially females).

Cinnamon Teal usually select nest sites in dense vegetation, such as grasses, weeds, bulrushes, and sedges in uncultivated land, meadowlands, marshes, swales, and grain fields, and on dikes and islands (Bent 1923, Dawson 1923, Palmer 1976a, Bellrose 1980). Females usually scratch out a shallow depression on dry land that they line with dead grasses and plant stems. They also frequently establish marsh nests and, more commonly than other species of dabbling ducks, nests over water. Marsh nests are bulkier baskets or platforms made of dried cattails, sedges, or marsh grasses. These nests may be under dense matted vegetation of the previous year's growth, may be

reached by a tunnel burrowed out by the female, or may be suspended over water in emergent vegetation. If threatened by rising water levels, females sometimes raise ground nests by adding materials. Although nests range from directly over water to 220 yards away from it, most are within 75 yards of water. The best brood habitats are small bodies of water, such as ponds, ditches, and canals, with plentiful submerged aquatic vegetation for feeding and emergent vegetation for protective cover (Bellrose 1980). The hen may move broods as far as a mile in a few days, but, if cover and feeding conditions are good, their activities may involve only a few acres (Palmer 1976a).

Marin Breeding Distribution

During the atlas period, the Cinnamon Teal, next to the Mallard, was the second most widespread breeding duck in Marin County. Although some breeding Cinnamon Teal were scattered throughout the county, most were concentrated in coastal and bayshore wetlands. Representative breeding locations included the pond at the Drake's Beach visitor's center, PRNS (FL 5/27/80 –DS); McGinnis Park, San Rafael (FL 6/3/80 –DS); and Laguna Lake, Chileno Valley (FL 6/28/81 –DS). Numbers of Cinnamon Teal in early spring belie actual breeding abundance since there is a peak migratory period from February through April with numbers falling to summer levels by May (Shuford et al. 1989).

115

Historical Trends/Population Threats

Cinnamon Teal were not reported historically from Marin County as breeding birds (G&W 1927, S&P 1933, G&M 1944), probably because of limited observer coverage or an author's impression that such records lacked

regional significance. Numbers of Cinnamon Teal were relatively stable on Breeding Bird Surveys in California from 1968 to 1989 (USFWS unpubl. analyses).

NORTHERN SHOVELER *Anas clypeata*

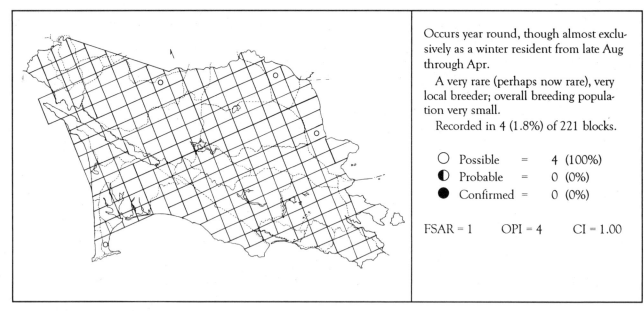

Occurs year round, though almost exclusively as a winter resident from late Aug through Apr.

A very rare (perhaps now rare), very local breeder; overall breeding population very small.

Recorded in 4 (1.8%) of 221 blocks.

○	Possible	=	4 (100%)
◑	Probable	=	0 (0%)
●	Confirmed	=	0 (0%)

FSAR = 1   OPI = 4   CI = 1.00

Ecological Requirements

With such an outsized bill, one might expect the "Spoon-bill" to ply its trade in waters of a different ilk, but, like many of the dabbling duck clan, its breeding haunts are shallow ponds and open marshy areas with shallow waterways and abundant aquatic vegetation (along with surrounding dry meadows). Soft, slimy mud is another requisite (Palmer 1976a). Shovelers do not appear to care if the water is clear, clean, muddy, flowing, or stagnant; and they nest near fresh, alkaline, brackish, or estuarine waters. Breeding Shovelers are the most territorial of the prairie-nesting dabbling ducks, presumably because of their need to secure high-quality feeding sites for reproduction (Ankney & Afton 1988). Shovelers select a home range with a "core area" or "waiting area," a nest site, and several (3–13) "peripheral" ponds (Poston 1974). Pairs spend 60%–90% of their time on the core area, which appears to supply the basic resources for nesting and pair isolation. The core area is a restricted portion of the home range, such as a pond, a section of a pond, or several adjacent small ponds. It contains a loafing area (the waiting area) and feeding areas. The male waits at the core area for the return of the female during incubation and defends it

against other intruding Shovelers at all times from the onset of laying until the waning of the pair bond or until the female hatches the brood, whichever comes first. Home ranges overlap, with neighboring pairs sharing "neutral" areas of nesting cover, peripheral ponds, and sometimes core areas in the absence of the residents. Nest sites are usually close to core areas but may be at some distance.

The Shoveler's large, spatulate bill with well-developed lamellae is designed for filter feeding. Shovelers often feed in very shallow water, continuously moving slowly about with their heads and necks partly or fully submerged. Thus engaged, they sweep their bills from side to side, skimming above the bottom or filtering the water to obtain small animal life and seeds (Palmer 1976a, Bellrose 1980). A number of Shovelers will feed socially in this manner, paddling rapidly together in a circular or elliptical orbit on the water, apparently stirring up the plankton-laden waters and straining it through the lamellae of the bill. In breeding areas in Alberta, Shovelers prefer to feed in the shallows of ponds containing submergent and surface vegetation (Poston 1974). They also feed in deeper water than most dabbling ducks do, by swimming along, with the bill slightly submerged, skimming and filtering the surface waters (Palmer 1976a, Bellrose 1980). Shovelers gather in large numbers to feed in this manner on sewage ponds. They also filter below the surface by tipping up, but infrequently compared with other dabblers; they seldom go to fields to forage. Like most others dabblers, they rarely dive. On warm summer nights, hens and broods feed after dark on emerging midges and mayflies and on water fleas making vertical migrations to the water's surface (Swanson & Sargeant 1972).

The diet of North American birds (fall to spring) is roughly 66%–72% vegetable matter, including seeds and soft parts of grasses, sedges, pondweeds, waterlilies, algae, and smartweeds. The remaining 28%–34% of the diet is animal matter, especially mollusks (mostly freshwater univalves), insects (water boatmen, backswimmers, water tigers, dragonfly nymphs, flies, and caddisfly and mayfly larvae), small crustaceans (ostracods, copepods), and crayfish and fish (probably rare); in certain areas, animal matter may predominate in the diet (Martin et al. 1951, n = 101; McAtee in Palmer 1976a, n = 70). The bill is particularly well adapted for feeding on microscopic phytoplankton and zooplankton, but these food items are rapidly digested, hence their importance is undoubtedly underestimated in many diet studies (Bellrose 1980). In one study of post-breeding Shovelers, their diet was 78% animal matter, of which 90% was zooplankton (Dubowy 1985). Like other dabbling ducks, Shovelers change their diet seasonally and rely more on animal matter in summer. In North Dakota, females (n = 15) consume 99% animal matter (mostly microcrustaceans and small snails) during laying when the need is high for protein and calcium for egg formation (Swanson et al. 1979, Krapu 1979). Ankney and Afton (1988) reported that prelaying (n = 14) and laying (n = 23) female Shovelers in Manitoba ate over 90% animal matter, again mostly snails and crustaceans. They concluded that while protein intake is important to nesting birds that the size of fat reserves is the factor limiting clutch size of Shovelers and probably also other dabbling ducks, such as Wood Ducks and Mallards. During the prelaying period, male Shovelers ate a similar proportion of animal matter to that consumed by females but only 67% (n = 10) during the laying period.

Northern Shovelers usually nest in dry upland sites, sometimes in moist meadowland, and, rarely, in wet marshes. Nesting cover is typically grasses (especially short varieties and salt grass), sometimes hay, and, rarely, weeds, bulrushes, sedges, or woody vegetation, such as willows, poplars, or rosebushes; concealment can be minimal, especially early in the season (Bent 1923, Dawson 1923, Poston 1974, Palmer 1976a, Bellrose 1980). The nest is a hollow, lined with dead grasses, weeds, or broken reeds, and, of course, down. Apparently females sometimes relocate nests to higher ground when threatened by rising waters (Poston 1974). Although they may range up to a mile from water, most nests are from about 75 to 300 feet from water; nests immediately adjacent to water are usually on islands or levees (Poston 1974, Palmer 1976a, Bellrose 1980). In the prairies of Canada, broods seldom remain on one pond longer than seven to ten days, and they may move with the hen up to a mile through a series of ponds in about two weeks (Poston 1974). Younger broods are kept in shallow shoreline areas near emergent vegetation; older broods prefer larger bodies of permanent water (Palmer 1976a).

Marin Breeding Distribution

During the atlas period, we obtained circumstantial evidence of breeding via sightings of a male at McGinnis Park, San Rafael, on 3 June 1980; a male at the Bahia Drive ponds near the Petaluma River mouth, Novato, on 7 June 1980; two to three birds on outer Point Reyes from 16 to 18 June 1981; and a female on Laguna Lake, Chileno Valley, on 19 July 1982 (all DS). Subsequently, breeding was confirmed at the Las Gallinas sewage ponds, San Rafael, with the observation of a female with downy young from 28 May to 7 July 1985 (DT, CLF, DAH); Shovelers also bred there at least in 1986, 1987, and 1988 (ABN).

Historical Trends/Population Threats

Formerly, Northern Shovelers were not known to breed in Marin County (G&W 1927, S&P 1933, G&M 1944), but they may have gone undetected because of limited observer coverage since small numbers did breed then nearby on San Francisco Bay (G&W 1927, G&M 1944). Recent increases in the number of breeding Shovelers, and their broods, at Grizzly Island Wildlife Area, Solano County, have coincided with increases in the number and total acreage of summer ponds following extensive flooding in 1983 and subsequent management for summer water (M.R. McLandress pers. comm.). Shoveler numbers increased on Breeding Bird Surveys in California from 1968 to 1989 but were relatively stable from 1980 to 1989 (USFWS unpubl. analyses).

GADWALL *Anas strepera*

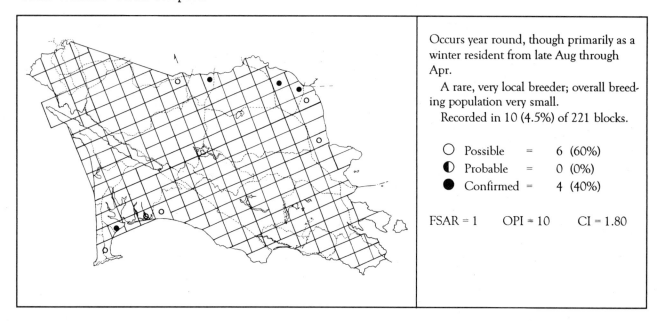

Occurs year round, though primarily as a winter resident from late Aug through Apr.

A rare, very local breeder; overall breeding population very small.

Recorded in 10 (4.5%) of 221 blocks.

○ Possible = 6 (60%)
◑ Probable = 0 (0%)
● Confirmed = 4 (40%)

FSAR = 1   OPI = 10   CI = 1.80

Ecological Requirements

The Gadwall's subtle yet striking beauty graces Marin County's shallow freshwater ponds and marshes, sluggish streams, and brackish marshes, which abound in submerged aquatic plants. During the breeding season, it avoids woods or thick brush (and waters with such borders) and, along with the Shoveler, uses alkaline or brackish waters more than other dabbling ducks do (Palmer 1976a). Breeding pairs often use areas that include a broad stretch of open water as well as small ponds. Like other dabbling ducks (see accounts), Gadwall usually occupy a home range with a nest site, waiting area, and feeding areas that may overlap with those of neighboring pairs; aggression of the male centers around a smaller defended area or just the mate (Gates 1962, Dwyer 1974, Palmer 1976a). When nesting densities are very high on islands, intense aerial-pursuit activity causes territorial defense of a female or section of habitat to break down (Duebbert 1966). Under these conditions, hens leaving nests for relief periods may be forced to fly more than a mile to feed and rest free of pursuing drakes.

Gadwall usually feed on shallowly submerged and floating vegetation, and more often in open water than other dabblers do (Palmer 1976a). They feed at all hours of the day and after dark on abundant supplies of emerging midges and water fleas making vertical migrations to open surface waters. Gadwall feed mostly by dabbling, tipping up, and picking, and by filtering from the surface or while swimming with their heads immersed; they apparently do not feed directly on the bottom (Serie & Swanson 1976).

Small planktonic crustaceans are most frequently ingested by filtering (though not as effectively as Shovelers do), and most insects and filamentous algae are obtained by surface picking or tipping up. Gadwall are adept at separating small midges and beetle larvae from a substrate of algae and detritus. Sometimes they feed from shore on windrowed detritus or concentrated plankton. While feeding, Gadwall spend more time moving than tipping up and move slowly over long distances between bouts of tipping up (Eadie et al. 1979). They also dive well for food when necessary (though infrequently), occasionally forage in grain stubble, and, rarely, forage in woods for acorns (Palmer 1976a).

Like wigeon, but unlike most dabbling ducks, Gadwall generally prefer the succulent leaves and stems rather than the seeds of aquatic plants. Filamentous algae are very common in Gadwall diets, making the Gadwall somewhat unique among ducks (Serie & Swanson 1976, Swanson et al. 1979, M.R. McLandress pers. comm.). The North American fall and winter diet is about 98% vegetable matter and 2% animal matter (Martin et al. 1951, n = 371; Mabbott in Palmer 1976a, n = 362). Like other dabblers, Gadwall depend more on animal matter in summer. During breeding on saline lakes in North Dakota, the diet of adults is 46% animal and 54% vegetable matter; females consume more animal matter than males do (Serie & Swanson 1976, n = 107). Consumption there of animal matter (mostly aquatic insects and crustaceans) by females in both freshwater (n = 35) and saline lakes (n = 20) reaches a peak at 72% of the diet during laying when demand is high for calcium and protein for egg formation (Serie & Swanson 1976, Krapu 1979, Swanson et al. 1979). Throughout North America, animal matter consumed includes aquatic insects (larvae and adults of midges, caddisflies, beetles, other flies, true bugs, dragonflies, damselflies, and grasshoppers), crustaceans, mollusks (mostly snails), and a few fish. Vegetable fare consists primarily of leaves, stems, rootstocks, and, sparingly, seeds (important locally or seasonally) of grasses, sedges, pondweeds, and other aquatic plants, including algae. Preflight young initially eat chiefly surface invertebrates but gradually switch to aquatic invertebrates and plants until, by three weeks of age, they are essentially herbivores; important invertebrates to young are midges, aquatic beetles, water fleas, and water boatmen (Palmer 1976a).

Although widely distributed in nesting habitat, Gadwall show a tendency toward colonial breeding (on islands, especially where surrounded by open water) (Palmer 1976a). Exceptionally, on islands, many nests may be within a few feet of each other, some less than one foot apart (Duebbert 1966). Gadwall nest a month to a month and a half later than Mallards (M.R. McLandress pers. comm.). This may be related to their dependence on nesting in dry and dense upland herbaceous vegetation, which becomes increasingly available as spring advances (Gates 1962). Late nesting may also be due to a dependence on insects that develop later in the season in semipermanent wetlands (Serie & Swanson 1976). Gadwall usually select nest sites on well-drained or, occasionally, damp ground, but rarely in emergent or matted floating vegetation. Reports of most nests being within 100 yards of water (sometimes nearly a mile from water) may be because of the tendency of Gadwall to nest on small islands, dikes, and channel banks with requisite cover (Gates 1962, Palmer 1976a, Bellrose 1980). At Grizzly Island in the Suisun Marsh, highest nest densities were about one-half mile (or as far as possible) from water (M.R. McLandress pers. comm.). For nesting, Gadwall favor transitions in habitat, such as the interface of water and land, breaks or openings in cover, patches or clumps within uniform stands of vegetation, or sites near mounds, stones, or other landmarks (usually within 10 ft.). Gadwall generally seek taller and more leafy vegetation for nesting than do other dabbling ducks and do not nest in stubble fields unless other herbaceous vegetation is growing there (Palmer 1976a, Bellrose 1980). The cover they select is usually dense, coarse herbaceous vegetation (especially nettles and thistles), taller grasses, alfalfa or hay, sedges, bushes, or willows. The nest is a hollow lined with dry grasses, weed stems, or strips and pieces of reeds, and, of course, down;, it is usually arched over by vegetation or is beneath leafy, herbaceous plants (Bent 1923, Dawson 1923, M.R. McLandress pers. comm.). Females sometimes build up the nest to escape rising water (Palmer 1976a). An exceptional nest site was one in a crow's nest in a tree. On islands, females sometimes lay their eggs in nest bowls of the preceding year(s?) (Duebbert 1966). Broods do not remain long on small water bodies; instead, they prefer open-water areas of moderate to large size having submerged aquatic plants for food and deep channels for escape by diving (Palmer 1976a). Females may lead broods as much as 500 yards across open water or over a mile from upland nest sites to favorable deep-water marshes or impoundments (Gates 1962, Duebbert 1966). In Utah, the distance that hens moved their broods during the rearing period averaged 0.56 miles (range 0.26–1.15 mi.) (Gates 1962, n = 13).

Marin Breeding Distribution

During the atlas period, Gadwall bred locally in Marin County along the San Pablo Bay shoreline and, occasionally, on Point Reyes and in the interior of the county. Representative breeding locations included San Antonio Creek, W of Point Reyes–Petaluma Rd. (FL 5/6/79 –SG); Bahia Drive ponds near the Petaluma River mouth, Novato (FL 6/20/80 –DS); and Horseshoe Pond, E of the Drake's Beach visitor's center, PRNS (FL 7/8 & 8/15/81 –DS).

Historical Trends/Population Threats

Historically, Gadwall were not known to breed in Marin County or the San Francisco Bay Area (G&W 1927, S&P 1933, G&M 1944). Subsequent confirmation of breeding in these areas (Gill 1977, ABN, records above) may partly reflect increased observer coverage or the dramatic continentwide post-1950s rise in breeding and wintering populations (Johnsgard 1978, Bellrose 1980). Wintering numbers have also increased on Point Reyes since the early 1970s (Shuford et al. 1989). Gadwall numbers increased on Breeding Bird Surveys in California from 1968 to 1989 (USFWS unpubl. analyses).

COMMON MERGANSER *Mergus merganser*

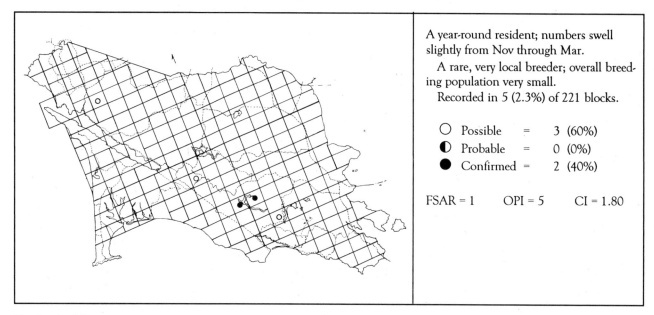

A year-round resident; numbers swell slightly from Nov through Mar.

A rare, very local breeder; overall breeding population very small.

Recorded in 5 (2.3%) of 221 blocks.

○ Possible = 3 (60%)
◗ Probable = 0 (0%)
● Confirmed = 2 (40%)

FSAR = 1   OPI = 5   CI = 1.80

Ecological Requirements

Along the northern California coast, these "fish-hounds" ply the cool, clear waters of rivers, large streams, lakes, and, particularly toward the south, reservoirs. Because visibility plays such a large part in the pursuit of their fish prey, Common Mergansers are generally absent from turbid or weed-choked waters. Foraging birds work relatively shallow waters, varying from riverine rapids to quiet backwaters, more or less following shorelines. They feed mostly near the bottom in about 6 feet of water, but their efforts may take them to 40 feet in depth (Palmer 1976b). Birds may initiate searches for prey by swimming along with their heads submerged. Mergansers propel themselves underwater with their feet only (stroked in unison), except perhaps in unusual circumstances, and they randomly search among, and under, submerged rocks or other objects where fish might hide. The diet of adults is overwhelmingly fish, but occasionally they eat fish eggs, aquatic salamanders, shrimp, and mussels or other mollusks (Palmer 1976b). Common Mergansers consume at least 50 species of North American fish, eating what is locally available roughly in proportion to their abundance and vulnerability. Studies of captive birds indicate Mergansers first eat smaller fish if available. The upper limit in size of fish they can eat probably ranges from 5 to 6½ inches in *girth* (Latta & Sharkey 1966). Ducklings at first feed entirely on insects caught mostly beneath the surface but soon catch small fish; they will also eat some green vegetation (Palmer 1976b).

Common Mergansers are cavity nesters and prefer hollow trees when available; as many as four nests have been found in different cavities in the same tree (Palmer 1976b). The height of tree cavities does not appear to be important (Palmer 1976b), but most are at moderate heights and range to 100 feet or more above the ground (Dawson 1923). Nest sites are used repeatedly, probably by the same female (Palmer 1976b). When suitable tree cavities are in short supply, Common Mergansers will nest in a variety of well-protected holes and dark recesses. Among the alternate sites reported are cavities on cliff faces, ledges under low fir bushes, among the undercut roots of standing trees, in remote crevices among loose boulders, under dense tangles of gooseberry bushes and nettles on the tops of islands, in old nests of hawks or crows, in large nest boxes, and in buildings (Bent 1923, Dawson 1923, Palmer 1976b, Bellrose 1980). Common Mergansers sometimes descend chimneys or otherwise enter unoccupied buildings. Nests in human structures include ones in between loosely piled bales of hay in an abandoned ice house, in depressions scraped in the dirt floor of an abandoned lighthouse, and underneath the supports of a covered bridge. In Sweden, people provide entrance holes to attics, and they have noted up to four nests in an attic. Some authors have reported that, in addition to a thick layer of down, the nest is also lined with weeds, grasses, rootlets, moss, or leaves (Bent 1923, Dawson 1923). However, Palmer (1976b) claimed that no vegetation is added to the nest. Perhaps the vegetation reported in some nests was material already present in the cavity before it was occupied by a Merganser. The young climb to the entrance of the cavity and tumble to the ground while the female calls from nearby. Most nest sites are situated near or over water, but females will bring broods down small tributaries to main waterways or will lead them overland as much as 200 yards; one female and her brood were found almost a mile from water (Palmer 1976b). Once on the water, part of the brood will sometimes ride on the mother's back. As the season progresses, adults and young tend to move downstream and, if available, to larger bodies of water, such as lakes and estuaries.

Marin Breeding Distribution

During the atlas period, Common Mergansers were confirmed breeding only at Kent Lake. A female with a brood was seen there on 27 June 1981, as were two females with broods in the summer of 1982 (GFMc). An estimated two pairs have bred at Kent Lake in most subsequent years through 1988 (JGE). A high count of seven adult females with 10+ chicks on 7 June 1985 (JGE) may have included the previous year's young as Mergansers are known to have "gang" broods, and probably extended families and delayed maturation (M.R. McLandress pers. comm.). Sightings of four females or immatures at Alpine Lake on

1 August 1981 (DS, ITi), one to three females on Walker Creek about one mile east of Hwy. 1 on 1 May and 12 June 1982 (DS), and one to five birds on Papermill Creek just northwest of Tocaloma on 26 March and early April 1982 (GMk) suggest the possibility of nesting at these sites. A more recent nesting confirmation came from the discovery of a two-to-three-week-old Common Merganser (one eye damaged) near Bon Tempe Lake on 23 July 1991 (JBa et al. *fide* RMS).

Historical Trends/Population Threats

Formerly, Common Mergansers were not known to breed in Marin County or elsewhere in the San Francisco Bay Area (G&W 1927, S&P 1933, G&M 1944). Because of their scarcity as breeders here, they may have been overlooked. On the other hand, the creation of large, forest-bordered reservoirs, such as Kent and Alpine lakes, may have allowed wintering birds to pioneer new breeding habitat. Numbers of Common Mergansers increased on Breeding Bird Surveys in California from 1980 to 1989 (USFWS unpubl. analyses).

RUDDY DUCK *Oxyura jamaicensis*

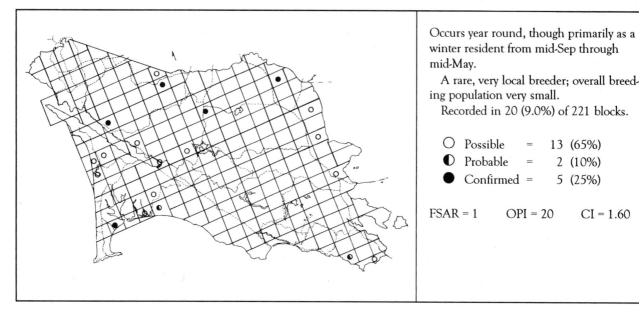

Occurs year round, though primarily as a winter resident from mid-Sep through mid-May.

A rare, very local breeder; overall breeding population very small.

Recorded in 20 (9.0%) of 221 blocks.

O	Possible	=	13 (65%)
◐	Probable	=	2 (10%)
●	Confirmed	=	5 (25%)

FSAR = 1   OPI = 20   CI = 1.60

Ecological Requirements

The rusty hues of male Ruddy Ducks in breeding plumage, with their brilliant, sky-blue bills, smartly accent Marin County's freshwater marshes and marsh-edged ponds. For breeding, Ruddies select permanent wetlands in semiarid environments that support rich concentrations of benthic invertebrates for foraging and emergent vegetation for nest construction, support, and concealment (Siegfried 1976a, Gray 1980). Nesting habitat and food do not appear to be limiting factors, and breeding males do not defend a well-defined territory or restrict themselves to discrete areas with fixed boundaries. Instead, males are highly mobile in search of food and females and defend an area that extends about ten feet around their mate, on or off the nest. Males tend to stay close to their mates before and during laying but will continue to court other females and copulate with them if the opportunity arises. During periods of nest relief, paired females are escorted by males to favorable open-water feeding areas, while unpaired females behave secretly and feed near emergent vegetation to avoid harassment by courting males (Gray 1980).

Ruddy Ducks procure their food mostly by diving and straining items from the soft muddy ooze on the bottoms of ponds as they move along (Siegfried 1973). They also skim items from the water's surface with the head and neck stretched out and moving from side to side, the bill halfway immersed, and the tongue making rapid pumping movements. Rarely, they pick at items on the surface. Ruddy Ducks forage during the day, but nonincubating birds, at least, also feed at night (Siegfried et al. 1976), and perhaps females and ducklings do as well (see Swanson & Sargent

1972). The year-round diet of Ruddy Ducks in North America is about 72% vegetable and 28% animal matter (Cottam in Palmer 1976b, n = 163). Martin et al. (1951) reported animal matter varying from a low of 21% of the diet in winter (n = 60) to 41% in summer (n = 25); but others have found almost complete dependence on animal matter during breeding (see below). The vegetable fare is mostly the seeds, tubers, and leafy parts of pondweeds and sedges, with some wild celery and algae. Animal matter consists largely of insects (mainly midge larvae; also caddisfly larvae, water boatmen, predaceous diving beetles, and nymphs of dragonflies and damselflies), along with small numbers of mollusks, crustaceans (mostly amphipods), leeches, and miscellaneous items, such as marine worms, water mites, bryozoans, fish, sponges, and hydroids.

In the breeding season in Manitoba, animal matter accounts for 90% of the diet of adult males (82% midge larvae and pupae, n = 23), 95% of adult females (63% midges, 22% mollusks; n = 19), and 88% of ducklings (73% midges, n = 18) (Siegfried 1973). At Tule Lake in California, five major invertebrates represent 94% (by volume) of the diet of breeding adults (Gray 1980). Midges comprise 79% of the diet of males (n = 22), 83% of females (n = 22), and 80% of ducklings; snails are consumed only by egg-laying females (5%, n = 7). Breeding females consume more midge larvae than males at every stage of the breeding cycle except incubation. At Tule Lake, the first peak, or "bloom," of midges in open water coincides with the period of prereproductive fattening of females. Most clutches are initiated about two weeks after numbers of midge larvae reach a peak in the nesting area. Midge densities decline in the breeding areas through the incubation and hatching periods and increase in open water. Highest prey densities are in open water immediately following peak hatching of young and coincide with the movement of females with broods out of the nesting area. Young initially seek shelter in shallow water and emergent vegetation but usually within a week move to open-water areas of high food availability. Although Ruddy Duck broods generally do not move overland to different ponds (Siegfried 1977) and brood movement over water is minimal when nests are located within favorable brood-rearing localities (Joyner 1977a), in large wetlands broods may move over three miles from nesting areas to open water (Gray 1980). Occasionally, Ruddy Ducks raise two broods. Females remain with young only until they are half grown; males accompanying females with broods are attracted to the female rather than to the young.

Ruddy Ducks preferentially nest around permanent marsh areas in the fringe of dense to moderately dense emergent vegetation of bulrushes, cattails, sedges, and rushes (Bent 1923, Low 1941, Palmer 1976b, Siegfried 1976b, Bellrose 1980). The height of nests above water or distance of nests from open water can, of course, vary because of seasonal and yearly changes in water levels. In Iowa, nest sites vary from 1 to 133 yards (av. 32 yds.) from open water free of emergent vegetation (Low 1941). Nests there also vary from about ½ to 3½ feet above the mud. Average nest heights above water in various habitats range from about 1 to 2 feet (Low 1941, Siegfried 1976b). Ruddies build nests up from the marsh bottom to above the water, use broken and matted emergent vegetation, or attach the nests, floating, to surrounding vegetation. The choice of nest sites is governed to a large extent by water depth at the time of nesting; therefore, the predominant species of plant cover used varies from year to year and during the course of the nesting season (Low 1941, Siegfried 1976b). In some studies, Ruddies were found to use predominantly green vegetation for nests (Siegfried 1976b), whereas in others they used mostly dried residual vegetation from the previous year (Low 1941, Joyner 1977b). Siegfried (1976b) suggested that Ruddies delayed breeding until there was enough new plant growth to satisfy nesting requirements, but Gray (1980) felt that food availability played an important role in determining the onset of breeding.

The female first constructs a flat platform of reeds, bulrushes, cattails, or marsh grasses on which she lays her outsized eggs (largest, relative to body size, of any waterfowl) (Bent 1923, Low 1941, Palmer 1976b, Siegfried 1976b, Bellrose 1980). When the clutch is complete, she adds a rim, forming a bowl-shaped nest, and begins incubating. She may or may not add a sparse lining of finer bits of marsh plants or down. Fresh materials are constantly being added to the nests to compensate for a gradual settling caused by the decomposition of the underparts of the nests (Low 1941). Varying numbers of nests are equipped with overhead canopies of bent vegetation for concealment and ramps or runways of matted vegetation for entering or leaving the nest (Bent 1923, Low 1941). Alternate nest sites include abandoned nests of Coots and Redheads, muskrat houses or feeding platforms, and the hollow side of a floating log (Bent 1923).

Ruddy Ducks are also noted for their habit of sometimes parasitically laying eggs in nests of other Ruddies and other marsh-nesting species (such as other ducks, grebes, American Bitterns, American Coots, and Common Moorhens) or dropping them on the ground (Bent 1923; Low 1941; Joyner 1973a,b; Palmer 1976b; Siegfried 1976b). Ruddy Ducks may respond to loss of nesting habitat and to drastically fluctuating water levels (high or low) by abandoning nest sites; building up the bases of their nests to compensate for rising water levels; increasing rates of inter- and intraspecific nest parasitism; and producing platform nests (flattened emergent vegetation) into which they deposit "unwanted" eggs (Joyner 1977b).

Marin Breeding Distribution

During the atlas years, Ruddy Ducks bred at scattered sites throughout Marin County. Numbers of breeding birds here are not as large as they might at first seem because fair numbers of birds oversummer on both salt and fresh water (Shuford et al. 1989). Representative breeding locations included the pond at Drakes's Beach visitor's center, PRNS (FL 7/10/82 –JGE); fish-breeding ponds near the Cheese Factory, Hicks Valley (FL 6/15-7/14/82 –ScC, DS); and Bahia Drive ponds near the Petaluma River mouth, Novato (FL 6/28/80 –DS).

Historical Trends/Population Threats

Grinnell and Miller (1944) reported a decline in the California population caused by loss of breeding habitat. Numbers were relatively stable on Breeding Bird Surveys in California from 1968 to 1989 (USFWS unpubl. analyses). Tule Lake was an important area of Ruddy Duck production in the 1970s, but now few broods survive (M.R. McLandress pers. comm.). This loss of production may be the result of large numbers of predators (raccoons) or perhaps the effect of pesticides from agricultural runoff.

Does innate courage or naïveté propel downy Wood Ducks, fluttering, from their lofty nest holes?
Drawing by Keith Hansen, 1989.

New World Vultures
Family *Cathartidae*

TURKEY VULTURE   *Cathartes aura*

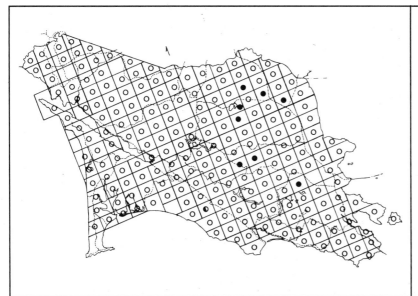

A year-round resident.

A fairly common, nearly ubiquitous breeder; overall breeding population large.

Recorded in 213 (96.4%) of 221 blocks.

○	Possible	=	204 (96%)
◑	Probable	=	1 (0.5%)
●	Confirmed	=	8 (3.5%)

FSAR = 3   OPI = 639   CI = 1.08

Ecological Requirements

The "tippy-glider," wings held in a slight V, soars gracefully over virtually all of Marin's landscape, circling and teetering gently in response to the vagaries of the air currents. Once aloft, it flaps leisurely but infrequently as it exploits the earth's envelope in its far-ranging searches for animals that have met their fate. TVs are usually seen in the air singly or in small groups except when congregating at or leaving roosts or during migration. In Marin County, they feed in virtually any habitat where they are able to reach the ground easily. Although TVs, unlike other North American vultures, forage efficiently beneath the forest canopy (Houston 1986, Jackson 1988), apparently they descend to the forest floor in Marin County only at nest sites. They feed here most often in open agricultural country that affords an abundance of grazing animals and easy sighting of dead "prey" from the air. They also feed frequently along open road corridors on animals cut down by fast-moving vehicles and along estuarine shores and beaches on carcasses of wave-cast birds and marine mammals.

Turkey Vultures are primarily solitary breeders, although nesting birds sometimes cluster near concentrated food sources (Jackson 1988). They choose secluded nest sites consisting of little more than a cleared, trampled

area within a relatively dark recess. Although nest sites are usually at ground level, some are high in tree cavities, in caves, under rocks on ledges of cliffs, in old tree nests of other raptors or herons, or in upper rooms of buildings (Tyler 1937; Jackson 1983, 1988). Prominent forest breeding habitats are bottomland hardwoods and thickets. When available, cliffs are also favored, primarily because of cave nesting sites and perhaps because updrafts make departures from the nest site easy. Ground nests may be in potholes, in crevices among rocks, under or beside logs, inside hollow logs, at the base of hollowed-out trees, and in thickets, tangles of vines, brush heaps, and clumps of chaparral with narrow entrance ways. Sometimes nest sites are below ground in caves or in hollows of rotten stumps. There appear to be no records of Turkey Vultures nesting in old tree nests of other species or in buildings in California (P.H. Bloom pers. comm.). In the West, about 77% of nests are in caves and 10% on cliff ledges or among rocks (Jackson 1983, 1988; n = 324). In the East, nest sites are more varied, with about 34% in hollow trees, stumps, or logs; 28% in thickets; 13% in caves; 8% on cliff ledges or among rocks; and 5% in buildings (n = 418). The choice probably reflects site availability rather than regional preference. In many heavily forested regions of the West, nest sites probably are more like those in the East, and Marin County is no exception (see records below). Turkey Vultures lay their eggs on the ground, on bare stone, in rotten wood chips, or sometimes in other debris. Although they usually make little or no effort to prepare the nest site, one bird using a tree cavity pulled off dry rotten wood from the walls of the cavity with its beak, tore it into bits, and spread it on the floor (Tyler 1937). TVs often use nest sites again in successive years or at intervals (Jackson 1988). Since 1920 there have been fewer nests found in the East in tree cavities and more in thickets, apparently because of changing forest management practices and the proliferation of exotic vines. For obvious reasons, nest sites in buildings must have also increased historically.

Roosting is a ritual aspect of Turkey Vulture existence. In spring and summer, some birds roost singly; others roost in aggregations year round (Jackson 1988). Roosting congregations are generally near stable food resources and often near or over water. Turkey Vultures often remain at roosts well past sunrise, perhaps for thermoregulatory reasons as well as to await favorable winds or updrafts for flight. Departure time from roosts is correlated with ambient wind speeds, but not with temperature or cloud cover. TVs can lower their body temperatures markedly at night, thus reducing energy expenditures (however, see Hatch 1970). At or near the roost, perching birds are statuesque with wings outspread, feathers raised, and backs to the sun. This behavior may facilitate a return to normal diurnal body temperature. In inclement weather, they may remain at roosts for as long as two days, foregoing meals until suitable flying conditions return.

Communal roosting appears to be an adaptation for increasing the efficiency of individuals foraging on a dispersed, unpredictable food supply (Rabenold 1983). The scavenging lifestyle is one of extended search and patience, since these weak-clawed, weak-billed raptors cannot select their victims. Birds forage widely and do not patrol a fixed breeding range (Houston 1986). Most feeding is done from midmorning to midday. Rabenold (1983) speculated that birds circle to higher altitudes later in the day to search for the next meal, to which they return the following day. The degree to which sight and smell guide Turkey Vultures in finding their meals has long been the subject of much debate. Unlike most birds, Turkey Vultures have a well-developed olfactory sense. In tropical forests, Turkey Vultures mostly use smell to locate carrion. Vision plays a minor role, for they find completely hidden food as quickly as visible bait (Houston 1986). Birds cannot detect fresh carcasses, probably because they do not yet give off a strong odor, but do prefer comparatively fresh meat if given a choice. Nevertheless, vision plays an important role (Jackson 1988) and seems to be of great aid in very open country. Turkey Vultures also watch each other and other

scavengers, such as ravens and crows, that have located food. They may sight scavengers on the ground or other vultures circling over carcasses in a distinct "verification pattern" (Rabenold 1983). Having located a seemingly dead animal, the Turkey Vulture approaches it cautiously with a gawky gait to see if it has breathed its last. Smaller, thin-skinned carcasses are torn open immediately. Vultures usually "attack" carcasses through available orifices—eyes, mouth, and anus (Rabenold 1983). For larger, thicker-skinned carcasses, the Vultures gather in numbers and wait patiently until other scavengers make the first incisions or until time and decay make the carcasses soft and ripe. If large animals are set upon immediately, they usually cannot be finished while fresh, but putrification works fast and the naked cathartid head is well adapted for avoiding disease while plunging into a body in an advanced state of decomposition.

Turkey Vultures are primarily carrion feeders, and the diet reflects what is available. The main items are mammals, birds, turtles, snakes, and fish. Occasionally Turkey Vultures eat insects, such as grasshoppers and mormon crickets; dead tadpoles in drying ponds; cow dung (perhaps deriving benefit from the beetles it contains); and seal, sea lion, or human excrement (Tyler 1937, Jackson 1988). Turkey Vultures will also occasionally take live prey, usually vulnerable young or incapacitated adults. They have killed newborn pigs, young and weakened chickens, tethered or otherwise entrapped birds, and the young of colonial waders. In addition, they sometimes batter nestling Great Blue Herons, forcing them to disgorge; wade into water to stab live fish; and peck out the eyes of cows or horses mired in bogs. When hard pressed, Turkey Vultures will eat vegetable matter, such as pumpkins and palm nuts. Paterson (1984) found plant material in about 25% of all pellets collected in Virginia in autumn. Vegetation comprised as much as 70% of one pellet, suggesting it was consumed directly, not inadvertently. TVs will also eat salt from blocks left in pastures for cattle.

Marin Breeding Distribution

During the atlas period, the Turkey Vulture was perhaps the most wide ranging of Marin's breeding birds, seen soaring over virtually every square inch of the county. But because of the difficulty of finding nests, the atlas map of this species is one of the least satisfying in terms of documenting the *details* of breeding distribution. Because of the limited numbers of stable cliffs or caves in Marin County, most Turkey Vultures seem to nest here in forested areas. Representative nesting locations were inside a burned out hollow at the base of a redwood (shielded by small branches and debris) on the ridge north of San Geronimo (NY 5/29-7/11/82 –DS); under a rock overhang among boulders in chaparral off the Yolanda Trail, Mt. Tamalpais (NE-NY 4/?-6/5/82 –ITi); inside the hollowed-out trunk of a living oak near Stafford Lake, Novato (NE 5/6/79 –KH); in a burned-out redwood stump in a canyon of Big Rock Ridge above Stafford Lake (NY 5/?/82 –ScC); and in a crack in serpentine rock under oaks on Mt. Burdell, Novato (NE 5/?/79 –ScC). Prior to the atlas period, a nest was found under a horizontal log in a logged bishop pine forest on Inverness Ridge (NE 5/7-11/73 –RH).

Historical Trends/Population Threats

Although not well quantified, some population trends are evident. Overall, Turkey Vultures seem to have been widespread and numerous in North America in the 1800s (Wilbur 1983, Jackson 1988). Subsequently, they declined in numbers with the depletion of populations of bison and other large herbivores. They later increased with the availability of road-killed animals along our expanding highway system but decreased again as forest breeding sites were cleared, organochloride pesticide contamination increased, and environmental laws required burial of animal wastes.

Grinnell and Miller (1944) reported that Turkey Vultures were "thought to be less numerous now than formerly" in California. Based on Christmas Bird Count (CBC) data from 1950 to 1973, Brown (1976) detected a decline in wintering populations of Turkey Vultures in the United States. California was the only state to show an apparent increase, but this was because of a large population on CBCs (Drake's Bay and Pt. Reyes) reported only in later years. Garrett and Dunn (1981) suggested that Turkey Vultures have declined as breeders in coastal southern California. Turkey Vultures were on the Audubon Society Blue List for 1972 and 1980, with concern in southern California (Tate 1981). They were also on their list of Special Concern in 1982 (Tate & Tate 1982), and on their list of Local Concern in 1986 (Tate 1986). Numbers of Turkey Vultures on Breeding Bird Surveys in California were relatively stable from 1968 to 1989 (USFWS unpubl. analyses).

Turkey Vulture eggshells were 11% thinner in California in the pesticide era (post-1947) than previously, but this degree of thinning is not of the magnitude generally associated with major declines of productivity in other species (Wilbur 1978). Other potential contaminants that might affect Vultures are systemic organophosphate pesticides applied topically to livestock and ingested from carcasses, and perhaps heavy metals (Pattee & Wilbur 1989). Turkey Vultures face additional threats today. Urbanization may limit food supplies and nest sites. Although road kills provide supplemental food, the Vultures themselves also fall victim to speeding vehicles. Recent changes in grazing practices and husbandry techniques have meant that fewer animal carcasses are left on the range to be eaten by Vultures (Wilbur 1983). Tree cavity sites, in which birds have high nesting success, may now be limited by forest management practices (Jackson 1983). Trees large enough to harbor suitable cavities are generally about 150 to 200 years old and are increasingly rare today. Also these trees must be injured before fungus invades to rot out cavities, and fire suppression makes this less likely. Although Turkey Vultures do not lead a charming lifestyle, these gentle creatures deserve our admiration and protection.

Although the Turkey Vulture is one of Marin County's most widespread and conspicuous birds, who among us has been honored with even a glimpse of the intimacies of its home life? Drawing by Keith Hansen, 1989.

Hawks and Eagles
Family *Accipitridae*

OSPREY *Pandion haliaetus*

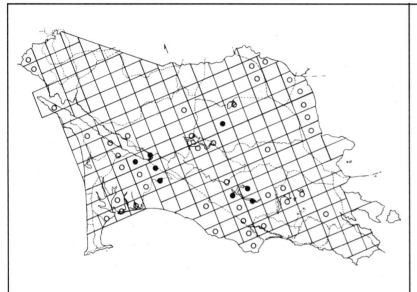

Occurs year round, though primarily as a summer resident from Feb through Sep.

An uncommon, local breeder; overall breeding population very small (numbers increasing).

Recorded in 49 (22.2%) of 221 blocks.

○	Possible	=	41 (84%)
◖	Probable	=	0 (0%)
●	Confirmed	=	8 (16%)

FSAR = 2   OPI = 98   CI = 1.33

Ecological Requirements

This cosmopolitan raptor haunts the fish-producing waters of bays, estuaries, reservoirs, and large streams or rivers. Marin County's breeding birds are concentrated within a few miles of the coast, where they forage primarily in estuaries, in the ocean near the surf, and in reservoirs. Overall, the coastal California breeding population is concentrated along rivers, streams, and bays. Marin County's Kent Lake is the only coastal reservoir currently used for nesting. In the interior of the state, 72% of the birds nest by lakes and reservoirs and 28% on rivers (Henny et al. 1978).

Ospreys nest solitarily or semicolonially. Most nests in Marin County are over, or within a half mile of, water and are situated about 40 to 120 feet up in Douglas fir, coast redwood, or bishop pine. Tree characteristics, elevation, slope, distance from water, and isolation from predators are likely the main factors influencing the choice of nest sites. From 1981 to 1990, 53 nest sites at Kent Lake were almost evenly split between Douglas fir (53%) and coast redwood (47%) and between dead (51%) and live (49%) trees; 10 of the 26 live trees had dead crowns (Evens 1991, in press). Of 25 sites in use from 1981 to 1984, 76% were in Douglas firs and 24% were in redwoods; of 28 sites

established since 1984, 32% were in Douglas firs and 68% were in redwoods. The reason for this shift in tree species use is unclear (Evens 1991, in press), but it may reflect the changing availability of suitable nest sites as prime sites become occupied. In this regard, it should be noted that the period of increasing use of redwoods as nest sites coincided with the most rapid growth of the Kent Lake Osprey population (Evens 1991, in press; Table 18). Of 18 nest sites in 1990 in the Tomales Bay area (from Five Brooks north to Mt. Vision), 10 were in bishop pines (7 dead, 3 live), 5 in Douglas firs (all dead), and 3 on artificial structures. The greater use of bishop pine reflects the dominance of this pine along almost all of Inverness Ridge adjacent to Tomales Bay, except at the south end of the bay, where it is replaced by Douglas fir.

Ospreys may prefer dead trees with a minimum of lateral branches because such trees deter climbing predators (Evens 1985). Nest sites at Kent Lake range from over water to about 0.56 miles (av. 209 yds.) from shore (Evens 1987, n = 42). One Marin nest in the early 1960s was on a rocky coastal bluff. Of the three nests constructed on artificial structures at Tomales Bay in recent years, two were on duck blinds and one was on an active power pole.

Table 18. Numbers of nests and productivity of Ospreys in Marin County, California, at Kent Lake from 1981 to 1990 and at Tomales Bay in 1989 and 1990 (Evens 1991, in press). Numbers for Kent Lake in parentheses represent adjustments (using the ratio of productive to occupied nests of 1:1.4 in subsequent years) for 1982 data to account for underestimation of occupied nests because of late season nest counts in that year.

KENT LAKE

YEAR	Occupied[1] Nests	Active[2] Nests	Productive[3] Nests	Total Young	Number of Fledglings per/		
					Occupied	Active	Productive
1981	15	11	11	23	1.53	2.09	2.09
1982	16(20)	15	14	20	1.25(1.0)	1.33	1.43
1983	20	14	13	24	1.20	1.71	1.85
1984	18	14	11	19	1.06	1.36	1.73
1985	22	20	19	37	1.68	1.85	1.95
1986	24	22	19	37	1.54	1.68	1.95
1987	31	27	23	41	1.32	1.52	1.78
1988	30	26	23	36	1.20	1.38	1.56
1989	32	28	26	48	1.50	1.71	1.85
1990	35	25	22	31	0.89	1.24	1.41
Mean					1.32(1.29)	1.59	1.76

TOMALES BAY

YEAR	Occupied[1] Nests	Active[2] Nests	Productive[3] Nests	Total Young	Number of Fledglings per/		
					Occupied	Active	Productive
1989	14	12	9	13	0.93	1.08	1.44
1990	15	11	8	11	0.73	1.00	1.38
Mean					0.83	1.04	1.41

[1] Occupied nest = a large apparently complete nest attended by one or two Ospreys during the breeding season.
[2] Active nest = an occupied nest with an incubating adult.
[3] Productive nest = an occupied nest from which at least one young fledged.

In 1989, the latter nest was carefully moved during the incubation period to a platform specifically constructed about 150 feet away, but the occupants abandoned it (J.G. Evens pers. comm.). In coastal California as a whole, Ospreys nest almost exclusively in trees, whereas in the interior of the state about 79% use trees and 21% use artificial structures (Henny et al. 1978). Tree nests are located at the top, exposed to the sky (Henny 1988). Elsewhere, Ospreys nest in a wide variety of sites in varying proportions, occasionally as much as two to three miles from water. Nest height is not as important as inaccessibility from mammalian predators and seclusion from disturbance. Nests over water are generally at lower heights than those over land, and ground nests, which tend to be on or near a prominent object, are prevalent on small islands. All nests have relatively unobstructed views of the surroundings and at least one perch nearby. Other nest sites include power towers, unused chimneys or windmills, sheds or buildings, channel markers, pilings, road signs, boats (sunk or aground), piles of fence rails, fences or walls, old stumps, cacti, tops of rock pinnacles, rocks or boulders (on land or in water), piles of seaweed, driftwood, or other debris on beaches, and even the crossed poles of a tepee and a 1000-pound bomb (Bent 1937, Henny 1988)! Ospreys readily adapt to nest sites provided for them and often have greater nesting success on nest platforms than at natural sites (Henny 1988).

Ospreys construct large, bulky nests primarily of sticks, but they also may use sod, seaweed, cornstalks, bird wings or corpses, bones, cow dung, and a wide variety of other natural and human debris. They line the nest with materials such as moss, lichen, eelgrass, grass, bark, and even mud. Nests can be very large because sticks are added throughout the breeding season, and old nests are refurbished and added to year after year. In some cases, nests have been continuously occupied for 45 years or more (Bent 1937). Pairs will sometimes have several alternative nests built within the territory over a period of years, one of which is active at a time (Henny 1988). Some birds (presumably subadults) build nests but do not lay eggs, and adults often build "frustration nests," generally not laying in them, after failing to rear young in their original nests.

The Osprey's mode of foraging combines plunging and grasping with its feet, the undersides of which are covered with pointed, prickly scales, or spicules, for retaining a grasp on slippery fish (Henny 1988). Ospreys generally cruise at a height of 50 to 100 feet and look into the water at an angle of 45° or less. When Ospreys see fish, they maneuver into position above, often hovering, waiting until the fish are close to the surface. From a long glide or brief hover, they plunge feet first, strike the water at about 20 to 45 mph, and penetrate to a maximum depth of about three feet. Just before the Osprey enters the water, the feet are swung forward beyond the head and the wings are extended upward and back so that their tips extend past the tail. After capture, powerful forward and downward strokes of the wings raise the bird to the surface and clear of the water. Ospreys sometimes fly down at an oblique angle and catch fish while skimming along the water's surface (J.G. Evens pers. comm.). In flight, Ospreys adjust the fish so that its head points forward, and they often must fend off piratical forays from gulls. Ospreys take fish up to about two pounds, and, exceptionally, they will capture two fish, one in each foot, on the same dive!

The Osprey diet is almost exclusively live fish, but occasionally dead ones are taken. A wide variety of freshwater and saltwater species are secured, but benthic-feeding fish of shallow waters are easier to capture, suggesting that they are selected over piscivorous fish when equally available (Swenson 1979). Larger fish are brought back to the nest later in the nesting cycle, not because the larger females first begin to forage for young then, but because fish have grown in size as the season progresses (DeSante & Scriven 1977). The increase in fish size is advantageous to adults then feeding the older, more demanding Osprey young. In Marin County, the few prey remains found under Osprey nests at Kent Lake were freshwater carp (W.C. Follet *fide* GFMc, Evens 1985), but in fact, Kent Lake breeders appear to feed much more extensively on saltwater species at Bolinas Lagoon and on the outer coast (Evens 1985, 1991, in press). Inverness Ridge breeders also appear to feed primarily in salt water. Ospreys also occasionally prey on small rodents or rabbits, small to medium-sized birds, snakes, frogs, turtles, and invertebrates (Bent 1937, Tait et al. 1972, Wiley & Lohrer 1973, Henny 1988). Presumably such prey are taken when fish are scarce; when foraging is hampered by inclement weather or murky water; when young Osprey lack fishing skill; or when crippled, captive, or concentrated alternative prey are too attractive to pass up.

Historical Trends/Population Threats/Marin Breeding Distribution

Osprey populations have declined seriously in historic times. In California, Grinnell and Miller (1944) reported that the species was "originally common and widespread," but by 1944 was "much reduced in number." Continentwide, but most severely in the East, a drastic population reduction began to be noticed in the 1960s (Ames & Mersereau 1964). This decline was attributed largely to eggshell thinning from the accumulation of pesticide residues, exacerbated by encroachment of humans on nesting sites and by shooting (Henny 1977, Ogden 1977). In California, the Channel Island population disappeared from 1917 to 1968, while concurrently the population on the central and southern mainland declined virtually to extinction (Diamond 1969). The southern California population disappeared long before the pesticide era, and this decline may be attributable to removal of nesting trees, degradation of lake and river quality, boating on nesting lakes, and shooting (Remsen 1978). With the banning of DDT, dieldrin, and other pesticides, Ospreys have begun a comeback, though the southern California population still remains close to extirpation (Henny et al. 1978, Garrett & Dunn 1981, Henny & Anthony 1989). Pesticide contamination and eggshell thinning were still occurring in California from 1973 to 1984, but apparently were not major mortality factors at that time (Littrell 1986). Ospreys appear to have increased in the West after the creation of reservoirs (Swenson 1981, Henny 1983), but it seems unlikely that this has completely counterbalanced the loss of spawning beds of anadromous fish from reservoir construction or the effects of pollution, disturbance, or shooting. In the San Francisco Bay Area, the loss of anadromous fish has been offset to some degree by the introduction, beginning in the 1870s, of fish from the East and Midwest that now make up the bulk of our warm-water fish populations (Skinner 1962).

Although historical sightings existed for Lake Lagunitas and Tomales Bay (Mailliard 1900, S&P 1933), there were no reports of nesting Ospreys in Marin County as of 1943 (G&M 1944). Given the limited historical coverage of the area, the former "abundance" of the species in California, and the current breeding distribution, it seems likely that Ospreys formerly bred here (though perhaps in smaller numbers) but were overlooked. From 1962 to 1963, Ospreys nested on the cliffs at Double Point on the Point Reyes peninsula (Chan 1979). In 1953, Kent Lake was constructed in the Lagunitas Creek watershed north of Mount Tamalpais. Although one of several reservoirs in that area, it was the largest and most remote. A fire that swept the slopes adjoining Kent Lake in 1945 left many large snags—prime nesting habitat—in an open Douglas fir-coast redwood forest. Many dead redwoods that now border the lakeshore apparently were drowned by the rising of the dammed waters (Evens 1985). The first Osprey nest was found at Kent Lake in 1967 (S. Cammiccia pers. comm.; Evens 1991, in press). Ospreys may not have nested there until then because of the time necessary for colonization and because copper sulfate was added to the lake in 1964 to kill carp, thus reducing or eliminating the food supply. The Kent Lake population increased rapidly to about 8 "active" nests in 1973 (C. Zumwalt pers. comm.), and an estimated 7 occupied nests in 1975 (Henny et al. 1978). Osprey studies at Kent Lake from 1981 to the present have documented a continued dramatic increase of the population to 35 occupied nests in 1990 (Evens 1991, in press; Table 18). The fact that the Kent Lake population expansion began before the ban on DDT in 1972 may be because this isolated watershed was

free of DDT residues. Currently, breeding Ospreys also concentrate in Marin County along central and northern Inverness Ridge and the fringes of the south end of Tomales Bay, where there were 15 occupied nests in 1990 (Evens 1991, in press). This population expanded greatly in the last decade. A sighting of an Osprey in the Tomales Bay area in the mid-1970s was considered a red-letter day, whereas now it is rare *not* to see an Osprey in this area on a summer day. The first known nest on Inverness Ridge was established above the town of Inverness in 1978, but pairs had been noted in the area for two or three years before that (Evens 1991, in press). Since most Ospreys nest within about 20 miles of where they were raised (Henny 1977), the Inverness Ridge population may have expanded by recruitment from the Kent Lake population.

During the atlas period, new information was added on the distribution of Ospreys breeding away from Kent Lake. Without a thorough systematic search just for Osprey nests, a minimum of 5 occupied nests were located on Inverness Ridge in 1982 (DS et al.). In 1981 and 1982, there was also a single nest on top of a duck blind over water at the southeast end of Tomales Bay (NY each year 1981–89 —JGE), another on Big Rock Ridge above Stafford Lake (NY 5/20/82 —ScC), and 16 occupied nests at Kent Lake (McCurdy 1983). Because nest surveys at Kent Lake in 1982 were not initiated until mid-June, perhaps after some nesting failures earlier in the season, there may have been up to 20 occupied nests at Kent Lake that year (Evens 1985). Using the conservative survey figures for Kent Lake and random observations from elsewhere in the county, there were a minimum of 23 occupied nests in Marin County during the last summer of atlas field work in 1982. The continued increase of the Kent Lake population (Table 18) and more thorough searches on Inverness Ridge, whose population is perhaps also still increasing, have produced a high count of 50 occupied nests in Marin in 1990 (Evens 1991, in press). The Marin County breeding population is currently the most southerly stronghold for the species in California, although a sizable population occurs in Baja California and the Gulf of California (Henny & Anderson 1979, Henny & Anthony 1989).

Numbers of Ospreys recorded on Breeding Bird Surveys in California were relatively stable from 1968 to 1989 (USFWS unpubl. analyses), but these multispecies surveys are not well suited for detecting population trends of semicolonial raptors. Surveys solely of Ospreys indicate that on the whole their numbers are increasing and the breeding range is currently expanding in northern California (Gould & Jurek 1988, Henny & Anthony 1989). Nonetheless, the Osprey is still a Bird Species of Special Concern in California (Remsen 1978, CDFG 1991b).

BLACK-SHOULDERED KITE *Elanus caeruleus*

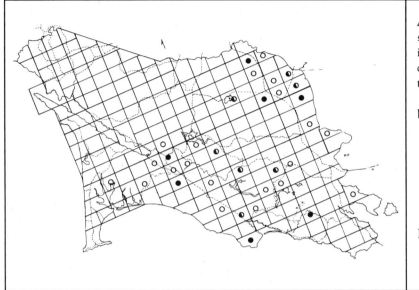

A year-round resident; numbers generally swell from Sep through Mar but vary irregularly between seasons and years, depending on fluctuating vole populations.

An uncommon, local breeder; overall breeding population very small.

Recorded in 34 (15.4%) of 221 blocks.

○ Possible = 20 (59%)
◐ Probable = 7 (21%)
● Confirmed = 7 (21%)

FSAR = 2   OPI = 68   CI = 1.62

Ecological Requirements

These elegant graceful kites inhabit Marin County's open lowland valleys and low, rolling foothills. They forage in moist meadows, grasslands, low marsh vegetation, riparian edges, irrigated pastures, and cultivated fields or orchards that provide the requisite prey base. Although the surrounding terrain may be semiarid, Kites often reside near water sources, where prey are more abundant. The particular characteristics of the nesting site do not appear to be as important as its proximity to a suitable food source (Hawbecker 1942). With open foraging country nearby, Kites often build nests in isolated trees or clumps of trees, although they sometimes place them in dense stands on steep slopes. They nest in a wide variety of trees of moderate height and sometimes in tall bushes. Native trees used in California are live and deciduous oaks, willows, cottonwoods, sycamores, maples, toyons, and Monterey cypress (Pickwell 1930; Hawbecker 1940, 1942; Dixon et al. 1957). Kites also use introduced trees, such as orchard varieties and eucalyptus. Unlike most tree-nesting hawks, Kites do not build their nests in a firm crotch next to a trunk or at a limb fork, but instead among the slender branches of the crown of the tree (Pickwell 1930). The nest is typically screened from view from below but is open above, affording easy access to the occupants and aerial predators. The nest is usually deep enough in the tree, however, to provide at least dappled shade when the young are left for long periods (Hawbecker 1940). Heights of tree nests range from 15 to 75 feet (most 20–50 ft.) above the ground (Pickwell 1930, Bent 1937, Hawbecker 1942). At

Grizzly Island in the Suisun Marsh of Solano County, Kites nest commonly in coyote brush about 6 to 8 feet high (D. Fortna pers. comm.). In this area, they nest in bushes even though there are many eucalyptus groves nearby in which Red-tailed Hawks and Great Horned Owls nest. Although sometimes frail looking, most nests are well-built platforms varying from a shallow to a deeply hollowed bowl (Pickwell 1930, Bent 1937, Hawbecker 1942). Nests tend to flatten out as the young develop (Hawbecker 1942). Kites build their nests of dry sticks and twigs and line them with materials such as grass, straw, rootlets, stubble, weed stems, lichen, moss, strips of inner bark, and perhaps a few feathers (Pickwell 1930, Bent 1937). Unlike many hawks, Kites generally build a new nest for each clutch. Occasionally, they will build on top of old nests of other birds, such as Cooper's Hawks and American Crows (Dixon et al. 1957). Rarely, they will rebuild in the exact spot in the following year after removal of a nest, refurbish the last year's nest, re-lay in the same nest if the eggs are taken, or use one of their nests from a previous year for a second brood (Barlow 1897, Hawbecker 1942).

Kites traverse their foraging grounds in buoyant, airy flight. They typically hunt while hovering at about 100 feet with legs dangling down. Birds generally face into the wind and maintain their position by slowly flapping their upstretched wings or remain aloft, "kiting," by the force of the wind alone. When prey are spotted, they raise their

133

wings even higher in a sharp V and then slowly descend, accelerating in the last few yards when actually making a strike from a diagonal or vertical fall.

Although hunting Kites may range up to about 2 miles from perches, they forage mostly within 100 yards (primarily males near nest sites) and secondarily up to 0.6 miles from perches (Warner & Rudd 1975). At all seasons, Kites forage mostly early and late in the day. From the initiation of incubation until the young approach fledging, the male provides food for both his mate and the young. (See Warner and Rudd 1975 for further details of seasonal, temporal, or sexual differences in hunting behavior, hunting success, and strike efficiency.) Rodents and birds are commonly decapitated before delivery to the nest (Palmer 1988a). The male usually transfers food to the female at or near a perch or the nest. If she declines, the male eats the prey or sometimes stores it in a shallow hollow of a limb or in a split limb of a tree (Dixon et al. 1957). The female may eat prey at a perch, but when she delivers it to the young she initially tears it into pieces to feed them (Palmer 1988a). Later in the season, she drops the prey at the nest, and the young are able to dismember it themselves.

Based on analysis of prey remains from their relatively large, owllike pellets, Kites in California eat small mammals almost exclusively (Bond 1940, 1942; Hawbecker 1940, 1942; Moore & Barr 1941; Stoner 1947; Cunningham 1955; Dixon et al. 1957; Waian & Stendell 1970; Stendell & Meyers 1973; Warner & Rudd 1975; Meserve 1977; Palmer 1988a). Prey must be diurnally active, have a minimum body weight (usually about 1 oz.), and occur in some minimal abundance (Meserve 1977). In most instances, the meadow mouse *(Microtus californicus)* overwhelmingly dominates the diet, accounting for 50%–100% (usually 70%–90%) of the prey items (references above). At times, feral house mice *(Mus musculus)* may be equally important or even the dominant prey. Instances of *Mus* accounting for 85%–90% of the diet are from prey remains of nonbreeding groups of Kites or from communal winter roosts (Meserve 1977). Because of their much smaller size (three times less by weight) than *Microtus*, *Mus* may not provide sufficient energy for Kites to nest successfully. In two California studies, numbers of *Microtus* prey were highest during summer and lowest in winter, and vice versa for *Mus* (Warner & Rudd 1975, Stendell in Meserve 1977). The harvest mouse *(Reithrodontomys megalotis)* is a distant third in dietary importance, occurring in about 5%–10% of the pellets. Other small mammal prey of minor importance are pocket gophers, pocket mice, kangaroo rats, white-footed mice, shrews, and the young of cottontail rabbits, woodrats, and ground squirrels. Rarely, small ground-dwelling birds, snakes, frogs, lizards, and large insects are taken. Kites occasionally scavenge (Warner & Rudd 1975).

Since Black-shouldered Kites exploit cyclic populations of meadow mice (Krebs 1966) and irregularly irrupting populations of house mice (Pearson 1963), they exhibit many adaptations to an abundant but temporally and spatially fluctuating food supply. Although Kites may nest in an area for many successive years, they generally are nomadic seasonally, and their breeding populations may increase locally and their nest spacing may decrease with increasing vole populations (Palmer 1988a). Most birds breed successfully in spring during the peak of vole populations, but some will double brood during periods of plentiful food (Dixon et al. 1957). In addition, clutch size increases with prey density, and the number of successful nests and the number of young raised are related to the percentage of voles in the Kites' diet (B.A. Wright in Palmer 1988a). Eggs hatch asynchronously, and the length of the nesting period varies with the food supply (Palmer 1988a). Also, as noted above, food is stored when plentiful.

Marin Breeding Distribution

During the atlas years, breeding Black-shouldered Kites were concentrated in Marin County in two general areas: (1) the valleys and low hills in the south-central coastal sector and (2) similar terrain near Novato. This distribution pattern was similar to that of the Red-shouldered Hawk and may reflect the productivity of lowland areas that remain relatively moist during the summer dry season and therefore support abundant prey in the respective habitats used by these two species. The lack of atlas breeding records in the northern part of the county near Tomales may have been because of overgrazing, which eliminates extensive potential *Microtus* habitat. The limited breeding population on Point Reyes is puzzling. Although much of this area is overgrazed, it supports extensive areas of seemingly suitable marshy grassland and coastal swale habitat. A representative Marin breeding locality was Bolinas (NB 4/14/77 –DS, CA).

Because Kites tend to be nomadic and to decrease or increase rapidly with fluctuating vole populations, future atlasers should be very cautious in interpreting any changes they detect when they repeat the Marin atlas at a later date.

Historical Trends/Population Threats

Early historical breeding records for Marin County are from near Novato in 1901 and 1902 (Ray 1904, G&W 1927) and from Kentfield in 1917 (Squires 1917). Stephens and Pringle (1933) considered Kites "rather rare" in Marin County. However, those authors and Stephens (1945) together list 15 records for the county from 1920 to 1945. This seems a rather respectable total, considering the very limited observer coverage at that time.

Much has been written about historical population decreases, a more recent dramatic upswing in the U.S. population, and a major range extension into Central America (Eisenmann 1971). Grinnell and Miller (1944) reported that Kites were common and widespread in appropriate habitat in California prior to 1885, but by 1943 they were rare in, or extirpated from, many sections, despite a slight recent trend of recovery. Several authors have since speculated that the species reached a nadir in the late 1920s and 1930s and have stated or implied, based on limited evidence, that the species was close to extinction at the time (Waian & Stendell 1970, Warner & Rudd 1975, Larson 1980, Pruett-Jones et al. 1980). However, Williams (1940) reviewed 109 published accounts and 136 records from correspondence and interviews and concluded that "no statement as to its actual increase or decrease is justified at the present; nor could we say whether the bird is holding its own." For the period 1935 to 1939 alone, Williams assembled records of 32 definite and 39 probable California breeding pairs. Considering the few observers then and the lack of systematic surveys, these data suggest that the species was not in imminent danger of extinction as a breeder in California at that time, despite its obvious serious decline earlier in the century.

Despite the problems of tracking population trends of a species tied to rapidly fluctuating food supplies, analyses of Christmas Bird Count data documented a rapid increase of the California population from the mid-1940s through the mid-1960s (Fry 1966, Waian & Stendell 1970, Eisenmann 1971, Larson 1980). Subsequent data suggest an increase continuing through the mid-1970s (Larson 1980, Pruett-Jones et al. 1980), but the population since the mid-1960s might just have been fluctuating markedly from year to year in response to prey populations. Numbers of Kites on Breeding Bird Surveys in California were relatively stable from 1968 to 1989, though data suggested a slight decrease from 1980 to 1989 (USFWS unpubl. analyses).

Early declines were apparently caused by shooting, habitat loss, and perhaps by overzealous egg collectors. The eggs were highly prized because of their scarcity, because of the variability between egg sets, and because Black-shouldered Kite eggs are among the most beautiful of those of all North American birds. Illegal egg collecting continued until at least 1940 despite laws passed in 1905 to protect the birds and their nests (Williams 1940); further protection was afforded by legislation in 1957. California's Kite population has apparently increased because of the birds' ability to tolerate habitat fragmentation caused by agricultural practices, to exploit increased *Microtus* populations thriving in fields irrigated year round (Eisenmann 1971, Warner & Rudd 1975, Pruett-Jones et al. 1980), and to reproduce at a high rate. A clutch size of four to five eggs and the ability to double brood in a single year are both unusual adaptations for a hawk (Hawbecker 1940, Eisenmann 1971). Martin (1989) noted that the amount of irrigated agricultural land in California increased by 42% from 1944 to 1978, coinciding with the period of dramatically increasing Kite numbers.

The great year-to-year fluctuations in Kite numbers appear, at least in part, to be tied to similar changes in the prey base influenced by rainfall. Pruett-Jones et al. (1980) found a significant positive correlation between Kite numbers and rainfall. This perhaps is explained by the fact that microtine rodents need standing water to reproduce (Church 1966) and that their numbers are usually reduced in a drought. The decline in Kite numbers in California during the 1975–76 to 1976–77 drought and the substantial increase in numbers in Oregon at that time, including their first breeding record (Henny & Annear 1978), further suggests a link between rainfall, vole populations, and Kite populations.

NORTHERN HARRIER *Circus cyaneus*

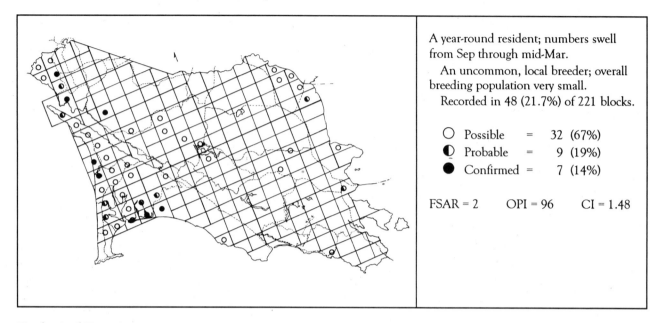

A year-round resident; numbers swell from Sep through mid-Mar.

An uncommon, local breeder; overall breeding population very small.

Recorded in 48 (21.7%) of 221 blocks.

○	Possible	=	32 (67%)
◐	Probable	=	9 (19%)
●	Confirmed	=	7 (14%)

FSAR = 2   OPI = 96   CI = 1.48

Ecological Requirements

The Northern Harrier is quick to attract attention with its conspicuously low foraging flights and the loop-the-loop antics of its roller coaster–like breeding display dives. Marin County's breeding Harriers inhabit freshwater marshes, coastal swales, wet meadows, moist grasslands, salt marshes, and hayfields. Throughout their breeding range, Northern Harriers occupy a variety of open terrain that typically has herbaceous cover, often intermixed with woody growth (Palmer 1988a). They generally occur in moist or wet areas, which are more likely to provide adequate nesting cover and a good prey base. In addition to marshland, swampland, or grain field habitats, they sometimes occupy fallow weed fields, cut woodlands, young stands of planted conifers, and sagebrush steppe far from water. In general, however, they nest in wetter, less exposed sites than their crepuscular ecological equivalent, the Short-eared Owl.

Harriers select ground nest sites in grassy areas, in cattails, in mixtures of herbaceous and woody growth, in weed patches, among low brush or close beside bushes or trees, or in grain fields or other low cultivated croplands. They also occasionally nest on muskrat houses in water or on accumulated floating vegetation; exceptionally, birds have located their nests on haystacks or, once, 20 feet up in a willow in an old Swainson's Hawk nest (Palmer 1988a). Ground nests tend to be well concealed, at least from the sides, in densely vegetated areas within a marsh or field; rarely, they are fully exposed.

The nest is generally a shallow, slightly hollowed platform situated on the ground, perhaps in a depression, or on top of flattened, low vegetation (Dawson 1923, Bent 1937, Palmer 1988a). It may be simply a hollow lined with grasses, or, particularly in damp places, it may be built up with sticks, straw, reeds, and weed stems and lined with finer vegetative parts and perhaps a little moss or feathers. The height of the nest wall varies with the height of water in tidal areas, and nests in wet areas often act as bulky, floating rafts. Harriers sometimes use nests several years in a row and add new materials annually (Palmer 1988a). Young over five days old usually leave the nest if disturbed or to seek shade in covered portions of runways. The young usually return to the nest when the female returns with food. With time, these hideouts often become crude platforms that the female sometimes uses as a distribution center for prey. At wet sites, the young are less likely to leave the nest before they can fly.

Northern Harriers may be colonial, even within tracts of apparently similar habitat (Palmer 1988a). Although rather opportunistic feeders, their distribution seems to be tied closely to the presence of small, diurnal, primarily grassland rodents (mostly microtines) and perhaps birds to some extent. In addition to their tendency toward colonial nesting, Harriers also exhibit a strong bent toward bigamy, or even harem polygamy with males sometimes mated with up to seven females. Polygamy tends to be practiced by older birds, especially in dense Harrier populations when voles are abundant.

The male typically caches and delivers all the food during incubation and early brood life. About five days after the eggs hatch, females begin short hunting flights, which they increase and extend throughout the remainder of the nesting cycle. Monogamous males generally tend to supply food for nestlings longer than polygamous males, which often cease prey deliveries to less favored nests. This can lead to instances of female attempts to intercept and snatch prey from the talons of a male going to feed another female, and to piracy attempts between females mated to the same male. More typically, the female flies up to seize food dropped by the male upon delivery. Food transfers usually occur within 100 yards of the nest, though some may occur over 0.6 miles away. The altitude or method of prey transfer may vary depending on the stage of the nesting cycle, the weather, the size of prey delivered, or pesticides accumulated by the adults. Before delivery, the male typically beheads the prey, sometimes eviscerates it, and, if it is a bird, more or less plucks it. Frogs are skinned, and the fur of voles is stripped off and discarded. On recovering the prey, the female will, if need be, prepare it and return to the nest to feed the young; she sometimes first eats a portion. The talons of Harriers are best adapted for seizing and holding prey. Consequently, much killing is done with the beak, often incidentally as the bird begins feeding on the neck and throat of prey. Harriers eat prey piecemeal and usually consume everything but the gastro-intestinal tract.

Northern Harriers exhibit marked overlap in their home ranges or hunting areas, especially away from nests (Palmer 1988a). These areas are not hunted uniformly, as birds again and again fly routes that enable them to surprise prey, sometimes hunting as little as 20%–30% of their territory. This results in particular prey species composing a significant portion of the diet for a short period, and then possibly not recurring. In one study, radio-tagged birds had a daily cruising radius of 1.25 x 1.75 miles; they used certain areas near the nest much more than others, and they departed in the same direction from which they had returned with prey.

The Northern Harrier is our only raptor that seeks small and medium-sized prey by low-level, lineal scanning (Palmer 1988a). Hearing is also an integral aid to hunting. Harriers have angular acoustic resolution within the range known for owls and at least four times as great as that of "typical" diurnal raptors (Palmer 1988a). Notably, Harriers are our only diurnal raptor with well-developed facial discs. In the field they are able to locate vole squeaks accurately and to attack prey successfully without the aid of visual or olfactory cues. Harriers typically hunt from buoyant, sustained, tilting flight, generally less than ten feet above the vegetation. They do not usually hunt while soaring or gliding. Harriers quarter to and fro over short distances over fields and marshes, making numerous sharp turns

and, occasionally, doubling back to reinvestigate likely spots. While quartering over dense vegetation, they often hover persistently, or stall midair and drop lower. In such instances, they frequently reach down with their legs and foot-stab in an effort to force prey from cover. This technique is used particularly against songbirds in bushy vegetation and against rails hiding in wracks of floating debris. Harriers will fly from one stranded debris wrack to another, hovering and sometimes landing in apparent attempts to flush prey. Flying prey are usually taken on the first attempt and are not pursued if they flee. Another common hunting technique is "border following," in which Harriers fly purposefully along ridges and vegetation discontinuities, such as fencerows, ditches, or roadsides, in efforts to surprise mobile prey.

Capable of remarkably quick maneuvering at close range, Harriers pounce directly on prey from flight, after hovering, or they "hook-pounce" in a three-quarter turn after overshooting prey (Palmer 1988a). They also make slower, deliberate pounces on microtine nests. Males tend to border-follow and nest-pounce more and hook-pounce less than females do. Generally, males tend to fly lower and faster and catch more passerines than females, which catch fewer, larger prey. The males' coloration may serve as an advantage in hunting sharp-eyed prey in open terrain.

Harriers also hunt while perched on the ground or, occasionally, from stumps or fence posts (Palmer 1988a). Rarely, they plunge, Ospreylike, to catch fish in ponds or make horizontal passes along the top of streams of flying bats. It is unclear whether large birds captured on the water are sometimes drowned deliberately or inadvertently. Harriers also opportunistically take advantage of songbird nests uncovered in newly mown hayfields. Additionally, they hunt in association with foxes, along the edges of fires, and even near targets in active bombing ranges! Harriers also pirate food from other species of raptors and vice versa. Both sexes appear to hunt throughout the day, but activity peaks among locations and years may reflect various activity periods of major prey species taken. Daily hunting activity varies with weather, prey activity, competition, and other factors. Harriers perch more in rainy weather, tend to hunt more birds when windy, and feed on carrion and rob prey more in severe winter weather.

For North America as a whole, the yearly Harrier diet by weight is about 58% mammals, 34% birds, and 8% other prey (Clark & Ward in Palmer 1988a). In another summary based on number of prey items (n = 2362), Snyder and Wiley (1976) reported the North American diet was 47.7% birds, 34.8% mammals, 15% invertebrates, and 2.5% lower vertebrates. Harriers, however, exploit whatever prey are readily available to their hunting techniques, resulting in great dietary variation among seasons and localities. For examples, Errington and Breckenridge (1936), reporting on the diet of nesting birds

137

in the Midwest, found that mammals accounted for 96% of the dietary items during a vole outbreak, but only 37% at another site during a drought year. Selleck and Glading (1943) reported that birds made up 80.6%, mammals 18%, and reptiles 1.4% of the total prey items (n = 438) at four nests in San Luis Obispo County, California. The main prey there were blackbirds, House Finches, other passerines, California Quail, and brush rabbits; there was considerable variation in the prey delivered to various nests.

Mammal prey may range from shrews to skunks and jackrabbits (especially voles and small to medium-sized rodents), but, except for their young, larger species are probably incapacitated or dead. Bird prey range from small sparrows to upland game birds, ducks, and American Bitterns, consisting mostly of small to medium-sized birds from sparrows to Mourning Doves; again, larger species taken are usually young birds or those found injured or dead. Short-eared and Screech owls are occasional prey, as are small diurnal raptors such as Sharp-shinned Hawks and American Kestrels. Other miscellaneous prey items include snakes, lizards, toads, frogs, fish, crayfish, large insects (especially grasshoppers), and spiders. Young Harriers may supplement their diet with slow, weak insects and snakes that they themselves can catch. In some instances, adults catch larger prey for older young. In fall and winter, voles and carrion are more important in the diet (especially to juveniles). Harriers take the greatest variety of prey items in spring and summer when young mammals, young and adult birds, and cold-blooded prey are more prevalent.

Marin Breeding Distribution

During the atlas period, nesting Harriers were concentrated in two sections of Marin County. The stronghold was the coastal lowlands, particularly on outer Point Reyes, where the extensive grassland and dune system are replete with coastal swale marshland. To a lesser degree, breeding Harriers concentrated in bayshore marshes and reclaimed marshland converted to grain agriculture, particularly in the vicinity of the Petaluma River near Novato. Representative breeding localities were the marshy/brushy border of salt marsh at Limantour Estero (NE 4/5/78 —AM); swale near McClure's Ranch, Point Reyes (NE 5/11/82 —DS); and swale near Brazil Ranch, SE of Dillon Beach (NY 6/3/82 —DS).

Historical Trends/Population Threats

Mailliard (1900) and Stephens and Pringle (1933) considered the "Marsh Hawk" a winter resident in Marin County, but nesting had been documented on Point Reyes as

early as 1917 (NE 6/20/17 —G&W 1927). The earlier ascriptions of winter residency probably reflected the influx of Harriers at that season and the limited exploration of the favored breeding haunts of Point Reyes and bayside marshes, rather than any subsequent change in status. In fact, much evidence points to declining, rather than increasing, populations of breeding Harriers in recent decades.

Grinnell and Miller (1944) noted that breeding Harrier populations had been greatly reduced by habitat loss in "late years." Although there is no numerical documentation, Harriers must have continued to decline sharply during the period of great human population growth and intense diking and filling of the greater San Francisco Bay marshes just before and after World War II (Atwater et al. 1979). As much as 95% of that estuary's tidal marshes have been leveed or filled since the Gold Rush, and Harrier populations must have plummeted accordingly. Using Christmas Bird Count data from 1952 to 1971, Brown (1973) documented a continentwide decline in wintering Harrier numbers from the early 1950s to the early 1960s, when populations leveled off and then increased somewhat, particularly in California. From 1968 to 1989, numbers of Harriers were relatively stable on Breeding Bird Surveys in California (USFWS unpubl. analyses). Concern over Harrier population declines has resulted in inclusion of the species on the Audubon Society's Blue List every year from 1972 to 1986 (Tate 1981, 1986; Tate & Tate 1982); as of 1986 Harriers were considered "down or greatly down nearly everywhere." Similar concerns resulted in listing the Northern Harrier as a Bird Species of Special Concern in California (Remsen 1978). Martin (1989) noted the mixed results of reports on population trends of Harriers. Though cautioning against the difficulty of interpreting population trends of the species, he felt that Harrier numbers appeared to be stable or increasing slightly in the West. In addition to habitat loss, Harriers have also been troubled by eggshell thinning from pesticide accumulations (Anderson & Hickey 1972). Although biocides were implicated in declines, at least early on, supporting evidence could be stronger. Other postulated causes of declines are grazing (Remsen 1978) and, at least formerly, shooting (Palmer 1988a). Despite encouraging signs in California, continued concern for the fate of this species is clearly warranted, as indicated by retention of the Northern Harrier on the state's recent list of Bird Species of Special Concern (CDFG 1991b).

SHARP-SHINNED HAWK *Accipiter striatus*

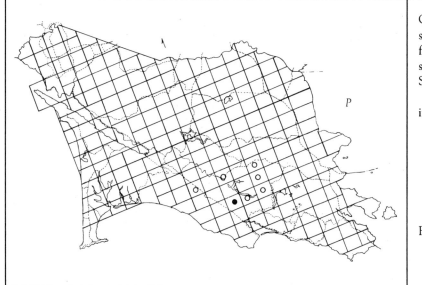

Occurs year round, though almost exclusively as a winter resident and transient from Sep through Apr; numbers swell substantially during fall migration from Sep through mid-Nov.

A rare, very local breeder; overall breeding population very small.

Recorded in 7 (3.2%) of 221 blocks.

○	Possible	=	6 (86%)
◑	Probable	=	0 (0%)
●	Confirmed	=	1 (14%)

FSAR = 1   OPI = 7   CI = 1.29

Ecological Requirements

This dashing miniature bird-hawk is such a rare breeder in Marin County that it is difficult to describe its habitat preferences here. The only breeding confirmation for the county was of a family group of adults and recently fledged young residing in a dense stand of second-growth Douglas fir and coast redwood. This forest had an understory of mostly small to medium-sized tanbark oaks, a few sapling firs and redwoods, and scattered ground cover of sword ferns. Regardless of the dominance of conifers, this habitat was noticeably denser than the stands of mixed evergreen forest where Cooper's Hawks breed here.

Grinnell and Miller (1944) knew of few actual nesting records for California and hence, apparently based on limited evidence, described breeding habitat as "either deciduous or coniferous woodland, not dense forest but at edges or where broken." Continentwide, most birds nest in stands of dense young conifers in conifer or mixed conifer-deciduous forests; where deciduous trees are the dominant cover, they usually select insular conifer stands for the actual nest site. Although some authors mention a preference for nesting sites near openings (Bent 1937, G&M 1944, Palmer 1988a), Sharp-shins nest both in broken forests, fragmented naturally or by timber harvests, and in large blocks of continuous pristine forests (Reynolds 1989). Based on extensive surveys in Oregon's conifer forests, the three species of *Accipiter* breeding there all select dense stands that provide screening from predators and a shady, mild environment (Reynolds et al. 1982, Reynolds 1983). In contrast to Cooper's Hawks and Goshawks, most Sharp-shins in Oregon use denser, younger

(25- to 60-year-old), even-aged stands for nesting (see Coopers account for comparison). These stands have shallow, single-layered, dense canopies (mean crown closure 68%–80%), an abundance of dead limbs on trunks beneath the live crowns, and ground cover of patches of ferns, mosses, grasses, and low shrubs. A few Sharp-shins nest there in dense (mean closure 90%), old-growth (200+ years) stands with multi-layered canopies and sparse ground cover; occasionally, a pair nests in a stand of stunted quaking aspen. Sharp-shins there chose nests sites on gentle to moderate slopes (av. 25%, range 8%–47%), and, unlike Coopers and Goshawks, which prefer northerly facing slopes, they do not prefer any particular slope aspect. Nest sites tend to be near springs or quiet streams, but this may have been an artifact of choosing dense forests that tend to be in moist situations.

In Oregon, Sharp-shins place their nests in the denser portion of the lower canopy on horizontal branches against the trunk or in a crotch of a double or split trunk (Reynolds et al. 1982). Nest heights there range from 10 to 80 feet above the ground, averaging 75 feet in mature sites and 39 feet in second-growth sites. Elsewhere, nests are placed in similar situations, ranging from 6 to 90 feet above the ground (Bent 1937). The nest is a shallow platform of interlaced dead conifer twigs lined with finer twigs or outer tree bark (Bent 1937, Palmer 1988a). Sharp-shins build most nests in conifers but, occasionally, select deciduous trees for nest sites. Unusual nest sites include an old Blue Jay nest 6 feet up in a sapling; in a hole in a cave; in a "hollow prong" of a broken sycamore branch; on high

139

rocks; on an old, collapsed magpie nest; and on top of a pile of tumbleweed (Bent 1937, Palmer 1988a, Reynolds 1989). Sharp-shins sometimes reoccupy nest sites the following year, usually building a new nest or, rarely, building on top of the previous year's nest (Reynolds & Wight 1978, Reynolds 1983, Palmer 1988a). In Oregon, Sharp-shins reoccupy 40% of nest sites the following year, but none thereafter; they build new nests within 100 yards of old nests (Reynolds 1983).

Breeding Sharp-shinned Hawks forage in a wide variety of coniferous, mixed, or deciduous forests and woodlands (Reynolds 1989). In Oregon, they forage primarily in the forest canopy, but in Alaska they also forage extensively in the ground-shrub and shrub-canopy zones (Reynolds 1989). Sharp-shinned Hawks are experts at reckless sneak attacks on unsuspecting prey. From concealing foliage, usually well up in the forest canopy, they dash out to seize small birds and vanish (Bent 1937, Palmer 1988a); or they drop low to the ground from perches and alternately flap and glide, concealing themselves behind vegetation or landforms, then pounce on quarry by surprise. Sharp-shins do not hesitate to dash fearlessly through dense tangles of trees and underbrush in pursuit of prey. They also pursue prey on the ground, sometimes jumping or running in open areas or through weeds and bushes. The male captures all the food for his mate and offspring until the midnestling phase, when the female resumes hunting (Palmer 1988a). Males will hunt up to nine-tenths of a mile from the nest site. Upon capturing prey, they begin tearing and plucking at the base of the skull. Favored plucking sites (stumps, logs, or horizontal limbs) in Oregon average 134 feet from nest trees (range 69–171 ft.; Reynolds et al. 1982, Reynolds 1983). Prey is often beheaded before delivery to the female or nestlings.

The Sharp-shinned Hawk diet is over 90% small birds, the remainder small mammals, reptiles, amphibians, and insects (Palmer 1988a). Snyder and Wiley (1976) reported that 93.1% of prey items (n = 1343) were birds, 4.2% invertebrates, 2% mammals, and 0.6% lower vertebrates. Sharp-shins take birds up to quail size, mostly sparrows, finches, warblers, thrushes, vireos, and swallows. They take mammals up to tree squirrels in size, mostly mice and voles, small rabbits, shrews, and bats. Cold-blooded prey include frogs, snakes, lizards, and insects, especially grasshoppers, dragonflies, crickets, beetles, large butterflies and moths, and caterpillars. During the breeding season, when males forage for the family, mean prey size for three sites in Oregon and Utah ranged from 0.4 to 1 ounce (Reynolds 1989). On average, Sharp-shins tend to take smaller prey than Cooper's Hawks, but there is controversy as to whether female Sharp-shins take larger prey than conspecific males (Balgooyen 1976, references in Palmer 1988a).

Marin Breeding Distribution

The few sightings of Sharp-shinned Hawks during the breeding seasons of the atlas period were primarily from ridges in the Kent Lake area north of Mount Tamalpais. The only confirmed breeding record was of the sighting of two fledglings accompanied by adults on the east side of Bolinas Ridge above Kent Lake on 28 and 30 July 1982 (GFMc, DS). Although Sharp-shins are definitely localized and very scarce breeders here, the true status of the species may be masked by its retiring habits and its preference for remote areas during the breeding season.

Historical Trends/Population Threats

Mailliard (1900) and Stephens and Pringle (1933) considered the Sharp-shinned Hawk a winter resident in Marin County. Grinnell and Miller (1944) reported only a few breeding records for the San Francisco Bay Area, none of which were from Marin. Although the species was scarce during the period of intensive field work during the atlas project, confirmation of breeding then suggests it was overlooked as a nesting species in Marin County in earlier times.

Grinnell and Miller (1944) did not report any population declines in California. Based on limited circumstantial evidence, Remsen (1978) felt that breeding populations had declined greatly since that time, resulting in placement of the species on the state's list of Bird Species of Special Concern, where it still remains (CDFG 1991b). Populations were apparently reduced early in the century by shooting, particularly in the East (Palmer 1988a). Sharp-shin populations declined drastically (mostly in the East) starting in the 1940s, apparently from pesticide accumulation and eggshell thinning, documented in the West (Snyder et al. 1973). The species was on the Audubon Society's Blue List every year from 1972 to 1986 (Tate 1981, 1986; Tate & Tate 1982). Based on Christmas Bird Counts, continentwide declines leveled off in the mid-1960s and swung upward by the late 1960s, largely from increases in California (Brown 1973). North American breeding populations were relatively stable from 1965 to 1979 (Robbins et al. 1986). Numbers increased in California from 1968 to 1979, but the trend was relatively stable when the analysis was extended to 1989 (USFWS unpubl. data). Currently, the most important regional threat to Sharp-shinned Hawks is the reduction of nesting and foraging habitat from logging (Reynolds 1989).

COOPER'S HAWK   *Accipiter cooperii*

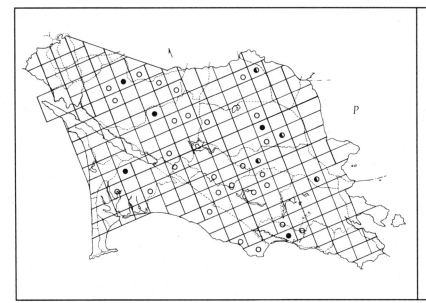

Occurs year round, though primarily as a winter resident and transient from Sep through Apr; numbers swell substantially during fall migration from Sep through mid-Nov.

A rare, local breeder; overall breeding population very small.

Recorded in 36 (16.3%) of 221 blocks.

○	Possible	=	27	(75%)
◑	Probable	=	4	(11%)
●	Confirmed	=	5	(14%)

FSAR = 1   OPI = 36   CI = 1.39

Ecological Requirements

The penetrating red eyes and the harsh, cackling alarm calls of a Cooper's Hawk defending its nest site are not quickly forgotten by the observer lucky enough to stumble upon such forest magic. In Marin County, most Cooper's Hawks breed in secluded stands of closed-canopied mixed evergreen hardwoods, usually dominated by coast live oak, California bay laurel, and madrone (see records below); rarely, they breed here in alder-dominated riparian forest or woodland. Although Grinnell and Miller (1944) emphasized the importance of riparian-deciduous habitat, Cooper's Hawks in California breed primarily in live oak woodlands (mixed evergreen forests), though they also inhabit coniferous forest to a limited degree (Asay 1987). Most California nests are in closed-canopied stands of six or more trees (rarely in isolated trees) with a subcanopy of vertical tree trunks and large branches with few small branches or leaves; ground cover is absent or consists of short grass and/or poison oak or a few other shrubs (Asay 1987, n = 52). Dense canopy cover (about 65%-95% closure) is a consistent vegetative characteristic of Cooper's Hawk nest sites throughout their range; also, understories at nest sites are often relatively open (Palmer 1988a). Marin County nest sites resemble the structure of those elsewhere in California, though the dominant trees and saplings, shrubs, and ferns in the sparse understory/ground cover differ (see records below). Most California nest trees (79%) are in flat areas, usually bottomlands between hills, and the rest (21%) are on steep hillsides (Asay 1987). The flat areas appear most favorable for growth of tall live oak trees.

Cooper's Hawks also breed in coniferous (typically second-growth) or mixed forests (Reynolds 1989). In Oregon's conifer forests, most pairs of three species of *Accipiter* nest in dense stands on gentle to moderate slopes with northerly exposures that provide screening and protection from predators and a shady, mild environment (Reynolds et al. 1982, Reynolds 1983). Most nest sites there are also near quiet, ephemeral streams or springs. Cooper's Hawks probably select for dense forest growth rather than for particular factors (such as water) that promote it. These coexisting species use habitats with different structures at the nest site associated with the age of the forest stand used. Sharp-shinned Hawks use 25- to 60-year-old even-aged stands; Cooper's Hawks use 30- to 80-year-old even-aged stands with somewhat larger and more widely spaced trees and deeper crowns; and Goshawks use 150+-year-old mature stands ranging from closed canopies with few shade-tolerant understory trees to stands with more open canopies with many understory trees. Cooper's Hawk nest sites in Oregon have an average canopy closure of 69% (range 15%-100%, n = 9), many dead limbs below the live crowns, and sparse to moderate ground cover. The slope gradient at nest trees there averages 17% (range 0%-80%). In Oregon, yearling females nest in younger successional stages than older females do, or in stands that have undergone selective overstory removal (Moore & Henny in Palmer 1988a).

In California's evergreen hardwood forests/woodlands, Cooper's Hawks select nest trees that are generally some of the most mature trees in the stand, in an area with the highest canopy cover and the sparsest ground cover (Asay 1987). Of California nests, 75 of 77 were in live oaks *(Quercus agrifolia* and *Q. wislizenii).* Cooper's Hawks here build nests in or just below the canopy and, depending on the growth form of the tree, either in a fork of the main trunk or out on a branch away from the trunk. Cooper's Hawks place their nests from three-quarters to four-fifths of the way up the tree; the average nest height of 48 California nests is 33 feet (range 19-46 ft.). Estimated heights of 5 Marin County nests ranged from about 25 to 50 feet above the ground (records below). In Oregon's conifer forests, Cooper's Hawks place their nests either immediately below the crown or in the lower crown of the nest tree; nest height of 33 nests there averaged 48 feet (range 25-100 ft.) above the ground (Reynolds et al. 1982). Most Cooper's Hawk nests there are placed on horizontal limbs against trunks; and a few are placed out on limbs or in crotches of double trunks. In eastern Oregon, many of these hawks nest in deformed trees infected with dwarf mistletoe and having heavy foliage, "witches brooms," or double trunks. Yearling females in Oregon use mistletoe as a nest structure significantly less often (50%) than older females (70%) do (Moore & Henny in Palmer 1988a). Throughout North America, average nest heights range from 26 to 50 feet above the ground (Palmer 1988a); nests may be as low as 10 feet or perhaps, exceptionally, on the ground (Bent 1937). Some nests are built on squirrel, crow, or woodrat nests, or on rubble in the fork of a tree; others may be incorporated in masses of mistletoe, grapevines, or the abnormal, densely branched growth of a limb (Bent 1937, Palmer 1988a).

The nest is a broad, shallow platform of clean, dry sticks and twigs, lined with flakes of bark added throughout egg laying and incubation. Greenery, usually one or two conifer sprays, is added to the nest intermittently. In evergreen hardwood habitat in California, the rate of nest site reoccupancy was 80% (Asay 1987, n = 41). Birds reused the previous year's nest in 32% (11 of 34) of the nesting areas occupied in consecutive years; half of all nesting attempts were in rebuilt nests. In conifer habitat in Oregon, Cooper's Hawks reoccupied 27% of nest sites in the second year and 11% in the third year (Reynolds 1983). If they reused a nest site, they usually built a new nest; a few birds irregularly used alternate nest sites. In another Oregon study, 10 of 17 (59%) nest sites were reused in the following year, and only successfully nesting females over two years old returned to the same site (Moore & Henny in Palmer 1988a).

Cooper's Hawks forage in a variety of cover types—from openings to dense forests—though one study in Utah showed a preference for foraging in dense stands of small to medium-sized trees (Reynolds 1983, 1989). A suggestion that these hawks forage mostly in edge situations may be an artifact of the ease with which they are seen in open

settings. On the other hand, prey is usually more abundant in edge situations than deep in dense forests. In Oregon, at least, the Cooper's Hawk is more of a generalist than the Sharp-shinned Hawk and captures prey in the ground-shrub, shrub-canopy, and canopy zones (Reynolds 1989).

Cooper's Hawks are efficient predators, capable of very rapid flight over short distances. Their rounded wings and long tails give them great maneuverability, which enables them to fly dexterously through dense brush (Brown & Amadon 1968, Palmer 1988a). They rely on concealment and surprise to capture quick and agile prey. Cooper's Hawks often hunt from a perch and fly down with a sudden burst of speed to seize unsuspecting prey (Brown & Amadon 1968, Palmer 1988a). Leaving the perch, they often fly low, taking advantage of the contours of the land or vegetation for cover, and may fly higher after flying quarry. In a typical strike, they stop flapping 12 to 15 feet from the prey and begin swinging the feet forward at about 5 feet (Palmer 1988a). Just before impact, they set their wings in a braking movement, thrust the pelvis forward, and rapidly extend the feet chest-high, seizing the prey with both or, occasionally, only one foot. Cooper's Hawks pursue and catch many birds that fly by the trees in which they are perched. On occasion, they also fly through swarms of bats leaving a cave, singling out one and following its every twist and turn. Coopers sometimes hunt from higher flight, stooping falconlike at pigeons in the open. They also pursue prey into bushes, stalk or pursue it on the ground (by walking, hopping, or half running and half flying), and even attempt to flush it from cover. Cooper's Hawks use their hearing to stalk quail. They are known to down prey in water and hold it underwater until it ceases to move.

Males feed their mates occasionally before egg laying and are their sole providers during incubation (Palmer 1988a); females rarely hunt during the first three weeks of the nestling period but do hunt increasingly thereafter (Kennedy & Johnson 1986). The amount of time and the time of day the male spends hunting may depend on the activity patterns of the prey, and especially the demands of the young, which increase to the point requiring hunting throughout the day. Males forage out to one and one-half to two miles or more from the nest (Reynolds 1983, Palmer 1988a). The male usually eats the head and viscera and does much of the plucking at the kill site (Palmer 1988a). He brings the prey to stumps, logs, or large horizontal limbs used as plucking sites, where he continues to pluck and partially dismember the prey. In Oregon, the most frequently used plucking site averaged 177 feet from the nest tree (range 138-282 ft.; Reynolds et al. 1982). When the young are small, the prey is well plucked, headless, and eviscerated, but by the fourth or fifth week, the male brings prey only three-quarters plucked and whole (Palmer 1988a). The female flies out to receive the prey at the plucking site and feeds herself there or at the nest. The female initially flies out to the plucking site to retrieve food for the young, but later, if she is absent, the male delivers prey to the nest. If the male brings more food than is needed it is stored for future use on an old nest nearby (Brown & Amadon 1968). Dead chicks may be eaten, but probably larger young do not attack smaller siblings unless they are very hungry from a shortage of prey (Palmer 1988a).

The Cooper's Hawk diet is about 70.4% birds (mostly medium-sized, such as jays, thrushes, and flickers), 17.9% small mammals, 8.9% reptiles (mostly) and amphibians, and 2.1% insects (Jones in Palmer 1988a). In the East, birds account for over 80% of the diet, but in the West, birds comprise only about 47%–74% of the diet. Cooper's Hawks capture larger birds than Sharp-shinned Hawks do, although mean weight of birds in the Cooper's Hawk diet is highly variable among studies—from 1.5 ounces in the eastern U.S. to 4.3 ounces in eastern Oregon (Reynolds & Meslow 1984, Reynolds 1989). Cooper's Hawks take birds as large as pheasants, grouse, small owls, American Kestrels, Merlins, and crows, and as small as nestling goldfinches. Important mammal prey are chipmunks, young hares, cottontails, tree and ground squirrels, woodrats (in Calif.; P.H. Bloom pers. comm.), voles, deer mice, and shrews. Mean weight of mammal prey at three sites in Oregon and Utah ranged from 5.2 to 10.4 ounces (Reynolds 1989). Some Coopers will specialize in certain types of prey. For example, in the southern Sierra foothills, a breeding pair brought to the nest 63.4% lizards, 29.3% birds, and 7.4% mammals (Fitch et al. 1946, n = 41). There is controversy as to whether females do (e.g., Storer 1966) or do not (e.g., Kennedy & Johnson 1986) take larger prey than males do.

Marin Breeding Distribution

During the atlas period, Cooper's Hawks were scattered widely throughout the forested regions of Marin County in the breeding season. The status as indicated by the atlas map is probably deceptive, though, considering that Cooper's Hawks are very retiring while breeding and prefer areas away from human presence. Observers equipped with a knowledge of the species' habits and a willingness to get off the trail in hilly terrain would likely be able to discover many more breeding sites. For example, one atlas observer stumbled upon four nests in one breeding season—at three of them the hawks were seen only at the immediate nest site. Contrary to popular belief, the Cooper's Hawk may be a more numerous breeder in Marin and other coastal counties than the Red-shouldered Hawk. The latter species is much more easily detectable than the Cooper's Hawk because it resides primarily in lowland areas, where observers are concentrated, and because it is very vocal and visible when displaying or hunting.

Representative breeding records are listed with fairly detailed nest site descriptions because of the paucity of such information for California beyond those found in Asay (1987): (1) Bolinas Ridge near Bolinas Lagoon, 6/2/81 (ARo et al.), NE about 25 ft. up in coast live oak in mixed forest of coast live oak, bay laurel, and coast redwood with a brushy understory on the edge of a redwood-dominated canyon slope; (2) N end of Inverness Ridge, 4/29/82 (DS), NE about 50 ft. up in bishop pine in a mixed coast live oak, bishop pine, and bay laurel forest with a moderate understory of huckleberry, poison oak, and hazelnut; (3) on north-facing slope off Marshall-Petaluma Rd., 6/21/82 (DS), NY about 45 ft. up in a bay laurel in a forest almost exclusively of that species with sparse ground cover mostly of sword ferns; (4) Chileno Valley, 7/2/82 (DS), NY about 45 ft. up in a California buckeye, in a buckeye, bay laurel, and coast live oak forest with sparse understory/ground cover; and (5) canyon off Big Rock Ridge, 7/4/82 (DS), NY about 45 ft. up in a bay laurel in a mixed forest of about equal proportions of bay laurel, coast live oak, and madrone with a sparse understory of sword ferns and hazelnut.

Historical Trends/Population Threats

For Marin County, Mailliard (1900) reported the Cooper's Hawk was a "common winter resident"; Grinnell and Wythe (1927) listed Inverness as a station of summer residence; and Stephens and Pringle (1933) considered the Cooper's Hawk a permanent resident, "fairly common, more numerous in winter." Prior to the atlas work, summer reports were few for the county, and the only breeding record was of a nest in an alder grove at Muddy Hollow, near Limantour Estero in the early 1970s (JH *fide* GWP). Prior data are not sufficient to compare with the status in Marin today. Since Grinnell and Miller's (1944) monograph on California's avifauna, the population of Cooper's Hawks breeding in the state has declined to an unknown degree, resulting in its listing as a Bird Species of Special Concern (Remsen 1978, CDFG 1991b).

Based on migration counts, Christmas Bird Counts, and incidental reports, Cooper's Hawk populations declined continentwide, but mostly in the East, from the 1920s to 1960s (Palmer 1988a). The Cooper's Hawk was on the Audubon Society's Blue List from 1972 to 1981 and in 1986, and on their list of Species of Special Concern in 1982 (Tate 1981, 1986; Tate & Tate 1982). From 1965 to 1979, North American breeding populations were low but relatively stable (Robbins et al. 1986); the California Foothills had one of the highest densities.

143

The California population was relatively stable from 1968 to 1989, though data suggested a slight decrease from 1980 to 1989 (USFWS unpubl. analyses).

Early declines may have been from extensive shooting, but declines since the late 1940s appear to be caused by DDT accumulation (Henny & Wight 1972, Snyder et al. 1973). Populations in the East declined much more than in the West. Eastern Cooper's Hawks carried higher concentrations of DDE than those in the West did, apparently because of the greater reliance of the eastern birds on avian prey (see above). California birds have been somewhat contaminated with pesticides; the decline of the California breeding population probably was caused mostly by habitat destruction (Remsen 1978). Today, nesting and foraging habitat loss from logging remains the main threat to breeding populations in the U.S., though indirect human disturbance at nest sites and the taking of nestlings by falconers pose additional threats (Remsen 1978). Pesticide accumulation, loss of wintering habitat, and shooting still pose threats in Mexico (Reynolds 1989).

RED-SHOULDERED HAWK *Buteo lineatus*

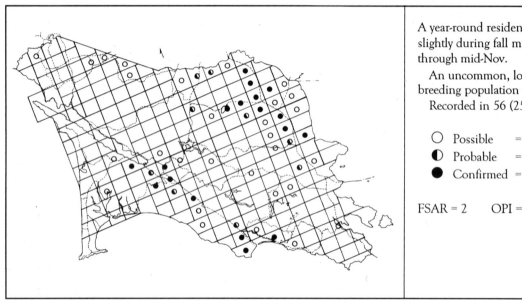

A year-round resident; numbers swell slightly during fall migration from Sep through mid-Nov.

An uncommon, local breeder; overall breeding population very small.

Recorded in 56 (25.3%) of 221 blocks.

○ Possible   = 29 (52%)
◑ Probable   =   9 (16%)
● Confirmed = 18 (32%)

FSAR = 2   OPI = 112   CI = 1.80

Ecological Requirements

This resplendent woodland hawk inhabits Marin County's well-timbered lowland drainages and, secondarily, adjacent upland slopes. Prime areas include stretches of dense riparian forest or woodland, oak-dominated mixed evergreen forest, oak woodland, or eucalyptus groves, adjacent to or interspersed with openings clothed with soft and luxuriant but relatively low vegetation of moist grasslands, meadows, swales, or marshland. Forests or woodlands provide nest sites, shelter, and some foraging opportunities. Although nesting habitat is usually near open water, this is not essential as long as moist upland openings are available for foraging. The haunts of Red-shouldered Hawks here contrast with the drier, more open upland habitats frequented by Red-tailed Hawks (see account).

Red-shouldered Hawks place their nests in large trees in stands of mature timber, often near openings; there may or may not be a well-developed understory at the nest site (D. Shuford pers. obs.). Red-shoulders generally situate nests more than halfway up the tree, below the canopy crown; Red-tails generally build much higher (Palmer 1988a). The average height of 274 widespread nest records is 47 feet, with a range of 8 to 110 feet (Apfelbaum & Seebach in Palmer 1988a); exceptional nests have been found on the ground (Palmer 1988a). Nests are generally placed in a main fork where the trunk divides into three or more branches (Bent 1937). They are seldom built on a horizontal branch against the trunk and very rarely in the fork of a branch. The nest is a substantial, well-built structure filling the crotch to a considerable depth. Red-shoulder nests are smaller than Red-tail nests and contain more soft material than those of accipiters. Red-shoulders sometimes use nests built by Cooper's Hawks or nests previously occupied by owls; they also will build over old squirrel nests. Red-shoulders build the nest from sticks or twigs mixed with strips of bark, dry leaves, lichens, mosses, and twigs of evergreens with needles attached. They line it with fine shreds of bark, soft mosses or lichens, fresh conifer sprays, and, as incubation progresses, downy feathers. Decorative greenery or other "symbolic" materials added to the nest (months before egg laying through the nestling stage) may function to indicate active attachment to a site (Palmer 1988a). Later, eggs and young would seem adequate notice of occupation. An apparent increase in the addition of greenery through the nestling phase (Portnoy & Dodge 1979) may support Bent's (1937) contention that this material may be for sanitary rather than ornamental purposes. Greenery or its substitutes may include conifer sprays, green leaves, whole plants, blades of cornstalks, dried tent caterpillar webs, ears of corn or corncobs, tissue paper, and nests of various passerines (Bent 1937, Palmer 1988a). Red-shoulders tend to build new nests each year, but occasionally they use them for two or three successive years or, more often, return to the old, alternative nest after a lapse of two or more years (Bent 1937).

The Red-shouldered Hawk sometimes hunts by gliding just over the tops of the forest, through the woods, or flying low over marshes or meadows (Bent 1937). It can slip upon prey at close range in trees or pounce on smaller, slower prey on the ground (Bent 1937), relying on surprise more than speed (Palmer 1988a). Red-shoulders are most frequently observed waiting patiently on relatively low perches on trees, utility poles, wires, or fence posts, from which they drop or swoop down on prey. In California, in more than 6000 hours of observation including over 250 prey capture attempts, Red-shoulders always initiated attacks from a perched position (P.H. Bloom pers. comm.). This hawk's hearing is extremely keen, and it may rely on hearing as much as sight for hunting (Dixon in Bent 1937 and Palmer 1988a).

As the moist habitats frequented and the hunting techniques used suggest, the Red-shouldered Hawk concentrates on cold-blooded vertebrates and, in some places, seasonally, on small mammals (Palmer 1988a). Snyder and Wiley (1976) reported that prey items (n = 1413) consisted of 55.6% invertebrates, 21.2% lower vertebrates, 20.2% mammals, and 2.8% birds. In southern California, small rodents are the principal prey (P.H. Bloom pers. comm.). Dietary items include snakes, toads, frogs, or other amphibians up to bullfrog size; mammals mostly from shrew (more than voles) to chipmunk size; small lizards and young turtles; a few small to medium-sized birds; a few small fish; a few crayfish; considerable numbers of insects, usually cricket and large-grasshopper size; and the odd centipede, earthworm, or snail. Red-shoulders are able to transport, sometimes drag, or eat in place, surprisingly heavy prey, such as small herons, full-grown squirrels, ducks, opossums, and muskrats. They also occasionally eat carrion.

Marin Breeding Distribution

During the atlas period, Marin County's breeding Red-shouldered Hawks were concentrated in two general areas: in the San Andreas fault zone, primarily of the Olema Valley; and, more extensively, in the lowlands around Novato. The paucity of Red-shoulders in the lowlands of the northwestern sector of the county may have reflected the lack of appropriate moist grassland and meadow edges to riparian areas there caused by heavy grazing. Representative nesting sites were in a Douglas fir in Inverness (NY May–early Jun 1982 –A&JWe); in Olema Marsh (NB 2/25/81 –DS); in an alder grove at Stinson Gulch (NE 4/26/82 –DS); in a eucalyptus along Novato Creek in O'Hare Park, Novato (NE 4/26/82 –ScC, DS); and in a valley oak along San Jose Creek, E of Hwy. 101, Novato (NB-NY 2/19-6/7/78 –MGN).

Historical Trends/Population Threats

Mailliard (1900) considered the "Red-bellied Hawk" an "occasional winter visitant" in Marin County, and Stephens & Pringle (1933) considered it a "rather rare" resident here. Compared with the current status, this would suggest an increase in numbers historically, whereas instead numbers have probably decreased. In earlier times, the status of this species was apparently underestimated because of the limited ornithological attention focused on the Point Reyes area or on the northern sectors of the county, including Novato, areas where the Red-shouldered Hawk is most numerous today. Although information is lacking, Red-shoulders have likely been displaced in recent times from former breeding areas in the moist lowlands of the now heavily developed Highway 101 corridor in eastern Marin.

Grinnell and Miller (1944) reported that the species was greatly reduced throughout California and even extirpated locally "due to progressive human occupancy of the land." In reviewing the recent status in California, Wilbur (1973a) concluded that despite local displacement, extirpation had not occurred in any major segment of the original range. A major population decline in the Central Valley (Wilbur 1973a, Gaines 1974) has reversed itself recently (S.A. Laymon pers. comm.). Suggestions of increases in some coastal counties (Wilbur 1973a) may reflect rebounds from former declines or, alternatively, an artifact of increased observer effort. In southern California, these hawks are reoccupying parts of the Los Angeles basin where mature trees now provide nesting habitat in certain residential areas, parks, and cemeteries; they have also expanded into date palm plantations in the Mohave Desert

(Harlow & Bloom 1989). On the whole, Red-shouldered Hawk numbers increased in California from 1968 to 1989 but were relatively stable from 1980 to 1989 (USFWS unpubl. analyses). Caution is still warranted, though, as the ongoing expansion of the human population in low-land corridors puts additional pressure on this species (despite its ability to adapt to some residential situations.

From the late 1950s to the early 1970s, eggshell thickness of Red-shouldered Hawk populations in southern California was reduced by 3%–14% from the accumula-tion of pesticide residues (Anderson & Hickey 1972, Wiley 1975). Reproductive success in southern California between 1972 and 1987 appeared to be normal, and the eggshell thinning is currently being investigated (Harlow & Bloom 1989). The loss of riparian and oak woodland nesting habitat is the most serious factor currently affecting the species in California.

RED-TAILED HAWK *Buteo jamaicensis*

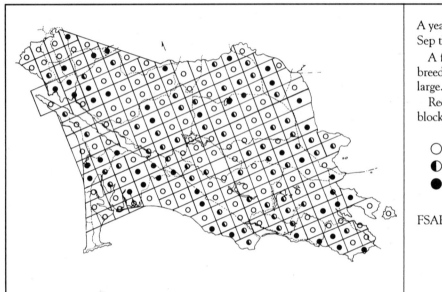

A year-round resident; numbers swell Sep through Feb.

A fairly common, nearly ubiquitous breeder; overall breeding population large.

Recorded in 213 (96.4%) of 221 blocks.

O	Possible	=	111 (52%)
◑	Probable	=	56 (26%)
●	Confirmed	=	46 (22%)

FSAR = 3   OPI = 639   CI = 1.70

Ecological Requirements

The Red-tailed Hawk is a bird of myth, song, and legend, but even more a part of everyday reality as it soars gracefully overhead on outstretched wings. Even our jays, for unknown reasons, pay homage to the Red-tail by their imperfect screeching vocal imitations. In Marin County and elsewhere, Red-tails are primarily birds of forest or woodland edges. Here they hunt mostly in open, relatively dry upland grasslands that host suitable foraging perches, which may be exposed limbs of isolated trees, trees in clumps, woodlots, edges of woodland or forest, utility poles, or large rock outcrops. Foraging perches are usually scattered throughout the territory, though certain ones are favored (Palmer 1988b). Nest site requirements are iso-lation from disturbance, a commanding view, and un-obstructed access. Red-tails typically nest high in the open crown of a tree taller than those surrounding it and generally within view of several perch sites. Chosen trees

are often well up a slope or on a ridge or hilltop, in a clump or grove of trees, in a woodlot, or, occasionally, in an extensive forest. Tree nests are usually situated at the junction of large limbs with the trunk or in crotches formed by two or more large limbs (Bent 1937). Red-tails also nest on the crossbeams of utility poles. Although preferring lofty views, Red-tails select varying nest sites, and in the West, nest heights range from a few feet (in desert habitats) to 120 feet (Bent 1937). The average height of 22 nests in sycamores in San Diego County was 55 feet, ranging from 43 to 75 feet (Dixon in Bent 1937); this is probably fairly typical of most of the wooded sections of California. Red-tails use a wide variety of trees for nesting. In Marin County, they appear to prefer eucalyptus, particu-larly in open ranchlands, and coast live oaks. Red-tails also use cliff ledges for nest sites, particularly in arid areas where trees are scarce. Red-tails sometimes nest in unused aeries of Golden Eagles; in nests of ravens, crows, and other species of buteos; and in nests previously used by owls; or they will build on the platforms of old squirrel nests (Bent 1937, Palmer 1988b). They may build a nest each year for at least several years, reuse a nest during successive years, or leave a nest vacant for a year or more and then reuse it (Palmer 1988b). The nest is a large, bulky affair made of sticks and twigs, lined with items such as strips of bark, small twigs, and lichens. For a period of weeks, before laying to late incubation, Red-tails add greenery or "decoration" to the nest in the form of conifer sprays, deciduous twigs and leaves, corncobs, cornhusks, cornstalks, willow and aspen catkins, a variety of other plant material, various rubbish, and even oriole nests! It is not always clear what is "decoration" and what is nest lining. The addition of decorative material appears to be a behavioral derivation of prey capture and delivery that serves to indicate active attachment to a site (Palmer 1988b).

As might be expected for a numerous and widespread species, Red-tails are versatile, opportunistic hunters (Palmer 1988b). Most frequently they hunt from an erect or forward-leaning stance, high on a perch, waiting for prey to reveal itself. For close prey, Red-tails glide downward at an angle with few wingbeats; for more distant prey they approach with a few rapid wingbeats alternating with glides. Watching for movements of the intended prey, on the final gliding approach at about a ten-foot distance, they extend the legs forward and spread the toes. The strike is usually made with one foot farther forward. A number of aerial foraging tactics are also used. Generally at an altitude under 200 feet, Red-tails will flap and glide, quartering over terrain to catch prey in the open; they may dodge among trees, brush, or rock outcrops, remaining concealed until coming upon their prey at close range. Occasionally, they also maneuver through thick stands of trees, accipiterlike, usually striking prey on or near the ground. Red-tails also swoop down from hovering flight or from an immobile position while facing into the wind on set wings (Dunne et al. 1988). When streams of bats are departing from caves, Red-tails sometimes stoop downward on them with half-closed wings or fly parallel and veer sharply toward them (Palmer 1988b). Red-tails may actually run on the ground when attacking (especially when the prey is large), and bound from one to another in pursuit of grasshoppers, crickets, or other small, relatively slow prey Two Red-tails, presumably paired, sometimes hunt cooperatively with one on each side of a tree attempting to catch tree squirrels. Red-tails will also pirate from other hawks, such as Northern Harriers, and will eat fresh carrion. Upon capture, they carry small prey to a feeding perch, which is lower than a hunting perch. Voles are swallowed whole; larger mammals may be beheaded and the fur partially discarded; small birds are beheaded and plucked. Heavy prey, which may struggle and crawl into cover, may

be dragged a short distance to a suitable spot, where it is plucked and fed on; the remains may be carried to an elevated perch.

The bulk of the Red-tail diet, up to 80% in some studies, is mammals (Palmer 1988b). Birds make up much of the remainder, but the menu also includes snakes, lizards, frogs and toads, salamanders, fish (mostly dead), turtles, crayfish, various insects, centipedes, spiders, and some carrion. Snyder and Wiley (1976) reported that prey items (n = 2224) in the North American diet consisted of 50.5% mammals, 36.8% invertebrates, 8.5% birds, and 4.2% lower vertebrates. The diet of Red-tails in the Sierra Nevada foothills (excluding arthropods probably taken accidentally, n = 507) is 73.7% mammals (mostly small to medium-sized ones, such as ground squirrels, pocket gophers, and rabbits), 21.6% snakes and lizards, and 4.7% birds (Fitch et al. 1946, n = 4154). Some Red-tails there specialize on larger prey than other individuals do.

Marin Breeding Distribution

During the atlas period, the Red-tailed Hawk was the most widespread of all of Marin County's breeding diurnal raptors and one of our most widespread breeding birds overall. Red-tails appeared to be most numerous as breeders in the central and northern sections of the county, where lowland valleys and rolling hills are dominated by grassland interspersed with broken woodland and forest or extensive tree plantings. Representative breeding localities were the eucalyptus grove along Hwy. 1 about 1 mi. S of Sonoma County border (NB 2/11/78 –SJ, DS); the eucalyptus grove at Brazil Ranch, SE of Dillon Beach (NE 4/28/82 –DS); and the eucalyptus grove near SE corner of Abbott's Lagoon (NE 5/11/82 –DS).

Historical Trends/Population Threats

The planting of cypresses and especially eucalyptus (used as hunting perches and nest sites by hawks) in the once nearly treeless northwestern part of Marin County apparently has enabled breeding Red-tails to expand locally in historical times. This expansion has probably been offset by displacement in parts of the heavily developed areas of Marin, particularly along the Highway 101 corridor, as has been noted elsewhere in California (G&M 1944). Red-tailed Hawk numbers appeared to increase slightly on Breeding Bird Surveys in California from 1968 to 1989 but were relatively stable from 1980 to 1989 (USFWS unpubl. analyses). Personnel of wildlife agencies responding to questionnaires felt that Red-tailed Hawks were declining in California. The authors summarizing that survey data indicated that most of the state's populations were stable, though local populations, such as on the southern coast, were declining rapidly, primarily from housing developments and fire (Harlow & Bloom 1989).

147

GOLDEN EAGLE *Aquila chrysaetos*

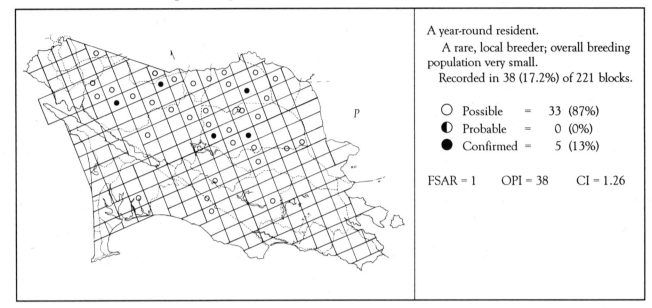

A year-round resident.
A rare, local breeder; overall breeding population very small.
Recorded in 38 (17.2%) of 221 blocks.

○ Possible = 33 (87%)
◑ Probable = 0 (0%)
● Confirmed = 5 (13%)

FSAR = 1   OPI = 38   CI = 1.26

Ecological Requirements

When watching soaring Golden Eagles at close range it is easy to fathom why they inspire folklore, creation myths, and, most of all, respect. These aerial masters range from the arctic tundra to desert regions. Breeding requisites include solitude, extensive open-ground foraging areas, and suitable nest sites nearby (Palmer 1988b). In Marin County, breeding Golden Eagles inhabit expansive interior grasslands and oak savannah interspersed with a mosaic of forests or woodlands in adjoining canyons or on nearby slopes.

Depending on availability, Golden Eagles build their nests in large trees, on niches or shelves of cliffs or steep earthen banks, on boulders, on human structures, or, rarely, on the ground (Bent 1937, Palmer 1988b). Tree nests range from about 20 (rarely 10) to 100 feet above the ground and the species most often used in California are pines, oaks, sycamores, eucalyptus, and redwoods (Bent 1937). Active nests in Marin County during the atlas period were in planted pines, Douglas firs, and redwoods. Ideally the nest site should be where an eagle burdened with prey can arrive without hindrance on a favorable wind or updraft, and where currents allow landing at slow speeds (Dixon 1937, Palmer 1988b). Depending on the region, nests are often oriented to provide shelter from excessive heat or cold (Palmer 1988b). Pairs frequently have additional nests (up to 12 total), and they may nest in one nest for a number of consecutive years or alternate nest sites; there is no obvious pattern of occupancy among

various pairs (Palmer 1988b). Certain nest sites are magnets attracting a succession of owners over perhaps hundreds of years or more.

These eagles' nests are very large, bulky affairs that vary considerably in size, depending on the amount of material added when reused. The body of the nest consists of large, dry sticks; the lining is typically of finer material, such as coarse roots, leaves, moss, lichens, rabbit fur, dry grass, and sprigs of bush or tree greenery. Some nest lining oddities are cow bones, deer antlers, barbed wire, burlap bags, newspapers, stockings, and other rubbish, including a cowboy hat (but no sign of cowboy, horse, or boots)! As is typical of raptors, Golden Eagles bring small branches or twigs of greenery (pine, deciduous, or other) to the nest throughout the reproductive cycle (sometimes to all nests in a territory) and at other times (Palmer 1988b). Greenery may function to advertise ownership or reinforce attachment to the territory.

Golden Eagles usually hunt early and late in the day, mostly when in flight (Palmer 1988b). Soaring birds sweep and circle high above the ground, descend upon spotting prey, then fold their wings and plunge headfirst. About three yards above ground, they check their flight, follow the quarry, and grasp it with one or both feet. These eagles also fly low to the contours of the ground, keeping out of sight, seizing prey they surprise away from cover. Less frequently, eagles hunt from perches, swooping down on prey that they spot moving into the open. They also stoop on or chase birds in the air. Rarely, if an eagle misses a squirrel, it may wait on the ground until the squirrel surfaces from a burrow, then take wing and catch it. Birds also feint at snakes to make them uncoil and tire, then seize them behind the head with one foot and grasp them farther behind with the other. Golden Eagles may hunt cooperatively in pairs (usually later in the nesting cycle) or in groups of up to four (Palmer 1988b). One member of a pair usually makes the initial attempt at capture. If unsuccessful, it may flush the intended victim (during the initial stoop or after landing and walking about on the ground), which is then caught by the other bird, which has been soaring above (Carnie 1954, Palmer 1988b). Groups of eagles sometimes cooperate to catch large prey, such as foxes, Wild Turkeys, or deer and antelope (disabled by snow or in poor condition) (Palmer 1988b).

Overall, the Golden Eagle's diet is about 83.9% mammals, 14.7% birds, 1.0% reptiles, and 0.4% fish (Olendorff in Palmer 1988b). In terms of biomass, the main prey of Golden Eagles are rodents (ground squirrels, prairie dogs, marmots), hares, and rabbits (Palmer 1988b). Goldens sometimes prey on full-grown deer or pronghorns, but probably only when the quarry is already injured or handicapped. They also take deer fawns or the young of other large mammals, adult and young foxes and coyotes, and a wide variety of small mammals (in addition to those already mentioned), including opossums, skunks, muskrats, tree squirrels, woodrats, and others in size down to deer mice and voles. Locally, Golden Eagles do occasionally prey on very young sheep (rarely other livestock or domestic animals), but consumption is mostly of stillborn young or other carrion. Birds also eat carrion of a variety of other species, particularly road-killed hares and rabbits. Bird prey range in size from cranes, swans, Wild Turkeys, and Great Blue Herons down to, rarely, larks and sparrows. Important bird prey are open-country game birds (grouse and pheasants) and magpies. Golden Eagles also eat small numbers of fish, snakes, tortoises and turtles, large insects such as grasshoppers and Mormon crickets, and the odd frog. In the interior central Coast Range of California, the Golden Eagle's diet is 77.3% mammals (mostly jackrabbits, ground squirrels, and black-tailed deer fawns), 13.5% medium- to large-sized birds (mostly Yellow-billed Magpies, Western Meadowlarks, and Great Horned Owls, but also such large species as Great Blue Heron, Mallard, Turkey Vulture, Red-tailed Hawk, Greater Roadrunner, and American Crow), 5.6% snakes, and 3.6% fish (Carnie 1954, n = 503). The considerable variation in the diet there of pairs hunting close together was apparently due to preference for, or specialization on, certain types of prey.

Males feed females during incubation and, early in the nestling phase, supply food for both their mates and the nestlings (Palmer 1988b). Incubating females leave their nests to obtain food brought by their mates to nearby plucking sites. When nestlings hatch, males prepare food at plucking sites by removing feathers from birds and decapitating or dismembering mammals and more or less removing their fur. Males then deliver food items to their nests, or females come to get them. When the young are small, generally a great excess of food accumulates at the nest. Hence the aerie serves as a food cache against possible shortage when hunting becomes difficult during prolonged periods of inclement weather. When the young get inadequate food, stronger eaglets sometimes attack weaker ones, eventually causing death, and they may sometimes eat them.

Marin Breeding Distribution

During the atlas period, Golden Eagles nested only in the northern interior of Marin County, but the exact locations are masked on the atlas map (see Content of Species Accounts p. 73). The relatively even spacing of nests, the scattered sightings between nest sites, and the fact that home ranges in San Diego County range from 19 to 59 square miles (av. 36; Dixon 1937) suggest that the total breeding population in Marin County was about five pairs. In 1982, we found four active nests and a fifth unoccupied nest used in previous years, which may have been an alternative nest of one of the other four pairs (ScC, DS, HBa —data on file). The lack of breeding Golden Eagles in the extensive grassland areas of the Point Reyes peninsula and the Marin Headlands may have been because of a lack of ground squirrels and low numbers of jackrabbits there.

Historical Trends/Population Threats

Pressure on Golden Eagles, especially through degradation or total loss of habitat, became serious in the West only in the present century (Palmer 1988b). Grinnell and Miller (1944) noted that the species had been reduced in numbers or extirpated in areas of California closely settled by humans, but elsewhere in the state numbers were close to normal. The Golden Eagle is currently listed in California as a Bird Species of Special Concern (Remsen 1978, CDFG 1991b) and as "Fully Protected" (Harlow & Bloom 1989). Thelander (1974) estimated there were 500 breeding pairs in California, and Olendorff et al. (in Palmer 1988b) estimated the state's wintering population at about 5046 birds. Numbers of Golden Eagles appeared to increase slightly on Breeding Bird Surveys in California from 1968 to 1989 but were relatively stable from 1980 to 1989 (USFWS unpubl. analyses); other observations suggest declines in the state, particularly on the southern coast (Harlow & Bloom 1989).

In the West, ranchers have put intense pressure on Golden Eagle populations because of reputed extensive predation on sheep, though the facts indicate such predation is limited and local. Golden Eagles were shot from airplanes as early as fall to spring of 1935–36, when over 200 birds were killed by "sportsmen" in Tehama County (Dale 1936). At least 20,000 (perhaps 40,000) eagles were killed, mostly from aircraft, from 1940 to 1962 in the sheep-raising country of west Texas and New Mexico alone (Spofford 1964, Palmer 1988b). Golden Eagles were given legal protection in 1963. Permits were still issued for livestock protection, though eagles could not be taken from aircraft or by poison. Hundreds were still being killed illegally in the early 1970s, but the enlightened efforts of

Audubon societies and state and federal agencies have greatly lessened the problem. Accidental electrocution on power lines has also been a problem but has been reduced in some areas by the redesign of transmission structures. Golden Eagles have also experienced eggshell thinning, death, and contamination from pesticides (Reichel et al. 1969, Palmer 1988b) and have picked up lead concentrations from the environment (Harlow & Bloom 1989). Golden Eagles are very sensitive to disturbance; watching of nests (even with telescopes at long range) is best avoided.

A Golden Eagle looks over its territory from its formidable nest. Photograph by Ian Tait.

Falcons
Family *Falconidae*

AMERICAN KESTREL *Falco sparverius*

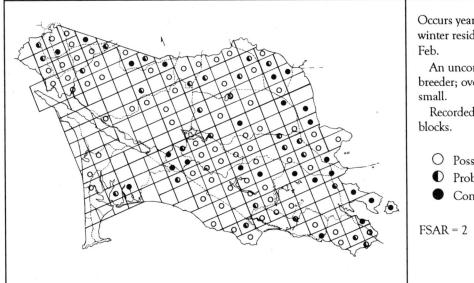

Occurs year round, though primarily as a winter resident from mid-Aug through Feb.

An uncommon, fairly widespread breeder; overall breeding population small.

Recorded in 122 (55.2%) of 221 blocks.

○	Possible	=	71	(58%)
◑	Probable	=	26	(21%)
●	Confirmed	=	25	(20%)

FSAR = 2   OPI = 244   CI = 1.62

Ecological Requirements

It is common to see these dainty, boldly marked falcons emphatically pump their tails or bob their heads after alighting in hunched posture on perches in open country. Elevation, moisture, or particular plant communities exert little influence on Kestrel distribution, as they range from sea level to timberline and from deserts to moist forest fringes. Kestrels are edge adapted and inhabit the margins of a wide variety of forests and woodlands bordering on low, open vegetation of grasslands, meadows, and scattered brush; open or burned forests or woodlands; and even urban-suburban settings. In Marin County, American Kestrels breed along the edges of, or within extensive openings in, all the major forest or woodland communities bordering on grasslands, open weed fields, or meadows; around isolated woodlots, windbreaks, and ranchyards in expansive pasturelands; or in similar urban-suburban environments. In winter, the sexes segregate by habitat—females mostly use expansive open habitats with few trees, and males mostly use clearings in habitats with more trees and brush (Koplin 1973, Mills 1976, Stinson et al. 1981). These differences may reflect the dominant females' forcing the males into less suitable habitats, thereby reducing competition for food, or sexual differences in preferred habitats harboring preferred prey. Smallwood (1988) attributed sexual habitat segregation on the wintering grounds to earlier migration of females, which occupy habitats of superior foraging quality first, leaving poor-quality habitats to later-arriving males. A suggestion that habitat separation may also be widespread in summer (to a lesser extent than in winter; Mills 1976) is countered by the knowledge that females initially center most activities around the nest site and are fed by their mates, which range widely throughout their territories, and that, in some areas at least, there is no sexual separation in the foraging niches of breeding birds (Balgooyen 1976). The main requirements for breeding Kestrels are low, open vegetation for ground foraging, suitable foraging perches (high preferred to low), an adequate prey base, and available nest cavities (Balgooyen 1976, Palmer 1988b).

Nest sites in particular can limit Kestrel density. A suggestion that Kestrels breed almost colonially or socially where there is an abundance of cavities (Palmer 1988b) may be an exaggeration, as territoriality will limit Kestrel numbers before nest sites are exhausted in such a situation (Balgooyen 1976). Unlike most raptors, Kestrels prefer natural tree cavities or those excavated by large woodpeckers (particularly Northern Flickers) for nesting (Bent 1938, Balgooyen 1976, Palmer 1988b). They also use holes in cliffs or eroded stream banks (natural or excavated by kingfishers), cavities in buildings, chimneys, drainpipes, hollowed-out fence posts, old pigeon boxes, magpie nests, and bird boxes. Kestrels add little, if any, material to the cavities and lay their eggs on the bare floor or on whatever the previous occupant has left behind (Bent 1938). Nest heights range from less than three feet above the ground to as high as suitable cavities exist—in one case over 350 feet up in a 22-story building (Palmer 1988b). Roest (1957) reported nest heights at various locations in North America ranging from 4 to 50+ feet above the ground (most 10-35 ft.) and Balgooyen (1976) reported 43 nests in the Sierra Nevada ranging from 7 to 80 feet (av. 26 ft.).

Balgooyen (1976) found most nests in the eastern Sierra in the lower reaches of basins, presumably because these sites were sheltered from weather and allowed easy flights back to the nest with food. In Marin County, most Kestrels nest in lowland areas because of the greater availability of open areas and, apparently, nests sites there, and probably because of a greater prey base in fertile lowland valleys. In the Sierra, Balgooyen (1976) found that both the slope exposure of the nest tree and the nest entrance tended to face east, providing protection from storms and the advantage of early morning sun. Raphael (1985) confirmed the easterly orientation of Kestrels' nest trees and nest cavities in Balgooyen's study area; Kestrels there chose these sites despite the availability of cavities oriented in other directions. Interestingly, woodpeckers in the same area, which might similarly benefit from the thermoregulatory advantages of easterly oriented nest cavities, tended to choose northerly facing cavities even though suitable decay was randomly oriented. Kestrels nesting in the tropics may avoid heat by selecting nest sites facing into prevailing winds and away from direct sunlight (Balgooyen 1990).

Kestrels hunt more or less regularly and continuously throughout the day and may or may not show peaks of foraging activity (Palmer 1988b). They seek visible and vulnerable prey in short, sparse vegetation, where they capture most prey on or near the ground and take most flying prey on the wing (Balgooyen 1976, Palmer 1988b). These falcons mostly hunt from perches (when available) and secondarily hover and hawk. Birds use a wide variety of foraging perches, including dead branches and trees, stumps, rock outcrops or cliffs, fence posts, telephone and power poles, transmission lines, and an array of artificial structures. Average perch height in the Sierra Nevada is 22 feet (n = 328); birds forage from lower perches in high winds (Balgooyen 1976). From perches, birds face into the wind and scan terrain for prey by rotating or tilting the head, then snap the head into a fixed position upon locating prey and fly down to make the capture. In the Sierra, effective capture distance from the perch extends to

900 feet, with 86% of captures from 0 to 164 feet (av. 112 ft.). In areas lacking perches, Kestrels face the wind with their bodies angled head upwards and hover with shallow wingbeats and tail fanned. Sometimes they hang motionless, then plummet directly down or drop lower and hover again before the final attack. Kestrels hover mostly from heights of 40 to 100 feet and dive headfirst after mammals and feet first after insects (Balgooyen 1976, Palmer 1988b). During dives, the birds may partly close their wings or flutter downward, checking and controlling their descent (Palmer 1988b). Whether hunting from perches or hovering, Kestrels modify their attacks, depending on the type of prey (Balgooyen 1976). They directly attack frogs, lizards, and small mammals from flight. Kestrels track the flight of grasshoppers, and after they land, the birds fly to the spot, brake, and usually flush the insect and make the kill on the wing. If grasshoppers remain still, Kestrels land and walk about, crisscrossing the area to attempt to raise the insect. From flight, Kestrels also, rarely, pick large insects or lizards deftly from tree trunks or rocks (Balgooyen 1976, Palmer 1988b). Sometimes they fly rapidly, low to the ground, in pursuit of flying prey (Palmer 1988b). Birds also hawk insects by flying directly out (up to 35 ft.) from perches (Balgooyen 1976) or by soaring and flapping upward and away from perches, then stalling and diving abruptly at their targets (Palmer 1988b). They sometimes dart out from a perch, tilt their bodies, attempt to strike down dragonflies with their wings, then drop to the ground to seize their prey (Palmer 1988b). Birds may eat prey at the capture site, while transported aerially, or on arrival at a nearby perch.

Kestrels sometimes catch birds in flight and secure bats from the bark of trees or by diving down on them or from behind in straight flight (Balgooyen 1976, Palmer 1988b). Rarely, these falcons obtain small nonflying insects, spiders, or worms with their beaks while running (occasionally flapping to gain speed) or jumping on the ground. Kestrels sometimes persistently rob nests and return to get the rest of a brood (Palmer 1988b). They have plundered burrows of Bank Swallows and nests of Cliff Swallows, Barn Swallows, phoebes, bluebirds, and House Sparrows by hanging upside down and reaching in with one foot or by ripping off the top of the nest. Infrequently, Kestrels take birds captured in mist nests or ground traps and hunt along the smoky windward edges of fires. Rarely, Kestrels eat fresh or decayed carrion. One Kestrel foraged on the ground for bread (initially with feral pigeons).

Kestrels usually capture prey in the talons and kill them by biting them with the beak in the head or neck (Balgooyen 1976, Palmer 1988b). They usually crush the head and discard the wings, legs, and other extraneous parts of insects; pluck feathers from birds; discard some rodent hair and ingest much; and discard large hard parts and alimentary canals of birds and mammals.

Kestrels are generalized predators of invertebrates and small vertebrate animals. Prey items consist of 95.7% invertebrates, 2.4% mammals, 1.2% birds, and 0.7% lower vertebrates (Snyder & Wiley 1976, n = 9242). Prey taken can vary considerably with locality, season, or the tendency of individuals to concentrate on one particular type of prey (Balgooyen 1976, Palmer 1988b). Principal prey are large insects (especially grasshoppers, Jerusalem crickets, dragonflies, beetles, and caterpillars); small mammals (from shrew to ground squirrel or rabbit size—especially voles); birds (from hummingbird to Mourning Dove or quail size, but mostly moderate size); and reptiles and amphibians (small lizards, snakes, frogs, tadpoles, and toads). Miscellaneous prey items include crayfish, centipedes, scorpions, spiders, earthworms, and snails. The Kestrels' diet by weight in the Sierra Nevada is 31.7% insects (mostly grasshoppers), 26.0% reptiles, 25.7% mammals, and 16.6% birds; by occurrence, it is 88.4% insects, 8.1% reptiles, 2.1% mammals, and 1.4% birds (Balgooyen 1976). In the early season or during inclement weather, Kestrels in the Sierra Nevada concentrate on birds and mammals. Later on, they rely more on lizards and insects and even more so on insects from midseason until fall departure. In Humboldt County, Kestrels feed on voles and shrews in the absence of insect prey (Collopy in Palmer 1988b). Although the sexes generally take the same kinds of prey in about the same proportions, there are some exceptions. In the Sierra Nevada, breeding males and females choose similar-sized prey (Balgooyen 1976), but in southern California, breeding males usually choose smaller prey than breeding females (Bryan in Palmer 1988b).

Males forage in areas of the territory away from the immediate nest site and bring females food from four to five weeks before egg laying until one to two weeks after hatching of the eggs (Balgooyen 1976). Males transport prey to perches near the nest site, where they transfer the food to females with their beaks (Balgooyen 1976, Palmer 1988b). Both sexes may cache surplus vertebrate prey by wedging or pushing it with the beak into a suitable site. Cache sites may range from the ground up to 65 feet and include grass clumps, hollow railroad ties, tree roots, bushes, fence posts, building gutters, tree limbs and holes, and tops of power poles or burned stumps. Although food caching may serve to hide prey, the main function is to store it as a reserve for times of inclement weather or low prey availability or to meet the demands of growing young. Cached food is usually eaten within a few hours or within 2 or 3 days; some food is held as long as 6 or 7 days. The young are initially fed by the female via the male for 7 to 10 days after hatching, then by both sexes separately (Balgooyen 1976). Through the first 7 to 14 days, the female initially removes all extraneous material from prey and feeds the young only flesh. Thereafter, prey are delivered to the young whole and unprepared.

Marin Breeding Distribution

During the atlas period, Kestrels bred widely in Marin County, though breeding numbers were substantially smaller than winter numbers. Breeding Kestrels were sparse or lacking on much of Point Reyes because of the dense forest or scrub cover on most of Inverness Ridge, and perhaps because of limited nest sites and small populations of large insects in the fog-shrouded, windswept grasslands of the outer Point Reyes peninsula. The reasons for their spotty distribution elsewhere in Marin, particularly in the grassland-dominated hills east of Tomales Bay where large numbers of Kestrels winter, is less clear. Nest sites may be a limiting factor: 40% of the blocks east of the Point Reyes peninsula that lack breeding Kestrels also lack breeding Northern Flickers, which typically provide many Kestrel nest cavities. Representative breeding localities of American Kestrels were Bear Valley, PRNS (FY 4/22/76 —RMS); Ignacio area (FY 5/27/77 —RMS); and Carson Ridge (DD 3/9/85 —ITi).

Historical Trends/Population Threats

Grinnell and Miller (1944) did not comment on any trends in California populations, but Palmer (1988b) reported that "widespread deforestation and land development have facilitated a continentwide population increase of this remarkably adaptive species." Numbers of breeding Kestrels decreased on Breeding Bird Surveys in California from 1980 to 1989 (USFWS unpubl. analyses). Eggshell thinning in Kestrels has been correlated with increasing levels of DDE (Risebrough & Monk 1989), but even though chemical contaminants have caused deaths, there have been no drastic declines in Kestrel numbers as a result (Palmer 1988b). There currently are no major threats to western populations (Platt & Enderson 1989).

PEREGRINE FALCON *Falco peregrinus*

Formerly a year-round resident and breeder until the 1970s, when extirpated as a nesting bird. Now occurs year round, though primarily as a winter resident and transient from mid-Sep through mid-Apr. Following a statewide increase after a ban on DDT pesticides and the implementation of a captive breeding program, summer sightings have increased in Marin and breeding attempted in 1990 and 1991 (successfully).

Ecological Requirements

These swift, spirited falcons inhabit open country, where their speed and feather-raising pursuit dives strike fear in the hearts of the avian populace. Peregrines hunt in the air—over oceans, forests and woodlands, marshes and wetlands, chaparral, and cities—and very rarely take ground prey. In coastal areas, Peregrines hunt a great deal around estuaries and seabird colonies. Ideally, they select nesting aeries that command a wide view, are near water, have plentiful bird prey in the vicinity, and are seldom disturbed (Palmer 1988b). Peregrine Falcons formerly nested in Marin County on cliffs overlooking the ocean (see below). In contrast, Prairie Falcons, which have never nested here, tend to inhabit more arid environments, select lower, more sheltered nest sites, and feed lower to the ground and considerably more on mammals than do Peregrines (Palmer 1988b). Peregrine Falcons will nest in deserts if near marshes, lakes, or rivers, and both Peregrine and Prairie falcons may nest on the same cliffs or switch ownership of nest sites in different years.

Peregrines typically select cavities or ledges on cliffs, often with a sheltering overhang, for nest sites (Palmer 1988b). They generally lay their eggs on a fairly level spot at least two feet in diameter—a larger space is advantageous so the young can move about as they grow. Peregrines make a nest scrape in debris, such as soil or rocks, and sitting birds may pull some of this material toward them to form a rim sufficient to keep the eggs from rolling away. In North America, cliff nest sites are usually unmodified or may contain old nests of Common Ravens, Rough-legged Hawks, Golden Eagles, Red-tailed Hawks, or cormorants. Historically, raven nests were often used in Marin County (B.J. Walton pers. comm.). Substitutes for cliff nests include church towers, castle ruins, bridges, quarries, raised platforms, and assorted buildings (mostly urban). In very open country, such as tundra, Peregrines will nest in recesses or level spots at or near the top of eroded riverbanks or on boulders, hills, slopes, dunes, bog hummocks or islets, or even on ground with no topographical relief. One pair nested in the straw packing inside a barrel cast up in salt marsh in San Francisco Bay near Redwood City, San Mateo County (Dawson 1923); other birds reportedly bred in bay marshes in Santa Clara County (G&W 1927).

Peregrines will also appropriate solid (rarely flimsy) stick nests (usually disused) of a variety of large birds placed in dead or living trees (Palmer 1988b). The use of stick nests in trees is only widespread in Australia, and there are only one or two such records in North America (occupation of Bald Eagle nests in British Columbia). On the whole, the use of tree cavities, including hollow tops where limbs have broken off, is even rarer, though slightly more frequent in North America than the use of stick nests in trees. Peregrines often use alternative nest sites within the same territory—one or two is common, and birds have used up to seven in 16 years. If several sites or ledges are available along a cliff, individual pairs may change about in different years or shift to different cliffs. If alternative sites or ledges are not available, pairs tend to stay put. Birds robbed of their eggs commonly move to alternate sites, and birds may move and re-lay after breeding failure. Use of particular sites may also alternate between Peregrines and other species of cliff-nesting raptors. Despite birds' switching to alternative sites, some Peregrine territories in Britain have been occupied at least since the 13th century.

The Peregrine Falcon is a very fast, extremely agile, and versatile raptor specialized for capturing aerial prey. In level flight, Peregrines normally fly at 25 to 35 mph and usually do not exceed 60 mph; in vertical stoops, they usually make strikes at about 100 mph and from a height of 5000 feet would reach a terminal velocity of 230 to 240 mph (Palmer 1988b). Breeding males may hunt throughout the day, but mostly early in the morning and secondarily toward evening. Timing of hunting may depend on the activity patterns or the size of prey. Peregrines living within colonies of nocturnal, burrowing seabirds hunt such prey (and bats) around their aeries in near darkness. Individuals specializing on waterfowl must hunt two times a day, and those hunting small shorebirds must hunt three to four or even five to six times per day. Hunting demands peak when males are feeding both females and growing young.

Often, probably when already satiated, Peregrines pursue flying birds seemingly for the pleasure of the chase (Palmer 1988b) or perhaps to hone hunting skills or tactics (B.J. Walton pers. comm.). At other times, they turn deadly serious in their attempts. Hunting birds launch

154

attacks from a stationary position on a prominence or tall tree, or from flight. If the quarry is below them, they may make a shallow stoop or climb higher and stoop at tremendous speed. If their initial strikes fail, Peregrines rise rapidly and stoop again, making repeated attempts if necessary. When prey near cover, Peregrines sometimes get beneath them, turn over, and seize them from below. If quarry are initially high overhead or are forced upward, these falcons spiral upward spectacularly to get above them. Fast birds try to keep above falcons or to outdistance them in straight-away flight, whereas slower fliers try to keep above their pursuers. As a last resort, quarry may plummet earthward, but they are closely pursued and generally captured quickly. If the prey reaches ground but fails to find concealing cover, it may be killed. Peregrines may launch attacks from circling flight, stooping at lower targets or spiraling up after higher prey. Smaller prey are often grasped in the air and carried to earth. Larger victims are often struck with such speed (with either or both feet) that falcons slash the victim with the rear talon(s) and rip right through without holding on. Feathers fly, and the prey may be dead as it falls earthward. Peregrines then half-circle and alight, and whether the prey is alive or not they bite it near the base of the brain, breaking the neck with their specialized double-notched beak, adapted for this purpose. Mated pairs may hunt cooperatively and may stay together year round in Marin. There is some evidence that females may maneuver the quarry into a favorable position for the male to strike from a greater height, coming out of the sun (B.J. Walton pers. comm.).

Peregrines also hunt flying low to the ground, keeping out of sight as best they can behind vegetation and irregularities of the terrain (Palmer 1988b). Some low flying is done deliberately to flush potential prey from vegetation. Peregrines also seek the shelter of waves when pursuing marine birds at sea. If the quarry escapes by diving, a falcon may wait overhead and pick the prey from the surface after it emerges exhausted after repeated dives. In forested regions, Peregrines take exposed prey crossing water or clearings. Peregrines usually flush standing or swimming birds before seizing them, but, very rarely, they do take some prey from or on the ground or water. Mammals (other than bats), usually found in Peregrine nests, are probably those pirated from other raptors (B.J. Walton pers. comm.). Relatively large mammals, such as full-grown ground squirrels, may be killed by a series of stoops at the head and neck that stun or blind the individual or fracture its skull. Lemmings are reportedly hunted afoot, but many are probably snatched by flying falcons. Ground hunting is more frequent in inexperienced young Peregrines, which catch insects, large slugs, fiddler crabs, and other suitable prey by this method. Adults sometimes hawk flying insects leisurely. These falcons also follow people, dogs, or harriers to catch birds they flush. Peregrines capture bats by cutting through flocks departing from caves or ambush individuals returning to them. They also catch fish breaking the surface, pirate them from Ospreys, and perhaps take stranded or dead ones. Peregrines also pirate food from other raptors of Harrier to Kestrel size. Peregrines eat some smaller prey on the wing. They probably at least partially dismember, then eat during flight, prey such as bats, voles, and insects, which are unsuitable for plucking. Birds captured at sea may also be eaten in flight. These falcons generally partially pluck and feed on heavy prey where they strike them down, though typically they carry food to one or more plucking sites or perches. They pluck wings and tail and eat the head to make prey aerodynamically efficient for carrying (B.J. Walton pers. comm.). The beaks and feet of larger prey often are not eaten.

Peregrines defend a small area around the aerie. Food supply probably determines the size of the much larger hunting range, which in the breeding season may be over 40 square miles; the total feeding areas of breeding pairs frequently overlap (Palmer 1988b). Some foraging is done from the aerie or nearby perches, but foraging flights during breeding in California range up to 4 to 5 miles (mostly 2 to 3 miles). The male feeds the female during prelaying and incubation. After hatching, he feeds both the brood and his mate, but the female hunts progressively more as her brooding declines. The male delivers prey (fresh or retrieved from a cache) to a nearby perch, and the females gets it there; or she may meet him in the air and obtain it in an aerial food pass or drop. Females may retrieve food cached by the male and again cache and retrieve any uneaten portion. Food caching also occurs at other seasons (B.J. Walton pers. comm.). Caching assures a supply of food during bad weather when hunting is difficult and at least sometimes is triggered by an abundance of prey. Sometimes the male delivers food to the young directly, especially when the female is absent. Avian prey are almost always, and mammals are frequently, headless when delivered to the aerie. Males may subsist largely on heads at this time, but they apparently consume some whole prey away from the breeding territory.

Peregrines prey principally on fast-flying birds in the open and worldwide have captured well over 250 species (Palmer 1988b). These range in size, rarely, from prey heavier than the predator (loons, herons, cormorants, geese, and large gulls) down to very small passerines. Most important prey are usually small to medium-sized birds—blackbirds, swallows, shorebirds, seabirds, pigeons, doves, etc. The bulk of the prey taken in an area usually consists of a few common open-country species. Individuals sometimes specialize on certain prey species, but less so when feeding a growing brood. In California, Peregrines usually do not deliver a predominance of any one prey species to a nest—prey remains usually mirror the array of the most numerous species of appropriate size recorded in the territory (B.J. Walton pers. comm.). About 25+ prey species is typical at California nests, and many prey items are represented at every nest. Coastal Peregrines often specialize on seabirds during the breeding season and on shorebirds and waterfowl in winter (Palmer 1988b). Seasonal changes in diet likely reflect availability of common prey species. Rock Doves are a preferred food, especially in cities. Mammals are extremely rare fare, but a wide variety are consumed, including shrews, bats, rabbits and young hares, pikas, tree squirrels, chipmunks, ground squirrels, lemmings, rats, and voles. In California, mammal prey include only bats and very small mammals, often pirated from Black-shouldered Kites and Red-tailed Hawks (B.J. Walton pers. comm.). Extremely rarely, Peregrines eat invertebrates, insects, and carrion (not recorded in California). Evidently males and females eat prey of the same average size (Palmer 1988b).

Historical Trends/Population Threats

Peregrine Falcons formerly nested in Marin County on precipitous seacliffs (G&W 1927, G&M 1944). Known former nesting sites include the cliffs between the Golden Gate Bridge and Point Bonita, the north side of Muir Beach, Bear Valley, Drake's Bay, the Point Reyes headlands, Kehoe Beach, McClure's Beach, and Tomales Point (B.J. Walton pers. comm.). Peregrines also formerly nested on Red Rock in San Francisco Bay, but it is unclear if the aerie(s) were on the small Marin County portion of that island. In the 1930s, there were seven pairs of Peregrines nesting in Marin County in one year, but by the 1960s there were only one or two pairs (B.J. Walton pers. comm.). In the 1970s, there were no documented pairs; in the 1980s, circumstantial evidence suggested at least one pair may have nested here, though confirmation is lacking. In 1990, a pair began nesting on a cliff at the Marin Headlands, but the attempt failed soon after the young hatched (Golden Gate Raptor Observatory). In 1991, this same pair apparently nested farther north along the southern Marin coast and, unassisted by humans, successfully fledged four young. Breeding Peregrines may become reestablished here via management efforts or from recruitment from natural population expansion/recovery. Young Peregrines were released at hack sites at Muir Beach from 1983 to 1988 and at Tomales Point in 1987 and 1988 (Linthicum 1988). One of the birds released at Muir Beach is now nesting on the San Francisco–Oakland Bay Bridge (B.J. Walton pers. comm.).

Grinnell and Miller (1944) noted for California at the time that Peregrines were "fairly common for a hawk" and that, except locally, numbers were holding fairly constant. North American populations also were relatively stable up to that time, but rather suddenly, beginning in the late 1940s, here and in Europe, Peregrine populations began to decline dramatically. This led to a severe population crash by the early 1960s, which bottomed out by 1973 to 1975 (Hickey 1969, Kiff 1988). Although other factors have affected Peregrines—mortality from collisions with wires, shooting on wintering grounds, habitat loss, egg collecting, taking young for falconry, disturbance at nest sites, and human encroachment affecting prey species—this decline was clearly linked to pesticide pollution. Because of their position high on the food chain, Peregrines readily concentrate contaminants from their prey. Population crashes in North America (and elsewhere) were primarily from reproductive failure caused by DDE-induced eggshell thinning (Cade et al. 1988, Peakall & Kiff 1988, Risebrough & Peakall 1988), though adult mortality from dieldrin or other organochlorines may also have been an important factor (Cade et al. 1988, Nisbet 1988). In California, Peregrine eggs analyzed to date have *extremely high* levels of DDT, DDE, PCBs, and dioxin (B.J. Walton pers. comm.).

The size of the historic Peregrine population in California is unknown. Herman et al. (1970) estimated that 100 California aeries were producing young until at least the mid-1940s. The actual number of aeries active in a given year at the turn of the century may have been as many as 300; extensive searching of historical records has now revealed about 200 pre-DDT era breeding sites, and many probably went unrecorded (B.J. Walton pers. comm.). From 1946 to 1950, there were definite signs of reproductive problems, but no evidence of serious population decline; from 1950 to 1960, there was a precipitous decline in the number of pairs producing young; and from 1961 to 1969, there were sporadic nesting success and further declines, leaving fewer than 10 known breeding pairs in the state in 1969 (Herman et al. 1970). By 1970 the state breeding population did not exceed 5 successful pairs—a reduction of 95% from the estimated level in the mid-1940s (Herman 1971). Because of these declines, Peregrines were placed on both federal and state Endangered species lists (USFWS 1989a, CDFG 1991a). Use of offending pesticides was greatly restricted in the United States in 1972 (Kiff 1988). Since these bans, populations have expanded through natural recovery and management activities, which have included manipulation of eggs and young at nest sites in California beginning in 1977 (Walton & Thelander 1988). Recent increases in the number of known active nest sites in California are also, in part, a result of increased efforts to find them (Walton et al. 1988). Since the 1970s, Peregrines have reoccupied only 35 of California's 200 known historic (pre-DDT era) nest sites, though they also have occupied over 100 sites not previously known (B.J. Walton pers. comm.). Many seemingly suitable sites remain vacant, and the process of population expansion has been slow (Walton et al. 1988), increasing at an average of 8% (6.8 breeding pairs) per year since 1975 (Monk et al. 1989). As of 1989, researchers knew of only 90 active nest sites in the state (Monk et al. 1989). The Coast Ranges north of San Francisco to the Oregon border currently support the largest number of nesting pairs in the western United States and about two-thirds of California's nesting population (Walton et al. 1988, Monk et al. 1989). Between 1971 and the mid-1980s, no Peregrines were known to have nested along the coastline north of San Francisco, an area with over 30 historic nest sites. In the late 1980s, Peregrine sightings along the north coast increased, and at least one pair nested successfully (B.J. Walton pers. comm.). With management help, Peregrine populations on the central California coast (from San Francisco to Santa Barbara counties) have increased from 1 pair at Morro Rock in the 1960s and 1970s to 12 pairs, many of which are located on the Big Sur coastline. The central coast contains about 65 historical nesting sites. The historical population of over 40 pairs on the southern California coast and Channel Islands was extirpated but has since recovered to about 8 pairs, 3 of which were established on large buildings or bridges in the Los Angeles basin by release programs; the island population is expanding rapidly (5 pairs in 1989). Interior populations have always been less densely spaced, and currently there are fewer than 6 active sites in river canyons of the Cascades and Sierra Nevada, including 3 pairs in Yosemite National Park.

Although nesting productivity of wild pairs is improving, it is still compromised by accumulations of pesticides remaining in the fatty tissues of these long-lived birds, augmented by further accumulations of pesticides still circulating in the environment (B.J. Walton pers. comm.). Eggshell thinning continues at critical or near critical levels throughout California (Walton et al. 1988), necessitating an aggressive management effort to maintain and increase the rate of recovery of the state's breeding population (Walton & Thelander 1988). In fact, one or both adults at nearly 50% of known nesting sites were born at the Peregrine Fund's facilities at Santa Cruz. There are three methods of "hands on" management of Peregrines: (1) fostering—placing in active Peregrine nests young produced from thin-shelled eggs removed from the wild and incubated in captivity, or from eggs laid and hatched by captive birds; (2) cross-fostering—placing captive reared young in the nests of Prairie Falcons, which raise them to independence; and (3) hacking—placing in a hack box at an appropriate nest site captive-reared young that are released, fed, and monitored through independence by concealed biologists.

Possible sources of currently accumulated DDE include (1) residues in soils, air, and water; (2) contaminants in other legal pesticides; (3) residues in migrant prey species; (4) illegal pesticide use; and (5) legal use for emergency applications (Walton & Thelander 1988, Risebrough & Monk 1989). Scientific studies indicate that Peregrines are accumulating pesticides mostly from the United States rather than from Mexico and South America, where there is little restriction of pesticide use. Although chlorinated hydrocarbon pesticide use is restricted in this country, other toxins, such as dioxin, still pose serious threats to Peregrines (B.J. Walton pers. comm.). Whether Peregrines can ever again maintain large natural populations in California without human assistance is an acid test of our resolve and ability to cope with environmental degradation and, perhaps, of the chances of long-term survival of our species on the planet. Even with a complete solution to the pollution problem, Peregrines will never reach historical levels because of extensive habitat loss, particularly of wetlands (Kiff 1988).

Pheasants and Quail
Family *Phasianidae*

RING-NECKED PHEASANT *Phasianus colchicus*

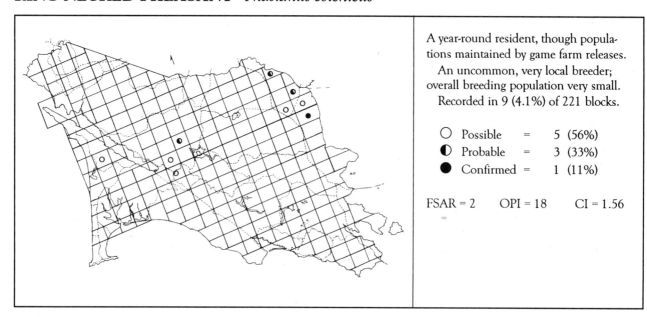

A year-round resident, though populations maintained by game farm releases.
An uncommon, very local breeder; overall breeding population very small.
Recorded in 9 (4.1%) of 221 blocks.

○ Possible   =   5 (56%)
◑ Probable   =   3 (33%)
● Confirmed   =   1 (11%)

FSAR = 2   OPI = 18   CI = 1.56

Ecological Requirements

This resplendent native of eastern Asia has been introduced widely in California and has taken hold in fertile, irrigated agricultural lands. The most important Pheasant habitats are cultivated fields of grain, such as rice, barley, and wheat, but irrigated pastures and hayfields may also be prominent locally. In Marin County, Ring-necked Pheasants occupy areas dominated by hay and alfalfa crops, but their population here is apparently not self-sustaining, as are those in similar habitat in nearby Sonoma, Napa, and Solano counties (Calif. Dept. Fish Game). Irrigated farmland is crucial to Pheasants for food. It provides the best habitat for them when it is interspersed with vegetation that also meets their requirements for nesting and cover (Olsen 1977, Johnsgard 1986).

In winter, birds form temporary mixed or unisexual flocks. For breeding, the polygynous males break off singly to attract harems of about three to ten females. The males select ill-defined crowing territories that include patches of varied, interspersed habitat. They avoid all but the edges of large blocks of monotypic vegetation and prefer a blending of food patches with herbaceous, meadow, marsh, brush, and tree clump habitats. Pheasants use moderately dense herbaceous and brushy cover for roosting, loafing, and

nesting. For nesting early in spring, they prefer permanent residual cover of dry grasses and forbs persisting from the previous year; with continued plant growth, birds shift to farm crops and new spring vegetation. Nesting habitats include hayfields, small grain crops, strip cover, pastures, wetland and woodland edges, and, to a lesser extent, fallow fields, gravel pits, lakeshores, farmyards, stubble fields, plowed fields, and orchards. Strip cover, which is also important for roosting and loafing, generally consists of low-growing vegetation parallel to roadways, railroads, drainage ditches, irrigation canals, streams, dikes, and fence lines. Pheasants prefer wider strips to narrower ones, and moderate-sized fields to small, narrow, or large ones. Males apparently adjust their crowing territories to include the nest sites of females.

Pheasants place most nests in shallow depressions scooped out of the earth or in natural hollows. Occasionally, they raise their nests slightly above the ground, for example, atop wind-drifted cornhusks or on tussocks in a marsh; rarely, they locate nests well above ground in straw stacks or in the old nests of other birds or squirrels. Nests are lined with dried grasses or leaves, weed stalks, fine twigs, or cornhusks taken from the immediate vicinity of the nest; a few feathers from the hen Pheasant may sometimes be found in the nest. The nest site microhabitat generally has a greater density of vegetative cover (particularly to the side of the nest) than does the broader surrounding nesting habitat (Wood & Brotherson 1981). The height of vegetative cover (within a general range of about 10-100 in.) does not seem to be as important as vegetative density (Olsen 1977, Wood & Brotherson 1981); but see Hanson (1970). Canopy cover can vary from leaving the nest completely exposed from above to providing partial or complete concealment. Although nesting cover appears to provide protection from predators, perhaps more importantly it furnishes a microclimate of lower temperature and higher humidity than is found at similar heights in surrounding vegetation (Francis 1968, Hanson 1970, Wood & Brotherson 1981). In California, brood cover consists primarily of grain, rice, natural cover areas, and plowed fields (Olsen 1977). In the fall, Pheasants tend to drift toward stream bottoms, swales, and swampy edges; ungrazed hayfields, wild grass, weeds, brushy woodlots, fencerows, and stubble fields provide additional cover. At all seasons, Pheasants require a source of water close by.

Ring-necked Pheasants are primarily grain eaters, though leafage can be important in their diets seasonally; they take animal matter in small amounts from spring through fall. In California, the diet varies greatly among habitat types, locally as well as geographically and seasonally (Grenfell et al. 1980). In grain-growing regions of the Sacramento and San Joaquin valleys, cultivated grains, such as rice, barley, wheat, oats, and grain sorghums, are the most important foods year round and may constitute as much as 80% of the whole diet in a given season. In the Sacramento Valley grain regions, at least, Pheasants increase their use of green forb and grass leafage in spring and of forb and grass seeds in spring and summer; animal foods account for only about 3%-7% of the spring through fall diet. In contrast, in an area of extensive irrigated pastureland in the San Joaquin Valley, the spring to fall diet consists of about 60%-90% grass and forb seeds. The amount of green leafage in the diet there shifts dramatically to over 60% in winter and drops to slightly over 25% in spring; cultivated crops reach a maximum of only about 17% of the diet in summer. Based on limited samples, the spring through fall diet in the Modoc Plateau and Great Basin regions varies seasonally from 75%-96% cultivated crops; winter diet (data available only from Modoc) is over 50% leafage, secondarily grass and forb seeds, and lastly cultivated grains. In spring, birds in the Modoc region use over 85% cultivated grain, whereas those in the Great Basin rely on over 50% leafage and about 40% grass seed; animal foods in these areas account for as high as 23% of the diet in summer. Pheasants also eat limited amounts of corms and roots, fleshy fruits,

flower buds and flowers, and mast; additionally, they do some damage to tomato, melon, and potato crops (Ferrel et al. 1949, Leach et al. 1953, Grenfell et al. 1980). Little appears to have been written on the foraging tactics of Pheasants, but they are primarily ground foragers and must uncover some items. Johnsgard (1986) indicated that the birds' short toes, strong claws, and sharp bills are all well adapted for digging and scratching. Edminster (1954), on the other hand, reported that they pick and root in the ground better with their beaks and do not use their feet for scratching out food. Pheasants appear to take most cultivated grain as waste grain from the ground, but they also take some from the plants before harvest (Ferrel et al. 1949). The fact that Pheasants browse on flower buds, flowers, and leafage suggests they also procure some weed seeds directly from the plants. In the Sacramento Valley, Pheasants consume 18 orders of insects and other invertebrates, grasshoppers being the most important; occasionally, they take mice (Ferrel et al. 1949). The diet of week-old chicks is exclusively insects; by 8 weeks of age it decreases to about 50% insects; and by 13 weeks it resembles that of adults. Chicks initially take small insects, such as beetles, and later larger ones, such as grasshoppers. Females appear to eat more insects than do males, and they frequently take calcium-rich snails, which presumably are important for egg formation (Korschgen 1964).

Marin Breeding Distribution

Although there were a few atlas sightings toward the coast, most were in the vicinity of agricultural hay and alfalfa fields near marshlands along San Pablo Bay near Novato. The only confirmation of breeding was a hen with a half-grown chick in reclaimed marshlands east of Ignacio on 13 May 1979 (Anonymous *fide* DS). Despite such evidence, the Marin population is not viable but depends upon the release by hunt clubs of game farm–reared birds (G. Thomsen, J.R. Slosson pers. comm.).

Historical Trends/Population Threats

Ring-necked Pheasants were first introduced to California in Santa Cruz, San Mateo, and Marin counties prior to 1889 by private parties (Grinnell et al. 1918; G&M 1944; Hjersman 1947). Birds were first released by the Fish and Game Commission in 1889 in a number of counties, including coastal Marin and Monterey; a year or two after 1894, they were also released in Humboldt and Santa Clara counties. Introductions began in earnest in 1908 from breeding stock from the newly established State Game Farm. By 1916, Pheasants had been released in 37 of the state's 58 counties, and they appeared to be established in the wild in coastal counties at Eureka and Fortuna, Humboldt County; Napa, Napa County; Watsonville, Santa Cruz County; Pacific Grove, Monterey County; and especially in the Santa Clara Valley north of

San Jose, Santa Clara County. Based on the current distribution of Pheasants, it is unclear whether viable populations really existed in all these areas. Pheasants may have been extirpated locally on the coast by changing agricultural practices rather than by inherently low fecundity. A hunting season was first opened in Inyo and Mono counties in 1925 and then statewide in 1933 (Hjersman 1947, Nelson & Hooper 1976, Mallette & Slosson 1987). By 1944, Pheasants had been planted in every county in the state except Alpine, and they had been persistently replanted in most of the seemingly "suitable" parts of the state (G&M 1944, Hjersman 1947). It appears that Pheasants never established themselves in Marin County (G&W 1927, S&P 1933, G&M 1944).

Although Pheasants were initially successful along certain sections of the coast, their most important populations there (in the Santa Clara Valley) declined in the early 1920s because of changing farm practices (Hjersman 1947). The heart of the state's Pheasant population switched to the Central Valley following the introduction of rice culture there during World War I. Nelson and Hooper (1976) and Mallette and Slosson (1987) reported that the state's Pheasant populations have declined in recent years from the advent of "clean farming" practices, which eliminate bordering weedy and brushy vegetation, and from the continued encroachment of urban-suburban sprawl. Although many naturalists might not mourn the decline of an alien species such as the Pheasant, it should be remembered that the Pheasant's demise would surely be paralleled by that of native species that also depend on the marginal refuges in large tracts of human-manipulated habitat. Breeding Bird Surveys, on the other hand, suggest that Pheasant numbers in California were relatively stable from 1968 to 1989 (USFWS unpubl. analyses).

Remarks

California birds were first obtained from China and Oregon (where they were first introduced in America in 1881; Bent 1932), but thereafter came largely from game farms (G&M 1944, Hjersman 1947). Although most California birds are of the race *P. c. torquatus*, other closely related races have been released, as well as crosses between some of them.

California Quail must be extremely vigilant if they are to raise all of their young to maturity. Drawing by Keith Hansen, 1989.

CALIFORNIA QUAIL *Callipepla californica*

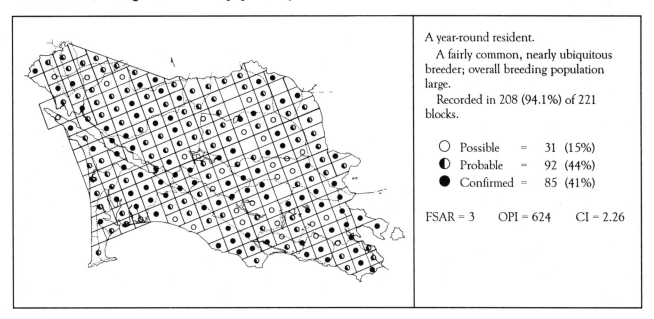

A year-round resident.

A fairly common, nearly ubiquitous breeder; overall breeding population large.

Recorded in 208 (94.1%) of 221 blocks.

○ Possible = 31 (15%)
◑ Probable = 92 (44%)
● Confirmed = 85 (41%)

FSAR = 3   OPI = 624   CI = 2.26

Ecological Requirements

From prominent lookouts, cocks stand sentry duty for wary coveys of "Valley Quail" before they break up into pairs in spring and scatter widely to breed. California Quail stick close to the brushy edges of, or openings in, all of Marin County's major scrub, woodland, and forest habitats where they border on pasturelands, weedy fields, meadows, and unkempt lawns and yards. In dense, extensive tracts of coastal scrub and chaparral, Quail frequent the edges or openings along trails, fireroads, localized burns, or other open disturbed sites. California Quail prefer edge situations with interspersed low protective cover, open-ground foraging areas, and water sources (Sumner 1935, Emlen & Glading 1945, Leopold 1977). Cover provides shade, shelter from inclement weather, and, perhaps most importantly, refuge from predators for adults and broods. Cover can consist of small or extensive patches of bushes, bramble and briar thickets, trees, thick clumps of weed stalks, rough outcrops of rock, or brush piles that are dense at ground level and impervious to penetration by avian predators. Such cover provides a daytime loafing area and a sanctuary for escape. At night, California Quail normally roost off the ground in dense evergreen trees or tall shrubs out of reach of ground predators and concealed from hungry owls. Quail foraging areas ideally provide a sparse to moderately dense growth of annual grasses and particularly forbs, with a duff or litter layer that harbors fallen seeds. California Quail generally forage within about 50 feet of escape cover. In dry areas in late summer and fall, they will venture several hundred yards into the open to forage until the arrival of the first migrant Cooper's Hawks,

when they again retract their foraging radius to the close proximity of cover. For much of the year, Quail can obtain water from succulent greenery, but in the hot and dry months of summer and early autumn, they usually need a dependable source of water close to cover, be it only a drip, seep, or puddle. This is less of a summertime problem along the fog-shrouded coastline. If hard pressed, Quail can live without drinking water, provided they have at hand heavy dew, berries, or succulent vegetation (Sumner 1935).

The absence of Mountain Quail in Marin County appears to be a fluke of geography, since suitable habitat is available here. They occur in coastal counties to the north and south and probably did not reach Marin because of habitat barriers to foot-powered dispersal. In coastal California, Mountain Quail inhabit coniferous forest with a shrubby understory, mixed evergreen forest, and chaparral. Although they overlap in habitat somewhat with California Quail, Mountains generally occur at higher elevations, on steeper slopes, and spend most of their time inside chaparral thickets or beneath the forest canopy (Gutiérrez 1980).

California Quail generally prefer nest sites that are in the open away from a continuous canopy of shrubs or trees (Leopold 1977). Early-season nest sites may be far from water when green vegetation is at a peak; even chicks can derive their water needs from succulent vegetation. Quail may avoid nesting close to streams (fenced or unfenced) or water troughs where overgrazing has destroyed nesting cover. With the diminution or disappearance of greenery

161

in midsummer, Quail must nest within about 400 yards (the cruising radius of chicks) from water (Sumner 1935, Leopold 1977). California Quail typically conceal their nests on the ground in dense clumps of grass or weeds, often sheltered at the base of bushes, fallen trees or limbs, vines, brush piles, or fencerows. Other nests are sheltered beneath overhanging rocks, in rock crannies, in niches in narrow gullies, or under piles of scrap lumber (Grinnell et al. 1918, Dawson 1923, Bent 1932, Glading 1938, Leopold 1977). The nest is usually a hollow in the ground lined sparsely with grasses, leaves, weed stems, and perhaps a few feathers; usually nests are roofed over, at least during the early part of incubation, by vegetation, or sometimes by overhanging rocks. Occasionally, birds build a crude but more substantial nest of the same materials on a log or stump, in a brush pile, on a bale of hay or the side of a haystack, or among vines on a trellis. Rarely, they place nests up in trees at the broken or decayed ends of limbs or at an intersection of two large branches. One pair nested in a garden on a rooftop. Exceptionally, these Quail may lay eggs in the nests of other birds on or above ground.

California Quail forage primarily on the ground by grazing on annual plants and by scratching in the soil and litter; occasionally, they jump to reach blossoms and climb into shrubbery. Mountain Quail also forage by these methods, jump for flowers and seeds more frequently, climb trees and shrubs to procure berries and fruits more readily, dig *beneath* the soil for bugs, and shell acorns (Gutiérrez 1980). Like other gallinaceous birds, both species pick up grit to grind seeds. California Quail generally forage mostly right after dawn and during a second burst of activity in the evening (Sumner 1935, Leopold 1977). In hot weather, they usually go to water daily and generally lead chicks to drink after the morning feeding bout and often at other times. During breeding, adults subsist on short rations: the male because of time spent defending against intruders, guarding the female and nest, and protecting the young; the female because of intermittent feeding during incubation and time spent tending the young. When Quail double brood, females desert their families after about three weeks to find new mates and nest again, leaving the original males to rear the first brood (Leopold 1977).

California Quail eat primarily forb seeds and green leafage, but also fruits, berries, buds, blossoms, catkins, acorn fragments, plant galls, and waste grain (Browning 1977, Leopold 1977, Grenfell et al. 1980). They consume about 1%-7% animal matter only in spring and early summer and more in wet than dry years. Animal foods include insects, millipedes, mites, spiders, snails, and sowbugs. The seeds of annual broadleaved forbs are a staple throughout the year and, along with minor amounts of grass seeds, constitute about 95% of the diet in summer, 90% in fall, 70% in winter, and over 55% in spring (Leopold 1977). In the Coast Ranges, bur clover is perhaps

the most important single food plant, though other legumes (various clovers, lotuses, and lupines) and filaree can be equally important locally. Other key seed-bearing forbs are fiddleneck, turkey mullein, geranium, vetch, various thistles, popcorn flower, chickweed, miners lettuce, red maids, buttercup, buckthorn weed, windmill pink, tarweeds, California poppy, vinegar weed, and gamble-weed (Browning 1977, Leopold 1977). Generally, the annual grasses that now dominate California's grasslands are *not* important Quail foods and in fact compete with and displace the more favored broadleaved annuals. Quail also browse extensively on green leafage, mostly of the seed-bearing annual forbs mentioned above. They regularly eat small amounts of green grasses but feed on them extensively only when the seeds and green foliage of forbs are scarce or absent. Consumption of greens begins with the appearance of new growth after the first fall rains (even in years of seed abundance), peaks in winter and spring, and generally ceases when annual plants die in late spring and summer and the new crop of seeds becomes available. Usage of greenery climbs from a low of about 2% in summer and 10% in fall to a peak of about 30%-44% in winter and 35%-40% in spring (Browning 1977, Leopold 1977). Use of greens in winter may vary between locations from as much as 75% to as little as 0%-3%. Acorn fragments can be an important component of the diet in fall or winter (as much as 35%) and even in spring, in some localities and in certain years (Browning 1977). In addition, Quail take limited amounts of the fruits of other woody perennials, such as poison oak, manzanita, ceanothus, mistletoe, acacia, and black locust. In summer and fall, Quail may eat some waste grains left after harvest, especially wheat, oats, barley, corn, or even rice, kafir, or safflower.

Quail chicks are born with a substantial residue of original egg yolk enclosed within the abdomen. This serves the vital function of tiding over the precocial young during the critical period when they are learning to feed, or during periods of rain or fog when foraging is difficult or impossible (Leopold 1977). Chicks a few days old live mostly on insects (Grenfell et al. 1980). At one site, chicks one to three weeks of age ate mostly seeds and only about 11% insects (n = 47) and at four to six weeks about 9% insects (n = 66); thereafter, insect consumption fell rapidly to a trace (Leopold 1977). Chicks start with small food items and, as they grow, graduate to larger ones (Sumner 1935, Grenfell et al. 1980).

Marin Breeding Distribution

The California Quail was one of the most widespread of Marin County's breeding birds, occurring in virtually every block during the atlas period. Quail were absent locally only on the tops of some of the higher ridges, such as the peak of Mount Tamalpais, and in a few areas without brushy cover. Representative breeding sites were Marshall (NE 6/15/76 –GJK); near Three Peaks (FL 6/17/82 –DS); and Pine Gulch Creek, Bolinas Lagoon (FL 6/14/80 –DS).

Historical Trends/Population Threats

Grinnell and Miller (1944) reported that the California Quail had declined in the state in the previous 35 years, though it was still numerous in favorable territory where not "shot out." Many authors attributed this decline primarily to intense market hunting (e.g., Grinnell et al. 1918). Settlers turned to Quail for food after the Gold Rush depleted supplies of edible large mammals (Leopold 1977). Quail hunting for the San Francisco market began in Marin County in the 1860s (Welch 1928). During the late 1880s and 1890s, millions of Quail were shot, trapped, and sold in California. In 1895-96, hunters sold 177,366 Quail in the open markets of San Francisco and Los Angeles alone. Because of decreases in the Quail population, laws were passed in 1880 that prohibited trapping and in 1901 that fixed a bag limit and outlawed the sale of Quail (Welch 1928, Leopold 1977). Bootleg operations continued to circumvent the laws, and by 1925 only a pitiful remnant of the state's bountiful supply of Quail remained.

Sumner (1935), on the other hand, concluded that the decline was due to a combination of overhunting and various other factors, such as "clean farming" practices, that eliminate cover and increase erosion, overgrazing, man's usurpation of water sources, fire control that promotes growth of impenetrable brush that chokes out Quail food, and poisons set out for rodents. Despite the depredations of hunters, Leopold (1977) felt that the decline in Quail numbers was mainly from a decrease in the production of Quail food caused by changing land use. He envisioned a population peak at the start of the market hunting era that was greater than in presettlement times. Quail numbers may have been increased at the time by the breaking up of native bunch grasses allowing the intrusion of seed-bearing forbs; by the planting of grains and hedgerows; and by the opening up of woods—factors that provided a mosaic of Quail habitat and, along with the virgin fertility of the soils, fueled increased production of preferred Quail foods. Leopold concluded that the subsequent decline in numbers was caused by the loss of soil fertility from intensive agriculture and overgrazing and by the invasion of alien annual grasses, which replaced the preferred Quail foods of native and introduced forbs. The trend toward large landholdings and mechanized agriculture has eliminated much cover, leading to further habitat deterioration. Although clearing and logging have opened up some habitat in certain areas of California, the overall trend here has been toward a reduction in the extent and quality of Quail habitat (Sumner 1935). Quail numbers were relatively stable on Breeding Bird Surveys in California from 1968 to 1989 (USFWS unpubl. analyses).

Rails, Gallinules, and Coots
Family *Rallidae*

BLACK RAIL *Laterallus jamaicensis*

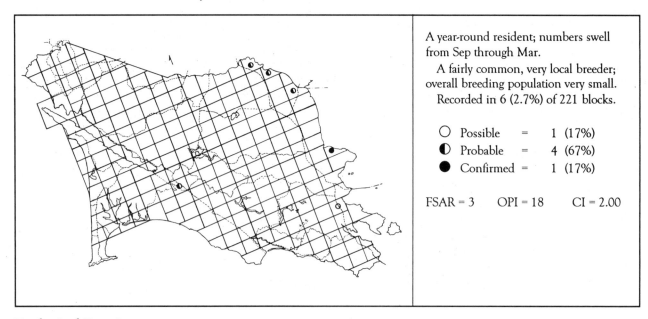

A year-round resident; numbers swell from Sep through Mar.

A fairly common, very local breeder; overall breeding population very small. Recorded in 6 (2.7%) of 221 blocks.

○	Possible	=	1 (17%)
◑	Probable	=	4 (67%)
●	Confirmed	=	1 (17%)

FSAR = 3   OPI = 18   CI = 2.00

Ecological Requirements

This furtive little rail inhabits tidal salt and brackish marshes and, to a lesser extent, freshwater marshes. Black Rails prefer areas of high marsh at the upper limit of tidal flooding with a dense cover, usually of pickleweed *(Salicornia virginica)* or sedges (*Scirpus* spp.) (Manolis 1978; Evens et al. 1989, 1991). The tidal marshes Black Rails inhabit in Marin County are either dominated by *Salicornia*, have a preponderance of *Salicornia* with *Scirpus* on the borders or in small patches within the *Salicornia* matrix, or are a mosaic of *Salicornia* and *Scirpus* (Evens et al. 1989). At Marin County's largest freshwater marsh, Olema Marsh, Black Rails have occurred in stands of cattail *(Typha)* or bulrush *(Scirpus)* that mix with other freshwater marsh or coastal swale plant species and border on willow or alder riparian forest (D. Shuford pers. obs.).

Black Rails are patchily distributed in tidal marshes. A suite of factors interact to determine the suitability of habitat, though no single factor or combination of factors is sufficient to predict Black Rail occurrence (Evens et al. 1989, 1991). The most important factors influencing Black Rail distribution are tidal regime, marsh elevation, and freshwater influence; marsh age (maturity) and size, degree of channelization, soil and water salinity, and plant

composition may also bear on rail habitat preferences (Evens et al. 1989, 1991). Black Rails are more numerous in marshes with unrestricted tidal flow than with restricted tidal flow; they are extremely rare in diked marshes. They inhabit the upper reaches of marshes where there is emergent vegetation at high tides and avoid marshes dominated by salt grass *(Distichlis spicata)*. The importance of a mix of tidal and freshwater influence is suggested by the concentration of Black Rails in the northern sections of the greater San Francisco Bay estuary where freshwater inflow is greatest. There Black Rails are most plentiful in large, broad tidal marshes bordering major rivers. In bayshore marshes, these rails are most numerous at the mouths of sloughs, creeks, and rivers, and at some *Salicornia*-dominated marshes rails cluster at clumps of *Scirpus*, indicators of freshwater influence (often from seeps). Ultimately, Black Rail habitat must provide cover, nest sites, and suitable food. Since predation by natural enemies such as Great Egrets, Great Blue Herons, and Northern Harriers can be severe (Evens & Page 1986), dense cover is important, especially during high tides. There is also speculation that Black Rails may avoid areas with large densities of Clapper Rails since the latter species may prey on small birds (JM *fide* JGE). To support Black Rails, marshes should grade gradually into weedy or brushy upland vegetation where the rails can retreat at extremely high tides.

Black Rails usually conceal their nests completely from view in the dense growth of *Salicornia*, grasses, sedges, or other marsh vegetation, which they also use to construct their nests; rarely, they leave them open to view from above (Bent 1926). They place most nests from one to several inches above the mud, but sometimes nests are built on the ground or up to 10 to 12 inches above ground. Nests vary greatly in structure from thin, frail platforms to, rarely, ground nests five inches thick; they may be flat or deeply cupped. Often the rails interweave surrounding vegetation over the nest to give it the appearance of a domed-over meadowlark nest with a side entrance. Thicker nests are usually built up from the ground, and thin ones are usually placed on convenient shelves of matted vegetation. Of six nests observed in the San Francisco Bay system, all were of the thin, raised type and lacked a dome of interwoven vegetation (J.G. Evens pers. comm.).

Because of their elusive nature, very little is known of the food habits of Black Rails (Wilbur 1974). Apparently they feed on insects or other arthropods (Bent 1926); presumably they pick or glean their meals from the muddy substrate or from the surface of marsh plants. Black Rail occurrence is positively associated with insect and spider abundance and negatively associated with amphipod abundance in marshes (Evens et al. 1986). It is unclear whether insects and spiders are a primary food source for Black Rails and whether these arthropods are more abundant in tidal marshes diluted by fresh water (Evens et al. 1989). What is clear is that much still needs to be learned of the habitat preferences and lifestyles of these secretive black gnomes.

Marin Breeding Distribution

In Marin County, Black Rails breed along the San Francisco and San Pablo bayshores from Corte Madera Marsh north to the Petaluma marshes, and on the outer coast, along the fringes of Bolinas Lagoon, at the south end of Tomales Bay, and, perhaps sporadically, at Olema Marsh. We recorded Black Rails in five atlas blocks on the bayside tidal marshes. The atlas work and subsequent more intensive rail censuses (Evens et al. 1986, 1989, 1991) revealed breeding Black Rails at Corte Madera Marsh, China Camp, Gallinas Creek, Novato Creek, Day Island, Black John Slough, the Petaluma marshes, in addition to the spots on the outer coast mentioned above. During the atlas period, breeding was confirmed only at China Camp. A nest was located at the upper edge of a salt marsh about eight inches above the mud in a patch of arrowgrass (*Triglochin* sp., presumably *T. maritima*) at a freshwater seep (NE 5/20/80 —ITa). In 1982, five additional nests were found in the same vicinity in *Salicornia*, again at the

upper edge of the marsh near freshwater seeps (ITa, JGE, GWP). Subsequently, during extensive surveys (Evens et al. 1986), Black Rails were confirmed breeding at Day Island near Novato with the observation of newly hatched chicks on 30 May 1986 (JGE) and at Black John Slough in the Petaluma marshes with the location of a nest with egg fragments on 8 May 1986 (GWP, NW). During the atlas period, we recorded Black Rails away from the bayside marshes only at Olema Marsh (up to four calling 6/17-7/30/80 —JGE, DS). Birds have not been recorded there since the early 1980s, perhaps because of extensive siltation during the intense flooding of 1982. Previously, breeding had been confirmed at a brackish marsh along Tomales Bay south of Inverness with the observation of an adult and chicks in the summer of 1976 (GB). A high count of seven calling birds was recorded at the south end of Tomales Bay on 16 May 1986 (JGE). A record of a bird calling on the west shore of Bolinas Lagoon on 10 and 11 March 1979 (RS et al.) may have been a breeder, a winter visitant, or a migrant. Probable evidence of breeding at Bolinas Lagoon is provided by records of one to two birds calling at the Pine Gulch Creek delta from 2 March to 20 May 1987 (DDeS, DAH) and one to two calling on the east shore on various dates from 29 March to 11 July, 1983 to 1986 (CCu et al.). Surveys at Schooner Bay, Drake's Estero, in spring 1986 and 1988 and at Richardson Bay in spring 1988 did not reveal any Black Rails (Evens et al. 1986, 1989).

Historical Trends/Population Threats

Until recently, the status of breeding Black Rails in northern California was clouded by the lack of adequate field work needed to detect such a secretive species. Early authorities had stated or implied that the species moved north to northern California in the fall after the breeding season (Bent 1926, AOU 1957). Incidental sightings from the late 1950s to the present (ABN) and, particularly, recent thorough surveys (Jurek 1976; Manolis 1978; Evens et al. 1989, 1991) have documented the occurrence of a substantial breeding population in tidal marshes around San Pablo and Suisun bays and smaller numbers in the Sacramento-San Joaquin Delta as far inland as Lodi, San Joaquin County. Kiff (1978) documented the first breeding record for northern California from the reidentification of an egg set collected on 10 April 1911 at Newark, Alameda County, in south San Francisco Bay, where today the species is a very rare or sporadic breeder. The greater San Francisco Bay estuary supports the bulk (80%) of the Black Rail population of the West, with the remainder along the lower Colorado River (<150 individuals); at the Salton Sea, canals, and lakes of the Salton Trough (<50 individuals); at Morro Bay; and at the Point Reyes sites described above (Evens et al. 1991).

Because tidal marshes in the San Francisco Bay system have been reduced by 60%–95% (Nichols & Wright 1971, Josselyn 1983), Black Rail populations there must also have declined drastically (Evens et al. 1989, 1991). Black Rails no longer breed in salt marshes on the California coast south of Morro Bay (Garrett & Dunn 1981, Unitt 1984). The California Black Rail *(L. j. coturniculus)* is currently listed as Threatened in California (CDFG 1991a) and is a Candidate (Category 2) for listing as federally Threatened or Endangered (USFWS 1991). Saltmarsh habitat was lost through diking, filling, and conversion to agricultural lands, salt ponds, and urban development. Because of its proximity to human habitation and agricultural land, high marsh habitat is most susceptible to conversion. Intensive alteration of high marsh habitat in south San Francisco Bay and apparent subsidence of remaining marshes may explain the near

absence of breeding Black Rails there (Manolis 1978; Evens et al. 1989, 1991). Most marsh habitat in the South Bay is completely flooded at high tide since remaining marsh abuts directly on salt pond dikes and roadways; formerly the marsh graded gradually into upland habitat. Further loss or degradation of marshes, possible rising sea level, and diversion of freshwater inflow to the North Bay potentially pose ongoing threats to Black Rail habitat (Evens et al. 1989, 1991). In addition, these rails face higher predation pressures from the lack of transitional upland vegetation in many marshes and possibly from introduced Norway rats, which are known to a be serious threat to Clapper Rail nests (Harvey 1980a). It is unknown whether toxic substances are affecting Black Rails, but there is increasing evidence of their effects on other birds in San Francisco Bay (Ohlendorf & Fleming 1988).

CLAPPER RAIL *Rallus longirostris*

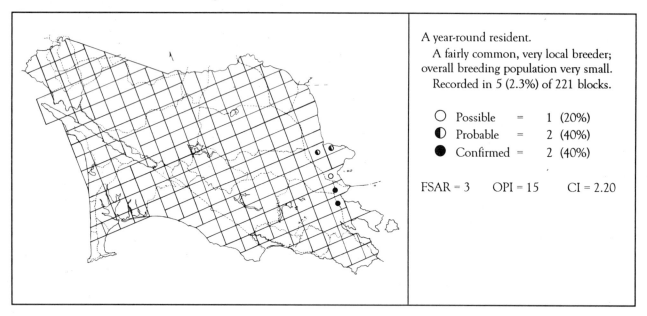

A year-round resident.
A fairly common, very local breeder; overall breeding population very small.
Recorded in 5 (2.3%) of 221 blocks.

○ Possible = 1 (20%)
◑ Probable = 2 (40%)
● Confirmed = 2 (40%)

FSAR = 3   OPI = 15   CI = 2.20

Ecological Requirements

California Clapper Rails *(Rallus longirostris obsoletus)* are at home in the ebb and flow of salt marshes intersected by numerous tidal channels. The vegetation of these marshes is usually dominated by cord grass *(Spartina foliosa)*, pickleweed *(Salicornia* spp.), and salt grass *(Distichlis)*; gumplant *(Grindelia)* provides important cover in some marshes (Gill 1979, Evens & Page 1984). During the breeding season, Clapper Rails also occupy brackish tidal marshes in those parts of south San Francisco, San Pablo, and Suisun bays that are dominated by bulrushes (*Scirpus* spp.)

and other low, salt-tolerant marsh plants (Gill 1979, Harvey 1980b). During the winter, Clapper Rails leave brackish marshes and contract into favored areas of *Spartina* salt marsh, further suggesting that brackish marshes may be suboptimal breeding habitat (P.R. Kelly pers. comm.). Their concentration in south San Francisco Bay (see below) also suggests they can tolerate higher salinities and a wider tidal range than Black Rails. Perhaps salinities and the degree of tidal inundation affect the distribution of these rails via vegetation structure and/or food resources.

Important factors for breeding Clapper Rails are (1) well-developed sloughs and secondary tidal channels; (2) extensive (dense, tall, lush) cord grass stands (though not all are used); (3) dense saltmarsh vegetation for cover, nest sites, and brooding areas; (4) intertidal mudflats, gradually sloping banks of tidal channels, and cord grass beds for foraging; (5) abundant invertebrate food resources; and (6) transitional vegetation at the upland edge of the salt marsh as a refuge during high tides (Evens & Page 1984, Harvey 1987, P.R. Kelly pers. comm.). These rails do occur where there are few stands of cord grass, as at Corte Madera Marsh in Marin County (J.G. Evens pers. comm.). At Corte Madera, the minimum channel size used by Clapper Rails averaged about 14 inches deep by 25 inches wide (Evens & Page 1983, n = 8). They avoid large channels that have undercut banks and small channels that are overgrown with vegetation. Clapper Rails may use all parts of the marsh during the year, but in winter, at least in the South Bay, they tend not to use extensive areas of pickleweed and instead concentrate then in cord grass in the lower marsh (P.R. Kelly pers. comm.). Unlike Black Rails, they are not restricted to high upper marsh for breeding. In Corte Madera Marsh, all nests found were in the upper marsh (J.G. Evens pers. comm.); in the South Bay, many nests are located in both the lower and higher marsh (Harvey 1980a).

Although there is much intersite variation in nest placement, Clapper Rails generally tend to locate their nests on raised ground near the tidal sloughs that intersect marshes (Harvey 1980a, 1987; Evens & Page 1984). Birds usually build their nests under the dense, sheltering vegetation of pickleweed, cord grass, gumplant, or salt grass; on occasion, or sometimes commonly (in the South Bay), they nest under a canopy of wrack or debris stranded on top of the marsh vegetation. At Corte Madera Marsh, 14 nests were under dense gumplant bushes on the elevated natural levees of tidal sloughs, and 3 late-season nests were under dense clumps of pickleweed (Evens & Page 1983). In the South Bay, nest concentrations vary from areas dominated by pickleweed and tidal wrack to those dominated by cord grass; nests are sheltered by pickleweed, cord grass, gumplant, salt grass, or tidal debris; and generally nests are associated with sloughs or the open bay edge (Harvey 1980a, 1987). Mean canopy height of nesting cover in the South Bay is 22 to 23 inches (Harvey 1980a). At Corte Madera Marsh, most nests are within 5 feet, and none were more than 10 feet, from a tidal channel (Evens & Page 1983, n = 17). In the South Bay, mean distances of nests to the nearest channel range from about 20 to 36 feet (Harvey 1980a, n = 50). Clapper Rails may prefer nesting in the cord grass zone of the lower marsh because nests there are better protected from terrestrial predators and because nests made of *Spartina* float during high tide. Variations in nest site distribution may reflect intersite

differences in plant succession and abundance, tidal gradients, or predation pressures. Nest placement may also vary seasonally (more use of wrack or gumplant early in the season before *Spartina* growth occurs) and yearly (more use of *Salicornia* nest sites in years of severe high tides).

Clapper Rails lay their eggs in the hollow of a bulky platform of dry cord grass, pickleweed, salt grass, or other marsh vegetation built up three to six inches above the sodden ground (Dawson 1923, Bent 1926, Harvey 1980a, Evens & Page 1984). Cord grass is the preferred nest material in the South Bay, perhaps because the hollow stems float and thus provide better protection for eggs during high tides (Harvey 1980a). Rails usually approach the nest site via a runway or tunnel through the matted vegetation (Dawson 1923). While one parent broods newly hatched chicks and incubates the remaining eggs, the other sometimes leads the first-hatched chicks up to 50 feet from the nest (Adams & Quay 1958). During their first few days, chicks are brooded almost continually either on the original nest, on brood nests, or on floating drift. In North Carolina, adults construct up to six brood nests of buoyant *Spartina* that float with the rising tide and provide dry places for refuge; brood nests there are like egg nests without canopies.

Clapper Rails forage mostly when tidal flats and channel banks are exposed. From within or near cover, they obtain food by probing and digging in the mud, picking from the surface, or rapidly seizing or chasing down more mobile prey. They often wash their food before eating it, peck open or dismember larger items before consuming them, and usually swallow small items whole (Williams 1929). The diet is predominantly invertebrates and small amounts of cord grass seeds. The main animal foods are ribbed mussels, clams, amphipods, shore crabs, spiders, along with occasional snails, nereid worms, and insects; minor items are small vertebrates, such as mice, fish, frogs, brush rabbits (probably carrion), and (for other races besides *obsoletus*) birds (Moffitt 1941, Evens & Page 1984). Stomach samples of 18 birds collected near Palo Alto, Santa Clara County, on 4 February 1939 were composed (by volume) of 85% animal matter and 14.5% cord grass seeds and hull fragments (Moffitt 1941). The summer diet may include more insects and less vegetable matter; vegetable foods at any season may be more important during tidal regimes where the mudflats are exposed for only limited periods. Parental care (including feeding of young) extends into the fifth or sixth week after hatching (Adams & Quay 1958).

Marin Breeding Distribution

In Marin County, breeding Clapper Rails are restricted to salt marshes along the shorelines of San Francisco and San Pablo bays. During the atlas period, Clapper Rails were confirmed breeding at Corte Madera Ecological Reserve,

Greenbrae (NE 3/25-6/30/82 —JGE, GWP). Other recent breeding records exist for Richardson Bay in 1972 (SFBCDC & Harvey 1983) and for Creekside Park along Corte Madera Creek, Greenbrae (FL 8/23/84 —HoP). Historical breeding records exist for Manzanita in 1930 and near Greenbrae in 1931 (Gill 1979). Other sightings for Marin are from Muzzi Marsh, Triangle Marsh, and San Clemente Creek, Corte Madera; Tiscornia Marsh, San Rafael; from the mouth of San Rafael Creek upstream approximately 0.6 miles; China Camp SP; Santa Venetia marshes; Las Gallinas Creek to the mouth of Novato Creek; Novato Creek upstream to 1.2 miles north of Hwy. 37; Day Island; and Black John Slough (Evens & Page 1984, J.G. Evens pers. comm.).

Gill (1979) estimated that for the period 1971 to 1975, the average yearly population in Marin was 153 birds (range 102-204), though his estimates for the entire San Francisco Bay system at that time were probably much too high (see below). Page and Evens (1987) estimated a population of about 40 birds at Corte Madera Ecological Reserve in both 1982 and 1987. Estimates from censuses at other Corte Madera marshes in 1987 were 15 birds at Muzzi Marsh, 3 birds at San Clemente Creek, and 1 bird at Triangle Marsh. The 59 birds inhabiting the Corte Madera marshes represents an unknown portion of the entire Marin population. Because of continuing dramatic declines in the South Bay and threats to the entire San Francisco Bay system population (see below), periodic censuses should be made of *all* Clapper Rail habitat in Marin County. With these declines, the Corte Madera and Gallinas Creek populations, in particular, are taking on increasing importance to the California Clapper Rail population as a whole (P.R. Kelly pers. comm.).

Historical Trends/Population Threats

The California Clapper Rail was formerly a resident of coastal salt marshes from Humboldt Bay south to Morro Bay, with the greatest population in San Francisco Bay (G&M 1944, Gill 1979, Evens & Page 1984). Populations have declined drastically since the late nineteenth century. The California Clapper Rail is now restricted to San Francisco, San Pablo, and Suisun bays and is listed as Endangered by both state (CDFG 1991a) and federal governments (USFWS 1989a). Although formerly recorded in Marin County at Tomales Bay, it is unclear if it ever bred there (Evens & Page 1984, Shuford et al. 1989). Intensive rail surveys from 1984 to 1986 at the south end of Tomales Bay failed to reveal any birds (JGE, GWP). Marin populations along San Francisco and San Pablo bayshores have surely declined over historical levels.

Gill (1979) estimated that 4200 to 6000 birds inhabited greater San Francisco Bay, with 55% of the population in the South Bay and 38% in the Napa Marsh. Logistical restraints limited Gill's ability to census many of the bay's

marshes, and his use of extrapolations probably greatly overestimated the size of the population (Harvey 1987, P.R. Kelly pers. comm.). Based on more thorough high-tide censuses in winter, the population of the entire San Francisco Bay system from the time of Gill's work up until about 1985 was about 700 Clapper Rails, with approximately 90% in the South Bay (P.R. Kelly pers. comm.). As of the winters of 1988-89 and 1989-90, the population had declined dramatically to under 500 birds, apparently mostly because of predation by introduced red foxes that appeared in South Bay marshes by at least 1983 (P.R. Kelly pers. comm.). Winter censuses in 1990-91 revealed continuing declines that leave only 300 to 400 rails still inhabiting the Bay (P.R. Kelly pers. comm.). Surely historical numbers greatly exceeded these recent population estimates.

Gill (1979) speculated that Clapper Rails had colonized the Napa Marsh in numbers since the 1930s because of increasing salinity there from reduced freshwater inflow into the Bay. The lack of many Clapper Rail sightings in the Napa Marsh before 1940 parallels the absence of records of breeding Black Rails in San Pablo Bay prior to the late 1950s. This is probably from very limited observer coverage in these areas rather than recent dramatic changes in these populations, which is further supported by the small numbers of Clapper Rails found in the Napa Marsh in the 1980s (P.R. Kelly pers. comm.). Gill (1979) suggested that local population fluctuations were from changes in production and biomass of *Spartina*—in dry years, populations were reduced because of increasing intraspecific competition for nesting territories. Greater use of *Salicornia* for nest sites in the South Bay in recent years, perhaps because of successional changes in marshes, suggest other factors may be responsible for population fluctuations (Harvey 1980a).

After, and in concert with, initial reductions from market hunting (Grinnell et al. 1918), habitat loss has been the primary cause of decline and failure to return to historical levels (Gill 1979, Evens & Page 1984). Gill (1979) summarized data on market hunting in the South Bay around the turn of the century. At that time, it was not uncommon for individual hunters to kill 30 to 50 rails a day. One newspaper account referred to 5000 rails killed in a one-week period alone in 1897—ten times today's total population in greater San Francisco Bay! Outcries led to passage of protective laws in 1913, and numbers began to rebound with recolonization of areas of local extirpation (G&M 1944). This population resurgence was short lived. Steady habitat destruction from human development has resulted in a loss of 60%-95% of the former saltmarsh habitat around the San Francisco Bay estuary (Nichols & Wright 1971, Josselyn 1983) and about 90% around Humboldt Bay (MacDonald 1977). Clapper Rails face a host of problems, including further habitat loss and degradation from human encroachment as summarized for the Black Rail (see account). Additional threats are recent losses of potential habitat formerly suitable for restoration, an increase in brackish marsh at the expense of salt marsh in the South Bay from dramatic increases in sewage outfall since the early 1970s, and the introduction of red foxes as noted above (Harvey 1983, 1987; P.R. Kelly pers. comm.). Restoration of large tracts of former salt marsh offers the best hope for offsetting other immediate threats.

VIRGINIA RAIL *Rallus limicola*

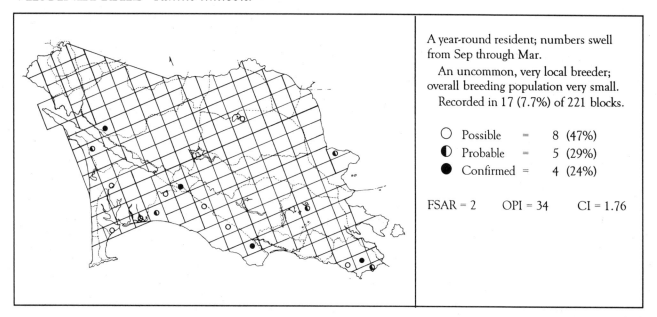

A year-round resident; numbers swell from Sep through Mar.

An uncommon, very local breeder; overall breeding population very small. Recorded in 17 (7.7%) of 221 blocks.

○ Possible = 8 (47%)
◑ Probable = 5 (29%)
● Confirmed = 4 (24%)

FSAR = 2   OPI = 34   CI = 1.76

Ecological Requirements

Eerie cackling or hiccupping calls betray the presence of Virginia Rails in their Marin County breeding haunts of freshwater marshes, coastal swales, wet meadows, and, perhaps, brackish marshes. In the winter, some Virginias disperse to tidal salt marshes, which they shun during the breeding season here, but not in some other parts of the range (Zimmerman 1977). Important needs of breeding birds are shallow standing water; dense marsh vegetation for cover, nest sites, and brooding areas; and a suitable supply of invertebrate food. Virginia Rails overlap considerably in habitat preference with Soras. Virginias are more widespread here and appear to have less stringent nesting requirements, though the differences in habitat needs between the two species are not easily explained. In Colorado, both Virginia Rails and Soras prefer breeding marshes with water less than 6 inches in depth (Griese et al. 1980). In Missouri, migrant Virginias, at least, inhabit areas of marsh with shallower water than Soras, though both species prefer similar vegetation density and height (Sayre & Rundle 1984). Migrant Virginias in Missouri prefer saturated to shallowly flooded sites less than 2 inches deep and are usually flushed near the interface of standing water and soil; Soras prefer water depths from 2 to 6 inches but use saturated sites more often than those with 18 inches of water. In Iowa, breeding Virginia Rails and Soras show little evidence of distinct niche segregation. Soras there are most numerous at nearshore sites with relatively shallow water, diverse vegetation, and many seed-producing plants, while Virginias are more evenly distributed across various marsh types (Johnson & Dinsmore 1986). Marsh areas with floating residual plants may be important to Soras because such cover provides good substrate for invertebrates that are kept near the surface within reach of these short-billed rails. The availability of preferred foods and the species' ability to exploit them, as reflected by bill shape, may be more important than water depth per se in explaining the difference in habitat preferences of these two species.

Virginia Rails conceal their nests in dense marsh vegetation where they usually suspend them in, and intertwine them with, emergent plant stalks (Townsend 1926, Walkinshaw 1937). Water depths around nest sites at the beginning of incubation range from about 3 to 10 inches (Walkinshaw 1937, Berger 1951, Zimmerman 1977, Griese et al. 1980). Sometimes Virginias build nests from the ground up that may reach seven or eight inches in height

(Townsend 1926). Glahn (1974) reported that Virginias locate most of their nests within tall vegetation near discontinuities with shorter vegetation, water, or mud along territory boundaries. Virginia Rails usually build their shallow platform nests from pieces of coarse rushes, sedges, or grasses and line them with finer materials of the same types (Townsend 1926, Walkinshaw 1937). When the vegetation allows, the nest is usually arched over with a canopy of rushes and sedges. Birds approach their nests via a sloping runway. At the first sign of rising water, these rails add material to raise the eggs above harm's way. The eggs hatch asynchronously, and one parent leads the first chicks away from the nest while the other continues to incubate the remaining eggs. Young feed with parental assistance the first day but are self-sufficient foragers by the end of the first week of life (Zimmerman 1977).

Virginia Rails use their slender curved beaks to probe and, presumably, to peck and glean for food along the muddy interface of standing water and marsh vegetation and in openings between plants. Breeding birds in Iowa consume 84.6% animal matter and 15.4% vegetable fare (Horak 1970, n = 37). Continentwide, the diet ranges from 97% animal matter in summer (n = 20) to 68% in fall (n = 69) (Martin et al. 1951). Animal matter is predominantly insects, along with spiders, snails, crayfish, bryozoans, slugs, small fish, frogs, and small snakes (Townsend 1926, Martin et al. 1951, Horak 1970). Seeds of marsh plants and duckweed are important plant foods.

Marin Breeding Distribution

Virginia Rails are patchily distributed in Marin County, reflecting the availability of suitable marshes, found mostly near the outer coast. Representative nesting sites were Olema Marsh (FL 5/1/80 —DS) and Cypress Grove, near Marshall, Tomales Bay (FL 5/23 & 6/6/78 —FMa, BTy).

Historical Trends/Population Threats

Grinnell and Miller (1944) noted a decline in Virginia Rail numbers in California from habitat loss. Subsequently, numbers must have continued to decline for the same reason. Because of its proximity to human endeavors, freshwater marsh habitat must have decreased to an even greater degree than tidal marsh habitat, which has been reduced in the San Francisco Bay system by 60%–95% from historical levels (Nichols & Wright 1971, Josselyn 1983).

SORA *Porzana carolina*

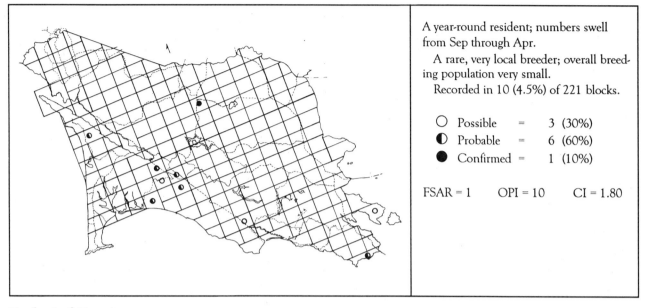

A year-round resident; numbers swell
from Sep through Apr.
  A rare, very local breeder; overall breeding population very small.
  Recorded in 10 (4.5%) of 221 blocks.

○	Possible	=	3 (30%)
◑	Probable	=	6 (60%)
●	Confirmed	=	1 (10%)

FSAR = 1   OPI = 10   CI = 1.80

Ecological Requirements

The Sora is another shadowy recluse of the moist soils and
shallow waters of freshwater marshes, coastal swales, wet
meadows, and, perhaps, brackish marshes. Some Soras
disperse to winter in tidal salt marshes, from which they
are absent during the breeding season. Important needs of
breeding birds are standing fresh water; dense marsh
vegetation for cover, nest sites, and brooding areas; and a
suitable supply of seeds and invertebrate foods. Differences
in habitat preferences between Soras and Virginia Rails are
subtle, though Soras are less widespread here and appear
to have more stringent requirements (see Virginia Rail
account).

Soras usually nest in dense marsh vegetation and, occasionally, in somewhat open surroundings. Whether in tall
or short vegetation, Soras tend to locate their nests near
discontinuities with vegetational borders, water, or mud
along territory boundaries (Walkinshaw 1940, Glahn
1974). They build nest platforms or well-built baskets of
rushes, sedges, or grasses raised up from the marsh floor
or suspended and interwoven with surrounding vegetation
(Bent 1926, Walkinshaw 1940). Nests are lined with finer
marsh vegetation and are usually more or less concealed
with an arched-over canopy of grasses, reeds, or cattails.
There is often a slanting runway of nest materials leading
to and from the nest. Nests are generally raised an average
of about three to seven inches above the water (Bent 1926;
Walkinshaw 1937, 1940; Berger 1951; Griese et al. 1980).
Birds usually complete the nest after they start laying and
will add materials to raise the nest when water levels rise

(Walkinshaw 1940). Eggs hatch asynchronously and one
parent leads the first chicks away while the other incubates
the remaining eggs.

With their stubby bills, Soras pick or glean from the
marsh substrate or water's surface and strip seed heads
from marsh plants (Bent 1926, Walkinshaw 1940, Sayre
& Rundle 1984). Breeding birds in Iowa consume 80.8%
vegetable matter, mostly the seeds of aquatic plants (Horak
1970, n = 19). Continentwide the diet ranges from 60%
(n = 109) animal matter in spring and summer to 31%-
32% (n = 223) animal matter in fall and winter (Martin et
al. 1951). In Missouri, spring and fall migrants consumed
63% (n = 18) and 82.5% (n = 20) vegetable matter, respectively, with sedge seeds predominant in spring and grass
seeds in fall (Rundle & Sayre 1983). In Connecticut, the
fall diet was 98% seeds in freshwater marshes and 91%
insects in brackish marshes (Webster 1964 *fide* Odum
1977). Animal foods are various aquatic insects, snails,
crustaceans, and small tadpoles or fish (Bent 1926, Martin
et al. 1951, Horak 1970, Odum 1977).

Marin Breeding Distribution

During the atlas period, Soras were found breeding at only
scattered sites in Marin County. Their distribution was
similar to, but more restricted than, that of Virginia Rails.
Most Soras were found on the outer coast. Nevertheless,
the only confirmed breeding record was of a nest (with ten
eggs) on the marshy edge of a fish-breeding pond inland in
Hicks Valley from 1 to 21 May 1982 (ScC, ITa).

171

Historical Trends/Population Threats

Grinnell and Miller (1944) reported no change in the aggregate numbers of Soras in California except as caused by reclamation of marshes, which up to that time and since must have been great (see Virginia Rail account).

COMMON MOORHEN *Gallinula chloropus*

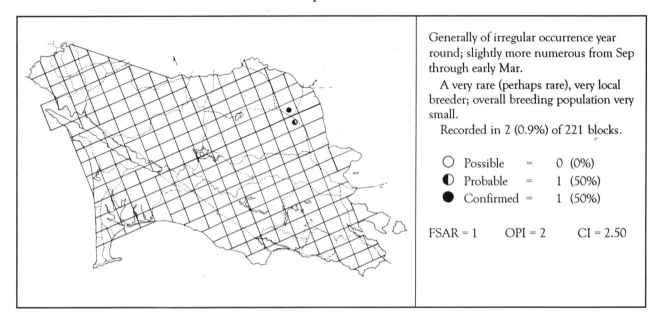

Generally of irregular occurrence year round; slightly more numerous from Sep through early Mar.

A very rare (perhaps rare), very local breeder; overall breeding population very small.

Recorded in 2 (0.9%) of 221 blocks.

○	Possible	=	0	(0%)
◑	Probable	=	1	(50%)
●	Confirmed	=	1	(50%)

FSAR = 1   OPI = 2   CI = 2.50

Ecological Requirements

In both appearance and habits, the Common Moorhen bridges the gap between our typical small rails and their cousin the American Coot. In Marin County, breeding Moorhens inhabit freshwater marshes with some open water, natural or artificial ponds, and drainage or irrigation ditches, though lakes or slow-flowing streams edged with emergent vegetation suffice elsewhere in California. The main breeding requirements seem to be robust emergent vegetation for cover, nest sites, and brood rearing; some open standing or slow-moving fresh water; and an adequate food supply. Moorhens typically use deeper-water marshes and prefer centrally placed emergents rather than the bordering vegetation of shallow-water marshes used by Virginia Rails and Soras (Weller & Fredrickson 1973, Byrd & Zeillemaker 1981). Moorhens keep more to cover and less to open water than do Coots.

In marshes of variable water depth, Moorhens select nest sites in areas of deeper water (Byrd & Zeillemaker 1981). In the managed shallow water of irrigated taro fields in Hawaii, Moorhens choose nest sites where the water depth averages 2.6 inches; elsewhere in the breeding range, they may nest over waters 1 to 6.5 feet deep. Moorhens

usually attach their nests to emergent or broken-down aquatic vegetation; nests range from near floating up to six inches, or, rarely, two or three feet above water (Dawson 1923, Bent 1926, Fredrickson 1971, Strohmeyer 1977, Roselaar 1980, Byrd & Zeillemaker 1981). They may build more nests than they use for egg laying (Bent 1926). Less frequently used nest sites include among scattered submerged bushes; under weeds on a floating island; on mobile, semisubmerged logs; high on a mass of cattails tangled by the wind; on top of a dead stump two feet from the water and surrounded by willows; on banks amid thick tangles of briars, grasses, and vines within a few feet of water; and in a low crotch of a bush near water (Bent 1926). Birds usually conceal their nests within stands of vegetation and only rarely nest in exposed situations. In Iowa, nests averaged 11 feet (range 0–59 ft.) from an edge of vegetative change or water and 15 feet (range 7–92 ft.) from open water (Fredrickson 1971); easy access to open water is probably important.

Moorhens build their shallow nest baskets from the dead leaves and stalks of cattails, bulrushes, grasses, or other coarse aquatic plants. They may preferentially select for nest building certain plants among those available (Byrd & Zeillemaker 1981). Often the nest is screened from above by a canopy of aquatic plants. It usually has an inclined runway of nest material used to leave or enter the nest (Bent 1926). Nest building continues through egg laying and incubation, and birds will add additional nest material to raise the nest above rising water (Bent 1926, Fredrickson 1971). The first clutch normally hatches synchronously; replacement and second clutches hatch asynchronously (Roselaar 1980). Within hours after hatching, the young are fed by the parents (Fredrickson 1971). Moorhens brood their young on brood platforms (with ramps) they build or on platforms built by Coots or muskrats. One adult brings food to the brooding mate, which transfers it to the young. Groups of Moorhens occasionally contain two adults along with both downy and nearly fledged young (Roselaar 1980, Byrd & Zeillemaker 1981). The older chicks of these "multiple brood family units" will sometimes feed and brood younger chicks, incubate eggs if the pair has not yet hatched the second clutch, and make nest repairs.

These aquatic rails feed while swimming, walking on floating vegetation, or walking on land, nodding their heads and perking their tails as they go (Dawson 1923, Bent 1926, Roselaar 1980). They obtain food by dipping the head underwater, by surface picking or sifting, and, rarely, by diving. Birds also up-end and snatch food from other birds. In addition, they pick food items off the ground and off plants, often by clambering over leaves and balancing on stems by flapping their wings. Moorhens often feed in dense cover, threading their way through the reeds, and also range onto grass on the dry borders of marshes, though seldom beyond easy reach of cover. The diet is omnivorous, with varying proportions of plant and animal matter; little quantitative work has been done, so changes in diet with season and locality are unknown (Bent 1926, Roselaar 1980). Animal matter in the diet consists of snails and other small mollusks, adult and larval insects, spiders and harvestmen, earthworms, amphibian tadpoles, and, rarely, small fish. Moorhens also eat carrion and birds' eggs up to those of Mallards' in size. Vegetable foods include the seeds, roots, and soft parts of succulent aquatic plants, and berries and fruits. Birds also feed on vegetable peelings and scraps. Initially, parents apparently feed chicks mostly aquatic insects, such as dragonfly and mayfly nymphs (Fredrickson 1971).

Marin Breeding Distribution

During the atlas period, Moorhens were recorded in the breeding season in small marshes in only two atlas blocks near Novato. Breeding was confirmed at a pond off Highway 37 with the presence of adults with small young on 2 June 1977 (RMS). There is a prior breeding record from Olema Marsh (FL 8/31/67 —CJR) and more recent ones from the Bolinas sewage ponds (FL 7/12/83 —JGE) and from a pond near Rush Creek, Novato (FL 7/21/84 —HoP). See Shuford et al. (1989) for additional records suggestive of breeding elsewhere on Point Reyes.

Historical Trends/Population Threats

Earlier avifaunal accounts lacked records of Moorhens breeding in Marin County (G&W 1927, S&P 1933) or, for that matter, along the coast north of the Golden Gate (G&M 1944). The recent breeding records in Marin County probably reflect greater observer coverage rather than any recent expansion of the breeding range. Grinnell and Miller (1944) felt that numbers had declined because of habitat loss, which was offset somewhat by the development of irrigation. Continued destruction of marshland since that time has surely reduced numbers substantially (see other rail accounts). Numbers of Common Moorhens were relatively stable on Breeding Bird Surveys in California from 1968 to 1989, a period after most habitat destruction had occurred, though numbers increased from 1980 to 1989 (USFWS unpubl. analyses).

AMERICAN COOT *Fulica americana*

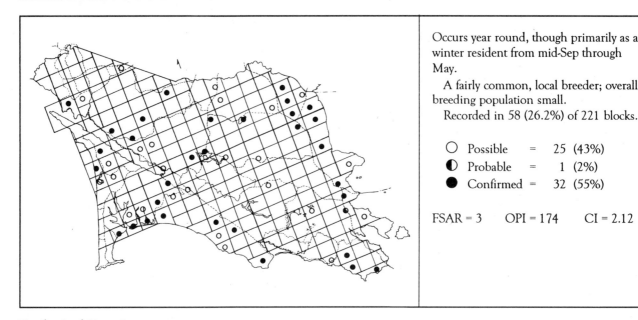

Occurs year round, though primarily as a winter resident from mid-Sep through May.

A fairly common, local breeder; overall breeding population small.

Recorded in 58 (26.2%) of 221 blocks.

○ Possible   =   25 (43%)
◑ Probable   =   1 (2%)
● Confirmed   =   32 (55%)

FSAR = 3   OPI = 174   CI = 2.12

Ecological Requirements

The "Mud-hen," though of humble mien, is perhaps our most adaptable nesting waterbird. Breeding Coots inhabit Marin County's freshwater ponds, lakes, reservoirs, marshes, sewage ponds, and irrigation channels. Prime breeding habitat has a good mix of open water and dense emergent vegetation, particularly tules or cattails. Robust emergents provide nest sites, nest materials, and cover for adults and broods; open water provides foraging habitat. Coots will nest where open water is patchily or continuously edged with emergent vegetation, but in Iowa, at least, Coots reach highest densities where there is a 50:50 mix of open water and emergent cover (Weller & Fredrickson 1973). Coots tend to occupy microhabitats with shallower water than do Pied-billed Grebes (Nudd 1982).

In the San Francisco Bay Area, breeding Coots build from seven to nine structures associated with nesting—including display platforms, egg nests, and brood nests (Gullion 1954). Elsewhere, Coots build fewer structures (except egg nests) when naturally occurring platforms, such as those built by muskrats, are available (Fredrickson 1970). Display platforms are composed of coarse cattail stems and leaves and are built on a foundation such as a floating board or stick or a heap of broken-down cattails (Gullion 1954). Display platforms are usually thoroughly water soaked and after the copulation period are allowed to disintegrate, though up to that point nonincubating birds may use them as roost sites. Egg nests are shallow baskets, usually with a floating foundation, attached to emergent vegetation over various depths of water (Bent 1926, Gullion 1954, Fredrickson 1970, Fredrickson et al.

1977). Most nests are partially or well hidden in emergent vegetation, though sometimes they are in plain sight at the edge of vegetation, in an isolated clump, or in an entirely open situation without concealment. Usually overhead cover is naturally provided. Coots do not build canopies above the nest (Gullion 1954). In the Bay Area, all structures are located close (usually 2 to 3 ft., or a maximum of 4 ft.) to open water. Throughout the range, exceptional nest sites are on dry ground; two feet above ground on a platform of dead cattails; and four feet above ground in the lower branches of an apple tree following receding floodwaters (Bent 1926). These odd records suggest nests were built at times of unusual water conditions (Gullion 1954). Coots often build more than one nest structure before finally selecting one in which to lay the eggs (Gullion 1954). Coots usually build their nests—starting with coarse materials and progressively adding finer materials—from dry or green stems and leaves of cattails or other marsh plants; they sometimes also use willow leaves and small sticks. The cup is composed of fine dry leaves. Coots enter and leave the nest via a ramp of coarse stems laid lengthwise and incorporated into the side of the nest. They may begin laying eggs while the nest is still under construction but finish the nest and line it before the clutch is complete (Bent 1926, Gullion 1954). Since egg nests are actually elaborate rafts, Coots must constantly add material to them to keep them from settling below the surface (Gullion 1954). Pairs of Coots may either build new egg nests or reuse display platforms or brood nests used previously by them or other pairs. When the eggs hatch, Coots usually construct a new, larger brood nest, or convert an egg nest to a brood nest. Brood nests frequently lack a cup, or, if present, it is usually obscured in the restructuring process. Brood nests are distinguished from egg nests by the wet materials worked into the final lining and by the presence of feces in and about the nest.

Since eggs hatch asynchronously, one parent takes over the major share of incubation while the other seeks food for the young already hatched (Gullion 1954). Initially one adult collects food and presents it to the incubating bird, which in turn feeds the chicks (Fredrickson 1970). Usually the male incubates during this period and also broods the young not feeding with the female (Gullion 1954). The female returns frequently to the nest with food. Two- and three-day-old chicks leave the nest, swim out to be fed by the female, then return to the nest and the protection of the incubating male. Three or four days after hatching, the female broods the older, more active young at night on the brood nest while the male incubates the remaining eggs and the newly hatched young on the egg nest. When a sufficient number (about eight) of young have hatched, both parents turn their attention to the care of the young and either desert the remaining eggs or dump them out of the nest. At about five days of age, the young begin to spend most of the day following their parents on foraging excursions in the emergent vegetation and later in open water. At dusk, when broods move to platforms, the male appears to assume the responsibility of caring for most young (Fredrickson 1970).

Coots obtain their food by dabbling and grazing from or near the surface of the water, by grazing or picking items from the surface of moist or dry land along or well back from the shore, and by diving to moderate depths (Bent 1926). While swimming or walking, they nod their heads in rhythm to their foot movements. Coots clip off green grasses in meadows, pastures, or lawns and sometimes grain (particularly rice) in cultivated land. They also steal some aquatic plant food from ducks and eat grain set out to attract ducks. Continentwide, the annual diet is about 89.4% plant matter and 10.6% animal matter and varies little by region (Jones 1940, n = 792). Plant foods make up about 98% of the diet in fall and winter (n = 658), 84% in spring (n = 82), and 56% in summer (n = 36) (Martin et al. 1951). Coots prefer the foliage, stems, fleshy rootstalks, and, secondarily, seeds of a wide variety of marsh and aquatic plants, especially pondweeds, sedges, algae, and grasses (Jones 1940, Martin et al. 1951). The main animal foods are insects (especially beetles, true bugs, and dragonfly and damselfly larvae and nymphs), mussels, and snails; infrequent items are spiders, crustaceans, and, rarely, small fish and amphibians. Initially, the young are fed exclusively animal matter, mostly in the form of aquatic insect larvae of dragonflies and damselflies; by the time they are eight days old, young Coots consume considerable quantities of vegetable food (Gullion 1954).

Marin Breeding Distribution

During the atlas period, Coots bred widely, though patchily, throughout the lowlands of Marin County. They were somewhat more prevalent breeders on the outer coast and along the San Pablo and San Francisco bayshores. Representative nesting locations were Olema Valley (FL 6/11/82 –BiL); Bolinas sewage ponds (FL 5/5/80 –DS); pond at ocean end of Tennessee Valley (FL 9/11/82 –DS); Hicks Valley (FL 6/21/82 –DS); and McGinnis Park, San Rafael (FL 6/3/80 –DS).

Historical Trends/Population Threats

Grinnell and Miller (1944) reported that Coot numbers had held up over the years, but historically they must have declined dramatically with the drainage of most of the state's wetlands. Marin County has few natural lakes and ponds, so Coot numbers may have increased here over the years because of the impoundment of water in municipal reservoirs, stock ponds, and sewage ponds. On the other hand, some marshes have been drained; others, such as Olema Marsh, have been lost to Coots as they have choked with emergent vegetation from poor drainage, apparently caused by road building and diking. Numbers of Coots wintering on Pt. Reyes have declined since 1976, apparently because of two periods of widespread drought in California (Shuford et al. 1989). On the whole, Coot numbers were relatively stable on Breeding Bird Surveys in California from 1968 to 1989 (USFWS unpubl. analyses), a period after most habitat loss had occurred. Numbers decreased from 1980 to 1989 (USFWS unpubl. analyses), perhaps because much habitat dried up during the three years of drought at the end of that period.

Plovers
Family *Charadriidae*

SNOWY PLOVER   *Charadrius alexandrinus*

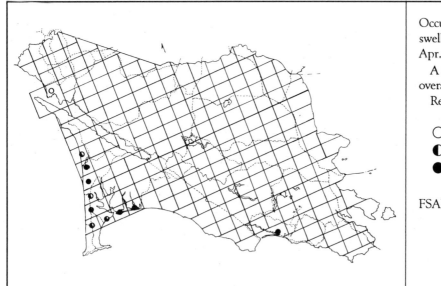

Occurs year round, though numbers swell considerably from Jul through early Apr.

A fairly common, very local breeder; overall breeding population very small. Recorded in 11 (5.0%) of 221 blocks.

○	Possible	=	1	(9%)
◐	Probable	=	4	(36%)
●	Confirmed	=	6	(55%)

FSAR = 3   OPI = 33   CI = 2.45

Ecological Requirements

An illusory movement is all that betrays a tiny sand-colored plover as it stealthily slips off its nest amid coastal dunes. On the mainland California coast, Snowy Plovers scatter widely to breed on sandspits, dune-backed beaches, lagoon and estuarine margins, around salt evaporators, and on small pocket beaches (Stenzel et al. 1981). Sandspits and bars, with their low topographic relief of well-developed hummocks and dunes, separate the ocean from coastal wetlands. Bordering wetlands enhance the spits as plover habitat. They provide tidal flats and other barren open areas in marshes that afford alternate, often productive, feeding areas and also refuge from human disturbance on the beaches. Frequent plover movements between beaches, tidal flats, and salt pans illustrate the attractiveness of a suite of favorable habitats close at hand. Dune-backed beaches are usually interrupted by rivers, creeks, ponds, lagoons, or salt pans, and the sections of these beaches that abut such wetlands hold disproportionate numbers of nesting plovers relative to the availability of the habitat. In Marin County, Snowy Plovers nest primarily on spits or on dune-backed beaches, but also on the margins of Abbott's Lagoon and occasionally on bluff-backed beaches (i.e., south end of Pt. Reyes Beach). Elsewhere on the coast,

plovers also nest in or on the margins of estuaries and lagoons, in naturally open or disturbed areas, such as salt pans in salt marshes or bay fill. At a few sites, plovers breed commonly at commercial or abandoned salt evaporators, where they nest on low dikes separating evaporator ponds and on the floors of dried ponds. Only small numbers of plovers nest at the mouths of coastal creeks and lagoons— on small pocket beaches that are set off by high bluffs or rocky points and usually lacking in dunes or hummocks.

Snowies prefer to nest in flat or gently undulating open areas devoid of, or sparsely covered with, low-growing vegetation, driftwood, or other debris (Stenzel & Peaslee 1979, Stenzel et al. 1981). In coastal areas, these may include sand beaches; sand flats among the dunes; salt or alkali flats in marshes, on lagoon or estuarine margins, or in evaporator ponds; low, unvegetated dikes; or, rarely, wind-eroded sandy bluffs or sandy dredge islands (Stenzel et al. 1981, D. Shuford pers. obs.). Coastal nest sites are usually within 100 yards of water but occasionally, when there is not a formidable barrier between the nest and water, are several hundred yards away from it (Stenzel et al. 1981). Openness of nesting habitat seems a key require-ment—for visual security from predators while the birds are

176

incubating eggs, for foraging, and for leading plover chicks from nesting sites down to shoreline foraging areas. For breeding, Snowies eschew beach areas that are heavily littered with driftwood, are back in dunes with steep dune faces perpendicular to the shoreline, or where there is moderate to dense vegetation, since any of these hinder movement of chicks to low-lying foraging grounds. Snowies also avoid breeding in areas very heavily used by humans.

During courtship, a male uses his belly and feet to make a series of shallow nest scrapes in soft substrate, only one of which the female selects for egg laying (Page et al. 1985). The nest scape may or may not be lined with bits of broken shell, fish bones, small stones, salt crystals, bits of wood, or other debris (Bent 1929, D. Shuford pers. obs.). Snowies typically continue to add nest material to the scrape throughout incubation (G.W. Page pers. comm.). They often select nest sites next to an object, such as driftwood, kelp, other stranded flotsam or jetsam, or a clump of vegetation (Stenzel & Peaslee 1979, Stenzel et al. 1981, Page et al. 1985). In California, 68% of 136 nests were within six inches of such an object (Page et al. 1985); objects selected are usually small rather than large ones (G.W. Page pers. comm.). Nearby objects possibly serve as concealment for incubating plovers, or they may function in unknown ways in courtship activities; observations suggest that objects do not function as windbreaks, to provide shade, as cues to nest location, or to conceal eggs or adults coming from or going to them (G.W. Page pers. comm.). At Mono Lake, the disruptive effects of nearby objects did not reduce predation, as did overhead cover (Page et al. 1985). The situation there may be anomalous, because objects are not numerous as they are at coastal sites; at the latter, searches by predators for plovers' nests beside objects might prove fruitless. In California, the Snowy Plover breeding system is one of serial polyandry—that is, in the same season, females nest in succession with different males (Warriner et al. 1986). A few days after the hatching of the first clutch, the female leaves the precocial young to the care of the male and departs to search for a new mate.

Snowy Plovers forage in open areas on outer-coast beaches, from the water's edge back to the fore edge of the dunes, and on tidal, sand, or alkali flats of estuaries, lagoons, salt marshes, river mouths, and evaporator ponds. They forage on beaches, mostly on wet sand or higher up where invertebrates concentrate around cast-up wrack. Like most plovers, Snowies are visual predators that primarily search for prey in a robinlike style—by walking or running several steps, peering down, and then picking items from the surface. Foraging birds run along in a halting zigzag fashion, stopping frequently to peck at prey items (Swarth 1983). Snowies also probe into the surface of the mud for wriggling prey they detect visually. They commonly charge, open mouthed, into mats of brine flies and twist their heads and snap at airborne flies. Infrequently, they wade into shallow water to feed on invertebrates. Rarely, they vibrate one foot on a solid surface to make prey move and reveal themselves (Johnsgard 1981). Snowy Plovers breeding at inland sites feed on a great variety of ground-dwelling arthropods, primarily flies and beetles (Swarth 1983). At Mono Lake, California, they feed primarily on brine flies and a species of carabid beetle; brine flies are also important at coastal salt evaporation ponds. A small stomach-pumped sample (n = 3) from birds at Limantour Estero, Point Reyes, indicates that coastal birds eat polychaete worms, insects, various small crustaceans, and an occasional clam (G.W. Page unpubl. data).

Marin Breeding Distribution

During the atlas period, Snowy Plovers bred on the outer coast of Point Reyes at the Seadrift/Stinson Beach spit at Bolinas Lagoon, Limantour Estero spit, Drake's Beach spit, Point Reyes Beach, and Abbott's Lagoon (Stenzel et al. 1981). Occasionally they may also breed at the mouth of Tomales Bay, at Sand Point at the south end of Dillon Beach, though documentation is lacking for that site.

Single-day surveys in the breeding season revealed 40 Snowies on Point Reyes in 1977 (Stenzel et al. 1981), 24 in 1989, and 25 in 1991 (PRBO unpubl. data). These are low estimates of the total breeding population as intensive studies of color-banded plovers at Point Reyes in 1989 documented that there were at least 32 adult Snowies breeding that year (Page et al. 1991). Representative breeding locations during the atlas period were the spit at Bolinas Lagoon (NE 5/11 & 12/77 –GWP et al.); Abbott's Lagoon (NE 4/14-27/77 –LES et al.); and Limantour Estero (NE 4/20-30/77 –SCP et al.).

Historical Trends/Population Threats

Grinnell and Miller (1944) noted declines in Snowy Plover numbers in the southern portion of the state. Page and Stenzel (1981) documented the decline in California's coastal breeding population. During statewide surveys from 1977 to 1980, plovers were not found breeding at 33 of 53 coastal sites with breeding records prior to 1970. It seems unlikely that plovers will breed again at 28 of the 33 sites because of habitat destruction or intense human use. The greatest losses are along the heavily urbanized southern California coast; this region, if left undisturbed, provides the best coastal breeding habitat. The coastal Oregon breeding population has also declined since 1979, and surveys in 1989 suggest that California's coastal population may still be declining (Page et al. 1991). Interior breeding populations may be declining as well, but population trend data for that region are difficult to interpret.

Numbers of Snowy Plovers wintering on the southern California coast also appear to have decreased since at least 1961 (Page et al. 1986).

Plover habitat has been degraded by industrial and residential development, intense recreational use by humans and their animals, off-road vehicle use, and grooming of beaches. Less noticeable but perhaps equally important are the indirect effects resulting from the planting for dune stabilization, and subsequent naturalization, of the introduced European beachgrass or marram grass *(Ammophila arenaria)*, which is now well established north of Point Conception. Natural dune systems along our coastline have a series of dunes that run perpendicular to the shoreline and are frequently interspersed with expanses of flat sand that extend back from the beach and provide excellent plover nesting habitat (Page & Stenzel 1981). *Ammophila*-dominated dunes usually have a continuous foredune running parallel with the shoreline that restricts access to the interdune sand flats. Additionally, *Ammophila* reduces the species diversity of native plants, increases plant cover, steepens the dunes (Barbour et al. 1976), and markedly depresses the abundance and diversity of sand dune arthropods (Slobodchikoff &

Doyen 1977). This reduction in potential prey may adversely affect the plovers since they frequently feed on insects well above the tide line (Stenzel et al. 1981). In northern California, degradation of plover habitat has been balanced to a large degree by the creation inside San Francisco Bay of salt evaporation ponds, which breeding plovers have used since at least 1918. For the whole coast, habitat degradation has far outweighed such enhancement (Page & Stenzel 1981).

Federal and state agencies and private conservation groups have expressed concern over the plover's declining populations. The Snowy Plover was on the Audubon Society's Blue List from its inception in 1972 to 1982 and on its list of Species with Special Concerns in 1986 (Tate 1981, 1986; Tate & Tate 1982). In California, this plover is currently a Bird Species of Special Concern (Remsen 1978, CDFG 1991b). Spurred by a petition by Page and Walter (1988), the coastal population of the Western Snowy Plover *(C. a. nivosus)* was finally listed by the U.S. Fish and Wildlife Service as federally Threatened in March 1993. Techniques to successfully hand-rear Snowy Plovers have been developed should the need arise (Page et al. 1989).

KILLDEER   *Charadrius vociferus*

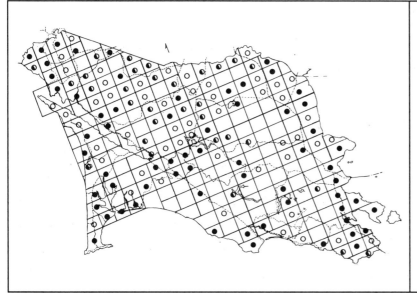

Occurs year round, though numbers swell greatly from Sep through Mar.

A fairly common, widespread breeder; overall breeding population fairly large.

Recorded in 146 (66.1%) of 221 blocks.

○ Possible   =   51 (35%)
◑ Probable   =   31 (21%)
● Confirmed =   64 (44%)

FSAR = 3   OPI = 438   CI = 2.09

Ecological Requirements

Whether described as plaintive or petulant, sonorous or strident, *vociferus* is aptly named. Killdeer are the first and most persistent of birds to raise the hue and cry when intruders invade their nesting haunts. Scantily vegetated open terrain that provides clear vistas at ground level characterizes both nesting and foraging areas. These include pastures; plowed or uncultivated fields; roadside margins; lawns and playing fields; the fringes of quiet shallow waters, such as stock or sewage ponds, lakes, lagoons, estuaries, and streams; and other disturbed sites. Killdeer select barren or sparsely vegetated, often gravelly nesting sites with an ample supply of nest material at hand (Bunni 1959). Lawns, even if close cropped, are rarely used for nesting unless they offer bare spots. Preferred gravelly areas often arise from erosion or stream flooding or from construction of roadsides, dikes, or railroad right-of-ways. Nest sites are usually in close proximity to water used for bathing, cooling in hot weather, and foraging. Rarely, nest sites may be 1.5 to 2 miles from water; irrigated lawns or fields may sometimes substitute for standing shallow water (Townsend 1929, G&M 1944, Bunni 1959). Nest sites frequently are elevated slightly on mounds, knolls, hills, or slopes, giving incubating birds a wide view of their surroundings and affording protection from flooding by rainwater (Bunni 1959). Nest scrapes and nests are often placed beside an object, such as a stone, plant, log, manure pile, or dirt mound, which perhaps provides concealment from predators. In the absence of such an object, the cryptically colored eggs blend with uneven surfaces or the coloration or texture of the substrate to afford protection. If these methods fail, Killdeer often resort to their classic broken-wing displays to lure potential predators away from nests or vulnerable young.

During courtship ceremonies, males construct with their feet several shallow scrapes, into the last of which their mates lay eggs; additional scrapes sometimes serve as reserve nests when eggs are lost (Bunni 1959). Killdeer avoid digging scrapes in hard substrates or in soft or muddy substrates where the pits might collapse. Availability close at hand of small, loose objects for nest building is important, since Killdeer obtain materials by tossing them with their bills toward the nest, usually from less than three feet. Typically, the bottom of the nest scrape is formed of stones that protect the nest from flooding by allowing water to percolate down; a fringe of nest material outside the nest protects from erosion. Killdeer prefer flat or angular stones from 0.2 to 0.4 inches (secondarily up to 0.6 in.) in length that are easily flipped. Birds select weed stems, twigs, and wood or bark chips in the 0.2- to 0.8-inch (secondarily up to 2.4-in.) size range over stones for lining the nest. White objects are preferred over black ones, though size and shape considerations will override color in the selection process. Almost any flat, lightweight object will do for nest material; these can include shells, lichens, manure, small bones, crayfish armor, dry shells of melon seeds, dead leaves, cornhusks, and rubbish such as peanut shells, paper matches, cigarette butts, dry chewing gum, bits of paper, plaster chips, or charcoal. Rarely, a nest on an area of sparse grass on a lawn is made mostly of grass, and sometimes eggs are laid in a bare scrape without nest materials. Killdeer sometimes nest on the gravel or crushed stone roofs of one- to four-story buildings (Bunni 1959, Demaree 1975). Chicks that don't succeed in tumbling safely from the roofs to the ground often succumb to dehydration. Killdeer have also nested three feet off the ground in a depression of semidecayed wood on a log (Bunni 1959). Killdeer sometimes begin to lay before the addition of much nest material, and birds typically continue to add nest material throughout incubation. During one nesting season, females will sometimes lay successive clutches successfully in the same scrape.

Killdeer forage in a variety of open habitats, particularly in pastures, plowed fields, lawns, and on the muddy, sandy, or marshy margins of shallow still or slow-moving water. Like most plovers, Killdeer are visual predators that forage robinlike by walking or running in a zigzag pattern, then stopping and peering intently in search of hidden prey, which they pick from the ground (Bunni 1959). They also pull earthworms from the ground and wade into shallow water to feed. A Killdeer will sometimes cleanse its prey by dropping it into water several times and picking it up, or by rinsing it with sideways movements of the bill. After the precocial young hatch, adults lead them to the nearest feeding area. The Killdeer diet is about 97.7% insects and other animal matter and 2.3% vegetable matter, chiefly weed seeds (McAtee & Beal 1912, n = 228). Important animal foods are beetles, grasshoppers, caterpillars, ants, true bugs, caddisflies, dragonflies, flies, centipedes, spiders, ticks, nereid worms, earthworms, snails, crabs, and other crustaceans. The diet of upland-feeding birds undoubtedly varies considerably from that of birds foraging on freshwater margins or tidal flats.

Marin Breeding Distribution

During the atlas period, Killdeer bred widely throughout the lowlands of Marin County. Representative breeding locations were the head of Schooner Bay (NE 3/22-4/7/81 —DS); near the mouth of Estero Americano (NE/NY 7/12/82 —DS); near Chileno Creek, Chileno Valley, on a gravel wash formed by the 1982 flood (NE 5/5/82 —PA); and Bahia Drive ponds near the Petaluma River mouth, Novato (NE 5/7/78 —DS). Of interest was an earlier sighting of a pair that successfully raised two or three broods on the roof of the Inverness Motel (NE-FL 3/29-8/3/67 —PL).

Historical Trends/Population Threats

Grinnell and Miller (1944) felt that the augmentation of favorable Killdeer habitat in California because of irrigation had more than compensated for reductions in "natural" territory. This may be the case, but it is difficult to judge the skimpy facts available regarding the effects on wildlife of the tremendous changes brought by the state's extensive agricultural and urban development. Killdeer numbers decreased on Breeding Bird Surveys in California from 1968 to 1989 but were relatively stable from 1980 to 1989 (USFWS unpubl. analyses).

Oystercatchers
Family *Haematopodidae*

BLACK OYSTERCATCHER *Haematopus bachmani*

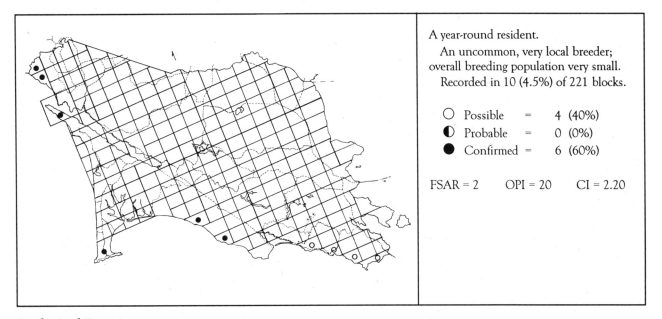

A year-round resident.

An uncommon, very local breeder; overall breeding population very small. Recorded in 10 (4.5%) of 221 blocks.

○ Possible	=	4	(40%)
◑ Probable	=	0	(0%)
● Confirmed	=	6	(60%)

FSAR = 2   OPI = 20   CI = 2.20

Ecological Requirements

Boisterous, effusive piping greets any meddler in Oystercatcher affairs along the wave-battered, sea-sprayed rocky shoreline of Marin County's outer coast. Black Oystercatchers inhabit rocky reefs, offshore islets, and sea stacks on promontories and stretches of exposed coastline. Their breeding requisites include nest sites sheltered from high tides, spray from crashing waves, prevailing winds or storms, and mainland ground predators; and suitable rocky intertidal foraging grounds (Webster 1941a, Hartwick 1974). Oystercatchers avoid nesting near high densities of gulls (Hartwick 1974). In British Columbia, the distance from nest sites to foraging areas varies from about 40 to 200 feet (Hartwick 1974). Nest sites and feeding territories are usually contiguous, but sometimes a nest site is isolated from the feeding area by water or the territories of other birds. Nest sites are often on shelves just above the sea, but they may range up to 90 feet or more above the tide line on the exposed shoulders of great rocks (Dawson 1923, Webster 1941a).

During the ten days to two weeks before egg laying, Oystercatchers build several "play nests," which are usually inferior in construction to the one finally chosen for the eggs (Webster 1941a). A typical egg nest is a platform or bowl of rock flakes, rounded pebbles, or bits of shell placed in a cranny of bare rock (Dawson 1923, Bent 1929, Webster 1941a, Hartwick 1974). Oystercatchers also lay their eggs in hollows scraped from soil pockets in irregularities of the rock or from weedy turf on ledges, lining these nests with similar materials to those in bare rock. Exceptionally, they build bowls of grass or dried moss similar to a gull's nest or lay their eggs in a hollow scooped in a gravel or shell beach. Birds add nest material throughout incubation (Webster 1941a). When the nonincubating bird is not foraging, it stands on lookout on a rock eminence, usually at or below nest level and within about 5 to 25 yards of the nest. After chick hatching, adults make initial foraging trips by flying, but after a few days they begin to walk; occasionally they continue to fly to feeding grounds distant from the defended territory (Webster 1941a, Hartwick 1974).

Black Oystercatchers forage mostly in the rocky intertidal zone. There they hop about rocks and wade in tide pools, pounding, prying, and cutting mollusks from their protective armor and anchorages and picking or probing in hiding places for unshelled prey (Webster 1941b, Hartwick 1976). At the Farallon Islands, 70%–95% of feeding

181

activity occurs during the lower half of the tidal cycle, depending on shoreline exposure and swell height (Morrell et al. 1979). Oystercatchers there feed during the high half of the tidal cycle, mostly in late summer, when adults are feeding large, rapidly growing chicks, and in fall, when fledglings require more time to feed themselves until they master their apprenticeship. Adults may concentrate in particular areas of the intertidal. For example, adults feeding chicks may spend considerable time foraging at the bottom edge of mussel beds, where a certain species of crab lives (Hartwick 1976). At the Farallon Islands, Oystercatchers also probe in the soil of a nontidal marine terrace for tenebrionid beetle larvae (Morrell et al. 1979), and at Vancouver Island they also feed in mussel beds on tidal mudflats, particularly in winter (Hartwick & Blaylock 1979).

An adult Oystercatcher's sturdy, bright vermillion, laterally compressed bill is an essential tool for mining the abundant (though tightly fastened and armored) invertebrate fauna of rocky reefs. Birds seek recently exposed or slightly inundated, hence partially relaxed, mollusks since these are the only ones they have a reasonable chance of opening (Webster 1941b, Hartwick 1976). Because of the short period when gaping mussels are available, Oystercatchers move quickly, often pass over small food items, and appear to cover greater distances while foraging on mussels than when seeking a greater array of prey (Hartwick 1976). In search of gaping mussels, Oystercatchers walk over reefs with their heads directed forward and their "chisel-tipped" bills poised to strike a sharp blow on the dorsal border oblique to the long axis of the mussel (Webster 1941b, Hartwick 1976). Such a blow depresses the valve, forming an abnormal gap that will admit the tip of the bird's bill. Birds also search for mussels already opened wide enough to permit entrance of their bills. In either case, the bill is then stabbed down into the mussel with a number of forceful and rapid jerks until the deepest part of the bill lies lengthwise between the margins of the valves. Next the mussel is opened by rapid levering and biting that severs the adductor muscle; sometimes the shell is fractured in the process. In rare instances, when a mussel sits with its ventral byssal fissure exposed, Oystercatchers work from that juncture to open the mussel by the above methods. Birds sometimes detach the mussel after opening it and carry it to a more convenient location to remove the meat. Many mussels are also located by probing in the mud and then usually are opened from the vulnerable ventral side. Oystercatchers remove the flesh by first tearing larger pieces and then laying the bill flat on the shell like scissors and pushing it forward as the points snip away the adherent flesh.

Oystercatchers loosen limpets from their moorings by first delivering one or more sharp strokes of the bill from a low angle (Webster 1941b, Hartwick 1976). This will remove small limpets but only weakens the grip of larger ones and sometimes chips their shells. As needed, this is followed by firm pushing, lateral head swaying, or to-and-fro rotation of the bill. If this does not complete the job, the bird forces the bill under the shell and levers it free. The Oystercatcher then seizes the limpet and carries it to a niche or rock crevice to remove the meat. Placing the limpet shell down, the bird rapidly bites around the edge of the shell and finally picks the body up, shakes the shell off, and swallows the meat in one gulp. Oystercatchers attack chitons in the same way as limpets, but unless they topple small ones with the first stroke, further quick work is needed (Webster 1941b). Birds push the tip of the bill under one corner of the leathery shell, breaking the vacuum set up by the muscular foot of the mollusk. Then they usually slip the bill under, flat side against the rock, and cut the animal loose by sawing strokes of the bill. Oystercatchers obtain barnacles by sharply tapping one valve, levering the valves apart by circular leverage, and then pulling out the bite-sized body whole. Oystercatchers obtain many smaller prey, such as small limpets and sea cucumbers, by probing and moving aside seaweed (Hartwick 1976).

The Black Oystercatcher diet consists primarily of mussels, limpets, and chitons, along with smaller amounts of barnacles, marine worms (annelids, nemerteans, and sipunculids), crabs, snails, young abalone, isopods, echinoderms, and sometimes insects (Webster 1941b, Hartwick 1976, Morrell et al. 1979). At the Farallon Islands, the diet is primarily the California mussel *(Mytilus californianus)*, several species of limpets, beetle larvae, and marine (nemertean and polychaete) worms; crabs are also taken (Morrell et al. 1979). The diet at the Farallones varies among territories, depending on the topography of the shoreline—sloping shoreline supports mussel beds, whereas steep shoreline does not. At nests where mussels comprise 40% or more of the prey remains, the diet is more varied than at nests where mussels comprise 30% or less of the diet. Presumably this reflects a greater diversity of prey in mussel beds. In any case, when mussels are available there, they are preferred over limpets as a food for chicks (Morrell et al. 1979).

Unlike most precocial shorebirds, Oystercatcher young initially are not able to feed themselves because their underdeveloped bills and feeding skills are no match for armored prey. Very young chicks usually remain close to the nest, and the parents take turns guarding the chicks and carrying food items singly to them from the intertidal zone (Webster 1941a, Hartwick 1974, Groves 1984). Adults may hold food in the bill before chicks or drop items and point to them on the ground (Hartwick 1976). One adult may also pass the food to the other adult, who prepares it and presents it to the chick while the first adult returns to foraging duties. In British Columbia, adults feed chicks at nests mostly mussels (larger than average sized) and limpets of large size or species (Hartwick 1976). Chicks are also fed quite large chitons and crabs. Crabs may be a special part of the chick diet since adults there do not prey on them until they begin feeding their chicks. In contrast to chicks, adults then are eating less profitable items—small to medium-sized limpets, smaller mussels, and a lot of small unshelled food items. Chicks move with foraging parents to the littoral zone in stages (Hartwick 1974). Young may reach the feeding area as early as two days after hatching but usually not until the third to fifth week (Webster 1941a, Hartwick 1974), depending on the difficulty of descent to feeding areas (Webster 1941a). Sometimes gulls prevent adults from moving their chicks to the intertidal zone, and so the young remain near the nest site until fledging (Hartwick 1974). Chicks that remain at the nest for long periods are fed an increasing proportion of mussels (Hartwick 1976). Although prefledging chicks that move to the littoral zone are able to capture small prey items, they still depend on adults for the most profitable ones (Hartwick 1976, Groves 1984). When young begin to move to foraging areas with parents, one adult often remains higher in the intertidal guarding the chicks and feeding them smaller items, while the other adult hunts farther down and carries mussel meat and other larger items to the chicks. It does appear, though, that feeding becomes a teaching process, as progressively more and more work is left to the chicks. The diet during this period shifts away from a dependence on mussels to more limpets and smaller unshelled items. At the Farallon Islands, marine worms and beetle larvae make up as much as 57% (by number) of the diet fed to 1- to 40-day-old chicks (Morrell et al. 1979). When chicks there are old enough (67–100 days) to forage with their parents in the littoral zone, limpets are the major prey item (60%–85%), whether fed to a chick by a parent or captured by a chick itself. The diet of newly independent chicks is mainly limpets, marine worms, and beetle larvae, since the young birds have not yet developed the skill to open mussels. Adults have been observed feeding adult-sized young at Point Lobos, Monterey County, as late as 3 November (Williams 1927), and fledglings are not fully adept at opening mussels or prying barnacles or chitons from rocks until they are three to four months old (Webster 1941a).

Marin Breeding Distribution

During the atlas period, Black Oystercatchers bred at a number of spots at irregular intervals along Marin County's outer coast where suitable stretches of rocky shoreline exist (Table 14, Figure 14). Representative breeding locations were Double Point, PRNS (NE summer 1978 –SGA); about ½ mi. NW of the mouth of Bear Valley, PRNS (FL 7/3/80 –DS); and near the mouth of Estero de San Antonio (FL 6/24/82 –DS). In 1988, Rauzon and Carter (1988) documented Black Oystercatchers breeding on West Marin Island inside San Francisco Bay; two Oystercatchers were also present there during USFWS surveys in 1990 (Carter et al. 1992).

Historical Trends/Population Threats

In surveys of selected sites in 1969 to 1972, Ainley and Whitt (1973) estimated 14 Oystercatchers were breeding at three sites on the Marin County coast. From complete surveys, Sowls et al. (1980) estimated 30 birds were breeding at eight sites on Marin's outer coast in 1979, and Carter et al. (1992) estimated 27 birds were breeding at nine sites there in 1989. Even numbers from the more recent surveys are probably low, considering the difficulty of counting this scattered, solitary-nesting species from boats.

From surveys in 1979 to 1980, Sowls et al. (1980) estimated a total of 462 Oystercatchers were breeding on the central and northern California coast. In 1989, Carter et al. (1992) recorded 575 birds in surveys of the same region (plus 6 in S.F. Bay in 1990); their numbers would have been even greater than those of the prior survey if they had rounded numbers to represent breeding pairs as was done previously. They concluded that the higher 1989 figures (rounded or not) may be indicative of better viewing conditions during the later survey and slightly different definitions of breeding birds between the surveys, rather than a true population increase.

Oystercatchers have held up well to human pressures in California, except locally at the Farallon Islands and at San Pedro, Los Angeles County (G&M 1944). Ainley and Lewis (1974) claimed that Oystercatchers disappeared from the Farallones in the 1860s, probably because of too much disturbance from humans and domestic animals. That population has subsequently recovered. Although it seems clear that the Farallon population did decline, it is hard to imagine the species totally disappearing there because the island harbors inaccessible intertidal areas where Oystercatchers could have taken refuge from disturbance. Near-shore oil spills potentially could decimate the littoral food resources upon which Oystercatchers depend (Sowls et al. 1980).

Stilts and Avocets
Family *Recurvirostridae*

BLACK-NECKED STILT   *Himantopus mexicanus*

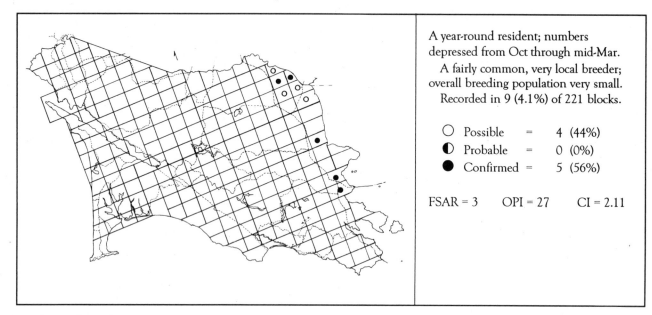

A year-round resident; numbers depressed from Oct through mid-Mar.

A fairly common, very local breeder; overall breeding population very small. Recorded in 9 (4.1%) of 221 blocks.

○ Possible   =   4 (44%)
◐ Probable   =   0 (0%)
● Confirmed   =   5 (56%)

FSAR = 3   OPI = 27   CI = 2.11

Ecological Requirements

These dainty black and white shorebirds perched on out-landishly long pink legs cast surreal reflections in the waters of a variety of shallow freshwater, brackish, and alkaline wetlands. In Marin County, Stilts breed in the reclaimed or altered bayshore saltmarsh habitats of diked (tidal and nontidal) brackish ponds, sewage ponds, and ephemeral freshwater ponds. Although they often overlap in habitat preferences with American Avocets, Stilts tend to prefer fresher water and more emergent vegetation, and they feed more in marshes, than do Avocets (Hamilton 1975). Observations at agricultural evaporation ponds in the San Joaquin Valley suggest that prey *availability* is the primary limiting factor for both of these shorebirds. Regardless of salinity and alkalinity, both Stilts and Avocets are numerous in evaporation ponds when suitable invertebrate prey are abundant and available to them via their respective foraging techniques (G. Gerstenberg pers. comm.). Hence, the habitat choices of these species seem to reflect the likelihood of finding suitable prey resources rather than a selection for particular water chemistry.

Stilts generally nest as close as possible to accessible feeding areas. They prefer rather open habitat, where they generally congregate in small, loose colonies, often mixing with Avocets. Birds choose nest sites on bare to moderately vegetated flat terrain; on the flat or irregular surfaces of low rises on dry land; at the water's edge; or, less frequently, built up in shallow water (Bent 1927, Palmer 1967, Hamilton 1975). When Stilts nest in vegetated areas, they tend to select sites on the edge of the vegetation with good visibility of their surroundings (Hamilton 1975). In the Bay Area, Stilts most often nest on unvegetated or sparsely vegetated dikes and levees of salt ponds, and occasionally in openings in salt marsh (Gill 1972, 1977; Hamilton 1975; Rigney & Rigney 1981). At San Francisco Bay salt evaporators, Stilts concentrate in the interior of pond complexes away from the bayshore. Most nests there are on discontinuous levees, insular levee fragments, or small dirt mound islands; few nests are on continuous or well-traveled dikes. Hamilton (1975) noted that Stilt nests tended to be located on the leeward side of saltpond dikes and on the side toward favored feeding areas; birds may also select nest sites with reference to the direction of human approach. Nests located on the centers of dikes usually are constructed downwind of small natural objects, which may serve as windbreaks.

Depending on the availability of materials and the nest location, Stilt nests vary from shallow scrapes in bare earth with hardly a vestige of nest material to elaborate raised platforms (Dawson 1923, Bent 1927, Palmer 1967, Hamilton 1975). Nest materials include pebbles, shells, plant stems, twigs, large feathers or dried bird carcasses, dry mud chips, bones, cow dung, and grasses. Sometimes Stilts add substantial amounts of material to nests to avoid rising waters. Normally, birds continue to occasionally add small amounts of nest material throughout incubation (Hamilton 1975). After the newly hatched precocial young obtain mobility, they are led to shallow-water feeding areas, preferably with low vegetative escape cover.

The extremely long legs of Black-necked Stilts are perfectly suited for wading well out into shallow water. Stilts are primarily visual foragers that obtain most of their prey from an immobile stance or while slowly walking (Hamilton 1975). Their main mode of prey capture is by pecking at the mud or from or near the water's surface without immersing the head. Stilts also capture terrestrial insects by pecking at the ground or vegetation. Less frequently, they plunge their heads or even necks or upper breast into water in pursuit of items, but apparently their bills do not reach bottom. Stilts also snatch flying insects from the air with their bills after running or fluttering toward them. Only very rarely do they forage by back-and-forth scythelike motions of the bill as Avocets commonly do (see account). On San Francisco Bay, Stilts often feed in marshes after their chicks hatch. Unlike Avocets, they use grass-bordered ephemeral pools, and in the rare instances when they feed on tidal mudflats, they do so close to shore. Hamilton (1975) compared the foraging niches between the sexes and between Stilts and Avocets. Male Stilts, with their longer legs, tend to feed in deeper water than do females. Although male Stilts can feed in deeper water than do Avocets, both species concentrate their foraging in "ankle-deep" water. On the other hand, female Stilts do tend to feed in shallower water than do Avocets. The niches are further separated by Avocets feeding more commonly by plunging below the surface than do Stilts; by feeding at greater depths; and by Avocets using a number of tactile foraging methods (see account).

The Black-necked Stilt diet is about 98.9% animal matter and only 1.1% vegetable matter in the form of a few seeds of aquatic or marsh plants (Wetmore 1925, n = 80). The animal foods are primarily aquatic forms of true bugs (water boatmen, water striders, waterbugs, and backswimmers) and beetles, along with lesser amounts of flies (types with aquatic larvae), snails, caddisflies, small fish, dragonfly and mayfly nymphs, crustaceans, miscellaneous insects, and, rarely, small frogs. Brine shrimp and brine flies are important food in south San Francisco Bay salt ponds (Hamilton 1975), as they may also be at alkali lakes in the interior.

Marin Breeding Distribution

There is no evidence that Stilts occurred in Marin County through the breeding season prior to the atlas period. During the atlas years, they bred at a few scattered diked wetlands along the San Pablo and San Francisco bayshores, with the stronghold of the population in the Rush Creek/Bahia Drive ponds area of Novato. Probably fewer than 50 pairs have nested recently in Marin each year, even under the most favorable conditions. Stilts were first discovered nesting in Marin County in 1978 at the Spinnaker wetlands, San Rafael (FL 7/2/78 —ARa); a high count of five nests was recorded there in 1983 (NE-FL May & Jun 1983 —HoP). In 1980 at least 32 pairs nested at the Bahia Drive ponds near the Petaluma River mouth, Novato (NE-FL 6/7-26/80 —DS), and 7 pairs attempted nesting at McGinnis Park, San Rafael, in an ephemeral wetland created by a broken dike (DD 5/10 & 6/3/80 —DS). Nesting failed at the latter site because it had dried up by late June. Since 1985, Stilts have bred each year at the Las Gallinas sewage ponds (ABN:DAH et al.) just north of McGinnis Park. Stilts also occasionally have bred at the Shorebird Marsh by the Village Shopping Center, Corte Madera (DD 3/17/87 —JGE, FL 8/3/89 —LES).

Historical Trends/Population Threats

Stephens and Pringle (1933) considered the Black-necked Stilt a rare winter visitant in Marin County based on a record in Grinnell and Wythe (1927). The latter authors reported that Stilts at that time occurred in limited numbers in the immediate vicinity of San Francisco Bay in summer and fall, and that stragglers were present only rarely in winter. Sibley (1952) considered the species an uncommon summer resident and a rare winter visitant to the south San Francisco Bay region. The Black-necked Stilt increased steadily in saltpond habitat in south San Francisco Bay in the 1950s and 1960s, and the species is now considered a common breeder and a regular winter visitor there (Gill 1972, 1977). Breeding probably did not begin in the North Bay until after the mid-1960s (R.E. Gill, Jr., *fide* GWP), and the number of breeders there still appears to be increasing (ABN). An increase in the estimated number of Stilts breeding in south San Francisco Bay, from 400 to 500 pairs in 1971 (Gill 1977) to 600 to 650 pairs in 1981, is attributed to more extensive observer coverage in the more recent survey (Rigney & Rigney 1981). In the Monterey Bay area, the wintering population has increased at least since 1959 (Roberson 1985). The coastal breeding population is still increasing, as indicated by the recent breeding records in Marin, the first breeding records for Sonoma County and coastal San Mateo County in 1977 (AB 31:1184), and the extension of the breeding range north to near Humboldt Bay in 1985 (AB 39:958).

It is not clear what is fueling the increase of coastal Stilt populations. Although evaporation ponds support the bulk of the Bay Area breeding population, these ponds have been in operation and available to shorebirds starting in the 1860s, suggesting that other factors are responsible for recent increases. Perhaps the coastal population is being augmented by recruitment of young from productive interior populations, or by adults fleeing from drought-diminished interior wetlands. Although the increase of the coastal Stilt population is encouraging, it should be remembered that populations in the interior, particularly in the Central Valley, have been reduced drastically in historical times by the draining of wetlands (G&M 1944, Cogswell 1977). These losses have been at least partially offset by irrigation (especially rice fields), agricultural drainage ponds, and sewage ponds. On the other hand, concentrations of pesticides, heavy metals, and other contaminants in agricultural and urban waters may ultimately have severe adverse effects on shorebirds. Selenium from agricultural drainage waters that concentrated in the food chain was the most likely cause of complete reproductive failures of Stilts and Avocets at Kesterson Reservoir, Merced County, in 1984 and 1985 (Williams et al. 1989). On the whole, Stilt populations were relatively stable on Breeding Bird Surveys in California from 1968 to 1989, despite an increase in numbers from 1980 to 1989 (USFWS unpubl. analyses).

An adult Black Oystercatcher solemnly surveys its rocky realm. Photograph by Ian Tait.

AMERICAN AVOCET *Recurvirostra americana*

Occurs year round, though almost exclusively as a winter resident from late Aug through late Apr. A rare breeder (postatlas) only since 1984.

Ecological Requirements

Although the hues of their burnt orange heads and necks and pastel blue legs bear little resemblance to the attire of Black-necked Stilts, Avocets inhabit a similar variety of shallow freshwater, saline, brackish, and alkaline wetlands. Despite the tendency for Avocets to be more partial to saline and alkaline (versus freshwater) habitats than are Stilts (Hamilton 1975), prey *availability* may be the factor most directly affecting distribution of these shorebirds (see Stilt account). Avocets avoid grass-bordered ephemeral freshwater ponds, where Stilts often feed and breed, and because of their affinity for barren habitat, Avocets feed less in salt marshes (but do so on exposed mud) than do Stilts. Avocets generally breed in loose colonies, often with Stilts, in proximity to suitable foraging areas (Gibson 1971, Hamilton 1975). Along the coast, Avocets breed primarily around diked brackish ponds, especially salt evaporators, and at sewage ponds. Although both Avocets and Stilts feed in these ponds, only Avocets also feed extensively on bay mudflats. There they feed mostly on the water's edge far from shore or in supersaturated mud or in shallow saltwater puddles left on the flats (Hamilton 1975, D. Shuford pers. obs.).

The type and location of territories that Avocets defend change with the stage of the nesting cycle (Gibson 1971). Prior to egg laying, pairs defend a feeding area. During incubation, pairs defend the nest site and either a contiguous or distant feeding area. Birds whose nests are close to the primary feeding area may also defend a more distant secondary feeding area, whereas birds with separate feeding areas and nest sites defend only one feeding area. After the chicks hatch, the territory becomes chick centered and mobile.

Other than a tendency to distribute their nests more irregularly than Stilts do (Hamilton 1975), Avocets build their ground nests of similar materials and in nearly identical locations to those of Stilts (see account and references). Gibson (1971) noted that Avocets choose nest materials available in the immediate vicinity of the nest. Avocet nests are distinguished from those of Black-necked Stilts by the larger size of Avocet eggs.

Like Stilts, Avocets also feed extensively by pecking at or just below the water's surface (and at mud), but Avocets plunge their heads or necks below the water much more frequently than do Stilts (Hamilton 1975). Avocets snatch flying insects from the air with their bills after running or fluttering in pursuit of their prey. They also run up hastily and strike at mats of brine flies on the mud with lateral sweeping motions of their bills (Wetmore 1925). Another rarely used method of visual feeding is for birds to rapidly open and close their bills while simultaneously moving them erratically along the water's surface (Hamilton 1975). Unlike Stilts, Avocets make extensive use of tactile methods of foraging. In shallow pools over mudflats, Avocets filter mud by rapidly opening and closing their bills slightly while at the same time moving them apparently at random over the mud. Birds also scrape mudflats by placing the recurved lower tip of the bill on the mud directly in front of them and then moving it forward and backward by stretching the neck. Avocets are perhaps best known for their scythelike, side-to-side feeding movements in mud or water. Leaning down, birds progress forward a step at a time, placing the slightly opened, recurved tip of the bill flat on the substrate to one side and rapidly moving it to the other side. They pause to raise the head and swallow and then repeat the process on the other side with the next step; infrequently, birds make multiple side-to-side movements (the first is longest) before pausing to swallow. Mostly outside the breeding season, birds sometimes congregate in large groups to forage in this manner, swaying back and forth as they progress forward in unison, apparently herding prey in front of them. From a swimming or breast-wading position, Avocets will tip up like dabbling ducks and make similar sideswipes of their bills on the mud below the surface while maintaining their position with backward-kicking legs. See the Black-necked Stilt account (above) for other differences in the foraging niche of these two species. Hamilton (1975) compared foraging between male and female Avocets at an inland site where they only used pecking and plunging. Males there had a much greater tendency to plunge-feed than females did, perhaps because of their longer but less curved bills.

Overall, the Avocet diet is about 65.1% animal matter (aquatic and shoreline forms) and 34.9% vegetable matter (Wetmore 1925, n = 67), the latter a very high percentage for a shorebird. Vegetable matter is primarily the seeds but also the leaves and stems of aquatic and marsh plants. Animal fare is primarily flies, beetles, crustaceans, true bugs, miscellaneous insects, and, rarely, snails, small fish, and salamanders. In fall and winter at south San Francisco Bay salt ponds, Avocets feed on brine flies, brine shrimp,

187

water boatman beetles, polychaete worms, plant stems, and a few small mollusks (Anderson 1970). Martin et al. (1951) reported little variation in the proportion of animal and vegetable matter in the diet between spring and fall.

Marin Breeding Distribution

There was no evidence of Avocets breeding in Marin County during, or prior to, the atlas period. Subsequently, the progress of a pair nesting on a tiny island at Spinnaker Lagoon, San Rafael, was followed during the breeding season of 1983 (NE-FL 5/18-6/12/83 —HoP). Avocets also attempted to nest at the Las Gallinas sewage ponds in 1987 but were unsuccessful (ABN:DAH, CLF).

Historical Trends/Population Threats

Both coastal wintering and breeding populations of Avocets have increased historically. Formerly, the American Avocet was considered an irregularly common fall and winter visitor to San Francisco Bay (G&W 1927), where nesting was first recorded in 1926 (Gill 1977). Although Avocets began to use Bay Area salt ponds by at least 1899 (Grinnell et al. 1918), not until the early 1940s did their population begin to expand there to include large numbers of wintering and breeding birds (Storer 1951; Gill 1972, 1977). By 1952, the Avocet was considered a common resident (more numerous in winter) of the south San Francisco Bay region (Sibley 1952). A decrease in the estimated number of Avocets breeding in south San Fran-

cisco Bay, from 1800 pairs in 1971 (Gill 1977) to 650 pairs in 1981, apparently represents different calculation methods rather than an actual population decline (Rigney & Rigney 1981). Winter numbers have also increased in Humboldt Bay since 1958, especially from 1961 to 1968 (Gerstenberg 1972), and at Bolinas Lagoon, particularly since 1974 (Shuford et al. 1989). First breeding records for Sonoma County in 1981 (AB 35:974) and Marin County in 1984 (above) document continued range expansion of breeding Avocets in the San Francisco Bay Area. See Black-necked Stilt account for comments on the increase of coastal breeding populations, which also apply to Avocets. Avocet populations in California's interior decreased early in this century because of extensive loss of marshlands (G&M 1944). This habitat loss has been offset at least partially by the addition of irrigation ponds, agricultural drainage ponds, and sewage ponds. On the other hand, these waters may be very harmful to shorebirds because they concentrate pesticides, heavy metals, and other contaminants. Selenium from agricultural drainage waters that concentrated in the food chain was the most likely cause of complete reproductive failures of Avocets and Stilts at Kesterson Reservoir, Merced County, in 1984 and 1985 (Williams et al. 1989). For California as a whole, numbers of Avocets appeared to decrease slightly on Breeding Bird Surveys from 1968 to 1989 (USFWS unpubl. analyses).

Sandpipers
Family *Scolopacidae*

SPOTTED SANDPIPER *Actitis macularia*

Occurs year round, though primarily as a winter resident and transient from Jul through May. Only two (nonatlas) breeding records.

Ecological Requirements

Wasting no time in taking on the airs of their elders, fluffy newborn Spotted Sandpipers teeter and bob as they test their spindly legs on the shifting sands and gravels of their breeding haunts. In California, Spotted Sandpipers nest from sea level to 11,000 feet—widely in higher and moister mountains and less extensively in coastal lowlands. Breeding habitats in the state include slow-moving streams and rivers, freshwater lakes, tarns, saline and alkaline lakes, and, rarely, coastal lagoons (G&M 1944, D. Shuford pers. obs.). Because Spotted Sandpipers have bred only twice in Marin County (see below), there is little to say about habitat preferences here.

Throughout the range, nest sites are usually on open or semiopen shoreline beaches or on offshore islands or gravel or sandbars. Nests are usually concealed in grassy or herbaceous cover and sometimes are placed next to or under logs, driftwood branches, rocks, bushes, or trees (Dawson 1923, Tyler 1929, Grinnell et al. 1930, Miller & Miller 1948). Where the vegetation is low and open, these sandpipers often nest well back from the shoreline, but otherwise they often nest just above the wave-cast debris line. One nest in the mountains of California was on the floor of an open yellow pine woodland over 150 feet back from and about 50 feet above a beachless lakeshore (Grinnell et al. 1930). On one island on a lake in Minnesota, a number of nests were from 65 to 165 feet back from the shoreline under a dense canopy of bushes and trees (Oring & Knudson 1972). Nests are saucer-shaped depressions in sand, gravel, or turf that are thinly to well lined with grasses, pine needles, leaves, twigs, bits of wood, or feathers (Dawson 1923, Tyler 1929, Grinnell et al. 1930). A frequent mating strategy of Spotted Sandpipers is serial polyandry—females nest successively with up to four males, leave the care of the precocial young to each male, and help incubate only the last clutch of eggs (Hays 1972, Oring & Knudson 1972, Oring et al. 1983). Sometimes females are monogamous, and, rarely, they pair with two males at the same time (Oring & Maxson 1978).

No detailed work apparently has been done on the diet of Spotted Sandpipers, but birds are known to prey on larval and adult forms of a variety of land and aquatic insects, assorted invertebrates, and, occasionally, on fish (Tyler 1929, Palmer 1967, Kuenzel & Wiegert 1973). Spotteds forage on aquatic shorelines and also in adjacent open upland grass and sedge covered beaches and meadows. While walking along, they capture prey by rapid downward pecks; by forward horizontal thrusts of the bill from a slow, crouched approach; or by snapping insects from the air. Also, they wade in the water and jump into deeper water to seize floating prey (Palmer 1967). Spotted Sandpipers sometimes immerse insects several times in water before swallowing them (Tyler 1929).

Marin Breeding Distribution

Bracketing the atlas period, there were two breeding records for Spotted Sandpipers in Marin County: an adult with three downy young at the "Canal Street Pond," San Rafael, on 9 July 1971 (WMP, ABu); and an adult with young at Rush Creek marsh off Binford Rd., Novato, on 21 June 1985 (GWP, BHe). No breeding confirmations or strongly suggestive breeding evidence was recorded during the atlas period. The loosely overlapping spring and fall migration periods of Spotted Sandpipers and the presence of occasional oversummering individuals here, patterns typical of many shorebirds, make it difficult to determine breeding status unless direct evidence of nesting is observed.

Historical Trends/Population Threats

Formerly, Spotted Sandpipers were not known to breed in Marin County (G&W 1927, S&P 1933, G&M 1944). It seems best to attribute the recent breeding records to increased observer coverage detecting irregular breeding rather than to a range expansion. Spotted Sandpiper numbers appear to have changed little in California in historical times (G&M 1944). Hydraulic mining on rivers may have

189

scoured out some nesting habitat, but then again, to the species advantage, it must have deposited much silt and gravel on beaches and bars. Increasing recreational use of rivers and lakes must displace some breeding sandpipers but does not appear to have had a marked effect on the population. Numbers of Spotted Sandpipers were relatively stable on Breeding Bird Surveys in California from 1968 to 1989 (USFWS unpubl. analyses).

The prim and proper appearance of a Western Gull on its nest belies its otherwise piratical, aggressive, and resourceful tendencies when in pursuit of food, any food. Photograph by Ian Tait.

Gulls
Family *Laridae*

WESTERN GULL *Larus occidentalis*

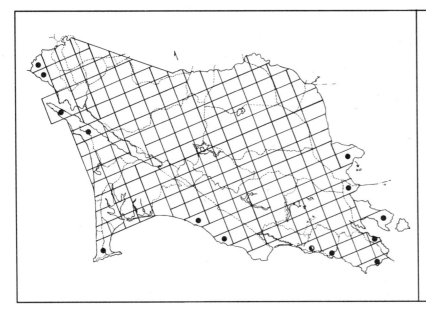

A year-round resident; gulls occupy Farallon Island (and probably Marin) breeding colonies almost year round, except the short period from mid-Sep until late Oct or early Nov.

A common, very local breeder; overall breeding population very small.

Recorded in 14 (6.3%) of 221 blocks (see Methods).

○ Possible	=	0	(0%)
◑ Probable	=	1	(7%)
● Confirmed	=	13	(93%)

FSAR = 4   OPI = 56   CI = 2.93

Ecological Requirements

What better avian symbol of seaside existence than the graceful, versatile, yet rapacious Western Gull. Our only breeding gull inhabits a wide variety of habitats ranging from the open sea, to coastal bays, estuaries, lagoons, tidal reefs, and beaches—it exploits more of the coastal marine environment than any other local breeding seabird (Ainley & Boekelheide 1990, Chap. 3). At sea, Western Gulls are confined largely to waters over the continental shelf and are rare more than 15 miles seaward of the edge of the shelf break (Briggs et al. 1987). Foraging areas for Farallon Island breeders vary yearly with ocean conditions (Ainley & Boekelheide 1990, Chap. 3). In years of high food availability in the ocean, birds forage mostly offshore near the Farallon colony. In years of reduced food availability, birds forage more in inshore waters, and they may fly 60 miles or more to feed at garbage dumps. Western Gulls are very rare inland except within a mile or two of the coastline, where they bathe at freshwater ponds or lakes or forage at dumps.

Western Gulls nest in large colonies, scattered aggregations, or, occasionally, isolated pairs on islands, offshore rocks, inaccessible mainland cliffs, and human structures, such as bridges and pilings. At the Farallon Islands, they

exploit a greater range of nesting habitat than any other surface-nesting seabirds (i.e., cormorants and murres) and are the most willing to nest near people (Ainley & Boekelheide 1990, Chap. 7). Western Gulls generally favor moderate slopes with rocky cover but also nest on open island terraces, steep hillsides, rocky slopes, ledges of cliff faces, and exposed summits of rocks (Bent 1921; Dawson 1923; Schreiber 1970; Harper 1971; Coulter 1973; Ainley & Boekelheide 1990, Chap. 7). Nests are usually situated in depressions on the ground out in the open on bare soil, grass, or low matted vegetation; near sparse low bushes; nestled in natural hollows among rocks; in niches in bare rock; or on human structures. Western Gulls construct small to bulky nest cups of grasses, weeds, seaweed, or other natural debris, including carcasses of dead birds or small mammals. In addition, they may incorporate into or "decorate" the nest with plastic or other refuse from our throwaway society. Sometimes nests are just a scrape in soil and accumulated guano with a few feathers or pebbles scattered about (Harper 1971). The young are semiprecocial—wandering from the nest after a few days—and are fed by regurgitation.

191

Western Gulls are consummate generalists, opportunistic foragers capable of searching large areas for mobile prey. Although well known for their scavenging habits, Farallon breeders apparently exploit primarily live marine prey, principally fish, from the ocean's surface (Ainley & Boekelheide 1990, Chap. 3). They apparently forage mostly early and late in the day and little at midday. Western Gulls usually feed in conspecific flocks, especially during warm-water years when food presumably is less available. They also commonly forage in mixed-species flocks (usually with Brandt's Cormorants), where they can play a catalyst role, attracting other birds to the site. Western Gulls are accomplished kleptoparasites, stealing prey from other successful birds of any species in a variety of settings (see below). On their own, they apparently follow schools of fish, hovering and screaming, and feed at the surface by dipping, seizing, or making shallow plunges, usually barely immersing themselves. In addition, they scavenge on beaches and mudflats; pick prey from tide pools; follow boats or wait at wharfs and seaside restaurants for cast-off fish offal, handouts, or garbage; pick through refuse at garbage dumps; and eat the eggs and young of other seabirds or their own species (Bent 1921, Pierotti 1981). Along the shoreline, it is not uncommon to watch a Western Gull sauntering along with a starfish protruding from its overstuffed maw. At seabird colonies, one can see a single gull with the feet of a seabird chick, about to be swallowed whole, pointing skyward from its open beak; several gulls tearing apart a chick or a small seabird, such as a Cassin's Auklet, in a merciless tug of war is a frequent occurrence as well. Western Gulls also carry clams, mussels, or sea urchins aloft to drop them on hard ground or rocks to break them open. They also detach morsels of carrion by seizing the body in the bill, dragging it away, and shaking their heads until a piece breaks off.

Although Western Gulls consume a great diversity of food items and will capitalize on irregularly abundant food sources, certain marine organisms predominate in the diet at the Farallon Islands, where chicks are fed about 60%–80% fish, 15%–20% garbage, 5%–7% marine invertebrates, and 1%–2% birds (Ainley & Boekelheide 1990, Chap. 3). In warm-water years, the diet diversifies, and adults eat (and feed to young) more garbage. Hence, in those years, they exploit the same resources as roosting, nonbreeding gulls normally do. Juvenile rockfish are the dominant fish prey, though cusk-eels, Pacific hake (as offal from fishing boats), and midshipmen are also important. Since many of the fish in the gulls' diet occur in waters deeper than they can exploit, they may obtain them from scavenging fish that cormorants regurgitate at sea, by exploiting fish driven to the surface by cormorants or other predators (Ainley & Boekelheide 1990, Chap. 3), or by stealing fish from cormorants or other seabirds at their nest sites (Bent 1921, L.B. Spear pers. comm.). The main

invertebrate foods at the Farallones are barnacles and euphausiids, along with lesser quantities of mysid shrimp, miscellaneous decapods, squid, limpets, mussels, and a few terrestrial invertebrates (primarily beetles).

Western Gulls sometimes feed on sea lion placentae and fecal matter (Schreiber 1970) and on other birds, such as Rock Doves, or small mammals (Annett & Pierotti 1989). Western Gulls at Santa Barbara Island in the Channel Islands feed their chicks mostly anchovies, other schooling fish, and squid, and a few intertidal invertebrates (Hunt & Hunt 1976). During the period of extremely warm ocean waters in the winter and early spring of the 1982-83 El Niño, Western Gulls at the Channel Islands were apparently feeding primarily, or perhaps solely, on pelagic red crabs (Stewart et al. 1984), as they also were then at the Farallon Islands (PRBO unpubl. data). Early in the nesting season, Western Gulls at Alcatraz Island in San Francisco Bay feed predominately on garbage (mostly chicken). They switch mostly to fish to feed their young at the time they hatch, *not* when fish are first available (Annett & Pierotti 1989). Adult males feed on larger food items and apparently travel longer distances to forage than do females (Pierotti 1981). Only males pirate food from neighboring gulls trying to feed their young, and they do so more in years of poor oceanic productivity. Preying on the eggs and young of other seabirds and neighboring gulls also increases in years of poor ocean food supplies (Ainley & Boekelheide 1990, Chap. 8; PRBO unpubl. data).

Marin Breeding Distribution

During the atlas period, Western Gulls were breeding at 13 sites along the outer coast of Marin County (Sowls et al. 1980; Table 14, Figure 14). At that time, they were also nesting at at least four sites in San Francisco or San Pablo bays, but bay waters were incompletely surveyed (Sowls et al. 1980; Marin atlas map). Representative breeding locations during the atlas period were the rocks near the mouth of Bear Valley (FL 7/3/80 –DS); Point Reyes Lighthouse (FL 6/21/81 –DS, RSt); Bird Rock off Tomales Point (FL 6/15/82 –DS); both West and East Marin islands off San Rafael (NE 5/22/82 –HPr); and a channel marker in Richardson Bay between Sausalito and Belvedere (NE 5/22/82 –HPr).

In 1989, Carter et al. (1992) found Western Gulls nesting at 16 sites on the outer coast of Marin County, including all 13 sites where they had been nesting in 1979 and 3 new sites (Table 14, Figure 14). Their baywide surveys in 1990 revealed about 230 Western Gulls nesting at 12 sites in the Marin County portions of San Francisco and San Pablo bays: Yellow Bluff (2), Sausalito Point Area (4), Peninsula Point and Cone Rock (6), Angel Island (6), Bluff Point to Paradise Cay (4), Point San Quentin (6), Marin Islands (64), The Sisters and Point San Pedro (96), Rat Rock (2), Southwest San Pablo Bay Duck Blinds (16),

Marin County–West San Pablo Bay Ship Channel (14), and Richmond–San Rafael Bridge (10). Boat counts tallied 45 gull nests on West Marin Island in 1990 and 48 in 1991 (H.M. Pratt pers. comm.) and on-site counts in the same years revealed 50 and 47 nests, respectively (R.L. Hothem/USFWS pers. comm.).

Historical Trends/Population Threats

Ainley and Whitt's (1973) preliminary surveys of selected sites along the Marin coast probably underestimated the county's Western Gull population at 186 breeding birds. Sowls et al. (1980) estimated 426 Western Gulls were nesting on the outer coast of Marin County in 1979 to 1980, and Carter et al. (1992) estimated 590 were nesting there in 1989. Carter et al.'s (1992) surveys of seabirds inside the San Francisco Bay estuary provided the first estimates of the number of Western Gulls breeding in that region of Marin County (see above); prior information was fragmentary (Sowls et al. 1980).

In historic times, numbers of Western Gulls in California have changed most dramatically at the Farallon Islands. In the mid-1800s, the population was about 20,000, close to today's size, but earlier had probably been smaller before the reduction of pinniped populations provided additional gull nesting habitat (Ainley & Boekelheide 1990, Chap. 7). The Farallon gull population was reduced by disturbance from humans and domestic animals and reached a low ebb around the turn of the century (Ainley & Lewis 1974). The greatest impact on the gull population was caused by commercial egg collectors gathering Common Murre eggs from 1848 to the early 1900s. Fearing compe-

tition from the gulls for murre eggs, collectors stepped on gull eggs and young. It is unknown if the disturbance caused many gulls to abandon breeding on the Farallones and, if so, if this affected nearby mainland breeding populations of gulls by increasing competition for nest sites. The Farallon population rebounded from a low of at most 6000 gulls to reach a plateau by 1959 and from then until the present has ranged from 22,000 to 25,500 breeding birds (Ainley & Lewis 1974; Ainley & Boekelheide 1990, Chap. 7). The 1979 PRBO estimate of 32,000 breeding gulls reported by Sowls et al. (1980) was subsequently revised to 25,500 by Ainley and Boekelheide (1990).

Sowls et al. (1980) compared their data with earlier surveys along the California coast and suggested that Western Gulls had been increasing since at least about 1970. Like many species of gulls, Westerns may have increased and reached all-time-high population levels by taking advantage of garbage and fish offal produced by an expanding human population, thus enhancing the gulls' winter survival (Ainley & Lewis 1974, Sowls et al. 1980, Spear et al. 1987). The recent closing of many San Francisco Bay Area dumps may reverse this trend. Estimates of the number of gulls breeding on the outer coast of central and northern California range from about 39,202 birds at 147 colonies in 1979 to 1980 (Sowls et al. 1980) to 30,534 birds at 205 colonies in 1989 (Carter et al. 1992). The estimate of 3270 Western Gulls nesting in the San Francisco Bay estuary in 1990 is 10% of the total of 33,804 birds nesting in the entire region in 1989 to 1990; the estimate of the Farallon population at 22,278 birds is 66% of the regional total.

Auks, Murres, and Puffins
Family *Alcidae*

COMMON MURRE *Uria aalge*

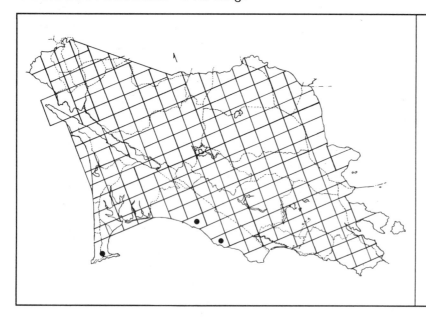

A year-round resident; numbers on ocean waters swell from Oct through Mar. Murres occupy Farallon Island (and probably Marin) breeding colonies irregularly starting in late Oct (rarely starting mid-Dec) and regularly from late Dec through departure from Jul to mid-Aug. Fewer murres nest, and some desert colonies, in extremely poor food years.

A very abundant, very local breeder; overall breeding population very small.

Recorded in 3 (1.4%) of 221 blocks (see Methods).

○ Possible   =   0 (0%)
◐ Probable   =   0 (0%)
● Confirmed =   3 (100%)

FSAR = 7   OPI = 21   CI = 3.00

Ecological Requirements

These penguin look-alikes are our most numerous breeding seabird. At sea, Common Murres primarily inhabit inshore and offshore ocean waters out to the edge of the continental shelf. Most birds concentrate over the inner shelf, usually in waters from about 200 to 500 feet deep (Wahl 1975, Briggs et al. 1987). During nesting, over 75% of the Murres at sea off California are within 25 miles of a colony, though they may range to 45 miles or more during warm-water years. Areas of concentration in over-shelf waters vary both seasonally and annually, with changes in food supply related to water temperatures (Ainley & Boekelheide 1990, Chap. 3). During early spring, Farallon Island breeders frequent deep waters along the continental shelf near the islands. Some birds range north along the continental slope almost 40 miles to the Cordell Bank, though most feed much closer. During May and June in cold-water years, they contract closer to the islands (and mainland colonies); in warm-water years, they spread out, especially over the shelf toward the mainland. By June in cold-water years, they occupy waters of a variety of temperatures and salinities but prefer turbid waters near colonies (Briggs et al. 1988). Perhaps Murres are better able to approach and prey upon relatively mobile fish when water clarity is low, or perhaps the turbid waters have the highest

abundance of fish prey (Briggs et al. 1988). In July in many years, they begin to exploit nearshore waters along the Marin and San Francisco shorelines (Ainley & Boekelheide 1990, Chap. 3). This shift occurs earlier in warm-water years. Inshore movement in July and August is evident by the distribution of dependent young and their parents—mostly inside the 90-foot depth contour (Ainley & Boekelheide 1990, Chap. 8). Inshore, Murres feed where the surface estuarine outflow of San Francisco Bay is underlain by cold, salty water, probably upwelled along the outer continental shelf (Briggs et al. 1988). By September, Murres, including fathers with chicks, have spread out south along the coast 60 miles or more to Monterey and beyond (Ainley & Boekelheide 1990, Chap. 3). Little is known of the seasonal habitat shifts of birds breeding at mainland colonies on Point Reyes.

Murres are highly gregarious, nesting shoulder to shoulder on islands, offshore rocks, and inaccessible mainland cliffs. The densely packed colonies usually range in size from groups of tens to thousands of pairs. Murres select nesting terrain varying from terraces, gradual slopes, and shoreline promontories to the narrow ledges and shelves of cliffs, steep slopes, grottoes, and sea caves (Bent 1919; Ainley & Boekelheide 1990, Chap. 8). The majority of

Murres in California nest on gentle slopes and flat areas at the base of slopes or on rounded hilltops (Takekawa et al. 1990). Murres lay a single egg on bare rock or soil, occasionally placing a few small stones around the egg. They almost always nest facing a vertical face, which they lean against while incubating (Ainley & Boekelheide 1990, Chap. 8). Lacking true nests, Murres lay pyriform (pear-shaped) eggs that roll in a circle, an adaptation that keeps eggs from easily plummeting off precipices to smash on rocks or fall into the sea. Unlike other alcids at the Farallon Islands, the young depart from the nesting ledge when they attain only 20%–25% of adult weight at about 22 to 25 days of age. Depending on the terrain near the nest site, chicks waddle to the shoreline or jump off cliffs to the sea below (W.J. Sydeman pers. comm.). Most departure occurs in the evening or just after nightfall on calm days (Ainley & Boekelheide 1990, Chap. 8). Unable to fly, chicks swim with one parent (the male) to feeding areas some distance from the breeding colony. The male accompanies and feeds the chick until it is fully grown and capable of flight.

Like other alcids, Murres pursue their prey underwater, propelled by partly folded wings. They apparently forage mostly early and late in the day and little during midday. Murres most often feed in large single-species flocks or occasionally in mixed flocks, especially with Brandt's Cormorants and Western Gulls (Ainley & Boekelheide 1990, Chap. 3). They are very efficient divers and can descend to depths of almost 600 feet, or perhaps even deeper (Piatt & Nettleship 1985). Early in the nesting season, prior to the period of intense coastal upwelling, adult Murres foraging on the outer continental shelf near the Farallones feed on euphausiids (Briggs et al. 1988; Ainley & Boekelheide 1990, Chap. 3). Chicks are not fed euphausiids, presumably because they provide insufficient nutrition relative to the high cost to adults of delivering them one by one to young. Generally Murres feed their young food items of high caloric value that can be easily carried lengthwise in the bill—these are usually midwater schooling organisms (fish and squid) about 1.5 to 6 inches long. Farallon breeders feed their chicks predominantly juvenile rockfish, anchovies, nightsmelt, and market squid, though the diet varies both seasonally and annually (Ainley & Boekelheide 1990, Chap. 3, n = 20,427). In cold-water years, rockfish account for 85% and anchovies for 7% of the early-season diet, but the diet diversifies later as Murres move to inshore feeding areas. In warm-water years, prey diversity is greater, and the percentage of rockfish in the diet declines (from 20% to 13% of the diet) from early to late season, while the percentage of anchovies increases (from 40% to 70%). The greater seasonal change in diet in warm-water years reflects the early movement of Murres inshore. Croll (1990) also documented seasonal and annual shifts in the Murre diet in Monterey Bay. It is likely that seasonal

movements and diet of Murres breeding on the mainland at Point Reyes may differ from that of Farallon breeders, as suggested by dietary differences between offshore and inshore colonies of Rhinoceros Auklets in British Columbia and Washington (Vermeer & Westrheim 1984, Wilson & Manuwal 1986). See Ainley & Boekelheide (1990, Chap. 3), for possible size differences in prey selected by Murres, Pigeon Guillemots, and Tufted Puffins at the Farallon Islands. Elsewhere Murres eat mostly fish of a variety of species and euphausiids; they eat minor amounts of amphipods, isopods, decapods, cephalopods, and polychaete worms (Johnsgard 1987).

Marin Breeding Distribution

During the atlas period, Common Murres were breeding at three large colonies along the Marin County coast: Point Reyes Lighthouse, Point Resistance, and Double Point Rocks (Sowls et al. 1980; Table 14, Figure 14). In 1989, these three colonies were still active, as was a small one established at Millers Point Rocks at least by 1982 (Carter et al. 1992).

Historical Trends/Population Threats

Preliminary surveys in 1969 to 1972 estimated 9440 Common Murres were breeding at the three sites where the bulk of the Marin County population has subsequently bred (Ainley & Whitt 1973); these estimates were probably low because the counts were not all taken from boats, as recent counts have been. Sowls et al. (1980) estimated that a total of about 37,000 Murres were breeding at three Marin County colonies in 1979 to 1980. Takekawa et al. (1990) documented declines from 1980–1982 to 1986 in numbers of breeding Murres in central California, including Marin County; total numbers in Marin fell to about 26,900 birds. Numbers dropped at Point Reyes Lighthouse by 53.5% (from 44,250 in 1982 to 20,590 in 1986), at Point Resistance by 59.8% (from 7540 in 1980 to 3030 in 1986), and at Double Point Rocks by 77.9% (from 14,870 in 1980 to 3280 in 1986). The declines had multiple causes (see below). In 1989, Carter et al. (1992) estimated that 23,495 Murres were breeding at Marin County colonies. A pattern of declines of this magnitude in a local area is best interpreted in a regional and historical context.

The history of the Farallon Murre colony is the best known of any in California. From a peak of 400,000 Murres in the 1850s, the Farallon population declined precipitously to about 60,000 birds at the end of commercial egg collecting just after 1900 (Ainley & Lewis 1974). By 1959, continued human disturbance and chronic oil pollution had further depressed numbers to a low of 6000 to 7000 birds. With protection and diminished oil pollution, the colony rebounded to 20,500 birds in 1972 (Ainley & Lewis 1974), peaked at 102,110 birds in 1982 (Takekawa et al. 1990), and dropped to 68,168 by 1989

(Carter et al. 1992). Despite such fluctuations, apparently numbers of breeding Murres in general have increased along the entire California coast throughout much of this century (Osborne & Reynolds 1971, Osborne 1972, Sowls et al. 1980, Briggs et al. 1987).

The entire population of Common Murres in California breeds along the state's central and northern coast. Sowls et al. (1980) estimated that 363,154 Murres bred at 19 sites in that region in 1979 and 1980; they did not include an estimate for the North Farallon Islands which then held about 51,540 birds (Carter et al. 1992). The state population peaked at about 520,000 in 1982 (Briggs et al. 1987). Between 1980-1982 and 1986, the central California breeding population declined overall by 52.6% (from 229,080 to 108,530 birds), while the northern California population remained relatively unchanged (Takekawa et al. 1990). The decline in the central coast population was caused by a high rate of incidental take of Murres during an intensive nearshore gill-net fishery, compounded by mortality from two major oil spills and a severe El Niño event in 1982-83. Declines at individual colonies ranged from 46%-100% and were most severe at colonies located nearest to areas of highest gill-net-fishing mortality. Declines along the Marin County coast, as detailed above, were among the most severe. From 1979 to 1987, gill-net fishing in central California waters killed roughly 70,000-75,000 Murres. Takekawa et al. (1990) estimated that gill-net mortality accounted for roughly 40%-45% of the 120,550 Murres lost from the central California population during this period. An estimated 4500 Common Murres were killed or debilitated in the Gulf of the Farallones in the November 1984 *Puerto Rican* oil spill (PRBO 1985) and about 7500 along the central California coast in the February 1986 *Apex Houston* oil spill (Page et al. 1990); a minimum (probably much higher) of 1100 Murres met a similar fate in the 1971 San Francisco oil spill (Smail et al. 1972). Carter et al. (1992) estimated 351,336 Murres were breeding at 23 sites in California in 1989; this number is only 3% fewer than the population estimate for 1979 to 1980, and the proportions of the population breeding in northern and central California were similar in both periods.

Murres at the Farallon Islands have also experienced eggshell thinning from pesticide residues (Gress et al. 1971), but no adverse effects on reproductive success have been detected (Ainley & Boekelheide 1990, Chap. 8). It is clear, though, that a species with such a history of population declines attributable to human causes should continue to be carefully monitored.

Subdued hissing sounds issue from the carmine mouths of Pigeon Guillemots scattered widely on rocky coastal sea cliffs.
Photograph by Ian Tait.

PIGEON GUILLEMOT *Cepphus columba*

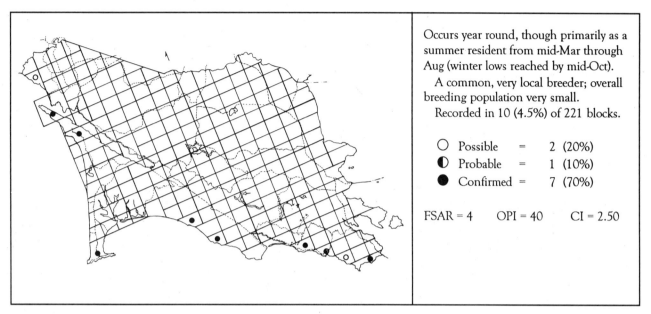

Occurs year round, though primarily as a summer resident from mid-Mar through Aug (winter lows reached by mid-Oct).

A common, very local breeder; overall breeding population very small.

Recorded in 10 (4.5%) of 221 blocks.

○	Possible	=	2 (20%)
◐	Probable	=	1 (10%)
●	Confirmed	=	7 (70%)

FSAR = 4 OPI = 40 CI = 2.50

Ecological Requirements

Our dapper "Sea Pigeons" inhabit nearshore ocean waters, over rocky substrate, usually within sight of land; sometimes they range up to three to (rarely) nine miles from mainland or island shores where they nest (Briggs et al. 1987; Ainley & Boekelheide 1990, Chap. 3). Guillemots nest solitarily or in small, loose colonies when suitable nest sites are clustered. They typically lay their eggs in shallow natural rock cavities in talus slopes, crevices in solid rocks of cliffs or crests of ridges, in sea caves, or among boulders on beaches (Bent 1919; Dawson 1923; Sowls et al. 1980; Ainley & Boekelheide 1990, Chap. 9). Nest sites range from the rocky shores at the water's edge up to the summit of precipitous cliffs. Guillemots also sometimes nest in burrows dug into clay or loose conglomerate rock, abandoned rabbit burrows, and artificial structures, such as rock walls, bridges, suitable wharf timbers, drainpipes, tires hung from pilings, or artificial nest boxes (Bent 1919; Sowls et al. 1980; Johnsgard 1987; Ainley & Boekelheide 1990, Chap. 9). The principal nest site requirement seems to be "a roof over their head" (Ainley & Boekelheide 1990, Chap. 9). Most cavities are slightly deeper than the length of an adult, thus allowing chicks refuge from predatory gulls. Even in deep cavities, suitable for Tufted Puffins or Rhinoceros Auklets (see below), Guillemots lay eggs and incubate near the entrance. Sometimes eggs laid under projecting ledges, boulders, or in spaces between piles of rocks can be seen from above (Bent 1919). In water-worn sea caves, Guillemots lay their eggs in various nooks and crannies about the walls or roof, in cavities under loose rock in the talus of crumbling walls, in open situations on flat rocks or shelfs, or even on the sandy floor of the cave, if beyond reach of daylight and water (Bent 1919, Dawson 1923).

Guillemots do not construct a true nest. Frequently the eggs repose upon a collection of small granite chips, pebbles, shell fragments, bones, or other natural or human debris, or sometimes on bare rock, gravel, or soil. It is unclear whether Guillemots just select hollows with accumulated debris or actually gather nest material, but at most sites they likely just scrape together whatever material is available within easy reach (Bent 1919). Availability of nest sites may limit Guillemot populations at some sites (Ainley & Boekelheide 1990, Chap. 9), but not at others (Kuletz 1983). At the Farallon Islands, some pairs may control more than one nest site within a few yards of the site being used and may perhaps alternate irregularly among them (Ainley & Boekelheide 1990, Chap. 9).

Pigeon Guillemots use wing-propelled dives to search for prey, primarily on or over rocky substrate of the subtidal zone (Follett & Ainley 1976; Ainley & Boekelheide 1990, Chap. 3). Guillemots are deep divers and probably descend to 330 feet or more (Ainley & Boekelheide 1990, Chap. 3). Once they reach the bottom, they "hover" by paddling their feet as they probe nooks and crannies for prey (Johnsgard 1987). Birds apparently forage mostly early and late in the day (Ainley & Boekelheide 1990, Chap. 3). In years of superabundant prey at the Farallones, small groups of Guillemots participate in multi-species foraging flocks preying on midwater-schooling rockfish, but otherwise they feed alone at submerged reefs

197

and hunt for solitary prey that hide in the rocks. In years of poor prey availability in rocky habitat, Guillemots apparently feed more on sandy bottoms, though probably near rocks.

Farallon breeders feed their chicks primarily juvenile rockfish and sculpins, along with small numbers of a variety of other fish, octopuses, and mysid shrimp (Ainley & Boekelheide 1990, Chap. 3, n = 2586). Adults bring food items one at a time, and prey are held crosswise in the bill, grasped by the head with the tail dangling out of one side (Johnsgard 1987). During cold-water years at the Farallones, rockfish are the principal prey, whereas in warm-water years, sculpins and other bottom-dwelling fish are more prevalent and dietary diversity is higher (Ainley & Boekelheide 1990, Chap. 3). Dietary overlap is high between Guillemots and Pelagic Cormorants, especially in years of rockfish abundance. In all years, the Guillemot diet diversifies toward the end of the chick-rearing period, when rockfish decrease and other species increase in importance. In warm-water years, the proportion of rockfish in the diet decreases from about 50% to 9% during the course of the nestling period, and in other years it decreases from about 80% to 50% during that period. In Alaska, individual Guillemots may display foraging site and prey preferences that are generally maintained within a season and between years; differences in diet between individuals appear to be correlated with laying date, habitat use, and possibly an acquired search image (Kuletz 1983). At the Farallones, individual Guillemots would more likely specialize in different prey in warm-water years, when overall dietary diversity is greater, than in cold-water years, when most individuals concentrate on rockfish (Ainley & Boekelheide 1990, Chap. 3). Apparently adults feed to a greater extent on invertebrates, such as crustaceans, mollusks, and marine worms, than is indicated by the food fed to chicks (Lewis & Briggs 1985).

Marin Breeding Distribution

During the atlas period, Pigeon Guillemots nested at scattered sites along the outer coast of Marin County endowed with rocky bluffs and sea stacks (Table 14, Figure 14). Representative breeding locations were Double Point/Allamere Falls (ON/FY 7/5/80 –DS, ITi) and the mouth of Cold Stream, just N of Slide Ranch (ON 7/26/82 –DS).

Historical Trends/Population Threats

In surveys of only selected portions of the Marin County coast, Ainley and Whitt (1973) estimated that 82 Pigeon Guillemots were breeding at four sites. In 1979, Sowls et al. (1980) estimated that 366 Guillemots were nesting along 15 stretches of the Marin coastline; this estimate is low because they only noted the presence of Guillemots, without reporting numbers, at four sites. In complete surveys, Carter et al. (1992) estimated that 1108 Guillemots were breeding along 14 stretches of the Marin coast. The most notable increase from 1979 to 1989 was from 120 to 616 birds at the Point Reyes headlands. Estimates for the entire Guillemot population breeding on the central and northern California coast ranged from 13,814 in 1979 to 1980 (Sowls et al. 1980) to 12,252 in 1989 (Carter et al. 1992).

Pigeon Guillemots declined on the Farallon Islands early in the 1900s because of oil pollution and disturbance from humans and domestic livestock (Ainley & Lewis 1974; Ainley & Boekelheide 1990, Chap. 9). Numbers have since increased, and the population estimate for most of the 1970s and early 1980s of 2000 to 2200 birds may be an all-time high because of the current availability of nest burrows formerly occupied by Tufted Puffins during their population peak on the islands early in this century. The population of Guillemots breeding at Southeast Farallon Island dropped to less than 100 birds during the 1982-83 El Niño event, but subsequently increased to 1867 birds in 1989 (Ainley & Boekelheide 1990, Chap. 9; Carter et al. 1992).

Oil pollution and disturbance continue to pose threats to Guillemot populations (Sowls et al. 1980). In the 1980s, many were also killed in gill nets along with Murres (H.R. Carter pers. comm.).

RHINOCEROS AUKLET *Cerorhinca monocerata*

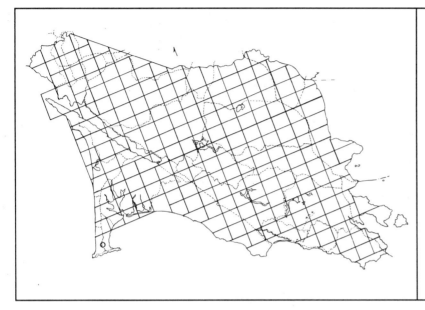

Occurs year round, though primarily as a winter resident from mid-Oct to mid-Apr; occupies Farallon Island (and perhaps Marin) breeding colonies mostly from Apr through Aug (extremes Feb-Sep).

An uncommon, very local breeder; overall breeding population very small. Recorded in 1 (0.4%) of 221 blocks.

○ Possible   =   1 (100%)
◑ Probable   =   0 (0%)
● Confirmed   =   0 (0%)

FSAR = 2   OPI = 2   CI = 1.00

Ecological Requirements

Despite a horny protuberance on its bill suggesting a superficial likeness to a rhinoceros and a surname claiming affinity to the auklets, this species is in fact a puffin. Nevertheless, by habit and fondness we are perhaps forever doomed to use the nickname "Rhino." Off California, these puffins inhabit inshore and offshore ocean waters over the continental shelf, but they are most numerous in deeper waters over the continental slope (Briggs et al. 1987). During the breeding season, most birds in California are found within about 30 to 35 miles of nesting colonies (Briggs et al. 1987; Ainley & Boekelheide 1990, Chap. 3). Birds disperse farther from colonies during warm-water years, when food is scarcer (Ainley & Boekelheide 1990, Chap. 3). In Marin County, Rhinoceros Auklets are seen in season on the water below the cliffs at the Point Reyes headlands and near Bird Rock—sites where they apparently breed—but the foraging range of these birds is unknown.

The generally small, loose breeding colonies on California's islands and steep mainland slopes (Sowls et al. 1980, Carter et al. 1992) contrast with the dense colonies of thousands of birds prevalent from Washington north to Alaska (Bent 1919, Sowls et al. 1978). Rhinoceros Auklets initially recolonizing the Farallon Islands were nesting in deep natural cavities or clefts in rocks, in caves, or in artificial nest boxes (Sowls et al. 1980; Sander 1986; Ainley & Boekelheide 1990, Chap. 11). As the population has continued to increase, some birds are now digging earthen nesting burrows under boulders in deep soil areas (W.J.

Sydeman pers. comm.). Rhinos also dig earthen burrows at Año Nuevo Island, San Mateo County, and Castle Rock, Del Norte County (H.R. Carter pers. comm.). Nest cavities on the Farallones are usually deeper than the average person's reach (Ainley & Boekelheide 1990, Chap. 11). In one Farallon cave, nests were found up to about 65 feet back from the opening (Sander 1986). Six of eleven nests inside the cave were located in one- to two-foot-deep rock crevices, while five were exposed on the surface of the cave floor; seven nests were lined with grass, and the remainder had no nesting material. Throughout most of the range, Rhinos visit nest sites only in the dark of night, but to a limited extent in California and Oregon, they move about their burrow entrances during daylight (Sowls et al. 1980; Ainley & Boekelheide 1990, Chap. 11). At the Farallones, their activities are largely crepuscular and nocturnal (Sander 1986). Nocturnal visitation may be an adaptation to reduce predation, to avoid kleptoparasitism by gulls while feeding chicks, or, perhaps more likely, to reduce interference by Tufted Puffins, with which Rhinos apparently compete for limited nest sites (Ainley & Boekelheide 1990, Chap. 11).

To the north in the heart of the breeding range, Rhinos nest primarily in earthen burrows on both forested and unforested islands (Bent 1919, Richardson 1961, Sowls et al. 1980, Wilson & Manuwal 1986). They select nest sites there on sea-facing slopes, cliffs, or level areas adjacent to edges of islands in terrain varying from forests with open understories to dense shrubbery, grassy slopes, or bare

199

earth. With their feet and bills, Rhinos excavate or reno-vate burrows from about 4 to 25 feet deep; average burrow lengths at different locations vary from 6-8 to 10-15 feet (Richardson 1961). Soil conditions, slope, and vegetation are important determinants of "Auklet" occupation and apparently burrow length. Rhinos prefer rather firm sandy soil held together by roots at the surface and avoid soil that is too loose and sandy or too hard and rocky. Rhinos usually dig roughly horizontal burrows into steep slopes or into the base of small banks in flatter areas. Burrows sometimes have one or more spurs or blind alleys, and the last few feet of the main passage tend to slope down, often dropping off an inch or two, to terminate in an enlarged dome-shaped nest chamber. Rhinos lay their single egg in a nest that varies from a depression in the dirt (with or without a little dried or green grass) to a shallow saucer-shaped nest of grass, leaves, twigs, moss, ferns, feathers, or other available material (Bent 1919, Richardson 1961). Dry grass often is added to the nest or is found in the burrow during the nestling stage. In all areas, Rhinos prefer nest sites with some slope or altitude close at hand, presumably to aid in both takeoffs and landings (Richard-son 1961, Wilson & Manuwal 1986). In general, Rhinos favor somewhat more gentle slopes and tolerate taller vegetation at nest sites than do Tufted Puffins (Vermeer 1979). In some areas, Rhinos make runways through dense vegetation from open takeoff and landing spots to the mouths of their burrows (Richardson 1961). Burrows may be used year after year, often by the same pairs. Chicks fledge at about 50%-70% of adult weight (Vermeer & Cullen 1982) and are barely able to fly from their burrows down to the water (Richardson 1961).

Rhinos' wing-propelled dives apparently carry them to intermediate depths—65 to 260 feet—in their pursuit of prey (Ainley & Boekelheide 1990, Chap. 3). They appar-ently feed mostly early and late in the day, alone or occasionally in small flocks. The diet fed to chicks at the Farallon Islands in 1986 (a warm-water year) was 74% juvenile rockfish, 22% Pacific saury, and 4% black cod (n = 27, Sander 1986; Ainley & Boekelheide 1990, Chap. 3). Ongoing diet studies at the Farallones from 1987 to 1989 indicate that rockfish, anchovies, sablefish, and salmon are in fact the main prey items and that the diet varies consid-erably with season and year (PRBO unpubl. data). Through-out the range, the diet fed to chicks is almost exclusively small fish (1.5 to 9.4 inches long)—particularly sandlance, anchovies, smelt, herring, rockfish, capelin, and Pacific saury—and sometimes small amounts of squid and octopus (Vermeer 1980, Hatch 1984, Vermeer & Westrheim 1984, Wilson & Manuwal 1986). Adults often carry many fish at a time crosswise in their bills to their chicks (Vermeer & Cullen 1982); later in the season they deliver one fish at a time (S.D. Emslie and W.J. Sydeman pers. comm.). The chick diet varies between nearby offshore and inshore colonies, latitudinally, and both annually and seasonally, apparently as affected by changes in the distri-bution and abundance of prey. At least in winter, adults also eat euphausiids (Ainley & Sanger 1979) and greater quantities of nonfish prey. In Monterey Bay, the winter diet can be as much as 70% market squid (Baltz & Morejohn 1977, n = 26).

Marin Breeding Distribution

Since at least 1977, up to 11 Rhinoceros Auklets at a time have been observed on the water below the Point Reyes headlands in May and June (ABN). These birds have been observed "billing" and in "passing flights," which suggest local breeding. Three of these "Auklets" were seen off Bird Rock, Tomales Point, on 5 June 1989 (Carter et al. 1992). Representative records during the atlas period included one to three birds just off the seabird nesting cliffs by the Point Reyes Lighthouse (6/11-24/80 —DS, JGE; 6/21/81 —DS, RSt) and four birds off Chimney Rock (6/20-7/16/77 —PRBO, JMR). The apparent establishment of breeding at Point Reyes is part of a much wider increase and range expansion of the breeding population described below.

Historical Trends/Population Threats

Rhinoceros Auklets were absent from the Farallon Islands from the 1860s (when perhaps eliminated by overzealous collectors) until the early 1970s (Ainley & Lewis 1974; Ainley & Boekelheide 1990, Chap. 3). Perhaps aided by the elimination of burrow-competing rabbits, by 1989 the Farallon population numbered 516 birds (Carter et al. 1992). Coincident with this recolonization, the population was increasing within the portion of the historic range from British Columbia to California and the breeding range expanded south to Point Arguello, Santa Barbara County (Scott et al. 1974, Sowls et al. 1980, Briggs et al. 1987, ABN), and recently to the San Miguel Island area of the Channel Islands (Carter et al. 1992). From surveys in 1979 to 1980, Sowls et al. (1980) estimated 362 Rhinoc-eros Auklets were breeding at six sites along the central and northern California coast. Continued rapid expansion of the population in that region is documented by estimates of 1750 breeding birds at 29 colonies in 1989 (Carter et al. 1992). The reasons for this range expansion and popu-lation increase appear to be unknown. Despite this upswing in the breeding population, the Rhinoceros Auk-let is still considered a Bird Species of Special Concern in California (Remsen 1978, CDFG 1991b).

Like other alcids, Rhinos are susceptible to oil pollution and human disturbance at nesting sites. About 1600 Rhinoceros Auklets were killed or debilitated along the central California coast in the *Apex Houston* oil spill in February 1986 (Page et al. 1990).

TUFTED PUFFIN *Fratercula cirrhata*

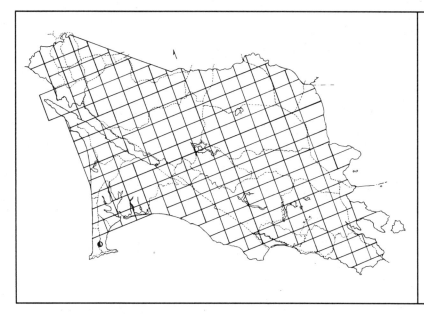

Occurs year round, though primarily as a winter resident from Oct through Apr. Puffins occupy Farallon Island (and perhaps Marin) nesting sites from mid-Mar (rarely starting early Apr) through Aug or early Sep.

An uncommon, very local breeder; overall breeding population very small. Recorded in 1 (0.4%) of 221 blocks.

○	Possible	=	0	(0%)
◐	Probable	=	1	(100%)
●	Confirmed	=	0	(0%)

FSAR = 2   OPI = 2   CI = 2.00

Ecological Requirements

At sea, the outlandish headgear of the solemn "Sea Parrot" enlivens the deep waters over the continental slope (Briggs et al. 1987; Ainley & Boekelheide 1990, Chap. 3). Near the Farallon Island breeding colony, Tufted Puffins most frequently forage in waters deeper than 260 feet between 30 miles south of the island to the Cordell Bank about 35 miles to the north (Ainley & Boekelheide 1990, Chap. 3). In warm-water years, breeders disperse farther from the island to feed. The foraging haunts of Point Reyes breeders are unknown but probably are similar to those of Farallon birds and probably involve longer commutes to and from nest sites.

Tufted Puffins breed on treeless islands, large offshore rocks and sea stacks, and steep mainland cliffs. In California, Tufted Puffins nest in small, loose colonies of up to 100 birds (Sowls et al. 1980), unlike the dense colonies of thousands of birds in Alaska (Sowls et al. 1978). Because the soil is generally shallow at the Farallones, Puffins there do not dig earthen nest burrows, as they do extensively elsewhere, but instead lay their single eggs in natural cavities or clefts in rock of steep terrain high on the island; some nest in artificial cavities of tile pipe and rock (Ainley & Boekelheide 1990, Chap. 11). Puffins probably breed in rock cavities at Point Reyes and other sites on the California coast, though at Castle Rock, Del Norte County, some birds dig burrows in hard soil (H.R. Carter pers. comm.). Lack of adequate nesting habitat may limit Tufted Puffins in California. Recently at the Farallones, nesting cavities are usually deeper than an average person's reach (Ainley & Boekelheide 1990, Chap. 11), but for-

merly, perhaps when nest sites were more limiting, many sitting birds and eggs were visible from outside (Dawson 1923). Some nesting sites then were "nothing more than the innermost recesses of niches and caves occupied by Murres." Throughout much of their breeding range, Tufted Puffins prefer grassy slopes, rocky slopes, boulder rubble, and cliff faces and edges as nesting habitat. There they nest mostly in earthen burrows dug with feet and bills three or four feet into soil or conglomerate rock; less frequently they use rock cavities (Bent 1919, Dawson 1923, Vermeer 1979, Johnsgard 1987). They prefer cliff tops and steep slopes clothed with low-growing or sparse vegetation (Vermeer 1979, Johnsgard 1987). Rarely, they drive tunnels through matted vegetation and deposit their eggs in the shade on the surface of the ground (Dawson 1923). Generally, Tufted Puffins favor steeper, more open terrain for nesting than do Rhinoceros Auklets; small numbers of Tufted Puffins nest on flat islands and run to take off on beaches below the vegetation (Vermeer 1979). Tufted Puffins may or may not line their nests scantily with leaves, grass, seaweed, or feathers (Bent 1919, Dawson 1923, Johnsgard 1987).

Tufted Puffins are deep divers, probably exceeding 330 feet in depth in their wing-propelled pursuit of prey (Ainley & Boekelheide 1990, Chap. 11). They apparently feed mostly early and late in the day, alone or occasionally in small flocks. Puffins hold many fish at a time crosswise in their bills, often in an alternating left- and right-handed manner, for delivery to young (Johnsgard 1987). At the Farallon Islands, the chick diet is mostly anchovies, rockfish, and squid (Ainley & Boekelheide 1990, Chap. 3, n = 728). Limited data suggest that rockfish predominate in cold-water years, when abundant in the diet of other Farallon breeding seabirds, and squid replace fish in warm-water years. The diet appears to diversify as the nestling period progresses, largely as a function of decreasing use of anchovies (which move inshore), increasing use of squid and unidentified fish (probably Pacific saury, which dwell in slope and pelagic waters), and stable use of rockfish. At the Farallon Islands, adult Puffins, like Murres, may also feed on euphausiids, but they do not feed them to chicks as they do to a limited degree at other locations (Hatch 1984). Elsewhere, Tufted Puffins feed mostly on a variety of fish—especially sandlance, rockfish, cod, prowfish, capelin, smelt, and herring—as well as euphausiids and polychaete worms (Vermeer 1979, Hatch 1984, Johnsgard 1987). The diet, of course, varies annually, seasonally, and with location.

Marin Breeding Distribution

Since 1976, Tufted Puffins have been seen almost annually in the vicinity of the Point Reyes headlands from mid-April through July (ABN). These birds have been observed in passing flights, gathering algae, and carrying food up to cliffs, but solid confirmation of breeding is lacking because the inaccessibility of the cliffs has impeded efforts to find nests. Representative records for the atlas period include up to seven birds on the water, diving to gather algae, and flying up to nearby cliffs at Chimney Rock from 12 June to 16 July 1977; and up to six birds on the water and in passing flights at the Point Reyes Lighthouse from 29 May to 30 June 1980 (many observers –ABN).

Historical Trends/Population Threats

Formerly, small numbers of Tufted Puffins came to the cliffs at Point Reyes during the nesting season (G&W 1927), and two pairs were "apparently nesting" on Bird Rock, Tomales Point, on 18 May 1930 (S&P 1933). A paucity of records until the mid-1970s (see above) may have indicated a decline and subsequent recovery, or perhaps just an upswing in sightings after a period of limited observer coverage drew to a close.

Numbers of Tufted Puffins breeding at the Farallones declined from about 2000 birds in 1911 to 26 in 1959 (Ainley & Lewis 1974). Subsequently the population has grown slightly and stabilized in the 1980s at about 80 to 100 birds, except for the short-lived decline to less than 10 birds during the 1982–83 El Niño event (Ainley & Boekelheide 1990, Chap. 11; PRBO unpubl. data). Ainley and Lewis (1974) speculated that the initial decline was caused by oil pollution and that Puffins had not made a full recovery because humans overexploited the Pacific sardine stock during the mid-1940s (see Double-crested Cormorant account). Tufted Puffins have also contracted their range and numbers more widely and no longer breed south of the Farallones (Sowls et al. 1980, Garrett & Dunn 1981) except at Prince Island in the Channel Islands (Carter et al. 1992). From surveys of the central and northern California coast, Sowls et al. (1980) estimated that 250 Puffins were breeding at 13 sites, and Carter et al. (1992) estimated 266 birds at 12 sites. The Tufted Puffin still faces threats from oil pollution and human disturbance (Sowls et al. 1980), and it remains a Bird Species of Special Concern in California (Remsen 1978, CDFG 1991b).

Pigeons and Doves
Family *Columbidae*

ROCK DOVE *Columba livia*

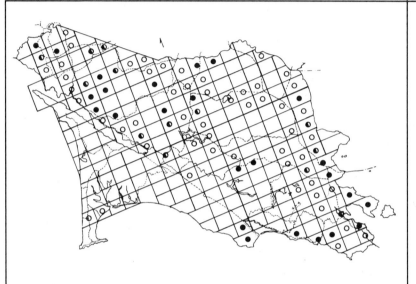

A year-round resident.

A fairly common, somewhat local breeder; overall breeding population small.

Recorded in 90 (40.7%) of 221 blocks.

○	Possible	=	52	(58%)
◐	Probable	=	13	(14%)
●	Confirmed	=	25	(28%)

FSAR = 3   OPI = 270   CI = 1.70

Ecological Requirements

Flocks of pigeons feeding tamely at city dwellers' feet are sometimes the only "wildlife" they get to know. North American Rock Doves are the feral descendants of domestic pigeons brought to this continent by European settlers. Today, most of our pigeon populations still depend directly or indirectly on humans for their survival, but some birds do exist in a semiwild state. Breeding Rock Doves require elevated, enclosed sites for nesting and roosting, foraging grounds that are bare or covered only with short or scattered vegetation, and water for drinking (Goodwin 1983, Cramp 1985). They avoid tall, dense vegetation of any kind, even grassland. Rock Doves are quite gregarious and commonly form flocks of varying size for virtually all activities away from their nesting territories. In the Old World, truly wild Rock Doves seek nest sites and shelter in cliffs (particularly on the coast) and feed in nearby treeless terrain. Today's feral birds are attached mostly to human settlements, where they nest in artificial structures and feed in open urban settings or in agricultural land. Most Rock Doves in Marin County inhabit urban centers or agricultural ranchland, though small numbers frequent coastal cliffs.

Although Rock Doves sometimes nest in solitary pairs, most breed in loose colonies. In large colonies, nests may be as close as 1.5 to 3.0 feet (Cramp 1985). They prefer to nest under cover in semidarkness (Goodwin 1983, Cramp 1985). Wild (Old World) birds or semiwild feral birds usually nest in caves on sheltered ledges or in niches; or in holes, niches, or deep crevices in coastal or inland cliffs; less frequently they may nest in clefts in other rocks or in ruined buildings. Their nests are often far back in caves or deep in potholes or wells; birds will nest on a cave floor if suitable ledges are already occupied. Feral birds, however, have mostly forsaken nesting in the wild for equivalent sites in or on farm buildings, church towers or steeples, large institutional buildings, large gabled houses, bridges, freeway underpasses, above-ground parking lots, and the like. Most nest sites are fairly high above ground. Although city-dwelling birds are tolerant of close human approach on the ground, they prefer abandoned buildings or inaccessible parts of structures for nesting. Rock Doves also nest in holes or hollows in trees, forks or depressions on large branches, or recesses in palm trees. Their nests are loosely constructed cups of roots, stems, and leaves, small

203

pieces of driftwood, seaweed, and feathers; there is no true lining (Cramp 1985). Most pairs use two nest sites alternately, though normally not the same site for successive broods. The majority of pairs also use the same or adjacent nest sites over several years.

Rock Doves form mainly communal, nocturnal roosts, though they sometimes roost singly or convene in the day during gloomy or stormy weather (Cramp 1985). Gregariousness at roosts is less pronounced among breeding birds, though off-duty males use communal roosts during incubation. The birds prefer roosts with cover all around, similar to nest sites. Although they prefer ledges that have broad overhangs and protection from the wind, they will use ledges more exposed to weather or artificial lighting. Roosts and breeding colony sites may be the same, or they may be separate; there also may be several alternative roost sites. The roost site chosen may be the closest to the place where the birds last fed, or possibly the choice may be dictated by weather. Roosts are often used by birds from different feeding flocks and perhaps function in part as foraging information centers. However, flocks in some areas are discrete units attached to specific nesting, roosting, and feeding areas, while elsewhere they are chance aggregations.

Rock Doves use exposed vantage points for long periods while surveying areas, waiting for feeding opportunities (Cramp 1985). Birds inhabiting agricultural or undeveloped lands often feed near their nest sites. Birds from settled areas may feed exclusively in urban centers, or they may nest and roost there and fly to nearby fields to forage (Goodwin 1983, Cramp 1985). Rock Doves commonly forage up to one-third mile from nest sites, but sometimes as far as 4 to 5 miles (Cramp 1985). Upon arriving at fields to feed, feral birds normally circle, gain height, and circle again before landing in open areas with good visibility. Foraging birds walk or run about, pecking at the ground. Although most birds forage on bare or sparsely vegetated ground, feral (but not wild) birds will forage, rarely, for vegetable fare on the ground in woodlands or up in trees, bushes, or vines (Goodwin 1983, Cramp 1985). Flocks frequently forage all at once, with some birds flying from the rear to the front; there is a dominance hierarchy in feral flocks, with central birds obtaining more food (Cramp 1985). In the country, Rock Doves feed around ranchyards, in arable land, and on land grazed by domestic livestock. In urban areas, they feed on paved squares, sidewalks, roads, vacant lots, parking lots, parks, and gardens. This species is adapted chiefly to a seed diet of cereal grains, legumes, weeds, and grasses (Goodwin 1983, Cramp 1985). In agricultural areas, cereal grains predominate in the diet over weed or grass seeds. Rock Doves occasionally eat acorns (usually broken or damaged), green leaves, buds, tender roots, flowers, berries, galls, and seaweed. In addition, they eat small amounts of inverte-

brate foods or small snails and mollusks, ticks and other arachnids, earthworms, slugs, moth larvae, and various insects. City-dwelling birds, on the other hand, subsist mostly on a wide variety of artificial foods offered to them by humans or obtained by scavenging. Of these, bread is a staple. Other foods include grains, peanuts, popcorn, cheese, cooked meat, fat, bacon rind, fish, apple, banana, potato, chocolate, and ice cream! Overall there is considerable variation in diet with season and locality. Rock Doves also collect small stones and grit to aid in digestion, and eat mortar, presumably for the calcium content.

Adults feed the young by regurgitation (Goodwin 1983, Cramp 1985). The diet of wild nestlings is similar to that of adults, but it includes a higher, though still minor, proportion of animal matter. "Crop (pigeon's) milk" is very important and is the sole food initially. At about four to five days of age, the young are fed morsels of soft food and small seeds. The importance of these and other solid foods in the diet increases until just before fledging, when the young consume only traces of crop milk. When their young are small, foraging adults take small seeds in preference to larger ones (Goodwin 1983). Although adults usually drink from the edge or in the shallows of water, they sometimes alight on the surface to drink or hover above it; young are brought water in the crop (Goodwin 1983, Cramp 1985).

Marin Breeding Distribution

Marin County's breeding Rock Doves were concentrated in the lowlands of the eastern urban corridor along Highway 101. They were scattered throughout the farm country of central and northern Marin but were relatively rare in ranchlands on the Point Reyes peninsula. Some of the birds in farming country were not truly feral, as some ranchers had built special lofts (dovecotes) for the birds and probably fed them. Representative nesting locations were ranch at E end of Clark Road, E of Tomales Bay (NE 5/13/82 —DS); abandoned building near quarry on N side of Marshall-Petaluma Rd. near Soulajoule Reservoir (NE 6/23/82 —DS); and nest in depression in decrepit straw mattress in abandoned ranch house, Hicks Valley (NY 5/16/82 —DS, W&ST). Birds frequented the sea cliffs north of Slide Ranch (south of Stinson Beach) in the nesting season, but because access is difficult, observers did not confirm breeding there.

Historical Trends/Population Threats

It seems likely that Rock Doves evolved in arid or semiarid and nearly treeless regions of Eurasia (Goodwin 1983), though the original distribution is obscure because of the long history of human domestication of the species for food, homing pigeons, and breeding of fancy varieties (Cramp 1985); these were apparently the very first domestic birds. Many have become feral, especially in urban areas, and these populations are still augmented by escaped birds. In the Old World, Rock Doves spread widely into many areas in response to the creation of suitable feeding grounds from agricultural and tree-cutting activities (Goodwin 1983). Domestic Rock Doves were brought to the New World, to Nova Scotia, as early as 1606, and later to other colonies along the eastern seaboard (Schorger 1952). Though they are now widespread (AOU 1983), the expansion of feral pigeons in North America appears to have been little documented.

Mailliard (1900) and Stephens and Pringle (1933), for Marin County, and Grinnell and Wythe (1927), for the San Francisco Bay Area, did not list the Rock Dove at all in their avifaunal summaries. It seems likely that Rock Doves occurred in these areas at the time but went unreported because of their domestic origins. Little additional

attention has been paid to these feral homesteaders. Grinnell and Miller (1944) gave only a skeletal account for this introduced species in California. They reported it "established in a free-living state about many cities." They did not mention its status in agricultural areas, its history of expansion, or the limits of its distribution at that time. A thorough search of historical archives would likely reveal the introduction of domestic pigeons to California at the time of Spanish missionaries or by enthusiasts during the Gold Rush. Rock Doves are now established throughout most settled and agricultural areas of California (McCaskie et al. 1979, Garrett & Dunn 1981). Breeding Bird Surveys indicated that Rock Dove populations were still increasing in the Central Valley from 1968 to 1979 (Robbins et al. 1986) and in California as a whole from 1968 to 1989 (USFWS unpubl. analyses).

BAND-TAILED PIGEON *Columba fasciata*

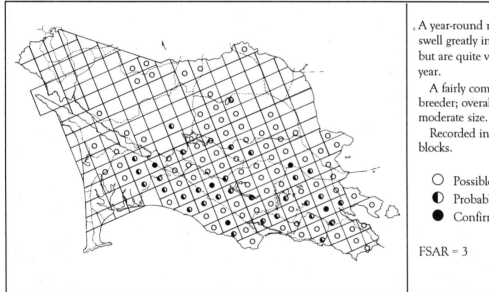

A year-round resident; numbers can swell greatly in winter (mostly Sep–Mar) but are quite variable then from year to year.

A fairly common, fairly widespread breeder; overall breeding population of moderate size.

Recorded in 117 (52.9%) of 221 blocks.

○	Possible	=	83 (71%)
◐	Probable	=	29 (25%)
●	Confirmed	=	5 (4%)

FSAR = 3 OPI = 351 CI = 1.33

Ecological Requirements

This gregarious wild pigeon lives in Marin County's conifer, mixed conifer, and broadleaved evergreen forests that provide ample mast, berry, and small fruit crops. Apparently the best Band-tailed Pigeon habitat is forest land well interspersed with various age classes of trees and with openings; oaks are of particular importance in California (Jeffrey et al. 1977). The birds usually nest as isolated pairs, frequently near permanent streams. Rarely (though apparently not in California), they breed in small, loose colonies; as many as 17 nests have been found in a single tree (Bent 1932, Neff 1947). Band-tails have nested in some part of

their breeding range in every month of the year, but breeding may (Gutiérrez et al. 1975) or may not (Michael 1928) be a response to abundant mast or berry crops.

Band-tailed Pigeons nest in a variety of trees or large bushes, and their nest heights range from 6 to 180 feet (most 15–40 ft.) above ground (Grinnell et al. 1918, Neff 1947, Glover 1953b, MacGregor & Smith 1955, Peeters 1962, Jeffrey et al. 1977). A sample of 33 nests in the Carmel area of Monterey County ranged from 12 to 95 feet (av. 36 ft.) above ground (MacGregor & Smith 1955). Rarely, these pigeons place nests on the top of a stump, on the ground, or in blowholes and on ledges in sandstone rimrock (Neff 1947); apparently no such records pertain to California. Most nests in coastal California are in conifers, oaks, alders, and occasionally in tall bushes, such as blue blossom *(Ceanothus thyrsiflorus),* or introduced trees near human habitation. Nests are usually placed in a fork, against a trunk, at variable distances out on a horizontal limb, or, infrequently, in dense branches. Tree nests are flimsy platforms constructed of dead coarse twigs of oaks, conifers, or other plant stems and forest litter (rarely, they are lined with pine needles); a ground nest was made of leaves and moss. Nest trees are frequently on a slope or adjacent to a small precipice and near a clearing, leaving room for incubating birds to exit the nest with a momentum-gaining dive (Neff 1947, Peeters 1962).

Band-tails feed singly or in flocks (even in the breeding season) and procure most of their food by plucking and gleaning from trees and shrubs and by gleaning from the ground. Birds searching in forest duff flip aside leaves and debris with horizontal movements of the bill (Smith 1968). Feeding flocks advance through the trees or across open ground by the progressive movement of individuals flying from the back of the flock to the front (Peeters 1962). Band-tails perform acrobatics while feeding in trees: they hang vertically by their feet from branches, half spreading their wings and tails to stabilize themselves as they reach for fruits and buds, then dropping to lower branches (Bent 1932, Peeters 1962).

Band-tailed Pigeons are almost exclusively vegetarians, specializing on mast, small wild and cultivated fruits and berries, grains, and other seeds; the few insects consumed appear to be taken incidentally. Band-tails tend to concentrate on abundant food sources to the exclusion of other available items, and their diet varies considerably with season and locality (Neff 1947, Smith 1968, Jeffrey et al. 1977, Grenfell et al. 1980). In California, acorns (especially of live oaks), consumed whole, are the staple of their diet from fall through spring, when they are supplemented by wild fruits, such as madrone and toyon, and cultivated grains. Band-tails tend to select the smaller of available acorns, particularly with respect to width and weight (Fry 1977). In spring, terminal buds, tender young leaves, and blossoms of oaks, madrone, and manzanita take on increasing importance. In summer and fall, fruits and berries become prominent dietary items. Important ones in California include elderberry, blackberry, raspberry, wild cherry and grape, dogwood, coffeeberry, salmonberry, thimbleberry, huckleberry, salal, chokecherry, and cascara. Cultivated grains, such as wheat, oats, and barley, are taken when sown in late winter and early spring, but particularly in summer and fall, when gleaned from stubble fields after harvest. Orchards supply buds, blossoms, and green fruit in spring and ripe fruits from spring through fall; plum, prune, apricot, peach, cherry, and almond orchards and

vineyards are the favorites in California. Crop damage caused by the pigeons is most severe in spring and early summer, when wild staples are scarce; locally, cultivated grains then may be the predominant item in the diet (Smith 1968, Grenfell et al. 1980). Band-tails will also readily "clean out" grain from bird feeders. Infrequently, they eat seeds of alders, pines, grasses, forbs, and galls.

For the first few days of life, adults feed the young exclusively "pigeon's milk," a fatty, yellow curdlike substance produced in glands of the adult's crop. Regurgitations from the parents' crops contain progressively more berries and seeds until the food of the young is nearly identical to that of adults (Neff 1947, MacGregor & Smith 1955, Jeffrey et al. 1977). Band-tails collect grit to help grind food and perhaps for its mineral content, and they need fresh water daily (Smith 1968). They frequently ingest mineral salts from upland deposits, estuarine borders, and the water of mineral springs. It has been suggested that the minerals may aid in digestion of mast (Smith 1968) or that they are a supply of calcium necessary for egg formation and crop gland function (March & Sadlier 1972).

Marin Breeding Distribution

The only previously published nesting record from Marin County was of a nest found at Lagunitas on 30 July 1912 (Mailliard 1912). During the atlas period, the distribution of nesting Band-tails in Marin closely approximated the distribution of conifer and dense mixed evergreen forest. A representative nesting location was Upland Ave., Mill Valley (NE summer 1980 or 1981 —KY).

Historical Trends/Population Threats

Unrestricted sport and market hunting in the past, particularly early in this century, led to a decline in the species and an outcry for legal protection (Chambers 1912, Grinnell 1913, Grinnell et al. 1918). In the winter of 1911–12, there was intense shooting at Band-tailed Pigeon concentrations in southern California. One hunter alone shipped 2000 birds to San Francisco and Los Angeles hotels, and a single trainload of some 100 "enthusiasts" shot an estimated 3000+ birds per day (Chambers 1912). A closed season was in effect in California from 1913 to 1932, and the fortunes of the pigeons rose accordingly (G&M 1944, Neff 1947, Smith 1968, Jeffrey et al. 1977). Numbers of Band-tailed Pigeons detected on Breeding Bird Surveys in California were relatively stable from 1968 to 1989 but decreased from 1980 to 1989 (USFWS unpubl. analyses).

Clear-cutting has destroyed vast expanses of suitable breeding habitat: this species nests only in forests at least 20 years old (Glover 1953b). Although favored berry- and fruit-producing trees and shrubs are abundant in the early stages of forest regeneration after logging or fire, these are often eliminated by herbicide spraying that targets broadleaved species and favors conifers (Grenfell et al. 1980).

MOURNING DOVE *Zenaida macroura*

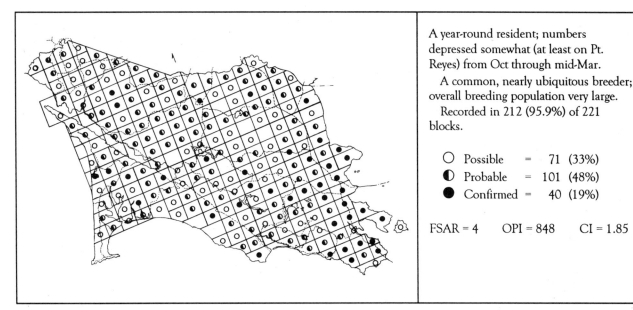

A year-round resident; numbers depressed somewhat (at least on Pt. Reyes) from Oct through mid-Mar.

A common, nearly ubiquitous breeder; overall breeding population very large. Recorded in 212 (95.9%) of 221 blocks.

○	Possible	=	71 (33%)
◑	Probable	=	101 (48%)
●	Confirmed	=	40 (19%)

FSAR = 4   OPI = 848   CI = 1.85

Ecological Requirements

These fast-flying, graceful doves are edge adapted. They forage in open country—grassland, pastureland, weed fields, croplands, roadside edges and ditches, and suburban yards and parks—and seek shelter and nesting sites in forest and woodland edges and woodlots. Although they may nest on the open edges of almost any of Marin's wooded habitats, they are most frequently found in oak woodlands, suburban plantings, riparian woodlands, and planted woodlots or windbreaks (particularly eucalyptus).

Mourning Doves build loose nest platforms of twigs, rootlets, and grass stems. They usually place them on a horizontal branch or in crotches of limbs. Nests range up to 40 feet high in trees, but most are about 10 feet above the ground. Birds also construct nests on the ground, in low bushes, in piles of bark, on shelves on cut banks, in used nests of other birds, and on wooden ledges of human structures (Bent 1932, Cowan 1952). Pairs usually nest solitarily. Nests may be grouped in close proximity in limited favored nesting areas in open country—for example, in isolated woodlots or windbreaks in expansive grasslands.

Mourning Doves feed almost entirely by pecking from the ground and only very rarely feed in trees. During breeding, foraging birds occur singly or in small flocks. The diet is almost exclusively grains (Browning 1962). A few insects are taken only incidentally, and small amounts of snail shells and bone fragments perhaps satisfy a physiological need of nesting birds for calcium. These latter items might also be a source of grit or may be mistaken for seeds

(Grenfell et al. 1980). Year round in California, seeds of 162 species of plants make up 99.9% of the diet—22 are principal food items that account for 10% of the total food in any month or region (Browning 1962, n = 1016). Mourning Doves obtain about two-thirds of their seeds from annual weeds and the remainder from cultivated grains. The diet varies somewhat with season and locality (Browning 1959, 1962). In the inner Coast Range of San Luis Obispo County, Mourning Doves use 55 species of plants, of which 10 are principal food items (n = 183). Early maturing annuals, such as buckthorn weed, red maids, miners lettuce, and California poppy, constitute about 70% of the April and May diet and together with Napa thistle and prostrate pigweed provide over 75% of the June and July diet. Turkey mullein is the most important item in late summer and early fall. Cultivated wheat and barley and, secondarily, milo are most important from late fall through winter, when they are taken as waste grain from fields after harvest. Other important annuals in the area are sunflower, hydra stickleaf, popcorn flowers, vinegar weed, vetch, filaree, phacelia, valley spurge, bur clover, and lambs quarters. Mourning Doves also take advantage of birdseed spread on the ground or at feeders.

As with other members of the pigeon and dove family, Mourning Doves initially feed their nestlings mostly "dove's (pigeon's) milk." At the age of 1 to 3 days, the young are fed 75%–90% dove's milk, but by 4 to 12 days, only 25%. Then regurgitated seeds form a progressively larger fraction of their diet (Browning 1959).

207

Marin Breeding Distribution

The Mourning Dove was one of Marin County's most widespread breeding birds. It reached its greatest abundance in lowland valleys of ranch and crop lands throughout the county and in suburban areas along the Highway 101 corridor in eastern Marin. Representative nesting locales were the long eucalyptus grove SE of Abbott's Lagoon (NE 6/20/82 —DS); S side of Nicasio Reservoir (NE on shelf on road cut 7/6/82 —DS); Mt. Burdell, Novato (NB-NE-NY 4/9–5/1/81 —DS); and Dominican College, San Rafael (NB 3/28/79 —DS). At the Abbott's Lagoon eucalyptus grove, six nests were found in less than a half-hour's search of a stretch of 100 to 200 yards (four were 1.5-4 ft. above the ground in stick and bark litter).

Historical Trends/Population Threats

In the early part of this century, there was limited evidence of local population declines in California (Grinnell et al. 1918). Mourning Doves appear to have increased greatly since that time, aided by human activities, such as cultivation, grazing, and ditch and roadside clearing, that have enhanced their food supply and created more of the disturbed areas they prefer for foraging (Grenfell et al. 1980). Although some of their habitat is currently being lost to increased herbicide use, clean farming, and urbanization, Mourning Doves adapt by exploiting recently cleared forests and new residential developments. Nevertheless, Mourning Dove numbers decreased on Breeding Bird Survey routes in California from 1968 to 1989 (USFWS unpubl. analyses).

Band-tailed Pigeons perform acrobatics that enable them to gobble up berries from dangling clusters. Drawing by Keith Hansen, 1989.

Roadrunners
Family *Cuculidae*

GREATER ROADRUNNER *Geococcyx californianus*

> Formerly a year-round resident; extirpated by at least the 1960s.

Ecological Requirements

This legendary ground-dwelling cuckoo inhabits arid open land with scattered brush and thickets, which in coastal northern California consists primarily of the interface between broken chaparral and oak savannah woodlands or grasslands. Historically, fires have probably done much to maintain this habitat mix. Roadrunners build bulky nest platforms of loosely interlaced sticks and twigs, lined (or not) with finer miscellany such as manure flakes, bark strips, grass tufts, leaves, roots, feathers, or snakeskin (Bryant 1916, Dawson 1923, Bent 1940). They usually place their nests about 3 to 10 feet above the ground in clumps or thickets of thorny shrubs (or cactus in other regions). Rarely, they locate them up to 20 feet above the ground in a tree, directly on the ground, in a cranny of a cliff, or on an artificial structure (Bryant 1916, Dawson 1923, Bent 1940). The birds situate their nests to receive full sun in the early morning hours, when adults are off hunting lizards, and partial shade in the heat of the day (Ohmart 1973).

Roadrunners usually forage on the ground by slowly stalking their prey, then making a short dash to finalize the capture. They also chase down mobile prey, jump up and snatch insects from the air, or glean insects from bushes, from the ground, or by climbing into shrubs (Bryant 1916, Bent 1940). In southern California, the diet of adults is 90% animal matter (by volume) and 10% fruit and seeds (Bryant 1916, n – 64). In the summer months, Roadrunners eat an even greater percentage of animal fare, consisting largely of insects, especially grasshoppers, crickets, and beetles, with lesser numbers of caterpillars, true bugs, flies, ants, bees, wasps, and scorpions. Vertebrates, including lizards, small birds, and small mammals, make up only about 10% (by volume) of the total diet (Bryant 1916); birds are probably taken to a greater degree in winter when cold-blooded prey are inactive (Zimmerman 1970). Snakes also are eaten (Bent 1940, Ohmart 1973). Even though the young are initially fed insects, by the time they are five to six days old they are fed mostly lizards. Through most of the nestling period, young are also fed a clear viscous liquid by regurgitation (Ohmart 1973). Eggs hatch asynchronously, and adults and young are occasionally cannibalistic on the smallest young in their nests. Females also lay larger clutches when prey are more available, for example during the rainy season in Arizona. These observations suggest that Roadrunners are adapted to a limited or irregular food supply (Ohmart 1973).

Marin Breeding Distribution/ Historical Trends/Population Threats

Roadrunners formerly lived in Marin County in small numbers (Mailliard 1900, S&P 1933) and undoubtedly bred here, though there is no documentation. The last reported sightings were at Homestead, Locust Station, Mill Valley, on 22 April 1939 (*Gull* 21, No. 5); at San Rafael Hill on 24 February 1941 (*Gull* 23, No. 3); and on Mount Tamalpais sometime in the 1950s (JW).

Grinnell and Miller (1944) noted declines or local extirpation from areas throughout California that had been thickly settled or heavily hunted. Roadrunners were widely persecuted at one time because (based on limited evidence) they were thought to prey heavily on the eggs and young of quail (Bryant 1916). Grinnell and Wythe (1927) noted a trend of increasing rarity of this species in the San Francisco Bay Area that has continued to this day, with Roadrunners now persisting in small numbers only in the hinterlands of the region. This decline has followed the intense development, habitat alteration, and disturbance attending a rapidly expanding human population. Verner et al. (1980) speculated that numbers in the Sierra foothills may have declined as chaparral-type habitats grew increasingly dense after decades of fire suppression activities. Numbers of Roadrunners were relatively stable on Breeding Bird Surveys in California from 1968 to 1989 but decreased from 1980 to 1989 (USFWS unpubl. analyses); this likely reflects trends largely in southern California, where the species is most numerous.

209

Barn Owls
Family *Tytonidae*

BARN OWL *Tyto alba*

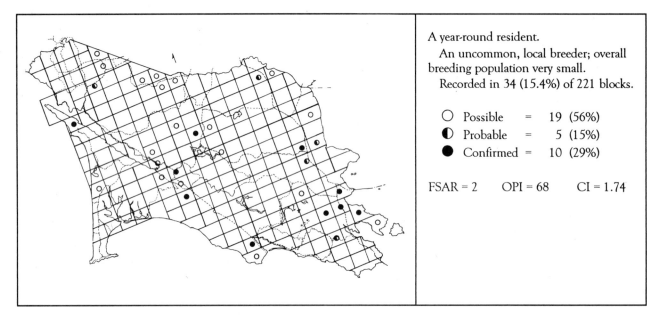

A year-round resident.

An uncommon, local breeder; overall breeding population very small.

Recorded in 34 (15.4%) of 221 blocks.

○ Possible   =   19 (56%)
◑ Probable   =   5 (15%)
● Confirmed =   10 (29%)

FSAR = 2   OPI = 68   CI = 1.74

Ecological Requirements

The whitish, ghostlike silhouette and eerie screeching calls of this monkey-faced owl of subtropical and tropical origins enlivens the darkness in a number of Marin County's open habitats. Barn Owls hunt in open ranchlands, grasslands, broken woodland and brushland, weedy fields, and marshes. They nest nearby in a wide variety of artificial and natural sites in wild, rural, or urban settings. Pairs usually nest solitarily, but nest sites are often limiting (Bloom 1979) and birds sometimes nest in loose colonies at particularly attractive sites (Smith et al. 1974). Nest sites provide a roof and usually at least a modicum of, if not pitch, darkness. Natural nest sites include clefts, holes, grottoes, and caves of rock cliffs, quarries, or mines; natural cavities or ground squirrel holes in earthen banks, roadcuts, or gullies; deserted badger burrows; and hollows of trees (Bent 1938, Johnsgard 1988, Voous 1988). In some areas where the earthen substrate is soft, Barn Owls perform much excavation themselves, using their feet (Johnsgard 1988). Though tree nests are becoming less numerous, Barn Owls still nest in cavities of sycamores and live oaks in California (Bloom 1979). Entrances to tree cavities in California range from 5 to 16 feet above the ground, and the height of actual nest sites varies from

ground level to about 40 feet. Unlike some large owls, Barns do not use abandoned nests of diurnal raptors, but on rare occasions they use deserted crow nests in California (Bent 1938, Voous 1988). Holes in cliffs and banks may have been the original nest sites, as the pale Barn Owl plumage blends well with sandstone cliffs and caves (Voous 1988). Also, the Barn Owl's elliptical egg seems better adapted to the flat bottoms of cave niches (where the round eggs, typically laid by other owls, would be in constant danger of rolling off) than to enclosed tree hollows.

In today's civilized surroundings, most Barn Owls nest in lofts, attics, and dark recesses of human structures, such as barns and farmhouses, church steeples, derelict buildings and sheds, large industrial plants, old deep wells, mine shafts, water pipes, windmills, discarded agricultural machinery, and haystacks both inside and outside of barns (Bent 1938, Bloom 1979, Johnsgard 1988, Voous 1988). Rarely, they will nest in an exposed, unprotected situation, such as the flat roof of an occupied dwelling. Barn Owls also readily nest in large wooden nest boxes, preferably placed inside barns, cabins, and lofts. Nests inside buildings are usually close to a ready exit.

Females lay their eggs in a crude shallow cup formed among dried pellets and heaps of broken bones or skull fragments, right on top of the hay in haylofts, or on wood chips or other natural debris in tree cavities (Bent 1938, Johnsgard 1988, Voous 1988). Favorable nest sites may be used for many successive years by the same or different pairs. Birds laying second clutches may deposit them in the same site as the first clutch, or they may choose a new site. Day roosts may be at nest sites, similar cavities or structures, or in the thick foliage of trees (including palms).

Barn Owls are highly nocturnal. They hide by day and typically become active and start hunting well after sunset and retire before dawn (Voous 1988). Observations of daytime hunting are rare and probably reflect unusual circumstances, such as a previous night of poor hunting because of inclement weather. Barn Owls are very versatile rodent hunters. With their acute hearing, they can strike and capture sound-producing prey in complete darkness (Johnsgard 1988, Voous 1988). Light, graceful, searching flights carry them over open country, where they bank, hover, and drop to the ground erratically (Bent 1938, Voous 1988). Barn Owls pursue prey on foot more than most owls do. To a limited degree, they also hunt from roadside poles (Voous 1988), drop from perches into bushes below to capture roosting sparrows, and catch bats flying out of caves (Smith et al. 1974). Barn Owls that bred at Castle Rock, Del Norte County, and fed extensively on Leach's Storm-Petrels (Bonnot 1928) must also have caught them on the wing. Foraging owls range about 0.6 to 1.9 miles from nest and roost sites (Johnsgard 1988, Voous 1988).

Barn Owls are restricted, rather than generalist, feeders like Great Horned Owls and prey primarily on small terrestrial rodents of field and marsh (Voous 1988). When alternative food items are available, shrews rather than birds (at least in Europe) are usually the main prey. This differs from Long-eared and Short-eared owls and most other rodent-hunting species, whose secondary prey is birds. The North American diet varies by prey numbers from 100% down to 70% mammals—mostly meadow voles and deer mice—with birds and large insects making up most of the balance (Voous 1988). Mammal prey range from a wide variety of small terrestrial rodents to pocket gophers, ground squirrels, moles, muskrats, jackrabbits, and skunks (Bent 1938). Bird prey in North America are mostly small songbirds but include rails, shorebirds, Coots, and Green-backed Herons, documenting that these owls do hunt over wet grasslands and marsh. Other vertebrate prey here include nocturnal lizards, turtles, frogs, toads, and fish. As might be expected, the diet varies geographically, seasonally, and year to year, depending on prey availability (Marti 1974, Voous 1988).

In California, 61% of prey numbers are small voles, 37% white-footed mice, 0.2% shrews, and 0.5% birds (Voous 1988), but another analysis showed 95% mammals, 3% birds, 2% insects, and less than 0.1% reptiles and amphibians (Jaksic et al. 1982, n = 8236). Mean weight of small mammal prey in California is 2.4 ounces (Jaksic et al. 1982, n = 7827). The diet of Barn Owls in the San Francisco Bay Area (including Marin County) is 99% small mammals (96% rodents). Meadow voles, pocket gophers, and deer mice account for 85% of the total, with the balance made up of various small mice, shrews, small rabbits, woodrats, moles, small birds, and a few Jerusalem crickets (Smith & Hopkins 1937, n = 338).

Barn Owls generally eat considerably smaller prey by weight than coexisting Great Horned Owls (Marti 1974, Knight & Jackman 1984) and somewhat larger prey than coexisting Long-eared Owls (Marti 1974). For example, in Colorado, mean prey weight is 1.6 ounces for Barn Owls, 6.2 ounces for Great Horned Owls, and 1.1 ounces for Long-eared Owls (Marti 1974). In some areas, Barns and Great Horns may capture prey of similar average weight, and they may overlap nearly completely in their food niches (Knight & Jackman 1984). Nonetheless, foraging separation occurs between the species (Rudolph 1978, Knight & Jackman 1984). Barn Owls are more nocturnal than Great Horns and can occupy more extensively open areas because they forage mostly on the wing rather than from perches. On the other hand, because of their greater size and strength, Great Horns generally capture a wider range of prey. Little is known of the dietary differences between male and female Barn Owls, but in Italy the food taken by females was more varied in species and size than that caught by males (Voous 1988).

Barn Owls are prolific breeders, and providing food for the young can be a prodigious accomplishment. They vary their clutch size with food availability and sometimes lay two or more clutches in a year (Voous 1988). Females begin incubation with the first egg, and consequently the difference in size between siblings is as large as or larger than for other owl species (Voous 1988). Females may begin laying the second clutch before the youngest owlets of the first brood have fledged (Johnsgard 1988). Males feed their mates, and in good years they stockpile food at the nest, sometimes even before the eggs are laid (Smith et al. 1974, Voous 1988). When the eldest nestlings are about three to four weeks old, the female resumes hunting, presumably because the dark, concealed nest site allows her to leave the young unprotected for periods of time (Voous 1988). During periods of food shortage, parents and larger young will eat smaller nestlings that behave abnormally or are already dead.

211

Marin Breeding Distribution

During the atlas period, Barn Owls bred at scattered sites throughout the lowlands of Marin County in both rural and urban-suburban settings. Representative breeding locations were Lower Pierce Ranch, Tomales Point (NY spring 1981 *fide* JGE); ranch north of the NW corner of Nicasio Reservoir (NY 7/24/82 −DS); Willow Ridge Stables, Point Reyes Station (NY 6/4/81 −JGE); Olema (NY 4/28/77 −RMS); and Rancho Baulinas, N of Bolinas Lagoon (NE-NY spring/summer 1977 & 1978 −JKip).

Historical Trends/Population Threats

Grinnell and Miller (1944) thought that Barn Owls had increased historically in California because of the increase in suitable nesting sites and the "reduction in numbers of owl-persecuting falconids." Numbers might also have been augmented by the clearing of land and the proliferation of rodents in agricultural areas. Times have changed, and, though still relatively abundant in parts of California, the species has declined steadily in recent years because of habitat loss from suburban and industrial developments (Bloom 1979). Barn Owls are now also virtually nonexistent in certain intensively cultivated agricultural areas of the Central Valley. Breeding Bird Surveys indicated that Barn Owl numbers were relatively stable in California from 1968 to 1989 but decreased from 1980 to 1989 (USFWS unpubl. analyses). These surveys are geared toward diurnal species, limiting their usefulness for detecting trends in highly nocturnal species like the Barn Owl. The species was on the Audubon Society's Blue List from 1972 to 1981 and on their list of Species of Special Concern since 1982 (Tate 1981, 1986; Tate & Tate 1982).

Traffic accidents are at present among the most serious human-induced mortality factors, as is readily evident from the carcass-littered roadsides of major highways, such as Interstate 5 in the Central Valley, that pass through prime Barn Owl country. Cases of poisoning by mercury, thallium, and organic biocides and thinning of eggshells have been recorded, but the extent of the threats posed to Barn Owls are unknown (Voous 1988, Marti & Marks 1989).

Typical Owls
Family *Strigidae*

WESTERN SCREECH-OWL   *Otus kennicottii*

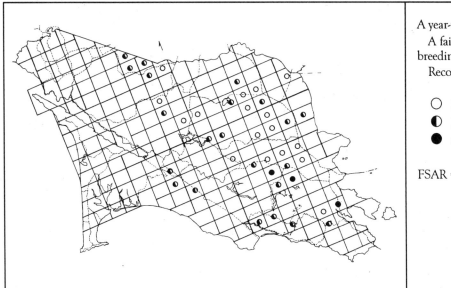

A year-round resident.
    A fairly common, local breeder; overall breeding population very small.
    Recorded in 42 (19.0%) of 221 blocks.

○	Possible	=	17	(40%)
◑	Probable	=	22	(52%)
●	Confirmed	=	3	(7%)

FSAR = 3   OPI = 126   CI = 1.67

Ecological Requirements

The bouncing-ball-like call of this tiny ear-tufted owl wafts softly through the night air in Marin County's oak woodlands and open broadleaved evergreen hardwood forests where there is little understory. Screech-Owls are absent from Marin's coastal riparian thickets, but further study is needed to determine if in the county's interior they occupy the limited amounts of riparian woodland, an important breeding habitat elsewhere in California's lowlands (G&M 1944). Screech-Owls typically nest in natural cavities of trees or stubs (elsewhere also saguaro cactus); old holes of large woodpeckers, such as Northern Flickers; and sometimes nest boxes (Dawson 1923, Bent 1938, Johnsgard 1988, Voous 1988), even those meant for Wood Ducks (S. Simmons pers. comm.). Birds have also used a bark-filled crotch of a eucalyptus tree, an old woodrat's nest, Black-billed Magpie nests, and even cliff cavities (Dawson 1923, Bent 1938). Screech-Owls sometimes nest in secluded recesses of buildings. Nests range from about 4 to 60 feet above the ground, but most are at moderate heights (Dawson 1923, Bent 1938, Marti & Marks 1989). Nest heights probably reflect the availability of suitable cavities and woodpecker holes rather than any preference

by the owls for particular heights. The owls do not make an actual nest but instead lay their eggs on the rotten wood chips, dead leaves, feathers, castings, or other debris accumulated at the bottom of the cavity (Dawson 1923, Bent 1938).

Screech-Owls are strictly nocturnal in their activities and retreat by day to roost in thick foliage, close against the camouflaging bark of trees, in tree hollows, in old buildings, or other secluded spots (Bent 1938, Johnsgard 1988, Voous 1988). Little has been observed of foraging behavior. The most frequently used hunting technique seems to be for an owl to swoop down from a perch on a twig projecting slightly from the foliage or beneath the canopy of a tree to capture prey on bare or grassy ground (Voous 1988). Many aspects of Screech-Owl biology are poorly known, but, like the Eastern Screech-Owl, males of the Western Screech-Owl probably bring food to incubating and brooding females and sometimes build up a store of food, such as voles, at the nest. The diet of Western Screech-Owls consists of varying amounts of insects and other arthropods, small birds, small mammals, crayfish, fish, and occasionally lizards, snakes, frogs, and salaman-

213

ders (Bent 1938, Johnsgard 1988, Voous 1988). Prey remains from nests in the San Joaquin Valley are mostly small mammals and birds, along with some fish and crayfish (S. Simmons pers. comm.). Reported invertebrate prey items include grasshoppers, crickets, locusts, Jerusalem crickets, mole crickets, walking sticks, praying mantids, roaches, sowbugs, waterbugs, large moths, caterpillars, cutworms, beetles, ants, scorpions, spiders, harvestmen, and centipedes. Among the vertebrate prey not already mentioned are voles, pocket gophers, pocket mice, deer mice, harvest mice, grasshopper mice, woodrats, kangaroo rats, shrews, and many small and medium-sized birds up to the size of Northern Flickers, Steller's Jays, and American Robins. Screech-Owls have also attacked and sometimes partially eaten Golden Pheasants, Ring-necked Pheasants, Bantam hens, and domestic ducks. Little is known of geographic or seasonal changes in diet, but birds to the south probably consume more insects and other cold-blooded prey, and birds in all regions probably eat less of these items in winter.

Marin Breeding Distribution

During the atlas period, we found Screech-Owls breeding primarily in the eastern and north-central, oak-dominated portions of Marin County. They were lacking from the grassland-dominated areas on outer Point Reyes and around Tomales and from most of the moist dense coastal forests, particularly where there was a thick understory. Representative breeding records were San Anselmo (NE in attic 5/4/79); Mill Valley (NY/FL 6/2/79); and Fairfax (FL 7/22/79). All these confirmed records were obtained years after the fact from California Center for Wildlife records (S. Hershon in litt.), hence the locations plotted on the atlas map are only approximate and observer names are lost to posterity.

Historical Trends/Population Threats

Grinnell and Miller (1944) felt the species may have increased in California in historical times from the "opening up" of heavy forests. On the other hand, many logged areas regrow with dense brushy understories that are unsuitable, while the clearing of areas of hardwoods for firewood, agriculture, or development must have had detrimental effects on the species. Further urban-suburban development is likely to displace some of these owls, though providing nest boxes might mitigate the loss of some habitat. Pesticide residues have caused slight eggshell thinning in wild Screech-Owls, but these pollutants apparently have not impaired reproductive success (Marti & Marks 1989).

GREAT HORNED OWL　*Bubo virginianus*

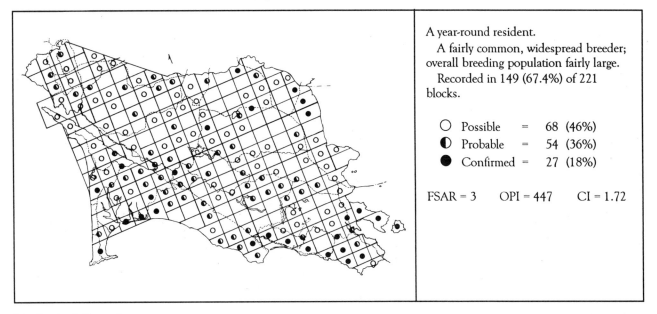

A year-round resident.

A fairly common, widespread breeder; overall breeding population fairly large. Recorded in 149 (67.4%) of 221 blocks.

○	Possible	=	68	(46%)
◑	Probable	=	54	(36%)
●	Confirmed	=	27	(18%)

FSAR = 3　　OPI = 447　　CI = 1.72

Ecological Requirements

This solemn, ferocious master of the night inhabits the edges of all Marin County's major woodland and forest habitats, as well as planted woodlots and windbreaks, where they border on open tracts of grassland, meadow, and field. Older stands of trees provide more potential nest sites and also offer more subcanopy flying room because they have few low branches (Johnsgard 1988). Elsewhere, Great Horned Owls also occupy extensive treeless areas with cliffs or rock outcrops for nesting and perches from which to hunt and regions ranging from boreal to tropical forests and deserts. Habitat preferences for a species that lives over such a broad latitudinal range are hard to define. The main requisites seem to be sheltered nesting and roosting sites, relatively open foraging grounds that supply a good mammal population, and suitable elevated hunting perches.

Great Horned Owls usually lay their eggs in an abandoned nest of a diurnal raptor (especially Red-tailed Hawks) in trees or sometimes cliffs; various species of raptor may alternate in their use of a given nest (Bent 1938, Johnsgard 1988, Voous 1988). Crow, raven, magpie, heron, or squirrel nests will also do as platforms for Great Horned Owl eggs. Other suitable nesting sites are ledges or caves in rocky cliffs, fissures of rocks, niches in cutbanks, rooms in Native American cliff dwellings, hollows in tree trunks and snags, depressions in the tops of old or dead trees, crotches in trees lacking debris or nest materials, a box in a tree filled with leaves, and occasionally lofts of barns. Rarely, these owls have nested on the ground next to a boulder or the base of a large tree, under a stump,

in a hollow log, in long grass near a windmill, under bushes in the desert, and in an old Canada Goose nest on a tussock of grass in a pond.

Great Horned Owls are mainly nocturnal but frequently hunt at dawn and dusk and occasionally during the day. They usually swoop down silently on their prey from an elevated perch in a direct, low, rapid flight (Marti 1974, Rudolph 1978). Typical perches include tall trees, telephone poles and wires, rock outcrops, and fence posts. Sometimes Great Horns hunt in harrierlike flights or catch bats in the air as they emerge from caves (Marti 1974). These owls also make night raids on the nests of other owls, hawks, and crows, and snatch crows from their night roosts (Voous 1988).

Great Horned Owls are generalized and opportunistic predators and feed on a wider range of prey than is known for any other owl or bird of prey in North or South America (Voous 1988). A complete listing of all the prey eaten is not necessary, but about 77.6% of prey numbers in North America are mammals, 6.1% birds, 1.6% other vertebrates, and the balance insects, spiders, scorpions, crabs, and other invertebrates (Voous 1988). Great Horns will also feed on carrion or trapped fur-bearing mammals, particularly in winter. Their largest prey are mammals like muskrats, porcupines, skunks, and foxes, and birds the size of grouse, pheasants, domestic poultry, ducks, geese, swans, herons, and gulls. Great Horns prey on a variety of diurnal raptors at least as large as Red-tailed Hawks and on just about any species of owl they encounter. In semiarid regions of California, the percentages of important prey (by

215

numbers) are 76.6% mammals, 15% insects (especially Jerusalem crickets), 4.2% birds, 1.6% reptiles, 1.8% arachnids, and 0.8% amphibians (Jaksic & Marti 1984, n = 2235 prey items). The most abundant prey in California are voles, woodrats, pocket gophers, and cottontails; their contribution to the diet by biomass is almost in the reverse order. In essence, they prey on almost all the available small mammals in a region, mostly those above 0.7 ounce in weight; diurnal, fossorial, and arboreal forms are mostly absent in the diet. In areas of overlap, Great Horns eat considerably larger prey on average than do Barn and Long-eared owls (Marti 1974). See Barn Owl account for information on food niche separation. In the Sierra foothills, Great Horns subsist mainly on small to medium-sized mammals (Fitch 1947). Cottontail rabbits and woodrats represent 79% of the diet there by weight; other important items are kangaroo rats, pocket gophers, gopher snakes, and ground squirrels (Fitch 1947, n = 654). Various mice, opossums, skunks, bats, small landbirds, quail, Screech-Owls, American Kestrels, Coots, snakes, lizards, toads, Jerusalem crickets, and beetles were also taken. As might be expected, there is regional variation in diet reflecting prey availability and both seasonal and long-term variation in the diet reflecting fluctuations in prey populations (e.g., Errington et al. 1940, Rush et al. 1972, Marti 1974, Jaksic & Marti 1984; see also Voous 1988). Although females are considerably larger than males, there are no data on average or absolute prey sizes between the sexes (Voous 1988). The male hunts for the incubating and brooding female and for the nestlings (Voous 1988). He usually provides an abundance of prey, which he deposits, and which may accumulate, at the nest. The size of food items brought to young increases with nestling age (Johnsgard 1988).

Marin Breeding Distribution

During the atlas period, the Great Horned Owl was the most widespread breeding owl in Marin County and perhaps the most widespread of our larger breeding birds. The atlas map shows many small gaps in the distribution, particularly away from roads. This apparently was mostly an artifact of our limited coverage of nocturnally active species. Complete coverage of owls would probably have revealed Great Horned Owls in almost every atlas block. Representative breeding locations were the Fish Docks, Point Reyes (FL 6/20/80 –DS); Morning Sun Ave., Mill Valley (NE-NY 3/5-5/15/81 –MC); and Tiburon (DD 5/27/82 –BiL).

Historical Trends/Population Threats

Grinnell and Miller (1944) reported that Great Horned Owls had become scarce locally in California but were holding up remarkably well, even in areas closely settled by people and despite much hunting of "vermin." This assessment is still valid today for this remarkably adaptable species. Numbers of Great Horned Owls were relatively stable on Breeding Bird Surveys in California from 1968 to 1989 (USFWS unpubl. analyses). Many owls are still shot, trapped, killed along highways by vehicles, and electrocuted by overhead powerlines (Voous 1988). Great Horned Owls have been poisoned by biocides, but this has not been as widespread or as well documented as for certain diurnal birds of prey.

NORTHERN PYGMY-OWL　*Glaucidium gnoma*

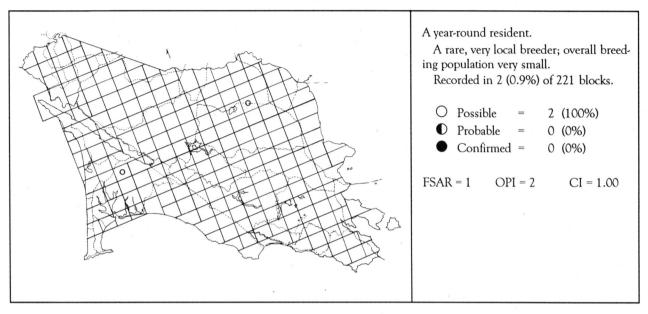

A year-round resident.
　A rare, very local breeder; overall breeding population very small.
　Recorded in 2 (0.9%) of 221 blocks.

○　Possible　　=　2 (100%)
◐　Probable　　=　0 (0%)
●　Confirmed　=　0 (0%)

FSAR = 1　　　OPI = 2　　　CI = 1.00

Ecological Requirements

Though in large part a creature of daylight, this midget of owldom still possesses the true spirit of that enigmatic clan, as one only rarely stumbles upon little *gnoma*, and then, likely as not, one beset by a mobbing, scolding throng of chickadees and nuthatches that advertises its presence far and wide. Because of the seeming rarity of Pygmy-Owls in Marin County, it is hard to determine habitat preferences here. Most encounters in Marin are of calling birds on the edges of Douglas fir forest or mixed evergreen forest dominated by Douglas firs or oaks. In California as a whole, Pgymy-Owls prefer open or broken forests or woodlands of conifers and oaks at low to mid-elevations (Skinner 1938, G&M 1944, Gaines 1988). Although the surrounding forest type may sometimes be moist and dense, the owls are strongly attracted throughout their range to forest edges along meadows, clearings, or other openings (Skinner 1938, Johnsgard 1988, Voous 1988). Meadows harbor a choice supply of small mammal prey, and forest edges are renowned for attracting a diversity and abundance of avian prey as well. Pygmy-Owls tend also to nest in forests or woodland edges close to these important open foraging grounds (Skinner 1938).

Pygmies lay their eggs in the bottom of abandoned woodpecker holes or natural cavities of trees or stumps in the scanty, naturally accumulated debris of wood chips, pine needles, twigs, feathers, and leaves, or the cast-off bones or beetle wings left from the previous year's dining (Skinner 1938). Pygmies sometimes nest in the same hole for several successive years. Known nest heights range from 5 to 75 feet above the ground (Skinner 1938), but

also probably as high as suitable cavities exist. Johnsgard (1988) reported an average nest height of 19 nests at 20.7 feet and a seeming preference for broadleaved trees over conifers for nest sites. It seems likely, however, that nest heights are largely determined by the availability of woodpecker holes and natural cavities. The same goes for the types of trees in which these cavities exist, though broadleaved trees may be more prevalent on forest edges where Pygmies tend to nest.

Northern Pygmy-Owls are active and hunt during daylight hours, especially near dawn and dusk, though they are not averse to snoozing at times during the day (Skinner 1938, Johnsgard 1988, Voous 1988). Foraging owls often perch on top of low to moderate-sized trees and snags in semiopen places. They travel from perch to perch shrike-like, dropping and buzzing along just above the ground, then rising sharply to the next perch. Pygmies are determined, no-nonsense predators that rely on speed and surprise, though their flight is more "noisy" than many other owls (Skinner 1938). They pounce from perches onto prey on the ground, seize birds from perches in trees while flying, and pull adult and young woodpeckers out of their nest holes. They also sometimes hunt mice in open barns and cabins. These plucky owls often attack relatively large prey. Sometimes they pounce on a rather large mammal that drags its captor along with it for a considerable distance before succumbing to the onslaught. One owl carried off an Olive-sided Flycatcher shot by a collector! As a rule, they grasp avian victims by the neck. The male does all the hunting and brings in the food to a perch near the nest, from which he calls his mate. The male typically decapitates and partly skins food before turning it over to the female. The female comes out to accept his offering and either remains to eat it or retires to the nest hole. Upon the hatching of the eggs, the male continues to bring food, first delivering small items to the young, and then larger items when the nestlings are more vigorous. There are suggestions in the literature of prey caching by this owl (Skinner 1938, Voous 1988), though this needs further documentation.

The diet of Northern Pygmy-Owls consists primarily of small mammals, small birds, insects, and other invertebrates, along with smaller amounts of cold-blooded vertebrates (Skinner 1938, Earhart & Johnson 1970, Snyder & Wiley 1976, Johnsgard 1988, Voous 1988). Insects and other invertebrates account for 61% of the prey items in the diet, mammals 23%, birds 13%, and reptiles and amphibians 3% (Snyder & Wiley 1976, n = 163). Mammals and birds undoubtedly are most important in terms of biomass. Earhart and Johnson (1970) reported that in a sample of 70 stomachs, 81% contained vertebrates and about one-third contained insects. Mammals are represented by various species of voles, deer mice, house mice, pocket gophers, chipmunks, and shrews. A wide variety of small birds (mostly passerines) are taken, including sizes up to American Robins, Steller's Jays, and sapsuckers. Pygmies occasionally take quail and chipmunks more than twice the size/weight of the owls. Amphibians and reptiles in the diet include toads, frogs, various lizards, and small snakes. Insect prey are grasshoppers, cicadas, beetles, crickets, Jerusalem crickets, katydids, dragonflies, butterflies, and large hawk moths. Geographical differences in the diet likely occur, with mammals probably taken more in the north and reptiles and insects more to the south. Reptiles are taken only in the spring and summer when available

(Earhart & Johnson 1970). On an annual basis, the larger females feed more on mammals (52% vs. 37%) and less on birds (21% vs. 34%) than do males. The smaller males presumably are more agile and better able to capture elusive avian prey than are females.

Marin Breeding Distribution

During the atlas period, Pygmy-Owls were recorded in Marin County in the breeding season on only single dates at three localities: on 17 May 1980 at the east end of Big Rock Ridge (P&MSh); on 9 May 1981 on Mt. Burdell, Novato (ScC); and on 23 March 1982 on Mt. Vision, Inverness Ridge (RS). Although they undoubtedly would have been found in more areas if more nighttime work had been done, the species is quite scarce during the breeding season in the county. In contrast, Pygmy-Owls are relatively numerous in bordering Sonoma County, whereas Northern Saw-whet Owls are uncommon there—the converse of the situation in Marin County. This difference defies easy explanation as broad areas of roughly similar habitat occur in both counties.

Historical Trends/Population Threats

Grinnell and Miller (1944) did not report on any trends in populations of this species in California. Johnsgard (1988) felt Pygmy-Owls generally were not seriously affected by human activities and, if anything, partial clearing of forests may improve hunting conditions for the species. This may be true, but conversely it seems that large-scale development, snag removal, or clear-cutting of forests may have detrimental effects on Pygmy-Owl populations. Pygmy-Owl numbers were relatively stable on Breeding Bird Surveys in California from 1968 to 1989 (USFWS unpubl. analyses).

BURROWING OWL *Speotyto cunicularia*

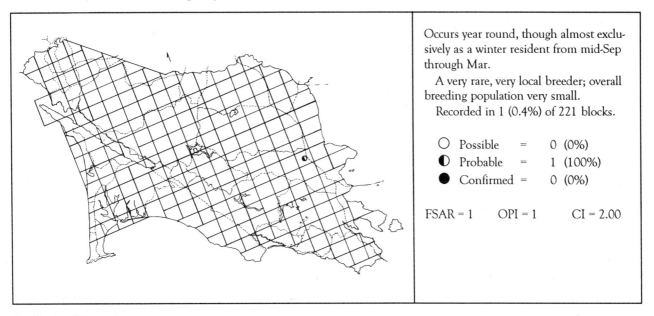

Occurs year round, though almost exclusively as a winter resident from mid-Sep through Mar.

A very rare, very local breeder; overall breeding population very small.

Recorded in 1 (0.4%) of 221 blocks.

○	Possible	=	0 (0%)
◑	Probable	=	1 (100%)
●	Confirmed	=	0 (0%)

FSAR = 1   OPI = 1   CI = 2.00

Ecological Requirements

A fleeting glimpse of an owl silhouette at dusk is one thing, but leisurely views of the antics of a family of long-legged "Billy Owls" (Dawson 1923) preening, sunning, bowing, and bobbing in front of their burrow in broad daylight is another—one long to be remembered by the person new to the world of birds. These diminutive, ground-dwelling owls inhabit relatively dry, flat, very open grasslands and disturbed areas with very short vegetation. Habitat preferences in Marin County are difficult to explain. Only one pair apparently bred here during the atlas period (see below). Elsewhere in northern California, Burrowing Owls occupy grasslands, pasturelands, edges of agricultural fields, abandoned fields and lots, and disturbed sites with sparse low-growing vegetation. Though receding before the tide of civilization, Burrowing Owls can tolerate a certain amount of noise and disturbance if certain other requirements are met, as evidenced by birds breeding at large airports, golf courses, and in small pockets of habitat in rapidly developing areas. The main requirements are adequate nest sites, productive open foraging grounds, and perching sites, such as raised rodent mounds, dikes or levees, fences, or utility poles and lines (Coulombe 1971, Voous 1988, Johnsgard 1988).

As their name implies, these owls usually nest inside the earthen burrows of mammals, or even tortoises and other animals (Voous 1988). Sometimes they select as nest sites burrows beneath rock faces, natural rock cavities (Rich 1986), drainpipes (Collins 1979), or, in South America, Inca ruins or derelict, abandoned houses (Voous 1988). In lowland northern California, they rely mostly on the exca-

vations of Beechy ground squirrels *(Citellus beecheyi)*, which they enlarge and improve (Thomsen 1971). The major factor controlling Burrowing Owl numbers appears to be the availability of suitable burrows (Coulombe 1971), though sometimes birds dig their own burrows from scratch using their feet and, to a limited extent, their beaks (Thomsen 1971, Martin 1973, Voous 1988). The importance of burrows to this owl's ecology is further emphasized by use of them as social centers, sites for food storage, refuges from predators, and as a stable, tempered environment during periods of extremely hot or cold weather (Coulombe 1971, Thomsen 1971). At the Salton Sea, temperatures at the entrances did not differ from those in the depths of the burrows. Humidities, though, were much higher inside burrows, which would reduce the water loss of owls there (Coulombe 1971). Tunnels usually slope down about 15° from the entrance and always have a sharp turn within about three feet of the surface (Coulombe 1971). Burrowing Owls also readily accept artificial burrows of wood or pipe, as long as the tunnel has one turn that maintains the nest chamber in complete darkness (Collins & Landry 1977, Collins 1979). Unlike most owls, Burrowing Owls transport nest materials and line the nest and the burrow entrance liberally with dried mammal dung, dried grasses, human litter, and divots from golf courses (Thomsen 1971, Martin 1973, Evans 1982, Johnsgard 1988, Voous 1988). Nest materials may function to provide insulation or to camouflage the owl's scent or that of its prey from mammalian predators (Martin 1973). The owls later remove nest materials from burrows, apparently during the early nestling phase (Thomsen 1971). Young Burrowing Owls make hissing and rasping sounds, which, as apparent vocal mimicry of rattlesnakes, may discourage prowling carnivores (Voous 1988); it should be noted that tree cavity–nesting Saw-whet Owl and Screech-Owl young also make similar-sounding begging calls (Thomsen 1971). When the young owlets (about two weeks old) first come to the mouth of the burrow, they (and their families) use nearby auxiliary burrows and usually use two or three different burrows in succession before they fledge (Evans 1982). Burrows invariably swarm with fleas (Collins 1979).

Burrowing Owls limit defense of their territories to the immediate vicinity of their burrows, and hence adjacent pairs often share mutual foraging areas (Coulombe 1971). In most parts of their range, Burrowing Owls are highly crepuscular, feeding mostly in the dim light near dawn and dusk (Coulombe 1971, Thomsen 1971, Collins 1979, Johnsgard 1988, Voous 1988). They also feed actively during daylight hours and at night; in some areas nocturnal foraging appears to increase in winter. Regional or seasonal differences in the timing of daily foraging activities may reflect those of their most frequent prey items or changes in environmental temperatures. Based on prey numbers, the Burrowing Owl diet is dominated by arthropods, mostly insects, but apparently small mammals are the most important prey in terms of biomass (Snyder & Wiley 1976, Jaksic & Marti 1981, Johnsgard 1988, Voous 1988). The North American diet by prey numbers is 90.9% invertebrates (mostly insects), 6.9% mammals, 2.0% reptiles and amphibians, and 0.3% birds (Snyder & Wiley 1976, n = 3564). The California diet by prey numbers is 70.6% insects, 23.6% mammals, 3.5% birds, 2.2% amphibians, 0.1% isopods, with trace amounts of reptiles, scorpions, and centipedes (Jaksic & Marti 1981, n = 3794). Beetles account for 49.2% and orthopterans (mostly Jerusalem crickets) for 50.3% of the invertebrate prey in California. Vertebrate prey here are dominated by voles (69.5% of total), followed by birds (12.1%), amphibians (7.4%), jackrabbits and cottontails (6.4%), pocket gophers (2.4%), house mice (1.0%), Norway rats (1.0%), bats (0.2%), and reptiles (trace). The diet of birds at the Oakland Airport, Alameda County, consists mostly of insects such as Jerusalem crickets and beetles and vertebrates such as meadow voles, young jackrabbits, pocket gophers, small to medium-sized birds, and toads; apparently a high percentage of vegetation in the pellets is consumed directly by the owls (Thomsen 1971). Near the Salton Sea in southern California, these owls feed primarily on arthropods and insects (earwigs, crayfish, crickets, and beetles) but also eat a few small mammals, birds, frogs, toads, snakes, and some carrion (Coulombe 1971). There is additional regional variation in the diet throughout the range and increasing use of mammals in winter and insects

in summer (Johnsgard 1988, Voous 1988). The mean weight of small mammal prey in California is 1.9 ounces (Jaksic & Marti 1981). Males provide food to incubating females, and they may temporarily cache food almost anywhere in their territory, usually within 100 feet of their burrows (Johnsgard 1988). A cache in southern California contained six freshly decapitated Mourning Doves, each of which represented 80%–84% of the body weight of a Burrowing Owl. Males bring most of the food to the young, and females help distribute it (Thomsen 1971); females begin to forage when the young are three to four weeks old (Martin 1973). Unlike most North American owls, male Burrowing Owls are slightly larger and heavier than females, but no difference has been found in average prey size between males and females (Voous 1988).

Because of their crepuscular and sometimes diurnal habits, Burrowing Owls probably locate most prey by sight (Voous 1988). Hearing must also play a role, though they have a *relatively* poor ability to locate prey in the dark compared with many North American owls. Burrowing Owls capture prey in their talons after short flights or glides to the ground from elevated perches; by flycatching sorties from perches; by direct aerial chases; by hovering (heights of about 25–50 ft.) or flying low over fields, then pouncing on prey on the ground; and by walking or running down prey on the ground (Coulombe 1971, Thomsen 1971, Martin 1973, Johnsgard 1988, Voous 1988). At Oakland, Alameda County, males performed 98% of hovering attempts (Thomsen 1971), perhaps because this is a spring and summer foraging method when males do most of the hunting. Birds probably also take insects that live in their burrows (Coulombe 1971).

Marin Breeding Distribution

The only evidence that Burrowing Owls bred in Marin County during the atlas period was the repeated observation of a pair in the Terra Linda area of San Rafael all spring (through May) in 1976 and 1977 (JSt). The near-absence of ground squirrels in West Marin may limit Burrowing Owl populations there, but where ground squirrels are more numerous in East Marin, other factors, perhaps extensive urbanization, must hinder them.

Historical Trends/Population Threats

Both Mailliard (1900) and Stephens and Pringle (1933) considered the Burrowing Owl a year-round resident in restricted areas of Marin County. Given the current status documented by the atlas work, Burrowing Owls appear to have declined historically in Marin County.

Grinnell and Miller (1944) reported that Burrowing Owls were becoming scarce in settled parts of California. This owl is currently on the state's list of Bird Species of Special Concern (Remsen 1978, CDFG 1991b). Data on recent trends in the population are conflicting. As of this writing, numbers of breeding Burrowing Owls continue to decline in the San Francisco Bay Area because of ongoing urban development (L. Feeney pers. comm.). Numbers also declined on Christmas Bird Counts throughout California from 1954 to 1986 (James & Ethier 1989) but were relatively stable on Breeding Bird Surveys in the state from 1968 to 1989 (USFWS unpubl. analyses). Widespread grid-based surveys are currently being conducted to better determine the status of the breeding population in lowland California (D.F. DeSante pers. comm.). The U.S. Fish and Wildlife Service has variously categorized the Burrowing Owl as "rare" in 1966, dropped that classification in 1968, and assigned it a status of "undetermined" in 1973 (Johns-

gard 1988). The species was on the Audubon Society's Blue List from 1972 to 1981 and has been on their list of Species of Special Concern since 1982, with the central and northern California population considered low or declining (Tate 1981, 1986; Tate & Tate 1982). This decline has been blamed mainly on rodent control programs that reduced nesting sites for the owls; on direct loss of nesting and foraging habitat to urban, industrial, and agricultural development; and perhaps to pesticides that have reduced food supplies and directly poisoned owls (Zarn 1974, Evans 1982, Johnsgard 1988, Marti & Marks 1989). Shooting has been an important source of mortality locally and in former times (G&M 1944, Evans 1982).

With a woodrat clutched tightly in its talons, an adult Spotted Owl gazes down on a dark-eyed, fuzzy youngster absorbing its new world. *Drawing by Keith Hansen, 1989.*

SPOTTED OWL *Strix occidentalis*

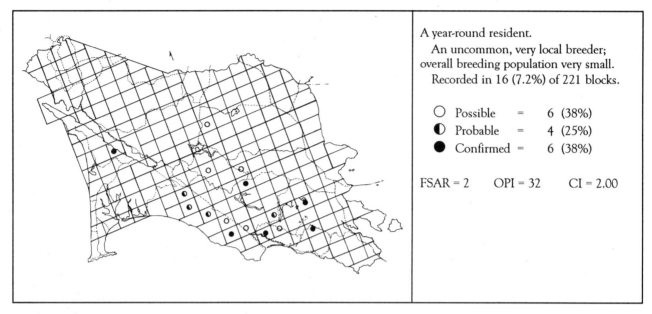

A year-round resident.
An uncommon, very local breeder;
overall breeding population very small.
Recorded in 16 (7.2%) of 221 blocks.

○	Possible	=	6 (38%)
◑	Probable	=	4 (25%)
●	Confirmed	=	6 (38%)

FSAR = 2   OPI = 32   CI = 2.00

Ecological Requirements

This recluse of the shadowy depths of ancient forests has in recent years been thrust into the national spotlight. The Spotted Owl symbolizes both the plight of vanishing old-growth ecosystems—supporting a fragile web of species coadapted over thousands of years of evolution—and the difficulty of overcoming political obstacles even when a species' existence hangs in the balance. Mounting concern over the owl's predicament, and the ensuing controversy surrounding the difficulties of meeting both the owl's and perceived human needs, spawned extensive research aimed at developing management strategies to ensure long-term survival of viable owl populations in remaining habitat (e.g., Forsman et al. 1984; Gutiérrez & Carey 1985; Dawson et al. 1987; Simberloff 1987; USFWS 1987a, 1989c; USFS 1988; Thomas et al. 1990).

Spotted Owls have long been known to breed in a variety of moist primeval conifer forests. In Marin County, at the southern limit of the range of the Northern Spotted Owl *(S. o. caurina)*, they breed mostly in forests dominated by coast redwoods, Douglas firs, and bishop pines and in forests where any of these conifers mix together or blend extensively with mixed evergreen hardwoods. These habitats are typical of those used in much of the species' range. Spotted Owls also breed to a limited extent in Marin's mixed evergreen hardwood forests, such as those at Tomales Bay State Park dominated by coast live oaks. Elsewhere in the state, some populations of the California Spotted Owl *(S. o. occidentalis)* also breed in riparian habitats dominated by oaks and other hardwoods in canyons of the

western Sierra Nevada (Neals et al. in Thomas et al. 1990) and in southern California (Gould 1977).

Recent research has demonstrated that superior Spotted Owl habitat is most commonly found in old-growth forests or mixed stands of old-growth and mature trees, usually 150 to 200 years old (Thomas et al. 1990). Throughout their range and in all seasons, Spotted Owls consistently concentrate their foraging and roosting in old-growth or mixed-age stands of mature and old-growth trees. They select nest sites primarily in old-growth trees, whether in old-growth stands or in remnant old-growth patches. The appropriate structural characteristics that suit the owls can sometimes be found in younger forests, particularly when they include remnants of earlier stands affected by fire, windstorms, or inefficient or selective logging. Nevertheless, with few exceptions, nest and major roost sites are located where elements of the earlier stands remain. That a particular suite of structural elements, rather than age of the forest, is important to the owls is demonstrated by habitat use in coastal redwood forests of northwestern California. There exceptional conditions lacking in most of the owls' range produce stands 50 to 80 years old that support relatively high numbers of owls. The combination of relatively high rainfall, a long growing season, the fast growth and stump sprouting abilities of redwoods, and the early intrusion of other conifers and hardwoods in the understory produce a structurally precocious forest with an abundant prey base. Although Spotted Owls in California depend on old growth at higher elevation sites dominated by Douglas fir or Douglas fir–true fir forests, this does not appear to be the case in the state's coastal redwood belt (G.I. Gould, Jr., in litt.).

The structural characteristics of superior forest habitat for the owls are moderate to high canopy closure (60%-80%); a multilayered, multispecies canopy dominated by large (30 in. diameter at breast height) overstory conifer trees and an understory of shade-tolerant conifers or hardwoods; a high incidence of large tall trees with large cavities, broken tops, dwarf mistletoe infections, or platforms of branches capable of accumulating organic matter suitable for use as a nest; numerous large standing dead trees; a forest floor with heavy accumulations of logs, dead limbs, and other woody debris to support abundant prey populations; and a canopy open enough to allow the owls to fly within and beneath it (Thomas et al. 1990). In California, 90% of the Spotted Owls surveyed by Gould (1977) inhabited forests with at least 40% canopy closure, and most favored northern exposures; 89% of their territories were on the lower slopes of canyons, and 90% were within 330 feet of a water course.

One reason Spotted Owls may prefer older forests is because the layered structure of the canopy provides a range of roosting environments and hence the most protection under a variety of weather conditions (Forsman et al. 1984). In Oregon, these owls roost in the day, primarily on limbs in trees or large woody shrubs, but also on limbs or logs on the forest floor. Owls there use large trees in the forest overstory for roosting during cool or wet weather and smaller trees or shrubs in the forest understory during warm weather. Despite the use of roosts low in the understory during warm weather, the majority of roost sites in spring and summer at one Oregon study area had southern exposures. During rainy or snowy weather, these owls tend to roost against the trunk or under the shelter of an overhead projection of the tree. In California, Spotted Owls tend to use the same roost trees repeatedly throughout the summer but shift roost sites frequently during winter (Barrows 1981). Spotted Owls there tend to select roosts in cooler microclimates in the lower portion of the canopy in summer, apparently to reduce heat stress (Barrows & Barrows 1978, Barrows 1981). Summer roosts in California tend to have dense canopies above and to be on north-facing slopes and in ravines; winter roosts are more variable and do not share these characteristics.

Like most owls, Spotted Owls do not build nests. Instead they lay their eggs in natural cavities or on elevated natural platforms (Bent 1938, Forsman et al. 1984, Johnsgard 1988, Voous 1988, Thomas et al. 1990). Nests typically are inaccessible and have well shaded, cool microclimates. Suitable cavities include those at the top of broken-off trees, ones lower in the trunk of live or dead conifers or hardwoods, potholes or cavities of rocky cliffs, shelves of larger caves, and washouts in clay banks. Some nest sites in cliffs are on the remains of abandoned Com-

mon Raven or Golden Eagle nests. Cliff nests are reported mostly from southern California and the Southwest, where tree cavity nests also seem frequent (Bent 1938). Truly exceptional nests were one on bare ground at the base of a large rock (Bent 1938) and another on a pigeon coop (Johnsgard 1988).

The platform nests the owls use in trees may simply be naturally accumulated debris. More often these are old nests of raptors (Red-tailed Hawk, Northern Goshawk, or Cooper's Hawk) or arboreal mammals (squirrels or woodrats), often built among the dense clusters of deformed limbs ("witches-brooms") of old trees infected with dwarf mistletoe (Forsman et al. 1984). Platform nests tend to be next to or close to the trunk. Within the range of the Northern Spotted Owl in Washington, Oregon, and northern California, there is geographical variation in the predominance of platform versus tree cavity nests, presumably reflecting regional availability of these types of sites (Forsman et al. 1984, Thomas et al. 1990). Spotted Owls in Marin County select both tree cavity and platform nests, but it is not established if one type is used here more often than the other. In Oregon, Forsman et al. (1984) reported that the height of tree cavity nests averaged 99 feet (range 38-181 ft., n = 30) and platform nests averaged 72 feet above the ground (range 33-123 ft., n = 17). Nests there tend to be located on the lower slopes of hillsides and within about 800 feet of water (Forsman et al. 1984), a pattern similar to that noted above for territories in California (Gould 1977), which also seems to hold for Marin County. It is unclear if the owls select nest sites close to water for use in drinking or bathing or whether other factors they select for coincidentally tend to occur near water. Johnsgard (1988) reported an average nest height of 31 feet for a small sample (n = 13) of sites, including cliff ledges or cavities, tree platforms, tree cavities, and one artificial structure.

Regardless of site, females scrape out a depression for the eggs, which may sit on bare soil; on debris such as rotted wood, conifer needles, pine cones, and small twigs left naturally or by the previous occupants; on bones, pellets, or feathers accumulated by the owls themselves; or on a mixture of the above (Bent 1938, Forsman et al. 1984). On rare occasions, females apparently will add a few sprays of green conifer needles to the nest (Forsman et al. 1984).

Spotted Owls dine on a wide variety of prey, but overall small arboreal or semiarboreal nocturnal mammals predominate in the diet, whether measured by numbers or biomass consumed (Thomas et al. 1990, n = 15,100+). Throughout the range, diet studies often reveal that 70%-90% of prey biomass is contributed by just two or three dominant species, such as northern flying squirrels, dusky-footed or bushy-tailed woodrats, and various hares or rabbits. Pocket gophers, red tree voles, and deer mice may be regionally important. Broad geographic differences in owl diets are manifest by a predominance of flying squirrels in moist conifer forests at relatively high latitudes or elevations and woodrats in drier conifer forests, mixed evergreen forests, or oak woodlands at relatively low latitudes or elevations. In California, woodrats, flying squirrels, deer mice, and red tree voles or other voles are the main prey items by numbers. After mammals, birds (including small owls) are the next most important group of prey. Birds contributed as much as 10%–18% of the number of prey items at 5 of 14 study sites in California. Various reptiles, amphibians, insects, arthropods, and other invertebrates are of minor importance to the diet; insects may be consumed in numbers in some areas but always represent only a small fraction of total prey biomass (Forsman et al. 1984, Thomas et al. 1990). In Marin County, 88% of 16 pellets found near Palomarin contained dusky-footed woodrats, 69% white-footed mice, 31% Band-tailed Pigeons, and 6% Steller's Jays; other observations indicate that brush rabbits and Sonoma chipmunks also serve as prey here (Beebe & Schonewald 1977).

Seasonal shifts in the diet in Oregon relate to changes in seasonal abundance or vulnerability of prey (Forsman et al. 1984). Various mammals are preyed on more during periods of juvenile dispersal or while juveniles of larger species are still of manageable size; insects are taken primarily in summer and early fall. Dietary composition at particular sites also appears to vary among years. Comparing both percent composition and mean prey weights, Forsman et al. (1984) found no difference in the diet of males and females at two sites in Oregon. Several studies (Barrows 1985, 1987; citations in Thomas et al. 1990) have shown a positive association between prey size and owl reproductive success (and breeding status), but it is unclear whether this reflects differential capture by the owls or merely differential transport of large prey to nests (Thomas et al. 1990).

Spotted Owls are primarily nocturnal predators that leave their roosts to hunt soon after sunset and return shortly before dawn (Forsman et al. 1984). They forage primarily in old-growth or mature timber, from the ground to the upper canopy. Beyond roosting, diurnal activity is usually restricted to occasional short flights to capture prey below the roost tree, to retrieve cached prey, to change roost trees, or to drink or bathe in nearby streams. Laymon (1991) found some pairs of owls in the Sierra Nevada hunting regularly in the daytime when feeding large dependent young that had already left the nest. He speculated that diurnal foraging may be a compensatory response of adults that are unable to meet the demands of feeding young owls solely by nocturnal foraging when food is limited. Just prior to and during incubation and when the

young are small, the male supplies all the food for the female, young, and himself. When young are two to three weeks old, females begin to forage for progressively longer periods and farther away from the nest each night (Forsman et al. 1984). The male initially brings food to the female (on or near the nest) and transfers the decapitated prey to her, beak to beak; later he will leave the food at the nest if the female is away. The female always feeds the young.

Whether capturing prey in trees or on the ground, Spotted Owls usually dive on their victims from an elevated perch (Forsman et al. 1984). After unsuccessful first attempts at catching squirrels in trees, the owls often hop or fly from limb to limb in pursuit of the fleeing animals. Insects are captured either on the ground or on limbs of trees (rather than in the air), usually by pouncing on them with the feet or by landing and picking them up with the beak. It seems likely that most birds or bats are taken when active, leaving or entering roost sites, rather than when concealed and asleep (S.A. Laymon pers. comm.). Spotted Owls hold vertebrate prey in the feet and kill them by crushing, tearing, or breaking the base of the cranium or neck (Forsman et al. 1984). They sometimes eat small prey whole, but usually they at least partially dismember animals larger than deer mice and consume the heads first. Year round, Spotted Owls regularly cache decapitated and partially eaten remains of excess prey and later retrieve them. They securely wedge the remains for storage on top of limbs in trees or on the ground beside logs, trees, or large rocks.

Marin Breeding Distribution

During the atlas years, Spotted Owls were found breeding primarily on Inverness Ridge, Bolinas Ridge, canyons of the Mount Tamalpais watershed, and nearby ridges north to the vicinity of San Geronimo and Tocaloma. This distribution mirrors that of Marin's old-growth and mature conifer and associated mixed evergreen forests. Representative breeding locations were Palomarin, PRNS (NE-NY 4/12-6/5/77 –GBe, SJ, BSo); near Phoenix Lake (ON-NY 3/14-4/18/76 –RMS); and Bolinas Ridge along Bolinas Lagoon (NY 6/2/81 –ARo, DS).

As part of a study of Spotted Owl vocalizations, Seth Bunnell in 1989 surveyed all of Inverness Ridge and limited parts of the remainder of West Marin for these owls. He located 19 pairs and knew of five other sites where they had been reported previously. He estimates that more complete surveys of all potential habitat in Marin would reveal at least 30 pairs of Spotted Owls (S. Bunnell pers. comm.). This compares with another recent estimate of 25 pairs in the county (USFWS 1987a).

Historical Trends/Population Threats

Early in this century, the true status of this owl was cloaked in mystery. Mailliard (1900) did not include the Spotted Owl among the owls listed in his avifaunal summary of Marin County's landbirds. Reporting on the San Francisco Bay region, Grinnell and Wythe (1927) considered the Spotted Owl "very rare," with only three records for the area, all from Marin County. Stephens and Pringle (1933) added four additional Marin County records, all from near Phoenix Lake, 1931 to 1933. With the accumulation of additional knowledge, Grinnell and Miller (1944) concluded that numbers of this owl in California were "nowhere large . . . at best to be rated as only fairly common." They further surmised that "no change in range or numbers [were] apparent from data in hand." Surely many of these owls had already been displaced at that time by the lumbering activities that now threaten the species' existence. Population decline has undoubtedly been greater in recent decades because most timber cutting in California has occurred since the end of World War II in 1945 (Thomas et al. 1990). From 1973 to 1977, Gould (1977) conducted the first statewide survey of Spotted Owls in California. He found evidence of 122 pairs of Northern Spotted Owls and 195 pairs of California Spotted Owls, largely within the range previously described by Grinnell and Miller (1944). Gould was unable to estimate the total size of the California population, but, applying conservative assumptions to data from resurveys of historical sites, he concluded that the state's population had declined a minimum of 28% over prior levels.

Based solely on inventories during the period 1985 to 1989, Thomas et al. (1990) documented a minimum of 2022 pairs of Northern Spotted Owls in Washington (360), Oregon (1129), and northern California (533). They suspected the true number was somewhere between 3000 to 4000 pairs. From 1973 to January 1991, 1392 Northern Spotted Owl territories and 1439 California Spotted Owl territories (1142 Sierra Nevada, 297 s. Calif.) have been located in California (G.I. Gould, Jr., in litt.). These figures do not represent breeding pairs, as they have not yet been adjusted for habitat loss at some sites, lack of surveys in about 20% of the range, intermittent occupation of some sites, sites maintaining only single owls, and territories with pairs that rarely breed. Because data are lacking on the size of the historic population, the true extent of the decline of the Northern Spotted Owl is unknown. Nevertheless, population reduction has been severe. Outspoken concern for the viability of the population ultimately led to protection in 1990 when the subspecies was finally listed as federally Threatened. The California Spotted Owl remains a Candidate (Category 2)

for federal listing as Threatened or Endangered (USFWS 1991) and a Bird Species of Special Concern in California (Remsen 1978, CDFG 1991b). Neither subspecies is in immediate danger of extinction in California, but there is major concern at the lack of a regulatory mechanism to ensure that continued habitat loss will not fragment the population into small isolated groups (G.I. Gould, Jr., in litt.). The population decline is attributed to habitat reduction from clearing for agriculture, urban development, natural events such as fire and windstorms, and most importantly from logging (Thomas et al. 1990). By some estimates (perhaps conservative), forest habitat of this owl has been reduced by 60% since 1800 (mostly since 1900) and continues to be lost at a rate of 1%–2% per year. Beyond habitat loss, forest fragmentation can lead to edge effects, such as increased blowdowns of large trees during storms; higher predation rates on Spotted Owls by Great Horned Owls; competition with Barred Owls now rapidly expanding into the Spotted Owl range; and potential loss of habitat or microhabitats that lessen the effects of weather, provide habitat for prey species, or serve as refugia during catastrophic events. Also, fragmentation can increase the risks of local extirpation because of the greater likelihood that small populations will exhibit or be affected by loss of genetic variability, deleterious demographic patterns (such as skewed sex or age ratios or poor reproductive success), environmental variation, or the inability of dispersing individuals to find and recolonize suitable habitat. Although most Spotted Owls here reside in protected parklands, isolation of the Marin County population, among others, is of concern for the above reasons (USFWS 1989c).

The Interagency Scientific Committee to Address the Conservation of the Northern Spotted Owl has proposed a management strategy based on a network of Habitat Conservation Areas throughout the subspecies' range (Thomas et al. 1990). Where possible, these areas should support 20 pairs of owls and should be separated from other areas by a maximum distance of 12 miles, features designed to minimize the effects of habitat fragmentation. Although the Forest Service has endorsed this strategy, it has yet to complete its own recovery plan. In the meantime, political forces are proposing plans more favorable to the timber industry and also attempting to weaken the Endangered Species Act (Liverman 1990). The outcome of this struggle is a true test of our society's ability to adequately cope with the stark and obvious realities that natural resources are limited and that we are not alone on this planet.

LONG-EARED OWL *Asio otus*

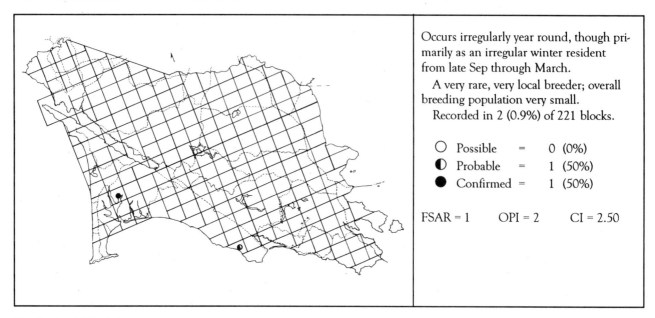

Occurs irregularly year round, though primarily as an irregular winter resident from late Sep through March.

A very rare, very local breeder; overall breeding population very small.

Recorded in 2 (0.9%) of 221 blocks.

○	Possible	=	0 (0%)
◑	Probable	=	1 (50%)
●	Confirmed	=	1 (50%)

FSAR = 1   OPI = 2   CI = 2.50

Ecological Requirements

Regardless of its uncanny ability to conceal itself during the day, this sleek medium-sized owl is one of the most elusive and puzzling of this mysterious clan. In some regions, it is numerous and breeds with regularity (Marks 1986); elsewhere, birds are nomadic, breeding when and where prey populations permit. Hence owl populations fluctuate markedly from year to year at some sites, and at others birds breed only irregularly (Voous 1988). Marin County appears to fall into the latter category. Long-eared Owls often hunt in open country of grasslands, meadows, and fields, where they seek small mammal prey, particularly microtine rodents. Apparently they also forage in open conifer stands or along their edges (Bull et al. 1989). Studies in Europe have linked fluctuations of Long-eared Owl population densities and clutch sizes to annual variations in microtine prey populations (Johnsgard 1988, Voous 1988). Such a link has not yet been documented in North America (Marks 1986), but, given dietary preferences here (see below), it undoubtedly will be with further work. Although no studies were conducted on their mammal prey, confirmed and apparent breeding of Long-eared Owls (and Short-eared Owls) in Marin County during the atlas period coincided with a population peak of voles *(Microtus)*. These mice were so abundant that year that observers often found them scurrying underfoot in the daytime (J.G. Evens pers. comm.). At the lone site where Long-eareds were confirmed breeding in Marin County during the atlas period, the owls nested in a nonnative pine plantation surrounded by grassland and scattered stands of open coastal scrub. They were also seen displaying at the edge of a coast live oak and California bay–dominated mixed evergreen forest bordering on open coastal scrub mixed with grassland. Hence, the main nesting requirements of Long-eared Owls are open or semiopen short-grass or sparsely vegetated foraging areas, an abundance of small mammal prey, and suitable nesting and day-roost sites on the edges of adjacent dense forests, thickets, or planted woodlots (Getz 1961, Marks 1986, Johnsgard 1988, Voous 1988). These owls do not select specific plant communities for breeding in California (G&M 1944). Nesting birds range from coastal lowlands to interior deserts and seem to favor riparian groves, planted woodlots, and belts of live oaks paralleling stream courses, perhaps because these habitats tend to occur in the fertile bottomlands most often used for foraging. Long-eareds probable also nest in conifer forests in California, as they do in Oregon (Bull et al. 1989). Dense cover is important to inhibit nest predation (Marks 1986, Bull et al. 1989) and predation of adults by Great Horned Owls (Voous 1988).

Long-eared Owls usually lay their eggs in vacant stick nests of crows, magpies, ravens, *Buteo* or *Accipiter* hawks, other birds, or squirrels in trees or large bushes (Bent 1938, Stophlet 1959, Craig & Trost 1979, Marks & Yensen 1980, Marks 1986, Johnsgard 1988, Voous 1988). In Oregon's conifer forests, they prefer to nest in dwarf mistletoe brooms (Bull et al. 1989). Rarely, they nest in shallow cavities in trees or stumps, in natural cavities in cliffs, in semiopen nest boxes or baskets constructed for other birds, or on the ground in sheltering vegetation (references above). There is limited evidence that Long-eareds occasionally modify nests by adding sticks or small amounts of nest lining (Bent 1938, Craig & Trost 1979, Voous 1988, Bull et al. 1989). Maximum nest height is about 61 feet, and average nest heights in various studies range from 7 to 32 feet (Stophlet 1959, Craig & Trost 1979, Marks & Yensen 1980, Peck & James 1983, Marks 1986, Johnsgard 1988, Bull et al. 1989) and probably vary locally with the stature of the vegetation and available stick nests or other nest sites. In Idaho, Long-eareds prefer partially canopied Black-billed Magpie nests over open magpie or crow nests, presumably because the former provide additional concealment (Marks 1986). Corvid nests used by the owls there tended to be wider and slightly higher above ground than unused corvid nests; wider nests provide ample room for eggs and young and probably better concealment from ground-based predators. Nests there are usually near midheight in trees, and in clumps of trees rather than in isolated trees or rows of trees. Nesting on the edge of clumps may reflect the availability of corvid nests (Marks 1986) and/or selection for proximity to open foraging areas. In Oregon's conifer forests, Long-eareds appear to nest in the smallest, most inconspicuous platforms that can accommodate them (Bull et al. 1989). There the average distance of nests from openings (2.5 acres in size) is 344 feet. Probably because birds do not defend foraging territories (Voous 1988), Long-eared Owls sometimes nest in loose "colonies" of three to ten pairs; nests are as close as 52 feet in Idaho (Marks 1985). Some owls return to reuse the previous year's nest site, particularly if they were successful the year before (Marks 1986).

Long-eared Owls are primarily nocturnal, but occasionally they hunt in daylight at far-northern latitudes, or when they are forced to by exceptionally short food supplies at the end of winter (Voous 1988). The owls typically start hunting 25 to 30 minutes after sunset and retire 30 to 45 minutes before sunrise, with peak activity in the few hours after activity starts and before it diminishes. These owls have very acute hearing and a highly perfected ability to locate prey by sound. With their light bodies and long wings, Long-eared Owls hunt from buoyant, mothlike flight resembling a nocturnal harrier. This enables them to hunt and hover efficiently low or high, and to capture prey in the short vegetation of open fields, farmlands, grasslands, marshes, and deserts (Marti 1976, Voous 1988). In winter, they sometimes hover over bushes to try to force out communally roosting landbirds (Voous 1988).

Long-eared Owls have a restricted diet. They specialize in capturing voles and mice, and, unlike some species, most Long-eareds leave the area to breed or winter elsewhere in times of food shortage (Voous 1988). Although the diet varies between locations and habitats, it typically consists of relatively few species of small mammals and varies little over time. Mammals (of 45 species) account for

98.2% of 23,888 prey items in North America and voles and deer mice make up 82.2% of the total; mammals as large as young rabbits are taken (Marti 1976). Voles account for 53.7% of total prey here and, as the dominant species, range from 29.8% to 94.4% of total prey items in local studies. Deer mice, pocket mice, pocket gophers, and kangaroo rats have also been the dominant prey in some studies here (Marti 1976, Craig & Trost 1979, Marks 1984, Barrows 1989, Bull et al. 1989). The preponderance of voles in the North American diet may be in part an artifact of limited data on the diet in deserts or conifer forests (Marks 1984, Bull et al. 1989). In the Great Basin Desert of Idaho, Long-eared Owls feed on a greater diversity of small mammals than in other North American studies and predominantly on three genera of mammals rather than on one or two, as is the case in studies elsewhere (Marks 1984). In the deserts of southern California, the diet of Long-eared Owls in winter is about 54% pocket mice and 32% kangaroo rats (Barrows 1989, n = 956). In Oregon's conifer forests, the diet of breeding Long-eareds is predominantly pocket gophers, with voles a distant second (Bull et al. 1989, n = 1123). Small to medium-sized birds represent 1.7% of North American prey items (35 species, Marti 1976), including birds as large as quail, Ruffed Grouse, and Mourning Doves (Bent 1938). Bats, reptiles, amphibians, fish, crayfish, and insects are very rarely taken (Marti 1976, Marks 1984). In Europe, birds may be important prey for Long-eared Owls in winter, with a higher proportion of birds taken in poor vole years (Voous 1988). Prey size of mammals rather than prey type may be the most important factor in prey selection (Marks 1984). In North America, most prey weigh less than 3.5 ounces (Marti 1976, Marks 1984), and average prey weight is 1.3 ounces (range 0.04–28 oz., Marti 1976, n = 23,888). In Colorado, average prey weight is 1.1 ounces for Long-eared Owls, compared with 1.6 ounces for Barn Owls, and 6.2 ounces for Great Horned Owls (Marti 1974). An increase in pocket mice in the postfledging diet in Idaho may reflect a corresponding increase in numbers of these mice in the environment from spring to summer, or, alternatively, young owls may have begun to capture prey at that time and either have a preference for smaller prey or have more difficulty catching other species of mice (Marks 1984). Insects, though rare in the diet, are more frequently taken in the postfledging period, suggesting they are captured by young owls. Although females are slightly larger and heavier than males and have much stronger and heavier talons, there is as yet no evidence of differential use of prey or hunting niches between the sexes (Earhart & Johnson 1970, Voous 1988).

Although the female may occasionally hunt early in the incubation period (Johnsgard 1988), the male does most of the hunting for the female and the young (Voous 1988). The eggs hatch asynchronously over an extended period—

up to 11 or 12 days in a nest with six owlets (Johnsgard 1988). As an adaptation to predation, the young leave the nest after about three weeks of age to climb about the branches, roosting solitarily in dense foliage until attaining flight and leaving the nest area at about five weeks (Marks 1986). Hence, where pairs nest close together, broods can mix and perhaps are sometimes fed by adults other than their parents (Marks 1985). On rare occasions, second clutches are reported (Voous 1988).

Marin Breeding Distribution

During the atlas period, Long-eared Owls were confirmed breeding by the observation on 12 May 1979 of three adults and a full-sized juvenile (with some down still in its plumage) at a pine plantation along the Estero Trail at the head of Home Bay, PRNS (JLo et al.). In addition, a territorial bird was at Palomarin, PRNS, from 9 May to 13 July 1979 (PRBO). Because of their almost strictly nocturnal habits, their propensity for irregular breeding, and the fact that winter visitant Long-eareds still gather at communal roosts at a time when local breeding birds are already incubating in March or early April (Voous 1988), it can be difficult to confirm breeding of this species. We likely would have confirmed breeding for this species in more blocks if we had concentrated our efforts at the first sign of the population explosion of voles on the Point Reyes peninsula in 1979, or soon after stumbling upon the one

nest that year. Subsequently, a nest with five eggs was found at the pine plantation at Home Bay on 3 May 1983 (CCu *fide* JE). The only known prior breeding record for Marin County was of a nest with eggs observed in an oak near Novato on 6 and 20 April 1904 (Ray 1904).

Historical Trends/Population Threats

Although they considered the species "common" or even "abundant" locally, Grinnell and Miller (1944) noted a reduction in Long-eared Owl numbers in California, apparently mostly because of the clearing of bottomlands for farming. Numbers have continued to decline, and the species is currently on the state's list of Bird Species of Special Concern (Remsen 1978, CDFG 1991b). This owl was also on the Audubon Society's Blue List in 1980 (Tate 1981). In addition to the destruction of riparian habitat, causes of the decline in California may be collisions with traffic, shooting and harassment at nest sites (Remsen 1978), and land use changes that have caused reductions of the small mammal prey base. Long-eared Owls have been lethally contaminated by heavy metals, insecticides, fungicides, rodenticides, and PCBs, but the overall effect on their populations has been less severe than in other species of owls and diurnal birds of prey, probably because, unlike buteo hawks, Long-eared Owls do not eat carrion (Voous 1988).

SHORT-EARED OWL *Asio flammeus*

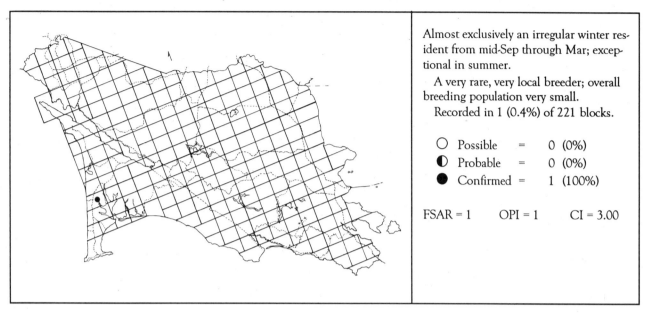

Almost exclusively an irregular winter resident from mid-Sep through Mar; exceptional in summer.

A very rare, very local breeder; overall breeding population very small.

Recorded in 1 (0.4%) of 221 blocks.

○ Possible   =   0 (0%)
◐ Probable   =   0 (0%)
● Confirmed =   1 (100%)

FSAR = 1   OPI = 1   CI = 3.00

Ecological Requirements

This arch nomad wanders and migrates only to settle where it finds high vole populations, gathering sometimes by the hundreds and staying to nest only as long as the food abundance lasts (Clark 1975, Voous 1988). Although Short-eared Owls are resident in some suitable marshlands, these habitats are increasingly rare; thus the species is an unpredictable migrant in most of its range. These owls occur irregularly in Marin County, and since they are known to have bred here only once (see below), it is difficult to describe local breeding habitat preferences. Though the exact site of the Marin breeding record is unknown, it was generally in an area where dunes, coastal swales, and grasslands intermingle on Point Reyes. In California, these owls breed in fresh, brackish, and salt marshes; in lowland meadows and moist grasslands; in irrigated fields; and in fallow or stubble fields (G&M 1944, D. Shuford pers. obs.). The main requirements for breeding are low nesting and resting cover and open foraging grounds supporting an abundance of small mammals, particularly voles (Clark 1975, Johnsgard 1988, Voous 1988).

Short-eared Owls defend breeding territories that vary inversely in size with prey abundance and sometimes nest close enough together to suggest the existence of nesting "colonies" (Clark 1975, Voous 1988). They typically lay their eggs in depressions on the ground, and, unlike most owls, they construct their own nests (Townsend 1938, Clark 1975, Johnsgard 1988, Voous 1938). Birds usually make a scrape in the substrate in open country and line it sparsely with grass stems, weed or stubble stalks, thin

twigs, or other vegetation, sometimes gathered at some distance from the nest. On occasion, nest sites may be mere scrapes in the ground or only the flattened or dead vegetation of the spot chosen. Nests may be entirely exposed to the light but more often are shielded by clumps of grasses, weeds, grains, or low-growing marsh vegetation. Short-eareds tend to pick drier sites for their nests than Northern Harriers do (Clark 1975). Very rarely, nests have been found in a patch of low bushes, on the top of a broken tree stump in a clearing, in old crows' nests, on a ledge, and apparently in burrows or cavities in the ground (Townsend 1938, Clark 1975, Voous 1988). Exceptionally, birds will nest in the exact site in successive years (Townsend 1938). As an adaptation of ground nesting to avoid predation, the young, after hatching asynchronously, leave the nest at the early age of 12 to 16 days, scattering around in the safety of "runs" they make in the vegetation (Clark 1975, Johnsgard 1988, Voous 1988). Chicks may disperse up to nearly 200 yards in four days.

Short-eared Owls are primarily crepuscular and secondarily nocturnal hunters, though they also forage more in the day than do most medium-sized owls (Clark 1975, Johnsgard 1988, Voous 1988). These owls apparently forage in the daytime mostly when they are unable to obtain enough preferred foods in the night, for example when feeding growing young; birds breeding at extreme northern latitudes must of necessity forage during daylight hours. Short-eared Owls seem somewhat less dependent on hearing for hunting than are Long-eared Owls, though their hearing is more acute than that of their diurnal

229

ecological counterparts, Northern Harriers (Voous 1988). The flight of Short-eared Owls seems even lighter, more buoyant and mothlike than that of Long-eared Owls. Short-eareds take most prey by surprise as they quarter low (mostly 1–6.5 ft., rarely over 10 ft.) over fields and marshes in slow tilting flight, alternately flapping and gliding on stiff wings (Townsend 1938, Johnston 1956b, Clark 1975, Johnsgard 1988, Voous 1988). In such coursing flights, the owls usually head into the wind and often hover momentarily before pouncing (Clark 1975). If they overshoot their prey, they frequently turn 180° and pounce, seemingly headfirst, heading downwind. With no wind, the owls seem to prefer to hunt into or away from the light rather than at right angles to the light. Short-eared Owls also hunt from extended ternlike hovering flight (about 6–100 ft. in height), maintaining themselves in one place by varying amounts of wing flapping. When hovering, the birds descend rapidly by raising the wings in a deep dihedral. This may be followed quickly by pouncing, or by checking the flight at a lower height before pouncing or flying elsewhere to hunt. Clark (1975) felt hovering was not a response to wind, but rather is used when prey is scarce. Occasionally these owls land on fence posts, tree stubs, grass tufts, or the ground and wait for their prey to appear before launching an attack. This technique is frequently used when weather conditions are unfavorable. In interspecific encounters with harriers, buteo hawks, and falcons, Short-eared Owls may rob them of their prey, or vice versa (Voous 1988).

Short-eared Owls specialize in catching voles, lemmings, and mice, though they adapt to a variety of other prey when local conditions dictate. The year-round diet (data mostly from winter) in North America is 94.8% mammals, 5.1% birds, and 0.1% insects, frogs, and lizards (Clark 1975, n = 9640). Voles *(Microtus)* account for 60.6% of the mammal prey, but pocket gophers, deer mice, pocket mice, brown lemmings, Norway rats, and numerous small terrestrial species are also taken. Clark (1975) thought that Short-eared Owls did not really prefer voles but instead opportunistically took whatever prey species were most available in open habitat. Colvin and Spaulding (1983), on the other hand, felt that the owls preferred the larger voles over smaller deer mice for energetic reasons and concentrated their hunting times during major periods of vole activity. In North America, at least 60 species of bird prey have been recorded, especially open-country and marsh species, such as Red-winged Blackbirds, Western Meadowlarks, Horned Larks, various sparrows, shorebirds, and rails. Many birds are probably captured at night (Clark 1975) or at least when there is little light. Birds are taken much more extensively during migration or in winter (e.g., Page & Whitacre 1975) and in coastal or island situations (Clark 1975). The owls sometimes prey on birds at seabird colonies (Townsend 1938, Voous 1988). Insect remains found in pellets of young in poor vole years are probably captured by the young while walking around. It is doubtful that parents would bother carrying insects to them (Clark 1975). Average prey weight of Short-eared Owls is about 1.2 ounces versus 1.05–1.1 ounces for Long-eared Owls (Voous 1988).

The male hunts for the female while she is involved in egg laying, brooding, and caring for the young (Clark 1975, Voous 1988). The female flies out to retrieve food from the male. Consumption of the prey is begun with the head. The female initially tears off pieces to feed to the begging owlets. The female usually begins foraging again when the chicks first scatter from the nest, well before fledging; in good vole years, when the male is apparently able to provide enough food for both the female and young, she remains close to the nest throughout nesting. When food is plentiful, surplus prey is often cached at the rim of the nest. Clutch size varies with the food supply, but birds only rarely lay second clutches and raise second broods, even in years of vole abundance.

Marin Breeding Distribution

During the atlas period, Short-eared Owls were confirmed breeding by the observation of up to seven owls, including three recently fledged young (with traces of white down in their plumage), near the north entrance to Point Reyes Beach, PRNS, from 24 to 26 June 1979 (S&MK et al.). This is the only known breeding record for Marin County and it coincided with the 1978–79 vole *(Microtus californicus)* outbreak on Point Reyes which also appeared to induce breeding efforts of Long-eared Owls nearby.

Historical Trends/Population Threats

Grinnell and Miller (1944) commented on a decline in winter numbers from shooting by duck hunters but made no mention of a change in status of breeding birds. Nevertheless, the elimination of 60%–95% of the former marshlands around San Francisco Bay (Nichols & Wright 1971, Josselyn 1983) and habitat loss elsewhere undoubtedly have greatly reduced both summer and winter numbers. The Short-eared Owl has been on the Audubon Society's Blue List from 1976 to 1986 (Tate 1981, 1986; Tate & Tate 1982). It is also currently on California's list of Bird Species of Special Concern (Remsen 1978, CDFG 1991b). Numbers of Short-eared Owls were relatively stable on Breeding Bird Surveys in California from 1968 to 1989 (USFWS unpubl. analyses). Grazing may be another factor responsible for the decline of the species in the state. Where Short-eared Owls nest in extensive farmlands, nests and young often are destroyed by mechanized farm equipment (Voous 1988). Pesticide residues have been found in tissues and eggs of Short-eared Owls, but the effects of these contaminants on owl populations are unknown (Marti & Marks 1989).

NORTHERN SAW-WHET OWL *Aegolius acadicus*

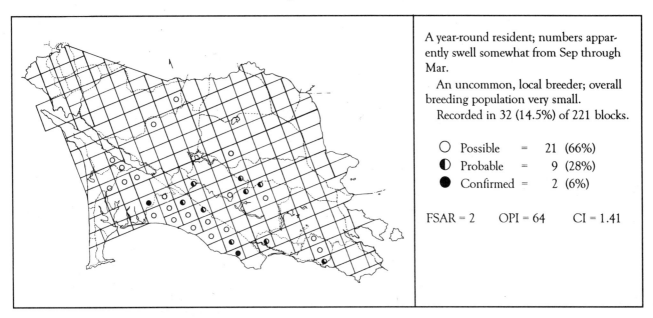

A year-round resident; numbers apparently swell somewhat from Sep through Mar.

An uncommon, local breeder; overall breeding population very small.

Recorded in 32 (14.5%) of 221 blocks.

○ Possible   =   21 (66%)
◑ Probable   =   9 (28%)
● Confirmed   =   2 (6%)

FSAR = 2   OPI = 64   CI = 1.41

Ecological Requirements

An observer imitating the repetitive, penetrating whistled calls of a Saw-whet Owl in the heart of its territory is likely as not to be aggressively dive-bombed as the occupant challenges the intruder. Saw-whet Owls inhabit Marin County's Douglas fir, bishop pine, coast redwood, and mixed evergreen forests and woodlands, as well as her alder riparian thickets. These habitats are all relatively moist and have diverse ground cover with variably open or fairly dense understories of shrubs and ferns. Mixed evergreen forests used by these owls vary from a mixture of dominant trees to pure bay laurel stands. Throughout their range, these owls are usually found in conifer-dominated zones, but often where there is a broadleaved component to the forest (Johnsgard 1988, Voous 1988).

Saw-whet Owls most frequently nest in deserted woodpecker cavities and also in natural tree cavities and nest boxes, including the spacious ones designed for Wood Ducks (Bent 1938, Johnsgard 1988, Voous 1988). Nest trees may be either broadleaved or coniferous species; cavities may be in snags or dead stubs of live trees. The woodpecker cavities used are those of the larger species— Northern Flickers, Pileated Woodpeckers, and Hairy Woodpeckers—with entrances at least 2.8 inches in diameter (Johnsgard 1988). Nest heights probably reflect what is available, principally from the dominant large woodpeckers in a given area; an extreme nest height was 63 feet above the ground (Bent 1938). In Ontario, the height of 13 nests ranged from 8 to 44 feet above the ground, with most from 12 to 20 feet (Peck & James 1983). Like most owls, Saw-whets do not build nests; instead they lay their

eggs on the bottoms of the cavities on wood chips, other naturally accumulated debris, or the nest materials of previous rodent occupants, mixed with feathers of the owls (Bent 1938, Johnsgard 1988, Voous 1988).

Saw-whet Owls are considered strictly nocturnal in their activity patterns. By day they roost in thick patches of forests in dense layers of foliage (or stranded debris) in tree canopies or under cover of vines in bushes (Bent 1938, Johnsgard 1988, Voous 1988). They generally prefer roost sites between 6 and 12 feet, though rarely as low as 6 inches, off the ground. Saw-whets forage at irregular intervals through the night, apparently largely within forests or woodlands or at their edges (Randle & Austing 1952, Forbes & Warner 1974, Johnsgard 1988, Voous 1988). Their highly developed hearing suggests that they can capture prey in total or near-total darkness (Johnsgard 1988). Saw-whets have bodies rather light in weight relative to the surface area of their wings, which provides for good maneuverability and allows them to hunt in somewhat shrub-dominated cover. There are few observations of actual foraging behavior, but apparently birds hunt mostly from relatively low perches and swoop down to the ground or, less frequently, into the foliage of trees to catch their prey.

The Saw-whet Owl diet is about 96.8% mammals, 1.6% birds, 1.4% insects, and 0.2% frogs (Snyder & Wiley 1976, n = 435). The mammal prey consists mostly of small terrestrial species, particularly woodland-inhabiting deer mice, voles, and shrews, but also other mice, small rats, young squirrels, flying squirrels, chipmunks, and bats

(Bent 1938, Johnsgard 1988, Voous 1988). The owls seem to take birds to a greater degree when their numbers increase during migration (Graber 1962, Catling 1971). Nesting Saw-whets at Silver Valley Lakes, San Mateo County, relied mostly on deer mice and stored extra mice in the nest (Santee & Granfield 1939). The diet varies between habitats and regions (Johnsgard 1988, Voous 1988). Mean prey weight is about 0.7 to 0.8 ounce (Voous 1988). Female Saw-whets are heavier than males, but differences between the sexes in average prey size or feeding habits have yet to be demonstrated. Since only the female incubates the eggs (Johnsgard 1988), the male must provide her with food at least during this period.

Marin Breeding Distribution

During the atlas period, Saw-whet Owls were found in the breeding season (Feb-Jul) mostly in various habitats on the moist conifer- and mixed evergreen-dominated coastal ridges, particularly Inverness Ridge, where it was the most common owl (large or small) in moderately dense and dense forests. Saw-whets were also found calling locally in dense mixed evergreen forests in the interior of the county. If more nocturnal field work had been undertaken, we undoubtedly would have recorded Saw-whets in more blocks, particularly on the conifer-dominated ridges of the

Mount Tamalpais and Lagunitas Creek watersheds. Saw-whets were most vocal in February and March at a time when local numbers are swelled by wintering birds; but territorial calling is apparently restricted to breeding birds, there being no evidence that these owls call in regions where they occur only as winter residents (Johnsgard 1988, Voous 1988). Saw-whets can be heard calling in almost every month of the year; a bird at a breeding site at Palomarin frequently called during the middle of the day (D.F. DeSante pers. comm.), though this is apparently unusual (J. Winter pers. comm.).

The only confirmed breeding records for Marin County were established during the atlas period. A pair successfully fledged seven young from a nest box on the edge of an evergreen hardwood forest at Palomarin, PRNS (ON-FL spring/summer 1979 —PRBO), and another pair occupied a nest hole on the edge of an alder riparian thicket at Laguna Ranch, PRNS (ON 5/2-24/79 —JGE et al.).

Historical Trends/Population Threats

No good information is available on any changes in status (G&M 1944, Johnsgard 1988, Voous 1988), but logging in California has likely reduced numbers of this forest- and woodland-inhabiting owl.

Poorwills
Family *Caprimulgidae*

COMMON POORWILL *Phalaenoptilus nuttallii*

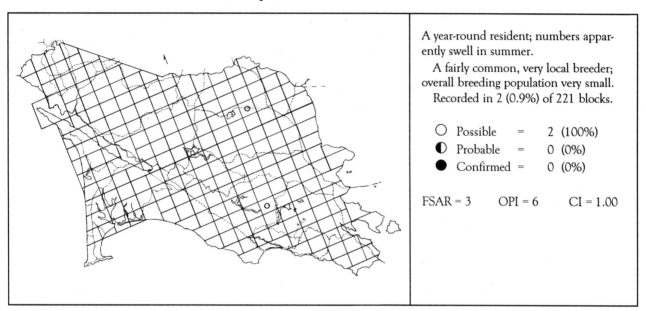

A year-round resident; numbers apparently swell in summer.

A fairly common, very local breeder; overall breeding population very small. Recorded in 2 (0.9%) of 221 blocks.

○ Possible	=	2	(100%)
◑ Probable	=	0	(0%)
● Confirmed	=	0	(0%)

FSAR = 3   OPI = 6   CI = 1.00

Ecological Requirements

The burning ember–like eyeshine and mellow self-descriptive whistled calls of breeding Poorwills are trademarks of relatively open chaparral in the Coast Range, including Marin County. Poorwills also nest on gravel streambeds, in proximity to Lesser Nighthawks (Unglish 1929), and likely use clearings in open dry pine forests, recently burned forests, and clearcuts. They lay their eggs on the ground on bare soil, gravel, sparse leaf and bark litter, moss, or flat rocks. They often locate their nests at the base of a bush, grass clump, or rock overhang, though they sometimes place them in the open (Aldrich 1935, Bent 1940, Swisher 1978). Undisturbed nestlings make short-distance movements (<10 ft.) from the nest site, presumably for thermoregulation (avoiding wet areas or direct sunlight) or concealment from aerial predators (Swenson & Hendricks 1983). Long-distance movement by young birds may be an antipredator adaptation triggered by disturbance.

Poorwills are primarily crepuscular and nocturnal feeders. They forage from the ground or from low perches—rocks or fence posts—in openings such as clearings or roads and capture prey by short, fluttery, mothlike flycatching flights, returning to the ground with their victims. Appar-

ently Poorwills capture some food on the ground (Bent 1940). Their diet is exclusively insects, primarily small night-flying types such as moths, beetles, chinch bugs, grasshoppers, and locusts.

Marin Breeding Distribution

During the atlas period, Poorwills were found in the breeding season in only two areas—on Mount Burdell, Novato, and on Carson Ridge. On Mount Burdell, a single bird was calling from a small patch of broken chaparral on 9 May 1981 (ScC). On Carson Ridge, up to six birds were calling in an extensive area of open serpentine chaparral on 21 May 1977 (JGE et al.). Though certainly not widespread in Marin, Poorwills would undoubtedly have been recorded in more locations if we had conducted more nighttime work in their rugged, relatively inaccessible breeding habitat. The only confirmed breeding record for Marin is of a nest found on 22 July 1908 "among some fragments of serpentine rock from which we had burnt the low, scrubby manzanita brush the previous winter" (Mailliard 1909a); the site was above San Geronimo, likely on or close to Carson Ridge. Recent controlled

233

burns in chaparral on Marin Municipal Water District lands in the Mount Tamalpais area should favor this species.

Historical Trends/Population Threats

Historical trends are unclear, though it is likely that fire suppression has reduced Poorwill habitat; conversely, log-ging, especially clear-cutting, has increased it. Horn and Marshall (1975) felt that clear-cutting had increased the species' range in Oregon. In California, Poorwill numbers were relatively stable on Breeding Bird Surveys from 1968 to 1989 but decreased from 1980 to 1989 (USFWS unpubl. analyses).

Swifts
Family *Apodidae*

VAUX'S SWIFT *Chaetura vauxi*

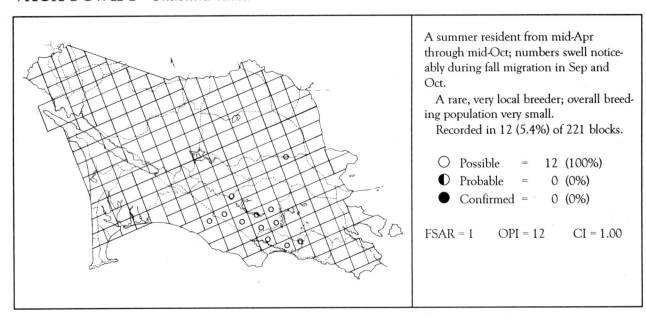

A summer resident from mid-Apr through mid-Oct; numbers swell notice-ably during fall migration in Sep and Oct.

A rare, very local breeder; overall breed-ing population very small.

Recorded in 12 (5.4%) of 221 blocks.

○ Possible	=	12 (100%)
◑ Probable	=	0 (0%)
● Confirmed	=	0 (0%)

FSAR = 1   OPI = 12   CI = 1.00

Ecological Requirements

On the coast, these airborne apparitions prefer redwood and Douglas fir forests, especially old-growth or fire-swept stands that provide decaying trees for nesting. Evidence from Oregon suggests that Vaux's Swifts may need old-growth forests to satisfy their nest site requirements (Bull & Cooper 1991).

Unlike closely related Chimney Swifts, Vauxes usually nest in natural settings and build their nests inside hol-lowed-out trees or stumps that are either heavily decayed or dead. In northeastern Oregon, 21 nests were found in 20 large-diameter old-growth grand fir *(Abies grandis)* trees (17 live, 3 dead); two nests were in one tree in separate chambers (Bull & Cooper 1991). All nest trees were hollowed-out by a fungus that decays the heartwood; entrance was made via holes excavated by Pileated Wood-peckers, as broken-topped trees, that sometimes provide swifts access to potential nest chambers, are scarce in most forests. Vaux's Swifts also nest in chimneys, water tanks, and even metal boilers on occasion (Taylor 1905, Bent 1940, Baldwin & Hunter 1963, Baldwin & Zaczkowski 1963). Tree nests are usually well below the top of the stub and sometimes are very close to the bottom of the cavity or

234

even below ground level if a stump has been undermined by fire (Dawson 1923, Bent 1940, Bull & Cooper 1991). In Oregon, 19 nests averaged 6.7 feet below the entrance hole used for access (some had two holes) and 5.2 feet from the bottom of the chamber; 2 nests were 1.3 and 8.2 feet *above* the entrance hole (Bull & Cooper 1991). Entrance holes averaged 39.4 feet above ground (range 26.2-60.0 ft.).

Vaux's Swifts construct compact and shallow nests that are narrow and saucer shaped. They use small pieces of twigs or conifer needles that they stick together and attach to the wall of the nest chamber with their gluey saliva. They sometimes line their nests with conifer needles. Birds apparently situate their nests inside chimneys or trees in locations providing protection from rain (Bent 1940).

Vaux's Swifts forage on the wing in open airways at variable heights. Their aerial domain appears to be the insect-productive air space over moist forested habitat, canyon bottoms, stream courses, and lakes. Birds propel themselves with a number of very rapid strokes, then sail or circle with their long, narrow wings curved backward and downward. The diet is poorly known as the only evidence appears to be from examining the gullets of young, in one nest, which contained mostly leafhoppers (Bent 1940). Presumably the diet is exclusively aerial insects of the general types taken by the Chimney Swift.

Marin Breeding Distribution

During the atlas years, Vaux's Swifts appeared to nest in Marin County only in small numbers. Most of the breeding season sightings then were from the vicinity of redwood or Douglas fir forest on the southern part of Bolinas Ridge. This species was seen most frequently near Kent Lake, where it probably nested upslope on Bolinas Ridge in an area replete with dead snags and stubs of redwood and fir that were charred by a 1945 fire. To the best of my knowledge, nesting of this species has never been confirmed in Marin, but breeding has been surmised from its nesting season occurrence here (Allen 1880, Mailliard 1900, S&P 1933, G&M 1944, this study). Representative locations of breeding season sightings during the atlas were ridge on S side of Lucas Valley Rd. (5/30/82 —BiL); Carson Ridge and vicinity of Kent Lake (4 on 6/5/82 —DS, ITi); and Garden Club Canyon along Bolinas Lagoon (2 on 7/4/82 —DS).

Historical Trends/Population Threats

Given that Vaux's Swifts nest inside large-diameter, decayed trees which tend to occur in old-growth stands, it is likely that numbers of breeding swifts have declined historically in Marin County (as well as in much of their range) because of extensive logging in the last century. The effect of fire suppression on availability of swift nest sites is unclear. Fire may damage trees that soon decay to leave hollow interiors. On the other hand, fire may kill many smaller trees that otherwise would have made good nest sites at maturity. Whether swifts will nest in forests opened by logging or fire, as long as suitable nests trees are left standing, or whether they require other characteristics of old-growth forests for nesting needs further study. Numbers of Vaux's Swifts were relatively stable on Breeding Bird Surveys in California from 1968 to 1989 (USFWS unpubl. analyses).

WHITE-THROATED SWIFT　*Aeronautes saxatalis*

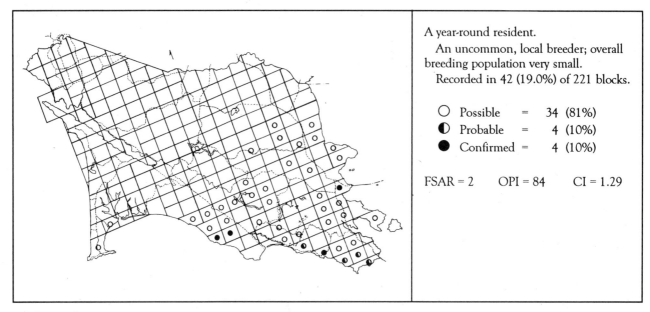

A year-round resident.

An uncommon, local breeder; overall breeding population very small.

Recorded in 42 (19.0%) of 221 blocks.

○　Possible　　=　34 (81%)
◑　Probable　　=　4 (10%)
●　Confirmed　=　4 (10%)

FSAR = 2　　OPI = 84　　CI = 1.29

Ecological Requirements

These masters of the air course over almost all terrains and habitats within foraging range of their breeding haunts. In California, they breed solitarily or in small colonies from near sea level probably up to 8000 or 9000 feet (Gaines 1988). Some traditional colony sites have a history of use of over 50 years (Dobkin et al. 1986), but many of these have probably been occupied by breeding swifts for much longer. White-throated Swifts usually nest in vertical or horizontal cracks or crevices in steep cliffs (Bent 1940). The main nest site requirements are narrow recessed nooks and crannies inaccessible to terrestrial predators. Proximity to good foraging areas is probably also important (Dobkin et al. 1986). Throughout much of their range they nest in granite cliffs, but also in a variety of other rock types. Granite occurs in Marin County only on the Point Reyes peninsula and is perhaps serviceable to White-throated Swifts only at the Point Reyes headlands; most White-throateds in Marin nest in other substrates. Elsewhere, these swifts also nest in caves, in dug-out Rough-winged Swallow holes (Bent 1940), and in recesses of buildings and wharves (Bailey 1907, Collins & Johnson 1982). Nests take the shape of the crack in which they are built and are made of feathers, plant down, weed stems, grasses, and bark, all glued together by the birds' saliva (Bent 1940).

White-throateds are considered the fastest of North American swifts (Bent 1940). They forage over a wide variety of habitats at variable heights. Their flight is more or less direct, but birds feeding hundreds of feet from the ground may dart and swoop erratically or alternately flap

and soar. Grinnell and Miller (1944) suggested that "possibly the daily cruising radius of these birds is greater than any other species, even the California Condor," though no data are available on how far that might be. Excluding the isolated Point Reyes sightings, all others made during the Marin atlas project were within five to seven miles of known breeding sites, in the southern and eastern part of the county. The White-throated Swift's diet is exclusively aerial insects, especially flies, beetles, bees, wasps, ants, and true bugs (Bent 1940).

Marin Breeding Distribution

Except for a nest site at a bayshore quarry, all confirmed and probable Marin County breeding records pertained to sea cliffs. Representative breeding locations were cliffs at Double Point (ON Apr-Jun 1977 –SGA) and a quarry at Larkspur Landing (ON/DD 5/30/82 –SSm). Three observations of aerial copulations near Palomarin (6/5/80 PRBO) were not recorded as confirmations because of the uncertainty of the actual blocks in which the birds were nesting; these may have been Double Point rather than Palomarin breeders.

Historical Trends/Population Threats

The White-throated Swift was unrecorded in Marin County by Mailliard (1900), whose ornithological exploration here focused mostly on the vicinity of San Geronimo. Stephens and Pringle (1933) considered it "very rare" in Marin County, and Grinnell and Wythe (1927) thought it was established in the San Francisco Bay Area only in the vicinity of Mount Diablo, Contra Costa County. Although our atlas data for Marin and casual coastal observations for the rest of the Bay Area (ABN) suggest White-throated Swifts are now more numerous, this most likely reflects increased observer coverage, resulting in the identification of more nesting sites of this local breeder. On the other hand, the nesting substrate of White-throated Swifts may inadvertently have been augmented by excavation of quarries and construction of buildings—sites that these birds increasingly use for nesting elsewhere. From 1968 to 1989, numbers of these swifts were relatively stable on Breeding Bird Surveys in California (USFWS unpubl. analyses).

Hummingbirds
Family *Trochilidae*

ANNA'S HUMMINGBIRD *Calypte anna*

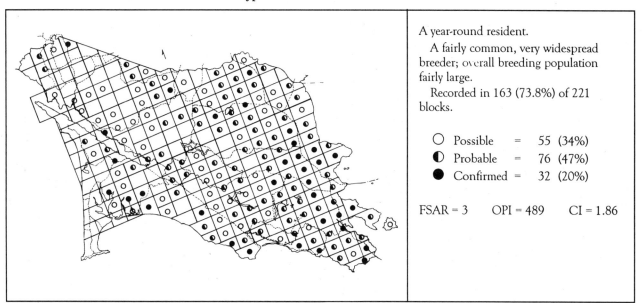

A year-round resident.

A fairly common, very widespread breeder; overall breeding population fairly large.

Recorded in 163 (73.8%) of 221 blocks.

○	Possible	=	55 (34%)
◑	Probable	=	76 (47%)
●	Confirmed	=	32 (20%)

FSAR = 3   OPI = 489   CI = 1.86

Ecological Requirements

In December, daredevil display dives punctuated by ground squirrel–like squeaks are signs that our only resident hummingbird, unique perhaps among our breeding landbirds, is initiating nesting activities while day length is yet decreasing. For breeding, Anna's hummers frequent oak woodlands, chaparral, broadleaved evergreen forests, riparian woodlands, coastal scrub, eucalyptus groves, and suburban plantings and gardens of Marin's hills and lowlands. Where they overlap with Allen's Hummingbirds near the coast, Annas generally avoid dense, moist habitats. Instead they prefer more open, sunny habitats with less understory, and they range into more upland situations. In the drier interior of the Coast Range (away from Marin), Annas are somewhat intermediate in habitat pref-

erence between Costas, which occupy very xeric and open habitats, and Black-chinned Hummingbirds, which frequent more mesic situations, particularly in or adjacent to riparian woodlands. The habitat preferences of Anna's Hummingbirds overlap those of Black-chins to a much greater degree than those of Costas (Stiles 1973).

Male Annas defend territories in broken vegetation of scattered trees or brush or of forest edges that provide a commanding view of their surroundings (Pitelka 1951a). The core area of the territory often consists of a patch of low shrubs of relatively uniform height, with taller bushes or trees all around, from each of which the male can scan most or all of the area (Stiles 1973). To maintain a vigorous and consistent territorial defense, breeding males also

237

require rich, dependable, and easily exploitable nectar sources. Preferably, floral sources are on the territory, but they may also be a considerable distance away; males may go about 55 to 765 yards or, rarely, as much as 0.6 miles for nectar sources. In coastal sage scrub and chaparral of southern California, the timing of establishment of breeding territories has evolved to coincide with the seasonal blooming of the chaparral currant *(Ribes malvaceum)*, which begins after the first heavy winter rains. Males' territories are often centered around patches of chaparral currant, particularly the later blooming *R. speciosum* (generally occurring on sheltered exposures in canyon bottoms and on northern and eastern exposures), though manzanita, eucalyptus, or profusely blooming ornamentals may be important, as local conditions dictate. Anywhere in their range, certain dominant flowering plants exert a profound influence on the local distribution of Anna's Hummingbird breeding territories.

Females nest mostly in shaded woodlands, especially of live oak and eucalyptus in this region, or in gardens. They apparently first locate a reliable nectar source, then situate the nest site nearby. Since incubating and brooding females do not conserve energy by entering nocturnal torpor, they must have a handy nectar source available at dawn and dusk, when insects are least available (Stiles 1973). Females defend the nest site and flower clumps, but once incubation begins, little time or energy is available for defending anything but the nest itself. Females also have one or more prominent perches in their regular rounds from which to launch insect-catching sallies.

Anna's Hummingbirds usually build their nests in trees or bushes on a large solid surface (Aldrich 1945, Legg & Pitelka 1956). Nest heights range from 1.5 to 30 feet above the ground in southern California (Chambers 1903), from 5 to 30 feet (most 11-15 ft.) in Santa Barbara (Pitelka 1951b), and from 10 to 50 feet (av. 28 ft.) in Santa Cruz (Legg & Pitelka 1956). Birds also select nest sites in orchards, in hanging vines on cliffs, and in artificial situations, such as insulated electrical wires hanging from service poles, light fixtures, hanging baskets, and coils of wire in outbuildings (Dawson 1923, Woods 1940). The nests of Anna's Hummingbirds are smaller and shallower than those of Allens, and they build them of plant down, shredded plant fibers, mosses, and plant stems bound with cobwebs. They line them with plant down or feathers and adorn them on the outside with lichens and plant seeds (Dawson 1923, Woods 1940, Legg & Pitelka 1956). Females may move early-season nests several times before they lay eggs (Legg & Pitelka 1956), and they may lay eggs when only a minimum of the cup is built, construction continuing during incubation (Dawson 1923, Woods 1940, Stiles 1973).

From hovering flight or perches, Annas secure carbohydrate food by probing tubular flowers for nectar or (less often during breeding) feeders for sugar solutions. Infrequently, they sip at sapsucker drillings and the juices of fruits pecked at by other birds (Woods 1940, Foster & Tate 1966). Although they use a wide variety of native flowering plants, important ones in the breeding season in California are currant *(Ribes)*, monkey flower *(Diplacus)*, sage *(Salvia)*, *Penstemon*, manzanita, and paint brush *(Castilleja)*. Annas use numerous cultivated varieties, and probably the most important naturalized species are tree tobacco *(Nicotiana)* and eucalyptus (Woods 1940, Stiles 1973). Insects are also a staple that birds procure by gleaning and probing trunks, limbs, and leaves in hovering flight; by flycatching from exposed perches; and by extracting entangled individuals from spider webs. From hovering flight, Annas also startle stationary insects into flight, then snap them up (Mobbs 1979). Gnats, small flies, ants, wasps, bees, true bugs, and spiders are the main prey (Woods 1940). Females spend much more time foraging for insects in the breeding season than do males, perhaps partly because males defend the best nectar sources and also because females have greater protein demands for egg laying and feeding the young (Stiles 1973). The female feeds the young by regurgitation. Females also apparently need additional minerals in the breeding season, which they procure from mortar, plaster, or sand (Woods 1940).

Marin Breeding Distribution

Although they bred widely in Marin County during the atlas period, Anna's Hummingbirds were more evenly distributed and more numerous in the eastern part of the county, where open woodlands are more prevalent. They were widespread and numerous in residential areas along the Highway 101 corridor. Representative nesting localities were Muddy Hollow, PRNS (NE 4/22/78 –JGE, DS et al.); Palomarin, PRNS (NY 3/1/78 –GBe); the ridge NE of Santa Margarita Valley-Los Gallinas area (NE 4/23/82 –BiL); E end Big Rock Ridge (NE 4/30/83 –BiL); and Cascade Canyon, Fairfax (NE-NY 4/11-5/12/77 –DS).

Historical Trends/Population Threats

California is one of the few areas on Earth that have undergone such an extensive and successful series of plant introduction and naturalizations. These changes have drastically altered the spatial and temporal array of flowers, causing far-reaching effects on the distribution, numbers, and movements, both local and long-distance, of hummingbirds (Stiles 1973). The establishment of exotic flowering species has enhanced the suitability of many breeding territories. It has also augmented the food supply and, hence, survival of migrants and particularly the survival of birds from late summer to early winter, when native flowers reach a low ebb in dry lowland areas. For these reasons, Anna's Hummingbirds have increased greatly in California in historical times (Woods 1940, G&M 1944, Stiles 1973). In the 1960s to early 1970s, Annas continued to expand considerably in range and abundance northward on the Pacific Coast (records to Alaska), particularly in California and Oregon, as they did throughout much of the Southwest and adjacent Mexico (Zimmerman 1973). Most expansion has been noted in suburban areas, again where ornamental and garden plants and a proliferation of

hummingbird feeders provide extensive nectar sources. The widespread expansion of the species may be the result of the birds' success in human-altered habitats in the core of the California range, ensuring a large population for continuing emigration and recruitment elsewhere. From 1968 to 1989, numbers of Anna's Hummingbirds were relatively stable on Breeding Bird Surveys in California (USFWS unpubl. analyses).

Allen's Hummingbirds bring enviable intensity and brilliance to coastal climes.
Drawing by Keith Hansen, 1989.

ALLEN'S HUMMINGBIRD *Selasphorus sasin*

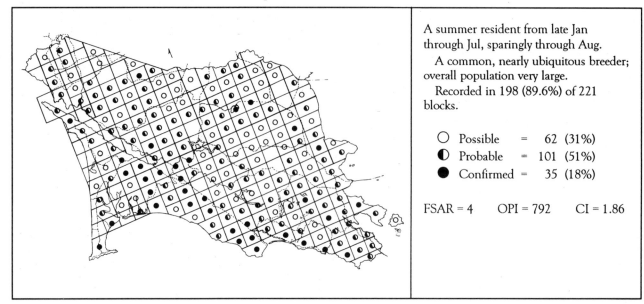

A summer resident from late Jan through Jul, sparingly through Aug.
A common, nearly ubiquitous breeder; overall population very large.
Recorded in 198 (89.6%) of 221 blocks.

○ Possible   =   62 (31%)
◐ Probable   = 101 (51%)
● Confirmed =   35 (18%)

FSAR = 4   OPI = 792   CI = 1.86

Ecological Requirements

With buzzing wings and feverish activity, Allen's Hummingbirds are harbingers of spring, arriving on the breeding grounds in late January and early February while winter rains still replenish the land. In Marin, females nest in riparian, mixed evergreen, Douglas fir, redwood, and bishop pine forests, as well as in moist north-facing coastal scrub, eucalyptus, and cypress groves, and to a limited extent oak woodland. In most habitats, they place their nests in dense understory vegetation, but this need not be the case in eucalyptus and cypress groves or in the rare instance when birds nest in oak woodland or in human structures. Nest sites are frequently near running water, where thickets and dense tangles abound. Males defend territories, separate from the females' nest sites, that are usually on the edge of the above habitats and adjoining scrub (especially coastal scrub). In narrow linear habitats such as riparian thickets or eucalyptus groves, males may establish territories above the females' nesting sites. Males rarely frequent the interior of dense shaded habitat, as they need a commanding view of their surroundings (Aldrich 1945, Legg & Pitelka 1956).

Nest heights usually range from 0.5 to 50 feet (rarely, to 90 ft.) above the ground (Bent 1940, Aldrich 1945) and generally are lower than those of Annas in areas of overlap. In Santa Cruz, Allen's Hummingbird nests ranged from 1.5 to 40 feet (av. 18 ft.) above ground, whereas those of Annas were from 10 to 50 feet (av. 28 ft.) (Legg & Pitelka 1956). Female Allens may nest in close proximity to each other, suggesting that where habitat is limiting, such as in cypress and eucalyptus groves, loose colonies may exist

(Bryant 1925, Aldrich 1945). Unlike Annas, which build on *top* of a solid support, Allens usually build with part of the supporting structure incorporated in the *sides* of the nest. These structures include limbs and twigs less than one inch in diameter as well as vine runners, fern stems and fronds, and the like (Aldrich 1945; see for further details on nest site selection and attachment). In Marin, Allen's Hummingbirds use many species of trees, especially eucalyptus and cypress, for nest support. In understory thickets, they prefer blackberry brambles and sword ferns. Females here also select artificial sites inside buildings—in rope or wire slings, on iron hooks, and under rafters (Mailliard 1913, PRBO nest records). They build tiny deep nest cups, using mostly moss on the outside and willow down and pappus from composite seeds in the lining. Other important nest materials are lichens (on the outside), feathers, shredded leaves, grass fibers, and hair. The females bind them all together and attach them to the supporting structure with spider webs (Aldrich 1945). As in the case of Annas, the female Allens also sometimes lays eggs on a mere platform that is completed later and typically adds nest material throughout nesting (Aldrich 1945).

Little has been written on the foraging and food preference of this species, but they appear to be quite similar to those of the Anna's Hummingbird (see account). When numbers of Allens first appear in Marin in February, they use *Ribes* flowers extensively. The timing of migratory movements may have evolved to coincide with the blooming of these shrubs.

Marin Breeding Distribution

During the atlas period, the Allen's Hummingbird was one of the most common and widespread of all of Marin County's breeding species, but it was in the zone of persistent summer fogs near the immediate coast that this species was most numerous and evenly distributed. Although some birds bred on moist ridges, most were concentrated in thickets of the lowlands and canyon bottoms. In the interior of Marin, most breeding activity centered around riparian thickets and eucalyptus groves; most forests in this region generally lack dense understory cover. Representative breeding locations were cypress grove at Mendoza Ranch, Point Reyes (NE 5/30/80 –DS); near stream at Bear Valley, PRNS (NE 3/22/81 –DS); cypress by streamside at Tennessee Valley (NE-NY 3/28-

4/25/77 –GMcM); and a live oak in open oak woodland on Big Rock Ridge near Marinwood (NE 3/24/79 –DS).

Historical Trends/Population Threats

It seems likely that the planting of early-blooming exotics and an increase in hummingbird feeders has benefited the species, especially early in the nesting season, when continuing winter rains curtail available food and foraging time. Allen's Hummingbirds have undoubtedly extended their range locally into areas where suitable nesting habitat formerly was limited but where eucalyptus and cypress have since been planted in grassland. Numbers of Allen's Hummingbirds were relatively stable on Breeding Bird Surveys in California from 1968 to 1989 (USFWS unpubl. analyses).

Kingfishers
Family *Alcedinidae*

BELTED KINGFISHER   *Ceryle alcyon*

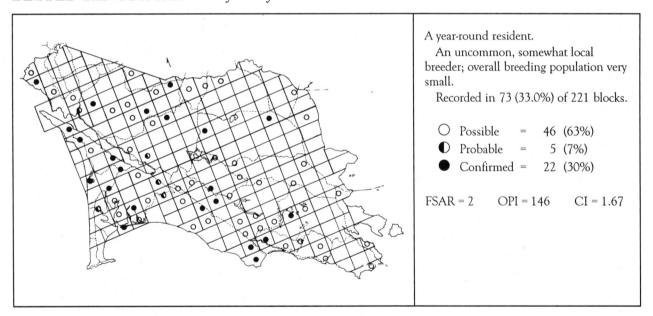

A year-round resident.

An uncommon, somewhat local breeder; overall breeding population very small.

Recorded in 73 (33.0%) of 221 blocks.

○	Possible	=	46	(63%)
◑	Probable	=	5	(7%)
●	Confirmed	=	22	(30%)

FSAR = 2   OPI = 146   CI = 1.67

Ecological Requirements

These dashing crested piscivores raise their rattling hue and cry along streams, freshwater ponds, and shallow estuarine margins that provide favorable food supplies. Kingfishers usually excavate nest burrows, using their bills and feet, in well-drained earthen banks with vertical or slightly overhanging faces that are bare or sparsely vegetated (Bent 1940, White 1953, Cornwell 1963). Often

these are naturally created by water erosion, but road cuts, gravel excavations, ditch banks, and other human modifications afford nest sites as well. Kingfishers may excavate burrows at any height but usually do so at least five feet from the bottom and not more than two feet from the top of the bank, to limit access by mammalian predators. They dig burrows that vary in length from about three to seven feet, shorter ones generally in harder substrates, and dig them on a horizontal plane unless they encounter obstacles (White 1953). The nest chamber is usually spherical or ovoid and somewhat flattened on the bottom, with the nest below the level of the tunnel. Females lay eggs either on bare earth or on the debris of regurgitated food pellets. When there is a limited supply of nest sites, Kingfishers occasionally nest in the open tops or decayed sides of stumps or trees and in earth adhering to roots of large upturned trees; they even nest in sawdust piles, though generally unsuccessfully (White 1953). A dead or dying tree or other suitable perch generally overlooks each nest site. Although most nests are over or near water, they may be up to a mile from a water source (Cornwell 1963).

Kingfishers feed either from perches or from hovering flight 20 to 50 feet in the air. They dive headlong, nearly vertically or at an angle, into relatively shallow and calm water, securing prey with their large bills. Kingfishers dive mostly in water less than two feet deep, and even in deeper water they probably do not catch prey below this depth (White 1953). They often subdue or stun prey before swallowing by whacking them against a perch. Foraging flights take the birds 0.5 to 5 miles from the nest site; most

trips are within a 1-mile distance, though daily flights of 2 miles are not uncommon (Cornwell 1963). Although the diet is often up to 90%–100% fish (Salyer & Laglar 1946, White 1953), at some sites crayfish occasionally predominate (White 1953, Eipper 1956). Other minor food items are large insects, other invertebrates, salamanders, frogs, lizards, young birds, mice, shrews, and even berries (Bent 1940, Salyer & Laglar 1946, White 1953). Small adult and larval insects found in Kingfisher pellets undoubtedly are from the ruptured stomachs of their fish prey (White 1953). Adults feed the young relatively large fish, such that one to three will fill the stomach of a single nestling.

Marin Breeding Distribution

Breeding Kingfishers were patchily distributed in Marin County during the atlas period because of limitations of suitable feeding and nesting sites. Breeders concentrated along the west side of Tomales Bay, where steep banks are almost continuous from Inverness north to Tomales Point. Representative nesting sites were Abbott's Lagoon (FL 6/14/82 –DS); near Sacramento Landing, Tomales Bay (FL 6/18/82 –DS); Salmon Creek along the Marshall-

Fish obscures face as this Belted Kingfisher brakes to enter its burrow and feed its growing young. Photograph by Ian Tait.

Petaluma Rd. (FY 6/21/82 —DS); and Stafford Lake, Novato (ON 5/?/82 —ScC).

Historical Trends/Population Threats

Numbers were formerly reduced (G&M 1944) by shooting resulting from fishermen's disfavor. After it was realized that Kingfishers help control some fish species destructive to trout's eggs and young, human persecution of Kingfishers decreased and the birds' populations increased. Fishermen's needs have also been met by covering rearing ponds with wire mesh. Although the creation of reservoirs may have increased habitat in areas such as Marin County, where natural lakes and permanent streams are few, elsewhere damming of year-round streams and riprapping for bank protection have probably more than counterbalanced these positive effects. Human depletion of fish resources upon which Kingfishers depend likely has also been to the species' detriment. Numbers of Kingfishers were relatively stable on Breeding Bird Surveys in California from 1968 to 1989 but decreased from 1980 to 1989 (USFWS unpubl. analyses).

Woodpeckers
Family *Picidae*

ACORN WOODPECKER *Melanerpes formicivorus*

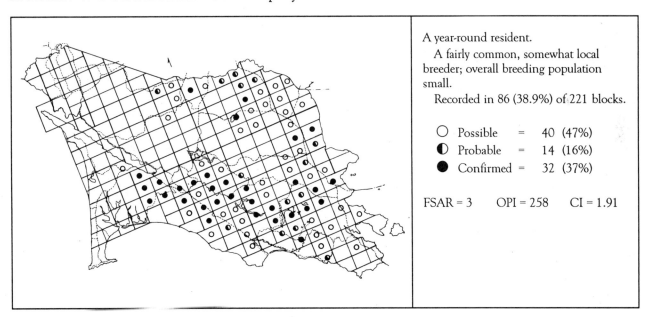

A year-round resident.

A fairly common, somewhat local breeder; overall breeding population small.

Recorded in 86 (38.9%) of 221 blocks.

○ Possible   =   40 (47%)
◐ Probable   =   14 (16%)
● Confirmed =   32 (37%)

FSAR = 3   OPI = 258   CI = 1.91

Ecological Requirements

As their name suggests, Acorn Woodpeckers are intimately dependent on the fruits of oak trees, mostly of the genus *Quercus*. They are permanent territorial residents in almost all California forests and woodlands with a reasonable density and diversity of oaks. In Marin County, their habitat includes oak woodlands and savannah; relatively open Douglas fir, redwood, mixed evergreen, and riparian forests; and residential areas where oaks have been preserved or planted.

Acorn Woodpeckers nest exclusively in cavities they excavate in living trees or dead snags, including pines, oaks, sycamores, and palm trees; they may also use utility poles. Holes are often reused for nesting and are also used for nocturnal roosting outside the breeding season.

Nesting, as well as all other phases of Acorn Woodpecker home life, is performed in groups, and up to 12 individuals may participate in incubation and feeding of nestlings (Ritter 1938, MacRoberts & MacRoberts 1976,

243

Koenig & Mumme 1987). Only one nest at a time is attended by a group. Within a group, up to three females may jointly lay eggs, and up to at least four males may compete for matings with the breeding females. These cobreeding sets of birds are almost always close relatives, usually siblings or else a parent and its offspring of the same sex. There is considerable competition among joint-nesting females within a group, and a female that lays her eggs first frequently has them removed from the nest and subsequently eaten by her cobreeding female relatives. Additional group members consist of offspring of both sexes that may remain in their natal group as nonbreeding "helpers" for one to five years prior to dispersal (Koenig & Mumme 1987). Breeding takes place in the spring and early summer (Apr to mid-Jul, with the peak of egg laying near the end of Apr), although in bumper acorn years it may also occur in the fall (Aug–Nov). The latest documented first-egg date is 23 September, at Hastings Reservation in Monterey County (Koenig & Mumme 1987).

Acorn Woodpeckers are critically dependent on mast. The birds store acorns or other mast, harvested directly from the trees in fall, one by one in individual holes drilled in communally defended storage trees or "granaries." Though granaries typically contain about 1000 to 4000 storage holes, they may host up to 20,000 or more! These storage facilities are usually in snags, dead limbs, thick bark, or structures such as the wooden eaves or roofs of houses. They may be in pines, oaks, sycamores, redwoods, Douglas firs, incense cedars, cottonwoods, fence posts, utility poles, palm trees (Ritter 1938), or, exceptionally, in large pine cones (Jehl 1979). The birds usually store acorns, but also, to a lesser degree, cultivated nuts (Ritter 1929), pine seeds (MacRoberts & MacRoberts 1976, Stacey & Jansma 1977), and such bizarre items as stones (Ritter 1938) and Douglas fir cones (W.D. Koenig pers. obs.). These latter items are probably secured by young birds that, in their zeal to store food, fail to discriminate between suitably shaped edible and nonedible items.

Stored acorns are eaten throughout the winter months and are critical to successful spring reproduction in at least some areas. Insect predators of acorns, especially weevil larvae, may also be eaten if encountered, but the myth that acorns are stored as "nurseries" for these insects is untrue (see MacRoberts 1974). Acorn Woodpeckers also eat diverse other foods that they capture with a variety of techniques (MacRoberts 1970). Flycatching is common at all seasons during good weather. Sapsucking occurs regularly in late summer (Jul and Aug) and late winter (Jan–Mar). Oak catkins are eaten in late winter and early spring, and bark gleaning occurs regularly. Finally, birds have even been recorded hovering and picking at wild oat seeds (MacRoberts & MacRoberts 1976). Major food items include acorns, sap, catkins, ants, beetles, bees, wasps, true bugs, and earwigs. Observers at Hastings Reservation occa-sionally have even seen Acorn Woodpeckers eating lizards (genus *Sceloporus*). Exceptionally, these birds prey on the eggs or young of other species of birds (Shuford 1985). They particularly prize crane flies as food for their nestlings but also feed the young a wide variety of insects, as well as acorn fragments (Beal 1911, MacRoberts & MacRoberts 1976, Koenig & Mumme 1987).

Marin Breeding Distribution

During the atlas period, Acorn Woodpeckers were wide-spread breeders in Marin County's forested regions and, as elsewhere in their range, were limited to extensive stands of oaks. Most coastal birds were dependent on coast live oaks, but valley oaks became increasingly important in the northeastern corner of the county near Novato. Acorn Woodpeckers were absent from the largely treeless tracts of land on outer Point Reyes and east of Tomales Bay, and they occurred only to a limited extent along the shore of San Francisco and San Pablo bays. Representative breeding localities were Mt. Burdell, Novato (ON 5/?/82 – ScC); Pioneer Park, Novato (ON 5/?/82 –ScC); and Olompali, Novato (ON 4/?/79 –ScC). Of interest is a small population of birds with golden, rather than red, crowns that was resident in the San Geronimo area up until at least 1980 (W.D. Koenig pers. obs.).

Historical Trends/Population Threats

Locally, birds are threatened by the loss of oaks to development, but often they are able to adapt well to exotic conditions as long as mast trees remain. Perhaps a more important long-term threat is the possible future loss of large stands of oaks because of a lack of recruitment of young oaks; the causes of this include grazing pressures of cattle and deer on seedlings and damage to acorns from insects and rodents (Griffin 1977). Although logging prac-tices tend to open up dense forests and favor hardwood trees such as oaks, these species are generally slow growing and are often removed by forest managers to favor econom-ically important conifers.

The only major hole competitor of the Acorn Wood-pecker is the introduced European Starling which can, at least occasionally, render breeding difficult for groups of woodpeckers by usurping their favored holes. However, the only study of competition between these species per-formed to date reported that reproductive success and group size of Acorn Woodpeckers were not affected by Starlings (Troetschler 1976). It remains to be seen whether this conclusion will hold at other study sites, or if Starlings continue to expand in California. Numbers of Acorn Woodpeckers on Breeding Bird Surveys in California were relatively stable from 1968 to 1989 but increased from 1980 to 1989 (USFWS unpubl. analyses).

WALTER D. KOENIG

244

RED-BREASTED SAPSUCKER *Sphyrapicus ruber*

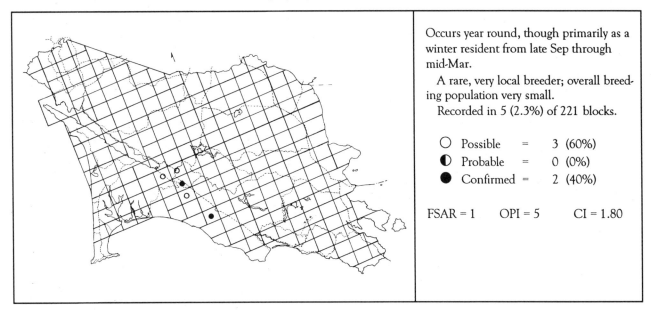

Occurs year round, though primarily as a winter resident from late Sep through mid-Mar.

A rare, very local breeder; overall breeding population very small.

Recorded in 5 (2.3%) of 221 blocks.

○	Possible	=	3 (60%)
◐	Probable	=	0 (0%)
●	Confirmed	=	2 (40%)

FSAR = 1   OPI = 5   CI = 1.80

Ecological Requirements

In California, the nasal breeding calls of Red-breasted Sapsuckers emanate primarily from moist conifer forests or woodlands, as well as bordering riparian zones dominated by aspens or alders (Shuford 1986). In Marin County, Red-breasted Sapsuckers breed in mixed evergreen woodlands or riparian groves of alders and willows adjacent to Douglas fir forests. They drill their nest holes from 4 to 70 feet above the ground; in the Sierra Nevada, average nest height of 49 nests was 42 feet (Raphael & White 1984). Birds use dead trees, limbs, stubs, or live trees for nesting; occasionally they occupy previously used holes (Lawrence 1967). Although they appear to prefer deciduous trees over conifers (Bent 1939, Howell 1952, Crockett & Hadow 1975), in the Sierra Nevada, Red-breasted Sapsuckers may select predominantly conifer snags (Raphael & White 1984). Sapsuckers find live aspens with tough outer shells of sapwood and centers decaying from "infection" by shelf fungi *(Fomes)* especially attractive; such sites provide better protection than dead trees do from the ravages of predators like raccoons (Bent 1939, Kilham 1971). Nest hole orientation appears to favor light and warmth, with a tendency for southern or eastern exposures, lower height in open surroundings, and location on the edges of clearings (Lawrence 1967, Inouye 1976).

Unlike most woodpeckers, these birds rarely, if ever, dig deep into decaying trees for wood-boring insects and larvae. Instead they primarily glean active exposed insects from trunks and limbs and, secondarily, flycatch against clusters of leaves or needles. They also make flycatching sorties into the air from perches, fly to the ground after

visible insects, and search for ants on the ground in the manner of flickers (Bent 1939, Howell 1952, Kilham 1977, Raphael & White 1984). They use conifers extensively for insect foraging. Although they pick many wild fruits from trees and bushes (and hang chickadeelike on branch tips to pluck off aspen buds), most vegetable matter that sapsuckers consume comes from the characteristic small square holes that they drill in trees, most frequently in series of horizontal and vertical rows (Tate 1973). Sapsuckers show a strong preference for drilling these holes in young trees in dense stands, in trees marked by previous sapsucker working, and in those already weakened or wounded in some manner (Kilham 1964, Lawrence 1967). In California, they drill them preferentially in native members of the willow and birch families, though they also use conifers to a lesser extent (Bent 1939, G&M 1944). They also use orchard trees extensively. The birds drink sap from the holes and also eat the soft inner bark, or cambium, of the trees. Although some authors feel that sapsuckers take many insects that are attracted to the oozing sap (Tate 1973), others feel this practice is infrequent (Kilham 1977).

Adults feed the young primarily insects (Howell 1952) and also some sap (Kilham 1977), though perhaps incidentally (Lawrence 1967). The size of insects they feed to young increases with the nestlings' age (Lawrence 1967). The

Some information on aspects of natural history were obtained from studies of the Yellow-bellied Sapsucker *(S. varius)*, formerly considered conspecific with the Red-breasted Sapsucker, whose habits do not appear to differ materially from its congener.

245

September-to-March diet of the Red-breasted Sapsucker (exclusive of sap) is 69% animal and 31% vegetable (Beal 1911, n = 34); in montane California, the birds' summer diet is 96% animal and 4% vegetable (Otvos & Stark 1985, n = 19); in the Sierra Nevada, its June-to-July diet is 88% animal and 12% vegetable (Dahlsten et al. 1985, n = 8). Animal fare is mostly made up of ants and scale insects along with smaller amounts of beetles, bees, wasps, aphids, termites, and miscellaneous insects. Vegetable fare consists of fruits and berries, cambium, and seeds; bark use peaks in spring (Tate 1973).

Marin Breeding Distribution

Red-breasted Sapsuckers were unknown as breeders in Marin County before the atlas project began (Mailliard 1900, S&P 1933, G&M 1944). We found them to be very local breeders in the Olema Valley and vicinity. Representative breeding locales were Bear Valley Headquarters, PRNS (NY 6/22/80 –DS) and Five Brooks, PRNS (FL 10/18/82 –EH, MAS). The young at the former site were

apparently destroyed by Acorn Woodpeckers (Shuford 1985). See Shuford (1986) for additional possible and probable breeding records for Marin County.

Historical Trends/Population Threats

Grinnell and Miller (1944) mapped the breeding distribution in coastal California as extending south as far as central Mendocino County. Shuford (1986) reviewed recent records and concluded that Red-breasted Sapsuckers breed continuously south to northern Sonoma County, with a small disjunct population in Marin County. A search of historical sources revealed that there had been very little ornithological investigation of any kind in the area of apparent range extension until recent years. This strongly suggested that sapsuckers previously had been overlooked in this region, rather than that they had expanded their breeding range. Current atlas work in Sonoma County is likely to add further details to the known breeding range.

NUTTALL'S WOODPECKER *Picoides nuttallii*

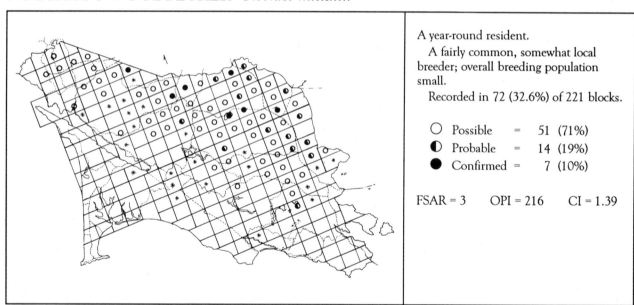

A year-round resident.

A fairly common, somewhat local breeder; overall breeding population small.

Recorded in 72 (32.6%) of 221 blocks.

○	Possible	=	51 (71%)
◑	Probable	=	14 (19%)
●	Confirmed	=	7 (10%)

FSAR = 3   OPI = 216   CI = 1.39

Ecological Requirements

The dry rattling calls of Nuttall's Woodpeckers resound from open, primarily deciduous oak woodlands, and bordering riparian groves, which may be especially attractive for nesting. In Monterey's Carmel Valley, Nuttalls usually center their home ranges around drainages (Miller & Bock 1972). In the interior of Marin County, they apparently also sometimes nest in open eucalyptus and cypress groves,

far from oak woodlands, but then usually near streamside vegetation. Elsewhere in California in ecological zones supporting oaks, Nuttall's Woodpeckers may also breed in open riparian forests devoid of oaks or where gray pines *(Pinus sabiniana)* mix with oaks. Nevertheless, throughout its range as a whole, perhaps the most consistent element of Nuttall's Woodpecker foraging habitat is a dominance of oak trees (Block 1991). Openness also seems to be a key character of Nuttall's Woodpecker habitat. In the breeding season these woodpeckers generally avoid Marin's coastal riparian habitat which tends to be dense and is never bordered by true oak woodland.

Although Nuttalls drill many of their nest cavities in oaks (Block 1991), they appear to prefer soft-wooded species of trees when available, perhaps because their foraging style leaves them ill-equipped for deep digging in hard wood (Miller & Bock 1972). Nest holes range from 3 to 45 feet (av. 17 ft., n = 54) above the ground and are usually in dead limbs or trunks.

Nuttall's Woodpeckers are much more versatile and acrobatic foragers than either Downy or Hairy woodpeckers (Miller & Bock 1972). Nuttalls forage for insects principally on the surface and shallow subsurface of trees mostly by light pecking and tapping, bark scaling, probing, gleaning, and foliage and twig scanning (Miller & Bock 1972, Jenkins 1979, Block 1991). To a limited degree, they drill and excavate extensively in classic woodpecker fashion, sapsuck, flycatch, and pick seeds from pinecones. At times, birds climb through foliage clusters, fluttering and balancing with their wings and hanging upside down to procure fruits (Miller & Bock 1972). Nuttalls generally glean more but peck and probe less during breeding than in the nonbreeding season (Block 1991). The proportional reliance on various foraging techniques also varies between habitats, as does use of foraging substrates. Across various habitats, Nuttall's Woodpeckers perform about 90% (n = 907) of their foraging maneuvers on branches or trunks; about 53% involve twigs and small branches (Block 1991). About 75% of foraging attempts are directed at live stems of trees and only about 2% at fruits, cones, and leaves. On average, trees used for foraging are larger in diameter and taller than those generally available; the size characteristics (height, trunk diameter, and canopy size) of trees used for foraging differs among study sites and between seasons and years. Nuttall's Woodpeckers tend to forage mostly about two-thirds up the height of the tree and 40%-70% of the distance from the center to the edge of the canopy, which corresponds to the location of small and medium-sized branches, the two most frequently used foraging substrates (Block 1991).

Although closely tied to oaks at all seasons, Nuttall's Woodpeckers vary their preference for foraging trees both among sites and between seasons, as indicated by selection of tree species out of proportion to their availability (Miller & Bock 1972, Block 1991). In the Carmel Valley during the breeding season—when deciduous oaks are newly leafed out—birds forage almost exclusively in oaks, primarily on and around branchlets and leaves (Miller & Bock 1972). At other times, birds there shift much of their foraging to live oaks, particularly during winter and early spring when other trees are bare. Block (1991) confirmed the tendency of Nuttalls to concentrate foraging in the breeding season on white (deciduous) oaks, but at some sites found that birds increased foraging in trees such as gray pines, rather than live oaks, during the nonbreeding season.

In one study in the Carmel Valley, Jenkins (1979) detected sexual differences in foraging behavior during the postbreeding season (Jun-Oct). There females fed primarily by gleaning. They foraged more frequently on smaller branches, twigs, and foliage, and used more obliquely oriented positions than did males. Males fed primarily by surface tapping and also fed lower in trees than did females. In contrast, Block (1991), working at two sites in the Sierra Nevada and one in the Tehachapi Mountains, found little variation between the sexes in either foraging behavior or foraging habitat during breeding (Apr-Jun) and nonbreeding (Nov-Feb) seasons. Males and females at his study sites used similar foraging maneuvers, substrates, and macrohabitats. The size of trees used by males and females differed slightly, and males tended to forage relatively higher in trees than did females (*contra* Jenkins 1979). These slight differences may have allowed the sexes to partition limited resources or may reflect dominance by one sex over the other (Block 1991).

The diet in California is 79% animal matter, primarily beetles, true bugs, caterpillars, and ants and other hymenopterans (Beal 1911, n = 53). Consumption of animal matter varies from about 87% of the diet in winter, to 80% in spring and summer, to 65% in fall (Martin et al. 1951, n = 52). Vegetable fare includes wild fruits and seeds, such as elderberry, blackberry, raspberry, poison oak, and acorns, along with cambrium and flower buds (Beal 1910, 1911). Sap is taken as the opportunity arises (Miller & Bock 1972).

Marin Breeding Distribution

During the atlas period, breeding Nuttall's Woodpeckers were concentrated in the northern interior of Marin County, especially around Novato. They were extremely rare on the immediate coast during the nesting season but occurred there with greater regularity during postbreeding dispersal, starting in mid- to late June (see atlas map). At that time, some birds shift to coastal eucalyptus and cypress groves and riparian woodlands. Representative nesting locations were Mt. Burdell, Novato (ON 5/?/82 –ScC); Stafford Lake, Novato (ON 4/?/82 –ScC); and Novato area (NY 5/6/77 –RMS). An old nesting record for Ross (see below) and a pair entering a nest hole at Bear Valley Headquarters, PRNS, on 11 May 1985 (DS) indicate occasional nesting in southern and coastal Marin County.

Historical Trends/Population Threats

In his annotated list of Marin County's landbirds, Mailliard (1900) considered the Nuttall's Woodpecker an "exceedingly rare visitant in major portion of county, but more numerous near northern boundary." Stephens and Pringle (1933) listed it as "uncommon" here, and a record of a pair feeding young at Ross on 16 June 1929 (*Gull* 11, No. 7) was considered noteworthy. These reports occurred

before much exploration of the Novato area, where we found the species numerous during the atlas period. From 1968 to 1989, numbers of Nuttall's Woodpeckers were relatively stable on Breeding Bird Surveys in California (USFWS unpubl. analyses).

DOWNY WOODPECKER *Picoides pubescens*

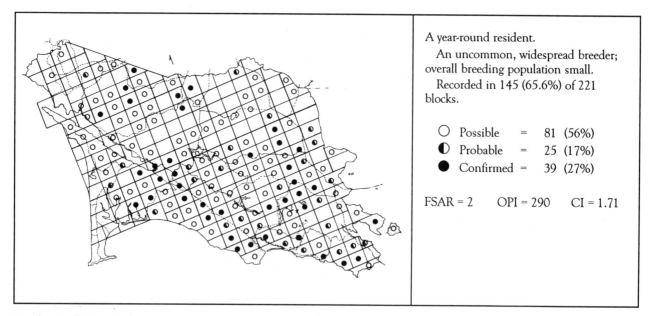

A year-round resident.
    An uncommon, widespread breeder; overall breeding population small.
    Recorded in 145 (65.6%) of 221 blocks.

O	Possible	=	81 (56%)
◑	Probable	=	25 (17%)
●	Confirmed	=	39 (27%)

FSAR = 2   OPI = 290   CI = 1.71

Ecological Requirements

This petite lively woodpecker inhabits Marin County's riparian tracts and moist mixed evergreen forests, especially those dominated by California bay trees. Downies also occasionally forage in adjacent shrubby habitats and tall weed fields. They overlap to a limited degree with the larger Hairy Woodpecker in broadleaved forests, but for the most part they avoid the conifer forests preferred by that species. Downies also overlap to a small degree with Nuttall's Woodpeckers in riparian groves or at the ecotone between broadleaved evergreen forests and oak woodlands, but the latter species prefers more open woodlands. Downies usually drill their nest holes in the soft wood of dead trees, dead branches of live trees, and stumps, and occasionally in live trees; most nest cavities are close to the tops of broken-off stubs of dead trees (Bent 1939, Lawrence 1967, Conner et al. 1975). Nest heights range from 3 to 50 feet or more above the ground (Bent 1939). Downies excavate their nest cavities in shorter, smaller-diameter trees and at lower heights than do Hairies (Conner et al. 1975; see Hairy Woodpecker account). Eleven Downy Woodpecker nests in Ontario ranged from 12 to 45 feet and averaged 29 feet above the ground (Lawrence 1967), whereas 19 nests in Virginia ranged from 4 to 38 feet and

averaged 16 feet above the ground (Conner et al. 1975). In some areas, nest holes appear to be oriented with respect to light and warmth and tend to have southern or eastern exposures and occur at lower heights in open surroundings (Lawrence 1967); elsewhere, a northeasterly orientation may provide shelter from wind and rain (Conner 1975, 1977). The slope of the trunk appears to be the most important factor in nest orientation (Conner 1975, 1977); nest holes facing slightly *downward* prevent rain from entering the cavity and aid in defense of the hole from predators.

Downies forage primarily by drilling and scaling but also by gleaning, probing, and occasionally by hovering and flycatching. They direct most foraging attempts at bark but do some gleaning from leaves and flower clusters. Though Downies forage more frequently in the lower zones of the canopy, they can feed from the tops of trees to the ground (Willson 1970, Williams 1975). Downies also exploit insects in galls on tall weed stalks (Confer & Paicos 1985); birds involved seem always to be males (Grubb & Woodrey 1990). Compared with the closely related but larger Hairy Woodpecker, Downies forage more on the smaller branches and twigs of trees; they probe and glean

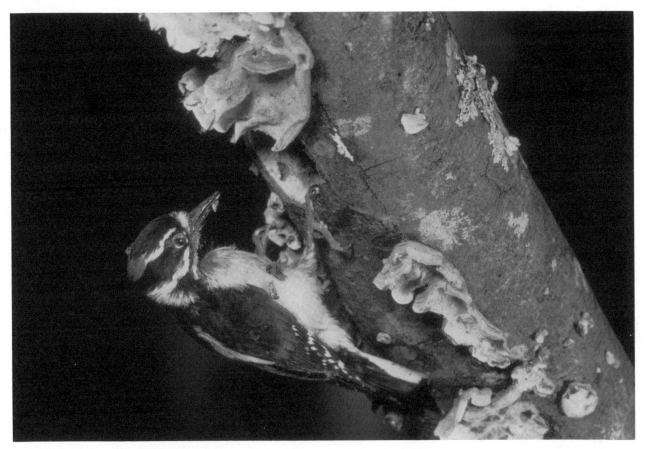

*Downy Woodpeckers often select nest holes on the downward-oriented side of leaning trees,
where gravity can hinder tree-climbing predators. Photograph by Ian Tait.*

to a greater extent; they do not drill as often or penetrate to as great a depth; and they feed on different tree species (Koplin 1969, Kisiel 1972, Conner 1981). See Nuttall's Woodpecker for comparison to that species.

It is well documented that the sexes of Downy Woodpeckers exploit different foraging niches. Males drill more on small branches and twigs than do females, which tend to forage more on larger branches and trunks (Jackson 1970; Kilham 1970; Willson 1970; Kisiel 1972; Williams 1975, 1980). Experimental studies suggest that males may choose the more productive portions of the forest and exclude females from these sites (Grubb & Woodrey 1990). On the whole, there is no consistent relationship between the vertical foraging distribution on trees of males versus females, as has been found in individual studies (Grubb & Woodrey 1990). Because of the above substrate preferences, males generally tend to forage more by drilling, females more on the surface by probing and gleaning (Jackson 1970, Kisiel 1972, Williams 1980). In winter, males feed more on dead substrates and on a wider array of tree species than do females (Williams 1980). In general, Downies forage more on live than on dead trees (Jackson 1970, Kisiel 1972, Williams 1975), though their use of

dead trees increases in winter when it can be roughly equivalent to their use of live trees (Jackson 1970). Since surface foraging techniques are more important on live trees and subsurface techniques on dead trees, Downies increase their drilling and decrease surface probing and gleaning in winter (Jackson 1970, Conner 1981). Travis (1977) also noted that in winter, Downies forage more on furrowed wood and larger trees and less on branches; see Conner (1981) for additional differences in seasonal foraging methods. Between-habitat foraging differences have also been noted (Williams 1975).

The annual diet of the Downy Woodpecker in California is 77% animal and 23% vegetable (Beal 1910, n = 80), which is remarkably similar to the species' continentwide diet of 76% animal and 24% vegetable (Beal 1911, n = 723). In the mountains of California (season unspecified), the diet of males (n = 12) is 95% animal and that of females (n = 17) 99% (Otvos & Stark 1985; see for further slight sexual differences in diet). In the East, reliance on animal matter varies from 86% in summer to 71% in fall and winter (Martin et al. 1951, n = 828). In Illinois in winter, females consume more homopterans and spiders than do males, presumably because they probe more in bark crevices and select rough-barked trees to forage in more than males do (Williams 1980). Males take more ants than do females, apparently because they peck into smaller limbs and are more adept at removing them with their larger tongues. The bulk of the species' animal food is insects, especially beetles (particularly wood-boring larvae), ants, caterpillars, and true bugs (scale and plant lice); other insects, spiders, millipedes, pseudoscorpions, sowbugs, and snails are taken infrequently. Although wood-boring beetle larvae are important to both Downy and Hairy woodpeckers, Downies eat only about half the amount that Hairies do, substantiating the fact that Downies peck into wood much less frequently (Beal 1911). The size of insects fed to young increases with nestling age (Lawrence 1967). The vegetable component of the diet is largely various fruits, mast, and seeds, though grain, galls, flower petals and buds, and cambium are eaten to a limited extent. Sap is also eaten occasionally (Foster & Tate 1966).

Marin Breeding Distribution

Although Downy Woodpeckers were distributed widely throughout the forested regions of Marin County during the atlas period, they occurred primarily in the lowlands and along moist drainages. Representative nesting locations were Chileno Valley (FY 5/30/82 –DS); along Miller Creek, E end Big Rock Ridge (FY 6/6/82 –BiL); near Alpine Lake (NY 6/5/82 –DS); and Panoramic Hwy., W of Pantoll (FY 6/2/81 –DS).

Historical Trends/Population Threats

Few prior data exist, but numbers of Downy Woodpeckers decreased on Breeding Bird Surveys in California from 1968 to 1989 (USFWS unpubl. analyses).

HAIRY WOODPECKER *Picoides villosus*

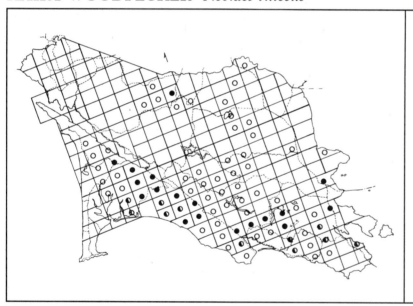

A year-round resident.

An uncommon, somewhat local breeder; overall breeding population small.

Recorded in 82 (37.1%) of 221 blocks.

○	Possible	=	54 (66%)
◑	Probable	=	10 (12%)
●	Confirmed	=	18 (22%)

FSAR = 2   OPI = 164   CI = 1.56

Ecological Requirements

Although near look-alikes except for subtle differences in size and plumage, Hairy and Downy woodpeckers are nonetheless quite distinct ecologically. The Hairy Woodpecker occupies Marin County's conifer, mixed conifer, and moist evergreen hardwood forests and coastal riparian thickets. In the latter two forest types, it overlaps to a limited degree with the Downy Woodpecker. Hairies excavate their nest cavities in live trees, dead trees, or dead parts of live trees. Some authors have reported that Hairies

prefer live trees for nesting (Kilham 1965, Lawrence 1967), but they use dead trees or dead portions of live trees more commonly in the Sierra Nevada (Raphael & White 1984). Nest holes range from 3 to 100 feet above the ground (Bent 1939) and on the average are in firmer wood, in larger trees, and higher above the ground than those of Downies (Conner et al. 1975). The heights of 11 Hairy Woodpecker nests in Ontario ranged from 15 to 45 feet and averaged 35 feet (Lawrence 1967); those of 10 nests in Virginia ranged from 8 to 65 feet and averaged 29 feet (Conner et al. 1975); and those of 19 nests in the Sierra Nevada averaged 16 feet (Raphael & White 1984). In some areas, nest holes appear to be oriented with respect to light and warmth, with most having a southern or eastern exposure and those in open surroundings occurring at lower heights (Lawrence 1967). Conner (1975, 1977) reported that the slope of the trunk appears to be the most important factor in nest orientation. Nest holes facing slightly downward prevent rain from entering the nest cavity, though locally a northeasterly orientation may also provide shelter from prevailing winds and rain. The downward orientation also aids in defense of the nest hole from predators. Lawrence (1967) reported that Hairy Woodpecker nest holes are often excavated near some sort of protrusion that provides camouflage and protection from weather.

Birds forage mostly by rapid drilling, pecking, probing, scaling, gleaning, and excavating on live and dead trees, stumps, downed logs, and occasionally on the ground; they sometimes hover and flycatch (Kilham 1965, Stallcup 1968, Kisiel 1972, Conner 1981, Raphael & White 1984, Lundquist & Manuwal 1990). Hairies sometimes take advantage of insects uncovered by Pileated Woodpeckers' prying off thick bark or digging deep holes (Maxson & Maxson 1981). In Virginia in winter, Hairies rely more on scaling and excavating and less on pecking (Conner 1981; see for additional seasonal differences). In the Washington Cascades, Hairies increase pecking, decrease probing, and eliminate gleaning from spring to winter (Lundquist & Manuwal 1990). Compared with Downies, they tend to drill more often and deeper and to forage more on larger branches and trunks and on different tree species (Koplin 1969, Kisiel 1972, Conner 1981).

Hairy Woodpeckers expand their foraging niche by the males and females working different species of trees, or by each sex using different proportions of various foraging techniques, substrates, or heights. Females tend to specialize in surface foraging methods on larger branches and limbs, whereas the males excavate deeper in dead trees and spend more time on smaller branches (Kilham 1965, Kisiel 1972). Morrison and With (1990) described the seasonal changes in the foraging niche of male and female Hairy Woodpeckers (relative to White-headeds) in the mixed conifer zone of the Sierra Nevada. In summer, males and females forage both in trees of similar height and at similar heights in these trees. Although both sexes forage at greater heights and in taller trees in winter, males exceed females in both categories then but still forage at the same *relative* height in trees as do females. Both sexes choose similar-diameter trees at both seasons. Males and females both concentrate their foraging on trunks at both seasons, but both sexes increase use of limbs during winter; they seldom use twigs in either season. Both sexes divide foraging activities relatively evenly between dead and live substrates in summer and winter. On the other hand, males make relatively even use of available tree species for foraging during both seasons, whereas females concentrate foraging on white fir and ponderosa pine in summer and incense cedar and black oak in winter. Males and females concentrate their foraging during the first five hours after sunrise in summer and the five to nine hours after sunrise in winter. Lundquist and Manuwal (1990) reported seasonal changes in Hairy Woodpecker foraging in the Washington Cascades but did not distinguish between the patterns of males and females.

The Hairy Woodpecker annual diet is about 78% animal and 22% vegetable (Beal 1911, n = 382). It varies little seasonally, with animal matter comprising 74%-76% in winter and fall and 80%-82% in spring and summer (Martin et al. 1951, n = 405). In the mountains of California (season unspecified), the diet is about 92%-93% animal matter (Otvos & Stark 1985, n = 69). The main animal foods are wood-boring beetle larvae, ants, caterpillars, weevils, true bugs, and scale insects, along with other insects, spiders, and millipedes. Although their diets are generally quite similar to Downies', Hairies consume about twice as many wood-boring beetle larvae, attesting to their more frequent and deeper drilling (Beal 1911). Compared with female Hairies, the males consume more wood-boring beetle larvae, bark beetles that inhabit thicker bark, and carpenter ants, again because the larger-billed males drill deeper; females consume more scale insects found under the loose, scaly bark of incense cedar (Otvos & Stark 1985, Morrison & With 1990). The size of insects fed to young increases with the age of nestlings (Lawrence 1967). Vegetable foods include fruits, seeds, grain, mast, cambium, and sap. In the nonbreeding season, mast and pine seeds may be important foods (Beal 1911, Stallcup 1968).

Marin Breeding Distribution

During the atlas period, the breeding distribution of the Hairy Woodpecker in Marin County was much more restricted than that of the Downy Woodpecker. Hairies were confined largely to Inverness Ridge, Bolinas Ridge, and the Mount Tamalpais watersheds. Breeding birds away from these areas were usually found in patchily distributed conifer or moist evergreen hardwood forests in canyons or on north-facing slopes. Representative nesting locations were Inverness (ON 5/2/80 –DS); Bear Valley, PRNS (NY 5/26/76 –RMS); Alpine Lake (FY 6/5/82 –DS); and Bon Tempe Lake (FY 5/12/76 –RMS).

Historical Trends/Population Threats

Few prior data exist, but numbers of Hairy Woodpeckers were relatively stable on Breeding Bird Surveys in California from 1968 to 1989, despite a decrease from 1980 to 1989 (USFWS unpubl. analyses).

NORTHERN FLICKER *Colaptes auratus*

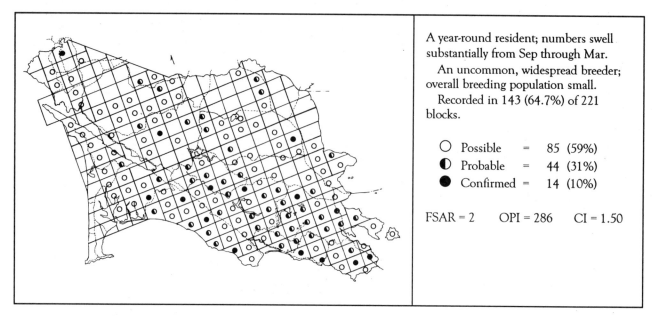

A year-round resident; numbers swell substantially from Sep through Mar.

An uncommon, widespread breeder; overall breeding population small.

Recorded in 143 (64.7%) of 221 blocks.

○ Possible   =   85 (59%)
◑ Probable   =   44 (31%)
● Confirmed =   14 (10%)

FSAR = 2   OPI = 286   CI = 1.50

Ecological Requirements

Once highly prized for ornamentation by Native Americans, the intermittently flashing, fiery orange-red flight feathers of Red-shafted Flickers still draw our admiration as birds course overhead in undulating flight. The Red-shafted subspecies of Northern Flicker, like its eastern counterpart, the Yellow-shafted Flicker, is wedded to grassland edges of forests or to woodlands or openings within them. Flickers nest in all of Marin's forests, woodlands, or planted groves as long as open ground for foraging is available either within the habitat, in nearby meadows, or in grasslands. Flickers excavate most of their nest holes in dead trees, dead limbs of live trees, or stubs, but they sometimes select sides of houses, posts, and earthen banks. They rarely use live trunks or limbs of trees, as Flickers prefer very soft wood for excavating (Raphael & White 1984). Nests range from ground level to 100 feet, though most are from 8 to 30 feet above the ground (Bent 1939). The height of 68 nests in the Sierra Nevada averaged 25 feet; some were enlarged nest cavities of other species of woodpeckers (Raphael & White 1984).

Of our woodpeckers, Flickers are least dependent on foraging on or beneath the bark of trees. They obtain much of their food by pecking and probing in the ground with their beaks, scratching the surface of the ground, and picking fruits from trees and bushes; they sometimes hang almost upside down from swaying branches to procure elderberries. Birds also pick items from the surface of the ground, dig (peck and tear) into rotten stumps or logs, glean insects from trees and bushes, and, rarely, flycatch (Bent 1939). In ponderosa pine forest in Arizona, North-

ern Flickers show annual variation in their use of foraging techniques and other resource-use behaviors (Szaro et al. 1990). The diet of the Red-shafted Flicker in California is about 54% animal food and 46% vegetable matter (Beal 1910, n = 118), compared with 61% and 39%, respectively, for the Yellow-shafted form of the East (Beal 1911, n = 684). The animal food is overwhelmingly dominated by ants, particularly ground-dwelling forms, though beetles, crickets, grasshoppers, caterpillars, miscellaneous insects, spiders, sowbugs, snails, and myriopods contribute minor amounts. Animal food may vary from 99% of the summer diet (n = 35) to only 33% in the fall (n = 48), when fruits predominate (Martin et al. 1951). Vegetable food consists primarily of small wild fruits, such as elderberries and gooseberries, cultivated fruits, acorns and other mast, poison oak seeds, grains, and, infrequently, cambium and weed seeds. Flicker young are fed by regurgitation (Lawrence 1967).

Marin Breeding Distribution

Although Flickers bred widely in Marin County during the atlas period, they were concentrated more toward the coast than the interior. The coastal area is more heavily forested and has generally thicker and moister soil in openings, which presumably aids ground foraging. Representative nesting locations were Laguna Ranch, PRNS (ON 7/20/79 –JGE), and beside a small pond near Soulajoule Reservoir (FY 6/17/82 –DS).

Historical Trends/Population Threats

Although data are lacking, it seems likely that Flickers have increased as breeding birds in historic times as a result of the opening up of dense coastal forests by clearing for human needs. Although placed on the Audubon Society's Blue List for 1971 (Tate 1981), based on recommendations from southern California and the central Rockies, numbers of Flickers were relatively stable on Breeding Bird Surveys in California from 1968 to 1989 and increased from 1980 to 1989 (USFWS unpubl. analyses).

PILEATED WOODPECKER   *Dryocopus pileatus*

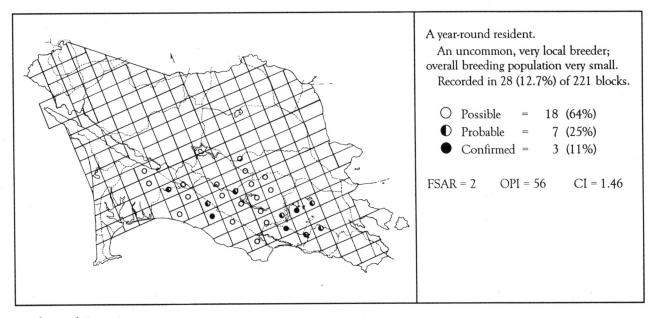

A year-round resident.

An uncommon, very local breeder; overall breeding population very small.

Recorded in 28 (12.7%) of 221 blocks.

○ Possible   =   18   (64%)
◑ Probable   =   7   (25%)
● Confirmed =   3   (11%)

FSAR = 2   OPI = 56   CI = 1.46

Ecological Requirements

This primeval-looking woodpecker inhabits Marin County's Douglas fir and redwood forests, moist mixed evergreen forests dominated by Douglas fir, and, to a limited degree, mixed bishop pine–hardwood forests. Pileateds are adapted to mesic forests with large-diameter trees, characteristic of ancient stands, but may not be dependent on old-growth forest since they use isolated patches of decay in highly productive conifer forests less than 75 years old (Harris 1982). Pileateds select structural features of nest trees and forest patches around their nests that are independent of the productivity or age of the stand. In California, stands of trees around nest sites are characterized by a high density of large trees and dead material, particularly clusters of dead trees (Harris 1982). Pileateds in California need about four 1-acre patches of dense, naturally occurring tree mortality per 247 acres of forest. Although they use stumps and logs for foraging, the densities and volume of these are variable around nesting sites and are therefore not good indicators of the suitability of a stand for nest location. Although Pileateds do not use the venerable remnant trees from older forests for nesting, such trees may be a crucial habitat feature since carpenter ant galler-ies, a prime food source, are usually found in large diameter logs, stumps, standing dead trees, and live trees with basal wounds (Harris 1982). Although Pileateds often select nest trees close to water (Harris 1982), or sometimes standing in it (Carriger & Wells 1919), this appears to be an artifact of the moist forests they inhabit rather than a factor the birds consider when choosing a nest site (R.D. Harris pers. comm.).

In California, Pileateds excavate nest cavities most frequently in conifers such as white fir, ponderosa pine, Douglas fir, red fir, coast redwood, and giant sequoia, as well as in broadleaved trees such as quaking aspen, black oak, madrone, black cottonwood, big-leaf maple, elm, and white alder (Harris 1982). In this state, they choose trees with an average diameter (at breast height) of 26 inches (range 20–36 in., n = 24) for nesting, even when larger snags are available; this compares with an average of 30 inches (range 15–47 in., n = 58) in Montana (McClelland 1979), 30 inches (range 23–39 in., n = 13) in Oregon (Bull & Meslow 1977), and 22 inches (range 13–36 in., n = 18) in Virginia (Conner et al. 1975). In the respective studies, nest hole heights averaged 59 feet above the ground in

California, 50 feet (range 18-98 ft.) in Montana, 43 feet (range 23-62 ft.) in Oregon, and 67 feet (range 24-120 ft.) in Virginia. Nest holes may rarely be as low as about 2 feet off the ground (Bent 1939). Of the California nest trees, those of the pine family were all snags, usually with broken tops (Harris 1982). Nests in trees with intact tops were located just above midbole, whereas those in trees with broken tops were near the top, where decay would be most likely. Of the remaining nest trees, five of ten hardwoods were alive, two giant sequoias were alive, and one of two redwoods was alive. Of the eight nest cavities in live trees, one was in a live portion of a redwood, while the others were in dead portions of the live trees. All of the California nests were in trunks (rather than limbs), had clear flight paths to the entrance, and were *not* consistently oriented with any specific compass directions. They tended to be located on the underside of the incline of a nest tree, as noted also in Virginia (Conner 1975), presumably because this affords protection from rain and predators. The entrance holes of Pileateds are larger relative to the bird's body size than holes of other California woodpeckers and are distinctly oblong from top to bottom, instead of round. Since the nest cavity is usually excavated through advanced decayed heartwood, the chamber shape follows that of the decayed portion of the wood; the sound sapwood around the cavity apparently provides protection from predators. Like other woodpeckers, in most cases Pileateds keep the bottom of the nest cavity practically bare, with only a few chips of wood left from excavation. One wonders if these woodpeckers bring in the sand or the few pebbles that on rare occasions are found on the floor of the nest chamber (Hoyt 1957). Pileateds often use nest trees in successive years in the East (Hoyt 1957), but not in California (R.D. Harris pers. comm.); only very rarely do they use a previous year's nest cavity again (McClelland 1979). Pileateds have been known to re-lay in the same cavity after the first set of eggs is taken (Carriger & Wells 1919, Bent 1939). In addition to nesting, snags are also important for roosting cavities (Bull & Meslow 1977).

Pileateds put their massive bills to good use by drilling gaping holes deep into the rotting timber of large snags, logs, and stumps or by scaling off large pieces of bark with glancing blows in search of sequestered prey. The home-spun name "stump-breaker" aptly fits birds working on downed logs, as they strike alternate blows from side to side in the manner of lumberjacks, sending wood chips several inches long flying in every direction. Birds also peck and probe on the wood's surface, tear up anthills on the ground, or swing by their feet, head down, like giant pendulums as they grasp branches and gobble berries. The annual diet is about 73% animal, primarily carpenter ants and wood-boring beetle larvae, and 27% vegetable, principally wild fruit, along with a few seeds, mast, and a little cambium (Beal 1911, n = 80). The diet varies with season,

as do the methods of procurement. Animal matter in the diet varies from 94% in spring (n = 15) to 51% in fall (n = 30) (Martin et al. 1951). During spring and summer, surface foraging methods predominate (Hoyt 1957, Conner 1981), and a wider variety of insects is eaten (Hoyt 1957). At least in areas with harsh winters, breeding birds forage more on fallen logs, low stumps, and the lower portions of snags and live trees, presumably because of insect sources newly available on these substrates after snowmelt (Hoyt 1957, McClelland 1979). Later in the fall, wild fruits and mast take on increased importance. In the winter, birds eat chiefly insects, especially carpenter ants (the main prey throughout their range), secured predominantly by excavating deep into the heart of trees, stumps, logs, power poles, and even decaying buildings (Bent 1939, Hoyt 1957, Conner 1981). Although decayed wood is a preferred foraging substrate, Pileateds also feed on live trees, particularly when infested with insects (Bull & Meslow 1977). In Oregon, prime feeding areas are dense mixed-species forests with high snag densities and more than 10% of the ground covered with logs (Bull & Meslow 1977); logs without limbs and bark are preferred, as are natural stumps over cut stumps. Pileateds forage in selectively logged areas, as long as substantial numbers of snags and logs are available (McClelland 1979), but rarely on logs and stumps in cut-over areas less than 40 years old—probably because dense shrub and sapling cover limit access to them (Mannan 1984).

Marin Breeding Distribution

In Marin County, Pileated Woodpeckers were restricted during the atlas period to the conifer forests of Inverness Ridge, Bolinas Ridge, and the Mount Tamalpais watersheds. A representative nesting record was Lake Lagunitas (NE-FL 4/10-5/28/79 —RDH).

Historical Trends/Population Threats

Unrecorded in Marin County by Mailliard (1900), the Pileated Woodpecker's range on the California coast was thought to extend "casually" south to Marin County at the time of Grinnell and Miller's (1944) comprehensive avifaunal summary. Knowledge of its status in Marin County then was apparently based solely on sightings by C. Hart Merriam at Larkspur and along San Geronimo Creek in the vicinity of Lagunitas "on various occasions between 1911 and 1918" (G&W 1927). Grinnell and Miller (1944) noted declines of the species in California following the expansion of lumbering operations.

Although the Pileated Woodpecker's range in Marin County today is probably similar to what it was early in this century, numbers may have increased since the era of intensive logging here. Harris (1982) noted that maintenance of Pileated populations was not incompatible with some logging. He felt that young-growth high-productivity sites now probably supported these woodpeckers because the harvest methods and management strategies in vogue 60 to 80 years ago left standing many large trees of low commercial value. He cautioned that today's intensive management practices may threaten to extirpate Pileateds from major portions of their California range, especially in

low-productivity sites where old-growth forest is the only suitable habitat. Despite these concerns, Pileated Woodpecker numbers on Breeding Bird Surveys in California increased in the period 1968 to 1979 (Robbins et al. 1986), increased slightly from 1968 to 1989, and were relatively stable from 1980 to 1989 (USFWS unpubl. analyses).

Tyrant Flycatchers
Family *Tyrannidae*

OLIVE-SIDED FLYCATCHER *Contopus borealis*

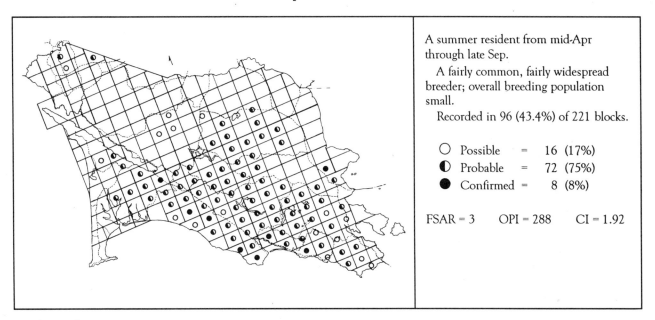

A summer resident from mid-Apr through late Sep.

A fairly common, fairly widespread breeder; overall breeding population small.

Recorded in 96 (43.4%) of 221 blocks.

○	Possible	=	16 (17%)
◖	Probable	=	72 (75%)
●	Confirmed	=	8 (8%)

FSAR = 3　　　OPI = 288　　　CI = 1.92

Ecological Requirements

The loud whistled calls of this sturdy flycatcher announce its presence in Marin County's open conifer and mixed conifer forests and near the coast in planted groves of eucalyptus and Monterey cypress. In addition to openings for foraging sallies, Olive-sideds apparently need some degree of coolness or moisture, as they do not use eucalyptus groves in the dry interior. These flycatchers construct their nests from 5 to 72 feet above the ground. In the West (more than in the East), their nests are often higher than 50 feet, rivaling their lofty foraging perches (Bent 1942). Olive-sideds prefer conifers as nesting trees, though they occasionally select broadleaved trees such as alders or oaks and, locally, eucalyptus. They usually place their nests well out on horizontal or drooping limbs, on cone clusters, or, rarely, in a crotch against a trunk. The nest itself is a

shallow cup constructed of dead twigs, coarse weed stems, dry grass, lichens, moss, rootlets, and dead pine needles and is lined with lichens and fine rootlets, grass, pine needles, or hair

Olive-sideds are born lookouts, having the highest foraging beat of any of our flycatchers. They normally perch on the uppermost branches, spires, or dead limbs of the tallest trees in the vicinity, ones that give a wide, open view of the airways. They forage solely by flycatching sallies of variable distance, mixed with tumbling aerial acrobatics when in hot pursuit of elusive prey, and the birds then return to the same or alternate perches. In the Colorado Rockies, Olive-sided Flycatchers forage primarily from dead perches and make longer sallies (mostly <50 ft.) than do Western Wood-Pewees (mostly <25 ft.) (Eckhardt

1979). Both species there prefer horizontal flights and, secondarily, downward (over upward) flights, unlike Pewees in California (see account).

The Olive-sided Flycatcher diet is almost exclusively animal food, of which 83% consists of bees and wasps, indicating a very high degree of specialization (Beal 1912, n = 69). Among other items they regularly eat are beetles, moths, true bugs, dragonflies, grasshoppers, and a few other miscellaneous insects. Interestingly, they are not known to eat caterpillars, spiders, and millipedes (regularly eaten by most flycatchers); thus Olive-sideds apparently eat only airborne flying insects.

Marin Breeding Distribution

During the atlas period, the distribution of this species in Marin County closely paralleled that of native conifer forests. An exception was where Olive-sideds occupied some groves of eucalyptus or cypress trees in the fog belt (e.g., near Tomales) far from conifer forests or, for that matter, from any stands of tall native trees. Representative breeding locations were eucalyptus-cypress grove in Bolinas (FL 7/25/82 —DS) and near Phoenix Lake (NB 5/21/77 —DS).

Historical Trends/Population Threats

For the south San Francisco Bay region, Sibley (1952) noted that Olive-sided Flycatchers had "rather recently invaded the lowland portions of the area, possibly following the extensive planting of conifers and eucalyptus." The birds appear to have expanded their range locally in Marin County, as well, by occupying planted eucalyptus and cypress as noted above. In the period 1968 to 1979, numbers of Olive-sided Flycatchers on Breeding Bird Surveys declined sharply in western North America but held their own in areas of the species' greatest abundance in California (Robbins et al. 1986). Survey numbers in California declined from 1968 to 1989 but were relatively stable from 1980 to 1989 (USFWS unpubl. analyses). A similar decline in Survey numbers in USFWS Region 1 (including California) led to placing the Olive-sided Flycatcher on the USFWS list of Migratory Nongame Birds of Management Concern (USFWS 1987b). In addition, Marshall (1988) documented the disappearance of this flycatcher from undisturbed climax forests of the southern Sierra and suggested the decline was caused by destruction of forests on the Central American wintering grounds.

WESTERN WOOD-PEWEE *Contopus sordidulus*

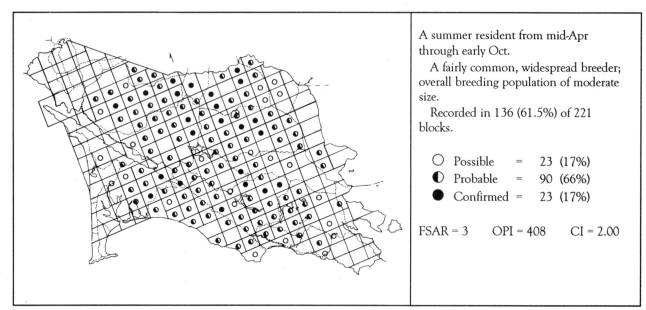

A summer resident from mid-Apr through early Oct.

A fairly common, widespread breeder; overall breeding population of moderate size.

Recorded in 136 (61.5%) of 221 blocks.

O	Possible	=	23 (17%)
◑	Probable	=	90 (66%)
●	Confirmed	=	23 (17%)

FSAR = 3   OPI = 408   CI = 2.00

Ecological Requirements

Emphatic breeding calls of the Western Wood-Pewee leap out from the hardwood stands of Marin County's mixed evergreen forests, and also from her riparian, mixed conifer, and conifer forests. Pewees usually frequent either relatively open stands or habitat edges in these forests. Nest heights range from 2 to 75 feet above the ground (mostly 15-30 ft.) in either live or dead trees (Bent 1942). Pewees usually build their nests in the open, on top of a limb or at the fork of a horizontal branch, though occasionally in an upright crotch. Their nests are shallow cups made of plant fibers, grasses, coarse weed straws, plant down, spider webs, shredded bark, lichens, and, rarely, green leaves (Bent 1942, Goodpasture 1953). Pewees artfully camouflage their nests by shape and color to give them the appearance of a bump or stub of the supporting limb, and they vigorously defend them against intruders.

In central coastal California, Western Wood-Pewees patrol their foraging beats mainly from perches such as treetops, outer tree canopies, and telephone wires (Verbeek 1975a). Although they prefer bare branches at middle to high elevations in the outer parts of trees, Pewees also perch on fences, downed trees, saplings, weed stalks, and occasionally inside tree canopies. Pewees there forage predominantly by hawking insects in the open air, generally away from vegetation and the ground, and more often in descending than in ascending or horizontal flight. They occasionally hawk inside the canopy, over grass, and under trees and, rarely, glean from branches and foliage in their hawking flight. Where they overlap with Pacific-slope Flycatchers and Black Phoebes, the height range of Pewees' foraging perches (1-115 ft.) is greater than that of the other two species, but the median height (18 ft.) is significantly different only from that of the Black Phoebe. In distance, Pewees' foraging flights range from 1 to 115 feet (median 12 ft.) and are significantly greater than those of Pacific-slope Flycatchers and Black Phoebes. In Colorado, Beaver and Baldwin (1975) found Pewees feeding mostly at mid-foliage portions of trees and in the air space immediately below; there and in California, they forage mostly at about 10 to 40 feet above ground (Verbeek 1975a, Beaver &

Baldwin 1975). Pewees generally forage from lower perches and make shorter sallies after prey than do Olive-sided Flycatchers (see account).

The Pewee's diet (Apr–Sep) is almost exclusively animal matter, consisting primarily of insects. The main items are flies, wasps, bees, ants, beetles, moths, butterflies, and caterpillars; minor items are true bugs, dragonflies, lace-winged flies, mayflies, termites, caddisflies, leafhoppers, and spiders (Beal 1912, n = 174; Beaver & Baldwin 1975, n = 69). In Colorado, lepidopterans accounted for only 13% of the diet by numbers, but 44% by dry weight (Beaver & Baldwin 1975).

Marin Breeding Distribution

Pewees bred widely in Marin County during the atlas period, and their distribution matched well that of forested areas here. Within the limits of this distribution, the species appeared to have no obvious geographical trend or center of abundance. More careful study might reveal that Pewees are most numerous in the central portions of the county, which provide more forests of moderately open character and likewise more edge situations. Representative breeding locations were Chileno Valley (NY 7/2/82 – DS); Laguna Ranch Canyon, PRNS (NE 6/?/80 –JGE); Cascade Canyon, Fairfax (NE 5/11/81 –DS); and Hick's Valley (NE 5/15/82 –ScC).

Historical Trends/Population Threats

Few prior data exist, but Pewee numbers declined on Breeding Bird Surveys in California from 1968 to 1989 (USFWS unpubl. analyses).

PACIFIC-SLOPE FLYCATCHER *Empidonax difficilis*

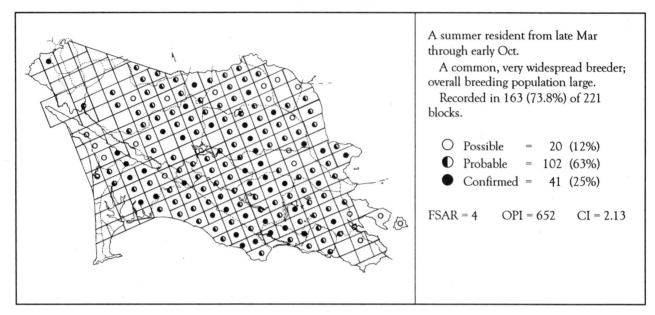

A summer resident from late Mar through early Oct.

A common, very widespread breeder; overall breeding population large.

Recorded in 163 (73.8%) of 221 blocks.

○ Possible   =   20 (12%)
◐ Probable   = 102 (63%)
● Confirmed =   41 (25%)

FSAR = 4   OPI = 652   CI = 2.13

Ecological Requirements

The warm olive and yellowish hues of our only breeding *Empidonax* flycatcher blend well with its Marin County nesting haunts—moist, relatively dense, and shaded forests of broadleaved evergreen, mixed broadleaved-conifer, conifer, and riparian trees. Within these habitats, Pacific-slope Flycatchers are most numerous in canyon bottoms near permanent or ephemeral streams. They place their nests in a wide variety of relatively open settings with the main requirements being support from below and behind and, often, shelter from above. Natural sites selected include forks of trees, cavities in trees or cutbanks, narrow shelves of banks or mossy cliffsides, behind loose flaps of bark, among the roots of upturned trees, the tops of low stumps, and abandoned Black Phoebe nests. Birds also nest commonly on human supporting structures both inside and outside buildings, on road cuts, on bridges, in flowerpots or fern baskets, and over porch lights. Nest heights range from ground level to 30 feet (av. about 11 ft.) (Bent 1942, Davis et al. 1963). Exceptionally, these flycatchers will construct a nest on flat ground (Reynolds 1942). They often use nest sites for successive broods in a single year and also in subsequent years; at least in the latter case the same individuals are sometimes involved (Sakai 1988). Since nest cups are usually placed against vertical surfaces, they are often triangular in shape or broadly oval, with the long side flattened (Davis et al. 1963). Pacific-slope Flycatchers often construct nests primarily of green mosses when available, but they also use bark strips, leaves, grasses, twigs, spider webs, and artificial materials found near buildings (Bent 1942, Davis et al. 1963). They usually line their nest cups with fine dried grasses, alone or with lichens and/or bark.

In riparian woodland on the central California coast, foraging Pacific-slope Flycatchers perch primarily within the middle and lower interior of trees, an area largely avoided by our other locally breeding flycatchers (Verbeek 1975a). To a limited extent, they also perch toward the outside and upper parts of trees, in understory trees and shrubs, on downed branches, and on buildings. Perch heights range from slightly less than 1 foot to about 55 feet (median 17 ft.). Although the range of their perch heights there is intermediate between those of Western Wood-Pewees and Black Phoebes, the median height is significantly different only from that of the Black Phoebe (it is higher). Pacific-slope Flycatchers there hawk insects from the air about 60% of the time; they make relatively short, quick darts, with ascending flights predominating; and they use hawking about equally in open air space and within the foliage and branchwork of trees. For the other 40% of their foraging, they make direct sallies or hovering flight to glean from the foliage and branchwork of trees and, to a limited extent, from the ground or buildings. The distances of their foraging flights range from about 1 to 26 feet (median 6 ft.)—significantly shorter than those of Western Wood-Pewees but not of Black Phoebes.

In Douglas fir-tanbark oak habitat in northwestern California, Pacific-slope Flycatchers change their foraging behaviors during the course of the breeding season. Generally, they capture their prey there during various stages of

*Necks extend and heads bob instantly as young Pacific-slope Flycatchers beg at the first
sensation of an insect-bearing adult alighting on their mossy nest rim.
Drawing by Keith Hansen, 1990.*

the breeding cycle, 72%-85% by hover-gleaning, 12%-27% by flycatching, and 1%-4% by gleaning (Sakai & Noon 1990). They hover-glean more than expected during preincubation and incubation but flycatch more than expected during periods with young in the nest. On the whole, these birds take their prey mostly from foliage; secondarily from the air, twigs, and small branches; and, rarely, from large branches and trunks. The proportion of prey captures from various substrates also varies among periods of the breeding cycle. A shift by foraging birds from extensive initial use of Douglas fir to heavy use of hardwoods later on is associated with decreasing reliance on overstory vegetation and increasing reliance on understory vegetation as the season progresses. Corresponding to the change in plant species use was a shift from favoring horizontal prey attack flights early on to increased use of vertical attack flights later in the season. Regardless of the direction of flights, the birds appeared to favor the shortest distance to capture prey during all breeding stages. The flycatchers did not change foraging position seasonally but remained at moderate heights and intermediate distances from the canopy edge throughout. Sympatric Hammond's Flycatchers there select taller trees and forage higher in the subcanopy than do Pacific-slope Flycatchers. Nevertheless, both species shift their seasonal use of substrate and foraging techniques in a corresponding manner, suggesting these changes in foraging behavior reflect changes in prey availability.

259

In Washington, Pacific-slope Flycatchers spend over 60% of their time foraging either within the tree canopy or in the air space below it; secondary foraging zones are brush, open air, the herb layer, and on the ground (Frakes & Johnson 1982). Foraging there is about equally split between hawking and gleaning, via hawking and hovering flight; foraging heights range from the ground to about 79 feet. Between Douglas fir and cottonwood-willow riparian habitats there, the flycatchers' foraging strategy differs in the relative amount of time spent foraging in various substrates, the proportion of gleaning directed at different substrates, height of foraging perches, and the directions and lengths of foraging flights.

Also in Washington, the foraging ecology of Pacific-slope and Willow flycatchers is more alike where they overlap in riparian habitat than where they occupy different habitats (Frakes & Johnson 1982). In riparian, they show little difference in frequency of hawking versus gleaning, in perch height, in flight length, in flight direction, or in frequency of return to the same perch. However, Pacific-slope Flycatchers feed more in the tree canopy, in the air space under the canopy, and in brush and less in the herb layer and in the open air than do Willows. They glean more from trunks and less from grass and herbs than do Willows. Willow Flycatchers also perch frequently in willows, grass, and herbs, which are rarely if ever used by Pacific-slope Flycatchers.

The Pacific-slope Flycatcher's diet is about 99.3% animal matter, the rest consisting of a few seeds and skins of fruit (Beal 1912, n = 157). The main components of the diet are bees, wasps, ants, flies, true bugs, moths, caterpillars, and beetles; a few other insects and spiders are also taken.

Marin Breeding Distribution

Pacific-slope Flycatchers were widespread breeders in Marin County during the atlas period, reflecting the extensive distribution of moist forests in this coastal county. They were most numerous and widespread toward the coast, where moist forests cover large continuous areas, and less numerous and more local toward the interior, where such forests are found only in narrow canyons or on north-facing slopes. Representative breeding locales were Inverness (NY/NE 7/10/82 —DNe); Skywalker Ranch, Lucas Valley Rd. (NY 7/17/82 —DS, HBa); Cataract Trail, Mt. Tamalpais (NE 5/8/82 —BiL); and Gloria Dr., San Rafael (NE 6/4/78 —ITi).

Historical Trends/Population Threats

Few prior data exist, but numbers were relatively stable on Breeding Bird Surveys in California from 1968 to 1989 (USFWS unpubl. analyses).

BLACK PHOEBE *Sayornis nigricans*

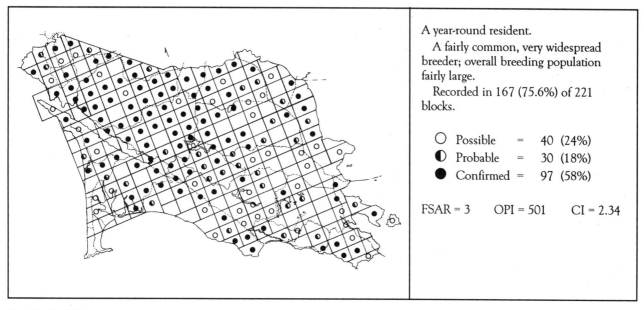

A year-round resident.

A fairly common, very widespread breeder; overall breeding population fairly large.

Recorded in 167 (75.6%) of 221 blocks.

○	Possible	=	40 (24%)
◑	Probable	=	30 (18%)
●	Confirmed	=	97 (58%)

FSAR = 3   OPI = 501   CI = 2.34

Ecological Requirements

In Marin County, as elsewhere, our nattily dressed Black Phoebes inhabit the edges of open country and maintain an intimate association with water. Individual Black Phoebes scout for insect prey from a series of well-spaced foraging perches on the margins of grasslands, weed fields, lawns, meadows, marshes, and woodland clearings. Breeding birds are usually found near streams and ponds, but cattle troughs, small seeps, or well-watered lawns will suffice as long there is a sufficient supply of insects and foraging perches, mud for nest building, and suitable nest sites. In presettlement times, Black Phoebes nested on the vertical surfaces of cliffs, boulders, steep banks, caverns, and, rarely, on dead trunks or limbs of trees. Today they select nest sites mostly on human structures, such as buildings, duck blinds, wells, and especially bridges and stream culverts (Woods 1942, Ohlendorf 1976). Nest heights can range from 15 feet below the ground (in wells) to 35 feet above the ground or water (Woods 1942, Ohlendorf 1976). In Texas, the average height of Black Phoebe nests was 10 feet (range 1-35 ft., n = 36), not significantly different from that of Say's Phoebes (Ohlendorf 1976) (but see Say's Phoebe account for other nest site differences). Black Phoebes plaster their nests, which are half-cup shaped, on vertical or nearly vertical surfaces that have an overhang above for protection. They construct their nest bowls of small pellets of mud mixed with lots of dry grass, weed fibers, or hair and line them with weed fiber, fine roots, bark, grass hairs, or wool (Woods 1942). Nests must be within carrying distance of

a mud source, found in Texas to be less than 50 feet (Ohlendorf 1976). Black Phoebes may reuse their nests for successive broods in the same year and also in subsequent years.

Black Phoebes forage from low perches such as fences, the outer lower tree canopy, fallen dead trees in meadows, weed stalks, rocks, buildings, and overhead wires (Oberlander 1939, Verbeek 1975a, Ohlendorf 1976). They tend to retire to shaded perches in the heat of the day (Verbeek 1975b). In coastal California, Verbeek (1975a) recorded perch heights of breeding birds ranging from about 2.5 to 33 feet (median 4 ft.). About 77% of prey capture attempts by breeding birds are by hawking, primarily in the open air or over grass. The rest are by gleaning from the ground, grass, buildings, or tree foliage, using darting and hovering flights. Unlike most flycatchers, Black Phoebes even perch on the ground to catch their prey. When open water is available, they may direct the preponderance of their flights at insects on or near the water (Oberlander 1939). When insects are scarce or less active (in winter, on rainy days, or on cold mornings), birds hover and glean more from grass and from building walls. Their foraging sallies tend to be relatively short (median 7 ft., range 1-49 ft.), with no flight direction predominant, and after prey capture, birds usually return to a different perch (Verbeek 1975a). However, Oberlander (1939) noted that toward dusk, Black Phoebes directed more foraging attempts upward, presumably because under these lighting conditions they could see

261

insects more easily against the pale sky. See Western Wood-Pewee and Pacific-slope Flycatcher accounts for comparison of foraging niches.

The Black Phoebe diet is about 99% animal matter, with the remainder consisting of a few seeds, fruit pulp, and "rubbish" (Beal 1912, n = 344; Ohlendorf 1976, n = 14). The main food items are bees, wasps, ants, flies, beetles, true bugs, moths, and caterpillars; minor items are grasshoppers, crickets, dragonflies, damselflies, termites, butterflies, and spiders. Insect hard parts are expelled as pellets (Oberlander 1939). Black Phoebes also occasionally dip their heads in water nearly to their eyes to catch minnows (Oberlander 1939)! In a portion of Texas, where Black and Say's phoebes coexist, the major food types in their diet overlapped by 77% based on orders, but only by 43% based on families (Ohlendorf 1976). By volume, dragonflies, damselflies, other water-associated insects, and termites were important for Black Phoebes, whereas grasshoppers, flies, and bees were most important for Say's Phoebes.

Marin Breeding Distribution

During the atlas period, Black Phoebes bred throughout most of Marin County but were patchily distributed here, as elsewhere, in response to the limitation of water sources and suitable nesting sites. Representative nesting locations were Olema Marsh at Whitehouse Pool (NE 4/22–5/3/81 –DS); Chileno Valley (NY 7/2/82 –DS); and San Jose Creek at Commercial Blvd., Novato (NY 5/7/78 –DS).

Historical Trends/Population Threats

Black Phoebes have probably increased historically in Marin County from construction of reservoirs, ranch ponds, and cattle troughs, which have increased the availability of water in the breeding season, augmenting both insect supplies and mud for nest building. Additionally, human structures have greatly increased suitable nest sites. Numbers of Black Phoebes increased on Breeding Bird Surveys in California from 1968 to 1989 but were relatively stable from 1980 to 1989 (USFWS unpubl. analyses).

SAY'S PHOEBE *Sayornis saya*

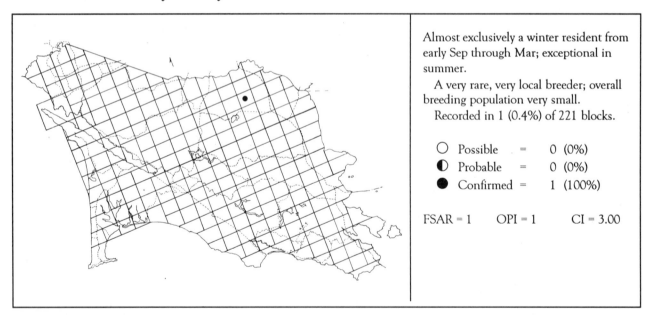

Almost exclusively a winter resident from early Sep through Mar; exceptional in summer.

A very rare, very local breeder; overall breeding population very small.

Recorded in 1 (0.4%) of 221 blocks.

○ Possible = 0 (0%)
◑ Probable = 0 (0%)
● Confirmed = 1 (100%)

FSAR = 1   OPI = 1   CI = 3.00

Ecological Requirements

Although Say's Phoebes are cheery and widespread members of Marin County's wintering avifauna, only one known pair has graced us with its presence in the breeding season. Hence, little can be said of its breeding habitat requirements in the county, except that the one nesting site adjoined arid grassland and open oak savannah—typical

habitat of the nearest breeding populations, in the interior Coast Range east of San Francisco Bay.

Unlike the vertical surfaces preferred by Black Phoebes, Says choose horizontal surfaces or shelves with protection from above on which to build their nests. Despite this difference—and the Black Phoebe's affinity for nearby water—both species place their nests in very similar situations that provide shade from midday heat. Natural nest sites for Say's Phoebes are crevices or shelves on cliffs or boulders, inside caves, in earthen banks, and in natural cavities of trees. They also use old or appropriated nests of Cliff and Barn swallows, Black Phoebes, burrows of Bank Swallows, and, rarely, American Robin nests in bushes (Bent 1942, Ohlendorf 1976). Today, however, most birds have adapted to building their nests on human structures, especially those that are abandoned or receive little use. Typical artificial sites include ranch buildings, outhouses, bridges, wells, mine shafts, and old mailboxes. Nest heights may range from 15 feet below the surface of the ground (in a well) to perhaps hundreds of feet high on cliffs (Bent 1942). The height of 112 nests in Texas ranged from 4 to 40 feet and averaged 9 feet; this was not significantly different from the height of Black Phoebe nests there (Ohlendorf 1976). Say's Phoebes make their nest cups of weed stems, dry grasses, other plant fibers, mosses, wool, spider webs, rags and the like near human habitation, and occasionally mud. They line them with wool or hair (Bent 1942). They may reuse nests for successive broods in one year and in subsequent years (Ohlendorf 1976).

Say's Phoebes forage from relatively low perches such as rocks, bushes, fences, and the corners of buildings. After sallying from a perch, they catch their prey in midair by hawking or by dropping to the ground directly or from hovering flight. The diet is 99.8%–100.0% animal matter, consisting primarily of insects; rarely, it includes a few seeds or fruits (Beal 1912, n = 111; Ohlendorf 1976, n = 23). The main food items are bees, wasps, grasshoppers, crickets, flies, beetles, moths, caterpillars, and true bugs; minor items are dragonflies, cicadas, nerve-winged insects, spiders, millipedes, and sowbugs. See Black Phoebe account for a discussion of differences in diet.

Marin Breeding Distribution

During the atlas period, there was one nesting record of the Say's Phoebe, a nest found under the eave of a building at the base of Mount Burdell, Novato, in June 1976 (ScC). This is the only known breeding record for Marin County and also the farthest north and most coastward breeding record for coastal northern California (McCaskie et al. 1979, ABN).

Historical Trends/Population Threats

Little prior information exists, but numbers of Say's Phoebes were relatively stable on Breeding Bird Surveys in California from 1968 to 1989, despite a decrease from 1980 to 1989 (USFWS unpubl. analyses).

ASH-THROATED FLYCATCHER *Myiarchus cinerascens*

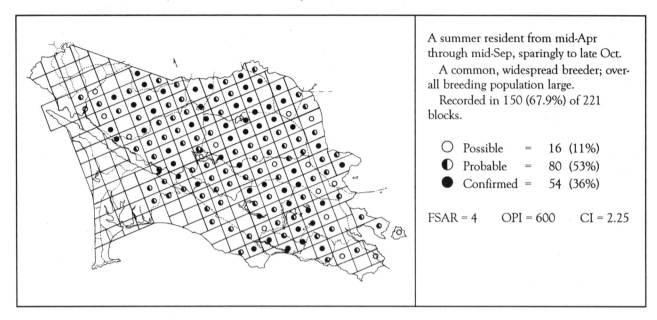

A summer resident from mid-Apr through mid-Sep, sparingly to late Oct.

A common, widespread breeder; overall breeding population large.

Recorded in 150 (67.9%) of 221 blocks.

○	Possible	=	16 (11%)
◑	Probable	=	80 (53%)
●	Confirmed	=	54 (36%)

FSAR = 4   OPI = 600   CI = 2.25

Ecological Requirements

The plucky Ash-throated Flycatcher dwells in Marin County's relatively open broadleaved evergreen forests, oak savannah woodlands, riparian forests, mixed conifer-broadleaved evergreen forests, and chaparral-edge habitats. Ash-throateds nest in natural tree cavities, woodpecker holes (sometimes usurped from the intended occupants), cavities behind the loose bark of trees, and, rarely, in old nests of other birds. They also readily adapt to bird boxes, hollow vertical or angled pipes, old tin cans or pots, old mailboxes, and the like. Nest cavities range from about 2.5 to 20 feet above the ground. The birds fill the bottom of these cavities with weed stems, rootlets, grass, or bits of dried cow or horse manure; they build the rest (most) of the nest from the hair and fur of animals and, rarely, snake and lizard skins (Bent 1942). The bulk of the nest varies considerably according to the size of the cavity.

Foraging at low to moderate heights, Ash-throated Flycatchers capture their prey by flycatching and fly gleaning (Block 1990). In foothill oak woodlands in California, these flycatchers direct prey capture attempts at leaves, twigs and small branches, air, ground, and, rarely, larger branches and trunks. Ash-throateds vary their foraging activities and substrates geographically (Block 1990, Petit et al. 1990). In California, the height of trees selected for foraging and foraging height of birds varied geographically, whereas the crown radius and diameter of trees selected for foraging and the crown position and relative height of foraging birds did not.

The diet (Apr–Dec) is about 92.3% animal and 7.7% seeds and fruits (Beal 1912, n = 91). The main articles of food are bees, wasps, true bugs, caterpillars and moths, flies, beetles, grasshoppers, and crickets; minor items are snakeflies, dragonflies, and spiders.

Marin Breeding Distribution

Although Ash-throated Flycatchers were widespread breeders in Marin County during the atlas years, they largely avoided the very open grasslands and dense moist forests along the immediate coast. Hence they were most numerous in the central and northeastern interior of the county (e.g., Big Rock Ridge), where moderately open broadleaved evergreen forests predominate. Representative breeding stations were Marshall-Petaluma Rd. about ½ mi. E of Marshall (NY/FY 6/11/82 –DS); Phoenix Lake (NY/FY 6/8/79 –ITi); vicinity of Rock Springs, Mt. Tamalpais (NY/FY 6/13/78 –ITi); and China Camp SP (ON 6/19/82 –BiL).

Historical Trends/Population Threats

Little prior information exists. Numbers of Ash-throated Flycatchers increased on Breeding Bird Surveys in California from 1968 to 1989, despite relative stability from 1980 to 1989 (USFWS unpubl. analyses).

CASSIN'S KINGBIRD   *Tyrannus vociferans*

Accidental breeder with only one record.

Ecological Requirements

Little can be said of Cassin's Kingbirds' habitat require-ments in Marin County since only one pair has strayed to nest here. These pioneers set up domestic duties on the outer coast near Palomarin, in a ranchyard treed with planted Monterey cypress and eucalyptus and surrounded by grassland, weed fields, and patchy coastal scrub. Struc-turally, this site must have struck a responsive chord in the *vociferans* psyche, but the climate of Marin's fog-shrouded coastline bears little resemblance to that of the dry inner Coast Range valleys of southern California where the species reaches its apex of abundance as a breeder in the state (G&M 1944). In the latter region, Cassins primarily inhabit grassland edges of broken oak woodlands and cottonwood-sycamore riparian groves (Dawson 1923, Pough 1957, G&M 1944).

In California, where Cassin's and Western kingbirds often nest side by side (Dawson 1923), the differences in habitat choice between the two species are particularly subtle. Garrett and Dunn (1981) stated that Cassins prefer habitat that is "less open" than Westerns'. Elsewhere, habitat separation between the two is more apparent, but they nonetheless overlap strongly in some areas. In the Southwest, Cassins prefer the denser habitats of pine-oak-juniper (on canyon sides), riparian, and oaks, while West-erns prefer more open desert shrub, dry creek washes, and farmland habitats (Hespenheide 1964, Smith 1966, Ohlendorf 1974, Blancher & Robertson 1984). A tend-ency of Cassins to occur at higher elevations appears to reflect the availability of preferred habitat. In the South-west, overlap of the two species is strong in open riparian and slight in dry creek washes, desert shrub, and planted trees.

Cassin's Kingbirds usually build their nests near the ends of horizontal branches of trees from about 8 to 80 feet above the ground (Bent 1942; references below). Nest heights vary with the height of available trees; mean nest heights among various habitats in the Southwest range from 15 to 53 feet (Ohlendorf 1974, Goldberg 1979, Blancher & Robertson 1984). Cassins tend to nest in the upper third of the canopy (Hespenheide 1964, Ohlendorf 1974, Blancher & Robertson 1984); in Arizona, relative height (nest height/tree height) ranges only between 0.73 and 0.78 (Blancher & Robertson 1984). Also in Arizona, Goldberg (1979) reported an average nest height of 53 feet (n = 34) in riparian habitat. Cassin's and Western king-birds exhibit only minor differences in nest height prefer-ences within the same habitats (Hespenheide 1964, Blancher & Robertson 1984). Cassins also occasionally nest in human structures—on utility poles, log fences, and farm gates (Bent 1942)—but not nearly as often as West-erns do (Ohlendorf 1974). Both species vigorously defend their nests against intruders. Cassins build bulky nest cups of twigs, rootlets, weed stalks, bark, and other plant fibers mixed with string, rags, or dry leaves (Bent 1942). They line them with fine rootlets, fine grasses, and perhaps a few feathers. Bent (1942) reported that Cassin's Kingbird nests "average somewhat larger and rather more firmly built" than those of Westerns, but Dawson (1923) and Blancher and Robertson (1985) noted great similarity between nests of these species.

Both species of kingbirds forage primarily by sallying off perches to catch flying insects and, secondarily, by flying down to pick insects off the ground (Blancher & Robert-son 1984). Rarely, they glean from vegetation, though Westerns do so more than Cassins do (Goldberg 1979). In general, intraspecific differences in foraging behavior between habitats are greater than any interspecific differ-ence in behavior in the same habitat. In riparian forest and open riparian habitats, Cassin's Kingbird average sally distances—respectively, 66 feet (n = 379) and 52 feet (n = 226)—are significantly different, as are their average perch heights of 39 feet (n = 382) and 25 feet (n = 225). In open riparian habitat, Cassins perch significantly lower than Westerns do, but the two species both pursue prey at heights from the ground up to about 164 feet and at similar average heights in this habitat. Average pursuit heights by Cassins of 49 feet (n = 390) and 36 feet (n = 229) in riparian forest and open riparian habitat, respectively, are significantly different. Goldberg (1979) noted interspecific differences in the tendency to return to the same perch after foraging and in the takeoff angle from the perch, but this did not result in differences in the height at which prey were taken.

In Texas, the respective diets of Cassin's and Western kingbirds are 94.6% (n = 79) and 97.5% (n = 48) insectiv-orous (Ohlendorf 1974). The main prey items by volume are grasshoppers, beetles, wasps, bees, true bugs, cicadas, butterflies, and moths; minor items are fleshy fruits, seeds, spiders, and flies. Beal (1912) reported that Cassins eat more vegetable food (as fruit) in North America than do any other tyrant flycatchers; but virtually all fruit is eaten in fall and winter. Both Ohlendorf (1974) and Blancher and

Robertson (1984) reported complete, or nearly complete, dietary overlap (at the level of insect order) between the two kingbird species. As with foraging behavior, there are greater intraspecific differences in diet between habitats than interspecific differences in the same habitat. In contrast to these similarities, males of both species take a greater proportion of hymenoptera than do their conspecific females (Goldberg 1979). Adults of both kingbird species feed grasshoppers of the same size to their young (Blancher & Robertson 1984); as Westerns' young grow, they are fed progressively larger grasshopper prey (data are unavailable for Cassins). Based on the great similarity in the ecology of these two kingbirds where they co-occur, Blancher and Robertson (1984) argued that it is unlikely that their habitat separation reduces their competition for food, as has previously been implied.

Marin Breeding Distribution

The sole Marin County breeding record of Cassin's Kingbird occurred prior to the atlas period. From 20 May to 14 July 1972, a pair was observed nesting at a ranch along Mesa Road, Bolinas, about one mile SE of Point Reyes Bird Observatory's Palomarin field station (*fide* RS, PRBO). The nest was situated about 40 feet up in a planted Monterey cypress. This extralimital breeding record is the northernmost for California. The species reaches the northern limit of its range in California in the interior of Alameda County, east of San Francisco Bay (McCaskie et al. 1979, ABN).

Historical Trends/Population Threats

Grinnell and Miller (1944) noted an apparent decline of the California population in the 50 to 80 years previous to 1944. From 1968 to 1979, the Cassin's Kingbird population increased in the "California Foothills" (Robbins et al. 1986), which includes coastal counties south of San Francisco Bay. From 1968 to 1989, though, it was relatively stable in California as a whole (USFWS unpubl. analyses).

WESTERN KINGBIRD *Tyrannus verticalis*

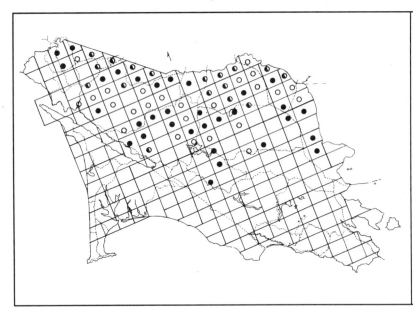

A summer resident from early Apr through Aug, sparingly to mid-Sep.

A fairly common, somewhat local breeder; overall breeding population small.

Recorded in 74 (33.5%) of 221 blocks.

○ Possible   =   25 (34%)
◐ Probable   =   17 (23%)
● Confirmed =   32 (42%)

FSAR = 3   OPI = 222   CI = 2.09

Ecological Requirements

In Marin County, these pugnacious tyrannids primarily inhabit the grassland edges of oak savannah, broken oak woodlands, open riparian, and planted windbreaks and woodlots (particularly eucalyptus). Although trees provide nest sites and foraging perches, Western Kingbirds avoid large blocks of woodland in favor of small isolated stands encircled by relatively dry, insect-rich grasslands. A trunk or two will suffice, and even these need not be present as long as tall bushes or artificial structures provide a few requisite foraging perches and a nest support.

Nests are usually placed in tall trees, if available, but bushes, tops of dead stumps, and, rarely, rocky cliffs or old nests of birds (such as robins or orioles) will do (Bent 1942). Artificial nest sites, such as utility poles, fence posts, and parts of buildings, are also readily used. Western Kingbirds most frequently build tree nests on horizontal branches, but sometimes they place them against trunks, in crotches, or on dead branches. Nest heights range from about 5 to 100 feet above the ground (Bent 1942, references below, D. Shuford pers. obs.). Average nest heights from a variety of habitats in the West range from 12 to 50 feet (Ohlendorf 1974, Goldberg 1979, MacKenzie & Sealy 1981, Blancher & Robertson 1984). Western Kingbirds tend to locate their nests in the middle to upper portions of the tree canopy; mean relative nest heights (nest height/tree height) in a variety of habitats range from 0.64 to 0.80 (Hespenheide 1964, MacKenzie & Sealy 1981, Blancher & Robertson 1984). See Cassin's Kingbird account for comparison of nest location with that species, and MacKenzie and Sealy (1981) for comparison with Eastern Kingbird. Westerns build compact nest cups of twigs, weed stems, plant fibers, and rootlets mixed with wool, plant down, string, hair, paper, and feathers (Bent 1942). The lining consists of animal hair, wool, cotton, or plant down.

Like Cassins, Western Kingbirds forage primarily by sallying off perches to catch flying insects and secondarily by flying down to pick insects off the ground (Blancher & Robertson 1984). Rarely, Westerns glean from vegetation, but more so than Cassins do (Goldberg 1979). In Arizona, Western Kingbirds' perch heights, sally distances, and heights of prey pursued were all significantly different between open riparian and desert habitats. Their perch heights averaged 30 feet (n = 363) and 15 feet (n = 791), respectively (Blancher & Robertson 1984). Their sally distances averaged 50 feet (n = 368) and 42 feet (n = 808), and the heights of prey pursued averaged 40 feet (n = 380) and 18 feet (n = 846) in open riparian and desert habitats.

For comparison of Westerns' and Cassins' foraging niches and for dietary information, see the Cassin's Kingbird account; see Beal (1912) and Dick and Rising (1965) for further information on diet.

Marin Breeding Distribution

Although Western Kingbirds bred on the Marin County coast along the shores of Tomales Bay during the atlas period, they primarily occupied lowland ranchlands, oak savannah, and oak woodland districts of the northern interior. The absence of breeding kingbirds on the grassland-swathed, fog-drenched Point Reyes peninsula may have reflected the low availability in this moist environment of large insects, such as grasshoppers, needed to supply the demands of voracious young. Suitable nest sites are surely available there, around ranchyards and windbreaks. Representative nesting locations were about 1 mi. N of Millerton Point, Tomales Bay (NE 6/27/82 –DS); Soulajoule Reservoir (NE 5/21/82 –DS); Hicks Valley (ON 5/?/82 –ScC); and Mt. Burdell, Novato (NE 4/29/81 –DS).

Historical Trends/Population Threats

Historically, numbers of breeding Western Kingbirds have no doubt increased in Marin County, at least locally in pastoral areas. The reason for this trend is the large increase in available nesting sites for the species from tree plantings (especially eucalyptus) in open country and from construction of artificial structures. On the whole, numbers of Western Kingbirds were relatively stable on Breeding Bird Surveys in California from 1968 to 1989, though they increased from 1980 to 1989 (USFWS unpubl. analyses).

Larks
Family *Alaudidae*

HORNED LARK *Eremophila alpestris*

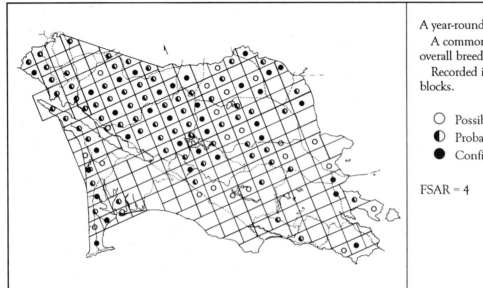

A year-round resident.
 A common, fairly widespread breeder; overall breeding population fairly large.
 Recorded in 123 (55.6%) of 221 blocks.

○	Possible	=	23 (19%)
◑	Probable	=	66 (54%)
●	Confirmed	=	34 (28%)

FSAR = 4   OPI = 492   CI = 2.09

Ecological Requirements

These aerial songsters inhabit Marin County's short-cropped grasslands of the flatlands or low rolling hills, sparsely vegetated sand dunes, barren disturbed fields, and summer-fallow stubble fields. The salient features of Horned Larks' breeding habitats are relative dryness and very sparse grass or weed cover. Pickwell (1931) found that, in a single season, growth and increase in vegetation during the first nesting effort caused abandonment of the initial site and selection of a more open site for the second nest. This emphasizes the importance to Horned Larks of very open ground for nesting.

Horned Larks usually build their nests flush to the ground in shallow cavities that females dig out with their bills and feet; less frequently they place them in natural depressions. A nest generally has a protective feature, such as a small rock or tuft of overhanging grass, on the side of the prevailing winds. On the opposite side there is a "pavement" covering the excavated dirt made of flattened pellets of dried mud, corncobs, cornstalks, or cow dung. This presumably serves as camouflage. The birds build their nest cups primarily of dried grasses and weed stems and line them with fine grasses, plant down, soft plant fibers, seed heads, wool, fur, rags, paper, string, or feathers

(Pickwell 1931, DuBois 1935, Verbeek 1967, Beason & Franks 1974).

Foraging Horned Larks walk and run, but never hop, between stops to pick items from the ground or low vegetation. The diet of the coastal and San Joaquin Valley breeding subspecies *(E. a. actia)* was found by McAtee (1905) to differ "remarkably" from those subspecies outside of California in the high percentage of vegetable matter consumed. Vegetable food composes 91% of the diet for California birds (n = 267) compared with less than 80% for those in the rest of the country. Of the vegetable food, 51% is weed seed and the rest is grain, both wild and cultivated varieties. Animal food comprises about 9% of the diet overall, with a peak of 28% in June, and consists of beetles, true bugs, ants, grasshoppers, caterpillars, other insects, and spiders (McAtee 1905, Beal 1910); adults, of course, feed the insects to their young.

Marin Breeding Distribution

During the atlas period, Horned Larks were concentrated in Marin County's low, rolling ranchlands of the central and northern sectors and along the western fringe of the Point Reyes peninsula. They avoided steep grassy hills

268

throughout their range here. Representative breeding localities were ranch on S side of Walker Creek about 1.5 mi. E of Hwy. 1 (FY 6/12/82 –DS); E side of Tomales Bay near Millerton Point (FY 5/13/82 –DS); Mt. Burdell, Novato (NY 4/29/81 –ITi); Redwood Dump, Novato (NE 5/17/78 –DS); Big Rock Ridge (FL 5/9/81 –DS).

Historical Trends/Population Threats

Few prior data exist, but numbers of Horned Larks were relatively stable on Breeding Bird Surveys in California from 1968 to 1989, despite a decline from 1980 to 1989 (USFWS unpubl. analyses). Historically, the intensive

changes to grasslands brought about by crop agriculture and grazing in California must have had a profound effect upon Horned Larks. Grazing likely has improved the Horned Lark's lot by keeping vegetation short and sparse. Crop agriculture likely has eliminated much habitat for breeding birds, but fallow fields may support larger winter populations than formerly. The California Horned Lark *(E. a. actia)* is currently a Candidate (Category 2) for federal listing as Threatened or Endangered (USFWS 1991), though the Marin population, at least, appears healthy.

Swallows
Family *Hirundinidae*

PURPLE MARTIN *Progne subis*

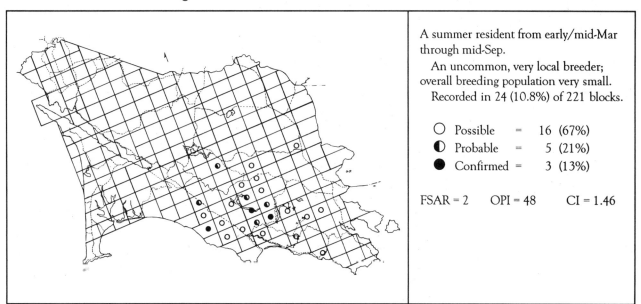

A summer resident from early/mid-Mar through mid-Sep.

An uncommon, very local breeder; overall breeding population very small.

Recorded in 24 (10.8%) of 221 blocks.

○	Possible	=	16 (67%)
◑	Probable	=	5 (21%)
●	Confirmed	=	3 (13%)

FSAR = 2   OPI = 48   CI = 1.46

Ecological Requirements

The largest of our swallows is also by far the most enigmatic. Of the two known colony sites in Marin County, one is in a large dead snag in a clearing in the Douglas fir forest atop Inverness Ridge. The other is on the eastern slope of Bolinas Ridge, above Kent Lake, where a fire in 1945 devastated the Douglas fir–coast redwood forest and left numerous large snags. The Marin County sites seem

typical of those in forested regions elsewhere in California and the West, where most Martins breed in natural clearings or those left by forest fires or lumbering activities (G&M 1944, Richmond 1953, Finlay 1975, Jackman & Scott 1975). Forests or trees per se are not required as long as suitable nest sites and foraging areas are present. Breeding sites are often near the insect-productive waters of ponds, lakes, reservoirs, and rivers (Richmond 1953, Jackson & Tate 1974, Jackman & Scott 1975, D. Shuford pers. obs.). However, these foraging habitats may be at some distance from the nest, since Purple Martins have a long daily cruising radius.

Martins, like many swallows, are cavity nesters. Formerly most Martins nested in natural situations, but populations east of the Rockies now nest mostly in artificial sites, particularly in Martin "apartment houses" (as many as 200 boxes) and in gourds hung from poles. Most western birds nest in natural sites, and they rarely use nest boxes, among artificial sites (G&M 1944, Richmond 1953, Phillips et al. 1964). Most natural nest sites are tree or stump cavities, usually abandoned holes of our larger woodpeckers. Other natural sites include cavities or crevices in cliffs, in lava tubes, or under boulders (Sprunt 1942, ABN). Artificial sites include cracks and crevices of buildings, undersides of bridges, and streetlights (Sprunt 1942, G&M 1944, Roberson 1985). Pristine surroundings are not the issue, as indicated by a Sacramento colony that habitually occupies the air vents on the underside of a freeway overpass above a transit bus parking lot. Nests have been recorded from 3 to 130 feet above ground or water (Sprunt 1942). In the East, Martins showed no preference for the various height intervals of nest boxes placed between 7 and 26 feet (Jackson & Tate 1974). Hence, Sprunt's (1942) report that most nests in houses are from 15 to 20 feet probably reflects the preference of the "landlords" rather than the tenants. My few observations of Martins' tree nest sites in California suggest that most are situated high in large dead snags. These large-diameter boles are likely to be most attractive to large woodpeckers and to have decayed first near their tops (see woodpecker accounts).

Martins construct nests sporadically for about a month prior to egg laying. Initially they add such materials as dead leaves, sticks, and paper but then lay down a relatively solid mat of sticks and mud to about the level of the entry hole. The mat slopes back to the rear and has a small, shallow cup for the eggs (Johnston & Hardy 1962). Other nesting materials might include grass, feathers, rags, pieces of rubber, string, or bark. Occasionally when the nest is open to the elements, the birds build a rim of mud in front of the nest (Sprunt 1942, Allen & Nice 1952). After completing the structure of the nest, the adults add green leaves and replace them as they dry out. The green leaves may possibly serve to supply moisture to the eggs during incubation (Taverner 1933), to cool the nest cavity by evaporation (Sprunt 1942), or to supply fumigant that acts against ectoparasites developing in the detritus of the nest (Johnston & Hardy 1962).

Martins forage almost exclusively on the wing. They fly with a rapid flapping of wings, alternating with periods of sailing in straight lines or long, sweeping arcs. They apparently feed occasionally on the ground for terrestrial insects (Sprunt 1942) or catch insects from the tops of weeds as they dart past (Beal 1918). Martins forage at heights from a few feet to greater than 500 feet, but most frequently between about 200 and 300 feet (Johnston & Hardy 1962)—generally higher than our other swallows. In Marin County, Martins apparently forage mainly above the higher ridges over terrestrial habitats. Birds also come down to feed in the lowlands, especially over ponds and coastal estuaries (in particular Bolinas Lagoon). Birds forage either singly or in groups, especially early in the spring, when insect food is localized (Johnston & Hardy 1962). The diet (Feb-Sep) is entirely animal, consisting primarily of insects (Beal 1918, n = 205). The main prey are bees, wasps, ants, flies, dragonflies, true bugs, beetles, and moths; minor items are grasshoppers, butterflies, mayflies, spiders, and sowbugs. In Alberta, the main prey fed to nestlings are dragonflies, flower flies, butterflies, and midges (Walsh 1978). The diet there varies with time of day, season, and weather. The size of prey fed to young increases as the young develop (Finlay 1971, Walsh 1978). Martins regurgitate pellets consisting of the hard parts of insects (Richmond 1953). They may need calcium, perhaps for egg formation, which they obtain from crushed bivalve shells, eggshells, grit, lime, or bones (Richmond 1953).

Marin Breeding Distribution

During the atlas years, Purple Martins were recorded in Marin County in the breeding season mostly around the southern portions of Inverness and Bolinas ridges. Many of these records could have pertained to birds foraging at some distance from the two known localized colonies described above and below. Confirmed nesting records were Inverness Ridge above Five Brooks (FY 6/?/77 – RMS; NB 5/31/80 –JGE); Kent Lake (NY 5/31/77 – RMS; FY 7/23/81 –GFMc); and Alpine Lake (FY 6/?/82 –ITi). The latter record may have involved birds that had moved from the vicinity of Kent Lake. In Marin County, breeding Martins were locally fairly numerous in the Kent Lake area and nearby on Bolinas and Carson ridges (e.g., 15 seen in this general area on 6/5/82 –DS, ITi). Most of these birds probably nested on the slopes of Bolinas Ridge above Kent Lake, but the steep terrain and difficult access have so far limited observer attempts to explore this area thoroughly. Since at least the late 1980s, Purple Martins have been seen regularly in the breeding season around the Seadrift spit at Bolinas Lagoon, suggesting that they may now nest there (K. Hansen pers. comm.). Elsewhere in Marin, breeding Martins were very infrequently encountered. The patchy distribution of breeding Purple Martins in Marin County and elsewhere in California and the West is puzzling. Although nest sites may limit their occurrence locally, the woodpecker holes upon which Martins depend are widespread. It may be that the combination of few nest sites and few suitable foraging areas limit them. In the arid West, conditions that favor adequate prey for these large aerial insectivores are probably much more localized than they are in the humid East—but still perhaps more widespread than the distribution of breeding Martins in the West suggests.

Historical Trends/Population Threats

Both early historical and recent accounts indicate that Purple Martins have always been very local breeders in Marin County and central California. Mailliard (1900) considered the Purple Martin "sparingly summer resident" in Marin County. Grinnell and Wythe (1927) reported only three sites in the San Francisco Bay Area where Purple Martins were "known to have remained through the nesting season." Two of these sites were in Marin County, at Olema and Nicasio. Stephens and Pringle (1933) considered the Martin an uncommon migrant or transient in Marin County; they made no mention of it breeding in the county. For California in general, Grinnell and Miller (1944) noted that, although Purple Martins are considered "fairly common . . . many suitable localities lack this swallow." In addition, they noted Martins spreading to some districts built up by people "in recent years" and that their numbers were probably increasing.

Because of declining populations, the Purple Martin is currently considered by the California Department of Fish and Game as a Bird Species of Special Concern (Remsen 1978, CDFG 1991b). Additionally, the Purple Martin has been on the Audubon Society Blue List from 1975 to 1981 and on their list of Species of Special Concern from 1982 to 1986 (Tate 1986). In California, though, Martins have declined substantially only in the southern region of the state (Remsen 1978, Garrett & Dunn 1981). Most reported declines in northern California (including Marin County) have involved only local areas and have been based largely on anecdotal evidence. Tate (1981) quoted one northern California observer who claimed that "the species no longer nests in forests in central California." This statement is far off the mark, as documented by the Marin County data and by incidental observations else-

where in northern California (ABN). Martin numbers on Breeding Bird Surveys were relatively stable from 1968 to 1989 (Robbins et al. 1986, USFWS unpubl. analyses). However, Breeding Bird Survey techniques may not be adequate to determine trends, in California or elsewhere, of species like the Martin that occur in low relative abundance and are patchily distributed. In California, it would be more effective to identify a large number of Martin colonies and monitor them on a regular basis.

Although North American Martin populations have been stable or increasing in recent years (Robbins et al. 1986), competition with European Starlings and House Sparrows has been widely reported as the cause of Purple Martin declines continentwide. Very few studies have addressed the problem specifically (Brown 1981). Jackson and Tate (1974) generally found an inverse correlation between the rates of Martin and of House Sparrow occupancy of apartment houses and gourds. They also concluded that House Sparrows were more serious competitors with Martins than were Starlings. They thought that House Sparrows repel Martins at small colonies and usurp their nests and destroy eggs at larger ones, and that Starlings are not serious nest site competitors but more a threat as predators on nestlings and eggs. Brown (1981), on the other hand, concluded that Starlings were the main threat to Martins and documented declines of Martins and increases in Starlings at unmanaged colonies. Both the House Sparrow and Starling likely have less effect on the more remote and patchily distributed Martin colonies in the West. More specific studies are needed to document the effects of these alien species on Martins and other native birds.

Prolonged periods of rain during the nestling phase may prove fatal to both young and adult Purple Martins and may produce dramatic changes in local populations (Robbins et al. 1986). This should be taken into account in any monitoring scheme. Although logging may open up some habitat to this species, it may also eliminate potential nest sites by snag removal, especially following forest fires, in areas that otherwise might be colonized by Martins.

TREE SWALLOW *Tachycineta bicolor*

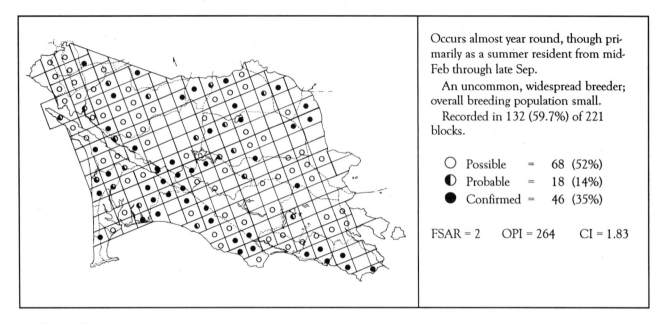

Occurs almost year round, though primarily as a summer resident from mid-Feb through late Sep.

An uncommon, widespread breeder; overall breeding population small.

Recorded in 132 (59.7%) of 221 blocks.

○	Possible	=	68 (52%)
◐	Probable	=	18 (14%)
●	Confirmed	=	46 (35%)

FSAR = 2   OPI = 264   CI = 1.83

Ecological Requirements

The dazzling metallic blue backs of breeding Tree Swallows inspire awe as the birds dip low over their favored foraging haunts of ponds, open streams, wet meadows, marshes, and irrigated fields. Of Marin County's swallows, Trees are the most closely wedded to moist habitats for feeding and nesting. Tree Swallows nest solitarily or only loosely colonially. When suitable nest sites are abundant, these birds choose not to nest close together; when nest sites are in close proximity, there is spatial and temporal spacing of nests enforced by territorial defense (Muldal et al. 1985). Tree Swallows are cavity nesters whose natural nest sites are decaying pockets in trees, such as hollow limbs, dead trunks, or old woodpecker holes. These are usually found at the heads of lakes, borders of freshwater marshes, and along river valleys, where whole stands of dead trees occur (Kuerzi 1941). The birds strongly prefer isolated nest sites or those in open stands; they avoid sites shaded by vegetation (Austin & Low 1932). Tree Swallows also readily adapt to nest boxes or cavities in the eaves of buildings. Suitable nest sites can be such a limiting factor that the erection of nest boxes may cause colonization far from moist habitats where ecological conditions are poor (Kuerzi 1941). Nest height ranges from about 2 to 50 feet (av. about 15 ft.) (Tyler 1942, Airola 1980, D. Shuford pers. obs.). The nest foundation is an accumulation of dry grass, straw, pine needles, or rootlets at the bottom of the nest cavity (Austin & Low 1932, Kuerzi 1941, Tyler 1942). A hollow for the eggs, either to one side or in the center, is lined thickly with feathers. The quills are buried in the

foundation or point away from the central hollow (Austin & Low 1932), and the feathers cover the eggs when left unattended (Stocek 1970). Older birds add most feathers to the nest before egg laying. Younger breeders tend to add fewer feathers, mostly as incubation progresses, and sometimes construct an incomplete foundation or lay eggs on the bare floor of a nest box (Kuerzi 1941). Reuse of nests by the same individuals in successive years has been low in some studies (Low 1933, 1934) and high in others (Chapman 1935, 1939).

Tree Swallows normally forage for aerial insects within 50 to 100 feet of the ground and often much lower, for instance while skimming close to the surface of ponds. Their flight is rapid and includes much swooping and darting, but infrequent soaring. They will also alight on the ground or on bushes to procure insects and vegetable matter, especially when aerial insects are unavailable (Tyler 1942, Erskine 1984). The diet overall consists of about 80.5% animal food and 19.5% vegetable (Beal 1918, n = 343). The animal food is primarily insects, along with a few spiders; the main items are flies, beetles, bees, wasps, ants, and true bugs; minor items are moths, caterpillars, grasshoppers, dragonflies, and mayflies. The diet differs from that of other swallows of this latitude in the appreciable quantity of vegetable food, in the form of fruits and seeds, consumed throughout the year. In the East, vegetable fare ranges from 1% in spring, to 21% in summer, to 30% in fall and winter (Martin et al. 1951, n = 362). Kuerzi (1941) reported that the normal foraging radius at a Connecticut colony is about a mile and sometimes up to three miles. Tree Swallows sometimes depart en masse from colonies on overcast days. On cold and cloudy days, they probably travel to lakes and ponds where the air over the water is warmer and more insect-productive (Chapman 1955). Birds forage much farther afield in rainy than in fair weather. During a period of inclement weather, a banded female was found five miles from her nest site at a Marin County colony (Stewart 1972). At such times, adults also resort to feeding on fruits for lack of insects (Chapman 1955). Although adults can subsist on vegetable fare, they do not feed it to their young. During periods of cold and rain there can be high nest failure (Stewart 1972), but, presumably by switching to fruit, adult Tree Swallows survive better under these conditions than do other species of swallows.

Marin Breeding Distribution

During the atlas period, Tree Swallows were widespread, but patchily distributed breeders in Marin County. They were concentrated somewhat along the coast where marshes and permanent streams are more prevalent. Many confirmed records for the interior of the county were near major roads that invariably paralleled streams. Representative breeding records were Muddy Hollow at Limantour Estero (FY 6/29/81 –DS); Palomarin (NB-NE 4/16–5/15/77 –SJ); Slide Ranch, S of Stinson Beach (ON 5/24/81 –DS); and Maggetti Ranch, Marshall-Petaluma Rd. (ON 5/27/82 –DS).

Historical Trends/Population Threats

Mailliard (1900) considered the Tree Swallow a summer resident that was "abundant" in Marin County's "white oak" regions. I suspect this was a typographic error as he also reported the Violet-green Swallow as "sparingly summer resident." Currently, the relative abundance of these species is roughly the reverse of that reported by Mailliard. Also, the Violet-green, not the Tree Swallow, is the swallow of the "white oaks." Tree Swallows were relatively stable on Breeding Bird Surveys in California from 1968 to 1989, despite an apparent slight decline from 1980 to 1989 (USFWS unpubl. analyses).

VIOLET-GREEN SWALLOW *Tachycineta thalassina*

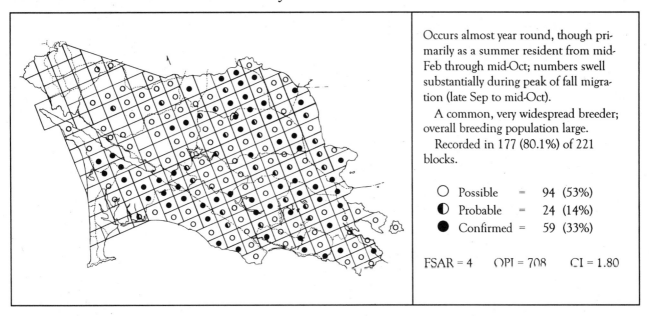

Occurs almost year round, though primarily as a summer resident from mid-Feb through mid-Oct; numbers swell substantially during peak of fall migration (late Sep to mid-Oct).

A common, very widespread breeder; overall breeding population large.

Recorded in 177 (80.1%) of 221 blocks.

○	Possible	=	94 (53%)
◐	Probable	=	24 (14%)
●	Confirmed	=	59 (33%)

FSAR = 4   OPI = 708   CI = 1.80

Ecological Requirements

This stunning beauty is our only truly widespread woodland- and forest-inhabiting swallow. The Violet-green Swallow, unlike the Tree, generally has no strong attachment to water, though it may prefer to nest near it in arid areas with an otherwise low prey base. In Marin County, it nests on the edges of, or in clearings in, all the major forest and woodland types, as well as in urban-suburban areas. Violet-greens here especially favor open oak woodlands for nesting. Locally, they select mostly old woodpecker holes or natural cavities in trees for nest sites, although birds will readily use nest boxes and crevices in buildings, such as those found under Spanish-style roof tiles. In some regions they nest more frequently in cracks or cavities in cliffs, in boulder piles, in tufa towers, and, rarely, in old Cliff

Swallow nests or Bank Swallow burrows (Bent 1942, Gaines 1988). Nest heights may range from ground level, as in boulder crevices, presumably up to a hundred feet or more in cliffs. Violet-greens make nests primarily of fine grass stems, twigs, and rootlets, and they line the cups thickly with feathers (Bent 1942, Edson 1943, Combellack 1954).

Violet-green Swallows forage at varying altitudes. They sweep low over ponds, fields, and marshes but often sail hundreds of feet above the ground, alternately flapping and gliding with their downcurved wings. They also land on the ground and hop about, presumably in search of insects (Erskine 1984). In contrast to Tree Swallows, Violet-greens are not inclined to forage only over moist habitats but will search for their aerial prey over virtually any terrain. The diet (Mar–Sep) is 100% insectivorous, with the most important items being true bugs, flies, wasps and bees, beetles, and ants; minor items are moths, caterpillars, and mayflies (Beal 1918, n = 110). Seasonal variation in the insect diet has been noted.

Marin Breeding Distribution

Violet-green Swallows bred widely in Marin County during the atlas period and appeared to be most numerous in the open oak woodlands in the Novato area. They were sparse or lacking as breeders in some of the grassland areas in the northwestern part of the county, presumably because of a paucity of suitable nesting locations. Representative breeding stations were Hick's Valley Rd., Novato (ON 4/?/82 –ScC); Mt. Burdell, Novato (NY/FY 4/2/81 –ITi); near Pine Mountain/Carson Ridge area (ON 6/5/82 –DS, ITi); and Cascade Canyon, Fairfax (ON 5/11/81 –DS).

Historical Trends/Population Threats

See comments under Tree Swallow. Numbers of Violet-green Swallows were relatively stable on Breeding Bird Surveys in California from 1968 to 1989, despite an apparent slight increase from 1980 to 1989 (USFWS unpubl. analyses).

Barn and Cliff swallows bustling about their domestic duties enliven ranchyards throughout most of Marin County. Drawing by Keith Hansen, 1990.

NORTHERN ROUGH-WINGED SWALLOW *Stelgidopteryx serripennis*

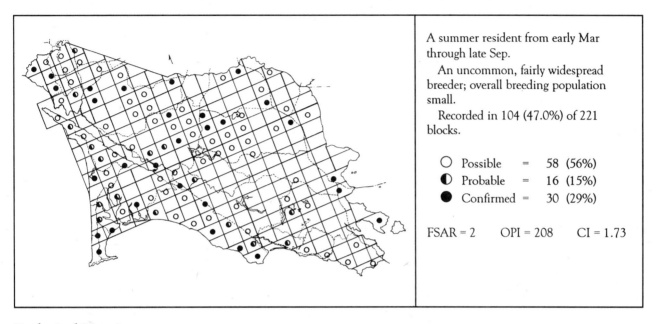

A summer resident from early Mar through late Sep.

An uncommon, fairly widespread breeder; overall breeding population small.

Recorded in 104 (47.0%) of 221 blocks.

○	Possible	=	58 (56%)
◑	Probable	=	16 (15%)
●	Confirmed	=	30 (29%)

FSAR = 2   OPI = 208   CI = 1.73

Ecological Requirements

Rough-winged Swallows, with their earth-tone plumages and guttural voices, usually breed around Marin County's streams, ponds, estuarine margins, and ocean bluffs that afford suitable nest sites. Water is not a strict requirement, though, as these birds are equally at home far from water where banks in gullies, road cuts, or similar settings serve their nesting needs. Although Grinnell and Miller (1944) recognized the breadth of moisture conditions over which Rough-wings are found, they emphasized their tolerance for and apparent choice of arid environments. To my mind, moisture conditions are of minor importance as long as suitable nest sites and very open terrain for foraging are available. Nest site preference appears to limit Rough-wing numbers, which in turn may allow their languid foraging style, effective in catching certain types of insects that occur over a range of moisture conditions but in no great abundance.

Rough-winged Swallows nest in isolated pairs or in small loose colonies, and their earthen hues blend well with their typical nest holes in vertical sand, dirt, or gravel banks. It appears that Rough-wings, unlike Bank Swallows, rarely if ever dig nest holes from scratch, although there is some controversy over this point (Lunk 1962). The holes Rough-wings occupy in earthen banks are usually made by kingfishers, rodents, and Bank Swallows. Although their predisposition not to, or inability to, dig burrows limits their numbers locally, Rough-winged Swallows generally are much more widespread than Bank

Swallows, which are restricted by their need for soft soil in which to dig burrows (Garrison et al. 1987). Rough-wings also nest in natural cracks and crevices in rock faces, cliffs, and caves, but only very rarely in trees. They also readily use artificial sites, such as crevices in buildings, ledges and crannies under bridges and culverts, air vents under freeway overpasses, drainpipes, gutters, and artificial nest tubes (Dingle 1942, Lunk 1962, D. Shuford pers. obs.). Nest holes may be 1 to 50 feet above the ground or water, and burrow length may range from nine inches to six feet (Dingle 1942). The nest foundation is an "indiscriminate pile" of material, but the nest cup itself is well shaped and lined with softer materials. The main nest materials are twigs, weed stems, rootlets, grass, leaves, bark shreds, plant fibers, flower parts, or dung. The lining is usually of fine grasses with a few green leaves or petals sometimes added as a final touch. In contrast to Bank Swallows, Rough-wings do not line their nests with feathers (Lunk 1962).

Rough-winged Swallows generally forage in rather slow, deliberate, often straight flight very low to the ground over ponds, streams, estuaries, fields, gullies, and dry arroyos; birds will occasionally land on the ground to procure food (Wolinski 1980, Sealy 1982). The diet (Apr–Sep) is virtually all animal matter, primarily insects (Beal 1918, n = 136). The main food items are flies, wasps, bees, true bugs, beetles, and ants; minor items are moths, caterpillars, dragonflies, mayflies, grasshoppers, spiders, and snails.

275

Marin Breeding Distribution

Breeding Rough-winged Swallows were patchily distributed throughout Marin County during the atlas years. They generally occupied lowland valleys, usually near water, and their presence reflected that of available nesting sites. Representative nesting locations were Abbott's Lagoon (ON 4/?/82 —JGE); low hills NE of Schooner Bay, Point Reyes (ON 4/20/82 —DS); near Tomales (NY 6/2/77 —RMS); base of Antonio Mountain, Chileno

Valley (FY 6/4/82 —DS, ScC); and pipes in seawall at Tiburon Fisheries Lab (ON several years during atlas period —BiL).

Historical Trends/Population Threats

Little historical data exist. Numbers increased on Breeding Bird Surveys in California from 1968 to 1979 (Robbins et al. 1986) but were relatively stable when analyses were extended from 1968 to 1989 (USFWS unpubl.).

CLIFF SWALLOW   *Hirundo pyrrhonota*

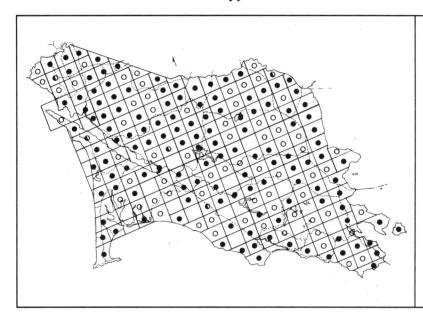

A summer resident from early/mid-Mar to early Sep.

A very common, nearly ubiquitous breeder; overall breeding population extremely large.

Recorded in 202 (91.4%) of 221 blocks.

○	Possible	=	67 (33%)
◑	Probable	=	5 (2%)
●	Confirmed	=	130 (64%)

FSAR = 5   OPI = 1010   CI = 2.31

Ecological Requirements

This swallow's name harkens back to days of former glory when most Cliff Swallow colonies looked out with commanding views over the untrammeled open spaces of the American West. Today, most Cliff Swallows have forsaken their ancestral haunts for the company of others of their kind that have taken up domestic duties in more "civilized" surroundings. The main requisites of nesting Cliff Swallows are vertical walls for nest attachment, a nearby source of mud for nest building, and open foraging areas (Emlen 1954). Vertical walls limit access of predators, and an overhang usually shields the nest from being dissolved by rains. Cliff Swallows are highly gregarious, and it is not uncommon to find hundreds or even thousands of nests at one site. Natural nest sites include cliffs, caves, sandbanks, and, very rarely, the undersides of large tree branches (Gross 1942). In addition, Cliffs sometimes take over and usually modify occupied or abandoned nests of

Bank or Barn swallows, Black Phoebes, and American Robins (Mayhew 1958). Today most Cliff Swallows nest on human structures. Perhaps the most common sites are under the eaves of buildings, especially barns; nests are usually on the outsides of barns but sometimes are inside, particularly in the East. In California, Cliff Swallows also nest abundantly under bridges and freeway overpasses, in stream or irrigation ditch culverts, and on dam faces. Unlike Barn Swallows, they will not enter buildings through tiny openings but must have a large entrance of at least about eight feet on a side (Samuel 1971).

There is no well-defined upper limit to the height of nests, as Cliff Swallows sometimes place them hundreds of feet above the ground on cliffs. At the lower end, though, they must have at least a three-foot clearance over water or an eight-foot clearance over land (Emlen 1954). A typical mud nest is gourd or retort shaped; the globular nest chamber extends forward into a short tubular entrance tunnel with the mouth directed downward (Emlen 1954). Since nests are often crammed together or built on top of each other, the shape varies. Birds may reuse or repair last year's nests, but these are usually not the same individuals that used the nests the previous year (Mayhew 1958). Gathering mud is a highly social activity that a group participates in together. To collect mud with their beaks, birds land at a favorable site and hold their wings partly or fully extended above their backs and fluttering slightly (Emlen 1954). They usually collect mud close to the colony, but birds may go up to a half mile or a mile to bring it back (Storer 1927, Emlen 1954). Nest building proceeds intermittently as successive layers of mud are allowed to dry before adding the next (Buss 1942, Emlen 1954). The lining of straw, grass, and leaves is often deposited, and eggs laid, before completion of the nest (Buss 1942); nest construction or repair may continue throughout the season. In the same areas as nesting Barn Swallows, Cliffs choose mud with a higher sand and lower silt content (Kilgore & Knudsen 1977), presumably because this mixture, though not as strong as less sandy ones, is more easily worked in construction of the Cliff Swallow's more complex nests.

This species often forages relatively low over meadows, fields, and open water, but in the warmth of the day, birds will soar at heights of 500 to 1500 feet over various habitats (Emlen 1952). Cliffs usually forage more than 100 feet high, consistently higher than Barn Swallows often foraging over the same area (Samuel 1971). Cliff Swallows mostly forage within a quarter mile of their colonies, but birds may go as far afield as four miles, especially during the warmer parts of the day (Emlen 1952). Their social tendencies extend to the feeding grounds, where most birds at any moment are loosely aggregated in a single foraging unit. The diet (Mar–Sep) is 99.4% animal food, primarily insects, along with a few spiders (Beal 1918, n = 375). The main food items are beetles, true bugs, bees, wasps, ants, and flies; minor items are moths, caterpillars, grasshoppers, dragonflies, mayflies, lace-winged flies, spiders, and snails. Vegetable food consists of a few berries.

Marin Breeding Distribution

The Cliff Swallow was one of the most common and ubiquitous breeding birds in Marin County during the atlas period. Most of its breeding sites were in the open

lowland valleys or rolling hills, where the vast majority of colonies were on human structures; scattered colonies occurred on ocean bluffs and a few small inland cliffs. Representative nesting locations were ocean cliff at Drake's Beach (NB 4/2/81 –DS); Red Barn, Bear Valley Headquarters, PRNS (ON 7/18/80 –DS); Kleiser Ranch, Walker Creek (ON 5/23/82 –DS); and Stafford Lake, Novato (ON 5/?/82 –ScC).

Historical Trends/Population Threats

With the spread of European settlers across the continent, Cliff Swallows were able to expand dramatically as suitable nesting sites increased and much of the land was opened up (Gross 1942). California was no exception (G&M 1944). In the arid West, irrigation and watering of lawns and gardens has also increased the availability of mud during the dry season, which coincides with most of the breeding season in California. In recent times, such advances have been offset to a limited degree by nest parasitism and ejection of the swallows' young and eggs by House Sparrows; by dense urban development, eliminating feeding areas; by the painting of barns, which reduces adhesion of the nests; and by destruction of nests by people concerned with the "unsightly and unsanitary" droppings under colonies. Concern over the cost of painting and maintenance of the Red Barn at the Point Reyes National Seashore Headquarters at Bear Valley prompted destruction of the nests there in 1981 and 1982. A compromise struck between the Park Service and local Audubon groups provided for fencing off some nest sites and allowing others to remain. Elsewhere, management for Cliff Swallows has been very effective in increasing local populations (Buss 1942, Gross 1942). Like other swallows, Cliff Swallow nestlings and adults may suffer high mortality when extended periods of cold or rainy weather depress their prey base of aerial insects (Gross 1942, Stewart 1972). Numbers of Cliff Swallows on Breeding Bird Surveys in California increased from 1968 to 1979 (Robbins et al. 1986) but were relatively stable when analyses were extended from 1968 to 1989 (USFWS unpubl.). These increases are almost certainly linked to ongoing development in the state that provides additional nest sites and also perhaps to continued expansion of the agricultural industry and its irrigation systems, which provide mud for nest building.

BARN SWALLOW *Hirundo rustica*

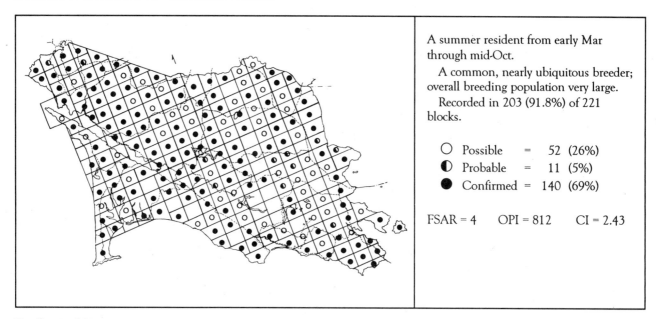

A summer resident from early Mar through mid-Oct.

A common, nearly ubiquitous breeder; overall breeding population very large.

Recorded in 203 (91.8%) of 221 blocks.

○ Possible   = 52 (26%)
◑ Probable   = 11 (5%)
● Confirmed = 140 (69%)

FSAR = 4   OPI = 812   CI = 2.43

Ecological Requirements

The graceful, fork-tailed profile of this sleek swallow is a familiar image of Marin County's open lowland ranch-lands, where the bird nests most commonly around barn-yards. Barn Swallows occur widely throughout unforested regions, even where developed, as long as there are suitable nest sites, nest material, and extensive insect-productive airways low to the ground. The latter occur over grasslands, marshlands, ponds, estuaries, meadows, weed fields, and beaches. Under natural conditions, Barn Swallows attach their nests to the ceilings or walls of shallow caves; to the inner walls of great hollow trees; or place them in niches, crevices, or fissures in rocky cliffs; on shelves or ledges of projecting rock with an overhang above; and in holes or natural cavities of cutbanks (Bent 1942, Speich et al. 1986). The most commonly reported natural nest sites are sea caves and ocean bluffs and, inland, cliffs and banks of rivers and lakes. Water does not appear to be a requisite; rather wave action or erosion often have produced suitable sites for nest attachment. In caves, Barn Swallows place nests on the walls, on small irregularities or niches, or on the ceiling on vertical faces, at cracks, or where pieces of rocks have fallen (Speich et al. 1986). Today their nests in the wilds are rare. They now nest mostly under the eaves of (or inside) barns and other buildings or under culverts, bridges, wharves, and boathouses. The tops of nests located in caves and culverts are usually within a couple of inches of the overhang of the ceiling (Grzybowski 1979, Speich et al. 1986). Unlike Cliff Swallows, Barns need only a small opening to enter an enclosed nest site, such as a building (Samuel 1971). In addition to their greater

availability, advantages of human structures as nest sites may be reduced risks of predation, substrates superior for long-term attachment of nests, more favorable thermal environments, and access to otherwise unexploited local-ized food sources (Speich et al. 1986). Barn Swallows are only loosely (passively) colonial with 1 to perhaps 30 or, exceptionally, up to 50 nests at a single site (Bent 1942). Barn Swallows are territorial and, unlike Cliff Swallows, maintain a minimum distance between nests. In New York, Snapp (1976) found that Barn Swallow nests in buildings were rarely less than about 10 feet apart, but in Oklahoma, Grzybowski (1979) found that 60% of the active nests in culvert colonies were closer together than that. These differences perhaps reflect the availability of suitable nest attachment sites.

A nearby source of mud is usually a requisite for nest building. The most common type of nest is an adherent mud nest in the shape of a half cone attached to a vertical surface under an overhang. As in Cliff Swallow nest sites, the vertical surface limits access of predators, and the overhang protects the mud nest from the dissolving effects of rain. Barn Swallows' mud gathering, unlike Cliff Swallows', is an individual activity, not a social one. Birds fly to the ground and stand around with their wings held at their sides (unlike Cliffs) and gather mud on or inside their bills (Samuel 1971). "In building their nests the barn swallows show themselves expert masons, but unlike the cliff swallows and like the ancient Egyptians they cannot make bricks without straw" (Bent 1942). Indeed, Barn Swallows incorporate straw, grass, and horse hair into the mud walls, apparently to aid in holding the mud together; this likely explains why their nests are more durable than those of Cliff Swallows (Kilgore & Knudsen 1977). See the Cliff Swallow account for differences in types of mud used. Barn Swallows typically line their nests with feathers and may add some of this lining even after eggs are laid (Samuel 1971). Nests placed on flat supporting structures are more circular and shallower than the cone-shaped nests attached to walls, and those in corners or crevices are built to fit the constraints of the space. Nests in narrow crannies or holes with supporting sides and floors may lack a mud foundation and may be made entirely of grasses, straw, feathers, or other available materials; some nests in sea caves are made and lined with seaweed (Bent 1942). Barn Swallows also nest in incomplete or abandoned Cliff Swallow or Black Phoebe nests. They may add to or rebuild nests from previous years or prior nests of the same season (Davis 1937, Bent 1942, Samuel 1971), with a high frequency of reuse by the original occupants (Shields 1984).

While foraging, Barn Swallows fly with rapid directed flight, with their wing tips sweeping back almost parallel to the body as they course low to the ground (cf. Cliff Swallow account). In addition to generally foraging at lower heights than Cliffs, Barns also tend to forage nearer their nest sites (within three-quarters of a mile of nest sites) (Samuel 1971). Barn Swallows may prefer to feed along edge habitats, such as woodland/field borders (Samuel 1971), where wind speeds are reduced and insects are more abundant than in adjacent fields (Grzybowski 1979), but they do forage extensively in very open terrain (D. Shuford pers. obs.). Birds also occasionally alight on the ground to catch food (Bent 1942). More often, especially on cool, foggy mornings when aerial insects are not about in numbers, they follow grazing animals or walking people as they disturb insects from damp grass (D. Shuford pers. obs.). The species' North American diet (Mar–Oct) consists of 99.8% animal matter, primarily insects, along with a few spiders; the little vegetable food eaten is mostly seeds (Beal 1918, n = 467). Barn Swallows' main food items are flies, true bugs, beetles, ants, bees, and wasps; moths, butterflies, caterpillars, grasshoppers, crickets, dragonflies, mayflies, spiders, and snails are of minor importance. Adult birds feed their young mostly food items smaller than 0.4 inch (Turner 1982). They tend to feed on larger items in that size range if available and feed larger items to their broods than they take themselves.

Marin Breeding Distribution

Like the Cliff Swallow, the Barn Swallow was one of Marin County's most ubiquitous breeders during the atlas period, and the two species had almost identical distributions. Most individuals of both species bred in the county's open lowland valleys or rolling hills and built nests in or on human structures. Small numbers of Barn Swallows still nest at scattered sites in ocean bluff sea caves, as detailed below. Representative nesting locations were six nests in sea caves along ocean bluffs just S of Estero Americano (NE/NY 7/12/82 –DS); Wildcat Beach, PRNS (NE in large crack on inside ceiling of sea cave 4/3/81 –DS); and Chileno Valley (NB 5/5/82 –DS).

Historical Trends/Population Threats

Like Cliff Swallows (see account), Barn Swallows have undoubtedly increased in historical times in California because of human activities. From 1968 to 1989, Barn Swallow numbers decreased on Breeding Bird Surveys in California (USFWS unpubl. analyses). Possible explanations of this recent trend are that fewer suitable nest sites exist on modern-day structures than on old barns and houses, and also that fewer low foraging areas exist in densely developed areas.

Jays and Crows
Family *Corvidae*

STELLER'S JAY *Cyanocitta stelleri*

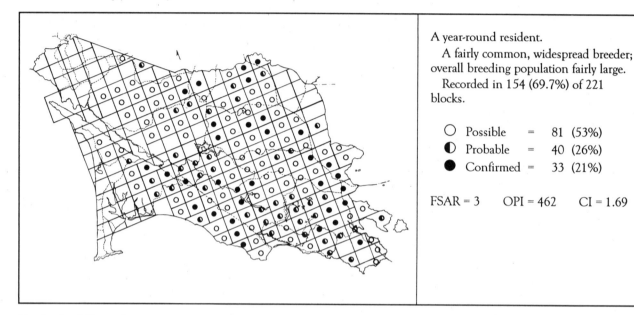

A year-round resident.
  A fairly common, widespread breeder; overall breeding population fairly large.
  Recorded in 154 (69.7%) of 221 blocks.

○	Possible	=	81 (53%)
◐	Probable	=	40 (26%)
●	Confirmed	=	33 (21%)

FSAR = 3   OPI = 462   CI = 1.69

Ecological Requirements

These crested firebrands inhabit Marin County's conifer, mixed conifer, broadleaved evergreen, and coastal riparian forests and bordering eucalyptus groves. All these habitats are generally moist and have relatively tall, closed, shaded canopies. As a rule, though, where forests are extensive, Steller's Jays are more numerous near breaks in the forest than deep within it (Goodwin 1986). Numerous openings, edges, and developed areas for foraging, and denser stands for nesting and shelter, presumably provide the optimal mix for breeding birds. Stellers overlap somewhat with Scrub Jays on the brushy edges of these habitats, especially along hardwood and riparian forests. The Scrub Jay is usually the dominant species when the two come into contact—except immediately around Steller's Jay nests (Brown 1963, 1964). Steller's Jays do not defend territories in the classic sense (Brown 1963, 1964). Instead they defend exclusive areas around their nests beyond which dominance over other Steller's Jays can be viewed as decreasing in a series of concentric circles as distance from the nest area increases. Steller's Jays build their nests in both conifers and broadleaved trees from 2 to 100 feet or more (most 8–25 ft.) above the ground. They usually place them on horizontal branches close to the trunk, less commonly well out on limbs, in holes or troughlike cavities in trees or stubs, or on shelves inside sheds (Bent 1946). The nest itself has a bulky foundation of large sticks reinforced with mud and dead leaves and a deeply hollowed interior of coarse rootlets, grasses, and pine needles.

Like most jays, Stellers are generalist foragers. They forage singly or in pairs, but many feed together at centrally located sources of food, such as at picnic areas and campgrounds. In Tilden Regional Park, Alameda and Contra Costa counties, about two-thirds of foraging occurs on the ground and the rest in trees; ground foraging occurs both beneath the canopy and in openings such as forest clearings or borders (Brown 1964). Steller's Jays obtain most of their food on the ground by hopping about, picking from the surface, and, secondarily, by inserting their bills in loose materials like leaf litter or soil, tossing them aside with sideways flips of the bill. In trees, they hop or fly short distances to procure acorns and fruits, forage on trunks, peel loose bark from branches, inspect old squirrel nests, and glean caterpillars and other insects from the foliage or branchwork. They break open hard objects such as acorns, bay laurel nuts, and sunflower seeds. Holding such an item in one or both feet, the bird raises its whole body and brings it down strongly, with its bill slightly open and the lower mandible making the initial puncturing blow. Acorns and seeds are stored throughout the year, primarily in the ground and in each jay's own dominance area (Brown 1963, 1964). A bird digs a hole with sideways flips of the bill, inserts the object, and covers it over with litter. By storing acorns, Steller's Jays, like Scrubs, are active agents of oak dispersal, particularly in the uphill direction (Grinnell 1936). Steller's Jays are known to steal the food caches of Clark's Nutcrackers and Gray Jays and are suspected of robbing the stores of Acorn Woodpeckers (Burnell & Tomback 1985). The incubating female is fed on and off the nest by the male (Goodwin 1986). The California diet is about 72% vegetable and 28% animal overall, though the latter fare increases considerably in the breeding season (Beal 1910, n = 93). Acorns provide the bulk of the vegetable food, though other fruits, nuts, grains, seeds, and galls are also eaten. Insects, especially bees, wasps, beetles, grasshoppers, crickets, caterpillars, and moths, predominate in the animal portion of the diet. Steller's Jays also eat other birds' eggs, nestling birds, small mammals, frogs, and spiders (Beal 1910). In settled areas, they also consume a wide variety of human foods, which may be very important in the diet locally, particularly at picnic sites and at bird feeding trays.

Marin Breeding Distribution

During the atlas period, Steller's Jays bred throughout Marin County wherever extensive shaded forests occurred. Hence they were absent from broad areas only in the low

rolling hills dominated by grassland, near Tomales and on the outer Point Reyes peninsula, and in the low-lying diked former marshlands around Novato. Most numerous on the conifer-dominated coastal ridges, Steller's Jays were much more localized in the county's interior and along its northern edge, where the birds occurred mostly in deep shaded canyons and on north-facing slopes. Representative nesting locations were Inverness (NB 4/18/82 —DS); Laguna Ranch, PRNS (FY 8/21/79 —JGE); and north slope of Mt. Burdell, Novato (FL 6/2/78 —RMS).

Historical Trends/Population Threats

Steller's Jays have held their own in California despite organized persecution by hunters in earlier times (Erickson 1937, Hooper 1938, G&M 1944). Any minor population decreases in Marin County and elsewhere in California that may have occurred from extensive logging or clearing for development have probably been offset by the effects of increased openings and edges for foraging and supplemental food sources from humans. While increasing elsewhere in the West from 1965 to 1979 (Robbins et al. 1986), Steller's Jay numbers remained relatively stable on Breeding Bird Surveys in California from 1968 to 1989 (USFWS unpubl. analyses).

SCRUB JAY *Aphelocoma coerulescens*

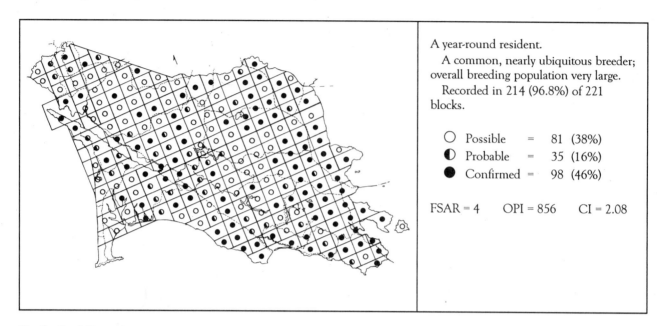

A year-round resident.

A common, nearly ubiquitous breeder; overall breeding population very large. Recorded in 214 (96.8%) of 221 blocks.

○	Possible	=	81 (38%)
◐	Probable	=	35 (16%)
●	Confirmed	=	98 (46%)

FSAR = 4   OPI = 856   CI = 2.08

Ecological Requirements

The inimitable Scrub Jay is the more open habitat-loving of our two jays in Marin County and is dominant where it overlaps with the Steller's Jay (Brown 1963, 1964). Scrub Jays inhabit Marin's open oak woodlands; drier, more open phases of her broadleaved evergreen hardwood forests; brushy edges of conifer forests; riparian thickets; chaparral; coastal scrub; eucalyptus patches with a scrubby understory; and, in the county's more urban areas, planted trees and shrubbery. The birds seem "especially abundant locally where woodland areas adjoin chaparral-covered [and coastal scrub-covered] slopes and ridges" (Pitelka 1951c); Verbeek (1970) noted that they hold territories in edge situations. Suitable habitats seem to have in common a mix (close at hand) of broken woodland and brush for nesting and cover and open ground areas for foraging.

Scrub Jays place their nests in a variety of trees, shrubs, and vines, but they choose oaks frequently, presumably because of their abundance in lowland California (where the species has been most thoroughly studied). J. W. Mailliard (1912) found 69 of 83 Marin County nests in oaks; Atwood (1980) reported that 121 of 172 nests in coast live oak woodland on Santa Cruz Island were in oaks; and Ritter (1983) reported that 84% of the nests in valley oak woodland of the Central Valley were either in California wild grape vine tangles, blue elderberry, interior live oak, or coffeeberry (all 19 nests in suburban habitats were placed in evergreen shrubs and trees). Nest heights range from 2 to 59 feet above the ground but vary, of course, with the structure of available habitat. Verbeek

(1973) reported an average nest height of five feet (range 2-8 ft., n = 25) in Monterey County; Ritter (1983) reported an average height of 11 feet (range 3-50 ft., n = 119) in the Central Valley; and Atwood (1980) reported an average height of 14 feet (range 3-59 ft., n = 171) on Santa Cruz Island. However, Atwood (1980) indicated average nest height on Santa Cruz Island varied from 4 feet (n = 5) in *Baccharis* thickets, to 10 feet (n = 45) in south-slope chaparral, and 17 feet (n = 36) in north-facing chaparral associated with live oak woodland. Atwood (1980) found nests on Santa Cruz Island were generally in dense brush and trees, where numerous twigs and small branches provided suitable support and concealment; most nests were placed in terminal branches. In plants lacking an abundance of small stiff divergent twigs, nests were usually supported by major branches or by the trunk. All nests were remarkably well concealed and normally visible only from below. Ritter (1983) found greater variation among nest sites in the Central Valley: there nests were situated in terminal branches, forks of branches, forks of tree trunks, on lateral branches, and in vines. Ritter (1983) found that Central Valley Scrub Jays built false nests prior to building complete, functional nests; Atwood (1980) found that Santa Cruz Island Scrub Jays did not. A typical functional nest is an open bulky structure composed of coarse sticks, occasionally mixed with

---

Information for this account is drawn only from studies of western races, since the behavior of the Florida Scrub Jay is quite different (Woolfenden & Fitzpatrick 1984).

moss and dry grass, and lined with finer twigs, rootlets, and sometimes grass or horsehair (Bent 1946, Atwood 1980). Exceptionally, Scrub Jays in California will breed in fall (Stanback 1991).

Scrub Jays forage in much the same ways as Steller's Jays do (see account), but they spend more time lower in trees and the scrub canopy, and more time in open areas. Scrubs use "anvil" sites to break open nuts. They store acorns in the ground with a thrust into loose soil or by hammering them in with their beaks and then covering them with dirt clods, rocks, or leaves (Michener & Michener 1945); they also wedge them into cracks or crevices in trees, stumps, and logs (Beal 1910). In their habit of ground storage of acorns, Scrub Jays are active agents of oak dispersal, particularly in the uphill direction (Grinnell 1936). Scrub Jays also remove the hairs from caterpillars by rubbing them in sand (Verbeek 1970). Where Scrub Jays overlap with Yellow-billed Magpies in Monterey County, Verbeek (1970) found that Scrub Jays were more generalists than were the Magpies. Scrub Jays there have a wider variety of feeding styles, a wider habitat range, and feed on a greater diversity of prey, including more vertebrates and plant material. Magpies tend to concentrate on pockets of abundant prey of a few species, whereas Scrub Jays search randomly for food. Overall, the Scrub Jay diet is about 27% animal and 73% vegetable matter; there is considerable seasonal variation, with animal food comprising up to 70% of the diet in April and as little as 5% in January (Beal 1910, n = 326). The animal matter includes insects (especially beetles, bees, wasps, ants, grasshoppers and crickets, and moths and caterpillars), spiders, eggs and nestlings of wild birds, eggs and chicks of domestic fowl, mice and shrews, lizards, snakes, and frogs. The vegetable food is primarily acorns and, to a lesser extent, wild and cultivated fruits, berries, and grain. Although Scrub Jays in Monterey County feed their young a wide variety of food, including most of the items listed above, invertebrates are of overwhelming importance to the nestling diet there (Verbeek 1970); the young are also fed some seeds and fruits, including acorns. Although there is great similarity between the families of invertebrates that Scrub Jays and Yellow-billed Magpies feed their nestlings, there is little overlap in the families most important to each species.

Marin Breeding Distribution

During the atlas period, the Scrub Jay was one of the most widespread breeders in Marin County. Its presence in the open grassland-dominated hills in the northwest sector of the county attested to its ability to subsist in small patches of scrub and trees in ravines. Scrub Jays were absent only from the extreme outer tip of Point Reyes, where these bare-minimum requisites were lacking. Representative nesting localities were Bear Valley Headquarters, PRNS (NB 5/11/81 —JGE); Tennessee Valley (FL/FY 5/21/82 —HPr); near Sleepy Hollow (NY 5/6/76 —RMS); E approach to Loma Alta (NB 5/2/82 —BiL); Terra Linda (FY 5/30/82 —BiL); and Kentfield (NB 4/3/82 —BiL).

Historical Trends/Population Threats

Scrub Jays have probably increased since the settlement of California as they colonized tree plantings in open valleys (G&M 1944), despite organized persecution by hunters in earlier times (Erickson 1937, Hooper 1938). At least as recently as 1968 to 1979, Scrub Jay populations increased significantly in parts of California that include the coastal region from the Monterey area northward (Robbins et al. 1986). Additional data suggest that numbers increased slightly on Breeding Bird Surveys in California as a whole from 1968 to 1989, but were stable from 1980 to 1989 (USFWS unpubl. analyses).

AMERICAN CROW   *Corvus brachyrhynchos*

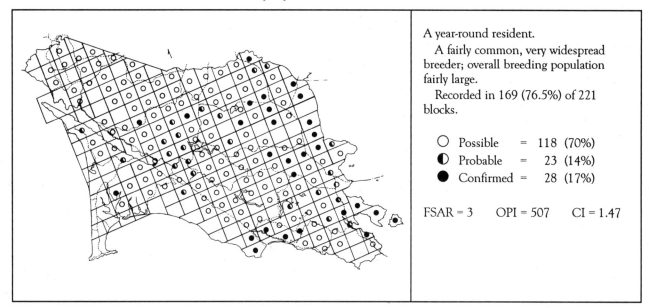

A year-round resident.

A fairly common, very widespread breeder; overall breeding population fairly large.

Recorded in 169 (76.5%) of 221 blocks.

○	Possible	=	118 (70%)
◑	Probable	=	23 (14%)
●	Confirmed	=	28 (17%)

FSAR = 3   OPI = 507   CI = 1.47

Ecological Requirements

These jet-black, gregarious corvids reside in Marin County's lowland valley grazing and agricultural lands, though they also frequent open disturbed areas, grassy playfields, and, to a limited extent, estuarine margins. Crows generally forage in open areas but retreat to forest and woodland edges, woodlots, planted windbreaks, or residential trees for nesting and roosting; orchards are common nesting grounds elsewhere in California. American Crows nest in pairs or loose colonies in a wide variety of trees, shrubs, and bushes (Emlen 1942, G&M 1944, Goodwin 1986). Although nests are usually well spaced (e.g., Emlen 1942), three occupied nests have been found in one small tree (Goodwin 1986). In the Central Valley, Emlen (1942) noted that early nests, built before leaves in trees were fully opened, were somewhat more centrally located in an orchard than later nests. Nest heights range from the ground (rarely) to 100 feet high (Bent 1946). Although most nests are generally about 20 to 60 feet above ground, in some areas most are under 20 feet. In a Central Valley orchard with trees about 20 to 30 feet in height, Emlen (1942) found that 80% of 111 occupied nests were from 16 to 24 feet above ground (range 6.5–29 ft.) and that they were placed about three-fourths of the way up the nest tree. Unusual nest sites are on the ground near a lake or marsh edge, in the hollow of an old stub, on top of a chimney, and on the crossarms of a telephone pole (Bent 1946). Crows build deep, wide nest cups, which they frequently place in the fork or crotch of a tree. Emlen (1942) noted that about one-third of orchard nests were in basal crotches or on branches greater than two inches in

diameter; most nests constructed after leaves had opened were peripheral in the tree, often in small terminal branches. The basal nest platform and frame are built of stout sticks that may be mixed, in varying degrees, with fine twigs, grasses, rope strands, rags, cornhusks, roots, moss, weed stems, and bark strips (Emlen 1942, Bent 1946). Later in the season, the nest foundation may be composed entirely of fine twigs and grasses (Emlen 1942). In most early nests in the Central Valley, mud is used to form a hard, firm floor; later nests generally contain little or no mud, perhaps because it is unavailable locally at that time (Emlen 1942). Crows usually line their nests with fine bark fibers, hair, wool, fur, or moss (Emlen 1942, Bent 1946). Rarely, they build false nests before completing functional nests (Goodwin 1986). In very rare instances, they will lay eggs in a nest before its completion and then continue construction for a few days (Emlen 1942). Old nests or nest platforms of previous seasons occasionally form the foundations for "new" nests, and sometimes birds use the same nest for renesting after destruction of the first eggs (Emlen 1942). Crows form large community roosts at night within nesting colonies, and occupied nests may be situated within the confines of the roosting area; by late May, the roosting flock may more than double, with the addition of neighboring birds from outside the nesting colony (Emlen 1942).

Crows are generalist foragers that feed singly or in flocks of varying size, even in the breeding season. They forage mostly on the ground by picking from the surface, by probing in soft soil, or by turning over sticks, clods of earth, or dung. They also alight in trees or bushes to procure both vegetable and animal matter. In some areas, American Crows forage on the shore and drop shellfish to break them (Goodwin 1986), but on the whole they are much less shore feeders than are Fish or Northwestern crows. Tame birds regularly hide food, but it is uncertain to what extent this occurs in the wild.

The Crow is omnivorous. Animal food comprises about 28% of its diet overall (up to 52% in May); vegetable food averages 72% but rises to 89% in the colder months when animal prey is less available (Kalmbach 1918, n = 1340). Undigestible items are regurgitated as pellets. The most important animal foods are insects (mainly beetles, grasshoppers, caterpillars, and true bugs), spiders, crustaceans, mollusks, fish, reptiles, amphibians, wild birds and their eggs, poultry and their eggs, small mammals, and carrion. The vegetable food consists primarily of corn, other grains, wild fruits, nuts, seeds, and cultivated fruits and nuts. In some instances, Crows can do serious economic harm to crops, but this is offset to some degree by their depredations on insect pests. They readily take scraps of human foods, and in some areas Crows habitually scavenge at refuse dumps and around slaughterhouses (Goodwin 1986). Crows are very wary and will desert a major food source when only a few of their kind have been killed with poisoned samples of the food in question.

Marin Breeding Distribution

American Crows bred widely in the lowlands of Marin County during the atlas period, but they just barely penetrated the fringes of the Point Reyes peninsula and Marin Headlands; over most of this area they were replaced by Common Ravens. A lack of breeding confirmations in the grassland-dominated ranchlands northeast of Tomales Bay suggested that summer fogs may have also reduced the appeal of this coastal region to Crows. Representative breeding locations were Home Bay, PRNS (FL 6/17/81 —DS); Bolinas (NB 3/21/81 —DS); San Marin High School, Novato (NE-FL May-Jun 1982 —ScC); north of Mt. Burdell, Novato (FL 6/2/78 —RMS); and Tiburon Fisheries Lab (NE 5/17/82 —BiL).

Historical Trends/Population Threats

Grinnell and Miller (1944) thought Crow numbers had remained fairly constant in California, as losses from "crow shoots" and bombings of winter roosts were balanced by gains from augmentation of their habitat in agricultural areas. The vast expansion of agriculture in California to the present day has likely added tremendously to the natural food supply of Crows, and we probably now see a far larger population compared with prehistorical times. Crow numbers were increasing on Breeding Bird Surveys in California from 1968 to 1989 (USFWS unpubl. analyses).

COMMON RAVEN *Corvus corax*

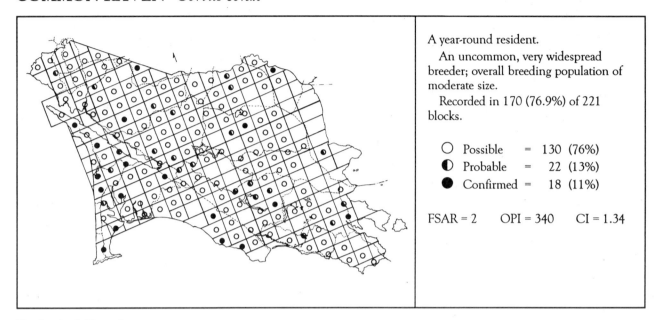

A year-round resident.

An uncommon, very widespread breeder; overall breeding population of moderate size.

Recorded in 170 (76.9%) of 221 blocks.

○ Possible   = 130 (76%)
◐ Probable   =   22 (13%)
● Confirmed =   18 (11%)

FSAR = 2   OPI = 340   CI = 1.34

Ecological Requirements

The largest of passerine birds, these masters of the air soar or dive in convoluted aerial acrobatics over almost any terrain and further command attention by their hoarse, resonant, croaking calls. In Marin County, Ravens reside primarily in open or semiopen country of low rolling grasslands, beaches, and estuarine margins. These habitats are especially attractive if they adjoin bluffs or ridges, since Ravens show a propensity for soaring on updrafts, like raptors (and unlike crows). They forage in open country at any elevation; they nest solitarily on seaside or inland cliffs, in trees on woodland or forest edges, or in planted wind-breaks or woodlots. Planted cypresses and pines provide important nest sites in Marin's coastal grasslands. Cliff nests can range up to 200 feet above the ground and are placed on ledges or inside cavities or crevices; they are usually protected from above by an overhang and below by a steep vertical face (Bent 1946, Hooper 1977). Tree nests can vary from a few feet up to 100 feet or more. They are usually in the tallest trees in the vicinity, are placed in a crotch, and are well concealed in the foliage (Bent 1946). Human structures such as oil derricks, windmills, the insides of abandoned houses and barns, high-tension poles, and railroad bridges will also suffice as nesting platforms. Of 87 nests in the Great Basin of eastern Oregon, 64 were on rimrocks, 20 in human structures, and 3 were in trees (Stiehl 1985). Nests there on rimrock ledges usually filled the space available, whereas those in buildings and trees were generally larger than ledge nests. Ravens use the same nests in successive years, but most pairs have two or more sites that they use alternately in

different years (Goodwin 1986). Ravens will also use old nests of raptors, such as Golden Eagles and Great Horned Owls (initially built by other raptors), and vice versa (Stiehl 1985).

Ravens build large, bulky nests. They construct the outer parts of branches, coarse sticks, twigs, mammal bones, or wire and reinforce them with lumps of earth and clumps of grass or moss; they use thinner sticks for the nest rim (Bent 1946, Stiehl 1985, Goodwin 1986). The central part of the nest is of thin sticks, twigs, clumps of earth, wool, hair, and similar material; the deep inner cup is lined with finer strands of wool, hair, fur, shredded bark, grass, and fine stems (Stiehl 1985, Goodwin 1986). Females sink the eggs deliberately in the nest lining before incubation and half bury the young in the soft lining in cold weather.

Like most corvids, Ravens are generalist feeders. Although they actually procure most of their food on the ground, they spend considerable time soaring in search of their meals. Ravens forage mostly while walking or, less often, hopping on the ground. They pick their food from the surface, probe in soft earth, turn over objects, pick through refuse at dumps, drop shellfish on hard surfaces to break them open, pounce on unsuspecting prey, attack sick or injured individuals of species normally left alone, and even force vultures to disgorge (Bent 1946, Goodwin 1986). Although Ravens are omnivorous, they tend to be more carnivorous than crows (Bent 1946, Harlow et al. 1975, Goodwin 1986). Mammals usually supply the staple of the diet, with most large and medium-sized ones taken as carrion while the smaller ones are preyed upon live;

286

afterbirth of large mammals is also eaten. Other important animal foods are birds and their eggs, insects, reptiles, amphibians, marine invertebrates, and garbage. Ravens' stomach contents suggest that when these birds visit rotting carcasses, they sometimes feed chiefly or entirely on blow fly maggots and beetles in and around them (Goodwin 1986). Ravens often are bold scavengers about human dwellings and encampments, and large numbers sometimes gather at garbage dumps, slaughterhouses, or other sources of abundant food. Vegetable foods include cultivated grains and wild fruits and berries; much vegetable matter may be ingested incidentally or comes from the stomachs of prey. Indigestible items are cast as pellets. Ravens habitually store surplus food. They preferentially store fat, even over foods they prefer to eat, except that breeding birds most eagerly store insects or other foods suitable for their young (Goodwin 1986). While feeding small nestlings, Ravens at first feed them small items; they kill and crush even small insects for the young, remove all hard parts and bits of bone from prey, and supply the young with soaked food by drinking water before feeding them. Adults bring the young water alone on hot days. During the nesting season, adult males feed females on or off the nest. In eastern Oregon, Stiehl (1985) noted a late-season (Jul) shift of the diet from carrion, small mammals, and eggs to insects, principally grasshoppers; presumably this reflected seasonal availability.

Marin Breeding Distribution

Common Ravens bred widely in Marin County during the atlas period. They were most numerous around the windswept bluffs and shorelines of the immediate coast, especially on the Point Reyes peninsula, and were sparse or absent in the lowlands bordering the San Francisco and San Pablo bayshores. Representative nesting localities were Upper Pierce Ranch, Tomales Point (NY 5/18/82 –DS); Abbott's Lagoon (NE 4/15/81 –DS); and Drake's Beach sea cliff (NE or NY 6/3/81 –DS).

Historical Trends/Population Threats

Grinnell and Miller (1944) noted historical declines or local extirpation of Raven populations in settled areas of California. DeSante and Ainley (1980) also implicate human disturbance as the cause of extirpation of breeding Ravens on the Farallon Islands. Recently these negative effects must have been offset to a certain degree by augmented food supplies from domestic livestock and by the proliferation of road kills with our expanding mobile population. From 1968 to 1989, Raven numbers increased on Breeding Bird Surveys in California, though the trend was less pronounced since 1980 (USFWS unpubl. analyses). At least from 1968 to 1979, the increase was concentrated in the foothills in areas including coastal counties from Monterey south and parts of those to the north (Robbins et al. 1986).

Titmice

Family *Paridae*

CHESTNUT-BACKED CHICKADEE *Parus rufescens*

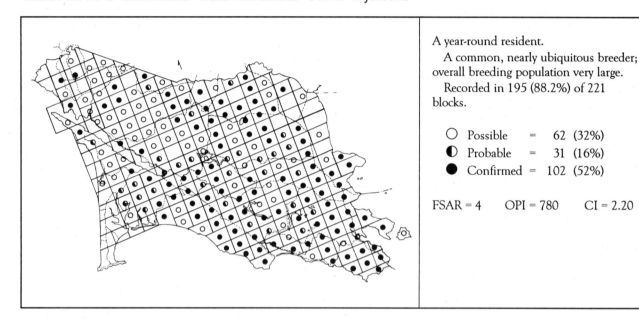

A year-round resident.

A common, nearly ubiquitous breeder; overall breeding population very large.

Recorded in 195 (88.2%) of 221 blocks.

○ Possible   =   62 (32%)
◐ Probable   =   31 (16%)
● Confirmed = 102 (52%)

FSAR = 4   OPI = 780   CI = 2.20

Ecological Requirements

The cheery calls of our only breeding chickadee ring out from virtually all of Marin County's moist, well-shaded forests. The Chestnut-backed Chickadee's main nesting haunts here are redwood, Douglas fir, bishop pine, mixed conifer, broadleaved evergreen, and willow and alder riparian forests. They also reside in extensive groves of planted pine, cypress, and eucalyptus and, sparingly, in the edges of oak woodlands.

Like most chickadees, Chestnut-backs nest in cavities in stumps, tree stubs, or decayed trees. The cavities may be natural, excavated in decayed wood by the birds themselves, or old woodpecker holes. Nest boxes, holes in buildings, old pipes (Bent 1946), or old Cliff Swallow nests (Dixon 1954) are used less frequently. Nest holes range from 1.5 to 80 feet above the ground, and the nest cavity is lined with soft materials such as mosses, fur, hair, small feathers, and rope fiber (Bent 1946).

Chestnut-backs forage mostly by gleaning from foliage and small twigs as they spiral through the canopy and subcanopy of the forest. They also glean from flowers, buds, fruits, and cones, less commonly from large branches and trunks, and, rarely, from the ground. While gleaning, they frequently hang upside down or sideways from twigs or from the corrugations of bark on large limbs.

Less frequently, they hover or flycatch in a "clumsy" manner (Dixon 1954, Root 1964, Smith 1967, Sturman 1968, Hertz et al. 1976). Compared to Plain Titmice, Chestnutbacks forage faster, hang beneath perches more often, hammer items held under their feet at "anvil" sites less often, and apparently eat smaller food items (Root 1964). Chestnut-backs also spend more time in mixed evergreen than live oak woodland, forage more in the foliage zone of the canopy than on large branches and limbs of the subcanopy, and go to the ground less frequently than Titmice do.

In a San Mateo County mixed deciduous–live oak woodland, Chestnut-backs forage at virtually the exact same levels, 0 to 39 feet (mostly 10–30 ft.), as both the Plain Titmouse and the Bushtit (Hertz et al. 1976). Resources there are partitioned by the type of substrate used within that zone: the Chestnut-backed Chickadee is a composite foliage and bark forager, intermediate between the foliage specialist Bushtit and the bark specialist Plain Titmouse. Chestnut-backs there forage on foliage about 60% of the time and stems about 40%. Although they only forage in shrubbery 7% of the time, they are intermediate in their use of that substrate compared with Bushtits (20%) and Titmice (2.5%). Also in San Mateo County, Wagner

288

(1981) found Chestnut-backs using evergreen (vs. deciduous) oaks more than Titmice but less than Bushtits. Chestnut-backs there show some seasonal and annual variation in the size of foraging perches they use.

In a live oak–mixed evergreen woodland in Contra Costa County, Root (1964) also found that Chestnut-backs rely more heavily on foliage and related substrates, Titmice predominantly on woody substrates; Titmice there concentrate on live oaks and chickadees on a wide variety of trees. However, in a live oak–bay laurel–eucalyptus woodland in Berkeley, Alameda County, Dixon (1954) reported the opposite trend—Chestnut-backs forage mostly in live oaks and Titmice in a variety of trees. Although Chestnut-backs there forage on foliage and stems in roughly equal proportions, Titmice forage in foliage overwhelmingly (87%).

In mixed conifer habitat in the Sierra, Chestnut-backs vary foraging techniques (and tree species use) seasonally (Brennan & Morrison 1990). Foliage use and gleaning peak there in spring and summer and decrease as twig use increases in late fall/early winter. In the Washington Cascades, these chickadees probe more in winter than spring and shift relative use of tree species in winter (Lundquist & Manuwal 1990).

In an area of overlap with Black-capped Chickadees in Vancouver, B.C., and Washington state, Chestnut-backs forage in slightly different manners on different substrates and at greater heights—from 0 to 140 feet (peak 45–50 ft.) versus 0 to 70 feet (mostly 0–5 ft.)—than do Black-caps (Smith 1967, Sturman 1968). In contrast to Black-caps, breeding Chestnut-backs are restricted mostly to conifer-dominated habitat and are stereotypically adapted to conifer foraging (Sturman 1968)—that is, they change their foraging strategy little when moving from conifers to hardwoods. Compared with Black-caps, Chestnut-backed Chickadees forage more often near the ends of branches; forage more often in the foliage of the canopy than in the branchwork of the subcanopy; choose perches on twigs more often than on large branches and trunks; forage more often on foliage, buds, and cones than on bark surfaces; and forage more on the upper surfaces of branches and twigs, from an upright stance. Black-caps forage more from a hanging than an upright stance, primarily because they increase the proportion of foraging by hanging when feeding in hardwoods while Chestnut-backs do not. As a rule, Chestnut-backs forage at greater heights (relative to tree height) than do Black-caps, even though Chestnut-backs forage at relatively lower heights in hardwoods than conifers and vice versa for Black-caps. Overall, Chestnut-backs are less diverse in their foraging style than Black-caps, but both forage in a greater variety of places in hardwoods than in conifers. Among seasonal differences, Chestnut-backs there forage more often on newly opened buds and cones early in the season, and they hang upside down more in winter.

The Chestnut-backed Chickadee diet in California is about 65% animal matter and 35% vegetable matter (Beal 1907). The main animal foods are true bugs, caterpillars, wasps, spiders, and beetles; this part of the diet naturally increases in the spring and summer. The vegetable foods are chiefly fruits and seeds, the latter primarily coniferous.

Marin Breeding Distribution

During the atlas period, Chestnut-backed Chickadees bred throughout Marin County but were most numerous and widespread on coastal ridges where denser, moister forests prevail. In the northern and interior sections of the county, Chestnut-backs were restricted to the moist drainages of narrow canyons, north-facing slopes, and the larger planted groves of eucalyptus, pine, or cypress. Representative breeding locations were eucalyptus grove at Upper Pierce Ranch, Tomales Point, (NY/FY 5/18/82 –DS); Palomarin, PRNS (NE-NY 4/23–5/15/82 –PRBO); and Mt. Burdell, Novato (NY 5/?/82 –ScC).

Historical Trends/Population Threats

Historically, tree plantings appear to have caused a local expansion of the breeding range of Chestnut-backed Chickadees in Marin County. This is most notable in the grassy ranchlands near Tomales that before European settlement apparently were essentially treeless except for low willows along streams. Chestnut-backs have also expanded their breeding range considerably in central coastal California since at least 1938 (G&M 1944; Dixon 1954, 1960), and chickadee populations in this region continue to increase (Brennan & Morrison 1991). Dixon postulated that following the growth of the human population, coastal Chestnut-backs were able to expand in range, via planted groves of shade and orchard trees, across areas formerly dominated by grassland and oak savannah. Chestnut-backs have also expanded their range south along the coast to Santa Barbara County (Garrett & Dunn 1981) and into and south along the Sierra Nevada (Crase 1976, ABN); at least in the Sierra, chickadee numbers have since stabilized (Brennan & Morrison 1991). Expansion into the Sierra Nevada may have been in response to an increase of Douglas fir—an important chickadee foraging tree—after extensive clear-cutting there around the turn of the century (Brennan & Morrison 1991). Perhaps Chestnut-backed Chickadee populations have also increased in Marin County for the same reasons following the extensive logging here in the nineteenth and early twentieth centuries. In contrast to these earlier and continued local increases, on the whole Chestnut-backed Chickadee numbers appeared to decrease slightly on Breeding Bird Surveys in California from 1968 to 1989, though they were relatively stable from 1980 to 1989 (USFWS unpubl. analyses).

PLAIN TITMOUSE *Parus inornatus*

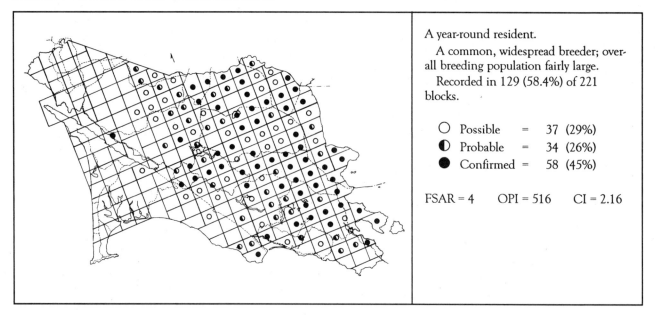

A year-round resident.

A common, widespread breeder; overall breeding population fairly large.

Recorded in 129 (58.4%) of 221 blocks.

○	Possible	=	37 (29%)
◑	Probable	=	34 (26%)
●	Confirmed	=	58 (45%)

FSAR = 4   OPI = 516   CI = 2.16

Ecological Requirements

Though drab in color, this crested parid is the voice and soul of the oaks. Titmice breed in Marin County's oak woodlands, oak savannah, open broadleaved evergreen forests, and open riparian woodlands. The broadleaved evergreen forests they inhabit are generally spacious, oak-dominated ones on south-facing slopes. Characteristic of these habitats are a predominance of hardwood trees with moderate to large boles and relatively open branchwork. Plain Titmice select nest sites from about 3 to 32 feet above the ground in natural (rotted-out) tree cavities, in hollows they excavate or partially excavate in decayed wood of trees, in old woodpecker holes, or in nest boxes (Bent 1946, Dixon 1954). More unusual nest sites are holes in earthen cliff banks, old Cliff Swallow nests, and human structures. Nest cavities are lined with soft materials such as fur, moss, hairs, fine grasses, weed stems and fibers, and a few feathers (Bent 1946, Dixon 1949).

In general, Plain Titmice forage much like chickadees do, but at a slower pace. They glean from bark and foliage, hang from twigs and trunks, or occasionally hover or flycatch. The Plain Titmouse is a bark specialist compared with the more generalist Chestnut-backed Chickadee and the foliage specialist Bushtit, but the three species generally forage at the same heights (Hertz et al. 1976). Compared with Chestnut-backed Chickadees, in oak woodlands Titmice generally spend more time in the subcanopy than the canopy and spend much more time gleaning from twigs, branches, limbs, and trunks than from foliage. They also go to the ground (or to low plants such as thistles) more frequently to gather fruits and nuts, use their larger bills

more for hammering and splitting open nuts and chipping off bark, do less hanging beneath perches, and apparently eat larger food items than Chestnut-backed Chickadees do (Root 1964, Hertz et al. 1976). Dixon (1954) observed that in live oak woodlands, Plain Titmice forage predominantly by gleaning from foliage and bark-glean infrequently. Titmice also come to feeders more readily than Chestnut-backed Chickadees do (B. Lenarz pers. comm.). See the Chestnut-backed Chickadee and Bushtit accounts for further details of niche separation among these species. In California's foothill oak woodlands, Titmice show seasonal, annual, and geographic variation in many aspects of their foraging ecology (Wagner 1981, Block 1990).

The California diet of Titmice (from areas encompassing orchards, which are not the main haunts of the species) is "43 percent of animal to 57 of vegetable" (Beal 1907). The animal food is primarily true bugs, caterpillars, beetles, wasps, ants, spiders, and other insects. Vegetable food consists of cultivated fruits and grains, wild fruits, seeds and nuts, leaf galls, oak and willow catkins, and leaf buds (Beal 1907, Dixon 1949).

Marin Breeding Distribution

During the atlas period, Plain Titmice bred primarily in the drier interior sections of the eastern part of Marin County, where open, oak-dominated broadleaved evergreen forests and oak woodlands predominate. The hills dotted with valley oaks around Novato are the mecca for Titmice in Marin. Titmice are rare and local on the Point Reyes peninsula and elsewhere on the immediate coast, where open oaks or open riparian woods are difficult to find amid the dense moist coastal forests. Representative nesting locations were Antonio Creek, near Point Reyes–Petaluma Rd. (NY/FY 5/12/77 –DS); near Stafford Lake, Novato (FY 5/6/79 –KH); E side Loma Alta (FY 5/30/82 –BiL); China Camp SP (ON 4/17/82 –BiL); and Peacock Gap, San Rafael (FY 4/27/76 –RMS).

Historical Trends/Population Threats

Grinnell and Miller (1944) noted retractions of the Plain Titmouse's range locally in California where oaks were cleared for agriculture and expansion of their range where trees had been planted in previously unoccupied areas. Titmice numbers appeared to decrease slightly on Breeding Bird Surveys in California from 1968 to 1989 and significantly from 1980 to 1989 (USFWS unpubl. analyses). In the future, oak woodland-dependent species such as this bird may experience extensive habitat loss, since seedling oaks are rare in these woodlands today (see Plant Community section). Removal of oak stands for firewood and to clear land for development is also a problem in the Sierran foothills (E.C. Beedy pers. comm.).

Beak crammed with insects, a Chestnut-backed Chickadee pauses before descending into its cavity to feed the clamoring young. Photograph by Ian Tait.

Bushtits
Family *Aegithalidae*

BUSHTIT *Psaltriparus minimus*

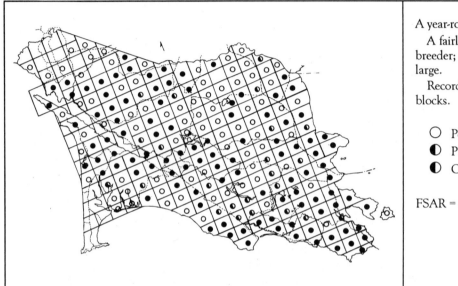

A year-round resident.

A fairly common, nearly ubiquitous breeder; overall breeding population large.

Recorded in 207 (93.7%) of 221 blocks.

○ Possible = 80 (39%)
◑ Probable = 23 (11%)
◑ Confirmed = 104 (50%)

FSAR = 3   OPI = 621   CI = 2.12

Ecological Requirements

These "bird children that never grew up" (Dawson 1923) frequent the mixed vegetation along sunny edges of all of Marin County's major forest, woodland, and scrub habitats, including planted woodlots, such as eucalyptus. Conifers themselves are little used, but Bushtits inhabit conifer forest edges and clearings with borders of live oaks, *Ceanothus*, coyote bush, and the like. The broadleaved evergreen vegetation of coastal scrub, chaparral, and oak woodland is most to their liking, though generally not in homogeneous stands: Bushtits seem to prefer a mixture of trees and shrubs, with somewhat open airways.

Unlike our other songbirds (except orioles), Bushtits build pensile nests. They hang them from 4 to 50 feet, but mostly less than 15 feet, above the ground in various trees or shrubs, both native and introduced (Bent 1946); live oak and *Ceanothus* are favorites on the coast. Bushtits generally conceal their striking nests in lichen-festooned dense foliage, but occasionally they build them in plain view. One wonders at the fate of an obvious nest. A nest is a long (about 7–10 in.), intricately woven, domed-over, pendant bag with a small entrance hole on one side near the top. The nest materials Bushtits use most frequently in the San Francisco Bay Area are mosses, lichens, oak leaves,

grasses, and the staminate flowers of coast live oak (Addicott 1938). In addition they use other flowers, fruits, plant down, conifer needles, bark fibers, insect cocoons, feathers, and bits of paper and string. They bind all these together with copious amounts of spider web.

Where they overlap with Chestnut-backed Chickadees and Plain Titmice in oak woodland on the central California coast, Bushtits forage at similar heights (see accounts) but have the broadest niche of the three species (Hertz et al. 1976). Bushtits there forage in a greater variety of trees and bushes and spend more time in bushes and vines (20%) than do the other two species. The 10% of foraging time Bushtits spend on honeysuckle vines indicates a strong preference for the vines, as they were the least abundant of the shrubby plants surveyed. Bushtits are foliage specialists, primarily of the canopy and subcanopy. They spend 90% of their time gleaning from foliage, the remainder from stems; nonfoliage foraging is directed at green twigs and petioles rather than woody surfaces.

Where Bushtits overlap with Plain Titmice in foothill oak-pine woodland in the central Sierra Nevada, both species vary monthly in their intraspecific use of foraging sites (plant species) and substrates, and yearly in their use

292

of foraging substrates (Hejl & Verner 1990). Despite overall tendencies of Bushtits to forage more often on buckbrush and Titmice on blue oak, both bird species show parallel use of various plants across the breeding season. Both species use live oak and buckbrush more, and blue oak less, in March; increase their use of blue oak in March; and increase their use of gray pine and other species in May. Bushtits and Titmice show different patterns of foraging substrate use across the breeding season. Paralleling phenological changes of plants, Bushtits forage mostly from buckbrush flowers in March, and from leaves and twigs of buckbrush and blue oak leaves in April and May. Substrate use by Titmice varies in a similar pattern, though they rely more on blue oak leaves in April and May. These within-season shifts in foraging behavior probably reflect changing prey availability with different stages of plant phenology.

Bushtits inhabiting mixed oak woodland on the central California coast forage more in evergreen and less in deciduous oaks, more from smaller perches, and more in bushes than either Plain Titmice or Chestnut-backed Chickadees do (Wagner 1981). A lack of seasonal or yearly differences in foraging behavior of Bushtits there may reflect limited sampling of these behaviors rather than a lack of variability of foraging patterns over time.

The Bushtit's diet in California is about 81% animal and 19% vegetable (Beal 1907, n = 353), with the latter increasing slightly in importance in autumn and winter (Beal 1907, Martin et al. 1951). Animal fare consists mainly of true bugs, beetles, butterflies and moths (mostly caterpillars), and spiders (Beal 1907); other insect taxa and pseudoscorpions are of minor importance. The vegetable matter includes fruit pulp, granules of poison oak, leaf galls, and seeds.

Marin Breeding Distribution

During the atlas period, Bushtits bred widely throughout Marin County. They did not exhibit any marked distributional patterns of abundance, except that they seemed to be somewhat less numerous in areas dominated by the coastal prairie on Point Reyes peninsula and around Tomales and by dense forest on Inverness and Bolinas ridges. Representative nesting areas were Inverness (NB 3/26/82 –DS); Chileno Valley (NE 5/5/82 –DS); Mt. Burdell, Novato (NB 4/21/81 –ITi); near Rock Springs, Mt. Tamalpais (NB 3/28/81 –DS); and Phoenix Lake (NB 4/19/80 –ITi).

Historical Trends/Population Threats

Grinnell and Miller (1944) felt that Bushtits had increased locally in "open valleys and plains" in parts of California, as habitat was enhanced by the planting of trees and shrubbery. It also seems likely that their numbers have increased in areas where clearing has opened up formerly dense forests, creating edge situations to the species' liking. Clearing of open oak woodlands, though, has probably been to their detriment. Breeding Bird Surveys revealed a fairly stable population in California from 1968 to 1989, though numbers decreased from 1980 to 1989 (Robbins et al. 1986, USFWS unpubl. analyses).

Nuthatches
Family *Sittidae*

RED-BREASTED NUTHATCH   *Sitta canadensis*

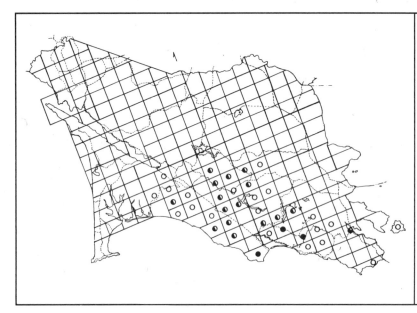

Occurs year round, though primarily as a fall transient and winter resident from Sep through Mar, when numbers vary greatly from year to year.

An uncommon, local breeder; overall breeding population very small.

Recorded in 39 (17.6%) of 221 blocks.

○	Possible	=	20	(51%)
◐	Probable	=	16	(41%)
●	Confirmed	=	3	(8%)

FSAR = 2   OPI = 78   CI = 1.56

Ecological Requirements

High-pitched, nasal, *ank-ank* calls betray the presence of breeding Red-breasted Nuthatches in Marin County's dense Douglas fir stands and may also resound from redwoods and planted pines and cypress. They are generally "replaced" in bishop pines by Pygmy Nuthatches. Red-breasted Nuthatches nest in cavities they excavate in the rotted interiors of live trees, tree stubs, or dead trees, or in old woodpecker holes or nest boxes. They use nest cavities in conifers or hardwoods at heights ranging from 2 to 120 feet above the ground (Tyler 1948a). In Yosemite, Michael (1934) found nest holes from 5 to 40 feet and estimated average height was probably 15 feet. In Sierra County, Airola (1980) reported nest holes averaging 30 feet in height (range 5–86 ft.). The nest cavity bottom may be just a deep layer of fine sawdust (Gunderson 1939), but more commonly it is lined with soft vegetable matter such as fine grasses, roots, or shredded bark (Tyler 1948a). A curious habit of this nuthatch, the function of which is unknown, is to liberally smear the entire circumference of its nest hole with pitch. Perhaps this serves to repel predators such as squirrels, as apparently do the chemical secretions spread at their nest entrances by White-breasted Nuthatches (see account).

Red-breasted Nuthatches tend to forage at intermediate heights and on different substrates compared with the Pygmy and White-breasted nuthatches (see accounts). Although they will forage throughout the crown (Stallcup 1968), Red-breasteds generally forage at medium heights relative to insect gleaners, and higher than most bark gleaners in mixed conifer forests in the Sierra Nevada (Airola & Barrett 1985, Morrison et al. 1987). They forage on a wide variety of substrates, including small branches, trunks, foliage, twigs, and medium branches. In general, Red-breasteds spend more time on the inner branches of the tree crown than in the outer canopy or on trunks, though they make more use of limbs and trunks and less of twigs in winter (Stallcup 1968, Morrison et al. 1985). In contrast, Pygmy Nuthatches tend to forage higher in conifers on peripheral foliage and branches, while White-breasted Nuthatches tend to forage lower down on the trunk and on larger branches. In Sierran mixed conifer forests, Red-breasteds change their relative use of various tree species for foraging between summer and winter (Airola & Barrett 1985, Morrison et al. 1987). There they forage over 80% of the time on live trees, but overall about 35% of the time on dead substrates of live or dead trees (Morrison et al. 1987).

Red-breasted Nuthatches forage primarily by gleaning, secondarily by probing and pecking, and to a limited extent by digging, flycatching, and hovering. They do flycatch frequently at the edges of clearings when suitable insect prey are abundant (D. Shuford pers. obs.). Like other nuthatches, Red-breasteds are experts at clinging to bark and hitching up or down trunks and along, under, or around limbs and branches in any plane. They chip or flake off pieces of bark, particularly in winter. In addition to tree foraging, they also fly to the ground or low vegetation for seeds or insects. In the Washington Cascades, Red-breasteds reduce gleaning and increase probing and pecking from spring to winter (Lundquist & Manuwal 1990). These nuthatches do *not* show substantial geographic variation in prey capture methods (Petit et al. 1990).

Red-breasteds pick some seeds and fruits from exposed sites. They also pry open cone scales and insert their bills to procure the seeds, which they frequently wedge in a crack or crevice to work upon. These nuthatches also occasionally suck sap from "the bleeding stumps of trees" (Tyler 1948a). They dine on insects (especially beetles, hymenoptera, true bugs, aphids, and caterpillars), spiders, conifer seeds, wild fruits, and buds (Tyler 1948a, Martin et al. 1951, Otvos & Stark 1985). In a study in Oregon, Red-breasteds ate negligible amounts of plant material except in winter, when seeds (mostly of sedge) accounted for 12%–17% of the menu (Anderson 1976). An increase in bark beetles and the inclusion of stink bugs and ladybird beetles in the winter diet there further suggests that Red-breasteds forage more on large proximal branches and trunks at that season.

Marin Breeding Distribution

The distribution of breeding Red-breasted Nuthatches in Marin County during the atlas period generally reflected the distribution of large stands of Douglas fir and coast redwood on Mount Tamalpais, Bolinas Ridge, and the southern part of Inverness Ridge. Representative breeding locales included Benstein Trail, Mt. Tamalpais (ON 5/19/76 –DS) and Bolinas Ridge N of Fairfax-Bolinas Rd. (NB 5/24/76 –DS). Although Red-breasted Nuthatches in California nest mostly above 2500 feet in elevation (G&M 1944), they nest close to sea level in Bolinas.

Historical Trends/Population Threats

Early accounts considered the Red-breasted Nuthatch a fall and winter visitant to this area (Mailliard 1900, S&P 1933, G&W 1927). It was first reported in Marin County in summer in June and July 1936 (Orr 1937), although it had probably been breeding here for a long time and had gone undetected until its breeding haunts were more thoroughly explored.

Population levels of Red-breasted Nuthatches are known to fluctuate dramatically in winter, when numbers of birds invade lowland areas on roughly a two- to three-year cycle as a result of poor conifer seed crops over large areas (Widrlechner & Dragula 1984). Grinnell and Miller (1944) also commented on "the vagrant tendency of the species, even as attempted or completed nesting." A graph of data from Breeding Bird Surveys in California from 1968 to 1979 (Robbins et al. 1986) also shows marked year-to-year variation in population levels, suggestive of long-term cycles. This might just as easily be explained by differential survival in winter between irruptive and non-irruptive years, rather than by irregular changes in breeding distribution. To my knowledge, a tendency for irruptive or irregular breeding is not substantiated by extralimital (confirmed) breeding records, or even by strong circumstantial evidence of shifting breeding populations. On the whole, numbers on Breeding Bird Surveys in California were relatively stable from 1968 to 1989, despite an increase from 1980 to 1989 (USFWS unpubl. analyses).

Logging practices that reduce conifer diversity or create monocultures are also likely to reduce numbers of this and other species that inhabit mixed conifer forests (Morrison et al. 1987).

WHITE-BREASTED NUTHATCH *Sitta carolinensis*

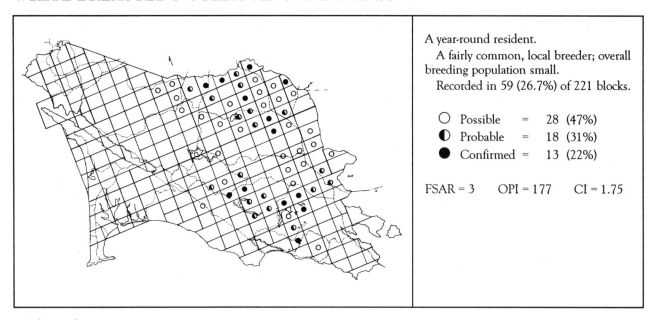

A year-round resident.

A fairly common, local breeder; overall breeding population small.

Recorded in 59 (26.7%) of 221 blocks.

○ Possible   =   28 (47%)
◐ Probable   =   18 (31%)
● Confirmed =   13 (22%)

FSAR = 3   OPI = 177   CI = 1.75

Ecological Requirements

In Marin County, as elsewhere, White-breasted Nuthatches are habitual "bark combers." They breed here primarily in open oak woodlands and oak savannah and only occasionally in mixed stands of Douglas firs and hardwoods. In California oak woodlands, they prefer deciduous oaks over live oaks for foraging (Wagner 1981, Block 1990). Overall, their main requirements seem to be trees with extensive rough bark surfaces and open branch-work for foraging (G&M 1944) and cavities for nesting.

In accordance with the nuthatch psyche, White-breasteds nest exclusively in cavities. They may use natural cavities, excavate their own, or modify preexisting ones; they may use cavities bored out by individuals of other species (usually woodpeckers) or by conspecifics or "make do" with nest boxes; excavation entirely by White-breasteds is rare (Tyler 1948b, Bent 1948, McEllin 1979a). Cavities are reused in successive years (Butts 1931, McEllin 1979a). Nest cavities can be in a variety of deciduous or coniferous trees, and nest heights can range from 1 to 61 feet above the ground (Bent 1948, Tyler 1948b). In Colorado, McEllin (1979a) found seven nests, all in live ponderosa pines and ranging from 12 to 56 feet in height (av. 35 ft.). All were in trunks, all but one had a large limb immediately below the entrance, and they tended to face east or south, away from the prevailing wind and rain from the west or north. In Minnesota, the height of five nests in deciduous trees ranged from 13 to 39 feet and averaged 20 feet (Ritchison 1981). Airola (1980) reported nest hole heights in Sierra County, California, averaging 19 feet and ranging from 4 to 61 feet.

The nest cavity is lined with fur, hair, shreds of bark, twigs, grasses, rootlets, dried earth, lumps of mud, a few feathers, or even coyote scat or pellets ejected by birds of prey (Bent 1948, Tyler 1948b). White-breasted Nuthatches are known to perch at the nest tree, swinging the whole body in an ark, and sweep insects and other objects held in the bill back and forth over the bark. Sweeping is concentrated inside and outside the nest entrance and at nearby protuberances and branch and trunk junctions. Since these nuthatches usually nest in relatively large natural cavities, for which they compete with tree squirrels, Kilham (1968) theorized that this bill sweeping makes use of the chemical defense secretions of insects to repel squirrels from approaching or entering their nest cavities.

As if to defy gravity, White-breasted Nuthatches use their sharp curved nails to cling to bark as they hitch up or, usually, down trunks or along, under, or around limbs and branches. Compared with our other nuthatches, White-breasteds forage mostly on extensive open bark surfaces (see Pygmy and Red-breasted nuthatch accounts). They concentrate their efforts mostly from the lower half of the tree crown downward and on the trunk and the inner portions of large limbs and branches (Stallcup 1968, Bock 1969, McEllin 1979b, Wagner 1981, Grubb 1982). They tend to forage relatively little on smaller branches (but see Block 1990), dead trees, stumps, logs, rocks, or the ground. White-breasted Nuthatches glean from the bark surface, peer and poke, probe fissures, scale and chip off small flakes of bark, and, rarely, flycatch. They take seeds from fallen cones on the ground (not from intact cones on trees) or from crevices in bark where previously cached by themselves or other species. Birds frequently wedge food items in crannies of horizontal branches and break them up or crush them with blows of the bill (Stallcup 1968). Males feed females at the nest (Ritchison 1981). In Colorado's ponderosa pine forests, McEllin (1979b) found that the sexes differed in their foraging niches. Female White-breasted Nuthatches foraged higher than males and more on limbs than trunks. During the breeding season, the sexes used significantly different foraging methods—males tended to scale more, females to peer and poke more. In winter in the deciduous forest in Ohio, Grubb (1982) found no difference between the foraging niches of the sexes. McEllin (1979b) noted that White-breasteds were specialists in the foraging substrates selected but generalists in the feeding behavior and food items taken. This suggested to him that they were preying on evenly distributed food items, in contrast with Pygmy Nuthatches (see account). Anderson (1976) also noted that White-breasteds were opportune feeders because they shift their diet more between habitats than do Red-breasted Nuthatches.

Broad-based comparisons indicate that neither of these nuthatches show substantial geographic variation in prey capture methods, and that White-breasteds have a relatively narrow foraging niche (Petit et al. 1990). On the other hand, White-breasted Nuthatches breeding in oak woodlands in California exhibit considerable geographic variation in their selection of *size* characteristics of trees and substrates for foraging, and foraging locations within the canopy (Block 1990). In ponderosa pine forests in Arizona, they show annual variation in foraging techniques and other resource-use measures (Szaro et al. 1990).

In the breeding season, White-breasted Nuthatches eat primarily animal foods, but they switch more to seeds and nuts in the colder months (Tyler 1948b, Martin et al. 1951). The main animal items are beetles, spiders, caterpil-

lars, true bugs, ants and other hymenoptera, along with some flies, grasshoppers, moths, and millipedes. Overall in North America, plant foods make up 68% of the winter diet (Martin et al. 1951, n = 45) whereas in Oregon they amount to 17% (sedge seeds) of the diet in oak habitat, and 8% (seeds and grass) in ponderosa pine forest (Anderson 1976). In Oregon, White-breasteds eat larger items in pines than in oaks (Anderson 1976).

Marin Breeding Distribution

The distribution of White-breasted Nuthatches in Marin County during the atlas period reflected the distribution of open oak woodland to the northeast around Novato, where the birds were most widespread and numerous, and that of open stands of mixed evergreen forests on Mount Tamalpais. Representative breeding localities were Mt. Burdell, Novato (NY/FY 4/21/81 —ITi) and Olompali, Novato (ON 6/?/82 —ScC).

Historical Trends/Population Threats

Early accounts stated or implied that the White-breasted Nuthatch was "rare" and occurred primarily as a winter visitant in Marin County, and a breeding record at Woodacre was deemed noteworthy (Mailliard 1900, G&W 1927, S&P 1933, G&M 1944). Today the species is a fairly widespread and numerous breeder in Marin County, but it is probable that the actual status has not changed much over the years. Mailliard (1900) stated that the species was "probably resident near Sonoma County line," but observers appear to have spent little if any time in that region until the period of the Marin atlas project. On the whole, White-breasted Nuthatch numbers increased on Breeding Bird Surveys in California from 1968 to 1989, though they were relatively stable from 1980 to 1989 (USFWS unpubl. analyses).

PYGMY NUTHATCH *Sitta pygmaea*

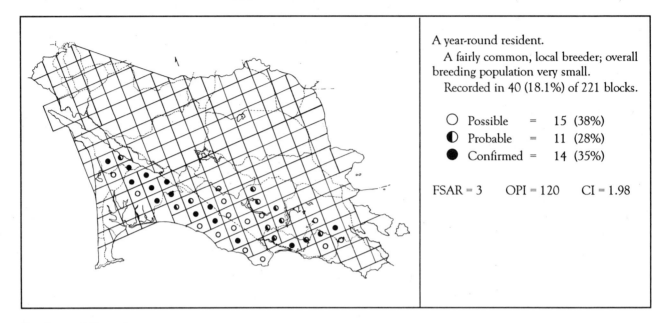

A year-round resident.

A fairly common, local breeder; overall breeding population very small.

Recorded in 40 (18.1%) of 221 blocks.

○ Possible = 15 (38%)
◑ Probable = 11 (28%)
● Confirmed = 14 (35%)

FSAR = 3   OPI = 120   CI = 1.98

Ecological Requirements

The Morse code–like calls of the Pygmy Nuthatch are a characteristic sound of Marin County's bishop pine forests. Pygmy Nuthatches breed here secondarily in Douglas fir and redwood forests and to a limited degree in groves of planted pines (particularly Monterey pine) and cypresses. They typically use conifer stands with relatively open canopies, branchwork, and foliage. Since they generally avoid densely foliaged, closed-canopied conifer forests, they occur much more locally here in Douglas fir and redwood forests than in bishop pine.

Pygmy Nuthatches are notoriously gregarious, feeding in flocks when not nesting and congregating in large communal roosts at night throughout the nonbreeding season (Norris 1958, Sydeman & Güntert 1983). Although most birds split off into pairs to breed, about 20%–30% of the nests are occupied by threesomes (Norris 1958, Sydeman et al. 1988, Sydeman 1989). The additional helpers at these nests are males, usually yearlings, and often the offspring or siblings of the birds they aid. The second male is intimately involved in the nesting effort and may help in nest construction, feeding the female during incubation and brooding, cleaning the nest, and feeding nestlings and fledglings; he also roosts in the nest cavity with the other birds.

Like our other nuthatches, Pygmies are exclusively cavity nesters. They may use natural cavities, excavate their own cavities, or modify preexisting ones made by other species (usually woodpeckers) or by conspecifics (Bent 1948, Norris 1958, McEllin 1979a); exceptionally, a nest may be

"under loose bark on a dead tree" (Bent 1948). Cavities are usually located in the trunks of snags, in lightning strikes or dead branches of live trees, or, occasionally, in the partly dead and rotten heartwood of a living tree (Bent 1948, Norris 1958, McEllin 1979a, Hay & Güntert 1983). Nest trees generally are in the stand of pines where the birds forage. Occasionally, nest cavities are in an adjacent stand of a different conifer where Pygmies do not forage, in isolated trees in brushland as far as 100 feet from mature conifer stands, or in stubs standing in water (Norris 1958). Although Pygmies most often choose pines for their nest cavities, they occasionally locate them in broadleaved oaks (W.J. Sydeman pers. comm.). Norris (1958) reported nest heights of coastal birds ranging from 6 to 60 feet (median 25 ft., n = 74), and those of interior montane birds ranging from 3 to 100 feet (median 22 ft., n = 52). Airola (1980) reported nest-hole heights in Sierra County averaging 16 feet (range 7-30 ft.). In Colorado, McEllin (1979a) reported heights of 26 nests ranging from 12 to 57 feet (av. 35 ft.). All of these nests had limbs near the cavity (23 below the entrance, 3 to the side) that birds used for perching or alighting before entering the nest. The nest openings faced south or east, away from the prevailing winds and rain from the west and north. In Arizona, Hay and Güntert (1983) reported the height of ten nests averaging 18 feet. Compared with roost cavities used in any season, nesting cavities there were lower in shorter trees. Nest cavities and winter roost cavities had smaller entrances and were predominantly in trunks compared

298

with summer and fall/spring roost cavities, which were situated about equally in trunks or branches. Placement of nest cavities lower in shorter and smaller-diameter trees may represent a response to wind. Generally the nest cavities are positioned to obtain a moderate angle of insolation, face east to receive morning sunlight, and are protected from prevailing westerly winds.

Pygmy Nuthatches line their nest cavities with materials with good insulative qualities. The materials they use most frequently are feathers, bark shreds or fibers, moss, fur, hair, and wool (Norris 1958). Snakeskin, plant down, cotton or cottony substances, string, grass blades, bits of cloth, lichen, cocoon fibers, papery material from yellow-jacket nests, and miscellaneous soft materials are used less often; decayed wood or wood chips are used to an unknown degree. Pygmies may add materials to the lining well into the egg-laying period, and perhaps throughout it. They may use nest cavities in successive years (Norris 1958, McEllin 1979a, W.J. Sydeman pers. comm.).

Pygmy Nuthatches are more likely to be heard than seen as they forage in boisterous groups of 5 to 15 birds, mostly in the upper half of live pines in peripheral branches and foliage, including needle clusters, cones, and young shoots (Norris 1958, Stallcup 1968, Bock 1969, Manolis 1977, McEllin 1979b). To a lesser extent, and more frequently outside the breeding season, they forage on larger inner branches and the trunk (Stallcup 1968, Manolis 1977). Minor foraging substrates include dead branches, trees, stumps, and logs; branches and foliage of live broadleaved trees or shrubs are used more often during the breeding season (Stallcup 1968). The range of foraging heights increases during the nonbreeding season (Manolis 1977, McEllin 1979b). Ground foraging varies seasonally (Manolis 1977, Stallcup 1968), apparently depending upon the availability of seeds in opened cones that have fallen singly or on limbs or boughs; seeds are also obtained from cones in the tree crown. In ponderosa pine forest in Arizona, Pygmies exhibit annual variation in foraging techniques and other resource-use measures (Szaro et al. 1990).

Pygmy Nuthatches forage mostly by probing the basal portions of pine needle clusters, pine cones, twigs, and small branches (Norris 1958, McEllin 1979b). To a lesser extent, they forage by peering and poking, probing fissures in bark, scaling or flaking off bark, and by hovering or flycatching. Like other nuthatches, they are adept at hitching along branches and limbs in any plane while searching for prey. They cache seeds in crevices or under flakes of bark on the trunk or branches of trees. To open the seeds, Pygmies wedge them in a crack or crevice on a horizontal branch and hammer them vigorously. Rarely, insects caught by flycatching are also cached under bark (Sealy 1984). Since food caching is energetically costly, it is most appropriate when a food resource is available periodically and/or unpredictably and is stimulated when food is in excess and can be stored for times of need.

Over much of their range, though not in Marin County, Pygmy Nuthatches overlap broadly in habitat use (but not foraging strategies) with White-breasted Nuthatches (Stallcup 1968, Bock 1969, McEllin 1979b; see White-breasted account). White-breasteds complement their specialization in foraging substrates by generalizing in their feeding behavior and in the food items they take (McEllin 1979b). Pygmies, on the other hand, are generalists regarding foraging substrates but specialists in feeding behavior and food items taken, though they specialize less in the non-breeding season. These patterns suggest that White-breasteds forage for evenly distributed food items, whereas Pygmies forage for patchy ones. Anderson (1976) also noted that Pygmies selected food from only a few taxa in the breeding season although many forms were available. See Bock (1969) and Manolis (1977) for comparison of foraging strategy with Mountain Chickadee.

Based on 31 stomachs, Beal (1907) reported that the diet of Pygmy Nuthatches in California was 83% animal matter and 17% conifer seeds. Norris (1958) felt Beal's samples were probably taken mostly in late spring or early summer, thus overestimating the animal proportion of the diet. Norris (1958) examined 73 stomachs taken throughout the year in Marin County and found that pine seeds made up 65% of the diet overall. May was the only month in which animal food exceeded 70%, and the April-to-July diet (weighted by month) averaged about 57% animal matter. In Marin County, from October to at least January, the monthly diet ranged from 86% to 99% pine seeds. However, a late-December sample (n = 8) from Howell Mountain, Napa County, averaged 61% animal matter. In Oregon, the winter diet in ponderosa pine was 96% animal matter and 4% seeds; the use of bark-dwelling insects increased there in winter (Anderson 1976). On the whole, Pygmies' main animal prey are wasps, ants, true bugs, spittlebugs, beetles, caterpillars, crickets, and spiders. Norris (1958) noted a much greater reliance on beetles and less reliance on hymenoptera than did Beal (1907). Adults foraging for young rarely travel more than 400 feet (av. 170 ft.) from the nest, with the average distance traveled varying inversely with the density of the forest (Norris 1958). Adults initially feed young nestlings tiny insects and spiders, but later, as they grow, adults feed them larger items. After removing the hard integument, adults sometimes feed pine seeds to well-developed nestlings. When young first fledge, they tend to remain high in pines, and adults forage largely then in the topmost branches and foliage. As the young mature, they often descend to the lower strata and are prone to visit open cones on fallen pines. Vegetable food is nearly as important to juveniles as it is to adults.

Marin Breeding Distribution

The distribution of Pygmy Nuthatches in Marin County during the atlas period reflected the distribution of open conifer stands on Inverness Ridge (the species' stronghold), Bolinas Ridge, and Mount Tamalpais. The distribution of Pygmy Nuthatches was similar to that of Red-breasteds, except the latter were absent in the bishop pines on the north end of Inverness Ridge, whereas the former were less widely distributed east of Bolinas Ridge in the Lucas Valley area, where dense conifer stands in narrow canyons are more prevalent. Representative nesting locations of Pygmy Nuthatches were near Tomales Bay SP (NY/FY 6/14/82 —DS; this cavity was shared with a pair of Starlings!); Tomales Bay SP (NB 4/13/77 —RMS); and Vedanta Trail, Olema Valley (ON 4/24/82 —JGE).

Historical Trends/Population Threats

Few prior data exist. Pygmy Nuthatch numbers appeared to increase slightly on Breeding Bird Surveys in California from 1968 to 1989 but were relatively stable from 1980 to 1989 (USFWS unpubl. analyses).

Its sturdy long toes and stiff tail feathers enable the Brown Creeper to cling effortlessly to its coarse-grained domain.
Photograph by Ian Tait.

Creepers
Family *Certhiidae*

BROWN CREEPER *Certhia americana*

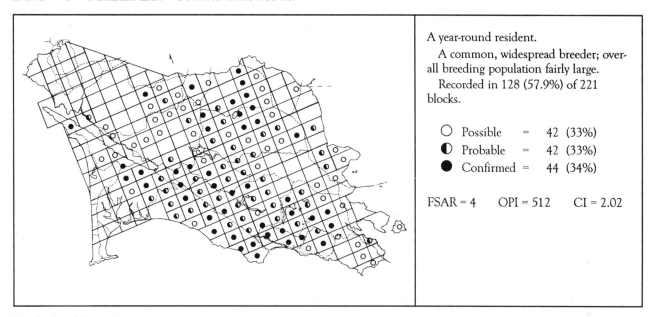

A year-round resident.

A common, widespread breeder; overall breeding population fairly large. Recorded in 128 (57.9%) of 221 blocks.

○	Possible	=	42 (33%)
◐	Probable	=	42 (33%)
●	Confirmed	=	44 (34%)

FSAR = 4   OPI = 512   CI = 2.02

Ecological Requirements

These bark brethren inhabit Marin County's moist, well-shaded, closed-canopied forests that provide moderate to large trunks and limbs for foraging. Breeding Creepers are particularly at home here in redwood, Douglas fir, bishop pine, mixed conifer hardwoods, and broadleaved evergreen forests; in the broadleaved evergreen realm, California bay laurels are important. To a limited extent, Creepers also frequent groves of planted cypresses and pines, and sometimes even eucalyptus. Creepers almost invariably place their nests in the cavities created by the bark separating from trees. Rarely, they locate them in knotholes, deserted woodpecker holes, on the tips of decaying stubs, or behind the shutters of a cabin (Tyler 1948c, Bent 1948). They situate nests in a variety of coniferous and deciduous trees but prefer dead or dying individuals or loose-barked species. Nests heights range from 1 to 60 feet, but most are less than 20 feet above the ground (Bent 1948, Davis 1978, Airola 1980). Airola (1980) reported that nest sites in the Sierra Nevada average 7 feet (range 1-21 ft.), whereas Davis (1978) reported that nest heights in Michigan average 10 feet (range 5-23 ft., n = 20). In Michigan, openings in the canopy permit light penetration to each nest site. The nest conforms to the shape of the cavity and is

attached to the rough bark (not the tree) with spider web cases and insect cocoons. The base, made of twigs and pieces of bark, is a hammock- or crescent-shaped structure that extends up on the sides in long narrow points or "horns" several inches above a centrally located nest cup. The cup is made of fine bark and wood fibers with lesser amounts of moss, feathers, or plant down.

Foraging Creepers procure most of their food by gleaning from the surface and by probing or pecking crevices, cracks, and fissures of the bark with their fine, slightly decurved beaks (Airola & Barrett 1985, Franzreb 1985, Morrison et al. 1987, Lundquist & Manuwal 1990). They very rarely hover-glean or hawk insects. Creepers use three basic patterns to scour bark surfaces while foraging (Franzreb 1985). They climb/hitch straight up trunks, carefully detouring around branches. They may also work up the trunk, then climb out branches clinging to the undersurface upside down. They then fly to the top of the branch, work their way back along the top of it to the trunk, and repeat the process as they advance up the tree. In addition, they may spiral around the trunk and branches as they move upward. Regardless of the method of upward movement, all birds generally work to within about 3 to 10

301

feet of the treetop. Then they fly to the base of a trunk of another tree, generally to within a few feet of the ground, and begin again their search for prey. Creepers tend to change trees when they reach a height where branch density increases to such a degree that maneuverability is impaired.

Birds prefer large trees for feeding because they have more foraging surface and tend to have bark with deeper and more numerous crevices for harboring prey. Foraging Creepers generally select more for tree height than for tree species (Airola & Barrett 1985, Franzreb 1985, Lundquist & Manuwal 1990). See Morrison et al. (1985, 1987) for seasonal changes in preferences for foraging on various conifers in the Sierra Nevada. Creepers forage almost exclusively on trunks and branches and only rarely on logs or the ground (Airola & Barrett 1985; Franzreb 1985; Morrison et al. 1985, 1987). Breeding birds choose trunks as their foraging substrate about 70%-90% of the time (Franzreb 1985; Morrison et al. 1985, 1987; Lundquist & Manuwal 1990). In the Sierra Nevada, birds increase trunk use from about 80% in summer to over 95% in winter (Morrison et al. 1985). In the Washington Cascades, by contrast, Creepers reduce trunk foraging from about 90% in spring to 70% in winter (Lundquist & Manuwal 1990). Airola and Barrett (1985) considered the Brown Creeper a medium-height forager in comparison to other insect-gleaning (mostly on foliage) birds in the Sierra Nevada. Working in the same forest, however, Morrison et al. (1987) found that Creepers foraged significantly lower than other bark gleaners. These differences probably reflect the wide range of heights at which Creepers forage, rather than a preference by the birds to forage low in trees. As noted above, Creepers forage where there are large, exposed bark surfaces, and by nature these tend to be distributed more on the lower trunks but can also occur at considerable heights in large trees. Creepers vary little seasonally or geographically in their prey capture methods (Lundquist & Manuwal 1990, Petit et al. 1990), or in their choice of spatial (horizontal or vertical) aspects of foraging locations (Lundquist & Manuwal 1990). Creepers forage predominantly on live trees (Airola & Barrett 1985, Morrison et al. 1987). In Arizona, Franzreb (1985) found

Creepers feeding on snags slightly more than would be predicted by their availability in the forest (Franzreb 1985). In Washington, Creepers use live and dead trees in proportion to their availability, regardless of season or forest age (Lundquist & Manuwal 1990).

What little is known of the Creeper diet indicates it is largely beetles, wasps, ants, true bugs, moths, caterpillars, spiders, pseudoscorpions, flies, and a few seeds (Beal 1907, Martin et al. 1951, Davis 1978, Dahlsten et al. 1985, Otvos & Stark 1985). Spiders may be an important Creeper food. In the Washington Cascades, spiders were found in all (n = 6) Creeper digestive tracts examined (Mariani & Manuwal 1990). Creeper abundance there was correlated positively with large Douglas fir trees (known for deeply furrowed bark) and the abundance of medium-size spiders. Spiders (all sizes) and soft-bodied arthropods were positively associated with bark furrow depth, which in turn was highly correlated with tree diameter.

Marin Breeding Distribution

The distribution of breeding Creepers in Marin County during the atlas period mirrored that of closed-canopied forests here. Creepers were most numerous and widespread in the forests in the fog zone of the immediate coastal ridges. In the northern interior, they were patchily distributed in narrow canyons or on north-facing slopes. Representative breeding locations were Upper Pierce Ranch cypress grove, Tomales Point (FY/NY 6/15/82 –DS); Mt. Burdell, Novato (NY/FY 5/25/81 –ScC, DS); and Cascade Canyon, Fairfax (NY/FY 5/11/81 –DS).

Historical Trends/Population Threats

Grinnell and Miller (1944) suspected that removal of old-growth forests had reduced the California population, particularly in the interior mountains. This likely also occurred at one point in the coastal region. Creeper populations did decrease in the Sierra-Trinity mountains of California during the period 1968 to 1979 (Robbins et al. 1986) but showed no trend for California as a whole from 1968 to 1989 (USFWS unpubl. analyses).

Wrens
Family *Troglodytidae*

ROCK WREN *Salpinctes obsoletus*

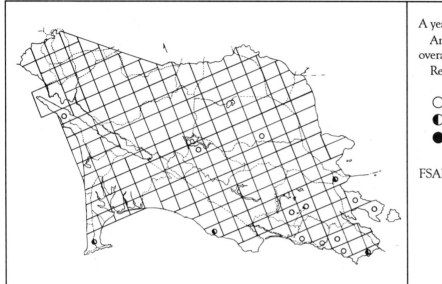

A year-round resident.

An uncommon, very local breeder; overall breeding population very small. Recorded in 15 (6.8%) of 221 blocks.

○	Possible	=	11	(73%)
◑	Probable	=	4	(27%)
●	Confirmed	=	0	(0%)

FSAR = 2   OPI = 30   CI = 1.27

Ecological Requirements

This spritely bouncy wren usually breeds in relatively barren rocky substrates, though in some regions, arroyos of hard sun-baked earth provide alternative habitat. Migrants and wintering birds may pause at small rock tumbles, cutbanks, or even at woodpiles or among the roots of upturned trees. Breeding birds, however, generally need a fair extent of broken or fractured rock or burrowed earth with numerous crannies and crevices for foraging and nesting sites. Rock Wrens flourish over a wide range of altitude, humidity, and temperature, factors that appear to have little overall influence on habitat selection in this species (G&M 1944). The broad tolerances of Rock Wrens are not matched by their cousins, Canyon Wrens. Where they overlap (not in Marin), these species are separated by slope and microclimate preferences. In Arizona, Tramontano (1964) found that where the two species breed sympatrically, Rock Wrens inhabit slopes of loose rock and scattered boulders whereas Canyon Wrens frequent precipitous outcroppings, cliffs, and canyon walls. Rock Wrens there choose nest sites on rocky slopes of any orientation except north facing, whereas Canyon Wrens choose nest sites invariably along north-, northwest-, or west-facing cliffs. In essence, Rock Wrens prefer more open, sunny exposures, Canyon Wrens cooler shaded ones.

Marin County is rather meagerly endowed with rocky cliffs or boulder piles and entirely wanting in inland talus slopes and lava flows. The few Rock Wrens that breed here inhabit coastal sea cliffs of Monterey shale and conglomerate and the odd quarry or serpentine outcrop. Although our sea cliffs are of wide extent, they provide few gentle or moderate slopes and are poorly outfitted with boulders, nooks, and crannies.

Rock Wrens usually place their nests inside cavities and small crevices among or under rocks, or in natural or rodent-excavated holes in earthen cutbanks. Less commonly, they build them in human structures, such as adobe walls of buildings or old stone reservoirs; in some areas, they even use fallen tree trunks (Dawson 1923, Bent 1948). The nest entrance is almost invariably paved with a runway of small flat stones, rock flakes, or pebbles (or, infrequently, similar human debris). The same materials underlie or are incorporated into the nest itself. The function of the paving is unknown, but it may aid in

303

preventing dampness inside the nest (Bent 1948). Alternatively, perhaps the rattling of the stones by a potential predator attracts the attention of the sitting bird and serves as a burglar alarm of sorts (Dawson 1923)! Rock Wrens sometimes use nest sites for successive broods (Tramontano 1964). The nest is a shallow saucer made of twigs, grasses, straw, weed stems, and rootlets. It is sometimes scantily lined with fine grasses, bark strips, rootlets, horsehair, sheep's wool, or perhaps a few feathers.

While foraging, Rock Wrens run with ease over open or broken rocky terrain, gleaning from the surface or probing cracks and crevices. They seldom hop or creep while foraging as Canyon Wrens commonly do (Tramontano 1964). Rock Wrens also occasionally fly-catch for insects, especially when breeding, and sometimes take aquatic insects from small pools of water. Rock Wrens spend nearly 90% of their foraging time in open or relatively uncovered situations. In contrast, Canyon Wrens spend 70% of their time foraging in relatively covered or secluded microclimates, for which their relatively longer, more slender bills and shorter tarsi are better suited. Rock Wrens commonly forage over rocky hillsides, open slopes, dry washes, and riverbeds, but only rarely along crevices of cliffs or steep canyon walls. They spend about 70% of their foraging time during breeding on south-, southeast-, or east-facing slopes. Breeding Canyon Wrens, on the other hand, are adapted to forage along steep but relatively cool exposed slopes. They spend about 60%-85% of their time foraging on cliffs or canyon walls and about 90%-95% of their time on north-, northwest-, or west-facing slopes. During breeding, males of both species feed the females at the nest.

The Rock Wren diet consists of a variety of primarily ground-dwelling insects in the 0.1- to 0.5-inch size range plus small amounts of seeds and other plant material (Tramontano 1964). The main animal fare is beetles, leafhoppers, ants, ant lions, moths and their larvae, true bugs, grasshoppers, and spiders.

Marin Breeding Distribution

Although recorded at scattered sites, Rock Wrens were not confirmed breeding in Marin County during the atlas period. The only known confirmed breeding record for Marin is of a nest with young discovered at Tiburon on 29 April 1933 (S&P 1933). Areas in Marin County where Rock Wrens were seen consistently in the breeding season were the Point Reyes headlands near the lighthouse (T 4/30-7/1/81 —DS); the Double Point cliffs (T Mar–Jun 1978 & 1979 —SGA); and a quarry near Larkspur Landing (T spring 1982 —SSm).

Historical Trends/Population Threats

Historically, breeding Rock Wrens have always occurred in limited numbers in Marin County, with most residing along ocean cliffs (Mailliard 1900, S&P 1933). The excavation of quarries in Marin may have slightly increased the number of breeding stations here. Rock Wrens have declined historically as breeders on the nearby Farallon Islands, though this appears to be a local phenomenon, perhaps attributable to predation by a rebounding Western Gull population (DeSante & Ainley 1980). An increase of Rock Wrens on Breeding Bird Surveys in California from 1968 to 1979 (Robbins et al. 1986) was not evident for the period 1968 to 1989 (USFWS unpubl. analyses).

BEWICK'S WREN *Thryomanes bewickii*

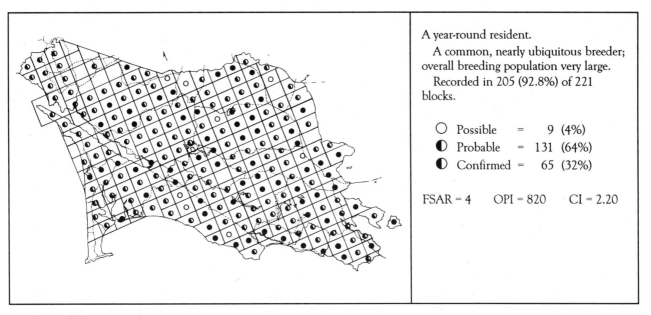

A year-round resident.

A common, nearly ubiquitous breeder; overall breeding population very large.

Recorded in 205 (92.8%) of 221 blocks.

○ Possible	=	9	(4%)
◑ Probable	=	131	(64%)
◑ Confirmed	=	65	(32%)

FSAR = 4   OPI = 820   CI = 2.20

Ecological Requirements

The boisterous song and petulant scolding calls of the Bewick's Wren are heard much more frequently than the bird is seen as it scurries through the underbrush of a wide variety of Marin County habitats. The Bewick's Wren generally occupies an intermediate position on the local habitat scale between the Winter Wren, which favors thick tangly growth under dense forests close to permanent creeks, and the House Wren, which dwells here in open woodlands with little or no understory. The strongholds of the Bewick's Wren in this region are the coastal scrub- and chaparral-covered hillsides. It also breeds commonly in riparian thickets; along the brushy margins of oak woodlands, mixed evergreen forests, and conifer forests; and in hedgerows and suburban plantings, including eucalyptus. Although Bewick's Wrens frequently use a mixture of trees and shrubs in these habitats, all they need is a moderately dense brush layer with some openings, as evidenced by their abundance in pure stands of coastal scrub and chaparral. In fact, they avoid a dense overstory, because light penetration to the shrub layer and ground is essential. In Oregon, territories of Bewick's and House wrens may overlap, although the species have distinctly different habitat preferences (Kroodsma 1973). There (as in Marin) Bewick's Wrens prefer a fairly dense understory, whereas House Wrens prefer an open one, and the two species coexist in heterogeneous habitat where patches suitable to each intermingle. In parts of coastal California, House Wrens sometimes defend territories that exclude Bewick's Wrens (Root 1969a). This is probably an infrequent occur-

rence, since habitat preferences alone usually separate these birds, except at edges of oak woodlands and some riparian woodlands.

Bewick's Wrens locate their nests from ground level to about 25 feet, though most are below 6 feet (Bent 1948). They are almost exclusively cavity nesters, but the variety of sites they use is somewhat astonishing (Bent 1948). Common nest sites are natural cavities in trees or stumps, holes in the ground or in low-cut banks, old woodpecker holes, the centers of dense clumps of brush, and spaces under the upturned roots of fallen trees. Less frequently used, and presumably less available, are sites under the peeled bark of a tree, in rock piles or cliff cavities, in bird boxes, at the mouths of Rough-winged Swallow burrows, or in old nests of birds such as orioles and mockingbirds. Bewick's Wrens also commonly use "artificial" sites in inhabited areas. These include deserted automobiles, cow skulls in pastures, tin cans, discarded cardboard cartons on the ground, the pockets of jackets hung on a wall, and inside the walls of a trailer (to name but a few). The nest itself is generally a bulky open cup conforming to the size of the cavity. Occasionally, if placed in a situation without a complete obstruction on all sides, nests are domed or arched over at the top, with a side entrance (E.V. Miller 1941). Nest materials include sticks and twigs, straw, coarse feathers, fine bark, weed stems, rootlets, moss, dead leaves, string, and other debris. The wrens mat these together with spider webs and cocoons and line the nests with fur, soft feathers, hair, wool, or cotton (E.V. Miller 1941, Bent 1948).

In various habitats in the Berkeley area, Bewick's Wrens forage from the ground to the tops of lofty trees, though mostly at the lower levels (E.V. Miller 1941). They gather most food there by gleaning and probing while hopping and flitting among the dense branches, limbs, and foliage of weeds, brush, and trees. They sometimes venture more into the open, clinging to tree trunks or the underside of branches. These wrens will also drop to the ground to pick from the surface or overturn leaves with their bill, but they do not scratch the litter or soil with their feet. On occasion, Bewick's Wrens will fly directly to, or flutter underneath, a branch to pick insects from it while airborne. In the early spring, the sexes seem to split the foraging niche in mixed habitat: males feed up in the trees, whereas females work within a foot or two of the ground (E.V. Miller 1941).

In oak woodlands in Arizona, Bewick's Wrens forage in the lower strata, mostly by probing and gleaning from branches, twigs, trunks, and leaves on the ground; rarely, they hawk or hover (Miles 1990). Over two years of study, probing represented 77%-82% of foraging attempts in May and June and 35%-46% in July; gleaning varied from 17% to 18% and from 54% to 64% of foraging attempts in the corresponding periods. Gleaning not only increased in July, but also shifted greatly then to the ground, presumably in response to the flush of annual plant growth (and insects) following summer rains. Bewick's Wrens there also varied their monthly and annual use of many other foraging substrates. Wagner (1981) found seasonal differences in substrate use and foraging height of Bewick's Wrens in one year of a two-year study in mixed oak woodland on the central California coast.

The diet of the Bewick's Wren in California is about 97% animal matter and 3% vegetable, the latter including a few seeds, galls, and "rubbish" (Beal 1907, n = 146). The animal food is primarily true bugs, beetles, ants, wasps, caterpillars, moths, grasshoppers, other insects, and spiders.

Marin Breeding Distribution

During the atlas period, the Bewick's Wren bred throughout most of Marin County. It was absent from only a few atlas blocks in grassland areas devoid of extensive brushy draws. Representative breeding locations were Limantour Spit (NY 4/27/80 –JGE); Kleiser Ranch, Walker Creek (NY above a headlight of a defunct Ford Falcon 5/23/82 –DS); Hick's Valley (NY 5/16/82 –DS et al.); Woodacre (FY 5/31/82 –BiL); and the ridge and valley W of Loma Alta (FL 6/4/82 –BiL).

Historical Trends/Population Threats

Few historical data exist. Bewick's Wren numbers were relatively stable on Breeding Bird Surveys in California from 1968 to 1989 but declined from 1980 to 1989 (USFWS unpubl. analyses).

HOUSE WREN   *Troglodytes aedon*

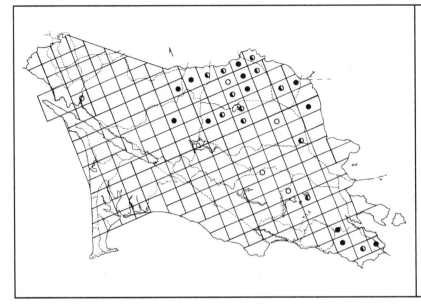

Primarily a summer resident from late
Mar through Oct; irregular through late
fall and early winter.

An uncommon, very local breeder;
overall breeding population very small.
Recorded in 29 (13.1%) of 221 blocks.

○	Possible	=	5 (17%)
◖	Probable	=	12 (41%)
●	Confirmed	=	12 (41%)

FSAR = 2   OPI = 58   CI = 2.24

Ecological Requirements

Those who know House Wrens well in Marin County
might consider their name an alias, as they are infrequently
seen here around human habitation. Most of our nesting
birds frequent open-canopied deciduous oak woodlands,
with little or no understory, or relatively open interior
riparian woodlands. Rarely, they set up domestic duties
here in open, mixed evergreen forests or eucalyptus groves.
Although House Wren territories do sometimes abut or
overlap those of Bewick's Wrens, the latter generally
choose woodlands or brushy habitats with denser tangles
(see account).

House Wrens are cavity nesters, and their choice of sites
is as varied and eccentric as that of Bewick's Wrens (see
account). Since House Wrens are less of a dooryard bird
in our area, and in the West in general, they nest here
mostly in natural cavities, crevices, or old woodpecker
holes in trees, stumps, or fallen logs. They also occupy nest
boxes and an array of artificial sites. In Marin County, a
House Wren once nested near San Geronimo "in the end
of the exhaust pipe of a temporarily idle stationary steam
engine attached to a large pump" (Mailliard 1936). Nest
heights can range from ground level to about 164 feet
(Bent 1948). An average nest height of 14 feet (range
2.5-42 ft., n = 21) in the Sierra Nevada (Airola 1980) is
probably representative of the species' predilections. Nests
are large bulky structures made mainly of small twigs or
sticks that generally fill the entire cavity except for the
nesting chamber. In the rare case in which an enclosed
cavity is not selected, the nest may be a conical or pyramid-
shaped pile of sticks, nearly closed at the top, with a tiny

entrance to admit the owner. The nest lining is usually of
feathers, grass, hair, or rootlets. A wide variety of other nest
materials may be used, including human artifacts and
snakeskin. Males are in the habit of building additional
"fake" or "dummy" nests either before or after the female
has begun incubation (Kendeigh 1941a, Bent 1948, Gross
1948). Although House Wrens have frequently been
reported destroying the nests, eggs, and young of other
birds, this trait has apparently not been found in the
western race (Bent 1948).

House Wrens forage by gleaning and probing cracks
and crevices as they scurry about on the ground, on the
trunks and limbs of trees, or in vine tangles, brush, or
downed branches. On occasion, they also hawk aerial
insects (Gross 1948). The diet in California is 97.5%
animal matter and 2.5% vegetable, though the latter is
mainly "rubbish" and probably swallowed accidentally
(Beal 1907, n = 36). The main animal foods are true bugs,
caterpillars, beetles, grasshoppers, ants and other hymenoptera, other insects, and spiders.

Marin Breeding Distribution

During the atlas period, Marin County's breeding House
Wrens were concentrated in the northeastern hills around
Novato, especially on Mount Burdell. This area supports
the county's most extensive deciduous oak woodlands. The
few House Wrens found in southern Marin were in open
mixed evergreen forest or eucalyptus groves. Representative
breeding localities included Mt. Burdell, Novato (NB-FY
4/24-5/9/81 —ITi); near Stafford Lake, Novato (ON

307

5/6/79 —KH; FY spring 1982 —ScC); and Nicasio (ON 5/9/81 —EV).

Historical Trends/Population Threats

Mailliard (1900) considered the House Wren a "common summer resident [and] not very abundant" in Marin County, whereas Stephens and Pringle (1933) considered it a "fairly common" summer resident here. It currently fits these rough verbal descriptions of abundance only in the Novato area, which suggests (but does not document) a decline here since the earlier part of this century. On the other hand, data from the Even Cheaper Thrills Spring Bird Count suggest that House Wrens were increasing in northeastern Marin from 1978 to 1987 (Appendix A). House Wren populations declined on Breeding Bird Surveys in the California Foothills, including coastal counties south of Monterey and parts of those to the north, from 1968 to 1979 (Robbins et al. 1986) but were relatively stable in California as a whole from 1968 to 1989 (USFWS unpubl. analyses).

The Marsh Wren's energy abounds as both a chatterbox and a prolific nest builder. Photograph by Ian Tait.

WINTER WREN *Troglodytes troglodytes*

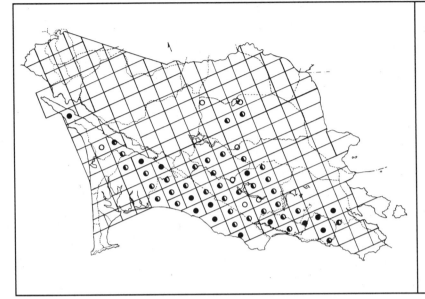

A year-round resident; numbers swell somewhat from mid-Aug to early Apr.
A common, local breeder; overall breeding population small.
Recorded in 56 (25.3%) of 221 blocks.

○ Possible = 7 (13%)
◑ Probable = 35 (62%)
● Confirmed = 14 (25%)

FSAR = 4   OPI = 224   CI = 2.12

Ecological Requirements

This stubby dark fidgety wren blends well with its breeding season surroundings in Marin County's dense, well-shaded, moist forests of conifers, mixed conifers and hardwoods, or broadleaved evergreen trees—forests that host a tangled understory of huckleberry, sword ferns, and mossy downed logs. Winter Wrens usually occupy canyons with permanent streams, where their loud bubbling song bursts forth over the sound of rushing water. Most Winter Wrens in Europe are polygynous breeders, but most in North America are monogamous (Horne & Bader 1990). Favorite nesting sites are in cubbyholes and crannies in the upturned roots of fallen logs, among the roots of trees overhanging gully banks, fire holes in half-burned stumps, in or under rotted stumps or downed logs, and in attached moss or crevices on rock faces or cliffs (Bent 1948). Less commonly, Winter Wrens will nest between the logs of an unoccupied log hut, in an old woodpecker hole, in the center of a baby fir, in the low drooping branches of a conifer, or in a clump of shoots growing from the trunk of an alder. Although nests in some areas have been found 100 feet above the ground, most nests in forested habitats range from the ground to about 12 feet. The nest proper is a globular, more or less bulky affair that fits the shape of the cavity and has a tiny side entrance. The outer part of the nest is mostly mosses with a base of (or reinforced with) grass, weed stems, fine twigs, and rootlets; the lining consists of fur, feathers, delicate roots, or fine filamentous lichens.

Winter Wrens forage by gleaning and probing low in the undergrowth, on the ground, and along stream edges (where they also occasionally dip their heads under water in pursuit of aquatic insects). In coastal Oregon, adults forage on virtually any substrate within about 10 feet of the ground, including shrubs, logs, and slash and litter on the ground itself (Horne & Bader 1990). In the East, Winter Wrens consume almost 100% animal matter; the main prey there are beetles, true bugs, spiders, caterpillars, and ants and other small hymenoptera (Bent 1948). Among the four taxa most commonly fed to nestlings in Oregon, spiders and adult beetles appear (based on fecal samples) to be preferred over lepidoptera (butterfly and moth) larvae and adult flies (Horne & Bader 1990). Adults wrens there select a higher number of larger prey than are randomly available and on average bring in larger arthropods to the young wrens as they mature. A proportional increase in beetles, and decrease in lepidoptera larvae, in the diet of maturing young, may reflect greater selectivity of adults (for caterpillars) early on when food demands and feeding rates are low, or the difficulty that small young have in digesting insects encased in hard chitinous shells.

Marin Breeding Distribution

The distribution of breeding Winter Wrens in Marin County during the atlas period closely paralleled the distribution of moist forests on the immediate coast. Strongholds were Inverness Ridge, southern Bolinas Ridge, and additional moist lower canyons of the Mount Tamalpais

309

watersheds. A few small isolated populations occupied north-facing slopes and canyons of Big Rock Ridge, more toward the interior of the county. Representative breeding records were Upper Pierce Ranch, Tomales Point (FY 5/18/82 –DS); ½ mi. S of Inverness (NB 4/19/77 – RMS); and Lake Ranch Gate, Inverness Ridge (FY/FL 5/?/76 –JGE).

Historical Trends/Population Threats

Little prior data exist. Numbers of Winter Wrens on Breeding Bird Surveys in California increased from 1968 to 1979 (Robbins et al. 1986); this was balanced by a decrease in numbers from 1980 to 1989, leaving no upward or downward trend for the entire period 1968 to 1989 (USFWS unpubl. analyses).

MARSH WREN *Cistothorus palustris*

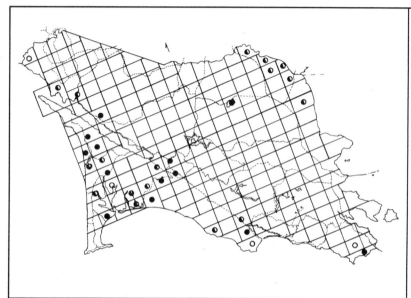

A year-round resident.
  A common, local breeder; overall breeding population very small.
    Recorded in 34 (15.4%) of 221 blocks.

○ Possible   =   4 (12%)
◑ Probable   =   17 (50%)
● Confirmed =   13 (38%)

FSAR = 4   OPI = 136   CI = 2.26

Ecological Requirements

The effervescent song of this high-spirited wren enhances Marin County's freshwater and brackish marshes and coastal swales. The basic requisites for breeding birds seem to be standing water or saturated soil and tall, dense marsh vegetation for concealment and placement of nests. In Marin County, Marsh Wrens almost always breed in fairly extensive tall stands of cattails and California tules. They are more choosy here about nesting in the low-growing marsh vegetation of coastal swales. Although Marsh Wrens use rush-dominated *(Juncus)* swales, that is not always the rule. Marsh Wrens typically avoid breeding in swales dominated by the low-growing bulrush *(Scirpus microcarpus)*—a habitat used by Common Yellowthroats, which generally have more stringent habitat preferences than Marsh Wrens.

Because Marsh Wrens are polygamous, males build multiple nests. They use these to attract females, which may choose one of them or initiate a new one, completed mostly by the male (Verner 1963, 1964, 1965). Verner and Engelson (1970) reported that the number of nests each

male built ranged from 10 to 50 and averaged about 25. Nests are domed ellipsoids with the single, round, wren-sized opening placed in the upper half (Welter 1935, Bent 1948, Verner 1965). Birds construct the outer shell of the nest by interlacing pliable, water-soaked cattail leaves, rushes, and stems and leaves of sedges and grasses and stuffing the latticework with cattail or other plant down. Display or dummy nests are devoid of a lining. To brood nests, the female adds a lining consisting of grass and sedge leaves and an insulating layer of cattail down, feathers, small rootlets, and shredded plant material. Marsh Wrens prefer to anchor their nests to cattails, in stands of moderate density, and less frequently use bulrushes, sedges, tall marsh grasses, and, rarely, small bushes or trees. They generally (but not always) nest in emergent vegetation; a preference for cattails may switch to bulrushes when water levels drop as the season progresses (Verner & Engelson 1970). Nest heights can range from 6 inches in low marsh vegetation to 15 feet in trees. A large sample (n = 629) of breeding and nonbreeding nests at various cattail-bulrush

310

marshes in Washington ranged in height from 12 to 77 inches and averaged 35.6 inches above the marsh floor (Verner 1965). Nest height varies in direct relation to the seasonal change in height of supporting cover caused by plant growth; early nests may be in the remains of the previous season's growth. Dummy nests, besides their use in courtship, also serve as nighttime roosts and secondary shelters for fledged young (Bent 1948, Verner 1965, Verner & Engelson 1970).

Marsh Wrens obtain most of their sustenance by gleaning from marsh vegetation, from bordering brushy willows, from the floor of the marsh, and near or from the surface of the water. They infrequently hawk flying insects. In Washington's cattail-bulrush marshes, Marsh Wrens prefer bulrushes for foraging. Presumably bulrushes promote higher productivity, because they are more thoroughly broken down in winter than are cattails, thus allowing more light to penetrate to the water's surface (Verner 1964). The California diet is 98% animal matter along with a few seeds of marsh plants (Beal 1907, n = 53). The main animal items are true bugs, caterpillars, beetles, ants, wasps, flies (especially crane flies and mosquitoes), grasshoppers, dragonflies, other insects, spiders, and snails. Marsh Wrens have long been known to occasionally prey on the eggs of other marsh-nesting birds (Bent 1948); this may affect habitat choice of other species in an area where the wrens are particularly abundant.

Marin Breeding Distribution

The patchy distribution of Marin County's breeding Marsh Wrens during the atlas period reflected that of their nesting marshes. Most breeding birds were found in the lowlands, especially on the Point Reyes peninsula and in marshes bordering San Pablo Bay near Novato. Representative nesting locations were Drake's Beach visitor's center, Point Reyes (FL 5/27/80 —DS); Olema Marsh (NE-NY Apr 1984-1988 —JGE); and Pine Gulch Creek, Bolinas Lagoon (NE/NY 4/24/77 —DS).

Historical Trends/Population Threats

Since these wee *Cistothores* are wedded to luxuriant marsh vegetation, they have undoubtedly declined dramatically with the clearing and draining of marshes for agriculture and development, especially around San Francisco Bay. Historically, there has been an estimated loss of 60%-95% of former tidal marsh habitat around San Francisco Bay (Nichols & Wright 1971, Josselyn 1983). The loss of *freshwater* marshland, with which the Marsh Wren is closely associated, has probably been even greater, as this plant community occupies the upland bayshore areas most prone to development. Numbers of Marsh Wrens were relatively stable on Breeding Bird Surveys in California from 1968 to 1989 (USFWS unpubl. analyses), a period after the greatest loss of wetlands.

Dippers
Family *Cinclidae*

AMERICAN DIPPER *Cinclus mexicanus*

Formerly a year-round resident; now occurs as an irregular winter resident, mostly from Oct through Mar.

Ecological Requirements

The celebrated water-ouzel truly embodies the spirit of swift and turbulent mountain streams. Although Dippers live on a variety of fast-flowing streams, creeks, and rivers, their favorites (at least in Colorado) are those with a rubble-strewn bottom (rocks 1–8 in. in size) and many emergent rocks harboring an adequate and easily obtainable food supply (Price & Bock 1983). In the breeding season, adequate nest sites are also a limiting factor. Dippers characteristically choose nest sites that are over, or nearly over, the edge of a stream; are sheltered from weather; and are inaccessible to predators (Hann 1950, Price & Bock 1983). Very rarely, they select sites set back as much as 28 feet from the water (Sullivan 1966). Dippers build their nests on narrow ledges or niches in vertical rock walls (often among mosses and ferns), under the roots of standing or fallen trees at streamside, under overhanging banks, on midstream rocks, on support beams of bridges or other buildings, or, rarely, in a cavity in the sloping top of a stream-edge stump (Bent 1948, Hann 1950, Bakus 1959, Price & Bock 1983). They also use artificial nest boxes on vertical faces over water (Hawthorne 1979).

Although nests may conform to the size of the available space and may occasionally be open at the top, most consist of a spherical or domelike outer shell made chiefly of mosses interwoven with a few grass stalks and roots; an inner cup-shaped lining of dry, coarse grasses; and a neatly arched opening at the bottom (Bent 1948, Hann 1950, Bakus 1959). Dippers may place their nests behind or near waterfalls, and if they situate them within the spray zone, the mosses of the nest stay green throughout the nesting season. Although generally solitary, monogamous breeders, Dippers are on occasion polygynous, with males mated simultaneously to two females with separate nests (Price & Bock 1973, 1983; Marti & Everett 1978).

To procure food, Dippers become one with their element. Although noted for their mastery of rapids and underwater dives, Dippers actually obtain most food where it is more readily available—from the slow-flowing water of pools, backwaters, stream edges, and lake margins (Thut 1970). In search of prey, ouzels run, walk, or hop (in rough or steep terrain) along rocky stream margins and wade into the water, clinging to slippery rocks with the aid of stout legs and sharp claws. Often a bird will stand on submerged rocks and, facing the current, hold its head under the water to glean prey from rock surfaces, probe among and under small stones, or catch items carried downstream by the current. Dippers also skim food from the surface as they traverse open water, paddling with their nonwebbed feet and flapping their wings. They will also frequently fly low in the air (less than 10 ft. above streams) to snatch airborne insects (Bent 1948, Hann 1950, Bakus 1959, Goodge 1959). These aquatic passerines show their true chutzpah by diving, usually against the current, from the air, from perches or emergent rocks, or from the water's surface. Once they make subsurface contact, they seemingly walk on the bottom, though rarely without lots of aid from flapping wings (Goodge 1959). The diet is predominantly aquatic insect larvae—particularly midges, caddisflies, stoneflies, mayflies, and mosquitoes—as well as adults of aquatic insects such as waterbugs and beetles, aerial insects, segmented worms, snails, and fish fry and eggs (Burcham 1904, Bent 1948, Bakus 1959, Thut 1970).

Marin Breeding Distribution/Historical Trends/Population Threats

Dippers were not found nesting in Marin County during the atlas period. In fact, the only historical breeding evidence is the report of Mailliard (1900) that "a pair formerly bred near the headwaters of Lagunitas Creek. None seen for some years." Historically, the American Dipper may always have been a rare and irregular breeder in Marin County because of the marginal suitability of local streams. The construction of a system of four dams and reservoirs in the Lagunitas Creek watershed from 1873 to 1953 probably sealed the fate of nesting Dippers in Marin County, though a sighting of a Dipper at Samuel P. Taylor State Park on 24 June 1966 (*Gull* 48:61) leaves hope for their occasional nesting. At present, American Dippers occur in Marin County only as rare and irregular winter residents on coastal streams of the Point Reyes and Mount Tamalpais watersheds (Shuford 1982, ABN). On the whole, Dipper numbers were relatively stable on Breeding Bird Surveys in California from 1968 to 1989, though they increased from 1980 to 1989 (USFWS unpubl. analyses).

Kinglets and Gnatcatchers
Family *Muscicapidae*
Subfamily *Sylviinae*

GOLDEN-CROWNED KINGLET *Regulus satrapa*

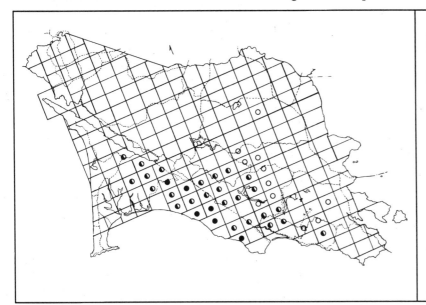

A year-round resident; numbers swell from mid-Oct through Mar.

An uncommon, local breeder; overall breeding population very small.

Recorded in 42 (19.0%) of 221 blocks.

○ Possible	=	11	(26%)
◑ Probable	=	25	(60%)
● Confirmed	=	6	(14%)

FSAR = 2   OPI = 84   CI = 1.88

Ecological Requirements

These diminutive Old World warblers are among the most difficult of small landbirds to see in the nesting season when they stay well concealed in closed- or open-canopy conifer forests dominated by trees with high needle density (Beedy 1981, Franzreb 1984). In Marin County, they breed almost exclusively in cool, shaded Douglas fir and redwood forests, but not in bishop pine forests.

Nest heights have been recorded from 4 to 64 feet above the ground, but because nests are generally well concealed in the upper canopy, extreme heights may be greater (Bent 1949, Galati & Galati 1985). In Minnesota, Galati and Galati (1985) found 19 nests that averaged 50 feet in height (range 27–64 ft.). In second-growth habitat in New Hampshire, Durfee (in Bent 1949) found 9 nests ranging from 8 to 46 feet in height, but except for the highest the rest averaged only 14 feet. Rathbun (in Bent 1949) reported a similar range of 9 to 45 feet for an unspecified number of nests near Seattle. Golden-crowned Kinglets generally attach their nests to the radiating twigs of conifer boughs at varying distances from, but usually near, the trunk. They conceal them so well that they are not visible to humans from above or at nest level and are only partly visible from

below. Dense overhanging foliage protects the nests from rain, sun, and wind. Protection from the wind is further ensured by placement of the nest on the leeward side of the tree (Galati & Galati 1985).

The nest is a deep globular or oblong cup, constricted or arched over slightly at the top. It is made chiefly of mosses bound by spider webs, parts of insect cocoons, and soft plant fibers. Kinglets interweave additional materials or ornamentation of lichens, dead leaves and grasses, and conifer needles into the mossy matrix. They line the cup with fine strips of bark, lichens, animal hair, feathers, fine rootlets, and other soft vegetable fibers (Bent 1949, Galati & Galati 1985).

The Golden-crowned Kinglet's elusiveness is more a function of the time it spends in dense foliage than its height above the observer. These kinglets forage throughout tall conifers but concentrate at middle elevations; they infrequently use pines, oaks, and snags (Franzreb 1984, Airola & Barrett 1985, Morrison et al. 1985). They expend most foraging effort at the tips of boughs in foliage, on small twigs and branches, and only rarely on trunks, cones, logs, or the ground. These kinglets capture prey

313

primarily by gleaning, secondarily by hovering, and infrequently by lunging, hawking, pecking or probing. The diet is predominantly adults, larvae, and eggs of arthropods, including wasps, ants, true bugs, flies, beetles, moths, butterflies, caterpillars, spiders, and pseudoscorpions (Beal 1907, n = 9; Bent 1949; Dahlsten et al. 1985); surprisingly, vegetable matter made up 27.5% of the diet of a small sample of breeding birds (n = 9) in the Sierra Nevada (Dahlsten et al. 1985).

Marin Breeding Distribution

During the atlas period, Golden-crowned Kinglets bred here primarily in the Douglas fir forests on Inverness Ridge and in the fir and redwood forests of the Bolinas Ridge, Mount Tamalpais, and Lagunitas Creek watersheds. An isolated population inhabited redwoods on the north slope of Big Rock Ridge in Novato. Representative nesting sites were Balboa Road, Inverness Ridge (NB 4/20/79 –DS); Glen Trail, PRNS (FL/FY 7/25/82 –DS); and Inverness Ridge above Five Brooks (NE or NY early 1980s –ITi).

Historical Trends/Population Threats

Early Marin County ornithologists were not aware that Golden-crowned Kinglets bred in the area (Mailliard 1900, S&P 1933), but the truth was uncovered by the time of Grinnell and Miller's (1944) classic work on California's avifauna. Marin's breeding population probably took a plunge at the time of extensive logging here early in this century but subsequently recovered with the regeneration of dense forests. Numbers of Golden-crowned Kinglets were fairly stable on Breeding Bird Surveys in California from 1968 to 1989 (USFWS unpubl. analyses).

BLUE-GRAY GNATCATCHER *Polioptila caerulea*

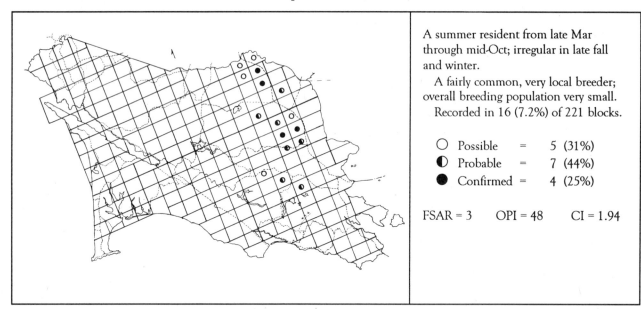

A summer resident from late Mar through mid-Oct; irregular in late fall and winter.

A fairly common, very local breeder; overall breeding population very small. Recorded in 16 (7.2%) of 221 blocks.

○	Possible	=	5 (31%)
◑	Probable	=	7 (44%)
●	Confirmed	=	4 (25%)

FSAR = 3   OPI = 48   CI = 1.94

Ecological Requirements

The somber hues of these lithe insectivores blend in well with their Marin County nesting haunts of deciduous and live oak woodlands interfacing with chaparral or brushy openings. Gnatcatchers here are particularly attracted to slopes with open stands of small valley oaks with adjacent patches of coast live oaks and openings with low brush. In Monterey County, Blue-gray Gnatcatchers prefer extensive stands of oaks varying from live oak woodland, mixed live oak–deciduous oak woodland, dense oak scrub, and open stands of mature deciduous oaks (Root 1967). Blue-grays there also nest in stands of large (about 9 ft. tall) arborescent chaparral resembling oak scrub but are absent in extensive stands of low chaparral, except where it adjoins oak woodlands. Rarely, they use open stands of streamside willows adjacent to chaparral and oak woodland. The fact that Gnatcatchers occupy some habitats with different physiognomy among those available while shunning others with similar structure to those occupied, suggests that, in addition to habitat structure, nest sites and particularly food abundance must also be important in habitat selection.

In-depth ecological study has revealed that Gnatcatchers shift their habitat use, reflected in their almost continual realignment of territorial boundaries, in response to changes in the seasonal distribution and abundance of their arthropod prey (Root 1967, 1969b). When birds first arrive in Monterey County in March and April, they concentrate their foraging efforts in the evergreen foliage of live oaks and chaparral. By late April, when deciduous oak foliage is well developed, they shift most foraging to these woodlands and center it there through July. Fledglings are led to stands of dense evergreen foliage, partly for protection from predators, and later they wander to nonbreeding habitats, such as adjacent riparian groves. By August, adults and juveniles leave deciduous oak woodlands for adjacent live oak woodlands and chaparral.

Gnatcatchers build deep cup-shaped nests, which they anchor to twigs and branches that they sometimes incorporate in the structure (Bent 1949; Root 1967, 1969b). They make the nest body from dried grasses and plant fibers, welded together with spider silk. Birds ornament the nest exterior with crustose lichens and an occasional grass seed hull, oak leaf, or feather, and they line the inside with plant down and feathers. Gnatcatchers place most nests in vertical forks (against a trunk or limb or at the splitting of large branches) or saddle them between upright branches or twigs on a horizontal branch; rarely, they build them in dense tangles of twigs. The same birds may use individual nest sites in different nest attempts in the same or subsequent years (Root 1967). Nests may or may not be screened by foliage. Concealment is based more on camouflage: Gnatcatchers' nests might easily be mistaken for weathered stubs or an accumulation of debris. The outer adornment of lichens is the standard camouflage, but in burned-over areas, pieces of scorched bark may serve the same purpose (Chamberlin 1901). Gnatcatchers build their nests in a variety of trees and bushes. In California, they situate most nests in oaks or chaparral shrubs but also in pines, alders, and even eucalyptus (Bent 1949). In the Monterey area, 90% of their nests are in deciduous oaks, reflecting the foraging beat at that season. The height of 66 nests there varied from about 3 to 34 feet above the ground with about 79% between 7 and 23 feet high (Root 1967). The few chaparral nests were near the top of the shrub, while oak nests were at least 3 feet below the top of the tree and usually at least a third of the way up the tree. Throughout California, nest heights range from 3 to 45 feet; one was 30 feet up in a pine but on a branch hanging over a gully and 60 feet above the ground. Extreme nest heights in the East can reach 70 to 80 feet (Bent 1949).

Gnatcatchers forage throughout the height of the vegetation but concentrate in the foliage zone; in chaparral they tend to use the subcanopy more. Foraging birds perch mostly on twigs and small branches, but occasionally they also perch on the upper surface of limbs and, rarely, on upright trunks and limbs, grass culms, or tree leaves (Root 1967). Gnatcatchers are rapid, energetic foragers. They typically hop rhythmically from perch to perch, stop

briefly, and cock their heads quickly from side to side to survey their surroundings for potential "victims." They capture prey by gleaning (directly or by leaning over with wings aflutter), lunging, hovering, and by acrobatic hawking in which birds rarely return to the same perch. Gnatcatchers also tumble, with wings checking their descent, in pursuit of insects that have dropped from the foliage. Rarely, they hang beneath perches like chickadees and titmice. When the sun is low, Gnatcatchers forage with other species in sunlit banks of foliage bordering openings.

Seasonal shifts in foraging preferences are evident, although most attempts occur on foliage (Root 1967). Early in the season, before deciduous foliage is well developed, attempts on twigs and branches predominate. Adults with young increase foraging on herbaceous plants and the ground. They make such attempts from perches low in trees or from downed limbs. Adults make aerial surveys up to 15 feet from such perches, hovering to inspect tall grass spikes for grasshoppers and other large insects not normally included in the adult diet. Gnatcatchers subdue large prey by beating them against branches. In July and August, when adults are feeding fledglings, they often forage while frequently opening and closing the tail rapidly. This action displays the white outer retrices with a flashing effect that presumably functions to flush insects from the foliage. Adults with young also do more hawking and hovering than adults without young. In June and July, there is a slight increase in the frequency of hawking irrespective of parental obligations, reflecting the characteristics of available prey. The March to August diet of California birds is exclusively small (0.1–1.2 in.) arthropods of 70 families (Root 1967, n = 58). The main groups, which may change seasonally, are true bugs, beetles, wasps and bees, moths and butterflies, cicadas and allies, flies, and spiders.

Marin Breeding Distribution

During the atlas period, Blue-gray Gnatcatchers bred in Marin County only on relatively dry ridges in the interior. They were most widely distributed on the eastern flanks of Mount Burdell and Big Rock Ridge and more locally on Blue Ridge near White's Hill and on Mount Tamalpais. Representative breeding stations were Mt. Burdell, Novato (NY 5/30/82 –ScC); Olompali, Novato (NY 5/20/82 –ScC); Big Rock Ridge near Blackstone Canyon (NY 5/25/77 –BBi, DS); and along the Yolanda Trail near Phoenix Lake (FL/FY 6/20/83 –MB).

Historical Trends/Population Threats

Blue-gray Gnatcatchers increased on Breeding Bird Surveys in the California foothill region, including coastal counties from Monterey south and parts of those to the north, from 1968 to 1979 (Robbins et al. 1986). For California as a whole, they increased from 1968 to 1989, though they stabilized from 1980 to 1989 (USFWS unpubl.

analyses). Counts on the Even Cheaper Thrills Spring Bird Count near Novato were relatively stable from 1978 to 1987 except for high counts in 1985 and 1987 that were well above the average for previous years (Appendix A).

Clearing of woodlands would tend to depress Gnatcatcher populations, whereas fires might open up habitat to their liking.

Thrushes
Family *Muscicapidae*
Subfamily *Turdinae*

WESTERN BLUEBIRD　*Sialia mexicana*

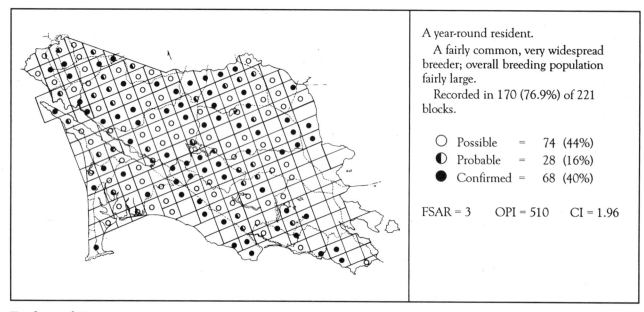

A year-round resident.

A fairly common, very widespread breeder; overall breeding population fairly large.

Recorded in 170 (76.9%) of 221 blocks.

○	Possible	=	74 (44%)
◑	Probable	=	28 (16%)
●	Confirmed	=	68 (40%)

FSAR = 3　　OPI = 510　　CI = 1.96

Ecological Requirements

The azure and rusty hues of Western Bluebirds add a tasteful tint to the borders of a wide variety of Marin County's habitats. Breeding birds require grasslands or very open brushlands, with suitable perch sites for foraging and nearby trees for shelter and nest sites. Our oak savannah or oak woodland edges are best outfitted with these requisites, although the edges of virtually all of Marin's forested habitats, planted windbreaks, or residential plantings will do—as long as they adjoin meadows, grasslands, weedy fields, or open scrub fields. Clearings in forests or very open woodlands may also suit this bluebird's needs. Western Bluebirds require more foraging perches and prefer somewhat denser ground cover than do Mountain Bluebirds (Pinkowski 1979); where they overlap (not in Marin), these two bluebird species are interspecifically territorial (Pinkowski 1979, Herlugson 1982).

Western Bluebird nests are simple and "carelessly" built affairs—made of dry grasses, a few feathers and other soft materials—placed from about 3 to 45 feet high in old woodpecker holes, natural tree cavities, bird boxes, cavities of buildings, or old Cliff Swallow nests (Bent 1949, D. Shuford pers. obs.).

The fundamental foraging strategy of Western (as well as Mountain and Eastern) Bluebirds is to search for ground-dwelling prey from a perch (Pinkowski 1979). Perch-foraging bluebirds prefer open, well-lighted areas containing low, sparse vegetation and little understory; tall vegetation would interfere in hunting for ground-dwelling prey. Birds usually sit motionless on a perch of low to moderate height that commands a wide view and carefully watch for prey. Typical perches are the upper and outer (preferably dead) branches of trees, isolated bushes, large rocks, coarse weed stalks, and a variety of artificial sites,

316

including fences and fence posts, utility poles and wires, buildings, highway signs, stakes, picnic tables, refuse cans, nesting boxes, and ground debris; bluebirds sometimes also perch horizontally on tree trunks. When they detect food from their vantage points, bluebirds drop, swoop, or flutter to the ground to seize prey in their bill. Small items are usually eaten on the ground, whereas larger ones are carried to a perch for "preparation" before consumption. Birds switch positions on the same perch or move to a new one when they have difficulty locating prey. Western Bluebirds also frequently make short, butterflylike flights from perches to hawk insects and may forage exclusively by this tactic when aerial prey are abundant. Less frequently, Western Bluebirds descend toward the ground and glean prey from low herbaceous foliage while remaining airborne or hover over it to catch flying insects they have disturbed. They sometimes also land to glean prey from the foliage and branches of trees and shrubs or from tree trunks. In addition, bluebirds hop along the ground feeding on items they encounter, particularly when seeking small prey or when foraging in areas containing few perches (Pinkowski 1979). When searching for prey on the ground, they do not work areas with much leaf litter and do not flip aside debris with the bill like other thrushes. Also when perches are few, they may hover with their wings flapping and tails spread or with the aid of strong breezes or updrafts, dropping to the ground quickly when prey is sighted. When feeding nestlings, adults increase their use of energy-costly foraging behaviors, such as hovering and hawking, and they feed the young larger (heavier) prey items (on average) than they eat themselves (Herlugson 1982). Because they are more dependent on perches, Western Bluebirds generally flycatch more and hover and flight-glean less than Mountain Bluebirds (Pinkowski 1979). However, bluebirds are opportunistic foragers, and there is more variation in foraging tactics of a given species between habitats than between different species in the same habitat. Block (1990) documented geographic variation of Western Bluebird's foraging techniques and locations in California oak woodlands, while Szaro et al. (1990) similarly demonstrated annual variation in foraging techniques and other measures of resource use in ponderosa pine forests in Arizona.

The Western Bluebird diet year round is about 80% animal matter (Beal 1915, n = 217). In California, animal matter ranges from 94%-100% of the diet in spring and summer to 74%-79% in fall and winter (Martin et al. 1951, n = 215). Dominant prey are grasshoppers and crickets, beetles, butterflies and moths, and caterpillars; secondarily, true bugs, ants and wasps, spiders, and cicadas; minor items are flies, earwigs, isopods, centipedes, myriopods, angleworms, snails, and sowbugs (Beal 1915, Herlugson 1982). In Washington, Herlugson (1982) noted that the adult diet in the prenestling phase is domi-

nated by beetles and lepidopterans. These items decrease in importance during the nestling phase, when ants, wasps, and true bugs increase in importance. Nestling diets of Western Bluebirds are dominated by grasshoppers, crickets, and beetles (Beal 1915, Herlugson 1982). Where Western and Mountain bluebirds overlap in Washington, the adult diets of the two species are similar in the prenestling phase, but overall they differ in the proportions of various food items consumed (Herlugson 1982); foods delivered to nestlings do not differ between species. Western Bluebirds obtain their vegetable fare of dry and succulent fruits and berries and, rarely, hard seeds, by picking them while they perch in vegetation (Pinkowski 1979). Important items are wild fruits such as elderberries and mistletoe, seeds of poison oak and various weeds, as well as cultivated fruits and berries (Beal 1915). These bluebirds most frequently consume vegetable items early on cool mornings, before temperatures rise and insects become active (Pinkowski 1979).

Marin Breeding Distribution

During the atlas period, Western Bluebirds bred throughout most of Marin County. They were sparse or absent on outer Point Reyes and absent from much of the corridor along Highway 101 and from steep ridges densely clothed with forests or chaparral. Although much of eastern Marin is urbanized, there are still large open spaces with seemingly suitable habitat where breeding Western Bluebirds are lacking (B. Lenarz pers. comm.). Representative nesting locations were eucalyptus grove outer Tomales Point (FY 6/15/82 –DS); cypress grove at Fish Docks, Point Reyes (NY 5/20/81 –DS); planted pine grove Marconi Ranch/Synanon (FY/FL 6/27/82 –DS); Mt. Burdell, Novato (NB 4/21/81 –ITi); and Carson Ridge (NY 6/5/82 –DS, ITi).

Historical Trends/Population Threats

Although Mailliard (1900) considered the Western Bluebird an "abundant resident" in Marin County, Stephens and Pringle (1933) considered it "common" but "present in winter only" here. The similar abundance categories but different seasonal status ascribed by these authors is puzzling. Grinnell and Wythe (1927) and Grinnell and Miller (1944) reported the species as breeding in the San Francisco Bay Area but listed no records from Marin County. Given the current status, it seems likely that Western Bluebirds were breeding regularly in Marin County throughout this period. Historically, Western Bluebirds likely have increased locally as breeders in the grasslands in the northwest corner of the county. This area was formerly devoid of large trees; consequently, planted windbreaks have created suitable nest sites and foraging perches, the latter further augmented by human structures such as fences and utility lines.

The Western Bluebird was on the Audubon Society's Blue List in 1972 and from 1978 to 1981, on its list of Special Concern in 1982, and on its list of Local Concern in 1986 (Tate 1981, 1986; Tate & Tate 1982). There is speculation that pesticide use, snag and decaying tree removal, changing agricultural practices, and competition for nest sites with European Starlings and House Sparrows have all had adverse effects on Western Bluebird populations (Elizroth 1983). Starlings are perhaps most often implicated in postulated declines of Western Bluebirds (e.g., Herlugson 1978). Although it is true that Starlings will aggressively displace other hole-nesting birds and

reduce their breeding populations, particularly if nest holes are in short supply (Weitzel 1988), it is not clear if this pressure has actually caused widespread declines of blue-birds in California. Western Bluebird populations in California appear to have declined only slightly from 1968 to 1989 while Starlings have been declining or stable (USFWS unpubl. analyses). On the other hand, the effects of Starlings may have been offset by human activities that open up forested habitats, making them more to this bluebird's liking, or by those that provide additional nest sites or perches in formerly open terrain.

SWAINSON'S THRUSH *Catharus ustulatus*

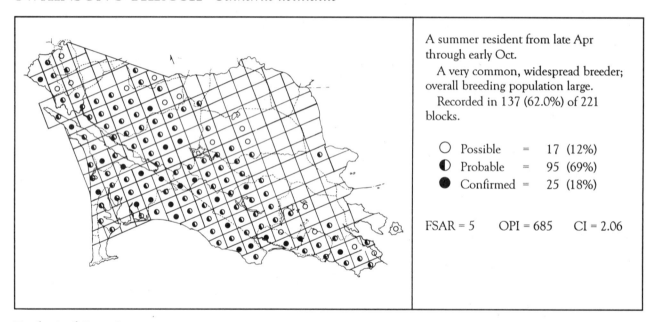

A summer resident from late Apr through early Oct.

A very common, widespread breeder; overall breeding population large.

Recorded in 137 (62.0%) of 221 blocks.

○ Possible = 17 (12%)
◑ Probable = 95 (69%)
● Confirmed = 25 (18%)

FSAR = 5　　OPI = 685　　CI = 2.06

Ecological Requirements

The haunting, upward-spiraling song of the Swainson's Thrush issues forth from Marin County's dense riparian groves, mixed evergreen forests on the lower slopes of stream drainages, locally from patches of north-facing coastal scrub, and from the moist intergradations of all these with other forested habitats. The unifying character-istic of these varied breeding haunts is the presence of a dense moist understory or shrub layer (cf. Wilson's War-bler). However, Swainson's Thrushes inexplicably do not breed in the dense understory of Douglas fir and bishop pine forests except along stream courses. In Marin County, the closely related Hermit Thrush breeds on shady forested slopes with an open understory (see account).

Swainson's Thrushes fashion attractive, well-made nest cups from dead leaves, mosses, twigs, fern stalks, and strips

of inner bark, all mixed with mud. They line the nest cup with dry grasses, fine rootlets, fine plant fibers, and skele-ton leaves. Swainson's Thrushes place their nests in the crotches of slender willows, in low-hanging dense branches of bushes, on top of fallen masses of dead bracken ferns, or, rarely, near the extremity of a limb of a tree (Bent 1949). Nest height varies from 6 inches to 40 or, rarely, perhaps 60 feet (most are 4–5 ft.).

Little has been published on the western forms of the Swainson's Thrush, but studies elsewhere shed light on their foraging habits. Like other members of this genus, the Swainson's Thrush is primarily a ground forager. The birds uncover savory morsels by flipping aside the debris of the forest floor with their bills, after which they progress to the next seemingly suitable spot by means of long springing hops (Dilger 1956). Swainson's Thrushes glean, lunge, and flycatch more in the foliage of trees and bushes than do Hermit Thrushes. The foraging beat is generally low to the ground. They also obtain fruits by plucking while perched in trees or bushes or by retrieving them from the forest floor. The spring to fall diet of adults in California is about 52% animal and 48% vegetable matter (Beal 1907, n = 157). For North America as a whole, the animal portion of the diet decreases from 92% in spring (n = 174) to 36% in fall (n = 129) (Martin et al. 1951). Animal food consists primarily of beetles, caterpillars, and ants, with smaller amounts of wasps, true bugs, flies, grasshoppers, other insects, spiders, and, rarely, salamanders (Beal 1907). Vegetarian fare includes elderberries, blackberries, raspberries, twinberries, coffeeberries, poison oak berries, and assorted cultivated fruits. As would be expected, the food fed to nestlings is overwhelmingly arthropods (92.6%), chiefly caterpillars, beetles, true bugs, ants and wasps, and arachnids (principally daddy-long-legs).

Marin Breeding Distribution

The breeding distribution of the Swainson's Thrush in Marin County during the atlas period closely paralleled that of the persistent penetration inland of the coastal summer fogs, which are requisite for the broad-scale devel-opment here of dense moist undergrowth. Most breeding birds occurred here within a few hundred feet of sea level, in conjunction with the distribution of moist dense shrub-bery. Representative nesting locations were moist coastal scrub at mouth of Estero San Antonio (FY 6/24/82 – DS); Vedanta Trail, Olema Valley (FY 6/15/81 –DS); and Marshall-Petaluma Rd., W of Gambonini Ranch (FY 6/23/82 –DS). The lack of breeding Swainson's Thrushes, at least locally, along permanent streams in the northeastern corner of the county may be due to the overgrazing of understory vegetation or the effects of high cowbird populations, or it may just reflect subtleties of habitat choice unseen by the human (but not the *Catharus*) eye.

Historical Trends/Population Threats

For unknown reasons, Swainson's Thrushes have de-clined dramatically since the 1920s on the west slope of the Sierra Nevada (Gaines 1988). On the whole, Swainson's Thrush populations appeared to decline slightly on Breed-ing Bird Surveys in California from 1968 to 1989 but were relatively stable from 1980 to 1989 (USFWS unpubl. analy-ses).

HERMIT THRUSH *Catharus guttatus*

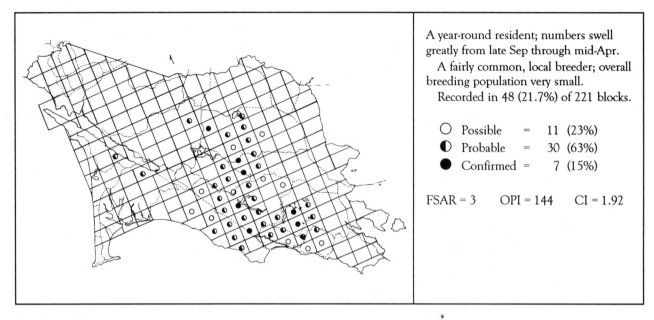

A year-round resident; numbers swell greatly from late Sep through mid-Apr.
A fairly common, local breeder; overall breeding population very small.
Recorded in 48 (21.7%) of 221 blocks.

○ Possible   =   11 (23%)
◑ Probable   =   30 (63%)
● Confirmed =   7 (15%)

FSAR = 3   OPI = 144   CI = 1.92

Ecological Requirements

Hermit Thrushes are common and widespread in Marin County in the winter, but wintering birds are replaced in the breeding season by a race *(C. g. slevini)* of more restricted distribution here (G&M 1944; AOU 1957, 1983). The transcendent, flutelike song of Marin's breeding birds rises from cool, shady redwood and Douglas fir forests with a sparse understory and, locally, from bishop pine forests of similar structure. The local requisites of breeding for Hermit Thrushes seem to be a conifer overstory, scattered saplings or bushes for nest sites and cover, and open ground with a well-developed leaf litter layer for foraging. Suitable forests occur here primarily on the midlevel to upper slopes of shaded canyons and north-facing drainages. Although coolness and moistness characterize the Marin County breeding haunts, these seem not to be of ultimate importance. The race *(C. g. polionota)* that breeds in the Great Basin of California occurs in arid, low-stature mountain mahogany *(Cercocarpus ledifolius)* woodlands (G&M 1944; AOU 1957, 1983), also with an open understory and an adequate leaf litter layer. In Marin County, the closely related Swainson's Thrush breeds more widely, primarily in lowland riparian and broad-leaved evergreen forests with a moist dense understory (see account).

Hermit Thrushes build compact, deeply cup-shaped nests fashioned from twigs, small branches of bushes, shredded bark, dead leaves, mosses, and rootlets (Bent 1949). They line them with fine shredded bark, fine rootlets, dried grasses, and decomposed leaves. Hermits

generally construct their nests in branches near the trunks of saplings or bushes, but may also place them in supporting branches and twigs of small intertwining trees or, rarely, well out on the limbs of tall conifers. Nest height varies from about 1.5 to 30 feet above ground (most 3-5 ft.).

As is the case with the Swainson's Thrush, the details of the foraging habits of western forms of the Hermit Thrush have not been well studied. In the East, the general foraging methods employed by the Hermit Thrush are similar to those of the Swainson's Thrush (see account), but the Hermit is considered more a ground forager and less a flycatcher (Dilger 1956). In one study, though, in an area of dense cover, Hermits spent only about one-fourth of their foraging time on the ground and far more in the foliage of saplings and the midstory of trees (Paszkowski 1984).

For the continent as a whole, the animal portion of the Hermit Thrush diet decreases progressively from 93% in spring (n = 171) to 40% in winter (n = 180) (Martin et al. 1951). The June to July diet of birds breeding in the Sierra Nevada is 98.7% animal and 1.3% vegetable (Dahlsten et al. 1985, n = 12), whereas that of birds wintering in lowland California is 56% animal and 44% vegetable (Beal 1907, n = 68). Principal animal foods are ants, true bugs, flies, beetles, scorpionflies, and caterpillars; incidental items are snails and salamanders (Beal 1907, Dahlsten et al. 1985). The main vegetable items in the diet are fruits and seeds. Important ones are mistletoe, seeds of the pepper tree, poison oak seeds, toyon, manzanita, pyracantha, and cotoneaster berries, and raspberries and other cultivated fruits (Beal 1907, G&M 1944).

Marin Breeding Distribution

During the atlas period, Hermit Thrushes bred in Marin County primarily at the southern end of Inverness Ridge, in the Mount Tamalpais and Lagunitas Creek watersheds, and on intervening ridges north to Big Rock Ridge. Although the central and northern sections of Inverness Ridge harbor suitable conifers, the dense understory shrub layer (dominated by huckleberry) precludes breeding by Hermit Thrushes except locally, where suitable openings in the shrub cover occur. Representative nesting locations

were W end of Big Rock Ridge (NY 6/21/82 –ScC); W end of Lucas Valley Rd. (FY 7/11/82 –DS); N side of the ridge N of San Geronimo and Forest Knolls (NY 5/29/82 –DS); and Bolinas Ridge below lower end of Kent Lake (FY 6/16/82 –BiL).

Historical Trends/Population Threats

Few historical data are available. On the whole, numbers of Hermit Thrushes were fairly stable on Breeding Bird Surveys in California from 1968 to 1989, though they appeared to increase slightly from 1980 to 1989 (USFWS unpubl. analyses).

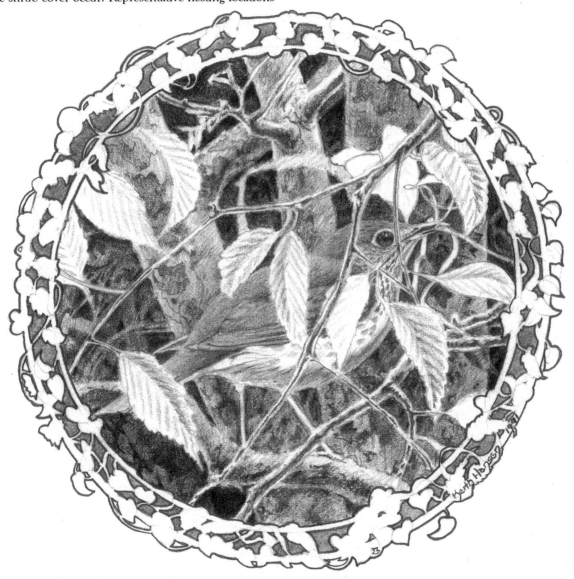

The haunting countersinging of Swainson's Thrushes rising from forest depths on a still, foggy evening is the pure essence of summer on the Marin County coast. Drawing by Keith Hansen, 1991.

AMERICAN ROBIN *Turdus migratorius*

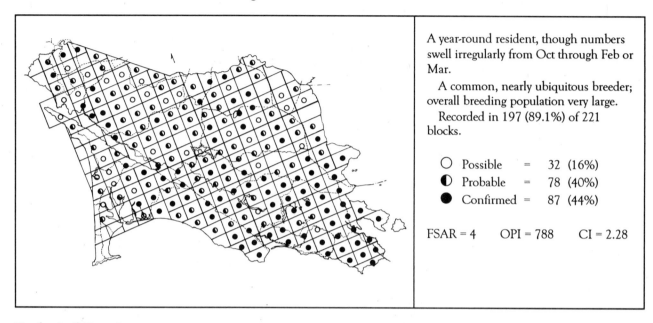

A year-round resident, though numbers swell irregularly from Oct through Feb or Mar.

A common, nearly ubiquitous breeder; overall breeding population very large.

Recorded in 197 (89.1%) of 221 blocks.

○ Possible   =   32 (16%)
◐ Probable   =   78 (40%)
● Confirmed =   87 (44%)

FSAR = 4   OPI = 788   CI = 2.28

Ecological Requirements

The American Robin is one of the best known North American birds and for good reason, since it is at home both in suburban neighborhoods and in the forested wilds. Another of our edge species, Robins use the borders of all of Marin County's forested habitats along moist grassy openings. They also favor human plantings around ranchyards, suburban yards, parks, and playing fields. Although Robins will occasionally nest well inside forests or woodlands, they must be in fairly close proximity to openings for foraging, and consequently most of them nest on edges or along clearings. Their basic requirements seem to be adequate nest sites and protective cover in trees, bushes, or human structures; moist open areas with sparse vegetation and soft soil for ground foraging; and mud for nest building.

Robins are remarkably adaptable in their choice of nest sites, though a variety of coniferous, broadleaved evergreen, or deciduous trees and bushes are their mainstays. Other natural sites include crevices in cliffs, ledges of rocks, among upturned roots of trees, in natural cavities or woodpecker holes in trees or stumps, or on top of old oriole, wren, or hornet nests. Robins will even nest on the ground, particularly where substantial vegetation is lacking; one bird laid its eggs on leaves near a house with no sign of a nest. Additionally, they will nest in a variety of artificial sites even when trees are at hand. These include beams inside and outside buildings, window ledges, eaves, gutters, bird boxes, fire escapes, fence rails, statues, chandeliers, and even movable sites, such as fence gates or train

signals. Although Robins seem to build many nests without regard to concealment, they usually partly conceal and elevate them beyond reach of predators. Most nests in conifers seem to have an overhanging branch to protect them from sun and rain (E.C. Beedy pers. comm.). Nest heights range from ground level to 80 feet, but most are about 5 to 20 feet above ground in trees and bushes (Howell 1942, Bent 1949, Tyler 1949, Young 1955, Klimstra & Stieglitz 1957, Knupp et al. 1977, Yahner 1983). Of 244 nests in New York (ranging up to 65 ft.), half were from 2 to 10 feet and only five were over 40 feet (Howell 1942). Average nest heights in Iowa and Illinois are 11 feet (range 5-45 ft.) and 15 feet (range 3-35 ft.), respectively (Klimstra & Stieglitz 1957); in Maine, 17 feet (Knupp et al. 1977, n = 60); and in Wisconsin, 7 feet (range 2-30 ft.; Young 1955, n= 202). Tree nests are usually supported by branches next to the trunk, but they may be placed well out on horizontal limbs and, rarely, in upright forks. In colder climates, Robins most frequently choose evergreens for first nests and deciduous trees for second nests. Sometimes they will use one nest to raise more than one brood in a season, and in successive years they may build nests over the foundation of the previous year's nest.

Robins generally build bulky, rough, usually bowl-shaped nests, though shape is governed to a large extent by the site chosen. They usually construct the outer wall of long, coarse dead grass stems, twigs, weed stems, paper, string, feathers, or rootlets; rarely, they also incorporate items such as snakeskin, dead leaves, cloth, lace, or other human artifacts (Howell 1942, Bent 1949, Tyler 1949). The birds plaster the inside of their nests with mud, which they may go up to a quarter of a mile to procure (Howell 1942). They will even make their own mud by entering water to wet their feathers and then shake it off to moisten dust; one bird was observed to fill its bill with dry earth and then dip it into a bird bath. Generally they will stop building for a day or two after adding the mud layer to let it dry. Robins sometimes substitute manure for mud; rarely, they omit the mud layer, particularly in drought conditions. Unusual nests have been composed solely of feathers, shredded paper, or just cotton and mud. The nest lining is composed mostly of dried grass blades, perhaps with a few grass stems or twigs. Other lining substrates are seaweed, cloth, string, cotton, paper, or horsehair.

Most people associate foraging Robins with their stop-and-go antics on lawns. Birds run or hop for short distances, pause in an upright stance and cock their heads from side to side, then secure their prey, once located, by probing, pecking, or gleaning. Almost everyone has seen the ensuing tug-of-war when an earthworm is rudely stretched from its protective burrow. Robins use visual rather than auditory or tactile cues when stalking earthworms (Heppner 1965). Robins specialize on earthworms when moisture brings them to the surface or at dawn and dusk when worms are foraging near the surface. They also pick up prey tossed up on wave-washed shorelines or plunge their bills into shallow water to secure more mobile prey. Although primarily ground foragers, Robins also glean or hawk large insects from the foliage or adjoining air space of trees and bushes, and they gobble up berries while perched or from hovering flight (Paszkowski 1982)

Robins have a varied omnivorous diet that can be weighted to over 99% animal life in midsummer in the Sierra Nevada (Dahlsten et al. 1985, n = 14). Continent-wide, animal foods range from 79% of the diet in spring to 19%-40% from summer to winter (Martin et al. 1951, n = 1423). Prominent animal items in the diet of western birds are caterpillars, beetles, earthworms, flies, grasshoppers and crickets, butterflies and moths, ants, centipedes, spiders, snails, and occasionally small fish (Bent 1949, Dahlsten et al. 1985). Common California fruits, which predominate in the diet later in the season, are berries of madrone, toyon, elderberry, coffeeberry, mistletoe, and blackberry; berries of ornamentals, such as pyrocantha, cotoneaster, eugenia, and camphor; and cultivated fruit where available (Bent 1949). Adults apparently feed the young by regurgitation for the first few days (Howell 1942).

Marin Breeding Distribution

During the atlas period, the American Robin was one of the most widespread breeding birds in Marin County because of its ability to exploit a variety of habitats from forest edges of the hinterlands to urban-suburban settings. Representative breeding localities were Bear Valley Trail, PRNS (NY 7/3/80 –DS); Walker Creek, near Hwy. 1 (NB 5/1/82 –DS); Miwok Park, Novato (NY 5/?/82 –ScC); and Mt. Burdell, Novato (NB 4/11/81 –DS).

Historical Trends/Population Threats

The American Robin was not always a widespread, numerous breeder here. Mailliard (1900), Storer (1926), and Stephens and Pringle (1933) all considered Robins to be only winter visitants in Marin County. However, Grinnell and Wythe (1927), in their authoritative book on the avifauna of the San Francisco Bay region, stated that prior to 1915 Robins reached the southern limit of their coastal breeding range in Sonoma and Marin counties. They list San Geronimo and Inverness as stations of record for permanent resident Robins before 1915. Starting in 1915, American Robins were first reported nesting in San Francisco. Further breeding reports quickly surfaced elsewhere in the Bay Area and the Sacramento Valley, areas formerly devoid of breeding Robins (Storer 1926). These Robins were colonizing lowland areas rendered suitable by human irrigation and settlement, and they continued to do so (G&M 1944, Sibley 1952). The planting of lawns and irrigation of orchards provided moist foraging habitat in the normally bone-dry summers of much of lowland California; tree plantings augmented nesting sites. Although Robins were breeding in the moist, fog-drenched coastal ridges of Marin County prior to their colonization of much of the Bay Area, they surely also expanded in the settled areas of Marin. Areas of Marin where Robins undoubtedly expanded greatly are the urban-suburban corridor along Highway 101 and the northern and eastern ranchlands. In the former region, expansion probably followed tree and grass plantings in some areas and tree clearing in others. In the ranchlands, Robins probably spread with watering in ranchyards and gardens and with the establishment of trees and buildings in formerly wide open terrain. Whether the expansion of concrete and asphalt will outstrip that of lawns and exotic tree plantings and cause a reversal of the trend in Robin populations remains to be seen. Perhaps it already has, as Robin numbers decreased on Breeding Bird Surveys in California from 1968 to 1989 (USFWS unpubl. analyses).

Wrentits
Family *Muscicapidae*
Subfamily *Timaliinae*

WRENTIT *Chamaea fasciata*

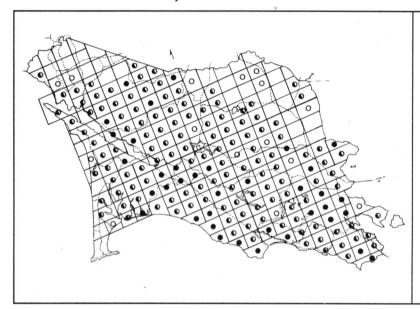

A year-round resident.

A common, very widespread breeder; overall breeding population very large.

Recorded in 182 (82.4%) of 221 blocks.

○ Possible   =   15 (8%)
◑ Probable   =   131 (72%)
● Confirmed   =   36 (20%)

FSAR = 4   OPI = 728   CI = 2.12

Ecological Requirements

The Wrentit is the sole representative of the Old World Babbler or Timalinae subfamily in North America. Its entire distribution is limited to the West Coast and is bounded to the north by the Columbia River, to the south by the deserts of Baja California, and to the east by the west slope of the Sierra Nevada (AOU 1983). In Marin County, it occurs in a variety of habitats with a dense continuous shrub layer and gaps no greater than a few meters across which Wrentits must fly. The preferred haunts here are mature chaparral and coastal scrub. Wrentits also breed widely in Marin in suitable scrub in riparian thickets, along the brushy borders of most other forested habitats, in successional scrub fields, and in suburban yards. They do inhabit conifer forests here to a degree but generally around sunny openings; they avoid dense huckleberry thickets under shaded Douglas fir forests.

Since 1979, the Wrentit has been one of three key species that have been the object of intensive research in Point Reyes Bird Observatory's study of the coastal scrub bird community at Palomarin. The average height above ground of 236 nests at Palomarin was 25.9 inches (range 6.7-53.9 in., G.R. Geupel unpubl. data). Wrentits there

built 88% of their nests in either coastal sage or coyote brush, and the remainder in blackberry, poison oak, bracken fern, sticky monkeyflower, coffeeberry, Douglas fir, lizard tail, and even rushes (PRBO unpubl. data). Elsewhere they use a wide variety of shrubs and, rarely, trees (Erickson 1938, Bent 1948). In coastal scrub at Berkeley, Erickson (1938) found 44 nests, of which 31 were in coyote brush. The height of 25 nests she measured ranged from 12 to 42 inches, but most were from 18 to 24 inches above ground. She also reported three unusual nests found by others from 12 to 15 feet up in live oaks or alders. Taking a week or longer, the male and female construct a tight, open-cupped nest that they normally conceal in the crotch of a dense shrub or, less frequently, in twigs of the leafy crown (Erickson 1938, G.R. Geupel unpubl. data). At Palomarin, Wrentits fashion the nest foundation from shreds of bark pulled off living coastal sage and coyote brush (G.R. Geupel unpubl. data), although they may use bark from a variety of other shrubs (Erickson 1938). They glue the bark strips together with balls of carefully collected cobwebs. Wrentits line the inside of the nest cup with fine shreds of bark or grasses and usually festoon the outside with small bits of lichens (Erickson 1938, G.R. Geupel pers. obs.). Near civilization, Wrentit nests sometimes contain string, tissue paper, and cigarette butts (G.R. Geupel pers. obs.). The importance of quality materials is indicated by the fact that if a nest fails or the pair decides to double brood, the first nest is usually dismantled and the materials are recycled in the next nest attempt (PRBO unpubl. data). It is not uncommon for a pair to complete a nest and then decide to move it to a new location before the first egg is laid. Wrentits normally conceal their nests well from above to avoid predation by Scrub Jays. Concealment from below does not seem to be as important, probably because Wrentits actively feign injury around their nest to distract snakes approaching from the ground (Geupel 1981). Despite a longer nesting cycle (33 days), Wrentits at Palomarin have higher nesting success than other species nesting in the same habitat (Geupel & DeSante 1983).

Wrentits actively glean larvae, insects, and spiders from the bark and, less frequently, from the green leaves or fruiting stems of the shrubbery (Erickson 1938, G.R. Geupel pers. obs.). Most items are within "peck range," but if the prey is high in the shrub, the Wrentit will quickly fly to it and just as quickly leap down. Sometimes individuals fly up and hang inverted while hunting among the leaves of live oaks, as a Bushtit or Plain Titmouse might do. Wrentits also hover briefly at sticky monkeyflowers and, rarely, will flycatch for butterflies or the like. Individuals attacking centipedes sometimes use both feet to subdue prey (Erickson 1938). Wrentits also consume great quantities of small fruits. If the fruit is small, it is swallowed whole; otherwise it is grasped with one foot, and small pieces are pulled off with the bill (Erickson 1938). Wrentits also eat grain and seeds when invertebrates and fruit become scarce in the winter. At Palomarin, traps baited with "chicken scratch" are normally successful only in winter and then only when placed in the tops of bushes (G.R. Geupel pers. obs.). Rarely do Wrentits forage on the ground.

The year-round diet of Wrentits in California is about 52% animal and 48% vegetable matter (Beal 1907, n = 165). Animal matter in the diet here ranges from a high of 94% in spring (n = 13) to a low of 36% in fall (n = 62) (Martin et al. 1951). The main animal foods are ants and wasps, beetles, caterpillars, moth cocoons, true bugs, and scale insects, along with various other insects and spiders (Beal 1907). In contrast to Bushtits, Wrentits consume a large proportion of ants and wasps and a small proportion of true bugs; the former items, at least, reflect the low

foraging beat of Wrentits. At Palomarin, small green geometrid (inchworm moth) larvae are the preferred forage brought back to nestlings (G.R. Geupel pers. obs.). This is in accord with Beal's (1907) report of the stomach contents of one brood that was largely caterpillars and secondarily spiders, true bugs, and beetles; all but the latter are very soft in nature. The vegetable fare is fruit such as elderberries, snowberries, coffeeberries, twinberries, blackberries, and poison oak seeds; the latter are especially important from August to February, when they make up one-quarter of the diet. A few weed seeds, leaf galls, and rubbish make up the remainder.

Marin Breeding Distribution

During the atlas period, Wrentits bred widely throughout most of Marin County. They were most numerous along the immediate coast where coastal scrub and other brush is prevalent and on selected drier interior hills and ridges, such as Mount Tamalpais and Carson Ridge, where chaparral is extensive. They were lacking in Marin only from the outer tip of Point Reyes, from sections of the grassland-dominated hills around Tomales, and from certain open, oak-studded hills or bayshore flatlands near Novato that generally lack suitable brush. Representative nesting locations were Palomarin, PRNS (NE-NY late Mar–late Jul 1979-1982 —PRBO); Limantour Spit, Point Reyes (NB 4/24/80 —DS); Ledum Swamp, Point Reyes (FY/FL 6/13/82 —DS); and China Camp SP (FY 6/19/82 —BiL).

Historical Trends/Population Threats

Grinnell and Miller (1944) did not mention any historical changes in Wrentit populations in California. Presumably this was because any changes were slight or because the positive and negative effects of human activities had been counterbalancing. Clearing of coastal scrub or chaparral for housing has been offset to a degree by the planting of suburban gardens, which Wrentits have invaded. Fire, agriculture, and other development are probably the main forces reducing Wrentit habitat. On the other hand, chaparral is fire adapted, and Wrentits normally reinvade the new vigorous growth within a few years. Extensive clearing of forests that are replaced by dense brushfields must have greatly benefited Wrentits in some areas. Analyses of Breeding Bird Survey data for 1968 to 1979 indicated Wrentits were increasing in California (Robbins et al. 1986), but not when extended to include data through 1989 (USFWS unpubl.).

GEOFFREY R. GEUPEL

Wrentits are very solicitous parents. Photograph by Ian Tait.

Mockingbirds and Thrashers
Family *Mimidae*

NORTHERN MOCKINGBIRD *Mimus polyglottos*

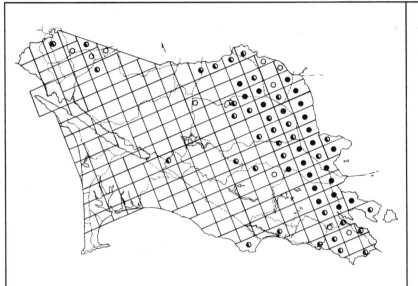

A year-round resident.

A fairly common, somewhat local breeder; overall breeding population small.

Recorded in 67 (30.3%) of 221 blocks.

○ Possible	=	10	(15%)
◑ Probable	=	34	(51%)
● Confirmed	=	23	(34%)

FSAR = 3   OPI = 201   CI = 2.19

Ecological Requirements

In California, the Northern Mockingbird originally inhabited desert wash scrub, broken chaparral, or open woodland edges in the southern part of the state (Grinnell 1911, Unitt 1984). With the expansion of human settlement, the Mockingbird has become predominantly a bird of residential and agricultural landscapes. In Marin County, these classy and highly visible vocal mimics largely dwell in urban and suburban yards or parks and, more sparingly, rural ranchyards. Important features of these habitats are a sparse cover of large bushes and densely foliaged trees for shelter and nesting, intervening open-ground foraging areas, and a supply of berry- and fruit-bearing trees. Mockingbirds are most numerous in residential areas with open lawns and scattered plantings. In 1981, Mockingbirds were breeding locally in a natural habitat of scattered stunted oaks and grassland at the end of San Andreas Road at the base of Mount Burdell, Novato (D. Shuford pers. obs.), but this area may soon be swallowed up by suburban sprawl.

Mockingbirds construct their bulky cup nests primarily of small twigs and line them with grass and rootlets. They may also incorporate various items—such as string, paper, foil, and trash—into the wall of the nest. Nest placement varies from about 1 to 40 feet above the ground (Bent 1948). In northern California, most nests are 3 to 15 feet up in vines, thickets, small trees, or even on fence posts or stumps (Harrison 1978). In Louisiana, average nest height of one sample of 108 nests was 6 feet (Joern & Jackson 1983), and of another of 151 nests was 8 feet (range 1.5-29 ft., Taylor 1965); in the latter study, nest height increased as the season progressed.

The Mockingbird diet is varied and, continentwide, the proportion of animal food ranges from a high of 73% in spring (n = 84) to a low of 33% in fall (n = 65) (Martin et al. 1951). The diet of the Mockingbird in southern California from late July to late August is about 23% animal matter and 77% vegetable (Beal 1907, n = 33). The vegetable matter is predominantly fruit and minor amounts of seeds. In Marin, wild blackberries, elderberries, and poison oak seeds would be included, as well as the berries of pyrocantha, cotoneaster, crataegus, and other fruits from ornamental and residential plantings. Mockingbirds spend much of their time feeding on the ground, and thus grasshoppers and ants constitute about 90% of the animal matter in the diet (Beal 1907). They eat smaller amounts of beetles, caterpillars, other insects, and spiders, and,

327

rarely, small lizards and snakes. Besides plucking berries from trees and bushes, Mockingbirds also glean some insects from the foliage. Home range sizes increase during the course of nesting (Biedenweg 1983), and abundant food sources such as feeding trays will attract many birds within a quarter-mile radius (Michener 1951). For their first six days, nestlings are fed almost all animal matter, predominantly small insects and spiders. After this they are fed more fruit, which, by 10 to 20 days after hatching, comprises 30%–35% of the nestling diet (Breitwiech et al. 1984). The switch occurs about the time the young are first able to regulate their own body temperatures. At this time, nestlings are fed greater proportions of fruit later in the day. This may be because fruit provides water, which is in greater demand during the heat of the day, or because the carbohydrates of fruit are needed later for energy demands in the cool hours of night (Breitwiech et al. 1984). Perhaps this also reflects daily changes in insect activity and hence availability (see Loggerhead Shrike account). The young are also fed small amounts of limestone bits or snail shells.

Marin Breeding Distribution

Mockingbirds now breed commonly in Marin County only in the urban-suburban environment along the Highway 101 corridor in the eastern portion of the county. During the atlas period, a small population appeared to be established in the rural Tomales area, as were marginal populations on the immediate coast in the Point Reyes Station (S 5/21–7/15/82 –DS) and Stinson Beach (singing bird 4/14/82 –HS) areas. Subsequently, there has been confirmed evidence of coastal breeding in Point Reyes Station (FY/FS "early summer" 1987 –RS) and at the RCA station near Bolinas (FY/FL "summers" of 1986 and 1987 –DDeS). Other representative nesting locations included the base of Mt. Burdell, Novato (UN 5/19/81 –DS; NY 5/?/82 –ScC); Novato (NY 5/25/78 –RMS); and Kentfield (NB 4/6/82 –BiL).

Historical Trends/Population Threats

Mockingbirds of both the western and eastern subspecies have been expanding their breeding ranges northward for many years. In California, the Mockingbird's breeding range has increased greatly in this century in concert with the expansion of the human population in urban, suburban, and rural agricultural areas, in the latter especially where orchards predominate (Arnold 1935, 1980). In 1911, the Mockingbird was spreading rapidly in the lowlands of southern California and the San Joaquin Valley (Grinnell 1911). In 1927, it was considered "a sparse winter visitant to the San Francisco Bay region" (G&W 1927), but at that time breeding had not yet been documented along the northern California coast. Nesting was established in the San Francisco Bay Area in 1928 and 1929, and Mockingbirds continued to expand their breeding range throughout the San Joaquin and Sacramento valleys (Arnold 1935, 1980; Sibley 1952). Although first recorded in Marin County at least by 1900 (Mailliard 1900), Mockingbirds were not seen with regularity here until about 1960, and then mostly in the fall and winter (ABN). Although the history of initial breeding in Marin County is unknown, it must have followed soon after their first influx, in the early 1960s. A breeding season record of a Mockingbird in Tiburon from 1 to 15 June 1958 was considered worthy of publication in the *Condor* (Stern 1959), but by the time of the atlas work from 1976 to 1982, Mockingbirds were breeding widely in eastern Marin County. Although Breeding Bird Surveys indicate that the Mockingbird population in California has been relatively stable from 1968 to 1989 (Robbins et al. 1986, USFWS unpubl. analyses), it is still expanding, at least locally, along the immediate coast north of the San Francisco Bay region (e.g., AB 34:929). It seems likely that the Mockingbird will continue to consolidate and expand its range in California in association with the burgeoning human population, though to a much more modest extent than in past decades.

JOHN R. ARNOLD

CALIFORNIA THRASHER *Toxostoma redivivum*

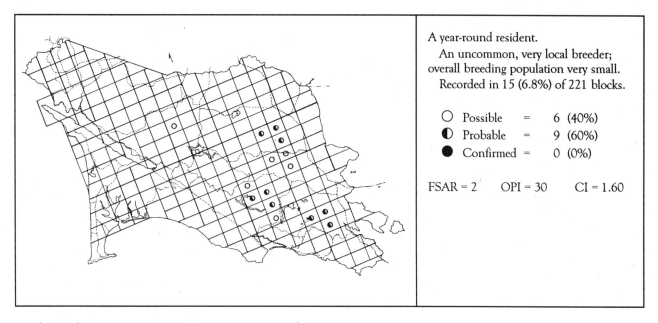

A year-round resident.
An uncommon, very local breeder;
overall breeding population very small.
Recorded in 15 (6.8%) of 221 blocks.

○	Possible	=	6 (40%)
◖	Probable	=	9 (60%)
●	Confirmed	=	0 (0%)

FSAR = 2   OPI = 30   CI = 1.60

Ecological Requirements

These voluble thrashers reside in Marin County only in tall dense chaparral on interior ridges shielded from the influence of persistent summer coastal fogs. Suitable chaparral is open next to the ground, while close overhead there is a strongly interlacing branchwork and an evergreen leafy canopy (Grinnell 1917). Tall protective brushy cover for concealment and nest sites, and loose, generally dry soil for foraging are the California Thrasher's main habitat requirements. Marin's breeding Thrashers do not inhabit coastal scrub along the immediate coast or suburban yards with appropriate shrubbery, as they do south of San Francisco, or thick riparian brush, as they do to a limited extent throughout much of their range.

California Thrashers build rough nest bowls of coarse interlaced sticks and finer twigs, and line them with dried grasses, rootlets, and bark strips (Dawson 1923, Woods 1948). They conceal their nests from about 2 to 12 feet above ground in the dense branchwork of bushes, scrubby trees, or hedges; nests are rarely found in live oaks or far from continuous brush cover (Grinnell 1917, Engels 1940, Woods 1948).

California Thrashers forage primarily on the ground in the litter and soil under chaparral cover, from which they rarely stray far. They do not employ their feet in scratching as do many ground foraging birds of brushy habitats. Instead, birds run swiftly or hop to suitable feeding grounds, where they use their long decurved bills to unearth prey, mostly by subsurface digging. With its legs well braced, the bird strikes its bill into the ground with

rapid strokes of its head and neck, and hooks the dirt back and out with a powerful pull of its neck. Frequently, its mandibles are slightly open when it digs, but usually not when dirt or litter is swept away with side-to-side motions of the bill (Engels 1940). Thrashers obtain fruit and berries from bushes or from the ground and presumably also secure some insect prey from the foliage (Grinnell 1917). California Thrashers are omnivorous, and their year-round diet in California is about 59% vegetable and 41% animal matter (Beal 1907, n = 82). Limited data (n = 7) suggest that animal matter comprises about 97% of the spring diet, but otherwise it constitutes only 34%-45% of the diet from summer through winter (n = 25-39/season) (Martin et al. 1951). Vegetable fare consists of wild and cultivated fruits and berries, including those of elderberry, coffeeberry, manzanita, poison oak, other *Rhus* bushes, raspberry, sumac, buckthorn, and grape (Beal 1907, Martin et al. 1951). Mast, weed seeds, leaf galls, rubbish, and grains are of secondary importance. The animal fare consists of beetles, ants, wasps, bees, caterpillars, cocoons, moths, true bugs, flies, grasshoppers, Jerusalem crickets, spiders, centipedes, and millipedes (Beal 1907).

Marin Breeding Distribution

During the atlas period, we found that California Thrashers had a restricted breeding distribution in Marin County. They bred here primarily on the top of Mount Tamalpais and on Carson and Big Rock ridges. Small populations inhabited isolated patches of chaparral in the hills near

Soulajoule Reservoir in north-central Marin. Thrashers have yet to be confirmed as breeders in Marin County, but because they are nonmigratory, permanent residents, there can be no doubt that they nest here regularly. Representative nesting locations based on presumed evidence of breeding were Dolcini Ranch near Soulajoule Reservoir (PO—seen 6/16/82 —DS); headwaters of San Jose Creek on Big Rock Ridge (PR–S 3/26-5/9/79 —DS); Carson Ridge (PR–S 2/26-6/14/80-82 —DS); near East Peak Mt.

Tamalpais (PR 5/14-6/11/82 —DSi); and Blithedale Ridge (PR 4/20 & 5/8/82 —DSi).

Historical Trends/Population Threats

There is little prior information, but Breeding Bird Survey data indicate that numbers of California Thrashers were declining in California from 1968 to 1989 (USFWS unpubl. analyses).

Shrikes
Family *Laniidae*

LOGGERHEAD SHRIKE *Lanius ludovicianus*

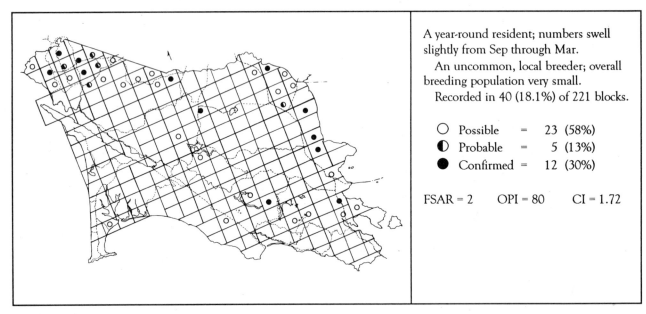

A year-round resident; numbers swell slightly from Sep through Mar.

An uncommon, local breeder; overall breeding population very small.

Recorded in 40 (18.1%) of 221 blocks.

○	Possible	=	23 (58%)
◑	Probable	=	5 (13%)
●	Confirmed	=	12 (30%)

FSAR = 2   OPI = 80   CI = 1.72

Ecological Requirements

These poised and efficient mandibular hunters inhabit Marin County's open lowland valleys of grasslands, fields, and broken woodlands. Like that of many grassland breeders here, the Shrike's preference for valley bottoms (over steeper hillsides) presumably reflects greater prey availability there. Shrikes do reside on relatively level ridgetops elsewhere in the Bay Area (S.L. Granholm pers. comm.). Shrikes center their activities in breeding territories around one to a few "headquarters" that provide adequate nest sites, nocturnal roosts, and lookout posts for scanning broad, open vistas where suitable prey abound (Miller 1931a, 1950). In Marin's ranching lands, foraging perches

such as fence posts and powerlines are common, but suitable nest sites may be limiting locally. Blackberry, rose, and willow thickets and eucalyptus groves provide nest sites in these areas.

Loggerhead Shrikes build nests of twigs, weed stalks, and grasses (Miller 1931a, 1950; Graber et al. 1973; Porter et al. 1975; Kridelbaugh 1983). They often place nests on the remains of old nests of Shrikes or other birds; occasionally they dispense with the base of sticks (Miller 1931a, 1950). The nest lining forms a thick warm felt whose margins frequently project an inch over the stick foundation. Lining materials are principally cottonlike substances such as plant down and wool, along with hair, feathers, rootlets, strips of bark, willow catkins, and string. One nest lining in Marin County of black-and-white skunk fur blended smartly with the Shrike's attire (D. Shuford pers. obs.). Shrikes conceal most nests at medium heights in dense bushes or small, thickly foliaged trees of various species (references above). Site selection is apparently based on the degree of protective cover rather than on a particular plant species; if several choices are readily available, trees with thorns seem to be used first (Porter et al. 1975). Atypically, Shrikes have nested in loose tangled bailing wire, between the upright boards of a support for telephone wires, in a brush pile, against a bank covered with creeping vines, or in the heart of a tumbleweed (Miller 1931a, 1950). Actual nest support in an arborescent setting is usually provided by crotches of large limbs or tangles of fine dense twigs (Miller 1931a, 1950), usually well within the periphery of the tree or shrub (Porter et al. 1975). Although nest height in western birds varies from 1.5 to 30 feet above ground, it is rarely less than 3 or more than 25 feet (Miller 1931a, 1950; Bent 1950); an exceptional nest in the East was at a height of 50 feet (Ford 1936). Reports of average overall nest height range from 7 to 10 feet, but vary from 2.5 feet in subsets of brush nests to 17 feet in second nests (vs. 9 ft. in first nests) (Porter et al. 1975, Kridelbaugh 1983).

With their large heads and powerful hooked beaks, Shrikes are admirably suited for a predatory existence. In the early morning and afternoon/early evening hours, breeding Loggerheads actively seek prey by scanning from low perches and quickly moving to the next perch (Miller 1931a, 1950). At midday, most birds forage in a passive manner from high perches, from which they infrequently sally forth after particularly inviting prey. Although attack rates in warm months are highest in early morning, attack rates in the winter are low in the morning and reach highest levels by midafternoon, reflecting the activity periods of cold-blooded prey (Craig 1978). Shrikes usually make short-distance flights between low perches by dropping down to a low, even flight, then abruptly rising at the next stop (Miller 1931a, 1950). Longer flights from high perches usually involve undulating finchlike flights. Morrison (1980) noted that Shrikes used higher hunting perches during breeding, perhaps because this allowed them better views over taller annual vegetation at that season. He found that 90% of attacks and captures were within about 30 feet of a perch during the prebreeding period and within 46 feet during breeding. He also noted that hunting perches during breeding were less than 50 feet from the nest, but Craig (in Morrison 1980) found Shrikes usually hunting from perches over 130 feet from nests. Shrikes make nearly vertical or diagonal plunges, either with set wings or rapid wing motion, in pursuit of prey on or close to the ground. They frequently hover at the end of an approach flight, and

they are adept at pursuing fleeing prey because of the maneuverability afforded them by their short rounded wings and long tails. Shrikes also hop actively on the ground or on the tops of bushes to scare up prey, and they flycatch from perches in the manner of clumsy kingbirds. Overall, ground attacks are more common, but air attacks increase during breeding, reflecting the greater availability then of flying prey (Morrison 1980). Although Shrikes usually take larger flying prey, such as butterflies, on or near the ground (Morrison 1980), they sometimes relentlessly chase and tire small birds (Graber et al. 1973). They characteristically seize prey with their strong beaks; for predatory birds, their feet are weakly developed. Loggerheads occasionally shift prey from their beaks to their feet in flight (Esterly 1917) and, rarely, catch larger prey with their feet (Caldwell 1967). Shrikes dispatch smaller prey with rapid biting motions of the bill, while for larger prey they aim at the vertebrae just below the base of the skull (Miller 1931a, 1950; Smith 1973). Shrikes are notorious for carrying larger prey (1.6 in., Craig 1978) to perches, where they impale them on a pointed projection or wedge them in a crotch to facilitate tearing them apart. Impaling stations are often within a few feet of the ground and seldom higher than 15 feet (Miller 1931a, 1950). Thorns, branch tips, and barbed wire fences are typical impaling spots. After satiation birds will cache their food there, returning later that day or on subsequent days to feed. Most authors consider the prime function of impaling and wedging to be facilitation of prey manipulation, since Shrikes' feet are of limited use in holding large prey (e.g., Miller 1931a, 1950; Wemmer 1969; Smith 1972; Craig 1978). Food storage is considered secondary, though, rarely, it may be of aid during prey shortage, especially in arid climates where impaled animals will dry without spoiling (Watson 1910). Alternatively, prey storage by males may reduce the energy demands of hunting on females, whose time might be more profitably devoted to incubating or brooding (Appelgate 1977). In support of this theory are observations of a female Shrike during breaks from incubation eating food cached on fences by her mate; of the female feeding the young mostly food cached by the male; and, in the evening, of the male presenting the brooding female with food partly from his caches. Smith (1972, 1973) noted that prey was usually impaled within 50 feet of capture and often considerably closer. The distance might be expected to vary with the availability of suitable impaling posts.

Although Loggerhead Shrikes have "an indiscriminate taste for all sorts of animal matter," the diet is primarily insectivorous (Miller 1931a, 1950). On a yearly basis, vertebrate food amounts to only 12% of the diet of the western races. Although Shrikes take prey ranging from insects 0.2 inches in length to mice or snakes weighing 0.9 ounce, most prey are in the 0.6- to 0.9-inch range (Craig

1978, Morrison 1980). Shrikes apparently prefer prey that is easy to catch over large prey (Slack 1975). In California studies, Craig (1978) and Morrison (1980) found that average prey size did not vary seasonally and Shrikes did not capture larger prey as a means of meeting food demands during breeding. Western birds apparently depend more on insects than do eastern birds. Shrikes most frequently take grasshoppers, crickets, Jerusalem crickets, locusts, beetles, larval and adult lepidopterans, bees, centipedes, millipedes, and spiders (Miller 1931a, 1950). They also consume lesser quantities of flies, dragonflies, mayflies, damselflies, termites, true bugs, and cicadas, and, rarely, gastropods or crustaceans. Vertebrate prey include small mammals such as harvest, white-footed and house mice, voles, kangaroo rats, and shrews; birds such as sparrows, finches, and warblers; a variety of snakes and lizards, and, rarely, tree frogs and minnows. Like most rapacious birds, Shrikes regurgitate pellets of undigested hard parts of prey, and the males feed the incubating and brooding females (Miller 1931a, 1950). Shrikes sometimes cannibalize young that die after winds blow them out of nests (Kridelbaugh 1983). Most of the vegetable matter Shrikes consume arrives fortuitously in the stomachs of larger prey, but 2%-3% of the diet appears to consist of seeds, debris, and other vegetable matter taken voluntarily (Miller 1931a, 1950).

Marin Breeding Distribution

During the atlas period, most Shrikes in Marin County bred locally in agricultural lands in the Tomales and Chileno Valley area and in fields and reclaimed salt marshes along the San Pablo Bay shoreline. Representative nesting localities were 2.5 mi. N of Tomales near junction of Hwy. 1 and Stemple Creek (NE 4/14-28/78 —SJ, DS); base of Antonio Mountain, Chileno Valley (FY/FL 6/4/82 —DS, ScC); and Hicks Valley (NE-NY 4/22-5/16/82 —DS). The absence of Shrikes as widespread

breeders in the ranchlands of the remainder of Marin County is puzzling. Miller (1931a) stated that they were lacking in many areas with fog or summer rain, which may partly explain their absence as breeders on fog-enshrouded Point Reyes. However, they are relatively widespread near Tomales, where summer fogs are frequent, but absent from many areas inland where fog is infrequent. Since perch and nest sites must be available over broad areas, a lack of an abundant food supply may be the main limiting factor.

Historical Trends/Population Threats

Loggerhead Shrikes have declined continentwide since at least the mid-1950s, most dramatically in the East (Morrison 1981a). The species has been on the Audubon Society Blue List every year since its inception in 1972 (Tate 1981, 1986; Tate & Tate 1982). The species is currently a Candidate (Category 2) for federal listing as Threatened or Endangered by the U.S. Fish and Wildlife Service (USFWS 1991) and is on their list of Migratory Nongame Birds of Management Concern (USFWS 1987b). Western populations generally have not declined dramatically, though the insular San Clemente Loggerhead Shrike *(L. l. mearnsi)* is listed as federally Endangered (USFWS 1989a). Christmas Bird Count data from 1955-56 to 1978-79 indicate the Pacific Coast population is stable or slightly declining (Morrison 1981a). From 1968 to 1979, Shrikes declined on Breeding Bird Surveys in the West as a whole, but not in California (Robbins et al. 1986). Further analysis of data from these surveys indicates that Shrike numbers were fairly stable in California from 1968 to 1989, despite a decline from 1980 to 1989 (USFWS unpubl.). Habitat loss and pesticide contamination have been suggested as possible causes of the overall decline (Anderson & Duzan 1978, Robbins et al. 1986, USFWS 1987b). This species bears close watching in Marin and throughout its range.

Starlings
Family *Sturnidae*

EUROPEAN STARLING *Sturnus vulgaris*

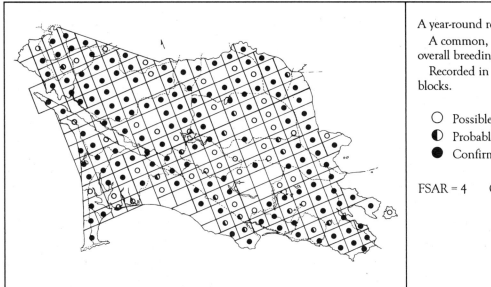

A year-round resident.

A common, nearly ubiquitous breeder; overall breeding population very large.

Recorded in 194 (87.8%) of 221 blocks.

○ Possible　　=　41　(21%)
◐ Probable　　=　15　(8%)
● Confirmed　=　138　(71%)

FSAR = 4　　OPI = 776　　CI = 2.50

Ecological Requirements

Although these aggressive invaders have called Marin County home for only about 40 years, they are now one of our most numerous and ubiquitous breeding birds in open surroundings. Essentially an edge species, Starlings feed in open habitats and seek shelter in open stands of almost any nearby woodland, forest, residential tree planting, or human structure that provides suitable nest sites and cover. Since Starlings breed colonially, good breeding habitat includes clumps of trees or buildings with a number of nest cavities and adjoining short-grassland feeding areas, where the birds can forage in loose flocks (Feare 1984). In Marin County as elsewhere, the prime foraging areas are grazed pasturelands, but lawns, playing fields, mowed hayfields, tilled farmland, salt marshes, and landfills are widely used alternative foraging sites. All foraging habitats are very open, providing Starlings with great mobility and good visibility.

Starlings show great adaptability in their choice of nest sites. Although they prefer natural cavities in trees and old or new holes of larger woodpeckers such as Northern Flickers, they also use a wide array of other sites (Bent 1950, Kessel 1957). Frequent domiciles are convenient cavities in or on barns, outbuildings, or deserted houses or schools; old drainpipes; church steeples and belfries; and crevices in cliffs and road cuts. Also used, perhaps less frequently, are mailboxes, holes in haystacks, old burrows of kingfishers and Bank Swallows, old dome nests of magpies, or the side of an Osprey nest. Other unusual sites are old rabbit holes, cracks in the ground, holes in rock piles, tins or boxes in rubbish heaps, the branches of trees, dense clumps of bushes, or ivy on the walls of buildings. In suburban areas of lowland California, Starlings also nest in cavities among the dead fronds in the skirts of Washington fan palms *(Washingtonia filifera)* (Troetschler 1976, D. Shuford pers. obs.).

Bent (1950) reported that nest heights range from about 2 to 60 feet, though most are from 10 to 20 feet high. In oak savannah in Santa Clara County, Troetschler (1976) reported that Starlings use suitable natural cavities at almost any height. Nest heights there averaged 26 feet (range 5-59 ft.). In the Sacramento Valley, Planck (1967) found that Starlings showed no preference as to the height, substrate, or the immediate terrain or other features of the habitat of nest boxes. They did show a preference for nest sites close to primary foraging areas and staging points along their flight lines to roosts. In one European study,

333

Verheyan (1980) noted a preference for high cavities facing east or southeast. Feare (1984) emphasized the insulative qualities of the nest cavity. In oak savannah, Troetschler (1976) reported that later in the season, as the weather warms, nest hole use decreased in dry areas, but more holes, including marginal older ones with large worn entrances, were used in moist areas that still could supply adequate nestling food. In the cool early spring only the better-insulated holes are adequate for nestling protection. Although Starlings often reuse nest holes in the same or successive years, individuals frequently switch nest holes and mates between successive broods in the same year and between years (Verheyan 1980).

Like many colonial and polygynous birds, male Starlings build rough nests as enticement to females to become their mate (Feare 1984). Along with incipient nest material, the male adds to the nest cavity petals of flowers or fresh green leaves, which he changes regularly. Once a pair bond is formed, the female usually takes the initiative and completes the nest and its lining, often first removing material placed by the male. The nest is a bulky structure of dry vegetation, mainly dry grasses and perhaps fine twigs, weed stems, dry leaves, rootlets, vines, or pine needles (Bent 1950, Kessel 1957, Feare 1984). The size of the nest reflects that of the cavity (Bent 1950), and the nest cup is always situated in that part of the nest cavity most remote from the entrance (Feare 1984). Starlings usually, though not always, line the nest cup with softer material of fine dry grasses and feathers, and also with artificial materials such as cloth, string, paper, cellophane, cotton wool, or even cigarette butts. When birds depart from the nest, they partially cover the eggs with leaves or other pieces of material.

Starlings are highly gregarious birds that breed colonially and synchronously. They appear to learn from each other the whereabouts and abundance of food and are more efficient in exploiting it by feeding in flocks (Tinbergen & Drent 1980, Feare 1984). Flocking behavior helps birds to discover and exploit localized transient patches of food and to feed at faster rates (up to a point) because of the lessened need of individuals to be vigilant toward predators.

During winter, Starlings forage in large inter- or intraspecific flocks, but during the breeding season they more often feed singly, in pairs, or in small flocks (Williamson & Gray 1975, Feare 1984). Males defend a small area around the nest site and during egg laying defend their mates to prevent them from mating with other males (Feare 1984). Consequently, at that time males and females travel as pairs to feeding areas (Dunnet 1955, Feare 1984). From colonies, birds fly to common feeding grounds that are usually within a few hundred yards of nest sites, though they may range up to a third- or half-mile away (Dunnet 1955, Feare 1984).

Starlings feed primarily in grasslands, where they take invertebrates (and, to a lesser extent, seeds) from the foliage, from the surface of the ground, and from the upper inch or so of the soil (Bent 1950, Dunnet 1955, Williamson & Gray 1975, Brownsmith 1977, Tinbergen & Drent 1980, Tinbergen 1981, Feare 1984). They probe into the soil with wide open or closed bills; they sometimes bore in with a closed bill, forcibly open it, and peer into the hole so formed for food. Starlings also glean insects from trees, flycatch from perches, and catch aerial insects in extended, graceful, swallowlike flights. They appear to flycatch more commonly in the autumn than other seasons (Dunnet 1955).

Starlings obtain fruit while perched in trees and bushes or from the ground along with grains; they may eat germinating grains in the soil or remove them by probing. Starlings sometimes feed in close association with livestock, whose disturbance of insects may benefit the birds; they also search for external parasites on the animals' backs.

Starlings are omnivorous, and their diet varies considerably both seasonally and geographically (Feare 1984). During the breeding season, they eat mostly invertebrates and, rarely, vertebrates such as newts, frogs, and lizards. Despite the variety in their diet, Starlings concentrate on only a few prey species while breeding. In most areas, these are larvae of beetles, moths, or butterflies that live on or just under the soil surface.

The diet in Texas (Russell 1971), which by geography and climate is likely to be similar to that in California, shows a much higher percentage of insects than found in the East (Kalmbach & Gabrielson 1921, Lindsay 1939). Year round, the diet in Texas is 73% animal food and 27% vegetable; animal food there increases to 85% in summer (Russell 1971, n = 200). In the East, animal food comprises 93% of the diet in spring (n = 249) and reaches a low of 32% in winter (n = 644) (Martin et al. 1951). The main insect prey of western birds are adult and larval beetles, moths, butterflies, grasshoppers, and crickets, with smaller quantities of ants, true bugs, flies, cicadas (and related species), along with a few spiders, isopods, and gastropods (Russell 1971, Moore 1986). The vegetable component consists principally of fruits and a few seeds, mostly in fall and winter (Russell 1971); in the West, wintering birds often feed on large quantities of grain from feedlots, corn silage, and garbage (Killpack & Crittenden 1952). Nestlings are fed primarily animal food, but their diets can vary with time of day, weather, nestling age (depending on prey availability and developmental requirements), and brood size; dietary diversity is greater for younger birds and, overall, for larger broods (Feare 1984, Moore 1986).

Foraging adults tend to select for large items for their young and eat small ones themselves (Tinbergen 1981).

Very small young generally receive soft-bodied insects, smaller caterpillars, and more spiders than older young. Caterpillars are quite important to fledged young, which spend much more time in trees than do adults (Feare 1984). Once their requirements for invertebrate foods relax, the fledglings' arboreal tendencies predispose them to switch to summer-ripening fruits. Although Starlings feed mostly in grasslands throughout the year, in winter they more readily use alternative sites and switch to plant foods, even when there is no apparent limitation on feeding on animal matter in grasslands. Perhaps it takes them less time to feed on grains than on invertebrates, allowing them more time for maintenance activities. With their seasonal shift in diet, in winter Starlings tend to feed more in urban areas, in gardens, at bird feeders, on household wastes, at dumps, dockyards, around warehouses, and on grain around farmyards and in cattle troughs. They readily enter buildings in pursuit of food. Males predominate at cattle troughs, but females may have to feed elsewhere to obtain a higher proportion of protein to maintain reserves for early breeding and to lay large clutches.

Marin Breeding Distribution

During the atlas period, the European Starling was one of the most widespread of Marin County's breeding birds. It was most numerous in the productive foraging grounds of lowland valleys and gently sloping hills of the ranchlands of Point Reyes and much of north and central Marin. Representative nesting localities were Upper Pierce Ranch, Tomales Point (FY/NY 6/1/82 –DS); Chileno Valley (FY 5/5/82 –DS); Bolinas Ridge above the lower end of Kent Lake (FY 5/21/82 –BiL); and Kentfield (NB 5/7/82 –BiL).

Historical Trends/Population Threats

Although a number of attempts were made to release Starlings in the East in the mid- to late 1880s, the 100 birds "liberated" in New York's Central Park in 1890 and 1891 were the core nucleus that spawned the hordes that have since spread far and wide over the entire continent (Bent 1950). Colonization was rapid and most pervasive to the south and west, in line with the species' traditional northeast to southwest movements in Europe. New areas initially were settled in the fall and winter, primarily by dispersing juveniles, followed roughly five years later by the establishment of breeding populations (Bent 1950). Starlings first reached northeastern California in 1942 (Jewett 1942) and were reported breeding there by 1949 (Ball & Koe *fide* DeHaven 1973). They were first reported on the coast of northern California on Point Reyes in 1949 (Gullion 1949), and hundreds were seen there by 1954 (*Gull* 36:17, 37:3, 38:2); over 2000 were seen in Novato on 12 February 1956 (*Gull* 38:11). Although first reported

nesting on the southern California coast in 1958 (Howard 1959), Starlings were not reported nesting on the northern coast (in San Francisco) until 1964 (Tenaya & Tenaya 1966). Given the pattern of establishment elsewhere, Starlings likely nested in these areas earlier and went unreported. Starling populations on Christmas Bird Counts in northern California increased slowly at first, then expanded rapidly (DeHaven 1973). Numbers began to swell quickly in the mid-1950s. They exploded beginning in 1961, with an increase of about 1600% in the next ten years despite extensive control efforts at feedlots and other areas in 1964 and 1967 (DeHaven 1973). Starlings increased on Breeding Bird Surveys in California from 1968 to 1979, while for the West as a whole they increased sharply from 1968 to 1973, with signs of stabilization thereafter (Robbins et al. 1986). Extension of data analysis indicates that Starling numbers generally decreased as breeding birds in California from 1968 to 1989, despite a relatively stable trend from 1980 to 1989 (USFWS unpubl.).

The rapid range expansion and numerical increase of Starlings has caused alarm because of their aggressive usurpation of nesting holes of woodpeckers, swallows, bluebirds, Wood Ducks, and other cavity nesters, and because of the potential effect of competition for food between Starlings and species that overlap with them in diet requirements (Bent 1950). Although Starlings have undoubtedly had a negative effect on California's native birds, the extent of that effect is unknown. It is clear, though, that Starlings do aggressively displace other hole-nesting birds, particularly if nest sites are in short supply (Weitzel 1988). From 1968 to 1974, during the rapid increase of the Starling's population in California, Troetschler (1976) studied the interactions of Acorn Woodpeckers and Starlings in Santa Clara County. Her data suggest that Starlings did *not* affect the reproductive success or group size of Acorn Woodpeckers there. She suggested, though, that long-term success of the Acorn Woodpeckers might be compromised by the extra energy they had to spend on hole defense and drilling new holes, energy that might be expended more profitably on adequate acorn storage and defense. Even if Acorn Woodpeckers are flexible enough to adapt to Starling competition, other species may not be. The Purple Martin may be a case in point (see account). Although Starling impacts on native birds seem not to be as drastic as some doomsayers predicted, the long-term interactions of this alien with our native fauna should be carefully monitored.

The Starling's effect on human interests have been well documented, and expensive control efforts have been undertaken (Howard 1959, Palmer 1973, Wright et al. 1980, Feare 1984). Damage to agriculture has been reported since c. 200 B.C. and continues to be the main complaint (Feare 1984). Starlings do considerable harm by consuming soft fruit crops, winter-sown cereal grain crops as they germinate, and livestock feed (which they also foul), especially of cattle. In California, locally reared juveniles inflict most damage to spring and summer fruit crops (Palmer 1973). On the other hand, adults and subadults (mainly migrants) cause most of the damage to livestock and poultry feed in fall and winter (Palmer 1973). Additional complaints lodged against Starlings include their roosts causing unsightly contamination of buildings, breaking of tree limbs, and killing of trees from the accumulation of droppings; possible transmission of animal and human disease; and noise. Extensive control efforts have had only limited and temporary local success (Wright et al. 1980, Feare 1984). With their flexible nest site requirements, mating system, and foraging strategies (Feare 1984), Starlings are the rats of the bird world and are here to stay.

Why are Loggerhead Shrike populations declining sharply in the East, and will California populations be so affected?
Photograph by Ian Tait.

Vireos
Family *Vireonidae*

SOLITARY VIREO   *Vireo solitarius*

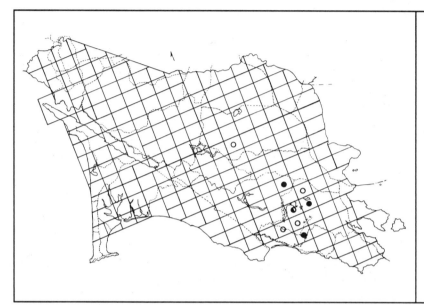

A summer resident from late Mar through mid-Oct.

An uncommon, very local breeder; overall breeding population very small. Recorded in 8 (3.6%) of 221 blocks.

○ Possible = 4 (50%)
◑ Probable = 1 (12%)
● Confirmed = 3 (38%)

FSAR = 2   OPI = 16   CI = 1.88

Ecological Requirements

The attentive listener hears the call-pause-and-response song of this "greenlet" only locally in Marin County during the breeding season. It issues forth from relatively dry, open mixed evergreen forests dominated either by broad-leaved hardwoods or Douglas fir mixed with a hardwood component. In comparison with Hutton's Vireos, which prefer moister, denser hardwood woodlands, Solitaries select those with a more open canopy. Although some birds nest near water, it is not essential on their nesting territories; instead, streamsides may provide the only hardwood elements in some forest areas dominated by conifers. For nesting areas, Solitary Vireos prefer shaded glades along woodland openings, meadow edges, and trailsides.

Solitary Vireos build semipensile basket nests that are somewhat bulkier and looser than those of most other vireos (Dawson 1923). They weave them of vegetable fibers, grasses, dead leaves, and bark strips. They lash these materials to limb forks by vegetable fibers and a little spider silk, and ornament them extensively with spider cases, flower petals, catkin bits, lichens, paper, and the like (Dawson 1923, Bent 1950). Solitaries line their nests with dry grass stems, grass heads (with seeds removed), small leaf stems, and horsehair. Western birds place their nests toward the end of horizontal or drooping branches of small

hardwoods, conifers, or understory bushes. Nest height varies from about 4 to 40 feet, but most nests are almost or quite within reach from the ground (Bent 1950).

In the mixed conifer zone of the Sierra Nevada, Solitary Vireos forage at medium heights mostly by slow pause-and-search gleaning from foliage, twigs, and, to a lesser degree, branches (Airola & Barrett 1985). They also hover, fly-catch, and occasionally lunge for prey. These vireos show substantial geographic variation in their use of various prey capture methods (Petit et al. 1990), but Szaro et al. (1990) found no annual variation in use of foraging techniques and only moderate annual variation in other measures of resources use in ponderosa pine forests in Arizona. The diet of California birds (Apr–Nov) is over 98% animal, consisting of true bugs, caterpillars and moths, wasps and ants, and beetles, along with a few miscellaneous insects and spiders (Beal 1907, n = 46; Dahlsten et al. 1985, n = 6). Solitaries also eat a few leaf galls and poison oak seeds (Beal 1907).

Marin Breeding Distribution

During the atlas period, Solitary Vireos bred locally in Marin County, primarily in the Mount Tamalpais and Lagunitas Creek watersheds. They resided at elevations

337

and exposures where the open quality of the conifers and associated hardwoods results from a lack of significant moisture from summer fog. Representative nesting localities were Phoenix Lake (NY 6/8/79 –ITi); Rock Springs, Mt. Tamalpais (FL/FY 7/8/78 –BGM et al.); and Cascade Canyon, Fairfax (FL/FY 6/19/80 –DS).

Historical Trends/Population Threats

Solitary Vireos have been sighted in the breeding season in the Ross/Phoenix Lake area regularly since at least 1931

(*Gull* 13, No. 7); nesting was confirmed at Ross on 13 June 1937 (NY; *Gull* 19, No. 7). From 1968 to 1979, Solitary Vireos increased on Breeding Bird Surveys in the California Foothills, which include the coastal counties from Monterey south and part of those to the north (Robbins et al. 1986); from 1968 to 1989 they increased in California as a whole (USFWS unpubl. analyses).

HUTTON'S VIREO *Vireo huttoni*

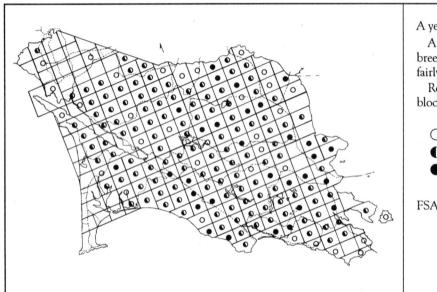

A year-round resident.
   A fairly common, very widespread breeder; overall breeding population fairly large.
   Recorded in 184 (83.2%) of 221 blocks.

○ Possible   =   33 (18%)
◑ Probable   =   121 (66%)
● Confirmed =   30 (16%)

FSAR = 3   OPI = 552   CI = 1.90

Ecological Requirements

The Hutton's Vireo has aptly been called "the spirit of the live oak tree" (Van Fleet 1919). Lichen-draped coast live oaks are the principal component of the broadleaved evergreen forests where this vireo dwells locally. It prefers evergreen forests of moderate to dense crown closure dominated by live oaks over dense north-facing bay laurel stands or open oak woodlands. In the breeding season, this vireo also frequents Douglas fir and bishop pine (where they mix with hardwoods), willow riparian groves, the edges of tall chaparral, and, sparingly, planted eucalyptus, cypress, and pine groves.

   Hutton's Vireos construct round, deeply cupped nests primarily of strands of the gray-green hanging lichen (*Ramalina reticulata*), where available, which they lash together with cobwebs (Van Fleet 1919, Bent 1950). They may use other nest materials, such as plant down, hair, and

bark, and they usually line the nest with fine grasses and perhaps some hair or feathers. They attach their nests in trees and bushes from about 4 to 75 feet above the ground, but mostly at moderate heights. Coast live oak is the preferred, though not exclusive, nesting tree in this region. Nests are usually ensconced in twigs, forks, or foliage near the ends of branches, and they are camouflaged by naturally growing lichens of the type from which the nest is made.

   Hutton's Vireos forage primarily by gleaning, hovering, and, to a limited degree, flycatching in the foliage and subcanopy of the forest and occasionally in the herb layer below it (Root 1967). Within these zones, they secure most prey on foliage and flowers; secondarily on twigs, lichens, and fruits; and lastly on herbs. Foraging birds make long pauses to inspect the foliage for prey before moving rapidly to another spot. While extracting prey from dense terminal sprigs of foliage they often hang upside down, chickadee-like, for a moment. The diet is over 98% animal matter along with a few seeds and galls (Beal 1907, n = 54; Chapin 1925, n = 70; Root 1967). The animal menu consists primarily of true bugs, caterpillars, moths, butterflies, beetles, bees, wasps, and ants, as well as a few miscellaneous insects and spiders.

Marin Breeding Distribution

During the atlas period, Hutton's Vireos bred widely in Marin County's extensive mixed evergreen forests. They were absent or scarce only on the outer tip of Point Reyes and in the low rolling grasslands around Tomales. Repre-

sentative breeding stations were Bolema Trail, Olema Valley (NY 5/?/77 –JGE); near Stafford Lake, Novato (NB 5/6/79 –KH); Mt. Burdell, Novato (NB 5/17/81 –HoP, DS; NY 5/?/82 –ScC); China Camp SP (FL 6/19/82 –BiL); and Camino Alto, between Corte Madera and Mill Valley (FL 6/12/82 –BiL).

Historical Trends/Population Threats

Hutton's Vireo numbers increased on Breeding Bird Surveys in California from 1968 to 1979 (Robbins et al. 1986), but further analysis indicated a fairly stable population in the periods 1968 to 1989 and 1980 to 1989 (USFWS unpubl.).

A male Warbling Vireo singing on the nest attests to its ebullient nature. Photograph by Ian Tait.

WARBLING VIREO *Vireo gilvus*

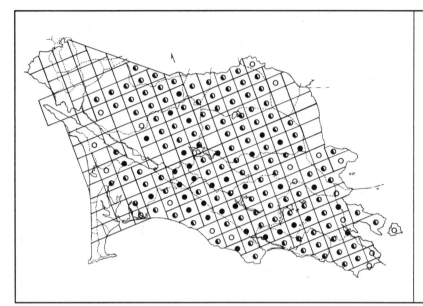

A summer resident from late Mar through early Oct.

An abundant, very widespread breeder; overall breeding population extremely large.

Recorded in 164 (74.2%) of 221 blocks.

○ Possible　　=　19 (12%)
◐ Probable　　=　112 (68%)
● Confirmed　=　33 (20%)

FSAR = 6　　OPI = 984　　CI = 2.08

Ecological Requirements

What this vireo lacks in distinctiveness of plumage it makes up for with one of the brightest, most persistent and ubiquitous songs in all of Marin County. Males are so loquacious that they sing even while incubating eggs on the nest! Locally, the Warbling Vireo's breeding stronghold is the complex of moist, shady, broadleaved evergreen forests dominated by coast live oak and California bay laurel; it also includes willow and alder riparian groves. Although exhibiting a predilection for moderately tall evergreen or deciduous broadleaved trees, Warbling Vireos also inhabit Douglas fir, bishop pine, and, sparingly, redwood, particularly where they mix with hardwoods. These birds' forest haunts are generally denser than those of Solitary and Hutton's vireos, though they overlap extensively with Huttons, particularly in live oaks, and narrowly with Solitaries in mesic drainages.

Like our other vireos, Warblings tend a hanging, cup-shaped nest that is lashed to a fork of a branch or twig well out from the trunk. They build the body of the nest from grasses, plant down, bark strips, leaves, bits of string and lichen, and vegetable fibers (Rust 1920, Dawson 1923, Bent 1950). They often ornament the outside with lichens and catkins, and they line the inside with fine grasses, bark from weed stalks, horsehair, and, rarely, plant down. Nests of western birds range from about 4 to 40 feet, but mostly 15 to 25 feet, above ground. Warbling Vireos orient their nests to overhanging foliage that provides shade from the afternoon sun, rather than to a thermally favorable side of a tree indicated by a certain compass direction (Walsberg 1981).

Relative to our other two vireos, Warblings are more active foragers. In coastal oak woodlands and in the mixed conifer zone of the Sierra Nevada, Warbling Vireos forage at moderate heights by gleaning, hovering, and hawking from twigs, foliage, branches, and, rarely, herbs (Root 1967, Airola & Barrett 1985). They feed more in the outer foliage zone than do Hutton's Vireos (Root 1967). On the whole, Warbling Vireos show considerable geographic variation in foraging behavior (Petit et al. 1990). The diet of California birds (Apr–Oct) is over 97% arthropods consisting of caterpillars, moths, butterflies, true bugs, beetles, leafhoppers and allies, along with spiders and miscellaneous insects (Beal 1907, n = 110; Dahlsten et al. 1985, n = 6). Plant material consists of a few elderberry, poison oak, dogwood, and snowberry seeds, and galls, mostly taken in late summer and fall (Beal 1907, Martin et al. 1951).

Marin Breeding Distribution

During the atlas period, Warbling Vireos were slightly less widespread in Marin County in the breeding season than were Hutton's Vireos, though Warblings were much more numerous overall. Warbling Vireos were absent as breeders from some areas with scrubby oaks on the Point Reyes peninsula and east of Tomales Bay and from drier oak woodlands near Novato, both of which were suitable to Hutton's Vireos. In the drier interior portions of Marin County, Warbling Vireos were restricted primarily to moist narrow canyons and north-facing slopes. Representative nesting localities were Laguna Ranch, PRNS (NE

340

5/21/80 —JGE); Millerton Gulch, east side of Tomales Bay (NB 5/27/82 —DS); O'Hare Park, Novato (NE 5/19/82 —ScC); northeast side of Big Rock Ridge (NE 5/16/82 —BiL); Bolinas Ridge above lower end of Kent Lake (FL 6/16/82 —BiL); and Cascade Canyon, Fairfax (NE 5/7-18/77 —DS).

Historical Trends/Population Threats

The Warbling Vireo was on the Audubon Society's Blue List from 1978 to 1980 and on their list of Local Concern in 1982 (Tate 1981, Tate & Tate 1982). In California, Warbling Vireos have declined historically as breeders on the southern coast (Garrett & Dunn 1981), in the Central Valley (Gaines 1974), and at least locally in the Sierra Nevada (Rothstein et al. 1980, Verner & Ritter 1983, Gaines 1988). They generally appear to be holding their own in coastal northern California. Breeding Bird Surveys indicate that on the whole Warbling Vireos were increas-

ing in California from 1968 to 1989 (USFWS unpubl. analyses). Based on long-term banding data from PRBO's Palomarin field station, DeSante and Geupel (1987) documented a total reproductive failure of Warbling Vireos in 1986 in central coastal California. A large number of other species failed to reproduce partially or totally as well. Although it may be highly coincidental, the timing of these reproductive failures coincided remarkably well with the passage of a radioactive "cloud" from the Chernobyl nuclear power plant accident and associated rainfall. However, the number of adults remained at normal levels at Palomarin that year, as they did on Marin's Even Cheaper Thrills Spring Bird count in both 1986 and 1987 (Appendix A). Whether radiation was responsible for the reproductive failures requires further field and laboratory investigation. Nevertheless the population trends of Warbling Vireos and other species with reduced reproductive success should be monitored closely.

A female Yellow Warbler will soon be dwarfed by the Brown-headed Cowbird youngster she instinctively feeds.
Photograph by Ian Tait.

Wood-Warblers
Family *Emberizidae*
Subfamily *Parulinae*

ORANGE-CROWNED WARBLER *Vermivora celata*

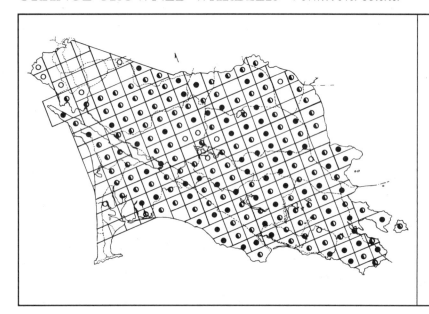

Occurs year round, though primarily as a summer resident from late Feb/early Mar through Sep.

A very common, nearly ubiquitous breeder; overall breeding population extremely large.

Recorded in 191 (86.4%) of 221 blocks.

O	Possible	=	14 (7%)
◑	Probable	=	113 (59%)
●	Confirmed	=	64 (34%)

FSAR = 5   OPI = 955   CI = 2.26

Ecological Requirements

Arriving in numbers on the breeding grounds in early March before our other parulids, the Orange-crowned Warbler's trilling song rises from riparian thickets, oak woodland, coastal scrub, chaparral, and openings in Douglas fir and bishop pine forests where there is sufficient ground cover. Coastal scrub breeders prefer moist, dense drainages, especially adjoining willows and alders, or other forest edges. Chaparral breeders are fond of oak woodland borders, and postbreeding movements greatly swell this species' ranks in extensive stands of pure chaparral. A moderately closed canopy or understory and dense ground cover for concealing nests seem to be breeding requisites.

The Orange-crowned Warblers that breed extensively on the California coast *(V. c. lutescens)* may build their nests up to 6 feet high in bushes or trees, but they generally place most of them in depressions on the ground under concealing vegetation. In contrast, the race that breeds on the Channel Islands and patchily on the southern California mainland *(V. c. sordida)* builds most nests up to 15 feet high in bushes and small trees, with ground nests the exception (Bent 1953). Ground nests may be on level terrain or in earthen crevices of trailside banks, road cuts,

or under uprooted trees. A profusion of annual growth, dried weeds and ferns from the previous season, or understory bushes usually shield ground nests from above. Nests in vines, clumps of ferns, bushes, or trees are usually well screened by leaf debris, lichen sprays, or thick leaf clusters. Orange-crowns construct neat but rather bulky nest cups from dried grasses, leaves, bark strips, and vegetable fibers. They line them with fine grasses and hair; an occasional nest in an earthen hollow will lack a lining (D. Shuford pers. obs.).

Orange-crowned Warblers forage primarily by gleaning from the surface of foliage and, to a limited extent, from the bark of twigs and branches; they hover and flycatch only sparingly (Root 1967). Although wedded to the earth for nesting, foraging birds spend most of their time in the canopy and small amounts in the subcanopy or herb layers. They move rapidly through the trees and tall bushes, probing their bills into leaf clusters, and they characteristically lean, stretch, or hang momentarily from perches to peck at nearby foliage. The diet of California birds is about 91% animal matter, consisting primarily of true bugs, beetles, caterpillars, wasps, ants, and spiders

(Beal 1907, n = 65). The consumption of these items and a minimal amount of flies suggests that Orange-crowns are most successful at capturing sluggish game (Beal 1907, Root 1967). Vegetable fare includes fruit, leaf galls, and seeds, presumably taken mostly in the fall and winter.

Marin Breeding Distribution

During the atlas period, Orange-crowned Warblers bred widely in Marin County. They were scarce or absent only on the outer tip of Point Reyes and in the low rolling grassland-dominated hills near Tomales. Representative breeding localities were near Palomarin (NE 5/6/77 –SJ; garter snake coiled up in nest!); O'Hare Park, Novato (FL 6/15/81 –ScC); Lucas Valley Rd. (FY 6/8/82 –BiL); Woodacre (FY 5/31/82 –BiL); Deer Park School, Fairfax (NY 5/10/76 –RMS); and China Camp SP (NB 4/17/82 –BiL).

Historical Trends/Population Threats

Orange-crowned Warblers have probably not changed markedly in abundance in Marin County in historical times. Development has undoubtedly destroyed some habitat, as has grazing by eliminating or degrading the understory of riparian groves. On the other hand, clearing of forests may have encouraged the growth of brush or ground cover suitable for nesting needs. Numbers of this warbler were relatively stable on Breeding Bird Surveys in California from 1968 to 1989 (USFWS unpubl. analyses).

NORTHERN PARULA *Parula americana*

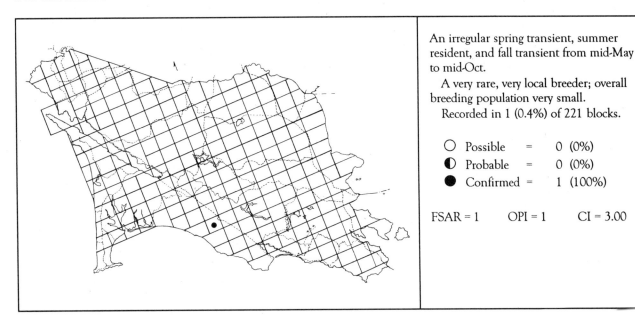

An irregular spring transient, summer resident, and fall transient from mid-May to mid-Oct.

A very rare, very local breeder; overall breeding population very small.

Recorded in 1 (0.4%) of 221 blocks.

○	Possible	=	0 (0%)
◑	Probable	=	0 (0%)
●	Confirmed	=	1 (100%)

FSAR = 1   OPI = 1   CI = 3.00

Ecological Requirements

In the East, this dainty warbler breeds in a wide variety of habitats from boreal spruce forests to sweet gum–oak swamps (Bent 1953, Morse 1967). In northern spruce it is primarily a species of the forest edge, while in southern lowland hardwood forests it is primarily a bird of the unbroken forest canopy. In mixed forests in Minnesota, Parulas locate their nests in forest to forest-edge habitat with variable numbers of large deciduous and coniferous trees and a relatively open canopy (Collins 1981). Foraging studies suggest that Northern Parulas are primarily adapted

to deciduous forests and that competition with kinglets and "spruce-woods warblers" restricts them to the edge of conifers (Morse 1967). The few nesting birds found in California have been in habitats that fall within the range described for the East. In Monterey County, one nest was situated in a rather open stand of mature Monterey pines interspersed with a few live oaks near a pasture (Williams et al. 1958). The understory consisted of low, dense evergreen and deciduous shrubs. A second nearby nest was in a somewhat denser stand of these pines with a rather

343

sparse understory of small, scattered live oaks and a few shrubs. In San Mateo County, Parulas nested in a coastal riparian forest in a narrow canyon with an open Douglas fir–mixed evergreen forest on the slopes above (P.J. Metropulos pers. comm.). Parulas have nested in Marin County on the edge of Douglas fir forests interspersed with mixed evergreen forest and in proximity to riparian habitat.

Nesting distribution in the East generally coincides with the distribution of plentiful nest sites and materials. In the Northeast, most birds build their nests in and of "old man's beard" lichen *(Usnea sp.)*, whereas in the Southeast they build them primarily in a flowering plant, "Spanish moss" *(Tillandsia usneoides)*. Both of these grow epiphytically on the trees of humid forests. Although distribution and abundance over broad areas may mirror that of the preferred nesting substrates (Bent 1953), Morse (1967) found no direct relationship between this warbler and lichen densities at a Maine study site. This suggests other factors are also important. The few California nests have been built from the lichen *(Ramalina reticulata)* that hangs profusely from the limbs of trees in coastal conifer, mixed evergreen, and riparian forests. This lichen resembles the typical eastern nesting substrates in superficial appearance and drooping manner of growth and also has been used for nesting to a limited degree in the Mississippi Valley (Williams et al. 1958). In areas of *Usnea* abundance, Parulas usually suspend and conceal their semipensile, oriolelike nests inside a festoon of free-hanging lichen, which sometimes trails a foot or more below the nest (Wilde 1897, Graber & Graber 1951, Bent 1953).

Parulas weave or felt their generally compact nests almost exclusively from the lichen strands to which they are attached or from those brought from outside. The festoon generally provides a cylindrical curtain above and around the nest. The birds come and go through one (or occasionally two or more) side entrances through the lichen, situated at or slightly above the level of the nest cup rim. They may incorporate a few pine needles or fine grass stems into the nest, probably for support or attachment purposes. Rarely, the nest is open from above and suspended from twigs, branches, foliage, or between a trunk and a lichen tuft. In the Southeast, Parulas most often conceal the nest near the branch from which long filaments of "Spanish moss" hang. They may make these nests from the flower or fine decaying inner fiber of "Spanish moss" or from thistledown. Rarely, where *Usnea* and *Tillandsia* are scarce, Parulas build nests in hanging clusters of twigs, ivy vines, and in bunches of leaves or other rubbish deposited by freshets on branches over streams (Bent 1953). In such situations they construct nests from fine dry grasses, fine bark shreds, box elder blossoms, spider webs, plant down, and leaves. Throughout the range, Parulas line their nests scantily with fine materials, including shreds of lichen, grasses, pine needles,

horsehair, down from the stems of swamp ferns, "Spanish moss" fiber, rootlets, twigs, and strips of weed stems; rarely, they line them elaborately with plant down. Parulas build nests in dead or live conifers, deciduous trees, or bushes, and they situate them against the trunk to well out on outstretched or drooping branches. Nests have been reported from 5 inches to over 100 feet above the ground, but they range from 1 to 20 feet (av. 5 ft.) in New Jersey (Wilde 1897, n = 33) and 26 to 40 feet in Quebec (Mousley in Bent 1953). Two nests in Monterey County were 15 and 30 feet up in the dead branches of Monterey pines (Williams et al. 1958). Nest height and situation is perhaps most dependent on the distribution and abundance of the lichen and "Spanish moss" nesting substrate.

In conifers, Parulas forage at the forest edge at medium heights (range 5–60 ft., av. 33 ft., Morse 1967). In the absence of competition on coastal Maine islands, Parulas exhibit plasticity by expanding their range of foraging heights and using a greater diversity of foraging stations. In southern deciduous forests, they forage uniformly throughout the breadth of the forest but primarily in the canopy above 49 feet. In general, males tend to forage at greater heights than do females (Morse 1971). The need to satisfy the increasing energy demands of young approaching fledging appears to explain the expansion at that time of conifer-foraging adults to nearby deciduous growth and of deciduous foragers to the understory (Morse 1967). Despite the above differences, Parulas in both habitats forage on similar substrates by similar methods. They feed primarily on the extreme tips of foliage, secondarily on small live twigs, and to a limited extent on dead twigs, branches, and epiphitic growth. They capture most prey by gleaning, with limited use of flycatching, hovering, hoverwalking, stretching, and hanging. Their habit of clinging to the underside of foliage while foraging spawned the name *parula*, reflecting the warbler's likeness to its larger parid cousins, titmice and chickadees, which characteristically forage in this manner. Parulas also forage, rarely, on the ground or by clinging to tree trunks (Bent 1953). Compared to other treetop warblers, Parulas are overall more sedate and deliberate in their movements as they hop, creep, or flit from twig to twig.

The diet appears to be almost exclusively insectivorous. The only quantitative work (from Puerto Rico) indicates Parulas eat about 97.7% animal matter and 2.3% vegetable matter, in the form of seeds of small berries (Bent 1953). The principal animal fare is beetles, spiders, true bugs, flies, planthoppers, caterpillars, moths, and a few ants and other small hymenopterans.

Marin Breeding Distribution

The only Marin County atlas breeding record, and the second for California, involved at least three Parulas at Five Brooks Pond in the Olema Valley in 1977. A singing male was first discovered there on 2 June (JM). The male was rediscovered on 4 June, and on 5 June two males and a female were present (SJ et al.). On the latter date, careful observations of the female carrying nesting material revealed a nest about 25 to 30 feet up in a lichen-draped *(Ramalina reticulata)* blue blossom *(Ceanothus thrysiflorus)* tree (SJ). The ceanothus was at the base of a Douglas fir-dominated slope, where it graded into a patch of red alders, just west of the pond. The following observations document further incidents at the nest site: 10 June—female still carrying nest material; 12 June—2 males, female not incubating; 17 June—male singing, female incubating; 27 June—male and female feeding young and female remaining on nest after feeding (brooding recently hatched young?); 5 July—two fledglings seen (ITa); 6 July—male scolding Steller's Jay; 7 July—male and female present; 16 July—male last seen (EYM).

A second confirmed Marin County breeding record was of a male and female feeding a fledgling one-half mile north of Inverness Park from 9 to 16 June 1984; the juvenile was still present on 26 June (MFe, SEF et al.). A male and a female were feeding a juvenile in the vicinity on 28 and 29 July 1984 (RHa), suggesting that a second pair had also bred; an adult male was present through 9 August. In 1985, observations suggestive of breeding were recorded at Bear Valley Headquarters, PRNS, and at Five Brooks Pond. At Bear Valley, a pair was seen from 1 to 4 June, with the male at least to 28 June (RMS et al.), while at Five Brooks a pair was recorded on 19 June, with the female present to the 29th (RS, SEF). In 1991, Parulas again nested near Five Brooks; a pair was seen from 16 June to 10 July and the female was carrying food (RS, DaS). Also that year, a singing male was present north of Bear Valley Headquarters, PRNS, from 26 May until early July (DaS et al.). The number of breeding season sightings of Parulas at Five Brooks and Bear Valley probably reflects greater coverage of these sites rather than any particular affinity of the warblers, as such habitat is widespread on Point Reyes.

Other than the Monterey and Marin records, the only other confirmed breeding record of Northern Parulas in California is from Gazos Creek, San Mateo County, in 1991. Two singing males and a female were first found there on 1 June; nest building was underway on 2 June; and adults were observed from 15 to 30 June repeatedly carrying food to (and removing fecal sacs from) a site where a nest was apparently hidden (BS, PJM et al.).

Historical Trends/Population Threats

Since the discovery of the first California nest, increased field work has revealed that Northern Parulas occur on the northern California coast annually as vagrants, in small numbers in May and June and irregularly from September to early October (ABN). Most of these birds apparently perish or continue on their off-course, long-distance journeys. Since a few have remained to breed, all sightings in suitable potential nesting habitat should be followed up to determine their nesting status. Whether Northern Parulas will establish a regular breeding population in California bears watching. If they do so, it will likely be on the immediate northern California coast, where vagrants "concentrate" and where moist, *Ramalina*-draped forests occur. At least in the period 1965 to 1979 the Northern Parula "showed a strong and continuing population increase" in the East (Robbins et al. 1986). Increases such as this would be likely to provide extra "pioneers" to potential breeding habitat in California.

YELLOW WARBLER   *Dendroica petechia*

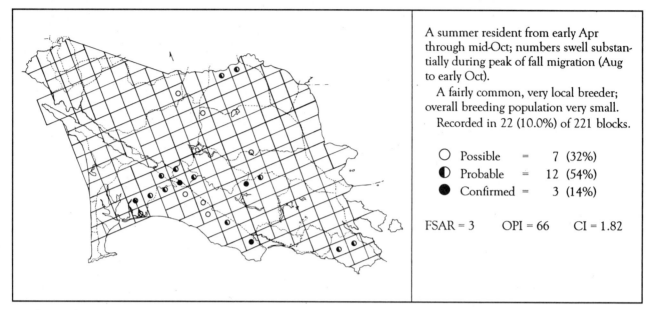

A summer resident from early Apr through mid-Oct; numbers swell substantially during peak of fall migration (Aug to early Oct).

A fairly common, very local breeder; overall breeding population very small.

Recorded in 22 (10.0%) of 221 blocks.

○	Possible	=	7	(32%)
◑	Probable	=	12	(54%)
●	Confirmed	=	3	(14%)

FSAR = 3   OPI = 66   CI = 1.82

Ecological Requirements

In Marin County, we hear the uplifting song of the Yellow Warbler rising from willow and alder riparian thickets—usually ones in relatively early stages of succession. Yellow Warblers seem to prefer willows here, perhaps because alder groves frequently lack a dense brushy understory, apparently an important feature noted in other studies (e.g., Morse 1973). In fact, in the Sierra Nevada they sometimes nest far from water in dry montane chaparral with scattered trees (Beedy & Granholm 1985, Gaines 1988). Although birds sometimes nest in predominantly brushy areas, they generally require taller trees for foraging (Kendeigh 1941b).

Yellow Warblers usually build their nests in bushes and saplings from about 1 to 15 feet above ground (most 3-8 ft.), or infrequently from 40 to 60 feet in tall trees (Bent 1953). They weave their well-formed nest cups around the branches of an upright fork or crotch, or in taller trees they sometimes attach them on lateral branches against the trunk. Nests are generally deeper than wide, and in narrow crotches may be cone-shaped (Schrantz 1943, Bent 1953). Yellow Warblers construct their nests of plant fibers, grasses, plant down, and bark shreds, and they line them with plant down, fine grasses, hair, and occasionally feathers; rarely, they make a nest entirely of wool or chicken feathers! The Yellow Warbler is one of the species most frequently parasitized by Brown-headed Cowbirds (Friedmann 1929, 1963). The warblers usually respond by deserting the nest or by covering the cowbird eggs with a

second nest built atop the first; in some cases Yellow Warblers have constructed six layers over successively laid cowbird eggs (Bent 1953)!

Yellow Warblers forage primarily by gleaning, and secondarily by hawking and hovering, from foliage and small branches (Morse 1973, Busby & Sealy 1979, Hutto 1981). The relative importance of hawking versus hovering varied among these studies, and in general the species shows much geographic variation in prey capture methods (Petit et al. 1990). Busby and Sealy (1979) studied sexual differences in Yellow Warblers' foraging in Manitoba. They found that females hovered more and foraged at lower heights, in smaller trees and more in bushes, and more in the lower and inner parts of trees. Females also moved shorter distances while foraging and foraged less in willows than did males. Morse (1973) also noted females foraging at lower heights; while in several instances he found females hovering more than males, this was not always the case. These foraging differences appear to reflect the differential roles of the sexes in nesting activities, rather than partitioning of the food resource, since both sexes eat similar prey species and sizes (Busby & Sealy 1979). The fact that males forage higher, in the outer canopy, in more open willows, and over longer distances, is apparently a function of the time they spend in display and territorial establishment and maintenance while moving about in conspicuous positions in the canopy. It would seem more advantageous from an energetic viewpoint for them to forage in display areas rather than fly elsewhere to forage and then return to greater heights to defend territories.

Since females are tied more to nesting duties, it appears beneficial for them to feed lower and more inconspicuously in the inner parts of denser trees and bushes. Females foraging over shorter distances and hovering more apparently are maximizing food intake while minimizing the time off the nest by feeding with rapid and varied movements. Generally, these foraging differences were the greatest during the early breeding season and decreased as the season progressed. After the cessation of nesting activities, both sexes foraged higher, a fact also noted for the species as a whole by Hutto (1981).

Overall, Yellow Warblers tend to feed relatively high in riparian habitat (Busby & Sealy 1979, Hutto 1981). In Wyoming riparian, Yellow Warblers forage at a greater absolute height than Wilson's Warblers, Common Yellowthroats, and MacGillivray's Warblers (Hutto 1981). Although absolute foraging height varies greatly among habitats and seasons in the West, the height these four species forage relative to each other remains constant; all four species forage a bit higher in August after the cessation of nesting activities. Of this group, Yellow and Wilson's warblers are relatively high foragers, and the other two species are relatively low foragers. Between Yellow and Wilson's warblers, absolute foraging height was the only significant difference in foraging strategy; relative foraging height, vegetation density, position in the canopy, foraging substrate, and feeding techniques were similar for both species; there was a slight tendency for Yellow Warblers to feed more in the outer, more open foliage and to hawk less for insects. See Morse (1973) for comparison of Yellow Warbler and American Redstart foraging. In areas of brush, Yellow Warblers may move up to 0.3 of a mile off their territories to forage in taller trees (Kendeigh 1941b).

The summer diet of California birds consists of over 97% animal matter, including ants, bees, wasps, caterpillars, beetles, true bugs, flies, spiders, and miscellaneous insects; vegetarian fare includes fruit pulp and an occasional seed (Beal 1907, n = 98). In general, Yellow Warblers are diverse and unspecialized arthropod feeders that take prey in proportion to their availability (Busby & Sealy 1979); see Busby & Sealy (1979) and Frydendall (1967) for dietary information elsewhere in the West.

Marin Breeding Distribution

During the atlas period, Yellow Warblers were patchily distributed as breeders in Marin County. They were most prevalent in the Olema Valley and near Limantour Estero. Representative breeding localities were Olema Marsh (NB 5/10/80 –JGE); Pine Gulch Creek, Bolinas Lagoon (NE/NY 5/21/77 –GBe et al.); and Lagunitas Creek, Tocaloma (NB 5/6/85 –JGE).

Historical Trends/Population Threats

Mailliard (1900) and Stephens and Pringle (1933), respectively, considered the Yellow Warbler to be a "common" and "fairly common" summer resident in Marin County; it is unclear, however, to what, if any, degree these assessments were colored by status in the fall migration when, at least currently, the Yellow Warbler is the most numerous warbler in Marin County (D. Shuford pers. obs.). A comparison of the historical status of the Yellow Warbler with that of the Orange-crowned and Wilson's warblers provides additional insight on the relative abundance of these species in former times. Mailliard (1900) considered both the Orange-crowned and Wilson's warblers "abundant" summer residents. Stephens and Pringle (1933) considered the Orange-crowned Warbler "common and abundant" and the Wilson's Warbler "fairly common" summer residents. These impressions suggest that, formerly, the Yellow Warbler was a somewhat less numerous breeding bird than Orange-crowned and Wilson's warblers, though not greatly so. Currently, Yellow Warblers are much less widely distributed (atlas maps) and much less numerous (Appendixes A and B) than either of these two other species. This suggests, but does not confirm, a historical decline of Yellow Warblers in Marin County. Grinnell and Wythe (1927) considered the Yellow Warbler a "common" summer resident in the Bay Area, and Grinnell and Miller (1944) considered it "common" or "even abundant locally" in this role for California as a whole. Although neither of the latter two authors indicated any historical change in the Yellow Warbler population up to that time, the species undoubtedly must have declined considerably by then, from the extensive destruction of riparian habitat that had already precipitated a major decline of California's riparian-obligate Yellow-billed Cuckoo (G&M 1944); the latter decline has continued to this day (Gaines & Laymon 1984, Laymon & Halterman 1987). Declines in Yellow Warblers in the Central Valley and elsewhere in the state led to the inclusion of the species on Fish and Game's list of Bird Species of Special Concern in California (Remsen 1978, CDFG 1991b; see also Garrett & Dunn 1981). These declines were apparently caused by the clearing of riparian habitat, for development and agriculture, and by the effects of cowbird parasitism. In addition, in Marin County and elsewhere in California, cattle grazing has drastically altered much riparian habitat, making it unsuitable for Yellow Warblers and other species. It is encouraging that, given the chance, Yellow Warblers can make rapid recovery once grazing impacts are lessened by reductions in cattle numbers or by fencing off sensitive areas (Taylor & Littlefield 1986). The Yellow Warbler was on the Audubon Society's Blue List for 10 of the first 11 years since its inception in 1972 (Tate 1981, Tate & Tate 1982), with particular concern for both northern and southern California breeding populations. It currently is on the Audubon Society's list of Species of Special Concern (Tate 1986). Yellow Warblers declined on Breeding Bird Surveys from 1965 to 1979 in the "Far Western States" but not in California and the West as a whole (Robbins et al. 1986); through 1989 the California population remained stable (USFWS unpubl. analyses). These conclusions should be viewed cautiously, as riparian habitats in many areas are patchily distributed and therefore are difficult to census with broad-scale techniques. Addition-

ally, stable trends where the species is most numerous may mask local declines where the species is less numerous. Conservationists have begun restoring riparian habitat to help stop, and perhaps reverse, the decline of the Yellow-billed Cuckoo in California (Laymon & Halterman 1987). This work should be extended where it can help other riparian species whose populations have also been reduced, though less critically.

YELLOW-RUMPED WARBLER *Dendroica coronata*

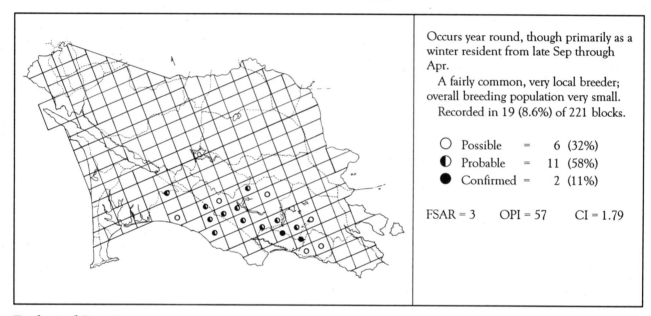

Occurs year round, though primarily as a winter resident from late Sep through Apr.

A fairly common, very local breeder; overall breeding population very small. Recorded in 19 (8.6%) of 221 blocks.

○ Possible = 6 (32%)
◑ Probable = 11 (58%)
● Confirmed = 2 (11%)

FSAR = 3   OPI = 57   CI = 1.79

Ecological Requirements

A mainstay of mixed species foraging flocks in winter in a variety of relatively open habitats, the Audubon's form of the Yellow-rumped Warbler also breeds sparingly in relatively open stands of Marin County's mixed evergreen forests dominated by Douglas fir and in pure Douglas fir forests. Audubons here favor meadow or grassland edges and generally avoid the dense interiors of these forests. They also have bred in planted Monterey pine, both in Marin County (Kelly 1942) and elsewhere in the Bay Area (Seibert 1942), but this is apparently of irregular occurrence. Audubons locate their nests from about 4 to 80 feet, but mostly from about 12 to 30 feet above the ground (Dawson 1923, Bent 1953). They often place them well out on limbs but sometimes against the trunk or at the tips of branches; rarely, they situate a nest behind a loose piece of bark or in a hollow or cavity in a tree. Audubons prefer conifers for nest supports in California, but occasionally they use deciduous trees. Their nests are deep, cup-shaped structures composed of twigs, fine grasses, pine needles,

weed stems or tops, fine shredded bark, or even string, flower pedicels, catkins, and other plant fibers, any of which may be mixed with feathers. The nest cup is heavily lined with feathers (which often curve upward and inward to partially conceal the eggs), along with horse, cattle, or deer hair or other fine fibers.

Yellow-rumps, or "Butter-butts" as they are often fondly called, are active and conspicuous as they go about making their livelihood. They generally forage at mid- to high elevations in the canopy, with a preference for open, less dense foliage, but they may feed at almost any level and on the ground. In a Sierran mixed conifer forest, Airola and Barrett (1985) found that Yellow-rumps forage by gleaning about 75% of the time, by hovering and hawking about 20%, and for the rest by lunging; they perform aerial maneuvers more than any other species in the insect-gleaning guild of that forest except the Western Tanager. Audubons there direct foraging attempts mostly at foliage and secondarily at twigs, air, trunks, and branches. In an

348

Arizona mixed conifer forest, Franzreb (1983b) reported that Yellow-rumps spend about 87% of their time gleaning and the rest hovering and hawking. The males there tend to forage in both taller trees and at greater heights than females, likely because males forage closer to song posts and females closer to nest sites, thereby reducing energy expenditures and maximizing fitness of the respective sexes. Where Yellow-rumps breed in Minnesota, males also forage higher than females (Hanowski & Niemi 1990). Species of trees they prefer for foraging vary among habitats (Franzreb 1983b, Airola & Barrett 1985) and between the sexes (Franzreb 1983b). Yellow-rumps in logged forests appear to select smaller trees, and forage at lower heights, than birds in unlogged areas. Also, in logged areas, they apparently are more generalized in tree species use, tree height preferences, and foraging heights (Franzreb 1983a). Yellow-rumped Warblers wintering in various oak woodlands in California do not vary geographically in the foraging activities they use to capture prey; they do vary among habitats in use of foraging substrate, foraging perches, position in tree, and species and tree height use (Block 1990). Despite such variation, on the whole Yellow-rumps show little geographic variation in use of foraging techniques and substrates (Petit et al. 1990).

The diet of Yellow-rumped Warblers in California from July through May is about 85% animal matter and 15% vegetable (Beal 1907, n = 383). In the West as a whole, the fall and winter diet ranges from 72% to 76% animal matter (Martin et al. 1951, n = 210). A small sample for the West (n = 20) suggests 100% reliance on animal matter in spring and summer (Martin et al. 1951), but the contents of three stomachs from the Sierra Nevada suggest a summertime diet of 81% animal and 19% vegetable matter (Dahlsten et al. 1985). The most important animal items in the diet are wasps and ants, true bugs, flies, hemipterans, caterpillars, and beetles (Beal 1907); spiders and pseudoscorpions are also taken (Dahlsten et al. 1985,

Otvos & Stark 1985). Vegetable foods are primarily weed seeds and small wild fruits, particularly poison oak (mostly the waxy outer coating), elderberry, grape, wax myrtle, and peppertree (Beal 1907, Martin et al. 1951).

Marin Breeding Distribution

During the atlas period, Yellow-rumped Warblers bred in Marin County on Mount Tamalpais, Bolinas Ridge, and other nearby ridges of the Lagunitas Creek watershed, as well as on Inverness Ridge. This distribution was similar to that of the Black-throated Gray and Hermit warblers, except for the extension of the Yellow-rump's range on the southern part of Inverness Ridge. Representative breeding records were the first meadow NW of Rock Springs, Mt. Tamalpais (FY/FL 7/10/81 —DS) and the junction of the Cataract and Helen Mark trails above the SW corner of Alpine Lake (FY/FL 8/1/81 —DS). Apparently the only other confirmed Marin County breeding record prior to the atlas period is of a pair feeding young on the grounds of the College of Marin, Kentfield, on 14 June 1942 (Kelly 1942). Other historical reports for June and July are from Rock Springs, Mount Tamalpais (Orr 1937) and from Ross (Kelly 1944). Audubons breed here mostly above about 700 feet elevation, but the Kentfield and Ross records were presumably close to sea level.

Historical Trends/Population Threats

Audubon's Warblers were first suspected of breeding in Marin County on Mount Tamalpais in 1936 (Orr 1937). This discovery very likely was a result of more thorough coverage of a poorly explored or unexplored area, rather than a range extension.

For California as a whole, Yellow-rumped Warblers were generally increasing on Breeding Bird Surveys from 1968 to 1989, despite relative stability from 1980 to 1989 (USFWS unpubl. analyses).

BLACK-THROATED GRAY WARBLER *Dendroica nigrescens*

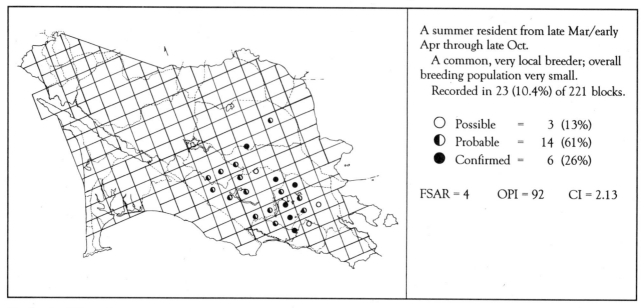

A summer resident from late Mar/early Apr through late Oct.

A common, very local breeder; overall breeding population very small.

Recorded in 23 (10.4%) of 221 blocks.

○	Possible	=	3 (13%)
◐	Probable	=	14 (61%)
●	Confirmed	=	6 (26%)

FSAR = 4   OPI = 92   CI = 2.13

Ecological Requirements

Breeding haunts of Marin County's Black-throated Grays are the relatively dry, open mixed evergreen forests usually dominated by Douglas fir but generously mixed with coast live, canyon live, or tanbark oaks or other broadleaved evergreen trees, saplings, or shrubs. Especially favored areas are those where more continuous Douglas fir cover mixes with oaks and saplings along meadow edges or where the firs grade into mixed or serpentine chaparral. Chaparral may even dominate as long as there are a few relatively tall firs for song posts. Black-throated Grays also breed here sparingly in relatively moist but open mixed woodlands of black oak, madrone, and live oaks. Black-throated Grays overlap here to a limited degree with Hermit Warblers, where the above-mentioned habitats grade into the denser Douglas fir preferred by the latter species (see account). In mixed Douglas fir–oak forest in Oregon, Black-throated Grays use habitat with a relatively heavy deciduous tree cover, primarily of small oaks in high density (Morrison 1982). In Oregon, at least, they show a general though not significant tendency to avoid conifers; their habitat there also has a relatively high vegetative cover in lower layers up to about 30 feet.

Black-throated Grays place their nests from 1.5 to 50 feet above the ground in deciduous, broadleaved evergreen, or coniferous growth. They secure them in concealing foliage in vertical crotches low in dense bushes or relatively open saplings, or higher on horizontal branches of conifers (Dawson 1923, Bent 1953). Black-throated Grays build deeply cupped nests of dead and often frayed

grasses, weed stalks or bark, flower stems, and perhaps other fine plant fibers, a few leaves, moss, catkins, string, or thread. They may bind their nests firmly with spider webs and decorate them with numerous bits of spider cocoons. Birds line nests with fine grasses, feathers, and fur or hair from deer, rabbit, cow, or horse.

Black-throated Grays generally forage at moderate heights in forest and woodland habitat. They search for prey with rather methodical, deliberate movements, at times leaning way over to peer under leaves or reaching up to twigs overhead in search of insects. They forage more than 80% (often 90%–100%) of the time by gleaning, and, infrequently, by hovering and flycatching (Morrison 1982, Miles 1990). In Arizona oak woodlands, most gleaning is from leaves and secondarily from small branches and twigs, though the proportion of prey capture attempts directed at these substrates varies seasonally and annually (Miles 1990). Morrison (1982) found consistent differences in foraging substrates and heights between sexes in Black-throated Grays and between that species and Hermit Warblers in a mixed Douglas fir–oak habitat in Oregon. Black-throated Gray males forage at greater heights than females in both firs and oaks, and in taller firs (but not oaks) than do females. Males forage mostly in relatively tall Douglas firs that are scattered throughout their otherwise oak-dominated territories. Females concentrate their foraging activities in oaks and on longer limbs than do males, but both sexes forage toward the tips of branches. On the whole, the sexual differences found in foraging presumably resulted from males concentrating their efforts near where they sang from tall Douglas firs, and females focusing their activities nearer the nest site.

Where they overlap, Black-throated Grays tend to forage lower than Hermit Warblers. The former species' relatively short blunt wings may enhance foraging in the lower denser vegetation of oaks. Hermit Warblers' relatively longer, more pointed wings may promote ease of movement within and between the trees and less dense foliage of their preferred conifer forests. Female Black-throated Grays tend to use longer branches than do female Hermits, but males of the two species use branches of similar length (Morrison 1982). Both sexes of both species use similar foraging tactics in the same relative proportions. Little is known of the Black-throated Gray diet, but it appears to be mainly, if not entirely, insects (Bent 1953, Dahlsten et al. 1985); oak worms and other green caterpillars appear to be favorites (Bent 1953).

Marin Breeding Distribution

During the atlas period, Black-throated Gray Warblers restricted themselves as breeders to the drier Douglas fir- and oak–dominated ridges and slopes from Mount Tamalpais north to Lucas Valley. The appropriate habitats are sheltered from persistent summer fogs, either by being high enough on Mount Tamalpais to be above the usual level of the summer inversion layer of warmer air or by being east or north of the first major coastal ridges that block the penetration of summer fog. Black-throated Grays did *not* occur in the extensive moist, dense Douglas fir habitat on Inverness Ridge. Representative breeding locales were Lucas Valley Rd., about ¼ mi. E of "Bull Tail Valley" (FY/FL 7/26/82 —DS); Cascade Canyon, Fairfax (FY/FL 6/19/80 —DS); Lake Lagunitas (NY about 15 ft. up in big-leaf maple 6/5/82 —DnB); Benstein Trail, Mt. Tamalpais (NB 15-20 ft. up in coast live oak 5/4/77 —DS); Simmons Trail, Mt. Tamalpais (FY/FL adult BTG feeding fledgling Brown-headed Cowbird 7/6/81 —DS); and south end of Potrero Meadow, Mt. Tamalpais (NY 12 ft. up in 16-ft. sapling tanbark oak 7/6/81 —DS).

Historical Trends/Population Threats

Black-throated Gray Warblers were first widely suspected of breeding in Marin County based on the publication of observations from the breeding season of 1936 on Mount Tamalpais (Orr 1937). Adults of this species, though, had already been seen feeding young near Phoenix Lake on 21 and 28 June 1931 (*Gull* 13, No. 7). These observations and others elsewhere in the Bay Area from the 1930s onward (Seibert 1942, Sibley 1952; cf. Grinnell & Wythe 1927) appear to be the result of more thorough coverage of a region where the species is patchily distributed, rather than of a change in breeding status or range.

Black-throated Gray Warblers appeared to increase slightly on Breeding Bird Surveys in California from 1968 to 1989 but were relatively stable from 1980 to 1989 (USFWS unpubl. analyses).

HERMIT WARBLER *Dendroica occidentalis*

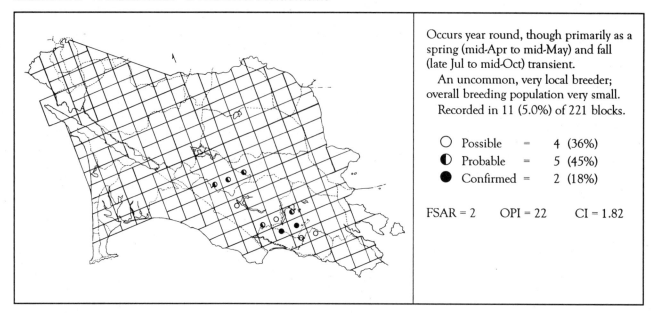

Occurs year round, though primarily as a spring (mid-Apr to mid-May) and fall (late Jul to mid-Oct) transient.

An uncommon, very local breeder; overall breeding population very small. Recorded in 11 (5.0%) of 221 blocks.

○	Possible	=	4 (36%)
◑	Probable	=	5 (45%)
●	Confirmed	=	2 (18%)

FSAR = 2   OPI = 22   CI = 1.82

Ecological Requirements

The Hermit Warbler adds a touch of the high mountains to Marin County's moderately dense Douglas fir forests, where it resides in relatively pure stands and also in mixed stands with coast redwoods and moderate numbers of live oak or other broadleaved trees. Hermits here do not inhabit dense, very moist pure stands of Douglas fir or redwood. Elsewhere, Hermits are found in moderately dense conifer stands, especially of Douglas fir, true firs *(Abies),* and large pines (G&M 1944, Morrison 1982, Chappell & Ringer 1983, Airola & Barrett 1985). In Washington, Hermits occupy second-growth as well as mature and old-growth forests with a mean canopy cover of 70% (Chappell & Ringer 1983). Deciduous trees are frequently codominant there in the understory or are a minor component of the canopy, especially in young stands; variable shrub cover seems to have little effect on habitat choice, as Hermits concentrate their activities in the canopy. Hermits tend to occupy denser and more conifer-dominated forests than Black-throated Grays, but the two species do overlap at the ecotone between their respective habitats. Where they co-occur with Black-throated Grays in Oregon, Hermits prefer habitat with relatively heavy total conifer cover and relatively low deciduous cover (Morrison 1982). Hermit habitat there also has relatively little vegetative cover up to about 30 feet above the ground and relatively greater cover above about 60 feet.

Hermit Warbler nests have been found as low as 2.5 feet up in a sapling, but most are saddled on a good-sized horizontal or upturned limb of a conifer well out from the trunk and about 20 to 45 feet above the ground (Bent

1953); exceptionally, nests have been found on the ground at the base of a bush (Munson & Adams 1984) and as high as 125 feet above the ground (Bent 1953). The nest is a compact cup composed mainly of herbaceous plant fibers and weed stalks, fine dead twigs, pine needles, lichens, dry moss, and plant down. All of these materials may be wadded together, rather than woven, and securely bound with cobwebs and other woolly substances (Barlow 1899, Bent 1953). The lining is made of fine grasses, the soft inner bark of conifers, and horse or wild animals' hair.

Breeding Hermit Warblers generally avoid deciduous growth and concentrate over 90% of their foraging activities in conifers (Morrison 1982, Airola & Barrett 1985). Foraging birds glean 80%–95% of the time, and hover, flycatch, and lunge only to a limited degree. In a Douglas fir–oak forest in Oregon, Hermits concentrate foraging activities near the center of limbs in contrast to Black-throated Grays, which focus toward the tips (Morrison 1982). In a Sierran mixed conifer forest, Hermits forage about 60% of the time on foliage and secondarily on twigs and branches (Airola & Barrett 1985). Hermits in both habitats forage mostly at mid- to high elevations (roughly 15–80 ft.) though they do range from near the ground to over 100 feet. Males forage considerably higher in conifers and use slightly longer limbs than do females (Morrison 1982). See the Black-throated Gray account for further habitat and foraging comparisons.

The diet of the Hermit Warbler is poorly known, but a small sample (n = 6) from the Sierra Nevada indicates the summer diet is about 92% animal and 8% vegetable

(Dahlsten et al. 1985). The Hermit is apparently unique among western warblers in its consumption of pine seeds (Martin et al. 1951). Animal foods include true bugs, beetles, homopterans, bees and wasps, other flying insects, caterpillars, and small spiders (Martin et al. 1951, Bent 1953, Dahlsten et al. 1985).

Marin Breeding Distribution

During the atlas period, Hermit Warblers bred locally in Marin County from Mount Tamalpais north to the ridges of the Lagunitas Creek watershed. This distribution was very similar to that of Black-throated Grays except that Hermits were more restricted to deeper canyons and more easterly or northerly exposures. Representative breeding

locations included the Cataract Trail, Mt. Tamalpais (FY/FL 7/10/81 –DS) and the Dipsea Trail near Laurel Dell, Mt. Tamalpais (FL 7/3/82 –BiL).

Historical Trends/Population Threats

Grinnell and Wythe (1927) and Stephens and Pringle (1933), respectively, considered the Hermit Warbler primarily a transient in the Bay Area and in Marin County. Subsequent confirmation of breeding in the Santa Cruz Mountains (G&M 1944, Sibley 1952) and during the Marin atlas period appear to be a result of more thorough observer coverage rather than of a true range extension.

From 1968 to 1989, Hermit Warblers appeared to increase slightly on Breeding Bird Surveys in California (USFWS unpubl. analyses).

MACGILLIVRAY'S WARBLER *Oporornis tolmiei*

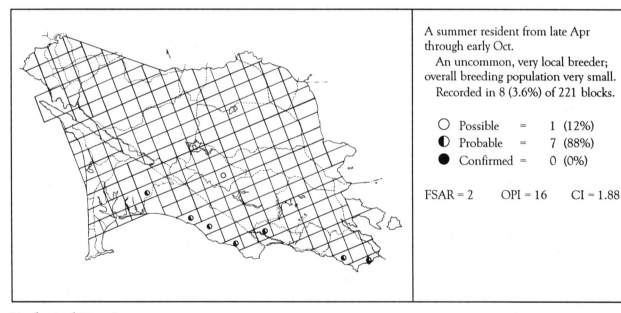

A summer resident from late Apr through early Oct.

An uncommon, very local breeder; overall breeding population very small.

Recorded in 8 (3.6%) of 221 blocks.

○	Possible	=	1 (12%)
◐	Probable	=	7 (88%)
●	Confirmed	=	0 (0%)

FSAR = 2   OPI = 16   CI = 1.88

Ecological Requirements

In Marin County, this inveterate skulker breeds sparingly in the moist dense shrubbery of riparian thickets, especially where they adjoin the moist phase of coastal scrub. Riparian forest or woodland is not true MacGillivrays' habitat: these birds avoid deciduous trees for foraging and are drawn to shrubbery (Morrison 1981b). Their occupation of fog-shrouded lowland scrub in the vicinity of streams and their avoidance of dry foothill chaparral suggest that MacGillivrays have an affinity for moisture here. However, these warblers do breed in *montane* chaparral in California's higher mountains (e.g., Beedy & Granholm 1985).

MacGillivray's Warblers construct bulky loose nest cups, which they place in the upright forks of bushes or saplings or around the ascending stems of rank herbage (Dawson 1923). Nest height varies from a few inches off the ground to about five feet, with most under three feet (Dawson 1923, Bent 1953). MacGillivrays construct their nests from coarse grasses, weed stalks, rootlets, and bark shreds and line them with fine grasses, small rootlets, and horsehair. Four species of breeding warblers overlap in riparian habitat in Wyoming but are separated by absolute foraging height (Hutto 1981). The MacGillivray's Warbler and the Common Yellowthroat forage at low levels, almost

353

exclusively by gleaning, while the Wilson's and Yellow warblers forage higher, by a combination of gleaning and sallying. MacGillivrays forage somewhat higher than Common Yellowthroats but mostly below three feet and only occasionally to about ten feet (Hutto 1981, Morrison 1984). MacGillivray's Warblers and Common Yellowthroats show significant differences in absolute and relative foraging height, foraging position, and foraging substrate. MacGillivrays glean about 70% from bark, 20% from foliage, and 10% from the ground, whereas Yellowthroats feed from these substrates in nearly equal proportions. MacGillivrays also tend to forage more in the inner parts of the vegetation than do Yellowthroats. Yet these two species forage by the same method and in vegetation of similar density.

The June to July diet of MacGillivray's Warblers in California is exclusively insects, including true bugs, homopterans, beetles, flies, bees, wasps, and ants (Dahlsten et al. 1985, n = 15).

Marin Breeding Distribution

During the atlas period, MacGillivray's Warblers were very patchily distributed as breeding birds in moist drainages along Marin County's outer coast. The only confirmed breeding records for the county (pre- and post-atlas) were

near San Geronimo (NE 5/7/08 —Mailliard 1909b); at Palomarin (FY/FL 6/29/69 —RMS); and Mt. Wittenberg, Inverness Ridge (FY 6/26/89 —JGE). Other representative breeding areas based on presumptive evidence during the atlas period were Laguna Ranch, PRNS (S/T 4/22-6/14/78 —JGE et al.) and Volunteer Canyon, Bolinas Lagoon (S through June 1980 —ARo).

Historical Trends/Population Threats

Mailliard (1900) considered the MacGillivray's Warbler "sparingly summer resident," while Stephens and Pringle (1933) reported it here as "uncommon" through the summer. Its status during the atlas period suggests there has been little historical change in the Marin population. The species does appear to have declined as a breeder in Monterey County (Roberson 1985). For the coast as a whole, any such decline has probably been offset greatly in the north coast mountains by increases as the species expanded into the relatively moist, low, second-growth shrubbery that regenerates after logging.

MacGillivray's Warblers generally increased on Breeding Bird Surveys in California from 1968 to 1989, despite relative stability from 1980 to 1989 (USFWS unpubl. analyses).

COMMON YELLOWTHROAT *Geothlypis trichas*

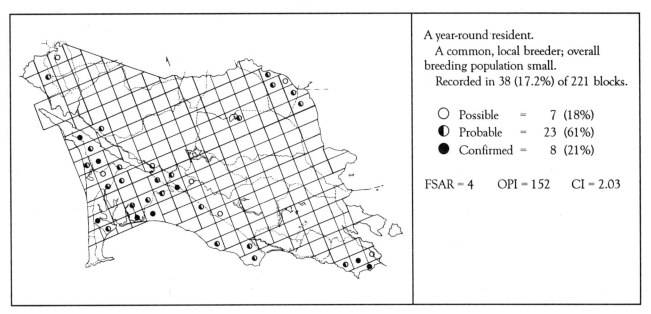

A year-round resident.
 A common, local breeder; overall breeding population small.
  Recorded in 38 (17.2%) of 221 blocks.

○	Possible	=	7	(18%)
◑	Probable	=	23	(61%)
●	Confirmed	=	8	(21%)

FSAR = 4   OPI = 152   CI = 2.03

Ecological Requirements

These perky masked warblers inhabit Marin County's freshwater marshes, coastal swales, swampy riparian thickets, brackish marshes, salt marshes, and the edges of disturbed weed fields and grasslands that border on these soggy habitats. About 80% of Marin's Yellowthroats breed in freshwater marsh, coastal swale, and riparian thickets and swamps, with the remainder in brackish marsh, salt marsh, and upland habitats (Hobson et al. 1986, D. Shuford pers. obs.). In the San Francisco Bay region as a whole, about 60% breed in brackish marsh, 20% in riparian woodland/swamp, 10% in freshwater marsh, 5% in salt marsh, and 5% in upland vegetation (Hobson et al. 1986). In this region, Yellowthroats frequently use the borders between these various plant communities. In brackish marsh, they rarely occupy pure stands of alkali bulrush *(Scirpus robustus)*; instead they frequent areas where this bulrush mixes with other marsh and upland plants. In salt marsh, Yellowthroats center their activity in taller vegetation, such as gumplant and coyote brush on the raised border of sloughs and levees, though they often forage in pickleweed. Territories also commonly straddle the interface of riparian corridors and freshwater marsh, or the ecotone between freshwater or tidal marshes and the upland vegetation of weed fields and grassland. Some Yellowthroats here do inhabit the interiors of riparian swamps such as Olema Marsh. Low, dense, rather lush, tangled vegetation appears to be the primary requisite. Although a source of free water promotes this type of growth, it does not appear to be absolutely essential (Kendeigh 1945). Yellowthroat territories usually include

open water or damp ground, but not always, especially in drought years (Hobson et al. 1986). In California, Yellowthroats sometimes breed up to 300 yards from a source of water, even after a very wet winter (Johnson 1904). The dense ground cover provides concealment for nests, teetering young, and foraging adults. There must be other subtle habitat needs. During intensive Bay Area surveys of the Saltmarsh Common Yellowthroat *(G. t. sinuosa)*, Hobson et al. (1986) sometimes found birds absent in what appeared (to the human eye, at least) to be suitable breeding areas.

Nest sites are varied and may be adjacent to, above, or well away from water. Nests are well concealed, mostly on or near the ground in grass tussocks, low herbaceous vegetation, cattails, tules, and bushes generally to about five feet above the ground, though many are below six inches (Kendeigh 1945, Gross 1953, Stewart 1953). Yellowthroats less frequently place their nests in trees such as willows, alders, eucalyptus, orchard trees, black oaks (in thick branches of mistletoe), and cypress up to about 23 feet above the ground (Johnson 1904). Unusual nest sites include an old nest of a Red-winged Blackbird 3.5 feet up in an emergent willow sapling, in grain fields, in a cultivated rose trained against the side of a house, and in one of a pair of shoes left on the back stoop of a house (Johnson 1904). Yellowthroats wedge the cup-shaped nest among, or lash it to, concealing vegetation. The nest varies from compact to loosely woven and bulky; sometimes loosely attached materials extend above the main rim, partially or completely roofing over the structure (Kendeigh 1945,

Gross 1953, Stewart 1953). The nest may have three distinct layers of material, increasing in fineness from the outside in (Stewart 1953). Birds generally construct the outer layers from coarse grass, dead leaves, weed stalks, cattail blades, rush and sedge stems, strips of bark, willow catkins, and dead ferns. They line the nest with fine grasses and sedges, tendrils, delicate bark fibers, hair, and occasionally fine rootlets or moss.

Yellowthroats gather their insect prey on or near the ground by gleaning from low herbaceous vegetation, bushes, and small trees or from the surface of the mud. They forage mostly within 5 to 6 feet of the ground or water's surface (Kendeigh 1945, Gross 1953). Of four warbler species breeding in riparian habitat in Wyoming, the Common Yellowthroat and MacGillivray's Warbler are a pair that forage at low levels, almost exclusively by gleaning, while Wilson's and Yellow warblers forage higher by a combination of gleaning and sallying (Hutto 1981). While breeding, Yellowthroats there do 90% of their foraging below 1 foot, and the remainder below 2 feet in height. After relief from nesting duties in August, while

foraging, they range about eight times higher, up to 16 feet. Yellowthroats there glean from bark, foliage, and the ground in roughly equal proportions. See the Mac-Gillivray's Warbler account for a comparison of foraging strategies.

Year round, Yellowthroats in California eat 99.8% animal matter (n = 114); the few seeds and miscellaneous vegetable matter in their stomachs were probably taken incidentally (Beal 1907). The main items in the diet of California birds are ants, wild bees and wasps, true bugs, beetles, caterpillars and moths, flies, grasshoppers, and spiders. Elsewhere, Yellowthroats have also been noted to consume damselflies, dragonflies, caddisflies, mayflies, and a few small mollusks (Gross 1953).

Marin Breeding Distribution

During the atlas period, Marin's breeding Yellowthroats were concentrated in the moist coastal and bayshore lowlands around the periphery of the county. The areas of their greatest abundance were on Point Reyes (in the Limantour Estero drainage, near the road between

Table 19. Numbers of breeding *pairs* of Saltmarsh Common Yellowthroats *(Geothlypis trichas sinuosa)* in Marin and other San Francisco Bay Area counties in 1985. Data from Hobson et al. (1986).

County	Location	Number of Breeding Pairs
Marin	Point Reyes peninsula	6
	Abbott's Lagoon	25
	Limantour Estero	74
	Olema and Bear Valley marshes	25
	Bolinas Lagoon and Dogtown marsh	5
	Rodeo Lagoon and Tennessee Valley	6
	Novato Creek	7
	Petaluma Point	9
	Black John Slough	11
	Marin Total	168
Sonoma		81
Napa		63
Solano		31
Contra Costa		0
Alameda		37
Santa Clara		118
San Mateo		57
San Francisco		14
	Bay Area Total	569*

* Foster (1977) found 166 pairs in these counties in a less complete survey in the drought year of 1977.

Abbott's Lagoon and Kehoe Beach, and at Olema and Bear Valley marshes) and along the sloughs and bayshore marshes from Novato north along the Petaluma River drainage (Table 19). Breeding Yellowthroats were absent from interior sites except for a probable breeder(s) at Stafford Lake, Novato. In the interior of the county, freshwater marshland is scant and riparian groves are generally sparsely vegetated because of the drier climate and intensive cattle grazing.

Representative breeding localities were Tomales Point, north side of tule elk fence (FY 5/31/82 –DS); gully SW of head of Barries Bay, Drake's Estero (FY 6/9/82 –DS); and Olema Marsh (NB 4/29/81 –DS). A more recent record of an active nest is of one found at Glenbrook drainage behind Limantour Estero (NE 5/6/85 –DS, BoB).

Historical Trends/Population Threats

The extent of tidal marshes in the San Francisco Bay ecosystem has been reduced by 60%-95% over historical levels (Nichols & Wright 1971, Josselyn 1983), and freshwater marsh probably has been reduced to an even greater degree because of its greater proximity to upland development. Yellowthroats have declined markedly because of this extensive habitat loss. Grinnell & Miller (1944) did not report a decline in Yellowthroat populations, though one must have been well underway at that time from loss of habitat. Foster (1977) estimated that the number of Saltmarsh Common Yellowthroats in the San Francisco Bay Area had declined by about 80%-95% in the last 100 years. However, her data were collected during drought years and may not be valid for comparison with historical

estimates from the few sites for which these are available. In 1985, Hobson et al. (1986) conducted more extensive surveys and recorded over three times the number of Yellowthroats found in 1977. Despite the increase in numbers because of better wetland conditions and more thorough coverage, they found Yellowthroats at only 4 of 16 sites where they were reported only prior to 1970, and at only 15 of 34 sites where they were reported from 1970 onward. Although it will never be possible to determine with numerical precision the extent of the decline of the Yellowthroat population of the San Francisco Bay Area, it is clear that this decline has been of major proportions. The 1985 figures provide a solid baseline against which to compare future trends. The species is still imperiled with further declines from habitat loss, degradation, and fragmentation from various sources ranging from land development to flood control management. Its population in this region can only be augmented substantially by concerted habitat restoration efforts.

On the whole, numbers of Yellowthroats (all subspecies) increased on Breeding Bird Surveys in California from 1968 to 1989, though perhaps only slightly from 1980 to 1989 (USFWS unpubl. data). Still it should be noted that the Common Yellowthroat was on the Audubon Society's Blue List in 1973 and 1974 (Tate 1981) because of concern in northern California (AB 27:945). The Saltmarsh Common Yellowthroat currently is a Candidate (Category 2) for federal listing as Threatened or Endangered (USFWS 1989b, 1991) and is a Bird Species of Special Concern in California (CDFG 1991b).

WILSON'S WARBLER   *Wilsonia pusilla*

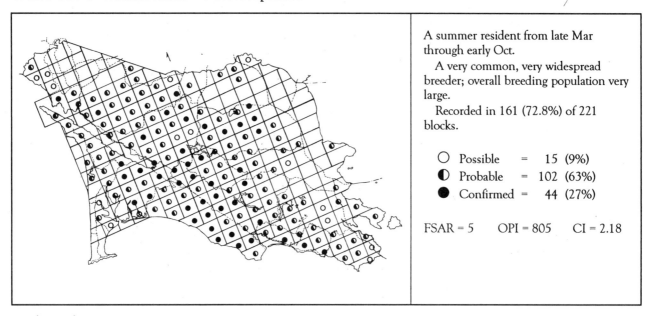

A summer resident from late Mar through early Oct.

A very common, very widespread breeder; overall breeding population very large.

Recorded in 161 (72.8%) of 221 blocks.

○ Possible   =   15 (9%)
◐ Probable   =   102 (63%)
● Confirmed =   44 (27%)

FSAR = 5   OPI = 805   CI = 2.18

Ecological Requirements

County breeding haunts of the perky "Pileolated Warbler" are moist, primarily forested habitats with a relatively dense understory, principally willow and alder riparian, red-wood, bishop pine, Douglas fir, mixed conifer, and broad-leaved evergreen forests. The importance of the understory is illustrated by the fact Wilson's Warblers also breed locally in coastal scrub (which by nature has no overstory of trees) where it is north-facing and dominated by sword fern or salal.

The breeding biology of Wilson's Warbler in California has been investigated in two different areas of sharply contrasting topography and climate, though at the same latitude: near sea level at Palomarin on the Point Reyes peninsula (Stewart 1973) and at 10,000 feet at the crest of the Sierra Nevada at Tioga Pass, Mono County (Stewart et al. 1977). These are among the few comparative studies of passerines at the extremes of their climatic ranges, and they reveal a number of important differences in the ecology of the species with respect to breeding areas.

Arrival dates on the breeding ground and mean dates of initiation of egg laying in the two locales differ by two months: males arrive in late March on the Point Reyes peninsula and in late May at Tioga Pass. In some years of extremely high snow pack, Sierran birds will not breed at higher altitudes at all. Territory size of Sierran birds averages about twice that of coastal birds, though vegetation volume is probably similar between these areas because of the taller stature of most coastal habitat. On the coast, Wilson's Warblers typically conceal and support their nests in understory vine tangles, small bushes, ferns, or tall

annual plants. Of 111 nests from 13 coastal California counties, 74% were built in blackberry vines, 9% in ferns, 6% in nettle, and 2% in wild rose (Stewart et al. 1977). Blackberries offered the advantages of horizontal runners for nest support, overhanging leaves for nest concealment, and a dense tangle of brambles serving to deter predators (Stewart 1973). Only 4% of the nests were on the ground, and the average height of above-ground nests was 20 inches (Stewart et al. 1977). Coastal nests at Palomarin ranged from 13 to 32 inches above the ground (av. 27 in., n = 11). Coastal birds build bulky nest cups composed of leaves, twigs, and small branches of blackberry, nettle, and oak and line them with animal hair interwoven with fine stems, moss, and deteriorated leaves (Stewart 1973). In contrast, Sierran birds build nests with much smaller nest cups, situated at ground level or sunk slightly below it in depressions; concealment is provided by location at the base of horizontal willow branches and by a thick growth of perennial herbs (Stewart et al. 1977). The difference in nest position on the coast versus the high Sierra appears to reflect differences in the growth form of vegetation most suitable for concealing the nest from predators in the respective habitats. Nest placement at ground level may also provide greater insulation needed in the colder sub-alpine environment. See White-crowned Sparrow account for discussion of similar differences in nest placement with respect to altitude or latitude and of the tailoring of nest size and external appearance to the microclimate of the nest site.

With a longer breeding season, 18% of individuals in the coastal population successfully raise two broods, while Sierran birds never make more than a single nesting attempt (Stewart et al. 1977). Although hatching success is similar in both areas, nesting success is much higher in the Sierra (71%, n = 45) compared with the coast (33%, n = 18), probably because of differences in predation rates between the habitat types. In the Sierran population, 26% of the males (n = 27) are polygynous, while on the coast all are monogamous. Note that polygyny is very rare among wood warblers, and only about 5% of all passerine birds in North America are known to be regularly polygynous (Verner & Willson 1969). The Sierran population of Wilson's Warblers, occupying a transient habitat and unpredictable climate with rain, hail, or snow occurring at any time, has evolved this strategy to maximize reproduction. The coastal population, inhabiting mature forests with a well developed understory and more predictable, stable climate, has evolved a strategy of a lower but more constant reproductive rate.

Wilson's Warblers feed actively on small-bodied, winged insects. They forage mostly at low to moderate heights in both understory and trees, but generally not higher than about 5 feet below the roof of the canopy. In coastal broadleaved evergreen forest, they frequently forage from about 30 to 55 feet up in the overstory (Stewart 1973). Overall in California, gleaning accounts for about 49% of foraging attempts, followed by hovering (46%) and fly-catching (5%), with some variation between habitats (Stewart et al. 1977, n = 244). In a variety of coastal habitats, adults make 97% of food-catching attempts (n = 70) on leaves and the remainder on small twigs. In riparian habitat in Wyoming, Wilson's Warblers forage more in the upper half and outer portions of the canopy, in vegetation of moderate to open density, and they direct foraging attempts roughly equally toward foliage, bark, and the air, and, rarely, toward the ground (Hutto 1981). Wilson's Warblers there forage 57% by gleaning, 37% by sallying, and 6% by hovering (n = 219).

The diet in California is about 93% animal matter and less than 7% vegetable matter (Beal 1907, n = 52). The main animal foods are true bugs, wasps and ants, beetles, and flies, with small numbers of caterpillars and spiders; the vegetable fare is almost entirely fruit pulp consumed in fall. In the Sierra Nevada, vegetable matter accounts for 3% of the summer diet (Dahlsten et al. 1985, n = 8). In Wyoming, Wilson's Warblers take beetles, mayflies, stone-flies, flies, and wasps (and somewhat larger prey) in greater proportion than their availability. Preferred prey tend to be noncryptic and patchily distributed (Raley & Anderson 1990). Some groups that rank low in preference are, nevertheless, still important in the diet because of their abundance in warbler foraging habitat; for example, leaf-hoppers comprise 16% of the diet and miscellaneous larvae 30%. Nonpreferred prey are generally those that exhibit cryptic coloration, a choice of camouflaging substrate, or good escape behavior.

Marin Breeding Distribution

During the atlas period, Wilson's Warblers bred throughout much of Marin County but occurred in greatest abundance on Inverness Ridge on the Point Reyes peninsula. Toward the interior, breeding populations were smaller and generally restricted locally to narrow canyons and north-facing slopes with moist dense understory vegetation. Wilson's Warblers were absent as breeders over substantial areas only in flatlands along the San Pablo Bay shoreline, in oak woodland–dominated areas near Novato, and in an area east of Tomales where grasslands prevail. These areas generally lack the topographic relief that provides microclimates conducive to the development of dense understory vegetation, or else they have riparian habitat without a suitable understory. Representative breeding locations were Tomales Bay SP (NE-NY 5/7-6/5/76 –RMS); Inverness Ridge (NE-NY 5/15-6/15/76 –RMS); Palomarin, PRNS (NE-NY 4/28-6/1/76 –RMS); and Big Rock Ridge above Stafford Lake (NY 5/?/82 –ScC).

Historical Trends/Population Threats

Although no clear trends are evident, it seems likely that Wilson's Warblers have decreased locally in some areas of riparian habitat along the California coast because of clearing for development and agriculture and from degradation of the understory by cattle grazing and trampling. At present, Breeding Bird Surveys from 1968 to 1989 indicate that Wilson's Warbler numbers are relatively stable in California (Robbins et al. 1986, USFWS unpubl. data).

ROBERT M. STEWART

YELLOW-BREASTED CHAT *Icteria virens*

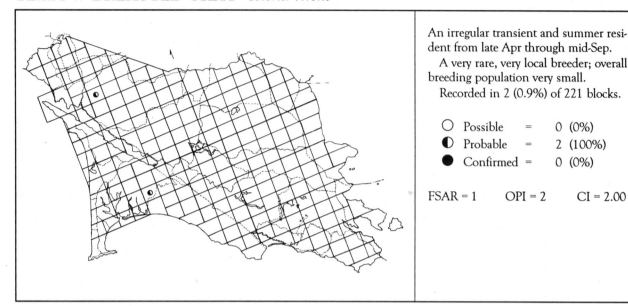

An irregular transient and summer resident from late Apr through mid-Sep.

A very rare, very local breeder; overall breeding population very small.

Recorded in 2 (0.9%) of 221 blocks.

◯ Possible   =   0 (0%)
◐ Probable   =   2 (100%)
● Confirmed   =   0 (0%)

FSAR = 1   OPI = 2   CI = 2.00

Ecological Requirements

This furtive but ebullient songster is an inhabitant of dense riparian understory tangles with small trees, tall weeds, blackberry thickets, brush, and vines. Dense low cover in a moist setting seems essential.

Chats build bulky nests, which they place precariously from about 1.5 to 5 feet (rarely to 8 ft.) high in the thick cover of small trees and bushes (Dawson 1923, Bent 1953). They construct their nests of dead leaves, coarse grasses, weed stems, and small vines, and line them sparingly with fine grasses, weed stems, weed bark, and horse-hair.

Apparently no detailed foraging studies of Chats exist, presumably because of the difficulty of observing them. Birds probably forage mostly below 10 feet (G&M 1944) by gleaning from foliage, branches, and the ground. The diet consists mainly of animal matter, but even in summer wild fruits may make up a substantial portion of the menu. The diet of birds in spring averages 2% plant food (n = 9), whereas that of birds in summer averages 35% plant food (n = 19) (Martin et al. 1951). Regularly occurring food items include caterpillars, moths, butterflies, grasshoppers, locusts, beetles, true bugs, ants, weevils, bees, wasps, mayflies, and a few spiders and crustaceans (Martin et al. 1951, Bent 1953). Western birds eat wild fruits such as madrone, thimbleberry, sumac, dogwood, and nightshade (Martin et al. 1951).

Marin Breeding Distribution

During the atlas period, there were only two records of probable breeding of Yellow-breasted Chats in Marin County. Single individuals were heard singing over a

period of time at Laguna Ranch, PRNS (S 5/20–6/4/82 —SCP) and along Walker Creek about 1.5 miles upstream from Hwy. 1 (S 5/1–6/12/82 —DS). Chats have been recorded only casually in Marin County in potential breeding habitat from April to July, and most have apparently been transients (Stephens 1936, Kinsey 1945, ABN). No confirmed breeding records for the county are known. In fact, the atlas records above represent the reports of longest seasonal occupation of a particular site here. It seems logical to conclude that Marin County's riparian habitat is only marginally attractive to Chats.

Historical Trends/Population Threats

Mailliard (1900) considered the Yellow-breasted Chat a "rare spring visitant" to Marin County, and Stephens and Pringle (1933) repeated his assessment. Prior to 1944, Kinsey (1945) had encountered Chats only three times from July to September "during twenty years of residence and extensive field work" in Marin County. From 23 April to about 14 June 1944 at Manor (near Fairfax), he and his wife trapped three males and saw another individual of unknown sex. On 6 May 1945, they captured, banded, and placed in an aviary a "pair" of Chats. Despite this spate of war-time records, it is clear that historically in Marin County, Chats were rare at any season. Although earlier observers may have missed some breeding Chats in unexplored regions of Marin County, it is clear that this species has long been scarce here. If Chats did once have local viable breeding populations in Marin County, it seems unlikely they would return now without management efforts, considering that much of our riparian habitat has been destroyed or degraded.

Yellow-breasted Chat populations have declined in recent decades on the northern California coast, at least from the Bay Area south (Remsen 1978, Roberson 1985). Because of a more widespread decline, the Yellow-breasted Chat is on California's list of Bird Species of Special Concern (Remsen 1978, CDFG 1991b). Declines in California are attributed to habitat destruction and perhaps cowbird parasitism or other factors. The Yellow-breasted Chat was listed on the National Audubon Society's Blue List or on its list of Species of Special Concern from 1976 to 1981, and on its list of Local Concern in 1982 (Tate 1981, Tate & Tate 1982). From 1968 to 1989, Breeding Bird Surveys suggested that Chats might be increasing slightly in California, though numbers were relatively stable from 1980 to 1989 (USFWS unpubl. analyses). Continued monitoring of Chat populations is warranted, considering this history and the continued threats to riparian habitat from our expanding human population.

Viewed from a window through a tangle of blackberry, salal, and reeds, a Wilson's Warbler stealthily approaches its nest. Photograph by Ian Tait.

Tanagers

Family *Emberizidae*
Subfamily *Thraupinae*

WESTERN TANAGER   *Piranga ludoviciana*

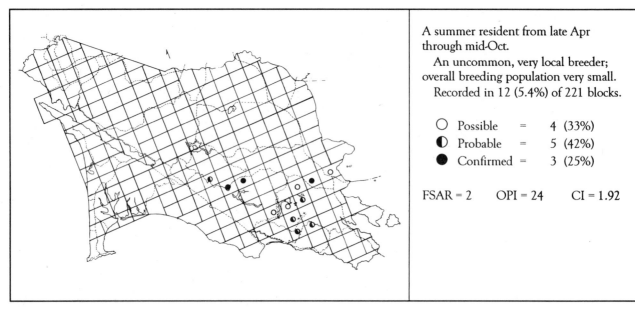

A summer resident from late Apr through mid-Oct.

An uncommon, very local breeder; overall breeding population very small.

Recorded in 12 (5.4%) of 221 blocks.

○	Possible	=	4 (33%)
◑	Probable	=	5 (42%)
●	Confirmed	=	3 (25%)

FSAR = 2   OPI = 24   CI = 1.92

Ecological Requirements

These flashy birds have been dubbed the "Sunset Tanager" by their human admirers. The blazing males stake out their territories in Marin County's mixed conifer forests where Douglas fir, or, sparingly, redwoods, mix with coast live, canyon live, and tanbark oaks. To a limited extent, they also use mixed woodlands of live oaks, black oak, and big-leaf maple along streams. Western Tanagers here prefer relatively open mesic mixed forests for nesting. They avoid dense pure stands of Douglas fir, redwoods, oaks or bays, and drier, very open stands of oaks. Shy (1984) measured habitat variables of 21 Western Tanager territories at various locations in the West. Canopy cover averaged 66.6%, "ground cover" averaged 38.8%, and the number of tree species averaged 4.1. This documents the relative openness and mixed character of Western Tanager breeding habitat.

Western Tanagers customarily settle their nests in the enveloping foliage of horizontal branches of conifers (usually near the tips) or, less frequently, in broadleaved trees or large shrubs; nest heights vary from about 6 to 65 feet above the ground (Dawson 1923, Hayward 1935, Wiggins

& Wiggins 1939, Sibley 1955, Bent 1958, Tatschl 1967). Tatschl (1967) reported that nest trees in New Mexico are usually in "open areas," though this could use additional confirmation. Exceptionally, Western Tanagers have nested on the ground under an overhanging rock ledge (Wiggins & Wiggins 1939). Western Tanagers construct substantial but rather roughly assembled nest cups of twigs, weed stems, rootlets, long pine needles, leaves, and moss. They line them somewhat heavily with fine rootlets, horse or cow hair, grasses, lichens, or other soft material (Dawson 1923, Wiggins & Wiggins 1939).

Western Tanagers use a variety of foraging techniques, including gleaning, hawking and, to a lesser extent, hovering and lunging. They not only take nearby insects of all sizes by gleaning, but they also search for large insects at greater distances. In Sierran mixed conifer forests, Western Tanagers devote about 47% of their efforts to gleaning and about 38% to hawking; they hawk for insects about three times more than any other species in the insect-gleaning guild of that forest (Airola & Barrett 1985). These birds hawk large slow insects from exposed perches, often between bouts of gleaning. They direct most foraging activities at the foliage or air, and only a minor amount at twigs and branches. Western Tanagers forage mostly at middle to upper heights of trees, perhaps because these layers are more open, making hawking maneuvers easier. Western Tanagers search foliage in a deliberate manner and often remain motionless except for moving the head from side to side while scanning the air for prey (Isler & Isler 1987). As with many bird species, they change the height of flycatching efforts in trees by moving from the treetops downward in the morning, then back upward in the afternoon, following insect activity that is stimulated by the ascending and descending sun (Bent 1958). Western Tanagers also feed on the ground, for refuse in logging camps (McAllister & Marshall 1945) and in campgrounds (E.C. Beedy & S.L. Granholm pers. obs.).

Between April and September, the diet of Western Tanagers is about 82% animal and 18% vegetable in the form of fruit and trace amounts of conifer seeds (Beal 1907, n = 46). Their reliance on vegetable fare probably increases with the ripening of fruits in late summer and fall. Their animal foods are predominantly hymenopterans (mostly wasps and some ants), followed by beetles, true bugs, grasshoppers, and caterpillars (Beal 1907); termites, homopterans, snails, and spiders are also eaten (Dahlsten et al. 1985). A wide variety of wild and cultivated fruits and berries is eaten, generally the smaller types, as Western Tanagers prefer to swallow their "dessert" whole (Beal 1907). Wild fruits eaten include elderberries, mulberries, raspberries, blackberries, and serviceberries (Beal 1907, Martin et al. 1951). Migrant Western Tanager "swarms" have been known to inflict severe damage on lowland cherry crops (Beal 1907, Bent 1958). These tanagers also occasionally eat new buds and sip the sweet liquid that exudes from some flower blossoms.

Marin Breeding Distribution

During the atlas period, breeding Western Tanagers were restricted primarily to mixed conifer forests at mid- to high elevations on the slopes of Mount Tamalpais and northward along the Lagunitas Creek watershed. These areas have moderate to high rainfall but are out of the zone of persistent summer fog, which is either blocked by intervening ridges or by an inversion layer of warmer air higher on the slopes of Mount Tamalpais. Tanagers may also breed occasionally in mixed oak woodlands on Mount Burdell, Novato, but this needs verification. An adult male was briefly seen to feed a female or immature Western Tanager in a moist oak drainage on Mount Burdell on 26 June 1980 (DS), but it seems best to consider this *probable* breeding evidence at best. A representative breeding locality was San Geronimo (FL summer 1976 —BTr).

Historical Trends/Population Threats

The Western Tanager was first confirmed breeding in Marin County in 1945 (FY 7/7/45, 2000 ft. at extreme headwaters Lagunitas Creek, 1.5 mi. SW of West Peak, Mt. Tamalpais —Miller 1946). Previous workers (Mailliard 1900, G&W 1927, S&P 1933, G&M 1944) were not aware of Western Tanagers breeding in Marin County, but this most likely reflects limited field work at the time.

Western Tanager numbers appeared to increase slightly on Breeding Bird Surveys in California from 1968 to 1989 but were fairly stable from 1980 to 1989 (USFWS unpubl. analyses).

Cardinaline Grosbeaks and Buntings
Family *Emberizidae*
Subfamily *Cardinalinae*

BLACK-HEADED GROSBEAK   *Pheucticus melanocephalus*

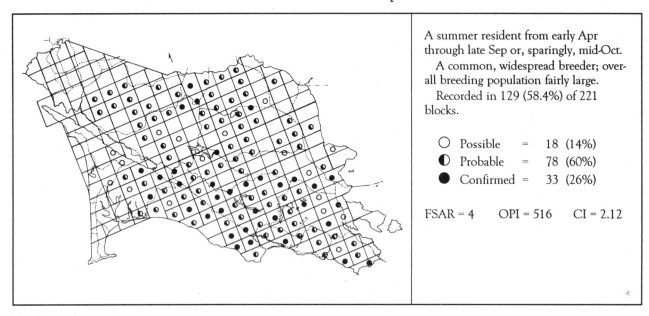

A summer resident from early Apr through late Sep or, sparingly, mid-Oct.

A common, widespread breeder; overall breeding population fairly large.

Recorded in 129 (58.4%) of 221 blocks.

O	Possible	=	18	(14%)
◑	Probable	=	78	(60%)
●	Confirmed	=	33	(26%)

FSAR = 4   OPI = 516   CI = 2.12

Ecological Requirements

At dawn on a spring day, the vibrant song of the Black-headed Grosbeak drowns out that of almost all other birds in Marin County's willow and alder riparian thickets and her relatively open moist broadleaved evergreen forests. Locally, Black-headed Grosbeaks breed sparingly on the edges of conifer forests where they border on openings and mix with broadleaved trees. The bulk of the population occurs near stream courses. Black-headeds are absent in dense closed stands of bay, mixed bay and live oak, and conifers. Grinnell and Miller (1944) thought that perhaps important factors to Black-headed Grosbeaks were the local diversity of plant growth and extensive "edge" conditions, hinting these were necessary because of the birds' varied diet. Comparing the habitat of three age classes of males in New Mexico, Hill (1988) found that the prime habitat of older males was the most heterogenous, had the greatest vertical vegetation structure, had many large trees, and was generally open.

Black-headed Grosbeaks fashion bulky loose nests that vary in shape from saucerlike platforms to ones resembling cups (Weston 1947). They ordinarily construct them of slender twigs, plant stems, and rootlets and line them with fine stems and rootlets. Black-headeds usually build their nests in deciduous bushes and trees bordering streams, but also occasionally in closed woods, dense brushland, and parklands away from water. The nest plants they most commonly use in California are willow, coast live oak, alder, big-leaf maple, blackberry, cottonwood, and elderberry. The height of 163 California nests ranged from 3 feet to 32 feet; average height was 10 feet, and two-thirds of the nests were between 4 feet and 12 feet above the ground (Weston 1947). The height of 21 nests in Utah ranged from about 7 feet to 23 feet and averaged 13 feet (Ritchison 1983). The nest support usually consists of a crotch or fork in a group of horizontal or vertical secondary branches at variable locations within a tree or bush (Weston 1947).

In Sierran mixed conifer forests, Black-headeds forage (and sing) mostly high in trees (Airola & Barrett 1985), but in coastal riparian and mixed evergreen forests, they forage throughout the trees and even occasionally on the ground (Weston 1947, D. Shuford pers. obs.). In the mixed conifer forests, foraging Black-headed Grosbeaks prefer black oaks and pines. Birds usually glean while foraging for insects, but they also appear to search below them for large insects at greater distances within the crown (Airola & Barrett 1985). Upon locating larger flying or stationary prey up to about 10 feet away, they lunge down upon it. Black-headeds use lunging about four times more frequently than any other species in the insect-gleaning guild of mixed conifer forest birds. These grosbeaks hawk flying insects on fewer than 10% of their foraging attempts. Airola and Barrett (1985) also found that Black-headeds forage primarily on foliage, secondarily on twigs, and to only a minor extent on branches or in the air. They will also cling head down from a slender twig to procure rolled up leaves with caterpillars inside them (Austin 1968). After retiring to a perch, they open the leaf with a few quick movements of the beak, subdue the caterpillar by biting it along its length, then swallow it whole.

The California diet from April to September is about 57% animal and 43% vegetable (Beal 1910, n = 225). Reliance on vegetable foods increases from spring to fall, paralleling the availability of fruits (Beal 1907, Martin et al. 1951). The animal component is predominantly beetles, scale insects, and caterpillars, with only minor amounts of hymenoptera (bees and wasps and a few ants), other true bugs, flies, grasshoppers, other insects, and spiders (Beal 1910); rarely, snails and small fish are eaten (McAtee 1908, Beal 1910). A small June–July sample (n = 7) from the mixed conifer zone of the Sierra Nevada indicates a diet of over 98% animal matter (Dahlsten et al. 1985). This may reflect grosbeaks' concentration on animal food while feeding nestlings, a period of low fruit availability, or regional differences in food availability and hence diet. Vegetable foods include a wide variety of wild and cultivated fruits, weed seeds, buds, flowers, catkins, and pine seeds. Elderberry and blackberry are important food plants, and additional ones in the Berkeley hills include wild oats, black mustard, thimbleberry, wild rose, cotoneaster, wild plum, locust, red-stem filaree, poison oak, coffeeberry, cow parsnip, fiddlenecks, and various thistles (Weston 1947). Seasonal changes in the vegetable diet begin with an initial focus on soft succulent matter such as leaf buds, flowers, and flower buds, as well as early-forming fruits (Weston 1947). There is a gradual shift to fruits as

these mature and then, with their disappearance, mainly to seeds found in bushes and on the ground. Nestlings are initially fed a soft, pale green mash, but soon they are introduced to soft animal matter such as caterpillars. Soft animal foods decline in importance as hard insect matter such as beetles (and vegetable matter, too) increase in the diet (Beal 1910, Weston 1947).

Marin Breeding Distribution

During the atlas period, Black-headed Grosbeaks bred widely in Marin County. Their distribution here coincided with that of riparian thickets of the lowland valleys and open, broadleaved evergreen forests of the hillsides. Black-headeds were absent as breeders in the grassland-dominated areas of outer Point Reyes and near Tomales; on some drier interior ridges (especially near Novato); and throughout much of the sedimentary plains bordering San Francisco and San Pablo bays. Representative breeding locations were Inverness (NE 7/3/82 –LP); O'Hare Park, Novato (FL 6/23/82 –ScC); Cascade Canyon, Fairfax (NE 5/12/77 –DS); and Phoenix Lake, Ross (NY 5/21/77 –DS).

Historical Trends/Population Threats

Historically, Black-headed Grosbeaks appear to have held their own in Marin County and California in general (Mailliard 1900, S&P 1933, G&M 1944, Robbins et al. 1986, USFWS unpubl. analyses). In 1986, though, based on long-term banding data from PRBO's Palomarin field station, DeSante and Geupel (1987) documented a total reproductive failure of Black-headed Grosbeaks in central coastal California. Partial or total reproductive failure occurred in a large number of other species as well. Although it may be highly coincidental, the timing of the reproductive failure coincided remarkably with the passage of a radioactive cloud from the Chernobyl nuclear power plant accident and the associated rainfall. This relationship bears further investigation, and the population trends of Black-headed Grosbeaks and other species that reproduced poorly in 1986 should be watched closely.

A Black-headed Grosbeak launched in flightsong and display energizes the airways. Drawing by Keith Hansen, 1989.

LAZULI BUNTING *Passerina amoena*

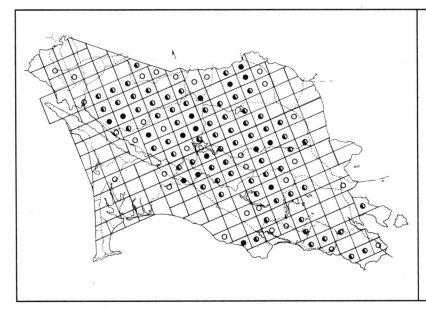

A summer resident from late Apr through late Sep.

A fairly common, fairly widespread breeder; overall breeding population of moderate size.

Recorded in 115 (52.0%) of 221 blocks.

○	Possible	=	31 (27%)
◐	Probable	=	67 (58%)
●	Confirmed	=	17 (15%)

FSAR = 3   OPI = 345   CI = 1.88

May hybridize with Indigo Bunting *(P. cyanea)*—an irregular spring transient, summer resident, and fall transient mostly from mid-May through late Sep.

Ecological Requirements

Another archetypal edge species, the Lazuli Bunting breeds on the brushy borders of Marin County's mixed evergreen forests, oak woodlands, Douglas fir forests, riparian groves, chaparral, coastal scrub, and planted cypress groves—where these communities interface with grasslands, meadows, and weed fields. In these situations, large clumps of introduced thistles are especially attractive to Lazuli Buntings. Brush and trees provide nest sites, cover, and song posts, while grassland and thistle patches provide good foraging grounds. What constitutes the proper vegetative mix is imprecisely known, as Lazulis are often absent in seemingly suitable edge situations. In areas of overlap with Indigos in Utah, Lazulis prefer areas with higher shrub density and lower ground cover (Whitmore 1975); Lazulis also seem to prefer more xeric sites (Wauer 1969).

Lazuli Buntings generally lash their nests to the supporting stalks of weeds, bracken ferns, and thistles, or settle them in forks of bushes, berry vines, or low in trees (Dawson 1923, Erickson 1968). Nest height usually varies from 1.5 to 4 feet, and exceptionally reaches 10 feet above the ground (Erickson 1968). Lazulis weave their coarse nest baskets out of dried grass (especially the leafy portions), weed stalks, strips of bark, small twigs, and fibrous roots (Dawson 1923, Erickson 1968). They line them with fine grasses, horsehair, or plant down.

Lazuli Buntings forage for insects by gleaning or lunging in foliage and branches and by occasional flycatching or hovering (Erickson 1968). Often they strip grassheads of seeds while they perch on the stout stems. But sometimes a bird takes a whole seed head in its bill after a short

hovering flight, returns to a perch holding the still-attached seed head in its foot, and then picks out the seeds. The diet of western birds (primarily in California) varies in animal content from about 64% in spring to 53% in summer (Martin et al. 1951, n = 46). Important insects are grasshoppers, caterpillars, beetles, true bugs, bees, and ants. Vegetable fare includes wild oats, miners lettuce, needlegrass, canarygrass, annual bluegrass, and small amounts of melicgrass, velvet grass, filaree, and chickweed.

Marin Breeding Distribution

During the atlas period, Lazuli Buntings bred widely in the central interior of Marin County. They were scarce to absent on the Point Reyes peninsula, in the grassland-dominated rolling hills around Tomales, in the eastern urban corridor, and along the San Pablo and San Francisco bayshores. Representative breeding stations were upper Millerton Gulch, E of Tomales Bay (NB 5/27/82 –DS); old Cerini Ranch near Marshall (NY 6/29/82 – DS); Nicasio Reservoir dam (FL 6/15/82 –ScC); Bolinas Ridge above Olema (NB 5/29/82 –DT); and Skywalker Ranch, Big Rock Ridge (NY/NE 7/8/82 –ITi, DS).

Historical Trends/Population Threats

Because of their fondness for open edge habitat, Lazuli Buntings were already expanding their local distribution in Humboldt County at the turn of the century by invading areas opened up by logging (Fisher 1902). Because of the continuation and expansion of logging practices, Lazulis have most likely increased in the coastal mountains in recent decades. The detrimental effects of overgrazing on grassland seed sources may have been offset by the spread and encouragement of introduced thistles. Lazuli Bunting populations were relatively stable on Breeding Bird Surveys in California from 1968 to 1989 (USFWS unpubl. analyses). In Marin County, they appeared to increase on the Even Cheaper Thrills Spring Bird Count from 1978 to 1987 (Appendix A).

Remarks: Hybridization with Indigo Buntings

Lazuli and Indigo buntings were formerly isolated from contact with each other by the Great Plains. As the population of European settlers expanded in that area, the planting of trees and shrubs in shelterbelts, control of fires, the demise of the buffalo, and an amelioration of climate all caused an increase in suitable bunting habitat. Indigos and Lazulis invaded this area from the east and west, respectively, and in the 1950s occupied a zone of overlap and hybridization as great as 400 miles wide (Sibley & Short 1959). The spread of Indigos westward has been more dramatic than that of Lazulis eastward and may have been fueled by a large increase in Indigos' population because of the opening of the eastern deciduous forest by agriculture, logging, and burning (Wells 1958). The western spread of Indigos has continued at the expense of Lazulis (Emlen et al. 1975).

Although the expansion and contact of these species were first noted early in the century, the first reports of hybrids and of breeding Indigo types in the far West occurred in the 1940s and 1950s (Sibley & Short 1959). The first confirmed breeding record in California of an apparent male Indigo with a female Lazuli was documented in 1956 (NE 6/10/56 Soledad Canyon, Los Angeles Co. —Bleitz 1958). Sibley and Short (1959) have cautioned that all recent records of *cyanea* west of the Great Plains are likely to be hybrids and that sight records are not satisfactory as the basis for records of "pure" Indigos, because hybrid characters may not be apparent in the field. This would make it extremely difficult to document the breeding of a pure pair of Indigos, which would be necessary before adding that species to the breeding avifauna of the state. On the other hand, the small percentage of hybrids in the zone of overlap in recent studies (Emlen et al. 1975) suggests that most apparent Indigos reaching California are of "pure" stock.

In Marin County, an apparent "pure" Indigo was seen on territory at Olema Marsh from 6 June to 15 July 1976 (AB 30:1001) and was sighted there again for short periods in 1977 and 1979 (ABN). An obvious hybrid male (dark blue with prominent white wingbars and white belly) was seen at the same site on 22 June 1979 with Lazulis (AB 33:895), suggesting that a successful hybrid breeding had occurred there in a previous year. In 1984, a male "Indigo" was first observed near the town of Olema on 7 July, and on 12 July a nest with two young was found, attended by a female Lazuli with which the "Indigo" was mated (RMS). The male was seen with food in his bill in the vicinity of the nest and accompanying the female on foraging trips in nearby fields. Although "Indigos" are recorded annually in May and June as rare transients in coastal northern California (ABN), the above records and single ones from Mendocino (AB 33:895) and San Mateo (AB 40:1253) counties are the only indications of breeding between these species in this region.

The breeding biology of Lazuli and Indigo buntings is very similar, and the reader is referred to the accounts of Indigos by Taber and Johnston (1968) and Ellison (1985).

Emberizine Sparrows
Family *Emberizidae*
Subfamily *Emberizinae*

RUFOUS-SIDED TOWHEE   *Pipilo erythrophthalmus*

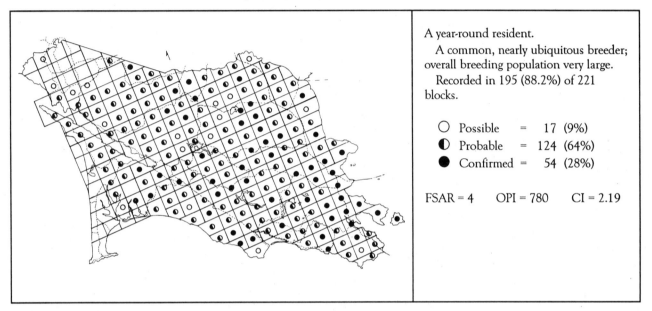

A year-round resident.

A common, nearly ubiquitous breeder; overall breeding population very large. Recorded in 195 (88.2%) of 221 blocks.

○	Possible	=	17	(9%)
◑	Probable	=	124	(64%)
●	Confirmed	=	54	(28%)

FSAR = 4   OPI = 780   CI = 2.19

Ecological Requirements

The plumage of western "Spotted Towhees" may serve as cryptic coloration against their sun-dappled backdrop beneath woody shrubs without extensive arboreal cover. These haunts contrast with the more mesic forested habitats of their eastern counterparts. In Marin County, Rufous-sided Towhees are conspicuous breeders in coastal scrub, chaparral, brushy riparian thickets, and on the shrubby edges or openings of the remaining forest or woodland plant communities. They also use suburban plantings of suitable structure. Rufous-sided Towhees avoid dense shrubbery when it occurs within the heart of Marin's closed-canopy conifer or mixed evergreen forests. Because they require a well-developed leaf litter and humus layer in which to forage, they prefer chaparral and brushy areas bordering on trees (particularly oaks) that provide fallen or windblown leaves (Davis 1957).

Although Rufous-sided Towhees nest mostly on the ground, they place nests occasionally in bushes or vine tangles up to six feet high (Baumann 1959, Davis 1960). They typically build their nests in depressions with the rim flush or slightly above ground level, invariably in sites protected from above by overhanging bushes, vines, or clumps of grass. Characteristic nest sites are grassy and/or leaf-littered areas on the edges of thickets or near isolated shrubs or trees. Some Rufous-sided Towhees place their nests on the ground between the branches of fallen oak limbs. They construct their cup-shaped nests with a framework of strips of inner bark, dead leaves, and coarse grass, and an inner lining of fine dry grass stems or rootlets. Rufous-sided Towhees are inveterate ground foragers, but they specialize more in scratching for their subsistence than do California Towhees (Davis 1957; see California Towhee account). Prime foraging areas are deep leaf litter and humus under vegetative cover. Rufous-sided Towhees rarely forage in areas not screened from above by overhanging vegetation, or in bare or sparsely covered soil. Unlike California Towhees, Rufous-sideds scratch from a perky upright posture with the head high, knees moderately flexed, and the tail in line with the back or more frequently cocked. They toss leaf litter and soil behind them with their long claws, by vigorous backwards thrusts of both feet simultaneously, and follow this with a short hop forward

369

to regain the original position and initiate the next scratching maneuver. Rufous-sided Towhees obtain most of their food from the middle or lower layers of the leaf litter and humus or in the upper layers of the soil proper where it is gleaned or pecked after uncovering. Rufous-sideds will also scratch for food above ground level—on top of woodrat nests built in trees or in accumulations of leaves or debris in crotches or cavities of oaks. They usually travel between scratching in a series of short hops. From spring to fall, Rufous-sideds will also peck and glean insects from the leaves, branches, and lichens in bushes and trees (especially oaks). Rarely, birds will also make vertical flycatching attempts to about two feet off the ground, and they will run through the grass pursuing grasshoppers. In the East, Greenlaw (in Smith 1978) noted that males made flycatching attempts more often than females. Rufous-sided Towhees also take fruits and berries from trees or bushes while perched or from hovering flight. They also sometimes visit feeders.

Year-round, the diet of California birds is about 24% animal and 76% vegetable (Beal 1910, n = 139). In the Pacific states (mainly California), the Spotted Towhee diet varies from 49%-62% vegetable matter in spring and summer (n = 66) to 91%-92% in fall and winter (n = 84) (Martin et al. 1951). A small sample (n = 6) from the Sierra Nevada indicates the summer diet there is about 84% animal (Dahlsten et al. 1985). Arthropod fare includes beetles, true bugs, ants, bees, wasps, caterpillars, and moths, along with a few grasshoppers, flies, miscellaneous insects, spiders, millipedes, and sowbugs. Insect food fed to the young shifts from mostly larvae early in the season to mostly grasshoppers later on (Davis 1960). Important vegetable foods are weed seeds, wild and cultivated fruits and berries, acorns (already opened), and grain. In spring,

Rufous-sideds feed on the seeds, seed capsules, and bracts of miners lettuce, young valley oak leaves, and blossoms of gooseberry and blackberry (Davis 1957). In California, the wild fruits and berries that they feed on most frequently in the late summer and fall are elderberries, coffeeberries, hollyleaf redberries, snowberries, gooseberries, poison oak drupes, blackberries, toyon, honeysuckle, manzanita, twinberries, and madrone (Beal 1910, Davis 1957).

Marin Breeding Distribution

During the atlas period, the Rufous-sided Towhee was a widespread breeder in Marin County, and its distribution overlapped that of the California Towhee with only a few exceptions. Although California Towhees can subsist in the sparse cover of ranchyards in the grasslands around Tomales, Rufous-sideds cannot. On Tomales Point, Rufous-sideds occupied the dense east-facing brushy gullies where California Towhees were absent. Both species were lacking on the grass- and dune-dominated tip of Point Reyes. Representative breeding stations were Chaparral Hill near Mt. Burdell, Novato (NE 5/?/79 —ScC); ridge N of San Geronimo (FL 7/11/81 —DS); Carson Ridge (NE 5/28/79 —ITi); and Mt. Tamalpais (FY 4/27/81 —DS).

Historical Trends/Population Threats

In the past, clearing of forests, with the subsequent intrusion of brush, and planting of cover in residential areas may have favored Rufous-sided Towhees, whereas fire suppression or extensive development may have harmed them. Rufous-sided Towhee numbers generally were fairly stable on Breeding Bird Surveys in California from 1968 to 1989, despite increasing from 1980 to 1989 (USFWS unpubl. analyses).

CALIFORNIA TOWHEE *Pipilo crissalis*

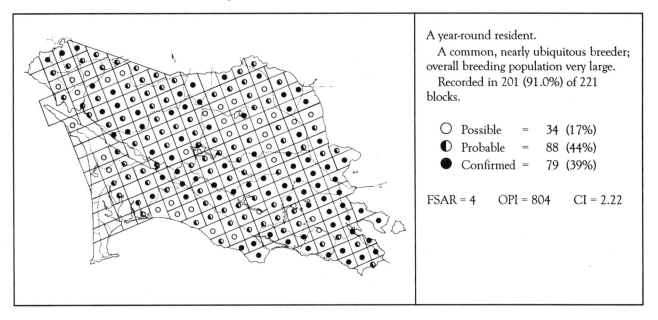

A year-round resident.

A common, nearly ubiquitous breeder; overall breeding population very large.

Recorded in 201 (91.0%) of 221 blocks.

○	Possible	=	34 (17%)
◑	Probable	=	88 (44%)
●	Confirmed	=	79 (39%)

FSAR = 4   OPI = 804   CI = 2.22

Ecological Requirements

A common dooryard bird, taken for granted by most, the California Towhee is one of the most characteristic birds of lowland California. A die-hard edge species, this towhee occupies Marin County's broken chaparral and coastal scrub, the brushy edges or clearings of all the major forest and woodland types (especially oak woodland and riparian), ranchyards, and particularly suburban plantings and lawns. Its main requisites are open ground for foraging and brush or trees for cover and nesting.

California Towhees construct bulky, well built nests that they conceal in the dense foliage of bushes, trees, or, rarely, on the ground. Although nests may range up to about 35 feet above the ground, most are from about 2.5 to 12 feet (Davis 1951, Childs 1968). California Towhees fashion nest cups from twigs, weed stalks, dry grass, or inner bark and line them with fine grass, plant stems, hair, or wool (Childs 1968). Reports of unusual nest sites include a cleft five feet up on the face of a rock wall, on top of an old mockingbird nest, in an accumulation of bark in a eucalyptus tree, and in a berry basket ten feet inside a barn (Davis 1951, Childs 1968).

California Towhees forage primarily on the ground in open areas near (or less frequently under) trees and brush. They glean food items from the soil surface or obtain them by scratching in the leaf litter, humus, or upper layers of exposed soil. Although California Towhees will forage alongside Rufous-sided Towhees in leaf litter under vegetation, they seldom penetrate far into very dense brush, where the latter species frequently feeds. In the open, California Towhees feed in bare soil or in sparse or

modified grassland; tall continuous grassland is used only when broken by animal trails or other interruptions. California Towhees usually forage in pairs. They utilize both pecking and two-footed scratching techniques extensively, unlike Rufous-sideds that use primarily scratching. California Towhees characteristically crouch with knees deeply bent and head and tails down when gleaning or scratching. They scratch less vigorously than do Rufous-sideds. When foraging or seeking cover, California Towhees travel on the ground by one- or two-footed hopping or by running for longer distances. In the summer months, they also procure insects from vegetation: in trees and bushes they peck at leaves, branches, oak catkins, and lichens, while on the ground they glean insects from grasses and low annuals. In the late summer and fall they pick elderberries, coffeeberries, poison oak, and other fruits and berries; they forage on these foods while perched or, less frequently, from hovering flight. California Towhees also jump up and bend grass seed heads down to strip the seeds, and they eat blades of freshly sprouted grass or garden vegetables, small mushrooms, newly grown plant buds or oak leaves, and, occasionally, opened acorns on the ground. California Towhees frequently visit bird feeders.

The year-round diet of birds in California is about 86% vegetable and 14% animal matter (Beal 1910, n = 399). Consumption of animal food reaches a peak of 38% in spring (n = 34) and a low of 4%–8% in fall and winter (n = 177) (Martin et al. 1951). The main vegetable foods are weed seeds, wild fruits and berries (mentioned above), cultivated fruits usually found on the ground, and grain.

371

Animal fare includes beetles, ants, bees, wasps, true bugs, caterpillars, grasshoppers, and crickets. Nestlings start out on a diet entirely of insects, particularly grasshoppers and caterpillars, but they graduate to consume as much as 8% vegetable matter before fledging.

Marin Breeding Distribution

During the atlas period, California Towhees bred widely in Marin County, particularly in the lowlands and toward the drier interior. Broadly, they were sparse or lacking only in the windswept grasslands on the tip of Point Reyes. Locally, they were scarce or absent on steep slopes, in thick forests, and in extensive grasslands. Representative breeding localities were Point Reyes Station mesa (NB 7/12/81 –JGE); Slide Ranch, 3 miles S of Stinson Beach (NE

5/24/81 –DS); Mt. Burdell, Novato (NB 4/27/81 –DS); ridge on south side of Lucas Valley Rd. (FY 6/18/82 –BiL); and near Phoenix Lake (NE 5/10/76 –RMS).

Historical Trends/Population Threats

Although some of man's activities have made parts of the California Towhee's original haunts uninhabitable, this has been more than compensated for by expansion of gardening and ranching into formerly barren lowland terrain (G&M 1944). Undoubtedly the clearing of some forested areas has also opened up habitat to this towhee's liking. From 1968 to 1989, California Towhee numbers were relatively stable on Breeding Bird Surveys in California (USFWS unpubl. analyses).

RUFOUS-CROWNED SPARROW *Aimophila ruficeps*

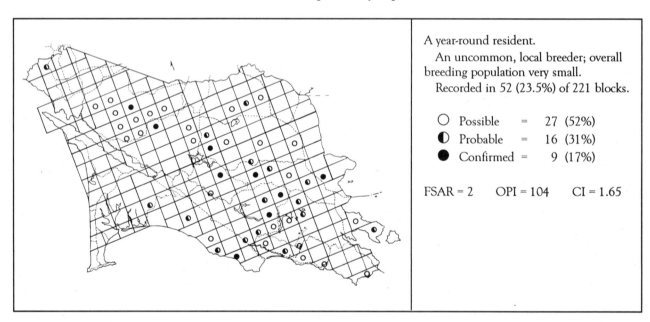

A year-round resident.
An uncommon, local breeder; overall breeding population very small.
Recorded in 52 (23.5%) of 221 blocks.

○ Possible = 27 (52%)
◑ Probable = 16 (31%)
● Confirmed = 9 (17%)

FSAR = 2   OPI = 104   CI = 1.65

Ecological Requirements

This rusty-capped skulker occupies a restricted niche. In Marin County, Rufous-crowned Sparrows generally occur on steep, sunny, south- or west-facing slopes with patchy or open coastal scrub dominated by coastal sage; in low, broken serpentine chaparral or short, sparse recently burned chaparral; along tall chaparral edges; or in rocky gullies with a few scattered shrubs. Their main requirements seem to be low sparse brush cover for protection and grass or forb ground cover for foraging; although rock outcrops are frequently present, they are not essential. The broken scrub or chaparral that Rufous-crowns favor is

found most widely on Marin's steep dry slopes, but it also occurs extensively on the flat or low rolling ridgetops on Mount Tamalpais and Carson Ridge, where the chaparral grows low and open on harsh serpentine soils.

In coastal California, Rufous-crowned Sparrows characteristically build their nests flush with the ground—in hollows under clumps of grass or at the bases of bushes—in open brush or on grassy slopes in proximity to scrub or chaparral. Elsewhere, they more frequently place their nests in low bushes up to three feet off the ground or, rarely, under low ledges on a hillside or inside a tin can

(Austin 1968). Nest cups vary from compact to loosely woven affairs made of coarse grass, fine twigs, bark, and vegetable fibers and lined with fine grasses or horsehair.

The diet is poorly known, but it appears to vary with season and availability. The summer diet of birds in California is 21% animal and 79% vegetable matter (Martin et al. 1951, n = 25). Reliance on animal matter generally decreases from summer to winter (Austin 1968). Arthropod food consists of grasshoppers, ants, bees, wasps, beetles, true bugs, leafhoppers, caterpillars, flies, spiders, and miscellaneous insects. The young are probably fed just insects. Vegetable matter is principally small grass and forb seeds, fresh grass stems, and tender plant shoots. Wild oats, filaree, miners lettuce, chickweed, dock, and pigweed are important plant foods in California (Martin et al. 1951). These sparrows apparently forage by gleaning and pecking as they hop slowly about, over, or through the herbaceous layer close to the ground; they may occasionally forage in taller shrubs or low oak trees.

Marin Breeding Distribution

During the atlas period, Rufous-crowned Sparrows were distributed patchily throughout Marin County, as is the combination of slope and shrub cover that suits their needs. They avoided lowland valleys and plains, rolling grassy hills, and heavily forested areas. Rufous-crowned Sparrows were somewhat more numerous in the interior of the county than on the immediate coast. Areas of particular concentration included serpentine chaparral on Carson Ridge along the Pine Mountain fire trail and

coastal sage–dominated slopes of the Walker Creek canyon. Representative breeding stations were Palomarin, PRNS (NY 4/25/78 –SJ); near Soulajoule Reservoir (FY 5/21/82 –ScC, DS); ridge W of Loma Alta (FL 6/11/82 –BiL); and Carson Ridge (NY 5/13/77 –DS, GBe).

Historical Trends/Population Threats

Their habitat preferences for sparse brush suggests that Rufous-crowned Sparrows are short-distance colonizers, adapted to invade areas swept by fire or other disturbances that open up the cover. Conversely, they will abandon an area if the brush becomes too dense. Consequently, Rufous-crowned Sparrow populations are probably always undergoing upward or downward trends in abundance over the short term in local areas. Because it allows chaparral to grow in dense decadent stands, long-term fire suppression since the turn of the century has likely reduced numbers of Rufous-crowned Sparrows in California. Development may occasionally open up (or destroy) habitat, though man's activities are usually restricted on the steep slopes that Rufous-crowns often occupy. From 1968 to 1989, numbers of Rufous-crowned Sparrows were relatively stable on Breeding Bird Surveys in California (USFWS unpubl. analyses), though these surveys were conducted decades after policies of fire suppression had been in place. The Southern California Rufous-crowned Sparrow *(A. r. canescens)* is currently a Candidate (Category 2) for federal listing as Threatened or Endangered (USFWS 1991).

CHIPPING SPARROW *Spizella passerina*

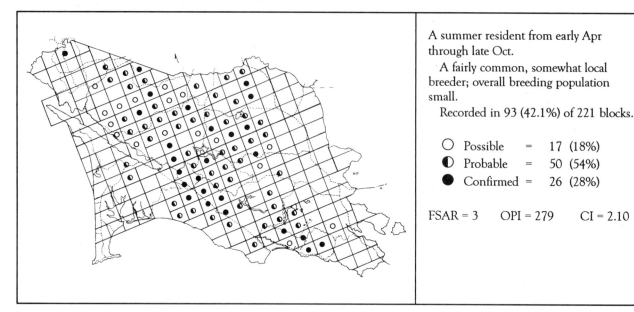

A summer resident from early Apr through late Oct.

A fairly common, somewhat local breeder; overall breeding population small.

Recorded in 93 (42.1%) of 221 blocks.

○ Possible   = 17 (18%)
◐ Probable   = 50 (54%)
● Confirmed = 26 (28%)

FSAR = 3   OPI = 279   CI = 2.10

Ecological Requirements

In Marin County, the dry buzzy trill of breeding Chipping Sparrows can be heard on the edges of oak woodlands, mixed evergreen, Douglas fir, bishop pine, and redwood forests and, sparingly, in cypress and eucalyptus groves where these habitats border on gently sloping grasslands or meadows of open character. Trees and brush provide cover and nest sites. Grassland and woodland edge appear to be this species' principal foraging beat. Chipping Sparrows generally locate their nests in trees or bushes from about 2 to 57 feet above ground. Occasionally they place them on the ground in grass or in odd settings—on a mowing machine in a semiopen tool shed, on the side of old straw stacks, in a moss-filled hanging basket on a stoop by a door, in pepper plants hung to dry in a shed, or six inches down at the bottom of a Hairy Woodpecker winter roost hole (Walkinshaw 1944, Stull 1968, Reynolds & Knapton 1984). Chipping Sparrows usually conceal arboreal nests in dense foliage, from close to the trunk to well out on horizontal branches (Walkinshaw 1944). Nest height seems to increase through the summer (Walkinshaw 1944). At least in some areas, nests are oriented on the south or east side of trees, where they catch the early morning sun and are protected from the prevailing winds and rain (Reynolds & Knapton 1984). Chipping Sparrows construct compact or loose nest cups made of rootlets, dead grass, and weed stalks, and line them with fine rootlets, fine grasses, or hair (Walkinshaw 1944, Stull 1968, Reynolds & Knapton 1984).

Chipping Sparrows are primarily ground foragers that take most of their food within about three feet of the

ground (Allaire & Fisher 1975). They peck or glean grass and weed seeds from the ground while hopping around in low, sparse vegetation or they pick them from the tips of grass or weed stems while reaching out from perches in brush piles, fallen trees, and barbed wire fences. While searching for insect prey, these birds actively move among low perches, from which they peer down to the ground or herbaceous vegetation and then fly down to catch prey in their bills. They also occasionally flycatch; they apparently feed on insects and new buds in trees in the spring (Stull 1968). Chipping Sparrows show no annual variation in use of foraging techniques and the least variation in other measures of resource use of nine species breeding in ponderosa pine forests in Arizona (Szaro et al. 1990).

The April through October diet of birds in California is about 45% animal and 55% vegetable food (Beal 1910, n = 96), though reliance on vegetable matter peaks at 98% of the diet in fall and winter (Beal 1907, Martin et al. 1951). Continentwide, animal matter accounts for 59%–66% of the diet in spring and summer (Martin et al. 1951, n = 336). Arthropod prey are caterpillars, ants, beetles, grasshoppers, true bugs, flies, leafhoppers, planthoppers, spiders, wasps, and a few moth pupae. Vegetable matter is dominated by weed seeds with only small amounts of grain and a trace of fruit. Important plant foods in the West are filaree, pigweed, bristle grass, panic grass, oats, and chickweed, along with needlegrass, bluegrass, red maids, and miners lettuce (Martin et al. 1951).

In Michigan, breeding Chipping Sparrows feed on a greater diversity of insects and seeds in summer than in spring (Evans 1964). The young are fed mostly on insects, and the vegetable matter they consume is usually leaf or stem tissue or, rarely, seeds. Adults feed the young many lepidopteran larvae and spiders, which adults themselves seldom eat. Adults also feed the young more rapid-flying insects and sluggish larvae than they consume themselves; both adults and young eat ground-dwelling insects and in the same proportion. The types of food the young consume suggest that in searching for food for young, adult Chipping Sparrows spend less time on the ground and more time in active flight or in the higher strata of vegetation.

Marin Breeding Distribution

During the atlas period, Chipping Sparrows were most numerous and widespread in central Marin County where edge habitats predominate. They were sparse or absent in densely forested areas on moist coastal ridges, in grassland

areas on Point Reyes and near Tomales, and in a relatively broad strip along the eastern urban corridor and bayshore. Representative breeding localities were Synanon Ranch, Walker Creek (NY 5/15/82 –DS); the south side of Nicasio Reservoir (NB 7/6/82 –DS); and Rock Springs, Mt. Tamalpais (NB 5/19/76 –DS).

Historical Trends/Population Threats

Historically, Chipping Sparrows have likely increased in California, as they have in the East, as logging and clearing of woodlands and forests have provided additional edge and open habitats (Stull 1968). From 1968 to 1989, however, for unknown reasons, population levels of Chipping Sparrows decreased on Breeding Bird Surveys in California (Robbins et al. 1986, USFWS unpubl. analyses).

Like other songbirds, young Chipping Sparrows avoid fouling the nest by depositing fecal sacs which the parents carry away.
Photograph by Ian Tait.

BLACK-CHINNED SPARROW *Spizella atrogularis*

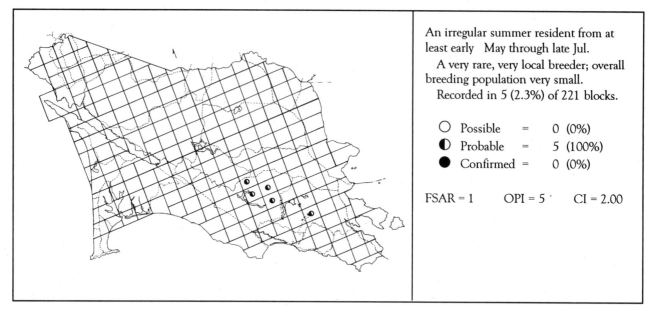

An irregular summer resident from at least early May through late Jul.

A very rare, very local breeder; overall breeding population very small.

Recorded in 5 (2.3%) of 221 blocks.

○ Possible   =   0   (0%)
◑ Probable   =   5   (100%)
● Confirmed   =   0   (0%)

FSAR = 1   OPI = 5 '   CI = 2.00

Ecological Requirements

Black-chinned Sparrows inhabit a wide variety of primarily arid brushland habitats in the western United States. In Marin County, birds irregularly occupy chaparral vegetation and, to a lesser extent, coastal sage scrub. Typical plant species in suitable chaparral habitat include chamise, scrub oak, and several species of ceanothus and manzanita, whereas coyote brush and coastal sage are prevalent in suitable coastal scrub habitat. All habitats occupied by Black-chins have the following characteristics: (1) shrub composition is a mixture of several species; (2) shrub cover is moderate to dense, but the canopy usually has openings exposing either the soil or small rock outcrops; (3) the vegetation is fairly young and is not a decadent stand that has not burned for a long period; (4) trees, large shrubs, or boulders are scattered throughout breeding territories and are used as song perches; (5) topography is gently to steeply sloping hillsides; and (6) the hillside is relatively dry and frequently south facing.

The typical nest of a Black-chinned Sparrow is a cup composed on the exterior of dry grasses and possibly a few weed stems. The interior usually is lined with fine grasses, shredded plant fibers, hair, or a few feathers. Nest structure has been described as compact (Dawson 1923) or "sometimes fairly compact but usually of rather loose construction" (Newman 1968). The nest generally is placed out of view in the interior branchwork of a large shrub and from 0.5 to 4.0 feet above the ground (Pough 1957).

The Black-chinned Sparrow is one of the least studied sparrows in North America, and little is known about its foraging habitats and diet. Grinnell and Miller (1944)

reported that foraging birds moving through the brush fly near the ground, through alleyways, and over bushtops. However, nothing is known about the microhabitat(s) in which Black-chins forage or the extent of seasonal variation in their foraging habits. Presumably, they eat seeds, fruits, and insects like most other sparrows, and the proportion of insects in the diet is higher in the breeding season. The only direct observations of their food items have been sightings of individuals carrying insects, presumably to nestlings (Johnson et al. 1948, Hardy 1949).

Marin Breeding Distribution

Black-chinned Sparrows "invade" Marin County at irregular intervals and during these "invasions" are usually reported for two to three consecutive years as either rare migrants or as a rare breeding species. Records from Palomarin and the Carson Ridge/Pine Mountain area give a good indication of the frequency of "invasions," since intensive censuses of landbirds in coastal scrub have been conducted annually at Palomarin since 1972 and Carson Ridge has been checked most years from 1976 until at least the mid-1980s. The dearth of records from other sites is likely a result of limited observer coverage.

The first records for the county were of up to six singing males at PRBO's Palomarin field station from 17 May 1972 through at least June of that year. Breeding was confirmed there by the presence of a nest with young 1.2 feet up in a coastal sage bush from 4 to 10 June 1972 (RMS). Subsequently, birds were recorded singing at Palomarin from 18 to 24 May 1973 and on 15 May 1974, but apparently they did not remain to breed. Black-chins next appeared at Palomarin in 1984, when a male and/or female were present from 15 May to at least 4 July, and two nests were discovered. One was found empty (preyed upon or abandoned) 23 inches up in a coastal sage bush on 15 June. The other was located 12 inches up in a sticky monkey flower bush and was followed from nest building on 12 June until 4 July, when the young were found dead and the nest abandoned. Both nests were at the interface between mature and disturbed south-facing coastal scrub dominated by coastal sage and sticky monkey flower. A singing bird at Laguna Ranch, PRNS, on 4 June 1972 (AP) represents the only record for coastal scrub away from the Palomarin site.

The Carson Ridge/Pine Mountain area has been another focus for recent Marin records since Black-chins were discovered there in 1976. A singing male was recorded there from 27 May to 13 June 1976 and on 13 May 1977 (DS). One bird was there on 6 May 1984, and nesting was confirmed with the observation of a fledgling begging food from a female on 23 July 1984 (DT et al.). One to two birds were recorded there from 18 April to 26 June 1985 (DT et al.) and two on 22 May 1986 (DAH).

Two birds were detected aurally on Big Rock Ridge on 17 May 1980 (PSh et al.) and also sometime in May 1981 (PCo).

Historical Trends/Population Threats

Like most aspects of the natural history of Black-chinned Sparrows, little is known about population status. Nearly all authors classify Black-chins as rare, erratic, and locally distributed in their California range (e.g., G&M 1944, Roberson 1985), and our ability to understand population trends is confounded by these characteristics. For example, the Black-chinned Sparrow was unrecorded in Marin County early in this century (Mailliard 1900, S&P 1933, G&M 1944), at a time of limited observer coverage. We now know, as noted above, that the species currently occurs only irregularly in Marin, even in areas with continuous observer coverage. Since the first half of this century, the known breeding range of Black-chinned Sparrows has continually expanded northward along the eastern and western edges of the Central Valley. Grinnell and Miller (1944) reported breeding records as far north as Contra Costa County on the western edge and Mariposa County on the eastern edge. More recent records have confirmed or strongly suggested breeding at scattered sites ringing the northern end of the Sacramento Valley in Lake, Glenn, Trinity, and Butte counties (ABN). This increase in known range could be interpreted as a true range expansion in the last 40 years, but it much more likely indicates better coverage by observers over a longer period. On the other hand, occupancy of the northern reaches of the range undoubtedly is highly erratic and might be restricted to "invasion" years. Populations of Black-chinned Sparrows decreased on Breeding Bird Surveys in California from 1968 to 1989, despite relative stability from 1980 to 1989 (USFWS unpubl. analyses). Because of the erratic nature of this species, less confidence should be placed in these trends than in those for most species. Bailey et al. (1987) speculated that the erratic nature of Black-chinned Sparrow populations is a response to dry conditions, but the factors controlling the distribution and abundance of this species have not been investigated and remain unknown.

A. SIDNEY ENGLAND

LARK SPARROW   *Chondestes grammacus*

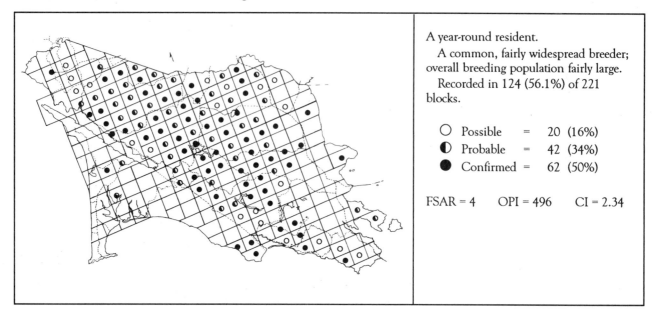

A year-round resident.

A common, fairly widespread breeder; overall breeding population fairly large.

Recorded in 124 (56.1%) of 221 blocks.

○ Possible   =   20 (16%)
◐ Probable   =   42 (34%)
● Confirmed   =   62 (50%)

FSAR = 4   OPI = 496   CI = 2.34

Ecological Requirements

In Marin County, this handsome sparrow is at home in sparse to moderately dense, relatively arid grasslands. Lark Sparrows are edge species, though. They also need the relief of trees, bushes, or rock outcrops for song perches, cover, and sometimes nest sites. Breeding birds are seldom found in expansive grasslands without these features. In Marin, Lark Sparrows most commonly inhabit grasslands bordering oak savannah, oak woodland, and mixed evergreen forest.

Lark Sparrows place their nests in shallow depressions in the ground (usually but not always shaded by a grass clump or a lone broadleaved plant) or in small trees or bushes generally to about 7 feet or, exceptionally, to 25 feet above the ground (Dawson 1923, Baepler 1968). They sometimes locate them from 5 to 10 feet high in crevices of cliffs of small rock mesas (Markle 1946). Ground nests are thick-walled but coarsely built cups of grass lined with fine grasses or horsehair. Elevated nests are sturdy deep cups of stout grasses, weed stems, string, or trash placed on a foundation of twigs and lined with fine grasses, horsehair, or rootlets.

The foraging habits of Lark Sparrows have been little studied, but they appear to feed primarily on the ground. They glean or pounce on insects on the earth or on annual vegetation, or they glean or pick seeds from the ground or from plants. Birds feed singly or in small flocks in the breeding season. The diet in spring and summer is about equal parts of animal and vegetable matter, the latter

increasing in importance through fall to account for about 98% of the menu in winter (Martin et al. 1951). Grasshoppers are the most important insect food, followed by locusts, beetles, and caterpillars (Martin et al. 1951, Baepler 1968). Vegetable fare is almost entirely grass and weed seeds and waste grain. Important seed plants for California birds are red maids, oats, knotweed, wheat, tarweed, turkey mullein, filaree, chickweed, and pigweed (Martin et al. 1951).

Marin Breeding Distribution

During the atlas period, Lark Sparrows were widespread breeders in central Marin County. They were sparse or absent on the Point Reyes peninsula, in the grasslands around Tomales, and in the lowlands of the eastern urban corridor and bayshore. Representative breeding localities were Chileno Valley (NE 7/2/82 —DS); Mt. Burdell, Novato (NE 5/29/78 —ScC; NB-NE 4/21–5/9/81 —ITi); Carson Ridge (FY/FL 6/8/81 —DS); and Potrero Meadows, Mt. Tamalpais (FY/FL 7/6/81 —DS).

Historical Trends/Population Threats

Little historical information is available, but Lark Sparrow populations were relatively stable on Breeding Bird Surveys in California from 1968 to 1989 (USFWS unpubl. analyses).

SAGE SPARROW　*Amphispiza belli*

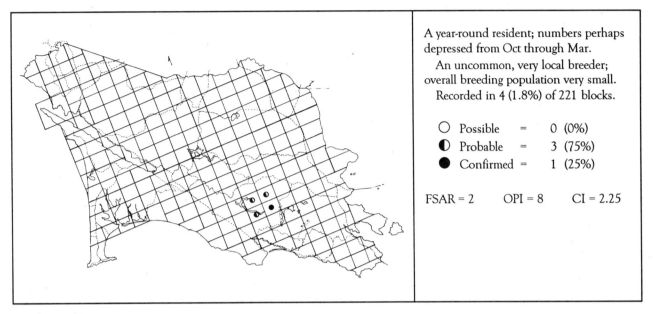

A year-round resident; numbers perhaps depressed from Oct through Mar.

An uncommon, very local breeder; overall breeding population very small. Recorded in 4 (1.8%) of 221 blocks.

○	Possible	=	0 (0%)
◑	Probable	=	3 (75%)
●	Confirmed	=	1 (25%)

FSAR = 2　　　OPI = 8　　　CI = 2.25

Ecological Requirements

In Marin County, the Sage Sparrow is a rare resident in stands of relatively dry chaparral brushlands. As the name implies, Sage Sparrows inhabit stands of big sagebrush *(Artemisia tridentata)*; this is the case for most interior races, but not for the one that breeds in Marin County and the rest of coastal California *(A. b. belli*, formerly recognized as a separate species called Bell's Sparrow). This race typically occupies relatively homogeneous stands of chaparral vegetation dominated by chamise *(Adenostoma fasciculatum)*. All ages of chamise chaparral may be used by Sage Sparrows, but the birds occur in highest numbers in relatively young, vigorous stands recovering from recent fire and with little accumulated dead material.

Sage Sparrows usually build a well-concealed cup nest placed less than three feet above the ground in a crotch between shrub branches (Miller 1968). The nest occasionally may be placed in a shallow depression on the ground beneath a shrub. Typical cup nests are composed of small twigs and dry stalks of grasses and weeds and are lined with fine dry plant material, shredded bark, hair, and occasionally feathers.

While foraging, the Sage Sparrow is a ground dweller that gleans for insects and seeds on the ground, in leaf litter, and by reaching up from the ground into the lower portions of shrubs (G&M 1944, Miller 1968, Ryser 1985). It may scratch the leaf litter in towhee fashion, but this is not common (Miller 1968). Another unusual foraging technique is gleaning insects at the tops of chaparral shrubs three to five feet above the ground. In early spring, the tips of chamise branches are young and succulent and

may support relatively dense populations of herbivorous insects, such as inchworms. During this short period, these insects may be the dominant item in the Sage Sparrow's diet, and birds may regularly be seen foraging well above the ground (A.S. England unpubl. data). However, foraging Sage Sparrows are relatively shy birds, typically observed moving about quickly on the ground beneath or between shrubs searching for food.

The Sage Sparrow diet includes seeds, insects, and succulent vegetation. Seeds are the most important food during winter (Martin et al. 1951, Miller 1968, A.S. England unpubl. data). In spring, the diet includes seeds but is dominated by insects such as beetles, caterpillars, ants, spiders, and grasshoppers (Miller 1968, Rotenberry 1980, A.S. England unpubl. data). Succulent vegetation and insects are important dietary components during the hot months of summer and fall when free water may not be accessible (Moldenhauer & Wiens 1970). The moisture in these foods enables Sage Sparrows to inhabit dry sites without available surface water (Moldenhauer & Wiens 1970, Weathers 1983).

Marin Breeding Distribution

Marin County's breeding Sage Sparrows are restricted to stands of chamise-dominated chaparral, which occur on relatively xeric south-facing slopes of interior ridges. The ridges that support chaparral vegetation generally have thin, dry soils, in part because of the limited penetration inland of coastal summer fog. This moisture is blocked either by intervening ridges or by an inversion layer of warmer air that generally keeps the tops of higher peaks such as Mount Tamalpais fog-free.

During the atlas period, all breeding season sightings were from the Carson Ridge/Pine Mountain area. Breeding was confirmed there with the observation of nest building on 19 April 1980 (KeHo) and a nest under construction one foot up in a bush on 25 May 1980 (DSi). Formerly, Sage Sparrows were reported from "Nicasio" and from Mount Tamalpais, where nesting was confirmed on the east slope west of Larkspur by the observation on 2 June 1917 of "several young just leaving the nest and hardly able to fly" (Squires 1917); they were reported also from the summit of Mount Tamalpais (G&W 1927). A record of a Sage Sparrow was reported without comment in a list of birds sighted on a 14 March 1926 Audubon Society trip to Point Bonita (*Gull* 8, No. 4); it was subsequently cited by Stephens and Pringle (1933) and Grinnell and Miller (1944), with the suggestion of residence or breeding. This record is anomalous and may pertain to an

early migrant; the brushy habitat in that area consists of coastal scrub, in which there is no evidence of breeding Sage Sparrows in the county.

Historical Trends/Population Threats

The trends in Sage Sparrow populations on the California coast are unclear. Long-term fire suppression may cause populations to be reduced or eliminated locally, but the species will return shortly following either natural or human-caused fires. Perhaps the greatest threat to the species is extensive residential development of chaparral hillsides, particularly in southern California. Sage Sparrow populations increased on the whole on Breeding Bird Surveys in California from 1968 to 1989, but less so from 1980 to 1989 (USFWS unpubl. analyses). Nevertheless, the Bell's Sage Sparrow (*A. b. belli*) is currently a Candidate (Category 2) for federal listing as Threatened or Endangered (USFWS 1991).

A. SIDNEY ENGLAND

SAVANNAH SPARROW *Passerculus sandwichensis*

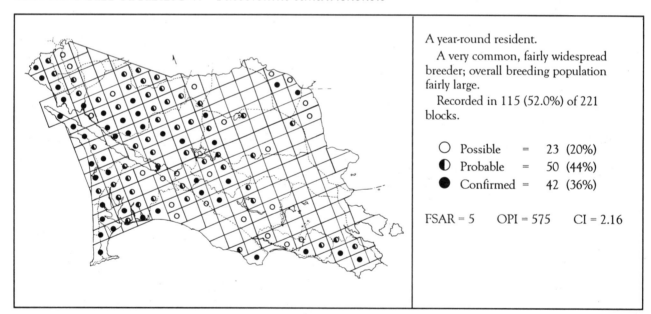

A year-round resident.

A very common, fairly widespread breeder; overall breeding population fairly large.

Recorded in 115 (52.0%) of 221 blocks.

○ Possible   = 23 (20%)
◐ Probable   = 50 (44%)
● Confirmed   = 42 (36%)

FSAR = 5   OPI = 575   CI = 2.16

Ecological Requirements

In Marin County, the insectlike song of the Savannah Sparrow can be heard rising from ground level on coastal hills clothed in grassland and also in lowland coastal and bayshore salt marshes. The grasslands this species frequents are relatively moist ones in the zone of persistent summer fogs. They generally have scattered forbs and a fairly dense ground layer of grasses and accumulated litter (Wiens 1969). Moisture is required only as it influences

the density of low vegetation, and birds will breed in drier upland sites if their vegetation requirements are met. Unlike saltmarsh-breeding Song Sparrows, Savannah Sparrows are found nesting in the older and higher parts of the marsh (5–10 ft. above mean sea level), where pickleweed less than one foot high grades into moist grassland (Marshall 1948; Johnston 1956a, 1968a). In Marin's moist upland grasslands, Savannah Sparrows overlap broadly with Grasshopper Sparrows. Habitat differences between the species are subtle, but Savannah Sparrows generally prefer shorter and less diverse grasslands than do Grasshopper Sparrows (see account).

Savannah Sparrow nest sites tend to be in denser cover and to have much more litter associated with them than those of the Grasshopper Sparrow (Wiens 1969, 1973). Savannahs usually conceal their nests inside grass tussocks or under matted grasses or weeds. Nineteen of 27 nests in Wisconsin were either partially domed over or were placed under overhanging litter; 14 (75%) of these opened north or east. Although birds of some other races may occasionally place their nests in small bushes or cacti up to four feet from the ground (Austin 1968), Savannahs on the central California coast *(P. s. alaudinus)* invariably place them on the ground or raise them up to about four inches on supporting grass or pickleweed (Johnston 1968a). Even in tidal marshes, birds place most nests directly on the ground. Grassland nests are often sunk in depressions at the base of grass clumps and are coarsely made cups of dried grass and fine weed stems lined with finer grasses and horsehair (Austin 1968). Saltmarsh nests are tightly formed, relatively deep cups composed of dead grass stems, pickleweed stalks, hair, and occasionally eelgrass *(Zostera).*

Savannah Sparrows forage primarily on the ground in low grass or marsh cover. Generally they feed more around grass clumps and less in open unvegetated areas than do Grasshopper Sparrows (Wiens 1973). In salt marshes, Savannahs will forage on marsh mud and in tangles of salt grass, pickleweed, and gumplant. They usually glean seeds from the ground or occasionally pick them from grass stems. Birds move by hopping, and they may scratch the ground like towhees do. Savannah Sparrows generally glean insects from the ground or herbaceous vegetation, but, infrequently, birds will jump in the air after them (Austin 1968). Although the diet of upland birds is about equally divided between plant and animal food, Savannah Sparrows are generally more insectivorous than other sparrows (Martin et al. 1951, Austin 1968). Animal matter peaks at about 74% of the menu in summer (n = 39) and drops to as little as 8% in winter (n = 118) (Martin et al. 1951). Animal food may be of greater importance in winter in tidal marshes, where it is more readily available. Important animal prey of upland birds are beetles, caterpillars, grasshoppers, ants, true bugs, flies, miscellaneous insects, spiders, and snails. In salt marshes, intertidal invertebrates such as small crustaceans, crabs, snails, and other gastropods are important foods. Vegetable matter is almost exclusively grass and weed seeds. Seed plants important to these sparrows in California are knotweed, turkey mullein, pigweed, oats, canarygrass, annual bluegrass, rabbitfoot grass, ryegrass, miners lettuce, chickweed, bromegrass, barley, red maids, sheep sorrel, and tarweed (Martin et al. 1951).

Marin Breeding Distribution

During the atlas period, Savannah Sparrows bred widely in Marin County's moist coastal upland grasslands in the fog zone, where they overlapped broadly with Grasshopper Sparrows. They were of local occurrence in salt marshes on the outer coast and along the bayshore near Novato. They were sparse or absent as breeders in the somewhat drier grasslands in the eastern portion of the county and in bayshore marshes south of Novato. Representative nesting locations were Abbott's Lagoon (NY 4/19/82 —KeHo, DS); Hall Ranch, Point Reyes (NE 6/11/81 —ECB, DS); former Synanon Ranch, Walker Creek (NE 5/15/82 — DS); end of Clark Rd., east side Tomales Bay (NY 7/7/82 —DS); and Bolinas Ridge above Olema (NY 5/11/77 —DS).

Historical Trends/Population Threats

Grinnell and Miller (1944) gave no hint of a population decline of this species, but the population breeding in salt marshes must have declined dramatically with the historic loss of about 60%–95% of the tidal marshlands of the San Francisco Bay system (Nichols & Wright 1971, Josselyn 1983). Walton (1978) estimated that, historically, Song Sparrow populations breeding in marshlands of the San Francisco Bay system had been reduced by 50%–75%, primarily from habitat loss. Saltmarsh-breeding Savannah Sparrows were probably reduced to an even greater extent, since they inhabit the upper reaches of the marshes more subject to being filled, diked, or developed. The Belding's Savannah Sparrow, breeding in southern California salt marshes, remains on the state Endangered list, though its numbers have increased recently (CDFG 1991a).

Upland breeding populations of Savannah Sparrows have fared better, and they are currently numerous in moist grassland. It should be noted that the structure of our grasslands has been drastically altered, from domination by native bunch grasses to domination by introduced Mediterranean annuals (Shuford & Timossi 1989; see Plant Communities section this volume). The moist coastal grasslands where Savannah Sparrows are numerous today still retain much of the native flora. Drier inland grasslands, on the other hand, are now almost entirely composed of introduced annual grasses. Have these changes had an effect on populations of Savannah Sparrows or other grassland species? Probably, but we don't know to what extent. Savannah Sparrow populations were relatively stable on Breeding Bird Surveys in California form 1968 to 1989 (USFWS unpubl. analyses).

GRASSHOPPER SPARROW   *Ammodramus savannarum*

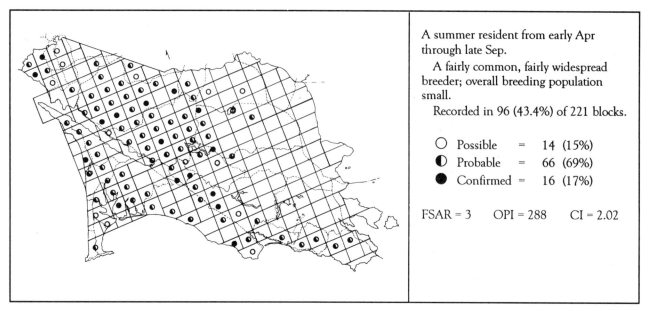

A summer resident from early Apr through late Sep.

A fairly common, fairly widespread breeder; overall breeding population small.

Recorded in 96 (43.4%) of 221 blocks.

○ Possible   =   14 (15%)
◑ Probable   =   66 (69%)
● Confirmed =   16 (17%)

FSAR = 3   OPI = 288   CI = 2.02

Ecological Requirements

This phantom grassland waif inhabits Marin County's moist coastal prairie grasslands, especially where native bunch grasses are prevalent. Along the immediate coast, Grasshopper Sparrows' typical habitat has scattered clumps of bracken ferns and the low-growing form of coyote bush *(Baccharis pilularis)*; these may be absent, and they generally drop out toward the county's interior. Overall, the species prefers short to middle-height grasslands (Smith 1963, 1968; Whitmore 1981). These generally have a fairly thick but low cover of grasses and a variety of taller forbs and usually occur on dry upland sites (Wiens 1969). "Optimum" habitat of the eastern subspecies *(A. s. pratensis)* is about 28% grass cover, 73% litter cover, and 28% bare ground (Whitmore 1979b).

Grasshopper Sparrows overlap broadly in habitat use with Savannah Sparrows here in Marin County and elsewhere in the two species' range. Compared with other grassland breeders, both species frequent generally intermediate conditions along a gradient of vegetation height, density, and litter (Wiens 1969), yet studies of eastern birds have shown subtle habitat differences between the two species. These distinctions are greatest at the time when birds initially occupy breeding areas, but habitat overlap increases seasonally with vegetative growth (Whitmore 1979a). Compared with Savannah Sparrows, Grasshopper Sparrows occupy grasslands with less grass cover and more bare ground but with greater "effective grass height," vertical and horizontal diversity, vertical and overall grass density, and forb cover (Wiens 1973, Whitmore 1979a). The frequent reference to the semicolonial nature

of the Grasshopper Sparrow may reflect individuals clumping in patches of structurally suitable grassland rather than any social tendencies of the species. Grasshopper Sparrows also tend to sing from higher perches than do Savannahs (Wiens 1969, 1973).

Although Grasshopper Sparrow nests tend to be situated in more open cover than those of Savannah Sparrows, they are usually well concealed in depressions at the base of grass clumps with the rim level at or slightly above ground level (Smith 1968, Wiens 1973, Whitmore 1981). Wiens (1969) found 15 nests in Wisconsin, all of which were domed over to some extent, and most (64%) faced north or northeast. Grasshopper Sparrow nest sites tend to have less litter and somewhat taller and more widely dispersed forbs than those of Savannah Sparrows (Wiens 1969). Nests are built of stems and blades of grass, lined with fine grass, rootlets, and occasionally horsehair and are usually arched or domed over at the back, giving an ovenlike appearance.

Little has been written on the foraging habits of Grasshopper Sparrows but the birds apparently hop and run through low herbage gleaning and picking insects and seeds from the ground or from low in the vegetation. Grasshopper Sparrows forage more frequently in open unvegetated areas than do Savannah Sparrows (Wiens 1973). Continentwide, the diet of the Grasshopper Sparrow from February to October is about 63% animal and 37% vegetable (Judd in Smith 1968, n = 170). The animal portion of the diet decreases from 60% in spring and summer (n = 126) to about 29% in fall (n = 17) (Martin et al. 1951). Animal fare is primarily grasshoppers, beetles, caterpillars, ants, and true bugs, along with a few spiders, snails, and miscellaneous invertebrates. The vegetable menu includes the seeds of grasses, weeds, and sedges. Important seed plants in California in fall are knotweed, campion, oats, and pigweed (Martin et al. 1951).

Marin Breeding Distribution

During the atlas period, the Grasshopper Sparrow bred widely in Marin County's moist coastal prairie grasslands, primarily within the zone of frequent summer fog toward the immediate coast. Its distribution overlapped remarkably well with that of the Savannah Sparrow, except in salt marshes, where the Grasshopper Sparrow was absent. In contrast to Marin, for the south San Francisco Bay region, Sibley (1952) noted that most breeding records were from the dry inner Coast Range, 20 to 25 miles from the coast. This may have reflected observer coverage, because most records of Grasshopper Sparrows for coastal northern California counties in the last two decades have been from the coastal slope and nearby ridges within about ten miles of the coast (ABN). Besides being widespread in Marin County, Grasshopper Sparrows are also relatively numerous here. One observer recorded a minimum of 150 birds while conducting extensive atlas surveys in the low rolling hills of northern Point Reyes and east of Tomales Bay in the spring and summer of 1982 (AB 36:1014). Representative breeding stations were north of McClure's Ranch, Point Reyes (FY 7/13/82 –DS); old Cerrini Ranch opposite Cypress Grove, east shore of Tomales Bay (FY 6/29 & 7/20/82 –DS); off Marshall-Petaluma Rd. near former Synanon Walker Creek Ranch (NE/NY 6/23/82 –DS); and Bolinas Ridge above Olema (NE 5/20/78 –ITi, RMS).

Historical Trends/Population Threats

Until recently, the Grasshopper Sparrow was considered a rather uncommon or rare breeding species in California. Mailliard (1900) reported it as "sparingly summer resident" in Marin County. Stephens and Pringle (1933) listed it in their "rare visitant" category for Marin, but they quoted mostly from Grinnell and Wythe (1927). The latter authors considered Grasshopper Sparrows "rare . . . locally" in the San Francisco Bay region, but they did list four localities for the species in Marin County, which up to that time had been relatively poorly explored. For California as a whole, Grinnell and Miller (1944) considered the Grasshopper Sparrow a "sparse and irregularly distributed resident" and "variable in occurrence from year to year." Even recently, McCaskie et al. (1979) considered the species rare to very uncommon along the California coast.

These reports are at odds with what we found in the Marin County atlas project, in which the Grasshopper Sparrow was recorded in over 40% of *all* the blocks in the county, many of which do not have extensive grassland. This difference could be due to at least one of three reasons: a historical increase in the species; year-to-year variability, with the atlas years corresponding to a high point in the population cycle; or the much more thorough coverage during the atlas project.

Although formerly considered scarce, Grasshopper Sparrow populations generally increased on Breeding Bird Surveys in California from 1968 to 1989, but were fairly stable from 1980 to 1989 (USFWS unpubl. analyses); continentwide, their numbers declined from 1965 to 1979 (Robbins et al. 1986). The Grasshopper Sparrow was on the Audubon Society Blue List from 1974 to 1986 (Tate 1986). Regarding year-to-year variability, some authors have felt that Grasshopper Sparrow populations fluctuate markedly between years in spite of available and suitable habitat (Smith 1963, 1968). Others feel that Grasshopper Sparrows choose patches of grassland with a particular suite of structural characteristics along the vegetation continuum, perhaps not readily evident to the human eye. In this light, populations appear to fluctuate in response to structural changes in the grassland community, brought about by succession, grazing pressure, variable rainfall, fires, and other disturbances (Wiens 1974, Whitmore 1979b). Hence, populations may be shifting spatially to take advantage of the changing suitability of the habitat, with population size fluctuating to an unknown degree. Because grasslands are climax communities over much of California, grazing intensity and year-to-year variation in the highly seasonal winter rainfall are the factors most likely to affect the structural characteristics of grasslands here. Although fires could have a marked effect on grassland structure, they are rare in the moist coastal grasslands with bunch grasses, where Grasshopper Sparrows are most frequent. Influxes of birds to Marin in June, in some years at least (J.G. Even & D. Shuford pers. obs.), may reflect sparrows changing habitat in midbreeding season in response to vegetational changes. For example, these late-arriving birds may represent a shift after first nesting attempts from interior grasslands, by then parched, to the still-moist grasslands of the coastal fog zone (AB 43:534).

Although some variability in population levels has been noticed in Marin over the years (D. Shuford pers. obs.), the species is seen here year after year at many traditional roadside sites, for example near Nicasio Reservoir. It was not until the atlas years that most of Marin's grasslands were first explored for breeding birds. Given the reliability of the species at traditional sites in prior years, it seems unlikely that the greater extent of sightings during the atlas years was due to just a coincidental population peak at that time. It seems much more likely that the thorough coverage revealed the true status of the species as a fairly numerous and widespread breeder in coastal grasslands. The Grasshopper Sparrow was almost "preadapted" for being overlooked, since it is a relatively inconspicuous and weak songster that dwells in a habitat typically infrequently checked because of its low bird diversity.

Those intimate with the Grasshopper Sparrow know that besides its typical insectlike buzz it also, infrequently, sings a quiet but bubbly Winter Wren–like song. Drawing by Keith Hansen, 1990.

SONG SPARROW *Melospiza melodia*

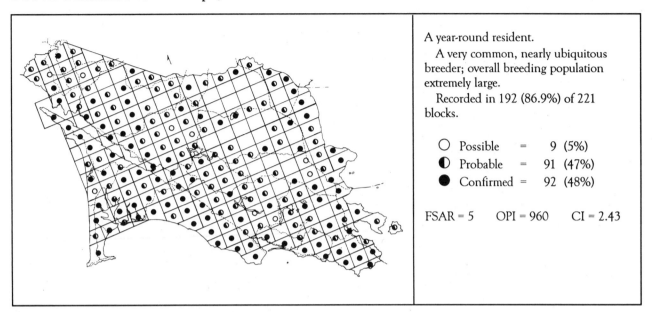

A year-round resident.

A very common, nearly ubiquitous breeder; overall breeding population extremely large.

Recorded in 192 (86.9%) of 221 blocks.

○	Possible	=	9 (5%)
◐	Probable	=	91 (47%)
●	Confirmed	=	92 (48%)

FSAR = 5　　　OPI = 960　　　CI = 2.43

Ecological Requirements

These perky sparrows inhabit Marin County's coastal scrub; salt, fresh, and brackish marshes; riparian groves; dense phases of dune scrub; and the moist brushy and weedy edges of these habitats. Marshall's (1948) detailed observations provide insight into the critical factors of these habitats to Song Sparrows. Coastal scrub is most suitable where the growth is divided into small clumps of bushes and separate tangles of vines; bordered by small grasses, ferns, and flowers; and separated by bare ground that is wet. Song Sparrows use only the moist phases of coastal scrub. They are absent where the brush forms a continuous high canopy and where it penetrates woodlands or forests as an understory. In salt marshes, Song Sparrows concentrate along the tidal sloughs in the taller vegetation of cord grass, pickleweed, or gumplant. They avoid areas where the cord grass is 18 inches or less in height and also the broad belt of pickleweed less than a foot tall in the highest upland portions of the marsh. In both salt and brackish marshes, Song Sparrows shun habitat where the tidal flow is cut off by diking and the water is stagnant and foul, even though the vegetation has the growth form they usually prefer. In fresh or brackish marshes, Song Sparrows prefer tall rank growth of cattails and bulrushes, particularly along the edges or where mixed with a variety of smaller plants and openings. The understory growth of riparian habitat is important, as Song Sparrows are absent where it is removed by the grazing and trampling of cattle or other factors. Song Sparrows are also absent from riparian that is roofed over by large trees (e.g., at Muir Woods where redwoods tower over the riparian),

even though the riparian vegetation shows no other marked change from that outside the higher canopy. Willows themselves limit Song Sparrows when they grow in a continuous dense canopy. Song Sparrows avoid the more open or drier phases of dune scrub or areas where the succulent vegetation between the lupines has been removed by overgrazing.

From these observations, Marshall (1948) concluded that the main habitat requirements of Song Sparrows are (1) moderately dense vegetation for nest sites, hiding places, and concealment during most foraging (dense vegetation is tolerated if it is somewhat open near the ground because of water flow or mammal runways); (2) a source of standing, running, or tidal water or, in coastal scrub or dune scrub, constant moisture from fog, dew, or seepage; (3) plenty of light (as evidenced by the lack of Song Sparrows in moist brush under closed forest canopies); and (4) exposed ground or leaf litter for foraging

Song Sparrows build substantial nest cups of weed stems, grasses, dead leaves, bark strips, ferns, and twigs. They line them with fine dry grasses, rootlets, and horsehair or other animal hair (Dawson 1923, Austin 1968). Song Sparrows place many of their nests in depressions in the ground under the concealing vegetation of grasses, weed stalks, ferns, brush piles, or fallen trees. They frequently situate ground nests on ditch banks or on low cliff faces. These sparrows often build nests in low marsh vegetation, bushes, and vine tangles, mostly below three feet in height. In San Francisco Bay salt marshes, Song Sparrows place all their nests above the ground in clumps of pickleweed, cord grass, salt grass, or gumplant bushes to avoid flooding by summer high tides (Johnston 1956a). The saltmarsh vegetation there averages less than 2 feet high, and nests on the average are elevated 9.5 inches in the marsh as a whole and 12 inches in the lower marsh; nests below 5 inches are flooded by the tides. In the Petaluma Marsh, vegetation must be at least 21 inches high to provide safety to nest sites and nests (Collins & Resh 1985). Nests there (often built in suspended litter) must be 8 inches high to avoid tidal flooding. In both upland and saltmarsh habitats, nest height tends to increase through the nesting season in conjunction with the growth of concealing vegetation (Nice 1937, Johnston 1956a, Austin 1968). Less often, high spring lake levels cause nest place-ment to be high early in the season, with a general decrease in nest height as water levels fall (Austin 1968). Infre-quently, Song Sparrows build nests in saplings or trees up to 28 feet from the ground (Austin 1968). They commonly build bush or tree nests in stranded flood debris and often build them over water. More unusual nest sites include cavities in trees or hollow logs, in unoccupied buildings such as wood sheds, in nest boxes, in a roll of wire on the ground, in the side of a paper wasp nest in a tree, and in the previous year's nest of a Swainson's Thrush (Nice 1937, Austin 1968).

Song Sparrows forage primarily on the ground. They pick their food from the bare ground or leaf litter under or at the base of bushes, under twig or branch piles, along runways beneath ground cover and pickleweed mats, and from floating marsh plants (Marshall 1948, Austin 1968). They also search the mud, ooze or shallow water between the stems of marsh plants, along stream, pond, or marsh margins, and in the recesses beneath undercut stream and slough banks. In typical foraging bouts, Song Sparrows progress slowly by short hops in a jerky manner with the head up, accompanied by wing and upward tail flicks and punctuated by frequent pecks at food items (Marshall 1948, Johnston 1956a). When pursuing airborne prey reachable from the ground, they make a rapid series of hops with the head and tail held low or run with the tail elevated and wings half outstretched. They frequently scratch vigorously with both feet to expose invertebrate and plant food within and under the surface litter. Song Spar-rows occasionally climb tules nuthatchlike to glean insects, feed on caterpillars high in willows, seize and devour minnows, and flycatch from exposed perches (Marshall 1948, Austin 1968, Johnston 1968b). In British Colum-bia, Smith (1978) noted that males flycatch much more frequently than do females. He suggested this was a result of greater opportunities afforded the males who spend much of their time on high perches singing or looking out for intruders. In contrast, females seldom use high perches, often move about inside dense thickets, and spend much time incubating. Additionally, Song Sparrows

feed finchlike on peeled gumplant seeds while perched on the top of flowering stalks, and, more frequently in the fall, they feed on cord grass flowers and the fleshy fruits and seeds of pickleweed by alighting on the stems (Marshall 1948, Austin 1968, Johnston 1968b). Foraging for insects in grass, brush, and trees apparently increases in the spring and summer (Austin 1968).

The year-round diet of Song Sparrows in California is about 21% animal matter and 79% vegetable matter (Beal 1910, n = 321). Animal prey rise from a from a low of 3% of the diet in September to over 71% in May. Important animal items include beetles, caterpillars, bees, ants and wasps, true bugs, and flies, along with miscellaneous insects, spiders, and snails. Saltmarsh birds appear to feed more heavily on invertebrates (particularly snails, nereid polychaete worms, and insects) than do upland birds (Marshall 1948), presumably because these foods occur in greater year-round abundance in the marshes. The chief plant food of the Song Sparrow is weed seed, whereas fruit and grain make only a minor contribution (Beal 1910). The important weed seeds used by Song Sparrows in California are rough pigweed, knotweed, mayweed, night-shade, chickweed, miners lettuce, and filaree (Beal 1910). Most of these are apparently picked from the ground (Marshall 1948). Other seeds of importance to the diet are those of tules in brackish marshes, pickleweed seeds from the surface of saltmarsh mud, and the other saltmarsh plants mentioned above (Marshall 1948, Johnston 1968b).

Marin Breeding Distribution

During the atlas period, Song Sparrows bred widely in Marin County's lowlands. Their populations were densest along the immediate coastline where coastal scrub vegeta-tion prevails and along the bayshore salt marshes. In the drier interior of the county, Song Sparrows were restricted to stream drainages and lake and pond borders. Represen-tative breeding localities included Bear Valley Trail, PRNS (NB 3/22/81 –DS); O'Hare Park, Novato (FL 5/16/82 –ScC); Miller Creek at Hwy. 101 (FY 6/6/82 – BiL); Phoenix Lake (NB 4/19/80 –ITi); Corte Madera Creek, Kentfield (FL 5/22/82 –BiL); and Corte Madera Ecologi-cal Reserve (NE 3/?/82 –JGE).

Historical Trends/Population Threats

The Song Sparrow has been considered a model of evolu-tionary divergence, because it has the greatest number of genetically distinct populations of any bird species in North America. Of the 31 subspecies recognized, 13 breed in California and 9 are endemic to the state (G&M 1944, AOU 1957). Of the 6 breeding subspecies found in coastal northern California, the 3 inhabiting salt and brackish marshes around the shores of San Francisco, San Pablo, and Suisun bays are of particular interest (*M. m. pusillula,*

M. m. *samuelis*, and M. m. *maxillaris*). These relatively small but distinct populations have apparently evolved because of the spatial isolation of segments of the marshes, separated by open water and ranges of hills; only narrow corridors connect saltmarsh populations to upland populations (Marshall 1948). Differentiation was encouraged not only by the geographic isolation of the populations, reinforced by the species' sedentary nature, but by different ecological conditions.

Grinnell and Miller (1944) considered these three races "abundant." However, since 1850, these marshland populations have been fragmented and reduced by an estimated 50%-75% (Walton 1978). Among other things, the San Francisco Bay ecosystem has been altered by increasing salinity; by increasing domestic and industrial sewage; by decreasing circulation, tidal action, and dissolved oxygen; and by a lowering of its water table. Marshland Song Sparrow populations have declined mainly because of habitat loss from landfilling, diking, dredging, and land subsidence (Walton 1978). M. m. *pusillula* has been severely reduced in south San Francisco Bay between the San Mateo and Dumbarton bridges and especially on the east side of that bay from Richmond south to Hayward. M. m. *samuelis* also has been severely reduced, particularly in the southern part of its range in Marin and Contra Costa counties. Reductions of these populations have amounted to extermination along three- to six-mile

stretches of bayshore that have been highly industrialized. Habitat for M. m. *maxillaris* has been reduced by 90% and currently supports only about 8% of the original population (Marshall et al. 1988). The most recent estimates of the size of the remaining populations are 2320 pairs for M. m. *pusillula*, 4599 for M. m. *samuelis* (Walton 1978), and 5666 for M. m. *maxillaris* (Marshall et al. 1988). Although mosquito control ditches are not optimal habitat, their development has increased suitable habitat for M. m. *samuelis* in the Petaluma Marsh by 300%, thus adding an estimated 2000 Song Sparrow territories in remaining marshlands (Collins & Resh 1985). All three races currently are Candidates (Category 2) for federal listing as Threatened or Endangered (USFWS 1989b, 1991), and all are currently considered Bird Species of Special Concern in California (CDFG 1991b). A petition submitted to list *maxillaris* as Endangered at the state level (Marshall et al. 1988) was turned down in late 1989; a petition for federal listing is currently under review. Although small populations of Song Sparrows are likely to survive in the bay marshes, the continued existence of the three distinct races remains uncertain because of additional habitat loss and the possible effects of habitat fragmentation. On the whole, Song Sparrow populations—mostly interior or upland forms—were relatively stable on Breeding Bird Surveys in California from 1968 to 1989 (USFWS unpubl. analyses).

The natural response when first seeing an adult White-crowned Sparrow feeding an outsized, begging Brown-headed Cowbird fledgling is, "What's wrong with this picture?" Drawing by Keith Hansen, 1992.

WHITE-CROWNED SPARROW *Zonotrichia leucophrys*

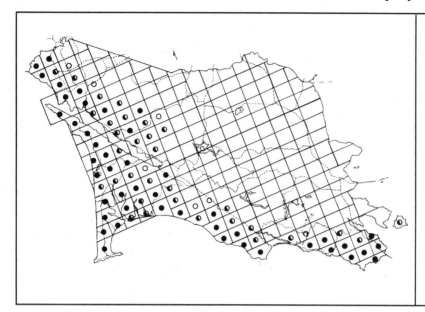

A year-round resident; numbers (migratory races) swell from mid-Sep through mid-Apr, particularly east of Point Reyes.

A very common, somewhat local breeder; overall breeding population of moderate size.

Recorded in 85 (38.5%) of 221 blocks.

○	Possible	=	7 (8%)
◐	Probable	=	33 (39%)
●	Confirmed	=	45 (53%)

FSAR = 5   OPI = 425   CI = 2.45

Ecological Requirements

The Nuttall's White-crowned Sparrow *(Z. l. nuttalli)* is a characteristic resident of coastal terraces and adjacent shrubby ridges of Marin County. In February and March, resident White-crowns break out of winter flocks to take possession of their breeding territories in coastal scrub, dune scrub, and brushy forest edges and woodland clearings on the immediate coast. Denser, mature (vs. open, disturbed) coastal scrub is preferred, as indicated by the predominance of adults over immature breeders in that habitat (D.F. DeSante pers. comm.). White-crown territories invariably have a patchy mixture of dense shrubbery, bare ground, and grass in the right proportions to permit ground foraging with quick escape to shelter (DeWolfe 1968). Dense shrubbery provides concealment for nests and for adults moving to and from them.

At PRBO's coastal scrub ecology study site at Palomarin, White-crowns almost always conceal their nests well in bushes or vine tangles, although "nonconformist" *nuttalli* will, very rarely, nest on the ground (D.F. DeSante pers. comm.). On Point Reyes peninsula, these sparrows nest most frequently in coyote brush, poison oak, coastal sage, and bush lupine. Almost any dense bush will do, though, as White-crowns nest widely in ornamentals in suburban areas and occasionally use nonwoody plants as well (Grinnell & Linsdale 1936, Kern 1984). Nest heights average 3.5 feet (range 1.5-11 ft.) at Berkeley, Alameda County (Blanchard 1941, n = 31); 1.8 feet (range 1-4 ft.) at Point Lobos, Monterey County (Grinnell & Linsdale 1936, n = 16); 1.3 feet near Lompoc, Santa Barbara County (Kern 1984, n = 54); and 1.5 feet (range 0-4.8 ft.) at Palomarin

(D.F. DeSante pers. comm., n = 226). Although Nuttall's White-crowned Sparrows rarely nest on the ground (Blanchard 1941), other races often do so, generally with increasing frequency with increasing altitude or latitude (DeWolfe 1968, Kern 1984). Atypical *nuttalli* nest sites include 35 feet up in a cypress, in the outer drooping branches of an acacia tree, and in an ivy vine on a building (Blanchard 1941). In Berkeley, White-crowns build most nests only a few inches inside the tips of dense new growth in a mass of low shrubbery, and no more than arm's length from one edge of a clump. They locate a few in small isolated trees, but always within a yard or so of more extensive shrubbery. Nests are deep, cup-shaped affairs of weed stems, grasses, fine twigs, dead ferns, bark strips, rootlets, dead leaves, and sometimes paper, rags, or other debris (Dawson 1923, DeWolfe 1968, Kern 1984). They are lined with fine grasses, weed stems, leaves, flower heads, rhizomes, mammal hair, feathers, or perhaps bits of waxed paper. Although the nests of the various races are similar in structure, they differ considerably in size and external appearance, and apparently are tailored to the microclimate at the nest site (Kern 1984). Above-ground nests generally have much thicker walls and floors, presumably because they are subjected to greater convective cooling and lack the additional insulation of vegetation and soil around ground nests.

White-crowns are principally ground foraging granivores. The main fare of these sparrows year round in coastal California is dried seeds of such plants as red maids, filaree, knotweed, chickweed, and various grasses

(DeWolfe 1968). Fresh vegetable matter such as flower blossoms, immature leaf and fruit buds, leaves, and leafy vegetables are also important items on the White-crown menu. After the dry summer and early fall of the coastal climate, White-crowns readily shift from seeds to newly sprouted grass shoots upon the commencement of winter rains (Grinnell & Linsdale 1936, D.F. DeSante pers. comm.). They less frequently consume fruit pulp, willow pollen, and sap (DeWolfe 1968). They pick most food from the ground or low herbaceous vegetation and, sparingly, from bushes or trees. Insects form only a minor part of the adult diet, even in the breeding season, and apparently are absent in *nuttalli* stomachs from September to February. The insects White-crowns eat most frequently are ants, wasps, caterpillars, beetles, and weevils. They pick or glean them from the grass or ground or catch them as they rise to escape. White-crowns also occasionally flycatch for or jump into the air after insects. Adults, of course, feed nestlings mostly insects.

Marin Breeding Distribution

During the atlas period, Marin's White-crowned Sparrows bred only in a narrow strip about three miles wide along the immediate coast. This region corresponds to the zone of intense, persistent summer fog and includes most of the county's extensive tracts of coastal scrub vegetation. Breeding White-crowns occurred slightly farther inland in the low hills east of Tomales Bay than they did where the steeper Inverness and Bolinas ridges provided more of a barrier to the inland penetration of coastal fog. A tiny part of the breeding population, however, has "spilled over" Inverness Ridge into the Olema Valley between Dogtown and Five Brooks. Representative breeding localities were Tomales Point (NB 4/13/82 –DS); Drake's Beach, PRNS (FY/FL cowbird 8/15/81 –DS); Fish Docks, Point Reyes

(NY 4/25/77 –DS); Limantour Spit (NY 5/1/80 –JGE); Palomarin, PRNS (NE-NY multiple nests each year 1976-1982 –PRBO); and Five Brooks (FY/FL 6/6/78 –RMS).

Historical Trends/Population Threats

Little prior data exist. White-crowned Sparrow populations decreased on Breeding Bird Surveys in California from 1968 to 1989 but were relatively stable from 1980 to 1989 (USFWS unpubl. analyses).

Remarks

The White-crowned Sparrow is one of the best studied species of songbirds in the world. Research on Point Reyes has investigated reproductive physiology and phenology (Mewaldt et al. 1968, Mewaldt & King 1977), effect of age on breeding success (Ralph & Pearson 1971), home range and site fidelity (Baker & Mewaldt 1979), and longevity (Baker et al. 1981), to name but a few. Particularly fascinating are the localized song dialects of the resident White-crowns in coastal California (Blanchard 1941). From work on Point Reyes, Milligan and Verner (1971) showed that sonograms from Marin White-crowns differ from those of birds resident in Berkeley and at Sunset Beach in Santa Cruz County. Using song dialects, Baptista (1975) compared the White-crowns of Marin County with those of San Francisco, and with the fragmented populations just east of San Francisco Bay. His findings suggest that the Golden Gate channel is an effective water barrier to dispersal and thus to the exchange of genes between Marin populations and those of the rest of the San Francisco Bay Area. More recently, Baker and Thompson (1985) have described the geographical limits of six populations on the basis of their dialects, all on the Point Reyes peninsula between Bolinas and Tomales Point. Although they all sound delightfully alike to most of us, these White-crowns have much to tell those who pause to learn their language.

DARK-EYED JUNCO   *Junco hyemalis*

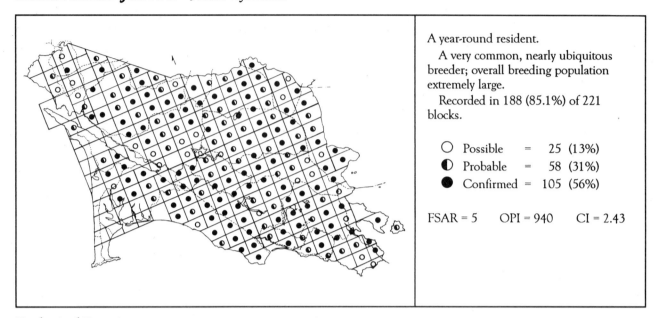

A year-round resident.

A very common, nearly ubiquitous breeder; overall breeding population extremely large.

Recorded in 188 (85.1%) of 221 blocks.

○ Possible   =   25 (13%)
◑ Probable   =   58 (31%)
● Confirmed = 105 (56%)

FSAR = 5   OPI = 940   CI = 2.43

Ecological Requirements

The handsomely dressed Oregon form of the Dark-eyed Junco breeds widely in Marin County, around the openings and edges of moist, shaded mixed evergreen, Douglas fir, bishop pine, and coast redwood forests and, to a lesser extent, Monterey pine and eucalyptus plantings. Although Juncos will breed in almost any shaded forest with some ground cover that remains green through the summer, they are particularly attracted to meadow/forest edges and moist places in general (Miller 1941, White 1973). Relatively open ground is important for foraging, sufficient ground cover or logs are necessary for concealing nests, while bushes and trees provide shelter and limited foraging substrate.

Juncos place most nests in cup-shaped depressions in the ground that are usually hidden under a low canopy of large forbs, ferns, grasses, vine tangles, bushes, seedlings, downed limbs or logs, overhanging rocks, or boards or sheet metal; rarely, they place nests inside tin cans (Phelps 1968, White 1973, D. Shuford pers. obs.). Juncos sometimes locate their nests off the ground in crevices of road cuts, rock ledges, walls of shallow caves, and appropriate recesses in the eaves and rafters of buildings. Relatively often, particularly in coastal California, they build nests up to 20 feet high in trees, either in dense foliage or in the open well out on large limbs or, rarely, in deserted woodpecker holes. Nests are sturdy, usually tightly woven cups of grasses, weed stems, leaves, other coarse herbage, bark, conifer needles, and perhaps moss (Phelps 1968, White 1973). They are lined with finer grasses, herbage, animal hair, or porcupine quills. Some Juncos make a great effort

to integrate the living stems, roots, and leaves of surrounding plants into the nest cup (White 1973). Although Juncos often renest close to the same site, they do not use the actual nest site or materials of the first nest; rarely, they will use the same depression in successive years.

Breeding birds usually feed singly or in pairs, although mated territorial males in meadow habitat often feed together in small groups, particularly during incubation (White 1973). Oregon Juncos feed mostly on the surface of the ground by pecking and picking up objects, but only infrequently by scratching in the litter to expose food items. On the ground, Juncos feed mainly among the plants but occasionally peck at insects or seeds on plants. Juncos also glean insects from the foliage and branches of trees and bushes and, rarely, flycatch for airborne insects by making short sallies or hops from the ground, large rocks, or trees; rarely, they procure seeds from cone-laden trees (Hagar 1960, Phelps 1968, White 1973). In the Sierra Nevada, White (1973) investigated the foraging habits of Oregon Juncos breeding along meadow edges and in adjacent forests. She found that meadow-nesting birds foraged over 96% of the time on the ground; this time was about evenly distributed on litter, on vegetation, and under shrubs (and, infrequently, under trees). The remainder of the time was spent mostly gleaning in trees and bushes. Meadow birds increased foraging under trees and shrubs in August and September because of increased seed numbers there. In contrast, forest-nesting birds forage about 78% of the time on the ground, about half of this in the open (not under a canopy) and feeding upon needle litter. The remainder of ground foraging was more evenly distributed under trees, shrubs, and in other open substrate. Overall, forest-dwelling birds spent about 20% of their time gleaning in trees. Time spent gleaning in trees decreased as the summer progressed, reaching a low of 5% in August. Juncos breeding in ponderosa pine forests in Arizona exhibit annual variation in their use of foraging techniques and in other resource-use measures (Szaro et al. 1990).

Year-round, the diet is about 50%–80% vegetable matter, but in the summer it varies from about 60% to 95% animal matter (Beal 1910, Martin et al. 1951, Gashwiler & Ward 1968, White 1973, Smith & Anderson 1982, Dahlsten et al. 1985). In the Sierra Nevada, White (1973) noted that the volume of seeds in the diet increased steadily from 4% in June to 52% in September; Gashwiler and Ward (1968) noted a similar trend. Animal foods consumed included beetles, ants, caterpillars, leafhoppers and other homopterans, true bugs, and lesser numbers of grasshoppers, spiders, wasps, flies, and miscellaneous insects (references above). Plant matter is almost exclusively seeds of weeds, grasses, conifers (particularly Douglas fir), and berry-producing bushes. Seeds eaten may be dormant, germinating, or still attached to freshly sprouted seedlings. Important plant foods to Juncos in California in summer are chickweed, red maids, miners lettuce, and Cryptantha (Martin et al. 1951).

Marin Breeding Distribution

During the atlas period, Oregon Juncos bred widely throughout Marin County. They were sparse or absent only on the outer reaches of the Point Reyes peninsula and in some extensive grassland areas around Tomales. They were most numerous in the conifer and associated mixed evergreen forests in the coastal fog zone and were somewhat more restricted inland to shaded, north-facing slopes and narrow canyons. Representative breeding localities were eucalyptus grove SE of Abbott's Lagoon (FY/FL 6/20/82 –DS); Mt. Burdell, Novato (NE 4/14/81 –DS); Big Rock Ridge, Novato (FL 6/15/82 –ScC); China Camp SP (FL/FY 6/19/82 –BiL); and Ross (NE-NY 4/9-18/76 –PLW).

Historical Trends/Population Threats

Breeding Juncos have increased locally in residential plantings in the Bay Area since at least 1917 (Allen 1933, 1943; Miller 1941:294). Like many widespread numerous species, Juncos are adaptable, and their populations have probably fluctuated within reasonable bounds even with large-scale habitat changes brought on by humans. Although populations can increase in some early successional stages after logging (Hagar 1960), they decline where living trees are few and brush stands are dense (White 1973). Dark-eyed Junco populations appeared to decrease slightly on Breeding Bird Surveys in California from 1968 to 1989, despite relative stability from 1980 to 1989 (USFWS unpubl. analyses).

New World Blackbirds and Orioles
Family *Emberizidae*
Subfamily *Icterinae*

RED-WINGED BLACKBIRD   *Agelaius phoeniceus*

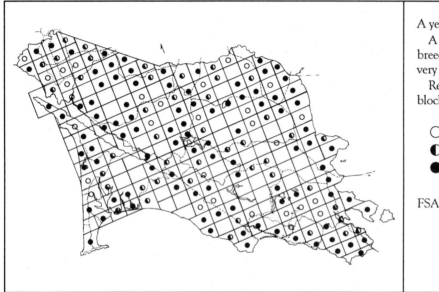

A year-round resident.

A very common, very widespread breeder; overall breeding population very large.

Recorded in 172 (77.8%) of 221 blocks.

○	Possible	=	30 (17%)
◑	Probable	=	44 (26%)
●	Confirmed	=	98 (57%)

FSAR = 5   OPI = 860   CI = 2.40

Ecological Requirements

The marsh-side stroller on a spring morning would have to be lost in the depths of inner contemplation not to notice the male Red-winged Blackbird, both feet firmly planted on the swaying vertical stalk of a cattail or tule, epaulets puffed and ablaze, and throat aquiver with a full-tilt gurgle. Breeding Red-winged Blackbirds inhabit Marin County's fresh and brackish marshes, coastal swales, brush and weed fields adjoining marshy aquatic habitats, roadside ditches, and irrigated meadows, fields, and croplands. They apparently prefer edge habitat on the periphery of fields or wetlands (Albers 1978), though they do sometimes nest in the center of dense cattail stands. Where Red-wings overlap with Yellow-headed Blackbirds (not in Marin), Red-wings are excluded from the outer marsh that borders open water and therefore are concentrated in the denser vegetation on the periphery of the marsh close to shore (Willson 1966). Hordes of Tricolored Blackbirds can also displace Red-wings to upland sites and marsh edges (E.C. Beedy pers. comm.).

Red-winged Blackbirds weave neat but rather bulky nest cups from the leaves of marsh plants (worked while wet), grasses, or weed bark. They fill the interstices with rotten wood, marsh-grass roots, fibrous peat, or mud, and they line the nests with fine dry grasses or slender rushes (Dawson 1923, Bent 1958). Rarely, Red-wings will build deep pensile nests reminiscent of those of orioles, will use and reline year-old Northern Oriole nests, or will place their nests in holes in trees or in bird boxes (Bent 1958, Orians 1980). Red-wings usually lash their nests to the upright stalks of emergent vegetation, or they place them in weeds, bushes, or trees, either over water or in upland sites sometimes far from water. They prefer nesting areas with erect residual vegetation and sturdy tall dense vegetation (Albers 1978). Nest placement can range from the ground, supported by surrounding vegetation, up to 30 feet in trees, but most nests are situated from about 1 to 8 feet high. Nest height, of course, varies with habitat. Late-season nests tend to be higher because of the seasonal growth of vegetation (Allen 1914, Bent 1958). However, in one upland area, there was a seasonal shift from tree, bush, or raspberry vine nests to lower nesting sites, as low herbaceous growth became suitable for support and cover (Holcomb & Twiest 1968). Red-wings will also switch their preference for certain plants or nest sites seasonally, relative to their availability or proximity to changing water levels (Case & Hewitt 1963, Albers 1978).

In the breeding season, Red-winged Blackbirds feed singly, in small groups, or sometimes in large flocks. They have a polygynous breeding system, and both males and females feed extensively off as well as on their territories (Orians 1961, 1980). Red-wings nesting in aquatic habitats forage primarily in marshes at midday, during the peak of aquatic insect emergence, and also in upland sites, during early morning and late afternoon (Orians & Horn 1969, Orians 1980). Wilson (1978) noted that where Red-wings were nesting in a marsh adjoining a grassy field the males fed much more frequently in the field than did females. This may have reduced competition for food by allowing the females to gather food for nestlings in the more productive marsh that tended to harbor large prey items. Although Red-wings frequently forage by gleaning insects from the vertical stalks of emergent vegetation, they are also adept at foraging in hay, alfalfa, or weed fields, and in upland bushes and trees. Compared with Yellow-headed or Brewer's blackbirds, Red-wings forage more extensively in bushes and trees (Orians 1980). There female Red-wings work inside the branchwork, rather than from below or on top of the canopy as the male Red-wings and other species of blackbirds do. Although most arboreal foraging consists of vireolike gleaning, Red-wings occasionally hover to grab insects from leaves and sometimes to pick samara seeds or extract pine cone seeds (Bent 1958). In calm warm weather, Red-wings (particularly the males) catch insects on the wing (Orians 1961). In open fields and on marsh edges, Red-wings uncover prey by flipping over sticks, rocks, cow patties, and other floating or stationary debris with gaping movements of their bills (Orians 1961, 1980). Gaping is also used in cattails, grasslands, and tree foliage, the bill being inserted into vegetation and then opened to expose any insects and seeds within. Ground-foraging birds intersperse bouts of scratching (particularly for seeds) with digging fairly deep holes with their bills. However, while foraging for nestlings, they move more rapidly, never pursue mobile prey, and do not dig or flip over objects. Bendell and Weatherhead (1982) reported that Red-wings selectively prey on cryptically colored, slow-moving foliage insects rather than on more mobile forms.

The diet of Red-winged Blackbirds year round in California is roughly 10%–30% animal matter and 70%–90% vegetable fare (Beal 1910, Soriano 1931, Crase & DeHaven 1978). Because these studies have focused on potential crop damage in the state's agricultural valleys, where very large concentrations of blackbirds winter, they

may not reflect the true range of dietary preference. There is considerable variation in the diet, both on a broad geographic scale and between aquatic- and upland-feeding birds (Orians 1980). In Manitoba, for example, Bird and Smith (1964) found that breeding birds from marshes were eating 100% insects, whereas those in agricultural areas were eating only 70% insects. In the breeding season, California birds may eat as much as 91% animal matter (Beal 1910). Adults feed nestlings almost exclusively insects (Beal 1910, Orians 1980) but also, rarely, small quantities of grain (Bendell & Weatherhead 1982). Important animal foods in California include beetles, caterpillars, and grasshoppers, along with lesser numbers of dipterans, true bugs, ants, wasps, moths, miscellaneous insects, and spiders. If dietary work had concentrated around aquatic systems, damselflies, dragonflies, mayflies, and caddisflies would probably have been more important (Orians 1980). In Quebec, Bendell and Weatherhead (1982) noted seasonal changes in the insect diet fed to young. The early-nesting birds concentrated on lepidopteran larvae, whereas later ones fed on slow-moving adult grasshoppers. Wilson (1978) noted that nestlings were fed a much greater proportion of nymphs and larvae, relative to their availability, than adult insects. This may have reflected their ease of capture or the fact they are assimilated fast, promoting nestling growth. Young were also fed a high proportion of larger food items relative to their availability. Important vegetable foods in California are cereal grains, including rice, oats, wheat, barley, corn, and sorghum, and wild seeds such as watergrass (strong preference), smartweed, pigweed, filaree, and Johnson grass. Crase and DeHaven (1978) noted historical changes in the diet that reflected changes in the importance of various grain crops in California's Central Valley. In areas of sympatry, breeding Red-winged Blackbirds overlap extensively in their diet with Yellow-headed and Brewer's blackbirds, but they feed their young more diverse prey than Yellow-headeds do. Foraging differences between these species are expressed largely through temporal and habitat patch use differences (Orians 1980; see other accounts). Sexual foraging differences indicate that males eat more rice, cultivated grain, and plant matter and less wild seed than do females (Crase & DeHaven 1978—see also for additional information on dietary differences between the various species of blackbirds).

Marin Breeding Distribution

During the atlas period, Red-winged Blackbirds bred widely in the lowlands of Marin County. The few gaps in the distribution primarily reflected their absence from steep or heavily forested terrain. Representative breeding locales were Tomales Point (NB 4/13/82 –DS); Olema Marsh (NE 4/30/81 –DS); E end of Chileno Valley (NE

6/4/82 —DS); Hicks Valley (NB 4/22/82 —DS); Stafford Lake, Novato (NE-FL 5/?-6/15/82 —ScC); and Mt. Burdell, Novato (NE 4/21/81 —ITi).

Historical Trends/Population Threats

Because Red-wings are such common breeders in California, it is tempting to think that their status has changed little historically. However, the elimination of over 90% of the marshland around San Francisco Bay and the draining of marshes in interior valleys has undoubtedly caused large local declines in breeding numbers. Irrigation, the planting of grain crops, and the establishment of cattle feed lots have offset these declines to an unknown degree by increasing alternative habitats or enhancing winter survival. Red-wing populations increased on Breeding Bird Surveys in California from 1968 to 1979 (Robbins et al. 1986), but the trend was stable when analysis extended from 1968 to 1989 (USFWS unpubl. analyses).

TRICOLORED BLACKBIRD   *Agelaius tricolor*

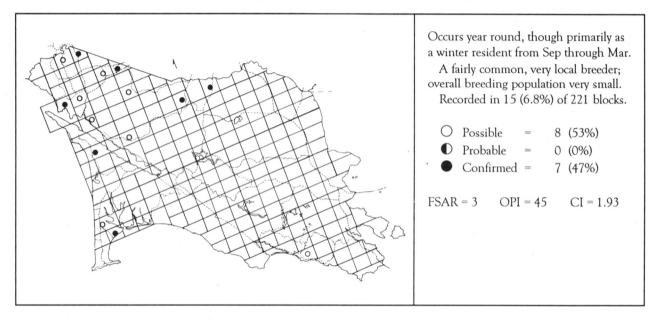

Occurs year round, though primarily as a winter resident from Sep through Mar. A fairly common, very local breeder; overall breeding population very small. Recorded in 15 (6.8%) of 221 blocks.

○	Possible	=	8 (53%)
◑	Probable	=	0 (0%)
●	Confirmed	=	7 (47%)

FSAR = 3   OPI = 45   CI = 1.93

Ecological Requirements

Roving bands of Tricolored Blackbirds nest colonially in the vicinity of fresh water, especially in marshy areas in emergent cattails and tules. As freshwater marsh habitats have declined, an increasing proportion of Tricolor nesting colonies have been found in vegetation such as blackberries, willows and other riparian fringes, thistles, nettles, mustard, mulefat, and planted grains (Orians 1961, DeHaven et al. 1975a, Hosea 1986, Beedy et al. 1991). Although Tricolored Blackbirds may overlap in nesting habitat with marsh-nesting Red-winged or Yellow-headed blackbirds, on average they nest in denser vegetation and will sometimes successfully displace these icterids—by sheer numbers rather than by aggression (Payne 1969). Suitable nesting sites for Tricolors must be surrounded by expanses of open feeding grounds (Orians 1961). Wide-ranging flocks of Tricolors forage at freshwater marshes, pastures, pond margins, agricultural fields, feed lots, riparian fringes, ditch banks, roadsides, weed and brush piles, and, occasionally, scrub habitats (Orians 1961, Beedy & Hayworth in press). Hence the factors necessary for Tricolored Blackbirds to nest successfully are (1) proximity (within four miles or less) to a large productive source area of insect food; (2) protection from potential predators at the nest site, provided by emergent or other vegetation surrounded by a moat of water or by naturally armored plants such as blackberries, thistles, or nettles; (3) a dense sturdy nesting substrate; (4) proximity to fresh water of limited or greater extent (E.C. Beedy, R. DeHaven, & J. Skorupa pers. obs.).

Tricolored Blackbirds usually bind their nests to upright plant stems from a few inches to a few feet above water or ground (Harrison 1978), but they occasionally build them on the ground (Neff 1937). Their deep cup nests are constructed with outer layers of long leaves (such as cattail thatch) woven tightly around supporting stems, whereas the inner layers are coiled stems of grasses and soft plant down (Harrison 1978). A little mud is sometimes added to the inside of the nest (Payne 1969). Tricolor nests are more loosely built than Red-wing nests, and their lining is of green rather than dried grass (Orians 1961, Payne 1969). In the Central Valley, the nests of different breeding colonies vary, but most pairs within the same colony make use of similar locally abundant plant material (Beedy & Hayworth in press).

The Tricolored Blackbird's nomadic, colonial social organization is one of the most unusual ecological adaptations among California's avifauna. This gregarious, gypsy-like lifestyle evolves most frequently in semiarid regions of great climatic fluctuation (Orians 1961). Climatic instability in lowland California is due to the great annual variation in winter rainfall and the extent of flooding. The Tricolored Blackbird is the most intensely colonial of all North American passerine birds (Orians 1980). Under favorable conditions, colonies can host staggering numbers of breeding birds. As many as 20,000 to 30,000 nests have been recorded in an area of ten acres or less (Neff 1937, DeHaven et al. 1975a). One expansive colony was estimated to contain 200,000 nests (Neff 1937)! The difficulty of estimating the number of breeding individuals in a tightly packed colony of this polygynous species is compounded by the fact that many birds that initially attempt to settle may not breed (Orians 1961, Payne 1969), and birds may switch nesting sites within a colony (E.C. Beedy pers. obs.). The colonial nesting of Tricolors evolved as a strategy to maximize exploitation of a locally abundant food supply and perhaps secondarily to avoid predation (Orians 1961, Payne 1969). The evolutionary pressure for predator avoidance has probably increased greatly with the loss and fragmentation of our once vast marshlands.

Since the territories of males average only a yard or two in radius (Orians 1961, 1980) and part of the available nesting habitat generally is left unoccupied, territorial behavior does not limit colony size (Orians 1961). Instead, the size of colonies appears to be related to the availability of food (Orians 1961, Payne 1969). Colony sizes are generally much larger in the heart of the species' range in the Central Valley, where marshlands and rice culture are extensive (Neff 1937, DeHaven et al. 1975a). Colonies tend to be much smaller in the Coast Range, and those in Marin County are no exception. From year to year throughout the range, colony size is unpredictable, many sites are not occupied, and centers of breeding abundance shift substantially (Orians 1961, Payne 1969, DeHaven et al. 1975a, Beedy et al. 1991). Banding studies provide additional evidence of nomadic behavior, indicating that nesting birds are unlikely to breed at sites where they were hatched or where they have nested in previous years (DeHaven et al. 1975b). Evidently Tricolors can move from one colony to another and renest less than ten days after deserting an unsuccessful nest (Payne 1969).

Nomadism and a short nesting cycle enable Tricolors to exploit unoccupied habitats when high-quality food resources become temporarily abundant (Orians 1961, Payne 1969). Although the initiation of nesting often coincides with rainfall or the flooding of fields for planting rice (Payne 1969), nesting appears to be triggered by an abundance of food (Orians 1961, Payne 1969). Evidence suggests that during the first few days of colony establishment, an assessment is made of the food supply available in the surrounding environment by means of mass feeding flights. These feeding flights form the most conspicuous activity around colonies at this time. Male Tricolors do not establish territories until the morning of the day breeding begins; nest building by females takes only four days; and nesting is usually highly synchronous, as all nests within a colony are typically constructed within the period of one week (Orians 1961). Tricolors react quickly to any changes in the surrounding environment affecting food availability, and food sources are apparently communicated to others by the direction from which incoming birds approach the colony. To support large numbers of young, Tricolor adults may travel up to four miles from colonies and exploit 30 square miles of land (Orians 1961); feeding areas also may be shared by birds nesting in different colonies (Payne 1969). Because of the great energy expenditure needed for food gathering, the Tricolor colonial system demands more favorable environmental conditions than the Red-winged Blackbird system (Orians 1961). These more exacting requirements may explain the peculiarly spotty breeding distribution of Tricolors. In addition, the Tricolored Blackbird is one of very few California birds that breed in both spring and, very rarely, fall, although nesting success of autumnal breeding is very low (Orians 1960, 1961; Payne 1969; DeHaven et al. 1975a).

Tricolors forage in large flocks and occasionally mingle with other blackbirds. Although they often fly long distances to seek food, Tricolors typically exploit locally abundant and changing food supplies and minimize the distance of their foraging flights (Crase & DeHaven 1977). They glean insects and seeds from dry ground, flooded fields, mudflats, floating algae mats, and low vegetation; occasionally they hawk insects in midair (Beedy & Hayworth in press). Flocks feeding in grasslands progress smoothly over the ground as birds from the rear fly over the rest of the flock to the front (Orians 1961). In one instance, birds from a Marin colony repeatedly fed by probing into eucalyptus flowers, oriole style (D. Shuford pers. comm.). In breeding season foraging studies in the San Joaquin Valley, animal matter made up 91% of the food volume of nestlings and fledglings (n = 95), 56% of that of adult females (n = 107), and 28% of that of adult males (n = 27) (Skorupa et al. 1980). The animal taxa most often consumed were beetles (63%), lepidopterans (35%), and flies (14%). Plant foods eaten most often included oats

(27%), chickweed (15%), and filaree (9%). Important plant foods in the Sacramento Valley are rice, watergrass, sorghum, and oats (Crase & DeHaven 1978). Payne (1969) reported that at one upland colony two species of rangeland grasshopper accounted for 47% of nestling food. Tricolors appear to be particularly well adapted to take advantage of irregular locust plagues (Orians 1961, Payne 1969). In fall and winter, Tricolors forage in large nomadic flocks and eat about 90% weed seeds and waste grain from agricultural fields (Crase & DeHaven 1978, n = 142).

Colonial breeding and declining wetlands make Tricolors vulnerable to disturbance, and mass desertion of breeding colonies have been reported. DeHaven et al. (1975a) reported that 10%–50% of colonies are partially or completely abandoned each year. These desertions have been attributed to various factors, including bird, mammal, or snake predation (Heermann 1853, Mailliard 1914, Evermann 1919, Neff 1937, Lack & Emlen 1939); excessive wind and rain (Neff 1937, Payne 1969); flooding of marshes; large European Starling roosts' usurping nesting areas (Payne 1969); decreased food supplies (Orians 1961, Payne 1969); poisoning (McCabe 1932, Hosea 1986); and human disturbance (Beedy & Hayworth in press). Recent studies in the Central Valley suggest that contamination by trace elements (such as selenium) are also potential causes of Tricolored Blackbird nesting failures (Grau et al. 1987, Beedy & Hayworth in press). Although nesting failure can occur throughout the breeding season, it is more prevalent early and late in the year, suggesting a relationship to insufficient food supplies for the breeding birds and their young (Orians 1960, 1961; DeHaven et al. 1975a).

Marin Breeding Distribution

Tricolored Blackbirds apparently breed every year in Marin County in small numbers, but, true to their nomadic tendencies, they usually do not breed at the same sites here in consecutive years. Most breeding colonies have been established in the moister ranchlands towards the coast in the general vicinity of Tomales and on the Point Reyes peninsula. Representative breeding locations during the atlas period included: tule marsh at pond at Drake's Beach visitor's center, PRNS (NB-FL 6/8–7/15/80 –JM, LCB, DS); blackberry and thimbleberry thicket in coastal swale at Brazil Ranch, SE of Dillon Beach (NB/DD 4/28/82 –DS); and by a pond near the junction of the Marshall-Petaluma Rd. and Wilson Hill Rd. (NB 5/2/77 –RMS). Post-atlas, Tricolored Blackbirds nested in a freshwater marsh at Cypress Grove near Marshall on Tomales Bay (NB-NE-NY 5/19–6/21/88 and 5/20–6/14/89 –JPK et al.). In 1989, about 85% of that colony was abandoned between 30 May and 2 June.

Historical Trends/Population Threats

It seems safe to assume that, historically, Tricolored Blackbirds have always been relatively uncommon breeders in Marin County. Mailliard (1900) and Stephens and Pringle (1933) considered Tricolors migrants or transients in Marin County. Grinnell and Wythe (1927) reported that they were irregular residents or vagrants in a few parts of the San Francisco Bay region and were "nesting," among other places, on Point Reyes. Their account may refer to Booth's (1926) observation of a colony building nests in a dense growth of raspberry bushes "a short distance north of Point Reyes, Marin County," sometime between 17 and 20 April 1926. Neff (1937) also reported a breeding colony at White's Gulch, Tomales Point, on 14 May 1933. Although the historical record is sketchy, it seems likely that the status of such nomads in peripheral parts of the range, such as Marin County, would be tied to the fortunes of the species in the heart of its range.

Grinnell and Miller (1944) considered Tricolors locally "common to abundant" throughout their California range. They also noted population declines in southern California and increases in the Sacramento Valley "as a result of human management of water supplies." This latter suggestion of increase is apparently traceable to Neff (1937) who had conducted the only major survey of the species up to that time. He felt the species had reached a low ebb after massive draining and reclamation of marshes in the late 1800s and early 1900s, only to later rebound with the establishment of rice culture and extensive irrigation. He felt that by the 1930s Tricolors might have been more abundant than in earlier times because of the recent benefits of irrigation that included an increased food supply, a regaining of lost marshland, and an extension of suitable habitat into formerly arid areas. Surveys conducted from 1969 to 1972 indicated that the breeding range and major nesting areas were unchanged from conditions described by Neff (1937) and other historical workers. Despite a fourfold increase in the previous 30 years in the acreage under rice cultivation, however, the valley population had declined by perhaps more than 50% (DeHaven et al. 1975a). If rice culture and irrigation had been beneficial, it must have been more than offset by other deleterious factors, such as draining of natural marshlands and applications of pesticides and herbicides in agricultural areas.

A recent survey of the Tricolored Blackbird's historical and current status revealed that its population declined by more than 72% from the 1970s to the 1980s and overall by about 89% from the 1930s to 1989 (Beedy et al. 1991). Losses of colonies in the Sacramento and San Joaquin valleys, the heart of the species' historical range, account for much of the overall population decline. Because of this dramatic decline, the Tricolored Blackbird is now a Candidate (Category 2) for federal listing as Threatened or

Endangered (USFWS 1991) and is a Bird Species of Special Concern in California (CDFG 1991a). Tricolored Blackbirds may continue to decline in the future as continued loss of wetlands and other nesting habitat forces them into confined areas, where they are vulnerable to predation, contamination, and other mortality factors. Because the

species relies on patchy superabundant food, the *quality*, not just the extent, of remaining habitat is of paramount importance.

EDWARD C. BEEDY

WESTERN MEADOWLARK *Sturnella neglecta*

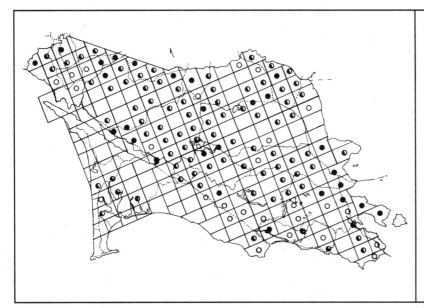

A year-round resident; numbers swell on Pt. Reyes from late Sep through Apr.

A common, widespread breeder; overall breeding population fairly large.

Recorded in 135 (61.1%) of 221 blocks.

○	Possible	=	26 (19%)
◑	Probable	=	83 (62%)
●	Confirmed	=	26 (19%)

FSAR = 4   OPI = 540   CI = 2.00

Ecological Requirements

The rich, powerful flutelike song of the Western Meadowlark penetrates the daydreams of the motorist rolling down the back roads of Marin County's grassy hill country. Since the county's agricultural base is primarily ranching, Meadowlarks breed here mostly in pasturelands and to a limited extent in cultivated fields or weed fields. They prefer lowland valleys and gently rolling hills covered with relatively tall, dense grass. The alluvial soil there presumably is more easily probed for food by their long bills, and dense grass provides protective nest sites. Soil texture appears to be most important, as steep ridges with compact soil, even when luxuriantly clothed with grasses, are generally avoided for breeding. Throughout California, pasturelands are Western Meadowlarks' preferred nesting habitat (Bryant 1914a). Observations elsewhere in California indicate that birds will also nest where grasses and forbs mix with low open brush. Like many other icterids, Western Meadowlarks are polygynous breeders (Lanyon 1957).

Meadowlarks choose shallow depressions in the ground in thick tufts of grass or at the base of bushes for their nest sites. They typically build dome-shaped nests with arched-

over canopies constructed of grasses or the fibers of bark or plant stems, which they may weave into the surrounding grass (Bryant 1914a, Bent 1958). Meadowlarks usually reach the round entrance hole on the side of the nest via a one- to five-foot runway through the grass. Nests are variable, however, and they range from open nests without runways to completely roofed nests with elaborate entrance tunnels (Lanyon 1957). Meadowlarks make their nests proper of dried grasses and line them with finer specimens of the same material. In Wisconsin, Lanyon (1957) found that nests tended to be oriented toward the north or east, in concert with the depression of vegetation in those directions by the prevailing winds.

The diet of Western Meadowlarks in California year round is about 63% animal and 37% vegetable (Bryant 1914a, n = 1920). In the breeding season, food of animal origin accounts for over 95% of the diet, whereas vegetable food, mostly grain, approaches that level of importance from December to February. Adults feed nestlings almost exclusively insects and only an occasional weed seed. Important items of the animal menu are beetles, grasshoppers, crickets, caterpillars, ants, bees and wasps, true bugs, flies, and spiders, along with a few miscellaneous insects, sowbugs, and snails. Meadowlarks also eat carrion when hard pressed (Hubbard & Hubbard 1969). Vegetable fare consists principally of grain, largely wild oats *(Avena fatua)*; Meadowlarks consume lesser amounts of other weed seeds (particularly in Sep and Oct) and occasional grape seeds. Other important grains in California are barley and wheat. Important weed seeds are filaree, tarweed, mustard, tumbleweed, Napa thistle, pigweed, amaranth, canarygrass, Johnson grass, foxtail, sunflower, bur clover, turkey mullein, and nightshade.

Western Meadowlarks forage almost exclusively on the ground. They pick grains and seeds from the ground, not from seed heads, and probe the ground near the base of sprouts to obtain the grain kernel, which may be eaten or just crushed for the "milk." Meadowlarks glean some insects from the surface of the ground and grass and from underneath flipped-over dirt clods or manure. They procure others by probing in the soil (Bryant 1914a). When probing the earth, Meadowlarks first set aside previously obtained food on the ground (Orians & Horn 1969). They then thrust their bills in and open them against the resistance of the soil (Beecher 1951).

Marin Breeding Distribution

During the atlas period, Western Meadowlarks bred widely in Marin County. They avoided the steeper, drier grassy ridges and they inexplicably shunned much of the grassland habitat on Point Reyes for breeding, although they were numerous there in winter. Representative breeding stations were near Tomales (FY 6/8/78 –RMS); Mt. Burdell, Novato (NE 5/?/79 –ScC); and the grassy upland border of Rush Creek marsh, Novato (NY 5/19/81 –DS).

Historical Trends/Population Threats

Historically, Western Meadowlarks may have increased as breeders locally along the San Pablo bayshore where diked marshlands have been converted to grain fields. Conversely, they may have decreased in lowland valleys in eastern Marin that have been transformed by massive development. Western Meadowlark populations decreased on Breeding Bird Surveys in California from 1968 to 1989 (Robbins et al. 1986, USFWS unpubl. analyses).

BREWER'S BLACKBIRD *Euphagus cyanocephalus*

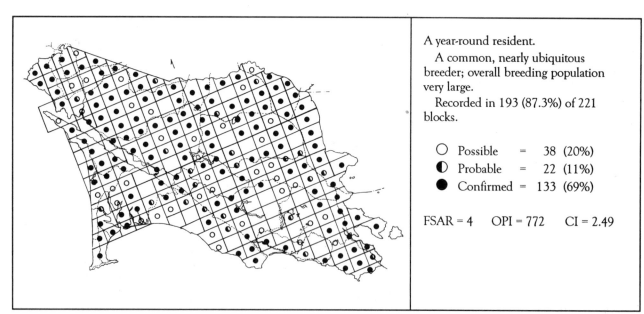

A year-round resident.

A common, nearly ubiquitous breeder; overall breeding population very large.

Recorded in 193 (87.3%) of 221 blocks.

O	Possible	=	38 (20%)
◐	Probable	=	22 (11%)
●	Confirmed	=	133 (69%)

FSAR = 4   OPI = 772   CI = 2.49

Ecological Requirements

This long-legged blackbird is a creature of the wide open spaces. Brewers forage in almost any conceivable open habitat, wet or arid, though they prefer the edges of streams, lakes, and marshes. Foraging areas must have bare or sparsely vegetated ground and very open or non-existent canopies. In the rural areas of Marin County, Brewers forage in grasslands, oak savannah, meadows, streams, lakes, or marsh edges, irrigated croplands, plowed fields, beaches (both above and at the high-tide debris line), weedy fields, feed lots, horse corrals, highway shoulders, campgrounds, picnic areas, and trailhead parking lots. In more developed regions, they inhabit lawns, playing fields, golf courses, abandoned lots, sidewalks, gutters, shopping center and fast-food parking lots, or anywhere else they are likely to get human handouts or inadvertent crumbs. Besides open foraging areas, breeding birds need adequate nesting sites with relatively high perches—such as trees, cliffs, or telephone wires—adjoining them (Horn 1968). Brewers usually nest in small, isolated colonies, but single nests sometimes do occur (Horn 1970). Brewers are polygynous, but unlike Red-winged, Yellow-headed, and Tricolored blackbirds, they do not defend traditional territories (Williams 1952). Multiple nests of a polygynous male may be widely spaced among nests of other males in the colony. Aggressive defense behavior centers around the nest, which the female guards more carefully than the male, and around the perches where males stand guard during nest building and incubation. Although males will defend nests to a degree, they devote most of their energy to the protection of females from the advances of other males. Coloniality in this species has apparently evolved as an adaptation to the exploitation of food resources that are intensely clumped in space and time (Horn 1968). For this reason, nesting colonies are often localized even where potential nesting sites may occur over broad areas. In other instances, colonies are found in isolated stands of suitable breeding habitat.

Although Brewer's Blackbirds sometimes conceal their nests on dry or damp ground in low dense vegetation, they most frequently build them in bushes or trees. Tree nests are usually at moderate heights, though, exceptionally, they may be over 150 feet from the ground (Williams 1958). Nest placement among Brewer's Blackbirds varies considerably, both geographically and between habitats (e.g., Walkinshaw & Zimmerman 1961). In Monterey County, the average height of nests in Monterey pine trees was 25 feet (range 7.5–42 ft., Williams 1958, n = 72). Brewer's Blackbirds usually locate tree nests in dense foliage on horizontal limbs or towards the tips of branches of a wide variety of native and ornamental species (Williams 1958). Rarely, they place nests in trees in cavities at the tops of broken-off stubs or in enlarged abandoned woodpecker holes (Williams 1958, Ritter & Purcell 1983). On occasion, they even choose nest sites in crevices and on ledges of cliffs (Furrer 1975). Besides typical dry-land sites, nests may also be placed over water in bushes, downed brush clumps, or even on wharf pilings (Williams 1958). A variety of other artificial sites have also been used, including support beams, wooden ledges, fence posts, telephone poles, haystacks, and a road grader; such sites seem to be used chiefly early in the season when they offer better concealment than some natural sites (Butler 1981). Brew-

ers appear to favor bushes affording better concealment, and they usually build their nests in the densest parts of bushes (Furrer 1975). Nest sites in bushes over water, though, may apparently trade concealment for lessened accessibility to land predators. In dry uplands, Brewers usually place ground nests near or under small bushes, whereas on moist or even wet ground they usually build them on small hummocks and conceal them in fresh lush vegetation. Although these blackbirds often use several nest types simultaneously, there is generally a predominance of one type in a colony. In sagebrush habitat in Washington, Furrer (1975) found two-thirds of a colony's nests in bushes in dry uplands and the remainder almost equally split between ground sites and bushes over water. He also noted seasonal and yearly differences in proportions of the various nest types. As the season progressed, the number of bush nests declined whereas those in moist ground sites increased, presumably because of the growth and hence availability of concealing herbaceous vegetation. Upland ground nests were of rare occurrence late in a dry year but not in a wet year, apparently because of the persistence of dense vegetation in the latter case. These patterns illustrate the behavioral flexibility of Brewer's Blackbirds in nest site selection in a heterogeneous and unpredictable environment.

Nests are sturdy structures of interlaced twigs, weed stems, grasses, or pine needles that may or may not be mixed with manure and mud that hardens to form a firm plasterlike cup; the nest lining is made of coiled rootlets or hair (Williams 1958, Hansen & Carter 1963).

Of the many foraging habitats mentioned above, Brewers prefer the rich edges of lakes and streams that are devoid of emergent vegetation (Orians 1980). When these aquatic habitats are available, they forage there primarily during midday at the peak of aquatic insect emergence; they forage in dry upland sites in the early morning and late afternoon (Horn 1968, Orians & Horn 1969). Brewers are principally ground foragers. They walk with short forward jerks of the head, picking insects from the ground or from low grasses or sedges. They also forage on relatively flat emergent vegetation or walk or hop with the aid of wings in belly-deep water (Williams 1958). Compared to Red-winged and Yellow-headed blackbirds, Brewers move at a more rapid and steady rate and seldom dig in the turf for hidden prey, scratch, or use their bills in gaping movements to flip over sticks, rocks, or dried dung in search of food (Orians 1980). When foraging in open brushy areas, Brewers either walk under bushes and leap up to secure prey from the branches or walk on top of the shrub canopy, picking visible insects (Orians & Horn 1969, Orians 1980). To a limited extent, Brewers also glean insects from the foliage of their nest trees, flycatch from exposed elevated perches or in short flights from the ground, or hover over the water, snapping food from the surface (Williams 1958). Most foraging takes place in areas adjacent to the colony, but these blackbirds occasionally make feeding flights up to a mile or more from the colony (Walkinshaw & Zimmerman 1961, Horn 1968). When a number of foraging areas are available near a colony, birds usually concentrate in one area at a given time, presumably the most productive one; individuals follow other success-ful birds to prime feeding areas (Horn 1968). Where Brewers occur together with Red-winged and Yellow-headed blackbirds, dietary overlap is high. However, there are temporal differences and considerable separation in the habitat patches used for foraging, with Brewers being the most terrestrial of the three species (Orians & Horn 1969, Orians 1980).

Brewer's Blackbirds are relatively omnivorous, and their diet varies considerably geographically according to habitat and food availability. The diet year round in California is about 32% animal matter and 68% vegetable fare; nest-lings are fed about 89% animal and 11% vegetable food, the latter increasing with nestling age (Beal in Williams 1958, n = 312). For the West as a whole, animal matter ranges from 82% of the diet in summer (n = 453) to 22% in winter (n = 150) (Martin et al. 1951). Important animal foods include caterpillars, flies, grasshoppers, beetles, damselflies and dragonflies, ants, and spiders; items of minor importance are miscellaneous insects, centipedes, sowbugs, and snails (Soriano 1931, Beal 1948, Horn 1968, Orians & Horn 1969, Crase & DeHaven 1978).

Vegetable food in California consists of wild oats, watergrass, cereal grains (especially rice and wheat), and wild forb seeds such as amaranth, fiddleneck, chickweed, sorghum, filaree, knotweed, and currant (Soriano 1931, Crase & DeHaven 1978). In urban-suburban settings, Brewer's Blackbirds readily and widely exploit crumbs and castoffs from the human larder.

Marin Breeding Distribution

During the atlas period, the Brewer's Blackbird was one of the most widespread breeders in Marin County. It concen-trated here in the lowland valleys and was sparse or absent in steep, hilly, or heavily forested terrain. Representative breeding locales were near Abbott's Lagoon (NE 5/11/82 —DS); the edge of Tomales Bay SP (NE 4/29/82 —DS); Chileno Valley (NB 5/5/82 —DS); and Marshall-Petaluma Rd. (NE 5/12/82 —DS).

Historical Trends/Population Threats

Historically, Brewer's Blackbirds have apparently increased considerably in California as a result of clearing of brush and trees, cultivation of crops, irrigation, and livestock husbandry (G&M 1944, Williams 1958). They probably also increased in the past in urban-suburban areas because of the amenities inadvertently provided. On the other hand, populations of this blackbird decreased on Breeding Bird Surveys in California from 1968 to 1989 (USFWS unpubl. analyses).

BROWN-HEADED COWBIRD *Molothrus ater*

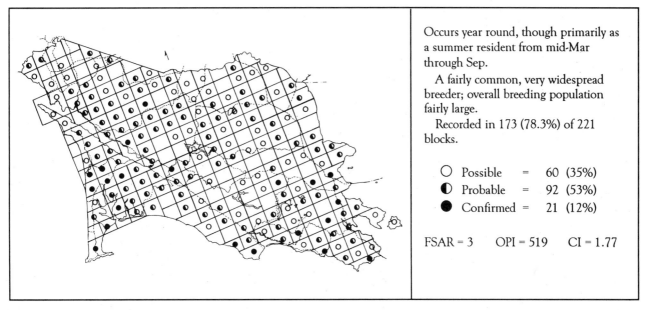

Occurs year round, though primarily as a summer resident from mid-Mar through Sep.

A fairly common, very widespread breeder; overall breeding population fairly large.

Recorded in 173 (78.3%) of 221 blocks.

○ Possible   =   60 (35%)
◑ Probable   =   92 (53%)
● Confirmed =   21 (12%)

FSAR = 3   OPI = 519   CI = 1.77

Ecological Requirements

As with many facets of the Brown-headed Cowbird's biology, its use of various habitats is shaped by its parasitic mode of reproduction. Because breeding Cowbirds are not tied to a particular nest where they must deliver parental care, they are free to carry out different daily activities in widely disjunct areas (Rothstein et al. 1986). In the morning, Cowbirds are dispersed throughout a wide variety of habitats where potential hosts are common. The greatest morning abundance occurs in riparian vegetation (Rothstein et al. 1980), but Cowbirds are likely to spend the morning in almost any habitat, including freshwater marshes, grasslands with occasional trees or shrubs, or even suburban and urban areas such as the San Francisco Bay region. While they are rare in unbroken stands of chaparral and dense forests, they commonly use forest edges or open woodland. Female Cowbirds spend their morning time in these habitats searching for host nests, while males try to court females and compete with one another for social dominance (Rothstein et al. 1984). Relatively little feeding is done during the morning. Females and some males occupy the same morning home range throughout the breeding season and even in successive seasons (Dufty 1982). Many males, however, seem to wander over large areas. These may be mostly subordinate yearling males prospecting for potential breeding sites.

Most individuals leave their morning breeding ranges between 10 a.m. and 1 p.m. and commute up to 4 miles or more to feeding sites, where they forage in flocks of 25 or more through the rest of the day (Rothstein et al. 1984). Most feeding sites consist of artificial habitat, such as horse corrals, feed lots, bird feeders, lawns, and campgrounds. As their name implies, Cowbirds have a strong preference for foraging near livestock (Friedmann 1929), which, as foraging associates, provide Cowbirds with several sources of food—insects attracted by livestock and their manure, insects flushed by livestock feeding in short grass, and grain and hay at corrals and feedlots. Cowbirds sometimes perch on cows or horses and, on occasion, feed on insects and possibly ticks in the fur of these associates. They also feed on table scraps at campgrounds. Most feeding occurs on the ground, but Cowbirds will readily visit bird feeders well above the ground. They usually catch insects while walking on the ground, often after dashing after these prey. Cowbirds rarely glean insects from foliage, but they occasionally flycatch. Grasshoppers seem especially prevalent in their diet, although the long list of arthropods consumed (Friedmann 1929) suggests that Cowbirds will eat anything they can catch. Plant matter in their diet consists mostly of the seeds of grasses and other plants. Fruit is eaten rarely. In the winter, the diet is mostly plant matter, and there is a shift to animal matter during breeding. This shift is much more pronounced in females, for whom the animal proportion may greatly exceed 50% (Ankney & Scott 1980). The dietary shift is related to the female's increased need for protein while laying eggs. Females also seem to make special efforts to consume calcium-rich food items, such as snails, probably to secure material for eggshells. In the few observations available, females ate the eggs they took from host nests, and this may also be an important source of protein and calcium.

401

The Cowbird's commuting behavior means that it is abundant at some sites, such as horse corrals, in the afternoon, yet totally absent from the same site in the morning. The total daily home range of many Cowbirds, including breeding and feeding sites used, is enormous and ranges up to 990 acres or more, compared with the 2.4 to 7.4 acres used by most birds of their size (1-1.8 oz.) (Rothstein et al. 1984). Even the morning ranges alone can average nearly 170 acres and can extend for more than 0.6 to 1.2 miles. In areas with little artificial foraging habitat, a single site, such as a horse corral, can provide food for the hundreds of Cowbirds breeding over a surrounding area of more than 90 square miles. But Cowbirds are not limited to using the commuting pattern (Rothstein et al. 1986). In areas where there are many feeding sites (e.g., backyard feeders), Cowbirds may feed and breed in the same locality. In such cases, one rarely sees large afternoon flocks. In short, breeding Cowbirds are remarkably opportunistic in their use of space (Rothstein et al. 1986, 1987) and have an extraordinary ability to find feeding sites. In the nonbreeding season, they tend to occur in large flocks, often with other blackbirds and Starlings. These flocks are usually located near the same type of feeding sites that Cowbirds prefer during the breeding season.

The enormous literature on the Cowbird's use of hosts has been summarized by Herbert Friedmann and his associates (Friedmann 1929, 1963; Friedmann et al. 1977; Friedmann & Kiff 1985). Throughout its North American range, the Cowbird has been known to parasitize 220 species and to have its chicks reared successfully by 144 of these. Generalizations regarding host use are often difficult to make because there is considerable geographic variation in this parameter. For example, Cowbirds heavily parasitize Red-winged Blackbirds on the Great Plains but rarely in California. Perhaps the strongest generalization is that Cowbirds may parasitize any passerine in their breeding range, except the larger corvids. Intensively parasitized species range in size from *Empidonax* flycatchers to meadowlarks. Although cavity nesters are occasionally parasitized, most hosts are open cup-nesting species of tyrant flycatchers, thrushes, vireos, wood warblers, orioles and blackbirds, tanagers, sparrows, and finches. There are even occasional bizarre cases of Cowbird eggs being found in the nests of certain ducks and hawks, species that could never rear a Cowbird. This extremely generalized host use extends even to the individual level: the best evidence to date, based on biochemical data, shows that a single female will parasitize several species during a season (Fleischer 1985). Host use has been studied much more extensively in the Midwest and the East than in California. In California, the best data on recorded host species and the percentage of nests parasitized within certain samples of nests or family groups come from the Sierra Nevada (Friedmann et al. 1977, Gaines 1977, Rothstein et al. 1980, Verner &

Ritter 1983, Airola 1986). In suburban Santa Barbara, Hooded Orioles are parasitized much more heavily than any other species (S.I. Rothstein pers. obs.). As for coastal northern California, frequent hosts include Pacific-slope Flycatcher, Warbling Vireo, Common Yellowthroat, Wilson's Warbler, Song Sparrow, and White-crowned Sparrow (Friedmann 1963, R.M. Stewart & D. Shuford pers. obs.).

Cowbird parasitism is usually detrimental to the host's own reproductive output. The adult females remove one host egg for each one to two eggs they lay (Friedmann 1963). The Cowbird nestling is usually larger than its host nestmates and therefore outcompetes them, both as a result of its larger size and of its relatively short (11-12 day) incubation period. Small hosts with long incubation periods, such as *Empidonax* flycatchers and some vireos, rarely fledge any of their own young if parasitized. Larger hosts such as the Hooded Oriole, Brewer's Blackbird, and Song Sparrow—or small ones with short incubation periods such as the Yellow Warbler—often succeed in raising some of their own young. Because the great majority of passerines feed their young the same diet of small, usually soft-bodied insects, dietary quality is seldom a critical variable in Cowbird-host dynamics. However, diet is a major factor for Cowbirds among those few host passerines that use fruit or seeds to feed their young, most notably the cardueline finches. Cowbird nestlings usually starve to death in the nests of species such as the House Finch.

Cowbird parasitism is a potent evolutionary pressure on most host species, and some such as the American Robin and Northern Oriole have evolved rejection of Cowbird eggs. Nearly all individuals of these "rejecter" species (or at least the females) eject Cowbird eggs from their nests (Rothstein 1975, 1977). But most species are "accepters" and show nearly 100% tolerance of Cowbird eggs, even if these are highly divergent in size and coloration from their own eggs. A few species, such as the Yellow Warbler, are somewhat intermediate and only reject Cowbird eggs laid early in their nesting cycle (in this warbler's case, by burying the Cowbird egg under nesting material, Clark & Robertson 1981). Another possible defense against parasitism is to drive away Cowbirds before they can lay in a nest. Some hosts seem to recognize Cowbirds and are particularly aggressive toward them (Robertson & Norman 1977). It is unclear whether such aggression is effective for small hosts because it may draw attention to host nests, thereby increasing the risk of parasitism (Smith et al. 1984). In California, host aggression seems especially strong in the Western Wood-Pewee, American Robin, Northern Oriole, and Red-winged Blackbird (S.I. Rothstein pers. obs.).

Female Cowbirds lay eggs on 60%-80% of the days during their two- to three-month breeding season for a total of 35 or more eggs. This number of eggs laid far surpasses that for any other species of wild bird (Scott & Ankney 1983), except possibly one of the other four species of parasitic Cowbirds. The high laying rate has been found in all three subspecies of the Cowbird and in a wide variety of habitats ranging from lowland agricultural areas to the High Sierra (Rothstein et al. 1986). The huge egg mass each female lays may impose slight physiological costs (Keys et al. 1986, Fleischer et al. 1987) but is achieved without depletion of major body reserves of calcium, protein, and other resources (Ankney & Scott 1980). Their great reproductive effort may explain why females have higher mortality rates than males (Darley 1971), which in turn explains why males are one and a half to three times more numerous than females. Males may *seem* to be even more than three times as abundant as females, because the latter are very secretive in the morning.

Cowbird parasitism has the potential to limit or even extirpate host populations. Declines in a number of California songbirds, especially the Bell's Vireo and Willow Flycatcher, are correlated with increases in Cowbird abundance (Gaines 1974). Other species affected in the state include the Yellow Warbler, Yellow-breasted Chat, Blue Grosbeak, Warbling Vireo, and, particularly in southern California, Wilson's Warbler. Current efforts to save California's endangered Least Bell's Vireo include extensive control programs to remove large numbers of Cowbirds from the host's few remaining breeding sites. It is important to note, though, that all the California species that now seem endangered by Cowbird parasitism were reduced to small populations by humans' massive habitat destruction during this century. Loss of habitat, rather than Cowbird parasitism, may be the main culprit in the decline of species such as the Bell's Vireo. On the other hand, the Cowbird may be delivering the coup de grace to these species; other riparian nesters, ones less susceptible to Cowbird parasitism, are not threatened with extirpation (the exception is the Yellow-billed Cuckoo). Cowbird control should be viewed as a stopgap measure to be employed until the more difficult goal of habitat restoration is achieved. In any event, it may prove to be surprisingly difficult to control Cowbird numbers in some areas (Rothstein et al. 1987). Furthermore, the longest-running Cowbird control program has produced mixed results. The tens of thousands of Cowbirds that have been killed on the Michigan breeding grounds of the endangered Kirtland's Warbler since 1972 may have kept the warbler from extinction, but its population has shown no increase (Kelly & DeCapita 1982). See Laymon (1987) for further discussion of Cowbird management options in California.

Marin Breeding Distribution

Cowbirds are now widespread breeders in Marin County. During the atlas period, the greatest concentrations occurred in the lowland valleys and gentle rolling hills of ranchlands on the Point Reyes peninsula and to the east in the central and northern sections of the county. Representative breeding stations were Fish Docks, Point Reyes (FL/FY by White-crowned Sparrow 5/29/81 –DS); Drake's Beach, Point Reyes (FL/FY by White-crowned Sparrow 6/30/80 –DS); Bolinas (FL/FY by Song Sparrow 8/9/82 –DS); and Simmons Trail, Mt. Tamalpais (FL/FY by Black-throated Gray Warbler 7/6/81 –DS).

Historical Trends/Population Threats

As is true for all of North America (Mayfield 1965), Cowbirds in California have increased in abundance and distribution more than any other native bird species (Rothstein et al. 1980). Before this century, Cowbirds in California were apparently limited to the Colorado River, where the Dwarf Cowbird *(M. a. obscurus)* occurred, and parts of the Great Basin (Modoc Plateau, Mono Lake area, and possibly the Owens Valley), where the Sage Brush Cowbird *(M. a. artemisiae)* occurred. The latter population has undergone a small increase on the east side of the Sierra-Cascade axis, while the former has colonized virtually all of California west of the Sierra-Cascade crest. While generally absent from the crest itself, Cowbirds appear to disperse across it resulting in so much interbreeding between the two subspecies that these are now less distinct than earlier in the century (Fleischer & Rothstein 1988, Fleischer et al. 1991).

The first breeding records for Los Angeles and Ventura counties, respectively, are from 1905 and 1904 (Willett 1912), and Cowbirds were common in the Los Angeles basin by the 1930s (Willett 1933). Cowbirds increased in the Central Valley by 1927, if not earlier (G&M 1944). In coastal northern California, breeding was first documented near Irvington, Alameda County, in 1922, and there were a number of additional records in the next few years (G&W 1927, Sibley 1952). Although not reported in Stephens and Pringle's (1933) summary of the county's avifauna, Cowbirds were first recorded in Marin on 15 October 1930 on the Tennessee Cove Road, and Cowbird eggs were found in an American Goldfinch nest at Point Reyes Station sometime prior to 1936 (*Gull* 18, No. 6). Another early Cowbird record for Marin was of a sighting at Inverness on 13 May 1934 (Stephens 1936). Grinnell and Miller (1944) reported a phenomenal increase in the population in the San Francisco Bay region (and elsewhere), and Pray (1950) reported continued expansion of breeding numbers there. Laymon (1987) reported that after the first records in an area there is generally a 10-year lag until the first major influx is noted and 20 years until population saturation is reached. Rothstein et al. (1980) documented the expansion of Cowbird populations in the Sierra Nevada since 1930 and indicated that increases were probably still occurring. This contention was supported by continued population increases on Breeding Bird Surveys in California from 1968 to 1979 (Robbins et al. 1986), though numbers were relatively stable when analysis extended to the period 1968 to 1989 (USFWS unpubl.). Cowbirds may still find opportunities to increase in coastal California, especially in the more remote forested regions, as human developments begin to encroach on wild lands. See Laymon (1987) for further details of historical changes in California.

Much and possibly all of this phenomenal increase was caused by habitat alterations by humans. Just about every environmental change inflicted on California, other than the paving over of downtown urban areas, has made the environment more favorable for Cowbirds. Such changes include the irrigation of arid regions, the dispersal of free-ranging livestock, and the establishment of horse corrals in wilderness areas. While the widespread destruction of riparian vegetation has taken away some prime breeding habitat for Cowbirds, the equally widespread planting of trees in fruit orchards and around houses, as in the Central Valley and perhaps some coastal valleys, has created new habitat in areas that previously could support few Cowbirds.

Remarks

Besides its range extension and interactions with host species, other facets of the Cowbird's biology have prompted numerous studies. Studies of the development

and use of the male's song have shown that Cowbirds have a complex society (West et al. 1981). Studies of another male vocalization, the flight whistle, have demonstrated a well-defined system of local dialects (Rothstein & Fleischer 1987). Despite the lack of parental care, Cowbirds in California are monogamous, and the females seem to be more faithful to their mates than is the case in most nonparasitic songbirds (Yokel 1986, Yokel & Rothstein 1991). Cowbirds have a strange behavior in which they suddenly run up to other birds and then freeze in a head-bowed posture (Selander & LaRue 1961, Rothstein 1980). If the other bird is of another species, it often then preens the Cowbird. Even birds such as Red-winged Blackbirds, though not known to preen members of their own species, will preen Cowbirds. Although Cowbirds sometimes give this display to other Cowbirds, it almost never results in preening then. This display is most easily seen in wintering flocks while Cowbirds are perched in trees or bushes.

While the Cowbird will not win any popularity contests, its spectacular range expansion, its adaptations for parasitism, and its highly social nature have made it one of the most frequently studied North American birds. Surely it is one of the most interesting birds in any region in which it occurs.

STEPHEN I. ROTHSTEIN

HOODED ORIOLE *Icterus cucullatus*

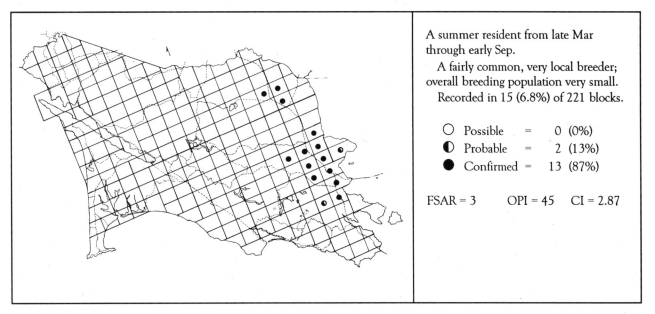

A summer resident from late Mar through early Sep.

A fairly common, very local breeder; overall breeding population very small. Recorded in 15 (6.8%) of 221 blocks.

○	Possible	=	0	(0%)
◑	Probable	=	2	(13%)
●	Confirmed	=	13	(87%)

FSAR = 3   OPI = 45   CI = 2.87

Ecological Requirements

Though near opposites in vocal ability and intensity of plumage, the Hooded Oriole and Northern Mockingbird share a common thread of history—a spectacular northward expansion in California following the planting of ornamental, shade, and fruit trees in settled areas. Formerly, Hooded Orioles bred in parts of southern California in broadleaved woodlands—of native fan palms, willows, cottonwoods, and especially sycamores—along watercourses, canyons, and dry arroyos (G&M 1944). These orioles still nest in native fan palms in southern California deserts, but coastal breeders now seldom breed in the sycamore groves they originally favored there (Pleasants 1979, Unitt 1984). Instead, coastal birds have colonized residential areas and parks in urban and suburban centers and, to a lesser extent, orchards and trees about rural dwellings. In these developed areas, fan palms are the overwhelming choice of these orioles for nest sites and nest materials. Hooded Orioles began to colonize central and northern California in the 1930s, again establishing themselves primarily in urban and suburban areas well supplied with planted fan palms (G&M 1944).

In Marin County, studies from 1976 to 1991 confirmed the marked dependence here of Hooded Orioles on Washington fan palms for nest sites and, particularly, nest materials (H. Peake unpubl. data). The distribution and density of Hooded Orioles in Marin is closely tied to the availability of suitable fan palms in residential yards and gardens, parks, and along roadways. In fact, nearly all Hooded Oriole nest sites here can be referred to by street address. The orioles prefer nest palms that have nearby,

but not touching, trees that serve as approach and departure routes. Palms are rarely used as nest sites if they stand in isolation from other trees or if they touch other trees, wires, or buildings that might provide access for terrestrial predators. The male stands sentry in nearby trees to guard the nest tree during the month-long incubation and nestling period. After the female has begun nest building, the male rarely lands on the nest palm until joining in the feeding of newly hatched young. Other ornamental (and sometimes native) trees and bushes provide cover for adults and fledged young, substrate for insect foraging, nectar-producing flowers, and fruit. Sugar-water feeders furnish an additional energy source, and bird baths are attractions for bathing rather than drinking.

Based on several hundred nests found in Marin County from 1977 to 1991, the preferred nest tree here is the California fan palm *(Washingtonia filifera)*. This native palm of the state's southern deserts harbors an abundance of blond filaments that fray from the edges of leaf segments. The use of these filaments as the basic ingredient for nest building explains much of the Hooded Oriole's local nesting patterns. Females that nest in palms without fibers, or in other types of trees, will carry back to their chosen nest trees filaments from other suitable palms up to several hundred yards away. The second choice for nest trees here is the Mexican fan palm *(Washingtonia robusta)*, but only some individuals of this palm sparingly produce filaments. The third choice for nest sites in Marin is the Canary (Island) date palm *(Phoenix canariensis)*, a feather rather than a fan palm, which lacks leaf filaments. Fourth

405

choice is the fortune or windmill palm *(Trachycarpus excelsa),* a fan palm from China, which also lacks leaf filaments but has a coarse, hairlike covering on its seemingly inverted trunk (smaller at the base and wider at the top). The season's first nests are often on the east side of the selected palm, the second nest on the west side; successive nests sometimes are built on adjoining leaves. In only one known instance (in San Francisco) did orioles reuse a nest that earlier in the season had produced young (H. Peake pers. obs.).

Females here appear to always start the season by nesting in palms, but sometimes they later switch to other infrequently used nest trees. In Marin County, less than 20 nests were found in nonpalm trees including blue gum eucalyptus *(Eucalyptus globulus),* American elm *(Ulmus americana),* monkey puzzle tree *(Araucaria imbricata),* western catalpa *(Catalpa speciosa),* green dracena *(Coryline australis),* and cypress. Conceivably, competition for available California fan palms might lead to the orioles' selecting alternative trees, but breeches of security seem to be the most frequent reason, especially during nest construction. Females in San Rafael that built three or four nests in one season apparently did so because perceived threats (including this observer) made them reject their original nest site and sometimes select nest trees other than California fan palms. The height of the several hundred nests observed in Marin County ranged from 6 feet in a young *filifera* to 90 feet in a mature *robusta,* though most were built 35 to 40 feet up in mature *filifera.*

No matter what the tree species selected as a nest site, virtually all Marin nests were made solely from the blond leaf filaments of Washington fan palms. Of a dozen or so nests examined closely, coarser fibers were used for the outside of the nest and finer filaments for the lining. The one exception to the exclusive use here of palm leaf filaments for nest construction was a female that built two nests in a fortune palm using the hairy fibers from its trunk. In fan palms, the new growth of leaves emanates vertically from the bud at the top of the trunk like a slow motion fountain from the top of an upright pipe. The palm fronds bend out and curve down more each year until they dry, turn tan, and clasp against the palm trunk, forming a skirt of dead leaves. Females typically select nest sites in the lower half of tree crowns, where the broad green palm leaves have assumed a somewhat horizontal, umbrella-like arc that protects the nests from sun, rain, and overhead predators. Fan palm leaves are pleated and split from the tip to the midpoint into 50 to 70 narrow pointed leaf segments with filaments fraying from the edges. The female typically builds the nest on the underside of the unsplit part of a green palm leaf. The lower browning leaves are rarely used, though females occasionally place their nests under the dried leaves of the palm skirt. In San Rafael, one brood was lost when the female chose for the first nest a

leaf that was turning brown. A June heat wave appeared to hasten the leaf's drying, causing it to clasp down tight against the trunk three or four days before the young would have left the nest under more favorable circumstances. Female orioles at Dominican College in San Rafael tend to build nests in palm skirts more frequently than do females at other sites in Marin, perhaps because the leaf crowns there are more open and provide less protection than those elsewhere. Marin's "100-year freeze" of December 1990 and January 1991 killed the palm leaves in the lower half of most palm tree crowns, the area where the orioles prefer to nest. Consequently, in the 1991 nesting season, most orioles used for nest sites the second choice, dried leaf skirts hanging down against *Washingtonia filifera* trunks (H. Peake pers. obs.).

In typical nest construction in Washington fan palms, the female flies up under the selected green leaf and clings like a fly on a ceiling. She pokes holes up through the leaf, using her sharp slender beak both as punch and awl, twisting her head left and right to enlarge these holes. Flying to another palm leaf on her tree, or often to another *filifera,* she plucks a blond filament. Returning to her nest leaf, she pokes and pushes the filament up through a hole, then flying to the upper side of the leaf, pulls some length of the filament up, then pokes the end down through another hole, literally sewing the nest anchors to the leaf. Upon completion, the anchoring threads suspend the elongate, semipensile nest hammocklike, snug to the underside of the leaf. Arrival and departure is made through two, or occasionally only one, open sides of the nest close to the palm leaf. Females building in Canary date palms stitch less and wrap more of the filaments around the stems of the leaf segments to secure the nest. Females nesting in other trees that lack the strong petioles (stems) of the Washingtonia palms stitch two or more leaves together with filaments to provide the protective "awning" for the nest. Such is the case with nests in fortune palm, blue dracena, American elm, common catalpa, and young blue gum eucalyptus.

Throughout most of California, Hooded Orioles now select fan palms overwhelmingly as their nest tree of first choice, though formerly other tree species must also have been important when the birds nested extensively in broadleaved woodlands. Other trees these orioles have used as nest sites in California, in addition to those mentioned above, include pepper, walnut, live oak, banana plant, tree yucca, cottonwood, fig, sycamore, maple, mesquite, olive, ash, acacia, umbrella tree, and avocado; exceptional nests were one in ornamental vines on a porch and another suspended from a single fiber strand wedged in a crack under the eaves of a house (Illingsworth 1901, Bailey 1910, G&M 1944, H.W. Grinnell 1944, Huey 1944, Bent 1958, Unitt 1984, S. Fitton in litt.). Hurd (in Bent 1958) noted, contrary to observations in Marin County, that Hooded Orioles in Riverside selected mostly eucalyptus trees for first nest attempts and palm trees for second nest attempts. In the Arcata/Eureka area along the moist coast of Humboldt County, where Washington fan palms are few and less well developed than at most interior sites where Hooded Orioles breed, the orioles nest almost exclusively in date palms, usually on the leeward side (S. Fitton pers. comm.). The growth form of date palms in Humboldt County is such that often fronds touch each other, providing protected areas where nests are built.

No matter what nest tree they select in California, these orioles almost exclusively prefer palm leaf filaments, primarily from Washington fan palms, for nest material. The Arcata/Eureka area again is an exception. Females there frequently use (singly or in combination) both Washington fan palm filaments and fibers hammered loose from the fronds of date palms; one nest there was made entirely from grass (S. Fitton in litt.). Other nest materials Hooded Orioles have used infrequently in California are the white hairs of "old man" cactus *(Cephalocerus senilis)*, dodder (an orange-colored parasitic vine) (H.W. Grinnell 1944, Bent 1958), and, as mentioned above, the hairy fibers from the trunks of fortune palms; other coarse fibers, such as those of yucca, used elsewhere in the species' range, are probably also used here on occasion. California nests are usually either lined with finer palm fibers or are left unlined; occasionally they are scantily lined with felted vegetable down or a few feathers (Dawson 1923). On one rare occasion, a female in San Rafael landed on the ground to procure some tissue paper, presumably for nest material (H. Peake pers. obs.).

Nest sites and nest materials in California vary considerably from those in Arizona and Texas. In these latter states, palm (or palmetto) trees are used for nest sites and materials less frequently than in California, and nesting is usually concentrated in deciduous woodlands along lowland stream courses (Bent 1958, Phillips et al. 1964, Oberholser 1974). In Texas, Hooded Orioles frequently build their nests in and of Spanish moss *(Tillandsia)*; nests may be placed in living trusses of this plant or in the lower limbs and drooping outer branches of undergrowth where pieces of Spanish moss are brought for nest construction. Nests there are also built in bushes using a black hairlike moss or in yuccas using the tough fibers from the trunk, also used in Arizona. In Arizona, nests are often placed in deciduous trees (frequently secured in clumps of mistletoe), and wiry grasses are favorite nest materials (Bent 1958); one nest in the desert was built entirely of horsehair (Huey 1944). The lining of nests seems to be more commonly practiced in Arizona and Texas; lining materials include dry moss, grasses, wool, horsehair, yucca fibers, Spanish moss, plant down, and sometimes a few feathers.

Where studied in San Rafael, Hooded Orioles forage mostly from 5 to 40 feet above the ground, methodically gleaning insects and caterpillars from the foliage and branchwork of trees and bushes. Rarely, they flycatch from a perch and at dusk pursue insects attracted to porch lights, catching their prey in flight (H. Peake pers. obs.). Although consumption of grasshoppers (Bent 1958) suggests they forage on the ground, this behavior has never been observed in Marin County (H. Peake pers. obs.), though elsewhere it apparently occurs rarely (Bent 1958). The diet is poorly documented, though a variety of insects, caterpillars, and probably spiders are consumed (Bent 1958). Hooded Orioles probe or puncture tubular flowers for nectar and drink sugar water from hummingbird type feeders regularly; they also consume fruit, especially figs and loquats, in season. These foods appear to be eaten by the young only after leaving the nest. In San Rafael on 10 November 1990, a female Hooded Oriole hungrily ate seeds while resting on her belly at a backyard feeder (H. Peake pers. obs.). This atypical feeding behavior was probably a reaction to food stress at a time when most of these orioles are wintering in Mexico.

Marin Breeding Distribution

During the atlas period, Hooded Orioles were found breeding only in the urban corridor along Highway 101 from Novato south to the Corte Madera/Larkspur area. This distribution matched that of extensive plantings of palm trees in the county's least fog-shrouded suburban and urban areas. Representative nesting locations during the atlas period included Warren Court, San Rafael (NY/FY 5/7/82 —HoP); Greenwood Ave., San Rafael (NY/FY 8/3/82 —HoP); and Lamont Ave., Novato (NE 5/6/79 —DS et al.).

In Marin County, Hooded Orioles concentrate in east and west Corte Madera and in central and northern San Rafael. In one week in May 1983, a search of much of central and southern Marin located 50 active nests—10 in Corte Madera and 40 in San Rafael (H. Peake unpubl. data). Distribution was determined by the availability of preferred palm nesting sites—42 nests were in *Washingtonia filifera*, 5 in *W. robusta* (a.k.a. *gracilis*), and 3 in the Canary (Island) date palm. Only a handful of Washington fan palms were scattered south of Corte Madera. To the north, when palms were clustered, nests were separated by 100 feet or more, except in one instance in which single nests were in two palms 30 feet apart. Areas of greatest oriole density were old (central) San Rafael and around Dominican College, where 22 active nests were located in an area of about two square miles; and Terra Linda with 13 active nests and Santa Venetia with 5 active nests, the two areas totalling about one square mile. Potential nesting sites with fan palms in Marinwood, Hamilton Field, Bel Marin Keys, and Novato were not included in the survey.

Hooded Orioles have nested in two areas with fan palms in Novato, one west of Highway 101 south of Delong Avenue and a second east of Highway 101 and south of Atherton Avenue (D. Shuford pers. comm.); there are few fan palms elsewhere in Novato, though it has a suitable climate. Veteran Marin nurserymen suggested that the limited distribution of palms in Novato was perhaps due to its development mostly in the post–World War II era, when landscape budgets were reduced and people were discouraged from planting palms on small lots because of the difficulty of the necessary tree care. Fan palms, especially *W. filifera*, are generally unsuccessful in moist and foggy coastal climates because of their susceptibility to crown rot (Maino & Howard 1955). This probably explains the scarcity of *filifera* in Mill Valley, Sausalito, and the outer coast and, hence, the lack of nesting Hooded Orioles in these areas as well.

Historical Trends/Population Threats

During this century, the Hooded Oriole has spread spectacularly northward as a breeder in both Arizona (Phillips et al. 1964) and California (G&M 1944, Sibley 1952, ABN). In California's San Joaquin Valley, notable sightings were in Fresno, Fresno County, in 1915 and in Modesto, Stanislaus County, in 1937 (G&M 1944). In the 1920s, Hooded Orioles reached the main limit of their breeding range on the California coast at Santa Barbara (Dawson 1923). These orioles were initially reported in the San Francisco Bay Area in Alameda, Contra Costa, and Santa Clara counties in 1930; first nesting records were from Santa Cruz in 1932 and San Leandro, Alameda County in 1939 (G&M 1944, Sibley 1952). There were no records for Marin County as of 1933 (S&P 1933), but breeding was first reported here at Larkspur on 22 May 1941 with the observation of a nest with young (*Gull* 23:21). Hooded Orioles continued to increase around the Bay Area with first reports for San Francisco in 1939

(Sibley 1952) and Napa and Solano counties in 1948 (AFN 2:187). Reports in *Audubon Field Notes* and *American Birds* documented widespread increases of the oriole population in the 1950s and 1960s along the coast and in the San Joaquin and Sacramento valleys. These orioles made a notable northward expansion on the coast by colonizing Humboldt County and breeding in Ferndale in 1972 (Yocum & Harris 1975, AB 26:903). Nesting was attempted in Arcata, Humboldt County, in 1981 (AB 35:977) and by 1985 a search of the Arcata/Eureka area revealed 40+ birds (AB 39:961). Expansion also continued northward in the Central Valley, highlighted by the discovery of 24 birds in the Anderson/Redding area of Shasta County from 26 to 31 May 1985 (AB 39:348). Such expansions are now of limited extent, as indicated by relatively stable numbers of Hooded Orioles on Breeding Bird Surveys in California from 1968 to 1989 (USFWS unpubl. analyses). In the coming years, Hooded Orioles will likely continue to expand locally as palm plantings increase in suburban and urban areas, and they will likely consolidate their holdings at the edge of their range as well. It is unlikely that they will expand much farther to the north, though, as they have now reached the limit of extensive palm plantings.

On a local scale, at least, numbers of Hooded Orioles breeding in Marin County declined steadily over the course of the five-year drought from 1986-87 to 1990-91. Presumably because of the combination of the heavy freeze in the winter of 1990-91 and the fifth year of a drought, Hooded Oriole numbers in San Rafael in 1991 reached there lowest point since studies began there in 1976, and apparently no young were produced (H. Peake unpubl. data). It will be interesting to see if nesting numbers rebound when wetter climatic conditions return.

HOLLY PEAKE

NORTHERN ORIOLE *Icterus galbula*

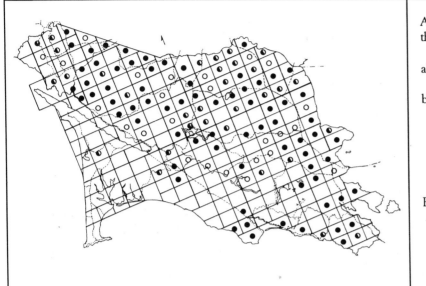

A summer resident from late Mar through early Sep.

A common, widespread breeder; overall breeding population fairly large.

Recorded in 129 (58.4%) of 221 blocks.

○ Possible	=	25 (19%)
◐ Probable	=	32 (25%)
● Confirmed	=	72 (56%)

FSAR = 4　　OPI = 516　　CI = 2.36

Ecological Requirements

These brightly colored "blackbirds" are inhabitants of Marin County's native oak savannah, oak woodland, and willow riparian habitats in valleys or gently rolling terrain, especially where trees are well spaced or in isolated clumps. They now also nest commonly in planted eucalyptus groves; along the fog-bound coast, they are found breeding almost exclusively, though sparingly, in this habitat. In suburban areas and ranchyards away from the fog belt, they sometimes nest in other introduced plantings with tree spacing similar to their other natural habitats. Marin and California's nesting birds are of the western, Bullock's form of the Northern Oriole.

Nests are situated in a variety of tree species, both native and introduced but locally are most frequently found in deciduous oaks (especially the valley oak), eucalyptus, and willows. Although often found in riparian areas, nests may be built far from available surface water. Concentrations of nesting birds along stream courses and valleys may reflect the appropriate spacing of nest trees and proximity to upslope foraging areas.

While Northern Orioles have been known to build their nests as low as 5 feet and as high as 80 feet or more above the ground, they usually place them between 15 and 50 feet high. The long pendulous nests are most often attached to small hanging branches on the outside of the canopy or alongside vertical or horizontal branches near the top of the canopy of the tree. Mean nest height of Northern Orioles at 20 sites on the Great Plains and in Canada ranged from 12 to 36 feet (mean of means = 26 ft., Schaefer 1976, n = 516). These orioles show geographic variation in nest placement unrelated to taxonomic differences in populations. Nest placement is most easily explained by geographic differences in vegetation. Regionally, though, where squirrel predation is a problem, some nests may be placed high in trees, and in some localities they may be placed on the leeward side of trees to reduce nest damage or loss from strong winds.

Northern Orioles also show geographic variation in the insulative qualities of nests correlated with local temperatures: nests are better insulated from heat in hotter climates (Schaefer 1980). The female weaves the nest of a variety of materials, commonly including grasses, fibers stripped from the stems of a variety of plants (often nettles), and *Ramalina* lichens. Northern Orioles will build their nests almost entirely of horsehair if it is available, and they are attracted by artificial fibers of all kinds, building nests of fishing line, string, yarn (often in bright colors), or even plastic Easter grass, when available.

Nests can occur in clusters, with 20 nests recorded within a 2.5-acre area of oak savannah and up to 5 nests in a single tree. Pairs do not always nest so densely in savannah habitat, and when they settle areas at lower densities, they seem to defend larger territories (Miller 1931b). In areas with a dense canopy and/or understory vegetation, their nests are predictably more dispersed, often with no other pairs or only one other pair in the vicinity. Birds may cluster their nests even when there is no apparent limitation on the availability of suitable nest sites (Williams 1982, 1988). At some sites where only a few trees are available, though, nest-site limitation may force colonial nesting as suggested by Pleasants (1979).

Northern Orioles defend only the immediate vicinity of their nest, and, although they are rarely seen foraging in groups, a number of pairs may overlap in foraging areas away from their nests. Radiotelemetry studies in the Carmel Valley, Monterey County, indicate that solitary nesting females tend to forage alone and near their nests, whereas females with near neighbors may forage up to 985 yards away from their nests at group foraging sites (Williams 1988, 1990). Although Northern Orioles glean insects extensively from the foliage and flowers of trees, they also spend considerable amounts of time foraging in shrubs and grassland. They use a technique common to many species in the subfamily Icterinae, that of "gaping." This technique entails poking the bill into vegetation or the body of an invertebrate and then opening the bill to allow extraction of hidden prey from the crevices of plant tissues or removal of soft tissue from an inedible shell (such as the urticating hairs on the body of a tent caterpillar). They will also remove the stinger from a honey bee before consuming it.

Northern Orioles' diet in California from April to August is about 79% animal matter and 21% vegetable fare (Beal 1910, n = 162). For the West as a whole, their consumption of animal food peaks at 92%–98% in spring and fall (n = 87) and reaches a low of 81% in summer (n= 213) (Martin et al. 1951). Principal food items include caterpillars and lepidoptera pupae—63% of the diet in April but only 8% in July (Beal 1910); beetles, including the cotton boll weevil (Howell 1906)—35% of diet (Beal 1910); bees and ants—15% (Beal 1910); many species of orthopterans, including grasshoppers (Bryant 1914b), camel crickets and species in the genus *Timema*; hemipterans, such as scale insects, stink bugs, leafhoppers, and treehoppers; earwigs (only available since the 1920s); as well as some spiders and, rarely, lizards or mollusks. Vegetable fare includes fruits (mainly in the summer months, especially July), sap, and nectar (Emerson 1904).

Marin Breeding Distribution

During the atlas period, Northern Orioles were widespread breeders in most of Marin County, but they nested at only a few scattered sites on the Point Reyes peninsula. Although there was a general trend of increasing abundance from the coast toward the drier interior, Northern Orioles were numerous breeders in eucalyptus groves even along the shores of Tomales Bay. Representative breeding localities were Bear Valley Headquarters, PRNS (FY 6/1/81 –DS); Bolinas Community Gardens (FY 6/4/76 –DS); Chileno Valley (NB 5/5/82 –DS); Magetti Ranch, Point Reyes–Petaluma Rd. (NY 5/27/82 –DS); Mt. Burdell, Novato (NE 4/21/81 –ITi); and San Antonio Creek, just W of Hwy. 101 (NE 5/17/80 –DS).

Historical Trends/Population Threats

The planting of eucalyptus groves appears to have greatly increased the breeding distribution of Northern Orioles in Marin County in historical times, especially in the low rolling hills and valleys of the grassland-dominated ranchlands to the east and north of Tomales Bay. Besides providing suitable nesting sites and cover in areas formerly largely devoid of trees, eucalyptus also furnish these orioles with a rich source of nectar from their profusely blooming flowers. Populations of Northern Orioles were relatively stable on Breeding Bird Surveys in California from 1968 to 1989 (USFWS unpubl. analyses).

PAMELA L. WILLIAMS

Cardueline Finches
Family *Fringillidae*
Subfamily *Carduelinae*

PURPLE FINCH   *Carpodacus purpureus*

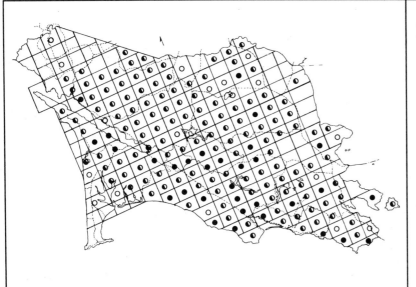

A year-round resident; winter numbers variable—may swell (usually) or decrease from late Sep through Mar.

A common, very widespread breeder; overall breeding population large.

Recorded in 177 (80.1%) of 221 blocks.

○	Possible	=	18	(10%)
◑	Probable	=	127	(72%)
●	Confirmed	=	32	(18%)

FSAR = 4   OPI = 708   CI = 2.08

Ecological Requirements

The wild watery trill of the Purple Finch rolls forth from Marin County's conifer, mixed conifer, broadleaved evergreen, and riparian forests and dense eucalyptus groves. Less dependent on ground foraging than the other *Carpodacus* finches, Purples occupy denser moister forests than their congeners. They also inhabit open woodlands and, frequently, forest edges, though not as dependent on these features as are Cassin's Finches (which breed in distant higher, cooler, and drier mountains). Also in comparison with Purples, House Finches are strongly edge-dependent. House Finches frequent relatively arid open habitats, where they forage in grasslands and weed fields and seek shelter or nest sites in adjoining trees, brush, or human edifices. Purple Finches generally respond indirectly to moisture through its effects on vegetation structure, but metabolic studies have shown that at high temperatures they need a huge percentage of moist food or an easily available supply of drinking water for use in their efficient cooling systems (Salt 1952).

In California, Purple Finches build their nests from about 5 to 50 feet above the ground in coniferous, broadleaved evergreen, and deciduous trees, generally on a horizontal or ascending branch well out from the trunk (Dawson 1923, Bent 1968a). Nests are well-built cups made of twigs and rootlets and lined with moss, *Ramalina* lichens, fine grasses, string, horsehair, wool, or other soft materials.

Based on a small sample (n = 7) of birds from the Sierra Nevada, the summer diet is about 42% vegetable and 58% animal in origin, the latter consisting of beetles, aphids, caterpillars, hymenopterans, and spiders (Dahlsten et al. 1985). In the spring and summer, Purple Finches rely heavily on blooming trees and bushes, from which they pick the flowers, trim off the petals, and eat the ovaries, stamens, and pistils (Salt 1952, Bent 1968a). They also eat large quantities of buds, berries, fruits, willow catkins, and seeds. They glean insects from the foliage or branches of bushes and trees and pick vegetable fare largely from the

411

branch- and twig-work while perched. Purple Finches revert to an almost exclusively vegetarian menu in the winter.

Marin Breeding Distribution

During the atlas period, Purple Finches were widespread breeders in Marin County but were most evenly distributed where moister denser forests prevail, toward the immediate coast. In the interior of the county, they were restricted largely to forests and woodlands in the vicinity of permanent streams, in narrow shaded canyons, and on north-facing slopes. Areas of marginal occurrence or absence were the grassland-dominated terrain of outer Point Reyes, around Tomales, and bordering the bayshore near Novato. Representative breeding stations were Tomales Bay SP (NB 4/29/82 —DS); Pike County Gulch, Bolinas Lagoon (NB 6/15/80 —DS); and near Barnabe Mountain (NB mid-May 1982 —BTr).

Historical Trends/Population Threats

Prior data are limited, but Purple Finches were relatively stable on Breeding Bird Surveys in California from 1968 to 1989 (USFWS unpubl. analyses).

HOUSE FINCH *Carpodacus mexicanus*

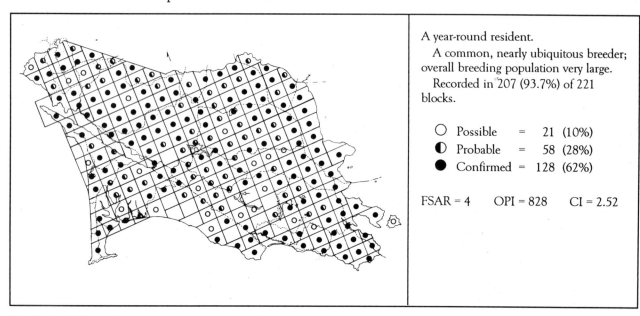

A year-round resident.

A common, nearly ubiquitous breeder; overall breeding population very large. Recorded in 207 (93.7%) of 221 blocks.

○ Possible   =   21 (10%)
◐ Probable   =   58 (28%)
● Confirmed = 128 (62%)

FSAR = 4   OPI = 828   CI = 2.52

Ecological Requirements

One of our most familiar birds and another classic edge species, the House Finch occupies the open or brushy borders of all of Marin County's major forest, woodland, or brushland plant communities but is nowhere more common than about human dwellings. With the spread of civilization, House Finches have adapted remarkably to ranch- and farmyards, as well as urban and suburban settings. They do not frequent forests, woodlands, or scrublands that offer a continuous canopy but prefer the edges that adjoin sparse grasslands or weed fields or where the latter habitats are interspersed with scattered shrubs or clumps of trees. Primarily ground foragers in open habitats, House Finches also need tall perches, such as trees, buildings, or transmission lines, to fly up to for safety's sake. They are hesitant to venture far into grasslands or weed lots without high perches close at hand. A nearby source of fresh water is also an important requisite (Salt 1952).

Nest sites are extremely varied and range from the ground up to about 50 feet (Dawson 1923, Salt 1952, Evenden 1957, Thompson 1960, Woods 1968); they are almost always either covered or shaded by vegetation or some other structure (Salt 1952). Around homes, barns, and outbuildings, any support or odd cubbyhole will serve as a nest site. House Finches frequently use supports under eaves, on drainpipes, on beams, or amid ivy clinging to walls. They also commonly build their nests in the dense foliage or in the open interiors of native, cultivated, or

412

ornamental trees and hedges. Sometimes they place them in thistle patches or on the ground under weeds. When a lack of nest supports on human structures forces birds to resort to bushes or shrubbery, they usually choose one as close to the building as possible. House Finches will, of course, nest far from buildings. Other nest sites include cavities in walls, trees, and cliffs, tin cans hanging on fenceposts, mailboxes, old hats, stovepipes, haystacks, and old woodpecker cavities. House Finches also occupy old bird nests and usually reline them. In California, abandoned nests of "Bullock's" and Hooded orioles, Barn and Cliff swallows, and Black Phoebes are the prime candidates for House Finch use. House Finches are not strongly territorial. Male defense, centering around the female as well as a space around the nest, wanes during incubation (Thompson 1960). Consequently, House Finches sometimes place their nests within a few feet or even inches of each other (Thompson 1960, Woods 1968). They may reuse nests for successive broods in a season and often reuse nest sites in successive years. "Choice of nest materials is as catholic as that of nest sites," and includes almost anything soft; often nest cups are constructed of a single material (Dawson 1923). Nest materials include such items as straw, grass, weed stems, flower heads, string, wool, soft paper, cotton, plant down, bark strips, moss, lichens, leaves, rootlets, hair, frayed cigarette filters, and, rarely, feathers. The nest lining is of finer materials of these sorts.

In the breeding season, males feed in flocks along with some nonincubating females; flocking, of course, increases at other seasons (Thompson 1960). House Finches are much more dependent on ground foraging for seeds than are the other *Carpodacus* finches. They also pick seeds or flowering heads from plants while hanging onto stems or branches and eat fruits attached to trees or, less frequently, when they have fallen to the ground (Salt 1952, Woods 1968). Additionally, in the spring they eat leaf and blossom buds from bushes and trees and sip sap oozing from cut branches of pruned trees. House Finches also readily obtain seeds from feeding trays. They probably glean a few insects from foliage, branches, and fruit, but some authors suspect they take them incidentally with vegetable matter (Thompson 1960).

The diet of House Finches in California is about 97.6% vegetable matter and 2.4% animal matter (Beal 1907, n = 1206). Animal food is principally plant lice, small caterpillars, and a few beetles. House Finches will also eat fat, especially suet. The vegetable portion of the diet consists of weed seeds (86.2% of the annual total), fruit (10.5%), and miscellaneous vegetable matter (0.9%). The proportion of weed seeds in the diet decreases and that of fruit increases over the course of summer. The most important weed seeds in California are Napa thistle, black mustard, wild

radish, filaree, knotweed, amaranth, and turkey mullein. The fruits that House Finches eat are largely the large soft-bodied cultivated types, such as apples, apricots, avocados, raspberries, cherries, figs, grapes, peaches, pears, plums, and strawberries (Woods 1968, Palmer 1973); they prefer these over small berries eaten by mockingbirds and waxwings. House Finches are almost exclusively vegetarian in fall and winter. Agriculturists consider the House Finch one of the most destructive bird "pests" in California, and they spend considerable money for control efforts (Palmer 1973). Other vegetable matter eaten includes very small quantities of flower parts, grain, and leaf galls (Beal 1907). Salt is also eaten (Woods 1968). House Finches are a notable exception to the rule that most fringillid finches eat a considerable quantity of insects in the breeding season and initially feed their young almost exclusively insects (Beal 1907, Woods 1968). Adult House Finches feed their young, by regurgitation, the same vegetarian diet they themselves eat. Males also feed incubating females (at least in the early stages) by regurgitation when females fly up from the nest or, less frequently, on the nest (Thompson 1960).

Marin Breeding Distribution

During the atlas period, the House Finch was one of the most widespread breeders in Marin County and had no large gaps in its distribution here. Because of their adaptations to more arid, open, and human-influenced habitats than those preferred by Purple Finches (Salt 1952), House Finches were more common in the low rolling hills and lowland valleys of Marin's interior ranching country and in the urbanized corridor along Highway 101. Representative breeding locales were Abbott's Lagoon (NE 6/20/82 –DS); the Fish Docks, Point Reyes (NB 5/13/80 –DS); Chileno Valley (NE 5/6/82 –DS); and Bolinas Ridge above Olema (NB 4/28/77 –DS).

Historical Trends/Population Threats

With the coming of civilization, the House Finch occupied new habitats and increased the density of its populations within its original range (Woods 1968). Although Grinnell and Miller (1944) did not comment on population trends in California, the species undoubtedly had increased dramatically in the state up to that time, and continued to do so along with the vast expansion of agricultural and suburban habitats. More recently, House Finch populations decreased on Breeding Bird Surveys in California from 1968 to 1989 (USFWS unpubl. analyses), despite stability from 1980 to 1989. Still, California has far and away the highest densities of House Finches of any state or province on the continent (Robbins et al. 1986).

RED CROSSBILL *Loxia curvirostra*

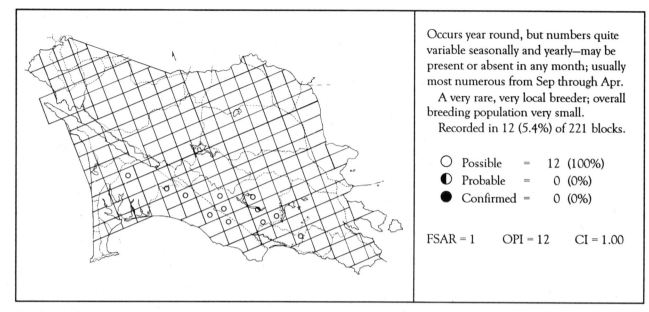

Occurs year round, but numbers quite variable seasonally and yearly—may be present or absent in any month; usually most numerous from Sep through Apr.

A very rare, very local breeder; overall breeding population very small.

Recorded in 12 (5.4%) of 221 blocks.

○ Possible	=	12	(100%)
◐ Probable	=	0	(0%)
● Confirmed	=	0	(0%)

FSAR = 1   OPI = 12   CI = 1.00

Ecological Requirements

Renowned for its fantastic bill and erratic seasonal wanderings, the Red Crossbill is one of our most enigmatic breeding birds. Crossbills are apparently indifferent to temperature, humidity, or altitude (Griscom 1937) within the conditions that give rise to cone-bearing trees, their lifeblood. Crossbills prefer to breed in mature forests with tall well-spaced trees—the stage at which these forests yield the most cones (Newton 1973). At all seasons, Crossbills are closely wedded to the conifer forests to satisfy their seed-dependent diet, and their movements, lacking in predictable seasonal periodicity, appear to be largely reliant on the fortunes of the cone crops, which are by nature irregular. The birds depart rapidly from areas depleted of seeds, no matter what the season or reason, and they will travel long distances in almost any direction in search of cone-heavy conifers. Length of occupancy of a particular area depends on the number of types of conifers and the synchrony and abundance of cone crops in the habitat (Benkman 1987a).

Crossbill movements and breeding attempts are predicated on maximizing seed intake rates, given the vagaries of spatially and temporally fluctuating cone crops (Benkman 1987a). This necessitates a religious attention to changes in this highly unpredictable food source, as conifer crops at a site can vary several orders of magnitude between years with intervals of 2 to 10 years between good cone crops. Likewise, cone crops fail over large regions every 2 to 4 years, forcing irruptive movements of Crossbills from their "normal" range. The *rate* of food intake (profitability) derived from a particular conifer depends on cone struc-

ture, timing of cone opening and seed release, and seed mass. Profitability generally peaks as cones first open, when there are high numbers of seeds per cone that are readily accessible, and declines as seeds are shed from cones. The timing of cone ripening varies from year to year—cool moist conditions may delay cone opening and unseasonal warm weather can cause seeds to be shed rapidly (Benkman 1987a, 1990). Although seeds of all conifers form in late summer, cones do not mature and open until 3 to 22 months later, depending on the species of conifer (Newton 1973). Consequently, to maximize profitability, Crossbills shift their use of various conifers to match the seasonal patterns of cone opening among conifer species, though they often hedge their bets by foraging on more than one conifer species at a time. Furthermore, as cone crops are depleted Crossbills must emigrate to take advantage of the great geographic variation in cone crop abundance, cone opening pattern, and seed mass.

The timing of breeding is equally unpredictable, since Crossbills will nest in any month of the year (Bailey et al. 1953, Bent 1968b). They have even been known to have three distinct breeding periods in six months at the same location (Griscom 1937)! In general, Crossbills breed most commonly in late summer and early autumn (Aug-Oct) and in late winter and early spring (Jan–Apr), when snow-rimmed nests are not uncommon (Griscom 1937, Bailey et al. 1953, Bent 1968b, Newton 1973, Benkman 1990). In a given region, though, birds rarely breed in the same month in consecutive years. Year-to-year variability in breeding is also great at any particular location within a region. Birds may nest for several successive years and then vanish, or they may arrive one year, breed, and then not be seen again for many years. Generally, Crossbills are rarely numerous in the same area two years in succession. Not only does the time of breeding vary from year to year in the same forest type, but some birds may breed in different types of conifer forest in successive years (Newton 1973). In the mountains of Colorado, Crossbills are known to progressively shift breeding upslope into different conifer zones from early winter to summer (Bailey et al. 1953). Crossbills may also abruptly cease breeding and emigrate if seed intake rates decline from natural perturbations, such as weather-induced seed shedding or insect outbreaks that decimate developing seed crops (Benkman 1990).

Although it has long been known that Crossbills need an abundant cone crop to nest, it is just now being appreciated that they initiate (or terminate) breeding in response to both the levels and *rates* of change of seed intake (Benkman 1990). Seed intake must be sufficient for egg formation and, particularly, the more energy-demanding nestling phase of reproduction. Birds that start nesting at high seed levels will abandon if intake rates decline, indicating that energy intake will be insufficient at the nestling stage. Conversely, birds will start nesting at seed intake rates just necessary for egg formation if these rates are increasing, suggesting that energy intake will later be adequate to meet nestling demands.

In Marin County, the main cone-producing trees attractive to Crossbills are Douglas fir and bishop pine. Crossbills here frequent these and also coast redwoods, planted Monterey pines and cypress, and occasionally alder thickets. Exactly what the Crossbills' preferences are in the "breeding season" in Marin County are not well known, because no nests have been found here.

Elsewhere, Crossbills typically build their nests at heights from about 10 to 90 feet (most under 40 ft., Bent 1968b). In Colorado, 16 nests in yellow pines averaged 31 feet (range 15-48 ft.) above ground (Bailey et al. 1953). There nests were located in fairly open conifer groves or in semi-isolated groves of trees rather than in densely timbered areas. A nest tree is often close to a dead or dying pine that the male uses for singing, preening, and a cautionary stopping place before entering or leaving the nest area; territories are maintained only during nest site selection. Crossbills usually saddle their nests on horizontal branches close to or, more commonly, well out from the trunk and often conceal them in thick tufts of cones and needles, clusters of branchlets, or cups of lichen; only rarely can nests be seen from below (Bailey et al. 1953, Bent 1968b). Crossbills tend to place their nests on the south side of trees where they receive the warmth of the sun and are sheltered from north winds (Bailey et al. 1953, Newton 1973). Crossbill nests are bulky, comparatively deep cups of conifer twigs, rootlets, bark strips, decayed

wood, weed stalks, dried grass, moss, lichens, and perhaps a few pine needles, stiff feathers, or picnic litter (Bailey et al. 1953, Bent 1968b). They are thickly (warmly) lined with finer materials such as hair, fur, fine rootlets or grass, lichens, moss, shredded bark, and a few feathers (Lawrence 1949, Bent 1968b). Crossbills tend to build bulkier and more thickly lined nests in winter than in summer (Newton 1973). In one case in Colorado, birds reused the same nest for a second breeding attempt (Bailey et al. 1953).

While breeding, Crossbills generally tend to forage in loose knit flocks—composed of males feeding incubating females, pairs feeding nestlings, and birds with fledglings in tow—that constantly fluctuate in size as birds move to and from nests (Bailey et al. 1953). On some days, no foraging flocks form and then birds work in isolated pairs or family groups. Crossbills derive the bulk of their sustenance from the seeds of conifers, obtained by first prying open the cone scales with their crossed mandibular tools and then extracting the seeds with their tongues. Crossbills are adept at climbing around conifer branches using both their bills and feet in parrot-fashion (Bent 1968b, Newton 1973). While reaching for nearby cones, they may hang by both feet, chickadee-like, or just by the bill or only one foot. Cones may be worked in situ, or they may be cut off and carried in the bill or claws to a perch, where the bird holds the cone against a branch with its feet and extracts the seeds in a leisurely fashion. Crossbills insert their partly opened bills between, and parallel to the long axis of, cone scales and separate the scales primarily by sideways movements of the mandibles (Torduff 1954, Newton 1973, Benkman 1987b). Regardless of the sex of Crossbills, the direction in which the tips of the mandibles cross is roughly evenly divided in the population, as the lower mandible curves upward and slightly either left or right. Consequently, birds are either "right- or left-handed" in their attempts to open pine cones (Torduff 1954). Feeding on the cone with the long axis of its head at right angles to the axis of the cone, the bird orients the tip of the lower mandible on the side toward the distal end of the cone. After an initial gap is created by a biting motion of the upper mandible, the jaws are spread sideways. The lower jaw is abducted laterally in the direction that its tip points, pressing and pivoting against the distal scale while the side of the upper mandible pushes the basal scale open (Benkman 1987b). If need be, the upper mandible may be driven further between the scale gap and the rest of the process repeated until the gap between scales widens and deepens, enabling the bird to reach the seed. Then the Crossbill protrudes its long, agile tongue using the spoon-shaped tip to scoop the seed back to the bill to be husked.

Although conifer seeds are their mainstay, Crossbills will also eat the tender buds or soft green cones of conifers; the seeds and buds of deciduous trees such as birches, alders, box elders, elms, willows, and poplars; and the seed heads of ragweed, hemp, dandelions, and other weeds. Crossbills will eat these items in place or, like seeds and nuts occasionally procured from the ground, will eat them after flying to a perch. It appears that a Crossbill scoops seeds from seed heads with its saliva-covered tongue, which is then used to manipulate the seed into position and crack it between the cutting edges of the bill (Sutton 1976). Crossbills may also hold large seeds with their feet, bite the end with the tips of the mandible, insert the mandibles in the crack, pry the shell open with lateral movements, and again extract the contents with the tongue (Torduff 1954). They also forage for fresh, dried, and frozen fruits (Lawrence 1949), but stomach contents indicate that just the seeds are eaten after extraction from the pulp (Sutton 1976). Anything more than a passing reliance on alternative foods is usually necessitated by cone crop failures' forcing irruptive movements beyond the range of conifer forests (Newton 1973). Then fruits as large as apples may be split open for their seeds. Although Crossbills are almost exclusively vegetarians from fall through spring (n= 225), their summer diet includes about 18% animal matter (n = 30) (Martin et al. 1951). Benkman (1990) remarked that in the East insect larvae may make up a major portion of the diet in late June and July. The main animal food items are spiders, caterpillars, plant lice, aphids, beetles, ants, and larvae of other insects (Martin et al. 1951, Bent 1968b). Crossbills awkwardly glean some insects from foliage or cones or pry them from crevices or from beneath bark with their bills or tongues. They may also use their tongues to procure insects after using their bills in scissor-like fashion to cut open curled leaves or after inserting their open bills into leaf galls until the mandibles are practically closed and crossed, and a slight twist of the head splits open the gall. It is also well established that Red Crossbills have a fondness for salt or salty substances. They may obtain these from natural mineral deposits, from salt spread to melt snow, from poured-out soapy dishwater, and even from snow discolored by dog urine (Aldrich 1939, Bent 1968b); they sometimes secure scrapings from bleached deer bones (Bailey et al. 1953). Like many seed-eating finches, the female is fed on the nest by the male, and the young are fed by regurgitation. The initial pabulum proferred to nestlings is a watery or dark viscid substance, suggesting a composition of animal matter, and later a thicker substance of sodden pine seeds transferred in soft balls (Lawrence 1949, Bailey et al. 1953, Snyder 1954).

Marin Breeding Distribution

The unpredictable, "unseasonal" breeding habits of Crossbills present formidable challenges to atlas work. Although confirming breeding on a case-by-case basis is apparently no more difficult than for other finches, it is nigh impossible if observers are looking for evidence in a season during which Crossbills may not nest in the years of the atlas project. For this reason, the Marin County atlas map of Crossbills is probably incomplete, since most of our data collection was done from April through July. Conversely, other studies suggest we may have recorded birds that had no intention of breeding here at the time. Johnston and Norris (1956) observed up to 40 birds in bishop pine forest on Inverness Ridge from 15 March to 11 June 1954, but of the total of 9 birds they collected on 31 May and 11 June, *none* were in breeding condition. As a consequence, our distribution map of Crossbills is not really comparable to that of a regular nesting species with a well-defined, spring to summer breeding season. The atlas records *do* all occur in areas of Marin with extensive conifers, and the long-term breeding range of the Red Crossbill here is probably equivalent to the combined breeding distribution of the Red-breasted and Pygmy nuthatches, two obligate conifer breeders. The only indications of Crossbill breeding in Marin County predate the atlas period. A female was observed "gathering grass" on Inverness Ridge on 23 April 1960 (GMi) and another female "carrying nest material" at Tomales Bay State Park on 29 April 1973 (PRBO).

Historical Trends/Population Threats

Population trends of an obligate nomad such as the Red Crossbill are extremely difficult to document and may just as easily be affected by very distant conditions as by local ones. It is unclear what effect extensive logging of California's conifer forests has had on Red Crossbills. It is worth noting that the subspecies from northeastern North America *(L. c. neogaea)* may have been brought to the brink of extinction near the turn of this century by extensive lumbering activities (Dickerman 1987). Nevertheless, Red Crossbill populations increased on Breeding Bird Surveys in California from 1968 to 1989, despite relatively stable numbers from 1980 to 1989 (USFWS unpubl. analyses).

PINE SISKIN *Carduelis pinus*

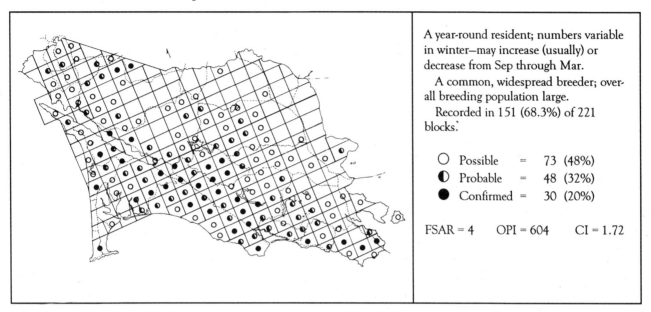

A year-round resident; numbers variable in winter—may increase (usually) or decrease from Sep through Mar.

A common, widespread breeder; overall breeding population large.

Recorded in 151 (68.3%) of 221 blocks.

○	Possible	=	73 (48%)
◑	Probable	=	48 (32%)
●	Confirmed	=	30 (20%)

FSAR = 4   OPI = 604   CI = 1.72

Ecological Requirements

These plain-looking but exuberant "goldfinches" are closely linked, but not tied, to Marin County's conifer forests. Siskins breed here in extensive bishop pine, Douglas fir, and coast redwood forests and also in extensive or small isolated stands of planted Monterey cypress, Monterey pine, and eucalyptus. Although Siskins feed here in alder and willow thickets during the winter and in the breeding season, they apparently do not nest in these habitats. Siskins nest most commonly in open forests or woodlands and along openings of (or borders with) grasslands, weed fields, and thistle patches.

Siskins may breed solitarily or semicolonially in the same tree, and they typically conceal their nests well out on densely foliaged horizontal limbs (Palmer 1968). Nest heights range from about 3 to 50 feet but mostly from 10 to 20 feet. Although Siskins place most nests in conifers, in the western states, birds also occasionally use box elders, maples, oaks, cottonwoods, and lilacs. On the California coast, Siskins nest primarily in native conifers but also in planted conifers, particularly Monterey cypress, and eucalyptus (Carriger & Pemberton 1907, Palmer 1968). Their nests are shallow compact cups made of twigs, rootlets, grass, weed stems or bark, leaves, and tree moss or lichens. They are lined with fine rootlets, hair, fur, plant down, or, rarely, feathers (Carriger & Pemberton 1907, Dawson 1923, Palmer 1968).

Siskins maintain their gregarious proclivities in the breeding season, when they continue foraging in flocks—albeit smaller ones—up to about six birds. Flocks or single birds feed in trees, bushes, weeds, thistles, and on the ground. Siskin flocks typically forage from the top of a tree downward, but they also move up through trees or horizontally from one tree to another (Rodgers 1937). Like crossbills or chickadees, they often hang upside down from cone or catkin clusters. Siskins frequently cling to thistle heads, pull out the cottony seed tufts, and dexterously and rather rapidly work their bills along to the seed, which they then remove, throwing the fluff to the breeze (Palmer 1968). They are less well adapted for ground foraging and walk with very short steps and occasional hops. Like other seed eaters, they need a reliable source of water. Siskins glean insects from foliage or even the walls of houses. They also obtain insects by shelling galls from the underside of oak leaves and by breaking off twig ends to get at the larvae of twig-boring insects. Males initially feed incubating and brooding females by regurgitation. The females in turn feed the young up to the seventh or eighth day in a like manner; insects are important to the developing young (Palmer 1968).

Although Siskins are primarily seed eaters, their diet is composed of up to 81% animal matter in summer (n = 19), but only 10% in winter (n = 142) (Martin et al. 1951). Siskins consume copious amounts of seeds from conifers, alders, willows, eucalyptus, thistles, dandelions, and other weeds (Palmer 1968). They take the seeds in place or after they have fallen to the ground. Siskins also eat flower and leaf buds, blossoms, leaves of garden seedlings, the sweet liquid inside eucalyptus flowers, and (rarely) the sap from sapsucker drillings. About one-sixth of the Siskin's yearly diet is insects (McAtee in Palmer 1968). Important ones

417

are caterpillars, plant lice, scale insects, true bugs, fly larvae, and grasshoppers; spiders are also eaten and suet is an occasional supplement. Siskins are also fond of salt and clay from mineral deposits, ashes, gravel and sand mixed with chloride, and newly set cement.

Marin Breeding Distribution

During the atlas period, Pine Siskins bred widely in the moister, most coast-influenced areas of Marin County that are dominated by conifer, mixed conifer, and broadleaved evergreen forests. Representative breeding localities were Fish Docks, Point Reyes (NE 5/13 & 29/80 –DS); Abandoned Ranch, Point Reyes (NB 5/13/80 –DS); vicinity of Tomales Bay SP (NB 4/29/82 –DS); and Bolinas (NB 4/14/77 –DS).

Historical Trends/Population Threats

Historically, Pine Siskins have expanded their range locally on outer Point Reyes and around Tomales, where cypress and eucalyptus groves have been planted for windbreaks in extensive areas of grassland. While grassland birds generally may have suffered from overgrazing, Siskins have probably benefitted from the introduction and spread of otherwise noxious thistles. Whether clearing of forests has affected them is unclear. Siskin populations decreased on Breeding Bird Surveys in California from 1968 to 1989 (USFWS unpubl. analyses).

LESSER GOLDFINCH *Carduelis psaltria*

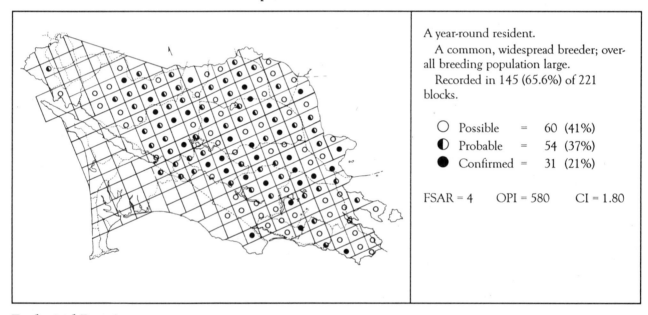

A year-round resident.
A common, widespread breeder; overall breeding population large.
Recorded in 145 (65.6%) of 221 blocks.

○	Possible	=	60 (41%)
◑	Probable	=	54 (37%)
●	Confirmed	=	31 (21%)

FSAR = 4   OPI = 580   CI = 1.80

Ecological Requirements

Small frisky bands of "Green-backed" Goldfinches inhabit the edges of Marin County's relatively dry oak savannah and oak woodland, chaparral (including Sargent cypress woodland/brushland), riparian woodland, and, more sparingly, the edges of broadleaved evergreen, conifer, and eucalyptus forests. These goldfinches prefer warm south- and west-facing slopes, and they forage extensively in grasslands and weed fields of pastures, roadsides, and hill slopes adjoining the cover where they nest and seek protection. They also forage extensively in trees and bushes. American Goldfinches overlap to a limited degree with Lessers along the edges of interior riparian stretches, but they generally breed in moister coastal situations. Lawrence's Goldfinches, on the other hand, generally frequent

the warmest and driest habitats of our three species of goldfinches and are of irregular occurrence in Marin County. Where Lawrences overlap extensively with Lessers, they exhibit subtle differences in habitat use, nest sites, and food preferences (see below and Lawrence's Goldfinch account). In southern California, at least, *breeding* Lawrences primarily occupy oak woodland edges, whereas Lessers use both oak woodland and chaparral extensively (Coutlee 1968a).

The large winter flocks of all three species of goldfinch disintegrate at the time of pair formation. But unlike many passerines, goldfinches do not establish territories until after they choose nest sites (Coutlee 1968a). Lesser Goldfinches maintain small territories centered around the nest tree, and birds tend to nest semicolonially, leaving many areas of apparently suitable habitat unoccupied (Coutlee 1968a). Lessers place their nests in a wide variety of trees and bushes, especially oaks. They tend to locate them in dense foliage or lichen clumps and, more often than not, toward the tips of drooping or horizontal branches (Linsdale 1957, 1968a; Coutlee 1968a). Nests are small compact cups made of a wide variety of materials, including dried grass, plant fibers, fine tree or weed bark, lichens, plant down, wool, thread, cotton, leaves, catkins, and cocoons. Nests have a thin lining of fine plant fibers or down, hair, or feathers. Nest heights range from about 2 to 30 feet, and although nest sites are similar to those of Lawrences, those of Lessers average lower in height (Linsdale 1957, Coutlee 1968a).

Like their congeners, Lesser Goldfinches forage in small flocks of about four to six birds in the breeding season and travel about one-quarter to one-half mile from their nest sites (Coutlee 1968a). Although they feed on the flowers, buds, catkins, and new leaves of trees such as oaks and willows, much of their food is seeds and dried fruits gathered from low bushes and tall herbaceous plants (Linsdale 1957, 1968a). The importance of a good seed crop is indicated by the abundance of Lessers observed in a profusion of herbs and annuals following a fire (Linsdale 1957). These goldfinches generally take vegetable matter while perched in the seed- or fruit-bearing plant or in one nearby from which they can reach the food. Herbaceous plants often bend under the goldfinches' weight, and the birds reach up or down or hang upside down to obtain their meals, picking off the seeds and fruits and mandibulating them to remove hulls or pappus. They swallow small seeds and dried fruits whole but pick at the pulp of fleshy fruits, such as those of coffeeberry and madrone, probably just for the juice. Birds sometimes forage on the ground for fallen seeds or on low, nearly horizontal stems. Lessers also glean a few insects from foliage. In California, the year-round diet is abut 98.3% vegetable matter and 1.7% animal matter (Beal 1910, n = 476). Although almost exclusively granivorous at other seasons, in summer Lesser Goldfinches eat enough insects to account for 9% of the diet (Martin et al. 1951, n = 459). Animal foods are mostly plant lice (woolly aphids), caterpillars, and a few miscellaneous insects (Beal 1910, Martin et al. 1951). The main vegetable fare is weed seeds, which account for 96% of the yearly diet; grain, fruit, and miscellaneous vegetable material are of minor importance. Throughout California, the most important food item is Napa or bur thistle, with groundsel, pigweed, tarweed, and turkey mullein also taken in considerable quantities (Beal 1910). Studies at Hastings Reservation, Monterey County, revealed that Lessers fed on 55 species of plants, of which Napa thistle, chamise, common fiddleneck, and vinegarweed were the most prominent (Linsdale 1957, 1968a). In that area,

Lawrences fed on only 20 species of plants, about 70% of them plants also eaten by Lessers. Linsdale (1957) noted that in mixed flocks these two species persistently and exclusively fed on one single kind of seed. The lower number of plant species in the Lawrence's Goldfinch diet may have been due to their lower population size (Linsdale 1957) or to bill size and shape differences and differing foraging strategies (Coutlee 1968b). Lessers have bills that are considerably longer and more pointed than Lawrences and therefore may be able to handle larger seeds and extract seeds more easily, enabling them to use a greater variety of plants (Coutlee 1968b). Laboratory experiments indicate that Lawrences feed in longer bouts than do Lessers and may spend more time searching out rich food sources where they can remain and feed for several minutes. In contrast, Lessers may feed for shorter periods on isolated stalks, enabling them to exploit a greater variety of plants in a broader range of sites, as well as in areas where Lawrences have already fed (Coutlee 1968b). Like other cardueline finches, Lessers need a reliable source of water to help soften the dry, hard seeds and fruits they eat; they also show a fondness for salt and grit (Linsdale 1957). During incubation and the first four days after the young hatch, males feed females on the nest by regurgitation. The young apparently are fed entirely regurgitated seeds, initially from the female via the male.

Marin Breeding Distribution

During the atlas period, Lesser Goldfinches bred widely in the eastern and north-central sections of Marin County and reached their greatest abundance in the oak woodlands and oak savannah around Novato. The contrast between this distribution and the American Goldfinch's indicates that, in general, Lessers are adapted to a drier climate and more open vegetation. Representative breeding locations were Three Peaks (DD 6/17/82 –DS); Chileno Valley (NB 5/5/82 –DS); Mt. Burdell, Novato (NE 5/17/80 –DS); Sargent cypress grove, Carson Ridge (NE 6/5/82 –DS); and Cataract Trail, N of Rock Springs, Mt. Tamalpais (FL/FY 8/1/81 –DS).

Historical Trends/Population Threats

Although population trends of this species are difficult to detect because of marked year-to-year variability (Robbins et al. 1986), numbers were relatively stable on Breeding Bird Surveys in California from 1968 to 1989 (USFWS unpubl. analyses). On Spring Bird Counts around Novato from 1978 to 1987, highest numbers of Lesser Goldfinches were recorded in the drought year of 1987, and second highest numbers in 1984 (Appendix A). These two dry years were also the only ones when Lawrence's Goldfinches were recorded on these counts (see account).

LAWRENCE'S GOLDFINCH   *Carduelis lawrencei*

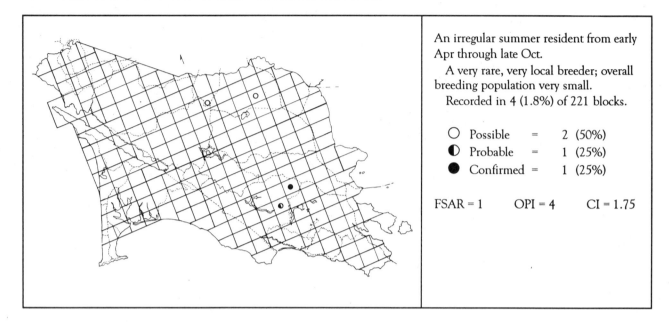

An irregular summer resident from early Apr through late Oct.

A very rare, very local breeder; overall breeding population very small.

Recorded in 4 (1.8%) of 221 blocks.

○   Possible   =   2   (50%)
◐   Probable   =   1   (25%)
●   Confirmed   =   1   (25%)

FSAR = 1   OPI = 4   CI = 1.75

Ecological Requirements

"Larry's" Goldfinch is the archgypsy. Even in the heart of its breeding haunts in the dry interior Coast Range of southern California, birds may be abundant at a locality one year and sparse or absent the next. Its distribution is "notably discontinuous" and movements are "erratic" (G&M 1944). The species' irregular movements are apparently tied to fluctuations in the kinds and amounts of the seed crops upon which it depends (Linsdale 1957). Although they range more widely in the off season, particularly into chaparral, breeding Lawrence's Goldfinches confine themselves largely to the grassy and weedy edges of oak savannah and oak woodland (Linsdale 1957, Coutlee 1968a). Rather than a particular habitat, the determining factors appear to be the structure of the edge habitat of open woodland or brushland that borders on grasslands, as well as the suitability of seed crops; these goldfinches have also bred in cypress groves and in native conifers (Linsdale 1957). Lawrence's Goldfinches are so irregular in Marin County that it is hard to discuss habitat preferences here. They have occurred on only two of ten Even Cheaper Thrills Spring Bird Counts that center around Novato (Appendix A), an area of Marin that most resembles the dry interior Coast Range. Most breeding season occurrences in Marin County have been along the edges of oak savannah and oak woodland or in open broadleaved evergreen forest bordering or intermixed with grassland. Birds have nested here in planted cypress, though, and on the edge of Douglas fir forest near the coast. Regardless, on

a scale of preference for climatic moistness, Lawrences generally fall at the driest end, with Lessers intermediate, and Americans on the moist end.

For nesting, oaks are generally the bungalows of choice, but a variety of trees and bushes are also used. At Hasting's Reservation, Monterey County, Lawrences prefer small lichen-festooned blue oaks as nest sites (Linsdale 1957). Birds choose nest sites there on the higher parts of the hills, about one-half mile from the best food-producing areas on flats along a creek and on open ground on a hilltop (Linsdale 1957). In a southern California canyon, where foliose lichens are absent, they often use sycamores and mistletoe clumps early on, but as the season progresses they use oaks more and more commonly (Coutlee 1968a). Lawrence's Goldfinches usually build their nests in dense vegetation or lichen clumps toward the tips of branches. Nest height ranges from 3 to 40 feet and averages about 15 to 25 feet—higher than that of sympatric Lessers (Linsdale 1957, Coutlee 1968a). Lawrences occasionally nest in the same tree with Lessers, but generally both species have small, mutually exclusive territories around the nest tree; Lessers are dominant over Lawrence's Goldfinches (Coutlee 1968a). Lawrences also tend to nest semicolonially. As many as ten nests have been observed in two adjoining trees in an isolated stand of cypress (Linsdale 1957, 1968b). Nests "are exquisite creations, highly varied in construction and sometimes quite picturesque" (Dawson 1923). The small compact cups are made of weed stems and leaves, lichens, flower stalks, grass, flower blossoms, leaves, and buds. They are thinly lined with fine plant fibers, fine bark strips, hair, feathers, or cotton (Linsdale 1957, Coutlee 1968a).

Breeding Lawrence's Goldfinches search in small single- or mixed-species flocks (with Lessers and House Finches) for patches of low, seed-bearing herbaceous plants and shrubs (Linsdale 1957, 1968b). They apparently are entirely granivorous (Martin et al. 1951). Both Lawrences and Lessers feed on these seeds, at least superficially, in an identical manner (see Lesser account). Although Lawrences concentrate on chamise seeds in chaparral in winter, in the breeding season they are primarily found around oak woodlands and at Hastings Reservation are highly dependent on patches of fiddleneck (Linsdale 1957, Coutlee 1968a). At Hastings, they feed on at least 20 kinds of plants, especially natives (Linsdale 1957, 1968b). Other important plants there besides fiddleneck are red maids, red-stem filaree, annual bluegrass, common peppergrass, and shepherd's purse. In addition, Lawrences feed to a limited degree on berries (pecking at the pulp) and greens in gardens; exceptionally, they eat Mourning Dove eggs and jumping galls in (and on the ground below) infested valley oaks (Linsdale 1957, 1968b). See the Lesser Goldfinch account for a comparison of the foraging niche. Like the other goldfinches, Lawrences need a source of fresh water to aid in digesting seeds, and they have a fondness for salt and grit. Males feed females at the nest by regurgitation during incubation and the first few days of the nestling phase, and the young are fed a diet of regurgitated seeds, initially from the female via the male (Linsdale 1957, Coutlee 1968a).

Marin Breeding Distribution

Lawrence's Goldfinches were observed in only four blocks during the atlas period: two in the Mount Tamalpais watershed and two near Novato. The only atlas breeding confirmation was of a nest under construction, observed at Elliott Nature Preserve in Fairfax on 21 May 1977 (BSp et al.). Surprisingly, but probably because of the preatlas distribution of observer coverage, all other Marin breeding records are from coastal sites: Tennessee Cove (NY 6/15/24 *Gull* 6, No. 7; S&P 1933); in the Abandoned Ranch and RCA cypress groves, Point Reyes ("nesting" early June 1972 —DDeS); and in Douglas fir at Bear Valley Headquarters, PRNS (NB 6/3/72 —M&LG).

Historical Trends/Population Threats

Mailliard (1900) reported that the Lawrence's Goldfinch was "abundant" in some years and "rare" in others in Marin County. Stephens and Pringle (1933) considered it uncommon here. Lawrence's Goldfinches were recorded on only two of ten Even Cheaper Thrills Spring Bird Counts from 1978 to 1987 (in the dry years of 1984 and 1987), and on one of three South Marin Spring Bird Counts (in the drought year of 1977) (Appendix A). These years also corresponded to the highest totals of Lesser Goldfinches on both these counts. The marked year-to-year variability in Lawrence's Goldfinch populations makes it difficult to detect population trends even over broad areas (Robbins et al. 1986). Nevertheless, their numbers were fairly stable on Breeding Bird Surveys in California from 1968 to 1989 (USFWS unpubl. analyses).

AMERICAN GOLDFINCH *Carduelis tristis*

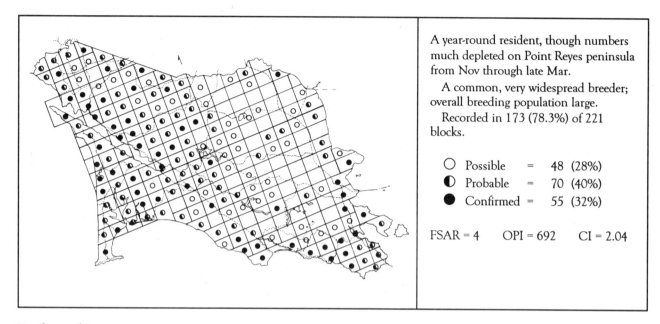

A year-round resident, though numbers much depleted on Point Reyes peninsula from Nov through late Mar.

A common, very widespread breeder; overall breeding population large.

Recorded in 173 (78.3%) of 221 blocks.

○ Possible = 48 (28%)
◐ Probable = 70 (40%)
● Confirmed = 55 (32%)

FSAR = 4   OPI = 692   CI = 2.04

Ecological Requirements

Although the California form of this cheery finch has been called the "Willow Goldfinch," it is by no means restricted to the vicinity of willows. Like our other goldfinches, it is edge adapted and in the breeding season frequents the open brushy and weedy borders of riparian thickets, freshwater marshes, open coastal scrub, dune scrub, planted cypress and eucalyptus groves, weed fields, and brushy roadside margins. Compared with Lesser and Lawrence's goldfinches, Americans occupy relatively moist habitats in proximity to permanent water or in areas of high humidity within the influence of coastal summer fog. Presumably these moist conditions nourish the plants upon which this goldfinch depends for seeds. The other two species of goldfinches will also nest near water but generally adjacent to arid surroundings. Unlike their Eastern relations, which begin breeding in July, American Goldfinches in California initiate nests in late April or May, probably because of the earlier maturation of seed-bearing plants in our winter-wet Mediterranean climate.

American Goldfinches place their nests in a wide variety of bushes, saplings, trees, stout herbaceous plants, and even ferns. In some areas, at least, they increase their use of forbs as nest sites as the season advances (Stokes 1950). Americans cradle most of their nests in upright forks, with several points of attachment. They also place some between two parallel uprights with no support beneath, and some in tufts of small upright twigs growing from horizontal branches (Nickell 1951). They saddle others over and around horizontal branches or wedge them

between horizontal forks where they resemble the semipensile nests of vireos. Nests sites are generally in open sunny situations and, though seldom well concealed, usually have some protection from the leafy canopy or shrub cover (Stokes 1950). Nest heights range from 1 to 60 feet, but nests over 30 feet high are rare (Walkinshaw 1938; Batts 1948; Stokes 1950; Nickell 1951; Berger 1957, 1968; Austin 1968; Holcomb 1969; Middleton 1979). Nest heights, of course, vary with habitat. Nests in shrubs, thistles, and forbs are by far the most numerous, and average heights from various studies range from about 4 to 6 feet above the ground; average heights in trees are roughly between 12 and 20 feet. Nest territories often have a taller tree used for song and territorial defense. Because birds defend limited territories around the nest tree and forage in flocks in nondefended areas, nesting may be semicolonial with concentrations around favorable nest sites and food supplies.

In upright forks, American Goldfinches usually fill the crotches beneath their nests with supporting materials such as thistle or cattail down or dry willow catkins. They construct the outer basketwork of the nest mostly of the thin outer bark of shrubs, bark or fiber strips of weed stalks, or grasses, and perhaps a few twigs or rootlets. These are held in place by small amounts of fine fibers, spider silk, cocoons, caterpillar webs, and dried froth of spittlebugs, apparently aided by some moistening secretion of the bird (Nickell 1951). The compact nest cups are so thickly lined they may hold water. The matted lining is made mostly of thistle down or other plant down or pappus, and sometimes small amounts of willow or cottonwood catkins, fine grasses, feathers, or moss. Within the lining there is a supportive layer of hairlike fibers consisting of finely shredded shrub bark or, more rarely, roots or animal hair. Although they collect most nest materials near the nest site, females will go up to one-half mile or more, if necessary, to the nearest source of thistle down (Drum 1939). Females will also salvage nest materials from other birds such as Northern Orioles or Yellow Warblers, from old nests after failure of initial attempts, or even from active neighboring goldfinch nests (Nickell 1951).

American Goldfinches eat principally seeds of wild plants and have a particular fondness for thistles (Beal 1910). They generally pluck seeds while perched in the seed-bearing plant or from a nearby support, and, like the other goldfinches, they may stretch in acrobatic contortions to reach pensile or swaying seed heads. In California, the annual diet is about 95% vegetable and 5% animal, the latter consisting of a few caterpillars, plant lice, and larval flies taken from spring to fall (Beal 1910, n = 84). Continentwide, animal foods account for 4% or less of the diet from summer through winter (n = 82), but up to 49% in spring (n = 41) (Martin et al. 1951). The birds glean insects from foliage or branches or obtain them by opening oak galls or infected seeds (Austin 1968). The principal seed plants identified in California are bur thistle, filaree, sunflower, and groundsel (Beal 1910). American Goldfinches also eat flower and leaf buds, young leaves, and, rarely, fruit or berries. They may obtain these in the treetops, particularly in late winter and spring (G&M 1944).

Observers have variously identified this species' foraging range from the nest site as invariably less than 200 to 350 yards and mostly 100 yards or less (Nickell 1951); at times within one-quarter but up to one-half mile (Coutlee 1967); and up to a mile or more (Drum 1939). Like other goldfinches, Americans need a source of fresh water to aid in seed digestion (Beal 1910). The males feed the females on the nest by regurgitation during incubation and up to about the fifth to eighth day of the nestling phase (Drum 1939). The young are fed primarily regurgitated seeds that are provided initially by the female via the male.

Marin Breeding Distribution

During the atlas period, American Goldfinches bred widely in Marin County. They were most numerous along the moist immediate coast and occurred sparingly around permanent water in the lowland valleys of the drier northeastern and north-central portions of the county. Representative breeding localities were eucalyptus grove at Abbott's Lagoon (NB 6/20/82 –DS); cypress grove at Abandoned Ranch, Point Reyes (NE 5/29/80 –DS); Brazil Beach near Lawson's Landing, Tomales Bay (NE 6/3/82 –DS); and Old Cerini Ranch, E of Hwy. 1 at Cypress Grove, Tomales Bay (NE 7/20/82 –DS).

Historical Trends/Population Threats

Populations of American Goldfinches generally decreased on Breeding Bird Surveys in California from 1968 to 1989, despite relative stability of numbers from 1980 to 1989 (USFWS unpubl. analyses). On one hand, grazing has stimulated the growth of seed-bearing thistles, but on the other hand, it has degraded nesting and foraging habitat of riparian edges by trampling.

Old World Sparrows
Family *Passeridae*

HOUSE SPARROW *Passer domesticus*

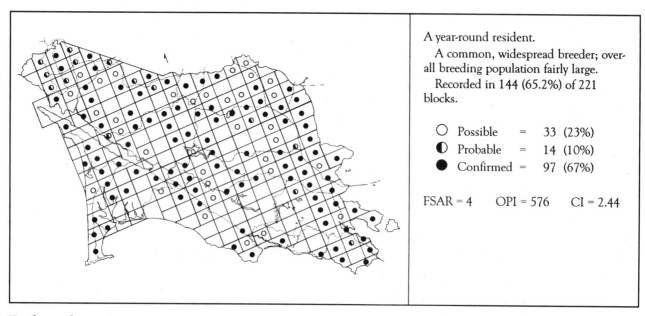

A year-round resident.

A common, widespread breeder; over-all breeding population fairly large.

Recorded in 144 (65.2%) of 221 blocks.

○ Possible   =   33 (23%)
◑ Probable   =   14 (10%)
● Confirmed =   97 (67%)

FSAR = 4   OPI = 576   CI = 2.44

Ecological Requirements

As its name implies, the House Sparrow has an intimate relationship with humans that spans more than 10,000 years since the development of cereal grain monoculture and the attendant long-term storage and use of these staples as an overwinter food supply for people and live-stock (Johnston & Klitz 1977). As this relationship solidi-fied in the Fertile Crescent of the Near East, the House Sparrow expanded its range widely in the Old World following the spread of agriculture. It has since been introduced broadly on other continents and is now almost certainly the most widespread landbird on Earth (Sum-mers-Smith 1963). House Sparrows inhabit a wide variety of agricultural and urban-suburban environments, but particularly places where occupied buildings and associ-ated trees are close together and interspersed with patches of open ground (Summers-Smith 1963). Such situations generally afford a regular source of food supplied by humans, supplemented to a limited degree by natural sources. These conditions are best met in cities and towns and in highly populous arable lands, particularly where chickens, pigs, and other livestock are kept. Because of their sedentary habits, House Sparrows reach their highest densities only where buildings and open farming areas

occur side by side: food, nest sites, and roost sites must be in close proximity. House Sparrow populations are usually not as dense in less populated farm districts, even when there is considerable cereal grain production, presumably because high year-round food supplies and other requisites are not as easily met there. Although concentrated by association with humans and buildings, House Sparrows form distinct breeding colonies, so some suitable breeding places are not occupied. Their colonial habits appear to be an adaptation to nesting in close proximity to concentrated food supplies.

In Marin County, the incessant, unmusical chattering and aggressive antics of House Sparrows are characteristic of urban parks, sidewalks and gutters, shopping mall and fast-food parking lots, suburban backyards (especially those with bird feeders), and the ranchyards and barnyards of the pastoral cattle and sheep country—that is, virtually every-where they can obtain intentional or unintentional hand-outs of food and protected nest sites.

House Sparrows build their bulky loose nests in a variety of situations (Weaver 1939, Bent 1958, Summers-Smith 1963). In most areas, the majority of nest sites are in and about buildings, in crevices and crannies such as under eaves, on rafters, beneath adobe tiles, in rain spouts, and in bird boxes. House Sparrows will also nest in ivy and other vines on buildings and in the dense branchwork of trees. They use a variety of deciduous and coniferous trees, but palms are a particular favorite in California. To a lesser degree, House Sparrows also use natural cavities in trees, old woodpecker holes, Cliff Swallow nests, the lower portions of hawk nests, Bank Swallow holes, caves, and holes in cliffs, earthen banks, or stone walls. As a rule, House Sparrows prefer hole and cavity nests and normally use open tree sites only when other sites are unavailable. They appear to use tree sites more commonly in warmer parts of the species' range. Nests in trees are globular in shape, are domed over, and have a side entrance or, less frequently, a top or bottom one (McGillivray 1981). House Sparrows will use open-cup nests of other species of birds as foundations that they dome over. One enterprising pair of sparrows used a hornet nest, pulling out a large part of the comb and substituting their usual nest materials for it (Bent 1958). Birds construct the outer layer of the nest with coarse hay, dried weeds, or straw and line it with softer materials, especially feathers, as well as string, leaves, cotton, cloth, paper, hair, frayed rope, plastic, or other debris. Females lay eggs before the final lining is added (Weaver 1939). Cavity nests vary in size according to the space available, which is filled up with nest material; cavity nests may not be domed over and may consist of just the lining materials. House Sparrows nest colonially and defend small territories just around the nest site. Nevertheless, a few compound nests have been found—one was a large ball of hay with three small openings leading to separate nest chambers. Nest heights range from a few inches off the ground (most above 8 to 10 ft.) to 50 feet. House Sparrows select larger and denser trees for "open" nests, which they typically build next to the main trunk (McGillivray 1981). In colder climes, they tend to position tree nests more centrally in tree rows, lower in trees, and with south-facing entrances, all for protection from strong north winds early in the season; later in the season they tend to build nests with north-facing entrances to take advantage of the cooling effects of wind (McGillivray 1981). Nest sites are frequently occupied by different individuals in successive nesting attempts in the same season (Weaver 1939, 1943; Sappington 1977).

The House Sparrow's diet consists primarily of seeds, especially grains, but it varies locally and regionally (e.g., Kalmbach 1940, Southern 1945, Summers-Smith 1963, Grün 1975, Wiens & Dyer 1977). Kalmbach's (1940) exhaustive study revealed that the diet in the U.S., overall by volume, is about 97% vegetable matter and 3% animal matter. About 78% of the vegetable fare is cereal grains, such as cracked corn, oats, wheat, grain sorghums, barley, buckwheat, and rice. Grass and weed seeds comprise about 17% of the diet, and important plants include ragweed,

crabgrass, smartweed or knotgrass, pigweed, and amaranth. The remainder of the vegetable menu includes mast and wild fruit, cultivated fruits and vegetables, and miscellaneous vegetable matter. Consumption of animal matter in the U.S. varies from none in winter to 12% at the peak of breeding in May. However, these figures mask the fact that House Sparrows will sometimes exploit abnormal abundance of insects. The main animal items in their diet are weevils and various other beetles, grasshoppers and crickets, caterpillars and moths, hymenopterans, and flies, along with miscellaneous insects, spiders, millipedes, earthworms, snails, and garbage. Near the sea, House Sparrows also take mollusks and crustaceans (Summers-Smith 1963).

Sappington (1977) found that, in addition to the parents, nest helpers also fed young at a majority of nests in Mississippi. The nestling diet decreases from nearly all animal matter (about 85%-100%) in the first few days of life (when fed partly by regurgitation) to about 20%-30% at fledgling, with a corresponding increase in vegetable food (Kalmbach 1940, Summers-Smith 1963). The consumption of soft-bodied insects decreases with age, whereas that of hard chitinous insects increases until vegetable foods become predominant; a higher frequency of spider consumption at early ages may be due to their easier digestibility (Kalmbach 1940) or perhaps to their greater energy or nutritive value (Wieloch 1975). In addition to other seasonal and age- or sex-related dietary differences, Pinowska (1975) found that females engaged in egg laying ate more insects (protein) and weed seeds (mineral salts and vitamins); increased consumption of grit may aid in digestion of hard insects or satisfy the changing requirements of females for mineral salts. The general consumption of eggshells, mortar, and salt may serve similar purposes (Summers-Smith 1963).

House Sparrows forage mostly on or close to the ground. They pick up waste grain after harvest, grain spread on the ground as livestock feed, semidigested grain from the droppings of livestock, seed from bird feeders, and food dropped or offered directly by humans (Barrows 1889, Bent 1958, Summers-Smith 1963). They also scratch up planted or sprouted seeds, clip off or pull up tender new shoots, cut out the embryo fruit of flower buds, clip vegetable leaves, eat undeveloped vegetable seeds, and peck fruits on the vine or in trees. House Sparrows will alight on stalks to pluck grain from the fruiting heads or to shake the kernels down to the ground to be picked up later; occasionally, they will hover next to a seed head to obtain the seeds. Grass and weed seeds are obtained by stripping the head. Animal food is also obtained in a variety of ways. Birds will methodically search for slow-moving insects, which they glean from the ground, bushes, tree trunks, and the undersides of tree foliage. They also take flies and other insects from under eaves where caught in cobwebs or from the grills of parked cars, and they catch moths attracted to lights. House Sparrows catch active insects using clumsy flycatching maneuvers from perches or the ground, by pouncing down from low flight, or by darting up from the ground to bushes. They also hover kestrellike, tails depressed and fanned and legs dangling, to obtain insects from buildings or foliage. Rarely, House Sparrows also flush prey from trees by grasping a twig in their feet and vigorously flapping their wings (Guillory & Deshotek 1981). Sometimes House Sparrows follow American Robins and European Starlings foraging on lawns for worms and grubs, to rob them of their catch (Bent 1958).

Nesting House Sparrows generally range only up to about 200 to 500 yards, or rarely a mile, from nest sites when foraging (Summers-Smith 1963, Wieloch 1975). In the summer, flocks of primarily immature birds form. Large numbers of birds roost communally at night in tall, densely foliaged trees in the countryside or in cities near nesting locations, and they commute out to feed in grain-fields during the day (Summers-Smith 1963, North 1973, Dyer et al. 1977). These flocks generally commute less than two miles, or rarely up to three to four miles, from roost sites to foraging areas. While foraging in grainfields they only venture about five yards from cover (Summers-Smith 1963).

Marin Breeding Distribution

During the atlas period, House Sparrows bred widely in Marin County, but their distribution was most continuous in the urban-suburban corridor along Highway 101 in eastern Marin. In the remainder of the county, they were more patchily distributed in association with the human population in small towns and around ranches on coastal bluffs, inland valleys, and low, rolling hills. They avoided areas that lacked human occupation, which generally coincided with steep and densely vegetated ridges. On Point Reyes, for example, House Sparrows concentrated on the outer peninsula around dairy ranches and in or near the Olema Valley, from the small communities of Inverness to Bolinas, but they shunned most of Inverness Ridge. Representative breeding records included Maggetti Ranch, E side Tomales Bay (NB 5/27/82 –DS); Chileno Valley (NB 6/4/82 –DS); Hicks Valley (FL 6/?/82 –ScC); and Novato (NB 5/27/78 –RMS).

Historical Trends/Population Threats

The introduction of House Sparrows and their rapid spread in North America is fairly well documented (Barrows 1889, Bent 1958, Robbins 1973). House Sparrows were introduced on this continent because European immigrants longed for the familiar birds of their homeland and because they believed the sparrows would be useful in controlling insect pests. House Sparrows were first liberated in New York City from 1851 to 1853. In the following

decades, scores of other introductions were made in the East (varying from 5 to over 1000 birds each), primarily of stock from Great Britain and, to a lesser extent, Germany. The spread of the House Sparrow population was also aided greatly by transplants to other areas of birds already established in the United States. Up until 1886, the only known successful introductions west of the 100th meridian were at San Francisco (1871 or 1872, origin unknown), at Stockton, California (1883, from San Francisco), and at Salt Lake City (1873 or 1874, from Europe). Initially, introductions and transplants took on the proportions of a "craze," with hordes of enthusiastic "benefactors" urging introductions in increased numbers and aiding and abetting birds already established, to the point of legal protection. From 1855 to 1870, there was only weak resistance to the introductions by a few enlightened naturalists and by citizens who had previous experience controlling the sparrows in Europe. A gradual turn in the tide of opinion against the sparrows became marked by 1880, especially among agriculturalists. Even with increasing opposition, sparrow enthusiasts were still providing "nesting boxes by the thousands" and "food by the barrel" (Barrows 1889). Control efforts had little effect except to lessen numbers locally. After the initial rash of introductions, which lasted about 35 years, little was recorded of further releases. The spread of House Sparrows continued at a rapid pace, with birds moving out from cities and towns to the agricultural areas. In addition to dissemination by purposeful release, House Sparrows expanded their range by following highways, where they could pick up grain dropped by passing vehicles or semidigested grain from the droppings of horses, and by unintentional long-distance dispersal via grain or cattle cars. The latter method was particularly effective in the West. By 1900, House Sparrows had extended their range across the Great Plains to the base of the Rockies, but they had spread only slightly from the western colonies (Bent 1958, Robbins 1973). By 1910, House Sparrows occupied nearly all of the United States except central Nevada, southern California, and the northern Rockies. By 1915 they were present, at least locally, even in these areas. All of the U.S. and a large part of southern Canada were colonized by 1969, with expansion and consolidation still occurring on the edge of the range. Some observers felt that the House Sparrow population had reached a peak in the East by 1890 and declined thereafter coincident with the shift from horse to automobile transportation. They speculated that the decline was due either to a decrease in grain supplies and grain spilling from nosebags and found in horse dung or to a natural decline typical of many rapidly spreading species that overshoot their limits.

Although birds arriving in San Francisco in 1871 or 1872 apparently came from transplants from the East, it has been suggested that the species repeatedly entered

California unintentionally via railroad lines (G&M 1944). By 1886, House Sparrows had appeared generally throughout the San Francisco Bay region and at Eureka, Stockton, and Hollister. By 1915, the species occupied virtually all sections of the state, at least sparingly. Although not reported in Marin County at the turn of the century (Mailliard 1900), House Sparrows were considered "very common" here by 1933 (S&P 1933). A decrease in the California population was noted locally in the two decades prior to 1944 (G&M 1944), perhaps for the same reasons suggested for the eastern population. House Sparrow populations were relatively stable on Breeding Bird Surveys in California from 1968 to 1989 (USFWS unpubl. analyses).

The House Sparrow's great success as a colonizer can be attributed to its preadaptation to a niche not previously occupied by other native birds, its great tolerance for extremes in environmental conditions, its varied feeding methods, its choice of a variety of nest sites, its ability to quickly exploit new food sources, and its tolerance of human disturbance (Summers-Smith 1963). Food supply seems to be the main factor in controlling House Sparrow numbers at present. Changes in the thrust of human endeavors will continue to affect House Sparrows, with various factors such as increased human populations augmenting numbers and others, such as increasing mechanization of harvest methods, depressing them.

Remarks

The House Sparrow has been accused, to varying degrees, of a multitude of transgressions to human interests, including economic damage to grain and other agricultural crops, fouling water, spreading parasites and disease in poultry and livestock, clogging drain pipes with their nests, and marring statues, buildings, or trees with their "filth" (Barrows 1889, Kalmbach 1940, Southern 1945, Bent 1958). Perhaps their greatest "fault" is their aggressive interactions with native birds. House Sparrows frequently defend and use nest sites before other species arrive and actively displace other species to the point of destroying or throwing out their eggs and young. The species most affected are the cavity nesters such as swallows, bluebirds, and wrens, though attacks also extend to open nesters such as American Robins and House Finches. Efforts at House Sparrow control have proven effective on only a local scale, but considering all of the problems humans have caused native birds, the least that can be done is to protect them from the offenses of introduced birds when possible. In the case of the House Sparrow, this can be most effective by eliminating the food supply that attracts them and, secondarily, by removing their nest materials before they are well established.

Although the introduction of the House Sparrow has had an overwhelmingly negative effect, on a positive note it has allowed the study of rapid evolution of geographic variation in body size and dimensions, plumage, the onset and duration of the breeding season, clutch size, and various physiological characteristics (see Murphy 1978).

SPECIES OF UNCLEAR BREEDING STATUS OR POTENTIAL BREEDERS

The following accounts describe what we know of species with equivocal historical or recent breeding evidence in Marin County, or of species that have bred elsewhere around San Francisco Bay and potentially could breed in Marin County. Some of these species may formerly have bred in Marin County at a time of very limited observer coverage and may have gone undetected before extirpation.

EARED GREBE
Podiceps nigricollis

Eared Grebes have bred irregularly in the San Francisco Bay Area (in Alameda, Santa Clara, and Sonoma counties) since 1983 (AB 37:1022, ABN, B. Burridge pers. comm.). Potential breeding habitat of shallow-water marshlands could be created for the species in Marin County's historic bayside marshlands, much of which is now diked off from the bay; the paucity of Bay Area breeding records suggests such habitat might be used only under unusual circumstances though. Eared Grebes now occur in Marin almost exclusively as winter residents (or migrants) from October through May (Shuford et al. 1989).

WESTERN GREBE
Aechmorphorus occidentalis
CLARK'S GREBE
A. clarkii

"Western" Grebes (when the above two species were considered one) formerly bred on Lake Merced in the city and county of San Francisco (G&W 1927, G&M 1944). Western and Clark's grebes occur in Marin County year round, though primarily as winter residents from September through May (Shuford et al. 1989). Despite summer occurrence here on salt water, it seems only remotely possible they will ever colonize some of Marin County's marsh-bordered lakes, all of which are probably too small to provide adequate nesting habitat.

FORK-TAILED STORM-PETREL
Oceanodroma furcata

The nearest known breeding colony of Fork-tailed Storm-Petrels is in northern Humboldt County (Sowls et al. 1980, Carter et al. 1992). Intriguing was the capture of an adult Fork-tailed Storm-Petrel with a bare brood patch on 27-28 May 1990 at the Farallon Islands (Carter et al. 1992, PRBO unpubl.). Although it is possible that a few of these petrels may nest on the Farallones, it is more likely the captured bird was on an extended foraging trip from a distant colony. Even though this petrel may never breed in Marin County, it does appear that some breeding birds at least rarely visit our offshore or pelagic waters. The Fork-tailed Storm-Petrel is currently a Bird Species of Special Concern in California (Remsen 1978, CDFG 1991b).

LEACH'S STORM-PETREL
Oceanodroma leucorhoa

Leach's Storm-Petrels breed nearby on the Farallon Islands and at Gull Rock, Sonoma County (Carter et al. 1992), suggesting that they could possibly nest in Marin County, perhaps at Bird Rock, where Ashy Storm-Petrels breed.

LITTLE BLUE HERON
Egretta caerulea

Up to two adult Little Blue Herons were seen in or near the West Marin Island heron and egret rookery off San Rafael in the breeding seasons of 1965, 1968, 1969, 1970, and 1971 (Unitt 1977). Observers suspected Little Blues were breeding there or hybridizing with Snowy Egrets, but neither was ever confirmed. A specimen at the California Academy of Sciences from the West Marin Island colony thought possibly to be a young Little Blue Heron is of uncertain identity (J. Morlan pers. comm.). Subsequently, they have probably been breeding or hybridizing with Snowy Egrets in south San Francisco Bay since at least 1981 (Morlan & Erickson 1988, AB 42:1336), but breeding was not confirmed there until 1988 (P. Woodin pers. comm.).

CATTLE EGRET
Bubulcus ibis

The Cattle Egret has spread rapidly in California since its arrival in the state in 1964 (McCaskie 1965). Nesting was first observed in southern California in 1970 (AFN 24:716) and in northern California in 1978 (AB 32:1204). Among other sites, the species now breeds in small numbers in Santa Clara County in south San Francisco Bay (AB 39:345), the closest colony to Marin County. Cattle Egrets occur in Marin County primarily as late fall and winter dispersants from mid-October to mid-January; breeding season records are few for the county (Shuford et al. 1989). The observation of one Cattle Egret at the Audubon Canyon Ranch heron and egret rookery on 16 April 1974 (MSd) is the only evidence of nest site prospecting by this species in the county. The Cattle Egret may still possibly become established here, especially if the California breeding population continues to expand.

FULVOUS WHISTLING-DUCK
Dendrocygna bicolor

Whistling-Ducks formerly bred (probably sporadically) near Mountain View, Santa Clara County in south San Francisco Bay (G&M 1944). Grinnell and Miller (1944) considered records in Marin County prior to 1895 (Mailliard 1904) to represent the occurrence of vagrants or migrants, though the true seasonal status was probably poorly known because of limited observer coverage. Numbers of breeding Fulvous Whistling-Ducks have since declined drastically in California, leading to their being listed in the state as a Bird Species of Special Concern (Remsen 1978, CDFG 1991b). The population in the Southwest (including California) is also a Candidate (Category 2) for federal listing as Threatened or Endangered (USFWS 1991). It is unlikely that they will return to breed in the Bay Area in the foreseeable future.

WATERFOWL

Several other species of ducks—Green-winged Teal *(Anas crecca)*, American Wigeon *(Anas americana)*, Canvasback *(Aythya valisineria)*, Redhead *(Aythya americana)*, and Lesser Scaup *(Aythya affinis)*—have bred sporadically or accidentally around San Francisco Bay, though as a group they occur there (and in Marin County) primarily as winter residents from September or October through March or April (G&M 1944, ABN). All these species have been seen in Marin County for short or extended periods (though irregularly) in summer (Shuford et al. 1989, ABN) and potentially could breed here.

CALIFORNIA CONDOR
Gymnogyps californianus

Although California Condors formerly occurred as far north as southern British Columbia, breeding was confirmed only as far north as Monterey and San Benito counties, California (Koford 1953). Wilbur (1973b) speculated that they may once have bred as far north as the Pacific Northwest but went undetected before the species began its rapid decline toward extinction. Apparently the only solid Marin County record of Condors is of at least a dozen birds from the mountains near Fairfax in July of 1847, though a specimen from the "mountains north of San Francisco" perhaps was collected in Marin (Koford 1953). The locality designated as "San Rafael" where eggs were collected prior to 1869 (G&M 1944) refers to a site in Monterey (not Marin) County (Koford 1953). It is possible that California Condors once bred in Marin before any ornithological exploration of the county.

Because this federal and state Endangered species was teetering on the brink of extinction, a controversial captive breeding program was initiated in 1980, and by 1987 the last remaining Condors were all in confinement. As of September 1991, there were 52 condors in captivity—27 brought in from the wild as adults, chicks, or eggs, and 25 raised from eggs laid in captivity (R. Mesta pers. comm.). Given the burgeoning development and increase in human numbers in the country's most populous state, it seems unlikely we will ever see free-flying Condors on a regular basis in the Bay Area, even if the captive rearing program is highly successful by today's standards. Two young captive-reared California Condors were released in January 1992 in the Sespe Condor Sanctuary, Ventura County (R. Mesta pers. comm.). Only time will tell if these birds embodying the soul and spirit of wild California will rise again or fall to the onslaught of so-called progress.

BALD EAGLE
Haliaeetus leucocephalus

Although there are no known nesting records for Marin County (G&W 1927, S&P 1933, G&M 1944, Detrich 1986), the county is clearly within the historic breeding range. Bald Eagle bones have been identified in shell middens of aboriginal people along the shore of San Francisco Bay at Alameda County (Howard 1929), indicating the species was present in the Bay Area in prehistoric times. In historic times, Bald Eagles were "formerly common and widely distributed" along the entire length of California, but by the 1940s they were nearly extirpated as breeders (G&M 1944). Detrich (1986) suspected that the near absence of breeding records of Bald Eagles in the San Francisco Bay Area was a gap in the record rather than in the original range of the species. The closest known coastal nesting records are from near Guerneville, Sonoma County, in 1904 (Detrich 1986) and near La Honda, San Mateo County, about 1915 (G&W 1927). The least populated western sectors of Marin County, where conifer-clad ridges overlook a series of near-pristine estuaries, would seemingly have provided suitable nesting habitat. In the mid-1880s, Point Reyes and other parts of Marin County supported "the greatest dairy operations in the state" (Mason 1970), in an era when predators, especially eagles, were routinely subjected to severe persecution by ranchers and stockmen (Detrich 1986). A newspaper report of a "bald head eagle" shot at Camp Taylor on 17 August 1868 (*Marin Journal*, 22 Aug 1868), suggests that a resident population may have been extirpated. The species is currently a rare and irregular winter visitant to Marin County, mostly from October through March.

The Bald Eagle is currently listed as state and federally Endangered in California. A proposal to introduce 32 Bald Eagles into the Point Reyes National Seashore over three years in the early 1990s in hopes of establishing a breeding population has met with resistance from some local biologists and conservationists. They question the wisdom of introducing a species—currently expanding on its own—into an area with no known historic breeding population because of the potential detrimental effects on already naturally established Ospreys, heron and egret colonies, or other potential prey of the eagles. Once data are in on population size and reproductive success from the 1991 breeding season, the U.S. Fish and Wildlife Service will give consideration to downlisting the Bald Eagle from Endangered to Threatened in parts of its range (P. Detrich pers. comm.). Although our national symbol can use all the help it can get, introductions or reintroductions should be done only after careful studies have evaluated any possible effects that might upset the finely tuned balance of the ecosytem in question.

PRAIRIE FALCON
Falco mexicanus

A sighting of a Prairie Falcon flying south from Sonoma County to Marin County over Estero Americano about 1.5 miles east of its mouth on 1 July 1982 (DS) is the only known breeding season record for the county. This bird likely represented a postbreeding dispersant or a non-breeder. An open country-inhabiting raptor such as a Prairie Falcon would most likely have been seen at least with some regularity during the years of intensive atlas work if in fact the species was breeding here. Prairie Falcons typically occur in Marin as rare winter residents (or migrants), mostly from mid-August through February (ABN). Prairie Falcons do breed in drier portions of the interior Coast Range in some San Francisco Bay Area counties (Garrett & Mitchell 1973, ABN). The habitat in

Marin County most similar to breeding habitat elsewhere in the Bay Area is found around Novato, but it appears to lack suitable breeding cliffs. The Prairie Falcon is a Bird Species of Special Concern in California (Remsen 1978, CDFG 1991b).

WILD TURKEY
Meleagris gallopavo

Wild Turkeys are not native to California, but they have been released and now wild, free-ranging resident populations inhabit large areas of the state (G&M 1944, Harper & Smith 1973, Graves 1975, Mallette & Slosson 1987). Although Wild Turkeys raised in Marin County were sold in San Francisco in 1883 (Schorger 1966), there appears to have been no effort to establish a wild population here until recently. In February 1988, California Department of Fish and Game personnel released 17 Wild Turkeys on the ridges south of Big Rock Ranch off Lucas Valley Road. These were wild-trapped Rio Grande Turkeys (*M. g. intermedia*) taken from populations established in Napa County, originally captured in the native range of the subspecies (F. Botti pers. comm.). If these birds enjoy the success of other populations now established in much of the Coast Range, they will probably be widely distributed in oak woodlands and oak savannah in northeastern Marin within a few years. The evidence to date suggests that the Marin birds are doing well. The population is expanding and sightings span from at least Alameda del Prado, Ignacio, on the north, south to the Loma Alta and Sleepy Hollow areas near Sir Francis Drake Boulevard (F. Botti & B. Beard pers. comm.). From 1988 to 1991, many adults with broods have been seen (e.g., two adults with 12 large young crossing Lucas Valley Rd. on flats E of Big Rock Ranch 7/17/91 —DS et al.).

WILSON'S PHALAROPE
Phalaropus tricolor

In California, this species breeds in the short vegetation of freshwater marshes and wet meadows, primarily east of the Cascade-Sierra axis, though formerly it bred irregularly (or at least in smaller numbers) in the central San Joaquin Valley (G&M 1944). Extralimital confirmed breeding records have been reported for the coast from Lake Talawa, Del Norte County (FL 7/10-8/5/77 —RSW) and from the Cader Lane Ponds in Petaluma, Sonoma County (FL 6/26/82 —RLe et al.); a few additional records suggestive of coastal breeding have been reported as well (ABN). In Marin County, Wilson's Phalaropes were seen in one of the marshy diked Bahia Ponds in Novato on 17 May, 7 June, and 26 June 1980 (GiT, DS). Although the timing of these records and the proximity to the Cader Lane Ponds (3-4 mi.) is tantalizing, the overlap, or near overlap,

431

in the timing of spring and fall migration on the coast (Shuford et al. 1989) clouds interpretation of this and other potential coastal breeding records. Direct confirmation of breeding of this species is the only way to add it to the main list of breeding species for a coastal California county.

HEERMANN'S GULL
Larus heermanni

From 1979 to 1981, Heermann's Gulls attempted to breed on Alcatraz Island, San Francisco, about 775 miles north of the nearest Mexican breeding colony at San Benitos Islands (Howell et al. 1983). This truly exceptional breeding record is not likely to be repeated, especially since the Alcatraz birds were unsuccessful in their attempts. But if successful, it is remotely possible that Heermann's Gulls might select a breeding site on one of Marin County's islands in San Francisco Bay. Heermann's Gulls occur in Marin County primarily as fall and early winter dispersants, mostly from June through November (Shuford et al. 1989).

CALIFORNIA GULL
Larus californicus

California Gulls began to breed in salt pond habitat in south San Francisco Bay near Alviso, Santa Clara County, in 1980 and near Newark, Alameda County, in 1984 and are continuing to expand, at least in the former county (PWo for S.F. Bay Bird Obs.). This is the only known breeding area on the Pacific Coast; they nest primarily in the Great Basin Desert and the northern Great Plains. As with the three species of terns (see below), the California Gull nucleus in the South Bay might possibly provide colonizers for Marin County if suitable habitat were available here in diked wetlands along the shorelines of San Pablo and San Francisco bays. California Gulls currently occur in Marin County year round, though mostly as fall dispersants and winter visitants from September (numbers drop by mid-Jan) through May (Shuford et al. 1989). This gull is a Bird Species of Special Concern in California (Remsen 1978, CDFG 1991b).

TERNS

Caspian *(Sterna caspia)* and Forster's *(S. forsteri)* terns and the state and federally Endangered Least Tern *(S. antillarum)* all breed at scattered sites around San Francisco Bay in disturbed or human created habitats. It seems very likely that one or more of these species might breed in Marin County if suitable nesting sites were provided in diked ponds or marshes along the shorelines of San Francisco and San Pablo bays.

MARBLED MURRELET
Brachyramphus marmoratus

The Marbled Murrelet is a year-round resident along the northern California coast that nests in old-growth forests up to 25 miles inland and forages in nearshore ocean waters, mostly within a mile or so of land (Carter & Erickson 1988). Although birds have been seen off the outer coast of Marin County in the breeding season (1 Apr–1 Sep, Carter & Erickson 1988), a lack of nearshore records from 2 May to 30 June and a total lack of inland records suggests that Marbled Murrelets do not breed regularly in Marin County despite the availability of seemingly suitable nesting habitat on conifer-clad coastal ridges. Local July and August records probably pertain to postbreeding dispersants from elsewhere; the species occurs in nearshore waters off Marin County mostly from August to March (ABN). Marbled Murrelets may once have bred in Marin County before the era of intense observer coverage and before logging eliminated extensive nesting habitat along the coast. The California population has probably declined mainly because of the destruction of old-growth forests (Carter & Erickson 1988). Recent reviews of the species' status have prompted government agencies to list this murrelet as state Endangered in California and federally Threatened.

YELLOW-BILLED CUCKOO
Coccyzus americanus

Mailliard (1900) listed the status of the Yellow-billed Cuckoo in Marin County as "Doubtful. Some reported as having been seen at Olema in 1898, but no specimens taken." Stephens and Pringle (1933) reported a record of an injured bird captured at "Point Reyes" on 19 July 1919. Marin County is within the overall historic breeding range of Yellow-billed Cuckoos in California—they formerly ranged north on the coast to the vicinity of Sebastapol, Sonoma County (G&M 1944). Populations of this riparian obligate declined drastically in the state in later years because of habitat loss, and the species is now listed as state Endangered (G&M 1944, Gaines & Laymon 1984, Laymon & Halterman 1987). It is plausible that cuckoos may once have bred here, perhaps at Olema Marsh currently the county's largest riparian forest, but went undetected before extirpation. In recent years, Yellow-billed Cuckoos have occurred irregularly in June and July as very rare vagrants on Marin's outer coast away from suitable breeding habitat.

CHIMNEY SWIFT
Chaetura pelagica

A record of a Chimney Swift at Bolinas Lagoon on 19 July 1975 (AB 29:1027) suggests the possibility of breeding in Marin County. The species has bred along the southern California coast (Garrett & Dunn 1981) and to the north in Mendocino County (AB 29:1027, McCaskie et al. 1979).

BLACK-CHINNED HUMMINGBIRD
Archilochus alexandri

A female hummingbird, identified as a Black-chinned, was observed at Ross, Marin County, from the time of nest building on 13 May 1941 until three days after the fledging of her young on 26 June (Stephens 1941). Grinnell and Miller (1944) cast doubt on the authenticity of this record. On the other hand, the extended period of observation by a number of bird students (including two of the region's most prominent–Laura A. Stephens & Junea Kelly), coupled with their knowledge of the rarity of the species at any season in Marin County (S&P 1933), suggests that it may have been a correct identification and valid breeding record. It seems best to leave the question open until another record is documented, although other species characteristic of the dry interior Coast Range, such as Say's Phoebe and Cassin's Kingbird, occasionally have nested in the more humid clime of Marin County. Black-chinned Hummingbirds currently occur very rarely/irregularly in Marin from mid-July to mid-September (ABN).

WILLOW FLYCATCHER
Empidonax traillii

Although never known to breed in Marin County (Mailliard 1900, S&P 1933), Willow Flycatchers formerly bred as close as the south San Francisco Bay region (G&M 1944). The Willow Flycatcher is now listed by the California Department of Fish and Game Commission as state Endangered, and the U.S Forest Service considers it a sensitive species in California (USFS 1984). A singing bird about one mile northeast of Wildcat Camp, Point Reyes National Seashore, on 5 July 1980 (DS, ITi) represents the only known midsummer record for Marin County, though this individual may have been a late migrant. On the other hand, this bird may have been prospecting for a breeding site, although there are only sporadic recent nesting records for lowland northern California (McCaskie et al. 1979, Roberson 1985, Harris et al. 1987). Willow Flycatchers occur in Marin mostly from mid-August to early October and irregularly from mid-May to early July (ABN).

BANK SWALLOW
Riparia riparia

The former status of this species in Marin County is puzzling. Mailliard (1900) reported the Bank Swallow was "an abundant summer resident in favorable localities." Stephens and Pringle (1933) list the Bank Swallow under their category of birds "present through the summer only," but then list only four spring records (22 Mar–12 Apr) and one early fall record for 25 July. Intimations of breeding at Nicasio (G&W 1927, Laymon et al. 1987) apparently pertain solely to a record from that locality on 19 March 1876 by C. A. Allen that was reported by Belding (1890) with no details of numbers of birds or nesting status. No Marin County sites are listed by Grinnell and Miller (1944) among their "definitely known" locations of nesting in California. The Bank Swallow is currently listed as Threatened in the state. This swallow now occurs in Marin irregularly in spring from late March though late May and in fall from mid-August to late September (ABN).

CEDAR WAXWING
Bombycilla cedrorum

In California, Cedar Waxwings breed with regularity only on the north coast in Del Norte County and south to the vicinity of Eureka, Humboldt County (G&M 1944, ABN). Extralimital breeding records exist for the interior of northern California and for the coast down to southern California (Garrett & Dunn 1981). Birds breed or oversummer irregularly in central California (e.g., AB 41:1485). Cedar Waxwings occur annually in Marin County in variable numbers as winter residents/visitants, mostly from late August through early June. The lack of records between late June and early August suggests that a record of an adult feeding immatures at Inverness on 31 August 1959 (GMi) represented birds that had migrated or dispersed some distance before arriving in Marin County. Birds in juvenile plumage are frequently seen as migrants.

AMERICAN REDSTART
Setophaga ruticilla

The American Redstart was first confirmed breeding on the northern California coast in 1972 (Binford & Stallcup 1972), and additional observations of confirmed or probable breeding suggest it is an irregular breeder on the coastal slope of Humboldt and Del Norte counties (ABN). The species typically occurs along the California coast as a rare but regular vagrant in spring and fall. In Marin County, it occurs mainly as a rare vagrant in spring from early June to early July and in fall from mid-August to early November (ABN). Two intriguing records suggest that redstarts may occasionally breed in Marin County. A bird

433

identified as a hatching-year male was banded at PRBO's Palomarin field station on 7 July 1982 (RJRy), suggesting it may have been raised from a nest somewhere in Marin. A first-year male was singing one-half mile north of Inverness Park 27 May–11 June 1984 (A&WG), but good observer coverage revealed no signs of breeding.

BOBOLINK
Dolichonyx oryzivorus

Bobolinks have long been suspected of breeding in California in the Surprise Valley, Modoc County, in the extreme northeastern corner of the state, but breeding confirmation has not yet been obtained (Dawson 1923, Mailliard 1924a, G&M 1944, Morlan & Erickson 1988). This area is relatively close to a regular breeding colony at Malheur National Wildlife Refuge in eastern Oregon (Wittenberger 1978). Along the California coast, Bobolinks occur as rare or irregular vagrants in spring from mid-May to mid-July and in fall in September and October (McCaskie et al. 1979). The possibility of extralimital nesting in Marin County was suggested by the presence of up to two males and one female Bobolink at the RCA station on Point Reyes from 5 to 19 June 1983 (AB 37:1025). Singing, displaying, and copulation were observed, but mowing of the field they were occupying eliminated the possibility of a nesting attempt. It remains a mystery whether these birds were fulfilling hormonal urges on migration or were actually attempting to nest. Del Norte County records—of adults feeding young on the coast near Fort Dick in July 1977 (undocumented, *fide* R.A. Erickson) and one to three singing males at Klamath from 5 to 19 June 1982 (AB 36:1014, R.A. Erickson pers. comm.)—add further intrigue to the possibility of occasional extralimital nesting on the coast.

YELLOW-HEADED BLACKBIRD
Xanthocephalus xanthocephalus

Yellow-headed Blackbirds were formerly rare breeders in the San Francisco Bay Area with nesting records for Sonoma, Contra Costa, Alameda, and Santa Clara counties (G&W 1927, G&M 1944). Recently, breeding was suspected at Skaggs Island, Sonoma County (T 25 adult males 5/28/86 –DRu et al.), and breeding was confirmed at the town of American Canyon, Napa County (T, NB, FY 5/24–6/29/91 –ESa et al.). Apparent migrants/vagrants, such as a male seen at a pond near the mouth of Novato Creek along the San Pablo Bay shoreline on 16 April 1988 (DS et al.), potentially might provide colonizers that would breed in Marin if conditions were right at the time of their arrival. Yellow-headed Blackbirds currently occur in Marin irregularly in spring in April (one June record) and in fall from mid-September to early October (ABN).

GREAT-TAILED GRACKLE
Quiscalus mexicanus

Expansion of the breeding range of Great-tailed Grackles in southern California (Garrett & Dunn 1981, AB 40:1257, AB 42:1341) probably explains the small but growing number of records of this species in northern California. A male Great-tailed Grackle found in San Francisco in 1978 was joined by a female in 1979 and they have attempted to nest since 1980, but without success (Morlan & Erickson 1988). A record of a Great-tailed Grackle at the Marin Headlands from 15 to 17 June 1988 (AB 42:1338) suggests the possibility that the species may some day attempt to breed in Marin County as well.

APPENDIXES

APPENDIX A.
Data from three Spring Bird Counts conducted in Marin County from 1977 to 1987.

Since 1977, three Spring Bird Counts have been conducted in Marin County: Even Cheaper Thrills—partly in Sonoma County, Marin County (southern), and Point Reyes Peninsula. These counts were patterned after Christmas Bird Counts published in *American Birds* and use the same 15-mile diameter count circles. In addition to recording numbers of individuals, observers on count day assign each species they encounter one of three general breeding categories—Possible, Probable, and Confirmed (or nonbreeder)—used in the Marin County Breeding Bird Atlas Project (see Table 5). On the Spring Counts the category S (singing male present) is considered as probable breeding if the bird in question is in a habitat where it normally breeds, despite the lack of evidence of longterm occupancy of a site. Data for all these counts are presented below in tabular form. Bold-faced names or numbers indicate species that are very rare in this area year round or for the season in question, or represent high counts. Descriptions of rare bird sightings are on file with the author. Standard data on weather and observer coverage are listed for each count; a participant list summarizes names of all counters for all years of each count.

When comparing counts, please bear in mind that count dates range from early May until early June. On early season counts, there are more migrant species and more individuals of species that occur here both as breeders and migrants. On later season counts, there should be more individuals of breeding species since both adults and fully independent young are counted. This increase in population size from recruitment of young may be offset by a seasonal decline in song by which many individuals of passerine species are tallied.

MARIN COUNTY (SOUTHERN), CALIFORNIA.

37°55'N 122°34'W, center 1.5 mi n.w. of Mill Valley; elevation 0 to 2600 ft; count circle and habitat coverage as described 1976 for the CBC of the same name (AB 30:592). Coverage 1977, 1982, and 1983.

1) 21 May 1977, 0430 to 1900. Partly cloudy, locally foggy in a.m., patchy overcast in p.m. Temp. 48–63° F. Wind Werly 3–15 m.p.h. Although numbers of individuals and species were compiled immediately, the data on party-miles, party-hours, and observers were not tallied until 1984 and consequently data were not complete. Observers were not recorded for 1 of 12 areas and party-hours and party-miles were not available for 3 areas. The latter were estimated by taking an average for the 12 areas from which data were available and applying it to the 3 questionable areas. About 60 observers in about 16 parties. Total party-hours, about 185 (169 on foot, 16 by car), total party-miles about 248 (144 on foot, 104 by car).

2) 5 June 1982, 0430 to 1915. Fog in a.m. coastally and on higher ridges, clearing to sunny with few clouds. Temp 39–71° F. Wind NWerly 0–10 m.p.h. Sixty-four observers in 23 parties. Total party-hours, 224.5 (201.5 on foot, 23 by car) plus 8 night hours. Total party-miles, 385.5 (159.5 on foot, 226 by car).

3) 4 June 1983, 0500 to 1800. Clear, sunny all day. Temp 45–78° F. Wind NWerly 0–5 m.p.h. Forty-six observers in 26 parties, plus one feeder watcher. Total party-hours, 207 (188 on foot, 19 by car) plus 1 feeder hour and 4 night hours. Total party-miles, 306 (145 on foot, 161 by car).

Participants: Peter & Julia Allen, Jane Anderson, Betty Beade, Dennis Beall, Max Beckwith, Gordon Beebe, Betty Bossi, Herb Brandt, Kate Brennan, Pat Briggs, Courtney Buechert, Jean Burnett, Betty Burridge, Jean Canepa, Scott Carey, Janice Chism, Carolyn & Frank Christian, Harold Conner, Rosamond Day, Larry Desmond, John Dillon, Mary During, Doug Ellis, Jules & Meryl Evens, Mary Farr, Carter Faust, Ann Gilbert, Tony Grady, Helen & Paul Green, Ann Gross, Kem Hainebach, Rita Halbeisen, Nancy Hanson, Roger Harris, Sheila Hershon, Laura Hines, Bob Hogan, David & Richard Holway, Alan Hopkins, Ken Howard, George Hugenberg, Stuart Johnston, Kathleen Jones, Doug Judell, Anne Knobloch, Bill & Paget Lenarz, Donna Lion, Susan Martin, Emmy Hill, Marie Mans, Gloria Markowitz, Grace (co-compiler 1982) & Mort McMichael, Bonnie & Woody Nackley, Michael Nelligan, Julie Numainville, Cynthia Oglove, Dana & Todd Olson, Lynda Orman, Kate Partridge, Charlotte & Chriss Poulsen, Lina Jane Prairie, Helen Pratt, Barbara Prince, Alton Raible, Faith Rendell, Inez Riney, Mary Lousie Rosegay, Ane Rovetta, Barbara Salzman, Don & Phyllis Samson, Marisela de Santa Anna, Phil (compiler

1977) & Margaret Schaeffer, Carol & Stuart Schneider, Bob & Ruth Scott, Betty Short, Dave Shuford (co-compiler 1982), Dianne Sierra (compiler 1983), Ann Spencer, Barry Spitz, Jean Starkweather, Lynne Stenzel, Bob Stewart, Don Stiver, Nick Story, Jim & Marta Sullivan, Gil Thomson, Carol & Noel Thoney, Irene Timossi, Dorothy Tobkin, Carol & Michael Trent, Pat Triggs, Phil Unitt, Keiko Yamane, Bob & Carol Yutzy, Jim Weigand, Janet Wessel, Jack Whetstone, Diane Williams, Summer Wilson, David Wimpfheimer, Jon Winter, Keiko Yamane, Jon Zablackis, Dianne Ziola, and various unidentified observers in 1977.

POINT REYES PENINSULA, CALIFORNIA.

38°08'N 122°53'W, center USC&GS triangulation point in Tomales Bay State Park; elevation 0 to 1470 ft; count circle and habitat coverage as described 1971 for CBC of the same name (AB 25:501). Coverage 1982 only.

1) 23 May 1982, 0600 to 1700. Partly cloudy all day. Temp. 44–94° F. Wind SEerly 1 m.p.h. Thirty observers in 14 parties. Total party-hours, 104 (78.25 on foot, 25.75 by car), zero night hours. Total party-miles, 178 (60 on foot, 118 by car). (In count area count week but not seen count day: Yellow-breasted Chat).

Participants: Ted Beedy, Betty Burridge, Scott Carey, Karen Cartier, Chris D'Orgieux, Dave DeSante, Jules Evens, Ben & Char Glading, Steve Granholm, Paul Green, Ruth Hawksley, Gregg Martinsen, Nancy Norvell, Paul O'Brien, Sabrina Patterson, Lina Jane Prairie, Cindy Reittinger, Elsie Richey, Susan Sanders, Dave Shuford (co-compiler), Bob Stewart, Sylvia Sykora, Dorothy Tobkin, Kent Van Vuren, Bob (co-compiler) & Carol Yutzy, Sally Walters, Bette Wentzel, Janet Wessel.

EVEN CHEAPER THRILLS, CALIFORNIA.

38°08'N 122°37'W, center the spring 1.4 mi n. of jct. San Marin Dr. and Novato Blvd., Novato; elevation 0 to 1887 ft; count circle and habitat coverage as described 1978 for the Arroyo Cheap Thrills, California CBC (AB 32:852). Coverage: 10 consecutive years from 1978 to 1987.

1) 7 May 1978, 0500 to 1830. Clear, sunny all day. Temp. 49–84° F. Wind Werly, 0–5 m.p.h. Twenty-nine observers in 11 parties. Total party-hours, 119 (88 on foot, 31 by car). Total party-miles, 303.5 (51.5 on foot, 252 by car).

2) 6 May 1979, 0445 to 1845. Scattered clouds and occasional showers in a.m., overcast with gentle rain (0.1 in.) in p.m. Temp. 46–64° F. Wind Serly, 1–12 m.p.h. Twenty-nine observers in 15 parties. Total party-hours, 153 (106.5 on foot, 44.5 by car, 2 by boat) plus 1 night hour. Total party-miles, 433 (75 on foot, 357 by car, 1 by boat).

3) 17 May 1980, 0200 to 1900. Clear, sunny all day. Temp 45–83° F. Wind W-SEerly, 0–8 m.p.h. Thirty-one observers in 14 parties. Total party-hours, 121 (91.5 on foot, 24.5 by car, 6 by boat) plus 6 night hours. Total party-miles, 416.5 (66 on foot, 342.5 by car, 8 by boat).

4) 9 May 1981, 0100 to 1830. Clear with haze on the horizon. Temp. 56–73° F. Wind NWerly 5–10 m.p.h. Twenty-nine observers in 12 parties. Total party-hours, 124.5 (100.75 on foot, 18.75 by car, 5 by boat) plus 11 night hours. Total party-miles, 360 (75 on foot, 275 by car, 10 by boat). (In count area count week but not seen count day: Cattle Egret, Black-chinned Sparrow).

5) 16 May 1982, 0300 to 1830. Local fog in a.m., clear/sunny for the rest of the day. Temp. 44–77° F. Wind NWerly 0–10 m.p.h. Twenty-six observers in 12 parties. Total party-hours, 118 (96.5 on foot, 12.5 by car, 9 by boat) plus 5.75 night hours. Total party-miles, 280 (56 on foot, 214 by car, 10 by boat).

6) 22 May 1983, 0400 to 1800. Sunny, with few scattered high cumulus clouds. Temp. 49–75° F. Wind NWerly 0–10 m.p.h. Twenty-one observers in 12 parties. Total party-hours, 112.5 (76 on foot, 30.5 by car, 6 by boat) plus 3 night hours. Total party-miles 467.5 (68 on foot, 391.5 by car, 8 by boat) plus 2 night miles.

7) 3 June 1984, 0430 to 1800. Mostly clear. Temp. 45–79° F. Wind Werly, 5–20 m.p.h. Twenty-five observers in 12 parties. Total party-hours, 108 (80.25 on foot, 21.75 by car, 6 by boat) plus 1.25 night hours. Total party-miles, 324.5 (49.5 on foot, 269 by car, 6 by boat) plus 3.5 night miles. (In count area count week but not seen count day: Cedar Waxwing).

8) 2 June 1985, 0430 to 1800. Overcast with drizzle in early a.m. clearing to sunny. Temp 52–74° F. Wind NWerly 0–10 m.p.h. Twenty-five observers in 13 parties. Total party-hours, 107.25 (84.5 on foot, 15.25 by car, 7.5 by boat), plus 9.25 night miles (0.25 on foot, 6 by car, 3 by boat) and 3.5 night hours (1 on foot, 0.5 by car, 2 by boat). Total party-miles 286.5 (50 on foot, 226.5 by car, 10 by boat).

9) 31 May 1986, 0430 to 1800. Patchy morning fog, otherwise sunny with scattered clouds. Temp. 55–70° F. Little wind. Twenty-two observers in 11 parties. Total party-hours 88.5 (54.75 on foot, 27.75 by car, and 4 by boat) plus 3.75 night hours. Total party-miles 188 (45 on foot, 137 by car, and 6 by boat) plus 11 night hours.

10) 31 May 1987, 0530 to 1800. Cloudy overcast in a.m., breaking to clear, sunny. Temp. 52–76° F. Wind NWerly 10–15+ m.p.h. Twenty-two observers in 12 parties. Total party-hours 101.75 (87 on foot, 14.25 by car, and 0.5 by bike) plus 0.5 night hours. Total party-miles 236 (66 by foot, 168 by car, and 2 by bike) plus 1 night mile.

Participants (* denotes counter for 5 or more years): Julia Allen, Jane Anderson, Terry Babineaux, Bob Baez, Bryant Bainbridge, Dennis Beall*, Max Beckwith, Gordon Beebe, Bob Boekelheide, Courtney Buechert, Pat & Trisha Bunsen, Betty Burridge*, Kurt Campbell (compiler 1983 & 1984), Scott Carey*, Mary Caswell, Diane Caualo, Peter Colasanti*, Pam Conley, Nancy Conzett, Chris Coulon, Dick Cunningham, Mark Delwiche, Larry Desmond, Beverly Ehreth, Doug Ellis*, Dick & Linda Erickson, Jules Evens*, Steve Gellman, Ed Good, Sarah Griffin, Nelson Hall, Janine Haller, Keith Hansen, Deyea Harper, Roger Harris, Tony Harrow, Luanna Helfman, Phil Henderson, Bob Hogan*, Ken Howard, Steve Howell, George Hugenberg*, Joanie Humphrey, Deborah Jacques, Debbie Johnston, Stuart Johnston, Bill* & Paget Lenarz, Robin Leong, Marc Liverman, Gloria Markowitz, Roger Marlowe, Gregg Martinsen, John McCormick, Joe McGee, Grace & Mort McMichael, Richard Merriss, Andrea Meyer, Charlene Modena, Derek Mooney, Gerry & Kathy Mugele, Bonnie & Woody Nackley, Adeene & Mike Nelligan, Dan & Wini Nelson, Cynthia Oglove, Todd Olson, Kate O'Neill, Gary Page, Chris Pattillo, Holly Peake, Susan Claire Peaslee, Teya Penniman, Nancy Petersen, Meghan Piercy, Lina Jane Prairie, Barbara Prince, Nancy Pullen, Bertha & Bob Rains, Ivana Roland, Louis Roth, Ruth Rudesill, Marisela de Santa Anna, Phil & Margaret Schaeffer, Jerry Scoville, Dave Shuford* (compiler all years except 1983 & 1984), Dianne Sierra*, Hank Skewis, Sue Smith, Eric Sorenson, Chris Spooner, Rich Stallcup, Lynne Stenzel, Bob Stewart, Chris Swarth, Ian Tait, Dan Taylor, Gil Thomson*, Irene Timossi*, Dorothy Tobkin, David Tomb, Susan & Wayne Trivelpiece, Betsy Utley, Ed Vine, Dave & Colleen Ward, Nils Warnock, Christine Weigen, Bette Wentzel, Janet Wessel, Jack Whetstone*, Pete White, Greg & Russ Wilson, David Wimpfheimer, Lori Withington, Keiko Yamane, Steve Yaninek.

Appendix A.

| | Marin County (Southern) | | | Point Reyes Peninsula | Even Cheaper Thrills | | | | | | | | | |

	21 May 1977	21 May 1982	4 June 1983	23 May 1982	7 May 1978	6 May 1979	17 May 1980	9 May 1981	16 May 1982	22 May 1983	3 June 1984	2 June 1985	31 May 1986	31 May 1987
Red-throated Loon	15	2	6	14	2	.	.	.	.	.	.	.	.	.
Pacific Loon	.	48	4	26	.	.	.	.	.	.	.	.	.	.
Common Loon	6	19	9	24	.	1	.	.	1	.	.	.	.	.
loon spp.	.	1	.	.	.	1	.	.	.	.	.	.	.	.
Pied-billed Grebe	10	6	6	2	20	18	13	23	19	10	22	18	27	10
Horned Grebe	40	1	.	.	.	.	.	1	.	.	.	.	1	.
Eared Grebe	.	.	6	4	1	18	15	4	19	4	.	.	1	.
Western/Clark's Grebe	264	457	60	97	3	.	7	.	5	8	5	2	1	2
American White Pelican	.	.	1	.	.	.	.	.	.	.	.	.	.	.
Brown Pelican	14	261	48	10	.	.	.	.	.	.	.	.	.	.
Double-crested Cormorant	6	45	55	120	45	26	4	47	1	9	1	6	25	12
Brandt's Cormorant	323	129	180	8	.	.	.	.	.	.	.	.	.	.
Pelagic Cormorant	46	63	52	97	.	.	.	.	.	.	.	.	.	.
American Bittern	.	.	.	1	.	4	.	.	.	.	1	.	1	.
Great Blue Heron	45	128	36	30	27	41	68	89	46	108	60	56	78	64
Great Egret	124	381	76	31	13	34	16	24	29	98	68	50	51	27
Snowy Egret	261	518	78	16	47	46	39	75	80	92	81	66	75	35
Green-backed Heron	.	.	.	3	1	.	3	4	1	1	3	7	7	5
Black-crowned Night-Heron	21	102	31	4	12	14	33	28	7	20	9	23	35	18
(Black) Brant	.	5	.	97	.	.	.	.	.	.	.	.	.	.
Ross' Goose	.	.	.	.	.	.	.	.	.	.	.	.	.	1
Canada Goose	.	4	.	.	1	1	1	2	.	.	.	10	3	21
Green-winged Teal	1	.	.	.	1	2	1	2	1	.	.	.	2	.
Mallard	320	410	403	51	114	130	119	183	295	144	149	339	244	406
Northern Pintail	.	2	7	1	7	7	13	25	7	17	12	18	27	23
Blue-winged Teal	.	.	.	.	.	1	5	.	.	2	6	4	1	5
Cinnamon Teal	6	14	8	23	63	42	52	98	62	52	99	91	81	135
teal spp.	.	.	.	.	.	1	.	.	.	.	.	.	.	.
Northern Shoveler	.	.	.	.	6	8	16	21	20	11	8	13	2	11
Gadwall	.	.	.	8	2	13	18	18	20	7	48	61	62	55
American Wigeon	.	1	.	2	3	.	.	1	.	.	.	.	.	1
Canvasback	7	1	.	.	7	5	2	3	1	.	.	1	1	3
Greater Scaup	292	75	5	6	17	42	23	10	92	6	6	16	5	22
Lesser Scaup	27	2	5	6	19	6	2	3	4	.	.	.	3	1
scaup spp.	.	227	25	5	75	19	500	.	.	.	.	7	.	10
Harlequin Duck	1	.	.	1	.	.	.	.	.	.	.	.	.	.
Oldsquaw	.	.	.	.	.	1	.	.	.	.	.	.	.	.
Black Scoter	.	5	.	20	.	.	.	.	.	.	.	.	.	.
Surf Scoter	35	108	49	191	2	.	4	.	.	.	22	.	.	1
White-winged Scoter	1	14	12	164	.	.	.	.	.	.	.	.	.	.
Common Goldeneye	.	.	.	.	.	.	.	1	3	.	.	.	2	2
Bufflehead	3	.	.	5	1	1	3	3	3	2	1	.	1	.
Red-breasted Merganser	7	2	.	24	.	1	.	.	2	.	.	.	.	.
Ruddy Duck	26	13	11	52	52	96	54	43	113	10	32	39	26	25
duck spp.	.	.	.	.	.	.	.	.	2	.	3	.	.	.
Turkey Vulture	181	226	182	124	149	208	167	187	209	210	200	154	194	155
Osprey	8	9	13	9	.	.	2	5	7	1	5	7	4	2
Black-shouldered Kite	5	.	.	3	2	7	9	11	2	3	7	15	14	10
Northern Harrier	1	.	3	13	1	3	9	11	7	3	2	7	7	3

Appendix A. (cont'd)   Marin County   Point Reyes   Even Cheaper Thrills
                              (Southern)   Peninsula

	21 May 1977	21 May 1982	4 June 1983	23 May 1982	7 May 1978	6 May 1979	17 May 1980	9 May 1981	16 May 1982	22 May 1983	3 June 1984	2 June 1985	31 May 1986	31 May 1987
Sharp-shinned Hawk	2	·	·	·	3	2	1	3	4	1	·	·	·	·
Cooper's Hawk	4	1	3	4	1	2	·	1	2	·	1	4	·	3
Accipiter spp.	·	·	·	·	1	·	·	1	·	2	2	·	·	·
Red-shouldered Hawk	2	9	8	6	6	9	14	13	12	9	12	15	6	8
Red-tailed Hawk	59	64	74	46	57	61	51	76	61	50	61	45	25	40
Golden Eagle	1(i)	·	3(2a,1i)	2(1a,1i)	2(u)	2(1a,1u)	3(a)	3(2a, 1i)	4(2a, 2i)	3(u)	5(2a, 3u)	5(4a, 1i)	·	3(a)
Peregrine Falcon	·	·	·	·	·	·	·	·	·	·	·	1	·	·
American Kestrel	15	21	21	5	19	32	30	25	20	20	22	21	10	18
Ring-necked Pheasant	·	·	·	1	11	6	7	6	9	8	5	2	4	8
Wild Turkey	·	·	·	·	·	·	·	·	·	·	·	8	·	·
California Quail	203	275	408	233	134	258	159	170	180	122	142	114	110	113
Black Rail	·	·	·	·	1	·	10	5	14	4	7	1	5	2
Clapper Rail	·	·	1	·	·	·	1	·	·	4	·	·	·	·
Virginia Rail	1	1	·	10	2	1	·	·	2	5	·	5	2	·
Sora	1	·	1	·	1	·	·	1	·	3	·	·	·	·
Common Moorhen	·	·	·	·	2	2	·	·	·	1	·	·	·	2
American Coot	7	51	81	17	103	80	86	96	86	68	49	25	56	44
Black-bellied Plover	8	14	4	13	8	7	15	4	31	·	·	·	·	·
Snowy Plover	·	·	2	5	·	·	·	·	·	·	·	·	·	**1**
Semipalmated Plover	1	·	1	·	33	101	·	12	1	·	·	·	·	·
Killdeer	91	71	90	47	128	97	84	128	91	62	136	110	102	104
Black Oystercatcher	1	3	1	4	·	·	·	·	·	·	·	·	·	·
Black-necked Stilt	·	2	5	·	15	23	59	55	56	9	81	40	47	36
American Avocet	·	·	3	·	·	10	30	13	12	5	21	65	4	27
Greater Yellowlegs	·	4	·	7	11	5	2	34	4	11	8	9	11	27
Lesser Yellowlegs	·	·	·	·	·	·	·	·	·	1	·	·	·	1
yellowlegs spp.	·	·	·	·	·	·	·	1	·	·	·	·	·	·
Willet	26	27	27	34	·	6	30	5	21	·	3	3	1	·
Wandering Tattler	·	·	·	1	·	·	·	·	·	·	·	·	·	·
Spotted Sandpiper	19	1	·	8	17	2	9	17	14	11	1	3	3	·
Whimbrel	·	9	3	86	36	15	1	1	4	·	·	·	·	·
Long-billed Curlew	2	·	7	5	·	6	1	5	2	2	·	·	18	·
"curlew" spp.	·	·	·	·	30	15	·	·	·	·	·	·	·	·
Marbled Godwit	6	33	20	93	1	141	5	26	10	·	·	·	3	5
Ruddy Turnstone	·	·	4	6	·	·	·	·	·	·	·	·	·	·
Black Turnstone	·	·	3	3	·	·	·	·	·	·	·	·	·	·
Red Knot	·	·	·	1	·	·	·	·	·	·	·	·	·	·
Sanderling	·	·	13	16	·	·	·	·	·	·	·	·	·	·
Western Sandpiper	62	·	·	3	97	247	·	3	3	4	1	·	·	·
Least Sandpiper	·	·	·	1	153	19	·	·	25	6	·	·	2	·
Dunlin	:	·	·	6	8	18	·	4	3	·	·	·	·	·
peep spp.	250	·	·	·	20	75	·	23	·	·	·	·	·	·
Short-billed Dowitcher	·	·	·	·	·	15	·	12	·	·	·	·	·	·
Long-billed Dowitcher	·	·	·	2	32	20	·	175	8	10	·	·	·	·
dowitcher spp.	·	·	·	·	·	110	3	68	3	·	1	·	·	·
Common Snipe	·	·	·	·	7	3	·	·	1	·	·	·	·	·
Wilson's Phalarope	·	·	·	·	·	·	2	·	5	2	4	3	10	2
Red-necked Phalarope	2	·	·	19	·	20	11	3	15	12	·	·	·	1
Red Phalarope	·	·	·	3	·	·	·	·	·	·	·	·	·	·
Bonaparte's Gull	1103	40	10	105	16	17	932	111	352	93	116	20	310	7

Appendix A. (cont'd)   Marin County (Southern)   Point Reyes Peninsula   Even Cheaper Thrills

	21 May 1977	21 May 1982	4 June 1983	23 May 1982	7 May 1978	6 May 1979	17 May 1980	9 May 1981	16 May 1982	22 May 1983	3 June 1984	2 June 1985	31 May 1986	31 May 1987
Heermann's Gull	·	·	2	·	·	·	·	·	·	·	·	·	·	·
Ring-billed Gull	31	43	48	28	8	50	7	182	10	15	17	4	55	5
California Gull	13	2	2	148	322	14	262	550	2	19	1	1	19	5
Western Gull	850	831	2235	992	308	78	22	93	50	234	94	1	63	14
Glaucous-winged Gull	3	8	6	38	5	17	1	11	3	2	2	2	3	3
gull spp.	·	54	96	11	123	75	1	101	40	·	44	41	16	21
Caspian Tern	101	90	74	34	35	40	31	6	10	45	15	38	30	37
Elegant Tern	·	25	6	·	·	·	·	·	·	·	·	·	·	·
Forster's Tern	358	81	87	76	23	30	11	8	22	12	3	13	25	5
Black Tern	·	·	·	·	**4**	·	·	·	·	·	·	·	·	·
Common Murre	213	92	32	49	·	·	·	·	·	·	·	·	·	·
Pigeon Guillemot	15	27	2	15	·	·	·	·	·	·	·	·	·	·
Rock Dove	32	356	169	29	164	161	168	294	179	179	190	92	98	157
Band-tailed Pigeon	199	294	169	69	34	82	41	72	109	37	44	52	84	2
Mourning Dove	251	467	315	146	175	126	156	196	215	135	142	237	109	171
Barn Owl	·	3	8	1	1	·	4	1	1	3	2	1	1	1
Western Screech-Owl	2	3	3	·	5	4	6	8	5	4	1	·	·	1
Great Horned Owl	7	12	6	2	8	11	11	17	14	6	9	7	3	3
Northern Pygmy-Owl	·	·	1	·	·	·	1	1	·	·	·	·	·	·
Spotted Owl	2	1	1	·	·	·	1	·	·	·	·	·	·	·
Northern Saw-whet Owl	1	·	·	·	·	·	·	1	·	·	·	·	·	·
Common Poorwill	4	·	·	·	·	·	·	1	·	·	·	·	·	·
Vaux's Swift	·	5	2	·	·	13	6	·	·	·	·	·	·	·
White-throated Swift	52	38	37	2	·	10	·	1	·	·	·	1	·	·
swift spp.	·	·	·	·	14	5	·	·	·	·	·	·	·	·
Anna's Hummingbird	135	153	105	25	24	40	48	43	66	65	18	42	40	81
Rufous Hummingbird	1	·	·	1	5	3	·	1	·	·	·	·	·	·
Allen's Hummingbird	219	173	188	76	34	49	42	41	33	38	23	22	9	24
Selasphorous spp.	·	30	9	·	5	·	5	8	·	19	17	18	4	·
hummingbird spp.	·	23	·	·	·	9	4	·	·	·	4	2	·	3
Belted Kingfisher	4	2	5	12	4	2	2	3	2	2	5	2	5	3
Lewis' Woodpecker	·	·	·	·	·	**7**	·	·	·	·	·	·	·	·
Acorn Woodpecker	62	73	71	27	19	73	48	28	33	29	34	34	14	31
Red-naped or Yellow-bellied Sapsucker	·	**1**	·	·	·	·	·	·	·	·	·	·	·	·
Red-breasted Sapsucker	·	·	·	1	·	·	·	·	·	·	·	·	·	·
Nuttall's Woodpecker	2	5	3	4	24	24	47	52	26	53	75	91	47	59
Downy Woodpecker	31	30	34	20	6	11	12	17	9	9	14	17	13	9
Hairy Woodpecker	6	15	17	6	2	2	5	·	·	·	1	2	5	2
Northern (Red-shafted) Flicker	46	48	37	14	4	5	4	8	9	3	8	7	6	6
Pileated Woodpecker	6	7	11	·	·	·	·	1	·	·	·	1	·	·
Olive-sided Flycatcher	53	76	76	6	8	18	9	11	8	2	12	9	18	7
Western Wood-Pewee	38	19	60	46	25	29	28	39	43	61	54	75	65	35
Willow Flycatcher	·	·	·	·	·	·	·	·	·	**1**	·	·	·	·
Pacific-slope Flycatcher	184	206	217	65	66	95	58	74	92	108	66	119	113	124
Empidonax spp. (non-Pacific-slope)	·	·	·	·	2	2	·	·	·	·	·	·	·	·
Black Phoebe	18	26	25	42	35	49	51	61	44	51	60	48	36	69
Ash-throated Flycatcher	72	88	75	24	56	67	88	151	118	124	69	119	79	130
Western Kingbird	·	·	2	16	77	44	67	52	30	50	58	60	46	65

Appendix A. (cont'd)   Marin County   Point Reyes   Even Cheaper Thrills
(Southern)   Peninsula

	21 May 1977	21 May 1982	4 June 1983	23 May 1982	7 May 1978	6 May 1979	17 May 1980	9 May 1981	16 May 1982	22 May 1983	3 June 1984	2 June 1985	31 May 1986	31 May 1987
Horned Lark	13	4	10	40	18	122	39	26	57	62	25	39	22	24
Purple Martin	9	24	4	.	.	3	.	.	.	.	.	1	.	.
Tree Swallow	44	41	72	76	64	111	83	54	48	31	49	64	77	42
Violet-green Swallow	103	230	263	54	95	334	213	380	230	275	169	140	156	239
N. Rough-winged Swallow	17	18	10	36	3	58	14	14	9	41	18	31	28	11
Bank Swallow	.	.	.	.	.	.	.	.	1	.	.	.	.	.
Cliff Swallow	384	1149	666	495	1035	2366	1103	1962	1794	2099	1385	1763	2343	1531
Barn Swallow	120	573	325	403	568	1022	634	537	355	454	472	463	418	544
Steller's Jay	175	192	154	24	43	47	34	63	46	48	59	56	45	61
Scrub Jay	469	457	370	174	155	146	173	204	165	129	178	170	89	193
American Crow	81	224	127	123	245	222	252	357	226	344	297	315	175	218
Common Raven	24	36	38	125	38	37	22	54	31	31	15	17	24	18
Chestnut-backed Chickadee	298	401	347	80	44	75	139	67	58	87	88	138	148	167
Plain Titmouse	166	72	89	17	74	122	176	99	84	78	110	105	109	216
Bushtit	597	336	417	78	108	171	217	182	88	223	205	294	238	228
Red-breasted Nuthatch	10	21	8	.	.	2	3	.	.	.	.	.	.	.
White-breasted Nuthatch	1	3	6	.	22	31	20	20	18	21	32	25	17	21
Pygmy Nuthatch	224	9	13	7	.	.	.	.	.	.	.	.	.	.
Brown Creeper	46	81	55	7	1	9	6	7	18	16	16	16	15	17
Rock Wren	4	3	.	.	.	.	1	.	.	.	.	5	2	2
Bewick's Wren	140	286	148	81	55	73	78	117	157	65	61	89	42	102
House Wren	.	2	5	.	3	9	6	23	18	27	17	41	17	29
Winter Wren	6	36	52	8	1	3	.	2	.	.	2	.	5	3
Marsh Wren	10	12	11	82	78	52	36	104	62	128	163	122	148	96
Golden-crowned Kinglet	20	35	41	.	.	4	.	1	1	.	.	.	.	1
Ruby-crowned Kinglet	.	.	2	.	8	1	.	.	.	.	.	.	.	.
Blue-gray Gnatcatcher	4	.	9	.	11	3	15	20	20	19	3	40	13	98
Western Bluebird	17	16	17	53	69	76	73	98	75	63	68	71	88	110
Swainson's Thrush	74	102	102	136	6	8	9	31	8	12	21	24	36	24
Hermit Thrush	7	37	55	.	1	.	.	.	5	3	7	3	2	1
Catharus thrush spp.	.	.	.	.	.	.	.	4	.	.	.	.	.	.
American Robin	259	272	319	55	48	106	77	65	65	61	40	57	73	44
Varied Thrush	.	1	.	.	1	.	.	1	.	.	.	.	.	.
Wrentit	373	385	265	171	17	30	41	59	74	34	30	37	23	65
Northern Mockingbird	125	119	101	2	61	57	99	70	41	81	90	59	53	59
California Thrasher	12	6	3	.	1	2	3	4	10	2	3	1	2	1
Water Pipit	.	.	.	.	2	1	.	.	.	.	.	.	.	.
Cedar Waxwing	361	65	.	29	56	190	87	65	98	.	.	.	.	2
Loggerhead Shrike	2	.	1	1	15	14	15	12	11	9	9	14	1	7
European Starling	675	417	794	436	380	1117	524	490	603	922	392	730	393	492
Solitary Vireo	10	10	10	.	4	5	2	4	1	1	2	2	.	3
Yellow-throated Vireo	.	.	.	.	.	.	.	.	.	.	.	.	.	**1**
Hutton's Vireo	92	63	58	21	33	52	72	53	59	65	21	60	36	58
Warbling Vireo	359	372	488	108	124	183	132	206	196	197	90	204	141	150
Orange-crowned Warbler	414	338	444	88	135	148	132	155	177	218	92	213	180	143
Nashville Warbler	1	1	.	.	2	.	.	.	.	2	.	.	.	.
Yellow Warbler	7	1	4	19	19	2	28	14	6	4	3	10	3	10
Yellow-rumped (Audubon's)	4	29	18	.	10	1	.	2	.	.	.	.	.	.
Black-throated Gray	20	27	34	.	.	6	.	.	1	3	1	1	3	1
Townsend's Warbler	7	.	.	.	13	5	29	8	10	.	.	.	.	.

Appendix A. (cont'd) Marin County (Southern) Point Reyes Peninsula Even Cheaper Thrills

	21 May 1977	21 May 1982	4 June 1983	23 May 1982	7 May 1978	6 May 1979	17 May 1980	9 May 1981	16 May 1982	22 May 1983	3 June 1984	2 June 1985	31 May 1986	31 May 1987
Hermit Warbler	·	3	·	·	3	·	4	5	·	·	·	1	3	·
MacGillivray's Warbler	1	3	·	3	·	·	1	·	·	·	·	·	·	·
Common Yellowthroat	27	14	16	22	5	4	6	8	27	3	15	12	12	12
Wilson's Warbler	72	110	83	135	95	76	75	63	70	33	34	47	36	50
Yellow-breasted Chat	·	·	·	·	1	·	·	·	·	·	·	·	·	1
Western Tanager	16	2	2	1	14	·	4	1	4	2	3	·	·	1
Black-headed Grosbeak	106	72	76	47	67	97	65	83	46	36	40	54	56	30
Rose-breasted Grosbeak	·	·	·	·	·	·	·	·	·	·	·	1	·	·
Lazuli Bunting	73	4	2	16	11	21	8	4	28	30	27	39	10	42
Indigo Bunting	·	·	·	·	·	·	·	·	·	·	1	·	·	·
Rufous-sided Towhee	308	336	313	65	88	119	145	120	143	124	70	98	153	121
California Towhee	241	374	243	105	122	112	142	108	103	133	125	119	169	126
Rufous-crowned Sparrow	25	17	5	1	·	·	2	5	1	3	2	2	1	5
Chipping Sparrow	28	36	18	8	22	36	19	22	22	30	21	25	35	12
Black-chinned Sparrow	**6**	·	·	·	·	·	2	·	·	·	·	·	·	·
Lark Sparrow	24	15	22	36	44	75	69	110	92	65	70	57	28	97
Sage Sparrow	6	3	3	·	·	·	1	·	·	·	·	·	·	·
Savannah Sparrow	11	27	43	246	9	11	20	9	31	22	37	11	37	18
Grasshopper Sparrow	4	1	3	9	2	1	5	2	3	5	3	16	9	9
Fox Sparrow	·	·	·	·	1	·	·	·	·	·	·	·	·	·
Song Sparrow	252	469	364	388	217	480	231	282	260	319	186	312	277	210
White-throated Sparrow	·	·	·	·	·	·	·	1	·	·	·	·	·	·
Golden-crowned Sparrow	1	·	·	·	10	4	·	·	·	·	·	·	·	·
White-crowned Sparrow	119	169	94	335	3	5	5	2	·	·	·	·	·	·
Dark-eyed (Oregon) Junco	204	266	290	49	65	148	201	180	150	187	98	168	189	187
Red-winged Blackbird	556	687	594	646	1250	2217	1628	1951	1049	989	1070	1867	1801	1395
Tricolored Blackbird	·	·	·	·	209	1	40	·	·	·	1	3	·	17
Western Meadowlark	92	93	57	94	167	202	200	186	171	137	115	156	98	146
Brewer's Blackbird	275	435	370	453	715	1652	651	469	830	791	687	1104	650	973
Brown-headed Cowbird	50	44	22	58	59	25	32	50	20	32	21	57	22	29
blackbird spp.	·	·	·	20	·	·	·	·	·	·	50	·	·	·
Hooded Oriole	10	12	17	·	1	5	1	1	1	1	·	2	2	4
Northern (Bullock's) Oriole	7	30	28	22	85	108	117	89	89	103	87	104	59	119
Northern (**Baltimore**)	·	1	·	·	·	·	·	·	·	·	·	·	·	·
Purple Finch	98	179	120	76	29	16	25	51	37	52	25	61	78	92
House Finch	927	1120	967	340	972	1517	732	1211	652	1035	564	1069	482	666
Red Crossbill	29	·	·	·	·	·	·	·	·	·	·	5	·	·
Pine Siskin	162	472	233	176	26	45	23	25	11	92	60	54	36	37
Lesser Goldfinch	182	147	74	22	74	107	125	191	129	122	153	110	123	286
Lawrence's Goldfinch	**4**	·	·	·	·	·	·	·	·	·	11	·	·	**25**
American Goldfinch	602	246	272	262	84	83	68	73	37	134	80	47	59	84
House Sparrow	207	250	183	111	321	571	219	299	427	312	324	431	120	209
Total Species	158	152	154	153	156	56	148	153	146	135	131	134	134	141
Total Individuals	17,482	19,455	16,869	10,884	11,710	18,233	13,444	15,390	12,645	13,299	10,823	14,119	12,426	12,625
Total Confirmed Breeders	64	69	68	30	47	40	49	45	45	46	48	57	51	46

Appendix B. Numbers of birds (means and ranges) tallied on two U.S. Fish and Wildlife Service Breeding Bird Survey routes conducted in Marin County from 1972 to 1986 (see Methods, p. 48). Besides breeding species, the list includes a number of oversummering nonbreeders and late migrants.

Species	Route 071 Point Reyes mean	Route 071 Point Reyes range	Route 083 Fairfax mean	Route 083 Fairfax range
Brown Pelican	-	-	15.88	0-100
Double-crested Cormorant	-	-	5.0	0-16
Great Blue Heron	0.6	0-2	18.7	8-38
Great Egret	0.6	0-4	66.4	31-143
Snowy Egret	-	-	5.0	3-12
Green-backed Heron	0.1	0-1	-	-
Black-crowned Night-Heron	0.1	0-1	3.6	0-11
Canada Goose	-	-	0.1	0-1
Mallard	0.1	0-1	8.0	0-44
Turkey Vulture	9.3	4-14	11.2	1-29
Osprey	0.1	0-1	1.5	0-7
Black-shouldered Kite	0.4	0-1	0.1	0-1
Cooper's Hawk	0.1	0-1	-	-
Red-shouldered Hawk	1.3	0-4	1.0	0-9
Red-tailed Hawk	2.9	1-4	3.4	1-7
American Kestrel	1.4	0-4	0.4	0-1
California Quail	13.7	5-24	16.2	5-35
Black Rail	0.1	0-1	-	-
American Coot	-	-	0.5	0-5
Killdeer	0.6	0-2	4.7	2-10
Spotted Sandpiper	-	-	0.3	0-2
Bonaparte's Gull	-	-	9.5	0-89
Ring-billed Gull	-	-	5.1	0-16
California Gull	-	-	0.2	0-2
Western Gull	0.1	0-1	14.1	0-47
Glaucous-winged Gull	-	-	0.4	0-2
Caspian Tern	-	-	1.9	0-11
Forster's Tern	-	-	0.4	0-4
Rock Dove	0.3	0-2	0.8	0-5
Band-tailed Pigeon	7.7	0-24	14.0	3-22
Mourning Dove	13.9	4-19	17.0	6-34
W. Screech-Owl	-	-	0.3	0-3
Great Horned Owl	0.4	0-2	0.4	0-1
N. Pygmy-Owl	0.1	0-1	0.1	0-1
Vaux's Swift	-	-	0.3	0-1
White-throated Swift	-	-	0.7	0-3
Anna's Hummingbird	2.3	0-7	2.7	0-9
Allen's Hummingbird	6.1	0-14	6.9	4-13
Belted Kingfisher	0.6	0-2	1.6	0-5
Acorn Woodpecker	14.4	7-25	19.9	14-28
Nuttall's Woodpecker	0.3	0-1	0.1	0-1
Downy Woodpecker	2.6	0-7	0.4	0-2
Hairy Woodpecker	0.9	0-5	1.6	0-6
Red-shafted Flicker	1.1	0-3	4.8	2-10
Pileated Woodpecker	0.7	0-3	1.2	0-7
Olive-sided Flycatcher	13.0	7-21	10.7	5-16
Western Wood-Pewee	8.7	4-19	2.8	0-9
Pacific-slope Flycatcher	25.9	8-66	17.2	9-31
Black Phoebe	1.3	0-5	0.4	0-2
Ash-throated Flycatcher	7.6	2-17	8.4	3-16
Western Kingbird	-	-	0.4	0-1
Horned Lark	-	-	0.9	0-3
Purple Martin	-	-	0.5	0-6
Tree Swallow	3.4	1-7	1.4	0-5
Violet-green Swallow	18.9	4-48	15.7	6-36
N. Rough-winged Swallow	0.9	0-3	2.6	0-20
Cliff Swallow	70.1	4-153	19.1	10-38
Barn Swallow	8.4	0-19	19.1	10-38
Steller's Jay	20.9	6-35	20.3	9-35
Scrub Jay	26.1	18-36	15.7	12-19
American Crow	20.9	3-53	11.1	5-19
Common Raven	5.6	0-11	4.9	0-14
Chestnut-backed Chickadee	57.3	20-81	21.2	6-38
Plain Titmouse	3.7	1-7	3.2	0-7
Bushtit	16.0	5-28	8.4	2-28
Red-breasted Nuthatch	-	-	3.0	1-5
White-breasted Nuthatch	1.1	0-5	0.5	0-2
Pygmy Nuthatch	0.9	0-6	1.4	0-7
Brown Creeper	12.6	0-28	3.8	0-9
Bewick's Wren	7.1	4-10	7.5	2-17
House Wren	0.7	0-3	-	-
Winter Wren	1.4	0-5	1.0	0-3
Marsh Wren	2.9	0-11	0.8	0-3
Golden-crowned Kinglet	1.7	0-6	1.6	0-8
Western Bluebird	4.4	1-7	1.8	0-5
Swainson's Thrush	47.0	33-65	6.0	1-15
Hermit Thrush	4.0	0-7	3.8	0-10
American Robin	28.1	13-52	12.4	4-19
Wrentit	7.4	0-17	16.3	5-39
Northern Mockingbird	0.3	0-1	0.1	0-1
California Thrasher	-	-	0.2	0-2
Cedar Waxwing	-	-	0.1	0-1
European Starling	24.4	0-52	21.4	6-54
Solitary Vireo	-	-	0.5	0-1
Hutton's Vireo	5.4	1-17	4.1	0-9
Warbling Vireo	39.9	22-78	36.5	18-55
Orange-crowned Warbler	16.6	10-36	25.8	17-35
Nashville Warbler	0.1	0-1	-	-
Yellow Warbler	2.0	0-8	-	-
Audubon's Warbler	0.3	0-2	2.4	0-7
Black-throated Gray Warbler	-	-	2.4	0-5
Hermit Warbler	0.1	0-1	0.7	0-3
MacGillivray's Warbler	0.1	0-1	-	-
Common Yellowthroat	2.9	0-8	0.1	0-1
Wilson's Warbler	31.1	15-63	9.4	5-17
Yellow-breasted Chat	0.1	0-1	-	-
Western Tanager	1.4	0-3	1.4	0-5
Black-headed Grosbeak	18.7	4-36	10.4	4-18
Lazuli Bunting	1.3	0-4	1.9	0-4
Rufous-sided Towhee	17.7	9-28	30.2	16-68
California Towhee	16.0	8-30	19.5	8-28
Rufous-crowned Sparrow	0.3	0-2	0.5	0-2
Chipping Sparrow	6.3	1-12	5.3	2-8
Lark Sparrow	1.1	0-6	2.7	0-6
Sage Sparrow	-	-	0.2	0-2
Savannah Sparrow	0.1	0-1	0.3	0-3
Grasshopper Sparrow	0.6	0-2	0.1	0-1
Song Sparrow	35.1	23-63	20.5	13-38
White-crowned Sparrow	6.7	0-29	2.7	0-7
Oregon Junco	18.6	4-40	17.8	8-30
Red-winged Blackbird	32.1	9-60	25.4	6-45
Tricolored Blackbird	-	-	0.4	0-5
Western Meadowlark	3.7	1-8	1.8	0-6
Brewer's Blackbird	65.6	33-88	28.2	8-79
Brown-headed Cowbird	7.1	2-22	3.3	0-11
Bullock's Oriole	2.7	0-7	0.3	0-3
Purple Finch	24.6	13-50	15.9	4-33
House Finch	31.1	8-56	27.5	10-62
Pine Siskin	28.1	9-71	53.0	21-91
Lesser Goldfinch	23.7	3-45	6.2	0-16
American Goldfinch	5.4	0-16	11.7	2-32
House Sparrow	13.3	3-29	2.0	0-5

APPENDIX C.
A list of Breeding Bird Censuses conducted in Marin County, California, 1951 to 1990.

Dates listed represent the actual year of each census. From 1951 to 1975, data were published in the same calendar year; thereafter, data were published in the following calendar year. The name and size of some plots have changed over the years—the most current data are listed.

1) **Bishop Pine Forest (A).** Location: 3.75 mi WNW of Inverness. Size: 10.5 ha = 26 acres. Coverage: 1951 & 1952 (AFN 6:312-314), 1953 (AFN 7:351), 1972 (AB 26:986), 1973 (AB 27:998-999), 1974 (AB 28:1039-1040), 1975 (AB 29:1126-1127), 1977 (AB 32:90).

2) **Bishop Pine Forest (B).** Location: 1.5 mi W of Inverness, 0.75 mi NW of Mt. Vision. Size: 8.5 ha = 21 acres. Coverage: 1972 (AB 26:985-986), 1973 (AB 27:999), 1974 (AB 28:1039), 1975 (AB 29:1127).

3) **Bishop Pine Forest (C).** Location: 1.7 mi W of Inverness, 1.1 mi NW of Mt. Vision. Size: 6.2 ha = 15.4 acres. Coverage: 1974 (AB 28:1038).

4) **Disturbed Bishop Pine Forest.** Location: 3 mi NW of Inverness Park. Size: 12.0 ha = 29.7 acres. Coverage: 1972 (AB 26:984-985), 1973 (AB 27:999-1000), 1974 (AB 28:1040), 1975 (AB 29:1127), 1977 (AB 32:90).

5) **California Bay–Bishop Pine Mixed Forest.** Location: 0.5 mi S of Inverness. Size: 11.7 ha = 29 acres. Coverage: 1972 (AB 26:981), 1973 (AB 27:997-998), 1974 (AB 28:1037-1038), 1975 (AB 29:1125-1126), 1976 (AB 31:72), 1977 (AB 32:87).

6) **Mature Douglas Fir Forest.** Location: 4 mi NW of Bolinas, 1.75 mi N of PRBO Palomarin Field Station. Size: 6.1 ha = 15 acres. Coverage: 1971 (AB 25:987-988), 1972 (AB 26:984), 1973 (AB 27:1001), 1974 (AB 28:1041), 1975 (AB 29:1128).

7) **Logged Douglas Fir Forest.** Location: 4.5 mi S of Olema, 200 yds S of east gate to Lake Ranch, PRNS. Size: 6.1 ha = 15 acres. Coverage: 1971 (AB 25:1004).

8) **Logged Douglas Fir Forest Reseeded with Monterey Pine.** Location: 4.5 mi S of Olema, about 0.5 mi E of east gate to Lake Ranch, PRNS. Size: 8.2 ha = 20.2 acres. Coverage: 1972 (AB 26:983-984), 1973 (AB 27:1000-1001), 1974 (AB 28:1040-1041), 1975 (AB 29:1127-1128), 1976 (AB 31:73-74), 1977 (AB 32:91).

9) **Mixed Evergreen Forest.** Location: Cataract Gulch, 400 ft E of Ridgecrest Blvd. Size: 6.1 ha = 15 acres. Coverage: 1966 (AFN 20:629-630), 1967 (AFN 21:629).

10) **Oak–California Bay–Buckeye Mixed Forest.** Location: 3.5 mi NW of Bolinas, just inside southern boundary of PRNS. Size: 4 ha = 10 acres. Coverage: 1972 (AB 26:979), 1973 (AB 27:995-996), 1974 (AB 28:1035), 1975 (AB 29:1123).

11) **Coastal Scrub.** Location: 4 mi NW of Bolinas, 0.5 mi inside southern boundary of PRNS. Size: 8.1 ha = 20 acres. Coverage: 1971 (AB 25:1003-1004), 1972 (AB 26:987), 1973 (AB 27:1004), 1974 (AB 28:1042), 1975 (AB 29:1129), 1977 (AB 32:98), 1979 (AB 34:80-81), 1980 (AB 35:93-94), 1981 (AB 36:94), 1982 (AB 37:95), 1983 (AB 38:129), 1984 (AB 39:114), 1985 (AB 40:71), 1986 (PRBO unpubl.), 1987 (PRBO unpubl.), 1988 (JFOs 60:56), 1989 (JFOs 61:69-70), 1990 (JFOs 62:78–79).

12) **Disturbed Coastal Scrub (A).** Location: 3.5 mi NW of Bolinas, just inside southern boundary of PRNS. Size: 4.7 ha = 11.6 acres. Coverage: 1972 (AB 26:987-988), 1973 (AB 27:1004), 1974 (AB 28:1042-1043), 1975 (AB 29:1129), 1977 (AB 32:100), 1978 (AB 33:91), 1979 (AB 34:81), 1980 (AB 35:94), 1981 (AB 36:94), 1982 (AB 37:95), 1983 (AB 38:129&134), 1984 (AB 39:114), 1985 (AB 40:71), 1986 (PRBO unpubl.), 1987 (PRBO unpubl.), 1988 (JFOs 60:54-55), 1989 (JFOs 61:68), 1990 (JFOs 62:79).

13) **Disturbed Coastal Scrub (B).** Location: 3.5 mi NW Bolinas, 0.16 mi inside southern boundary of PRNS. Size: 8.1 ha = 20 acres. Coverage: 1971 (AB 25:1002-1003), 1972 (AB 26:988), 1973 (AB 27:1004-1005), 1974 (AB 28:1043), 1975 (AB 29:1129), 1977 (AB 32:100), 1978 (AB 33:91), 1979 (AB 34:81), 1980 (AB 35:94), 1981 (AB 36:94), 1982 (AB 37:95-96), 1983 (AB 38:134), 1984 (AB 39:114), 1985 (AB 40:71), 1986 (PRBO unpubl.), 1987 (PRBO unpubl.), 1988 (JFOs 60:55), 1989 (JFOs 61:69), 1990 (JFOs 62:79-80).

14) **Burned Disturbed Coastal Scrub.** Location: 5.5 mi NW of Bolinas, 2 mi inside southern boundary PRNS. Size: 8.1 ha = 20 acres. Coverage: 1983 (AB 38:129).

15) **Coastal Riparian Marsh.** Location: Olema Marsh, 0.5 mi SW of Pt. Reyes Station. Size: 17.5 ha = 43.8 acres. Coverage: 1985 (AB 40:71), 1986 (ACR Report 85-1-2), 1987 (ACR Report 85-1-3), 1988 (ACR Report 85-1-4), 1989 (ACR Report 85-1-5), 1990 (JFOs 62:75–76).

16) **Coastal Freshwater Marsh.** Location: Livermore Marsh, 0.5 mi NW of Marshall. Size: 10.5 ha = 26.2 acres. Coverage: 1985 (AB 40:71), 1986 (ACR Report 85-1-2), 1987 (ACR Report 85-1-3), 1988 (JFOs 60:64), 1989 (JFOs 61:76), 1990 (JFOs 62:74–75).

17) **Coastal Prairie.** Location: 0.5 mi NW of Marshall. Size: 31 ha = 77.5 acres. Coverage: 1988 (JFOs 60:56-57), 1989 (JFOs 61:70-71), 1990 (JFOs 62:80).

LITERATURE CITED

A

Adams, D. A. and T. L. Quay. 1958. Ecology of the Clapper Rail in southeastern North Carolina. J. Wildl. Mgmt. 22:149-156.

Adamus, P. R. 1987. *Atlas of Breeding Birds in Maine, 1978-1983*. Maine Dept. Inland Fisheries and Wildl., Augusta.

Addicott, A. B. 1938. Behavior of the bush-tit in the breeding season. Condor 40:49-63.

Ainley, D. G. 1976. The occurrence of seabirds in the coastal region of California. W. Birds 7:33-68.

——. 1984a. Storm-Petrels. In D. Haley, ed. *Seabirds of Eastern North Pacific and Arctic Waters*, 58-63. Pacific Search, Seattle.

——. 1984b. Cormorants. In D. Haley, ed. *Seabirds of Eastern North Pacific and Arctic Waters*, 92-101. Pacific Search, Seattle.

——. 1990. Seasonal and annual patterns in the marine environment near the Farallones. In D. G. Ainley and R. J. Boekelheide, eds. *Seabirds of the Farallon Islands: Ecology, Dynamics, and Structure of an Upwelling-System Community*, 23-50. Stanford Univ. Press, Stanford.

Ainley, D. G., D. W. Anderson, and P. R. Kelly. 1981. Feeding ecology of marine cormorants in southwestern North America. Condor 83:120-131.

Ainley, D. G. and R. J. Boekelheide, eds. 1990. *Seabirds of the Farallon Islands: Ecology, Dynamics, and Structure of an Upwelling-System Community*. Stanford Univ. Press, Stanford.

Ainley, D. G. and T. J. Lewis. 1974. The history of Farallon Island marine bird populations, 1854-1972. Condor 76:432-446.

Ainley, D. G., S. Morrell, and T. J. Lewis. 1974. Patterns in the life histories of storm petrels on the Farallon Islands. Living Bird 13:295-312.

Ainley, D. G. and T. Osborne. 1972. A Marin County, California, breeding site for Ashy Petrels. Calif. Birds 3:71.

Ainley, D. G. and G. A. Sanger. 1979. Trophic relationships of seabirds in the northeastern Pacific Ocean and Bering Sea. In J. Bartonek and D. N. Nettleship, eds. Conservation of marine birds of northern North America. U.S. Fish Wildl. Serv. Wildl. Res. Rept. 11.

Ainley, D. G. and M. C. Whitt. 1973. Numbers of marine birds breeding in northern California. W. Birds 4:65-70.

Airola, D. A., ed. 1980. California Wildlife Habitat Relationships Program. Northeast Interior Zone. Vol. 3: Birds. Almanor Ranger District, Lassen Natl. Forest, P.O. Box 767, Chester, CA 96020.

Airola, D. A. 1986. Brown-headed Cowbird parasitism and habitat disturbance in the Sierra Nevada. J. Wildl. Mgmt. 50:571-575.

Airola, D. A. and R. H. Barrett. 1985. Foraging and habitat relationships of insect-gleaning birds in a Sierra Nevada mixed-conifer forest. Condor 87:205-216.

Albers, P. H. 1978. Habitat selection by breeding Red-winged Blackbirds. Wilson Bull. 90:619-634.

Aldrich, E. C. 1935. Nesting of the Dusky Poor-will. Condor 37:49-55.

——. 1939. Notes on the salt-feeding habits of the Red Crossbill. Condor 41:172-173.

——. 1945. Nesting of the Allen Hummingbird. Condor 47:137-148.

Allaire, P. N. and C. D. Fisher. 1975. Feeding ecology of three resident sympatric sparrows in eastern Texas. Auk 92:260-269.

Allen, A. A. 1914. The Red-winged Blackbird: A study in the ecology of a cattail marsh. Proc. Linn. Soc. N.Y. 24-25:43-128.

Allen, A. S. 1933. Arrival and departure of avian visitants in the San Francisco Bay region. Condor 35:225-227.

——. 1943. Additional notes on the birds of a Berkeley hillside. Condor 45:149-157.

Allen, C. A. 1880. Habits of Vaux's Swift. Bull. Nutt. Ornithol. Club 5:55-56.

——. 1881. Collecting on the Pacific Coast. Ornithologist and Oologist 6:18-19.

Allen, R. W. and M. M. Nice. 1952. A study of the breeding biology of the Purple Martin *(Progne subis)*. Am. Midl. Nat. 47:606-665.

American Ornithologists' Union. 1957. *Check-list of North American Birds*. 5th ed. Lord Baltimore, Baltimore.

——. 1983. *Check-list of North American Birds*. 6th ed. Allen Press, Lawrence, Kans.

Ames, P. L. and G. S. Mersereau. 1964. Some factors in the decline of the Osprey in Connecticut. Auk 81:173-185.

Anderson, D. W. and J. J. Hickey. 1972. Eggshell changes in certain North American birds. In K. H. Voous, ed. Proc. XVth Int. Ornithol. Congress, 514-540. E. G. Brill, Leider, Netherlands.

Anderson, S. H. 1976. Comparative food habits of Oregon nuthatches. Northwest Sci. 50:213-221.

Anderson, W. 1970. A preliminary study of the relationship of saltponds and wildlife—south San Francisco Bay. Calif. Fish Game 56:240-252.

Anderson, W. L. and R. E. Duzan. 1978. DDE residues and eggshell thinning in Loggerhead Shrikes. Wilson Bull. 90:215-220.

Andrle, R. F. and J. R. Carroll, eds. 1988. *The Atlas of Breeding Birds in New York State*. Cornell Univ. Press, Ithaca.

Ankney, C. D. and A. D. Afton. 1988. Bioenergetics of breeding Northern Shovelers: Diet, nutrient reserves, clutch size, and incubation. Condor 90:459–472.

Ankney, C. D. and D. M. Scott. 1980. Changes in nutrient reserves and diet of breeding Brown-headed Cowbirds. Auk 97:684–696.

Annett, C. and R. Pierotti. 1989. Chick hatching as a trigger for dietary switching in the Western Gull. Colonial Waterbirds 12:4–11.

Appelgate, R. D. 1977. Possible ecological role of food caches of Loggerhead Shrikes. Auk 94:391.

Arnold, J. R. 1935. The changing distribution of the Western Mockingbird in California. Condor 37:193–199.

———. 1980. Distribution of the Mockingbird in California. W. Birds 11:97–102.

Asay, C. E. 1987. Habitat and productivity of Cooper's Hawks nesting in California. Calif. Fish Game 73:80–87.

Atwater, B. F., S. G. Conrad, J. N. Dowden, C. W. Hedel, R. L. MacDonald, and W. Savage. 1979. History, landforms, and vegetation of the estuary's tidal marshes. In T. J. Conomos, ed. San Francisco Bay: The Urbanized Estuary, 347–386. Pacific Div., Am. Assoc. Adv. Sci., San Francisco.

Atwood, J. L. 1980. Breeding biology of the Santa Cruz Island Scrub Jay. In D. M. Power, ed. The California Islands: Proceedings of a Multidisciplinary Symposium, 675–678. Santa Barbara Nat. Hist. Mus., Santa Barbara.

Austin, O. L., Jr., ed. 1968. A. C. Bent et al.'s Life histories of North American cardinals, grosbeaks, buntings, towhees, finches, sparrows, and allies. U.S. Natl. Mus. Bull. 237 (Parts 1–3).

Austin, O. L., Jr. and S. H. Low. 1932. Notes on the breeding of the Tree Swallow. Bird-Banding 3:39–44.

Azevedo, J. and D. L. Morgan. 1974. Fog precipitation in coastal California forests. Ecology 55:1135–1141.

B

Baepler, D. H. 1968. Lark Sparrow. In O. L. Austin, Jr., ed. A. C. Bent et al.'s Life histories of North American cardinals, grosbeaks, buntings, towhees, finches, sparrows, and allies. U.S. Natl. Mus. Bull. 237 (Part 2): 886–902.

Bailey, A. M., R. J. Niedrach, and A. L. Baily. 1953. The Red Crossbills of Colorado. Denver Mus. Nat. Hist. Mus. Pictorial 9.

Bailey, F. M. 1907. White-throated Swifts at Capistrano. Condor 9:169–172.

———. 1910. The palm-leaf oriole. Auk 27:33–35.

———. 1928. Birds of New Mexico. New Mexico Dept. Game and Fish.

Bailey, S. F., R. A. Erickson, and K. F. Campbell. 1987. The spring migration: Middle Pacific coast region. Am. Birds 41:486.

Baker, M. C. and L. R. Mewaldt. 1979. The use of space by White-crowned Sparrows: Juvenile and adult ranging patterns and home range versus body size comparisons in an avian granivore community. Behav. Ecol. Sociobiol. 6: 45–52.

Baker, M. C., L. R. Mewaldt, and R. M. Stewart. 1981. Demography of White-crowned Sparrows (Zonotrichia leucophrys nuttalli). Ecology 62:636–644.

Baker, M. C. and D. B. Thompson. 1985. Song dialects of White-crowned Sparrows: Historical processes inferred from patterns of geographic variation. Condor 87:127–141.

Bakun, A. 1973. Coastal upwelling indices, west coast of North America, 1946–71. U.S. Dept. Commerce, NOAA Tech. Rept. NMFS SSRF-671.

Bakus, G. J. 1959. Observations on the life history of the Dipper in Montana. Auk 76:190–207.

Baldwin, P. H. and W. F. Hunter. 1963. Nesting and nest visitors of the Vaux's Swift. Auk 80:81–85.

Baldwin, P. H. and N. K. Zaczkowski. 1963. Breeding biology of the Vaux's Swift. Condor 65:400–406.

Balgooyen, T. G. 1976. Behavior and ecology of the American Kestrel (Falco sparverius L.) in the Sierra Nevada of California. Univ. Calif. Publ. Zool. 103.

———. 1990. Orientation of American Kestrel nest cavities: Revisited. J. Raptor Res. 24:27–28.

Baltz, D. M. and G. V. Morejohn. 1977. Food habits and niche overlap of sea birds wintering on Monterey Bay, California. Auk 94:526–543.

Baptista, L. F. 1975. Song dialects and demes in sedentary populations of the White-crowned Sparrow (Zonotrichia leucophrys nuttalli). Univ. Calif. Publ. Zool. 105:1–52.

Barbour, M. G., T. M. DeJong, and A. F. Johnson. 1976. Synecology of beach vegetation along the Pacific coast of the United States of America: A first approximation. J. Biogeogr. 3:55–69.

Barlow, C. 1897. Some notes on the nesting habits of the White-tailed Kite. Auk 14:14–21.

———. 1899. Nesting of the Hermit Warbler in the Sierra Nevada Mountains, California. Auk 16:156–161.

Barrows, C. W. 1981. Roost selection by Spotted Owls: An adaptation to heat stress. Condor 83:302–309.

———. 1985. Breeding success relative to fluctuations in diet for Spotted Owls in California. In R. J. Gutiérrez and A. B. Carey, eds. Ecology and management of the Spotted Owl in the Pacific Northwest. U.S. For. Serv. Gen. Tech. Rept. PNW-185.

———. 1987. Diet shifts in breeding and non-breeding Spotted Owls. J. Raptor Res. 21:95–97.

———. 1989. Diets of five species of desert owls. W. Birds 20:1–10.

Barrows, C. W. and K. Barrows. 1978. Roost characteristics and behavioral thermoregulation in the Spotted Owl. W. Birds 9:1–8.

Barrows, W. B. 1889. The English Sparrow (Passer domesticus) in North America. U.S. Dept. Agri., Div. Econ. Ornithol. and Mamm. Bull. 1.

Bartholomew, G. A., Jr. 1942. The fishing activities of Double-crested Cormorants on San Francisco Bay. Condor 44:13–21.

Batts, H. L., Jr. 1948. Some observations on the nesting activities of the eastern goldfinch. Jack-Pine Warbler 26: 51–58.

Baumann, S. A. 1959. The breeding cycle of the Rufous-sided Towhee, *Pipilo erythrophthalmus* (Linnaeus) in central California. Wasmann J. Biol. 17:161–220.

Beal, F. E. L. 1907. Birds of California in relation to the fruit industry (Part I). U.S. Dept. Agri. Biol. Surv. Bull. 30.

——. 1910. Birds of California in relation to the fruit industry (Part II). U.S. Dept. Agri. Biol. Surv. Bull. 34.

——. 1911. Food of the woodpeckers of the United States. U.S. Dept. Agri. Biol. Surv. Bull. 37.

——. 1912. Food of our more important flycatchers. U.S. Dept. Agri. Biol. Surv. Bull. 44.

——. 1915. Food of the robins and bluebirds of the United States. U.S. Dept. Agri. Bull. 171.

——. 1918. Food habits of the swallows, a family of valuable native birds. U.S. Dept. Agri. Bull. 619.

——. 1948. Some common birds useful to the farmer. U.S. Dept. Inter. Conserv. Bull. 18.

Beason, R. C. and E. C. Franks. 1974. Breeding behavior of the Horned Lark. Auk 91:65–74.

Beaver, D. L. and P. L. Baldwin. 1975. Ecological overlap and the problem of competition and sympatry in the Western and Hammond's flycatchers. Condor 77:1–13.

Beebe, G. D. and J. Schonewald. 1977. Spotted Owls near Palomarin. Point Reyes Bird Obs. Newsl. 43:6–7.

Beecher, W. J. 1951. Adaptations for food-getting in the American blackbirds. Auk 68:411–440.

Beedy, E. C. 1981. Bird communities and forest structure in the Sierra Nevada of California. Condor 83:97–105.

Beedy, E. C. and S. L. Granholm. 1985. *Discovering Sierra Birds: Western Slope.* Yosemite and Sequoia Natural History associations.

Beedy, E. C. and A. Hayworth. In press. Tricolored Blackbird nesting failures in the Central Valley of California: General trends or isolated phenomena? In D. Williams, ed. Proc. of the Symp. on Endangered Species of the San Joaquin Valley, Bakersfield, California, December 1987.

Beedy, E. C., S. D. Sanders, and D. A. Bloom. 1991. Breeding status, distribution, and habitat associations of the Tricolored Blackbird *(Agelaius tricolor),* 1850–1989. Jones & Stokes Associates Inc. (JSA 88–187), Sacramento. Prepared for U.S. Fish & Wildl. Serv., Sacramento.

Belding, L. 1890. Land birds of the Pacific district. Occas. Papers II. Calif. Acad. Sci., San Francisco.

Bellrose, F. C. 1980. *Ducks, Geese, and Swans of North America.* 2nd ed. Stackpole, Harrisburg, Penn.

Bellrose, F. C., K. L. Johnson, and T. U. Meyers. 1964. Relative value of natural cavities and nesting houses for Wood Ducks. J. Wildl. Mgmt. 28:661–676.

Bendell, B. E. and P. J. Weatherhead. 1982. Prey characteristics of upland-breeding Red-winged Blackbirds, *Agelaius phoeniceus.* Can. Field-Nat. 96:265–271.

Benkman, C. W. 1987a. Food profitability and the foraging ecology of crossbills. Ecol. Monogr. 57:251–267.

——. 1987b. Crossbill foraging behavior, bill structure, and patterns of food profitability. Wilson Bull. 99:351–368.

——. 1990. Intake rates and the timing of crossbill reproduction. Auk 107:376–386.

Bent, A. C. 1919. Life histories of North American diving birds. U.S. Natl. Mus. Bull. 107.

——. 1921. Life histories of North American gulls and terns. U.S. Natl. Mus. Bull. 113.

——. 1922. Life histories of North American petrels and pelicans and their allies. U.S. Natl. Mus. Bull. 121.

——. 1923. Life histories of North American wild fowl (Part I). U.S. Natl. Mus. Bull. 126.

——. 1926. Life histories of North American marsh birds. U.S. Natl. Mus. Bull. 135.

——. 1927. Life histories of North American shore birds (Part 1). U.S. Natl. Mus. Bull. 142.

——. 1929. Life histories of North American shore birds (Part 2). U.S. Natl. Mus. Bull. 146.

——. 1932. Life histories of North American gallinaceous birds. U.S. Natl. Mus. Bull. 162.

——. 1937. Life histories of North American birds of prey (Part 1). U.S. Natl. Mus. Bull. 167.

——. 1938. Life histories of North American birds of prey (Part 2). U.S. Natl. Mus. Bull. 170.

——. 1939. Life histories of North American woodpeckers. U.S. Natl. Mus. Bull. 174.

——. 1940. Life histories of North American cuckoos, goatsuckers, hummingbirds, and their allies. U.S. Natl. Mus. Bull. 176.

——. 1942. Life histories of North American flycatchers, larks, swallows, and their allies. U.S. Natl. Mus. Bull. 179.

——. 1946. Life histories of North American jays, crows, and titmice. U.S. Natl. Mus. Bull. 191.

——. 1948. Life histories of North American nuthatches, wrens, thrashers, and their allies. U.S. Natl. Mus. Bull. 195.

——. 1949. Life histories of North American thrushes, kinglets, and their allies. U.S. Natl. Mus. Bull. 196.

——. 1950. Life histories of North American wagtails, shrikes, vireos, and their allies. U.S. Natl. Mus. Bull. 197.

——. 1953. Life histories of North American wood warblers. U.S. Natl. Mus. Bull. 203.

——. 1958. Life histories of North American blackbirds, orioles, tanagers, and allies. U.S. Natl. Mus. Bull. 211.

——. 1968a. Eastern and California Purple finches. In O. L. Austin, Jr., ed. A. C. Bent et al.'s Life histories of North American cardinals, grosbeaks, buntings, towhees, finches, sparrows, and allies. U.S. Natl. Mus. Bull. 237 (Part 1): 264–280.

——. 1968b. Red Crossbill (various races). In O. L. Austin, Jr., ed. A. C. Bent et al.'s Life histories of North American cardinals, grosbeaks, buntings, towhees, finches, sparrows, and allies. U.S. Natl. Mus. Bull. 237 (Part 1): 497–526.

Berger, A. J. 1951. Nesting density of Virginia and Sora rails in Michigan. Condor 53:202.

——. 1957. Population density of Alder Flycatchers and Common Goldfinches in *Crataegus* habitats of southeastern Michigan. Wilson Bull. 69:317–322.

——. 1968. Clutch size, incubation period, and nestling period of the American Goldfinch. Wilson Bull. 85:494–498.

Biedenweg, D. W. 1983. Time and energy budgets of the Mockingbird *(Mimus polyglottos)* during the breeding season. Auk 100:149-160.

Binford, L. C. and R. W. Stallcup. 1972. American Redstart breeding in California. Calif. Birds 3:87-90.

Bird, R. D. and L. B. Smith. 1964. The food habits of the Red-winged Blackbird, *Agelaius phoeniceus*, in Manitoba. Can. Field-Nat. 78:179-186.

Blanchard, B. D. 1941. The White-crowned Sparrows *(Zonotrichia leucophrys)* of the Pacific seaboard: Environment and annual cycle. Univ. Calif. Publ. Zool. 46:1-178.

Blancher, P. J. and R. J. Robertson. 1984. Resource use by sympatric kingbirds. Condor 86:305-313.

——. 1985. Predation in relation to spacing of kingbird nests. Auk 102:654-658.

Bleitz, D. 1958. Indigo Bunting breeding in Los Angeles County, California. Condor 60:408.

Block, W. M. 1990. Geographic variation in foraging ecologies of breeding and nonbreeding birds in oak woodlands. In M. L. Morrison, C. J. Ralph, J. Verner, and J. R. Jehl, Jr., eds. Avian foraging: Theory, methodology, and applications, 264-269. Studies Avian Biol. 13.

——. 1991. Foraging ecology of Nuttall's Woodpecker. Auk 108:303-317.

Bloom, P. H. 1979. Ecological studies of the Barn Owl in California. In P. P. Schaeffer and S. M. Ehlers, eds. Proc. Natl. Audubon Society's Symp. on Owls of the West: Their ecology and conservation, 36-39. Western Education Center, Tiburon, Calif.

Bock, C. E. 1969. Intra- vs. interspecific aggression in Pygmy Nuthatch flocks. Ecology 50:903-905.

Bolander, L. Ph. and C. A. Bryant. 1930. Some notes on Point Reyes birds. Condor 32:70-72.

Bolin, R. L. and D. P. Abbott. 1963. Studies on the marine climate and phytoplankton of the central coastal area of California, 1954-1960. Calif. C.O.F.I. Rept. 9:23-45.

Bond, R. M. 1940. Food habits of the White-tailed Kite. Condor 42:168.

——. 1942. White-tailed Kites feeding on house mice. Condor 44:231.

Bonnot, P. 1928. An outlaw Barn Owl. Condor 30:320.

Booth, E. J. 1926. Observations in the San Francisco Bay region. Condor 28:271.

Breitwiech, R., P. G. Merritt, and G. H. Whitesides. 1984. Why do Northern Mockingbirds feed fruit to their nestlings? Condor 86:281-287.

Brennan, L. A. and M. L. Morrison. 1990. Influence of sample size on interpretations of foraging patterns by Chestnut-backed Chickadees. In M. L. Morrison, C. J. Ralph, J. Verner, and J. R. Jehl, Jr., eds. Avain foraging: Theory, methodology, and applications, 187-192. Studies Avian Biol. 13.

——. 1991. Long-term trends of chickadee populations in western North America. Condor 93:130-137.

Briggs, K. T., D. G. Ainley, L. B. Spear, P. B. Adams, and S. E. Smith. 1988. Distribution and diet of Cassin's Auklet and Common Murre in relation to central California upwellings. In H. Ouellet, ed. Acta XIX Congressus Inter-

nationalis Ornithologici, Vol I, 982-990. Ottawa, Canada, 22-29 June 1986. Natl. Mus. Nat. Sci., Univ. Ottawa Press.

Briggs, K. T., W. B. Tyler, D. B. Lewis, and D. R. Carlson. 1987. Bird communities at sea off California: 1975 to 1983. Studies Avian Biol. 11.

Brown, C. R. 1981. The impact of Starlings on Purple Martin populations in unmanaged colonies. Am. Birds 35:266-268.

Brown, J. L. 1963. Aggressiveness, dominance and social organization in the Steller Jay. Condor 65:460-484.

——. 1964. The integration of agnostic behavior in the Steller's Jay, *Cyanocitta stelleri* (Gmelin). Univ. Calif. Publ. Zool. 60:223-328.

Brown, L. and D. Amadon. 1968. *Eagles, Hawks, and Falcons of the World.* Vol 2. McGraw-Hill, New York.

Brown, W. H. 1973. Winter population trends in the Marsh, Cooper's and Sharp-shinned hawks. Am. Birds 27:6-7.

——. 1976. Winter population trends in the Black and Turkey vultures. Am. Birds 30:909-912.

Browning, B. M. 1959. An ecological study of the food habits of the Mourning Dove. Calif. Fish Game 45:313-331.

——. 1962. Food habits of the Mourning Dove in California. Calif. Fish Game 48:91-115.

——. 1977. Appendix B. Foods of the California Quail. In A. S. Leopold. *The California Quail,* 229-249. Univ. California Press, Berkeley.

Brownsmith, C. B. 1977. Foraging rates of Starlings in two habitats. Condor 79:386-387.

Bryant, H. C. 1914a. A determination of the economic status of the Western Meadowlark in California. Univ. Calif. Publ. Zool. 11:377-510.

——. 1914b. Birds as destroyers of grasshoppers in California. Auk 31:168-177.

——. 1916. Habits and food of the Roadrunner in California. Univ. Calif. Publ. Zool. 17:21-50.

——. 1925. Nesting of the Allen Hummingbird in Golden Gate Park. Condor 27:98-100.

Bull, E. L. and H. D. Cooper. 1991. Vaux's Swift nests in hollow trees. W. Birds 22:85-91.

Bull, E. L. and E. C. Meslow. 1977. Habitat requirements of the Pileated Woodpecker in northeastern Oregon. J. For. 75:335-337.

Bull, E. L., A. L. Wright, and M. G. Henjum. 1989. Nesting and diet of Long-eared Owls in conifer forests, Oregon. Condor 91:908-912.

Bunni, M. K. 1959. The Killdeer, *Charadrius v. vociferus* L., in the breeding season: Ecology, behavior, and the development of homoiothermism. Ph.D. thesis, Univ. Mich., Ann Arbor.

Burcham, J. S. 1904. Notes on the habits of the Water Ouzel *(Cinclus mexicanus).* Condor 6:50.

Burnell, K. L. and D. F. Tomback. 1985. Steller's Jays steal Gray Jay caches: Field and laboratory observations. Auk 102:417-419.

448

Busby, D. G. and S. G. Sealy. 1979. Feeding ecology of a population of nesting Yellow Warblers. Can. J. Zool. 57:1670–1681.

Buss, I. C. 1942. A managed Cliff Swallow colony in southern Wisconsin. Wilson Bull. 54:153–161.

Butler, R. W. 1981. Nesting of Brewer's Blackbirds on man-made structures and natural sites in British Columbia. Can. Field-Nat. 95:476–477.

Butts, W. K. 1931. A study of the chickadee and White-breasted Nuthatch by means of marked individuals. Part III. The White-breasted Nuthatch *(Sitta carolinensis cookei)*. Bird-Banding 2:59–76.

Byrd, G. V. and C. F. Zeillemaker. 1981. Ecology of nesting Hawaiian Common Gallinules at Hanalei, Hawaii. W. Birds 12:105–116.

C

Cade, T. J., J. H. Enderson, C. G. Thelander, and C. M. White, eds. 1988. Commentary—The role of organochlorine pesticides in Peregrine Falcon population changes. In Cade et. al., eds. *Peregrine Falcon Populations: Their Management and Recovery*, 463–468. The Peregrine Fund, Boise, Idaho.

Cadman, M. D., P. F. J. Eagles, and F. M. Helleiner. 1987. *Atlas of the Breeding Birds of Ontario.* Federation of Ontario Naturalists and the Long Point Bird Obs. Univ. Waterloo Press, Waterloo.

Caldwell, L. D. 1967. Attack behavior of a Loggerhead Shrike. Wilson Bull. 79:116–117.

California Department Fish and Game. 1991a. 1990 annual report on the status of California's state listed Threatened and Endangered plants and animals. Sacramento.

———. 1991b (January). Bird and mammal Species of Special Concern. Sacramento.

California Department Water Resources. 1978. Wind in California. Bulletin 185.

———. 1980. California rainfall summary monthly total precipitation, 1849–1979. Sacramento.

Carnie, S. K. 1954. Food habits of nesting Golden Eagles in the Coast Ranges of California. Condor 56:3–12.

Carriger, H. W. and J. R. Pemberton. 1907. Nesting of the Pine Siskin in California. Condor 9:18–19.

Carriger, H. W. and G. Wells. 1919. Nesting of the northern Pileated Woodpecker. Condor 21:153–156.

Carter, H. R. and R. A. Erickson. 1988. Population status and conservation problems of the Marbled Murrelet in California, 1897–1987. Final Rept. to Calif. Dept. Fish Game, contract FG7569(FY 1987-88), Sacramento.

Carter, H. R. and K. A. Hobson. 1988. Creching behavior of Brandt's Cormorant chicks. Condor 90:395–400.

Carter, H. R., K. A. Hobson, and S. G. Sealy. 1984. Colony-site selection by Pelagic Cormorants *(Phalacrocorax pelagicus)* in Barkley Sound, British Columbia. Colonial Waterbirds 7:25–34.

Carter, H. R., D. L. Jaques, G. J. McChesney, C. S. Strong, M. W. Parker, and J. C. Takekawa. 1990. Breeding populations of seabirds on the northern and central California coasts in 1989 and 1990. Draft Final Rept. U.S. Fish Wildl. Serv., Dixon, Calif.

Carter, H. R., G. J. McChesney, D. L. Jaques, C. S. Strong, M. W. Parker, J. E. Takekawa, D. L. Jory, and D. L. Whitworth. 1992. Breeding populations of seabirds in California, 1989-1991. Unpubl. Rept., U.S. Fish Wildl. Serv., Northern Prairie Wildl. Res. Ctr, Dixon, Calif.

Case, N. A. and O. H. Hewitt. 1963. Nesting and productivity of the Red-winged Blackbird in relation to habitat. Living Bird 2:7–20.

Catling, P. M. 1971. Spring migration of Saw-whet Owls at Toronto, Ontario. Bird-Banding 42:110–114.

Chamberlin, C. 1901. Some architectural traits of the Western Gnatcatcher. Condor 3:33–36.

Chambers, W. L. 1903. Early nesting of *Calypte anna* in the vicinity of Santa Monica, California. Condor 5:133.

———. 1912. Who will save the Band-tailed Pigeon? Condor 14:108.

Chan, G. L. 1979. Reconnaissance survey of the Double Point Area of Special Biological Significance. Draft #2. Rept. to Calif. Dept. Fish Game and State Water Resources Control Board.

Chapin, E. A. 1925. Food habits of the vireos: A family of insectivorous birds. U.S. Dept. Agri. Bull. 1355:1–44.

Chapman, L. B. 1935, 1939, 1955. Studies of a Tree Swallow colony. Bird-Banding 6:45–57; 10:61–72; 26:45–70.

Chappell, C. B. and B. J. Ringer. 1983. Status of the Hermit Warbler in Washington. W. Birds 14:185–196.

Childs, H. E., Jr. 1968. Brown Towhee (various races). In O. L. Austin, Jr., ed. A. C. Bent et al.'s Life histories of North American cardinals, grosbeaks, buntings, towhees, finches, sparrows, and allies. U.S. Natl. Mus. Bull. 237 (Part 2): 603–619.

Church, R. L. 1966. Water exchanges in California vole *(Microtus californicus)*. Physio. Zool. 39:326–340.

Clark, K. L. and R. J. Robertson. 1981. Cowbird parasitism and evolution of anti-parasitic strategies in the Yellow Warbler. Wilson Bull. 93:249–258.

Clark, R. J. 1975. A field study of the Short-eared Owl, *Asio flammeus* (Pontoppidan), in North America. Wildl. Monogr. 47.

Cogswell, H. L. 1977. *Waterbirds of California.* Univ. California Press, Berkeley.

Collins, C. T. 1979. The ecology and conservation of Burrowing Owls. In P. P. Schaeffer and S. M. Ehler, eds. Proc. Natl. Audubon Society's Symp. on Owls of the West: Their ecology and conservation, 6–17. Western Education Center, Tiburon, Calif.

Collins, C. T. and E. V. Johnson. 1982. Further records of White-throated Swifts utilizing manmade structures. W. Birds 13:25–28.

Collins, C. T. and R. E. Landry. 1977. Artificial nest burrows for Burrowing Owls. N. Am. Bird Bander 2:151–154.

Collins, J. N. and V. H. Resh. 1985. Utilization of natural and man-made habitats by the salt marsh Song Sparrow, *Melospiza melodia samuelis* (Baird). Calif. Fish Game 71: 40–52.

Collins, S. C. 1981. A comparison of nest-site and perch-site vegetation structure for seven species of warblers. Wilson Bull. 93:542–547.

Colvin, B. A. and S. R. Spaulding. 1983. Winter foraging behavior of Short-eared Owls *(Asio flammeus)* in Ohio. Am. Midl. Nat. 110:124–128.

Combellack, C. R. B. 1954. A nesting of Violet-green Swallows. Auk 71:435–442.

Confer, J. L. and P. Paicos. 1985. Downy Woodpecker predation at goldenrod galls. J. Field Ornithol. 56:56–64.

Connelly, D. P. and D. L. Chesemore. 1980. Food habits of Pintails, *Anas acuta*, wintering on seasonally flooded wetlands in the northern San Joaquin Valley, California. Calif. Fish Game 66:233–237.

Connelly, J., Jr. 1978. Trends in Blue-winged and Cinnamon teal populations in eastern Washington. Murrelet 59:2–6.

Connelly, J. W. and I. J. Ball. 1984. Comparisons of aspects of breeding Blue-winged and Cinnamon teal in eastern Washington. Wilson Bull. 96:626–633.

Conner, R. N. 1975. Orientation of entrances to woodpecker nest cavities. Auk 92:371–374.

——. 1977. The effect of tree hardness on woodpecker nest entrance orientation. Auk 94:369–370.

——. 1981. Seasonal changes in woodpecker foraging patterns. Auk 98:562–570.

Conner, R. N., R. G. Hooper, H. S. Crawford, and H. S. Mosby. 1975. Woodpecker nesting habitat in cut and uncut woodlands in Virginia. J. Wildl. Mgmt. 39:144–150.

Cornwell, G. W. 1963. Observations on the breeding biology and behavior of a nesting population of Belted Kingfishers. Condor 65:426–431.

Coulombe, H. N. 1971. Behavior and population ecology of the Burrowing Owl, *Speotyto cunicularia*, in the Imperial Valley of California. Condor 73:162–176.

Coulter, M. C. 1973. Breeding biology of the Western Gull, *Larus occidentalis*. M.S. thesis, Oxford Univ.

Coulter, M. C. and R. W. Risebrough. 1973. Shell-thinning in eggs of the Ashy Petrel *(Oceanodroma homochroa)* from the Farallon Islands. Condor 75:254–255.

Coutlee, E. L. 1967. Agonistic behavior in the American Goldfinch. Wilson Bull. 79:89–109.

——. 1968a. Comparative breeding behavior of Lesser and Lawrence's goldfinches. Condor 70:228–242.

——. 1968b. Maintenance behavior of Lesser and Lawrence's goldfinches. Condor 70:378–384.

Cowan, J. B. 1952. Life history and productivity of a population of Mourning Doves in California. Calif. Fish Game 38:505–521.

Craig, R. B. 1978. An analysis of the predatory behavior of the Loggerhead Shrike. Auk 95:221–234.

Craig, T. H. and C. H. Trost. 1979. The biology and nesting density of breeding American Kestrels and Long-eared Owls on the Big Lost River, southeastern Idaho. Wilson Bull. 91:50–61.

Cramp, S., ed. 1985. *Handbook of the Birds of Europe, the Middle East, and North Africa: The Birds of the Western Palearctic. Vol. IV: Terns to Woodpeckers.* Oxford Univ. Press, New York.

Crase, F. T. 1976. Occurrence of the Chestnut-backed Chickadee in the Sierra Nevada Mountains, California. Am. Birds 30:673–675.

Crase, F. T. and R. W. DeHaven. 1977. Food of nestling Tricolored Blackbirds. Condor 79:265–269.

——. 1978. Food selection by five sympatric California blackbird species. Calif. Fish Game 64:255–267.

Crockett, A. B. and H. H. Hadow. 1975. Nest site selection by Williamson and Red-naped sapsuckers. Condor 77:365–368.

Croll, D. A. 1990. Physical and biological determinants of the abundance, distribution, and diet of the Common Murre in Monterey Bay, California. In S. G. Sealy, ed. Auks at sea, 139–148. Studies Avian Biol. 14.

Cunningham, J. D. 1955. Notes on food habits of the White-tailed Kite in southern California. Condor 57:371.

Custer, T. W., G. L. Hensler, and T. E. Kaiser. 1983. Clutch size, reproductive success, and organochlorine contaminants in Atlantic coast Black-crowned Night-Herons. Auk 100:699–710.

D

Dahlsten, D. L., M. L. Morrison, D. L. Rowney, and M. Wilson. 1985. Bird diets and prey availability in the western Sierra Nevada, California. Calif. Fish Game 71:172–178.

Dale, F. H. 1936. Eagle "control" in northern California. Condor 38:208–210.

Darley, J. A. 1971. Sex ratio and mortality in the Brown-headed Cowbird. Auk 88:560–566.

Davis, C. M. 1978. A nesting study of the Brown Creeper. Living Bird 17:237–263.

Davis, E. M. 1937. Observations on nesting Barn Swallows. Bird-Banding 8:66–73.

Davis, J. 1951. Distribution and variation of the Brown Towhee. Univ. Calif. Publ. Zool. 52:1–120.

——. 1957. Comparative foraging behavior of the Spotted and Brown towhees. Auk 74:129–166.

——. 1960. Nesting behavior of the Rufous-sided Towhee in coastal California. Condor 62:434–456.

Davis, J., G. R. Fisler, and B. S. Davis. 1963. The breeding biology of the Western Flycatcher. Condor 65:337–382.

Davis, W. B. 1933. The span of the nesting season of birds in Butte County, California, in relation to their food. Condor 35:151–154.

Dawson, W. L. 1923. *The Birds of California.* South Moulton, San Diego.

Dawson, W. R., J. D. Ligon, J. R. Murphy, J. P. Myers, E. Simberloff, and J. Verner. 1987. Report of the Scientific Advisory Panel on the Spotted Owl. Condor 89:205–229.

DeHaven, R. W. 1973. Winter population trends of the Starling in California. Am. Birds 27:836–837.

DeHaven, R. W., F. T. Crase, and P. P. Woronecki. 1975a. Breeding status of the Tricolored Blackbird 1969–1972. Calif. Fish Game 61:166–180.

———. 1975b. Movements of Tricolored Blackbirds banded in the Central Valley of California 1965-1972. Bird-Banding 46:220-229.

Demaree, S. R. 1975. Observations on roof-nesting Killdeers. Condor 77:487-488.

Dement'ev, G. P. and N. A. Gladkov, eds. 1951-1954. *Birds of the Soviet Union. 6 Vols.* Sovetskaya Nauka, Moskow.

DeSante, D. F. and D. G. Ainley. 1980. The avifauna of the South Farallon Islands, California. Studies Avian Biol. 4.

DeSante, D. F. and L. F. Baptista. 1989. Factors affecting the termination of breeding in Nuttall's White-crowned Sparrows. Wilson Bull. 101:120-124.

DeSante, D. F. and G. R. Geupel. 1987. Landbird productivity in central coastal California: The relationship to annual rainfall, and a reproductive failure in 1986. Condor 89:636-653.

DeSante, D. F. and P. Pyle. 1986. *Distributional Checklist of North American Birds. Vol. 1: United States and Canada.* Artemisia Press, Lee Vining, Calif.

DeSante, D. F. and E. Scriven. 1977. Sexual size dimorphism in the Osprey—a new hypothesis. Abstract, 1977 Annual Meeting Northwestern Bird and Mamm. Assoc.

Detrich, P. J. 1986. The status and distribution of the Bald Eagle in California. M.S. thesis, Calif. State Univ., Chico.

DeWolfe, B. B. 1968. Nuttall's White-crowned Sparrow. In O. L. Austin, Jr., ed. A. C. Bent et al.'s Life histories of North American cardinals, grosbeaks, buntings, towhees, finches, sparrows, and allies. U.S. Natl. Mus. Bull. 237 (Part 3): 1292-1324.

Diamond, J. M. 1969. Avifaunal equilibria and species turnover rates on the Channel Islands of California. Proc. Natl. Acad. Sci. 64:57-73.

Dick, J. A. and J. D. Rising. 1965. A comparison of foods eaten by Eastern Kingbirds and Western Kingbirds in Kansas. Kans. Ornithol. Soc. Bull. 16:23-24.

Dickerman, R. W. 1987. The "old northeastern" subspecies of Red Crossbill. Am. Birds 41:189-194.

Dilger, W. C. 1956. Adaptive modifications and ecological isolating mechanisms in the thrush genera *Catharus* and *Hylocichla.* Wilson Bull. 68:177-199.

Dingle, E. v. S. 1942. Rough-winged Swallow. In A. C. Bent, ed. Life histories of North American flycatchers, larks, swallows, and their allies. U.S. Natl. Mus. Bull. 179: 424-433.

Dixon, J. 1924. Nesting of the Wood Duck in California. Condor 26:41-66.

Dixon, J. B. 1937. The Golden Eagle in San Diego County, California. Condor 39:49-56.

Dixon, J. B., R. E. Dixon, and J. E. Dixon. 1957. Natural history of the White-tailed Kite in San Diego County, California. Condor 59:156-165.

Dixon, K. L. 1949. Behavior of the Plain Titmouse. Condor 51:110-136.

———. 1954. Some ecological relations of chickadees and titmice in central California. Condor 56:113-124.

———. 1960. Additional data on the establishment of the Chestnut-backed Chickadee at Berkeley, California. Condor 62:405-408.

Dobkin, D. S., J. A. Holmes, and B. A. Wilcox. 1986. Traditional nest site use by White-throated Swifts. Condor 88:252-253.

Drobney, R. D. 1980. Reproductive bioenergetics of Wood Ducks. Auk 97:480-490.

———. 1982. Body weight and composition changes and adaptations for breeding in Wood Ducks. Condor 84:300-305.

Drobney, R. D. and L. H. Fredrickson. 1979. Food selection by Wood Ducks in relation to breeding status. J. Wildl. Mgmt. 43:109-120.

Drum, M. 1939. Territorial studies on the eastern goldfinch. Wilson Bull. 51:69-77.

DuBois, A. D. 1935. Nests of Horned Larks and longspurs on a Montana prairie. Condor 37:56-72.

Dubowy, P. J. 1985. Feeding ecology and behavior of post-breeding male Northern Shovelers and Blue-winged Teal. Can. J. Zool. 63:1292-1297.

Duebbert, H. F. 1966. Island nesting of the Gadwall in North Dakota. Wilson Bull. 78:12-25.

Dufty, A. M., Jr. 1982. Movements and activities of radio-tracked Brown-headed Cowbirds. Auk 99:316-327.

Duncan, D. C. 1987. Nest-site distribution and overland brood movements of Northern Pintails in Alberta. J. Wildl. Mgmt. 51:716-723.

Dunne, P., D. Sibley, and C. Sutton. 1988. *Hawks in Flight.* Houghton Mifflin, Boston.

Dunnet, G. M. 1955. The breeding of the Starling *Sturnus vulgaris* in relation to its food supply. Ibis 97:619-662.

Dwyer, T. J. 1974. Social behavior of breeding Gadwalls in North Dakota. Auk 91:375-386.

Dwyer, T. J., G. L. Krapu, and D. M. Janke. 1979. Use of prairie pothole habitat by breeding Mallards. J. Wildl. Mgmt. 43:526-531.

Dyer, M. I., J. Pinowski, and B. Pinowska. 1977. Population dynamics. In J. Pinowski and S. C. Kendeigh, eds. *Granivorous Birds in Ecosystems: Their Evolution, Populations, Energetics, Impact, and Control,* 53-105. Int. Biol. Progr. 12. Cambridge Univ. Press, London.

Dzubin, A. 1969. Comments on carrying capacity of small ponds for ducks and possible effects on Mallard production. Saskatoon Wetlands Seminar, 138-160. Can. Wildl. Serv. Rept. Ser. 6.

Dzubin, A. and J. B. Gollop. 1972. Aspects of Mallard breeding ecology in Canadian parkland and grassland. In Population ecology of migratory birds: A symposium, 113-152. U.S. Fish Wildl. Serv. Res. Rept. 2.

E

Eadie, J. McA., T. D. Nudds, and C. D. Ankney. 1979. Quantifying interspecific variation in foraging behavior in syntopic *Anas* (Anatidae). Can. J. Zool. 57:412-415.

Earhart, C. M. and N. K. Johnson. 1970. Size dimorphism and food habits of North American owls. Condor 72:251-264.

Eckhardt, R. C. 1979. The adaptive syndromes of two guilds of insectivorous birds in the Colorado Rocky Mountains. Ecol. Monogr. 49:129–149.

Edminster, F. C. 1954. *American Game Birds of Field and Forest: Their Habits, Ecology, and Management*. Charles Scribner, New York.

Edson, J. M. 1943. A study of the Violet-green Swallow. Auk 60:396–403.

Ehrlich, P. R., D. S. Dobkin, and D. Wheye. 1988. *The Birder's Handbook: A Field Guide to the Natural History of North American Birds*. Simon & Schuster, New York.

Ehrlich, P. R. and A. H. Ehrlich. 1990. *The Population Explosion*. Simon & Schuster, New York.

Eipper, A. W. 1956. Differences in vulnerability of the prey of nesting kingfishers. J. Wildl. Mgmt. 20:177–183.

Eisenmann, E. 1971. Range expansion and population increase in North and Middle America of the White-tailed Kite *(Elanus leucurus)*. Am. Birds 25:529–536.

Elizroth, E. K. 1983. Breeding biology and mortality of Western Bluebirds near Corvallis, Oregon. Sialia 5:83–87.

Elliott, H. W., III and J. D. Wehausen. 1974. Vegetational succession on coastal rangeland of Point Reyes peninsula. Madroño 22:231–238.

Ellison, W. G. 1985. Indigo Bunting. In S. B. Laughlin and D. P. Kibbe, eds. *The Atlas of Breeding Birds of Vermont*, 334–335. Univ. Press of New England, Hanover, N.H.

Emerson, W. O. 1904. *Icterus bullocki* as a Honey-eater. Condor 6:78.

Emlen, J. T., Jr. 1942. Notes on a nesting colony of Western Crows. Bird-Banding 13:143–153.

———. 1952. Social behavior in nesting Cliff Swallows. Condor 54:177–199.

———. 1954. Territory, nest building, and pair formation in the Cliff Swallow. Auk 71:16–35.

Emlen, J. T., Jr. and B. Glading. 1945. Increasing Valley Quail in California. Calif. Agri. Exp. Sta. Bull. 695.

Emlen, S. T., J. D. Rising, and W. L. Thompson. 1975. A behavioral and morphological study of sympatry in the Indigo and Lazuli buntings of the Great Plains. Wilson Bull. 87:145–179.

Engels, W. L. 1940. Structural adaptations in the thrashers (Mimidae: genus *Toxostoma*) with comments on interspecific relationships. Univ. Calif. Publ. Zool. 42:341–400.

Erickson, M. M. 1937. A jay shoot in California. Condor 39:111–115.

———. 1938. Territory, annual cycle, and numbers in a population of Wren-tits *(Chamaea fasciata)*. Univ. Calif. Publ. Zool. 42:247–334.

———. 1968. Lazuli Bunting. In O. L. Austin, Jr., ed. A. C. Bent et al.'s Life histories of North American cardinals, grosbeaks, buntings, towhees, finches, sparrows, and allies. U.S. Natl. Mus. Bull. 237 (Part 1): 111–132.

Errington, P. L. and W. J. Breckenridge. 1936. Food habits of Marsh Hawks in the glaciated prairie region of north-central United States. Am. Midl. Nat. 7:831–848.

Errington, P. L., F. Hamerstrom, and F. N. Hamerstrom, Jr. 1940. The Great Horned Owl and its prey in north-central United States. Iowa State Coll. Agri. Res. Bull. 277.

Erskine, A. J. 1984. Swallows foraging on the ground. Wilson Bull. 96:136–137.

Esterly, C. O. 1917. How does the shrike carry its prey? Condor 19:25.

Euliss, N. H., Jr. and S. W. Harris. 1987. Feeding ecology of Northern Pintails and Green-winged Teal wintering in California. J. Wildl. Mgmt. 51:724–732.

Evans, D. L. 1982. Status reports on twelve raptors. U.S. Fish Wildl. Serv. Spec. Sci. Rept. Wildl. 238.

Evans, F. C. 1964. The food of Vesper, Field, and Chipping sparrows nesting in an abandoned field in southeast Michigan. Am. Midl. Nat. 72:57–75.

Evenden, F. G., Jr. 1957. Observations on nesting behavior of the House Finch. Condor 59:112–117.

Evens, J. G. 1985. Monitoring the Osprey colony at Kent Lake, Marin County California: Five year summary, 1981–1985. Rept. to Marin Municipal Water District. PRBO Contrib. 331.

———. 1987. Reproductive success of Osprey at Kent Lake, California, 1987. Rept. to Marin Municipal Water District. PRBO Contrib. 381.

———. 1989. Reproductive success of Osprey at Kent Lake with notes on an incipient population at Tomales Bay, California, 1989. Rept. to Marin Municipal Water District. PRBO Contrib. 481.

———. 1991. Reproductive success of the Osprey population in Marin County, California, 1981–1990: A decade of growth. Rept. to Marin Municipal Water District. PRBO Contrib. 504.

———. in press. Growth and reproductive success of the Osprey population in western Marin County, California, 1981–1990. W. Birds.

Evens, J. G. and G. W. Page. 1983. The ecology of rail populations at Corte Madera Ecological Reserve: With recommendations for management. PRBO Contrib. 255.

———. 1984. California Clapper Rail *(Rallus longirostris obsoletus)*. Endangered Species Info. System, U.S. Fish Wildl. Serv.

———. 1986. Predation on Black Rails during high tides in salt marshes. Condor 88:107–109.

Evens, J. G., G. W. Page, S. A. Laymon, and R. W. Stallcup. 1991. Distribution, relative abundance, and status of the California Black Rail in western North America. Condor 93:952–966.

Evens, J. G., G. W. Page, L. E. Stenzel, R. W. Stallcup, and R. P. Henderson. 1989. Distribution and relative abundance of the California Black Rail *(Laterallus jamaicensis coturniculus)* in tidal marshes of the San Francisco Bay estuary. Rept. to Calif. Dept. Fish Game, Sacramento.

Evens, J. G., G. W. Page, L. E. Stenzel, and N. D. Warnock. 1986. Distribution, abundance, and habitat of California Black Rails in tidal marshes of Marin and Sonoma counties, California. Point Reyes Bird Obs. Sci. Rept.

Evermann, B. W. 1919. A colony of Tricolored Blackbirds. Gull 1:2–3.

452

LITERATURE CITED

F

Faber, R. A., R. W. Risebrough, and H. M. Pratt. 1972. Organochlorines and mercury in Common Egrets and Great Blue Herons. Envir. Pollution 3:111-122.

Fairley, L. 1987. *Mount Tamalpais: A History.* Scottwall Associates, San Francisco.

Feare, C. 1984. *The Starling.* Oxford Univ. Press, New York.

Ferguson-Lees, J. 1976. Foreword. In J. T. R. Sharrock, comp. 1976. *The Atlas of Breeding Birds in Britain and Ireland,* 9-11. British Trust for Ornithology, Tring, England.

Ferrel, C. M., H. Twining, and N. B. Herkenbaum. 1949. Food habits of the Ring-necked Pheasant *(Phasianus colchicus)* in the Sacramento Valley, California. Calif. Fish Game 35:51-69.

Findholt, S. L. 1984. Organochlorine residues, eggshell thickness, and reproductive success of Snowy Egrets nesting in Idaho. Condor 86:163-169.

Finlay, J. C. 1971. Breeding biology of Purple Martins at the northern limit of their range. Wilson Bull. 83:254-269.

——. 1975. Nesting of Purple Martins in natural cavities and in man-made structures in Alberta. Can. Field-Nat. 89: 454-455.

Fisher, W. K. 1902. The redwood belt of northwestern California. I. Faunal peculiarities of the region. II. Land birds. Condor 4:111-114, 131-135.

Fitch, H. S. 1947. Predation by owls in the Sierran foothills of California. Condor 49:137-151.

Fitch, H. S., B. Glading, and V. House. 1946. Observations on Cooper Hawk nesting and predation. Calif. Fish Game 32:144-154.

Fitch, H. S., F. Swenson, and D. F. Tillotson. 1946. Behavior and food habits of the Red-tailed Hawk. Condor 48: 205-237.

Fleischer, R. C. 1985. A new technique to identify and assess the dispersion of eggs of individual brood parasites. Behav. Ecol. Sociobiol. 17:91-99.

Fleischer, R. C. and S. I. Rothstein. 1988. Known secondary contact and rapid gene flow among subspecies and dialects in the Brown-headed Cowbird. Evolution 42:1146-1158.

Fleischer, R. C., S. I. Rothstein, and L. S. Miller. 1991. Mitochondrial DNA variation indicates gene flow across a zone of known secondary contact between two subspecies of the Brown-headed Cowbird. Condor 93:185-189.

Fleischer, R. C., A. P. Smyth, and S. I. Rothstein. 1987. Temporal and age-related variation in the laying rate of the parasitic Brown-headed Cowbird in the eastern Sierra Nevada, California. Can. J. Zool. 65:2724-2730.

Follett, W. I. and D. G. Ainley. 1976. Fishes collected by Pigeon Guillemots, *Cepphus columba* (Pallas), nesting on Southeast Farallon Island, California. Calif. Fish Game 62:28-31.

Forbes, J. A. and D. W. Warner. 1974. Behavior of a radio-tagged Saw-whet Owl. Auk 91:783-795.

Ford, E. R. 1936. Unusual nest site of the Loggerhead Shrike *(Lanius ludovicianus ludovicianus).* Auk 53:219.

Forsman, E. D., E. C. Meslow, and H. M. Wight. 1984. Distribution and biology of the Spotted Owl in Oregon. Wildl. Monogr. 87:1-64.

Foster, M. L. 1977. A breeding season study of the Salt Marsh Yellowthroat *(Geothlypis trichas sinuosa)* of the San Francisco Bay Area, California. M.A. thesis, San Jose State Univ.

Foster, W. L. and J. Tate, Jr. 1966. Activities and coactions of animals at sapsucker trees. Living Bird 5:87-113.

Frakes, R. A. and R. E. Johnson. 1982. Niche convergence in *Empidonax* flycatchers. Condor 84:286-291.

Francis, W. J. 1968. Temperature and humidity conditions in potential pheasant nesting habitat. J. Wildl. Mgmt. 32:36-46.

Franzreb, K. E. 1983a. A comparison of avian foraging behavior in unlogged and logged mixed-coniferous forest. Wilson Bull. 95:60-76.

——. 1983b. Intersexual habitat partitioning in Yellow-rumped Warblers during the breeding season. Wilson Bull. 95:581-590.

——. 1984. Foraging habits of Ruby-crowned and Golden-crowned kinglets in an Arizona montane forest. Condor 86:139-145.

——. 1985. Foraging ecology of Brown Creepers in a mixed-coniferous forest. J. Field Ornithol. 56:9-16.

Fredrickson, L. H. 1970. Breeding biology of American Coots in Iowa. Wilson Bull. 82:445-457.

——. 1971. Common Gallinule breeding biology and development. Auk 88:914-919.

Fredrickson, L. H., J. M. Anderson, F. J. Kozlik, and R. A. Ryder. 1977. American Coot *(Fulica americana).* In G. C. Sanderson, ed. Management of migratory shore and upland game birds in North America, 123-147. Int. Assoc. Fish Wildl. Agencies and U.S. Fish Wildl. Serv.

Friedmann, H. 1929. *The Cowbirds: A Study in the Biology of Social Parasitism.* C. C. Thomas, Springfield, Ill.

——. 1963. Host relations of the parasitic cowbirds. U.S. Natl. Mus. Bull. 233.

Friedmann, H. and L. F. Kiff. 1985. The parasitic cowbirds and their hosts. Proc. West. Found. Vert. Zool. 2:227-304.

Friedmann, H., L. F. Kiff, and S. I. Rothstein. 1977. A further contribution to knowledge of the host relations of the parasitic cowbirds. Smithson. Contr. Zool. 235.

Fry, D. K., Jr. 1966. Recovery of the White-tailed Kite. Pac. Discovery 19:27-30.

Fry, M. E. 1977. Acorn selection by Band-tailed Pigeons. Calif. Fish Game 63:59-60.

Frydendall, M. J. 1967. Feeding ecology and territorial behavior of the Yellow Warbler. Ph.D. thesis, Utah State Univ., Logan.

Furrer, R. K. 1975. Breeding success and nest site stereotypy in a population of Brewer's Blackbirds *Euphagus cyanocephalus.* Oecologia 20:339-350.

453

G

Gaines, D. 1974. A new look at the nesting riparian avifauna of the Sacramento Valley, California. W. Birds 5:61–80.

——. 1977. *Birds of the Yosemite Sierra: A Distributional Survey.* California Syllabus, Oakland.

——. 1988. *Birds of Yosemite and the East Slope.* Artemisia Press, Lee Vining, Calif.

Gaines, D. and T. Beedy. 1987 (revised). Checklist of the birds of Yolo County. Davis Audubon, Davis, Calif.

Gaines, D. and S. A. Laymon. 1984. Decline, status and preservation of the Yellow-billed Cuckoo in California. W. Birds 15:49–80.

Galati, B. and C. B. Galati. 1985. Breeding of the Golden-crowned Kinglet in northern Minnesota. J. Field Ornithol. 56:28–49.

Garrett, K. and J. Dunn. 1981. *Birds of Southern California: Status and Distribution.* Los Angeles Audubon, Los Angeles.

Garrett, R. L. and D. J. Mitchell. 1973. A study of Prairie Falcon populations in California. Wildl. Mgmt. Branch Admin. Rept. 73-2. Calif. Dept. Fish Game, Sacramento.

Garrison, B. A., J. M. Humphrey, and S. A. Laymon. 1987. Bank Swallow distribution and nesting ecology on the Sacramento River, California. W. Birds 18:71–76.

Gashwiler, J. S. and A. L. Ward. 1968. Oregon Junco foods in coniferous forests. Murrelet 49:29–36.

Gates, J. M. 1962. Breeding biology of the Gadwall in northern Utah. Wilson Bull. 74:43–67.

Gerstenberg, R. H. 1972. A study of shorebirds (Charadrii) in Humboldt Bay, California, 1968 to 1969. M.S. thesis, Humboldt State Univ., Arcata.

Getz, L. L. 1961. Hunting areas of the Long-eared Owl. Wilson Bull. 73:79–82.

Geupel, G. R. 1981. The unique Wrentit of California's coastal scrub. Point Reyes Bird Obs. Newsl. 56:9–10.

Geupel, G. R. and D. F. DeSante. 1983. Abstract, 101st meeting of the American Ornithologists' Union. New York, N.Y.

Geupel, G. R. and D. F. DeSante. 1990. Incidence and determinants of double brooding in Wrentits. Condor 92:67–75.

Gibson, F. 1971. The breeding biology of the American Avocet *(Recurvirostra americana)* in central Oregon. Condor 73:444–454.

Gill, R. E., Jr. 1972. South San Francisco Bay breeding bird survey. Wildl. Mgmt. Branch Admin. Rept. 72-6. Calif. Dept. Fish Game, Sacramento.

——. 1977. Breeding avifauna of the south San Francisco Bay estuary. W. Birds 8:1–12.

——. 1979. Status and distribution of the California Clapper Rail *(Rallus longirostris obsoletus).* Calif. Fish Game 65:36–49.

Gilliam, H. 1962. *Weather of the San Francisco Bay Region.* Calif. Nat. Hist. Guides 6. Univ. California Press, Berkeley.

Glading, B. 1938. Studies on the nesting cycle of the California Valley Quail in 1937. Calif. Fish Game 24:318–340.

Glahn, J. F. 1974. Study of breeding rails with recorded calls in north-central Colorado. Wilson Bull. 86:206–214.

Glover, F. A. 1953a. Nesting ecology of the Pied-billed Grebe in northwestern Iowa. Wilson Bull. 65:32–39.

——. 1953b. A nesting study of the Band-tailed Pigeon *(Columba f. fasciata)* in northwestern California. Calif. Fish Game 39:397–407.

Godfrey, W. E. 1966. *The Birds of Canada.* Natl. Mus. Canada Bull. 203. Ottawa.

Goldberg, N. H. 1979. Behavioral flexibility and foraging strategies in Cassin's and Western kingbirds *(Tyrannus vociferans* and *T. verticalis)* breeding sympatrically in riparian habitats in central Arizona. Ph.D. thesis, Univ. Ill., Champaign.

Goodge, W. R. 1959. Locomotion and other behavior of the Dipper. Condor 61:4–17.

Goodpasture, K. A. 1953. Wood Pewee builds with green leaves. Wilson Bull. 65:117–118.

Goodwin, D. 1983. *Pigeons and Doves of the World.* 3rd ed. British Mus. (Nat. Hist.). Comstock, Ithaca, N.Y.

——. 1986. *Crows of the World.* 2nd ed. British Mus. (Nat. Hist.).

Gould, G. I., Jr. 1977. Distribution of the Spotted Owl in California. W. Birds 8:131–146.

Gould, G. I., Jr. and R. M. Jurek. 1988. Osprey status review. Job Final Rept. II-19, W-65-R-4. Calif. Dept. Fish Game, Sacramento.

Graber, R. R. 1962. Food and oxygen consumption of three species of owls (Strigidae). Condor 64:473–487.

Graber, R. R. and J. W. Graber. 1951. Nesting of the Parula Warbler in Michigan. Wilson Bull. 63:75–83.

Graber, R. R., J. W. Graber, and E. L. Kirk. 1973. Illinois birds: Laniidae. Ill. Nat. Hist. Surv. Biol. Notes 83.

Granholm, S. L. 1989. Seasonal wetlands in San Francisco and San Pablo bays: Current status, projected losses, and cumulative losses since 1975. In Endangered habitat: A report on the status of seasonal wetlands in San Francisco Bay and a recommended plan for their protection, 7–43. National Audubon Society and others.

Grau, R., E. Richardson, G. M. Santolo. 1987. Toxicity of selenium to nestling Tricolored Blackbirds *(Agelaius tricolor).* Unpubl. Rept., 23 Oct 1987. Dept. Avian Sci., Univ. Calif., Davis.

Graves, W. C. 1975. Wild Turkey management in California. In L. K. Halls, ed. Proc. 3rd Natl. Wild Turkey Symp., 1–5. Texas Parks and Wildl. Dept., Austin.

Gray, B. J. 1980. Reproduction, energetics, and social structure of the Ruddy Duck. Ph.D. thesis, Univ. Calif., Davis.

Grenfell, W. E., Jr., B. M. Browning, and W. E. Stienecker. 1980. Food habits of California upland gamebirds. Wildl. Mgmt. Branch Admin. Rept. 80-1. Calif. Dept. Fish Game, Sacramento.

Grenfell, W. E., Jr. and W. F. Laudenslayer, Jr., eds. 1983. The distribution of California birds. California Wildlife/Habitat Relationships Program Publ. 4. Calif. Dept. Fish Game, Sacramento, and USDA For. Serv., San Francisco.

Gress, F., R. W. Risebrough, D. W. Anderson, L. F. Kiff, and J. R. Jehl, Jr. 1973. Reproductive failures of Double-crested Cormorants in southern California and Baja California. Wilson Bull. 85:197-208.

Gress, F., R. W. Risebrough, and F. C. Sibley. 1971. Shell thinning in eggs of the Common Murre, *Uria aalge*, from the Farallon Islands, California. Condor 73:368-369.

Griese, H. J., R. A. Ryder, and C. E. Braun. 1980. Spatial and temporal distribution of rails in Colorado. Wilson Bull. 92:96-102.

Griffin, J. R. 1977. Oak woodland. In M. G. Barbour and J. Major, eds. *Terrestrial Vegetation of California*, 383-415. John Wiley & Sons, New York.

Grinnell, H. W. 1944. The Hooded Oriole's choice of nesting sites in the settled portions of southern California. Condor 46:298.

Grinnell, J. 1909, 1924, 1939. A bibliography of California ornithology. Pac. Coast Avifauna 5, 16, & 26.

——. 1911. Distribution of the Mockingbird in California. Auk 28:293-300.

——. 1913. The outlook for conserving the Band-tailed Pigeon as a game bird of California. Condor 15:25-38.

——. 1917. The niche relationships of the California Thrasher. Auk 34:427-433.

——. 1936. Uphill planters. Condor 38:80-82.

Grinnell, J., H. C. Bryant, and T. I. Storer. 1918. *The Game Birds of California*. Univ. California Press, Berkeley.

Grinnell, J., J. S. Dixon, and J. M. Linsdale. 1930. Vertebrate natural history of a section of northern California through the Lassen Peak region. Univ. Calif. Publ. Zool. 35.

——. 1937. *Fur-bearing Mammals of California: Their Natural History, Systematic Status, and Relations to Man. Vols. I & II.* Univ. California Press, Berkeley.

Grinnell, J. and J. M. Linsdale. 1936. Vertebrate animals of Point Lobos Reserve, 1934-35. Carnegie Inst. Wash. Publ. 481.

Grinnell, J. and A. H. Miller. 1944. The distribution of the birds of California. Pac. Coast Avifauna 27.

Grinnell, J. and T. I. Storer. 1924. *Animal Life in the Yosemite.* Univ. California Press, Berkeley.

Grinnell, J. and M. W. Wythe. 1927. Directory to the bird-life of the San Francisco Bay region. Pac. Coast Avifauna 18.

Griscom, L. 1937. A monographic study of the Red Crossbill. Proc. Boston Soc. Nat. Hist. 41:71-210.

Gross, A. O. 1942. Northern Cliff Swallow. In A. C. Bent, ed. Life histories of North American flycatchers, larks, swallows, and their allies. U.S. Natl. Mus. Bull. 179:463-484.

——. 1948. Eastern House Wren. In A. C. Bent, ed. Life histories of North American nuthatches, wrens, thrashers, and their allies. U.S. Natl. Mus. Bull. 195:113-141.

——. 1953. Northern and Maryland yellowthroats, Florida Yellowthroat, Western Yellowthroat, and Salt Marsh Yellowthroat. In A. C. Bent, ed. Life histories of North American wood warblers. U.S. Natl. Mus. Bull. 203:542-577.

Groves, S. 1984. Chick growth, sibling rivalry, and chick production in American Black Oystercatchers. Auk 101:525-531.

Grubb, T. C., Jr. 1982. On sex-specific foraging behavior in the White-breasted Nuthatch. J. Field Ornithol. 53:305-314.

Grubb, T. C., Jr. and M. S. Woodrey. 1990. Sex, age, intraspecific dominance status, and the use of food by birds wintering in temperate-deciduous and cold-coniferous woodlands: A review. In M. L. Morrison, C. J. Ralph, J. Verner, and J. R. Jehl, Jr., eds. Avian foraging: Theory, methodology, and applications, 270-279. Studies Avian Biol. 13.

Grün, G. 1975. Die Ernährung der sperlinge *Passer domesticus* (L.) und *Passer montanus* (L.) untes verschiedenen Umweltbedingungen. Int. Studies Sparrows 8:24-103.

Grzybowski, J. A. 1979. Response of Barn Swallows to eggs, young, nests and nest sites. Condor 81:236-246.

Guillory, H. D. and J. H. Deshotek. 1981. House Sparrow flushing prey from trees and shrubs. Wilson Bull. 93:554.

The Gull. 1919-present. Golden Gate Audubon Society (formerly Audubon Assoc. of the Pacific) monthly bulletin. GGAS, 1250 Addison St., #107B, Berkeley, CA 94702.

Gullion, G. W. 1949. Starlings on Point Reyes peninsula, Marin County, California. Condor 51:273.

——. 1954. The reproductive cycle of American Coots in California. Auk 71:366-412.

Gunderson, A. 1939. Nesting habits of the Red-breasted Nuthatch. Condor 41:259-260.

Gutiérrez, R. J. 1980. Comparative ecology of the Mountain and California quail in the Carmel Valley, California. Living Bird 18:71-93.

Gutiérrez, R. J., C. E. Braun, and T. P. Zapatka. 1975. Reproductive biology of the Band-tailed Pigeon in Colorado and New Mexico. Auk 92:665-677.

Gutiérrez, R. J. and A. B. Carey, eds. 1985. Ecology and management of the Spotted Owl in the Pacific Northwest. U.S. For. Serv. Gen. Tech. Rept. PNW-185.

H

Hagar, D. C. 1960. The interrelationships of logging, birds and timber regeneration in the Douglas-fir region of northwestern California. Ecology 41:116-125.

Hamilton, R. B. 1975. Comparative behavior of the American Avocet and the Black-necked Stilt (Recurvirostridae). Ornithol. Monogr. 17.

Hancock, J. and J. Kushlan. 1984. *The Herons Handbook.* Harper & Row, New York.

Hann, H. W. 1950. Nesting behavior of the American Dipper in Colorado. Condor 52:49-62.

Hanowski, J. M. and G. J. Niemi. 1990. Effects of unknown sex in analyses of foraging behavior. In M. L. Morrison, C. J. Ralph, J. Verner, and J. R. Jehl, Jr., eds. Avian foraging: Theory, methodology, and applications, 280-283. Studies Avian Biol. 13.

Hansen, E. L. and B. E. Carter. 1963. A nesting study of Brewer's Blackbirds in Klamath County, Oregon. Murrelet 44:18-21.

Hanson, W. R. 1970. Pheasant nesting and concealment in hayfields. Auk 87:714-719.

Hardy, R. 1949. Ground Dove and Black-chinned Sparrow in southern Nevada. Condor 51:272-273.

Harlow, D. L. and P. H. Bloom. 1989. Buteos and the Golden Eagle. In National Wildlife Federation. Proc. Western Raptor Mgmt. Symp. and Workshop, 102-109. Natl. Wildl. Fed. Sci. and Tech. Ser. 12.

Harlow, R. F., R. G. Hooper, D. R. Chamberlain, and H. S. Crawford. 1975. Some winter and nesting season foods of the Common Raven in Virginia. Auk 92:298-306.

Harper, C. A. 1971. Breeding biology of a small colony of Western Gulls (Larus occidentalis wymani) in California. Condor 73:337-341.

Harper, H. T. and W. A. Smith. 1973. California's turkey stocking program. In G. C. Sanderson and H. C. Schultz, eds. Wild Turkey Management: Current Problems and Programs, 55-63. Univ. Missouri Press, Columbia.

Harris, J. H., S. D. Sanders, and M. A. Flett. 1987. Willow Flycatcher surveys in the Sierra Nevada. W. Birds 18:27-36.

Harris, R. D. 1982. The nesting ecology of the Pileated Woodpecker in California. M.S. thesis, Univ. Calif., Berkeley.

Harris, S. W. and R. J. Wheeler. 1965. Hybrid of Blue-winged Teal x Cinnamon Teal in northwestern California. Condor 67:539-540.

Harrison, C. 1978. A Field Guide to the Nests, Eggs, and Nestlings of North American Birds. Collins, Glasgow.

Hartwick, E. B. 1974. Breeding ecology of the Black Oystercatcher (Haematopus bachmani Audubon). Syesis 7:83-92.

——. 1976. Foraging strategy of the Black Oystercatcher (Haematopus bachmani Audubon). Can. J. Zool. 54:142-155.

Hartwick, E. B. and W. Blaylock. 1979. Winter ecology of a Black Oystercatcher population. In F. A. Pitelka, ed. Shorebirds in marine environments, 207-215. Studies Avian Biol. 2.

Harvey, T. E. 1980a. A breeding season survey of the California Clapper Rail (Rallus longirostris obsoletus) in south San Francisco Bay, California. Final Rept., U.S. Fish Wildl. Serv., S.F. Bay Natl. Wildl. Refuge, Newark.

——. 1980b. California Clapper Rail survey, 1978-1979. Job Final Rept., Job V-1.8. Calif. Dept. Fish Game, Sacramento.

——. 1983. Breeding season study of the California Clapper Rail in San Francisco Bay, 1982. Rept. for U.S. Fish Wildl. Serv., S. F. Bay Natl. Wildl. Refuge, Newark.

——. 1987. The California Clapper Rail: Biology, present status, and future trends. Manuscript of oral presentation given at A.O.U. meeting in San Francisco in 1987. Available from S.F. Bay Natl. Wildl. Refuge, Newark.

Hatch, D. E. 1970. Energy conserving and heat dissipating mechanisms of the Turkey Vulture. Auk 87:111-124.

Hatch, S. A. 1984. Nestling diet and feeding rates of Rhinoceros Auklets in Alaska. In D. N. Nettleship, G. A. Sanger, and P. F. Springer, eds. Marine birds: Their feeding ecology and commercial fisheries relationships, 106-115. Proc. Pac. Seabird Group Symp. Seattle, Wash., 6-8 Jan 1982. Canadian Wildl. Serv. for P.S.G.

Hawbecker, A. C. 1940. The nesting of the White-tailed Kite in southern Santa Cruz, County, California. Condor 42:106.

——. 1942. A life history study of the White-tailed Kite. Condor 44:267-276.

Hawthorne, V. M. 1979. Use of nest boxes by Dippers on Sagehen Creek, California. W. Birds 10:215-216.

Hay, D. B. and M. Güntert. 1983. Seasonal selection of tree cavities by Pygmy Nuthatches based on cavity characteristics. U.S. For. Serv. Gen. Tech. Rept. RM-99.

Hays, H. 1972. Polyandry in the Spotted Sandpiper. Living Bird 11:43-57.

Hayward, C. L. 1935. Observations of some breeding birds of Mount Timpanogos, Utah. Wilson Bull. 47:161-162.

Heermann, A. L. 1853. Catalog of the oological collection of the Academy of Natural Sciences of Philadelphia. Proc. Natl. Acad. Sci. 6:17.

Hejl, S. J. and J. Verner. 1990. Within-season and yearly variation in avian foraging locations. In M. L. Morrison, C. J. Ralph, J. Verner, and J. R. Jehl, Jr., eds. Avian foraging: Theory, methodology, and applications, 202-209. Studies Avian Biol. 13.

Heady, H. F. 1977. Valley grassland. In M. G. Barbour and J. Major, eds. Terrestrial Vegetation of California, 491-513. John Wiley & Sons, New York.

Henny, C. J. 1977. Research, management and status of the Osprey in North America. In R. D. Chancellor, ed. Proc. World Birds of Prey Conf., 199-222. Int. Council Bird Preserv., Vienna.

——. 1983. Distribution and abundance of nesting Ospreys in the United States. In D. M. Bird, N. R. Seymour, and J. M. Gerrard, eds. Biology and Management of Bald Eagles and Ospreys, 175-186. Proc. 1st Int. Symp. on Bald Eagles and Ospreys, Montreal, 28-29 Oct 1981. Harpell Press, Quebec.

——. 1988. Osprey. In R. S. Palmer, ed. Handbook of North American Birds. Vol. 4: Diurnal Raptors (Part 1), 73-101. Yale Univ. Press, New Haven.

Henny, C. J. and D. W. Anderson. 1979. Osprey distribution, abundance, and status in western North America: III. The Baja California and Gulf of California population. Bull. S. Calif. Acad. Sci. 78:89-106.

Henny, C. J. and J. T. Annear. 1978. A White-tailed Kite breeding record for Oregon. W. Birds 9:131-133.

Henny, C. J. and R. G. Anthony. 1989. Bald Eagle and Osprey. In National Wildlife Federation. Proc. Western Raptor Mgmt. Symp. and Workshop, 66-82. Natl. Wildl. Fed. Sci. and Tech. Ser. 12.

Henny, C. J., D. J. Dunaway, R. D. Mallette, and J. R. Koplin. 1978. Osprey distribution, abundance, and status in western North America: I. The northern California population. Northwest Sci. 52:261-271.

Henny, C. J. and H. W. Wight. 1972. Population ecology and environmental pollution: Red-tailed and Cooper's hawks. In Population ecology of migratory birds: A symposium, 229-250. Bur. Sport Fish and Wildl., Wildl. Res. Rept. 2.

Heppner, F. 1965. Sensory mechanisms and environmental cues used by the American Robin in locating earthworms. Condor 67:247-256.

Herlugson, C. J. 1978. Comments on the status and distribution of Western and Mountain bluebirds in Washington. W. Birds 9:21-32.

——. 1982. Food of adult and nestling Western and Mountain bluebirds. Murrelet 63:59-65.

Herman, S. G. 1971. The Peregrine Falcon decline in California. II. Breeding status in 1970. Am. Birds 25:818-820.

Herman, S. G., M. N. Kirven, and R. W. Risebrough. 1970. The Peregrine Falcon decline in California. I. A preliminary review. Aud. Field Notes 24:609-613.

Hertz, P. E., J. V. Remsen, Jr., and S. I. Zones. 1976. Ecological complementarity of three sympatric parids in a California oak woodland. Condor 78:307-316.

Hespenheide, H. A. 1964. Competition and the genus Tyrannus. Wilson Bull. 76:265-281.

Hickey, J. J., ed. 1969. Peregrine Falcon Populations: Their Biology and Decline. Univ. Wisconsin Press, Madison.

Hill, G. E. 1988. Age, plumage brightness, territory quality, and reproductive success in the Black-headed Grosbeak. Condor 90:379-388.

Hjersman, H. A. 1947. A history of the establishment of the Ring-necked Pheasant in California. Calif. Fish Game 33:3-11.

Hobson, K., P. Perrine, E. B. Roberts, M. L. Foster, and P. Woodin. 1986. A breeding season survey of Salt Marsh Yellowthroats Geothlypis trichas sinuosa in the San Francisco Bay region. S. F. Bay Bird Obs. Rept. to U.S. Fish Wildl. Serv., Contract 84-57.

Hobson, K. A. and H. R. Carter. 1988. Bill deformity in a Brandt's Cormorant chick. Calif. Fish Game 74:184-185.

Hoffmann, R. 1927. Birds of the Pacific States. Houghton Mifflin, Boston.

Holcomb, L. C. 1969. Breeding biology of the American Goldfinch in Ohio. Bird-Banding 40:26-44.

Holcomb, L. C. and G. Twiest. 1968. Ecological factors affecting nest building in Red-winged Blackbirds. Bird-Banding 39:14-22.

Hooper, E. T. 1938. Another jay shoot in California. Condor 40:162-164.

Hooper, R. G. 1977. Nesting habitat of Common Ravens in Virginia. Wilson Bull. 89:233-242.

Horak, C. J. 1970. A comparative study of the food habits of the Sora and Virginia Rail. Wilson Bull. 82:206-213.

Horn, H. S. 1968. The adaptive significance of colonial nesting in the Brewer's Blackbird (Euphagus cyanocephalus). Ecology 49:682-694.

——. 1970. Social behavior of nesting Brewer's Blackbirds. Condor 72:15-23.

Horn, K. M. and D. B. Marshall. 1975. Status of Poor-will in Oregon and possible extension due to clearcut timber harvest methods. Murrelet 56 (1):4-5.

Horne, B. V. and A. Bader. 1990. Diet of nestling Winter Wrens in relationship to food availability. Condor 92:413-420.

Hosea, R. C. 1986. A population census of the Tricolored Blackbird, Agelaius tricolor (Audubon), in four counties in the northern Central Valley of California. M.A. thesis, Calif. State Univ., Sacramento.

Houston, D. C. 1986. Scavenging efficiency of Turkey Vultures in tropical forest. Condor 88:318-323.

Howard, H. 1929. Avifauna of an Emeryville shellmound. Univ. Calif. Publ. Zool. 32:301-394.

Howard, W. E. 1959. The European Starling in California. Calif. Dept. Agri. Bull. 48:171-179.

Howell, A. H. 1906. Birds that eat the cotton boll weevil: A progress report. U.S. Dept. Agri. Bull. 25.

——. 1932. Florida Bird Life. Florida Dept. Game and Fresh Water Fish.

Howell, J., D. Laclergue, S. Paris, W. I. Boarman, A. R. DeGange, and L. C. Binford. 1983. First nests of Heermann's Gull in the United States. W. Birds 14:39-46.

Howell, J. C. 1942. Notes on the nesting habits of the American Robin (Turdus migratorius L.). Am. Midl. Nat. 28:529-603.

Howell, T. R. 1952. Natural history and differentiation in the Yellow-bellied Sapsucker. Condor 54:237-282.

Hoyt, S. F. 1957. The ecology of the Pileated Woodpecker. Ecology 38:246-256.

Hubbard, J. P. and C. L. Hubbard. 1969. Meadowlarks feeding on road-kills. Wilson Bull. 81:107-108.

Huey, L. M. 1944. Nesting habits of the Hooded Oriole. Condor 46:297.

Hunt, G. L., Jr. and M. W. Hunt. 1976. Exploitation of fluctuating food resources by Western Gulls. Auk 93:301-307.

Hunt, G. L., Jr., R. L. Pitman, M. Naughton, K. Winnet, A. Newman, P. R. Kelly, and K. T. Briggs. 1979. Distribution, status, reproductive ecology, and foraging habits of breeding seabirds. In Summary of marine mammal and seabird surveys of the Southern California Bight area, 1975-1978. U.S. Dept. Inter., Bur. Land Mgmt., Los Angeles.

Hutto, R. L. 1981. Seasonal variation in the foraging behavior of some migratory western wood warblers. Auk 98:765-777.

I

Illingsworth, J. F. 1901. The Bullock's and Arizona Hooded orioles. Condor 3:98-100.

Inouye, D. W. 1976. Non-random orientation of entrance holes to woodpecker nests in aspen trees. Condor 78:101-102.

Isler, M. L. and P. R. Isler. 1987. The Tanagers: Natural History, Distribution, and Identification. Smithson. Inst. Press, Washington, D.C.

Ives, J. H. 1972. Common Egret and Great Blue Heron nest study, Indian Island, Humboldt County, California 1971–72. Wildl. Mgmt. Branch Admin. Rept. 72-9. Calif. Dept. Fish Game, Sacramento.

J

Jackman, S. M. and J. M. Scott. 1975. Literature review of twenty-three selected forest birds of the Pacific Northwest. U.S. For. Serv., Portland.

Jackson, J. A. 1970. A quantitative study of the foraging ecology of Downy Woodpeckers. Ecology 51:318–323.

———. 1983. Nesting phenology, nest site selection, and reproductive success of Black and Turkey vultures. In S. R. Wilbur and J. A. Jackson, eds. *Vulture Biology and Management*, 245–269. Univ. California Press, Berkeley.

———. 1988. Turkey Vulture. In R. S. Palmer, ed. *Handbook of North American Birds. Vol. 4: Diurnal Raptors (Part 1)*. Yale Univ. Press, New Haven.

Jackson, J. A. and J. Tate, Jr. 1974. An analysis of nest box use by Purple Martins, House Sparrows and Starlings in eastern North America. Wilson Bull. 86:435–449.

Jaksic, F. M. and C. D. Marti. 1981. Trophic ecology of *Athene* Owls in Mediterranean-type ecosystems: A comparative analysis. Can. J. Zool. 59:2331–2340.

———. 1984. Comparative food habits of *Bubo* Owls in Mediterranean-type ecosystems. Condor 86:288–296.

Jaksic, F. M., R. L. Seib, and C. M. Herrera. 1982. Predation by Barn Owl *(Tyto alba)* in Mediterranean habitats of Chile, Spain and California: A comparative approach. Am. Midl. Nat. 107:151–162.

James, P. C. and T. J. Ethier. 1989. Trends in the winter distribution and abundance of Burrowing Owls in North America. Am. Birds 43:1225.

Jeffery, R. G. (Chairman) et al. 1977. Band-tailed Pigeon *(Columba fasciata)*. In G. C. Sanderson, ed. Management of migratory shore and upland game birds in North America, 210–245. Int. Assoc. Fish Game Agencies, Washington, D.C.

Jehl, J. R., Jr. 1979. Pine cones as granaries for Acorn Woodpeckers. W. Birds 10:219–220.

———. 1988. Biology of the Eared Grebe and the Wilson's Phalarope in the nonbreeding season: A study of adaptations to saline lakes. Studies Avian Biol. 12.

Jenkins, J. M. 1979. Foraging behavior of male and female Nuttall Woodpeckers. Auk 96:418–420.

Jewett, S. G. 1942. The European Starling in California. Condor 44:79.

Joern, W. T. and J. F. Jackson. 1983. Homogeneity of vegetational cover around the nest and avoidance of nest predation in Mockingbirds. Auk 100:497–499.

Johnsgard, P. A. 1978. *Ducks, Geese, and Swans of the World*. Univ. Nebraska Press, Lincoln.

———. 1981. *The Plovers, Sandpipers, and Snipes of the World*. Univ. Nebraska Press, Lincoln.

———. 1986. *Pheasants of the World*. Oxford Univ. Press, New York.

———. 1987. *Diving Birds of North America*. Univ. Nebraska Press, Lincoln.

———. 1988. *North American Owls: Biology and Natural History*. Smithson. Inst. Press, Washington, D.C.

Johnson, A. W. 1904. Notes on unusual nesting sites of the Pacific Yellowthroat. Condor 6:129–131.

Johnson, D. H., M. D. Bryant, and A. H. Miller. 1948. Vertebrate animals of the Providence Mountains area of California. Univ. Calif. Publ. Zool. 48:221–375.

Johnson, N. K. and C. Cicero. 1986. Richness and distribution of montane avifaunas in the White-Inyo region, California. In C. A. Hall, Jr. and D. J. Young, eds. Natural history of the White-Inyo Range, eastern California and western Nevada and high altitude physiology, 137–159. Univ. Calif. White Mtn. Res. Sta. Symp. Vol. 1, August 23–25. Univ. Calif. White Mtn. Res. Sta., Los Angeles.

Johnson, R. and J. J. Dinsmore. 1986. Habitat use by breeding Virginia Rails and Soras. J. Wildl. Mgmt. 50:387–392.

Johnson, S. R. and C. F. Yocum. 1966. Breeding waterfowl in the Lake Earl–Lake Talawa area, Del Norte County, California. Murrelet 47:1–5.

Johnston, D. W. and R. A. Norris. 1956. Observations on Red Crossbills in Marin County, California. Condor 58:77.

Johnston, R. F. 1956a. Population structure in salt marsh Song Sparrows. Part I. Environment and annual cycle. Part II. Density, age, structure, and maintenance. Condor 58:24–44, 254–272.

———. 1956b. Predation by Short-eared Owls on a *Salicornia* salt marsh. Wilson Bull. 68:91–102.

———. 1968a. Coastal Savannah Sparrow. In O. L. Austin, Jr., ed. A. C. Bent et al.'s Life histories of North American cardinals, grosbeaks, buntings, towhees, finches, sparrows, and allies. U.S. Natl. Mus. Bull. 237 (Part 2): 712–714.

———. 1968b. Song Sparrow: San Francisco Bay marsh subspecies. In O. L. Austin, Jr., ed. A. C. Bent et al.'s Life histories of North American cardinals, grosbeaks, buntings, towhees, finches, sparrows, and allies. U.S. Natl. Mus. Bull 237 (Part 3): 1547–1553.

Johnston, R. F. and J. W. Hardy. 1962. Behavior of the Purple Martin. Wilson Bull. 74:243–262.

Johnston, R. F. and W. J. Klitz. 1977. Variation and evolution in a granivorous bird: The House Sparrow. In J. Pinowski and S. C. Kendeigh, eds. *Granivorous Birds in Ecosystems: Their Evolution, Populations, Energetics, Impact, and Control*, 15–51. Int. Biol. Progr. 12. Cambridge Univ. Press, London.

Jones, J. C. 1940. Food habits of the American Coot with notes on distribution. U.S.D.I. Biol. Serv. Wildl. Res. Bull. 2.

Josselyn, M. N. 1983. The ecology of San Francisco Bay tidal marshes: A community profile. U.S. Fish Wildl. Serv., Div. Biol. Serv., Washington, D.C. FWS/OBS-83/23.

Josselyn, M. N. and J. W. Buchholz. 1984. Marsh restoration in San Francisco Bay: A guide to design and planning. Tiburon Center for Environmental Studies, San Francisco State Univ. Tech Rept. 3.

Joyner, D. 1973a. Effects of interspecific nest parasitism by Redheads and Ruddy Ducks. J. Wildl. Mgmt. 40:33-38.

——. 1973b. Interspecific nest parasitism by ducks and coots in Utah. Auk 90:692-693.

——. 1977a. Behavior of Ruddy Duck broods in Utah. Auk 94:343-349.

——. 1977b. Nest desertion by Ruddy Ducks in Utah. Bird-Banding 48:19-24.

Jurek, R. M. 1976. California Black Rail survey. Nongame Wildl. Invest. Job Progr. Rept., Proj. No. W-54-R-8, Job I-I-1.3. Calif. Dept. Fish Game, Sacramento.

K

Kalmbach, E. R. 1918. The crow and its relation to man. U.S. Dept. Agri. Bull. 621.

——. 1940. Economic status of the English Sparrow in the United States. U.S. Dept. Agri. Tech. Bull. 711.

Kalmbach, E. R. and I. N. Gabrielson. 1921. Economic value of the Starling in the United States. U.S. Dept. Agri. Bull. 868.

Kashiwagi, J. H. 1985. Soil survey of Marin County, California. Natl. Coop. Soil Surv., Soil Cons. Serv., U.S. Dept. Agri.

Kelly, I. 1978. Coast Miwok. In R. F. Heizer, ed. *Handbook of North American Indians. Vol. 8. California.* Smithson. Inst., Washington, D.C.

Kelly, J. W. 1942. Audubon Warbler nesting in Marin County. Gull 24:25-26.

——. 1944. Audubon Warblers at Ross. Gull 26:26.

Kelly, S. T. and M. E. DeCapita. 1982. Cowbird control and its effect on Kirtland's Warbler reproductive success. Wilson Bull. 94:363-365.

Kendeigh, S. C. 1941a. Territory and mating behavior of the House Wren. Ill. Biol. Monogr. 18:1-120.

——. 1941b. Birds of a prairie community. Condor 43:165-174.

——. 1945. Community selection by birds on the Helderberg Plateau of New York. Auk 62:418-436.

Kennedy, P. L. and D. R. Johnson. 1986. Prey-size selection in nesting male and female Cooper's Hawks. Wilson Bull. 98:110-115.

Kern, M. D. 1984. Racial differences in nests of White-crowned Sparrows. Condor 86:455-466.

Kessel, B. 1957. A study of the breeding biology of the European Starling (*Sturnus vulgaris* L.) in North America. Am. Midl. Nat. 58:257-331.

Keyes, G. C., R. C. Fleischer, and S. I. Rothstein. 1986. Relationships between elevation, reproduction, and the hematocrit level of Brown-headed Cowbirds. Comp. Biochem. Physiol. 83A:765-769.

Kibbe, D. P. 1986. Determining adequacy of coverage in statewide breeding bird atlas projects: When enough is enough. In S. M. Sutcliffe, R. E. Bonney, Jr., and J. D. Lowe, comps. Proc. 2nd Northeastern Breeding Bird Atlas Conference, 18-24. April 25-27, 1986. Lab. of Ornithol., Cornell Univ., Ithaca, N.Y.

Kiff, L. F. 1978. Probable Black Rail nesting record for Alameda County, California. W. Birds 9:169-170.

——. 1988. Commentary. Changes in the status of the Peregrine in North America: An overview. In T. J. Cade, J. H. Enderson, C. G. Thelander, and C. M. White, eds. *Peregrine Falcon Populations: Their Management and Recovery*, 123-139. The Peregrine Fund, Boise, Idaho.

Kilgore, D. L., Jr. and K. L. Knudsen. 1977. Analysis of materials in Cliff and Barn Swallow nests: Relationship between mud selection and nest architecture. Wilson Bull. 89:562-571.

Kilham, L. 1964. The relations of breeding Yellow-bellied Sapsuckers to wounded birches and other trees. Auk 81:520-527.

——. 1965. Differences in feeding behavior of male and female Hairy Woodpeckers. Wilson Bull. 77:134-145.

——. 1968. Reproductive behavior of White-breasted Nuthatches. I. Distraction display, bill sweeping and nest hole defense. Auk 85:477-492.

——. 1970. Feeding behavior of Downy Woodpeckers. I. Preference for paper birches and sexual differences. Auk 87:544-556.

——. 1971. Reproductive behavior of Yellow-bellied Sapsuckers. I. Preference for nesting in *Fomes*-infected aspens and nest hole interrelations with flying squirrels, raccoons, and other animals. Wilson Bull. 83:159-171.

——. 1977. Nesting behavior of Yellow-bellied Sapsuckers. Wilson Bull. 89:310-324.

Killpack, M. L. and D. N. Crittenden. 1952. Starlings as winter residents in the Uinta Basin, Utah. Condor 54:338-344.

Kingery, H. E. and W. D. Graul, eds. 1978. Colorado bird distribution latilong study. Colorado Field Ornithologists.

Kinsey, E. C. 1945. More records of the Chat in Marin County, California. Condor 47:269-270.

Kisiel, D. S. 1972. Foraging behavior of *D. villosus* and *D. pubescens* in eastern New York state. Condor 74:393-398.

Klimkiewicz, M. K. and J. K. Solem. 1978. The breeding bird atlas of Montgomery and Howard counties, Maryland. Maryland Birdlife 34:3-39.

Klimstra, W. D. and W. O. Stieglitz. 1957. Notes on reproductive activities of Robins in Iowa and Illinois. Wilson Bull. 69:333-337.

Knight, R. L. and R. E. Jackman. 1984. Food-niche relationships between Great Horned Owls and Common Barn-Owls in eastern Washington. Auk 101:175-179.

Knupp, D. M., R. B. Owen, Jr., and J. B. Dimond. 1977. Reproductive biology of American Robins in northern Maine. Auk 94:80-85.

Koenig, W. D. and R. L. Mumme. 1987. *Population Ecology of the Cooperatively Breeding Acorn Woodpecker.* Princeton Univ. Press, Princeton.

Koford, C. B. 1953. The California Condor. Natl. Audubon Soc. Res. Rept. 4.

Koplin, J. R. 1969. The numerical response of wookpeckers to insect prey in a subalpine forest in Colorado. Auk 71:436-435.

——. 1973. Differential habitat use by sexes of American Kestrels wintering in northern California. Raptor Res. 7:39–42.

Korschgen, L. J. 1964. Foods and nutrition of Missouri and Midwestern pheasants. Trans. N. Am. Wildl. Conf. 29: 159–181.

Krapu, G. L. 1974a. Foods of breeding Pintails in North Dakota. J. Wildl. Mgmt. 38:408–417.

——. 1974b. Feeding ecology of Pintail hens during reproduction. Auk 91:278–290.

——. 1979. Nutrition of female dabbling ducks during reproduction. In T. A. Bookhout, ed. Waterfowl and wetlands—an integrated review, 59–70. Proc. Symp. 1977 N. Cent. Sect., The Wildl. Soc.

——. 1981. The role of nutrient reserves in Mallard reproduction. Auk 98:29–38.

Krebs, C. J. 1966. Demographic changes in fluctuating populations of Microtus californicus. Ecol. Monogr. 36:239–273.

Kridelbaugh, A. 1983. Nesting ecology of the Loggerhead Shrike in central Missouri. Wilson Bull. 95:303–308.

Kroodsma, D. E. 1973. Coexistence of Bewick's Wrens and House Wrens in Oregon. Auk 90:341–352.

Kruckeberg, A. R. 1984. California serpentines: Flora, vegetation, geology, soils, and management problems. Univ. Calif. Publ. Bot. 73. Univ. California Press, Berkeley.

Kuenzel, W. J. and R. G. Wiegert. 1973. Energetics of a Spotted Sandpiper feeding on brine fly larvae (Parocoenia; Diptera; Ephydridae) in a thermal spring community. Wilson Bull. 85:473–476.

Kuerzi, R. G. 1941. Life history studies of the Tree Swallow. Proc. Linn. Soc. N.Y. 52–53:1–52.

Kuletz, K. J. 1983. Mechanisms and consequences of foraging behavior in a population of breeding Pigeon Guillemots. M.S. thesis, Univ. Calif., Irvine.

L

Lack, D. and J. T. Emlen. 1939. Observations on breeding behavior in Tricolored Red-wings. Condor 41:225–230.

Lack, P., ed. 1986. The Atlas of Wintering Birds in Britain and Ireland. British Trust for Ornithology and Irish Wildbird Conservancy. T. & A. D. Poyser, Calton.

Landers, J. L., T. T. Fendley, and A. S. Johnson. 1977. Feeding ecology of Wood Ducks in South Carolina. J. Wildl. Mgmt. 41:118–127.

Lanyon, W. E. 1957. The comparative biology of the meadowlarks (Sturnella) in Wisconsin. Publ. Nutt. Ornithol. Club 1.

Larson, D. 1980. Increase in the White-tailed Kite populations of California and Texas—1944–1978. Am. Birds 34:689–690.

Latta, W. C. and R. F. Sharkey. 1966. Feeding behavior of the American Merganser in captivity. J. Wildl. Mgmt. 30:17–23.

Laughlin, S. B. and D. P. Kibbe. 1985. The Atlas of Breeding Birds of Vermont. Univ. Press of New England, Hanover, N.H.

Laughlin, S. B., D. P. Kibbe, and P. F. J. Eagles. 1982. Atlasing the distribution of the breeding birds of North America. Am. Birds 36:6–19.

Lawrence, L. DeK. 1949. The Red Crossbill at Pimisi Bay, Ontario. Can. Field-Nat. 63:147–160.

——. 1967. A comparative life-history study of four species of woodpeckers. Ornithol. Monogr. 5.

Laymon, S. A. 1987. Brown-headed Cowbirds in California: Historical perspectives and management opportunities in riparian habitats. W. Birds 18:63–70.

——. 1991. Diurnal foraging by Spotted Owls. Wilson Bull. 103:138–140.

Laymon, S. A., B. A. Garrison, and J. M. Humphrey. 1987. Historic and current status of the Bank Swallow in California, 1987. Wildl. Mgmt. Div. Admin. Rept. 88-2. Calif. Dept. Fish Game, Sacramento.

Laymon, S. L. and M. D. Halterman. 1987. Can the western subspecies of the Yellow-billed Cuckoo be saved from extinction? W. Birds 18:19–25.

Leach, H. R., C. M. Ferrel, and E. E. Clark. 1953. A study of the food habits of the Ring-necked Pheasant on irrigated pasture in California. Calif. Fish Game 39:517–525.

Legg, K. and F. A. Pitelka. 1956. Ecologic overlap of Allen and Anna hummingbirds nesting in Santa Cruz, California. Condor 58:393–405.

Leopold, A. S. 1977. The California Quail. Univ. California Press, Berkeley.

Leopold, A. S., M. Erwin, J. Oh, and B. Browning. 1976. Phytoestrogens: Adverse effects on reproduction in California Quail. Science 191:98–100.

Lewis, D. B. and K. T. Briggs. 1985. Pigeon Guillemot. In California seabird ecology study: Synthesis of information, 126–138. Center for Marine Studies, Univ. Calif., Santa Cruz. Rept. for Pac. OCS Region Minerals Mgmt. Serv., U.S. Dept. Inter.

Lewis, H. F. 1929. The Natural History of the Double-crested Cormorant (Phalacrocorax auritus auritus L.). Ru-Mi-Lou Books, Ottawa.

Lidicker, W. Z., Jr. and F. C. McCollum. 1979. Canada Goose established as a breeding species in San Francisco Bay. W. Birds 10:159–162.

Lindsay, A. A. 1939. Food of the Starling in central New York state. Wilson Bull. 51:176–182.

Linsdale, J. M. 1957. Goldfinches on the Hastings Natural History Reservation. Am. Midl. Nat. 57:1–119.

——. 1968a. Green-backed Goldfinch. In O. L. Austin, Jr., ed. A. C. Bent et al.'s Life histories of North American cardinals, grosbeaks, buntings, towhees, finches, sparrows, and allies. U.S. Natl. Mus. Bull. 237 (Part 1): 474–486.

——. 1968b. Lawrence's Goldfinch. In O. L. Austin, Jr., ed. A. C. Bent et al.'s Life histories of North American cardinals, grosbeaks, buntings, towhees, finches, sparrows, and allies. U.S. Natl. Mus. Bull. 237 (Part 1): 486–496.

Linthicum, J., ed. 1988. Peregrine Falcon monitoring, nest management, hack site, and cross-fostering efforts, 1988. Rept. of Santa Cruz Pred. Bird Res. Group, Univ. Calif., Santa Cruz.

Littrell, E. E. 1986. Shell thickness and organochlorine pesticides in Osprey eggs from Eagle Lake, California. Calif. Fish Game 72:182–185.

Liverman, M. C. 1990. The (Endangered) Endangered Species Act: Political economy of the Northern Spotted Owl. Endangered Species UPDATE 7(10 & 11):1–4.

Lord, J. and D. J. Munns, eds. 1970. *Atlas of Breeding Birds of the West Midlands.* Collins, London.

Lovell, H. E. 1958. Baiting of fish by a Green Heron. Wilson Bull. 70:280–281.

Low, J. B. 1941. Nesting of the Ruddy Duck in Iowa. Auk 58:506–516.

Low, S. H. 1933. Further notes on the nesting of the Tree Swallow. Bird-Banding 4:76–87.

——. 1934. Nest distribution and survival ratio of Tree Swallows. Bird-Banding 5:24–30.

Lundquist, R. W. and D. A. Manuwal. 1990. Seasonal differences in foraging habitat of cavity-nesting birds in the southern Washington Cascades. In M. L. Morrison, C. J. Ralph, J. Verner, and J. R. Jehl, Jr., eds. Avian foraging: Theory, methodology, and applications, 218–225. Studies Avian Biol. 13.

Lunk, W. A. 1962. The Rough-winged Swallow *Stelgidopteryx ruficollis* (Vieillot): A study based on its breeding biology in Michigan. Publ. Nutt. Ornithol. Club 4.

M

McAllister, T. H., Jr. and D. B. Marshall. 1945. Summer birds of the Fremont National Forest, Oregon. Auk 62: 177–189.

MacArthur, R. H. and E. O. Wilson. 1967. *The Theory of Island Biogeography.* Princeton Univ. Press, Princeton.

McAtee, W. L. 1905. The Horned Larks and their relation to agriculture. U.S. Dept. Agri. Biol. Surv. Bull. 23.

——. 1908. Food habits of the grosbeaks. U.S. Dept. Agri. Biol. Surv. Bull. 32.

McAtee, W. L. and F. E. L. Beal. 1912. Some common game, aquatic, and rapacious birds in relation to man. U.S. Dept. Agri. Farmer's Bull. 497.

McCabe, T. T. 1932. Wholesale poison for the Red-wings. Condor 34:49–50.

McCaskie, R. G. 1965. The Cattle Egret reaches the West Coast of the United States. Condor 67:89.

McCaskie, R. G., P. DeBenedictis, R. A. Erickson, and J. Morlan. 1979. Birds of northern California: An annotated field list. 2nd ed. Golden Gate Audubon Soc., Berkeley.

McChesney, G. L. 1988. Mark-recapture population estimates and diet of Ashy and Leach's storm-petrels on Southeast Farallon Island, California, 1987. B.A. thesis, Univ. Calif., Santa Cruz.

McClelland, B. R. 1979. The Pileated Woodpecker in forests of the northern Rocky Mountains. In J. G. Dickson, R. N. Conner, R. R. Fleet, J. C. Kroll, and J. A. Jackson, eds. *The Role of Insectivorous Birds in Forest Ecosystems,* 283–299. Academic Press, New York.

McCurdy, G. F. 1983. The status of the Osprey at Kent Lake, Marin County, California. Rept. for the Marin Municipal Water District.

MacDonald, K. B. 1977. Coastal salt marsh. In M. G. Barbour and J. Major, eds. *Terrestrial Vegetation of California,* 263–294. John Wiley & Sons, New York.

McEllin, S. M. 1979a. Nest sites and population demographies of White-breasted and Pigmy nuthatches in Colorado. Condor 81:348–352.

——. 1979b. Population demographics, spacing and foraging behavior of White-breasted and Pygmy nuthatches in ponderosa pine habitat. In J. G. Dickson, R. N. Conner, R. R. Fleet, J. C. Kroll, and J. A. Jackson, eds. *The Role of Insectivorous Birds in Forest Ecosystems,* 301–331. Academic Press, New York.

McGillivray, W. B. 1981. Climatic influences on productivity in the House Sparrow. Wilson Bull. 93:196–206.

MacGregor, W. G. and W. M. Smith. 1955. Nesting and production of the Band-tailed Pigeon in California. Calif. Fish Game 41:315–326.

MacKenzie, D. I. and S. G. Sealy. 1981. Nest site selection in Eastern and Western kingbirds: A multivariate approach. Condor 83:310–321.

McLandress, M. R. and D. G. Raveling. 1981a. Hyperphagia and social behavior of Canada Geese prior to spring migration. Wilson Bull. 93:310–324.

——. 1981b. Changes in diet and body composition of Canada Geese before spring migration. Auk 98:65–79.

MacRoberts, M. H. 1970. Notes on the food habits and food defense of the Acorn Woodpecker. Condor 72:196–204.

——. 1974. Acorns, woodpeckers, grubs, and scientists. Pac. Discovery 27:9–15.

MacRoberts, M. H. and B. R. MacRoberts. 1976. Social organization and behavior of the Acorn Woodpecker in central coastal California. Ornithol. Monogr. 21:1–115.

Mailliard, J. 1900. Land birds of Marin County, Cal. Condor 2:62–68.

——. 1904. A few records supplementary to Grinnell's check-list of California birds. Condor 6:14–16.

——. 1909a. Nest of the Dusky Poor-will *(Phalaenoptilus nuttallii californicus).* Condor 11:45–47.

——. 1909b. Nest of the Tolmie Warbler. Condor 11:65–66.

——. 1911. Odds and ends. Condor 13:49–50.

——. 1912. Breeding of the Band-tailed Pigeon in Marin County, Calif. Condor 14:194.

——. 1913. Some curious nesting places of the Allen Hummingbird on the Rancho San Geromino. Condor 15: 205–207.

——. 1914. Notes on a colony of Tri-colored Red-wings. Condor 16:204–207.

——. 1924a. Some new records for northeastern California. Condor 26:213–217.

——. 1924b. Autobiography of Joseph Mailliard. Condor 26:10–29.

——. 1936. Poor selection of building sites. Condor 38:249.

Mailliard, J. W. 1912. Concerning nesting sites of the California Jay. Condor 14:42.

461

Maino, E. and F. Howard. 1955. *Ornamental Trees: An Illustrated Guide to their Selection and Care.* Univ. California Press, Berkeley.

Major, J. 1977. California climate in relation to vegetation. In M. G. Barbour and J. Major, eds. *Terrestrial Vegetation of California*, 11–74. John Wiley & Sons, New York.

Mallette, R. D. and J. R. Slosson. 1987. Upland game of California. Calif. Dept. Fish Game, Sacramento.

Mannan, R. W. 1984. Summer area requirements of Pileated Woodpeckers in western Oregon. Wildl. Soc. Bull. 12: 265–268.

Manolis, T. 1977. Foraging relationships of Mountain Chickadees and Pygmy Nuthatches. W. Birds 8:13–20.

——. 1978. Status of the Black Rail in central California. W. Birds 9:151–158.

——. 1991. Atlasing California's breeding birds—county by county. W. Birds 22:92–94.

March, G. L. and R. M. F. S. Sadlier. 1972. Studies on the Band-tailed Pigeon *(Columba fasciata)* in British Columbia, II. Food resource and mineral-graveling activity. Syesis 5:279–284.

Mariani, J. M. and D. A. Manuwal. 1990. Factors influencing Brown Creeper *(Certhia americana)* abundance patterns in the southern Washington Cascade Range. In M. L. Morrison, C. J. Ralph, J. Verner, J. R. Jehl, Jr., eds. Avian foraging: Theory, methodology, and applications, 53–57. Studies Avian Biol. 13.

Markle, J. M. 1946. A nesting site of the Lark Sparrow. Condor 48:245–246.

Marks, J. S. 1984. Feeding ecology of breeding Long-eared Owls in southwestern Idaho. Can. J. Zool. 62:1528–1533.

——. 1985. Yearling male Long-eared Owls breed near natal nest. J. Field Ornithol. 56:181–182.

——. 1986. Nest site characteristics and reproductive success of Long-eared Owls *(Asio otus)* in southwestern Idaho. Wilson Bull. 98:547–560.

Marks, J. S. and E. Yensen. 1980. Nest sites and food habits of Long-eared Owls in southwestern Idaho. Murrelet 61: 86–91.

Marshall, J. T. 1948. Ecological races of Song Sparrows in the San Francisco Bay region. Part I: Habitat and abundance. Part II: Geographic variation. Condor 50:193–215, 233–256.

——. 1988. Birds lost from a giant sequoia forest during fifty years. Condor 90:359–372.

Marshall, M. F., L. R. Mewaldt, M. F. Rippey, R. L. C. Leong, H. L. Cogswell, K. Dedrick, S. Gregory, H. T. Harvey, R. F. Johnston, and S. E. Senner. 1988. Petition to list the Suisun Song Sparrow *(Melospiza melodia maxillaris)* as Endangered. Submitted to Calif. Fish Game Comm.

Marti, C. D. 1974. Feeding ecology of four sympatric owls. Condor 76:45–61.

——. 1976. A review of prey selection by the Long-eared Owl. Condor 78:331–336.

Marti, C. D. and S. W. Everett. 1978. Polygyny in Utah Dippers. W. Birds 9:174.

Marti, C. D. and J. S. Marks. 1989. Medium-sized owls. In National Wildlife Federation. Proc. Western Raptor Mgmt. Symp. and Workshop, 124–133. Natl. Wildl. Fed. Tech. and Sci. Ser. 12.

Martin, A. C., H. S. Zim, and A. L. Nelson. 1951. *American Wildlife and Plants: A Guide to Wildlife Food Habits.* McGraw Hill, New York.

Martin, D. J. 1973. Selected aspects of Burrowing Owl ecology and behavior. Condor 75:446–456.

Martin, J. W. 1989. Harriers and kites. In National Wildlife Federation. Proc. Western Raptor Mgmt. Symp. and Workshop, 83–91. Natl. Wildl. Fed. Sci. and Tech. Ser. 12.

Mason, J. 1970. *Point Reyes: The Solemn Land.* North Shore Books, Inverness, Calif.

——. 1981. The Black Forest. Point Reyes Historian 6: 635–637, 640.

Mason, J. and H. V. C. Park. 1971. *Early Marin.* North Shore Books, Inverness.

——. 1975. *The Making of Marin.* North Shore Books, Inverness.

Maxson, S. J. and G. D. Maxson. 1981. Commensal foraging between Hairy and Pileated woodpeckers. J. Field Ornithol. 52:62–63.

Mayfield, H. 1965. The Brown-headed Cowbird with old and new hosts. Living Bird 4:13–28.

Mayhew, W. W. 1958. The biology of the Cliff Swallow in California. Condor 60:6–37.

Melbostad, G. W. 1969. A history of transportation, land use, and economic development in coastal Marin County, 1800–1900. M.A. thesis, Dominican College, San Rafael.

Meserve, P. L. 1977. Food habits of a White-tailed Kite population in central Chile. Condor 79:263–265.

Mewaldt, L. R., S. S. Kibby, and M. L. Morton. 1968. Comparative biology of Pacific coastal White-crowned Sparrows. Condor 70:14–30.

Mewaldt, L. R. and J. R. King. 1977. The annual cycle of White-crowned Sparrows *(Zonotrichia leucophrys nuttalli)* in coastal California. Condor 79:445–455.

Michael, C. W. 1928. Nesting time of Band-tailed Pigeons in Yosemite Valley. Condor 30:127.

——. 1934. Nesting of the Red-breasted Nuthatch. Condor 36:113.

Michaelson, J. C. 1977. North Pacific sea surface temperatures and California precipitation. M.A. thesis, Univ. Calif., Berkeley.

Michener, H. and J. Michener. 1945. California jays, their storage and recovery of food, and observations at one nest. Condor 47:206–210.

Michener, J. R. 1951. Territorial behavior and age composition in a population of Mockingbirds at a feeding station. Condor 53:276–283.

Middleton, A. L. A. 1979. Influence of age and habitat on reproduction by the American Goldfinch. Ecology 60: 418–432.

Miles, D. B. 1990. The importance and consequences of temporal variation in avian foraging behavior. In M. L. Morrison, C. J. Ralph, J. Verner, and J. R. Jehl, Jr., eds.

Avian foraging: Theory, methodology, and applications, 210-217. Studies Avian Biol. 13.

Millar, C. I. 1986. Bishop Pine (Pinus muricata) of inland Marin County California. Madroño 33:123-129.

Miller, A. H. 1931a. Systematic revision and natural history of the American shrikes (Lanius). Univ. Calif. Publ. Zool. 38:11-242.

——. 1931b. Notes on the song and territorial habits of Bullock's Oriole. Wilson Bull. 43:102-108.

——. 1941. Speciation in the avian genus Junco. Univ. Calif. Publ. Zool. 44:173-434.

——. 1946. Western Tanager summer resident in Marin County. Gull 28:33.

——. 1950. California Shrike. In A. C. Bent, ed. Life histories of North American wagtails, shrikes, vireos, and their allies. U.S. Natl. Mus. Bull. 197:157-179.

——. 1951. An analysis of the distribution of the birds of California. Univ. Calif. Publ. Zool. 50:531-644.

——. 1968. Sage Sparrow. In O. L. Austin, ed. A. C. Bent et al.'s Life histories of North American cardinals, grosbeaks, buntings, towhees, finches, sparrows, and allies. U.S. Natl. Mus. Bull. 237 (Part 2): 1004-1021.

Miller, A. H. and C. E. Bock. 1972. Natural history of the Nuttall Woodpecker at the Hastings Reservation. Condor 74:284-294.

Miller, E. V. 1941. Behavior of the Bewick Wren. Condor 43:81-99.

Miller, J. R. and J. T. Miller. 1948. Nesting of the Spotted Sandpiper at Detroit, Michigan. Auk 65:558-567.

Miller, M. R. 1983. Foraging dives by post-breeding Northern Pintails. Wilson Bull. 95:294-296.

——. 1987. Fall and winter foods of Northern Pintails in the Sacramento Valley, California. J. Wildl. Mgmt. 51:405-414.

Miller, R. F. 1942. The Pied-billed Grebe, a breeding bird of the Philadelphia region. Cassinia 32:23-34.

Milligan, M. M. and J. Verner. 1971. Inter-populational song dialect discrimination in the White-crowned Sparrow. Condor 73:208-213.

Mills, G. S. 1976. American Kestrel sex ratios and habitat separation. Auk 93:740-748.

Mobbs, A. J. 1979. Methods used by the Trochilidae when capturing insects. Avicul. Mag. 85:26-30. (Walsall, West Midlands, England.)

Moffitt, J. 1939a. Notes on the distribution of herons in California. Condor 41:81-82.

——. 1939b. Notes on the distribution of Whistling Swan and Canada Goose in California. Condor 41:93-97.

——. 1941. Notes on the food of the California Clapper Rail. Condor 43:270-273.

Moldenhauer, R. R. and J. A. Wiens. 1970. The water economy of the Sage Sparrow, Amphispiza belli nevadensis. Condor 72:265-275.

Monk, J. G., M. N. Kirven, and B. J. Walton. 1989. California Peregrine Falcon monitoring and management effort in 1989 with a discussion of population trend analysis. Appendix 6. In J. Linthicum, ed. Peregrine Falcon moni-

toring, nest management, hacksite, and cross-fostering efforts, 1989. Annual activity statement of the Santa Cruz Pred. Bird Res. Group, Univ. Calif., Santa Cruz.

Moore, J. 1986. Dietary variation among nestling Starlings. Condor 88:181-189.

Moore, R. T. and A. Barr. 1941. Habits of the White-tailed Kite. Auk 58:453-462.

Morlan, J. and R. Erickson. 1988. Supplement to the Birds of northern California, 1988. In R. G. McCaskie, P. DeBenedictis, R. Erickson, and J. Morlan. Birds of northern California: An annotated field list, 85-97. 2nd ed. Golden Gate Audubon, Berkeley.

Morrell, S. H., H. R. Huber, T. J. Lewis, and D. G. Ainley. 1979. Feeding ecology of Black Oystercatchers on South Farallon Island, California (abstract only). In F. A. Pitelka, ed. Shorebirds in marine environments, 183-186. Studies Avian Biol. 2.

Morrison, M. L. 1980. Seasonal aspects of the predatory behavior of Loggerhead Shrikes. Condor 82:296-300.

——. 1981a. Population trends of the Loggerhead Shrike in the United States. Am. Birds 35:754-757.

——. 1981b. The structure of western warbler assemblages: Analysis of foraging behavior and habitat selection in Oregon. Auk 98:578-588.

——. 1982. The structure of western warbler assemblages: Ecomorphological analysis of the Black-throated Gray and Hermit warblers. Auk 99:503-513.

——. 1984. Influence of sample size on discriminant function analysis of habitat use by birds. J. Field Ornithol. 55: 330-335.

Morrison, M. L., I. C. Timossi, K. A. With, and P. N. Manley. 1985. Use of tree species by forest birds during winter and summer. J. Wildl. Mgmt. 49:1098-1102.

Morrison, M. L. and K. A. With. 1987. Intersexual and interseasonal resource partitioning in Hairy and White-headed woodpeckers. Auk 104:225-233.

Morrison, M. L., K. A. With, I. C. Timossi, W. M. Block, and K. A. Milne. 1987. Foraging behavior of bark-foraging birds in the Sierra Nevada. Condor 89:201-204.

Morse, D. H. 1967. Competitive relationships between Parula Warblers and other species during the breeding season. Auk 84:490-502.

——. 1971. The foraging of warblers isolated on small islands. Ecology 52:216-228.

——. 1973. The foraging of small populations of Yellow Warblers and American Redstarts. Ecology 54:346-355.

Muldal, A., H. L. Gibbs, and R. J. Robertson. 1985. Preferred nest spacing of an obligate cavity-nesting bird, the Tree Swallow. Condor 87:356-363.

Munro-Fraser, J. P. 1880. History of Marin County, California. Alley, Bowen, & Co. Republished 1972 by C. B. Veronda, P.O. Box 505, Petaluma, CA 94952.

Munson, C. R. and L. W. Adams. 1984. A record of ground nesting by the Hermit Warbler. Wilson Bull. 96:301.

Murphy, E. C. 1978. Breeding ecology of House Sparrows: Spatial variation. Condor 80:180-193.

N

National Oceanic and Atmospheric Administration. 1982. Monthly normals of temperature, precipitation, and heating and cooling degree days 1951–80. Climatography of U.S. 81 (California).

Naylor, A. E. 1960. The Wood Duck in California with special reference to the use of nest boxes. Calif. Fish Game 46:241–269.

Neff, J. A. 1937. Nesting distribution of the Tri-colored Red-wing. Condor 39:61–81.

——. 1947. Habits, food, and economic status of the Band-tailed Pigeon. N. Am. Fauna 58:1–76.

Nelson, L. and J. Hooper. 1976. California upland game and their management. Leaflet 2720. Div. Agri. Sci., Univ. Calif., Davis.

Newman, J. D. 1968. Black-chinned Sparrow. In O. L. Austin, ed. A. C. Bent et al.'s Life histories of North American cardinals, grosbeaks, buntings, towhees, finches, sparrows, and allies. U.S. Natl. Mus. Bull. 237 (Part 2): 1241–1248.

Newton, I. 1973. *Finches.* Taplinger, New York

Nice, M. M. 1937. Studies in the life history of the Song Sparrow. Trans. Linn. Soc. N.Y. 4:1–246.

Nichols, D. R. and N. A. Wright. 1971. Preliminary map of the historic marshlands, San Francisco Bay, California. Open File Rept. Basic Data Contrib. 9. U.S. Geol. Surv., Menlo Park.

Nickell, W. P. 1951. Studies of habitats, territory, and nests of the eastern goldfinch. Auk 68:447–470.

Nisbet, I. C. T. 1988. The relative importance of DDE and dieldrin in the decline of Peregrine Falcon populations. In T. J. Cade, J. H. Enderson, C. G. Thelander, and C. M. White, eds. *Peregrine Falcon Populations: Their Management and Recovery,* 351–375. The Peregrine Fund, Boise, Idaho.

Norris, C. A. 1960. The breeding distributions of thirty bird species in 1952. Bird Study 7:129–184.

Norris, R. A. 1958. Comparative biosystematics and life history of the nuthatches *Sitta pygmaea* and *Sitta pusilla.* Univ. Calif. Publ. Zool. 56:199–300.

North, C. A. 1973. Population dynamics of the House Sparrow (*Passer domesticus* L.) in Wisconsin. In S. C. Kendeigh and J. Pinowski, eds. *Productivity, Population Dynamics, and Systematics of Granivorous Birds,* 195–219. Polish Sci. Publ., Warsaw.

Nudd, T. D. 1982. Ecological separation of grebes and coots: Interference competition or microhabitat selection? Wilson Bull. 94:505–514.

O

Oakleaf, B., H. Downing, B. and M. Raynes, and O. Scott, eds. 1979. Working draft of Wyoming avian atlas. Wyom. Game and Fish Dept., Lander.

Oberholser, H. C. 1974. *The Bird Life of Texas. Vol. 2.* Univ. Texas Press, Austin.

Oberlander, G. 1939. The history of a family of Black Phoebes. Condor 41:133–151.

Oberlander, G. T. 1956. Summer fog precipitation on the San Francisco peninsula. Ecology 37:851–852.

Odum, R. R. 1977. Sora (*Porzana carolina*). In G. C. Sanderson, ed. Management of migratory shore and upland game birds in North America, 57–65. Int. Assoc. Fish Wildl. Agencies and U.S. Fish Wildl. Serv.

Ogden, J. D., ed. 1977. Transactions of the North American Osprey Research Conference. USDI, U.S. Natl. Park Serv. Proc. Ser. 2, Washington, D.C.

Ohlendorf, H. M. 1974. Competitive relationships among kingbirds (*Tyrannus*) in Trans-Pecos, Texas. Wilson Bull. 86:357–373.

——. 1976. Comparative breeding ecology of phoebes in Trans-Pecos, Texas. Wilson Bull. 88:255–271.

Ohlendorf, H. M., T. W. Custer, R. W. Lowe, M. Rigney, and E. Cromartie. 1988. Organochlorines and mercury in eggs of coastal terns and herons in California, USA. Colonial Waterbirds 11:85–94.

Ohlendorf, H. M. and W. J. Fleming. 1988. Birds and environmental contaminants in San Francisco and Chesapeake bays. Marine Pollution Bull. 19:487–495.

Ohlendorf, H. M., E. E. Klaas, and T. E. Kaiser. 1978. Environmental pollutants and eggshell thinning in the Black-crowned Night-Heron. In Wading birds, 63–82. Natl. Aud. Soc. Res. Rept. 7.

Ohmart, R. D. 1973. Observations on the breeding adaptations of the Roadrunner. Condor 75:140–149.

Olsen, D. W. 1977. A literature review of pheasant habitat requirements and improvement methods: Annual performance report for Federal Aid Project. Publ. Utah Div. Wildl. Res. 77-7, Salt Lake City.

Orians, G. H. 1960. Autumnal breeding in the Tricolored Blackbird. Auk 77:379–398.

——. 1961. The ecology of blackbird (*Agelaius*) social systems. Ecol. Monogr. 31:285–312.

——. 1980. Some adaptations of marsh-nesting blackbirds. Monogr. Pop. Biol. 14. Princeton Univ. Press, Princeton.

Orians, G. H. and H. S. Horn. 1969. Overlap in foods and foraging of four species of blackbirds in the Potholes of central Washington. Ecology 50:930–938.

Oring, L. W. and M. L. Knudson. 1972. Monogamy and polyandry in the Spotted Sandpiper. Living Bird 11:59–73.

Oring, L. W., D. B. Lank, and S. J. Maxson. 1983. Population studies of the polyandrous Spotted Sandpiper. Auk 100:272–285.

Oring, L. W. and S. J. Maxson. 1978. Instances of simultaneous polyandry by a Spotted Sandpiper, *Actitis macularia.* Ibis 120:349–353.

Orr, R. T. 1937. Summer records of birds of Marin County, California. Condor 39:38.

Osborne, T. O. 1972. Ecology and avian use of the coastal rocks of Northern California. M.A. thesis, Humboldt State Univ., Arcata.

Osborne, T. O. and J. G. Reynolds. 1971. California seabird breeding ground survey. Wildl. Mgmt. Branch Admin. Rept. 71-73. Calif. Dept. Fish Game, Sacramento.

Otvos, I. S. and R. W. Stark. 1985. Arthropod food of some forest-inhabiting birds. Can. Ent. 117:971–990.

P

Page, G. W., F. C. Bidstrup, R. J. Ramer, and L. E. Stenzel. 1986. Distribution of wintering Snowy Plovers in California and adjacent states. W. Birds 17:145–170.

Page, G. W., H. R. Carter, and R. G. Ford. 1990. Numbers of seabirds killed or debilitated in the 1986 *Apex Houston* oil spill in California. In S. G. Sealy, ed. Auks at sea, 164–174. Studies Avian Biol. 14.

Page, G. W. and J. G. Evens. 1987. The sizes of Clapper Rail populations at Corte Madera Ecological Reserve, Muzzi Marsh, San Clemente Creek, and Triangle Marsh. Point Reyes Bird Obs. Rept. to Marin Audubon Soc. PRBO Contrib. 367.

Page, G. W., P. L. Quinn, and J. C. Warriner. 1989. Comparison of the breeding of hand- and wild-reared Snowy Plovers. Conserv. Biol. 3:198–201.

Page, G. W. and L. E. Stenzel, eds. 1981. The breeding status of the Snowy Plover in California. W. Birds 12:1–40.

Page, G. W., L. E. Stenzel, and C. A. Ribic. 1985. Nest site selection and clutch predation in the Snowy Plover. Auk 102:347–353.

Page, G. W., L. E. Stenzel, W. D. Shuford, and C. R. Bruce. 1991. Distribution and abundance of the Snowy Plover on its western North American breeding grounds. J. Field Ornithol. 62:245–255.

Page, G. W. and M. Walter. 1988. Petition to list the coastal population of the Western Snowy Plover as threatened. Point Reyes Bird Obs. Rept. to U.S. Fish Wildl. Serv.

Page, G. W. and D. F. Whitacre. 1975. Raptor predation on wintering shorebirds. Condor 77:73–83.

Palmer, R. S., ed. 1962. *Handbook of North American Birds. Vol. 1: Loons through Flamingos.* Yale Univ. Press, New Haven.

——. 1967. Species accounts. In G. D. Stout, ed. *The Shorebirds of North America*, 143–267. Viking, New York.

——. 1968. Pine Siskin. In O. L. Austin, Jr., ed. A. C. Bent et al.'s Life histories of North American cardinals, grosbeaks, buntings, towhees, finches, sparrows, and allies. U.S. Natl. Mus. Bull. 237 (Part 1): 424–447.

——, ed. 1976a. *Handbook of North American Birds. Vol. 2: Waterfowl (Part 1).* Yale Univ. Press, New Haven.

——, ed. 1976b. *Handbook of North American Birds. Vol. 3: Waterfowl (Part 2).* Yale Univ. Press, New Haven.

——, ed. 1988a. *Handbook of North American Birds. Vol. 4: Diurnal Raptors (Part 1).* Yale Univ. Press, New Haven.

——, ed. 1988b. *Handbook of North American Birds. Vol. 5: Diurnal Raptors (Part 2).* Yale Univ. Press, New Haven.

Palmer, T. K. 1973. The House Finch and Starling in relation to California's agriculture. In S. C. Kendeigh and J. Pinowski, eds. *Productivity, Population Dynamics, and Systematics of Granivorous Birds*, 275–290. Polish Sci. Publ., Warsaw.

Parsons, J. J. 1960. Fog drip from coastal stratus, with special reference to California. Weather (London) 15:58–62.

Paszkowski, C. A. 1982. Vegetation, ground, and frugivorous foraging of the American Robin. Auk 99:701–709.

——. 1984. Macrohabitat use, microhabitat use, and foraging behavior of the Hermit Thrush and Veery in a northern Wisconsin forest. Wilson Bull. 96:286–292.

Paterson, R. L., Jr. 1984. High incidence of plant material and small mammals in the autumn diet of Turkey Vultures in Virginia. Wilson Bull. 96:467–469.

Pattee, O. H. and S. R. Wilbur. 1989. Turkey Vulture and California Condor. In National Wildlife Federation. Proc. Western Raptor Mgmt. Symp. and Workshop, 61–65. Natl. Wildl. Fed. Sci. and Tech. Ser. 12.

Patton, C. P. 1956. Climatology of summer fogs in the San Francisco Bay Area. Univ. Calif. Publ. Geogr. 10:113–200.

Payne, R. B. 1969. Breeding season and reproductive physiology of Tricolored and Red-winged blackbirds. Univ. Calif. Publ. Zool. 90:1–114.

Peakall, D. B. and L. F. Kiff. 1988. DDE contamination in Peregrines and American Kestrels and its effect on reproduction. In T. J. Cade, J. H. Enderson, C. G. Thelander, and C. M. White, eds. *Peregrine Falcon Populations: Their Management and Recovery*, 337–350. The Peregrine Fund, Boise, Idaho.

Pearson, O. P. 1963. History of two local outbreaks of feral house mice. Ecol. Monogr. 44:540–549.

Peck, G. K. and R. D. James. 1983. *Breeding Birds of Ontario: Nidology and Distribution. Vol. I: Nonpasserines.* Royal Ontario Museum, Toronto.

Peeters, H. J. 1962. Nuptial behavior of the Band-tailed Pigeon in the San Francisco Bay Area. Condor 64:445–470.

Perring, F. H. and S. M. Walters. 1962. *Atlas of the British Flora.* Botanical Soc. British Isles. T. Nelson, London.

Peterson, R. T., G. Mountfort, and P. A. D. Hollom. 1954. *A Field Guide to the Birds of Britain and Europe.* Collins, London.

Petit, D. R., K. E. Petit, and L. J. Petit. 1990. Geographic variation in foraging ecology of North American insectivorous birds. In M. L. Morrison, C. J. Ralph, J. Verner, and J. R. Jehl, Jr., eds. Avian foraging: Theory, methodology, and applications, 254–263. Studies Avian Biol. 13.

Phelps, J. H., Jr. 1968. Oregon Junco, Pink-sided, Northwestern, and Point Pinos Oregon juncos. In O. L. Austin, Jr., ed. A. C. Bent et al.'s Life histories of North American cardinals, grosbeaks, buntings, towhees, finches, sparrows, and allies. U.S. Natl. Mus. Bull. 237 (Part 2): 1050–1089.

Phillips, A., J. Marshall, and G. Monson. 1964. *The Birds of Arizona.* Univ. Arizona Press, Tucson.

Phillips, J. C. 1922–1926. *A Natural History of the Ducks.* 4 vols. Houghton Mifflin, Boston.

Piatt, J. F. and D. N. Nettleship. 1985. Diving depths of four alcids. Auk 102:293–297.

Pickwell, G. 1930. The White-tailed Kite. Condor 32:221–230.

Pickwell, G. B. 1931. The prairie Horned Lark. St. Louis Acad. Sci. Trans. 27:1–153.

465

Pierotti, R. 1981. Male and female parental roles in the Western Gull under different environmental conditions. Auk 98:532-549.

Pinkowski, B. C. 1979. Foraging ecology and habitat utilization in the genus *Sialia*. In J. G. Dickson, R. N. Conner, R. R. Fleet, J. A. Jackson, and J. C. Kroll, eds. *The Role of Insectivorous Birds in Forest Ecosystems*, 165-190. Academic Press, New York.

Pinowska, B. 1975. Food of female House Sparrows *(Passer domesticus)* in relation to stages of the nesting cycle. Polish Ecol. Studies 1:311-325.

Pitelka, F. A. 1951a. Ecologic overlap and interspecific strife in breeding populations of Anna and Allen hummingbirds. Ecology 32:641-661.

——. 1951b. Breeding seasons of hummingbirds near Santa Barbara, California. Condor 53:198-201.

——. 1951c. Speciation and ecologic distribution in American jays of the genus *Aphelocoma*. Univ. Calif. Publ. Zool. 50:195-464.

Planck, R. J. 1967. Nest site selection and nesting in the European Starling, *Sturnus vulgaris* L., in California. Ph.D. thesis, Univ. Calif., Davis.

Platt, S. W. and J. H. Enderson. 1989. Falcons. In National Wildlife Federation. Proc. Western Raptor Mgmt. Symp. and Workshop, 111-117. Natl. Wildl. Fed. Sci. and Tech. Ser. 12.

Pleasants, B. Y. 1979. Adaptive significance of the variable dispersion pattern of breeding Northern Orioles. Condor 81:28-34.

Point Reyes Bird Observatory. 1985. The impacts of the T/V *Puerto Rican* oil spill on marine birds and mammal populations in the Gulf of the Farallones, 6-19 November 1984. Point Reyes Bird Obs. Spec. Sci. Rept.

Porter, D. K., M. A. Strong, J. B. Giezentanner, and R. A. Ryder. 1975. Nest ecology, productivity, and growth of the Loggerhead Shrike on the shortgrass prairie. Southwestern Nat. 19:429-436.

Portnoy, J. W. and W. E. Dodge. 1979. Red-shouldered Hawk nesting ecology and behavior. Wilson Bull. 91: 104-117.

Poston, H. J. 1974. Home range and breeding biology of the Shoveler. Can. Wildl. Serv. Rept. Ser. 2.

Pough, R. H. 1957. *Audubon Western Bird Guide: Land, Water, and Game Birds*. Doubleday, Garden City, N.Y.

Pratt, H. M. 1972. Nesting success of Common Egrets and Great Blue Herons in the San Francisco Bay region. Condor 74:447-453.

——. 1974. Breeding of Great Blue Herons and Great Egrets at Audubon Canyon Ranch, California, 1972-73. W. Birds 5:127-136.

——. 1980. Directions and timing of Great Blue Heron foraging flights from a California colony: Implications for social facilitation of food finding. Wilson Bull. 92:489-496.

——. 1983. Marin County California heron colonies: 1967-81. W. Birds 14:169-184.

Pray, R. H. 1950. Cowbirds in the Bay Area. Gull 32:38.

Prestt, I. and A. A. Bell. 1966. An objective method of recording breeding distributions of common birds of prey in Britain. Bird Study 13:277-283.

Price, F. E. and C. E. Bock. 1973. Polygyny in the Dipper. Condor 75:457-459.

——. 1983. Population ecology of the Dipper *(Cinclus mexicanus)* in the Front Range of Colorado. Studies Avian Biol. 7.

Pruett-Jones, S. G., M. Pruett-Jones, and R. L. Knight. 1980. The White-tailed Kite in North and Middle America: Current status and recent population trends. Am. Birds 34:682-688.

R

Rabenold, P. P. 1983. The communal roost in Black and Turkey vultures—an information center? In S. R. Wilbur and J. A. Jackson, eds. *Vulture Biology and Management*, 303-321. Univ. California Press, Berkeley.

Raley, C. M. and S. H. Anderson. 1990. Availability and use of arthropod food resources by Wilson's Warblers and Lincoln's Sparrows in southeastern Wyoming. Condor 92:141-150.

Ralph, C. J. and C. A. Pearson. 1971. Correlation of age, size of territory, plumage, and breeding success in White-crowned Sparrows. Condor 73:77-80.

Ralph, C. J. and C. L. Ralph. 1958. Notes on the nesting of egrets near San Rafael, California. Condor 60:70-71.

Randle, W. and R. Austing. 1952. Ecological notes on the Long-eared and Saw-whet owls in southwestern Ohio. Ecology 33:422-426.

Raphael, M. G. 1985. Orientation of American Kestrel nest cavities and nest trees. Condor 87:437-438.

Raphael, M. G. and M. White. 1984. Use of snags by cavity-nesting birds in the Sierra Nevada. Wildl. Monogr. 86.

Rauzon, M. J. and H. R. Carter. 1988. Observations of nesting waterbirds in the San Francisco Bay Area in 1988. Point Reyes Bird Obs. Rept., Contrib. 432.

Ray, M. S. 1904. Spring notes from bay counties. Condor 6:139.

Raynor, G. S. 1983. A method for evaluating quality of coverage in breeding bird atlas projects. Am. Birds 37: 9-13.

Reichel, W. L. et al. 1969. Pesticide residues in eagles. Pesticides Monitor Jour. 3:142-144.

Remsen, J. V., Jr. 1978. Bird species of special concern in California: An annotated list of declining or vulnerable bird species. Wildl. Mgmt. Branch Admin. Rept. 78-1. Calif. Dept. Fish Game, Sacramento.

Reynolds, J. D. and R. W. Knapton. 1984. Nest site selection and breeding ecology of the Chipping Sparrow. Wilson Bull. 96:488-493.

Reynolds, R. T. 1983. Management of western coniferous forest habitat for nesting *Accipiter* hawks. U.S. For. Serv. Gen. Tech. Rept. RM-102. Rocky Mtn. For. and Range Exp. Sta., Fort Collins, Colo.

——. 1989. Accipiters. In National Wildlife Federation. Proc. Western Raptor Mgmt. Symp. and Workshop, 92–101. Natl. Wildl. Fed. Sci. and Tech. Ser. 12.

Reynolds, R. T. and E. C. Meslow. 1984. Partitioning of food and niche characteristics of coexisting *Accipiter* during breeding. Auk 101:761–779.

Reynolds, R. T., E. C. Meslow, and H. M. Wight. 1982. Nesting habitat of coexisting *Accipiters* in Oregon. J. Wildl. Mgmt. 46:124–138.

Reynolds, R. T. and H. M. Wight. 1978. Distribution, density, and productivity of accipiter hawks breeding in Oregon. Wilson Bull. 90:182–196.

Reynolds, T. E. 1942. Unusual location. Gull 24:24.

Rice, D. L. and B. Peterjohn. 1986. Considerations in establishing adequacy of coverage standards. In S. M. Sutcliffe, R. E. Bonney, Jr., and J. D. Lowe, comps. Proc. 2nd Northeastern Breeding Bird Atlas Conference, 13–15. Lab. Ornithology, Cornell Univ., Ithaca, N.Y.

Rich, T. 1986. Habitat and nest-site selection by Burrowing Owls in the sagebrush steppe of Idaho. J. Wildl. Mgmt. 50:548–555.

Richardson, F. 1961. Breeding biology of the Rhinoceros Auklet. Condor 63:456–473.

Richmond, S. M. 1953. The attractions of Purple Martins to an urban location in western Oregon. Condor 55:225–249.

Rigney, M. and T. Rigney. 1981. A breeding bird survey of the south San Francisco Bay salt pond levee system 1981. Rept. by members of the South Bay Institute for Avian Studies for the S. F. Bay Natl. Wildl. Refuge, Newark.

Risebrough, R. W. and J. G. Monk. 1989. Toxic chemicals and birds of prey: A perspective in 1987. In National Wildlife Federation. Proc. Western Raptor Mgmt. Symp. and Workshop, 245–255. Natl. Wildl. Fed. Sci. and Tech. Ser. 12.

Risebrough, R. W. and D. B. Peakall. 1988. Commentary—The relative importance of the several organochlorines in the decline of Peregrine Falcon populations. In T. J. Cade, J. H. Enderson, C. G. Thelander, and C. M. White, eds. *Peregrine Falcon Populations: Their Management and Recovery.* The Peregrine Fund, Boise, Idaho.

Ritchison, G. 1981. Breeding biology of the White-breasted Nuthatch. Loon 53:184–187.

——. 1983. Breeding biology of the Black-headed Grosbeak in northern Utah. W. Birds 14:159–167.

Ritter, L. V. 1983. Nesting ecology of Scrub Jays in Chico, California. W. Birds 14:147–158.

Ritter, L. V. and K. Purcell. 1983. Cavity-nesting Brewer's Blackbirds. W. Birds 14:205.

Ritter, W. E. 1929. The nutritional activities of the California Woodpecker *(Balanosphyra formicivora).* Quart. Rev. Biol. 4:455–483.

——. 1938. *The California Woodpecker and I.* Univ. California Press, Berkeley.

Robbins, C. S. 1973. Introduction, spread, and present abundance of the House Sparrow in North America. In S. C. Kendeigh, chairman. A symposium on the House Sparrow *(Passer domesticus)* and European Tree Sparrow *(P. montanus)* in North America. Ornithol. Monogr. 14: 3–9.

——. 1982. Overview of international atlasing. In S. D. Laughlin, ed. Proc. of the Northeastern Breeding Bird Atlas Conference, 3–10. Vermont Inst. Nat. Sci., Woodstock, Vt.

Robbins, C. S., B. Bruun, and H. S. Zim. 1966. *Birds of North America.* Golden Press, New York.

Robbins, C. S., D. Bystrak, and P. H. Geissler. 1986. The Breeding Bird Survey: Its first fifteen years, 1965–1979. U.S. Fish Wildl. Serv. Resource Publ. 157.

Roberson, D. 1985. *Monterey Birds.* Monterey Peninsula Audubon Soc., Carmel, Calif.

Robertson, I. 1974. The food of nesting Double-crested and Pelagic cormorants at Mandarte Island, British Columbia, with notes on feeding ecology. Condor 76:346–348.

Robertson, R. J. and R. F. Norman. 1977. The function and evolution of aggressive host behavior towards the Brown-headed Cowbird, *Molothrus ater.* Can. J. Zool. 55:508–518.

Rodgers, T. L. 1937. Behavior of the Pine Siskin. Condor 39:143–149.

Roest, A. I. 1957. Notes on the American Sparrow Hawk. Auk 74:1–19.

Root, R. B. 1964. Ecological interactions of the Chestnut-backed Chickadee following a range extension. Condor 66:229–238.

——. 1967. The niche exploitation pattern of the Blue-gray Gnatcatcher. Ecol. Monogr. 37:317–350.

——. 1969a. Interspecific territoriality between Bewick's and House wrens. Auk 86:125–127.

——. 1969b. The behavior and reproductive success of the Blue-gray Gnatcatcher. Condor 71:16–31.

Roselaar, C. S. 1980. Moorhen. In S. Cramp, chief ed. *Handbook of the Birds of Europe, the Middle East, and North Africa: The Birds of the Western Palearctic. Vol. 2: Hawks to Bustards,* 578–588. Oxford Univ. Press, Oxford.

Rotenberry, J. T. 1980. Dietary relationships among shrub-steppe passerine birds: Competition or opportunism in a variable environment? Ecol. Monogr. 50:93–110.

Rothstein, S. I. 1975. An experimental and teleonomic investigation of avian brood parasitism. Condor 77:250–271.

——. 1977. Cowbird parasitism and egg recognition of the Northern Oriole. Wilson Bull. 89:21–32.

——. 1980. The preening invitation or head-down display of parasitic cowbirds: II. Experimental analyses and evidence for behavioural mimicry. Behaviour 75:148–184.

Rothstein, S. I. and R. C. Fleischer. 1987. Vocal dialects and their possible relation to honest status signalling in the Brown-headed Cowbird. Condor 89:1–23.

Rothstein, S. I., J. Verner, and E. Stevens. 1980. Range expansion and diurnal changes in dispersion of the Brown-headed Cowbird in the Sierra Nevada. Auk 97: 253–267.

——. 1984. Radio-tracking confirms a unique diurnal pattern of spatial occurrence in the parasitic Brown-headed Cowbird. Ecology 65:77–88.

Rothstein, S. I., J. Verner, E. Stevens, and L. V. Ritter. 1987. Behavioral differences among sex and age classes of the Brown-headed Cowbird and their relation to the efficacy of a control program. Wilson Bull. 99:322–337.

Rothstein, S. I., D. A. Yokel, and R. C. Fleischer. 1986. Social dominance, mating and spacing systems, female fecundity, and vocal dialects in captive and free-ranging Brown-headed Cowbirds. Current Ornith. 3:127–185.

Rothwell, B. S. 1959. Pioneering in Marin County. Unpubl. manuscript. California Room, Marin County Library, Civic Center, San Rafael.

Rudolph, S. G. 1978. Predation ecology of coexisting Great Horned and Barn owls. Wilson Bull. 90:134–137.

Rundle, W. D. and M. W. Sayre. 1983. Feeding ecology of migrant Soras in southeastern Missouri. J. Wildl. Mgmt. 47:1153–1159.

Rush, D. H., E. C. Meslow, P. D. Doerr, and L. B. Keith. 1972. Response of Great Horned Owl populations to changing prey densities. J. Wildl. Mgmt. 36:282–295.

Russell, D. N. 1971. Food habits of the Starling in eastern Texas. Condor 73:369–372.

Rust, H. J. 1920. The home life of a western Warbling Vireo. Condor 22:85–94.

Ryser, F. A., Jr. 1985. *Birds of the Great Basin: A Natural History.* Univ. Nevada Press, Reno.

S

Sakai, H. F. 1988. Breeding biology of Hammond's and Western flycatchers in northwestern California. W. Birds 19:49–60.

Sakai, H. F. and B. R. Noon. 1990. Variation in the foraging behaviors of two flycatchers: Associations with stage of the breeding cycle. In M. L. Morrison, C. J. Ralph, J. Verner, and J. R. Jehl, Jr., eds. Avian foraging: Theory, methodology, and applications, 237–244. Studies Avian Biol. 13.

Salt, G. W. 1952. The relation of metabolism to climate and distribution in three finches of the genus *Carpodacus.* Ecol. Monogr. 22:121–152.

Salyer, J. C. and K. F. Laglar. 1946. The eastern Belted Kingfisher, *Megaceryle alcyon alcyon* (Linnaeus), in relation to fish management. Trans. Amer. Fish Soc. 76:97–117.

Samuel, D. E. 1971. The breeding biology of Barn and Cliff swallows in West Virginia. Wilson Bull. 83:284–301.

San Francisco Bay Conservation and Development Commission and T. E. Harvey. 1983. Aquatic and wildlife resources of Richardson Bay. Special Area Plan Study. Sept. 1983.

Sander, T. G. 1986. Aspects of the breeding biology and recolonization history of Rhinoceros Auklets *(Cerorhinca monocerata)* on Southeast Farallon Island, California. Rept. of Point Reyes Bird Obs./Evergreen State Coll., Olympia, Wash.

Santee, R. and W. Granfield. 1939. Behavior of the Saw-whet Owl on its nesting grounds. Condor 4:3–9.

Sappington, J. N. 1977. Breeding biology of House Sparrows in north Mississippi. Wilson Bull. 89:300–309.

Sayre, M. W. and W. D. Rundle. 1984. Comparison of habitat use by migrant Soras and Virginia Rails. J. Wildl. Mgmt. 48:599–605.

Schaefer, V. H. 1976. Geographic variation in the placement and structure of oriole nests. Condor 78:443–448.

——. 1980. Geographic variation in the insulative qualities of nests of the Northern Oriole. Wilson Bull. 92:466–474.

Schorger, A. W. 1952. Introduction of the domestic pigeon. Auk 69:462–463.

——. 1966. *The Wild Turkey: Its History and Domestication.* Univ. Oklahoma Press, Norman.

Schrantz, F. G. 1943. Nest life of the eastern Yellow Warbler. Auk 60:367–387.

Schreiber, R. W. 1970. Breeding biology of Western Gulls *(Larus occidentalis)* on San Nicolas Island, California, 1968. Condor 72:133–140.

Scott, D. M. and C. D. Ankney. 1983. The laying cycle of Brown-headed Cowbirds: Passerine chickens? Auk 100:583–592.

Scott, J. M., W. Hoffman, D. Ainley, and C. F. Zeillemaker. 1974. Range expansion and activity patterns in Rhinoceros Auklets. W. Birds 5:13–20.

Sealy, S. G. 1982. Rough-winged Swallows scavenging adult midges. Wilson Bull. 94:368–369.

——. 1984. Capture and caching of flying carpenter ants by Pygmy Nuthatches. Murrelet 65:49–51.

Seibert, M. L. 1942. Occurrence and nesting of some birds in the San Francisco Bay region. Condor 44:68–72.

Selander, R. K. and C. J. LaRue, Jr. 1961. Interspecific preening invitation display of parasitic cowbirds. Auk 78:473–504.

Selleck, D. M. and B. Glading. 1943. Food habits of nesting Barn Owls and Marsh Hawks at Dune Lakes, California, as determined by the "cage nest" method. Calif. Fish Game 29:122–131.

Serie, J. R. and G. A. Swanson. 1976. Feeding ecology of breeding Gadwalls on saline wetlands. J. Wildl. Mgmt. 40:69–81.

Sharrock, J. T. R., ed. 1976. *The Atlas of Breeding Birds in Britain and Ireland.* British Trust for Ornithology, Tring, England.

Shields, W. M. 1984. Factors affecting nest and site fidelity in Adirondack Barn Swallows *(Hirundo rustica).* Auk 101:780–789.

Shuford, W. D. 1982. Field checklist of the birds of Marin County, Alta California. PRBO, 4990 Shoreline Hwy., Stinson Beach, CA 94970.

——. 1985. Acorn Woodpecker mutilates nestling Red-breasted Sapsuckers. Wilson Bull. 97:234–236.

——. 1986. Have ornithologists or breeding Red-breasted Sapsuckers extended their range in coastal California? W. Birds 17:97–105.

Shuford, W. D., G. W. Page, J. G. Evens, and L. E. Stenzel. 1989. Seasonal abundance of waterbirds at Point Reyes: A coastal California perspective. W. Birds 20:137–265.

Shuford, W. D. and I. C. Timossi. 1989. *Plant Communities of Marin County.* Calif. Native Plant Soc. Spec. Publ. 10.

Shy, E. 1984. Habitat shift and geographical variation in North American tanagers. Oecologia 63:281–285.

Sibley, C. G. 1952. The birds of the South San Francisco Bay region. Published by the author. Available at PRBO library, 4990 Shoreline Hwy., Stinson Beach, CA 94970.

———. 1955. Nesting of the Western Tanager in the Santa Cruz Mountains, California. Condor 57:307.

Sibley, C. S. and L. L. Short, Jr. 1959. Hybridization in the buntings (Passerina) of the Great Plains. Auk 76:443–463.

Siegfried, W. R. 1973. Summer food and feeding of the Ruddy Duck in Manitoba. Can. J. Zool. 51:1293–1297.

———. 1976a. Social organization in Ruddy and Maccoa ducks. Auk 93:560–570.

———. 1976b. Breeding biology and parasitism in the Ruddy Duck. Wilson Bull. 88:566–574.

———. 1977. Notes on the behavior of Ruddy Ducks during the brood period. Wildfowl 28:126–128.

Siegfried, W. R., A. E. Burger, and P. J. Caldwell. 1976. Incubation behavior of Ruddy and Maccoa ducks. Condor 78:512–517.

Simberloff, D. 1987. The Spotted Owl fracas: Mixing academic, applied, and political ecology. Ecology 68:766–772.

Sisson, R. F. 1974. Aha! It really works! Natl. Geogr. 145:143–147.

Skaar, P. D. 1967. Long range changes in the avifauna of the Bozeman, Montana region. Proc. Montana Acad. Sci. 27:55–66.

———. 1969. Birds of the Bozeman Latilong, Bozeman, Montana. Published by the author, 501 S. Third, Bozeman, Montana.

———. 1975, 1980. Montana Bird Distribution: Preliminary Mapping by Latilong. Published by the author, 501 S. Third, Bozeman, Montana.

Skinner, J. E. 1962. An historical review of the fish and wildlife resources of the San Francisco Bay Area. Water Projects Branch Rept. 1. Calif. Dept. Fish Game, Sacramento.

Skinner, M. P. 1938. Rocky Mountain, California, Vancouver, and Coast Pygmy owls. In A. C. Bent, ed. Life histories of North American birds of prey (Part 2). U.S. Natl. Mus. Bull. 170:401–434.

Skorupa, J. P., R. L. Hothem, and R. W. DeHaven. 1980. Foods of breeding Tricolored blackbirds in agricultural areas of Merced County, California. Condor 82:465–467.

Slack, R. S. 1975. Effects of prey size on Loggerhead Shrike predation. Auk 92:812–814.

Slobodchikoff, C. N. and J. T. Doyen. 1977. Effects of Ammophila arenaria on sand dune arthropod communities. Ecology 58:1171–1175.

Smail, J., D. G. Ainley, and H. Strong. 1972. Notes on birds killed in the 1971 San Francisco oil spill. Calif. Birds 3:25–32.

Smallwood, J. A. 1988. A mechanism of sexual segregation by habitat in American Kestrels (Falco sparverius) wintering in south-central Florida. Auk 105:36–46.

Smith, C. F. and C. L. Hopkins. 1937. Notes on the Barn Owls of the San Francisco Bay region. Condor 39:189–191.

Smith, C. R. 1982. Thoughts on adequate coverage, random sampling, auxiliary data collection, and data analysis for breeding bird atlas projects. In S. B. Laughlin, ed. Proc. Northeastern Breeding Bird Atlas Conference, 80–89. Vermont Inst. Nat. Sci., Woodstock, Vt.

———, ed. 1990. Handbook for Atlasing American Breeding Birds. Vermont Inst. Nat. Sci., Woodstock, Vt.

Smith, D. G., C. R. Wilson, and H. H. Frost. 1974. History and ecology of Barn Owls in Utah. Condor 76:131–136.

Smith, J. N. M. 1978. Flycatching by male Song Sparrows, Melospiza melodia. Can. Field-Nat. 92:195–196.

Smith, J. N. M., P. Arcese, and I. G. McLean. 1984. Age, experience and enemy recognition by wild Song Sparrows. Behav. Ecol. Sociobiol. 14:101–106.

Smith, K. C. and D. C. Anderson. 1982. Food, predation, and reproductive ecology of the Dark-eyed Junco in northern Utah. Auk 99:650–661.

Smith, R. L. 1963. Some ecological notes on the Grasshopper Sparrow. Wilson Bull. 75:159–165.

———. 1968. Grasshopper Sparrow. In O. L. Austin, Jr., ed. A. C. Bent et al.'s Life histories of North American cardinals, grosbeaks, buntings, towhees, finches, sparrows, and allies. U.S. Natl. Mus. Bull 237 (Part 2): 725–745.

Smith, R. L. and L. D. Flake. 1985. Movements and habitats of brood-rearing Wood Ducks on a prairie river. J. Wildl. Mgmt. 49:437–442.

Smith, S. M. 1967. An ecological study of winter flocks of Black-capped and Chestnut-backed chickadees. Wilson Bull. 79:200–207.

———. 1972. The ontogeny of impaling behavior in the Loggerhead Shrike, Lanius ludovicianus L. Behavior 42: 232–247.

———. 1973. A study of prey-attack behavior in young Loggerhead Shrikes, Lanius ludovicianus L. Behavior 44:113–141.

Smith, W. A. 1968. The Band-tailed Pigeon in California. Calif. Fish Game 54:4–16.

Smith, W. J. 1966. Communications and relationships in the genus Tyrannus. Nutt. Ornithol. Club Publ. 6.

Snapp, B. D. 1976. Colonial breeding in the Barn Swallow (Hirundo rustica) and its adaptive significance. Condor 78:471–480.

Snyder, D. E. 1954. A nesting study of Red Crossbills. Wilson Bull. 66:32–37.

Snyder, N. F. R., H. A. Snyder, J. L. Lincer, and R. T. Reynolds. 1973. Organochlorines, heavy metals, and the biology of North American accipiters. BioSci. 23:300–305.

Snyder, N. F. R. and J. M. Wiley. 1976. Sexual size dimorphism in hawks and owls of North America. Ornithol. Monogr. 20:1–96.

Soriano, P. S. 1931. Food habits and economic status of the Brewer and Red-winged blackbirds. Calif. Fish Game 17:361–395.

Southern, H. N. 1945. The economic importance of the House Sparrow, *Passer domesticus* L., a review. Ann. Appl. Biol. 32:57-62.

Sowls, A. L., A. R. DeGange, J. W. Nelson, and G. S. Lester. 1980. Catalog of California seabird colonies. USDI, Fish and Wildl. Serv. Biol Serv. Progr. FWS/OBS 37/80.

Sowls, A. L., S. A. Hatch, and C. J. Lensink. 1978. Catalog of Alaskan seabird colonies. USDI, Fish Wildl. Serv. FWS/OBS-80/37.

Spear, L. B., T. M. Penniman, J. F. Penniman, H. R. Carter, and D. G. Ainley. 1987. Survivorship and mortality factors in a population of Western Gulls. In J. L. Hand, W. E. Southern, and K. Vermeer, eds. Ecology and behavior of gulls, 44-56. Studies Avian Biol. 10.

Speich, S. M., H. L. Jones, and E. M. Benedict. 1986. Review of the natural nesting of the Barn Swallow in North America. Amer. Midl. Nat. 115:248-254.

Spofford, W. R. 1964. The Golden Eagle in the Trans-Pecos and Edwards Plateau of Texas. Audubon Conserv. Rept. 1. Natl. Aud. Soc., New York.

Sprunt, A. S., Jr. 1942. Purple Martin. In A. C. Bent, ed. Life histories of North American flycatchers, larks, swallows, and their allies. U.S. Natl. Mus. Bull. 179:489-509.

Squires, W. A. 1917. Some field notes for 1917. Condor 19:185-186.

Stacey, P. B. and R. Jansma. 1977. Storage of piñon nuts by the Acorn Woodpecker in New Mexico. Wilson Bull. 89:150-151.

Stallcup, P. L. 1968. Spatio-temporal relationships of nuthatches and woodpeckers in ponderosa pine forest of Colorado. Ecology 49:831-843.

Stanback, M. T. 1991. Autumnal breeding in the Scrub Jay. J. Field Ornithol. 62:94-96.

Stendell, R. C. and P. Meyers. 1973. White-tailed Kite predation on a fluctuating vole population. Condor 75:359-360.

Stenzel, L. E. and S. C. Peaslee. 1979. Part II: The California mainland coast. In G. W. Page and L. E. Stenzel, eds. The breeding status of the Snowy Plover in California, II-1 to II-23. Nongame Wildl. Invest. Rept. Calif. Fish Game, Sacramento.

Stenzel, L. E., S. C. Peaslee, and G. W. Page. 1981. Results II. Mainland Coast. In G. W. Page and L. E. Stenzel, eds. 1981. The breeding status of the Snowy Plover in California, 6-16. W. Birds 12:1-40.

Stephens, A. B. 1931. Audubon notes. Gull 13, No. 7.

Stephens, L. A. 1936. Birds of Marin County, California. Gull 18, No. 6.

——. 1941. June field trip. Gull 23:24-25.

——. 1945. White-tailed Kite. Gull 27:36-37.

Stephens, L. A. and C. C. Pringle. 1933. Birds of Marin County. Audubon Assoc. of the Pacific, San Francisco. Available at PRBO library, 4990 Shoreline Hwy., Stinson Beach, CA 94970.

Stern, R. J. A. 1959. Mockingbird observed on the southern tip of Tiburon Peninsula, Marin County, California. Condor 61:59.

Stewart, B. S., P. K. Yochem, and R. W. Schreiber. 1984. Pelagic red crabs as food for gulls: A possible benefit of El Niño. Condor 86:341-342.

Stewart, R. E. 1953. A life history of the Yellow-throat. Wilson Bull. 65:99-115.

——. 1975. *Breeding Birds of North Dakota*. North Dakota Inst. Reg. Studies, Fargo.

Stewart, R. M. 1972. Nestling mortality in swallows due to inclement weather. Calif. Birds 3:69-70.

——. 1973. Breeding behavior and life history of the Wilson Warbler. Wilson Bull. 85:21-30.

Stewart, R. M. and K. Darling. 1972. Breeding biology of the Wilson's Warbler in the high Sierra and on the coast. Point Reyes Bird Obs. Newsl. 24:3-5.

Stewart, R. M., R. P. Henderson, and K. Darling. 1977. Breeding ecology of the Wilson's Warbler in the high Sierra Nevada, California. Living Bird 16:83-102.

Stiehl, R. B. 1985. Brood chronology of the Common Raven. Wilson Bull. 97:78-87.

Stiles, F. G., III. 1973. Food supply and the annual cycle of the Anna Hummingbird. Univ. Calif. Publ. Zool. 97:1-109.

Stine, S. MS. Fat, furs, feathers, and flesh: The game trade in early California. Unpubl. manuscript.

Stinson, C. H., D. L. Crawford, and J. Lauthner. 1981. Sex differences in winter habitat of American Kestrels in Georgia. J. Field Ornithol. 52:29-35.

Stocek, R. F. 1970. Observations of the breeding biology of the Tree Swallow. Cassinia 52:3-20.

Stokes, A. W. 1950. Breeding behavior of the goldfinch. Wilson Bull. 62:107-127.

Stoner, E. A. 1934. Recent occurrences of the American Egret in the San Francisco Bay region. Condor 36:57-59.

——. 1947. Food of White-tailed Kites in Suisun Marsh. Condor 49:84-85.

Stophlet, J. J. 1959. Nesting concentration of Long-eared Owls in Cochise County, Arizona. Wilson Bull. 71:97-99.

Storer, R. W. 1951. The seasonal occurrence of shorebirds at Bay Farm Island Alameda County, California. Condor 53:186-193.

——. 1966. Sexual dimorphism and food habits in three North American accipiters. Auk 83:423-436.

Storer, T. I. 1926. Range extensions by the Western Robin in California. Condor 28:264-267.

——. 1927. Three notable nesting colonies of the Cliff Swallow in California. Condor 29:104-108.

Strohmeyer, D. L. 1977. Common Gallinule (*Gallinula chloropus*). In G. C. Sanderson, ed. Management of migratory shore and upland game birds in North America, 110-117. Int. Assoc. Fish. Wildl. Agencies and U.S. Fish Wildl. Serv.

Stull, W. D. 1968. Eastern and Canadian Chipping sparrows. In O. L. Austin, Jr., ed. A. C. Bent et al.'s Life histories of North American cardinals, grosbeaks, buntings, towhees, finches, sparrows, and allies. U.S. Natl. Mus. Bull. 237 (Part 2): 1166-1184.

Sturman, W. A. 1968. The foraging ecology of *Parus atri-capillus* and *P. rufescens* in the breeding season, with comparisons with other species of *Parus*. Condor 70: 309–322.

Sullivan, J. O. 1966. A Dipper nest away from water. Condor 68:107.

Summers-Smith, J. D. 1963. *The House Sparrow.* Collins, London.

Sumner, E. L., Jr. 1935. A life history study of the California Quail, with recommendations for conservation and management. Calif. Fish Game 21:167–256, 277–342.

Sutcliffe, S. M., R. E. Bonney, Jr., and J. D. Lowe, eds. 1986. Proceedings of the 2nd Northeastern Breeding Bird Atlas Conference. Lab. Ornithology, Cornell Univ., Ithaca, N.Y.

Sutton, G. M. 1976. On the feeding behavior of the Red Crossbill. Bull. Okla. Ornithol. Soc. 9:3–6.

Swanson, G. A., G. L. Krapu, and J. R. Serie. 1979. Foods of laying female dabbling ducks on the breeding grounds. In T. A. Bookhout, ed. Waterfowl and wetlands—an integrated review, 47–57. Proc. Symp. 1977, N. Cent. Sec., The Wildl. Soc.

Swanson, G. A., M. I. Meyer, and J. R. Serie. 1974. Feeding ecology of breeding Blue-winged Teals. J. Wildl. Mgmt. 38:396–407.

Swanson, G. A. and A. B. Sargeant. 1972. Observation of nightime feeding behavior of ducks. J. Wildl. Mgmt. 36: 959–961.

Swanton, H. 1933. The Snowy Egret in Marin County, California. Condor 35:73.

Swarth, C. W. 1983. Foraging ecology of Snowy Plovers and the distribution of their arthropod prey at Mono Lake, California. M.S. thesis, Calif. State Univ., Hayward.

Swenson, J. E. 1979. The relationsip between prey species ecology and dive success in Ospreys. Auk 96:408–412.

——. 1981. Status of the Osprey in southeastern Montana before and after the construction of reservoirs. W. Birds 12:47–51.

Swenson, J. E. and P. Hendricks. 1983. Chick movements in Common Poorwills. Wilson Bull. 95:309–310.

Swisher, O. D. 1978. Poor-wills nesting in southwestern Oregon. N. Am. Bird Bander 3:152–155.

Sydeman, W. J. 1989. Effects of helpers on nestling care and breeder survival in Pygmy Nuthatches. Condor 91:147–155.

Sydeman, W. J. and M. Güntert. 1983. Winter communal roosting in the Pygmy Nuthatch. In J. W. Davis, G. A. Goodwin, and R. A. Ockenfels, tech. coords. Snag habitat management: Proceedings of the symposium, 121–124. U.S. For. Serv. Gen. Tech. Rept. RM-99.

Sydeman, W. J., M. Güntert, and R. P. Balda. 1988. Annual reproductive yield in the cooperative Pygmy Nuthatch *(Sitta pygmaea)*. Auk 105:70–77.

Szaro, R. C., J. D. Brawn, R. P. Balda. 1990. Yearly variation in resource-use behavior by ponderosa pine forest birds. In M. L. Morrison, C. J. Ralph, J. Verner, and J. R. Jehl, Jr., eds. Avian foraging: Theory, methodology, and applications, 226–236. Studies Avian Biol. 13.

T

Taber, W. J. and D. W. Johnston. 1968. Indigo Bunting. In O. L. Austin, Jr., ed. A. C. Bent et al.'s Life histories of North American cardinals, grosbeaks, buntings, towhees, finches, sparrows, and allies. U.S. Natl. Mus. Bull. 237 (Part 1): 80–111.

Tait, W. W., H. M. Johnson, and W. D. Courser. 1972. Osprey carrying a small mammal. Wilson Bull. 84:341.

Takekawa, J. E., H. R. Carter, and T. E. Harvey. 1990. Decline of the Common Murre in central California, 1980–1986. In S. G. Sealy, ed. Auks at sea, 149–163. Studies Avian Biol. 14.

Tangren, G. V. 1977. Climatic effects on the seasonality of California's avifaunas. Am. Birds 31:960–965.

Tate, J., Jr. 1973. Methods and annual sequence of foraging by the sapsucker. Auk 90:840–856.

——. 1981. The Blue List for 1981: The first decade. Am. Birds 35:3–10.

——. 1986. The Blue List for 1986. Am. Birds 40:227–236.

Tate, J., Jr. and D. J. Tate. 1982. The Blue List for 1982. Am. Birds 36:126–135.

Tatschl, J. L. 1967. Breeding birds of the Sandia Mountains and their ecological distributions. Condor 69:479–490.

Taverner, P. A. 1933. Purple Martins gathering leaves. Auk 50:110–111.

Taylor, D. M. and C. D. Littlefield. 1986. Willow Flycatcher and Yellow Warbler response to cattle grazing. Am. Birds 40:1169–1173.

Taylor, H. R. 1905. The nest and eggs of the Vaux Swift. Condor 7:177 & 179.

Taylor, P. D. and S. M. Smith. 1986. Multi-species clusters of birds in southern Ontario. In M. D. Cadman, P. F. J. Eagles, and F. M. Helleiner, comps. *Atlas of the Breeding Birds of Ontario*, 576–580. Univ. Waterloo Press, Waterloo.

Taylor, W. K. 1965. Nesting heights of some Louisiana birds. Wilson Bull. 77:146–150.

Tenaya, K. and R. Tenaya. 1966. First report of the Starling in San Francisco, California. Condor 68:600.

Thelander, C. G. 1974. Nesting territory utilization by Golden Eagles *(Aquila chrysaetos)* in California during 1974. Wildl. Mgmt. Branch Admin. Rept. 74-7. Calif. Dept. Fish Game, Sacramento.

Thomas, J. W., E. D. Forsman, J. B. Lint, E. C. Meslow, B. R. Noon, and J. Verner. 1990. A conservation strategy for the Northern Spotted Owl. Rept. of the Interagency Sci. Comm. to Address the Conservation of the Northern Spotted Owl. U.S. For. Serv., Portland, Oregon; Bur. Land Mgmt.; U.S. Fish Wildl. Serv.; U.S. Natl. Park Serv.

Thompson, S. P., C. D. Littlefield, and R. A. Ryder. 1979. Historical review and status of colonial nesting birds on Malheur National Wildlife Refuge, Oregon. Proc. 1979 Conf. Colonial Waterbird Group 3:156–164.

Thompson, W. L. 1960. Agonistic behavior in the House Finch. Part 1: Annual cycle and display patterns. Condor 62:245–271.

Thomsen, L. 1971. Behavior and ecology of Burrowing Owls on the Oakland municipal airport. Condor 73:177–192.

Thut, R. N. 1970. Feeding habits of the Dipper in southwestern Washington. Condor 72:234–235.

Tinbergen, J. 1981. Foraging decisions in Starlings (*Sturnus vulgaris* L.). Ardea 69:1–67.

Tinbergen, J. M. and R. H. Drent. 1980. The Starling as a successful forager. In E. N. Wright, I. R. Inglis, and C. J. Feare, eds. *Bird Problems in Agriculture*, 83–101. Lamport Gilbert, Reading, Great Britian.

Titman, R. D. 1983. Spacing and three-bird flights of Mallards breeding in pothole habitat. Can. J. Zool. 61:839–847.

Torduff, H. B. 1954. Social organization and behavior in a flock of captive, nonbreeding Red Crossbills. Condor 56:346–358.

Townsend, C. W. 1926. Virginia Rail. In A. C. Bent, ed. Life histories of North American marsh birds. U.S. Natl. Mus. Bull. 135:292–301.

——. 1929. Killdeer. In A. C. Bent, ed. Life histories of North American shore birds (Part 2). U.S. Natl. Mus. Bull. 146:202–217.

——. 1938. Short-eared Owl. In A. C. Bent, ed. Life histories of North American birds of prey (Part 2). U.S. Natl. Mus. Bull. 170:169–182.

Tramontano, J. P. 1964. Comparative studies of the Rock Wren and the Canyon Wren. M.S. thesis, Univ. Ariz., Tucson.

Travis, J. 1977. Seasonal foraging in a Downy Woodpecker population. Condor 79:371–375.

Tremblay, J. and L. N. Ellison. 1979. Effects of human disturbance on breeding of Black-crowned Night Herons. Auk 96:364–369.

Troetschler, R. G. 1976. Acorn Woodpecker breeding strategy as affected by Starling nest-hole competition. Condor 78:151–165.

Turner, A. K. 1982. Optimal foraging by the swallow (*Hirundo rustica* L.): Prey size selection. Anim. Behav. 30:862–872.

Tyler, W. M. 1929. Spotted Sandpiper. In A. C. Bent, ed. Life histories of North American shore birds (Part 2). U.S. Natl. Mus. Bull. 146:78–97.

——. 1937. Turkey Vulture. In A. C. Bent, ed. Life histories of North American birds of prey (Part 1). U.S. Natl. Mus. Bull. 167:12–28.

——. 1942. Tree Swallow. In A. C. Bent, ed. Life histories of North American flycatchers, larks, swallows, and their allies. U.S. Natl. Mus. Bull. 179:384–400.

——. 1948a. Red-breasted Nuthatch. In A. C. Bent, ed. Life histories of North American nuthatches, wrens, thrashers, and their allies. U.S. Natl. Mus. Bull. 195:22–35.

——. 1948b. White-breasted Nuthatch. In A. C. Bent, ed. Life histories of North American nuthatches, wrens, thrashers, and their allies. U.S. Natl. Mus. Bull. 195:1–12.

——. 1948c. Brown Creeper. In A. C. Bent, ed. Life histories of North American nuthatches, wrens, thrashers, and their allies. U.S. Natl. Mus. Bull. 195:56–70.

——. 1949. Eastern Robin. In A. C. Bent, ed. Life histories of North American thrushes, kinglets, and their allies. U.S. Natl. Mus. Bull. 196:14–45.

U

Unglish, W. E. 1929. The Texas Nighthawk in Santa Clara County, California. Condor 31:223.

Unitt, P. 1977. The Little Blue Heron in California. W. Birds 8:151–154.

——. 1984. *The Birds of San Diego County*. San Diego Soc. Nat. Hist. Memoir 13.

U.S. Fish and Wildlife Service. 1987a. The Northern Spotted Owl status review. Portland, Oregon.

——. 1987b. Migratory nongame birds of management concern in the United States: The 1987 list. Office Migratory Bird Mgmt., USFWS, Washington, D.C.

——. 1989a. Endangered and threatened wildlife and plants. 50 CFR 17.11 and 17.12.

——. 1989b. Endangered and threatened wildlife and plants; animal notice of review. 50 CFR Part 17.

——. 1989c. The Northern Spotted Owl: A status review supplement. Portland, Oregon.

——. 1991. Endangered and threatened wildlife and plants; animal candidate review for listing as endangered or threatened species. 50 CFR Part 17.

U.S. Forest Service. 1988. Final supplement to the environmental impact statement for an amendment to the Pacific Northwest Regional Guide. Spotted Owl guidelines. 2 vols. USFS, Portland.

U.S. Weather Bureau. 1934. Climatic summary of the United States.

V

Van Fleet, C. C. 1919. A short paper on the Hutton Vireo. Condor 21:162–165.

Verbeek, N. A. M. 1967. Breeding biology and ecology of the Horned Lark in alpine tundra. Wilson Bull. 79:208–218.

——. 1970. Feeding ecology of two coexisting corvids. In N. A. M. Verbeek. The exploitation system of the Yellow-billed Magpie. Ph.D. thesis, Univ. Calif., Berkeley.

——. 1973. The exploitation system of the Yellow-billed Magpie. Univ. Calif. Publ. Zool. 99:1–58.

——. 1975a. Comparative feeding behavior of three coexisting tyrannid flycatchers. Wilson Bull. 87:231–240.

——. 1975b. Northern wintering of flycatchers and the residency of Black Phoebes in California. Auk 92:737–749.

Verheyan, R. F. 1980. Breeding strategies of the Starling. In E. N. Wright, I. R. Inglis, and C. J. Feare, eds. *Bird Problems in Agriculture*, 69–82. Lamport Gilbert, Reading, Great Britain.

Vermeer, K. 1979. Nesting requirements, food, and breeding distribution of Rhinoceros Auklets, *Cerorhinca monocerata*, and Tufted Puffins, *Lunda cirrhata*. Ardea 67:101–110.

——. 1980. The importance of timing and type of prey to reproductive success of Rhinoceros Auklets *Cerorhinca monocerata*. Ibis 122:343–350.

Vermeer, K. and L. Cullen. 1982. Growth comparison of a plankton- and a fish-eating alcid. Murrelet 63:34–39.

Vermeer, K. and S. J. Westrheim. 1984. Fish changes in diets of nestling Rhinoceros Auklets and their implications. In D. N. Nettleship, G. A. Sanger, P. F. Springer, eds. Marine birds: Their feeding ecology and commercial fisheries relationships, 96–105. Proc. Pac. Seabird Group Symp., Seattle, Washington, 6-8 Jan. 1982. Canadian Wildl. Serv. for P.S.G.

Verner, J. 1963. Song rates and polygamy in the Long-billed Marsh Wren. Proc. XIII Int. Ornithol. Congr. 1:299–307.

——. 1964. Evolution of polygamy in the Long-billed Marsh Wren. Evolution 18:252–261.

——. 1965. Breeding biology of the Long-billed Marsh Wren. Condor 67:6–30.

Verner, J., E. C. Beedy, S. L. Granholm, L. V. Ritter, and E. F. Toth. 1980. Birds. In J. Verner and A. S. Boss, tech. coordinators. California wildlife and their habitats: Western Sierra Nevada, 75–319. Gen. Tech. Rept. PSW-37. Pac. Southwest Forest and Range Exp. Stn., Forest Serv., Berkeley, Calif.

Verner, J. and G. H. Engelson. 1970. Territories, multiple nest building, and polygyny in the Long-billed Marsh Wren. Auk 87:557–567.

Verner, J. and T. A. Larson. 1989. Richness of breeding bird species in mixed-conifer forests of the Sierra Nevada, California. Auk 106:447–463.

Verner, J. and L. V. Ritter. 1983. Current status of the Brown-headed Cowbird in the Sierra National Forest. Auk 100:355–368.

Verner, J. and M. F. Willson. 1969. Mating systems, sexual dimorphism, and the role of male North American passerine birds in the nesting cycle. Ornithol. Monogr. 9.

Voous, K. H. 1960. Atlas of European Birds. Nelson, Amsterdam.

——. 1988. Owls of the Northern Hemisphere. M.I.T. Press, Cambridge, Mass.

W

Wagner, J. L. 1981. Seasonal change in guild structure: Oak woodland insectivorous birds. Ecology 62:973–981.

Wahl, J. R. 1975. Seabirds in Washington's offshore zone. W. Birds 6:117–134.

Waian, L. B. and R. C. Stendell. 1970. The White-tailed Kite in California with observations of the Santa Barbara population. Calif. Fish Game 56:188–198.

Walkinshaw, L. H. 1937. The Virginia Rail in Michigan. Auk 54:464–475.

——. 1938. Life histories of the eastern goldfinch, Part I. Jack-Pine Warbler 16:3–11, 14–15.

——. 1940. Summer life of the Sora Rail. Auk 57:153–168.

——. 1944. The eastern Chipping Sparrow in Michigan. Wilson Bull. 56:193–205.

Walkinshaw, L. H. and D. A. Zimmerman. 1961. Range expansion of the Brewer Blackbird in eastern North America. Condor 63:162–177.

Walsberg, G. E. 1981. Nest-site selection and radiative environment of the Warbling Vireo. Condor 83:86–88.

Walsh, H. 1978. Food of nestling Purple Martins. Wilson Bull. 90:248–260.

Walters, R. E., ed. 1983. Utah bird distribution—latilong study. 97 pp. mimeo.

Walton, B. J. 1978. The status of the salt marsh Song Sparrows of the San Francisco Bay system, 1974-1976. M.A. thesis, San Jose State Univ., San Jose.

Walton, B. J. and C. G. Thelander. 1988. Peregrine Falcon management efforts in California, Oregon, Washington, and Nevada. In T. J. Cade, J. H. Enderson, C. G. Thelander, and C. M. White, eds. Peregrine Falcon Populations: Their Management and Recovery, 587–597. The Peregrine Fund, Boise, Idaho.

Walton, B. J., C. G. Thelander, and D. L. Harlow. 1988. The status of Peregrines nesting in California, Oregon, Washington, and Nevada. In T. J. Cade, J. H. Enderson, C. G. Thelander, and C. M. White, eds. Peregrine Falcon Populations: Their Management and Recovery, 95–104. The Peregrine Fund, Boise, Idaho.

Warner, J. S. and R. L. Rudd. 1975. Hunting by the White-tailed Kite (Elanus leucurus). Condor 77:226–230.

Warriner, J. S., J. C. Warriner, G. W. Page, and L. E. Stenzel. 1986. Mating system and reproductive success of a small population of polygamous Snowy Plovers (Charadrius alexandrinus). Wilson Bull. 98:15–37.

Watson, J. R. 1910. The impaling instincts in shrikes. Auk 27:459.

Wauer, R. H. 1969. Recent bird records from the Virgin River Valley of Utah, Arizona, and Nevada. Condor 71:331–335.

Weathers, W. W. 1983. Birds of Southern California's Deep Canyon. Univ. California Press, Berkeley.

Weaver, R. L. 1939. Winter observations and a study of the nesting of English Sparrows. Bird-Banding 10:73–79.

——. 1943. Reproduction in English Sparrows. Auk 60:62–74.

Webster, C. G. 1964. Fall foods of Soras from two habitats in Connecticut. J. Wildl. Mgmt. 28:163–165.

Webster, J. D. 1941a. The breeding of the Black Oystercatcher. Wilson Bull. 53:141–156.

——. 1941b. The feeding habits of the Black Oystercatcher. Condor 43:175–180.

Weitzel, N. H. 1988. Nest-site competition between the European Starling and native breeding birds in northwestern Nevada. Condor 90:515–517.

Welch, W. R. 1928. Quail shooting in California today and fifty years ago. Calif. Fish Game 14:122–128.

Weller, M. W. and L. H. Fredrickson. 1973. Avian ecology of a managed glacial marsh. Living Bird 12:269–291.

Wells, P. V. 1958. Indigo Buntings in Lazuli Bunting habitat in southwestern Utah. Auk 75:223–224.

Welter, W. A. 1935. The natural history of the Long-billed Marsh Wren. Wilson Bull. 47:3–34.

Welty, J. C. and L. Baptista. 1988. The Life of Birds. 4th ed. Saunders, New York.

Wemmer, C. 1969. Impaling behaviour of the Loggerhead Shrike, *Lanius ludovicianus* Linnaeus. Z. Tierpsychol. 26: 208-224.

Werschkul, D. F., E. McMahon, and M. Leitschuh. 1976. Some effects of human activities on the Great Blue Heron in Oregon. Wilson Bull. 88:660-662.

West, M. J., A. P. King, and D. H. Eastzer. 1981. The cowbird: Reflections on development from an unlikely source. Amer. Sci. 69:56-66.

Weston, H. G., Jr. 1947. Breeding behavior of the Black-headed Grosbeak. Condor 49:54-73.

——. 1948. Spring arrival of summer residents in the Berkeley area, California. Condor 50:81-82.

Wetmore, A. 1925. Food of American phalaropes, avocets, and stilts. U.S. Dept. Agri. Bull. 1359.

Wheeler, R. J. 1965. Pioneering Blue-winged Teal in California, Oregon, Washington and British Columbia. Murrelet 46:40-42.

White, H. C. 1953. The eastern Belted Kingfisher in the Maritime Provinces. Fish. Res. Board Can. Bull. 97.

White, J. M. 1973. Breeding biology and feeding patterns of the Oregon Junco in two Sierra Nevada habitats. Ph.D. thesis, Univ. Calif., Berkeley.

Whitmore, R. C. 1975. Indigo Buntings in Utah with special reference to interspecific competition with Lazuli Buntings. Condor 77:509-510.

——. 1979a. Temporal variations in the selected habitats of a guild of grassland sparrows. Wilson Bull. 91:592-598.

——. 1979b. Short-term change in vegetation and its effect on Grasshopper Sparrows in West Virginia. Auk 96:621-625.

——. 1981. Structural characteristics of Grasshopper Sparrow habitat. J. Wildl. Mgmt. 45:811-814.

Widrlechner, M. P. and S. K. Dragula. 1984. Relation of cone-crop size to irruptions of four seed-eating birds in California. Am. Birds 38:840-846.

Wieloch, M. 1975. Food of nestling House Sparrows, *Passer domesticus* L., and Tree Sparrows, *Passer montanus* L., in agrocenoses. Polish Ecol. Studies 1:227-242.

Wiens, J. A. 1969. An approach to the study of ecological relationships among grassland birds. Ornithol. Monogr. 8.

——. 1973. Interterritorial habitat variation in Grasshopper and Savannah sparrows. Ecology 54:877-884.

——. 1974. Climatic instability and the "ecological saturation" of bird communities in North American grasslands. Condor 76:385-400.

——. 1989. *The Ecology of Bird Communities. Vol. 1: Foundations and Patterns. Vol. 2: Processes and Variations.* Cambridge Studies Ecol., Cambridge Univ. Press, Cambridge, England.

Wiens, J. A. and M. I. Dyer. 1977. Assessing the potential impact of granivorous birds in ecosystems. In J. Pinowski and S. C. Kendeigh, eds. *Granivorous Birds in Ecosystems: Their Evolution, Populations, Energetics, Impact, and Control,* 15-51. Int. Biol. Progr. 12. Cambridge Univ. Press, London.

Wiggins, I. L. and B. L. Wiggins. 1939. An unusual nesting site of the Western Tanager. Condor 41:80-81.

Wilbur, S. R. 1973a. The Red-shouldered Hawk in the western United States. W. Birds 4:15-22.

——. 1973b. The California Condor in the Pacific Northwest. Auk 90:196-198.

——. 1974. The literature of the California Black Rail. U.S. Fish. Wildl. Serv. Spec. Sci. Rept. Wildl. 179.

——. 1978. Turkey Vulture eggshell thinning in California, Florida and Texas. Wilson Bull. 90:642-643.

——. 1983. The status of vultures in the Western Hemisphere. In S. R. Wilbur and J. A. Jackson, eds. *Vulture Biology and Management,* 113-123. Univ. California Press, Berkeley.

Wilde, M. L. C. 1897. Nesting of the Parula Warbler *(Compsothlypis americana)* in Cape May County, New Jersey. Auk 14:289-294.

Wiley, J. W. 1975. The nesting and reproductive success of Red-tailed Hawks and Red-shouldered Hawks in Orange County, California, 1973. Condor 77:133-139.

Wiley, J. W. and F. E. Lohrer. 1973. Additional records of non-fish prey taken by Ospreys. Wilson Bull. 85:468-470.

Willett, G. 1912. Birds of the Pacific slope of southern California. Pac. Coast Avifauna 7.

——. 1933. A revised list of the birds of southwestern California. Pac. Coast Avifauna 21.

Williams, J. B. 1975. Habitat utilization by four species of woodpeckers in a central Illinois woodland. Am. Midl. Nat. 93:354-367.

——. 1980. Intersexual niche partitioning in Downy Woodpeckers. Wilson Bull. 92:439-451.

Williams, L. 1927. Notes on the Black Oyster-catcher. Condor 29:80-81.

——. 1940. The status and preservation of the White-tailed Kite in California. Gull 22:29-32.

——. 1942. Display and sexual behavior of the Brandt's Cormorant. Condor 44:85-104.

——. 1952. Breeding behavior of the Brewer's Blackbird. Condor 54:3-47.

——. 1958. Brewer's Blackbird. In A. C. Bent, ed. Life histories of North American blackbirds, orioles, tanagers, and allies. U.S. Natl. Mus. Bull. 211:302-334.

Williams, L., K. Legg, and F. S. L. Williamson. 1958. Breeding of the Parula Warbler at Point Lobos, California. Condor 60:345-354.

Williams, L. W. 1929. Notes on the feeding habits and behavior of the California Clapper Rail. Condor 31:52-56.

Williams, M. L., R. L. Hothem, and H. M. Ohlendorf. 1989. Recruitment failure in American Avocets and Black-necked Stilts nesting at Kesterson Reservoir, California, 1984-1985. Condor 91:797-802.

Williams, P. L. 1982. A comparison of colonial and non-colonial nesting by Northern Orioles in central coastal California. M.A. thesis, Univ. Calif., Berkeley.

——. 1988. Spacing behavior and related features of social organization in Northern Orioles of central coastal California. Ph.D. thesis, Univ. Calif., Berkeley.

——. 1990. Use of radiotracking to study foraging in small terrestrial birds. In M. L. Morrison, C. J. Ralph, J. Verner, and J. R. Jehl, Jr., eds. Avian foraging: Theory, methodology, and applications, 181–186. Studies Avian Biol. 13.

Williamson, F. S. L. 1956. The molt and testis cycles of the Anna's Hummingbird. Condor 58:342–366.

Williamson, P. and L. Gray. 1975. Foraging behavior of the Starling (Sturnus vulgaris) in Maryland. Condor 77:84–89.

Willson, M. F. 1966. Breeding ecology of the Yellow-headed Blackbird. Ecol. Monogr. 36:51–77.

——. 1970. Foraging behavior of some winter birds of deciduous woods. Condor 72:129–132.

Wilson, S. W. 1978. Food size, food type, and foraging sites of Red-winged Blackbirds. Wilson Bull. 90:511–520.

Wilson, U. W. and D. A. Manuwal. 1986. Breeding biology of the Rhinoceros Auklet in Washington. Condor 88:143–155.

Wittenberger, J. F. 1978. The breeding biology of an isolated Bobolink population in Oregon. Condor 80:355–371.

Wolford, J. W. and D. A. Boag. 1971. Food habits of Black-crowned Night Herons in southern Alberta. Auk 88:435–437.

Wolinski, R. A. 1980. Rough-winged Swallow feeding on fly larvae. Wilson Bull. 92:121–122.

Wood, A. K. and J. D. Brotherson. 1981. Microenvironment and nest site selection by Ring-necked Pheasants in Utah. Great Basin Nat. 41:457–460.

Woods, R. S. 1940. Anna's Hummingbird. In A. C. Bent, ed. Life histories of North American cuckoos, goatsuckers, hummingbirds, and their allies. U.S. Natl. Mus. Bull. 176:371–387.

——. 1942. Black Phoebe. In A. C. Bent, ed. Life histories of North American flycatchers, larks, swallows, and their allies. U.S. Natl. Mus. Bull. 179:154–164.

——. 1948. California Thrasher. In A. C. Bent, ed. Life histories of North American nuthatches, wrens, thrashers, and their allies. U.S. Natl. Mus. Bull. 195:402–410.

——. 1968. House Finch. In O. L. Austin, Jr., ed. A. C. Bent et al.'s Life histories of North American cardinals, grosbeaks, buntings, towhees, finches, sparrows, and allies. U.S. Natl. Mus. Bull. 237 (Part 1): 290–314.

Woolfenden, G. E. and J. W. Fitzpatrick. 1984. The Florida Scrub Jay: Demography of a cooperative-breeding bird. Monogr. Pop. Biol. 20. Princeton Univ. Press, Princeton.

Wright, E. N., I. R. Inglis, and C. J. Feare, eds. 1980. Bird Problems in Agriculture. Lamport Gilbert, Reading, Great Britain.

Y

Yahner, R. C. 1983. Site-related nesting success of Mourning Doves and American Robins in shelterbelts. Wilson Bull. 95:573–580.

Yocum, C. F. and S. W. Harris. 1975. Status, habits, and distribution of birds of northwestern California. Humboldt State Univ. Bookstore, Arcata, Calif.

Yokel, D. A. 1986. Monogamy and brood parasitism: An unlikely pair. Anim. Behav. 34:1348–1358.

Yokel, D. A. and S. I. Rothstein. 1991. The basis for female choice in an avian brood parasite. Behav. Ecol. Sociobiol. 29:39–45.

Young, H. 1955. Breeding behavior and nesting of the eastern Robin. Am. Midl. Nat. 53:329–352.

Z

Zarn, M. 1974. Burrowing Owl (Speotyto cunicularia hypugaea). Habitat management series for Endangered species. U.S. Bur. Land Mgmt. Tech. Notes 250.

Zimmerman, D. A. 1970. Roadrunner predation on passerine birds. Condor 72:475–476.

——. 1973. Range expansion of Anna's Hummingbird. Am. Birds 27:827–835.

Zimmerman, J. L. 1977. Virginia Rail (Rallus limicola). In G. C. Sanderson, ed. Management of migratory shore and upland game birds in North America, 46–56. Int. Assoc. Fish Wildl. Agencies and U.S. Fish and Wildl. Serv.

Zusi, R. L. and R. W. Storer. 1969. Osteology and myology of the head and neck of the Pied-billed Grebes (Podilymbus). Misc. Publ. Mus. Zool. Univ. Mich. 139.

INDEX

The Marin County Breeding Bird Atlas was composed into type using Ventura Publisher and a Hewlett-Packard LaserJet III printer with LaserMaster controller in Goudy Old Style set 10.5/11.5.

BUSHTIT BOOKS : BOLINAS, CALIFORNIA